W9-CEA-498

PSYCHOLOGY

Second Edition

PSYCHOLOGY

PETER GRAY

Boston College

Worth Publishers

To Anita and Scott

PSYCHOLOGY, ***Second Edition***

Printed in the United States of America

Library of Congress Catalog Card Number: 93-61159

ISBN: 0-87901-464-4

Printing: 2 3 4 5–98 97 96 95 94

Development editor: Susan Seuling

Design: Malcolm Grear Designers

Art director: George Touloumes

Production editor: Betsy Mastalski

Production supervisor: Barbara Anne Seixas

Layout: Matthew Dvorozniak

Picture Editors: June Lundborg Whitworth and Barbara Salz

Line art: Warren Budd and Demetrios Zangos

Composition and separations: TSI Graphics, Inc.

Printing and binding: Von Hoffmann Press, Inc.

Cover: Johannes Vermeer, *Head of A Young Girl* (detail), 17 c. Oil on canvas.

Mauritshuis, The Hague. Photo The Granger Collection, New York City.

Illustration credits begin on page IC-1 and constitute an extension

of the copyright page.

Worth Publishers

33 Irving Place

New York, New York 10003

ABOUT THE AUTHOR

During his undergraduate and graduate years, at Columbia and Rockefeller Universities, Peter Gray supported himself by teaching nursery school, coaching basketball at youth centers, supervising a summer program in biology for inner-city high school students, and teaching psychology courses at Hunter College and City College of New York.

Since 1972 Dr. Gray has been at Boston College, serving in the past as Psychology Department Chair. He has taught a wide range of courses in the undergraduate and graduate curricula while pursuing research in physiological psychology and (more recently) in child development, cognition, and their relation to education. He continues to teach the introductory course regularly, and has been active in a program designed to help students from disadvantaged educational backgrounds gain more from their college experience.

In order to write an introductory textbook that shows students how psychologists think and work, Dr. Gray has educated himself deeply in every area. For 15 years he has immersed himself in the literature and avidly followed developments in each subfield, from its roots up to work currently being done. This broad knowledge, acquired through curiosity and persistence, has given him a unique perspective on the whole field. Peter Gray's *Psychology* has the authority and currency of a textbook written by a team of experts, yet it has the advantages of a single authored book: continuity, logic, and personality.

Peter Gray brings to his readers an accessible book that is intelligent and thought-provoking, warm and engrossing. His enthusiasm for psychology is evident in every chapter and in the reason he gives for writing this book: "*Understanding, organizing, summarizing, and retelling to students what human beings have learned about human behavior is the most exciting task that I can imagine.*"

CONTENTS IN BRIEF

CONTENTS

PART 6
THE PERSON IN A WORLD OF PEOPLE 491

CHAPTER 14
SOCIAL COGNITION 493

CHAPTER 15
SOCIAL INFLUENCES ON BEHAVIOR 531

PART 7
PERSONALITY AND DISORDERS 563

CHAPTER 16
THEORIES OF PERSONALITY 565

PREFACE

My immodest goal has been to write an introduction to psychology that describes the main ideas of the field, and the evidence behind them, in as logically coherent and intellectually stimulating a manner as possible—one that will excite students' interest by appealing to their intelligence. As cognitive psychologists have shown repeatedly, the human mind is not particularly good at absorbing and remembering miscellaneous pieces of information. It is designed for thinking, figuring out, understanding; and it remembers what it understands. I want students to join you and me in *thinking about* behavior—its functions, causes, and mechanisms.

Toward achieving this goal, I have entered each domain of psychology with the aim of identifying its main questions, its main approaches to answering questions, and its most durable and interesting theories and findings. I have striven to describe these as clearly as possible and have provided concrete, real-life examples to help readers see their relevance. The book is organized around ways of thinking about behavior, in a manner that permits the development of extended arguments while still covering the traditional ground of the introductory course. Focus questions in the margins continuously call attention to the main ideas and lines of evidence. My aim throughout has been to depict the science of psychology as a human endeavor in which progress comes through the work of thoughtful, if fallible, people who make observations, conduct experiments, reason, and argue about behavior.

One of my dearest aims has been to achieve some small measure of the personal touch that William James accomplished so masterfully in *The Principles of Psychology*—the book that still stands, in my mind, as far and away the best introduction to psychology ever written. I hope that students will read my text—as anyone must read James's—not as Truth with a capital *T*, nor as an unbiased distillate of all of psychology, but rather as one person's honest attempt to understand the field and to convey that understanding as best he could. Toward that end, in writing the book I constantly imagined myself carrying on a dialogue with an inquiring, thinking, appropriately skeptical student.

I must also confess to sharing two of James's biases—rationalism and functionalism. As a rationalist, I am uncomfortable presenting findings and facts without trying to make sense of them. Sometimes in our teaching of psychology we overplay the methods for gathering and analyzing data and underplay the value of logical thought. I want students always to think about findings in relation to larger ideas and not to get the impression that the discipline is simply a piling of fact upon fact. As a functionalist, I want to know why, in terms of survival or other benefit, people (or animals) behave as they do. This latter bias does not dominate the book, but it certainly seeps through in many places. It is part of the reason why the first major unit (following the brief *Background to the Study of Psychology* unit) is entitled *Nature, Nurture, and Behavioral Adaptation* and deals with behavioral evolution and learning in back-to-back chapters. Natural selection and learning are the two reasons why behavior is functional, and I want students to know something about those processes, and their interaction, right from the start. This functionalist orientation also leads me, in the second half of the book, to pay more than the usual amount of attention to cross-cultural research and to behavioral processes as they operate in the contexts of people's everyday lives.

An issue faced by any textbook author is how much attention to pay to current as opposed to classic work. Clearly, the primary task of any introductory psychology text published today is to represent the field as it is today, but, in my view, that cannot be accomplished without a historical perspective. One cannot adequately depict psychology for the future by providing a snapshot of the present. Ideas and approaches in psychology or any scholarly field emerge and evolve over time, and a reasoned presentation must portray something of that evolution. This book contains plenty of current research, but it sets that research in the context of ideas that have been around for a long time and are associated with such names as Darwin, Pavlov, Piaget, Lewin, and Freud.

The Second Edition

The responses of instructors and students to the first edition convinced me not to modify the book's original goal, approach, style of writing, or overall organization. The second edition has the same chapters, in the same order, as the first, and the organization within chapters is only slightly changed. Yet substantial changes were made, for three purposes:

1. ***To keep the book current and lively*** To keep readers intellectually engaged, I have had to keep on learning, and therein lay most of the work and fun of revision. During the three-year revision period I skimmed thousands of research articles and chapters in every field of psychology, and read hundreds carefully, to determine which new developments warrant inclusion in the introductory course. The result was not so much the discovery of new ideas as the determination of how long-standing ideas are playing themselves out in current research and debate. The second edition contains nearly 600 new references, most of which are from the 1990s, in a total reference list of nearly 1,800. Of course that statistic means little by itself; the significance lies in whether the new references increase the vibrancy and accuracy of the book. Many of the choices were guided by user feedback. For instance, a number of adopters reported that their students would like to read more in the area of health psychology, and that request inspired a number of additions, most notably a new section in Chapter 17 entitled *Psychological Factors Affecting Medical Condition.* A more detailed description of changes made for the second edition can be found in the *Instructor's Resource Manual.*

2. ***To make the book even more accessible to the typical student*** Increased accessibility does not imply less depth or reduced emphasis on the logic and evidence behind ideas. A book becomes more accessible not by being "dumbed down" but by being "smartened up." The clearer the logic, and the more precisely it is expressed, the easier the book is to read and understand. From first page to last, the prose has been sharpened, tightened, and selectively trimmed.

   The second edition is also made more accessible through (a) *focus questions* in the margins (described more fully under *Features*) to encourage interactive reading; (b) additional illustrations closely integrated with the text; (c) a more liberal use of subheadings to provide more visual breaks and to help students see transitions from one idea to another; and (d) some reordering of topics to improve logical coherence, most notably the movement of split-brain research from Chapter 11 (Memory) to Chapter 6 (The Nervous System), and research on romantic love from Chapter 14 (Social Cognition) to Chapter 13 (Social Development).

3. ***To increase the emphasis on cultural influences*** The role of the cultural context in the development and workings of psychological processes, which was treated fairly thoroughly in the first edition, is emphasized even further in the second. This reflects the movement of psychology as a whole in a cross-cultural direction, is consistent with the book's overriding emphasis on the functions and ecology of behavior, and complements the book's considerable emphasis on the evolutionary bases of behavior. Cultural psychology is, in the second edition, introduced as a major psychological approach in Chapter 1 and treated as a dominant theme in Chapter 13 (*Social Development*). In many other chapters, new cross-cultural research is used to exemplify, qualify, or expand on an idea under discussion. Throughout the second half of the book (from Chapter 11 on) I have attempted to keep the reader aware of the cultural bases for what might from a parochial perspective seem to be "human nature."

General Organization

Over the decades, a relatively uniform way of dividing up and arranging topics has emerged and taken hold in introductory psychology. For the most part, I have followed that standard organization: It is comfortable; it fits reasonably well with the ways that research psychologists divide up the discipline; and it makes considerable logical sense. My slight departures reflect three developments in contemporary psychology: (1) Knowledge of heredity and evolution is increasingly recognized to be essential for understanding the origins and functions of basic psychological processes. (2) Developments in the study of basic learning processes (which has always been conducted largely with nonhuman animals) link that field more closely than ever to an evolutionary perspective. (3) Developments in cognitive psychology have strengthened the link between its componential model of the mind and the traditional psychometric model of the mind.

The book is divided into seven units, or parts, each of which consists of two or three chapters.

Part 1, *Background to the Study of Psychology*, has two relatively brief chapters. The first, on the history and scope of psychology, shows how some of psychology's most basic ideas and ways of conducting research have developed over time; and the second, on methods, lays out some general elements of psychological research that will be useful to students in later chapters. (If you prefer a more thorough discussion of statistics than Chapter 2 contains, you might supplement it with the first three sections of the Statistical Appendix.)

Part 2, *Nature, Nurture, and Behavioral Adaptation*, is devoted explicitly to two fundamental themes that reappear frequently in the book: (1) Behavioral mechanisms are formed through an interplay between genetic inheritance (nature) and environmental experience (nurture); and (2) behavior can be understood as adaptation to the environment, which occurs at two levels—the phylogenetic level (through natural selection) and the individual level (through learning). These themes are developed in three chapters. The first is on behavioral genetics; after laying out the fundamentals of the nature-nurture issue and the behavioral genetic approach, this chapter explores research on the heritability of intelligence and schizophrenia as well as various single-gene traits. The second chapter, on the evolution of behavior, includes the idea that even behaviors that are most highly prepared by evolution must develop, in the individual, through interaction with the environment. The third chapter, on basic processes of learning, includes the idea that learning mechanisms themselves are products of evolution.

Part 3, *Physiological Mechanisms of Behavior*, is a three-chapter discussion of the attempt to explain behavior in terms of the neural and hormonal mechanisms that produce it. The first chapter is a functional introduction to the nervous system and to the actions of hormones and drugs. The second is about basic mechanisms of motivation and arousal; here the ideas about the nervous system and hormones developed in the previous chapter are applied to the topics of hunger, sex, reward mechanisms, sleep, and emotionality. The third chapter is on sensory mechanisms, focusing mainly on hearing, vision, and pain. Although this unit emphasizes physiological mechanisms, it is not exclusively physiological. The discussions of motives and emotions pay ample attention to the role of environmental influences, and the discussion of sensation includes psychophysical methods and findings.

Part 4, *Cognitive Mechanisms of Behavior*, begins with a chapter on perception that flows logically from the chapter on sensation that concluded Part 3. Like the physiological approach, the cognitive approach attempts to explain behavior in terms of inner mechanisms; but it is concerned with mechanisms that are too complex to understand physiologically, and are therefore discussed in the metaphorical terms of information-processing models. The second chapter of this unit is on memory, the core topic of cognitive psychology, and the third is entitled *The Human Intellect.* This somewhat unusual chapter deals with three topics that are becoming ever more closely associated in contemporary psychology: (1) the structure of human intelligence, (2) the cognitive components of problem solving, and (3) the cognitive components of language, ability and the relation of language to thought. Throughout these chapters, the information-processing approach is highlighted but is tempered by ecological discussions that draw attention to the functions of each mental process and the environmental contexts within which they occur.

In sum, Parts 2, 3, and 4 are all concerned with basic psychological processes, and each part deals with those processes from a different explanatory perspective. Part 2 takes a functionalist, or adaptationist, perspective; Part 3 takes a physiological perspective; and Part 4 takes an information-processing perspective. This arrangement allows me to develop coherent arguments and to avoid the confusion that often comes when very different modes of explanation are mixed together. The remaining three parts are concerned with understanding the whole person and the person's relationships to the social environment.

Part 5, *Growth of the Mind and Person*, is a two-chapter unit on developmental psychology. The first chapter, on cognitive development, deals with the same large processes—thought and language—as did the last chapter of Part 4, but now from a developmental perspective. A major goal here is to show how the adult mind can be understood by identifying and describing the steps through which it is built in the developing child. The second chapter, on social development, is concerned with the changes in social relationships and life tasks that occur through the life span and with ways in which these relationships and tasks vary across cultures. This chapter also sets the stage for the next pair of chapters.

Part 6, *The Person in a World of People*, is a two-chapter unit on social psychology. The first chapter, on social cognition, is concerned with the mental processes involved in forming judgments of other people, perceiving and presenting the self in the social environment, and forming and modifying attitudes. The second chapter, on social influence, deals with compliance, obedience, conformity, cooperation and competition, group decision-making, and intergroup conflict. A theme running through this chapter is that of contrasting the normative and informational influences that stem from observing other people's behavior. The unit on social psychology is placed before the one on personality and mental disorders because the insights of social psychology—especially those pertaining to social cognition—are increasingly becoming incorporated into personality theories and approaches to understanding and treating mental disorders.

Part 7, *Personality and Disorders*, consists of three chapters on topics that students most strongly identify as "psychology" before they enter the course. The first chapter, on personality theories, focuses on the main explanatory concepts and lines of evidence underlying (a) Freud's theory, (b) post-Freudian psychodynamic theories, (c) humanistic theories, (d) social learning theories, and (e) trait theories of the person. The second chapter, on mental disorders, begins by discussing the problems involved in categorizing and diagnosing disorders, and then, through the discussion of specific disorders, emphasizes the notion of multiple causation and the theme that the symptoms characterizing disorders are different in degree, not in kind, from normal psychological experiences and processes. The final chapter, on treatment, offers an opportunity to recapitulate many of the main ideas of earlier chapters—now in the context of their application to therapy. Ideas from Parts 2, 3, 4, and 6 reappear in the discussions of biological, behavioral, and cognitive therapies, and ideas from the personality chapter reappear in the discussions of psychodynamic and humanistic therapies.

Although this ordering of topics makes the most sense to me, I recognize that other sensible arrangements exist and that time limits may prevent you from using the entire book. Therefore, each chapter is written so that it can be read as a separate entity, independent of others. Links are often made to material presented in another chapter, but most of these are spelled out in enough detail to be understood by students who have not read the other chapter. The only major exception falls in the physiological unit: Chapters 7 and 8, on motivation and sensation, assume that the student has learned some of the basic information presented in Chapter 6, on the nervous system. Specific suggestions for making deletions within each chapter can be found in the Instructor's Resources.

Features

The main pedagogical feature of this or any other textbook is, of course, the narrative itself, which should be clear, logical, and interesting. Everything else is secondary. I have avoided the boxes and inserts that are often found in introductory psychology texts, because such digressions add to the impression that psychology is a jumble of things that don't fit together very well. I have aimed, to the degree that the field allows it, to produce a logical flow of ideas.

One nondisruptive feature I have included is *focus questions*, located in the margins, which direct students' attention to the main idea, argument, or evidence addressed in the adjacent paragraphs of text. In a separate preface *To the Student* I offer advice for using the focus questions to help guide both the initial reading and the review of each chapter. The focus questions also offer instructors a means to make selective assignments within any chapter. The questions are numbered so instructors can easily let students know which issues will be fair game for exams. Many of the multiple-choice questions in the *Test Bank* are keyed by number to the focus questions. In my own course I will tell students that tests will contain brief essay questions that are *verbatim* selections from among the book's focus questions, along with multiple-choice questions that can be answered by those who can fully answer the focus questions.

Because the focus questions make a traditional end-of-chapter review unnecessary, the *Concluding Thoughts* section of each chapter expands on the broad themes of the chapter, points out relationships to ideas discussed in other chapters, and sometimes even offers a new idea or two for students to consider as they reflect on the chapter. *Concluding Thoughts* is followed by a brief section called *Further Reading*, which contains thumbnail reviews of several relevant and interesting books that are sufficiently nontechnical to be read by the first-year student. At the very end of each chapter, a tiny section called *Looking Ahead* is designed to entice the reader into the next chapter and to show its relationship to the chapter just read.

Supplements

An excellent study guide called *Focus on Psychology* has been prepared to accompany this text. Its author, Mary Trahan, is a cognitive psychologist at Randolph-Macon College who has a special interest in applying the insights of her field to the teaching of psychology. Trahan's guide is designed to be used in parallel with the reading of each textbook chapter, and its contents are linked to the textbook's focus questions. Students who used the first edition of the study guide praised it highly.

An extremely useful collection of *Instructor's Resources* has been prepared by Timothy M. Osberg, a specialist in developmental and clinical psychology, and Burt Thompson, a specialist in perception and learning, both at Niagara University. For each chapter of the textbook, Osberg and Thompson offer interesting class demonstrations and activities complete with handouts and transparency masters, provide writing exercises that test students' mastery of concepts, and suggest ways to elaborate on key ideas. I have contributed some general thoughts about teaching introductory psychology and some suggestions for using this text in a variety of time frames. Also provided in the *Instructor's Resources* are lists of recommended videos and software, including *The Mind* teaching modules, a comprehensive *Psychology Videodisc*, and the software package *PsychSim*, all available from Worth Publishers to accompany the text.

The Mind teaching modules are topic-specific videos edited from *The Mind* series by Frank Vattano at Colorado State University and produced by Worth Publishers in collaboration with WNET. There are 38 modules available on videocassette, with an Instructor's Guide that describes each module and offers suggestions for classroom use. There is also a two-sided CAV videodisc that includes 14 highlights from the modules, with a bar-coded Faculty Guide. The *Psychology Videodisc* offers video clips, still photographs, and illustrations covering all the major topics in the textbook. The accompanying Instructor's Guide describes the items and offers suggestions for using them to enhance lectures. A Computerized Index for the videodisc lets you preview the items available on any topic and assemble a Slide Show from the items you select. *PsychSim*, the award-winning interactive graphics simulations developed for Worth Publishers by Thomas Ludwig at Hope College, is a series of software modules in which students can play the role of researcher or subject and see how their decisions and responses affect the outcome of a given experiment. *PsychSim* is available for IBM PC, IBM with Windows 3.x, and Macintosh using Hypercard. An extensive set of acetate *Transparencies* includes illustrations from the textbook and other sources and is available on request.

A *Test Bank* of multiple-choice and essay questions has been prepared by Mary Trahan, with contributions by Timothy Shortell, Gregory R. McGuire, Norman R. Simonson, Peter R. Finn, William Prinzmetal, and me. We have keyed the test items to the focus questions in the text so that you can easily identify to your students the material they should concentrate on when studying for exams. The *Test Bank* is available paperbound and on disks in your choice of three test-generation systems: CompuTest (IBM, Apple), Brownstone (IBM), and Chariot (Macintosh).

Acknowledgments

Nobody writes a textbook alone. Hundreds of people contributed to the development and revision of this one, of whom I can list only a few here.

Herbert Terrace's inspiring introductory psychology course at Columbia University enticed me, at age 18, to turn away from a planned career in physics toward one in psychology. In graduate school at Rockefeller University, I was inspired and taught by Neal Miller, Jay Weiss, Bruce McEwen, William Estes, Peter Marler, and many others. My outlook has also been strongly influenced by my colleagues at Boston College, some of whom have contributed in very direct ways to the development of this book. They are (in alphabetical order) Dan Baer, Greg Ball, Ali Banuazizi, Norm Berkowitz, Hiram Brownell, Donnah Canavan, Randy Easton, Marc Fried, Murray Horwitz, Marianne LaFrance, Ramsay Liem, Michael Moore, John Mitchell, Gilda Morelli, Michael Numan, Nadim Rouhana, Bill Ryan, Karen Rosen, Jeanne Sholl, Kavitha Srivinas, Joe Tecce, and Ellen Winner. Of these, I owe special thanks to my friend Michael Moore, who worked closely with me on early drafts of the cognitive and developmental units, and who carefully read and brilliantly critiqued early drafts of the other units.

I thank, too, my friends Daniel and Hanna Greenberg, educational innovators and philosophers who have contributed greatly to my own thinking in both psychology and education. And, more than anyone else, I thank my wife, Anita, and my son, Scott, who have contributed immeasurably to my growth and to the development of the ideas in this book. It is dedicated to them.

Every draft of the manuscript was reviewed by experts in each area of psychology and notably successful teachers of the introductory course. I was greatly impressed by the seriousness with which the reviewers approached this task; they taught me a great deal, and each one influenced the final outcome. For their thoughtful, sometimes challenging, and always helpful reviews, I thank:

Michael L. Atkinson, *University of Western Ontario*
Ali Banuazizi, *Boston College*
Steve R. Baumgardner, *University of Wisconsin-Eau Claire*
Toni L. Blum, *Stetson University*
Galen Bodenhausen, *Michigan State University*
John L. Caruso, *University of Massachusetts, Dartmouth*
Patricia G. Devine, *University of Wisconsin, Madison*
Michael J. Dougher, *University of New Mexico*
Bruce Earhard, *Dalhousie University*
Peter R. Finn, *Indiana University*
Bennett G. Galef, Jr., *McMaster University*
Preston E. Garraghty, *Indiana University*
Jill M. Hooley, *Harvard University*
Justin M. Joffe, *University of Vermont*
Ronald W. Johnson, *St. Francis Xavier University*
Lloyd Kaufman, *New York University*
Theresa M. Lee, *University of Michigan*
Thomas W. Lombardo, *University of Mississippi*
Leonard S. Mark, *Miami University (Ohio)*
Merrill J. May, *Weber State University*
Sallyanne McColgan, *clinical psychologist*
Matt McGue, *University of Minnesota*
Patricia A. McMullen, *Dalhousie University*
Gilda A. Morelli, *Boston College*
Daniel D. Moriarty, Jr. *University of San Diego*
James L. Mosley, *University of Calgary*
Darwin Muir, *Queen's University*
Michael Numan, *Boston College*
Randy J. Nelson, *The Johns Hopkins University*
Elizabeth Weiss Ozorak, *Allegheny College*

Hal Pashler, *University of California, San Diego*
David G. Payne, *SUNY-Binghamton*
Sergio M. Pellis, *University of Lethbridge*
Ed L. Pencer, *St. Francis Xavier University*
Steve Anderson Platt, *Northern Michigan University*
David C. Rowe, *University of Arizona*
Irwin Silverman, *York University (Ontario)*
John J. Skowronski, *Ohio State University at Newark*
Kavitha Srinivas, *Boston College*
James R. Stellar, *Northeastern University*
Ross Thompson, *University of Nebraska, Lincoln*
William P. Wallace, *University of Nevada, Reno*
Gillian Watson, *University of British Columbia*
Mark Winter, *Southern Utah University*
Otto Zinser, *East Tennessee State University*

This edition of the text owes much to the reviewers who helped shape the first. Once again, I thank:

George W. Albee, *University of Vermont*
Lewis M. Barker, *Baylor University*
John B. Best, *Eastern Illinois University*
Sharon Brehm, *State University of New York, Binghamton*
Nathan Brody, *Wesleyan University*
Michael F. Brown, *Villanova University*
Robert B. Cialdini, *Arizona State University*
Stanley Coren, *University of British Columbia*
Katherine Covell, *University of Toronto*
Martin Daly, *McMaster University*
Richard B. Day, *McMaster University*
V. J. DeGhett, *State University of New York, Potsdam*
Timothy J. DeVoogd, *Cornell University*
Donald D. Dorfman, *University of Iowa*
David C. Edwards, *Iowa State University*
Gilles O. Einstein, *Furman University*
Nancy Eisenberg, *Arizona State University*
Owen R. Floody, *Bucknell University*
Janet J. Fritz, *Colorado State University*
Mary Gauvain, *Scripps College*
Don J. Gawley, *AT&T Bell Laboratories*
Daniel Gilbert, *University of Texas, Austin*
G. P. Ginsburg, *University of Nevada, Reno*
W. Larry Gregory, *New Mexico State University, Las Cruces*
Ed Haas
Benjamin Harris, *University of Wisconsin, Parkside*
Bryan Hendricks, *University of Wisconsin, Marathon Center*
Stephen P. Hinshaw, *University of California, Berkeley*
Jill M. Hooley, *Harvard University*
Valerye A. Hunt, *Fraser Valley College*
John C. Jahnke, *Miami University of Ohio*
Sybillyn Jennings, *Russell Sage College*
Saul M. Kassin, *Williams College*
Terry J. Knapp, *University of Nevada, Las Vegas*
Mary F. Lombard, *Regis College*
Alan Marks, *Berry College*
Donald H. McBurney, *University of Pittsburgh*
David B. Miller, *University of Connecticut, Storrs*
Douglas Mook, *University of Virginia*
Greg Moran, *University of Western Ontario*
Daniel D. Moriarty, Jr., *University of San Diego*
Harry G. Murray, *University of Western Ontario*
Lynn M. Musser, *Purdue University*
John B. Nezlek, *College of William and Mary*
Julie K. Norem, *Northeastern University*
Tibor Palfai, *Syracuse University*
Peter Platenius, *Queen's University*
Dennis R. Proffitt, *University of Virginia*
Leon Rappoport, *Kansas State University*
Marc Riess, *Middlebury College*
Joseph F. Rychlak, *Loyola University of Chicago*
Neil J. Salkind, *University of Kansas*
Steven M. Smith, *Texas A & M University*
Kathryn T. Spoehr, *Brown University*
James R. Stellar, *Northeastern University*
Ross Thompson, *University of Nebraska, Lincoln*
Mary Trahan, *Randolph-Macon College*
Eric Turkheimer, *University of Virginia*
Jonathan Vaughan, *Hamilton College*
W. Scott Wood, *Drake University*
Murray S. Work, *California State University, Sacramento*

I have been blessed by the opportunity to work with two outstanding developmental editors—Phyllis Fisher on the first edition and Susan Seuling on the second. Because I stubbornly insisted that they not change any of my writing, but only make suggestions, these two remarkably talented people had to become my teachers. They had to convince me of their views, to the point where their views became mine, in order to improve the book. In the process they helped me become a better thinker, psychologist, and writer than I was before. Phyllis, who has an extensive background in psychology as well as editing, helped shape the intellectual content of the book, for example by making me far more sensitive than I was before to issues of gender and culture. Susan showed me how to sharpen the thought in ways that make the book's logic clearer and more accessible. To both of them I am deeply grateful.

Many people at Worth Publishers deserve my heartfelt thanks. Betsy Mastalski, Barbara Anne Seixas, Demetrios Zangos, Patricia Lawson, Matthew Dvorozniak, and others worked diligently and skillfully to produce the book and make it a work of art.

Natick, Massachusetts
January 1994

Peter Gray

TO THE STUDENT

Welcome to your psychology textbook. I hope you will enjoy it. It is about a question that, to me, is one of the most fascinating anyone can ask: What makes people feel, think, and behave the way they do? That, really, is what psychology is about. In this book you will read, in different units, about different approaches to answering that big question; and you will discover dozens of specific findings and ideas that help to answer it.

I hope that as you read this book you will allow yourself to become intrigued by psychology; that you will not focus too narrowly on getting a good grade; that you will think about, challenge, and discuss with others the book's ideas; and that you will keep constantly in mind that ideas in psychology come from people who are basically no different from you—so your own insights, questions, and thoughts are legitimate. Psychology is a science, and the essence of science is this: We do not accept anything on authority. It doesn't matter *who* says that something is or isn't true; what matters is the *evidence*—the facts and logic upon which the ideas are based, which are open for evaluation by any thinking person. In this book I have tried to present both the main ideas in psychology and some of the evidence. Each page is offered for your consideration, not for your unquestioned acceptance.

Using the Focus Questions for Study and Review

To help you study and review the text, I have supplied for each chapter a set of *focus questions*, which can be found in the book's margins. Each question directs your attention to the main idea or line of evidence discussed in the paragraph or paragraphs that follow it. On page 3, for example, you will find that the first focus question of Chapter 1 is: ■ *How can psychology be defined, and what are three ways of expanding on that definition?* That question tells you exactly what the adjacent paragraphs are about. If you read it first, before reading the paragraphs, it will help you to focus your attention and to read actively—you will read to answer the question. The questions become even more effective in guiding your study if you turn them into your own words and spend a little time thinking about them before reading to answer them. For example, after reading the first question you might say to yourself, "OK, how does this author define psychology? Will his definition match my own view of what psychology is about? And what are his three ways of expanding on the definition?"

Single focus questions will often break down into several questions when you think about them. For instance, the second question of Chapter 1 is: ■ *How did Descartes' version of dualism help pave the way for a science of behavior?* When you think about that question, you might wonder, "What exactly is *dualism*? And what is

Descartes' specific version of it? And how did his version help provide the basis for the scientific study of behavior?" After posing those questions in your own words, you are ready to read and think about the answer presented in the adjacent paragraphs. Your thought about the answer presented there will help prepare you for the next focus question, which introduces a criticism of Descartes' theory.

After reading the paragraphs that answer a particular focus question, stop for a moment and think about the answer, and maybe jot down your own note in the margin concerning the answer. In later chapters you will discover that many focus questions ask about the evidence for or against some idea. Be sure to think especially carefully about the answers you read to those questions and ask yourself whether or not you find the evidence convincing. At first the focus-question approach to reading your textbook may seem awkward and annoying. Your natural tendency may be to read straight through the text and ignore the focus questions, or to glance at them without thinking about them as you read. But experience has shown that, with practice, the recommended way of using the questions becomes natural and pays big dividends in comprehension, enjoyment, and test performance. You may also apply this skill to your reading of textbooks in other courses. In those books you will probably not find focus questions already written for you, but you can use such cues as section headings and opening sentences to generate your own focus questions as you read. For more information about this study method you might turn to page 338, where textbook reading is discussed in the context of a more general discussion of ways to improve memory.

Although using the focus questions in the recommended way will probably increase the time you need to read each chapter the first time through, it will probably decrease the total time you need to learn and remember the chapter's ideas and lines of evidence. Your first reading will be more purposeful and thoughtful, so the time required for re-reading or review will be reduced. The focus questions are also a very useful aid in reviewing. To review each chapter read each focus question again and try to answer it. If you cannot answer a question fully, read that portion of text again, and if the question still gives you trouble mark it and ask your instructor or study companions to help you clarify it.

An excellent study guide called *Focus on Psychology* has been written by Mary Trahan and published as a separate volume to be used with this textbook. The contents of the guide are tied closely to the textbook's focus questions, so you can use the guide to supplement the method of study just described. The guide asks questions and provides exercises that help you to elaborate on the focus questions as you read, and it also contains review questions and practice tests that you can use at various points to assess your understanding. Students who used the study guide in the first edition praised it highly and credited it for improving their grade.

Using the Book's Other Features

In addition to the focus questions, you should also pay close attention to the *numbered figures* in each chapter. In some cases a figure will help you understand a point that would be difficult to grasp from words alone, and in other cases it will provide you with information that supplements or complements what is in the text. Whenever the text says, "see Figure _______," take a few moments to study that figure and read the caption. Many of the figures are graphs of data that back up an idea described in the text. If you have not had much experience reading graphs, please do not feel embarrassed about mentioning that to your instructor. He or she might then present some sample graphs in class and explain how to read them.

Another feature is the use of ***bold italics*** to highlight important terms. I suggest that you *not* devote much effort, on your first reading, to learning term definitions. Rather, read with the aim of understanding and thinking about the main *ideas* and the lines of evidence supporting or refuting them. In that process you will learn many of the terms, in the context of the ideas, without explicitly trying to learn them. The bold italics may be useful, however, in your later review. As you are reviewing the margin notes, look also for each of the bold italics terms and check your knowledge of its meaning. These terms are also defined in the *glossary* at the back of the book. If an important term has been defined in an earlier chapter, it is sometimes, but not always, defined again when it reappears. If it is not defined, you can use the glossary to find both the term's definition and the number of the page on which it was first used.

A feature that this book shares with other books and articles in psychology is the use of *reference citations,* which can be found in the narrative on nearly every page. Each citation consists of the name of one or more researchers followed by a year. Sometimes both the name (or names) and the year are in parentheses, such as *(Jones & Smith, 1984)* and other times, when the name or names are part of the sentence, only the year is in parentheses, such as *According to Alice Jones (1987)*. . . . In either case, the year refers to the year of publication of an article or book, by the person or persons named, which describes more fully the idea or the research study being mentioned or discussed. The full reference to that article or book can be found in the *References* section at the back of the textbook. At first you may find these citations disruptive to the flow of your reading, but you will soon learn to read right through them. Their purpose is to give credit to the people whose work or ideas are being described and to give you the opportunity to look up, and read more about, any ideas or research findings that intrigue you. In addition, at the end of each chapter, in a section called *Further Reading,* you will find brief reviews of several interesting books that you might use to supplement your study of specific areas of psychology.

And now—let's discuss psychology.

Peter Gray

Ben Shahn

BACKGROUND TO THE STUDY OF PSYCHOLOGY

PART 1

You and I stand at a moment in time preceded by Aristotle, Descartes, Freud, and millions less known. Psychology today is the accumulated and sifted ideas of all people before us and with us who have attempted to fathom the mysteries of the human mind. It is also, by its own definition, a science, using methods as objective as the subject matter will allow. In this background unit, we examine the history and methods of psychology.

Before Psychology: Preparing the Intellectual Ground

Philosophical Developments: From Spirit to Machine

Nineteenth-Century Physiology: Learning About the Machine

Darwin and Evolution: A New Unity of Person and Nature

The Evolution of Psychology: A History of Alternative Perspectives

Origins of Experimental Psychology: How Can the Mind Be Studied?

Developments in Zoological (Comparative) Psychology

Views from the Clinic: Understanding Individual Minds

Cultural and Social Psychology: The Social Nature of the Mind

The Rise of Modern Cognitive Psychology

Psychology as a Discipline and a Profession

The Connections of Psychology to Other Scholarly Fields

Psychology as a Profession

THE HISTORY AND SCOPE OF PSYCHOLOGY

CHAPTER 1

1. *How can psychology be defined, and what are three ways of expanding on that definition?*

Note to students: This is the first focus question of the book. A good way to study the book is to read each focus question before you read the adjacent paragraphs of text. After completing the paragraphs, you might then look back at the question to see if you can answer it. For more study ideas turn back to the book's preface, and consult "To the Student."

The human being, as far as any human being can tell, is the only creature that contemplates itself. We not only think, feel, dream, and act, but wonder why and how we do these things. Such contemplation has taken many forms, ranging from just plain wondering, to folk tales and popular songs, to poetry and literature, to formal theologies and philosophies. A little more than a century ago, human self-contemplation took a scientific turn, and we call that science *psychology*.

Psychology is the *science* of *behavior* and the *mind*. ***Behavior*** refers to the observable actions of an individual person or animal. ***Mind*** refers to an individual's sensations, perceptions, memories, thoughts, dreams, motives, emotional feelings, and other subjective experiences. As a ***science***, psychology endeavors to answer questions through the systematic collection and logical analysis of objectively observable data. The data in psychology are always based on observations of behavior, because behavior is directly observable and mind is not; but psychologists often use these data to make inferences about the mind.

Beyond the simple definition just presented, we can characterize psychology in many ways. Three have been particularly useful to me in developing this book:

1. ***Psychology is a set of questions.*** Psychology is the set of all questions about behavior and mind that are potentially answerable through scientific means. Some of the questions are very broad, with answers that are necessarily complex, qualified, or tentative: What is the nature of human intelligence? How are memories stored and retrieved? In what ways are people influenced by their perceptions of what other people think of them? Other questions are narrower, with more specific or definite answers: Why does a mixture of blue light and yellow light look white to people? What parts of the brain are most directly involved in the ability to understand and produce language? At what age do children begin to fear strangers? Each subfield of psychology probes a different set of broad and narrow questions.
2. ***Psychology is a set of procedures for answering questions.*** Psychology, like any science, has many theoretical perspectives, methods, and tools that guide and aid in the process of answering questions. Chapter 2 covers psychology's methods in a general way, and all the subsequent chapters are concerned with particular methods for answering particular questions.
3. ***Psychology is a product of history.*** Like any organized human endeavor, psychology is what it is today because of a historical evolution. Viewed this way, psychology is a set of questions, methods, perspectives, and tentative answers that have been passed on and modified through successive generations. To understand psychology today, it is necessary to know something of that history.

In reading this chapter on the history of psychology, think of history not simply as a record of the past but also as an explanation of the present.

Before Psychology: Preparing the Intellectual Ground

Before a science of psychology could come to pass, human beings had to conceive of and accept the idea that questions about human behavior and the mind can be answered scientifically. By the mid-nineteenth century, developments in philosophy, physiology, and evolutionary biology allowed this emerging idea to flourish.

Philosophical Developments: From Spirit to Machine

René Descartes

Descartes' speculations, in the seventeenth century, about reflexes and the interaction of the body and soul in controlling voluntary behavior were an important step in the direction of a scientific analysis of human behavior.

For the philosophical roots of psychology one could easily go back to the ancient Greeks, who speculated about the senses, the human intellect, and the physical basis of the mind in ways that often seem remarkably modern. But such ideas became dormant in the Middle Ages and did not begin to sprout again until about the fifteenth century (the Renaissance) or to take firm hold until the eighteenth century (the Enlightenment). A key thinker in the transition between prescientific and scientific views of the human being was the French scholar René Descartes (1596–1650). As a mathematician he developed what is still studied as Cartesian geometry, and as a philosopher he speculated about human behavior and the mind.

Descartes' Version of Dualism

Descartes inherited from earlier philosophers the theory of ***dualism***, the idea that each human being consists of two distinct entities—body and soul. The body is a purely physical machine, which operates according to natural law and can be understood by means of science. The soul, in contrast, is a spiritual entity, which operates according to free will rather than natural law and, therefore, cannot be understood by means of science. The radical aspect of Descartes' theory in the seventeenth century was not his belief in dualism but his emphasis on the body.

■ ***2. How did Descartes' version of dualism help pave the way for a science of behavior?***

Descartes contended that much of human behavior does not involve the soul at all. In his *Treatise of Man* (1637/1972), he offered detailed descriptions of the body's machinery to show how behavior might be controlled mechanically. Although little was known about the nervous system in his time, Descartes' basic idea about the mechanical control of movement is similar to our modern understanding of reflexes, which are involuntary responses to stimuli (see Figure 1.1). Descartes believed that even quite complex behaviors could be controlled by such means. In fact, in keeping with the doctrine that nonhuman animals do not have souls, he contended that all forms of behavior that we share with such animals can occur without involvement of the soul.

In Descartes' view the essential things humans do that other animals cannot are to think (defined by Descartes as conscious deliberation and judgment) and to use thoughts to guide our actions. But even when discussing thinking, Descartes placed more emphasis on the body than did previous philosophers. He suggested that the soul, though not physical, has a physical location; it resides in a small organ buried between the two hemispheres (halves) of the brain (see Figure 1.2). Threadlike structures, which we now call nerves, bring sensory information by physical means into the brain, where the soul receives the information and, by nonphysical means, thinks about that information. On the basis of those thoughts, the soul then wills movements to occur and executes its will by triggering physical actions in nerves that in turn act upon muscles. Because of such emphasis on the soul's interaction with the body, Descartes' version of dualism is called ***interactionism***.

■ ***3. Why is Descartes' theory, despite its intuitive appeal, unsuitable as a foundation for a complete psychology?***

Descartes' theory is appealing to many people even today, because it acknowledges the roles of sense organs, nerves, and muscles in behavior without violating people's intuitive feeling that at least some of their behavior results from their freely made decisions. But the theory has serious limitations, both as a philosophy

Figure 1.1 ***Descartes' depiction of a reflex***

Descartes believed that reflexes occur through purely mechanical means. In describing this figure, Descartes (1637/1972) suggested that the fire causes movement in the nearby particles of skin, pulling on a "thread" (marked CC) going to the brain, which in turn causes a pore to open in the brain, allowing fluid to flow through a "small conduit" to the muscles that withdraw the foot. What Descartes called a "thread" and a "small conduit" are today called nerves, and we now know that nerves operate through electrical means, not through physical pulling or the shunting of fluids.

and as a foundation for a science of psychology. As a philosophy it stumbles on the question of how a nonmaterial entity (the soul) can have a material effect (move the body), or how the body can follow natural law and yet be moved by a soul that does not (Campbell, 1970). As a foundation for psychology the theory sets strict limits, which few psychologists would accept today, on what can and cannot be understood scientifically. The whole realm of thought, and all behaviors that are guided by thought, are out of bounds for scientific analysis if they are the product of a willful soul.

Materialism and Empiricism

■ **4.** ***How did Hobbes's materialism and the subsequent development of empiricist philosophy help lay the ground for a science of psychology?***

At about the time that Descartes was developing his interactionist theory of dualism, an English philosopher named Thomas Hobbes (1588–1679) was going much further. Hobbes argued that spirit, or soul, is a meaningless concept and that nothing exists but matter and energy, a philosophy known as ***materialism.*** In Hobbes's view, all human behavior, including the seemingly voluntary choices that we make, can in theory be understood in terms of physical processes in the body, especially the brain. Conscious thought itself, he argued, is purely a product of the brain's machinery. Most of Hobbes's work was directed toward the implications of materialism for politics and government, but his ideas helped initiate a school of thought about the mind known as *British empiricism*, which was carried on by such English philosophers as John Locke (1632–1704), David Hume (1711–1776), and James Mill (1773–1836).

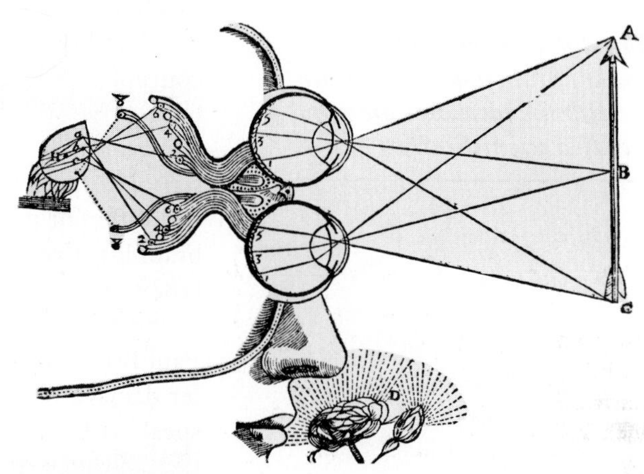

Figure 1.2 ***Descartes' depiction of how the soul receives information through the eyes***

Descartes believed that the human soul is housed in the pineal gland, depicted here as the tear-shaped structure in the center of the head. In describing this figure, Descartes (1637/1972) suggested that light from the arrow enters the eyes and opens pores in structures that we now know as the optic nerves. Fluid flows from the eyes through the opened pores, causing movement in the pineal gland, which, in Descartes' terms, "renders the idea" of the arrow to the soul.

Empiricism, in this context, refers to the idea that all human knowledge and thought ultimately derives from sensory experience (vision, hearing, touch, and so forth). The British empiricists' central idea was that the human mind consists of basic units, or elementary ideas (such as the idea of a chair), which originate from sensory experiences. These elementary ideas become associated (linked together) in certain ways based on the pattern of one's sensory experiences, and those links in turn provide the basis for the chaining together of ideas into the flow that we call *thought*. You will read more about empiricist philosophy in later chapters and see it contrasted with ***nativism***, the view that elementary ideas are innate to the human mind and do not need to be gained through experience. The important point for now is simply that the empiricist philosophers believed that thought is not a product of free will, but rather a reflection of one's experience in the physical world. From this point of view, thought can be studied scientifically.

Nineteenth-Century Physiology: Learning About the Machine

■ **5.** ***How did the nineteenth-century conception of the nervous system inspire a theory of behavior called*** **reflexology?**

The nineteenth century was a time of great advance in physiology, the science of the body's machinery. One especially important development for the later emergence of psychology was an increased understanding of reflexes. The basic arrangement of the nervous system—consisting of a central nervous system (brain and spinal cord) and peripheral nerves that connect the central nervous system to sense organs and muscles—was well understood by the beginning of the century. In 1811 in England, Charles Bell demonstrated that nerves entering the spinal cord contain two separate pathways, one for carrying messages into the central nervous system from the skin's sensory receptors, and one for carrying messages out to operate muscles. In experiments with animals, scientists began to learn about the neural connections that underlie simple reflexes, such as the withdrawal response to a pin prick, and also found brain areas that, when active, could either enhance or inhibit such reflexes.

Some of these physiologists began to suggest that all human behavior occurs through reflexes, that even so-called voluntary actions are actually complex reflexes involving higher parts of the brain. One of the most eloquent spokespersons for this view, known as ***reflexology***, was the Russian physiologist I. M. Sechenov. In a monograph entitled *Reflexes of the Brain*, Sechenov (1863/1935) argued that every human action, "[b]e it a child laughing at the sight of toys, or . . . Newton enunciating universal laws and writing them on paper," can in theory be understood as reflexes. All human actions, he claimed, are initiated by stimuli in the environment. The stimuli act on the person's sensory receptors, setting into motion a chain of events in the nervous system that culminates in the muscle movements that constitute the action. Reflexology was an important predecessor to a school of thought in psychology called *behaviorism* (to be discussed later).

■ **6.** ***How did discoveries of localization of function in the brain help establish the idea that the mind can be studied scientifically?***

Another important development in nineteenth-century physiology was the concept of ***localization of function*** in the brain—the idea that specific parts of the brain serve specific functions in the control of mental experience and behavior. In Germany, Johannes Müller (1838) published the idea that the different qualities of sensory experience come about because the nerves from different sense organs excite different parts of the brain. Thus, we experience vision when one part of the brain is active and hearing when another part is active. In France, Pierre Flourens (1824) performed experiments with animals showing that damage to different parts of the brain results in different kinds of deficits in animals' ability to move. And Paul Broca (1861), also in France, published clinical evidence that people who suffer damage to a very specific area of the brain's left hemisphere lose the ability to speak without losing other mental abilities. All such evidence concerning the relationships between mind and brain helped lay the groundwork for a scientific psychology because it gave substance to the idea of a material basis for mental processes. The discovery of localization of function also led to the idea that natural divisions may exist among various mental processes, and that the mind can be understood by identifying those basic processes and discovering how they interact. As you will see later, this is an idea that is especially important today in the psychological approach called *cognitive psychology*.

Darwin and Evolution: A New Unity of Person and Nature

■ 7. *How did Darwin's theory of natural selection offer a scientific basis for functional explanations of behavior?*

In 1859, the English naturalist Charles Darwin (1809–1882) published *The Origin of Species*, which was destined to revolutionize biology, mark a new age in philosophy, and provide, along with the developments in physiology, a scientific grounding for psychology. Darwin's fundamental idea was that living things have arrived at their present shape through a long evolutionary process involving natural selection, in which those individual organisms whose inherited characteristics were best adapted to their environment survived and reproduced while others died. Because of evolution, each part of any given plant or animal can be examined for the function it serves in allowing the individual to survive and reproduce in its natural environment. To understand, for example, why one species of bird has a stout beak and another has a slender beak, one must know what foods the birds eat and how they use their beaks to obtain those foods. The same principle that applies to anatomy applies to behavior. Through natural selection, living things have acquired innate predispositions to behave in ways that promote their survival and reproduction in their natural environment. A key word here is *function*. While the physiologists were concerned with the neural mechanisms of behavior, Darwin was concerned with the functions of behavior, that is, with the ways in which an individual's behavior functions to help the individual survive and reproduce.

The expression of emotion

There is no doubt about the emotion shared by these two members of closely related species. Research by contemporary psychologists supports Darwin's notion that expressions such as joy and sadness have an evolutionary basis. You will find a discussion of this topic in Chapter 4.

In *The Origin of Species* Darwin discussed only plants and nonhuman animals, but in later writings he made it clear that he viewed humans as no exception. Humans also evolved through natural selection, and human anatomy and behavior could be analyzed in the same terms used to analyze those of other living things. In a book entitled *The Expression of the Emotions in Man and Animals*, Darwin (1872/1965) illustrated how evolutionary thinking can contribute to a scientific understanding of human behavior. There he argued that the basic forms of human emotional expressions (such as laughing and crying) are inherited, as are those of other animals, and may have evolved because of survival advantages associated with the ability to communicate one's emotions or intentions to others of one's kind. Darwin, perhaps more than anyone else, helped convince the intellectual world that human beings, despite their pretensions, are as much a part of nature as any other creature and can be understood through the methods of science. The world was ripe for psychology.

The Evolution of Psychology: A History of Alternative Perspectives

Psychology became a recognized scientific discipline in the latter half of the nineteenth century. Then came an evolutionary period in which various competing schools of thought arose, each offering a new view on subject matter and methods appropriate to this new science. As in most intellectual disputes, a degree of truth lay on every side. Psychology today can be understood as a synthesis of what had seemed to be contradictory ideas in the turmoil of its development. Let us look at some of the schools of thought, or approaches in psychology, for what they can tell us about psychology today.

Origins of Experimental Psychology: How Can the Mind Be Studied?

The first research psychologists were Germans who were impressed by the success of laboratory methods in physiology and wished to apply similar methods to the study of the mind. Their view was that the proper place to begin this study was with the simplest kinds of mental processes—simple sensations, memories, and judgments. If these could be understood, then the science could progress to more complex processes. Among these first psychologists, the one most often credited as the founder of our science was Wilhelm Wundt (1832–1920).

Wundt and the Laboratory Dissection of the Mind

■ **8.** ***Why is Wundt considered the founder of scientific psychology? How are two of his key ideas illustrated by his reaction-time experiments?***

Although others had conducted psychological research before him, Wundt is considered the founder of scientific psychology for two reasons. First, he wrote the first textbook of psychology that defined the discipline as a science and systematically surveyed the psychological research that had been done (published in two parts, in 1873 and 1874). Then, in 1879, at the University of Leipzig, he opened the first university-based laboratory of psychology. Because this event represented the official acceptance of this new science by a respected university (Blumenthal, 1985), it is usually taken to mark psychology's birth as an independent science. The first official graduate students in psychology were Wundt's students.

Wilhelm Wundt

Wundt's opening of a laboratory of experimental psychology at the University of Leipzig in 1879 is often taken to mark the birth of psychology as a science.

Before starting his psychological research, Wundt had worked as an assistant to the eminent physiologist Hermann von Helmholtz on projects such as measuring the speed of neural impulses. From this work, Wundt acquired the insight that mental processes, as products of the nervous system, do not occur instantaneously but rather take time. One of his aims in psychology was to measure the speed of simple mental processes. The fastest-occurring processes would be the most elementary, the "atoms of the mind." After identifying these he could begin to test hypotheses about how these elements combine to form more complex mental processes.

One of Wundt's methods was to test people in two reaction-time tasks, one slightly more complex than the other, and to subtract the shorter time from the longer to determine the time required for the mental step or steps that differentiated the two tasks. Thus, in one experiment (Kendler, 1987), the simple task was to release a telegraph key, connected to an electrical timer, as quickly as possible when a light came on. This took an average of 0.20 second. In the more complex task, the person was to release one key, held down by the left hand, if the light was red, and a different key, held down by the right hand, if the light was green. The average reaction time for this was 0.29 second. Subtracting the former from the latter, Wundt determined that the time needed to categorize the color and decide which key to release was 0.09 second. By comparing this with times for other kinds of judgments, Wundt could rank different judgments in terms of their simplicity, where simplicity was defined as the quickness with which they could be performed. Wundt's idea that complex mental processes can be understood as sequences of more elementary processes and his idea that the elementary processes can be measured as reaction times are foundations for the field of research that today is called *cognitive psychology*.

Titchener's Structuralism and the Problem of Introspection

The school of psychological thought that descended most directly from Wundt's approach is called ***structuralism***, a term used not by Wundt but by one of his students, Edward Titchener (1867–1927). Titchener, an Englishman educated at Oxford, went to Leipzig to earn a Ph.D. degree in psychology under Wundt and then moved to the United States to head the newly established department of psychol-

Edward Titchener

A student of Wundt's, Titchener was one of the first psychologists in North America. His goal was to learn about the structure of the mind through the introspective analysis of its elements.

■ **9. *What was the goal of Titchener's structuralism? Why did his introspective approach to the structure of the mind fail as a scientific method?***

ogy at Cornell University. Like Wundt, Titchener believed that the proper goal of psychology is to identify the elements of the mind and to determine how they combine with one another. Titchener's aim was to learn about the *structure* of the mind through analyzing elementary conscious experiences, which he considered to be the mind's building blocks.

Titchener was influenced not only by Wundt but also by British empiricist thought. This led him to believe, unlike Wundt, that all of the elements of the mind could be tied directly to sensory experience. Thus, Titchener's goal was to identify the most elementary sensory experiences. His prime method was ***introspection***, a method that Wundt had occasionally used but had more often opposed as unscientific (Blumenthal, 1985). *To introspect* literally means *to look inward* to examine one's own conscious experience. Titchener believed that through careful training people could learn to introspect objectively and scientifically. He and his students would listen to simple sounds or look at simple sights and try to separate their experience of the sound or sight into its elements. Through such work, Titchener concluded that every sensation has four basic dimensions: quality, intensity, duration, and clarity (Kendler, 1987). Thus, he might describe the sensation produced by a particular flash of light as blue, strong, brief, and clear.

Today, nearly all psychologists agree that Titchener's method failed. Wundt had been right in warning about the limitations of introspection. Suppose that you, a student of Titchener's, look into your mind while gazing at a flash of light and decide that the sensation it produces has four elemental qualities, and that I, trained in introspection by another master, look into my mind while gazing at the same flash and decide that there are only three. To you, the clarity and intensity of the patch are two separate elements, but I claim they are one. How can we resolve our disagreement? Whose introspection is more accurate? Are we just using words differently, or do our two minds really differ in some fundamental way? I can't look into your mind to see what you see when you look at the flash, and you can't look into mine. The problem is that introspection is a private technique, and science requires public techniques. A public technique is one that produces data that can be observed by outsiders, not just by the individual user of the technique.

James's Functionalism

A contemporary of Titchener's, William James (1842–1910) held professorships at Harvard in both philosophy and psychology (the latter beginning in 1889). James is famous today as a great thinker, writer, and teacher who helped make psychology known to the intellectual world and who established some of its philosophical foundations. He had a small laboratory at Harvard, primarily for teaching purposes, but he was not by nature a laboratory scientist. In describing the work of the German experimentalists, James (1890/1950) wrote, only half in jest, "This method taxes patience to the utmost, and could hardly have arisen in a country whose natives could be *bored*." More important, James opposed Wundt and Titchener's view that one can understand the structure of the mind by analyzing its elementary parts. In one article, he compared their approach to that of a person attempting to understand a house by analyzing the content of each of its bricks (James, 1884). James argued that to understand a house or a mind one must first ask what it is for, and then must look at the whole thing and its larger parts to see how it fulfills its purposes. Because of his emphasis on the purposes and functions of the mind, James's psychological perspective is called ***functionalism***.

William James

A contemporary of Titchener's, James is considered to be the founder of the school of philosophical and psychological thought called *functionalism*. He believed that the main objective of psychology should be to understand the mind's functions, not its structures.

While the structuralists were most influenced by physiology, which attempted to understand the elementary machinery of behavior, James and other functionalists were most influenced by Darwin, who had shown that behavior can be understood in terms of its purposes without analyzing the elementary mechanisms

■ **10.** ***How was James's functionalism different from Titchener's structuralism? How did James's use of introspection differ from Titchener's?***

through which it occurs. To James, purposes or goals are the most important aspects of human consciousness and actions, which must be understood broadly and cannot be characterized as products of more elementary conscious experiences. To illustrate this perspective, in the first chapter of his classic textbook *The Principles of Psychology*, James (1890/1950) contrasted Romeo and Juliet's attraction to each other with that between iron filings and a magnet:

> Romeo wants Juliet as the filings want the magnet; and if no obstacles intervene he moves toward her by as straight a line as they. But Romeo and Juliet, if a wall be built between them, do not remain idiotically pressing their faces against the opposite sides like the magnet and the filings with the card. Romeo soon finds a circuitous way, by scaling the wall or otherwise, of touching Juliet's lips directly. With the filings the path is fixed; whether it reaches the end depends on accidents. With the lover it is the end which is fixed, the path may be modified indefinitely.

James was eclectic in his views about methods. He respected the experimental method, but his own contributions were more philosophical. He relied heavily on introspection, but used it more loosely and broadly than did Titchener, as a source of ideas rather than proof, and made no claim that he was being rigorously scientific. To develop a theory about emotions he looked into his own mind while in various emotional states and described what he was feeling; and to get ideas about the concept of the self (what people mean when they say *I* or *me*) he thought about the various meanings this concept had to him and the functions it served in his daily life. You will read more about James's view of emotions in Chapter 7 and his view of the self-concept in Chapter 14.

Figure 1.3 ***A pioneering woman in psychology: Mary Calkins***

In the nineteenth century women were barred from Ph.D. programs in psychology. In 1890, against the stern admonitions of Harvard's president, William James admitted Mary Calkins into his graduate seminar. When she joined the seminar, all of the other students dropped it, apparently in protest, and James tutored her alone. Calkins later completed the requirements for the Ph.D., outperforming all of the male students on the qualifying exams, yet Harvard refused to grant her the degree. Despite this obstacle she went on to a distinguished career as a researcher and professor at Wellesley College and became the first woman president of the American Psychological Association. (From Scarborough & Furumoto, 1987.)

James's functionalism did not lead to a lasting, unified school of thought in psychology, partly because it was based so heavily on introspection, but it provided a core of ideas that have since been pursued by others through more rigorous means. One of the many students inspired by James was Edward Thorndike (1874–1949), who studied under James for a while at Harvard and then went to Columbia University for a Ph.D. and a long career as a professor of educational psychology. Thorndike was one of the first psychologists to perform systematic experiments on the learning process, with both animals and humans. His main contribution was to develop an explicitly functionalist theory of learning, describing the learning process in terms of its value to the learner (discussed in Chapter 5). Another of James's students, who was a pioneer in another sense, is discussed in Figure 1.3.

Gestalt Psychology

■ **11.** ***How did a perceptual effect, the phi phenomenon, help promote Gestalt psychology as an alternative to structuralism?***

In 1912, two years after James's death, a German psychologist named Max Wertheimer (1880–1943) published an article on a perceptual effect that he labeled the *phi phenomenon*. The phenomenon can be described as follows: Take a single light and blink it at a certain rapid rate (about 20 times per second) against a dark background. What you see (no surprise) is a single blinking light. Now add a second light, near the first, and blink it at the same rate but in alternation with the first, so that when the first is on the second is off and vice versa. The sensory result is not what you would expect if you consider the two lights separately. You do *not* see two blinking, stationary lights, but rather a single, unblinking light moving rapidly back and forth. In his paper on this phenomenon, Wertheimer (1912) pointed out that it violates the atomistic view of perception favored by Wundt and Titchener. The two blinking lights together produce in the observer a sensory experience of movement that does not exist in the physical lights themselves or in the sensory experience that either light produces alone. The movement can be understood only as a sensory product of the whole complex stimulus—both blinking lights together.

■ **12. *How was the Gestalt school of thought applied to descriptions of perception and problem solving?***

Based on this and other studies that followed, Wertheimer and a group of other German psychologists—including Kurt Koffka, Wolfgang Köhler, and Kurt Lewin—founded a school called ***Gestalt psychology***. *Gestalt* is a German word that can be translated roughly as *organized shape*, or *whole form*. The premise of this new school was that the mind must be understood in terms of organized wholes, not elementary parts. A melody is not the sum of individual notes, a painting is not the sum of the individual dots of paint, an idea is not the sum of its elementary concepts. The meaningful units of consciousness are whole, organized constructs—whole melodies, whole scenes, whole ideas—that cannot be understood by analyzing elementary judgments and sensations of the sort that Wundt and Titchener studied.

Most early research in Gestalt psychology was in the area of perception (discussed in Chapter 9). In many laboratory demonstrations, Gestalt psychologists showed that in conscious experience whole objects and scenes take precedence over component parts. For example, when looking at a chair, people perceive and recognize the chair as a whole before noticing its arms, legs, and other parts. Moving away from the area of perception, Köhler (1917/1973) performed experiments on problem solving with chimpanzees. He argued that these animals hit upon solutions through sudden flashes of insight, in which the whole solution (such as moving a box to a position underneath a banana dangling on a string in order to reach it) comes at once rather than in bits and pieces. Other Gestalt psychologists, including Kurt Lewin, took their principles into the realm of social psychology in ways that are discussed in Chapters 14 and 15.

Art and perceptual experience

Long before Gestalt psychologists considered the question of part-whole relationships, artists were exploring this and other perceptual experiences. In his painting *The Garden*, Giuseppe Arcimboldo (1527–1593) takes advantage of the viewer's tendency to look at the whole. For a clearer impression of the parts, turn the book upside down.

Gestalt psychology started in Germany, but by the mid-1930s, with the increased threats against Jews and their sympathizers that accompanied German Nazification, all of its founders—including Wertheimer, Koffka, Köhler, and Lewin—had moved to North America and established research laboratories in various colleges and universities there (Ash, 1985). Gestalt psychology eventually lost its position as a discrete school of thought, but it became integrated into many different lines of psychological work.

Developments in Zoological (Comparative) Psychology

All the perspectives in psychology that we have considered so far defined the field as the science of the human mind—the normal, adult human mind at that (and some might add male and European to the list of adjectives). But other psychologists, at the same time, were developing broader conceptions of psychology. Psychologists studying nonhuman animals defined psychology as the science of all animal behavior, human and nonhuman. Their approach was influenced by Darwin, who had argued convincingly for the continuity of life. If humans are biologically related to other animals, then some principles of behavior that apply to other animals may likewise apply to humans.

The psychological study of nonhuman animals came to be called ***comparative psychology*** because it often entailed the comparison of various animal species (including humans) with each other. That label, though still used, is somewhat misleading because it does not indicate what is being compared (the term might be taken to refer to the comparison of different groups of people rather than different species of animals). Moreover, most studies of animal behavior, which are traditionally classed in the "comparative" category, are of one species only and are thus not truly comparative. A more accurate label that encompasses all psychological research on nonhuman animals is ***zoological psychology*** (Dewsbury, 1992).

John B. Watson

On the ground that the proper study of psychology is observable, verifiable behavior and not hidden mental processes, Watson founded the behaviorist approach to the science. The goal of *behaviorism* was to describe the environmental causes of behavioral effects.

Watson and the Development of Behaviorism

One of the most influential of the early zoological psychologists was John B. Watson (1878–1958). He began studying animals as a graduate student at the University of Chicago in 1901, and continued such research as a professor at Johns Hopkins University. Over the years, he performed experiments with monkeys, chickens, dogs, cats, frogs, and fish (Hothersall, 1990), but his usual research animal was the rat, which he studied in mazes and other testing apparatuses.

Watson was impressed with the amount he could learn about an animal's behavior with no consideration of the animal's mind. Laws of behavior could be described that related changes in behavior directly to changes in the environment to which the animal was exposed, with no mention of thought or other mental processes. For example, a rat's route and rate of movement through a maze toward food could be predicted on the basis of where food had been placed during previous trials, without reference to the rat's "knowledge," "perceptions," "decisions," or other mental events. In fact, Watson became convinced that any reference to the mind only obscured the explanation, because no direct way existed to observe the animal's mind. All one could observe were the external environmental conditions (such as the shape of the maze and the type of reward in its goal box) and the animal's actions. As he reflected on this, Watson also became convinced that mental constructs were of no value in explaining human behavior. A human has access to his or her own mind through introspection, but, like other critics of Titchener, Watson argued that introspection is not a scientific technique and can lead only to irresolvable debate. Science, argued Watson, must limit itself to what can be publicly observed.

■ **13. *What are principles of behaviorism, as set out by its founder, John B. Watson?***

Based on such considerations, Watson began to advocate a new perspective in psychology, which he called ***behaviorism***. In 1913, he published a manifesto entitled "Psychology as the Behaviorist Views It," the main ideas of which can be summarized as follows:

1. The proper subject of study in psychology is not the mind but *behavior*, defined as the observable actions of people and other animals.
2. The appropriate goal of psychology is to identify the environmental conditions that cause individuals to behave in particular ways.
3. The achievement of this goal does not require reference to the mind or to any unobservable events occurring within the individual. In fact, such reference should be avoided. It is enough simply to describe the lawful environment-behavior relationships.
4. No fundamental difference exists between human behavior and that of the animals, nor between the methods that should be used to study humans and other animals.

Many psychologists throughout North America responded enthusiastically to Watson's idea. They wanted to throw out the armchair philosophy and convoluted terminology that they saw as carry-overs from stuffy European traditions. Within a decade after Watson's 1913 article, behaviorism replaced Titchener's structuralism as the dominant school in North American psychology, and it remained in that position into the mid-1960s. Watson himself, however, was forced to leave the academic world before the school that he had founded reached full bloom. In 1920, an extramarital affair with his research assistant Rosalie Rayner became public, and the scandal was cause for Johns Hopkins University to fire him and for no other university to pick him up. He continued publishing books and articles on behaviorism, and he and Rayner (whom he later married) conducted some highly publicized research with nursery school children. But his main employment after 1920 was in the advertising world. In an autobiographical sketch, Watson (1936) wrote, perhaps wistfully, "I began to learn that it can be just as thrilling to watch the growth of a sales curve of a new product as to watch the learning curve of animals and men."

Watson (1924) argued that all of behavior is essentially reflexive. That is, he argued that all of behavior can be understood as behavioral reactions (responses) to events in the environment (stimuli). For this reason, his brand of behaviorism is often called *S-R psychology*, where *S* stands for stimulus and *R* for response. But not all of Watson's successors in behaviorism agreed with this reflex formulation of all behavior.

Skinner and a New Version of Behaviorism

Of the many behaviorists who succeeded Watson, by far the most influential was B. F. Skinner (1904–1990). As a graduate student at Harvard, Skinner developed a new kind of apparatus for studying learning in animals and a new way of describing the learning process. In 1938, he published a book entitled *The Behavior of Organisms*, which summarized his research and the ideas behind it. The book brought him instant fame among psychologists, and from not long after its publication until his death, more than 50 years later, he was the recognized leader of behaviorism.

■ **14. *How was Skinner's version of behaviorism similar to Watson's, and how was it different?***

Skinner agreed with the four tenets of Watson's behaviorism outlined above, but explicitly disagreed with Watson's idea that all, or even most, of behavior can be understood as reflexes. Skinner's emphasis was not on stimuli that precede responses, but rather on stimuli that are *consequences* of responses. He coined the term *operant response* to refer to any behavioral action that operates on the environment to produce some consequence (such as food, water, or electric shock). The founda-

Figure 1.4 ***B. F. Skinner and the Skinner box***

Skinner, who devoted a long career to the study of animal learning and to wide-ranging speculation about human behavior, was the acknowledged leader of behaviorism for the past four decades or so. To study operant responses in rats and other animals, he invented an apparatus widely known as a Skinner box.

tion of his theory lay in the simple observation that operant responses increase or decrease in frequency depending on their consequences. If a hungry rat receives a pellet of food each time it presses a lever, the rat will press the lever with increasing frequency (see Figure 1.4). Elaborating on this observation, Skinner and his followers discovered numerous reliable relationships between the rate at which an animal will produce an operant response and the nature, timing, and probability of the consequences of the response (discussed in Chapter 5).

In emphasizing the role of consequences in controlling behavior, Skinner was following in the footsteps of E. L. Thorndike, who, as noted earlier, was influenced by William James's functionalism. Skinner's behaviorism is grounded in functionalism. Its focus is not on the mechanics of behavior, but on the relationship between behavior and its beneficial or harmful effects upon the behaving animal. Skinner is frequently referred to as an *S-R* psychologist, like Watson, but he objected to that label (Epstein, 1991; Skinner, 1974). If the *S-R* label is taken to mean only that Skinner preferred to describe behavior in terms of observable stimuli and responses, without reference to the mind, then the label is apt. But if *S-R* is taken, as it usually is, to suggest a reflex theory of behavior ($S \rightarrow R$), then the label does not apply to Skinner.

Like Watson, Skinner had a knack for stating his case strongly, clearly, and sometimes in terms that seemed deliberately designed to provoke controversy. The mere title of one of his books, *Beyond Freedom and Dignity* (1971), elicited a storm of protest. His basic argument in that book was that concepts such as freedom and dignity, like all other concepts referring to the mind, have no explanatory value. Skinner's message was that human behavior is a product of the conditions in which a person grows and lives, and terms like *freedom*, *dignity*, *willpower*, *decisions*, and so on only obscure our understanding of the lawful relationships between behavior and its consequences. The hero is merely the person who has been rewarded often for actions we call "good," and the villain is the person who has been rewarded often for actions we call "bad."

Ethology

In the 1930s, at a time when behaviorism was flourishing in North America, a very different approach to the study of behavior was taking hold in Europe. The leaders of this movement—most notably Konrad Lorenz (1903–1989) in Austria and Nikolaas Tinbergen (1907–1988) in Holland—were genuine animal enthusiasts who studied animals for their own sake, not as substitutes for humans. Rather than focusing on domesticated breeds in laboratory settings, they preferred to study wild animals in their natural habitats—woods, fields, and ponds. Lorenz named this science ***ethology***, a term that today can be defined simply as the study of animal behavior in the natural environment (Gould, 1982). Ethology originated as a branch of zoology, not psychology. But neither nature nor good scientists respect the arbitrary disciplinary boundaries that universities establish for administrative purposes. Ethologists and psychology's behaviorists were studying the same thing, animal behavior, and it was inevitable that the two would begin to interact.

15. ***How did ethology and behaviorism differ? Why did they later begin to merge?***

At first the interactions between ethologists and behaviorists took the form of arguments. Both groups were studying animal behavior, but from entirely different points of view and with very different methods. The behaviorists were interested almost solely in learning. They brought to their work a philosophical bias, dating back to British empiricism, that behavior is a reflection of previous experience and the way to understand it is to understand learning. They were impressed by the degree to which they could train animals in the laboratory to behave in very unnatural ways by controlling the animals' experiences. Skinner even trained pigeons to play a version of Ping-Pong.

Konrad Lorenz and followers

Ethologists described a behavior known as *imprinting* in which newly hatched ducks or geese follow and become attached to the first moving thing they see or hear. These geese, which were hatched by Lorenz in an incubator, responded to him as if he were their mother. You will learn more about ethologists' research on mechanisms of learning in Chapter 5.

In contrast, ethologists were influenced most strongly by Darwin; they were impressed by the highly complex and adaptive behavior patterns that animals display without any apparent learning, at least not learning as defined by behaviorists. Lorenz studied courtship patterns in ducks and geese, and Tinbergen studied mating rituals in stickleback fish and various species of gulls. Their experiments showed that these behaviors occur in essentially normal form even in animals that had never previously observed the behaviors nor been rewarded for practicing them. Lorenz and Tinbergen developed the idea that many survival-related behavior patterns are "wired into" the animal's nervous system and are triggered at the appropriate time by the co-occurrence of specific stimuli in the environment (such as the sight of an appropriate mate) and events inside the body (such as the heightened production of sex hormones in the spring).

By the 1960s, however, developments in both ethology and behaviorism began to bring the two schools together in cooperative ways. Behavioral researchers were increasingly reporting biologically based constraints on animals' learning abilities and describing differences in the kinds of responses that different species could learn (Shettleworth, 1972). For example, they reported that migratory birds are biologically predisposed to learn landmarks that help guide their migratory flight, and that seed-eaters are predisposed to learn the locations of seeds. Behavioral researchers increasingly accepted the idea that learning itself is a set of processes that came about through evolution, and that quite different learning mechanisms may have evolved to serve different survival needs. At the same time, some ethologists began to turn their attention to mammals, and they found mammal behavior to be far more flexible and dependent on prior experiences than that of insects, fish, and birds, which had been the focus of earlier ethological studies. As you will see in Chapter 4, some ethologists even went on to study humans, and they helped develop new insights about the interactions between innate predispositions and environmental experiences in human behavior.

Physiological Psychology

As discussed earlier, the progress made during the nineteenth century in understanding the nervous system helped make possible a science of psychology. Once psychology emerged as a formal discipline, however, most researchers preferred to ignore the nervous system, which is extraordinarily complex and difficult to study, and concentrate instead on explaining behavior in terms of hypothetical mental processes or in terms of relationships between behavior and events in the environment, without worrying about how they are executed in the brain.

■ **16.** ***How did Lashley's early work in physiological psychology challenge Watson's behaviorism, and how did it help unite North American comparative psychology with European ethology?***

But not all early psychologists ignored the nervous system. One of several who did not was Karl Lashley (1890–1958), who had been one of Watson's graduate students at Johns Hopkins. Lashley learned a lot about observing animal behavior and constructing well-designed experiments from Watson, but he was not satisfied with Watson's *S-R* mode of explanation (Bruce, 1991). After receiving his degree in 1915, he went on to conduct numerous experiments with rats, monkeys, and other animals, aimed at identifying the neural bases of learning. His work led him to conclude that complex behavior does not consist of chains of reflexes, as Watson had believed, but rather is the output of complex neural programs in the brain, which are preformed by heredity and modified by experience (Lashley, 1930, 1951). His research showed that these programs can generate well-organized behaviors, such as running, jumping, or climbing, even without any sensory input. By providing evidence that learning operates not by piecing together new chains of reflexes but by modifying inherited neural programs, Lashley helped unite North American comparative psychology with the ethology that was developing in Europe.

Lashley was one of the pioneers in what we now call ***physiological psychology***—the attempt to understand the physiological mechanisms, in the brain and elsewhere, that organize and control behavior. As you will discover in Chapter 7, physiological psychology has been especially successful in learning about basic motivational and emotional mechanisms that we share with other animals, such as those involved in hunger, sex, fear, and aggression.

Views from the Clinic: Understanding Individual Minds

Simultaneously with early developments in experimental and comparative psychology, which were centered at universities, another important strand in the twine of psychology was developing in a very different setting—the offices and clinics of health professionals who were attempting to help people overcome psychological problems. The most influential of these clinical pioneers was Sigmund Freud (1856–1939).

Freud and Psychoanalysis

■ **17.** ***How did Freud arrive at his concept of an unconscious mind that influences conscious thought and behavior? In what ways was Freud's work different from that occurring in academic circles, and how did it broaden the range of psychological inquiry?***

Freud was a creative thinker whose work and ideas were outside of the mainstream of academic research and thought. Unlike the other pioneers we have been discussing, Freud was not a university professor. He was a physician who specialized in neurology and, from 1886 on, worked with patients at his private office in Vienna. He found that many people who came to him had no detectable medical problems but seemed to suffer from their memories, especially their memories of disturbing events in their early childhood. In many cases they could not recall such memories consciously, but cues in their behavior led Freud to believe that disturbing memories were present nevertheless, buried in what he referred to as the *unconscious mind.* From this insight, Freud developed a method of treatment in which his patients would talk freely about themselves, and he would analyze what they said in order to uncover the buried memories. The goal was to bring the memories to the patient's conscious attention, so his or her conscious mind could then work out ways of dealing with them.

Freud coined the term ***psychoanalysis*** to refer both to his method of treatment and to his theory of the mind (discussed in Chapters 16 and 17). The most funda-

Sigmund Freud

As a Viennese physician specializing in neural disorders, Freud came to believe that many of his patients' physical and mental problems originated as a way of keeping certain disturbing memories out of consciousness. He went on to develop a theory of the mind and an approach to psychotherapy called *psychoanalysis*. Here he is shown in his office in Vienna in 1938.

mental aspect of his theory was his concept of a dynamic unconscious mind. While Wundt, Titchener, James, Wertheimer, and others had defined the mind entirely in terms of conscious experience, Freud argued that the conscious mind is only the tip of the iceberg, and that the bulk of the mind is unconscious. The unconscious mind not only contains buried memories, but it is also the source of instinctive wishes or drives, particularly sexual and aggressive drives. Although the conscious mind has no direct access to the contents of the unconscious, it is nevertheless strongly affected by the unconscious. Conscious thoughts and wishes can be understood as products of the unconscious mind that have been modified to become acceptable to the conscious mind. For example, a child's wish to kill a parent might be so terrifying that it would be converted unconsciously into an obsessive conscious fear that the parent might die. The child would never be aware of the original wish unless it arose later in the course of psychotherapy.

Freud considered his methods to be scientific, but relatively few psychologists in academic circles have ever agreed with him on that. Most have argued that his approach leaves too much room for interpretation. So many alternative ways of putting the clues together exist that any given analysis is at least as much the analyst's creation as a true account of the mind of the person being analyzed. Still, many research psychologists today do accept Freud's general theory that unconscious mental processes influence conscious thought and action. Freud's work also helped bring psychology's attention to a wide range of issues that the field had previously ignored. The role of childhood experiences in later development, the sexual drive and its various manifestations, and the whole realm of irrational, emotional behavior and thought became appropriate subjects for psychological research.

Humanistic Psychology

After Freud, other clinically-based psychologists developed alternative theories (discussed in Chapter 16). Some of these were variations of Freud's psychoanalysis, but others were radically different. Included among the latter are those that make up ***humanistic psychology***.

18. *In what sense does humanistic psychology present an optimistic view of human nature? What is the goal of humanistic therapy?*

Humanistic psychology, led by such therapists and scholars as Carl Rogers (1902–1987) and Abraham Maslow (1908–1970), became most prominent in the 1960s. As a general theory, humanistic psychology presents an optimistic view of human beings. It centers on the idea that each person has an *actualizing tendency*, an inborn set of drives that go beyond basic animal needs and lead people to engage in creative activities, which contribute to their own satisfaction and to society at large (Maslow, 1970; Rogers, 1963). This actualizing tendency can be stunted, however, by parents, teachers, and others who criticize children's self-initiatives, thereby convincing them that they are unable or unworthy. Rogers (1951) and other early humanistic therapists reported that people who came to them for therapy usually had negative views of themselves, which prevented them from taking control of their lives. Unlike psychoanalysis, humanistic psychology focuses on people's conscious minds, not their unconscious minds. A central goal of humanistic therapy is to help people acquire positive self concepts.

Like psychoanalysis, humanistic psychology has had a major impact on the practice of psychotherapy, has influenced the way people in our culture think and talk about themselves and others, and has strongly influenced the views that nonpsychologists have about psychology. Research psychologists often criticize humanistic psychology as unscientific. Yet, as discussed in Chapter 16, this approach has generated some interesting research and, with its emphasis on people's conscious thoughts, has influenced the course of modern cognitive and social psychology.

Cultural and Social Psychology: The Social Nature of the Mind

Those of us who are products of Western cultures tend to think of the human mind as the property of the individual. You have your mind, I have mine. But think about that for a minute. Think about how much overlap exists between your mind and mine, and how dependent both of our minds are on the culture in which we live. Were it not for that overlap, I could not be writing to you and you could not make sense of what I am writing. We share knowledge and general ways of thinking and behaving because we are part of the same broad culture.

Leonard Doob (1990) has used the example of sneezing to illustrate the pervasiveness of social and cultural influences on human thought and behavior. At one level, sneezing is a simple, reflexive reaction to irritation in the nose. But Doob asked questions that carry us beyond the reflex level: "Will [the person who senses the urge to sneeze] try to inhibit this reflex action? What will he say, what will bystanders say, when he does sneeze? What will they think of him if he fails to turn away and sneezes in their faces? Do they and he consider sneezing an omen and, if so, is it a good or bad omen?" Clearly, to answer such questions, we would have to know about the social context in which the urge to sneeze occurred and the beliefs and customs of the culture in which the sneezer was raised.

As another illustration, imagine that you grew up on a deserted island without ever having contact with another human being. What kind of person would you be? You would lack the knowledge, ideas, values, and customs that characterize and unify people who live intertwined lives in other parts of the world. Even more important, you would lack language, and lacking that you would lack the ability for verbal thought, the kind of thought that uses words as mental symbols to represent objects, events, and ideas. Biologically, you would be a recognizable human being, but psychologically you would not. Aristotle was right when, 23 centuries ago, he declared that human beings are by nature social animals.

Cultural Psychology

The psychological perspective that emphasizes most strongly the dependence of the human mind on the culture in which it develops is ***cultural psychology*** (Shweder, 1990). It can be defined as the study of the psychological differences among people living in different parts of the world, and of the ways by which people's thoughts, feelings, and behavior are influenced by their culture. Only recently has this approach begun to take shape as a recognized field within psychology. Yet its basic premises go back to the very beginnings of the discipline.

■ **19.** ***What are the basic premises of cultural psychology as advocated by Wundt and Vygotsky?***

One of the first psychologists to advocate a cultural psychology was none other than Wilhelm Wundt, the same man who is credited with founding experimental psychology. Wundt argued that the experimental method he practiced in the laboratory was useful for understanding the elementary machinery of the mind, but could not, by itself, constitute a complete psychology (Blumenthal, 1985; Leahey, 1992). He claimed that the higher workings of the mind depend on culture—the language, knowledge, beliefs, and other forms of information that accumulate in a population over time and are passed from one generation to another. These cultural variables influence all aspects of motivation, emotion, thought, and action. To understand these influences, Wundt argued, psychologists would have to move out of the lab and observe people in different parts of the world as they engage in their normal, daily activities. Within any given culture, psychologists would also have to study history in order to understand how the culture evolved over time and affected the psychology of its people. Wundt himself read extensively about the languages, religions, and customs of people in different parts of the world, and between 1900 and 1920 he published a ten-volume work, *Völkerpsychologie*, on cultural psychology.

Another groundbreaker in cultural psychology was Lev Vygotsky (1896–1934). A leader of psychology in the Soviet Union during the early years after the revolution that formed that country, Vygotsky was strongly influenced by the ideas of Karl Marx. Like Marx, he considered the human mind to be a product of history. From this perspective, each culture, which has its own distinct history, has produced a somewhat different version of the human mind—for example, the "American mind" or the "Russian mind." Vygotsky's research focused on the ways in which children, through their social interactions with adults, acquire the mind of their culture. Some of his ideas on this issue are discussed in Chapters 12 and 13.

Social Psychology

In contrast with cultural psychology, ***social psychology*** is a well established, long accepted, large subfield of contemporary psychology (discussed in Chapters 14 and 15). Gordon Allport (1968) aptly defined this subfield as "an attempt to understand and explain how the thought, feeling, and behavior of individuals are influenced by the actual, imagined, or implied presence of others."

■ **20.** ***How does social psychology differ from cultural psychology? What role did Lewin play in the development of modern social psychology?***

Unlike cultural psychology, which emphasizes cross-cultural differences, history, and the long-term processes of human development, social psychology usually emphasizes the here and now. Its goal is to identify and understand general psychological processes through which people are influenced by other people at any given moment. Social psychology is concerned with such issues as conformity, obedience, the effects of others' expectations, and the ways by which people form impressions of other people and attitudes about social issues. Also unlike cultural psychology, social psychology relies heavily on experimental procedures, often conducted in university laboratories with college students as subjects. It is less concerned with cultural diversity than with general principles of social interaction that are presumed to cut across cultures. Cultural psychologists often criticize this approach on the grounds that the general principles it extracts from laboratory findings could be unique to the particular age group, cultural group, and time in history occupied by the subjects of such experiments.

One of the pioneers of social psychology as a laboratory science was Kurt Lewin (1890–1947). Originally a Gestalt psychologist working in Germany, Lewin emigrated to the United States in the early 1930s. As an observer of the early stages of Nazism and as an immigrant to a new country, he was profoundly aware of the powerful influence of the social environment, for good or ill, on the thinking and behavior of individuals. Lewin's Gestalt background led him to reject the *S-R* behaviorism that dominated much of American psychology at the time, but he embraced the experimental method. He developed a perspective in social psychology called *field theory* (discussed in Chapter 15), which centers on the idea that each human being, at any given moment, exists in a psychological "field" made up of forces that tend to push or pull the person in various directions (Lewin, 1951). These forces include the person's own goals and values, and the person's beliefs about what others expect him or her to do.

The Rise of Modern Cognitive Psychology

Psychologists often speak of a "cognitive revolution" occurring in the 1960s and '70s, during which ***cognitive psychology*** replaced behaviorism as the dominant school of thought in North American psychology. The term *cognition* refers to knowledge, and cognitive psychology can be defined as the study of people's ability to acquire, organize, remember, and use knowledge to guide their behavior. Although cognitive psychologists study the mind, they do so not through introspection but rather through inferences drawn from observable behavior. Cognitive psychologists develop models or theories about mental processes that mediate behavior, and test them in controlled situations where people would be expected to behave in one way if the model is correct and in a different way if it is incorrect.

■ **21.** ***What were some historical precursors to modern cognitive psychology?***

Although cognitive psychology began to come into its own in the 1960s, it was not suddenly born then. Years before, some research psychologists who called themselves behaviorists—such as Clark Hull (1882–1952) and Edward Tolman (1886–1959)—were in fact practicing what would now be called cognitive psychology. Their brand of behaviorism was sometimes called *S-O-R* behaviorism to distinguish it from Watson's *S-R* behaviorism. The *O* in this formulation stands for hypothetical processes occurring inside the organism, which mediate the relationship between stimuli and responses. Tolman (1948), for example, studied maze learning in rats and developed the view that rats acquire a *cognitive map*, a mental representation of the spatial layout of the maze, and use that inner map to guide their movements (discussed in Chapter 5). Going back still further, Wilhelm Wundt was clearly a cognitive psychologist whose laboratory methods and ideas were remarkably similar to those of cognitive psychologists today (Blumenthal, 1985).

Influence of the Computer

Perhaps the main stimulant for the blossoming of cognitive psychology in the past few decades has been the emergence of computer technology. In every age the concepts that people have of the brain and mind are influenced by the kinds of machines that are available as analogies (Rose, 1973). Descartes explicitly compared mechanical aspects of human behavior with the hydraulic mechanisms used to move the robot-like statues that decorated public gardens in seventeenth-century France. Nineteenth-century reflexologists compared the brain to the telephone switchboard, an analogy that was also implicit in the theories of some of the early twentieth-century behaviorists. Today the machine that most influences people's conception of the brain is the computer. A computer receives coded information (the input), reorganizes the information, compares it to other information stored in its memory, performs calculations on it, and uses the results to determine what signals to send to the computer's output system. All this is analogous to what the brain does: input is analogous to the receipt of information by sensory systems, output is analogous to behavioral action, and everything in between is analogous to thought.

■ **22.** ***How did the computer analogy contribute to the rise of modern cognitive psychology?***

The workings of a computer can be understood in two quite different ways. One is to learn about its hardware, that is, the electrical system through which the computer operates; this is analogous to learning about the physiology of the brain. The other is to learn about the computer's software, that is, its program or set of programs. A computer program can be understood as a set of clearly specified steps for operating on specific kinds of information. The steps have to be written in such a way that the machine can follow them, but they can also be translated into English. We can write them out in the form, "First do _______, then _______, then _______. . . ." When cognitive psychologists talk about understanding the mind, they are usually talking about something similar to specifying the steps of a computer program. They are asking: Through what steps is information transformed as a person perceives, remembers, thinks, and makes decisions? From this perspective, if you can program a computer to respond in the same way as a human does to a set of input stimuli, then you have provided a plausible explanation of the human's behavior (Simon, 1992).

Influences of Piaget and Chomsky

Aside from the role of computer technology, the cognitive revolution was also spurred by several interesting lines of research and theory about the mind. Among

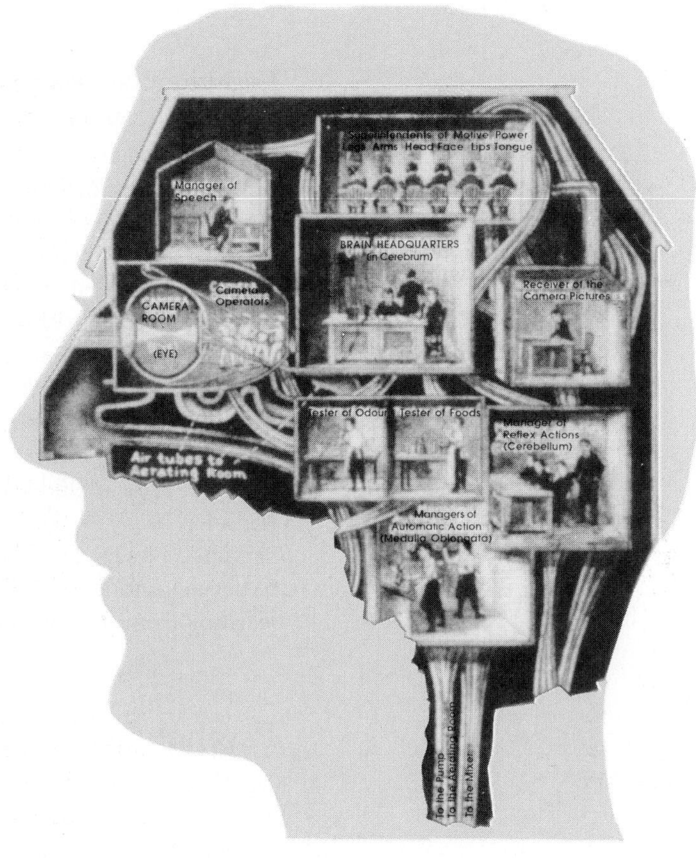

An early analogy

The use of analogies to understand the brain can go beyond machines. In the 1930s a children's encyclopedia used the notion of a factory to represent the complex information-organizing activities of the brain.

■ **23. *How did Piaget's and Chomsky's ideas influence the cognitive revolution?***

these was the work of Jean Piaget (1896–1980), a Swiss psychologist who studied children's reasoning abilities. Based on data collected in hundreds of experiments, Piaget developed the idea that children undergo a series of mental metamorphoses from infancy through adolescence, at each of which they become able to reason in a qualitatively different and more advanced way. He attempted to describe the manner of thinking that characterizes each stage of this development in terms of hypothetical mental constructs called *schemes*. Roughly, a scheme can be thought of as a blueprint for acting upon the world and for using information about the world to control those actions. By 1960 American psychologists were aware of Piaget's work, and many began to perform experiments to test some of his ideas. Although Piaget's specific, highly mathematical manner of describing schemes did not catch on, his general approach of trying to explain behavior in terms of internal mental constructs was widely adopted and contributed greatly to the cognitive movement.

A second name for special mention is that of Noam Chomsky (1928–), who is not a psychologist but a linguist. In 1957, Chomsky published a book entitled *Syntactic Structures*, which spurred a revolution in linguistics and had an enormous impact on psychology as well. In this book, and even more explicitly in later writings, Chomsky argued that language must be understood as a system of mental rules, not as stimulus-response chains as behaviorists had proposed. He also argued that these rules are constrained and partially predetermined by the innate capacities of the human mind. Thus, Chomsky attacked behaviorism on its two most vulnerable fronts at once: the cognitive front, in arguing that language must be understood in terms of mental rules, and the biological front, in arguing that these rules are in part wired into the brain as a result of evolution. Many psychologists eagerly began to test Chomsky's ideas experimentally. The results they published contributed to the rapid growth of *psycholinguistics* (the study of the psychological bases for human language), and this work was very much a part of the cognitive revolution.

Cognitive Psychology Today

Cognitive psychology cannot be described today as a single approach or school of thought. Rather, it is a constellation of approaches unified only in their attempt to explain observable behavior by reference to hypothetical mental structures or processes. Some cognitive psychologists, who call themselves *information-processing theorists*, use the computer analogy directly and try to spell out their theories of the mind in terms that a computer can follow. Others warn that the computer analogy can be misleading. The human being is not just an "information-processing device," but also a biological survival machine with motives and emotions that are foreign to computers but color all aspects of human thought and behavior. Some psychologists have even proposed that Freud's psychoanalytic theory falls within the range of cognitive psychology; they have argued that a full account of human behavior must include the irrational as well as the rational aspects of our behavior (Erdelyi, 1985). Moreover, cognitive psychology has in some ways merged with social and cultural psychology. Increasingly, cognitive psychologists are attempting to develop models that account for cultural differences and include special rules for learning from the social environment (Simon, 1992; Sternberg, 1985a).

Psychology as a Discipline and a Profession

Psychology today is an extraordinarily vast and diverse field. The historical account that you have just read describes not just an evolution but a mushrooming. Each school of thought brought with it new questions about the mind and behavior, and new techniques for trying to answer them. Psychology today is an amalgam of all of those questions and techniques.

The Connections of Psychology to Other Scholarly Fields

In concluding this chapter, you might think for a few minutes about the place of psychology among the spectrum of disciplines that form the departments of a typical college of arts and sciences. Figure 1.5 illustrates a scheme that I call (with tongue only partly in cheek) the *psychocentric theory of the university*. The disciplines are divided roughly into three broad areas. One division is the *natural sciences*, the sciences of nature—including physics, chemistry, and biology—shown in the left-hand side of the figure. The second is the *social sciences*, the sciences of society and the individual's relationships to society—including sociology, anthropology, political science, and economics—shown in the right-hand side of the figure. The third is the *humanities*—including languages, philosophy, art, and music—shown in the lower part of the figure. The humanities represent things that *humans* do. Humans, unlike other animals, talk to one another, develop philosophies, and produce art and music.

■ **24.** ***How does psychology link the three main divisions of academic studies?***

Where does psychology fit into this scheme? As shown in the figure, it fits right in the center, tied to all three of the broad divisions. On the natural science end it is tied strongly to biology by way of physiological psychology and ethology. On the social science end it is tied strongly to sociology by way of social psychology, and to anthropology by way of cultural psychology. In addition to bridging the natural and social sciences, psychology ties the whole spectrum of sciences to the humanities, through its interest in how people produce and understand languages, philosophies, art, and music.

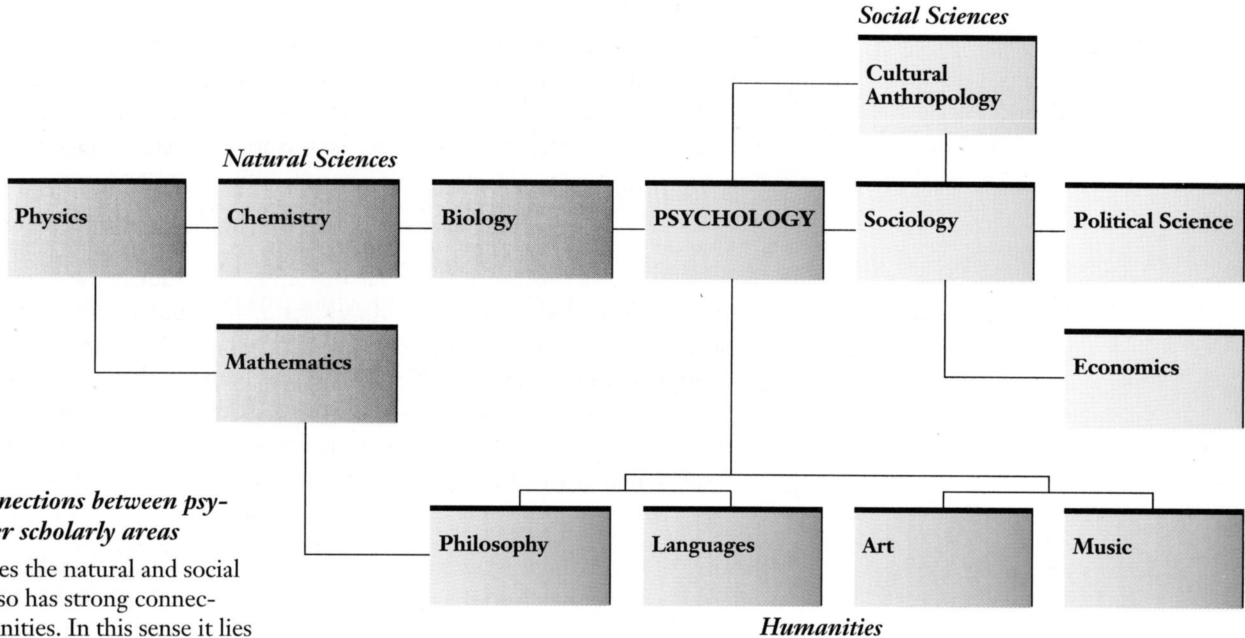

Figure 1.5 ***Connections between psychology and other scholarly areas***
Psychology bridges the natural and social sciences, and it also has strong connections to the humanities. In this sense it lies in the center of the academic pursuits of the university.

If you were to look at the research activities of psychologists, you would find that some behave like natural scientists. They have labs, wear white coats, perform experiments, and spend a good deal of time over in Biology, Chemistry, and Physics exchanging ideas and equipment. Others, you would find, behave more like social scientists. They use surveys, historical documents, and interviews as sources of data, and they find intellectual companionship in the various social science departments. The distinction between these two groups, however, is often a fuzzy one. Social psychologists often have labs and fancy data-collecting equipment, and zoological psychologists can be found whose data come mainly through their own two eyes, out in the field.

The link between psychology and the humanities is provided by people who ask questions about *how* and *why* people do such things as talk, reason, and create art or music. For example, consider the link between psychology and the study of languages. If you are interested in describing the structure of one or another of the world's languages, you are a *linguist*. But if you are interested in how people are able to learn and use that structure, and how this may affect other aspects of their behavior, you are a *psycholinguist* (a psychologist of language). Similarly, some psychologists are interested in how and why people respond to and create art, music, literature, and philosophies.

Psychology as a Profession

Psychology is not only an academic discipline but also a profession. As a profession, it includes both academic psychologists, who are engaged in research and teaching, and practicing psychologists, who apply psychological knowledge and ideas in clinics, businesses, and other areas. Approximately two-thirds of professional psychologists in the United States hold doctoral degrees in psychology, and most of the rest hold master's degrees (Stapp & others, 1985). The main settings in which they work and the kinds of services they perform in each are:

- ***Academic departments in universities and colleges*** Here psychologists are employed to conduct basic research and to teach psychology courses.
- ***Elementary and secondary schools*** School psychologists administer psychological tests, supervise programs for children who have special needs, and may help teachers develop more effective classroom techniques.
- ***Independent practice*** Most in this category are self-employed clinical or counseling psychologists, whose clients have psychological problems or disorders.
- ***Hospitals, mental health centers, clinics, and counseling or guidance centers*** Most here are clinical or counseling psychologists employed by an institution to work with people who have psychological problems or disorders.
- ***Business and government*** Psychologists are hired by businesses and government agencies for such varied purposes as conducting research, screening candidates for employment, helping design more pleasant and efficient work environments, and counseling personnel who have work-related problems.

The decision to major in psychology in college does not necessarily imply a choice of psychology as a career. Most students who major in psychology do so primarily because they find the subject fun to learn and think about. Most go on to careers in other fields—such as social work, law, education, and business—where they are quite likely to find their psychology background to be helpful (Woods, 1987).

Concluding Thoughts

At the end of each chapter I offer several "concluding thoughts," which in some cases might help you organize your review of the chapter and in other cases might add an insight or two to those that you generate yourself as you think about the chapter's contents. (Another useful way to review each chapter is to try to answer each of the guide questions that appear in the margins. Again, if you have not yet done so, I urge you to read the study suggestions in the section of the preface labeled "To the Student.") Here are two concluding thoughts for the chapter you have just read:

1. Ways to characterize the mind The history of psychology can be viewed in part as a history of alternative ways of characterizing the human mind. Most of the early psychologists were interested primarily in conscious, rational thought. Following the lead of philosophers before them, their broad question was, "How do people think?" Wundt and Titchener (structuralists), in their different ways, tried to understand thought in terms of its elementary parts. That tradition persists today in cognitive psychology's studies of the elementary processes involved in perception, memory, judgment, and so on. James (a functionalist), in contrast, felt that thought loses its very essence if it is broken down. He characterized thought as a continuous flow, which must be understood in terms of its broad goals or purposes rather than its parts. The Gestaltists also argued that thought must be understood in wholes rather than parts. Freud (a psychoanalyst) added a new twist to the problem, arguing that the study of conscious thought is insufficient; unconscious, irrational thoughts affect the conscious ones and also influence behavior in ways that bypass consciousness. Finally, Watson and Skinner (behaviorists) rejected the issue of thought entirely, changing the question from "How do people think?" to "How is behavior controlled by stimuli and consequences in the environment?"

2. The value of a historical perspective A temptation exists stronger today than in times past, to think of everything old as obsolete. In psychology, that temptation is manifest in the tendency to avoid reading the works of the early psychologists and other thinkers who set forth the questions and pioneered the methods that constitute the field of psychology as we know it today. But those who do read such works are often amazed by the breadth of mind, clarity of vision, and sheer intelligence of such pioneers as Charles Darwin and William James. Sometimes psychology seems to be a hodgepodge of specific facts, findings, theories, and techniques. Reading about the broader issues, in the original words of psychology's pioneers, can elevate one's vision about that jumble. One work to which I will refer occasionally throughout this book is William James's two-volume *Principles of Psychology*, first published in 1890. Take a look at that work in your library, or maybe even buy a copy (it's available in paperback). If you do buy it, you might very well enjoy reading it along with this textbook. As you go from topic to topic in this book, look up what James had to say on the topic and see if progress has occurred. On some topics you might be quite impressed with how far psychology has moved in a hundred years, and on others you might well decide that the field has barely begun to budge.

Further Reading

David Hothersall (1990). *History of psychology* (2nd ed.). New York: McGraw-Hill.

This lively historical account begins with the psychological theories of the ancient Greeks and ends with the behaviorism and neobehaviorism of the mid-twentieth century.

Gregory Kimble, Michael Wertheimer, & Charlotte White (Eds.) (1991). *Portraits of pioneers in psychology.* Hillsdale, NJ: Erlbaum.

This is a collection of short, lively, biographical sketches of twenty-two pioneers in psychology, including Titchener, James, Thorndike, Pavlov, Watson, Freud, Lashley, and Tolman.

Elizabeth Scarborough & Laurel Furumoto (1987). *Untold lives: The first generation of American women psychologists.* New York: Columbia University Press.

This book tells the story of courageous women who managed to break into the previously all-male ranks of academic psychology and to open the doors for other women to follow. Included are separate chapters on Mary Calkins, Milicent Shinn, Ethel Puffer, Margaret Washburn, and Christine Ladd-Franklin.

Paul J. Woods (Ed.) (1987). *Is psychology the major for you?* Washington, DC: American Psychological Association.

This booklet contains useful information about careers that psychology majors go on to both in and out of psychology; about preparing for graduate training in psychology; and about ways to maximize one's undergraduate education.

Looking Ahead

As you have seen, psychology has always been defined as a science. It became a formally recognized area of study when people accepted the idea that behavior and the mind can be studied by scientific methods. But what are scientific methods, and what special problems occur in applying such methods in psychology? These are the main questions of the next chapter.

METHODS OF PSYCHOLOGY

CHAPTER 2

In the last chapter, psychology was defined as the *science* of behavior and the mind. But what does it mean to say that psychology is a science? Science entails an organized effort to be objective and logical. In addition, it usually entails the systematic collection and analysis of publicly observable data. In psychology, the data are usually measures or descriptions of some form of behavior produced by human or animal subjects, collected in accordance with carefully prescribed procedures. Special problems exist in collecting such data and drawing conclusions from them.

This chapter is about scientific methods as applied to psychology. You will read sections on research strategies, statistical procedures, sources of error and bias, and ethical issues. But first, to ease ourselves into the topic, here is a story about a horse . . . and a psychologist.

Lessons from Clever Hans

This story, a true one, took place in Germany near the beginning of the twentieth century. The horse is Clever Hans, famous throughout Europe for his ability to answer questions, and the psychologist is Oskar Pfungst. I tell the story here because it contains some important lessons about scientific attitude and methods, but it would be worth telling even if it had no lessons. In a preface to the original account (Pfungst, 1911/1965), James Angell wrote, "Were it offered as fiction, it would take high rank as a work of imagination. Being in reality a sober fact, it verges on the miraculous."

The Mystery

Hans's owner, a Mr. von Osten, was an eccentric retired schoolteacher and devoted horseman who had long believed that horses would prove to be as intelligent as people if only they were given a proper education. To test his thesis, von Osten spent 4 years tutoring Hans in the manner employed in the most reputable German schools for children. Using flash cards, counting frames, and the like, he set about teaching his horse reading, arithmetic, history, and other scholarly disciplines. He always began with simple problems and worked to more complex ones and rewarded Hans frequently with praise as well as carrots. Recognizing that horses lack the vocal apparatus needed for speech, von Osten taught Hans to spell out words using a code in which the letters of the alphabet were translated into hoof taps, and to answer yes-no questions by tossing his head up and down for yes and back and forth for no. After 4 years of this training, Hans was able to answer practically any question that was put to him in either spoken or written German, whether about geography, history, science, literature, math, or current events.

Figure 2.1 ***Clever Hans at a mathematics lesson***
Mr. von Osten believed that his horse was intellectually gifted, and so did many other people until the psychologist Oskar Pfungst performed some simple experiments.

Remarkably, he could also answer questions put to him in other languages, even though he had never been trained in them.

Now you might think that von Osten was a charlatan, but he wasn't. He genuinely believed that his horse could read and understand a variety of languages, could perform arithmetical calculations, and had acquired a vast store of knowledge (see Figure 2.1). He never charged admission or sought other personal gain for displaying Hans, and he actively sought out scientists to study the animal's accomplishments. Indeed, many scientists, including some rather eminent zoologists and psychologists, came to the conclusion that von Osten's claims were true! Perhaps the most convincing evidence to them was that Hans could answer questions even when von Osten was not present, a finding that seemed to rule out the possibility that the horse depended on secret signals from his master. Moreover, several circus trainers, who specialized in training animals to give the appearance of answering questions, studied Hans and could find no evidence of trickery.

The Solution

1. ***How did Clever Hans give the appearance of answering questions, and how did Pfungst unveil his methods?***

Hans's downfall finally came when the psychologist Oskar Pfungst performed a few simple experiments. Pfungst (1911/1965) found that Hans could not answer any questions if he was fitted with blinders so that he could not see any of the people who were present, and that even without blinders he could not answer questions unless at least one person in his sight knew the answer. From this, Pfungst hypothesized that the horse obtained cues as to when to start and stop tapping by observing some subtle aspects of the behavior of the questioner or others who knew the answer. With further study, Pfungst discovered just what the signals were.

Immediately after asking a question that demanded a hoof-tap answer, the questioner and other observers would naturally turn their heads down just a bit to observe the horse's hoof. This, it turned out, was the signal for Hans to start tapping. To determine whether Hans would be correct or not, the questioner and other observers would then count the taps, and unintentionally make another response as soon as the correct number had been reached. This response varied from person to person, but a common component was a slight upward movement of either the whole head or some facial feature, such as the eyebrows. This, it turned out, was the signal for Hans to stop tapping. Hans's yes-no head-shake responses were also controlled by visual signals. Questioners and observers would unconsciously produce slight up-down head movements when they expected the horse to answer yes and slight back-forth head movements when they expected no, and Hans would shake his head accordingly.

All of the signals that controlled Hans's responses were so subtle that even the most astute observers had failed to notice them until Pfungst pointed them out. And Pfungst himself reported that the signals occurred so naturally that, even after he had learned what they were, he had to make a conscious effort to prevent himself from sending them after asking a question. For 4 years von Osten had believed that he was communicating scholarly information to Hans, when all he had really accomplished was to teach the horse to make a few simple responses to a few simple, though minute, gestures.

The Lessons

■ **2.** ***How does the Clever Hans story illustrate the value of skepticism, the value of controlled experimentation, and the need to rule out observer-expectancy effects?***

One lesson of this story has to do with human gullibility and the value of skepticism. People are naturally drawn to extraordinary claims and often act as if they want to believe them. This is as true today as it was in the time of Clever Hans. We have no trouble at all finding otherwise rational people who believe in astrology, psychokinesis, water divining, telepathy, or other occult phenomena, despite the fact that all such phenomena have consistently failed to occur when subjected to controlled tests (Singer & Benassi, 1981). Von Osten clearly wanted to believe that his horse could do amazing things, and so to a lesser degree may have the scholars who had studied the horse before Pfungst. Pfungst learned the truth partly because he was highly skeptical of such claims. Instead of setting out to prove them correct, he set out to prove them wrong. His skepticism led him to look more carefully, to notice what others had missed, to think of an alternative, more mundane explanation, and to pit the mundane explanation against the paranormal one in controlled tests.

Skepticism should be applied not only to extraordinary claims that come from outside of science, but also to the usually more sober claims or theories produced by scientists themselves. The ideal scientist always tries to disprove theories, even those that are his or her own. The theories that scientists accept as correct, or most likely to be so, are those that potentially could be disproved but have survived all attempts so far to do so.

A second lesson has to do with the value of careful observations under controlled conditions. Pfungst solved the mystery of Clever Hans by isolating the conditions under which the horse could and could not respond correctly to questions. He tested Hans repeatedly, with and without blinders, and recorded the percentage of correct responses in each condition. The results led him to hypothesize that the animal relied on visual signals. He then pursued this hypothesis by carefully observing Hans's examiners to see what signals they might be giving off. And when he had an idea what the signals might be, he performed further experiments, in various controlled ways, and recorded their effects on Hans's tapping and head-shake responses. Careful observation under controlled conditions is a hallmark of the scientific method.

A third lesson concerns *observer-expectancy effects*, which plague a great deal of psychological research (Rosenthal, 1965, 1976). A general problem in studies of humans and other sentient animals is that researchers may quite unintentionally communicate to the subjects their expectations as to how they "should" behave, and the subjects, intentionally or not, may respond by doing just what the researchers expect. The same is true in any situation in which one person administers a test to another. Have you ever taken an oral quiz and found that you could tell whether or not you were on the right track by noting the facial expression of your examiner? By tentatively testing various tracks, you may have finally hit upon just the answer that your examiner wanted. Clever Hans's whole cleverness depended on his picking up such cues. We will return to the issue of expectancy effects later, in a discussion of sources of error and bias in psychological research.

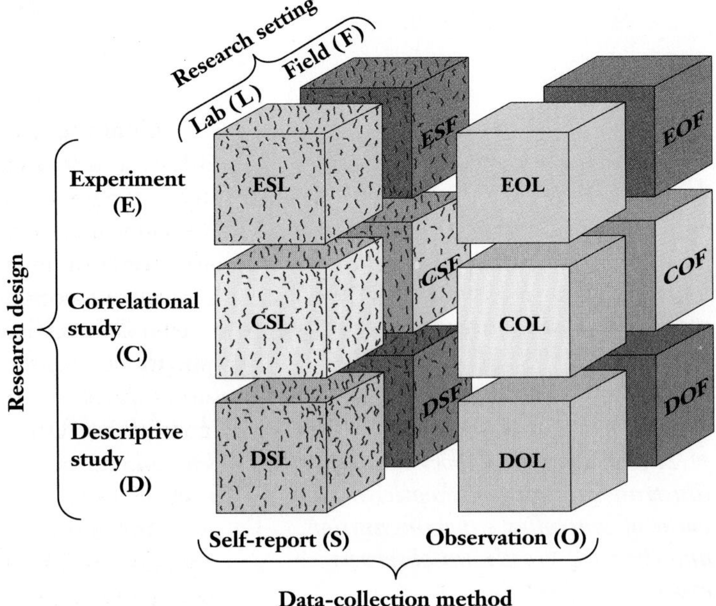

Figure 2.2 ***Three dimensions of research strategy***

The three categories of research designs, combined with two categories of data-collection methods and two categories of research settings, yield twelve different types of research strategies. (Adapted from Hendricks & others, 1990.)

A Taxonomy of Research Strategies

Throughout this book you will be reading about research evidence for or against one or another idea or hypothesis, and it will be useful to enter armed with some general knowledge of the different kinds of research strategies you will encounter. One approach to categorizing research strategies in psychology is to think of them as varying along three separate dimensions (Hendricks & others, 1990). One dimension is the *research design*, of which there are three basic types—experiments, correlational studies, and descriptive studies. The second dimension is the *data-collection method*, of which there are two basic types—observation and self-report. And the third dimension is the *setting* in which the study is conducted, of which there are again two basic types—laboratory and field. Each of these dimensions can vary independently of the others, resulting in twelve different varieties of studies, each defined by its combination of design, data-collection method, and setting (see Figure 2.2). We will first discuss the three types of designs, and then turn briefly to the other two dimensions.

Research Designs

Experiments

An experiment is the most direct and conclusive approach to testing a hypothesis about a cause-effect relationship between two variables (a variable is simply anything that can vary). In describing an experiment, the variable that is hypothesized to cause some effect on another variable is called the ***independent variable***, and the variable that is hypothesized to be affected is called the ***dependent variable***. The aim of any experiment is to learn how the dependent variable depends on the independent variable. In psychology, dependent variables are usually measures of behavior, and independent variables are factors that are hypothesized to influence those measures.

■ **3.** ***How does an experiment test causal hypotheses?***

More specifically, an ***experiment*** can be defined as a procedure in which a researcher systematically varies (manipulates) one or more independent variables while looking for changes in one or more dependent variables, while keeping all other variables constant. The reason for keeping other variables constant is to insure that any change observed in a dependent variable is really caused by the change in an independent variable, not by some other factor that happened to vary.

4. *What are the independent and dependent variables in (a) Pfungst's experiment with Hans and (b) the experiment on treatments for depression?*

Consider, for example, the variables in one of Pfungst's experiments with Clever Hans. To determine whether or not visual cues were critical to Hans's ability to respond correctly to questions, Pfungst tested the horse sometimes with blinders and sometimes without. In that experiment the independent variable was the presence or absence of blinders, and the dependent variable was the percentage of questions responded to correctly. The experiment could be described as a study of the effect of blinders (independent variable) on Hans's percentage of correct responses to questions (dependent variable). Pfungst took care to keep other variables, such as the difficulty of the questions, constant across the two test conditions. This experiment is an example of a *within-subject experiment*, because the different conditions of the independent variable were applied to the same subject (Hans).

As a second example, consider an experiment in clinical psychology conducted by Alberto DiMascio and his colleagues (1979). These researchers identified a group of patients suffering from major depression (defined in Chapter 17) and randomly assigned them to different treatments. One group received both drug therapy and psychotherapy, a second received drug therapy alone, a third received psychotherapy alone, and a fourth received no scheduled treatment (though they were assigned to a psychiatrist whom they could call when needed). The drug therapy consisted of daily doses of an antidepressant drug, and the psychotherapy consisted of weekly sessions with a psychiatrist focusing on the person's social relationships. After 16 weeks of treatment, the researchers rated each patient's degree of depression using a standard set of questions about mood and behavior. In this experiment, the independent variable was the kind of treatment given, and the dependent variable was the degree of depression after 16 weeks of treatment.

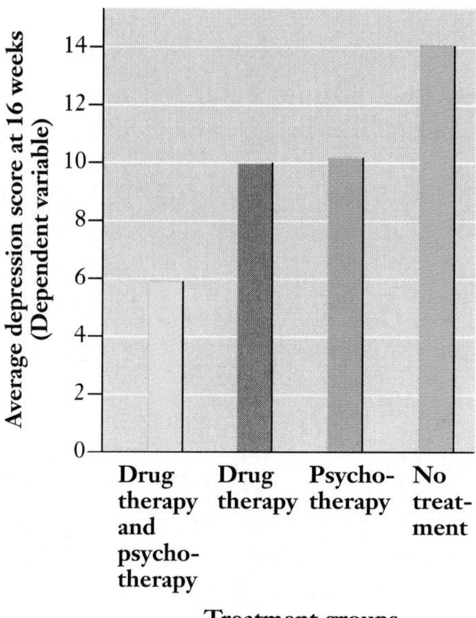

Figure 2.3 *Effect of treatment condition on depression*

The graph shows that those subjects who received both drugs and psychotherapy were the least depressed at the end of the 16-week treatment period (based on results of a standard interview procedure scored on a 17-point scale). In contrast, those who received neither treatment were the most depressed. (From DiMascio & others, 1979.)

This is an example of a *between-groups experiment*, because the different conditions of the independent variable (that is, the different treatments) were applied to different groups of subjects. Notice that the researchers randomly assigned the subjects to the different treatment groups. Random assignment is used in between-group experiments to prevent the biases that could result from other assignment methods. For example, if assignment had been made according to the subjects' own choices of treatment, those who were most likely to improve even without treatment might have disproportionately chosen one treatment over the others. Then we could not know whether greater improvement of one group compared to the others was due to the treatment or due to preexisting differences in the subjects.

The results of this experiment are shown in Figure 2.3. Following a common convention in graphing experimental results, to be used throughout this book, the figure depicts variation in the independent variable along the horizontal axis and variation in the dependent variable along the vertical axis. As you can see in the figure, those in the drug-plus-psychotherapy group were the least depressed after the 16-week period, and those in the no-treatment group were the most depressed. The results support the hypothesis that both drug therapy and psychotherapy help relieve depression, and that the two together have a greater effect than either alone.

Correlational Studies

In an experiment, as you have just seen, the researcher deliberately manipulates one variable (the independent variable) to determine its effect on another variable (the dependent variable). But many of the questions that psychologists ask are about relationships between variables over which the researcher has no reasonable means of control. In such cases an experiment is not possible, but a ***correlational study*** is. A correlational study can be defined as any study in which the researcher does not manipulate any variable, but observes or measures two or more variables to find relationships among them. Correlational studies can identify lawful relationships, but they do not tell us in any direct way whether change in one variable is the cause of change in another.

5. *How do correlational studies differ from experiments, and why must caution be exerted in inferring causal relationships from them?*

Sometimes correlational studies look quite similar to experiments and are analyzed statistically in the same way as experiments, but we must nevertheless be cautious about interpreting them in cause-effect terms. Consider, for example, a classic study by Diana Baumrind (1971) on the relationship between parents' discipline style and behavioral characteristics in their young children. Through questionnaires and home observations, Baumrind classified discipline styles into three categories: *authoritarian* (high exertion of parental power), *authoritative* (a more democratic style, but with the parents still clearly in charge), and *permissive* (parental laxity in the face of their children's disruptive behaviors). She also rated the children on various aspects of behavior, such as cooperation and friendliness, through observations in their nursery schools. The main finding was that children of authoritative parents scored better on the measures of behavior than did children of authoritarian or permissive parents.

Most people who read of Baumrind's study treat it as if it were an experiment and interpret the results in cause-effect terms. They assume that parental style was the independent variable and the children's behavior was the dependent variable and conclude that the differences in parental style caused the differences in the children's behavior, but this was not an experiment. Neither the parents' style of discipline nor the children's behavior was manipulated by the researchers; both were simply measured. Therefore, we cannot be sure what was cause and what was effect. Maybe the differences in parental style caused the differences in children's behavior, but you can probably think of some other possible ways to explain the correlation.

What causes what?
Although many correlational studies have found a relationship between the viewing of televised violence and aggressive behavior, such studies cannot tell us whether television inspires the aggressive behavior or whether aggressive individuals are more likely than others to watch violent television programs.

Maybe the differences in children's behavior caused the differences in parental style, rather than the other way around. Perhaps some children are better behaved than others for reasons quite separate from parental style, and perhaps parents with well-behaved children simply glide into an authoritative mode of parenting, while those with more difficult children fall into either of the other two modes as a way of coping. Or perhaps the causal relationship goes in both directions—parents affect children and children affect parents. Still another possibility is that a third variable influences both parental style and children's behavior. For example, anything that makes families feel good about themselves (such as having good neighbors, good health, and an adequate income) might promote an authoritative style in parents and, quite independently, also lead children to behave well. In many correlational studies one causal hypothesis may seem more plausible than others, but that is a judgment based on reasoning about possible causal mechanisms, or on evidence from other sources, not from the correlation itself.

In Baumrind's study, one variable (parental style) was used to place subjects into discrete groups and the other (children's behavior) was compared across those groups. Many correlational studies are analyzed in that way, but in many others both variables are measured numerically and neither is used to assign subjects to groups. In the latter case the data are assessed by a statistic called the *correlation coefficient*, to be discussed later.

Descriptive Studies

6. *How do descriptive studies differ from experiments and from correlational studies?*

Sometimes the aim of research is to describe the behavior of an individual or set of individuals without systematically investigating relationships between specific variables. A study of this sort is called a ***descriptive study***. Descriptive studies may or may not make use of numbers. As an example of one involving numbers, researchers might survey the members of a given community to determine the percentage who suffer from various mental disorders. This is a descriptive study if its aim is simply to describe the prevalence of each disorder without correlating the disorders to other characteristics of the community's members. As an example of a descriptive study not involving numbers, an ethologist might observe the courtship behavior of a duck species to describe the sequence of movements that are involved. Some descriptive studies are narrow in focus, concentrating on one specific aspect of behavior, and others are very broad, aiming to learn as much as possible about the habits of a particular group of people or species of animal. One of the most extensive and heroic descriptive studies in history is Jane Goodall's of the behavior of wild chimpanzees in Africa, which was conducted over a period of 30 years and provided a wealth of information about every aspect of these animals' lives.

Data-Collection Methods

We turn now from research design to the second dimension of the cube in Figure 2.2, the data-collection method. Two broad categories of data-collection methods exist: self-report and observational.

■ **7. *How do self-report methods, naturalistic observations, and tests differ from one another? What are some advantages and disadvantages of each?***

Self-report methods are those in which people are asked to rate or describe their own behavior or mental state in some way. This might be done through a ***questionnaire***, in which people produce self-descriptions either by checking off items on a printed list or by writing answers to essay questions. Or it might be done through an ***interview***, in which people describe themselves orally in a dialogue with the interviewer. An interview may be tightly structured, with the interviewer asking questions according to a completely preplanned sequence, or it may be more loosely structured, with the interviewer following up on the subject's earlier responses with additional questions. Researchers have developed numerical methods for scoring some structured interviews, as in the case of the method used to rate depression in the experiment depicted in Figure 2.3.

Observational methods include all procedures by which researchers observe and record the behavior of interest themselves rather than rely on subjects' self-descriptions. In one subcategory, ***naturalistic observation***, the researcher avoids interfering with the subject's behavior. For example, an ethologist might unobtrusively watch a duck's courtship behavior, or a developmental psychologist might watch children through a one-way window into a laboratory playroom. In the other subcategory, ***tests***, the researcher deliberately presents stimuli or problems for the subject to respond to. Examples include reaction-time tests, in which a person is asked to respond in a particular way as quickly as possible when a specific stimulus is presented, and problem-solving tests such as maze problems for animals or paper-and-pencil logic problems for people.

An observational technique

In most studies using a one-way window, subjects are informed that they are being watched. Nevertheless, they are less conscious of being observed, and behave more naturally when the observer is out of view than they would otherwise.

None of these data-collection methods is in any absolute sense superior to another. Each has its purposes, advantages, and limitations. Self-report methods can provide information that researchers would not be able to observe directly, but the validity of such information is limited by the subjects' honesty and ability to observe and remember accurately their own behaviors or moods. Naturalistic observations allow researchers to learn first-hand about their subjects' natural behaviors, but the practicality of such methods is limited by the great amount of time they take, the difficulty of observing ongoing behavior without disrupting it, and the difficulty of coding results in a form that can be used for statistical analyses. Tests are convenient and easily scored, but are by nature artificial, and the relationship between test results and everyday behaviors is not always clear. What is the relationship between a rat's ability to run a maze and the kinds of behaviors that rats engage in normally? What is the relationship between a person's score on an IQ test and his or her ability to solve the problems of daily living? These are the kinds of questions that psychologists must try to answer whenever they generalize from test results to behaviors beyond the test environment.

Research Settings

■ **8.** ***What are advantages and disadvantages of laboratory studies compared to field studies?***

The third dimension of research strategy shown in Figure 2.2 is the research setting, which can be either the laboratory or field. A ***laboratory study*** is any research study in which the subjects are brought to a specially designated area that has been set up to facilitate the researcher's ability to collect data or to control the environmental conditions. A ***field study*** is any research study conducted in a setting other than the laboratory. Laboratory and field settings offer opposite sets of advantages and disadvantages. The laboratory allows the researcher to collect data under more uniform, controlled conditions than are possible in the field. However, the strangeness or artificiality of the laboratory may induce behaviors in subjects that obscure those of interest to the researcher. A study of parent-child interactions in the laboratory, for example, might produce results that reflect not so much the subjects' normal ways of interacting as their reactions to a strange environment in which they know that they are being observed. To counteract such problems, some researchers combine laboratory and field studies. If the same conclusions emerge from tightly controlled laboratory studies and less controlled but more natural field studies researchers can be more confident that the conclusions are meaningful.

Experiments are most likely to be conducted in laboratories, and correlational and descriptive studies are most likely to be conducted in field settings. But any of the three research designs can be, and often are, carried out in either type of setting. For example, a *field experiment* can be conducted by manipulating some aspect of the natural environment in a controlled way. In one field experiment (discussed in Chapter 14), school teachers were instructed to praise some of their students, selected at random, about their ability in math and not to praise others, and the effect of this manipulation on the students' scores on subsequent math tests was observed (Miller & others, 1975). This is a field study because it was conducted in the children's regular classrooms. However, it is also an experiment, with an independent variable manipulated by the researchers (praise or no praise) and a dependent variable hypothesized to be affected by the independent variable (grades on subsequent math tests).

A field study

Social psychologist Harold Takooshian and his colleagues found that passersby rarely intervene when they observe a man apparently attempting to break into a car. Staged incidents are often part of field studies in social psychology.

Statistical Methods in Psychology

When the data in any research study have been collected, they must somehow be summarized and interpreted. Statistical procedures are mathematical aids for summarizing and interpreting data. Statistics can be divided into two categories: (a) ***descriptive statistics***, which are used to summarize a set of data, and (b) ***inferential statistics***, which help researchers decide how confident they can be in drawing specific conclusions (inferences) from the data. We will look here at some commonly used descriptive statistics and then at the rationale behind inferential statistics. A more detailed discussion can be found in the Statistical Appendix at the back of this book.

Descriptive Statistics

Describing the Central Tendency and Variability of a Set of Scores

■ ***9. How do the mean, median, and standard deviation help describe a set of numbers?***

Descriptive statistical procedures include all of the numerical methods for summarizing a set of data. If people in a study were classified according to whether or not they showed some specific behavior, we might summarize the data by calculating the percentage who showed it. If the original data were numerical in form (such as depression ratings), we might summarize them by calculating either the mean or median. The ***mean*** is simply the arithmetic average, determined by adding together the scores and dividing by the number of scores. The ***median*** is the center score, determined by ranking the scores from largest to smallest and finding the score that falls in the exact center of the list. (The Statistical Appendix explains when the mean or the median is more appropriate.)

The mean or median tells us about the central tendency of a set of numbers, but not about its variability. Variability refers to the degree to which the numbers in the set differ from one another or from their mean. In Table 2.1 you can see two sets of numbers that have identical means but different variabilities. In Set *A* the scores cluster close to the mean (low variability), and in Set *B* they differ widely from it (high variability). A common measure of variability is the ***standard deviation***, which is calculated by a formula (described in the Statistical Appendix) that takes into account the difference between each individual score and the mean. As illustrated in Table 2.1, the greater the average difference between each score and the mean, the greater the standard deviation.

Table 2.1 ***Two sets of data, with the same mean but different amounts of variability.***

Set *A*	Set *B*
7	2
7	4
8	8
11	9
12	14
12	16
13	17
Median = 11	*Median* = 9
Total = 70	*Total* = 70
Mean = 70/7 = 10	*Mean* = 70/7 = 10
Standard deviation = 2.39	*Standard deviation* = 5.42

Describing a Correlation

A descriptive statistic used in correlational studies is the ***correlation coefficient***, which measures the strength and direction of the correlation between two variables that have been measured numerically. Correlation coefficients are calculated by a formula (described in the Statistical Appendix) that produces a result ranging from +1.00 to –1.00. The sign (+ or –) indicates the direction of the correlation (positive or negative). A positive correlation is one in which an increase in one variable coincides with a tendency for the other variable to increase also, and a negative correlation is one in which an increase in one variable coincides with a tendency for the other variable to decrease. The absolute value of the correlation coefficient (from 0 to 1.00, irrespective of sign) indicates the strength of the correlation. A correlation is strong if the relationship between the two measures is very reliable, such that one variable can be used to predict quite accurately the other.

■ **10.** ***How does a correlation coefficient describe the direction and strength of a correlation?***

As an example, consider a study correlating high school students' scores on a standard intelligence test (IQ scores) with their grade point averages (GPAs), in which the raw data consist of an IQ score and a GPA for each of fifteen students. To visualize the results, the researchers might produce what is called a *scatter plot* in which each student's pair of scores is represented by a single point on a graph. The scatter plots for four different hypothetical sets of results are shown in Figure 2.4. Plot *A* illustrates a *moderate positive correlation*. Notice that each point represents both the IQ (marked on the horizontal axis) and GPA (marked on the vertical axis) for a single student. Thus, the point indicated by the red arrow represents a student whose IQ is 112 and GPA is 3.60. By looking at the whole constellation of points, you can see that, in general, higher GPAs correspond with higher IQs. This is what makes the correlation positive. Plot *B* illustrates a *strong positive correlation*. Notice that here the points fall very close to an upwardly slanted line. The closer the points are to forming a straight line, the stronger the correlation between the two variables. In this example, the stronger the correlation, the more accurately you could predict someone's GPA from his or her IQ, or vice versa. Plot *C* illustrates a *moderate negative correlation*. In this case, GPA tends to fall as IQ rises. Finally, Plot *D* represents *uncorrelated data*—a coefficient close to or equal to 0. Here the two variables are unrelated; knowing a person's IQ does not help you predict

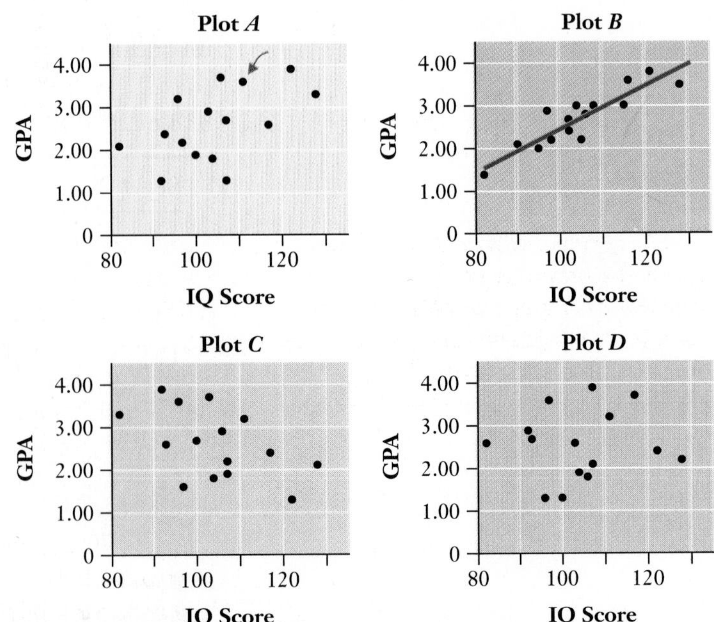

Figure 2.4 ***Scatter plots relating grade point average to IQ***

Plot *A* represents a moderate positive correlation, Plot *B* a strong positive correlation, Plot *C* a moderate negative correlation, and Plot *D* a correlation close to zero. (The actual correlation coefficients calculated for the data shown here are +0.52 for *A*, +0.89 for *B*, –0.52 for *C*, and +0.08 for *D*. The data are hypothetical.)

GPA, or vice versa. (In case you are curious, actual studies of the correlation between IQ and GPA usually produce moderate positive correlations, with coefficients ranging from about +0.30 to +0.70 in different studies [Jensen, 1980].)

Inferential Statistics

Any given set of data collected in any given research study contains some degree of variability that can be attributed to chance. In the experiment comparing treatments for depression shown in Figure 2.3, the different depression ratings obtained for the different groups reflect not just the effects of treatment, but also random effects caused by uncontrollable variables. For example, more people who were predisposed to improve could by chance have been assigned to one treatment group than to another. As another example, measurement error introduced by defects in the rating procedure could have contributed to differences in the depression scores. If the experiment were repeated several times, the results would be somewhat different each time because of these uncontrollable random variables. Given that results can vary due to chance, how confident can a researcher be in inferring a general conclusion from the study's data? Inferential statistical procedures are means to answer that question based on the laws of probability.

Statistical Significance

11. ***What might you infer about your hypothesis if your experimental results were statistically significant at the 5 percent level?***

The inference at issue in any given study can be called the ***research hypothesis***. In an experiment, the research hypothesis is usually that the independent variable has some consistent effect on the dependent variable. In a correlational study, the research hypothesis is usually that two measured variables are correlated in some way. Inferential statistical methods, applied to either an experiment or a correlational study, are procedures for calculating the probability that the data could have come out as they did if the research hypothesis is *wrong*. The lower that probability is, the more confident the researcher can be that the research hypothesis is correct. A long-standing convention in psychology is to label results as ***statistically significant*** if the probability is less than 5 percent that the data could have come out as they did if the hypothesis is wrong.

For an example of inferential statistics used in analyzing experimental results, look back at Figure 2.3. DiMascio and his colleagues (1979) reported that the effect of drug therapy was statistically significant at the 5 percent level. This meant that their inferential statistics revealed less than a 5 percent chance that a difference between the drug and nondrug groups, as large as or larger than that observed, could have occurred if the drug had no effect. Similarly, they reported that the effect of psychotherapy was also significant at the 5 percent level.

Elements in Tests of Statistical Significance

12. ***How is statistical significance affected by the size of the effect, the number of subjects or observations in each group, and the variability of the scores within each group?***

What are the elements that go into a test of statistical significance? One element clearly, is the *size of the observed effect*, as calculated by the descriptive statistics. Other things being equal, the larger the observed difference in the dependent variable between groups in an experiment, or the larger the correlation coefficient in a correlational study, the more significant the results. A second element is the *number of individual subjects or observations* in the study. Other things being equal, the greater the number of subjects or observations, the more likely the results are to be significant. If that number is huge, even very small effects will be statistically significant.

A third element, applicable when the data are numerical in form and are summarized as means, is the *variability* of the data within each group. Variability within the group can be thought of as a direct assessment of the degree of randomness operating on the dependent variable, or the degree to which the dependent variable is affected by uncontrolled variables. For example, in the experiment on the effects of treatments on depression, greater variability in depression scores within each treatment group would reflect greater randomness. Other things being equal, the lower the variability, the more likely the results are to be significant. Thus, the likelihood of finding statistical significance in a difference between group means increases as (a) the size of the difference between the means increases (b) the number of subjects in each group increases, and (c) the variability of the data within each group decreases. (We need not concern ourselves here with the exact formula by which these factors are mathematically combined in an inferential test, but, if you are curious, you can look up the formula for a *t*-test in any textbook in psychological statistics.)

The method for assessing the statistical significance of a correlation coefficient takes into account just two factors—the absolute size of the correlation coefficient (its distance above or below 0) and the number of pairs of correlated observations. As the number of subjects grows, the size of the correlation coefficient needed for statistical significance declines. For example, in the study correlating GPA and IQ, application of a standard formula reveals that a correlation coefficient of 0.30 would be statistically significant at the 5 percent level only if 47 or more students had been included in the study, but a coefficient of 0.70 would be significant at that level even if as few as 9 students had been included.

Statistical significance tells us that a result probably did not come about by chance, but it does not by itself tell us that the result has practical value. Don't confuse statistical significance with practical significance. If I were to test a new weight-loss drug on a thousand people, with a similar number in a control group, I might find a high degree of statistical significance even if the drug produced an average weight loss of only a few ounces. In that case, most people would agree that, despite the high statistical significance, the drug has no practical significance in a weight-loss program.

Sources of Error and Bias in Psychological Research

■ **13.** ***What is the difference between error and bias, and why is bias the more serious problem?***

Researchers must take care to minimize possible sources of error and bias in their studies. ***Error***, as a technical term, refers to increased randomness in results. The greater the error, the greater will be the random variability in the results, and hence the less will be the chance of obtaining statistical significance. ***Bias***, as a technical term, refers to nonrandom (directed) effects caused by some factor or factors extraneous to the research hypothesis. Bias is the more serious problem because it can lead to the false conclusion that the research hypothesis has been supported when in fact the results came out as they did for a different reason. Inferential statistics cannot tell us whether the results that they identify as significant stem from bias or from the truth of the research hypothesis. In psychological research, error and bias can result from problems in measurement, the expectancies of observers and subjects, and the drawing of generalizations from a nonrepresentative sample.

Problems in Measurement

An important limiting factor in psychological research is the ability to measure the behavior or characteristic that is of interest. A good measurement procedure is reliable, sensitive, and valid.

Measuring what babies see

Donald Duck is the lab assistant as researchers record the responses of this 7-month-old's brain to visual stimuli flashed on a screen. Donald keeps the infant's eyes directed toward the lights while the electric device on her head records her brain's responses. As you read about problems of measurement, think about how Donald's presence helps reduce error in this experiment.

■ **14.** ***How can lack of reliability and lack of sensitivity contribute to error?***

Reliability and Sensitivity

A measurement procedure is ***reliable*** if it yields similar results each time it is used with a particular subject under a particular set of conditions. Measuring height with an elastic ruler would not be as reliable as measuring it with a stiff ruler because the elasticity would cause the results to vary from one time to the next. A paper-and-pencil test of intelligence is not reliable if the answers depend more on the momentary whims of the subject than on something more stable about the person. Typically, the reliability of a measure is assessed by using the same measure (or different versions of it) at least twice with the same subjects and then calculating the test-retest correlation. If the correlation is high (meaning that each person tended to score about the same each time), the test is considered to be reliable.

A measurement procedure is ***sensitive*** if it can detect fine differences across individuals or test conditions. If a procedure detects no differences, it is completely insensitive. For example, if your psychology professor gave a midterm exam and everyone got the same score no matter how well they knew the material, the test would be completely insensitive. This is what would happen if every question was either so easy that everyone got it right or so hard that everyone got it wrong (in the latter case you might say that the test was insensitive in more ways than one). Low reliability and low sensitivity both are sources of measurement error, and hence both reduce the likelihood of finding statistical significance in a research study.

Validity

A measurement procedure is ***valid*** if it measures or predicts what it is intended to measure or predict. A procedure may be reliable and sensitive, and yet not be valid. For example, assessing intelligence in adults by measuring thumb length is highly reliable (you would get nearly the same score each time), moderately sensitive (people do differ on this measure), but almost certainly not valid (thumb length is almost certainly unrelated to adult intelligence). If common sense tells us that a measurement procedure assesses the intended characteristic, we say the procedure has *face validity*. A test of ability to solve logical problems has face validity as a measure of intelligence, but thumb length does not.

■ **15.** ***How can the validity of a measurement procedure be assessed, and how can lack of validity contribute to bias?***

A more certain way to gauge the validity of a measurement procedure is to correlate its scores with another, more direct index of the characteristic we wish to measure or predict. In that case the more direct index is called the *criterion*, and the validity is called *criterion validity*. Suppose, for example, that I defined intelligence as the quality of mind that allows a person to achieve greatness in any of various realms, including business, diplomacy, science, literature, and art. With this definition, I might use the actual achievement of such greatness as my criterion. I might identify a group of people who have achieved such greatness and a group who, despite similar environmental opportunities, have not, and assess the degree to which they differ on various potential measures of intelligence. The greater the two groups differ on any of the measures, the greater is the correlation between that measure and my criterion for intelligence, and the more valid is the test. If thumb length turned out to distinguish the two groups better than did the test of logic, I would have to conclude that thumb length has the greater criterion validity despite its lower face validity.

As you can see from this example, the assessment of validity requires a clear definition of the characteristic to be measured or predicted. If your definition of intelligence differs from mine, you will choose a different criterion than mine for assessing the validity of possible intelligence tests.

Lack of measurement validity is a source of bias. In other words, an invalid measure can produce the appearance of support for a hypothesis that is not true. Suppose, for example, that the interview procedure used in the depression study (illustrated in Figure 2.3) was not a valid measure of depression, but reflected subjects' desires to appear depressed or not. In that case the results would still be statistically significant, but the researchers' conclusion (that treatment affects depression) would be mistaken. A more accurate conclusion would be that some treatments lead to a stronger desire to appear not depressed than do others.

Biasing Effects of Observers' and Subjects' Expectancies

Observer-Expectancy Effects

■ **16.** ***What are two ways by which an observer's expectations can bias results? How does blind observation prevent such bias?***

Being human, researchers inevitably have wishes and expectations that can affect how they behave and what they observe when recording data. The resulting biases are called ***observer-expectancy effects***. A researcher who desires or expects a subject to respond in a particular way may unintentionally communicate that expectation and thereby influence the subject's behavior. As you may recall, Pfungst discovered that this sort of effect provided the basis for Hans's ability to answer questions. In a between-groups experiment, a researcher who expects subjects in one group to behave one way and those in another group to behave another way may send different unintentional signals to the two groups and thereby elicit the expected difference. In addition to influencing subjects' behavior, observer expectancy can also influence the observer's perception or judgement of that behavior. For example, an observer who expects to find that people smile more in one condition than in another may interpret an ambiguous facial expression as a smile in the one condition and as something else in the other.

The best way to prevent observer-expectancy effects is to keep the observer ***blind***, that is, uninformed, about those aspects of the study's design that could lead to differential expectations. Thus, in a between-groups experiment, a blind observer would be uninformed as to which treatment any given subject had received. Not knowing who is in which group, the blind observer has no basis for expecting a particular behavior from a particular subject. In the study of treatments for depression (illustrated in Figure 2.3), the clinicians who evaluated patients' depression at the end of the treatment period were blind to treatment condition. To keep them blind, patients were instructed not to say anything about their treatment during the evaluation interview.

Subject-Expectancy Effects

17. *How can subjects' expectancies bias the results of an experiment? How does a double blind procedure control both subjects' and observers' expectancies?*

Subjects also have expectations. If different treatments in an experiment induce different expectations in subjects, then those expectations may account for observed behavioral differences. Effects of this sort are called ***subject-expectancy effects***. For example, people who take a drug may subsequently behave or feel a certain way simply because they believe that the drug causes such behavior or feeling. Similarly, subjects receiving psychotherapy may improve simply because they believe that psychotherapy will help them.

Ideally, to prevent bias due to subject expectancy, subjects should be kept blind as to the treatment they are receiving. An experiment in which both the observer and the subjects are kept blind in this way is called a ***double blind experiment***. In double blind drug studies, subjects who do not receive the drug receive a ***placebo***, an inactive substance that looks like the drug, and neither subjects nor observers are told who received the drug and who did not. Consequently, any observed difference between those who got the drug and those who did not must be due to the drug's chemical qualities, not subjects' or observers' expectancies.

Subjects cannot always be kept blind concerning their treatment. For instance, you can't administer psychotherapy to people without their knowing it. As a partial control in some psychotherapy experiments, subjects in the nonpsychotherapy group are given a fake form of therapy designed to induce subject expectancies equivalent to those induced by psychotherapy. Incidentally, the subjects in the depression experiment described earlier were not blind concerning their treatment. Those in the nondrug groups did not receive a placebo, and those in the nonpsychotherapy groups did not receive fake psychotherapy. The results depicted in Figure 2.3 could, at least in theory, be placebo effects.

Problems in Generalizing from a Sample to a Larger Population

18. *Why did a telephone poll fail, and why must researchers be cautious about extending their conclusions beyond the group studied?*

The set of people or animals in any study are only a subset, or *sample*, from some larger population. If researchers want to make claims about the larger population, their sample should be representative of that population. A sample that is not representative of the population that the researcher thinks he or she is studying is called a ***biased sample***. A notorious example of research that went awry because of a biased sample was the *Literary Digest*'s poll of U.S. voters in 1936, which led the *Digest* to announce that Alf Landon would beat Franklin D. Roosevelt in the presidential election that year by a margin of 2 to 1 (Huff, 1954). It turned out that their conclusion could not have been more mistaken—Roosevelt won by a landslide. The *Digest* had conducted its poll by telephoning magazine subscribers. In 1936, in the midst of the Great Depression, people who could afford magazine subscriptions and telephones may indeed have favored Landon, but the great majority of voters, as the election showed, did not.

Psychological research very often employs college students as subjects, since most research is conducted on college campuses. For some studies, such as those of basic sensory processes, there is probably little problem in generalizing from college students to other groups. But for studies of values, goals, achievement motivation, and the like, what is true of college students may not be true of people in

Figure 2.5 ***A cross-cultural difference***
In most non-Western cultures, young children are kept much closer to their caregivers than in the West. This may provide a basis for cross-cultural differences found in studies of attachment.

general. Psychologists who wish to generalize their findings about such processes beyond the college population must often go to considerable trouble to study people in other settings. The same issue applies at an even broader level when psychologists wish to generalize their findings to other parts of the world. Because of cross-cultural differences, such as that illustrated in Figure 2.5, a psychological law that holds for people reared in North America or Western Europe may not apply to people reared in the Orient. You will find many examples of such cross-cultural differences in later chapters of this book.

Ethical Issues in Psychological Research

Because their research is with human beings and other sentient animals, psychologists must consider ethical as well as scientific issues in designing their studies. DiMascio and his colleagues (1979) might, from a scientific vantage point, have improved their study of treatments for depression by using a placebo in the nondrug conditions and a fake form of psychotherapy in the nonpsychotherapy conditions to reduce differences among the groups in subject expectancies. But the researchers felt that their subjects should know what form of treatment they were getting, so they could make an informed decision about whether or not to participate and could understand side effects that might arise as treatment progressed. The researchers also chose to change the treatment for any patient who by the end of 8 weeks had not shown evidence of reduced depression. In those cases they used the depression score at 8 weeks in the final data analysis (combining it with the 16-week data on the other subjects). These departures from ideal research protocol somewhat weaken the scientific merit of the study, but the researchers felt that the compromise was essential from an ethical standpoint.

■ **19.** ***What are the ethical concerns pertaining to privacy, discomfort, deception, and animal welfare? How do researchers strive to satisfy these concerns?***

In research with humans, ethical considerations revolve around three interrelated issues: (1) the person's right to privacy, (2) the possible discomfort or harm that a research procedure could produce, and (3) the use of deception that characterizes some research designs. Concerning the first two of these issues, the usual ethical safeguards include obtaining informed consent from subjects before they take part in a study, informing subjects that they can quit at any time (and respecting their right to do so), and keeping records and reports in a way that ensures subjects' anonymity. In addition, whenever a possibility of discomfort or harm exists, researchers are obliged to determine whether the same question could be answered in a study that involves less risk, and, if the answer is no, to demonstrate that the human benefits of the study outweigh any possible costs. In reality, the great majority of psychological studies involve completely harmless procedures, such as reading rapidly flashed letters, memorizing lists of terms, or carrying on a discussion with other subjects.

The most controversial ethical issue in human psychological research concerns deception. In a small minority of experiments the independent variable involves a lie. Subjects may be falsely told or led to believe that something is happening, or going to happen so that the researcher can study their reactions to that belief. Some psychologists are opposed to all use of deception on the grounds that deception (a) is intrinsically unethical and (b) undermines the possibility of obtaining truly informed consent (Carroll & others, 1985). Others, however, justify deception on the grounds that some psychological processes cannot be studied effectively without it. These psychologists further contend that (a) research deception usually takes the form of benign "white lies," which are cleared up when the researcher informs the subject of the true nature of the study after the session has ended, and (b) informed consent can still be obtained by telling subjects that some details of the study must be withheld until the data have been collected and by advising them of any realistic dangers that could be involved.

The use of nonhuman animals in research presents another area of ethical controversy. With animals one can employ procedures that cannot be employed with humans. One can breed them in controlled ways, raise them in controlled environments, and surgically intervene in their physiology. Basic biological mechanisms underlying animal behavior are similar to those underlying human behavior, so such research contributes to our understanding of humans as well as the species studied. Still, research on nonhuman animals can sometimes cause them to suffer, and any researcher employing animals has an ethical obligation to balance the animal's suffering against the potential benefits of the research. Animals must be well cared for and not subjected to unnecessary deprivation or pain. Some people question whether subjecting animals to pain or deprivation for research purposes is ever justifiable. But others, pointing to the enormous gains in knowledge and the reduction in human (and animal) suffering that has come from such research, have turned the ethical question around. In the words of one (Miller, 1986), "Is it morally justifiable to prolong human (and animal) suffering in order to reduce suffering by experimental animals?"

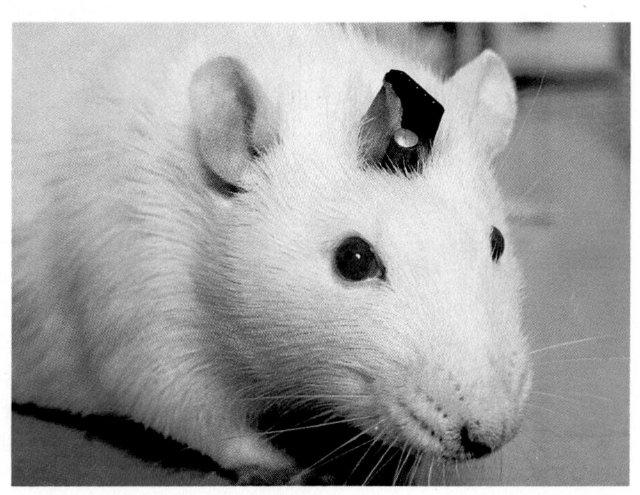

A rat with an electrode in its brain

Experiments in physiological psychology frequently involve operations on animal brains. For scientific as well as ethical reasons, conscientious researchers are scrupulous about minimizing discomfort to the animals. Discomfort can produce behaviors that interfere with those the researcher wishes to study.

The American Psychological Association (1981, 1982) has established ethical guidelines for psychological research. Moreover, in the United States and many other countries today, publicly funded research institutions are required by law to have ethics review panels, whose task is to review all proposed studies that have any potential for ethical controversy. Such panels often turn down research proposals that once were viewed as quite acceptable. A few studies that are now considered classics and are cited in most general psychology textbooks, including this one, would not have been approved today. As you read of some of the studies in the chapters to follow, questions of ethics may well occur to you from time to time. Such questions are always legitimate, as are questions about the scientific merit of a study's design and the validity or generality of its results. Psychology needs and usually welcomes people who raise those questions.

Concluding Thoughts

1. How does science compare to everyday observation and thought? No sharp distinction exists between science and the kinds of observation and thought that all of us use every day to learn about the world around us. In our everyday learning, we begin with the data of our senses, and we use those data to draw tentative conclusions (make inferences) about specific aspects of our world. For example, we might one day observe someone from Town X act politely and someone from Town Y act rudely and infer from those observations that people from X are more polite than people from Y. Most of us make such inferences all the time, often on scarcely more evidence than that. Science is simply the attempt to improve upon our natural ways of learning by systematizing the data-collection procedures, controlling conditions to be more certain which variables are having which effects, striving to eliminate sources of bias, deliberately thinking of alternative explanations, and using statistical procedures to assess the degree of confidence we should have in our tentative conclusions. As you review each of the main concepts discussed in the sections on research strategies, statistical methods, and sources of error and bias in this chapter, you might think about how that concept applies—somewhat less formally—to the distinctions between good and poor observation and thought in everyday life. We are observing and thinking poorly when we draw firm conclusions from too little evidence, or neglect to think about alternative explanations, or fail to see what is really there because of our biased expectations.

2. What is a science of psychology for? I remember, as a college freshman on a visit home, flaunting my pride a bit overbearingly about an *A* that I had received in calculus. My mother, hearing me brag and having a knack for reducing undue pride and putting things into perspective, asked a simple question: "What is calculus for?" I was floored. I could rattle off terms and equations about calculus, and I could solve the problems as they were given to me in the class, but I had no understanding at all of what calculus was for. Perhaps that is why, by a few months after the class had ended, I had completely forgotten the terms, the equations, and how to solve them. So what is a science of psychology for?

Some people think of psychology purely in applied terms, as a means of solving human problems. These people are likely to appreciate the study on treatments for depression (illustrated in Figure 2.3), but are less likely to understand Wundt's desire to measure the speed of human judgments or Lorenz's desire to describe the courtship behaviors of ducks (both noted in Chapter 1). The issue of pragmatism occurs in other sciences as well. What good does it do us to know what the other side of the moon looks like?

For the most part, people go into psychological research, or any other research field, because they are curious, or because they are thrilled by the prospect of being the first to uncover some mystery of nature, large or small. So psychology, like any other science, has two purposes: to solve practical problems and to satisfy the human quest for knowledge. It is hard to separate the two, however, because very often research done solely to satisfy curiosity reveals solutions to practical problems that at first seemed unrelated to the research. As you read the remaining chapters of this book, I hope you will allow yourself to become engaged by the questions for their own sake, regardless of whether you think they have practical applications. Each chapter contains mysteries, some solved, some not.

Further Reading

Keith E. Stanovich (1992). *Thinking straight about psychology* (3rd ed.). New York: HarperCollins.

This book deals with popular misconceptions about psychological phenomena, the faulty uses of evidence and logic that lead to such misconceptions, and the processes through which enduring psychological knowledge has been developed. The author's goal is to help readers acquire the tools needed for critical thinking in psychology.

Theodore X. Barber (1976). *Pitfalls in human research.* New York: Pergamon.

This slender volume outlines, and illustrates with specific examples, ten different categories of mistakes in designing and conducting a research study, each of which can lead researchers or consumers of research to false conclusions.

Darrell Huff (1954). *How to lie with statistics.* New York: Norton.

This witty paperback, filled with anecdotes and cartoons, has a serious message. It tells you how not to lie with statistics, and how to spot lies when they occur. It is guaranteed to make you a more critical consumer of statistical information. Don't be put off by its date; it is reprinted regularly and widely available.

Robert J. Sternberg (1988). *The psychologist's companion: A guide to scientific writing for students and researchers* (2nd ed.). Cambridge: Cambridge University Press.

Psychologists, like scholars in every field, must communicate their ideas and findings in writing. This book, by one of the most prolific writers among contemporary psychologists, is a very practical guide to the writing of psychological papers of all types, ranging from library papers and lab reports by first-year college students to papers for publication by full-fledged researchers.

Looking Ahead

This is not the only chapter of this book that deals with methods. In effect, all the chapters to follow are about methods, because our knowledge in every area of psychology is inseparable from our ways of knowing. Each chapter offers at least some discussion of the methods used to test the ideas being discussed. The concepts described in the present chapter that will be especially useful in chapters to follow are (a) the difference between an experiment and a correlational study; (b) the meaning of correlation coefficient, statistical significance, measurement validity, and double blind experiment; and (c) the problem of generalizing from a sample. Now, we move from background to the first chapter dealing substantively with the content of psychology. It is about the role of heredity in behavior.

Mary Cassatt

NATURE, NURTURE, AND BEHAVIORAL ADAPTATION

PART 2

We are the products of our genes and our environments. Our genes have been shaped by millions of years of evolution, adapting us to the general conditions of human life on earth. Through this process we have acquired, among other things, an immense capacity to learn. This unit consists of three chapters. The first examines the interplay between genes and environment in determining differences among individuals. The second has to do with inherited behavioral tendencies and with the attempt to understand those tendencies in terms of evolutionary history. The third deals with basic processes of learning, which constantly modify behavior to meet the unique conditions of each individual's life.

Principles of Gene Action and Heredity

How Genes Affect Physical Development and Behavior

Sexual Reproduction and Patterns of Heredity

Single-Gene and Chromosomal Effects on Behavior

Mendelian Inheritance of a Behavioral Trait in Dogs

Single-Gene Disorders in Humans

Chromosomal Disorders in Humans

Polygenic Effects on Behavior

The Concept of Heritability

Selective Breeding for Behavioral Characteristics in Animals

The Heritability and Environmentality of IQ

Genetic Influence on Risk for Schizophrenia

GENETICS OF BEHAVIOR

CHAPTER 3

In 1582, an English educator named Richard Mulcaster introduced into the world's literature a harmonious pair of terms, ***nature*** and ***nurture***, to refer to what he regarded as twin forces in the development of a child's mind (Teigen, 1984). By *nature* he meant the child's inborn biological endowment (what we would now call *genetic inheritance*), and by *nurture* he meant all the environmental conditions (including schooling) in which the mind develops. To Mulcaster, the poetic flow of this pair of terms captured the harmony in which these forces work together. In an essay on the education of boys, he wrote, "Nature makes the boy toward, nurture sees him forward" (Mulcaster, 1582). Some 30 years later, William Shakespeare used the same terms in a similar way in *The Tempest*. Then, in the second half of the nineteenth century, the English scientist Francis Galton (1822–1911) popularized the terms, but he seemed to pit them against one another rather than emphasize their harmony.

Galton was interested in differences of many sorts among people, but particularly differences in intellectual achievement. Reasoning that such differences could be caused by differences in biological inheritance (nature), or by differences in environmental conditions (nurture), he initiated a research program to determine which plays the larger role. Galton's research marked the start of the so-called ***nature-nurture debate***, which in various guises has continued throughout psychology's history. In essence, the subject of the debate is this: Are psychological differences among people primarily the result of differences in their genes or in their environments?

Scientists now know far more about genes than did Galton and his peers, and ***behavioral genetics***—the study of the effects of genes on behavior—is a large and rapidly growing subfield of contemporary psychology. This chapter is about behavioral genetics, and it consists of three main sections. The first provides a brief review of gene biology. The second discusses some of the most clear-cut effects of genes on behavior, cases in which behavioral differences among individuals can be attributed either to a single gene or to an abnormal number of chromosomes. The third discusses research on behavioral differences that are influenced by many genes. In the third section, we focus on intelligence (as measured by IQ tests) and susceptibility to schizophrenia (a class of mental disorder), as these have been the center of the most study and controversy concerning the relative importance of nature and nurture. The chapter emphasizes that the effects of genes on behavior are relative to the range of environmental conditions in which individuals develop. Mulcaster was right. Nature and nurture always work together. Neither can be fully understood independently of the other.

Principles of Gene Action and Heredity

How Genes Affect Physical Development and Behavior

Genes are the blueprint for the synthesis of *protein molecules*, on which all physical development depends. A class of proteins called *structural proteins* forms the structure of every cell in the body, and another class called *enzymes* controls the rate of every chemical reaction in every cell. We are what we are, biologically speaking, because of our proteins.

How do genes direct the synthesis of proteins? The answer has been worked out in wondrous detail by molecular biologists, but here a rough sketch will suffice. Physically, genes exist within extremely long molecules called DNA (deoxyribonucleic acid). DNA exists in the nucleus of every cell of the body, where it serves as a template (that is, a mold or pattern) for producing another molecular substance called RNA (ribonucleic acid). RNA, in turn, serves as a template for producing protein molecules. A protein molecule consists of a long chain of smaller molecules called *amino acids*. Twenty distinct amino acids exist, and these can be arranged in countless sequences to form different protein molecules. Thus, the main job of the gene is to control, through the RNA mediator, the sequence of amino acids in a protein molecule. DNA molecules contain the codes for many different protein molecules. From a molecular vantage point, a gene can be defined as the segment of a DNA molecule containing the code for one specific type of protein molecule.

■ 1. ***How do genes affect behavior?***

The key point here is that genes are able to affect behavior through one, and only one, means—the manufacture of proteins. Through building proteins they contribute to the anatomy and physiology of the body, and through that they affect behavior. Sometimes, as a sort of shorthand, people speak of genes "for" particular behavioral traits, but in reality there are no genes for behavioral traits that are separate from genes for anatomy and physiology. Thus, a gene might influence musical ability by promoting the development of a brain system that analyzes sounds, or by promoting certain physical aspects of the vocal cords. Similarly, a gene might affect aggressiveness by promoting the growth of systems in the brain that respond to irritating external stimuli and organize aggressive behavior. In a sense all genes that contribute to the body's development are "for" behavior, as all parts of the body are involved in behavior. Especially relevant for behavior, however, are genes that contribute to the development of sensory systems, the nervous system, and motor systems (muscles and other organs involved in movement).

■ 2. ***What are some ways by which the environment affects physical development and behavior?***

At every level of analysis, from biochemical to behavioral, the effects of genes are entwined with the effects of the environment. The term *environment*, as used in this context, refers to every aspect of an individual and his or her surroundings except the genes themselves. It includes the nourishing womb and maternal bloodstream before birth; the internal chemical environment of the developing individual; and all the events, objects, and other individuals encountered after birth. Foods—a part of the environment—supply genes with amino acids, which are needed to manufacture proteins. Environmental effects also turn genes on and off. For example, physical exercise changes the chemical environment of muscle cells in a way that activates genes that promote further growth of the muscle. One's body and behavioral capacities result from a continuous and highly complicated interplay between genes and environment (see Figure 3.1). In no sense is one more basic than the other.

Geneticists use the term ***genotype*** to refer to the set of genes that the individual inherits and the term ***phenotype*** to refer to the observable properties of the body and behavioral traits. The same genes can have different effects depending on the environment and the mix of other genes. Two people with the same genotype

Figure 3.1 ***Route through which genes affect behavior***

Genes build proteins, which form the body's physiological systems, which produce behavior. Each step in this process involves interaction with the environment. $Environment_1$ and $Environment_2$ represent internal chemical environments that affect gene and enzyme action, respectively; $Environment_3$ includes the external environment. The behavioral response in turn can affect each level of the environment.

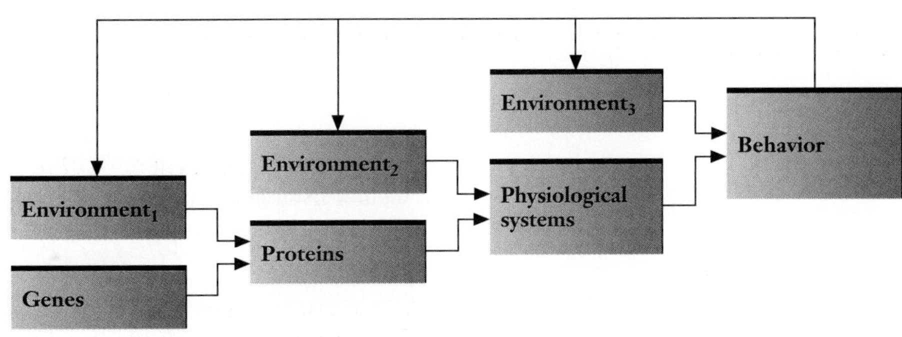

Identical twins

These 13-year-old girls have the same genes, but they obviously differ in at least one aspect of their phenotype.

can be quite different in phenotype. As an obvious example, identical twins (who have the same genes) will differ phenotypically in muscle strength if one exercises a lot and the other doesn't. You will see other examples as the chapter progresses.

Sexual Reproduction and Patterns of Heredity

The genes are not only templates for producing proteins, but are also the units of heredity. To understand patterns of genetic inheritance, it is useful to know something about the arrangement of genes in the cell and what happens to that arrangement in sexual reproduction.

Chromosomes

The genetic material (long strands of DNA) exists in each cell in structures called ***chromosomes***, which are usually dispersed throughout the cell nucleus and not visible. However, just prior to cell division the chromosomes condense into compact structures that can be stained, viewed with a microscope, and photographed. The photographic representation of chromosomes in a single cell is known as a ***karyotype***. As you can see in Figure 3.2, the normal human male karyotype consists of 23 pairs of chromosomes, 22 of which are called ***autosomes*** and numbered 1 through 22, from largest to smallest. The remaining pair, the ***sex chromosomes***, includes a large ***X chromosome*** and a much smaller ***Y chromosome***. The normal human female karyotype is identical to the male's except that it has two X chromosomes and no Y.

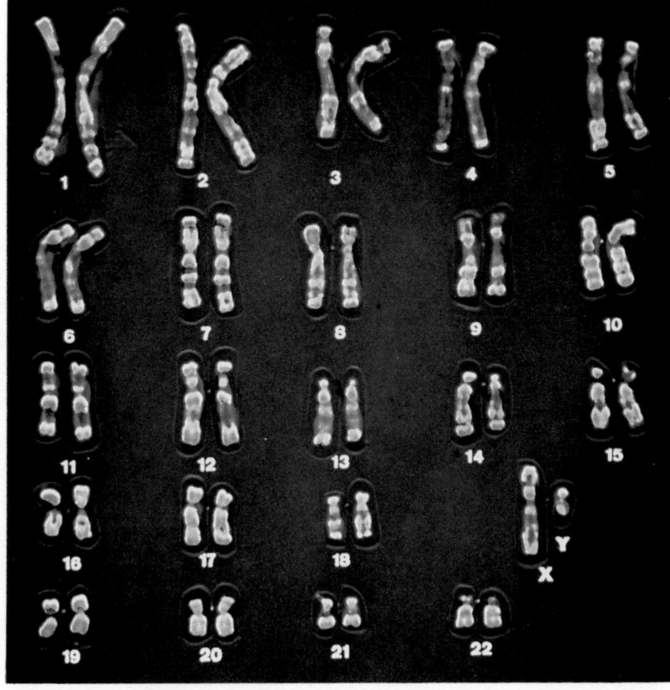

Figure 3.2 ***Normal human male karyotype***

The 22 numbered pairs of chromosomes are called autosomes, and the remaining 2, labeled X and Y, are called sex chromosomes. The female karyotype, not shown, is identical to the male's except for the existence of a second X and no Y.

Cell Division

Cells can divide (duplicate themselves) in two ways: mitosis, which is involved in normal body growth, and meiosis, which produces the egg and sperm cells used in sexual reproduction. In ***mitosis***, each chromosome precisely replicates itself and then the cell divides, with one copy of each chromosome moving into each of the two cells thus formed. Because of the faithful copying of genetic material in mitosis, all of your body's cells (except for egg or sperm cells) are genetically identical to each other. The differences among different cells in your body—such as liver cells and skin cells—arise from the differential activation of their genes, not from different gene content.

Meiosis, on the other hand, produces cells that are not genetically alike. Meiosis operates on precursor cells in the male's testes to produce sperm cells and in the female's ovaries to produce egg cells. At the beginning of meiosis, the two members of each pair of chromosomes in the precursor cell line up next to one another, and the DNA in each chromosome reproduces itself, resulting in sets of four identical-looking incomplete chromosomes called chromatids (see Figure 3.3). Then the cell divides, with two chromatids from each set of four going to each of the two cells thus formed. In the male, both of these new cells then divide again, after the chromatids have developed into full chromosomes, and one chromosome from each set goes to each of the new cells. The result is four sperm cells, each of which has half the normal number of chromosomes, one member of each original pair. Egg production is similar to sperm production except that only one of the four potential eggs derived from the two divisions survives the process.

■ 3. ***How does meiosis produce egg or sperm cells that are all genetically different from one another?***

A given person's egg or sperm cells look alike in terms of the number and shape of their chromosomes (except that half of the male's sperm cells have an X chromosome and the other half have a Y), but they are all different from one another in the genes they contain. To understand this, you must first realize that paired chromosomes, despite looking identical, do not have identical genes. During meiosis, after the chromosomes have reproduced but before the first cell division, sections of DNA are interchanged between chromosomes within each set of four in a random manner, a process called ***crossing over*** (illustrated in Figure 3.4).

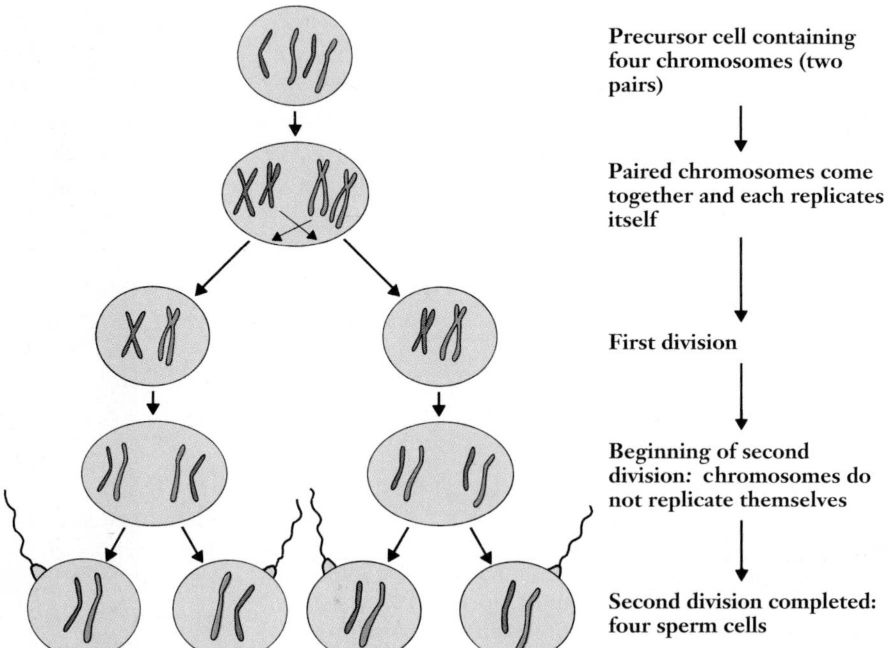

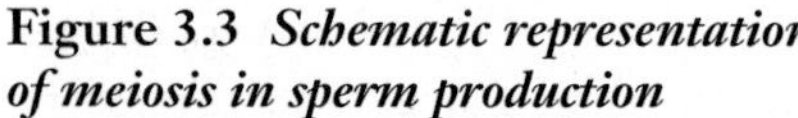
Figure 3.3 ***Schematic representation of meiosis in sperm production***

Each chromosome of the precursor cell reproduces itself once, but then the cell divides twice, resulting in four sperm cells, each of which has one member of each original pair of chromosomes. Meiosis in egg production is similar to that in sperm production, but only one of the two cells produced at each division survives.

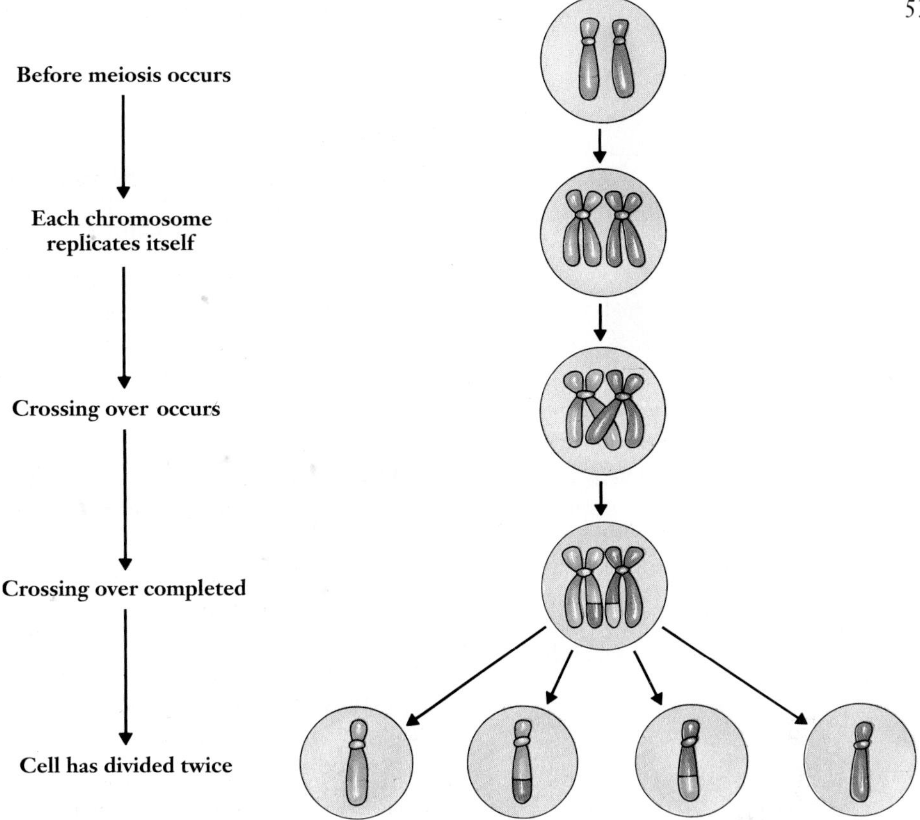

Figure 3.4 ***Schematic representation of crossing over during meiosis***

This drawing illustrates the effect of crossing over at one place on one pair of chromosomes. Crossing over actually occurs in multiple places. The result is that the chromosome in each cell is different from that in each other cell. (Adapted from Plomin & others, 1990.)

Then during each meiotic cell division, the chromosomes within each set are randomly divided between the new cells thus formed. Because of both crossing over and the random assortment of chromosomes, the DNA content of a precursor cell can be divided among the resulting egg or sperm cells in a virtually infinite number of ways. Thus, the chance that a person will produce two genetically identical eggs or sperm is, for all practical purposes, nil.

Genetic Diversity

It may seem ironic that the very cells you use for "reproduction" are the only cells in your body that cannot, in theory, reproduce you. They are the only cells in your body that do not have all of your genes. In sexual reproduction you are, of course, not really reproducing yourself. Rather, you are creating a new individual who is genetically different from, though in some ways similar to, both you and your partner. When a sperm and an egg unite, the result is a single new cell, the ***zygote***, which contains the full complement of 23 paired chromosomes, one member of each pair coming from each parent. The zygote then grows, through mitosis, eventually to become a new adult. Because each sperm or egg is different from any other sperm or egg (even from the same parent), each zygote is different from any other. The purpose of sexual reproduction—as opposed to asexual reproduction, or *cloning*—is to produce offspring that are genetically diverse. That is, sex is a contrivance that came about in the course of evolution because of the advantage inherent in genetic diversity. In a world where the environment keeps changing, genes have a better chance of surviving in the long run if they get rearranged at each generation in many different ways, to produce different kinds of bodies, than if they are all put into the same kind of basket, so to speak. If one kind of body can't survive a particular environmental change, another kind may.

■ **4.** ***What is the difference between identical and fraternal twins?***

The only people who are genetically identical to each other are ***identical twins***. They are formed when two bundles of cells separate from one another during the early mitotic divisions following the formation of a single zygote. Because they originate from one zygote, identical twins are also known as *monozygotic twins*.

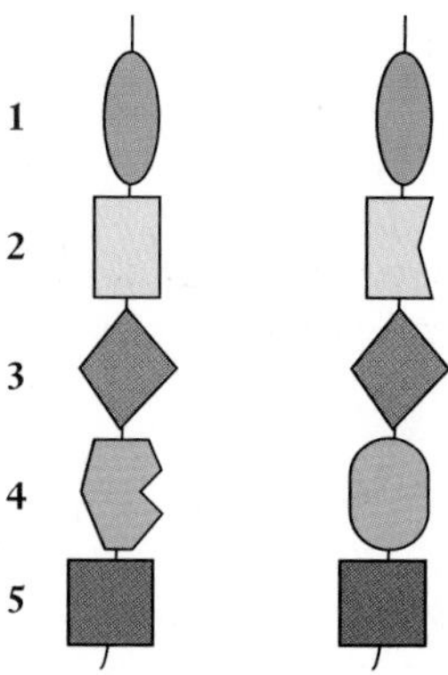

Figure 3.5 ***Schematic illustration of gene loci on a pair of chromosomes***
Successive genes are depicted here as beads on a string. This pair of chromosomes is homozygous at loci 1, 3, and 5 (the paired genes there are identical) and heterozygous at loci 2 and 4 (the paired genes there are not identical). Nonidentical genes that can occupy the same locus are called alleles.

Fraternal twins, or *dizygotic twins*, on the other hand, originate from two zygotes, formed when two different eggs are each joined by a different sperm. Fraternal twins are no more or less similar to one another genetically than are any pair of nontwin siblings. More will be said about these two classes of twins later in the chapter, as they provide a unique resource for studying both genetic and environmental contributions to variability in human characteristics.

Consequences of the Fact That Genes Come in Pairs

You have seen that genes exist on long DNA strands in chromosomes, something like beads on a string, and that chromosomes come in pairs. The two genes that occupy the same ***locus*** (location) on a pair of chromosomes are sometimes identical to one another and sometimes not. When they are identical the individual is said to be ***homozygous*** at that locus, and when they are not identical the individual is said to be ***heterozygous*** at that locus (see Figure 3.5). Different genes that can occupy the same locus, and thus can potentially pair with one another, are referred to as ***alleles***.

■ **5. *What is the difference between a dominant and a recessive gene (or allele)?***

For example, a gene for brown eyes and a gene for blue eyes in humans are alleles because they can occupy the same locus. If you are homozygous for brown eyes, you have two copies of a gene that manufactures an enzyme that makes your eyes brown. What if you were heterozygous for eye color, with an allele for brown eyes paired with one for blue eyes? In this case, you would have brown eyes, phenotypically indistinguishable from what would happen if you were homozygous for brown eyes. This fact is described by saying that the allele for brown eyes is ***dominant*** and the one for blue eyes is ***recessive***. A dominant gene (or allele) is one that will produce its observable effects in either the homozygous or the heterozygous condition, and a recessive gene (or allele) is one that will produce its effects only in the homozygous condition. But not all pairs of alleles manifest dominance and recessiveness. Some pairs blend their effects. For example, if you cross red four-o'clocks (a kind of flower) with white four-o'clocks, the offspring will be pink, because neither the red nor the white allele is dominant over the other.

■ **6. *What does it mean to say that you and a specific relative are X percent related?***

The fact that genes come in pairs provides the basis for calculating what geneticists call *percent relatedness*. Because you received one member of each of your paired genes from your mother, and the other from your father, you are said to be 50 percent related to each of your two parents. An extension of this reasoning can be used to calculate the percent relatedness of other classes of relatives (see Table 3.1). Percent relatedness is a useful index of the likelihood that any given rare gene that exists in one individual will also exist in a relative. Most genes are very common in the population, so any two people chosen at random share more than 50

Table 3.1 ***Genetic relatedness***

Relationship	Degree of relationship	Percent relatedness
Identical twins		100.00%
Parent/child Full brothers, full sisters Fraternal twins	First degree	50.00
Grandparent/grandchild Uncle or aunt/nephew or niece Half-brothers, half-sisters	Second degree	25.00
First cousins	Third degree	12.50
Second cousins	Fourth degree	6.25

percent of their total genes. But no matter how rare a particular gene is, if one of your parents has it, the chance that you will have it is at least 50 percent.

Mendelian Patterns of Heredity

You may already know of the famous experiments with peas conducted in the mid-nineteenth century by an Austrian monk named Gregor Mendel. In a typical experiment, Mendel would start with two purebred strains of peas, differing in one or more easily observed traits, and cross them to observe the traits of the offspring, called the F_1 (first filial) generation. Then he would breed the F_1 peas among themselves to produce the F_2 (second filial) generation. For example, in one experiment Mendel crossed a strain of peas that regularly produced round seeds with a strain that regularly produced wrinkled seeds. His famous findings were: (a) all of the F_1 generation had round seeds; and (b) three-fourths of the F_2 generation had round seeds and one-fourth had wrinkled seeds.

7. *Why do three-fourths of the offspring of two heterozygous parents show the dominant trait and one-fourth show the recessive trait?*

On the basis of our knowledge that genes come in pairs, how can we explain Mendel's finding? If we consider seed texture to be controlled by a single (paired) gene locus, with the allele for round dominant over that for wrinkled, Mendel's findings make perfect sense. Let us use the capital letter *R* to stand for the dominant, round-producing allele and the small letter *r* for the recessive, wrinkle-producing allele. The purebred round strain is homozygous for the "round" allele (*RR*), and the purebred wrinkled strain is homozygous for the "wrinkled" allele (*rr*). (A purebred strain is homozygous for all observed traits.) Since one allele must come from each parent, the only possible result for the F_1 generation, produced by crossing the two purebred strains, is the heterozygous condition (*Rr*). This explains why all of the F_1 peas in Mendel's experiment were round. On the other hand, when *Rr* peas are bred with each other to produce the F_2 generation, four equally likely results can occur: (1) an *R* from each parent (*RR*); (2) an *R* from the female parent and an *r* from the male (*Rr*); (3) an *r* from the female parent and an *R* from the male (*rR*); or (4) an *r* from each parent (*rr*). (See Figure 3.6.) Since only one of these possible outcomes (*rr*) is wrinkled, the expectation is that one-fourth of the F_2 generation will be wrinkled and the other three-fourths round. This, of course, is just what Mendel found.

It is important to note that although the *Rr* peas look the same as the *RR* peas, they are not genetically the same. In other words, though they have the same phenotype, they have different genotypes. An *Rr* pea plant, if crossed with either an *Rr* or *rr* variety, is capable of producing offspring with wrinkled seeds (*rr*). An *RR* plant, on the other hand, can produce only round-seeded offspring (*Rr* or *RR*) no matter what the variety with which it is crossed.

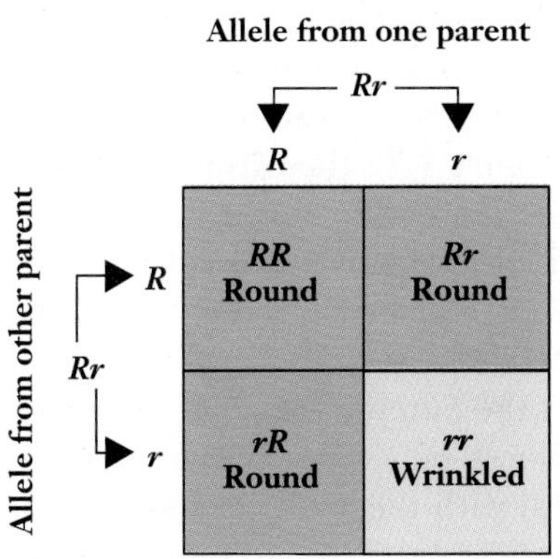

Figure 3.6 ***Explanation of Mendel's ratio***

When two pea plants that are heterozygous for round versus wrinkled seeds are crossbred four possible gene combinations occur. Here ***R*** stands for the dominant, round-producing allele, and ***r*** for the recessive, wrinkle-producing allele. In three cases the phenotype of the offspring will be round, and in one case wrinkled. This 3:1 ratio was Mendel's famous finding.

Single-Gene and Chromosomal Effects on Behavior

One approach in behavioral genetics is to look for behavioral characteristics or disorders that are either inherited in Mendelian fashion, indicative of single-gene control, or that are related to observable abnormalities in the karyotype. Such studies represent the most clear-cut demonstrations that genetic variation can affect behavior, and they also serve as a first step toward understanding the biochemical routes through which specific genes can affect behavior. In humans, research of this sort has focused mostly on behaviorally important genetic disorders or diseases, and in some cases it has led to effective treatments. In this section we will look first at a classic study of behavioral differences in dog breeds, and then at some genetic disorders in people.

Figure 3.7 ***Dogs used in Scott and Fuller's research***

At left are a male basenji and a female cocker spaniel; at right are two F_1 hybrids resulting from a basenji-cocker cross.

■ **8.** ***How did Scott and Fuller show that the difference between cocker spaniels and basenji hounds in fearfulness is controlled by a single gene locus with the "fear" allele dominant over the "nonfear" allele?***

■ **9.** ***Why would it be a mistake to conclude from Scott and Fuller's work that fear in dogs is due to a single gene, or due to genes and not environment?***

Mendelian Inheritance of a Behavioral Trait in Dogs

Some years ago, John Paul Scott and John Fuller (1965) performed an extensive study of the behavior of various breeds of dogs and their mixed-breed offspring. In one especially interesting series, they crossed cocker spaniels with basenji hounds. Basenjis are very timid dogs, showing fear of people until they have been much handled and gentled. Cockers, on the other hand, show little fear under normal rearing conditions. In a standard test with 5-week-old puppies, Scott and Fuller found that all of the basenji puppies yelped and/or ran away when approached by a strange person, whereas only a few of the cocker puppies showed these reactions. When cockers and basenjis were crossbred (see Figure 3.7), the offspring (F_1 hybrids) were like basenjis in this test: all showed signs of fear when approached. Since this was as true of hybrids raised by cocker mothers as those raised by basenji mothers, Scott and Fuller concluded that the effect stemmed from their genes and not from the way they were treated by their mothers.

The fact that the F_1 hybrids were as fearful as the purebred basenjis suggested to Scott and Fuller that the difference in fearfulness between the two purebred strains might be controlled by a single gene locus, with the allele promoting fear dominant over that promoting confidence. If this were so, then mating F_1 hybrids with each other should produce a group of offspring (F_2 generation) in which three-fourths would show basenji-like fear and one-fourth would show cocker-like confidence, the same ratios that Mendel had found with seed texture in peas. Scott and Fuller did this experiment, and in fact found ratios very close to those predicted. As additional evidence, they also *backcrossed* F_1 hybrids with purebred cockers. About half of the offspring of the backcrosses were basenji-like in fear and the other half were cocker-like in confidence—just as expected if the "fear" allele is dominant over the "nonfear" allele (see Figure 3.8).

Be careful not to misinterpret this finding. It concerns a difference between two breeds of dogs in certain behavioral tests. It would not be reasonable to conclude that fear in all of its various forms is controlled by a single gene. Thousands of different genes must contribute to building the complex neural structure needed to experience fear and express it in behavior. Scott and Fuller's work demonstrates only that the difference between cocker spaniels and basenji hounds in a particular test of fear is controlled by a single gene. Recognize also that their studies do not diminish the role of environmental effects. Scott and Fuller were able to detect the

Figure 3.8 ***Explanation of Scott and Fuller's results for back-crosses between basenji-cocker hybrids and purebred cockers***

The finding that half of these offspring were fearful and half not makes sense if fearfulness results from a dominant allele (*F*) and lack of fearfulness from a recessive allele (*f*). Because half of the offspring receive *F* from their hybrid parent and all receive *f* from the purebred parent, half of the offspring will be *Ff* (phenotypically fearful) and the other half *ff* (not fearful).

Allele from cocker-basenji hybrid: *Ff*

Allele from purebred cocker: *ff*

	F	*f*
f	*fF* Fearful	*ff* Not fearful
f	*fF* Fearful	*ff* Not fearful

effect of a specific gene pair because they raised all of the dogs in similar environments. In other research, Scott (1963) showed that any puppy isolated from people for the first four months of life will be fearful of humans. Had Scott and Fuller isolated the cockers from all human contact and given the basenjis lots of kind handling before the behavioral test, they might well have found the cockers to be more fearful than the basenjis despite the genetic predispositions toward the opposite.

Nancy Wexler

As part of her research on Huntington's disease, Wexler has spent every spring since 1981 in a remote region of Venezuela where the disease is rampant, to test those currently affected. She has traced the disease back 10 generations to one woman who died of it in the early 1800s. Wexler also lectures widely on the ethical dilemmas raised by knowledge gained from genetic research.

Single-Gene Disorders in Humans

Many human disorders that affect behavior are passed from generation to generation by single-gene inheritance. Some of these, such as Huntington's disease and PKU, are inherited in patterns like those that Mendel found for round or wrinkled peas. Others, such as red-green color blindness and Fragile X syndrome, have more complicated patterns of heredity.

Huntington's Disease: A Dominant Disorder

Huntington's disease is one of the relatively few debilitating single-gene disorders that are caused by a dominant rather than a recessive allele. Its symptoms usually first appear when the person is about 35 to 45 years old, at which time cells in the brain begin to decline in size and number, causing progressive debilitation in intellect, personality, and muscle control, and resulting in death within 10 or 20 years. Because the disorder stems from a dominant gene, the victim suffers the additional knowledge that each of his or her children has a 50 percent chance of inheriting it. Each child has a 50 percent chance of receiving the chromosome with the disordered gene, and every child who receives it will eventually manifest the disorder. Fortunately the gene is rare, occurring in about 1 person out of 15,000 (Wynbrandt & Ludman, 1991).

The time course of Huntington's disease illustrates an important point about dominant disorders. A lethal dominant disorder can be transmitted from one generation to the next only if it manifests its most debilitating effects after its victims have reached the age at which they can produce children. If Huntington's disease struck earlier, its victims would typically be too ill to have children, and the gene would not be passed on to the next generation. This fact is not true for recessive disorders; the genes for recessive disorders continue to be passed on from one generation to the next by healthy heterozygous carriers, regardless of how lethal the genes may be in the homozygous condition.

10. ***Why can lethal dominant disorders, unlike recessive disorders, persist in the population only if they manifest their effects after early adulthood?***

Using modern methods for mapping genes, geneticists discovered that the Huntington's gene is located near one end of chromosome 4. This in turn led to a means of determining if a person has the gene (Gusella & others, 1983). One member of the team that discovered the gene's location, Nancy Wexler, is herself the

Figure 3.9 ***Triplets, two with PKU and one without***

The two children at the right are genetically identical and have PKU. Their arm posturing is typical of severely affected PKU individuals. Because PKU is caused by a recessive allele, on average one out of every four children born to two parents who are heterozygous for the allele will have the disorder. Today the most severe effects of PKU are prevented by starting affected individuals on a diet low in phenylalanine immediately after birth.

daughter of a Huntington's victim. When the test became available, Wexler was faced with the same dilemma that now faces everyone with a Huntington's parent (Jaroff, 1992): Did she really want to know? Of course, she would want to know that she didn't have it, but what if she did have it? What would life be like knowing for sure that the disease would strike? Wexler's decision is private, but a recent follow-up study of people who chose to be tested found that even those who had the gene were, in general, happier to have that knowledge than to continue in doubt (Wiggins & others, 1992). One advantage of the test is that it can help a person at risk decide whether or not to have children. Researchers of course hope that before long their understanding of the gene will provide a basis not just for detecting it but also for preventing its harmful effects.

PKU: A Recessive Disorder

Phenylketonuria, usually called **PKU**, is an example of a disorder caused by a recessive gene pair. The disorder occurs in about 1 out of every 10,000 newborn babies. If untreated, it usually results in reduced brain size, poor motor coordination, and severe mental retardation, including, in many cases, an inability to speak or understand language (Hay, 1985). (See Figure 3.9.) The gene responsible for this disorder can be any of several different defective alleles of a gene that normally directs the synthesis of an enzyme that controls the body's use of phenylalanine (an amino acid present in milk and other protein-containing foods). The defective allele creates a defective enzyme, which is anywhere from 0 to 50 percent as effective as the normal enzyme in breaking down phenylalanine (Okano & others, 1991). In the absence of the normal enzyme, phenylalanine accumulates in the body and is converted to an acidic substance that, in high quantities, is poisonous to the brain and other tissues.

■ **11.** ***How has knowledge of the genetic basis of PKU led to an environmental treatment?***

Although inherited genetically, PKU can be treated by environmental means. Because scientists understand the biochemical basis for PKU, they can minimize the faulty gene's damaging effects by controlling the biochemical environment. Most hospitals today routinely test newborn babies for PKU and immediately place affected infants on a diet low in phenylalanine. With low phenylalanine intake, little of the poisonous acid is created, and the baby can grow up quite normally. The diet must be started soon after birth, because the most severe and irreversible effects of the acid on brain development occur in infancy. Later in life, PKU sufferers can be somewhat less diligent about their diet, though mild reduction in mental abilities can still occur if the phenylalanine level gets too high (Welsh & others, 1990). Also, pregnant PKU women must go back onto the diet to prevent brain damage to the fetus during prenatal development.

■ **12.** ***How does the paired nature of genes reduce the incidence of genetic disorders?***

To say that a PKU-producing allele is recessive is to say that its effects will not occur if it is paired with a normal, non-PKU-producing allele. Thus, a child can be born with the disease only if both parents carry the abnormal allele. Let's use the capital letter *P* for the dominant normal allele and the small letter *p* for any of the various PKU-producing alleles. If two parents who don't have PKU have a PKU baby, they must both be heterozygous (*Pp*) carriers of the disease, which in turn means that there is 1 chance in 4 that any future child they have will be born with PKU (as was shown in Figure 3.6 for wrinkled peas). Most single-gene disorders are like PKU in that they are caused by recessive alleles. In other words, most such disorders occur only if a faulty gene exists on both chromosomes at the same gene locus. It is fortunate that genes come in pairs. If one is defective, then its mate on the homologous chromosome can usually make up for the deficit. It's like carrying a spare tire. Only if *both* members of a gene pair are defective will the person be harmed.

Red-Green Color Blindness: A Sex-Linked Disorder

■ **13.** ***Why do males have more genetic disorders than do females?***

An exception to the rule that genes come in pairs exists for genes located on the X chromosome in males. The Y chromosome, which males have instead of a second X, is very small (look back at Figure 3.2) and does not contain genes to match all of those on the X. The interesting result is that males are more vulnerable to certain genetic disorders than are females. If a female has something wrong on one of her X chromosomes, the matched gene on the other X will usually be normal and produce a normal phenotype. But a male who has a defective gene on his X is in trouble. He has no spare.

Because they are far more likely to show up in men than in women, recessive traits controlled by the X chromosome are called ***sex-linked traits***. One relatively benign example is red-green color blindness (the inability, under certain conditions, to distinguish between red and green). Let's use *C* to stand for the dominant allele that promotes normal color vision, and *c* to stand for any of the various recessive alleles that promote red-green color blindness. Since this gene is located on the X chromosome, and a male has only one, a male can be genotypically either *C* or *c*. If 1 out of 10 X chromosomes in the population contains the recessive allele (a figure that is approximately accurate), then 1 out of 10 men will be red-green color blind. A female, in contrast, has two X chromosomes and can be genotypically *CC*, *cC*, *Cc*, or *cc*. Only in the last case (*cc*) will she show the trait phenotypically. If 1 out of 10 X chromosomes in the population contains the recessive allele, then the chance that both X chromosomes in a given female will contain the recessive allele is 1 out of 100. (The probability of two independent events occurring together is equal to the probability of one times the probability of the other. In this case, $1/10 \times 1/10 = 1/100$.)

Fragile X Syndrome: A More Complex Pattern of Inheritance

In the 1970s, researchers first began to learn that many cases of mental retardation are associated with a specific defect on the X chromosome. The defect can be observed as a break or tear on the X chromosome when it is studied under certain conditions in the laboratory, and, therefore, the pattern of physical and mental conditions associated with it came to be called ***fragile X syndrome***. The syndrome includes moderate to severe mental retardation manifested especially in tests that require the person to notice or remember the sequential order of items of information (Zigler & Hodapp, 1991). Perhaps because of this deficit in sequencing ability, people with this syndrome usually have great difficulty speaking or understanding multi-word statements, even though they have no particular difficulty with individual words (Dykens & Leckman, 1990).

■ **14.** ***How does the pattern of inheritance of fragile X syndrome differ from that for a typical sex-linked trait such as red-green color blindness?***

The specific gene on the X chromosome that produces fragile X syndrome has recently been identified and described in biochemical detail (Verkerk & others, 1991). It produces an unusual protein molecule that may interfere with brain processes in a variety of ways. Fragile X is now understood to be one of the most common of all varieties of mental retardation, occurring at a rate of about 1 per 1250 males and 1 per 2000 females (Davies, 1991). This pattern of somewhat greater frequency in males than in females suggests that the gene causing the syndrome is neither fully dominant nor fully recessive. Thus, unlike the case for red-green color blindness, a female who has the defective gene on one X chromosome is apparently only partly protected by the good gene on her other X chromosome. Depending on other unknown conditions, the partly protected female may or may not manifest the disorder. This explanation is also consistent with the observation that the degree of mental retardation in affected females is, on average, less than that in affected males.

From a genetic standpoint, the most unusual feature of fragile X syndrome is that the gene can exist in a completely inactive form for several generations and then be converted into an active form. Men and women who carry the inactive form of the gene show no sign of the disorder. The children of men who carry the inactive gene also do not show the disorder (the gene remains inactive in them), but the children of women who carry it often do show the disorder. Apparently, the gene can be converted from the inactive to the active form during egg production in women, but not during sperm production in men (Shapiro, 1991). The more general point to be made here is that patterns of heredity for single-gene disorders do not always coincide with Mendel's ratios, but may depend on unique biochemical aspects of the gene's activation and expression.

Chromosomal Disorders in Humans

15. ***How do abnormal numbers of chromosomes arise in meiosis?***

Some genetic disorders come not from single genes but rather involve whole chromosomes or relatively large chunks of chromosomes. Sometimes, in the process of meiosis, both copies of a chromosome end up in the same egg or sperm cell, leaving another egg or sperm cell with no copy of that chromosome. Other times a piece of a chromosome separates from the rest during meiosis, causing a portion of the chromosome to exist in duplicate in one egg or sperm cell and to be absent in another. Usually such egg and sperm cells are not viable; they either fail to form a zygote when they join with their complement, or they form a zygote so abnormal that it dies and is spontaneously aborted (miscarried). But a few chromosomal abnormalities are compatible with survival. About 1 out of every 200 infants is born with a detectable chromosomal abnormality, most of which involve either a sex chromosome or chromosome 21 (Plomin & others, 1990).

Living with Turner's syndrome

Barbara Tiemann, past president of the Turner's Syndrome Society, is shown on her way to work in Boston. Because women with Turner's syndrome look a little different and because their condition is called a "syndrome," many people mistakenly think that they are intellectually slow. The society serves as a support group to help members deal with this kind of prejudice.

Variations in the Number of Sex Chromosomes

As pointed out earlier, the normal female karyotype has two X chromosomes and the normal male has an X and a Y. The most common variations in sex chromosome number compatible with survival are: (a) XXX, (b) X0 (a single X chromosome and no complement—the 0 stands for the absence of a chromosome), (c) XXY, and (d) XYY. Since the absence or presence of a Y chromosome determines phenotype sex, XXX and X0 individuals develop as females, and XXY and XYY as males. In general, XXX females and XYY males undergo normal sexual development. They are usually fertile, and they have normal children because the extra chromosome is usually lost during gamete formation. On the other hand, X0 females and XXY males are usually underdeveloped sexually and infertile. The X0 disorder is also known as *Turner's syndrome*, and the XXY is known as *Klinefelter's syndrome*.

Most individuals with variations in the number of sex chromosomes fall within the normal range of mental development, though mild mental retardation occurs somewhat more often in XXX women and XXY and XYY men than in the general population (Evans & others, 1991). Also, for unknown reasons, X0 women as a group perform below average on tasks involving spatial ability (such as completing picture puzzles) but not on tasks involving verbal ability (such as defining terms), and XXY men show the opposite pattern—below average on verbal but not spatial tasks (Netley, 1983).

Down Syndrome

The most common chromosomal disorder that doesn't involve a sex chromosome is ***Down syndrome***, which occurs in about 1 out of every 700 live-born infants (Therman, 1986). Another name for this disorder is *trisomy-21*, reflecting the fact

An actor with Down syndrome

People with Down syndrome can benefit from a supportive and stimulating environment. Actor Chris Burke (center), who has Down syndrome, has achieved success in a highly competitive field. Here Burke and other cast members are rehearsing a dance for an episode of the television series *Life Goes On*.

that the abnormality in the karyotype is usually an entire extra chromosome 21 (a triplet rather than the usual pair), although sometimes only a portion of an extra chromosome 21 is present. Many physical ailments (especially heart abnormalities) accompany this disorder, which often reduce the life span. Most Down children can be recognized by their physical appearance. Typical (but not inevitable) signs include short stature; a thick, short neck; stubby hands and fingers; a flattened nose bridge; a protruding tongue; and a fold of skin over the inner corner of each eye. In the past, Down children were commonly considered uneducable and placed in institutions, where they were often neglected. This belief had the effect of a self-fulfilling prophesy: when neglected, most people with Down syndrome remained extremely retarded throughout their lives. It is now clear that such people do far better if raised in a supportive environment and given special education. With that support, some achieve IQs in the low normal range (70 or 80) and become able to care for themselves and find gainful employment (Cicchetti & Beeghly, 1988; Cohen, 1984).

■ **16.** ***What similarity between Down syndrome and Alzheimer's disease suggests that the same gene may be responsible for mental deterioration in both disorders?***

Recent research has shown that people with Down syndrome develop abnormal protein coats (called *amyloid plaques*) on nerve cells in their brain, and that the code for this protein lies at a specific gene locus on chromosome 21 (Loehlin & others, 1988). Although many different genes on the chromosome are responsible for the constellation of symptoms in Down syndrome, this gene may be most responsible for the mental retardation. The same gene is also apparently involved in Alzheimer's disease, a disorder involving severe mental deterioration that usually strikes in late adulthood. People with Alzheimer's develop the same kind of brain plaques as those with Down syndrome, and evidence exists that in both diseases the amyloid-producing gene is more active than normal (Delabar & others, 1987; Selkoe, 1991).

The incidence of Down syndrome, as well as certain other chromosomal disorders, increases with the age of the mother. The reason for this is uncertain, but possibilities include hormonal and other physiological changes that accompany aging, and the accumulated effects of years of exposure to environmental radiation, which may adversely affect the precursor cells that divide to form eggs (Therman, 1986). Although most attention has been paid to the mother, the father's age is also relevant. In about 20 percent of cases the extra chromosome 21 comes from the sperm, and the likelihood of this occurring increases with the father's age (Therman, 1986).

Polygenic Effects on Behavior

Thus far our concern has been with clear-cut genetic effects that result from variation at a single gene locus or from an abnormal karyotype. Though these are clinically important, and they illustrate basic principles of heredity, they tell us relatively little about normal variability in behavior. Most measurable differences among people cannot be explained in terms of single genes or abnormal numbers of chromosomes, but rather lie in the combined effects of many genes and their interactions with the environment.

■ 17. ***How does the distribution of scores for a polygenic trait differ from that usually obtained for a single-gene trait?***

For any measurable behavioral characteristic in any given group of individuals, one finds a certain range of variability. Some mice are more active than others, some rats learn mazes more quickly than others, some people score higher on IQ tests than others. The measured differences in such behaviors are not discrete, or step-like, as they would be if they were heavily influenced by a single gene. Rather, the differences are ***continuous***, meaning that any gradation within the observed range is possible. Most often the set of scores obtained on such measures approximates a ***normal distribution***, meaning that most scores fall near the middle of the range and the frequency tapers off toward the extremes (see Figure 3.10). Any characteristic that varies in a continuous way is presumably affected by many genes and hence is referred to as a ***polygenic characteristic*** (the prefix *poly-* means many). The same characteristics are also influenced by the environment, so the variability observed in a graph such as that in Figure 3.10 is due to a combination of genetic differences at many gene loci and a wide variety of environmental differences. A nonbehavioral example of a polygenic characteristic is height in humans. Many gene loci are involved in producing variations in height, and any given person's height depends on the relative number of alleles promoting tallness or shortness that occupy these loci, as well as on environmental factors (such as nutrition).

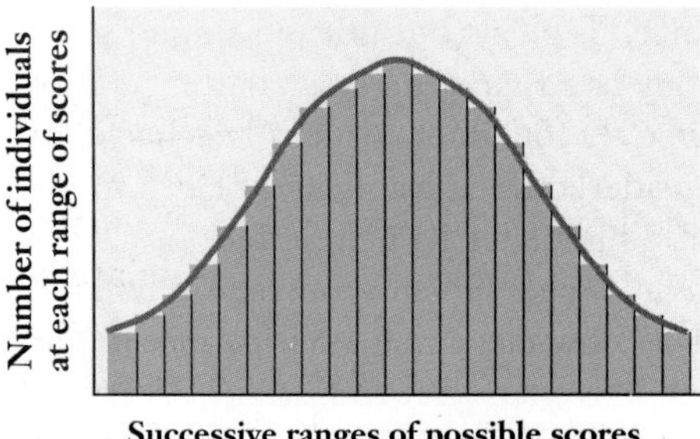

Figure 3.10 *Normal distribution*
When many individuals are tested for a polygenic characteristic, the majority usually fall in the middle of the range of scores and the frequency tapers off toward zero at the extremes. Mathematically, this defines a normal curve.

The behavioral-genetics study of polygenic effects is usually more abstract than that of single-gene or chromosomal effects. It is generally not possible, with present means, to identify the specific genes involved in such effects, to specify the biochemical routes through which they act, or to predict patterns of heredity within a family. Rather, behavioral geneticists attempt to understand the degree to which average differences among individuals in the phenotype characteristic are due to genetic as compared with environmental differences among the individuals. This approach is called *quantitative genetics*, because it relies on statistical methods and mathematical models (Plomin & others, 1990). Here we will consider only the overall logic of this approach, along with some of the main findings and controversies.

The Concept of Heritability

The central concept in quantitative genetics is that of ***heritability***. Heritability refers to the degree to which variation among individuals on a particular trait, in a particular population, can be attributed to genetic differences among those individuals. Coupled with other information, it is useful in predicting the extent to which offspring are likely to resemble their parents on the trait in question. Heritability is often quantified by a statistic called the ***heritability coefficient***, abbreviated h^2. This coefficient is technically defined as the proportion of the variance of a trait, in a population, that is due to genetic variation. As a formula, it can be written:

$$h^2 = \frac{\text{Variance due to genes}}{\text{Total variance}}$$

The denominator (total variance) is simply a measure of the degree to which the individuals being studied differ from one another in the characteristic that was

GROUP *A*

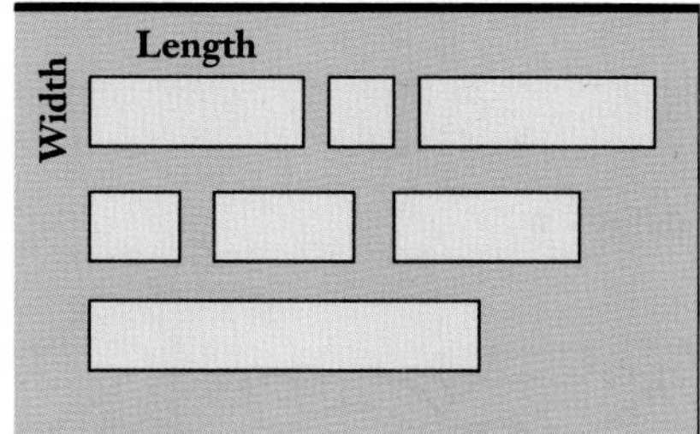

GROUP *B*

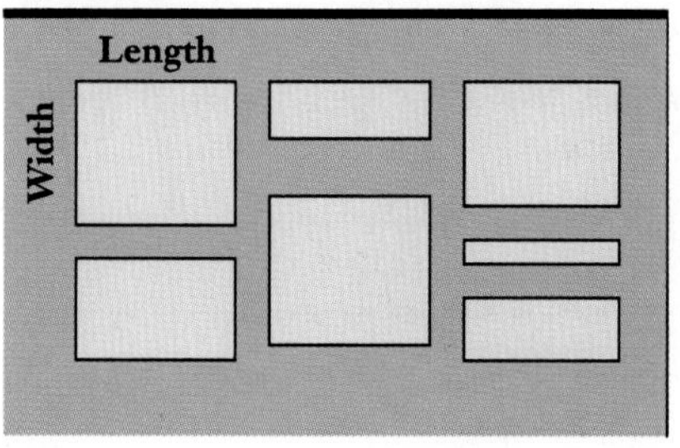

Figure 3.11 ***A geometric analogy to heritability***

It makes no sense to ask whether a given rectangle's area is due more to its width or its length. Shrink either to zero and the area goes to zero. But one can sensibly ask whether variation in area in a specific group of rectangles is due more to differences in their length than in their width. In Group *A* above, variation in area is due to differing lengths, and in Group *B* it is due to differing widths. Similarly, for variation in a characteristic such as IQ, one can imagine one group of people in which variation is due mostly to their differing genes and another in which it is due mostly to their differing environments.

■ **18.** ***In what sense does heritability apply to differences among individuals and not to a trait within an individual?***

measured. It can be calculated directly from the set of scores obtained from the individuals in the group (the formula for variance can be found in the Statistical Appendix). The numerator (variance due to genes), in contrast, cannot be calculated directly, but must be estimated by comparing sets of individuals who differ in their degree of genetic relationship to one another. Behavioral geneticists who work with animals use selective breeding (to be described later) as a means of estimating variance due to genes, and those who work with people use such procedures as comparing identical and fraternal twins (also to be described later). Examination of the formula shows that the heritability coefficient can in theory vary from 0.00 to 1.00. A coefficient of 0.00 means that none of the observed variance in the characteristic is due to genes (all of it is due to environmental differences), a coefficient of 1.00 means that all of the variance is due to genes, and a coefficient of 0.50 means that half of the variance is due to genes.

Because any method for calculating heritability depends on assumptions that may not be fully correct, a calculated heritability coefficient is at best a rough approximation. For that reason, some behavioral geneticists prefer not to use numbers to describe it. Yet, whether expressed quantitatively or not, the concept of heritability lies behind all studies aimed at comparing the extent to which genetic diversity and environmental diversity contribute to the observed variation in a characteristic. It is important, therefore, to understand what the concept means and what it *doesn't* mean.

Heritability Applies to Differences Among Individuals, Not to a Trait Within an Individual

Sometimes people mistakenly assume that heritability refers to the proportion of a particular characteristic within an individual that arises because of heredity as opposed to environment. For example, if they hear that the heritability for IQ scores for a set of people is 0.60, they might assume that 60 percent of a person's intelligence is caused by genes and the remaining 40 percent by the environment. But if you think about it, you will realize that such an assumption makes no sense. Genes and environment are both absolutely essential for intelligence to develop at all. With no genes there would be no person and hence no intelligence, and with no environment there would also be no person and no intelligence. Given that genes and environment are both absolutely essential for any trait to develop, it would be meaningless to say that one contributes more than the other to the trait. The same is true for any other characteristic of an individual. A useful analogy concerns the contribution of length and width to the area of a rectangle, as described in the caption to Figure 3.11 (suggested by Hebb, 1958).

To think about the point further, consider the trait of height in tomato plants. To estimate the degree to which any given plant's height is due to its genes or due to its environment would be absurd, because both are absolutely essential for the plant to grow at all. However, suppose you observe two plants and notice that one is taller than the other. It is not absurd to ask whether that *difference* is due more to differences in the plants' genes or more to differences in their environments (such as soil fertility). In the former case, heritability would be high and in the latter case, it would be low.

Heritability Increases as Genetic Diversity Increases

This statement follows directly from the definition of heritability and the formula for measuring it (h^2 = variance due to genes/total variance). The numerator in the formula can be high relative to the denominator only if the individuals in the group being studied differ from one another in their genes (look again at the formula). If you were to study heritability of height in a group of cloned (genetically identical) tomato plants, you would necessarily find a heritability coefficient of 0.00 (see top

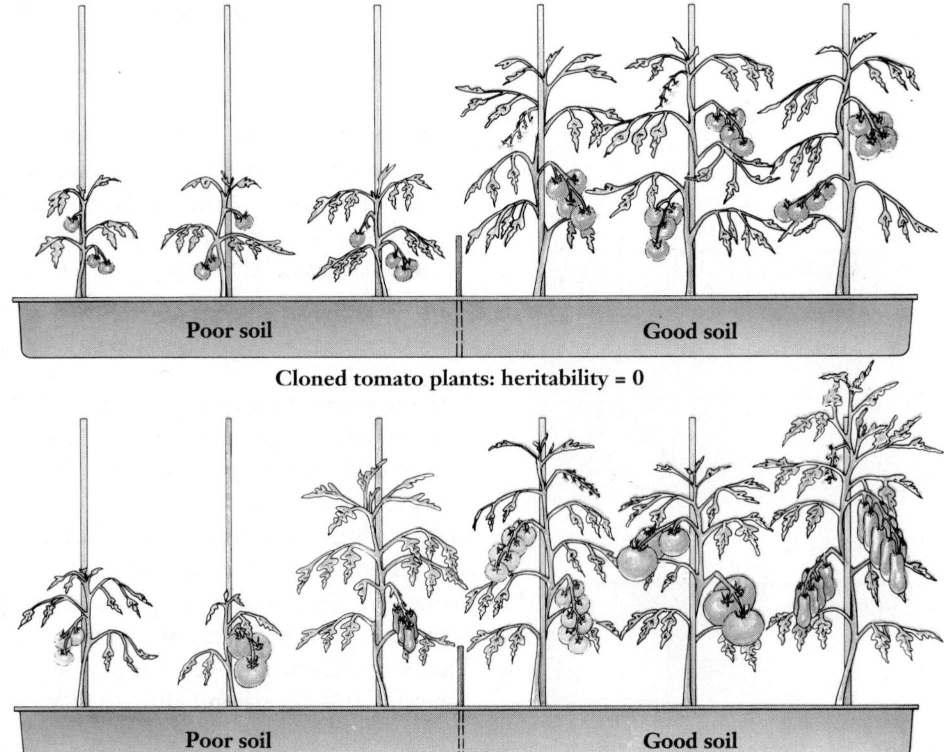

Figure 3.12 ***How genetic diversity affects heritability***

The differences in the cloned tomato plants (top) are due to environment alone. Because the plants are genetically identical, the numerator in the heritability formula must be 0.00, and heritability must be 0.00. In contrast, the differences among the genetically diverse tomato plants (bottom) are due to both genetic and environmental differences. Thus, the heritability coefficient for that group must be greater than 0.00 and less than 1.00.

■ **19.** ***How does heritability change with changes in the genetic or environmental diversity of the group studied, and why? (If you can answer this question, you understand heritability. If you can't, you don't.)***

half of Figure 3.12). That does not mean that their genes don't contribute to their height; it only means that the *differences* among the plants have to be due to environmental differences (such as soil fertility), because the genes do not vary from plant to plant. On the other hand, if you started with a genetically diverse group of tomato plants, you would find the heritability for height to be greater than 0.00 (see bottom half of Figure 3.12). The greater the genetic diversity, the greater is the numerator in the ratio that defines the heritability coefficient. The same applies for IQ scores in people or any other measurable characteristic.

Heritability Decreases as Environmental Diversity Increases

This statement also follows directly from the definition and formula for heritability. Increased environmental diversity adds to the denominator (total observed variance in the characteristic measured) without adding to the numerator (variance due to genes), thereby decreasing the heritability coefficient. If you raised a group of tomato plants under exactly the same environmental conditions (assuming that were possible), then whatever differences you found among them in plant height would have to be attributed to genetic differences; variance due to genes and total variance would be identical, and the heritability coefficient would be 1.00. In contrast, if you raised the tomato plants in highly diverse conditions—some in rich soil, others in sand, some with lots of moisture, others with little—these environmental differences would greatly increase the total variability in plant height, but would not increase the variability attributable to genes. Therefore the denominator of the heritability formula would increase, but not the numerator; and the heritability coefficient would decrease.

Environmentality Is the Complement of Heritability

Some researchers prefer not to use the term *heritability* because it focuses too much attention on genes and not enough on the environment. As we have seen, the heritability coefficient is actually as much a measure of the environmental contribution to variability as it is a measure of the genetic contribution. For example, a heritability coefficient of 0.40 means that 40 percent of the measured variance is due to genetic variation and 60 percent is due to environmental variation. To create greater equity in focus, some behavioral geneticists have proposed that the term ***environmentality*** be used to refer to the proportion of variance that is due to environmental variation (Fuller & Thompson, 1978). Thus, a heritability coefficient of 0.40 would correspond to an environmentality coefficient of 0.60.

A great pumpkin

With the right combination of genes and environment, anything is possible!

Selective Breeding for Behavioral Characteristics in Animals

Polygenic effects on behavior in nonhuman animals can be studied through ***selective breeding***, defined as the deliberate mating of individuals that score toward one end or the other on some measurable characteristic. The basic procedure of selective breeding is by no means new. For thousands of years before a formal science of genetics existed, plant and animal breeders used selective breeding to produce new and better strains of every sort of domesticated species. Grains were bred for fatter seeds, cows for docility and greater milk production, horses along separate lines for work and racing, canaries for their song. Dogs were bred along dozens of different lines for such varied purposes as following a trail, herding sheep (running around them instead of at them), and providing gentle playmates for children. The procedure in every case was essentially the same: Those members of each generation that best approximated the desired type were mated to produce the next generation, resulting in a continuous genetic molding toward the varieties that we see today.

In the hands of behavioral geneticists, selective breeding is, among other things, a tool for assessing the heritability of behavioral characteristics. To the degree that a characteristic is heritable, the offspring of selected parents should be more like their parents than like the general population, and to the degree that it is not heritable, the offspring should be more like the general population. Thus, the rate at which a behavioral characteristic can change over generations of selective breeding is one measure of its heritability. (The formula given previously for h^2 can be translated into a formula based on rate of change in selective breeding.)

Tryon's Classic Study of Maze-Learning Ability

■ **20.** ***How did Tryon produce "maze bright" and "maze dull" strains of rats, and how did he show that the difference was due to genes, not rearing?***

The first long-term, systematic study of selective breeding in psychology was begun in the 1920s by Robert Tryon (1942), partly in reaction to the claim of some psychologists that essentially all behavioral differences among individuals are environmental in origin. One of Tryon's goals was to show that a type of behavior frequently studied by psychologists could be strongly influenced by variation in genes.

Tryon began by testing a genetically diverse group of rats—formed by mixing breeds collected from various laboratories—for their ability to learn a particular maze. Then he mated those males and females that made the fewest errors in the maze to begin what he called the "maze bright" strain, and those that made the most errors to begin the "maze dull" strain. When the offspring of succeeding generations reached adulthood, he tested them in the same maze and mated the best-performing members of the "bright" strain, and worst-performing members of the "dull" strain, to continue the two lines. Some of his results are shown in Figure 3.13 on page 66. As you can see, with each generation the two strains became more and more distinct, until by the seventh generation there was almost no overlap between them. Almost all seventh-generation "bright" rats made fewer errors in the maze than even the best "dull" rats. To control for the possibility that the offspring were somehow learning to be "bright" or "dull" from their mothers, Tryon used a cross-fostering procedure, in which some of the offspring from each strain were raised by mothers in the other strain. He found that rats in the "bright" strain were equally good in the maze, and those in the "dull" strain equally poor, regardless of which mothers raised them.

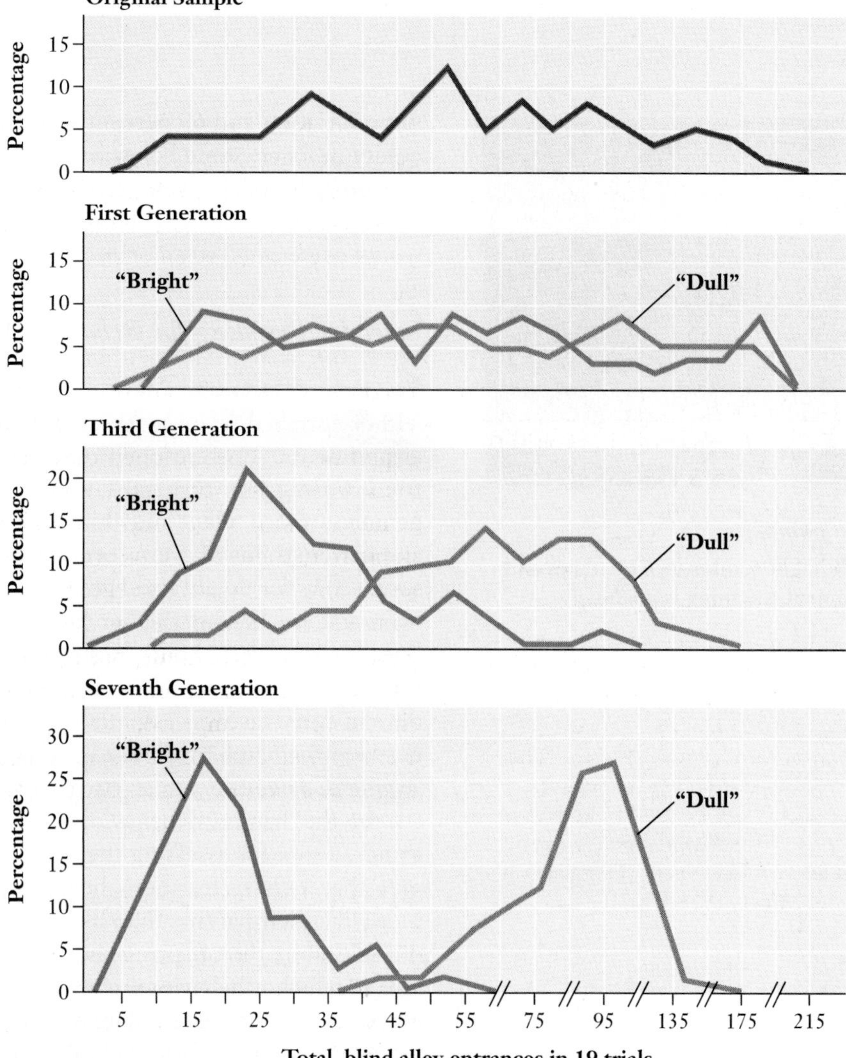

Figure 3.13 ***Selective breeding for "maze brightness" and "maze dullness" in rats***

The top graph shows the percentage of rats in the original parent stock that made each possible range of errors in the maze. Subsequent graphs show the percentage of "bright" and "dull" rats that made each possible range of errors. With successive generations an increasing percentage in the "bright" breed made few errors and an increasing percentage in the "dull" breed made many errors. (From Tryon, 1942.)

Tryon did not calculate a heritability coefficient from his data. He was satisfied to show that maze learning is to some degree heritable and that quite large differences can be produced over several generations of selective breeding. Since his time, behavioral geneticists have performed dozens of similar experiments on a wide variety of behaviors in various species. Fruit flies have been bred to move instinctively either toward or away from a source of light, mice to be either more or less likely to fight, rats to show either more or less fear in an unfamiliar environment, and so on (Broadhurst & others, 1974; Wimer & Wimer, 1985). On this basis, some behavioral geneticists have concluded that any behavioral characteristic that can be measured and that varies among members of a species can be affected by selective breeding. This is not really a surprising conclusion, as it follows logically from the fact that all behaviors depend in some way on sensory, motor, and neural structures, all of which are affected by heredity.

Later Studies That Affect Our Understanding of Tryon's Results

■ **21.** ***How did later studies show that effects of selective breeding can be specific to the bred-for task and the conditions of rearing?***

Once a strain has been bred to show some behavioral characteristic, the question arises as to what other behavioral or physiological changes accompany it. Tryon referred to his two strains as "bright" and "dull," but all he had measured was their performance in a particular type of maze. Performance in the maze no doubt depended on many sensory, motor, motivational, and learning processes, and specific changes in any of these could in theory have mediated the effects that Tryon observed. In theory, Tryon's "dull" rats could simply have been those that had less acute vision, or were less interested in the variety of food used as a reward, or were more interested in exploring the maze's blind alleys. In later studies, another re-

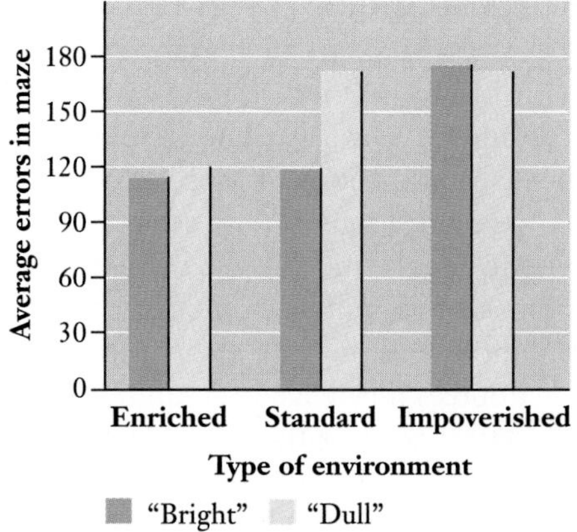

Figure 3.14 ***Interaction of genes and environment in maze performance***
Cooper and Zubek (1958) found that a difference between "maze bright" and "maze dull" strains of rats in maze learning occurred only when the rats were raised in standard laboratory cages. The breeds they used were not the same as those developed by Tryon, but were the result of another selective breeding program at McGill University. (Data from Cooper & Zubek, 1958.)

searcher found that Tryon's "dull" rats were as good as the "bright" ones, and sometimes even better, in other learning tasks (Searle, 1949).

In addition to the type of learning task employed, another important condition in Tryon's study was the environment in which he bred and raised his rats. Because genes express themselves through interaction with the environment, a change in environment could in theory change the relative performances of the two strains of rats. Some years after Tryon's study, R. M. Cooper and John Zubek (1958) compared the maze performances of other strains of rats that had been bred for "maze brightness" or "maze dullness." They raised some of each strain in cages that were either enriched or impoverished compared to the standard cages used in previous experiments. The enriched cages contained tunnels, ramps, and many other objects designed to stimulate activity and learning, and the impoverished cages contained nothing but a food box and water pan. The results of the experiment are depicted in Figure 3.14. As you can see, the "bright" strain outperformed the "dull" strain only when raised in the standard cages. With an enriched environment, both strains performed as well as the standard-environment "brights," and with an impoverished environment, both performed as poorly as the standard-environment "dulls." Stated differently, enriching the environment caused the "dulls" but not the "brights" to improve, and impoverishing the environment caused the "brights" but not the "dulls" to worsen. Thus, in this case, the effect of selective breeding might be described as a capacity to develop good maze-learning ability when raised in standard laboratory cages.

The Heritability and Environmentality of IQ

With humans, of course, the heritability of polygenic traits cannot be studied by selective breeding. Instead, it can be studied by selectively comparing pairs of people who differ in their degree of genetic relationship with one another. Using this method, researchers have studied the heritability of many human characteristics, but by far the most thoroughly studied and debated of these is intelligence, as measured by standard IQ tests. In fact, the whole issue of heritability first arose in relation to debates about individual differences in intellectual ability. Let's look at a bit of that history before turning to contemporary studies of the heritability of IQ.

Galton's Pioneering Research

As noted earlier, in the nineteenth century Francis Galton initiated a program of research on the nature-nurture question as applied to intellectual achievement. Inspired by the evolutionary theory that his half-cousin Charles Darwin had described in *The Origin of Species* (1859), Galton developed the idea that differences in human mental abilities may be inherited, and he set about trying to prove it. His basic question was this: Are the observed differences in people's intellectual achievement more the result of differences in their heredity (nature) or in their environments (nurture)? Or, in modern terms: Is heritability for intellectual achievement high or low?

22. ***What was Galton's evidence that intellectual ability runs in families, and how did he use adopted children and twins to buttress his argument for the strong role of nature?***

Using such sources as biographical dictionaries and historical texts, Galton identified about a thousand eminent men who had become famous through extraordinary achievements in such areas as diplomacy, science, literature, and art. In his book, *Hereditary Genius* (1869), he showed statistically that a disproportionate number of these men were related to one another. For example, in an analysis based on the male relatives of the 100 most eminent men on his list, Galton found that about 30 percent of the first-degree relatives (brothers, sons, and fathers) and 7 percent of the second-degree relatives (uncles, nephews, grandfathers, and grandsons) were themselves among the top 0.025 percent of the male population as a whole in degree of eminence.

Galton was aware that these results might be due partly to the privileged environments shared by eminent men and their relatives, but he argued that this effect of shared environment was relatively small. One of his most interesting arguments was based on his calculations concerning the eminence—or lack of it—achieved by the adopted kinsmen of Roman Catholic popes. Over the centuries, popes had adopted many boys and raised them as if they were their sons. These adoptees, according to Galton, were surrounded by eminent people and received the best of educations, yet, in contrast to the biological sons of eminent men, very few achieved eminence themselves. Galton's argument here is not particularly convincing (because the typical environment of papal adoptees may have been quite different from the typical environments of the biological sons of the eminent men in Galton's sample), but it is historically interesting as the first use of what today is called the ***adoptive method*** for studying heritability. This method involves comparing biological (birth) relatives with adoptive relatives. To the degree that a trait is heritable, greater similarity should be found between biological relatives than between adoptive relatives.

Like parents, like child

Eminent people often pass on more than genes to their offspring. Anthropologist Richard Leakey, shown here discussing a fossil with his father, has benefited from the genes and the wisdom of both his eminent parents—anthropologists Louis and Mary Leakey.

After publishing *Hereditary Genius*, Galton (1876) continued his research on nature and nurture by studying pairs of male twins. Using self-report questionnaires and other biographical materials, he studied many sets of twins and concluded that those who were "alike at birth" remained similar psychologically throughout their lives, even after they left home and entered different environments. By contrast, those who were "different at birth" remained dissimilar throughout their lives. From this, Galton argued that the degree of similarity of twins must be due more to nature than to nurture; otherwise all twins should grow more similar when they live in the same home and more different when they leave home and enter different environments. Galton was unaware of the full significance of his work, because the genetic basis for the distinction between two classes of twins was not yet known (Rende & others, 1990). Yet his work anticipated the behavioral genetics method that today is called the ***twin method***. In this method, as you will see later, the degree of similarity between identical twins is compared to that between fraternal twins in order to quantify the heritability of traits.

Galton, Mill, and the Political Aspects of the Nature-Nurture Debate

On the basis of his research, Galton (1907) wrote, "There is no escape from the conclusion that nature prevails enormously over nurture when the differences of nurture do not exceed what is commonly to be found among persons of the same rank in society and in the same country." Notice Galton's own qualification of his conclusion. He did not conclude that variability among any randomly chosen group of people is due more to nature (genes) than nurture (environment), but only that the variability found within a given range of environments is. More precisely, his conclusion might be restated as follows: psychological differences among upper-class British males are due more to differences in their genes than to differences in their environment.

23. ***How did Galton's socio-political writings about nature and nurture differ from his more cautious scientific conclusion?***

But in other writings, where he strayed from the data, Galton was not so circumspect. He often implied that differences between social classes, as well as within them, are due to genetic differences; and he advocated a program of *eugenics*—which essentially means selective breeding—to improve human stock (Fancher, 1985). In an article published in a popular magazine, Galton (1865) wrote enthusiastically of a future Utopia in which all young men and women would take an intelligence test. Those who scored highest would be encouraged by the state through monetary incentives to marry each other and produce many children, and those who scored low would be discouraged from marrying or having children. He even suggested that the low scorers might gladly pay taxes to help finance the education of the high scorers' children. Perhaps you can see why discussions of the heritability of intelligence have always been hotly tinged with emotion. From Galton's time until today the issues have never been purely scientific, but have been wrapped in political ideology about social class, measures of human worth, and appropriate routes to human betterment.

■ **24.** ***How did John Stuart Mill differ from Galton on the nature-nurture issue and in his politics?***

For the contrasting side of the nature-nurture debate, one need only look to another nineteenth century Englishman, John Stuart Mill (1806–1874). Mill was one of the British empiricist philosophers (mentioned in Chapter 1), and as such was interested in the ways that the human mind is built up through life's experiences. He was acutely aware of his own privileged environment, which included the opportunity to study and travel and a famous father (the philosopher James Mill) who took the time to tutor him throughout his childhood. James and John Mill were among the father-son pairs in Galton's study of hereditary genius, but, while Galton credited their shared genes, John Mill credited their shared environment (Fancher, 1985). Politically, Mill was an ardent democrat, who argued forcefully against the unequal conditions that society had established for different classes of people. He spoke strongly against slavery in the United States, and he wrote a lengthy essay, "The Subjection of Women" (1869/1980), that is still considered one of history's most powerful statements favoring gender equality. Mill's opinion of the political ideology favored by Galton is nicely captured in the following quote, written some years before Galton's first book (Mill, 1848/1978): "Of all the vulgar modes of escaping from the consideration of the social and moral influences on the human mind, the most vulgar is that attributing the diversities of human conduct and character to inherent original natural differences."

Prominent modern writings on the nature-nurture issue are imbued with much the same mix of science and politics as they were at the time of Mill and Galton. For a modern rendition of Mill's positions you might read *Not in Our Genes*, by R. C. Lewontin, Steven Rose, and Leon Kamin (1984); and for a modern rendition of Galton's you might read Richard Herrnstein's *IQ in the Meritocracy* (1971) or Hans Eysenck's *The Inequality of Man* (1973).

IQ Correlations in Twins

Politics aside (assuming we can set it aside), what do the data tell us today about the heritability of intelligence? Most studies of this issue have relied on standardized IQ tests as the measure of intelligence. The question of whether or not such tests are valid measures of intelligence is addressed in Chapter 11. For now it is sufficient to note that IQ scores do correlate moderately well with at least one aspect of life deemed important in our society, performance in school. The question at hand is this: To what extent are observed differences in IQ the result of differences in genes as compared to differences in the environment?

■ **25.** ***How do correlation coefficients for IQ, for various categories of relatives, provide evidence that IQ is to some degree heritable?***

In 1981, Thomas Bouchard and Matthew McGue summarized the results of all studies they were able to find in the world's literature on the heritability of IQ (omitting only those believed to be fraudulent). In each study, researchers had calculated correlation coefficients for IQ scores for various categories of pairs of relatives, such as identical twins, fraternal twins, and nontwin siblings, who were raised in the same home or adopted in infancy and raised in different homes. As you may recall from Chapter 2, correlation coefficients can run from 0.00 to either plus or minus 1.00. A correlation of 0.00 in this case would mean that the IQs for the pairs in the study are no more alike on average than those of two people chosen at random. A correlation of +1.00 would mean that their IQs are perfectly correlated; by knowing one person's IQ you could predict the other's exactly.

The results for some of the most interesting categories of relatives are summarized in Table 3.2. Taken at face value, they suggest a strong genetic component to

Table 3.2 ***Mean correlation coefficients for IQ, for various categories of pairs of relatives***

Type of relationship	Number of		Mean
	Separate studies	Pairs of relatives	correlation coefficient
Identical twins raised apart	3	65	0.72
Identical twins raised together	34	4,672	0.86
Same-sex fraternal twins raised together	29	3,670	0.62
Opposite-sex fraternal twins raised together	18	1,592	0.57
Nontwin siblings raised together	69	26,473	0.47
Unrelated (adopted) siblings raised together*	11	713	0.30

*This category consists of sibling pairs in which either one or both members were adopted and the genetic relationship was zero.

Source: T. J. Bouchard & M. McGue, 1981. "Familial studies of intelligence: A review," *Science* 212, pp. 1056–1057.

variation in IQ. For pairs of siblings raised in the same family, the closer the biological relationship the higher the IQ correlation: The correlations are +0.86 for identical twins, +0.62 for same-sex fraternal twins, and +0.30 for unrelated (adopted) siblings. Perhaps even more impressive, the average correlation for identical twins *raised apart* (+0.72) is higher than that for fraternal twins raised together (+0.62).

26. *What are two ways to estimate heritability coefficients from correlation coefficients for twins?*

The correlations for twins can be used to estimate the heritability coefficient for IQ. One method is simply to use the correlation for raised-apart identical twins itself as the estimate of heritability (Loehlin & others, 1988). In theory, this correlation would be 1.00 (identical IQs for each pair of twins) if all IQ differences were due to genes and 0.00 if all IQ differences were due to environment. By this measure, based on the data in Table 3.2, the heritability of IQ is 0.72. A more recent study, which adds greatly to the number of raised-apart identical twins studied so far, produced a very similar result—0.69 (Bouchard & others, 1990).

Another way to estimate heritability is to double the difference between the correlations for raised-together identical twins and raised-together fraternal twins of the same sex. The assumption here is that the environment is equally similar for the two categories of twins, so the difference in correlation between the two must be due to the difference in their degree of genetic relatedness. Because fraternal twins are half as genetically related to each other as are identical twins (look back to Table 3.1), the difference must be doubled to arrive at an estimate of the heritability coefficient. (For a more complete rationale for this and other methods to calculate heritability, see Plomin & others, 1990). By this method, using the data in Table 3.2, heritability = 2(0.86 – 0.62) = 0.48. The same calculation performed on studies conducted since 1981 puts the heritability coefficient somewhat higher, closer to the value found using raised-apart identicals (Loehlin & others, 1988). The great majority of estimates of IQ heritability, using the methods just described and other methods as well, fall within the range of 0.50 to 0.75, indicating that somewhere between 50 and 75 percent of the variance in IQ found in such studies is due to genetic variability (Plomin & others, 1990).

The Problem of Selective Placement

Many researchers (including Kamin, 1974, and Taylor, 1980) have challenged the use of IQ correlations for raised-apart identical twins to estimate heritability. Their challenge is based largely on the *selective-placement argument*. According to this ar-

27. *What is the selective-placement argument, and how did Bouchard and his colleagues address that argument with data from the Minnesota Twin study?*

gument, adoption agencies place children only in homes that meet certain requirements, and twins adopted through the same agency are especially likely to be placed into similar homes. Moreover, in some studies, some of the so-called "raised-apart" identicals were actually raised by relatives who lived near each other and visited frequently. Thus, according to the selective-placement argument, the high correlation for raised-apart twins is not just due to their genetic similarity, but is also due to their greater-than-average environmental similarity.

This challenge was recently addressed by Thomas Bouchard and his colleagues (1990) with data from the Minnesota Twin Study, one of the largest studies of raised-apart identical twins that has been conducted to date. They measured the similarity of the adoptive homes of each pair of twins along several dimensions, including the parents' socioeconomic status and the amount of intellectual amenities in the home, and they assessed the frequency with which the twins had met during childhood (ranging from never to often). They found no relation at all between these measures and the IQ similarities of the adoptive pairs of twins. In other words, the IQ correlation was as high (about +0.70) for identical twins raised in homes that were most different from one another as it was for identical twins raised in homes that were most similar to one another. The researchers concluded that, at least within the range of homes in which their sample of twins were raised, the degree of similarity of the homes did not affect the similarity of the twins' IQs. This, of course, does not mean that IQ differences would be unaffected by *extreme* differences in homes, differences greater than those in the Minnesota study.

IQ Correlations in Unrelated Children Raised Together

28. *What is the evidence that the effect on IQ similarity of living in the same home tends to disappear as children grow older? How might this change be explained?*

It seems reasonable to expect that the IQs of children raised in the same family would be more similar than average not just because of shared genes, but also because of shared environments. After all, such children are exposed to the same parents, the same neighborhoods, and the same schools. Early studies tended to confirm this reasonable expectation. As you can see in Table 3.2, the eleven studies of adopted, genetically unrelated sibling pairs raised in the same home produced an average correlation coefficient of +0.30, well above the 0.00 that would be expected for pairs of unrelated individuals chosen randomly. However, those studies were mainly of young children. What happens to the IQ correlation as the children get older? According to several reports, it declines eventually to zero (Plomin & Daniels, 1987). In one study, for example, Sandra Scarr and Richard Weinberg (1977, 1983) found that by age eighteen, the IQ correlation for genetically unrelated children raised in the same home was -0.03 (not significantly different from 0), compared to +0.35 for full genetic siblings raised in the same home. Other studies show that the correlation coefficients for all categories of children raised in the same home tend to decline as the children get older, but the greater the genetic relationship, the smaller the decline (Plomin & Daniels, 1987).

Based on such research, Scarr and Kathleen McCartney (1983) suggest that parents have a rather strong effect on their children's IQs when their children are young, but the effect fades as children grow older and increasingly choose their own activities. Even though they inhabit the same home, neighborhood, and school, two older children may live in effectively quite different environments. They may spend their free time in different activities, have different friends, and approach their studies in different ways. The differences may stem partly from their own active choices, partly from the fact that people treat them differently, and partly from random events in their lives. Scarr and McCartney emphasize the role of active choice and suggest that the more genetically dissimilar two raised-together children are, the more likely they are to create different environments for themselves.

Psychologists in the past have sometimes thought of the environment as more or less thrust upon children, and as quite similar for different children within the same home, but Scarr and other behavior geneticists (including Dunn & Plomin, 1990) challenge those assumptions. They argue that to a considerable degree (at least in our culture) people create their own environments, and that a person's genetic constitution plays an important role in the kind of environment he or she creates.

A damaging environment

When behavior geneticists speak of environmental effects, they don't just mean learning. Poor nutrition and lead poisoning are two of many ways a poor environment can slow intellectual development. Prior to lead paint laws, many children suffered brain damage from eating lead paint.

Cultural and Racial Studies of IQ

Many studies have shown average differences in IQ between members of different racial and cultural groups. For example, in the United States, Jews and Asian-Americans regularly score somewhat higher than other groups (Willerman, 1979). The differences that have attracted by far the most attention, however, are the lower average scores obtained by the lower compared to the upper socioeconomic classes in Europe, and by blacks compared to whites in the United States. Much debate has centered on whether such differences result partly from genetic differences between the groups or entirely from environmental differences.

An example of the argument for a genetic component to the differences can be found in an article published some years ago by Arthur Jensen (1969), an educational psychologist. Jensen's thesis—which elicited a storm of controversy—was that compensatory educational programs aimed at raising the academic achievements of blacks and other economically deprived groups are likely to fail because the differences are more genetic than environmental in origin. He admitted that he had no direct evidence for that claim, but rather was reasoning indirectly, primarily from family-relationship studies of the sort illustrated in Table 3.2. Others (such as Lewontin, 1970), however, were quick to respond to Jensen's article by pointing out that even if the heritability coefficients derived from family-relationship studies are accurate, they have nothing to do with differences between social or cultural groups. In family-relationship studies the correlations are between pairs of people who share relatively similar environments. The vast majority of the subjects in such studies were raised in white families in the upper two-thirds of the population in socioeconomic status (Bouchard & others, 1990; Scarr & McCartney, 1983).

■ **29. *How is it possible to have high heritability within groups and zero heritability across them?***

To understand how it is possible to have high heritability within groups and zero heritability across them, imagine planting a genetically diverse packet of tomato seeds in two different fields, A and B, which differ from each other in soil fertility. Within either field, differences in size of tomato plants could be entirely due to genetic differences among the seeds, leading to a heritability coefficient of 1.00. Yet, because the seeds planted in the two fields come from the same package, any average difference between the two fields in plant size would have to be due to the environmental difference—a heritability of 0.00. Those who argue that the IQ differences between whites and blacks, or between rich and poor, are entirely environmental in origin argue that the environments of the two groups are different enough to produce the IQ differences even if everyone came from the same "packet of seeds."

■ **30. *What are two lines of evidence supporting the view that IQ differences between racial or cultural groups are due to environmental differences?***

Some researchers have tested the genetic versus environmental explanations of group differences in IQ by looking at the IQ's of children adopted at an early age into a group different from that of their genetic parents. Findings from several studies of this type support the environmental explanation. In one study, in France, lower-class children who were adopted at an early age into middle- or upper-class families had an average IQ of 109, which was 14 points higher than the average for lower-class children raised by their biological parents and not significantly different from that for middle- and upper-class children overall (Schiff & others, 1978). In another study, in the United States, black children raised by white, middle- and upper-class adoptive parents had, at adolescence, IQs that were significantly higher than those of the black population overall and not significantly different from those of the white population overall (Weinberg & others, 1992).

In other studies of black-white IQ differences, researchers have compared the IQs of individuals who are socially defined as blacks, but who vary in their ratio of African compared to European ancestry. People in the United States are usually identified as black if they have any detectable African ancestry. Thus, their African ancestry may vary from a low of 25 percent or less up to 100 percent. If the genetic theory of race differences in IQ is correct, blacks who have high IQs should be found to have more European ancestry than those who have lower IQs. Many years ago Paul Witty and Martin Jenkins (1935) tested this hypothesis in a study of school children in Chicago. They identified black children who had IQs in the superior range (125 or better) and then interviewed their parents to see if they had more European ancestry than did the general black population. The results were negative. The proportion of European ancestry in the high-IQ black children was neither more nor less than that in the black population at large. (The highest IQ of all in that study, a whopping 200, was scored by a young black girl with 100 percent African ancestry.) More recently, Sandra Scarr and her colleagues performed a similar study, using modern biochemical methods to determine the degree of African and European ancestry in a group of socially defined blacks (Scarr & Carter-Saltzman, 1983). Like Witty and Jenkins, they found no relationship between ancestry and IQ, and they concluded that the *social* designation of black, not biological ancestry, is the critical variable in determining the black-white IQ difference.

To many people there is something disquieting about such research. Why all the fuss about race? The range of IQ scores within any group greatly outweighs the average difference between groups, so why should it matter whether small average differences between groups are or are not partly genetic in origin? To a large extent, the excitement generated by cultural and racial studies of IQ differences has always been more political than scientific in nature. The presence of average IQ differences between groups, coupled with a view that such differences are genetic in origin, has long been used, in various guises, to justify economic and social inequalities. Because of this, those who wish to eradicate inequalities between the rich and poor, or blacks and whites, are politically motivated to show that IQ differences are *due* to economic and social inequalities, and are not the cause of the inequalities. The Galton-Mill debate continues, and perhaps it will not abate until the world truly offers equivalent opportunities for all.

Genetic Influence on Risk for Schizophrenia

Another realm in which the nature-nurture controversy has been much apparent is that of mental or emotional disorders. Why do some people have psychological breakdowns while others don't? According to the nature side of the controversy, the answer lies in genes—some people are genetically more prone to such breakdowns than others. According to the nurture side, the answer lies in the environment—those who have breakdowns have been exposed to more stressful environments than those who don't. At this point you will perhaps not be surprised to learn that the weight of evidence, for almost every class of mental disorder that has been studied, indicates that both sides of the classic debate are partly correct, with lots of room for argument about degree.

By far the most extensive research in this realm has been concerned with ***schizophrenia***, a serious class of mental disorder that usually first appears in young adulthood and is characterized by disrupted perceptual and thought processes. Common symptoms include hallucinations (such as hearing voices that aren't there), delusions (clearly false beliefs, such as the belief that one's movements are controlled by radio waves), and either the absence of emotional responsiveness or inappropriate emotionality (such as laughing while describing a very sad event). Much more is said about the varied symptoms of schizophrenia and the problems of diagnosing it in Chapter 17. For the present our concern is with studies of its heritability.

■ **31.** ***Why doesn't the observation that schizophrenia runs in families prove, by itself, that schizophrenia is heritable?***

Researchers have long known that schizophrenia tends to run in families, though not in the same clear-cut pattern as single-gene disorders such as PKU or Huntington's disease. The chance that a child will eventually develop schizophrenia is less than 1 in 100 if the child has no close relatives with the disorder, but is about 1 in 10 if the child has a parent or sibling with the disorder and almost 1 in 2 if the child has two parents with the disorder (Gottesman, 1991). On the face of it, such results might seem to support a genetic explanation for variation in susceptibility to schizophrenia, but at least in theory the results could be explained purely environmentally. Members of the same family share similar environments, so they may be exposed to the same environmental factors that either produce or protect against schizophrenia. Moreover, parents with schizophrenia might provide a disorganized and stressful home, which might promote the disorder in their children. Clearly, other data are needed to decide whether the family-resemblance findings are due primarily to shared genes or shared environment. Those data, as in the case of studies of IQ heritability, have come from adoption and twin studies.

Adoption Studies of Schizophrenia

■ **32.** ***How did Kety and Rosenthal provide strong evidence for the heritability of schizophrenia, and how did they minimize the possibility of bias in diagnosis?***

If family similarity in the presence or absence of schizophrenia is due principally to shared genes, then adopted children should be more like their biological than their adoptive relatives in this characteristic; but if it is due principally to shared environment, the opposite should be true. Based on this rationale, Seymour Kety and David Rosenthal directed a study in Denmark—where birth, adoption, and mental-hospitalization records are more readily available than in the United States (Kety & others, 1976). They began by identifying thirty-three adults who had been adopted in infancy and who later (in adolescence or adulthood) were hospitalized for schizophrenia. For comparison, they also selected a control group of adoptees who did not have schizophrenia or any other diagnosed mental disorder but were similar to those in the schizophrenia group in other ways, such as age and socioeconomic class. Then they tracked down the biological and adoptive parents, siblings, and half-siblings of both groups and asked them to participate in an extensive psychiatric interview. The purpose of the interview (unknown to the interviewee) was to look for signs of schizophrenia. To prevent bias, the interviews were conducted and evaluated by a team of psychiatrists who were blind (uninformed) as to whether the interviewee was a biological or adoptive relative, or was related to an individual who did or did not have schizophrenia. The main results are shown in Figure 3.15. Only the biological relatives of the schizophrenic adoptees manifested significantly more evidence of schizophrenia than any other group, and they were about four times as likely as the others to show such symptoms.

■ **33.** ***Why did the Kety and Rosenthal study include relatives of adopted individuals who did not develop schizophrenia?***

You might wonder why Kety and Rosenthal included relatives of nonschizophrenic adoptees in this study. Suppose they had not, and had found (as they did) that the biological relatives of people with schizophrenia showed more signs of the disorder than did the adoptive relatives. In that case one could argue that their findings might be due to a difference between people who give up a child and people who adopt one. That is, perhaps people who give up a child are predisposed toward mental disorders, while those who adopt a child are especially healthy psychologically. As you can see in Figure 3.15, the results for the relatives of the control adoptees negate this explanation. The biological relatives of the control

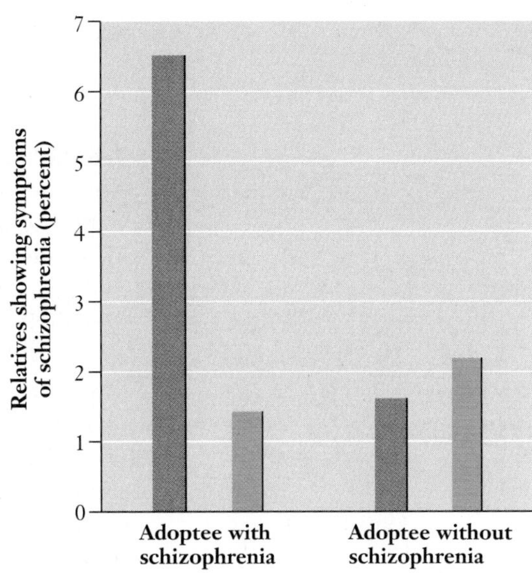

Figure 3.15 ***Results of an adoption study of the heritability of schizophrenia***

Kety, Rosenthal, and their colleagues looked for signs of schizophrenia in the biological and adoptive relatives of adoptees who either had or had not become schizophrenic. The results here are the percentage of relatives who showed either schizophrenia or a milder disorder now called *schizotypical personality disorder*. (Data from Kety & others, 1976.)

adoptees did not show more evidence of schizophrenia than did the adoptive relatives. All in all, Kety and Rosenthal's study provides compelling evidence that family resemblance with respect to schizophrenia is due more to genetic than environmental similarity. More recent adoption studies, involving additional controls to rule out bias or alternative explanations, have also strongly supported that conclusion (Gottesman, 1991; Kety, 1988).

Twin Studies of Schizophrenia

Another way to assess the role of genetic variation in determining who does or does not develop schizophrenia is to find people who have the disorder and who also have either an identical or fraternal twin. In studies of this sort, the original group identified as having the disorder are referred to as the *index cases*. The relatives of the index cases can then be studied to see what percentage of them have the disorder. This percentage is referred to as the ***concordance*** for the disorder, for the class of relatives studied. A separate concordance measure can be calculated for identical and fraternal twins (or any other class of relatives studied) and used to estimate heritability.

34. ***How did Gottesman and Shields find higher concordance for schizophrenia in identical than in fraternal twins?***

An exemplary and now classic study of this sort was directed by Irving Gottesman and James Shields (1966) in England. For a period of 16 years, all patients admitted to the psychiatric unit of the Maudsley Hospital in London were asked if they had a twin of the same sex. Those who did, and who themselves were diagnosed as having schizophrenia, constituted the index cases. Then the twins were tracked down, and those who could be found and were willing to participate (most of them) were studied to determine (a) if they were identical or fraternal twins of the index cases, and (b) if they showed symptoms of schizophrenia. Gottesman and Shields ended up with 22 pairs of identical and 33 pairs of fraternal twins. The judgments as to whether the twins of the index cases had schizophrenia or not were made on the basis of psychiatric tests and interviews by a team of psychologists and psychiatrists who did not know whether the person they were evaluating was a fraternal or identical twin of someone with schizophrenia. Of the 22 identical twins of index cases, 11 (concordance = 50 percent) were judged to have schizophrenia. Of the 33 fraternal twins, only 3 (concordance = 9 percent) were judged to have schizophrenia. Many other studies have since produced quite similar results. The average concordances found in such studies, for other relatives as well as for the two classes of twins, are shown in Table 3.3.

The twin studies, like the adoption studies, show strong evidence that genetic

Table 3.3 *Concordance rates for schizophrenia*

Relationship to a person who has schizophrenia	Average percentage found to have schizophrenia (concordance)
Relatives in same generation	
Identical twin	48%
Fraternal twin	17
Nontwin brother or sister	9
Half-sibling	6
First cousin	2
Relatives in later generation	
Child of two parents with schizophrenia	46
Child of one parent with schizophrenia	13
Grandchild of one person with schizophrenia	5
Niece or nephew of one person with schizophrenia	4

Source: I. I. Gottesman, 1991. *Schizophrenia genesis: The origins of madness*, p. 96. New York: Freeman.

■ **35.** ***How do twin studies show an environmental as well as a genetic contribution to variability in who does or doesn't develop schizophrenia?***

differences are significant determinants of who does or doesn't develop schizophrenia, but unlike the adoption studies they also point to an environmental influence. Of particular interest is the fact that the concordance for identical twins is much less than the 100 percent that would be predicted if genetic variation alone were involved. To some degree reduced concordance could come from misdiagnosis, because any errors in diagnosing either the index cases or their twins would reduce the measured concordance below its true value. But some pairs of discordant identical twins have been studied over many years, and no doubt exists in those cases that one manifests the disorder and the other does not (Wahl, 1976). Using statistical procedures too complex to describe here, some behavioral geneticists calculate from the sort of concordances shown in Table 3.3 that the heritability for the *liability* (risk) for schizophrenia is about 0.70 (Plomin & others, 1990). It is important to realize, though, that this refers to the heritability not of diagnosed schizophrenia but of a hypothetical underlying predisposition to it. Although some research has suggested that the inherited part of this risk might stem primarily from a single dominant gene, the bulk of the evidence now suggests that many genes are involved and that no single gene plays an overwhelming role (Fowles, 1992).

The Search for Prevention by Environmental Means

The studies just described indicate that in existing environments the development of schizophrenia depends to a great extent on genetic differences among people. Does this mean that it is useless to try to find environmental means to prevent the disorder? No, certainly not. To illustrate why, it would be instructive to consider some findings about the heritability not of schizophrenia but of tuberculosis (TB).

■ **36.** ***How does an analogy to TB suggest that schizophrenia could, in theory, be eliminated through purely environmental means?***

In the 1930s and early 1940s, when TB was much more common than it is today, F. R. Kallman performed an extensive study of twins and other relatives to assess the heritability of the risk for this disease. He found, incredible as it may seem, that 87 percent of the identical twins, 25 percent of the fraternal twins or ordinary siblings, and 11 percent of the half-siblings of index cases eventually came down with the disease (Roth, 1957). At the time of the study, 1.4 percent of the general population came down with TB at some time in their lives. The evidence was overwhelming that genetic differences among individuals, not environmental differences, played the largest role in determining who got sick and who didn't.

The Genain quadruplets

Nora, Iris, Myra, and Hester Genain are identical quadruplets who have all been diagnosed with schizophrenia. Two of the sisters have more debilitating forms of the disorder than do the other two. The differences among them must stem from environmental influences.

Should that have led scientists to conclude that the only way to solve the TB problem would be through genetic control? Certainly not. Today relatively few people get TB, because TB depends not only on genetic predisposition, but also on exposure to the TB bacillus, the germ that causes the disease. TB was reduced not by changing people's genes, but by cleaning up the environment to get rid of the bacillus. In the 1930s almost everyone was exposed to the TB germ, so determination of who got TB and who didn't depended more on genetic susceptibility than on exposure to the germ. But today most people are not exposed to the TB bacillus, so genetic susceptibility is less important. (Recently, however, drug-resistant strains of TB have arisen in some cities, so genetic susceptibility may again become a significant factor in incidences of the disease.)

Today a number of long-term studies of children who are genetically at risk for schizophrenia are underway in various parts of the world (Asarnow, 1988). One of the major goals of the studies is to identify environmental conditions that, in combination with genetic predisposition, bring on the disorder. The studies are not likely to bring an environmental solution as easy or as effective as that for tuberculosis, but they are turning up some helpful leads. They suggest that children predisposed to schizophrenia often have difficulty focusing their attention or dealing with more than one source of environmental input at a time and that these children may be more likely to develop overt symptoms of schizophrenia in highly stimulating, emotion-provoking, or disturbed homes than in those that are more orderly and calm (Fowles, 1992; Tienari & others, 1989). Research of this sort may eventually lead to an understanding of the different environmental needs of children with different inborn temperaments or tendencies. This is one of the most interesting future promises of the field of behavioral genetics.

Concluding Thoughts

Four themes that ran through the chapter are worth reiterating and elaborating upon here.

1. Genes influence behavior through protein synthesis. Sometimes when people talk about the role of genes in behavior they lose sight of how indirect that role is. Genes are not little demons that sit inside a person and pull strings to make the person act according to their wishes. They are simply DNA molecules, which provide the code for building the body's proteins. Variations in that code from person to person can affect behavior to the degree that they affect the sensory, motor, neural, and other physiological systems involved in behavior. Genetic effects on human behavior are most apparent when an abnormality in the code leads either to the absence of some important protein (as in the cases of PKU and red-green color blindness) or to the overabundance of a protein that produces harmful effects (as in the cases of fragile X syndrome and Down syndrome).

2. Single-gene effects can be inferred from patterns of heredity. The concept of the gene was formulated by Mendel at a time when nothing was known about DNA or protein synthesis. Mendel inferred the existence of genes and their paired nature from patterns of heredity. By assuming that genes come in pairs, that variations (now called *alleles*) can exist within a given pair, and that some variations are dominant over others in their effect, he was able to explain the ratios that he found in the inherited characteristics of hybrid peas. Since then, researchers—such as Scott and Fuller in their work with dogs—have used patterns of heredity to infer that single-gene differences underlie certain stepwise behavioral differences among individuals. The same is true for many genetic disorders in humans. In reviewing the chapter you might see if you can explain the patterns of heredity leading to the inference of (a) a single dominant gene located on an autosome, (b) a single recessive gene located on an autosome, and (c) a single recessive gene located on an X chromosome.

3. The nature-nurture debate is about heritability and has to do with populations, not individuals. Some people misinterpret the nature-nurture debate in a way that leads them to conclude that there is nothing to debate. They seem to assume that the debate is about which is more essential to the development of an individual's characteristics—genes or environment. The debate would be foolish indeed if that really were its question. Genes and environment are both absolutely essential for the development of any characteristic; neither can be more essential than the other. Rather, the debate is about the degree to which *differences* among individuals, say in maze learning or IQ or liability for schizophrenia, are due to genetic as opposed to environmental *differences*. That is a potentially answerable question, which quantitative geneticists address by calculating heritability coefficients from selective breeding studies with animals and adoption and twin studies with people. As you have seen, however, the answer is not fixed. Heritability depends not just on the characteristic studied, but also on the genetic and environmental diversity of the specific group studied. Heritability for any given trait might differ from Group A to Group B. If you understand the heritability concept you should be able to explain the differences between two groups that could lead to high heritability in one and low heritability in the other.

4. The optimal environment may be different for individuals who have different genes. The interplay of genes and environment in the development of behavioral characteristics becomes most apparent when a genetic effect on behavior is reduced or abolished through an environmental change. Infants with PKU become mentally retarded if they are fed the same diet on which most infants thrive, but they don't become retarded if fed a restricted diet. Cooper and Zubek found that their "maze dull" rats were less adept than the "maze bright" rats at learning a maze if both groups were reared in normal cages, but were not worse if both groups were reared in more stimulating cages. Apparently, as measured by maze-learning ability, the "dulls" benefitted more from extra stimulation than did the "brights." Returning to humans, most people can develop and function well in stimulating and emotion-provoking homes, but long-term studies of people genetically at risk for schizophrenia suggest that such people may need a calmer environment for optimal development. In more subtle ways, genetic differences among all of us may lead us each to seek those environmental conditions that are most conducive to our own development.

Further Reading

John Paul Scott & John L. Fuller (1965). *Genetics and the social behavior of the dog.* Chicago: University of Chicago Press.

In this fascinating book, two of the pioneers of behavioral genetics describe the methods and findings of their 13-year-long research project on genetics, social behavior, and learning in dogs. You can see here how one question leads to another in a long-term research program.

Raymond E. Fancher (1985). *The intelligence men: Makers of the IQ controversy.* New York: Norton.

This lively book, by one of the best writers among modern psychological historians, traces the history of the nature-nurture debate on IQ through biography, from Mill and Galton in the nineteenth century through Kamin and Jensen in our time.

Robert Plomin (1990). *Nature and nurture: An introduction to human behavioral genetics.* Pacific Grove, CA: Brooks/Cole.

Plomin is one of today's most prolific researchers and writers in the field of human behavioral genetics. In this brief book, available in paperback, he describes the basic methods of his field in prose that a beginning student can understand. He shows how the methods have been applied not just to IQ and schizophrenia but also to such characteristics as alcoholism, depression, emotionality, and sociability.

Irving I. Gottesman (1991). *Schizophrenia genesis: The origins of madness.* New York: Freeman.

Gottesman has devoted a long career to understanding the origins of schizophrenia, especially its genetic basis. In this sophisticated but highly readable book, available in paperback, he discusses the results of his and other researchers' work on that topic.

Looking Ahead

Behavioral genetics emphasizes the differences among individuals. But any two randomly chosen members of a species are far more alike than different, and genes are at least as responsible for the similarities as for the differences. If there is such a thing as human nature, spanning history and cultures, it stems from our shared genes, which build into us a common set of capacities, tendencies, and proclivities. Those genes have been acquired in the course of evolution, through a long weeding-out process: Genes that built bodies that survived and reproduced were passed along, and genes that didn't were not. In the next chapter we will look at the behavioral characteristics that unite and help define a species, and we will attempt to understand them in terms of evolution.

Figure 4.1 ***Light and dark peppered moths***

You have to look hard to see the light moth on the lichen-covered bark, or the dark moth on the dark bark. The evolution from light to dark (or back again) in this case involves change at just one gene locus, which is part of the reason why it can occur so rapidly. More complex evolutionary changes—such as in the evolution of an eye or a wing—involve an accumulation of the effects of many gene changes, each of which adds some degree of survival advantage.

tributed to Jean-Baptiste de Lamarck (1744–1829), though many other evolutionists, both before and after Lamarck, held the same view (Futuyma, 1986). Even Darwin did not reject that idea, but rather added to it the ideas of random change and natural selection. Now, however, with the modern synthesis, we know that evolution is based on genes alone, and we know that no amount of practice or experience can change an individual's genes. Random change followed by natural selection, not directed change stemming from individual experience, provides the basis for evolution.

The Role of Environmental Change in Evolution

If the environment did not change over time, organisms might become as adapted to it as possible and evolve no further. But the environment keeps changing. Climates change, sources of food change, predators change, and so on. When the conditions of life change, what was previously a useful characteristic may become harmful, and vice versa.

Consider, for example, the change in peppered moths living in and around London over the past 150 years or so (Bishop & Cook, 1975). Before the Industrial Revolution of the mid-nineteenth century, the moths were mostly light in color, the same shade and mottling as the lichen that covered the tree trunks on which they spent most of their time. Their coloring thus helped protect them from being seen and eaten by birds (see Figure 4.1). At each generation, a few dark-colored mutant moths would hatch; but, as experiments later showed, birds would easily have seen and eaten them, and their genes would have been eliminated from the gene pool (Kettlewell, 1973). After industrialization, however, the air in and around London became so polluted that the lichen could not grow and the trees took on the darker color of their bark. In this environment, the dark moths were more likely to survive and have offspring, while the light ones were gobbled up. By 1950, 90 percent of the peppered moths in and around London were of the dark variety. Now that antipollution laws have cleaned up the air in London, the lichen are growing again, and the light moths are making a comeback (Cook & others, 1986).

■ **3.** ***How does the example of the peppered moth illustrate the effect of environmental change on evolution?***

Darwin believed that evolution is a slow and steady process. But today we know that it can occur relatively rapidly, slowly, or almost not at all, depending on the rate and nature of environmental change and on the degree to which genetic variability already exists in the population (Gould & Eldredge, 1977). Environmental change spurs evolution *not* by causing the appropriate mutations to occur, but by promoting the process of natural selection. A change in the color of the tree trunks did not cause more mutations in the gene for moth color; rather it changed the selection criteria in favor of those moths with genes for the best camouflage.

Evolution Has No Foresight

4. *What are three mistaken beliefs about evolution, all related to the misbelief that foresight is involved?*

People sometimes mistakenly think of evolution as a mystical force working toward some planned end. One manifestation of this belief is the idea that evolution could produce changes for some future purpose, even though in the present environment these changes serve no function or are even harmful. But evolution has no foresight. Peppered moths could not have begun to evolve to a darker color in anticipation of the Industrial Revolution, or to a lighter color in anticipation of antipollution laws. Only those genetic changes that are immediately beneficial to the organism, in the sense of increasing survival and reproduction, can proliferate through natural selection.

Another manifestation of the belief in foresight is the idea that present-day organisms can be ranked according to the distance they have moved along a set evolutionary route, toward some planned end. For example, some may think of humans as the most evolved creatures, with chimpanzees next, and amoebas way down on the list. But evolution has no set route or planned end. The three just-named creatures have taken their different forms and behavioral characteristics because of chance events that led them to occupy different niches in the environment, where the selection criteria differed. The present-day amoeba is not an early step toward humans, but rather a creature that is at least as adapted to its environment as we are to ours. The amoeba has no more chance of evolving to become like us than we have of evolving to become like it.

A third manifestation of the belief in foresight is the idea that natural selection is a moral force, that its operation and its products are in some moral sense right or good. In everyday talk, people sometimes imply that whatever is natural (including natural selection) is good, and that evil stems from society or human contrivances that go beyond nature. But nature is neither good nor bad, moral nor immoral. To say that natural selection led to such and such a characteristic does not lend any moral virtue to that characteristic. As you will see later, fighting is as much a product of evolution as is cooperation, but that is no reason to consider them morally equivalent.

Natural Selection of Behavior-Producing Mechanisms

5. *Why does evolution apply as much to behavior as to anatomy?*

An organism's ability to survive and reproduce depends on its behavior, and, as you know from Chapter 3, behavior can be modified through selective breeding. Just as Tryon was able to breed rats, through artificial selection, to be better at learning a particular maze, natural selection breeds animals to become better at doing what they must to survive and reproduce in their natural environments. The consequence is that behavior evolves—or, to be more precise, the *mechanisms* for producing behavior evolve. These range from simple reflex mechanisms, such as that for the withdrawal response to a painful stimulus, on through the most complex learning mechanisms.

Your ability to read and make sense of these words is not just a result of natural selection, of course. You had to learn English, you had to come into contact with certain ideas, and so on. But the fact that you, given certain environmental conditions, can understand these words, while a chimpanzee or an amoeba could not do so under any conditions, *is* the result of natural selection. The massive human brain, with its billions of neurons and trillions of connections—which enable motivation, emotion, sensation, perception, language learning, and reasoning to occur, and to occur in certain ways and not others—is a product of evolution by natural selection. Our brain and the rest of our behavioral machinery came about for one and only one reason: to promote our ability to survive and reproduce in the environment in which we evolved.

Evolutionary Adaptation

■ **6. *What is meant by adaptation at the evolutionary, individual, and cultural level? How do individual and cultural adaptations depend on evolutionary adaptation?***

To ***adapt*** is to change to suit new conditions. We are, in this chapter, primarily concerned with *evolutionary adaptation*, in which natural selection changes the genetic makeup of organisms over generations as the environment changes. But adaptation also occurs at two other levels—individual and cultural.

Individual adaptation is the class of adaptive changes that occur within individuals during their lifetimes. It includes all the moment-to-moment and year-to-year adjustments that individuals make to the fluctuations in their environment. These adjustments include hormonal responses to environmental stresses; increased or decreased strength stemming from use or disuse of muscles; and, most important for psychology, the entire class of changes that are labeled *learning*.

A cultural tradition

Humans are not the only species that pass skills from generation to generation. Fishing for termites with carefully selected sticks is a skill that chimpanzees acquire at least partly by observing their elders.

Humans not only learn, but encode what they have learned into words, share it with one another, and pass it on from generation to generation. This has produced culture and the process of change called *cultural adaptation*. Human cultures consist of the ideas, tools, artwork, and institutions (such as governments and religions) shared by large numbers of interacting individuals. As these ideas and artifacts are passed from generation to generation, they are modified. Adaptation takes place at the cultural level when new ideas and artifacts gradually replace those that are older and less useful. This type of evolution proceeds much more quickly than biological evolution. Essentially all of the dramatic change that has occurred over the past 10,000 years or more in the way people live is due to cultural evolution. The amount of biological evolution that has occurred in humans in that time is minuscule.

Individual and cultural adaptation both depend upon evolutionary adaptation. The biological machinery that permits all forms of individual adaptation to occur and predisposes humans to live in groups and share their knowledge is itself the product of evolution. That machinery evolved because it enabled our ancestors to survive and produce offspring. Thus, an understanding of evolution is basic to understanding adaptive changes in individuals and cultures.

Thinking About Behavior in Terms of Its Function

Each level of adaptation promotes behaviors that serve specific purposes, though the behaving individual is generally not aware of those purposes. Natural selection leads to behavioral mechanisms that promote the individual's ability to survive and reproduce. Learning and other forms of individual adaptation make use of those mechanisms and help the individual surmount the specific obstacles and achieve the specific goals that present themselves in the course of a lifetime. And cultural evolution can lead to behaviors (such as practicing a particular religion) that may serve an individual's needs, the needs of those in power, or the needs of the culture as a whole.

■ **7. *What is the functionalist approach in psychology, and how is it applied at the evolutionary level?***

The ***functionalist approach*** in psychology—which today is not a distinct school of thought but is integrated into many areas of psychology (see Chapter 1)—is to try to understand specific behavioral actions or tendencies in terms of their adaptive functions. How does this or that behavior help promote (a) the long-term survival or reproduction of the individual (evolutionary adaptation), or (b) the individual's ability to solve a particular problem unique to its life (individual adaptation), or (c) the purposes of those in power in the culture in which the person lives (cultural adaptation)? This approach is often difficult to apply to human behavior, because it is often hard to disentangle the different levels of adaptation. What one person interprets as an evolutionary adaptation may be interpreted by another as cultural.

When applied at the evolutionary level, the functionalist approach in psychology is essentially the same as the functionalist approach in anatomy: Why do giraffes have long necks? Why do humans lack fur? Why do male songbirds sing in the spring? Why do humans have such an irrepressible ability to learn language? The anatomist trying to answer the first two questions, and the behavioral researcher or psychologist trying to answer the latter two, would look for ways by which each trait helped ancestral members of the species to survive and reproduce.

Ultimate and Proximate Explanations of Behavior

■ **8.** ***What is the difference between ultimate and proximate explanations of behavior?***

Biologists and psychologists who think in evolutionary terms find it useful to distinguish between two different kinds of explanations of behavior—ultimate and proximate. ***Ultimate explanations*** are functional explanations at the evolutionary level; that is, they are statements of the role that the behavior plays in the animal's survival and reproduction. ***Proximate explanations*** are explanations that deal not with function but mechanism; they are statements of the immediate conditions that bring on the behavior.

Consider, for example, why male songbirds (of many species) sing in the spring. An ultimate explanation might go something like this: Over the course of evolution, songbirds have adapted to a mating system that takes place in the spring. The male's song serves (a) to attract a female with which to mate and (b) to warn other males to stay away from the singer's territory in order to avoid a fight. In the evolution of these birds, males whose genes promoted such singing produced more offspring (more copies of their genes) than those whose genes did not promote such singing. A proximate explanation, in contrast, might go as follows: The increased period of daylight in the spring triggers, through the birds' visual system, a physiological mechanism that leads to the increased production of testosterone (a male hormone), which in turn acts on a certain area of the brain (which we might call the "song area"), promoting the drive to sing. Notice the complementarity of these explanations. The ultimate explanation states the survival or reproductive value of the behavior, and the proximate explanation states the stimuli and physiological mechanisms through which the behavior occurs.

A redwinged blackbird at home

This male's singing warns other males of the species to stay away.

Of course, it is one thing to offer an explanation that sounds plausible, and another to establish its scientific validity. To test any explanation scientifically, one must make systematic observations or perform experiments to see if specific predictions based on that explanation hold up. That is as true of ultimate explanations as it is of proximate explanations. The ultimate explanation offered in the example above is supported by experiments showing that recorded bird songs do indeed attract females and/or repel males of the same species (Yasukawa, 1981); and the proximate explanation is supported by physiological investigations of the sort to be discussed in Chapter 7.

Some Precautions Concerning Adaptational Thinking

It is easier to make up explanations (either ultimate or proximate) than it is to prove them. Richard Lewontin and Stephen J. Gould (1978) have referred to some of the ultimate explanations developed by biologists and psychologists as "Panglossian myths," named after the optimistic Dr. Pangloss of Voltaire's novel *Candide*, who believed that every detail of everything on earth was placed there to serve a useful function. For example, according to Pangloss, the human nose has its peculiar shape to enable us to wear glasses. To avoid creating Panglossian myths, it is important to base ultimate explanations on appropriate evidence and to realize that not every individual characteristic of humans or other animals is adaptive. Here are three reasons why characteristics cannot always be explained in adaptational terms.

Genetic Drift

When one finds a heritable difference between two populations of a given species that occupy different locations, a strong and often reasonable temptation exists to attribute the difference to natural selection. The differing locations set different selection criteria; as a consequence, evolution can take different directions for the two groups. But another possible explanation is simple chance. Individuals that appear in one location may by chance have an unusual set of genes compared to those in another location. If the genes are not strongly maladaptive, they will be passed along from generation to generation. Any change in the gene pool that is due to chance alone, without natural selection, is referred to as ***genetic drift***. Perhaps the most potent form of genetic drift is the ***founder effect***—the genetic difference between two populations that occurs when one was founded by a small group of individuals that migrated to a new area and happened to have some unusual genes.

9. ***How is the problem of distinguishing natural selection from genetic drift illustrated by the example of schizophrenia in northern Sweden?***

To understand the problem of distinguishing between natural selection and genetic drift, consider this: Schizophrenia exists at about a 1 percent rate among people in most parts of the world, but at about a 3 percent rate among people living north of the Arctic Circle in Sweden. Why? Three possible answers come to mind: (1) The difference may have nothing to do with genes. Perhaps the harsh conditions of the Arctic environment bring out the disorder in people who would not manifest it elsewhere. (As discussed in Chapter 3, the incidence of schizophrenia is affected by the environment as well as by genes.) (2) The difference may be due to natural selection (suggested by Huxley & others, 1964); that is, in the history of this group, people with a certain dose of the genes that promote schizophrenia may have been more likely to survive and produce offspring than those without those genes. Supporting this view, some research suggests that people with schizophrenia are unusually resistant to certain kinds of physical shocks, wounds, and diseases (Huxley & others, 1964; Vinogradov & others, 1991). (3) The difference may be due to the founder effect or some other type of genetic drift. The Arctic population was founded by a small group of Swedish migrants, who might by chance have had a higher proportion of schizophrenia-promoting genes than the population at large.

The first (environmental) possibility might be verified by determining if newer migrants to this part of the world, who have not interbred with the longer-established residents, also have an unusually high rate of schizophrenia. If they don't, that would tend to support either of the two genetic theories. Finding data that supports one of the two genetic theories over the other, however, would be difficult. One possibility would be to see whether an unusually high rate of schizophrenia also exists in other parts of the world where living conditions are similar to those in northern Sweden. If so, that finding (coupled with the evidence against the environmental theory) would tend to support natural selection as the explanation. A problem with this approach is that finding a part of the world where living conditions are exactly the same as in northern Sweden is impossible, so the approach can be used only if one has a reasonable hypothesis as to just what aspect of those conditions is critical. Thus, distinguishing the effects of natural selection from the effects of genetic drift often requires a two-step process. First, one must specify the environmental conditions that plausibly could provide the basis for selecting the trait in question. Then, one must compare several populations where those conditions exist with populations where they don't exist.

Correlates of Structure

Darwin was aware that often a particular characteristic can evolve as a nonadaptive side effect of some other adaptive change. He referred to such changes as ***correlates***

10. *How is the problem of distinguishing direct effects of natural selection from side effects illustrated with the female spotted hyena?*

of structure, implying that the nonadaptive and adaptive changes are linked in the organism's biological structure. An example that might be explained in these terms concerns a characteristic of the spotted hyena that has intrigued naturalists since the time of Aristotle (Gould, 1983). The female of this species has an enlarged clitoris, almost indistinguishable in size and shape from the male's penis. Why? Based on studies of the animals' behavior, Hans Kruuk (1972) proposed a possible ultimate explanation. He found that spotted hyenas live in clans but often separate and travel far distances alone. When two individuals meet they perform a greeting ceremony, which involves lifting a leg to exhibit the genital area, followed by sniffing and licking each other in that area. Kruuk suggested that this ceremony may help spotted hyenas recognize their kin and keep their clan together, and that the female's clitoris evolved over time so that she would have as conspicuous a structure as the male for initiating this ceremony.

But Gould (1983), looking at the same question, has suggested a different answer involving a correlate of structure. Most anatomical differences between males and females in any mammalian species are due to the presence or absence of a class of hormones called *androgens* (including testosterone) during fetal development and later. Spotted hyenas are unique in that the female produces as high a level of androgens as the male, and both female and male fetuses are exposed to high levels of androgens produced by their mother. That is the proximate explanation of the female's enlarged clitoris. Androgens in fetal life can make the clitoris in the female of any mammal grow large and look like a penis. Now the question becomes: Why does the female spotted hyena produce a high level of androgens?

Kruuk's explanation would hold that natural selection favored high androgens because they resulted in the enlarged clitoris. But Gould suggests what may be a more plausible scenario. Natural selection favored a high level of androgens because it increased the body size and muscular strength of the female spotted hyena, and enlargement of the clitoris was a side effect. The spotted hyena is one of the few mammals in which the female is larger than the male and leads the clan in hunts and aggressive encounters with other clans. If Gould is correct, that is the phenomenon that begs for an ultimate explanation. Why is it advantageous for female spotted hyenas to be large and strong relative to males? The point here is that an understanding of proximate mechanisms is often an essential step in developing plausible ultimate explanations.

On point

Sometimes the use of a structure for a purpose beyond those for which it evolved can be harmful. The foot can adapt to ballet positions, but ultimately that adaptation leads to physical deformity.

Putting an Organ to Use for Purposes Beyond Those for Which It Evolved

Suppose Gould is right, that the female spotted hyena's enlarged clitoris came about as a side effect. Even so, Kruuk's explanation could still be partly correct. Once the clitoral enlargement began to occur, the female may have found a use for it in the greeting ceremony, either through learning or through further evolutionary change. Whatever structures one has are part of the conditions of one's life, around which further adaptive change can occur.

11. *Why don't the current behavioral functions of an organ always correspond with the original functions for which it evolved?*

Now consider the human brain. The basic form of this organ certainly did not come about as a side effect. It must have evolved because the behavioral characteristics it made possible were valuable to the survival and reproduction of our ancestors. But that doesn't mean that everything people now do with their brains has a direct evolutionary, adaptational explanation. You may use your brain to understand computers, compose sonnets, or figure out your taxes, but that doesn't mean that the human brain evolved for those specific purposes. The brain evolved its complex characteristics and potentials to solve problems that were critical to survival and reproduction in an earlier time. Now that we have it, however, we can use it for all sorts of purposes that would never have occurred to our ancestors.

Ethology: The Study of Species-Specific Behavior Patterns

Suppose you saw an animal that looked exactly like a dog, but it went "meow," climbed trees, and ignored the mail carrier. Would you call it a dog or a cat? Clearly, we identify animals as much by their behavior as by their anatomy. Behavior patterns that are so characteristic of a given species of animal that they can be used to help identify that species are called ***species-specific behaviors***. Meowing, tree climbing, and acting aloof are species-specific behaviors of cats. Dam building is a species-specific behavior of beavers. Talking and two-legged walking are species-specific behaviors of humans.

The field of behavioral study that has concentrated most explicitly on species-specific behaviors is ***ethology***, which originated in Europe in the 1930s as a branch of zoology concerned with animal behavior in the natural environment (see Chapter 1). In contrast with psychologists, who studied animals in mazes and other artificial contrivances and who were looking for general principles of learning that cut across different species, ethologists were more interested in the behavioral differences among species, which they attributed to their different evolutionary histories. Ethologists were (and still are) interested in (a) identifying and describing species-specific behaviors, (b) understanding the environmental requirements for the development of such behaviors in the young animal, and (c) understanding the evolutionary pathway through which the genetic basis for the behavior came about.

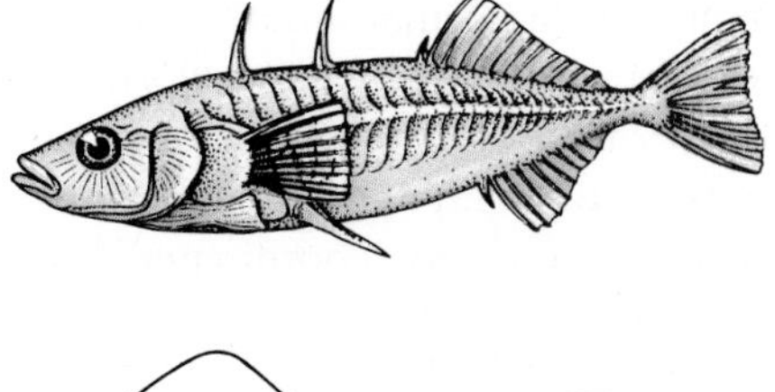

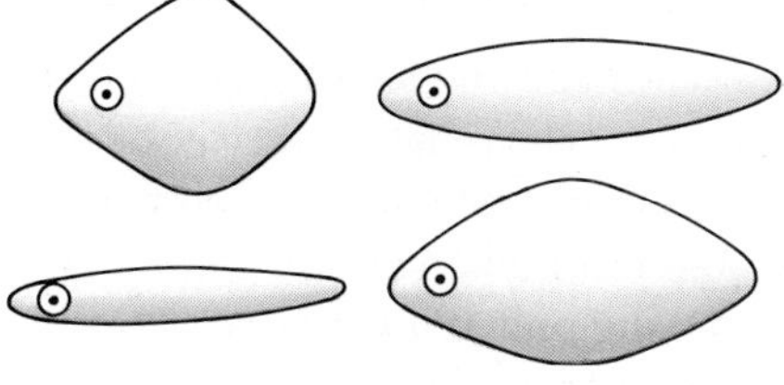

Figure 4.2 ***Stickleback models used in the test of sign stimuli***

Models that had a red belly (bottom four) provoked aggression in male sticklebacks no matter how crude they were, whereas even a perfect replica of a male stickleback with no red belly (top) did not. (From Tinbergen, 1951.)

■ **12.** ***How did Tinbergen identify the sign stimuli for the attack response and the zigzag dance in the male stickleback?***

Describing Species-Specific Behaviors

Fixed Action Patterns and Sign Stimuli

The early ethologists, including Konrad Lorenz and Nikolaas Tinbergen (the field's main founders), studied various species of insects, fish, reptiles, and birds, and found that these animals are quite predictable in many aspects of their behavior. Different members of the same species produce identical responses to specific environmental stimuli. The ethologists referred to such movements as ***fixed action patterns***, emphasizing the idea that the controlling mechanisms are "fixed" in the animal's nervous system by heredity and are relatively unmodifiable by learning. The ethologists also coined the term ***sign stimulus*** to refer to any stimulus that elicits a fixed action pattern. The relationship between a sign stimulus and a fixed action pattern is essentially reflexive, except that the response to a sign stimulus is usually more complex than that of a reflex and occurs only when the animal is in an appropriate physiological condition.

Tinbergen (1951, 1952) studied fixed action patterns and sign stimuli in a little European fish, the stickleback. During the breeding season, the male stickleback's belly turns from dull gray to bright red, and he builds a nest and defends the area around it by attacking other male sticklebacks that come too close. To determine what triggers the attack on other males, Tinbergen made stickleback models of varying accuracy and trailed them on thin wires through a male's territory. He found that any model with a red belly, no matter how little it resembled a real stickleback in other respects, would elicit a vigorous attack from the defending male (see Figure 4.2). A model without a red belly, no matter how much it resembled a real stickleback in other respects, failed to elicit an attack. Thus, Tinbergen showed that the red belly is the sign stimulus for the attack response in the male stickleback. (He even observed male sticklebacks attacking in the direction of a red van driving past their glass-walled aquarium.)

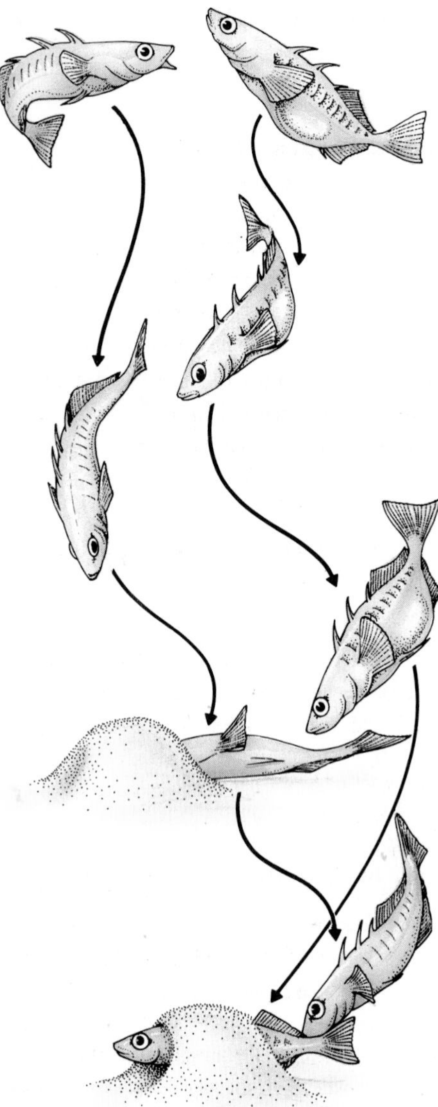

Figure 4.3 ***Courtship behavior of sticklebacks***

After performing the zigzag dance in her presence, the male stickleback leads the female into the nest he has constructed, where she lays her eggs. (Adapted from Tinbergen, 1951.)

■ ***13. Why are species-specific behaviors in mammals better characterized in terms of biological preparedness rather than in terms of fixed action patterns?***

■ ***14. Why is the concept of species-specific behavior relative rather than absolute?***

Tinbergen also determined the sign stimulus for another stickleback fixed action pattern, the *zigzag dance*, by which the male lures the female into his nest and prompts her to lay eggs where he can fertilize them (see Figure 4.3). Again using dummies attached to wires, Tinbergen found that the sign stimulus for this behavior is the female's swollen belly.

Biological Preparedness as the Basis for Species-Specific Behaviors

In their early writings, ethologists tended to describe all species-specific behaviors in terms of fixed action patterns and sign stimuli, but as they began to study mammals they found that many species-specific behaviors are more flexible in form and less tightly controlled by specific stimuli than is implied by those terms. This is particularly true of primates, and most especially humans. A scientist from outer space making a study of earthly life would almost certainly point to two-legged walking and use of a grammar-based language as among the species-specific behaviors of humans, but these are neither rigid in form nor tightly controlled by environmental stimuli, and they obviously involve a great deal of learning. At the same time, it is clear that humans are biologically predisposed to engage in these behaviors.

Regarding walking, evolution has provided humans with anatomical systems—such as strong hindlimbs with feet, weaker forelimbs without feet, and a short, stiff neck—that combine to make it more convenient for us to walk upright than on all fours. Moreover, we are born with neural systems in the brain and spinal cord that enable us to move our legs and other body parts correctly for coordinated two-legged walking, and neural structures that help motivate this behavior at the appropriate stage of our development. Consider the difference between two-legged walking in humans and in dogs. Dogs are capable of learning to walk on two legs, and much is made of that fact by circus trainers, but they are never very good at it. They do not have the appropriate muscular and skeletal systems to coordinate the behavior properly, and they have no natural impulse to walk in this manner. A dog, unlike a human child, will practice two-legged walking only if it receives immediate rewards such as food for doing so. Thus, two-legged walking is not a species-specific behavior in dogs.

The same is true for talking. Humans are born with anatomical structures (including a tongue and larynx) that can produce a wide range of sounds, and with a brain that has special neural centers for understanding and producing language (discussed in Chapter 11). Infants begin talking at a certain stage even if they receive little outside inducement (discussed in Chapter 12). Of course, to acquire a language a child must hear others use it and have others around with whom to speak it. But the fact that learning is involved does not negate the point that talking is a species-specific behavior. The natural environment of the human being, the one in which we have been evolving for millions of years, is one in which children are surrounded by adults who communicate through spoken language. Chimpanzees can be taught to simulate some aspects of human language, just as dogs can be taught to walk on their hind legs, but diligent training is required and they are never very good at it.

Having characterized the concept of species-specific behavior in terms of biological preparedness, I must now add that the concept is relative rather than absolute. No behavior stems just from biological preparation; some sort of experience with the environment is always involved. Conversely, any behavior that an animal can produce—no matter how artificial it may seem or how much training is necessary to produce it—must make use of the animal's inherited biological capacities. The concept of species-specific behavior is useful as long as we accept it as relative and do not get into arguments about whether one or another behavior really should or should not be called species-specific. *Big* and *little* are useful terms in our vocabulary, but there is no point in arguing about whether a bread box is properly called one or the other. Two-legged walking is more species-specific for humans than for dogs, as a bread box is bigger than a book of matches.

The question to ask when we study a particular behavior is not: Is this a species-specific behavior? Rather, the meaningful questions are: What are the environmental conditions needed for the full development of this behavior? What internal mechanisms are involved in producing it? What is its function in the individual's daily life? In the course of evolution, why would the genes that make this behavior possible have been favored by natural selection? These questions can in principle be asked of any behavior, whether the behavior is thought of as species-specific or not.

Development of Species-Specific Behaviors: The Role of the Environment

The Rationale of Deprivation Experiments

■ **15. *What is the purpose of deprivation experiments, and how is that purpose illustrated in studies of fighting in rats and of singing in white-crowned sparrows?***

After identifying various species-specific behaviors, ethologists wanted to learn about the development of such behaviors in the individual. What aspects of the animal's natural environment are needed for a behavior to develop in its typical, species-specific form? To answer this kind of question, they devised ***deprivation experiments***. By depriving young animals of selected aspects of their normal environment, the ethologists hoped to determine which environmental experiences are not essential to the development of the behavior.

In some cases such experiments have shown that a particular species-specific behavior can develop quite normally in animals that have had no opportunity to observe the behavior in others. For example, Irenäus Eibl-Eibesfeldt (1961)—one of the first ethologists to focus on mammals—found that rats raised in isolation from other rats, without ever seeing rats fight, nevertheless fought the very first time they were placed together and used the same postures and movements as do normally raised rats (see Figure 4.4). This result, of course, does not mean that fighting in rats is completely independent of experience. The isolated rats had experience moving and exercising their muscles in various ways in their cages, for example, which no doubt contributed to the development of their ability to fight. Rather, the study shows that the basic pattern of movements in rats' fighting is genetically prepared in such a way that it can occur without observational learning.

In other cases, deprivation experiments have helped pinpoint experiences that are necessary for a particular species-specific behavior to develop. For example, Peter Marler (1970) found that white-crowned sparrows develop the ability to sing their species-specific song only if they are permitted to hear that song during their first summer after hatching. Indeed, populations of the species living in different areas have somewhat different dialects, and a white-crowned sparrow learns to sing

(a)

(b)

(c)

Figure 4.4 ***Species-specific fighting postures of rats***

When aggressive rats meet, they (a) first circle one another with arched backs, and then (b and c) rise into a boxing-like position and push each other with their paws. They fight in this way whether raised in isolation or with other rats. (From Eibl-Eibesfeldt, 1961.)

the dialect of the adult that it hears. Yet the range of possible songs that the birds can learn is limited. No matter what environmental experiences it has, a white-crowned sparrow cannot learn to sing like a canary, or like any species other than a white-crowned sparrow.

Emlen's Study of Migratory Flight in the Indigo Bunting

My favorite example of a deprivation experiment is a study conducted by Stephen T. Emlen (1975) with indigo buntings. The indigo bunting is a small songbird that spends its summers in the eastern United States and Canada and its winters in the Bahamas and Central America. Like most songbirds, it migrates only at night. Without the sun as a guide, how does it know which way is north and which is south? That is the question that Emlen wished to answer.

Indigo bunting

Over the course of their evolution, indigo buntings have become genetically programmed to observe the night sky and learn which of the stars appears to move least. The tiny bird uses the northern hemisphere's most stationary star, currently Polaris, to guide its migratory flight.

16. ***How did Emlen discover that indigo buntings must learn which star is stationary? What is a possible evolutionary explanation of why they must learn it?***

If indigo buntings are kept in cages and exposed to natural seasonal changes in the daily hours of light, they get restless during the migrating seasons and make many futile movements to get out of their cages. Emlen found that if the birds are caged in such a way that the stars are in view, their restless movements are directed south in the fall and north in the spring. If the stars are not in view, their movements are directed randomly. Apparently, they use the stars to tell direction. Emlen next found that if he blocked from view the area of the sky that includes Polaris (the North Star) and the constellations around it, the birds directed their movements randomly; but if he blocked other portions of the sky, preserving the view of Polaris and the surrounding constellations, they directed their movements appropriately. Apparently, indigo buntings use Polaris as their guide. This is quite a "logical" choice, because Polaris is the only clearly visible star in the Northern Hemisphere that maintains a fixed compass position throughout the night. All of the other stars appear to move across the sky as the earth rotates on its axis.

So, buntings migrate away from Polaris in the fall and toward it in the spring. But how do they know that Polaris, and not some other bright star, should serve as their guide? Is this knowledge inborn, or do they somehow have to learn that Polaris is the one fixed spot in the night sky? This is where the deprivation experiment comes in.

Emlen raised three groups of indigo bunting nestlings in a laboratory, carefully controlling their visual experience. Group 1 was never exposed to any representation of the stars throughout the summer months. Group 2 was allowed to view a representation of the true night sky in a planetarium. Group 3, the most interesting group, was allowed to view, in the same planetarium, a false representation of the night sky, in which all of the stars rotated around Betelgeuse (a bright star in the constellation Orion) rather than Polaris. When the birds began to show migratory restlessness in the fall, all groups were placed in the planetarium with a representation of the true night sky. The results were that Group 1 showed no consistency in their orientation, Group 2 oriented directly away from Polaris as expected, and Group 3 oriented directly away from Betelgeuse! Thus, Emlen found that indigo buntings are not born (or rather hatched) with the knowledge that they must fly away from Polaris in the fall. Instead, their genes help equip them to know that (a) they must fly away from the fixed star in the fall, and (b) before that time they must learn, through observation, which star that is.

Why must each new generation of buntings learn the sky? Why haven't they evolved the innate knowledge to use Polaris as their guide? Emlen suggests an interesting answer to that question. The heavens are not fixed; each year the earth's axis of rotation changes very slightly. Over thousands of years, the North Pole pointed toward a succession of different stars, as explained in Figure 4.5. To accomodate this change, a flexible system for choosing the fixed star is apparently more effective than a rigid instinct to fly away from a particular star. If Emlen is correct,

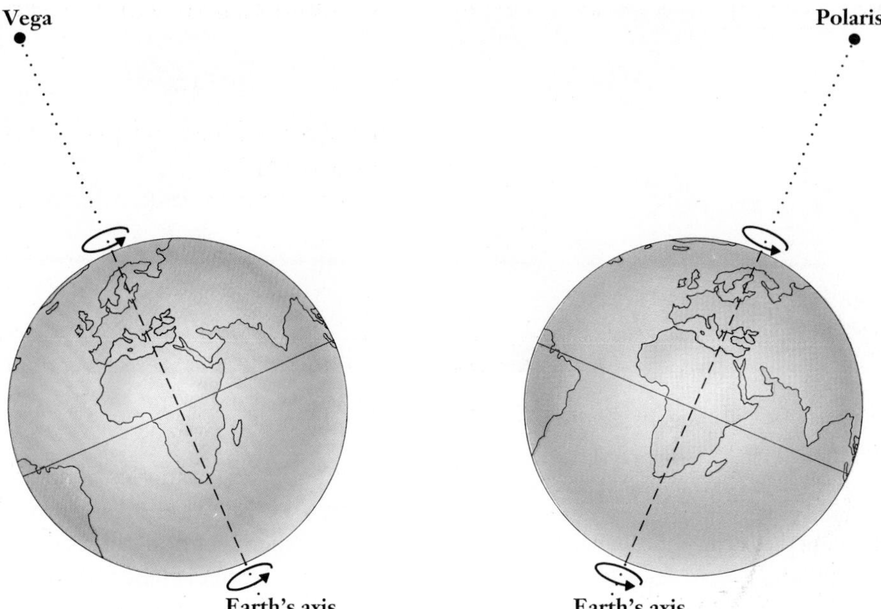

Figure 4.5 ***Evolutionary advantage of indigo buntings' learning which star is stationary***

Whichever star lies most directly over the earth's North Pole will be the most stationary star in the Northern Hemisphere, and hence the most reliable guide for migratory flight. Today that star is Polaris. But the earth spins on an axis that wobbles in a cycle that takes 26,000 years to complete. Thus, 13,000 years ago the most stationary star was not Polaris but Vega, and in the interim a succession of other stars have occupied that status. (Adapted from Emlen, 1975.)

ancestral buntings who held a genetically fixed image of the sky would, with time, have gone off course and perished, while those that had a more flexible system, allowing them to adjust which star to use as their guide, would have continued to make it to their southern destination. This nicely illustrates the ethologists' idea that specific learning mechanisms arose in evolution to meet specific survival problems that could not be met through less flexible means (a point to be pursued in Chapter 5).

Tracing the Evolution of Species-Specific Behaviors

Scientists interested in the origins of anatomical traits, especially bones, can dig up fossils and try to reconstruct the evolutionary pathway by comparing fossils of different ages. But behavior does not fossilize (except occasionally in remnants such as footprints, or, for humans, in products of behavior such as tools). How can ethologists make reasonable inferences about the evolutionary pathway of species-specific behaviors? The answer, as pointed out by Darwin and pursued by the pioneering ethologists, is through the systematic comparison of behaviors in present-day species.

Two Forms of Cross-Species Comparisons: Homologies and Analogies

■ **17.** ***What is the difference between a homology and an analogy, in behavior as well as anatomy?***

To understand the logic of comparing present-day species to infer an evolutionary pathway, we must distinguish between two conceptually different classes of similarities among species—homologies and analogies. A ***homology*** is any similarity between species that exists because of their common ancestry. If we look back far enough, all animals are related to one another, so it is not surprising that some homologies—such as in the basic structure of the DNA molecule and of certain enzymes—can be found between any two species. But the more closely related two species are, the more homologies they will show. An ***analogy***, in contrast, is a similarity that stems not from common ancestry but from *convergent evolution*. Convergent evolution occurs when different species, because of some similarity in their habitat or lifestyle, independently evolve some common characteristic.

As an illustration, consider some comparisons among different species that can fly. Flying has arisen separately in three different taxonomic groups—birds, some insects (such as butterflies), and some mammals (bats). Similarities across these three groups in their flying motions, and in the anatomical structures that permit

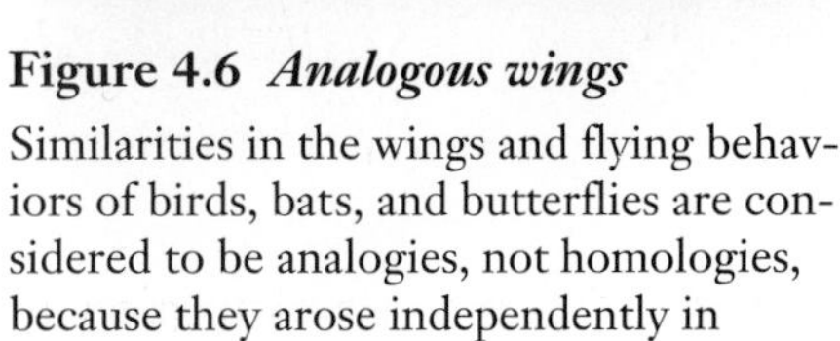

Figure 4.6 ***Analogous wings***

Similarities in the wings and flying behaviors of birds, bats, and butterflies are considered to be analogies, not homologies, because they arose independently in evolution.

such flight, are examples of analogies because they do not result from common ancestry (see Figure 4.6). However, similarities among species within any of these groups, such as among birds or butterflies, are likely to be homologies.

Aside from evidence based on already existing knowledge about the relatedness of the species being compared, analogies and homologies can often be distinguished by the nature of the similarity involved (Lorenz, 1974). Analogies entail similarity in function and gross forms coupled with lack of similarity in detail and underlying mechanisms. Thus, the wings of birds, bats, and butterflies are all similar in the sense that they provide broad, flappable surfaces, but they are very different in the details of their construction. Similarly, the specific movements involved in flight in these three groups are quite different in detail and are controlled by different neural mechanisms. In contrast, because homologies arise from shared genes, they entail similarities in the underlying construction and physiological mechanisms, even when, because of divergent evolution, large differences have emerged in gross form or function (for example, see Figure 4.7).

Analogies are useful as clues in understanding the evolutionary function of a species-specific behavior (as you will see later), but only homologies are useful in inferring the actual pathway of change through which it evolved. The pioneer in the use of this method was Darwin himself, so it seems most fitting to illustrate it by describing one of Darwin's studies, taken from his chapter on instinct in *The Origin of Species*.

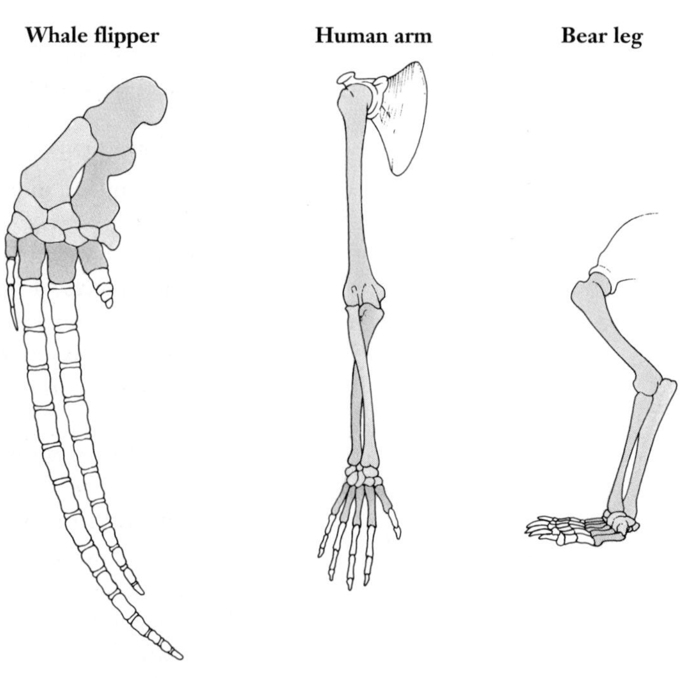

Figure 4.7 ***Homologous forelimbs***

Similarities in the forelimbs of different species of mammals are considered to be homologies because they arose from common ancestry. Though the limbs of the whale, human, and bear differ in function and gross structure, they are similar in certain of their structural details, as is characteristic of homologies. Behaviors too can be homologous, and a key to their homology is similarity in mechanism and detail, even when function differs. (Adapted from Lorenz, 1974.)

(a)

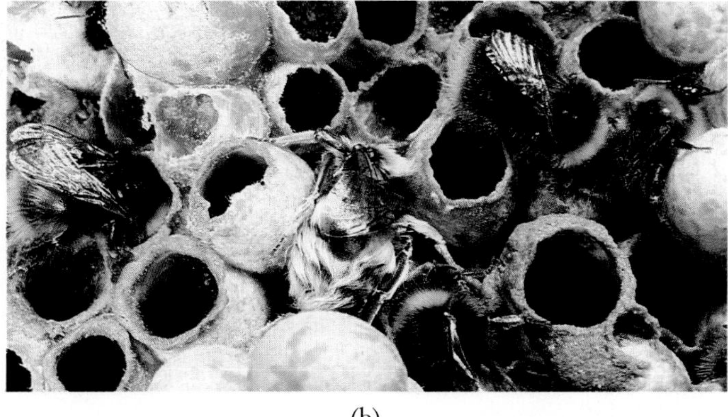
(b)

Figure 4.8 ***Cells built by honeybees and bumblebees***

The hexagonal cells of the honeybee's hive (a) are the optimal shape for storing large amounts of honey and larvae using the least amount of wax. Darwin suggested that ancestors to modern honeybees built their hives in a way similar to that of modern bumblebees (b), but through evolution, began placing their cells closer together, patching up the points of intersection, resulting eventually in the kind of hive they build today.

18. ***How did Darwin use comparison by homology to infer the evolutionary steps through which honeybees acquired their hive-making ability?***

Darwin's Study of Hive Building in Bees

Have you ever examined the hive that honeybees make? It is a marvelous piece of work, which the bees build with wax secreted from special glands in their bodies. Each comb in the hive consists of a double layer of thin-walled, hexagonally shaped cells, with their bases beveled to enable the two layers of cells to fit together perfectly (see Figure 4.8a). Mathematicians in Darwin's time had shown that this design is the most efficient possible; it allows for the storage of the greatest amount of honey and larvae with the least use of wax. The cells' exquisite design, plus the fact that the they look as if they would be extraordinarily difficult to build, was used as evidence in Darwin's time that a divine and unfathomable intelligence lay behind their construction. Darwin knew that for his theory of evolution to be accepted, he would have to show how such a marvelous behavior as this, in such a simple animal as the bee, could have come about through natural selection.

Darwin began his study of the honeybee's hive-building by surveying the types of storage structures built by other living bee species. He discovered that these structures could be arranged in a series from very simple to complex. The simplest, produced by bumblebees, consisted of small clusters of spherical cells (see Figure 4.8b). Darwin noted that spherical cells are easy to build, and that insects usually build them by sweeping their body, or some part of their body, compasslike around a fixed point. Another species of bee, *Melipona domestica*, which is anatomically more similar to the honeybee than is the bumblebee, builds much larger clusters of spherical cells that are more closely compacted than those of the bumblebee. Darwin noted that this species builds its cells in essentially the same way as does the bumblebee, but closer together, patching up intersecting cells with flat walls. This insight provided him with the key to explaining the honeybee's hive-building ability.

Darwin reasoned that if a group of honeybees began building spherical cells a certain distance apart (which they could do by using their own bodies as a measure), and then patched up the points of intersection between adjacent cells with flat walls, doing this in two layers, they would produce precisely the structures one finds in the honeybee hive. They would not have to calculate the sizes of the planes and angles of hexagonal prisms in order to build them, but would simply have to add another, not terribly complex step (that of building the cells equal distances apart) to the behaviors already present in the *Melipona* bees. Subsequently, Darwin developed a method to observe honeybees directly as they built their combs, and he confirmed that this indeed was how they worked.

Based on his comparisons of different bee species, Darwin proposed that the early ancestors of honeybees built spherical cells, as do present-day bumblebees, and that through evolution they gradually came to position their cells closer together, sharing more walls in common, until they arrived at the "perfect" form of the present-day comb. Each small step in this process would represent a selective advantage to the bees, allowing for the construction of more cells (so as to store more honey and house more larvae) with less expenditure of precious wax.

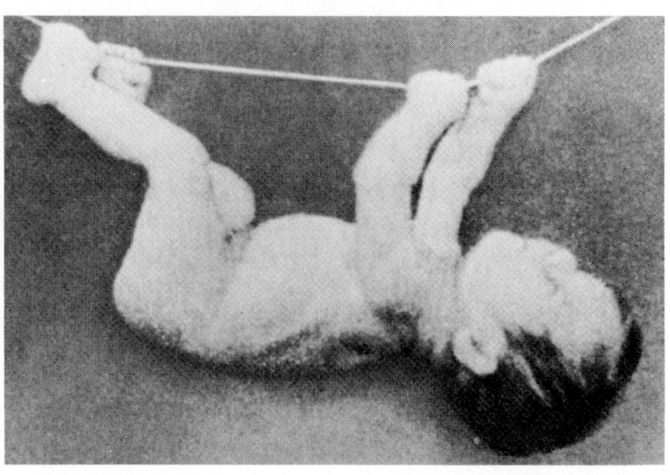

Figure 4.9 ***Premature infant clinging with hands and toes***
This ability may be a vestigial carryover from an earlier evolutionary time, when the infants of our ancestors would cling to their parents' fur.

Vestigial Behaviors

■ **19.** ***How can comparison by homology be used to infer the original function of a behavior that is now vestigial?***

Some species-specific behaviors do not make sense as adaptations to the present environment, but do make sense as adaptations to conditions present at an earlier time. These behavioral remnants of the past are called ***vestigial characteristics***, and they can often be understood through homologies. An interesting example is the *grasp reflex*, by which newborn human infants close their fingers tightly around objects placed in their hands. This reflex may well be useful in the development of the infant's ability to hold and manipulate objects, but that does not explain why prematurely born infants will grasp so strongly that they can support their own weight, or why they will grasp with their toes as well as their hands (see Figure 4.9), or why the best stimulus to elicit the response is a clump of hair (Eibl-Eibesfeldt, 1975). These aspects of the reflex make more sense when we observe the homologous behavior in other primates. To survive, infant monkeys and apes cling tightly to their mother's fur while she swings around in trees or goes about her other daily business. In the course of our evolution from ape-like ancestors we lost our fur, so our infants can no longer cling to us in this way, but the grasp reflex remains.

The issue of vestigial traits becomes quite important when we extend it from reflexes to our inherited drives or motives. Because of culture, our habitat and lifestyle have changed dramatically in just a few centuries, a speck of time compared to the time scale of biological evolution. The great bulk of our evolution occurred in a world that was very different from the one we inhabit today, and some of our inherited tendencies may be not only nonfunctional but harmful. An example is our taste for sugar. In the world of our ancestors sugar was a rare and valuable commodity. It existed primarily in fruits and provided energy needed for life in the wild, as we can see by looking at the diets of present-day monkeys and apes. But today, in our culture, sugar is readily available, and life (at least for most of us) is less physically strenuous. Yet our taste for sugar persists as strong as ever, despite such negative consequences as tooth decay and obesity.

Nonverbal Emotional Expressions as Species-Specific Behaviors

When Darwin turned his attention from other animals to humans, he focused especially on the category of behavior we now call ***nonverbal communication***, defined as communication without words. We, like other animals, regularly communicate our moods and behavioral intentions to each other through bodily postures, movements, and facial expressions. In 1872, Darwin published a book entitled *The Expression of the Emotions in Man and Animals*, making the case that (a) specific, objectively describable facial expressions reliably accompany specific emotional states in humans; (b) some of these expressions are universal, occurring in people of every age, race, and culture, and even in people who were born blind and thus could not have learned them through observation; and (c) the evolutionary origins of some of these expressions can be understood by comparison with expressions of other animals. In the past thirty years a number of ethologists and psychologists have picked up where Darwin left off, and the evolutionary analysis of nonverbal expressions has become a rather active area of research. We will start here with three general principles that Darwin outlined concerning the evolution of nonverbal signals, and then turn to studies of human emotional expressions.

20. ***How do communicative signals arise through ritualization, antithesis, and direct action of the nervous system?***

Principle 1: Ritualization

Darwin's first principle was that many signals evolved from behaviors that originally served functions other than communication. Darwin called this "the principle of serviceable associated habits," but today it is referred to as ***ritualization***. In this evolutionary process, behavior that originally served some noncommunicative function begins to serve a communicative function when other members of the species, seeing the initial movements of the behavior, use them as clues in predicting what the actor will do next. If that communicative function benefits the individual manifesting the behavior, natural selection modifies the behavior, along with associated anatomical structures, in a way that enhances its communicative function. Eventually the noncommunicative function of the behavior may decline or disappear, in which case the behavior finally functions either mostly or solely as a signal.

As an example, consider the evolution of aggressive signals, or threats, in animals. Darwin pointed out that the displays that most animals use to threaten one another contain obvious elements of the behavior patterns involved in fighting. An animal about to attack another animal must first face the other and expose its weapons (beak, antlers, teeth, claws, or whatever). Originally, facing the enemy and exposing the weapons were part of the act of attacking, but they evolved, in some species, into signals of threat (see Figure 4.10). Since there is an advantage in

Figure 4.10 ***Threat display shown by a northern gannet***

As a rule, the nonverbal signals with which animals threaten one another evolved from, and bear a physical resemblance to, the movements involved in actual fighting.

knowing when one is likely to be attacked, animals acquired the ability (through natural selection or learning or both) to recognize the cues that another animal is about to attack. This in turn resulted in a selective advantage to those individuals that manifested their aggressive intentions most clearly—for example, by staring for a longer time or showing their weapons more conspicuously—as they could best intimidate others into submitting or running away without actually fighting, and thereby get their way with minimal risk of injury. Thus, as evolution proceeded, what was initially a battle of tooth or claw increasingly became a battle of bluff, a way of communicating aggression and accomplishing one's aggressive ends with less actual fighting.

Ritualization can occur through learning and cultural tradition as well as through natural selection. Many human nonverbal signals that may or may not be entirely learned seem to be ritualized forms of behaviors that originally served purposes beyond signaling (see Eibl-Eibesfeldt, 1989). For example, the side-to-side shaking of the head to signal "no" may have originated from the movements by which an infant who has had enough to eat turns away from the mother's breast or another source of food. Similarly, tongue protrusion as a general signal of rejection may have originated from the tongue movements by which infants physically reject food that has been placed in their mouths.

Principle 2: Antithesis

If a species communicates a particular message with a particular movement or posture, natural selection or learning or both may lead the species to adopt the opposite movement or posture to communicate the opposite message. This is what Darwin called the principle of ***antithesis***. Among the best examples are signals of nonaggression, including signals of submission. To appear nonaggressive, one must first and foremost *not* appear aggressive, so natural selection would favor signals that involve hiding the signs of aggression or behaving in ways opposite to those of aggression. Thus, gulls that express aggression by pointing their beaks at one another express nonaggression by pointing their beaks directly away from each other (Tinbergen, 1960), and primates that signal aggression by a direct stare signal nonaggression by very conspicuously looking away (Redican, 1982). Darwin's own illustration of the principle, applied to dogs, is shown in Figure 4.11. In the submissive state, practically all moving parts of the dog are oriented in a direction opposite to the way they are in the aggressive state.

Figure 4.11 ***The principle of antithesis***
As depicted in this woodcut from Darwin (1872/1965), the hostile and submissive dogs show opposite postures and movements. The hostile dog has its ears forward, back up, hair up, and tail up; the submissive dog has its ears back, back down, hair down, and tail down.

Principle 3: Autonomic Responses

The response systems of the body can be divided into two classes: the *somatic* or *skeletal*, which includes the muscles attached directly to bones; and the *autonomic*, which includes glands and the muscles not attached to bones, such as the muscular walls of the heart, blood vessels, and digestive tract. Nonverbal signals that arise from ritualization or antithesis generally involve the skeletal muscles. Darwin pointed out that other signals arise from the involuntary autonomic responses that accompany physiological arousal. Trembling when frightened and blushing when ashamed are among the examples of human autonomic responses that are visible to another person and can signal one's emotional state. It is not clear to what extent such signals have been modified over evolutionary time explicitly to serve a communicative function, and to what extent they occur only as a side effect or because they serve other, noncommunicative functions. There has been relatively little research on autonomically mediated signals.

The Anatomy of Human Emotional Expressions

21. ***How can human facial expressions of emotion be described anatomically?***

Darwin believed that precise description is as important to the study of human facial expressions as to that of any other biological phenomenon. His book on emotional expressions includes descriptions of the muscles of the face and how they move during various expressions. The most thorough modern extension of Darwin's work along this line is that of American psychologists Paul Ekman and Wallace Friesen (1975, 1982). They produced an atlas containing both verbal descriptions and pictures of the facial expressions that accompany six basic emotions—surprise, fear, disgust, anger, happiness, and sadness. Ekman and Friesen developed the verbal descriptions by measuring the relative positions of the moveable parts of the face in photographs and films of dozens of people who were experiencing each emotion, and by using statistical means to find the positions that were most typical of each. Then, to produce standard pictures for their atlas, they asked models who were skilled at facial movements to contract just those muscles dictated by the verbal description. Figure 4.12 shows the full-faced expression of each of the basic emotions.

We rarely express emotions in the pure forms depicted in Figure 4.12. More commonly we feel and express several emotions at once, and ***blends*** of two or more may appear on our face. For any two of the six basic emotions, you can probably imagine a situation that would elicit both at once. For example, surprise can blend with fear, disgust, anger, happiness, or sadness, depending on whether the unexpected encounter is with a fierce bandit, a disemboweled pig, a despised enemy, a dear friend, or a loss of fortune. Even the seemingly opposite emotions of sadness and happiness can blend, as, for example, when reminiscing over the sweet, lost

Figure 4.12 ***Six basic human emotional expressions***

These expressions were produced by a model who was asked to move specific facial muscles in specific ways. As you study each figure, try to describe the positions of facial features for each expression. For example, surprise can be described as follows: (1) the brows are pulled upward, producing horizontal wrinkles across the forehead; (2) the eyes are opened wide, revealing white above the iris; (3) the lower jaw is dropped; and (4) no tension exists around the mouth.

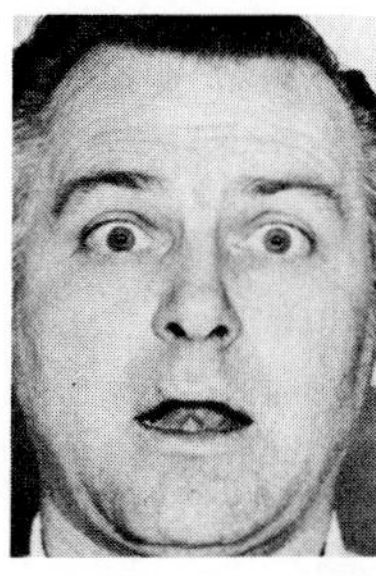
Surprise

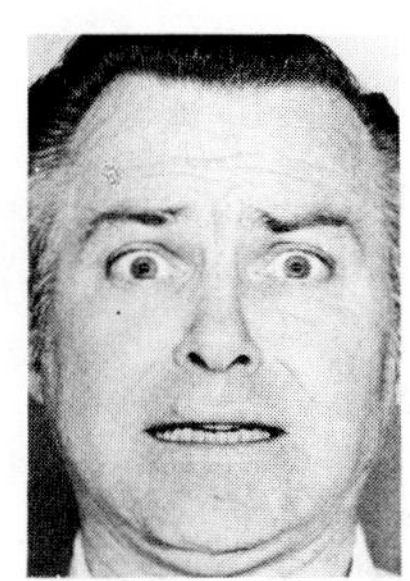
Fear

Disgust

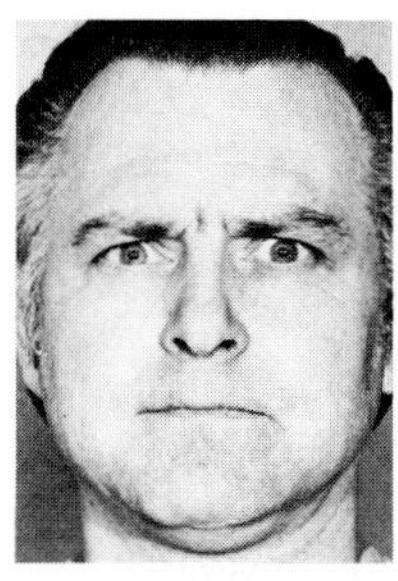
Anger

Happiness

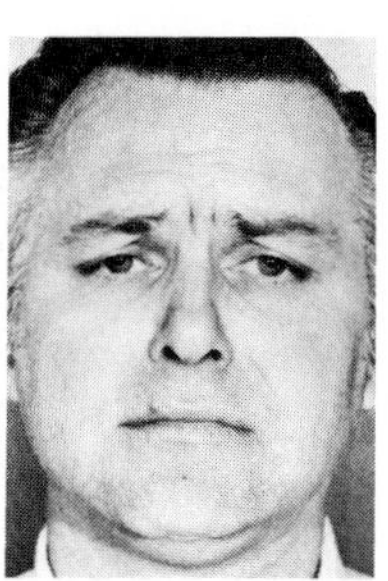
Sadness

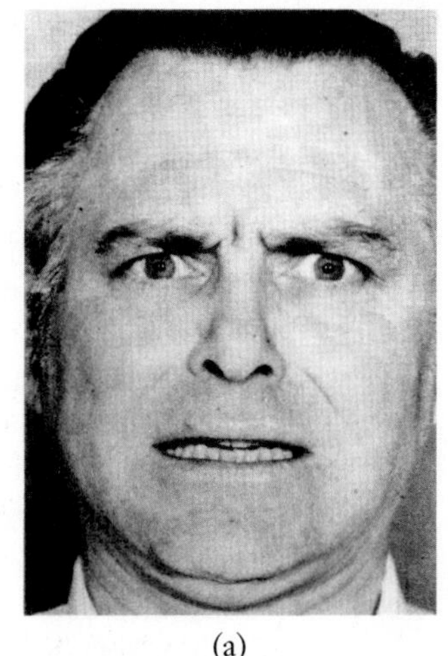
(a)

(b)

Figure 4.13 ***Blends of anger-fear and sorrow-happiness in humans***

People often show blends of emotions by manifesting one emotion in the upper part of the face and the other in the lower part, as illustrated here for (a) anger-fear and (b) sorrow-happiness, taken from Ekman and Friesen's atlas.

days of childhood. According to Ekman and Friesen (1975), blends are most often expressed by showing one emotion in the lower part of the face and the other in the upper part, as shown in Figure 4.13. Blends can also be found in the emotional expressions of other animals, as shown for the dog in Figure 4.14. (As a bicyclist, I find Figure 4.14 to be quite useful. I can scare away an attacking dog that has its ears back, but if the ears are forward, I pedal as fast as I can.)

The Universality of Emotional Expressions

■ **22.** ***What was wrong with Darwin's evidence for the universality of emotional expressions? How have modern researchers confirmed his general conclusion?***

Do people everywhere express emotions in the same basic ways? Darwin (1872/1965) attempted to answer that by surveying missionaries and government officials working in various parts of the world among people who had little if any previous contact with Europeans. His survey contained such questions as: (1) "Is astonishment expressed by the eyes and mouth being opened wide, and by the eyebrows being raised?" (2) "When in good spirits, do the eyes sparkle, with the skin around and under them a little wrinkled, and with the mouth drawn back at the corners?" From the responses to this survey, Darwin concluded that the basic emotional expressions are universal.

Darwin's study has justly been criticized because the questions he asked clearly described the results that he expected. Observers of behavior, particularly relatively untrained observers such as those that Darwin relied on in this study, often "see"

Figure 4.14 ***Blend of anger-fear in dogs***

Dogs also manifest emotional blends in their faces. Increasing hostility in the dog is shown here from left to right, and increasing fear from top to bottom. The lower right-hand dog is simultaneously strongly hostile and fearful. (From Lorenz, 1966.)

what they expect to see. This problem can be circumvented by using observers who are unaware of the hypothesis being tested. (Observer-expectancy effects and double blind methods are discussed in Chapter 2.) Recent cross-cultural studies have been conducted in ways that prevent observer bias, and these have generally confirmed Darwin's conclusion. For example, Ekman and his colleagues showed their atlas photographs to individuals in many different countries—including members of a preliterate tribe in the highlands of New Guinea who had little previous contact with other cultures—and found that in every culture people described each depicted emotion in a way that was consistent with descriptions in the United States (Ekman, 1973; Ekman & others, 1987). In a reversal of this procedure, they also photographed members of the New Guinea tribe who had been asked to act out various emotions and showed the photographs to college students in the United States. The college students were highly accurate in labeling the emotions portrayed by the New Guineans.

Another scientist who studies human nonverbal communication cross-culturally is ethologist Irenäus Eibl-Eibesfeldt. After spending the first half of his career studying nonhuman animals, he turned his attention to a worldwide study of species-specific behaviors in humans. One of his findings concerns a signal that he labeled the ***eyebrow flash***, a momentary raising of the eyebrows lasting about 1/6 of a second, usually accompanied by a smile and an upward nod of the head (see Figure 4.15). He observed this response in every culture he studied—including cultures in New Guinea, Samoa, and various parts of Africa, Asia, South America, and Europe—and concluded that it is a universal sign of greeting among friends (Eibl-Eibesfeldt, 1989). Raised eyebrows are also a component of the emotional expression of surprise (look back at Figure 4.12), so the eyebrow flash with its accompanying smile might be interpreted as a nonverbal way of saying, "What a happy surprise to see you."

Eibl-Eibesfeldt (1975) has also filmed children who were born blind, or both blind and deaf, and found that they manifest emotions in the same basic ways as

Figure 4.15 ***The eyebrow flash***

This universal signal of greeting is shown here in adjacent frames from films of a (a) French woman, (b) Yanomami man (of the Brazil-Venezuela border), (c) !Kung woman (of the central Kalahari, in Africa), and (d) Balinese man.

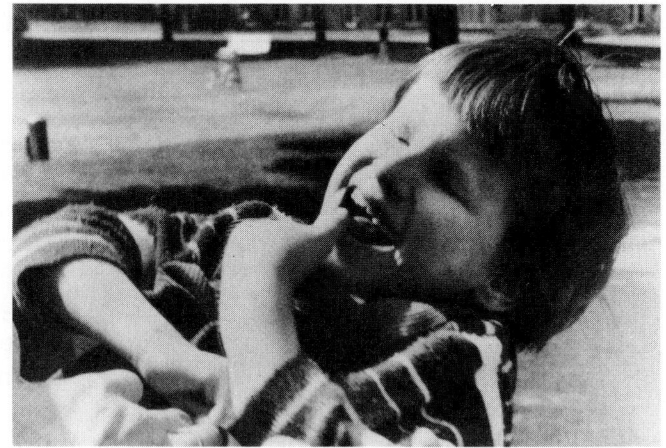

Figure 4.16 ***Some emotional expressions need not be learned through observation***

This young girl, manifesting joy, has been blind and deaf since birth.

sighted children do (see Figure 4.16). Such observations provide the most direct evidence that at least some human expressions do not have to be learned through observing them in others or hearing descriptions of them.

Taking all this evidence together, there can be little doubt that we come into the world genetically prepared to express certain emotions in certain species-specific ways. It is also clear that we come into the world genetically prepared to learn ways of controlling and modifying our emotional expressions and to learn new ones. Even researchers who focus on universal expressions are quick to point out many cross-cultural differences. For example, Eibl-Eibesfeldt (1975) found that despite its cross-cultural similarity in form and general meaning, large cultural differences exist in the use of the eyebrow flash. The Japanese, who are reserved in social expressions among adults, use it mainly when greeting young children, while Samoans, at the other extreme, greet nearly everyone in this way.

Possible Primate Homologies to Two Kinds of Smiles

Partly on the basis of his own observations at zoos, Darwin (1872/1965) pointed out many similarities between human emotional expressions and those of monkeys and apes. He suggested that these similarities represent homologies and can be used in making inferences about the evolution of human expressions, an idea borne out by subsequent research. Perhaps the best evidence concerns the smile.

23. ***How do the human happy and nonhappy smiles differ anatomically?***

The human smile is, of course, a component of the expression of happiness. It also serves as a greeting signal, even when the greeter is not happy. In the mid-nineteenth century, the French anatomist Duchenne de Bologne pointed out that the happy and nonhappy smiles are anatomically distinct from one another (Darwin, 1872). The happy smile involves not just a turning up of the lips, but also a pulling in of the skin around the eyes, which draws attention to the eyes and seems to make them sparkle. The nonhappy smile, in contrast, involves lips alone. This distinction has recently been confirmed in many studies for both adults and young children (Ekman, 1992). In one study, for example, 10-month-old infants smiled with eyes and mouth when approached by their mother (presumably a happy situation), but smiled with mouth alone when approached by a stranger (a possibly tense situation) (Fox & Davidson, 1988).

Ekman (1992) considers the mouth-alone smile to be a derivative of the happy smile. He emphasizes its use in masking one's true feelings and calls it a "false smile." Another possibility, however, is that the mouth-alone smile is a distinct expression, which arrived by a completely different evolutionary route. This idea is supported by studies of two smilelike displays shown by nonhuman primates (van Hooff, 1976).

One is the *silent bared-teeth display*, which may be homologous to the nonhappy greeting smile in humans. If you have ever watched macaque monkeys in a zoo, you

24. *How do studies of monkeys and apes support the view that the human greeting smile and human happy smile have separate evolutionary origins?*

have almost certainly observed this display, a grimace shown usually by the more submissive of two monkeys as it glances nervously toward the more dominant. A direct stare in macaques (and other primates) is an aggressive signal, which precedes attack and can precipitate an attack by the other, and the silent bared-teeth display seems to have evolved as a means for a more submissive monkey to look at a more dominant one without provoking a fight. If it could be translated into words, it might be rendered as, "I'm looking at you but I'm not going to attack, so please don't attack me."

J. A. van Hooff (1972, 1976) studied this display in chimpanzees (our closest animal relatives) and found that among them it takes on a new function, more similar to that of the human smile of greeting. *Both* the more submissive and the more dominant of two chimpanzees show the display upon meeting, and it usually precedes friendly interaction between them. From such observations, van Hooff proposed that the silent bared-teeth display originated in monkeys as a submissive gesture, but evolved in chimpanzees, and even further in humans, into a general form of greeting. As used by the less dominant individual it may retain its original meaning, "Please don't attack me," but used by the more dominant it may mean, "Rest assured, I won't attack," and by both it may mean, "Let's be friends."

The other primate smilelike response is the *relaxed open-mouth display*, which occurs mostly in young primates during playful fighting and chasing and is believed to be related to the smile that accompanies human laughter and happiness. In chimpanzees, it is often accompanied by a vocalized "ahh ahh ahh," which sounds like a throaty human laugh. Van Hooff believes that this display originated as a means for young primates to signal to each other that their aggressive-like behavior is not to be taken seriously; nobody will really get hurt. Interestingly, in human children, laughter accompanies playful fighting and chasing more consistently than any other form of play (Blurton-Jones, 1967); and even among us "sophisticated" adults, pie throwing, chase scenes, mock insults, and other forms of fake aggression are among the most reliable ways to elicit laughter. Thus, our laughter is not only similar in form to the relaxed open-mouth display of other primates, but at least in some cases seems to serve a similar function. The smile that accompanies non-laughing happiness in humans is similar in form to the smile that accompanies laughter, so it too may have originated from the relaxed open-mouth display (Redican, 1982). There is, it seems to me, some poetry in the thought that the smile of happiness may have originated from a signal indicating that, although the world can be a frightening and aggressive place, the aggression going on now is just in fun and we are safe.

(a)

(b)

Possible homologues to the human smile of greeting and the human laugh and smile of happiness

The silent bared-teeth display (a) is believed to be homologous to the human greeting smile, and the relaxed open-mouth display (b) is believed to be homologous to the human laugh and smile of happiness. The animals in both photos are pygmy chimpanzees.

Sociobiology: The Comparative Study of Animals' Social Systems

■ **25.** ***What kinds of questions do sociobiologists ask, and how do they use comparison by analogy to help answer them?***

An animal alone is in some ways not a complete animal. That is certainly true of the highly social species, from honeybees to humans. A bee without other bees cannot build a hive or tend a queen. A human without other humans cannot build a village or exchange ideas. Recognizing the close interdependence of animals with others of their own kind, many ethologists and other animal behaviorists have concentrated on the study of social systems in animals, a study called ***sociobiology***.

As a school of thought, sociobiology arose partly from ethology, but it has taken on a somewhat different flavor. While ethology has tended to focus on the specific movement patterns involved in species-specific behaviors, sociobiologists have focused more on the ultimate functions of such behaviors. Not surprisingly, they have paid most attention to patterns of mating, aggression, and cooperation—patterns that are central to the functioning of social groups and are quite clearly related to the individual's goal of survival and reproduction. Why do some animal species bond as male-female pairs for an extended period of time, while others don't? Why do some animal species spread themselves out over the available territory, while others live in concentrated groups? Why do animals sometimes compete and other times help one another in their struggle for survival? These are the kinds of questions that sociobiologists address.

A standard approach in sociobiology is that of comparison by analogy. If different species have independently evolved a similar social system, comparing them may reveal commonalities of habitat and lifestyle that made the system adaptive. In the following sections, we examine some sociobiological theories about the conditions of life that lead to particular patterns of mating, aggression, and cooperation.

Polygyny

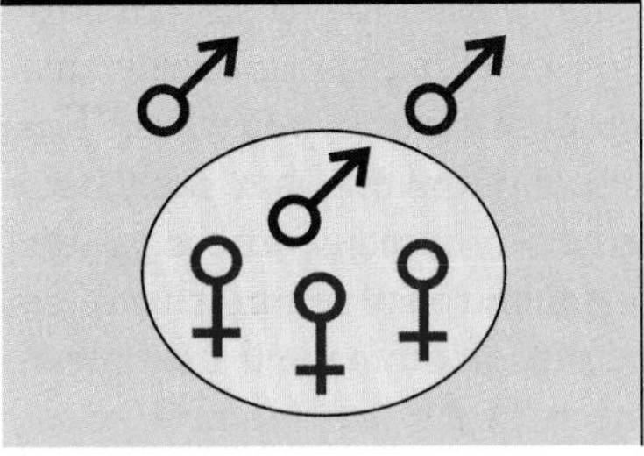

Polyandry

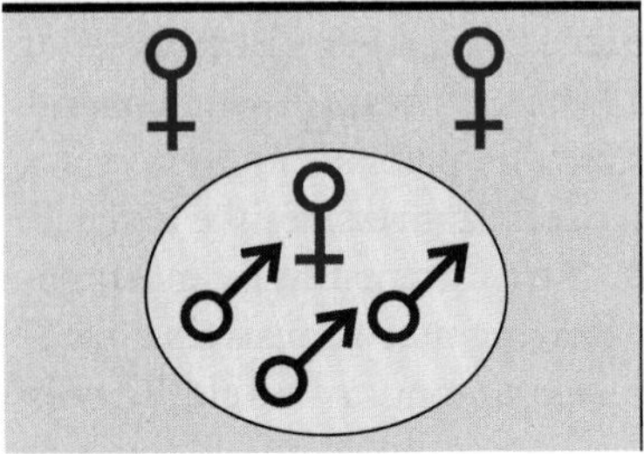

Monogamy

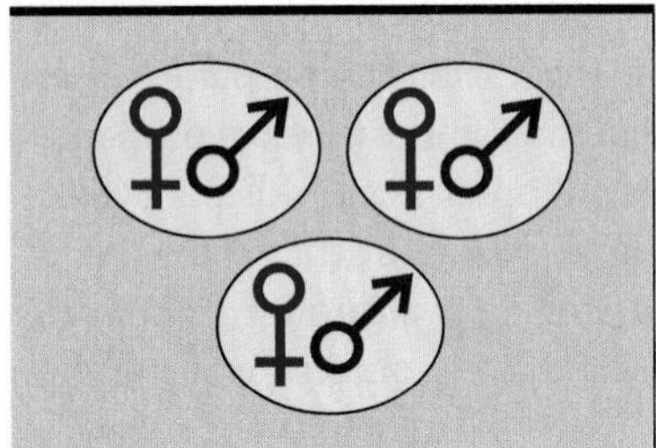

Polygynandry

Figure 4.17 ***Four mating systems***

In a polygynous system the unmated males represent a threat to the mated male, and in a polyandrous system the unmated females represent a threat to the mated female.

Patterns of Mating in Relation to Parental Investment

From an evolutionary perspective, sex is the prime reason for society. Were it not necessary for female and male to come together to reproduce, members of a species could, in theory, go through life completely oblivious to one another.

Countless varieties of male-female arrangements for sexual reproduction have evolved in different species of animals. One way to classify them is in accordance with the number of partners a male or female mates with over a given period of time, such as a breeding season. Four broad classes are generally recognized: (1) ***polygyny***, in which one male mates with more than one female; (2) ***polyandry***, in which one female mates with more than one male; (3) ***monogamy***, in which one male mates with one female; and (4) ***polygynandry***, in which a group consisting of more than one male and more than one female mate with one another (Rees & Harvey, 1991). (These terms are easy to remember if you know that *poly-* means many, *mono-* means one, *-gyn* means female, and *-andr* means male.) As illustrated in Figure 4.17, a feature of both polygyny and polyandry is that some individuals are necessarily deprived of a mating opportunity—a state of affairs associated with considerable conflict. Why have different species evolved these different mating systems, and how do these systems affect other aspects of their lives?

In one of the most frequently quoted papers in sociobiology, Robert Trivers (1972) outlined a theory relating courtship and mating patterns to sex differences in ***parental investment***. Parental investment can be defined roughly as the time, energy, and risk to survival that are involved in producing, feeding, and otherwise caring for each offspring. More precisely, Trivers defined it as the loss, to the adult, of future reproductive capacity that results from the production and nurturance of any given offspring. Every offspring in a sexually reproducing species has two parents, one of each sex, but the amount of parental investment from the two is usually not equal. The essence of Trivers's theory is this: *In general, for species in which parental investment is unequal, the more parentally invested sex will be (a) more vigorously competed for than the other and (b) more discriminating than the other sex when choosing mates.* To illustrate and elaborate on this theory, let us apply it, as many sociobiologists have (for example, Davies, 1991), to evolutionary thinking about the four classes of mating systems.

Polygyny Is Related to High Female and Low Male Parental Investment

26. Based on Trivers's theory, why does high female parental investment lead to (a) polygyny, (b) large size of males, and (c) high selectivity in the female's choice of mate?

Polygyny is the most common mating system in mammals, and Trivers's theory helps explain why. Mammals, for whatever reason, have evolved in such a way that the female necessarily invests a great deal in any offspring she produces. The young must first develop for a period of weeks or months within her body, and then, for at least some period after birth, must obtain nourishment from her in the form of milk. Because of her high investment, the number of offspring that a female mammal can produce in a breeding season or a lifetime is limited. For example, a female whose gestation and lactation periods are such that she can produce at most four young a year can produce no more than that number, regardless of whether she mates with one male or twenty. Things are different for the male, however. His involvement with offspring is, at minimum, simply the production of sperm cells and the act of copulation. These require little time and energy, so his maximum reproductive potential is limited not by parental investment but by the number of fertile females he mates with. A male that mates with twenty females, each of which can produce four young, can in theory produce eighty offspring a year. When a greater evolutionary advantage accrues to the male for multiple matings than to the female, a pattern evolves in which males compete with one another to mate with as many females as they can.

Among mammals, male competition for females often takes the form of one-on-one battles, which the larger and stronger of the males is more likely to win. This leads to a selective advantage for increased size and strength in males, up to some maximum beyond which the advantage of greater size in obtaining mates is

Who's bigger and stronger?

These male elephant seals are sizing each other up for possible battle over mating rights to the many females in the background. Because the larger combatant usually wins, male elephant seals have through natural selection become huge compared to the females.

outweighed by disadvantages, such as problems in finding sufficient food to support the large size. In general, the more polygynous a species, the greater is the average size difference between males and females. An extreme example is the elephant seal. Males of this species fight one another, sometimes to the death, for mating rights to groups of up to fifty females, and the males outweigh females severalfold. In the evolution of elephant seals, those males whose genes made them large, strong, and ferocious enough to defeat other males sent many copies of their genes onto the next generation, while their weaker opponents sent few or none.

For the same reason that the female mammal usually has less evolutionary incentive than does the male to mate with many individuals, she has more incentive to be discriminating in her choice of mate (Trivers, 1972). Because she invests so much, risking her life and decreasing her future reproductive potential whenever she becomes pregnant, her interests lie strongly in producing offspring that will have the highest possible chance themselves of surviving and reproducing. To the degree that the male affects the young, either through his genes or through other resources he provides, females would be expected to select males whose contribution will be most beneficial. In elephant seals, it is presumably to the female's evolutionary advantage to mate with the winner of battles. The winner's genes increase the chance that her sons will win battles in the future and produce many young themselves.

■ 27. ***How do sex differences in pipefish help confirm Trivers's theory?***

Polyandry Is Related to High Male and Low Female Parental Investment

Polyandry does not exist as the primary mating pattern in any mammal, but it is the primary pattern in many nonmammalian species. It is more likely to appear in species that lay eggs than in mammals, because in egg layers a smaller part of the reproductive cycle is tied to the female's body. Once eggs are released from the female they can be cared for by either parent, and, depending on other conditions, evolution can lead to greater male than female investment. For example, various species of pipefishes are polyandrous. The female pipefish deposits her eggs at special attachment sites on the body of the male, who fertilizes them and carries them with him until the young are ready to swim off on their own (see Figure 4.18). Because the female pipefish can produce far more eggs than one male can handle, the limit to her reproductive capacity is the number of males with which she mates. As a consequence, female pipefish are the more aggressive courters and males exert the greater selectivity in choice of mate (Rosenqvist, 1990). Several species of shorebirds also are polyandrous and show a pattern of greater size and courtship aggressiveness in the female than the male (Erckmann, 1983).

Figure 4.18 ***A pair of pipefish***

The male pipefish shown here is carrying a string of eggs along its belly, and the female is directly above him. Among pipefish, the male's parental investment is greater than the female's. In consequence, females compete for and have evolved to be larger than males.

Monogamy Is Related to Equivalent Male and Female Parental Investment

According to Trivers's theory, when the two sexes are approximately equal in parental investment, their degree of competition for mates will also be approximately equal. This is a condition conducive to monogamy. Equal parental investment, and hence monogamy, seems to come about in evolution when other aspects of the lifestyle or environment of a species make it difficult or impossible for a single adult to raise the young, but quite possible for two adults working together to raise them (Dewsbury, 1988). Under these conditions, if either the mother or the father abandons the young they may fail to survive, so there is selective pressure for the two parents to stay together and care for the young. Because neither sex is much more likely than the other to fight over mates, there is little selective pressure for sex differences in size and strength, and, in general, the males and females of monogamous animals are nearly identical to each other in these characteristics.

■ **28.** ***How does the high rate of monogamy among birds and carnivores help support Trivers's theory?***

Consistent with the view that monogamy arises from the need for more than one adult to care for offspring is the fact that over 90 percent of bird species are predominantly monogamous (Lack, 1968) compared to only about 3 percent of mammalian species (Kleiman, 1977). The reproductive system of birds is such that it would be much harder for a single adult to raise the young than is usually the case for mammals. Most bird species must incubate and protect their eggs until they hatch, and then guard the hatchlings and fetch food for them until they are able to fly. One parent alone would not be able simultaneously to guard the nest and leave it to get food, but two working together can. Thus, in the evolution of birds, genes leading both parents to stay together and care for the young would be passed along to their surviving young, while genes leading either to stray would die out as their young starved or fell victim to predators.

In mammals, monogamy seems to have arisen most often in species that are like birds in the sense that the young must be provided with food other than milk, of a type that the male is capable of providing. The best-known examples are certain carnivores, including foxes and coyotes (Malcolm, 1985). Young carnivores must be fed meat until they have acquired the necessary strength, agility, and skills to hunt on their own, and two parents are much better than one at accomplishing this task. But the need for care from more than one adult does not inevitably lead to monogamy. Some carnivores, such as lions, solve the problem by living in small groups in which closely related females, usually sisters, assist one another in the care of the young.

■ **29.** ***How might female strategies provide the basis for monogamy in certain species of primates?***

Monogamy is relatively common in primates, occurring in approximately 15 percent of all species of monkeys and apes (Rutberg, 1983). According to an analysis by Sarah Hrdy (1981), a shift from polygyny toward monogamy in these species can often be understood as a process initiated by females and, in a sense, forced upon males. Imagine a species of monkey in which the female can raise some young on her own, but could raise more young, or more fit young, with the help of a male. Any change in her reproductive strategy that would induce a male to stay and help care for the young would be to her evolutionary advantage. One possible strategy is to live separately from other females, defending a territory by aggressively driving other females away, and require the male to stay with her for a period of time before she will copulate with him. This system makes it harder for the male to find other females or to copulate with them, so it may now be to his advantage to shift some of his resources away from that strategy and toward some investment in child care. Once that begins to happen, the female can produce more or larger young than she could before, which she cannot raise on her own. Eventually, over evolutionary time, the male monkey finds himself in essentially the same situation as the male bird or fox. If he leaves the young they may die, so evolution leads further in the direction of male fidelity. Consistent with this analysis, Hrdy (1981) cites evidence that females of monogamous primates do typically defend separate territories and produce larger young than do polygynous species.

Few if any monogamous species are completely so. The bird, fox, or monkey that bonds with one individual will often take the opportunity to copulate with another if it arises. Such behavior may make evolutionary sense for the male, because the extra copulation produces little loss to him, and it could possibly produce viable offspring. This is especially true if the female is bonded with another male that will help care for those offspring. Such behavior may also make evolutionary sense for the female. Among other things, it may increase the genetic diversity of her offspring (Dewsbury, 1988). It may also reduce the likelihood that neighboring males will treat her offspring hostilely; males of some species may tend to behave toward the young of any female with which they have copulated as if they were their own (Hrdy, 1981).

Polygynandry Is Related to Investment in the Group

Our closest animal relatives are the chimpanzees (see Figure 4.19). Two species of these exist—*common chimpanzees* (usually referred to just as chimpanzees) and *pygmy chimpanzees* (also called bonobos). The basic social structure of both species is the colony, which consists typically of two or three dozen adult males and females and their offspring. When the female is sexually receptive, she develops on her rump a prominent pink swelling, which she actively displays to advertise her readiness to mate. During this time, which lasts about a week in common chimps and three weeks in pygmy chimps, she is likely to mate with most of the adult males of the colony (Goodall, 1986; Kano, 1989).

30. *How might polygynandry help prevent chimpanzee colonies from falling apart?*

An advantage of such promiscuity, for the female, may be that it prevents males from knowing which offspring are or are not their own (Hrdy, 1981). Because almost any male could be the father of almost any female's young, the male's evolutionary interest lies not in attacking any young but in helping to protect and care for the group as a whole. For males, the relative lack of fighting over sex may be critical in allowing them to stay together in the same colony. Moreover, among pygmy chimpanzees, sex—both heterosexual and homosexual—is regularly used to reduce tension at times when conflict could occur (Kano, 1990). Thus, the relatively free sex that occurs within chimpanzee colonies may be an evolutionary adaptation that helps in a number of ways to keep the colony together.

Just as monogamy rarely comes in a pure form, neither does polygynandry. For example, in chimpanzee colonies sometimes a male and female will form what researchers call a *consortship*, which can be thought of as a bit of monogamy inserted into a basically polygynandrous system (Goodall, 1986). Through frequent grooming and other favors given to the female, and actively driving off other males, a particular male may successfully monopolize the sexual activity of a particular female throughout an ovulatory cycle, and thus assure his paternity of her next offspring. Some chimps become specialists at consortships, while others do not attempt this difficult task at all. Goodall reminds us constantly that few hard-and-fast rules govern the behavior of our closest animal relatives. Individual differences exist within colonies, and different colonies may have different traditions passed on by learning rather than genes.

Avoidance of Incest

Animals of most species tend to avoid incest (mating with close genetic relatives), especially that between siblings or between parent and child. Incest conveys an

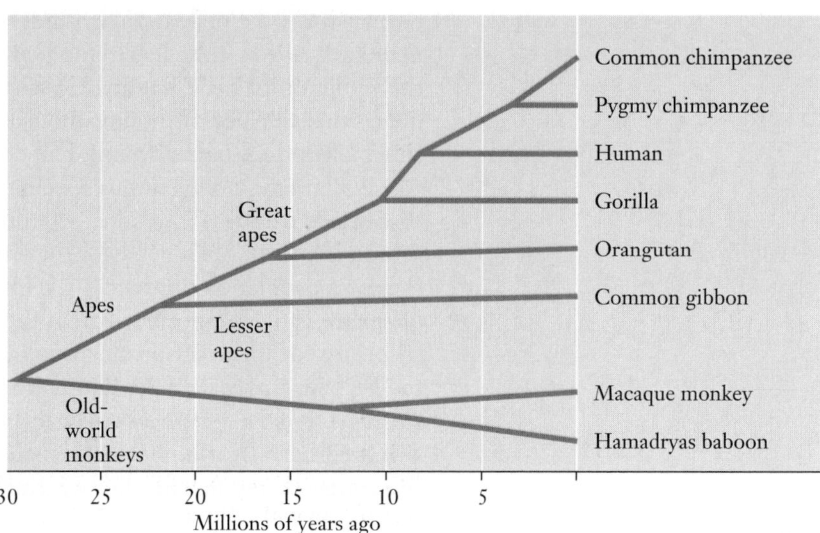

Figure 4.19 ***Relationship of various apes and monkeys to humans***

Our ancestral line split off from that leading to old-world monkeys 30 million years ago, and it split off from that leading to the two species of chimpanzees 8 million years ago (Data from Sibley & Ahlquist, 1984).

Jane Goodall and friend

For three decades, Goodall studied wild common chimpanzees in their natural East African environment. The mutual trust that is evident in this photograph permitted Goodall to uncover a wealth of information about chimpanzee social and emotional life.

■ **31.** ***What is the evolutionary disadvantage of incest, and how do chimpanzees avoid incest?***

evolutionary disadvantage. As pointed out in Chapter 3, genetic disorders often arise from recessive genes, which produce their harmful effects only if inherited from both parents. A closely related male and female are more likely to share the same defective genes than are an unrelated pair, so their offspring are more likely to inherit a genetic disorder. Thus, in the course of evolution, individuals with a genetic tendency to avoid incest would, on average, have produced healthier offspring than those without such a tendency.

Research has shown that a wide variety of incest-avoidance mechanisms have arisen in the animal world, most of which can be placed into two broad categories: (1) recognition of close relatives and rejection of them as sexual partners; and (2) migration of either males or females away from the place where they were born, making it unlikely that they would encounter kin of the opposite sex after reaching sexual maturity (Partridge & Halliday, 1984).

Goodall (1986) found that both of these mechanisms operate in chimpanzees. Even if a female chimp actively courts all of the other males in the colony, she will avoid her own brothers and adult sons, and successfully resist them in those rare instances in which they do attempt to copulate with her. The only incestuous mating that she cannot avoid by this strategy is that with her father, because daughters do not know which chimps their fathers are, and vice versa. Female chimps may to some degree avoid mating with males that are old enough to be their father (Pusey, 1980), but a more significant strategy is a general tendency for females to move out of their colony of birth and join a different colony when they become sexually mature. This process is aided by a complementary tendency, the *strange female effect*, for male chimps to be more attracted to females that have just entered their colony than to those that have always been with them (Goodall, 1986).

Patterns of Aggression

Aggression, as the term is used by ethologists and sociobiologists, refers to fighting and threats of fighting among members of the same species. Physiological mechanisms that enable aggressive behavior to occur have presumably evolved because they help animals acquire and retain resources needed for survival and reproduction. As already mentioned, a good deal of animal aggression centers on mating.

Polygynous males fight over females, polyandrous females fight over males, and monogamous individuals of both sexes aggressively drive potential sexual competitors away from their partners. Aggression can also serve to protect a feeding ground for oneself and one's offspring, to drive away individuals that may be a threat to one's young, and to elevate one's status within a colony. Here we will look briefly at two broad classes of aggressive behavior: territorial aggression and within-group aggression related to dominance.

Territorial Aggression

■ ***32. How do territorial signaling and the home-court advantage help reduce bloodshed in territorial animals?***

Many species of animals establish home territories, either permanently or for the duration of a breeding season, which they defend from others of their kind. Monogamous birds and mammals defend the territory around their nest or den partly to keep away potential sexual competitors, but also to preserve a feeding ground for themselves and their young. Animals that live in large groups—including wolves, macaque monkeys, and chimpanzees—often defend large feeding ranges, sometimes many square miles in size, from invasion by other groups of their kind. At times of food shortage or overpopulation, territorial battles can be bloody. But at other times life-threatening battles are avoided by a combination of territorial signaling, through which residents warn others not to enter, and a tendency to respect each other's signals and stay out of occupied territories.

Methods of territorial signaling vary from species to species. Such diverse groups as birds, crickets, and alligators loudly announce, by song, that they are home and defending their area. Territorial troops of monkeys often warn off other approaching troops by running up into trees and shaking the branches loudly. Certain other mammals mark their territories with odor trails deposited either in their urine (as in the case of bears and wolves) or from special scent glands (as in the case of badgers and rabbits). When you walk your male dog and observe him urinating on every lamppost and fire hydrant in the neighborhood, you are observing a vestige of the territorial-marking behavior of his wolf ancestors.

In some species, prolonged fights are also avoided through a tendency for individuals that find themselves in another's territory to become less aggressive and more inclined to flee than they would be in their own territory. When fights do occur, the territorial owner fights more viciously than the intruder and usually succeeds in driving the intruder out, even if the intruder is the larger of the two. As an example, Lorenz (1966) described the behavior of two cichlid fish in a tank. When first placed in the tank, Fish A, the bigger of the two, drove Fish B into a tiny corner near the surface (the most dangerous place for fish to live in nature, where predatory birds can attack them) and forced it to stay there for several days. Gradually, however, B expanded its territory until it occupied approximately half the tank. After that the two fish coexisted peacefully, fighting only when one by chance swam over the boundary into the territory of the other. When A swam into B's territory, B would drive A out, and when B swam into A's territory, A would drive B out. This example is typical of much (though not all) animal territorial aggression: the defender wins, the invader retreats, and no blood is spilled in the process.

Figure 4.20 ***Submissive response in a wolf***

Animals that live in groups have evolved signals to terminate or prevent fights, so that the loser need not flee and can remain in the group. Here a wolf shows its submissive status by rolling over on its back in a defenseless posture. Dogs also show submission in this manner.

Aggression and Dominance Within the Colony

Animals that live in large groups may appear to get along peacefully, but closer examination often reveals an enormous amount of within-group bickering. They squabble almost continuously over such resources as food, mates, and the best location in the group (the center is usually preferred because it offers the most protection from predators). When group members fight, they must have a means of terminating the fight other than one in which the loser flees to another territory. The loser's interest lies in remaining in the group and the winner's interest lies in

33. ***How do submissive signals and dominance hierarchies help reduce aggression within a colony?***

allowing the loser to remain (otherwise there would be no group, with its attendant advantages to each individual). To permit fights to terminate without the loser running far away, a variety of submissive signals have evolved that allow one animal to signal to another that it has lost and will no longer challenge the victor (see Figure 4.20).

Another great aid in reducing fighting within a colony is memory. Animals recognize other colony members and remember the results of their previous aggressive encounters. If A has previously beaten B in a fight, then B will be less inclined to challenge A the next time, and A will have established ***dominance*** over B. In some species, including barnyard chickens, rather strict ***dominance hierarchies*** are established, in which the individuals in the group can be ranked from highest to lowest, with each being dominant over those lower in rank and submissive to those higher. In other species, however, dominance hierarchies are not that rigid and are not always based on individual fighting ability. In chimpanzees, cleverness can play a role. Goodall (1988) observed a relatively small male chimp achieve dominance over the entire colony by charging at the other chimps while banging together empty kerosene cans, which he had stolen from Goodall's camp. In other cases, she saw chimps raise their rank by forming coalitions and challenging a more dominant chimp together.

34. ***How can a male chimpanzee achieve dominance through means other than his own fighting ability?***

In both common and pygmy chimpanzee colonies, females have a separate dominance hierarchy from males, and female dominance may play an important role in establishing the male hierarchy. In both species, mothers frequently come to the aid of their young sons during aggressive encounters with other young males (Goodall, 1986; Kano, 1990). The more dominant the female, the more successful she is in driving away those who threaten her son. Through this means, a dominant female teaches other young males not to attack her son. The lesson may last for a long time into adulthood and help her son to assume a high rank in the male hierarchy.

Figure 4.21 ***An alarm-calling ground squirrel***

When they spot a predator, female ground squirrels often emit an alarm call, especially if they are living in a group of close kin. Males are less likely to live near close kin and do not show this response.

Patterns of Helping

Animals of the same species bicker, fight, and sometimes kill one another in their competition for resources, but they also help one another. From an evolutionary perspective, ***helping*** can be defined as any behavior that increases the survival chance or reproductive capacity of another individual. Given this definition, it is useful to distinguish between two categories of helping—cooperation and altruism.

Cooperation occurs when an individual helps another while at the same time helping itself. This sort of helping occurs all the time in the animal world. It occurs when a mated pair of foxes work together to raise their mutual young, or a pack of wolves work together to kill an antelope, or a troop of macaque monkeys work together to repel a troop invading their territory. Most of the advantages of social living lie in cooperation. By working with others for common ends, each individual has a better chance of survival and reproduction than it would have outside of the social group. There is nothing anti-Darwinian about cooperation. It is selfish. It is a way of obtaining resources that one cannot obtain alone. Whatever costs accrue are more than repaid by the benefits.

Altruism, in contrast, occurs when an individual helps another while at the same time *decreasing* its own survival chance or reproductive capacity. Animals do sometimes behave in ways that at least appear to be altruistic. For example, some animals, including ground squirrels, emit a loud, distinctive call when they spot an approaching predator. The call warns others of the predator's approach and at the same time tends to attract the predator's attention to the caller (Sherman, 1977). (See Figure 4.21.) The selfish response would be to remain quiet and hidden, or to sneak off quietly, rather than risk one's own detection by warning others. How can such behavior be explained from an evolutionary perspective? As Trivers (1971) has pointed out, any evolutionary account of apparent altruism must operate by showing that from a broader perspective the behavior is not truly altruistic. Sociobiologists have developed two broad theories to account for apparent acts of altruism in animals—the kin selection theory and the reciprocity theory.

■ **35. *How do the kin selection and reciprocity theories take the altruism out of "altruism"?***

The ***kin selection theory*** holds that apparent acts of altruism come about evolutionarily because they are most likely to help close relatives, that is, most likely to help those that have the same genes (Hamilton, 1964). What actually survives over evolutionary time, of course, is not the individual but the individual's genes. Any gene that promotes the production and preservation of copies of itself can be a fit gene, from the vantage point of natural selection, even if it promotes the self-destruction of an individual carrier of the gene.

Imagine an individual ground squirrel with a rare gene that promotes the behavior of calling out when a predator is near. The mathematics of inheritance are such that, on average, one-half of the children or siblings of the individual with this gene would be expected to have the same gene, as would one-fourth of the nieces or nephews and one-eighth of the cousins (look back at Table 3.1). Thus, if the altruist incurred a small risk (Δ) to its own life, while increasing a child or sibling's chances of survival by more than 2Δ, a niece's or nephew's by more than 4Δ, or a cousin's by more than 8Δ, the gene would increase in the population from one generation to the next. Such a gene is clearly *fit* in the evolutionary sense.

Many research studies have shown that animals do help kin more than nonkin. Sherman (1977) found that ground squirrels living with kin are more likely to produce alarm calls than are ground squirrels living with nonkin. Goodall (1986) and Nishida (1990) found that chimpanzees are far more likely to help close kin than nonkin in all sorts of ways. In these examples, the helper presumably discriminates between kin and nonkin. In theory, however, altruistic behavior can evolve through kin selection even without such discrimination. A tendency to help any member of one's species, indiscriminately, can evolve if the animal's usual living arrangements are such that, by chance alone, a sufficiently high percentage of helping is directed toward kin.

The ***reciprocity theory*** provides an account of how apparent acts of altruism can arise even in situations where nonkin are helped as often as kin. According to this theory, behaviors that appear to be altruistic are actually forms of long-term cooperation (Trivers, 1971). Through computer simulations of evolution, researchers have shown that a genetically induced tendency to help nonkin can evolve if that tendency is tempered by (a) an ability to remember which individuals have reciprocated such help in the past, and (b) a tendency to refrain from again helping those individuals that failed to reciprocate (Axelrod, 1984; Nowack & Sigmund, 1992). The reason such behavior evolves is that it induces others to reciprocate. That is, the reward for helping is the increased likelihood of receiving help in the future. A considerable amount of behavior that fits this pattern seems to go on in the animal world. For example, vampire bats frequently share food with unrelated vampire bats who have returned that favor routinely in the past (Wilkinson, 1988; 1990).

Pitfalls to Avoid in Sociobiological Thinking About Humans

Can a sociobiological analysis—of the kind applied in understanding mating, aggression, and helping in nonhuman animals—shed any light on human social interactions? That question can raise considerable passion, especially among people who are aware of past misuses of evolutionary theory.

In the nineteenth and early twentieth centuries a philosophical movement called *social Darwinism* employed a rough analogy between biological evolution and capitalism to justify otherwise unconscionable practices. The principal philosopher of the movement, Herbert Spencer, popularized the phrase "survival of the fittest" and applied it to human social systems. In his view the fittest were those who rose to the top in unchecked capitalism, and the unfit were those who fell into poverty or starvation. He also believed that women are inherently inferior to men and are meant by nature to occupy subordinate positions in society (Hofstadter, 1955). Some years later, a still more perverted form of evolutionary thinking played a role in Nazi philosophy—the purification of humanity was to be achieved by eliminating inferior races. Because of its association with Nazi racial theories, analyzing human behavior in terms of evolution became distasteful for a period after World War II.

It would be unfair, however, to equate modern sociobiology with such abuses of evolutionary theory. The sociobiological analysis of human behavior—carried on by a growing group of responsible scientists, including women and men of every political stripe—is a fascinating intellectual endeavor that is no more affected by political bias than are other areas of psychology. We are animals; we have an evolutionary history; we have drives, behavioral tendencies, and learning mechanisms that were shaped by natural selection, just as is true of all other animals. The broad aim of human sociobiology is to understand human drives, tendencies, and learning mechanisms in terms of their roles in promoting our past and present abilities to survive and reproduce.

Most modern sociobiologists are well aware of the possible pitfalls of their approach and are quick to remind each other of them in their written work and debates. These pitfalls include the following widely recognized errors in logic:

The Deterministic Fallacy

■ **36. *How can the deterministic fallacy, the naturalistic fallacy, and the superficial analogy distort thought about human social behavior?***

All of psychology is concerned with the determinants of behavior. The deterministic fallacy is not that genes play a role in determining behavior. Rather, the fallacy is that genes determine behaviors in a rigid way that is essentially unaffected by the environment. Some popular books on human evolution have exhibited the deterministic fallacy when they have argued that one or another behavior—such as fighting for territories—is unavoidable because it is controlled by our genes. That sort of argument is untenable even when applied to nonhuman animals. Territorial birds, for example, defend territories only when the environmental conditions are ripe for them to do so. We humans have the capacity to control the environmental conditions in which we live. In that way we can either enhance or reduce the environmental ingredients needed for one or another behavioral tendency to develop and manifest itself.

Far from exhibiting the deterministic fallacy, many sociobiologists have chosen their line of work precisely because they believe that human behavior can be modified for the better. For example, in a recent sociobiological analysis of male violence against women, Barbara Smuts (1992) wrote: "Although an evolutionary analysis assumes that male aggression against women reflects selection pressures operating during our species' evolutionary history, it in no way implies that male domination of women is genetically determined, or that frequent male aggression toward women is an immutable feature of human nature. In some societies male aggressive coercion of women is very rare, and even in societies with frequent male aggression toward women, some men do not show these behaviors. Thus, the challenge is to identify the situational factors that predispose members of a particular society toward or away from the use of sexual aggression. I argue that an evolutionary framework can be very useful in this regard."

Figure 4.22 ***Male hamadryas baboon dominating three females***

Males of this species are much larger than females and often behave quite ruthlessly toward them. The bowed, turned-away head is a signal of submission. Hamadryas baboons also have rigid male dominance hierarchies and engage in between-troop battles over territories.

The Naturalistic Fallacy

The naturalistic fallacy is the view that whatever is "natural" is right (Alexander, 1987). Social Darwinists can be accused of this fallacy for assuming that, because natural selection can be construed as survival of the fittest, survival of the fittest is a moral principle that should guide our conscious choices about government and other social institutions. This reasoning equates nature with morality; but nature is neither moral nor immoral. Morality is a product of the human mind. We have acquired, in our evolution, the capacity to think in moral terms. We can develop moral philosophies that go in any of various directions, including directions that place constraints on individual self-interest for the good of the larger community.

The Misleading Use of Analogies

In the 1960s a number of books were published that made rather sweeping claims about human nature based on analogies to one or another species of animals. For example, in a book entitled *African Genesis*, Robert Ardrey argued that humans are by nature strongly impelled toward territorial conflict, male battles for status, and male dominance over females. He built his case largely on analogies between humans and hamadryas baboons. Why hamadryas baboons? He claimed that he chose this species because of evidence (now largely discredited) that it evolved under environmental conditions very similar to those of early humans. His critics, however, argued that he chose this species for a different reason: Hamadryas baboons, more than almost any other species of primates, fit his preconception of human nature (see Figure 4.22).

Comparison by analogy is a useful approach as long as its limitations are kept in mind. As we have seen, analogies based on comparisons across many species have produced some interesting generalizations. An example is the generalization that monogamy tends to occur in species in which the young need extensive care that one parent alone cannot provide, and that monogamy is associated with lack of sex differences in size. But those generalizations do not hold up for every species. Not all species solve the problem of providing multiadult care for the young through monogamy, and not all species in which the male and female are the same size are monogamous. Moreover, in some cases where the correlation does hold, the adaptive explanation may be different from that which applies in other cases. As

Tinbergen (1968) pointed out long ago, comparison by analogy provides no real short cut to understanding any particular species. It can be a basis for developing hypotheses, but the hypotheses must then be tested through detailed study of the species one wishes to understand.

Some Sociobiological Hypotheses About Humans

In their attempt to understand human nature, sociobiologists use both cross-cultural and cross-species comparisons. Groups of our species differ greatly from culture to culture, yet in many basic ways we are everywhere similar, and some of those similarities fit quite well with generalizations about natural selection that have come from studies of other species. Some of the cross-cultural similarities that sociobiologists find most interesting involve group living and patterns of helping, mating, and aggression.

The Tendency to Live in Communities

Humans seem to be strongly biased toward living in groups (Breuer, 1982; Chagnon & Irons, 1979). In no part of the world do people live like orangutans (an ape species for which the only social group is the mother and her children plus the occasional coming together of a male and female for mating). Human societies are more like the gregarious chimpanzee model. People everywhere live in at least moderately large communities, with smaller groupings of various types forming within the community. In non-Western, nonindustrialized cultures, most people live in tribes or villages consisting of a few dozen up to a few hundred individuals.

People everywhere feel lonely when alone too long, and loneliness drives them to seek other people much as hunger drives them to seek food. No population of human beings anywhere is unconcerned about making friends. Hermits exist, but are everywhere regarded as peculiar. It is uncertain what factors in our evolution led to our tendency to live in groups, but observations of present-day villages suggest that these include cooperation in hunting and gathering food; cooperation in child care; cooperation in building dwellings; cooperation in defense against predators; cooperation in defense against other groups of our own species; and, most human of all, the sharing, through language, of information that bears on all aspects of the struggle for survival.

Cooperation as a basis for community life

The human capacity to survive in an extraordinary range of environments depends not just on individual intelligence, but also on cooperation. These Turkana nomads in Kenya must work together to extract precious water for themselves and their cattle from the arid land.

The Tendency Toward Nepotism

In accordance with the kin selection theory, nonhuman animals usually help close relatives more than nonrelatives. In humans, the selective helping of kin is called *nepotism*, and cross-cultural research shows that such behavior occurs everywhere (Essock-Vitale & McGuire, 1980). If a mother dies or for other reasons is unable to care for a child, the child's grandmother, aunt, or another close relative is by far the most likely adopter (Kurland, 1979). Close kin are also most likely to share dwellings or land, hunt together, or form other collaborative arrangements. In communal societies deliberately designed to abolish or minimize the importance of blood ties, strong tendencies to slide back toward them frequently emerge (Spiro, 1979). On the other side of the same coin, studies in Western culture indicate that genetic kin living in the same household are less likely to be violent toward each other than nonkin living in the same household (Daly & Wilson, 1988); and studies in other cultures have shown that villages in which most people are closely related have less internal friction than those in which people are less related (Chagnon, 1979).

The Tendency Toward a Mix of Monogamy and Polygyny

37. ***What lines of evidence suggest that humans evolved as a moderately polygynous species?***

Though we live in groups a bit like chimpanzees, we do not appear anywhere to be quite as sexually promiscuous as chimpanzees. In every culture people tend to form mating bonds that are legitimized through some sort of culturally recognized marriage contract, and males in most cultures play at least some role in caring for their children (Dewsbury, 1988; Eibl-Eibesfeldt, 1989). Anthropological studies indicate that the majority of non-Western cultures, where Western influence has not made polygyny illegal, practice a mixture of monogamy and polygyny (Murdock 1981). In such cultures, men with sufficient wealth or status have more than one wife, while the majority of men have either one wife or none.

Cross-cultural research suggests that men are not only more likely than women to have more than one partner in marriage, but are also more likely to seek sex outside of marriage (Symons, 1979). Such observations fit well with the general mammalian pattern. Males can increase their number of offspring much more by mating with multiple partners than females can, so males have acquired through natural selection a stronger drive to do so. An alternative interpretation of the same findings, however, centers on the greater power that men have compared to women in virtually all human societies. Perhaps women are dissuaded from seeking sex with more than one partner less by inborn desire than by laws and customs that punish them more than men for doing so (Small, 1992). Such laws and customs may well reflect men's values more than women's. Perhaps the safest conclusion is that men everywhere have a strong drive to control the sexual behavior of their wives (Small, 1992; Wilson, 1989).

The moderate size difference between men and women is another piece of evidence that humans evolved as a moderately polygynous species (Dewsbury, 1988). As described earlier, among mammals in general, the degree to which males are larger than females correlates positively with the degree to which the species is polygynous. Cross-cultural observations of parental investment by men and women also fit the theory. In some societies, especially where monogamy is enforced, fathers are almost as invested in their children as are mothers, and in some societies they are much less invested; but nowhere are fathers routinely *more* invested than mothers (the condition that would promote polyandry).

The Tendency for Men to Be More Violent Than Women

Among the great majority of mammals, males are not only larger and stronger than females, but are more inclined to fight. Human beings are apparently no exception to this general pattern. Cross-cultural studies show that everywhere men are more violent, more likely to maim or kill, than women. In fact, in a survey of cross-cultural data on this issue, Martin Daly and Margo Wilson (1988) were unable to find any society in which the number of women who killed other women was even one-tenth as great as the number of men who killed other men. On average, in the data they examined, male-male killings outnumbered female-female killings by more than 30 to 1. One might construe a scenario through which such a difference in violence would be purely a product of learning, in every culture, but the hypothesis that the difference resides at least partly in inherited sex differences seems more plausible.

38. ***How do sociobiologists explain the link between sexual jealousy and violence in males?***

Moreover, according to Daly and Wilson's analyses, patterns of violence and homicide are very much in accord with sociobiological theory. For example, one of the leading motives for murder among men in every culture is sexual jealousy. In some cultures men are *expected* to kill other men who have sex with their wives (Symons, 1979), and in other cultures such murders are common even though they are illegal (Daly & Wilson, 1988). Why do men engage in such acts and not women? According to Daly and Wilson the ultimate explanation lies at least partly in the asymmetry of reproduction. Men tend to act violently toward sexual competitors because in the long run of evolution those who behaved that way fathered more children than those who didn't. Through most of history (and for most people today), the only way a man could be certain that his wife's children were also *his* children was to prevent her from having sexual intercourse with anyone else. Women never had that problem; they always knew that their children were theirs, regardless of who the father might be. Their reproductive interest lay more strongly in staying alive than in fighting with sexual competitors.

The Tendency to Avoid Incest

39. ***What is the evidence that humans have an aversion to incest, and how might the Westermarck effect serve as a proximate mechanism of that aversion?***

Reliable data on the actual incidence of sexual intercourse between human first-degree relatives (parent-child or brother-sister) is almost impossible to obtain. But cross-cultural studies indicate that the great majority of people in every culture view such unions as something to be either condemned or pitied (Berghe, 1983; Thornhill & Thornhill, 1987). This is true even in cultures that do not specifically outlaw such incest, and even where people have no knowledge that it can have deleterious effects on offspring.

What might be the proximate mechanism that promotes incest avoidance in humans? Long ago, the Finnish sociologist Edward Westermarck (1891) proposed that people develop a psychological aversion toward sexual involvement with anyone with whom they had prolonged, intimate contact in early childhood. This aversion is now called the ***Westermarck effect***, and its existence is supported by a considerable body of research (Berghe, 1983; Durham, 1991). For example, studies of Israeli kibbutzim—cooperative communities in which children are raised together somewhat as one big family—indicate that those who grow up together in the same kibbutz rarely date or marry each other, even though their elders may encourage them to do so (Tiger & Shepher, 1975). By their own preference, young kibbutzniks almost always look elsewhere for their boyfriends and girlfriends or husbands and wives. Another line of evidence comes from research in the United States showing that romantic attachment is far more likely to occur between a brother and sister who were raised in separate families, and who met as adults (knowing full well that they were brother and sister), than between those who were raised in the same family (Berghe, 1983). Most often, over the course of evolution, a person with whom one was raised in childhood (or a person one raised) would be one's genetic kin, so the hypothesis that the Westermarck effect is a biologically evolved adaptation that promotes incest avoidance seems quite reasonable.

Concluding Thoughts

To conclude this chapter, you might enjoy reflecting on some general lessons that have come to psychology from evolutionary thinking or from research inspired by such thinking. Here are four:

1. The value of studying behavior in the natural environment before dissecting it in the laboratory Behavioral mechanisms evolve and develop to deal with the problems that animals routinely face in their natural environments. When animals (including people) are tested in unnatural settings, their behaviors may make little sense. This is a point that the early ethologists often made in their arguments with psychologists, who often limited themselves to laboratory studies. If Tinbergen had begun his research on sticklebacks by testing them in isolated laboratory aquaria, his discovery that males attack any red object that they see would have simply been a source of puzzlement. But because he began the other way around, first learning all he could about their mating habits and other aspects of their natural lives, he was able to make sense of this behavior. People, too, have acquired their behavioral patterns in the contexts of their lives, and often those patterns don't make sense in the stark or strange conditions of the laboratory. Today psychologists, like ethologists, are increasingly concerned with the natural contexts and real-life meanings of the behaviors they study. The laboratory is a fine place to perform controlled experiments aimed at understanding proximate causal mechanisms, but not to learn about the real-life functions of behavior.

2. The value of careful descriptions of behavior The early ethologists thought of behavior as something like anatomy. They saw it as having form, and they were very concerned about describing that form in detail. By adopting this approach, psychologists Ekman and Friesen were able to produce a more objective description of people's facial expressions of emotions than had previously been produced, which enabled them to perform new studies of the universality of the expressions and the contexts in which they occur. Careful description is a valuable first step to further discoveries about any category of behavior.

3. The value of two kinds of cross-species comparison—homologies and analogies Psychologists have long studied the behavior of other animals as one route to understanding human behavior. Evolutionary thinking not only provides a general rationale for that enterprise, by pointing out our relatedness to other animals, but also to some degree helps us decide which comparisons to make. If we want to understand the underlying mechanism of some form of human behavior by studying it in an animal, we should choose an animal in which the behavior is homologous—not just analogous—to the human's. As you will see in Chapters 7 and 8, physiological psychologists have learned a great deal about basic motivational and sensory mechanisms in humans by studying their homologous forms in other mammals. Analogies are useful for developing hypotheses about the adaptive value of a form of behavior, but they are not so useful for learning about mechanisms, because convergent evolution can produce superficially similar behaviors through means that involve very different mechanisms.

4. The value of thinking about psychological mechanisms in terms of their adaptive functions The mechanisms that underlie motivation, emotion, sensation, perception, memory, and reasoning are all products of evolution by natural selection. They evolved because they enabled our ancestors to solve the kinds of real-life problems, in their real-life environments, that threatened their survival and reproduction. That insight can provide some guidance in the development of more specific theories about such mechanisms. We can expect motivational and emotional mechanisms to be biased toward survival-promoting and reproductive goals; and sensory, perpetual, memory, and reasoning mechanisms to be biased toward picking up and using information essential to achieving those goals. In the sociobiology discussion in this chapter you have seen examples of such thinking in a realm where it has been most controversial, theories about human social relationships. As we proceed through chapters on the psychological mechanisms just listed, you will see examples of evolutionary theories that are more widely accepted.

Further Reading

Charles Darwin (1859; reprinted 1963). *The origin of species.* New York: Washington Square Press.

Darwin was an engaging writer as well as a brilliant thinker. Why not read at least part of this important book? The most relevant chapter for the psychologist is Chapter 8, entitled "Instinct," which includes Darwin's research on hive building in bees, as well as many other insights about the behavior of both wild and domesticated animals.

Jane Goodall (1988). *In the shadow of man* (rev. ed.). Boston: Houghton Mifflin.

Goodall's 3-decade-long study of wild chimpanzees, begun in 1960, surely rates as one of the most courageous and scientifically important studies of animal behavior ever undertaken. This book, first published in 1971, provides an account of her early struggle to locate the animals and find ways of studying them, and of some of her pioneering findings about their behavior. For a more complete and scientific account of her research, I recommend Goodall's 1986 book, The Chimpanzees of Gombe.

Sarah Blaffer Hrdy (1981). *The woman that never evolved.* Cambridge, MA: Harvard University Press.

Despite its clever title, this is a serious analysis of the evolution of behavior in primates. In an attempt to counter the bias of many previous accounts, which focused on males and tended to treat females as passive carry-alongs in the evolutionary process, Hrdy centers her attention on females. She builds a case that female activities and strategies are most central to behavioral evolution, because females most directly control reproduction.

Martin Daly & Margo Wilson (1988). *Homicide.* New York: Aldine de Gruyter.

Many interesting and provocative books have examined various human behaviors from a sociobiological perspective, and this is one of them. Daly and Wilson look at worldwide data on homicide from a sociobiological vantagepoint, and they argue that the patterns that they find are consistent with sociobiological theories concerning such issues as sex differences, sexual jealousy, family relationships, and struggles for status.

Jerome Barkow, Leda Cosmides, & John Tooby (Eds.) (1992). *The adapted mind: Evolutionary psychology and the generation of culture.* New York: Oxford University Press.

In this compendium of modern evolutionary thought about human behavior, the chapters—each written by a different researcher or set of researchers—deal with such topics as cooperation, mating and sex, parenting, language, and aesthetic preferences.

Looking Ahead

Among the products of evolution are the basic mechanisms of learning, which allow people and other animals to benefit from experience and adapt to their environments within their lifetimes. The study of learning has long been one of the most central activities of psychology. We turn to it in the next chapter.

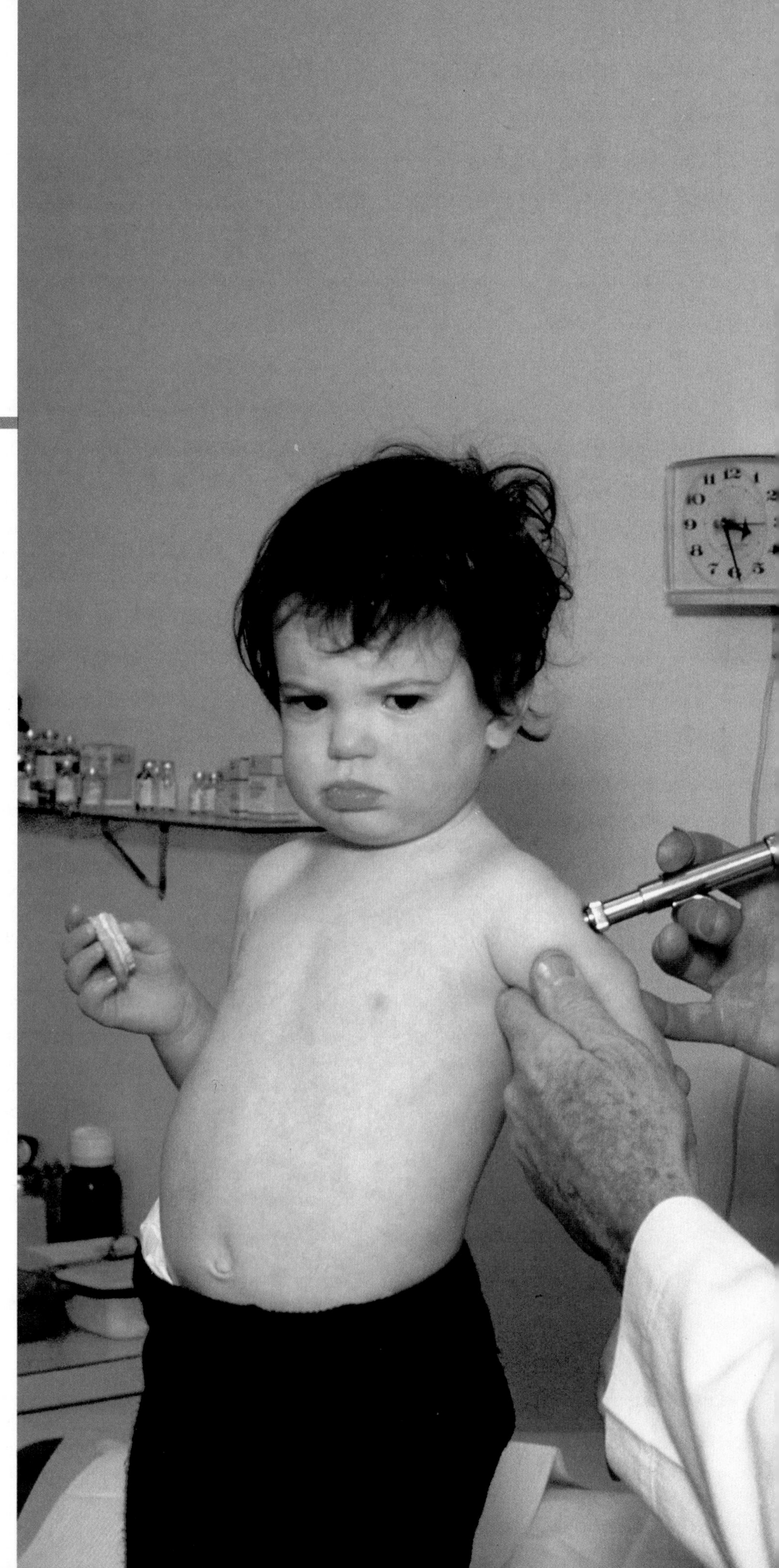

THE ADAPTIVENESS OF BEHAVIOR II: LEARNING

CHAPTER 5

Learning is a kind of adaptation to the environment that occurs within the lifetime of the individual. It can be defined as the process or set of processes through which experience at one time can affect an individual's behavior at a future time. *Experience* here refers to any effects of the environment that are mediated by the individual's sensory systems (vision, hearing, touch, and so on). *Behavior at a future time* refers to any subsequent behavior that is not part of the individual's immediate response to the stimuli during the learning experience. If I make a clicking sound and then flash a bright light in your eyes, your immediate response to the click or to the light (such as blinking) does not exemplify learning, but your increased tendency to blink to the click alone, the next time I present that sound, does exemplify learning.

Most of psychology is in one way or another concerned with learning. That is, most of psychology deals with effects of experience on behavior. Social psychologists try to explain people's beliefs and social behaviors in terms of their past experiences. Clinical psychologists try to explain people's emotional problems in terms of their past experiences. Cognitive psychologists try to understand the basic perceptual, memory, and thought processes that are involved in people's ability to learn. Thus, most of the chapters in this book, or in any other introductory psychology text, are in one way or another about learning.

In this chapter our concern is with the most basic attempts to characterize or describe the learning process. We will examine learning from three different perspectives: (1) the *behavioral perspective*, which characterizes learning in terms of observable stimuli and responses; (2) the *cognitive perspective*, which characterizes learning in terms of hypothetical mental entities, such as expectancies and cognitive maps; and (3) the *ecological perspective*, which identifies separate, specialized learning mechanisms that have been built through evolution to meet specific survival needs. As you will see, much of the research within each perspective has been conducted with nonhuman animals. That is partly because greater control can be exerted over their environments, and partly because basic learning mechanisms are assumed to be more easily uncovered in animals whose nervous systems and behavioral repertoires are less complex than ours.

The Behavioral Perspective: Acquiring New Responses to and for Stimuli

1. ***What is behaviorism, and what two classes of learning are identified by this perspective?***

Behaviorism, as described in Chapter 1, is the attempt to understand behavior in terms of relationships between observable *stimuli* (events in the environment) and observable *responses* (behavioral actions). The early behaviorists were in the forefront of the effort to make psychology an objective science, and, in support of objectivity, they proposed dropping from psychology terms that refer to unseen, inner, mental entities such as thoughts or feelings. As John B. Watson (1913), the acknowledged founder of behaviorism, put it, "In a system of psychology completely worked out, given the response the stimuli can be predicted, and given the stimuli the response can be predicted." Neither Watson nor other behaviorists after him denied the existence of processes inside the organism, but they believed that these are too obscure to be studied scientifically.

In addition to developing objective, stimulus-response descriptions of behavior, the early behaviorists established learning as their main explanatory concept. They maintained that a person's behavior at any given time is the product of that person's past experiences. In a famous boast illustrating this view, Watson (1924) wrote, "Give me a dozen healthy infants, well-formed, and my own specified world to bring them up in and I'll guarantee to take any one at random and train him to become any type of specialist I might select—doctor, lawyer, artist, merchantchief, and yes, even beggar-man and thief, regardless of his talents, penchants, tendencies, abilities, vocations, and the race of his ancestors." Of course, Watson did not mean his boast to be taken literally. He meant simply to dramatize his view that behavioral differences among people stem mainly from their varying experiences, mediated by learning.

As behaviorism developed, its main goal became to identify basic learning processes that could be described in terms of stimuli and responses. By 1938, B. F. Skinner, the successor of Watson as behaviorism's most recognized leader, was able to describe, in such terms, what he took to be two separate learning processes (Skinner, 1938). One, now most often called *classical conditioning*, is a process by which a stimulus that previously did not elicit a response comes to elicit a response, in reflexlike fashion, after it is paired for one or more trials with a stimulus that already elicits a response. Your blinking to a clicking sound that was previously paired with a bright flash of light is an example of classical conditioning. The other learning process, which Skinner emphasized most strongly and labeled *operant conditioning*, is a process by which the consequences of a response increase or decrease the likelihood that the response will occur again. Your increased rate of smiling at people if that behavior brings you favorable consequences is an example of operant conditioning. The main task of behaviorism throughout its history has been to discover and apply the principles associated with classical and operant conditioning. Let us look now at those principles.

Classical Conditioning

■ **2. *What is a reflex, and how can it change through habituation?***

Classical conditioning has to do with the learning of reflexes. A ***reflex*** is a simple, relatively automatic, stimulus-response sequence mediated by the nervous system. If your knee is tapped with a rubber mallet, your leg will jerk. If a bright light is flashed in your eyes, you will blink. If lemon juice is squirted into your mouth, you will salivate. If a loud alarm suddenly clangs, your muscles will tighten. In each of these examples, a particular, well-defined event in the environment, a *stimulus*, results in a particular, well-defined bit of behavior, a *response*. The tap on the knee, the flash of light, the squirt of lemon juice, and the sudden alarm are stimuli. The leg jerk, the eye blink, the salivation, and the tightening of muscles are responses. It is not surprising that behaviorists, early on, were interested in reflexes. With reflexes, the rather vague and wishy-washy statement "behavior is influenced by the environment" can be replaced by the more definite and stronger statement "a response is caused by a stimulus." Some early behaviorists hoped to be able to characterize all behavior in terms of reflexes.

To be considered a reflex, the response to a stimulus must be mediated by the

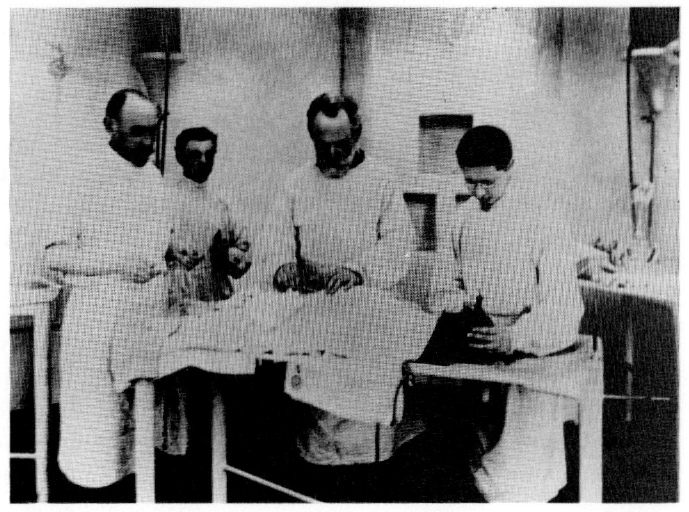

Ivan Petrovich Pavlov

The scientist (second from right) was a skilled surgeon who perfected his craft while carrying out studies of the physiology of digestion. In his conditioning research, he typically connected one of his dog's salivary ducts to a tube and measuring device. An early version of such a device is shown in Figure 5.1.

nervous system. Messages carried by nerves from the eyes, ears, or other sensory organs enter the spinal cord or brain and act there to produce messages in nerves running outward to muscles and glands. If something hits you and you fall down due to the direct force of the impact, that is not a reflex. But if something hits you and your muscles respond in a way that tends to keep you from falling down, that is a reflex. Because reflexes are mediated by the nervous system, they can be modified by experience.

One simple effect of experience is ***habituation***, defined as a decline in the magnitude of a reflexive response when the stimulus is repeated several times in succession. Not all reflexes undergo habituation. One that does is the startle response to a loud sound. You might jump the first time the sound occurs, but each time the sound is repeated you respond less and soon show no visible response at all. In some cases habituation persists over long periods, and thus can be considered to be a simple form of learning. Habituation does not produce a new stimulus-response sequence, but only weakens an already existing one. Classical conditioning, in contrast, is a form of reflex learning that does produce a new stimulus-response sequence. Classical conditioning was first described and most extensively studied by a Russian physiologist, Ivan Petrovich Pavlov.

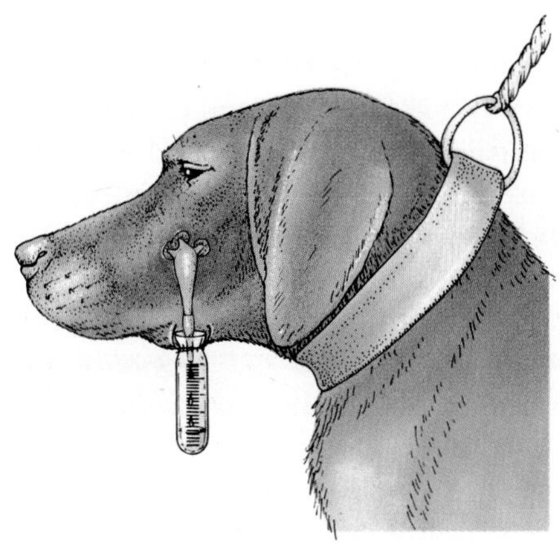

Figure 5.1 ***Pavlov's method for measuring salivation***

The dog's saliva drains directly into a glass tube. In his early experiments, Pavlov learned that dogs produce different salivary secretions in response to different kinds of food. Later he learned that the dogs could be conditioned to produce these secretions in response to stimuli that reliably precede the presentation of food. (Adapted from Yerkes & Morgulis, 1909.)

Pavlov's Discovery

Ivan Pavlov (1849–1936) was one of those scientists who inspire myths about the dedicated scientist. By the time of his most famous research on classical conditioning, he was in his fifties and had already earned a Nobel prize for studies of the reflexes involved in digestion. His research so engulfed his life that he is said to have hardly noticed such events as the Bolshevik Revolution of 1917, which transformed his country. One former co-worker (Gantt, 1975, as quoted by Hothersall, 1990) recalled, many years later, Pavlov's angry scolding of an assistant who arrived 10 minutes late to start an experiment: "But Professor," exclaimed the assistant, "there's a revolution going on with shooting in the streets." To which Pavlov replied, "What difference does that make when you've work to do in the laboratory? Next time there's a revolution, get up earlier!"

■ **3.** ***How did Pavlov discover the conditioned reflex? How did he then systematize the process of conditioning and name the relevant stimuli and responses?***

Pavlov's initial discovery of what we now call classical conditioning emerged from his earlier studies of digestive reflexes in dogs. Using permanently implanted tubes to collect salivary and stomach juices from dogs, he and his team of researchers found, for example, that a dog salivates differently when different kinds of food are placed in its mouth. Juicy meat triggers a very thick saliva, dry bread a wetter saliva, and acidic fluids a wetter one yet. In a fine-grained analysis, then, these represent three different reflexes, with three different stimuli eliciting three measurably different salivary secretions (see Figure 5.1).

In the course of these studies, Pavlov encountered a problem. Dogs that had been given food on previous occasions in Pavlov's experiments would begin to salivate *before* receiving food. Apparently, signals that regularly preceded food, such as sight of the food or the sound associated with its delivery, alerted the dogs to the upcoming stimulation and caused them to salivate. At first Pavlov was content to treat this simply as a source of experimental error. He called it "psychic secretion," implying that it was something outside of the physiologist's realm of study, and he attempted to eliminate it by developing ways to introduce the food into the dog's mouth without any forewarning. But then it occurred to Pavlov that this might well be a phenomenon that could be studied physiologically. Rather than call it psychic secretion, perhaps he could consider it a reflex and analyze it objectively, just as he had analyzed the reflexive salivary response to food in the mouth. It was this insight that eventually led Pavlov to his first experiments on conditioned reflexes (Pavlov, 1927/1960).

The Procedure and Generality of Classical Conditioning

To study this phenomenon, Pavlov deliberately controlled the signals that preceded food. For example, in one experiment he sounded a bell just before placing food in the dog's mouth. After several such pairings of a bell with food, the dog would salivate in response to the bell sound alone; no food was necessary. Pavlov referred to this new reflex as a ***conditioned reflex***, because it depended on the unique *conditions* present in the dog's previous experience—the pairing of the bell sound with the food-in-mouth stimulus. He referred to the stimulus in a conditioned reflex (the bell sound, in this case) as a ***conditioned stimulus***, and to the learned response to it (salivation) as a ***conditioned response***. Likewise, he referred to the original, unlearned reflex as an ***unconditioned reflex***, and to its stimulus (food placed in the mouth) and response (salivation) as an ***unconditioned stimulus*** and ***unconditioned response***. For a diagram of Pavlov's basic procedure, called ***classical conditioning***, see Figure 5.2.

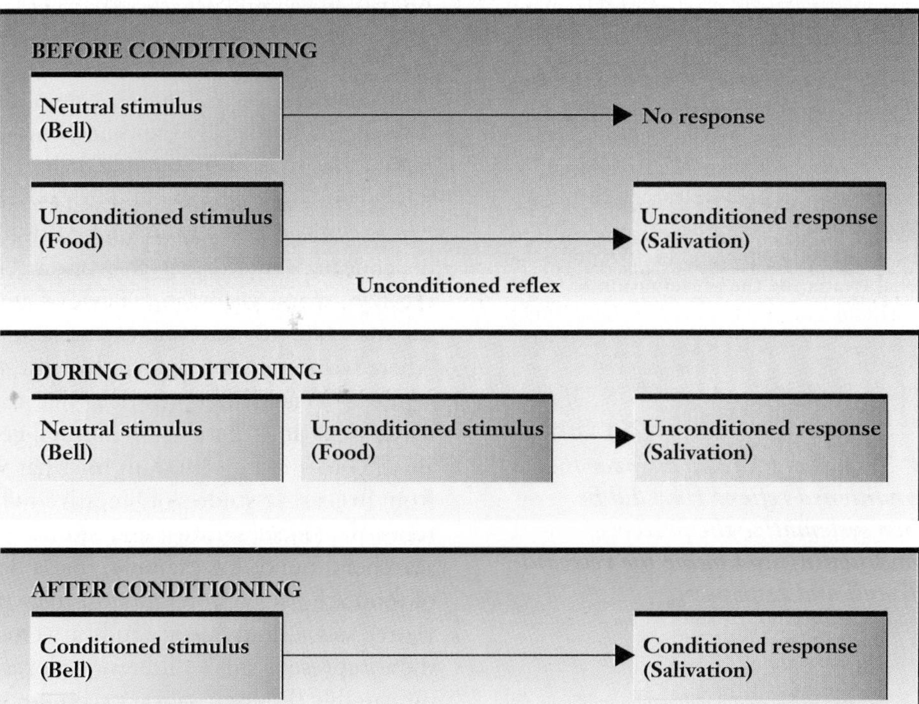

Figure 5.2 ***Classical conditioning procedure***

A neutral stimulus initially does not elicit a response. After it is paired for several trials with an unconditioned stimulus, however, it becomes a conditioned stimulus and does elicit a response.

Pavlov (1927/1960) was impressed in these studies by the similarity between the dog's salivary response to a conditioned stimulus and its response to the unconditioned stimulus. A sound that had previously been paired with meat elicited a thick saliva, similar to that elicited by meat; and a sound that had been paired with bread elicited a thinner, wetter saliva, similar to that elicited by bread. The same conditioned stimulus could result in different conditioned responses depending on the nature of the unconditioned stimulus with which it had been paired.

In other experiments, Pavlov and his colleagues varied the stimulus used as the conditioned stimulus. They concluded that essentially any environmental event that the animal could detect could become a conditioned stimulus for salivation. Sounds produced by bells, buzzers, metronomes, or tuning forks were highly effective and used most often because they were the easiest to control. But Pavlov's group also produced conditioned responses to visual stimuli, such as a black square or circle; to olfactory stimuli, such as the odor of camphor; and to tactile (touch) stimuli, such as pressing a particular point on the animal's skin. In each case, the stimulus initially did not elicit the salivary response, but it did after having been paired with food a number of times. Pavlov's team even found that a moderately painful stimulus, such as an electric shock or puncture of the skin, could be used as a conditioned stimulus for salivation. Such stimuli were initially unconditioned stimuli for vigorous withdrawal responses, but after repeated pairing with food the withdrawal stopped and the dog no longer seemed to experience pain (Pavlov, 1927/1960).

Conditioned fear

The events preceding an injection can be conditioned stimuli for a fear response because of their previous pairing with pain. By averting her eyes from these stimuli, this woman may be reducing her conditioned fear.

Of course, classical conditioning is not limited to salivary responses. Researchers have shown this in hundreds of laboratory experiments, and you have undoubtedly experienced it dozens of times in the course of your everyday life. The sound of a dentist's drill may elicit a conditioned cringing response because of its previous pairing with pain. The mere smell of coffee may help wake you up because of its previous pairing with coffee's effects. The sight of the toilet when you enter a bathroom to comb your hair may elicit a previously unfelt urge to urinate due to previous pairing of that sight with that urge. If you once had an automobile accident at a curve in the road on a wet day, each new encounter with such a curve, on such a day, may elicit a conditioned tensing of muscles. If you go through a day recording instances of conditioned responses, you will find that the list quickly becomes quite long.

The Importance of Pavlov's Discovery in the Emergence of a Science of Learning

■ **4. *How can classical conditioning be understood as an objectification of the philosophers' law of association by contiguity?***

To understand the importance of Pavlov's work on conditioning, it is useful to view it in the context of earlier, philosophical thought about learning. For centuries before Pavlov, one of the most influential ideas about learning was the ***law of association by contiguity***, originally proposed by Aristotle (Hothersall, 1990). *Contiguity* means closeness in space or time, and the law of association by contiguity can be stated as follows: If a person experiences two environmental events (stimuli) at the same time or one right after the other (contiguously), those events will become associated in the person's mind, such that the thought of one will, in the future, tend to elicit the thought of the other. If your thought *ice cream* is followed more often by the thought *spoon* than by the thought *pencil*, that is because in your past experience ice cream has been accompanied more often by a spoon than by a pencil. If the sound of the word *ball* evokes in a child's mind an image of a spherical object, that is because in the child's past experience that sound had been often paired with the sight of a spherical object. Thus, according to Aristotle and subsequent philosophers, association by contiguity plays a major role in determining the flow of a person's thoughts and is involved in all sorts of learning, including the learning of language.

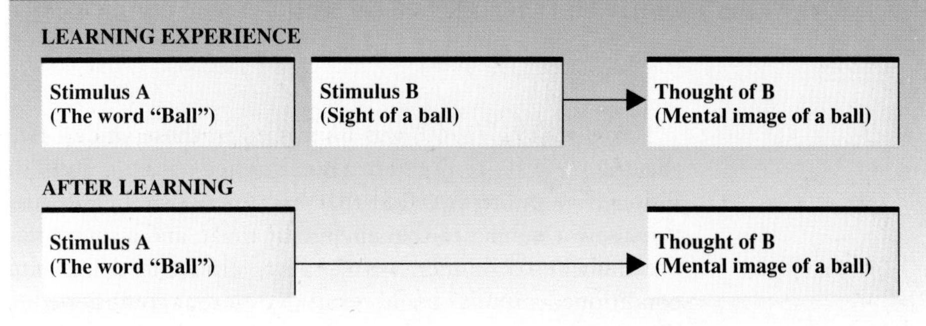

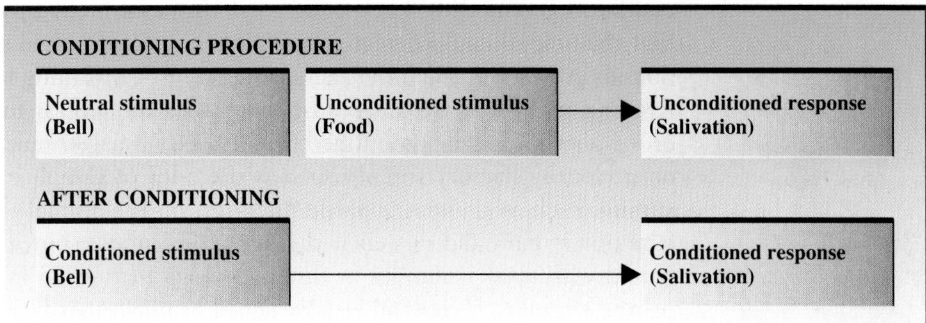

Figure 5.3 ***Comparison of the law of association by contiguity with the principle of classical conditioning***

Philosophers, from Aristotle on, argued that if two stimuli are paired in a person's experience, the recurrence of one will tend to elicit the thought of the other. Pavlov's principle of conditioning parallels the philosophers' law, with one important difference. Because Pavlov began with a stimulus (unconditioned stimulus) that reflexively elicited an observable response, he could measure learning objectively as the increased likelihood that the response would occur to the new stimulus (conditioned stimulus).

Now, consider the similarity between the philosophers' law of association by contiguity and Pavlov's principle of conditioning (outlined in Figure 5.3). Both propose that learning occurs when two stimuli are paired in a person's experience. The essential difference is that in the philosophers' formulation one stimulus comes to elicit a *thought* that was previously elicited just by the other, while in Pavlov's formulation one stimulus comes to elicit a *behavioral response* that was previously elicited just by the other. The great advantage of Pavlov's formulation is that a response is publicly observable, whereas a thought is not. A researcher using Pavlov's method can look at an animal or person and see the change in response and use it to chart the course of learning. Philosophers could only speculate about the association of thoughts, but Pavlov could do experiments. He could vary the conditions and objectively measure the effects on an individual's behavior. This idea, of course, was not lost on Watson and other American behaviorists. To them it was a step that helped make a *science* of learning possible.

Phenomena Associated with Classical Conditioning

Pavlov and his associates performed hundreds of experiments on classical conditioning and identified many phenomena related to conditioning that are still very important in psychology today. Let's look now at some of them.

Extinction and Recovery from Extinction

■ **5.** ***How can a conditioned reflex be extinguished? What was Pavlov's evidence that extinction does not return the animal to the untrained state?***

One question that interested Pavlov had to do with the permanence, or lack of permanence, of a conditioned reflex. Once a dog has learned to salivate to a bell, will this reflex continue to occur if the bell is sounded for many trials without the unconditioned food-in-mouth stimulus? Pavlov's group found that without food the bell elicits less and less salivation on each trial, and eventually none at all, a phenomenon that they labeled ***extinction***. But they also found that extinction does not return the animal fully to the unconditioned state. The mere passage of time following extinction can partially renew the conditioned reflex, a phenomenon now known as ***spontaneous recovery*** (see Figure 5.4). And a single pairing of the conditioned stimulus with the unconditioned stimulus can renew the conditioned reflex,

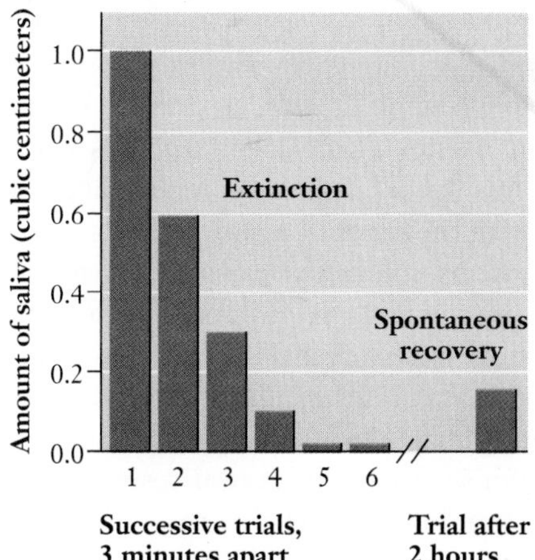

Figure 5.4 ***Extinction and spontaneous recovery of conditioned salivation***
The conditioned stimulus in this case was the sight of meat powder, presented repeatedly out of the animal's reach at 3-minute intervals. Extinction was complete by the fifth and sixth presentations, but when 2 hours were allowed to elapse before the seventh presentation, the reflex was partially renewed. (Data from Pavlov, 1927/1960.)

which can be abolished again only by another series of extinction trials. Based on such findings, Pavlov (1927/1960) reasoned that the conditioned reflex is not truly lost during extinction, but is somehow inhibited, and can be disinhibited by the passage of time or a single reinforced trial.

Subsequent research has shown that some conditioned reflexes are more difficult to extinguish than others. In particular, conditioned changes in heart rate, blood pressure, and certain other internal responses are much harder to extinguish than conditioned movements that involve the skeletal muscles (the muscles attached to bones). For example, electric shock to a person's arm produces an increased heart rate and a flinching away from the source of shock (a skeletal response), both of which can be conditioned to a new stimulus with just a few reinforced trials. Following such conditioning, the conditioned flinch disappears after only two or three extinction trials, but the conditioned heart-rate response usually persists even after dozens of such trials (Gantt, 1953). This may help explain why people can appear calm on the outside while experiencing turmoil inside, leading to such ailments as chronically high blood pressure and ulcers.

Generalization and Discrimination

■ **6.** ***What is generalization in classical conditioning, and how can it be abolished through discrimination training?***

After conditioning, stimuli that resemble the conditioned stimulus will elicit the conditioned response even though they themselves were never paired with the unconditioned stimulus. This phenomenon is called ***generalization***. The magnitude or likelihood of a response to the new stimulus is correlated with its degree of similarity to the original conditioned stimulus. Thus, a dog conditioned to salivate to a 1000 Hz (cycles per second) tone also salivated to tones of other frequencies. But the further the tone was in frequency from the original conditioned stimulus, the less the dog would salivate to it (Pavlov, 1927/1960).

Generalization between two stimuli can be abolished if the response to one is reinforced while the response to the other is extinguished, a procedure called ***discrimination training***. To illustrate this procedure, Pavlov's group used a dog whose conditioning to the sight of a black square had generalized to a gray square. After a series of trials in which presentations of the gray square were never followed by food and presentations of the black square were always followed by food, the dog stopped salivating to the gray square and continued to salivate to the black one. The researchers continued this procedure with ever-darker shades of gray, until they eventually conditioned the dog to discriminate a black square from a gray one that was so nearly black that a human observer had difficulty telling them apart (Pavlov, 1927/1960).

■ **7.** ***How can classical conditioning and discrimination training be used to assess an animal's sensory capacities?***

Classical conditioning coupled with discrimination training provides an excellent tool to study an animal's sensory capacities. A dog cannot tell you what it can or cannot hear, but you can find out by doing a conditioning experiment. If an animal can be conditioned to respond to a stimulus, we know it can sense that stimulus; and if an animal can be trained to respond to one stimulus and not to another, we know it can sense the difference between the two. Pavlov's team conditioned dogs to salivate to tones so high-pitched as to be inaudible to humans, and to discriminate between pitches less than one-eighth of a note apart. In one experiment with a dog that had previously been conditioned to discriminate between tones coming from the right or the left, the researchers cut the nerve fibers connecting the right and left halves of the higher parts of the brain. After the surgery, the dog continued to salivate to tones, but could no longer discriminate between tones coming from different locations, and could not be retrained to do so. From this, Pavlov (1927/1960) concluded that the ability to localize sounds depends on the integrated activity of the two halves of the brain. This sort of experiment on the physiology of perception would have been difficult without the conditioned reflex as a tool.

Higher-Order Conditioning

■ ***8. How can one conditioned reflex be used to produce a new one?***

Once a conditioned reflex has been established, it can be used, without the original unconditioned stimulus, to produce a new conditioned reflex, a process called ***higher-order conditioning***. As an illustration, Pavlov (1927/1960) and his team conditioned a dog in the usual way to salivate to a buzzer, and then conditioned the dog to salivate to a black square by pairing it with the buzzer on several trials without the food-in-mouth unconditioned stimulus. As you might expect, they found such *second-order conditioning* to be rather fragile, as each reinforced trial for the new stimulus (black square) was an extinction trial for the previous stimulus (buzzer). Can second-order conditioning provide a basis for conditioning to yet another stimulus? Pavlov's group were unable to obtain *third-order conditioning* with salivation, but did obtain it with another response, a leg-withdrawal response for which electric shock was the unconditioned stimulus. Even in this case, however, they were unable to obtain *fourth-order conditioning*.

Conditioned Emotional Responses

■ ***9. How did Watson demonstrate that an emotional reaction can be conditioned?***

We move temporarily from Pavlov's laboratory to that of John B. Watson. Watson was one of the first psychologists to describe human learning explicitly in Pavlovian terms, and he was also one of the first to demonstrate directly how an emotional response—fear—can be conditioned in human infants. Consistent with his behavioral perspective, Watson (1924) defined *fear* not as a feeling, but as a set of observable responses: "a catching of the breath, a stiffening of the whole body, a turning away of the body from the source of stimulation, a running or crawling from it." Based on this definition, Watson found two unconditioned stimuli for fear in young infants—sudden loud sound and sudden loss of support (as when a baby slips out of a person's hands). Other stimuli, he argued, come to elicit fear only as a result of conditioning.

In a classic demonstration of such conditioning, Watson and Rosalie Rayner (1920) conditioned an 11-month-old baby named Albert to fear laboratory rats. At first Albert played happily and fearlessly with a rat that was placed in front of him. To condition the fear, the experimenters struck a steel bar with a hammer to produce a loud sound on two different occasions when Albert was paying close attention to the rat. Each occurrence of the loud sound elicited the fear response, and after the second occurrence Albert showed the fear response each time he saw the rat even though the loud sound was not repeated. Thus, in the terminology of classical conditioning, the rat had become a conditioned stimulus for fear through being paired with a loud sound, which was an unconditioned stimulus for fear.

You might wonder about the ethics of this experiment. In fairness to Watson I should note that he was far more interested in how to eliminate unwanted fears

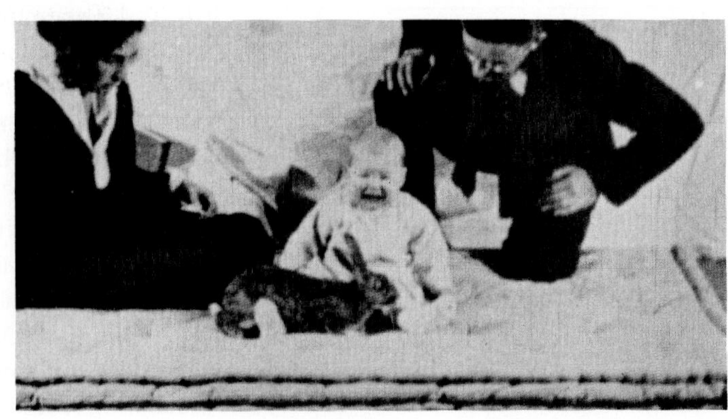

Little Albert with Watson and Rayner

After Albert was conditioned to respond fearfully to a rat, he also cried at the sight of other furry objects, including the rabbit shown here, thereby exhibiting generalization. Courtesy of Professor Benjamin Harris.

Forewarned is not necessarily forearmed

In natural environments, classical conditioning has functional value. The animal learns negative responses toward harmful stimuli and positive responses to those that are beneficial. In contrast, when advertisers attempt conditioning, the results may be harmful to unwary "subjects."

than in how to produce them. In Chapter 18, you will see how Watson's research and ideas helped lead to clinical methods to extinguish irrational fears through exposing the person to the fear-producing stimuli at gradually increasing magnitudes in a safe, relaxing context.

Fear, of course, is not the only emotional response that can be conditioned through Pavlovian procedures. When beer and car advertisers pair their products with scenes of beautiful people having wonderful times, they are trying to get you to drool with pleasure, like Pavlov's dogs, whenever you see their product.

Conditioned Drug Reactions

In one of their most intriguing experiments, Pavlov's group conditioned a dog to show a drug reaction to a nondrug stimulus. After repeated pairing of a tone with injection of a drug that elicited restlessness and vomiting, the dog began to exhibit those responses to the tone alone (Pavlov, 1927/1960). This discovery suggests that stimuli normally present when a drug is taken may, through conditioning, come to induce the symptoms of the drug. Because of conditioning, the sight of a coffee cup or the smell of coffee might give you a lift; and a visit to a hospital where you were previously given a sedative might make you feel sleepy.

Research conducted more recently has shown that conditioned effects of stimuli paired with some drugs are *opposite* to the most prominent unconditioned effects of the drugs. Morphine, for example, reduces sensitivity to pain. When rats are repeatedly injected with morphine in a distinctive environment, and then are placed in that environment without morphine, they become temporarily more sensitive to pain, not less (Hinson & others, 1986). What happens in such cases might be understood as follows (Siegel & others, 1988): The drug produces two effects—a direct effect (which in this case includes reduced sensitivity to pain) followed by a reflexive physiological response that tends to counteract the direct effect (tends to increase pain sensitivity). But only the reflexive counteractive effect becomes conditioned, so, when the cues are present without the drug, pain sensitivity increases rather than decreases.

■ **10.** ***Why is the conditioned response to a drug-related stimulus often opposite to the most direct effect of the drug?***

You might think of such conditioning as analogous to what would happen if a bell sound (conditioned stimulus) reliably preceded a shove from the front (unconditioned stimulus). The shove would tend to push you backward, but you would counteract that with a reflexive movement forward. Only the reflexive movement forward would be conditioned, so if the bell were sounded without the shove, you might fall on your face—a reaction opposite to the most direct effect of the shove. The body protects itself with counteractive reflexes to stimuli (such as shoves and drugs) that disrupt its normal functioning. The conditioning of those reflexes is normally useful because it allows the counteraction to begin even before the potentially harmful stimulus strikes.

The discovery of conditioned counteractive effects of drugs may help explain an important observation associated with human drug abuse. A study of heroin overdose cases revealed that quite often the "overdose" was not larger than the ad-

11. ***How does the conditioning of counteractive drug effects help explain why an addict's usual dose can sometimes be an "overdose"?***

dict's usual drug dose, but was taken in an unusual environment (Siegel, 1984). Apparently, when an addict takes a drug in the usual drug-taking environment, cues in that environment, because of past conditioning, produce a counteractive physiological reaction that allows the addict's body to tolerate a large dose of the drug. If the addict takes the same amount of the drug in a novel environment, where the conditioned cues aren't present, the full impact of the drug kicks in before a counteractive reaction begins—resulting in extreme illness or death. Consistent with this interpretation, rats that had previously received many morphine injections in a specific, highly distinctive cage were much more likely to survive a high dose of the drug if given to them in that same cage than if given in a different setting (Siegel, 1976, 1984). Similar effects have been shown in animal experiments using alcohol (Melchior, 1990) and various other drugs (Goudie, 1990).

Operant Conditioning

We are pulled as well as pushed by events in our environment. That is, we do not just react to stimuli; we also behave in ways that seem designed to *produce* or *obtain* certain environmental changes or stimuli. My dog rubs against the door to be let out. I flip a switch to illuminate a room, press keys on my computer to set up words on a screen, and say "please pass the potatoes" to get potatoes. Most of my day seems to consist of behaviors of this sort, and I expect that most of my dog's day would too if there were more things that she could control. Surely if Pavlov's dogs had some way to control the delivery of food into their mouths, they would have done more than salivate—they would have pushed a lever, or bitten open a bag, or done whatever was required to get the food.

Actions such as those just listed—which seem to be performed for the sake of their effect—are called *instrumental responses* because they function like *instruments*, or tools, to work some change on the environment. They are also called ***operant responses*** because they *operate* on the world to produce some effect. B. F. Skinner (1938) coined this term, as well as the term ***operant conditioning***, which refers to the learning process by which the consequence of an operant response affects the likelihood that the response will occur in the future. Although the term was Skinner's, the process now called operant conditioning was studied extensively before Skinner by other pioneers, most notably E. L. Thorndike.

Thorndike's Puzzle-Box Procedure

At the same time that Pavlov initiated his first studies of conditioning, a young American student of psychology, Edward Lee Thorndike (1898), published a report on his own learning experiments with various animals, including cats. Thorndike's training procedure was quite different from Pavlov's, and so was his description of the learning process. His apparatus was a *puzzle box*, a small cage that could be opened from inside by some relatively simple act, such as pulling a loop or pressing a lever (see Figure 5.5)

In one experiment Thorndike deprived cats of food long enough to make them hungry, and then placed them inside the cage, one at a time, with food just outside it. When first placed inside, the cat would engage in many behaviors—such as clawing at the bars or pushing at the ceiling—in an apparent attempt to escape the cage and get at the food outside. Finally, apparently by accident, the cat would pull the loop or push the lever that opened the door to freedom and food. Thorndike repeated this procedure many times with each cat. He found that on early trials they made many useless movements before happening on the one that released the latch, but, on average, they would escape somewhat more quickly with each successive trial. After about twenty to thirty trials, most cats would trip the latch to freedom and food almost as soon as they were shut in (see Figure 5.6). An observer who

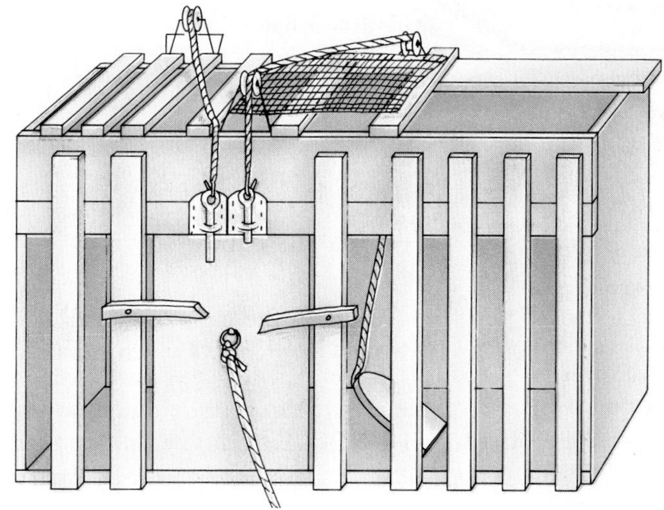

Figure 5.5 ***One of Thorndike's puzzle boxes***

A cat placed inside this box could open it by pushing the lever on the floor. Before each trial, the clips on either side of the door would be turned up and the left-hand bolt would be released. When the cat pressed the lever, pulling the right-hand bolt up, the door would fall forward. (From Thorndike, 1898.)

joined Thorndike on Trial 31 might have been quite impressed by the animal's intelligence; but, as Thorndike himself suggested, an observer who had sat through the earlier trials might have been far more impressed by the creature's stupidity than its intelligence. In any event, Thorndike came to view learning as a trial-and-error process, through which an individual gradually becomes more likely to make those responses that produce beneficial effects.

Thorndike's Law of Effect

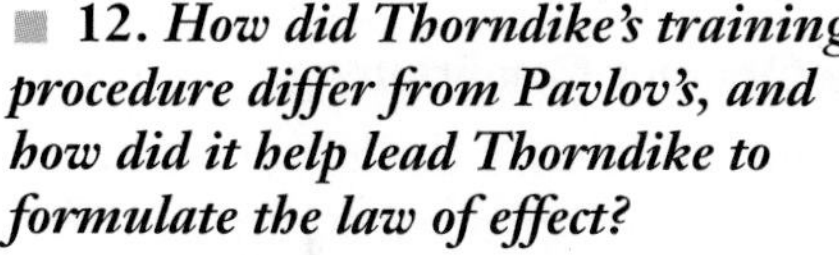

12. ***How did Thorndike's training procedure differ from Pavlov's, and how did it help lead Thorndike to formulate the law of effect?***

Thorndike's basic training procedure differed fundamentally from Pavlov's. Pavlov could directly *elicit* the response he wished to condition in his animal. For example, he could elicit salivation by putting food in the dog's mouth. His conditioning method was to pair a new stimulus with a stimulus that already elicited the response. Thus, Pavlov was concerned only with environmental events that *preceded* the response that he wished to condition, not with the effect or consequence of the response. With Pavlov's procedure, the animal can be thought of as a passive, responsive machine: Push button X and get response Y. Thorndike, in contrast, could not directly elicit the response he wished to condition. There was no known unconditioned stimulus, no button Thorndike could push, that would make the animal open the latch. With Thorndike's procedure, the animal has to be thought of as an active creature, one that produces or *emits* various responses, seemingly of its own accord. Most of the cat's initial movements in the box were ineffective, and Thorndike had to wait patiently until the animal emitted the correct one. To gain some control over the cat's behavior, Thorndike had arranged the environment in such a way that only one type of response would open the box. Thus, with Thorndike's method, the important environmental event (the opening of the box) was a *consequence* of the response, not something that occurred before the response.

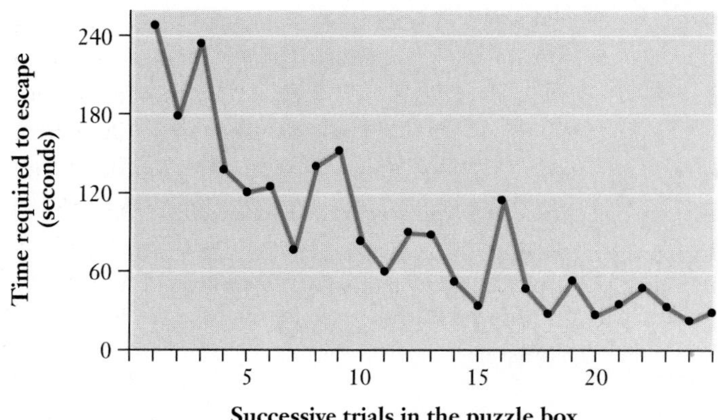

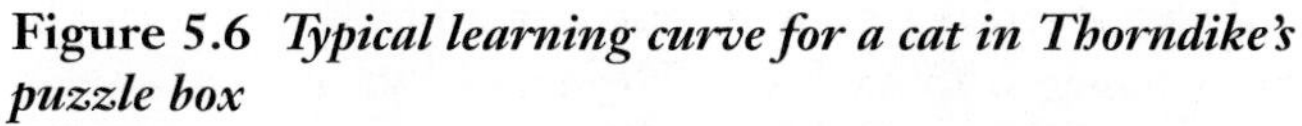

Figure 5.6 ***Typical learning curve for a cat in Thorndike's puzzle box***

As illustrated here for a single cat, Thorndike found that cats usually took less time to escape from the box on successive trials, though a great deal of variability occurred from trial to trial. (Adapted from Thorndike, 1898.)

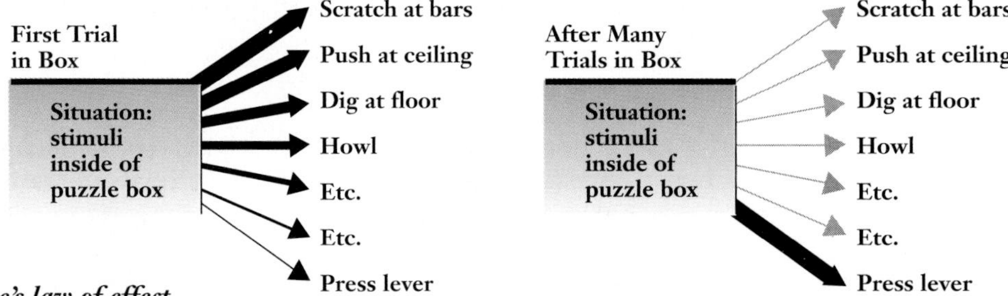

Figure 5.7 ***Thorndike's law of effect***

According to Thorndike, the stimulus situation (being inside the puzzle box) initially elicits many responses, some more strongly than others, but the satisfying consequence of the successful response (pressing the lever) causes that response to be more strongly elicited on successive trials.

Partly on the basis of his puzzle-box experiments, Thorndike (1898) formulated the ***law of effect***, which can be stated, in somewhat abbreviated form, as follows: *Responses that produce a satisfying effect in a particular situation become more likely to occur again in that situation, and responses that produce a discomforting effect become less likely to occur again in that situation.* In Thorndike's puzzle-box experiments, the *situation* presumably consisted of all the sights, sounds, smells, internal feelings, and so on that were experienced by the hungry animal in the box. None of these initially elicited the latch-release response in reflexlike fashion; rather, taken as a whole, they set the occasion for many possible responses to occur, only one of which would release the latch. Once the latch was released, the *satisfying effect*, including freedom from the box and access to food, caused that response to become more firmly bonded to the situation than it was before, so the next time the cat was in the same situation, the probability of that response's recurrence was increased (see Figure 5.7). Of the many different responses that initially occurred in the puzzle box, the one that changed the environment in a satisfactory way was more likely to occur the next time.

Skinner's Method of Studying and Describing Operant Conditioning

13. ***How did Skinner's method for studying learning differ from Thorndike's, and why did he prefer the term reinforcer to Thorndike's satisfaction?***

The psychologist who did the most to extend and popularize the law of effect for more than half a century is Burrhus Fredric Skinner. As a graduate student at Harvard around 1930, Skinner developed an apparatus for studying learning in animals that was considerably more convenient than Thorndike's puzzle boxes. His device, commonly called a Skinner box, is a cage with a lever or other mechanism in it that the animal can operate to produce some effect, such as delivery of a pellet of food or a drop of water (see Figure 5.8). The advantage of Skinner's apparatus is that the animal, after completing a response and experiencing its effect, is still in the box and free to respond again. With Thorndike's puzzle boxes and similar apparatuses such as mazes, the animal has to be placed back into the starting place at the end of each trial. With Skinner's apparatus the animal is simply placed in the cage and left there until the end of the session. Throughout the session there are no constraints on when the animal may or may not respond. Responses (such as lever presses) can easily be counted automatically, and the learning process can be depicted as change in the rate of responses (see Figure 5.9).

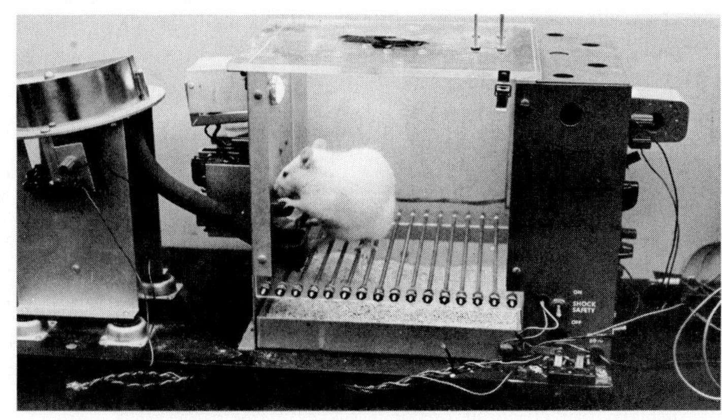

Figure 5.8 ***Skinner box, or operant conditioning chamber***

When the rat presses the lever, it activates an electrical relay system that causes the delivery of a food pellet or drop of water into the cup next to the lever. Each lever press can be automatically recorded to produce a cumulative record, such as that shown in Figure 5.9.

(assuming that the subject is motivated to succeed at the task) for the response of decreasing blood pressure. As was the case for the subjects in Hefferline's thumb-twitch experiment, the client need not discover or be aware of just how he is reducing his blood pressure for successful learning to occur. Using a similar method, biofeedback trainers have also reported success in teaching people with irregular heart rates to produce more regular heartbeats and people who suffer from headaches to reduce muscle tension in the scalp and thereby reduce the incidence of headaches (Duckro, 1991; Mercer, 1986).

■ **16.** ***How can operant conditioning be used to get an animal to do something that it presently doesn't do?***

Phenomena Associated with Operant Conditioning

Skinner and his followers identified and studied many behavioral phenomena associated with operant conditioning. Let's examine some of them.

Shaping

Suppose you put a rat in a Skinner box and it never presses the lever, or a cat in a puzzle box and it never pulls the loop. In operant conditioning, the reinforcer comes only after the subject emits the desired response. But what happens if that response never occurs? The solution to this problem is a technique called ***shaping***, in which successively closer approximations to the desired response are reinforced until the response finally occurs.

Imagine that you wish to shape a lever-press response in a rat whose initial rate of lever pressing is zero, or so low that you don't have the patience to wait for the response to occur. First you might present the reinforcer (such as a pellet of food) whenever the rat goes anywhere near the lever. As a result, the rat will soon be spending most of its time near the lever and occasionally will touch it. When that happens, you might provide the reinforcer only when the rat touches the lever, which will increase the rate of touching. Some touches will be more vigorous than others and produce the desired lever movement; when that has happened a few times you can stop reinforcing any other response—your animal has now been shaped. We all use this technique, more or less deliberately, when we teach new skills to people. For example, when teaching a novice to play tennis we tend at first to offer praise for any swing of the racket that propels the ball in the right general direction, and as improvement occurs we gradually reserve praise for closer and closer approximations to an ideal swing.

Partial reinforcement in daily life

Winning at slot machines occurs on a variable-ratio schedule, which produces a rapid, steady style of play. Success at reaching a previously busy telephone number occurs on a variable-interval schedule, which results in a slow and steady rate of redialing.

Extinction and Schedules of Partial Reinforcement

An operantly conditioned response declines in rate and eventually disappears if it no longer results in a reinforcer. Rats stop pressing levers if no food pellets appear, cats stop scratching at doors if nobody responds, and people stop smiling at those who don't smile back. The lack of reinforcement of the response, and the consequent decline in response rate, are both referred to as ***extinction***. Extinction in operant conditioning is analogous to extinction in classical conditioning.

■ **17.** ***How do the four schedules of partial reinforcement differ from one another, and what effect does each have on response rate and response steadiness?***

In many cases, both in the real world and in laboratory setups, a particular response only sometimes produces a reinforcer. This is referred to as ***partial reinforcement***, to distinguish it on the one hand from continuous reinforcement, where the response is always reinforced, and on the other hand from extinction, where the response is never reinforced. In initial training, continuous reinforcement is most efficient, but once trained an animal will continue to perform for partial reinforcement. Skinner and other operant researchers have described four basic *schedules* of partial reinforcement, each of which has a different, quite predictable effect on the rate and pattern of responding. As you read the description of each schedule, look also at the appropriate part of Figure 5.10, which depicts the typical response pattern of an animal that is reinforced on that schedule.

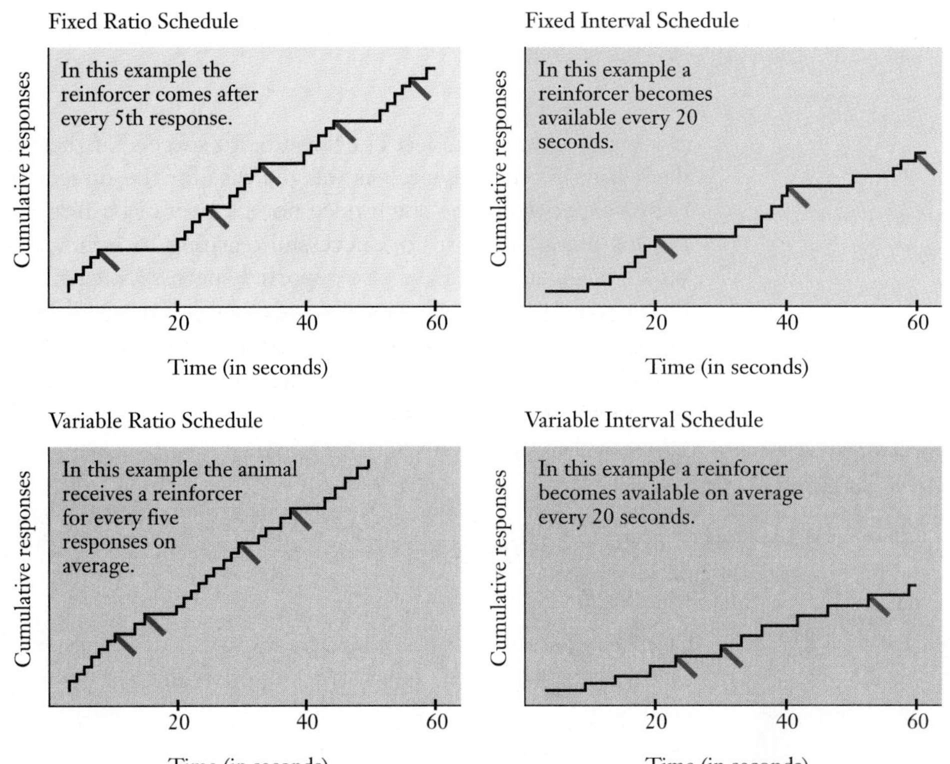

Figure 5.10 ***Typical cumulative response curves for rats well-trained on four different schedules of reinforcement***

As explained in Figure 5.9 each upward step represents one response. Here each slanted mark indicates the occurrence of a reinforcer. Ratio schedules (whether fixed or variable) typically produce faster response rates than do interval schedules; and variable schedules (whether ratio or interval) typically produce steadier response rates with shorter postreinforcement pauses than do fixed schedules.

- ***Fixed-ratio (FR) schedule*** With this schedule, the response must be emitted a certain fixed number of times before a reinforcer occurs. If a rat must make twenty lever presses before obtaining a pellet of food, the schedule is FR-20. If a garment worker must sew five dresses before getting paid, the schedule is FR-5. An animal on a fixed-ratio schedule in a Skinner box typically produces a burst of lever presses until the reinforcer appears, and then, after a pause that may sometimes be of considerable duration, produces another burst (see Figure 5.10). The response rate during the burst is usually constant, which is consistent with the idea that the animal is treating the series of lever presses required for each reinforcer as one behavioral act.
- ***Variable-ratio (VR) schedule*** With this schedule, the response must be emitted a certain *average* number of times before a reinforcer will appear, but the number needed on any given instance varies randomly around that average. If a rat must make an average of ten responses for each pellet of food, but the actual number required for a given pellet is unpredictable, the schedule is VR-10. Many human gambling systems can be described as variable-ratio schedules. For example, the reinforcement schedule for betting heads in a coin-flipping game is VR-2, and that for betting on a particular lay of a six-sided die is VR-6. Slot machines also operate on variable-ratio schedules. A variable-ratio schedule typically produces a high, steady rate of responding, with shorter postreinforcement pauses than occur with a fixed-ratio schedule (see Figure 5.10). Because one reinforcer sometimes comes immediately after another, this schedule provides greater incentive to resume responding right after receiving a reinforcer than does the fixed-ratio schedule. According to Skinner (1953), compulsive gambling occurs partly because people become hooked by the variable ratio. The very next response may pay off regardless of how long it has been since the last response paid off, so the gambler keeps responding.
- ***Fixed-interval (FI) schedule*** With this schedule, a fixed period of time must elapse after each reinforced response before another reinforcer can be obtained. Thus, if a rat must wait 30 seconds after receiving a pellet of food be-

fore a lever press will produce another pellet, the rat is on an FI-30-second schedule. Similarly, if you are baking cookies a batch at a time in a small oven, your response of checking the oven with each batch to see if they are done is reinforced after rather constant intervals. A fixed-interval schedule induces a regularly varying rate of responding; the subject pauses for a period of time after each reinforcer and then responds at an accelerating rate until the fixed interval is up and another reinforcer is received (see Figure 5.10). If your rate of study in college accelerates near midterm and finals time, that may indicate that the main reinforcers controlling your study are grades on tests that occur at those fixed intervals.

- ***Variable-interval (VI) schedule*** With this schedule, an unpredictable amount of time, varying around some average, must elapse between the presentation of one reinforcer and the availability of another. For example, if a pellet of food becomes available at unpredictable intervals averaging 30 seconds, the lever-pressing rat is on a VI-30-second schedule. A nonlaboratory example is that of repeatedly dialing a busy telephone number. At some point the line will become free and the call will go through, but there is no way to tell just when. Subjects well trained on a variable-interval schedule typically respond at a slow but steady rate (see Figure 5.10). Because reinforcement availability is based on time rather than the number of responses, and because a reinforcer may occur at any time, the slow and steady response rate is most efficient.

The different response patterns produced by the different schedules make sense from the viewpoint of adaptiveness. The high response rate observed with fixed and variable ratio schedules pays off because the number of reinforcers received is directly proportional to the number of responses made. A similarly high response rate would not pay off with interval schedules because the maximum number of reinforcers is set by the clock. The steady response rate, with short postreinforcement pauses, observed with variable schedules (ratio or interval) pays off because with them, unlike with fixed schedules, a reinforcer can come any time.

18. ***How can partial-reinforcement schedules be used to produce behavior that is very resistant to extinction?***

Compared to continuous reinforcement, partial-reinforcement schedules, especially variable-ratio and variable-interval, cause behavior to be more resistant to extinction. This phenomenon is known as the *partial-reinforcement effect*. If a rat is trained to press a lever only on continuous reinforcement, and then shifted to extinction conditions, it will typically make a few bursts of lever-press responses and then quit. But if the rat has been shifted gradually from continuous reinforcement to an ever-stingier variable schedule, and then finally to extinction, it will often make hundreds of unreinforced responses before quitting. So, quite often, will a human gambler, as many casino owners know full well. Subjects who have been reinforced on stingy variable ratios, or long variable intervals, have received reinforcers after long periods of no reinforcement, so they have learned (for better or worse) to be persistent.

Stimuli That Set the Occasion for Operant Behavior

The reinforcing stimulus in operant conditioning is a consequence of the response, but other stimuli precede and set the occasion for the response. A rat trained in a Skinner box has not merely learned to make a lever-press response, but has learned to make it in a particular *context*, which includes being inside the Skinner box. The rat does not go foolishly about making the lever-pressing movement in its home cage or in other places where the response has never been reinforced.

In his original formulation of the law of effect, Thorndike (1898) emphasized the importance of the *situation* in which the animal is trained, saying, "Of several responses made to the same situation, those which are accompanied or closely followed by satisfaction to the animal will, other things being equal, be more firmly connected with the situation, so that when it recurs, they will be more likely to recur." The set of stimuli inside a puzzle box or a Skinner box are examples of a Thorndikian situation (look back at Figure 5.7). Only in the presence of those stimuli is the response reinforced; therefore, the response becomes likely to occur when those stimuli are present.

■ **19.** ***How can a neutral stimulus be turned into a discriminative stimulus to control an operant response?***

Through *discrimination training* an operant response can be brought under the control of a more specific stimulus than the entire inside of a Skinner box. Discrimination training in operant conditioning is analogous to discrimination training in classical conditioning. The essence of the procedure is to reinforce the animal's response when a specific stimulus is present and extinguish the response when the stimulus is absent. Thus, to train a rat to respond to a tone by pressing a lever, a trainer would alternate between reinforcement periods with the tone on (during which the animal gets food pellets for responding) and extinction periods with the tone off. After considerable training of this sort, the rat will begin pressing the lever as soon as the tone comes on and stop as soon as it goes off. The tone in this example is called a ***discriminative stimulus***. A discriminative stimulus can be thought of as a cue; it is present when a particular response will be reinforced and absent when the response will not be reinforced. A discriminative stimulus in operant conditioning is similar to a conditioned stimulus in classical conditioning in that it promotes a particular response as a result of the subject's previous experience, but it does so in a less reflexive way. It *sets the occasion* for responding, rather than reflexively eliciting the response.

Operant discrimination training, like the analogous procedure in classical conditioning, can be a powerful tool for learning about the sensory abilities of animals and human infants who cannot describe their sensations in words. In one experiment, for example, researchers trained 1-day-old human babies to turn their heads in one direction—using a sip of sugarwater as the reinforcer—whenever a tone was sounded, and in the other direction whenever a buzzer was sounded (Siqueland & Lipsitt, 1966). This demonstrated, among other things, that newborns can hear the difference between the two different sounds. (You will read more about such experiments in Chapter 12.)

The Amazing Barnabus

Through the systematic process of chaining, Barnard College students trained an ordinary rat named Barnabus to climb a spiral ramp, push down a drawbridge, cross a moat, climb a staircase, crawl through a tunnel, enter an elevator, operate the elevator, raise a miniature Columbia University flag, and finally press a lever, all in the proper sequence for the ultimate reward of a pellet of food (Pierrel & Sherman, 1963).

Chaining, Secondary Reinforcement, and Tokens

Let's return to the rat that has been conditioned to press a lever whenever a tone comes on. Because the tone sets the occasion for receiving a reinforcer, the tone itself acquires reinforcing value. If the trainer arranges the environment so that the tone comes on whenever the rat pulls a string, the rat will learn to pull the string. After such training, the animal's behavior in the Skinner box consists of a chain of two operant responses linked by the tone, which serves as a reinforcer for one response (the string pull) and a discriminative stimulus for the next (the lever press):

string-pull response → tone → lever-press response → food

With further training, this chain could be extended by establishing a discriminative stimulus for the string-pull response (say, a green light) and then using that as the reinforcer for yet a new response (say, turning a wheel). By this stepwise procedure, rats have been trained to complete chains of as many as a dozen discrete responses in order to obtain in the end a pellet of food or a drop of water (Pierrel & Sherman, 1963). Similar techniques have been used to train severely retarded people to complete such response sequences as those involved in dressing themselves. First the person learns the last step in the sequence, for some reinforcer, and then new steps are added, each of which is reinforced by the opportunity it provides to perform the next step.

In a token economy

These volunteers at the Brooklyn Developmental Center (New York) wait on "customers" at the Center's "store." Staff members give tokens to their severely retarded clients to reward and motivate them for learning, maintaining, or improving a skill. Clients can then use the tokens to purchase different items at the store.

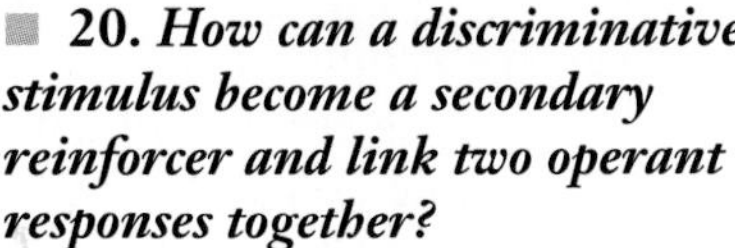

■ **20.** ***How can a discriminative stimulus become a secondary reinforcer and link two operant responses together?***

Through the procedure just described, almost any kind of stimulus can become a reinforcer. A ***primary reinforcer*** is a stimulus, such as food or water, that is reinforcing even without previous training, and a ***secondary reinforcer*** is a stimulus, such as the tone in the above example, that has acquired its reinforcing value through previous training. According to one widely accepted theory, the usual route by which a previously neutral stimulus becomes a secondary reinforcer is through first serving as a discriminative stimulus for some other reinforced response (Keller & Schoenfeld, 1950). In the example just discussed, the tone could be used as a secondary reinforcer for the string-pull response because it had been a discriminative stimulus for the lever-press response. From this perspective, a secondary reinforcer is reinforcing because it permits an individual to obtain a primary reinforcer. Operant theorists point out that much human behavior is reinforced by secondary reinforcers—such as money, certificates, grades, and praise—which have acquired their reinforcing value because in the past they have served as discriminative stimuli for other reinforced responses. If I have money in my hand, I can buy food; therefore, I will work for money:

work → money → buy food → food

In this chain, unlike the one described above for the rat, a considerable delay may occur between one response (working for money) and the next (using the money to buy food). A secondary reinforcer, such as money, which can be saved and turned in later for another reinforcer, is called a ***token***.

In a classic experiment with chimpanzees, J. B. Wolfe (1936) demonstrated that humans are not the only animals who can learn to work for tokens. Wolfe first trained chimpanzees to place poker chips into a machine that dispensed grapes. Because poker chips alone could activate the machine, they became discriminative stimuli for the response that led to grapes. Trained chimpanzees would not try to operate the machine unless they had a poker chip, and they would readily learn a new response to obtain poker chips, showing that these had become secondary reinforcers. Interestingly, the chimpanzees would work for poker chips even when the grape machine was not present and the chips could not be used immediately to get grapes, indicating that the chips now functioned as true tokens. The chimpanzees would save them and cash them in for grapes when the machine again became available.

■ **21.** ***How does negative reinforcement differ from positive reinforcement, and how does avoidance training differ from escape training?***

Negative Reinforcement and Avoidance Learning

In Skinner's terminology, ***reinforcement*** refers to any process that *increases* the likelihood that a particular response will occur. Reinforcement can be positive or negative. ***Positive reinforcement***, the type that you have been reading about so far, occurs when the *arrival* of some stimulus following a response makes the response

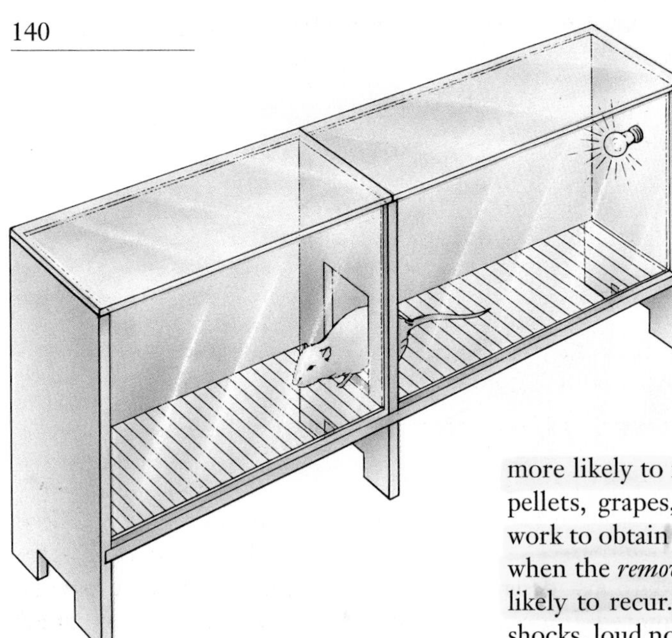

Figure 5.11 ***Two-compartment escape and avoidance apparatus***

Electric shocks can be provided to the floor of either compartment. If no signal precedes the shock, the animal learns to escape the shock by running from one compartment to the other when the shock comes on. If a signal (such as a light) precedes the shock in every trial, the animal learns to avoid the shock by running from one compartment to the other as soon as the signal comes on.

more likely to recur. The stimulus in this case is called a ***positive reinforcer***. Food pellets, grapes, money, words of praise, and everything else that organisms will work to obtain are positive reinforcers. ***Negative reinforcement***, in contrast, occurs when the *removal* of some stimulus following a response makes the response more likely to recur. The stimulus in this case is called a ***negative reinforcer***. Electric shocks, loud noises, unpleasant company, scoldings, and everything else that organisms will work to get away from are negative reinforcers. The one example of negative reinforcement discussed so far was Hefferline's thumb-twitch experiment. People learned to make the thumb-twitch response because each occurrence of that response resulted in temporary removal of unpleasant static. Notice that *positive* and *negative* here do *not* refer to the direction of change in the response rate—that increases in either case. Rather, they refer to whether the response causes a particular stimulus to arrive (positive) or be removed (negative).

An operant response that is reinforced by the removal of a negative reinforcer is called an ***escape response***. Psychologists often study escape learning in rats and other animals using a two-compartment apparatus such as the one depicted in Figure 5.11. When an electric shock comes on in the compartment where the rat is standing, the rat can escape by running into the other compartment. Most rats learn this response quite quickly. If conditions are then modified so that some signal, say, a light, comes on just before the shock, the animal will learn to run to the other compartment as soon as the light comes on, and before the shock is administered. The response is now an ***avoidance response***, because it enables the animal to avoid the shock entirely. Avoidance learning is extremely important in everyday life. We do not just learn to escape unpleasant or life-threatening situations that we find ourselves in, but we learn to avoid those situations in the future. Having capsized in rough seas and escaped, we learn to head for shore as soon as storm clouds appear, before the sea gets rough.

Punishment

■ **22.** ***How does punishment differ from reinforcement, and how do the two kinds of punishment parallel the two kinds of reinforcement?***

In Skinner's terminology, ***punishment*** is the opposite of reinforcement. It is the process through which the consequence of a response *decreases* the likelihood that that response will recur. As with reinforcement, punishment can be positive or negative. In *positive punishment*, the *arrival* of a stimulus, such as electric shock for a rat or scolding for a person, decreases the likelihood that the response will occur again. In *negative punishment*, the *removal* of a stimulus, such as taking food away from a hungry rat or money away from a person, decreases the likelihood that the response will occur again. Both types of punishment can be distinguished from extinction, which, you recall, is the decline in a previously reinforced response when it no longer produces any effect.

To picture the distinction between positive and negative punishment, and to see their relation to positive and negative reinforcement, look at Figure 5.12. The terms are easy to remember if you recall that the positive and negative always refer to the arrival or removal of a stimulus, and that reinforcement and punishment always refer to the direction of change in the likelihood that the response will recur.

Response causes stimulus to be	Response rate: Increases	Response rate: Decreases
Presented	**Positive reinforcement** (Lever press → Food pellet)	**Positive punishment** (Lever press → Shock)
Removed	**Negative reinforcement** (Lever press → Turns off shock)	**Negative punishment** (Lever press → Removes food)

Figure 5.12 ***Two types of reinforcement and two types of punishment***

Reinforcement (whether positive or negative) increases the response rate, and punishment (whether positive or negative) decreases the response rate. Positive and negative refer to whether the reinforcing stimulus arrives or is removed when the response is made.

The figure also makes it clear that the same stimuli that can serve as positive reinforcers when presented can serve as negative punishers when removed; and the same stimuli that can serve as positive punishers when presented can serve as negative reinforcers when removed. It is easy to think of the former as "desired" stimuli and the latter as "undesired," but Skinner urged us to avoid such mentalistic terms. He argued that the only way we can tell whether a stimulus is "desired" or "undesired" is by observing the manner in which it serves as a reinforcer or punisher to the individual in question, so the mentalistic terms add nothing to our understanding.

Punishment is interesting to many people because of its common use to control children's behavior. Skinner (1953) and many other psychologists (Newsom & others, 1983) have argued that caregivers would do better to make more deliberate use of positive reinforcement and less use of punishment.

■ **23.** ***What are some practical problems with the use of punishment to improve a child's behavior?***

Suppose a mother and father want to teach their child polite table manners. They might try to do this by punishing the child's impolite manners, but problems that could arise from this procedure include the following: (a) Punishment produces negative emotional reactions, such as anger or fear, which can lead to other unwanted behaviors at the dinner table or elsewhere. (b) Through classical conditioning, any stimuli present during the punishment—such as the parents themselves—may become conditioned stimuli for the negative emotions. This would be an unwanted side effect; parents certainly don't want their child to react negatively to them or to meals. (c) Through observational learning (to be described in the next section), the parents' use of punishment may inadvertently teach the child to use punishment to control others' behavior, which may have undesirable consequences. (d) Punishment may lead the child to refrain from those specific ill-mannered actions that have been punished, but it does not build well-mannered actions. The child may not show overtly rude manners, but may not behave very pleasantly, either. Thus, according to Skinner and others, a more effective method might be to provide positive reinforcement, such as praise or privileges, for showing increasingly good manners at each meal, until the bad manners are simply pushed out by the good.

Nevertheless, in some cases punishment can be an effective, perhaps necessary means to get rid of a particularly harmful form of behavior. As an example, Thomas Sajwaj and others (1974) have described a therapeutic use of punishment that enabled a baby girl to overcome a form of behavior called *rumination*, which involves compulsively moving the tongue to the back of the mouth to induce vomiting after swallowing any fluid or food. In other children, such behavior has sometimes led to death from dehydration or malnutrition. To get the baby girl to stop doing this, the therapists squirted lemon juice into her mouth (a mild, immediate punishment) each time she began to show the muscle movements that preceded vomiting. After several weeks of such treatment, she stopped producing those muscle movements and no longer vomited, and she eventually regained her health.

The Cognitive Perspective: Acquiring Information About the World

24. ***In the most general terms, how does the cognitive perspective differ from the behavioral perspective?***

The behavioral perspective, in the pure forms advocated by Watson and Skinner, avoids explanations in terms of unseen events in the mind or brain; it seeks instead to describe learning and other behavioral processes in terms of observable stimuli and responses. But many of Watson's and Skinner's contemporaries argued that unseen mental constructs that are inferred from observed behavior can be very useful in predicting and explaining what organisms will learn or do. They pointed out that many constructs in science—such as gravity and the idea of force—are not directly observable, but are inferred from the way things behave and are useful in predicting future behavior. Some of these contemporaries called themselves *liberalized behaviorists* or *S-O-R theorists*. The *O* in *S-O-R* stands for *organism*, or, more precisely, for some sort of interpretation of the stimulus that occurs inside the organism:

stimulus → interpretation → response

Today the approach advocated by those liberalized behaviorists is called ***cognitive psychology*** (see Chapter 1). Cognitive psychology is the attempt to understand the behavior of humans and other animals in terms of hypothetical mental entities that are inferred from observable behavior. You will read much more about cognitive psychology in later chapters (especially Chapters 9-14). The present discussion of this perspective concentrates on its contributions to the understanding of basic learning processes. First we will look at classical and operant conditioning from a cognitive perspective. Then we will turn to studies of place learning (learning where things are) and observational learning (learning by watching others).

Cognitive Views of Conditioning

According to cognitive theorists, many phenomena associated with classical and operant conditioning make sense only if we assume that a good deal of mental activity occurs before a response is made. This mental activity includes such events as interpretation of stimuli present, anticipation of future stimuli, and activation of knowledge about how to make certain stimuli appear. In the following paragraphs, we will look at some of the evidence for this way of thinking about conditioning.

The Cognitive Nature of Stimuli

As you have seen, a fundamental concept in the behaviorist's view of learning is that of the *stimulus*. But what precisely is a stimulus? Cognitive theorists argue that, to understand the role of stimuli in conditioning, one must consider not just their physical aspects but also their *meaning* to the individual being conditioned. To predict how a given individual will respond to a given stimulus, we must know how that individual will interpret that stimulus, and to know that is to know something about the structure of the subject's mind.

25. ***What is some evidence, from people and pigeons, that conditioned and discriminative stimuli are interpreted before they are responded to?***

Consider, for example, an experiment in classical conditioning conducted many years ago by Gregory Razran (1939), who used college students as subjects, a squirt of lemon juice into the mouth as the unconditioned stimulus, and printed words as conditioned stimuli. By pairing each word with a squirt of lemon juice, Razran conditioned students to salivate to the words *style*, *urn*, *freeze*, and *surf*. He then tested the students to see if the conditioned response would generalize to other words that had never been paired with lemon juice. Of most interest, he found that the students salivated more to the words *fashion*, *vase*, *chill*, and *wave* than to the words *stile*, *earn*, *frieze*, and *serf*! That is, the conditioned response generalized more to words that resembled the original conditioned stimuli in meaning than to words that resembled the originals in physical appearance or sound. Thus, the true conditioned stimuli were not the physical sights or sounds of the words, but the subjects' interpretation of them.

An even more dramatic demonstration of stimulus generalization based on word meaning was conducted by a Soviet psychologist (Volkova, 1953). First, a Russian schoolboy was conditioned to salivate to the Russian word for *good* and, by discrimination training, not to salivate to the word for *bad*. When the discrimination was well established, the boy was found to salivate copiously to such statements as *The Soviet Army was victorious*, and not at all to statements such as *The pupil was fresh to the teacher*. In other words, those statements that the boy interpreted as good elicited salivation, and those that he interpreted as bad did not. A child who had a different set of conceptions of what is good or bad might not have salivated to the statement about the Soviet Army, or might have salivated to the statement about the fresh student.

Figure 5.13 ***Tree pictures similar to those used to study concepts in pigeons***
Pigeons that had been trained to peck whenever a slide contained a tree, or part of a tree, pecked when they saw slides such as these and refrained from pecking when they saw similar slides that did not contain a tree.

Concepts in Pigeons

But we do not need to look to humans or language to make the point that stimuli are interpreted before they are responded to. Consider an experiment conducted by Richard Herrnstein (1979), who operantly conditioned pigeons to peck a key for grain, using slides depicting natural scenes as discriminative stimuli. Herrnstein divided the slides into two categories—those that had at least one tree or portion of a tree somewhere in the scene and those that didn't (see Figure 5.13). The pigeons received grain for pecking the key whenever a "tree" slide was shown and nothing when a "nontree" slide was shown. In the first phase, 80 slides were presented each day, 40 of which contained trees and 40 of which didn't. By the end of 5 days of such training—that is, after 5 presentations of all 80 slides—all of the birds were successfully discriminating between the two categories of slides, pecking when the slide contained a tree and not pecking otherwise.

Now, the question is, what did the pigeons learn in Herrnstein's experiment? Did they learn each slide as a separate stimulus, unrelated to the other slides, or did they learn a rule for categorizing the slides? Such a rule might be stated by a person in the following terms: "Respond whenever a slide includes a tree or part of a tree, and don't respond otherwise." To determine whether the pigeons had acquired such a rule, Herrnstein tested them with new slides and found that they immediately pecked at a much higher rate with new slides containing trees than with those that did not contain trees. In fact, the pigeons were as accurate with slides that they had never seen before as they were with slides that had been used during training. The birds had apparently based their responses on a ***concept*** of trees (Herrnstein, 1990). A concept, as the term is used here, can be defined as a rule for categorizing stimuli into groups. The pigeons' tree concept, in this case, must have guided their decision to peck or not to peck.

How might one describe the pigeons' tree concept? That is an interesting question, not easily answered. It is *not* the case, for example, that the pigeons simply learn to peck at slides containing a patch of green. Many of the nontree slides had green grass, and some of the tree slides were of fall or winter scenes in New England, where the trees had red and yellow leaves or none at all. In some cases only a small portion of a tree was apparent, or the tree was in the distant background. So the method by which the pigeons distinguished tree slides from nontree slides cannot be stated in *simple* stimulus terms, although ultimately it must have been based on the birds' analysis of the stimulus material (Astley & Wasserman, 1992). The point is that, even for pigeons and certainly for humans, to predict how an individual will respond to a stimulus one must know something of the concepts or rules by which the individual classifies stimuli into different groups.

S-R ***Theory of Classical Conditioning***

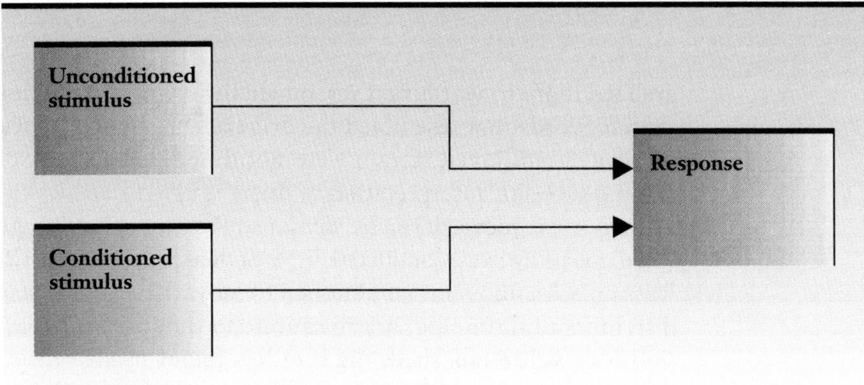

S-S ***Theory of Classical Conditioning***

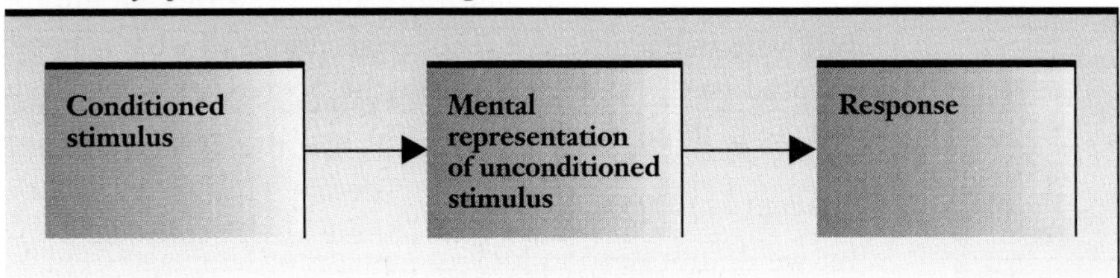

Figure 5.14 ***Comparison of*** **S-R** ***and*** **S-S** ***theories of classical conditioning***

According to the *S-R* theory, conditioning produces a direct bond between the conditioned stimulus and the response. According to the *S-S* theory, conditioning produces a bond between the conditioned stimulus and the unconditioned stimulus. Support for the *S-S* theory comes from experiments showing that weakening the unconditioned reflex (through habituation), after conditioning, also weakens the conditioned reflex.

Classical Conditioning Interpreted as Stimulus-Stimulus Association

What does an animal learn in classical conditioning? Watson (1924) and other early behaviorists believed that the animal learns a new reflex, that is, a new stimulus-response connection. From this view, Pavlov's conditioned dog salivated to the bell because of a direct, learned connection between the bell and salivation. This *stimulus-response (S-R) theory* of classical conditioning is diagrammed in the top part of Figure 5.14. Pavlov (1927/1960) himself, however, had a different theory. Consistent with the earlier associationist philosophers, Pavlov believed that the animal does not learn a direct stimulus-response connection, but rather learns a connection between two stimuli, the conditioned stimulus and the unconditioned stimulus. Because the bell and food have been paired in past experience, a physiological bond is formed between their representations in the brain, such that the sound of the bell now activates the part of the brain that was formerly activated by food, and that in turn elicits salivation. Using mental rather than physiological terms, we could say that the dog salivates to the bell because the bell sound elicits in the dog a mental representation of food (bell → mental representation of food → salivation). This *stimulus-stimulus (S-S) theory* of classical conditioning is illustrated in the bottom part of Figure 5.14.

■ **26.** ***How is it possible to test the*** **S-R** ***and*** **S-S** ***theories of classical conditioning, and how does an experiment involving habituation support the latter?***

Many experiments have been conducted over the years to test the *S-R* and *S-S* theories of classical conditioning, and the weight of evidence favors the latter, though both theories may be correct to some degree (Schwartz & Reisberg, 1991). As an illustration, consider an experiment conducted by Robert Rescorla (1973). Rescorla used rats as subjects, a loud sound as the unconditioned stimulus, and a signal light as the conditioned stimulus. The loud sound elicited freezing (a fear response in which the rats stand motionless) as an unconditioned response. By pairing the signal light with the loud sound, Rescorla conditioned the rats to freeze when the signal light came on. Now, the question was this: Did the rats freeze in response to the signal light because of a direct, learned connection between light and freezing, in accordance with the *S-R* theory (light → freezing)? Or did they freeze because of a learned connection between the light and the loud sound, in accordance with the *S-S* theory (light → mental representation of loud sound → freezing)?

To answer this question, Rescorla habituated the response to the loud sound in half of the conditioned rats. That is, he presented the loud sound many times without the signal light until they no longer froze in response to it. Then he again tested the rats with the signal light. Would the rats that no longer froze in response to the loud sound continue to freeze in response to the light? The *S-R* and *S-S* theories make different predictions. According to the *S-R* theory, the habituated rats should continue to freeze in response to the light because conditioning would have produced a direct connection between light and freezing. But according to the *S-S* theory, the habituated rats should not freeze in response to the light because conditioning would have produced a connection between the light and a representation of the loud sound, which itself no longer elicits freezing. Rescorla's results supported the *S-S* theory. Habituation to the sound greatly reduced the degree to which the rats froze in response to the light.

■ **27. *How does the construct of expectancy help explain the ways in which a conditioned response is different from an unconditioned response?***

Classical Conditioning Interpreted as Learned Expectancy and Prediction

The *S-S* theory of classical conditioning, by its nature, is more cognitive than the *S-R* theory. The *S-S* theory holds that the observed stimulus-response relation is mediated by an inner, mental representation of the original unconditioned stimulus. Cognitive theorists argue that the inner representation may be best understood as an *expectation* of the unconditioned stimulus. From this view, Pavlov's dog learned to *expect* food when it heard the bell.

The *expectancy theory* helps make sense of the observation that a conditioned response is often quite different from the unconditioned response. Consider again a dog being conditioned to a bell that precedes food. In response to food, the dog not only salivates, but also chews (if it is solid food) and swallows. Salivation becomes conditioned to the bell, but chewing and swallowing usually do not. Moreover, the bell comes to elicit not only salivation, but also responses that do not usually occur in response to the food-in-mouth stimulus—such as tail wagging, food begging, and looking in the direction of the usual source of food (Jenkins & others, 1978). According to the expectancy theory, all of these responses, including salivation, occur *not* because they were previously elicited by the unconditioned stimulus, but because they are the dog's responses to the *expectation* of food:

bell → expectation of food → tail wagging, food begging, salivation, etc.

Expectancy

There is nothing inscrutable about this young tiger cat. The sound of the can being attached to the opener permits her to predict the arrival of food. Her response is not identical to her response to food itself, but one of rapt attention.

Rescorla (1988) has summed up his cognitive view of classical conditioning with the following words: "[Classical] conditioning is not a stupid process by which the organism willy-nilly forms associations between any two stimuli that happen to co-occur. Rather, the organism is best seen as an information seeker using logical and perceptual relations among events, along with its own preconceptions, to form a sophisticated representation of its world."

Support for Rescorla's view comes from research showing that classical conditioning occurs only, or at least mainly, when the new stimulus provides information that the animal can use to *predict* the arrival of the unconditioned stimulus, and thereby prepare itself for that event. Here are three classes of such findings:

■ **28. *What are three different conditions in which the pairing of a new stimulus with an unconditioned stimulus does not result in classical conditioning? How do these observations support a cognitive view of conditioning?***

1. ***Ineffectiveness of simultaneous and backward conditioning*** Classical conditioning is most effective if the conditioned stimulus slightly precedes the unconditioned stimulus, and commonly doesn't occur at all if the conditioned stimulus comes either simultaneously with or just after the unconditioned stimulus (Schwartz & Reisberg, 1991). This observation makes sense if the animal is actively seeking predictive information; a stimulus that does not precede the unconditioned stimulus is useless as a predictor, and thus is ignored by the animal.
2. ***Ineffectiveness of conditioning to stimuli that have been presented often without the unconditioned stimulus*** Not all stimuli that are present just prior to an unconditioned stimulus become conditioned stimuli. Conditioning is much

more likely to occur to a *new* stimulus than to one that was previously presented many times in the absence of the unconditioned stimulus (Rescorla & Wagner, 1972; Rescorla, 1988). Thus, conditioning is not a function just of the pairing of the conditioned and unconditioned stimulus, but also of the reliability with which the former predicts the latter. It is as if the animal learns to ignore stimuli that have been unreliable predictors, and to attend only to reliable predictors and novel stimuli that may turn out to be reliable predictors.

3. ***Ineffectiveness of conditioning when the animal already has a good predictor*** A number of experiments have shown that if one conditioned stimulus reliably precedes an unconditioned stimulus, the animal will not become conditioned to a new conditioned stimulus that is presented simultaneously with the first one. This failure of conditioning is called the ***blocking effect***; the already-conditioned stimulus *blocks* conditioning to the new stimulus. For example, Leon Kamin (1969) showed that if a sound reliably precedes the onset of a shock, and on later trials a light is added so that both the light and sound come on simultaneously just before the shock, a rat does *not* develop a conditioned response to the light. A cognitive interpretation of this is that the rat has already solved the problem of predicting shock (by listening for the sound) and has no reason to learn a new way of predicting it. Only if the sound were to become an unreliable predictor would the animal look for another predictor, and in that case the animal does learn to respond to the light.

Cognitive psychologists often emphasize that their use of terms such as *expectation* and *prediction* does not imply anything mystical. To illustrate this, and to develop explicit theories of how such processes might work, some cognitive psychologists simulate the processes of expectation and prediction with computer models (Commons & others, 1991). The three classes of findings in the list above, for example, are actually rather easy to simulate with a computer (I have done it, just to convince myself that it is possible).

Operant Conditioning Interpreted as Means-End Knowledge

Historically, theories about operant conditioning have paralleled those about classical conditioning. According to the *S-R* theory, held by many behaviorists (Guthrie, 1952), operant conditioning entails the strengthening of a bond between the reinforced response and stimuli that are present just before the response is made (the discriminative stimuli). Thus, for a rat learning to press a lever in a Skinner box, the learned connection could be described as:

stimuli inside Skinner box → lever press

Or, if a more specific discriminative stimulus, such as a tone, is used, it could be described as:

tone → lever press

According to this view, the reinforcer, which follows the response, is involved in learning only insofar as it helps stamp in the connection between the antecedent stimuli and the response. Other theorists, however, have emphasized the importance of the learned *S-S* relationship between the discriminative stimuli and the reinforcer (Mowrer, 1960; Spence, 1956), or the learned *R-S* relationship between the response and the reinforcing stimulus (Mackintosh & Dickinson, 1979).

■ **29. *How can the view that operant conditioning involves means-end knowledge be experimentally tested? What are the results of one such test?***

Research now indicates that *all* of these relationships are learned and are integrated into the animal's store of information in a way that allows the animal to obtain reinforcers efficiently (Dickinson, 1989; Rescorla 1991). In an early cognitive description of operant conditioning, Edward Tolman (1959) discussed it as the learning of *means-end relationships*. A means-end relationship is the animal's knowl-

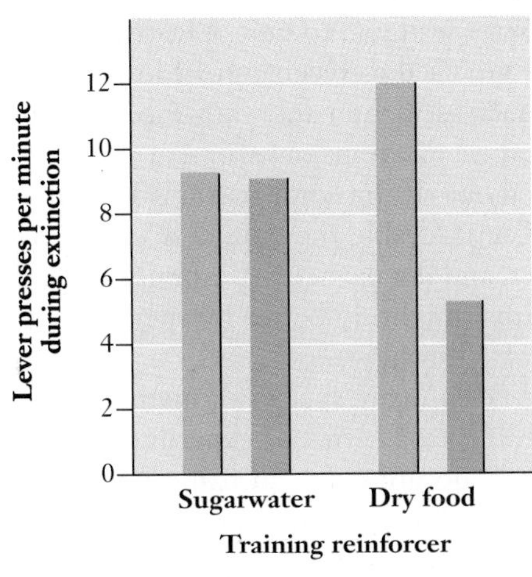

Figure 5.15 ***Evidence that rats learn what reinforcer a response produces***

All of the rats were trained to press the lever when hungry. Some had received drops of sugarwater as their training reinforcer, and others had received dry food pellets. When tested under extinction conditions (no reinforcer given), the animals that had been trained with sugarwater made about the same number of responses whether they were thirsty or hungry. In contrast, those that had been trained with food pellets made fewer responses when thirsty than when hungry. These results suggest that the rats had a conception of the reinforcer that the response would produce and knew whether it would satisfy both thirst and hunger or only hunger. (Adapted from Dickinson & Dawson, 1987.)

edge or belief that in a particular situation a particular response will have a particular effect. Thus, according to Tolman, if a rat is reinforced with a particular kind of food for pressing a lever when a tone is on, the rat acquires the knowledge that pressing the lever when the tone is on will produce that food. In the future, the occurrence of the tone does not automatically produce a lever press response as the *S-R* theory would hold, but rather activates the animal's knowledge that a lever press will bring a certain food. The animal can then press the lever or not, depending on its current disposition toward the food. Thus, in Tolman's view, the rat's behavior is best understood as follows:

tone → knowledge that lever press will now bring a certain kind of food → decision to press lever or not depending on whether the food is desired

In support of this cognitive view, animals that have learned an operant response have been shown to vary their response rate in ways that are predictable on the premise that the animals have learned a means-end relationship (Dickinson, 1989; Rescorla, 1991). For example, in one experiment, some hungry rats were trained to press a lever for sugarwater and others were trained to press a lever for dry food pellets as a reinforcer (Dickinson & Dawson, 1987). Later all rats were tested under extinction conditions (no reinforcer given), after having been deprived of either food or water. The interesting result was that when tested in the new drive state (thirst), those that had previously been reinforced with sugarwater (a substance that would satisfy thirst as well as hunger) pressed at a high rate, and those that had previously been reinforced with dry pellets (which would not satisfy thirst) pressed at a low rate (see Figure 5.15). The most direct way to explain this difference is to assume that the rats had acquired knowledge of the kind of reinforcer they would receive for pressing the lever and were able to use that knowledge to decide whether or not the reinforcer would satisfy their current drive state. As in all cognitive theories, there is no supposition here that the rats are conscious of such knowledge and decision, or that any mystical process is involved. A computer could be programmed to behave in the same way.

Reward Contrast Effects in Operant Conditioning

■ **30.** ***How are reward contrast effects explained from a cognitive perspective, and what is the evidence that they depend on brain structures not present in fish and reptiles?***

Many other phenomena associated with operant conditioning are consistent with the idea that subjects learn to expect a certain reinforcer for making a certain response. One class of these phenomena are *reward contrast effects*, which involve shifts in the response rate when the size of the reward changes. Suppose one group of rats is trained to press a lever for relatively large pellets of food as reinforcers, and another group is trained to press for smaller pellets. As you might predict, rats in the first group would typically respond at a somewhat faster rate than those in the second. So far, this is consistent with *S-R* theory. Presumably, the *S-R* connection built by the larger reinforcer is stronger than that built by the smaller reinforcer, resulting in faster response rates in the first group. But now suppose the rats receiving the large reinforcer are suddenly shifted to the small reinforcer. According to the *S-R* model, they should continue, at least for a while, to respond at a higher rate than the other rats, because of the stronger *S-R* connection built during the first phase of the experiment. But what actually happens is the opposite. Rats shifted from a large to small reinforcer show a sharp drop in their response rate, to a slower rate than shown by rats that had been in the small-reinforcer condition all along. This illustrates the ***negative contrast effect***. Conversely, rats shifted from a small to large reinforcer show an increase in their response rate, to a higher rate than that of rats that had been in the large-reinforcer condition all along. This illustrates the ***positive contrast effect***.

An analogy between these effects in animals and effects of pay shifts in people is easily drawn. If you have been getting $1 per page for typing term papers, you will probably be delighted to discover that your pay is now $2 per page, and you may type with renewed vigor; but if you have been getting $4 per page, that same discovery (that you are now only getting $2) may lead you to quit. Clearly, our experience of reward size is relative to what we are used to receiving. From a cognitive perspective, these contrast effects—in rats as in humans—are explained by assuming that the animal (a) has learned to expect a certain reward, and (b) is able to compare the present reward to the expected one. If the comparison is favorable, the animal increases its response rate, and if unfavorable the animal decreases its rate. The animal is constantly out to do better, and if a particular response leads to less reinforcement than it did before, the animal might do better by spending less time at it and more time looking for reinforcers elsewhere.

Reward contrast effects have been observed in many species of mammals and in pigeons (Flaherty, 1982). However, according to a series of experiments conducted by M. E. Bitterman (1975), such effects do not occur in fish and reptiles. For example, in one of Bitterman's experiments, fish trained to push a key for a large reinforcer (forty worms per response) and then switched to a small reinforcer (four worms per response) continued, after the switch, to respond at a faster rate than fish that were initially trained with the small reinforcer. In certain other ways, too, Bitterman found that the behavior of fish and reptiles conformed more closely to *S-R* predictions than did the behaviors of mammals and birds. Perhaps, in the evolution of mammals and birds from their reptilelike ancestors, changes occurred in the brain that permitted more complex cognitive processes, including the ability to compare present rewards with past ones, and these were added on to a basic *S-R* learning mechanism. This view finds support in an experiment showing that rats treated with amobarbital, a drug that reduces neural activity in some of the higher parts of the brain, failed, like Bitterman's fish and reptiles, to show the negative contrast effect, while undrugged rats clearly showed it (Rosen & others, 1967). The same is true of immature rats whose higher brain structures are not fully developed (Amsel, 1986).

Vacation reading

This young man's absorption in his book suggests that he deeply enjoys reading. Research on overjustification predicts that if he were rewarded for this activity, he might begin to see it as work.

31. ***How does the overjustification effect illustrate a limitation in the use of reward to promote certain behaviors in people?***

The Overjustification Effect

In humans, rewards can affect the likelihood of engaging in a particular form of behavior by changing the person's understanding of the meaning of that behavior. Consider an experiment conducted with nursery school children as subjects (Lepper & Greene, 1978). Children in one group were rewarded with attractive "Good Player" certificates for drawing with felt-tipped pens. This had the immediate effect of leading them to spend more time at this activity than did children in the other group (who were not rewarded). Later, however, when certificates were no longer given, the previously rewarded children showed a sharp drop in their use of the pens—to a level well below that of children in the unrewarded group.

Other researchers have found that the drop in performance due to a period of reward occurs only for tasks that are initially seen as ends in themselves, that is, as the kinds of activities that one engages in for one's own pleasure, rather than for some other end (Newman & Layton, 1984). This decline is called the ***overjustification effect*** because the reward presumably provides an unneeded justification for engaging in the behavior. The result, according to the usual cognitive interpretation, is that the person comes to see the task as work (the kind of thing that one does for external rewards) rather than play (the kind of thing one does for its own sake). The overjustification effect suggests that some rewards used in schools might have negative long-term effects. For example, rewarding children for reading might cause them to think of reading as work rather than fun, which would lead them to read less on their own. The broader point is that one must take into account the cognitive consequences of rewards in predicting their long-term effects.

Place Learning

Much of the early impetus for a more cognitive view of learning came from research by Edward Tolman and his students, using rats in mazes. Behaviorists at Tolman's time (the 1920s-1940s) often interpreted maze learning in stimulus-response terms. They believed that the animal learns a sequence of responses—such as turn right, go forward, turn left—each signaled by stimuli that are present at the critical choice points in the maze. Tolman's research led him to reject that view. He proposed instead that animals allowed to explore either a maze or a more natural terrain do not learn a specific sequence of responses, but rather acquire a ***cognitive map***—a mental representation of the spatial layout of the maze or terrain. He also proposed that animals acquire that representation just from exploring, whether they find any rewards or not.

■ ***32. How did Tolman show that rats use cognitive maps and that they learn such maps whether they are rewarded or not?***

Tolman's Evidence That Animals Learn Cognitive Maps

Tolman and his students showed that, when faced with a change in their starting place, or with blockades placed in their usual routes, rats behave *as if* they are able to consult a map and work out the best available route to the goal (Tolman, 1948). In one experiment, for example, Tolman and Honzik (1930a) used the maze depicted in Figure 5.16, which contains three possible routes from the start box to the goal box (and food). After sufficient experience, rats showed a strong preference for Route 1 (the shortest), a weaker preference for Route 2 (the next shortest), and weakest for Route 3 (the longest).

In the critical phase of the experiment, Route 1 was blocked at one of two points, as shown in Figure 5.16. When the block was at Point A, most rats ran down Route 1, reached the block, and then went back and took Route 2. But when the block was at Point B, most rats ran down Route 1, reached the block, and then went back and took Route 3, previously their least preferred route. By inspecting Figure 5.16 (which literally is a map), you can see that this is exactly what an intelligent individual with maplike knowledge of the maze would be expected to do in this situation. The block at Point B blocks Routes 1 and 2, so now only Route 3 leads to the goal. According to Tolman, such behavior—occurring as it did the first time the rats were faced with the blockade—cannot be interpreted in terms of learned stimulus-response habits, but must be understood as insight based on maplike knowledge of the maze.

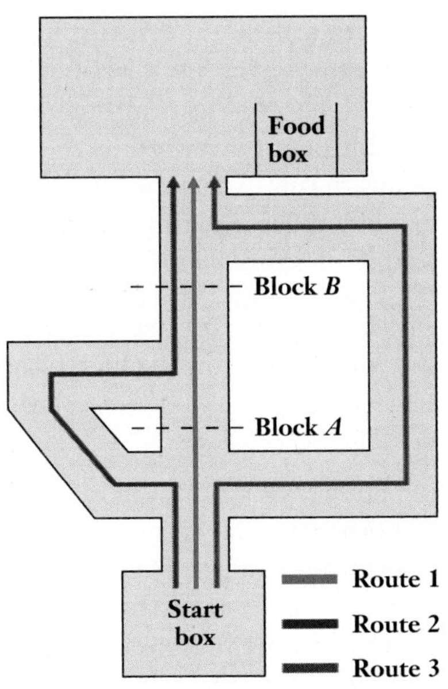

Figure 5.16 ***Maze used to demonstrate insightful use of cognitive maps***

Rats well trained in this maze normally took Route 1, the most direct route to the food. When a block was placed at Point *A*, they ran back and took Route 2, the shortest unblocked route. When a block was placed at Point *B*, rather than *A*, they ran back and took Route 3, the only unblocked route. Most rats made these adaptive responses on the first trial that the block appeared, which led Tolman and Honzik to conclude that the rats had spatial knowledge (a cognitive map) of the maze, which they could use intelligently. (Adapted from Tolman & Honzik, 1930a.)

Tolman's Evidence That Place Learning Does Not Require Reward

Do animals learn the spatial layout of their environment only when they receive some reward, such as food, for finding a particular location, or do they learn it even without such rewards? To answer that question, Tolman and Honzik (1930b) tested three groups of rats in a complex maze under different reward conditions. Group 1 received one trial per day in the maze with no food or other reward in the goal box. As expected, rats in this group showed little improvement from day to day in the time it took them to reach the goal box (the goal box contained no "goal" for them). Group 2 received one trial per day with food in the goal box. As expected, this group improved considerably from day to day. The most interesting group was Group 3. These rats received one trial per day with no reward for 10 days, like Group 1, but beginning on the eleventh day they received one trial per day with a food reward, like Group 2. These rats improved dramatically between Days 11 and 12. On Day 11 they were no better than the other unrewarded group (Group 1), but on Day 12, after just one experience with the reward, they were as fast at reaching the goal box as the rats that had been rewarded all along (see Figure 5.17).

On the basis of this and other experiments, Tolman (1948) argued that rewards affect what animals *do* more than what they *learn*. Animals learn the location of dis-

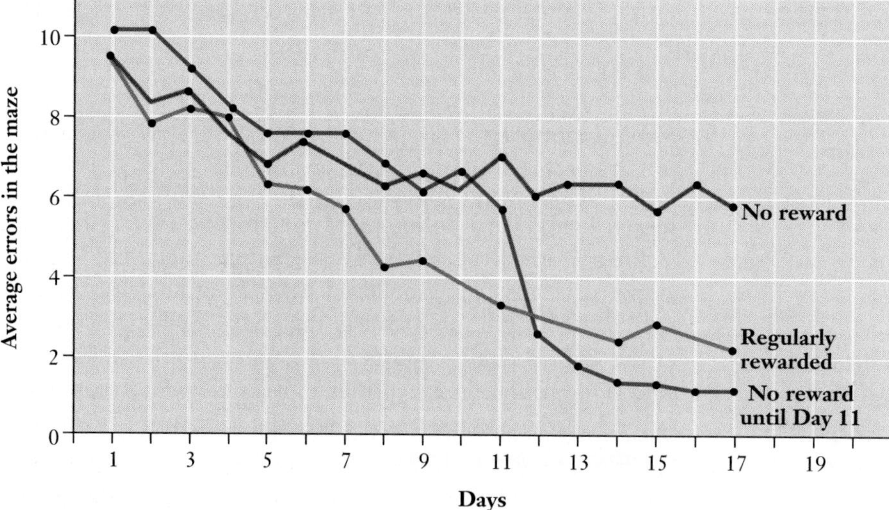

Figure 5.17 ***Latent learning of a maze***

Each rat received one trial per day in the maze, with or without a food reward in the goal box. The group that received its first reward on Day 11 performed as well on Day 12 (and thereafter) as the group that had received a reward every day. From this, Tolman and Honzik concluded that the rats had learned the spatial layout of the maze even without a reward, but the rats did not use that knowledge until the changed conditions made it worthwhile for them to do so. (From Tolman & Honzik, 1930b.)

tinctive places in their environment whether or not they have ever found rewards there, but they do not run directly to those places unless they have found rewards there. Tolman used the term ***latent learning*** to refer to learning that is not immediately demonstrated in the animal's behavior. In the experiment just described, the rats in Group 3 learned the maze in the first ten trials, but that learning remained *latent*, not manifested in their behavior, until the addition of a reward in the goal box gave the rats a reason to use their cognitive maps to run to that location.

Tolman's conclusion that animals acquire maplike representations of the terrains they explore has been confirmed in hundreds of subsequent experiments, with species ranging from insects to humans (Gallistel, 1990). We will consider some of this more recent research later, near the end of the chapter.

Observational Learning

A traditional drink

Chimpanzees in certain colonies crumple leaves to form efficient sponges for drinking water. This tradition apparently passes from generation to generation within a colony through observational learning.

If you look at learning as it occurs in everyday human life, you cannot help but notice that people learn to a great extent by watching other people. Imagine what life would be like if such skills as driving a car or performing surgery were learned purely by trial and error! Fortunately, people learn such skills partly by observing closely and mimicking the behavior of those who have already mastered them. On a grander scale, learning by watching others seems to be a prerequisite for human culture. The skills and rituals acquired by each generation are passed on to the next not so much because the older generation deliberately trains the younger (though that is part of it), but more because members of the younger generation intently observe their elders to learn to behave as they do. Learning by watching others is called ***observational learning***.

Observational learning is especially apparent in humans, but it can be seen to some degree in other creatures as well. It is well known that apes "ape" one another. Experiments have shown that kittens learn more quickly to press a lever for food if they have seen their mother do so than if they have not (Chesler, 1969), and that even octopuses can learn an operant discrimination task by watching an already-trained member of their species perform it (Fiorito & Scotto, 1992). Some researchers have argued that the mechanism of such learning is not the same as observational learning in humans (Galef, 1992), but nobody denies that animals do learn by observing others of their kind.

Observational Learning of Specific Skills and General Behavioral Styles

Albert Bandura (1977)—the psychologist who, over the years, has most vigorously studied observational learning in humans—has emphasized that people observe others to learn not just specific motor skills (such as driving a car or performing surgery), but also more general modes or styles of behaving. When you enter a new situation, you probably look around to see what others are doing before doing much yourself. When you do begin to act, you may mimic rather precisely some of the actions you have observed—such as the maneuvers required to coax a cup of coffee from the newfangled coffeemaker in the room. But beyond that (unless you are a clown) you probably don't imitate many of the exact actions of others. Rather, you adopt a general style of behavior that fits with what seems to be acceptable in the setting.

■ **33.** ***How did Bandura demonstrate two different functions of observational learning in experiments with children?***

Bandura has demonstrated both of these functions of observational learning—acquiring specific actions and learning general styles of behavior—in experiments with kindergarten children. In one experiment, one group of children observed an adult behaving very aggressively toward a large inflated Bobo doll (Bandura, 1969). The aggressive actions included specific verbal insults and physical acts, such as banging the doll with a mallet, hurling it down, kicking it, and bombarding it with balls. A second group watched the adult model behave in a gentle manner toward the doll; and a third group was not shown any model. Later, when each child was allowed to play in the room with a variety of toys, including the Bobo doll, those in the first group behaved more aggressively, and those in the second group behaved more gently, than those in the third group. The children in the first group not only mimicked many of the same aggressive actions that they had observed in the adult model, but also improvised many new aggressive actions of their own, and directed them toward other toys as well as toward the Bobo doll. The children had learned not only specific ways of being aggressive, but also the more general message that an appropriate way to play in this particular playroom is to act aggressively.

"The Far Side" cartoons by Gary Larson are reprinted by permission of Chronicle Features, San Francisco.

Bandura's Cognitive Theory of Observational Learning

Bandura's theory of observational learning is an explicitly cognitive one. Just as Tolman posited that rats actively explore mazes to develop cognitive maps, Bandura (1977, 1986) proposes that people actively observe the behavior of other people to gain knowledge about the kinds of things that people do. Bandura theorizes that, to understand observational learning, one must consider four interacting mental processes. These are: (1) *attention*—the learner must perceive the model and, for one reason or another, find the model to be interesting; (2) *memory*—the learner must encode the information obtained from observing the model in a form that can be used at a later time; (3) *motor control*—the learner must be able to use this coded information to guide his or her own actions; and (4) *motivation*—the learner must have some reason or inducement to perform the modeled actions. These processes must be involved in *any* complex form of behavior that depends on information gained from the environment. The four components of the theory—attention, memory, motor control, and motivation—are discussed extensively in later chapters.

■ **34.** ***How does Bandura's theory illustrate the idea that learning cannot be understood in isolation from other mental processes?***

The Ecological Perspective: Filling the Blanks in Species-Specific Behavior Patterns

■ **35.** ***How does the ecological perspective differ from the behavioral and cognitive perspectives?***

The behavioral and cognitive approaches to learning both emphasize processes that are assumed to operate across a wide range of learning situations, and for that reason they are both considered to be part of a *general-process perspective*. Behaviorists have looked for general laws related to classical and operant conditioning, expressible in terms of stimuli and responses, that apply to all sorts of learning situations. And cognitivists have tried to describe general mental constructs, such as expectancies, that likewise apply to all sorts of learning situations. The alternative to the general process perspective is sometimes called the *specific-process perspective*, though it is more often called the ***ecological perspective*** (Johnston & Pietrewicz, 1985)

According to the ecological perspective, learning must be understood in relation to the natural environment, or ecology, in which a species evolved. Through natural selection, different species of animals acquired different instinctive species-specific behavior patterns (discussed in Chapter 4) that help them survive and reproduce in their natural environments. The mechanisms that promote many such behaviors evolved in such a way that they are not rigid, but can be modified in response to specific aspects of the animal's experience. Thus, the abilities of animals to find food, avoid predators, find mates, raise their young, and do whatever else they must to survive and reproduce depend on inherited behavioral tendencies coupled with inherited means to modify or refine those tendencies. The latter, taken together, make up the collection of mechanisms called *learning*. Many learning mechanisms evolved to meet specific survival-related purposes, and to understand how these mechanisms work we must think about them in relation to those purposes.

In Chapter 4 the white-crowned sparrow's ability to learn its parents' song and the indigo bunting's ability to learn the night sky were cited as examples of specific learning mechanisms designed to supplement specific instinctual tendencies. In Chapter 12 the idea that human language is acquired through a unique, specialized learning ability will be discussed. Now we will look at the learning of food aversions and preferences, and then, more briefly, at a few examples of other specialized learning mechanisms.

Learning What to Eat

For some animals, learning what to eat is not a problem. Koalas, for instance, eat only the leaves of eucalyptus trees. Through natural selection, Koalas evolved a food-identifying mechanism that tells them eucalyptus leaves are food and everything else is not. That simplifies their problem of food selection, but if eucalyptuses were to vanish so would the koalas. Other animals are more flexible in their diets. Most flexible of all are omnivorous creatures, such as rats and humans, which treat almost all organic matter as potential food and must *learn* what is safe to eat. Such animals have, through natural selection, acquired special mechanisms for learning to identify healthful foods and to avoid potential poisons.

Food-Aversion Learning

If rats become ill after eating some novel-tasting food, they will subsequently avoid that food (Garcia & others, 1972). In experiments demonstrating this, researchers induce illness by adding a toxic substance to the food or by administering a drug or a high dose of x-rays after the food is eaten. Similarly, people who by chance get sick after eating some unusual food often develop a long-term aversion to the food (Bernstein & Borson, 1986; Logue, 1988). For years as a child, I hated the taste and smell of a particular breakfast cereal, because one of the first times I ate it happened to precede, by a few hours, my developing a bad case of a stomach flu. I knew, intellectually, that the cereal wasn't the cause of my illness, but that didn't help. The learning mechanism kicked in automatically and made me detest that cereal.

■ **36. *What are two ways in which food-aversion learning differs from typical examples of classical conditioning?***

Many psychologists choose to describe such cases of food-aversion learning in terms of classical conditioning. In those terms, the x-ray treatment (or whatever else is used to induce illness) serves as the unconditioned stimulus for the feeling of illness or nausea, and the taste and smell of the food become conditioned stimuli for that feeling. But John Garcia, the researcher who has most actively studied food-aversion learning over the past 25 years, argues that such learning is quite different from standard cases of classical conditioning (Garcia & others, 1989).

For example, in typical cases of classical conditioning, such as those studied by Pavlov, conditioning occurs only when the unconditioned stimulus follows immediately (within a few seconds) after the conditioned stimulus. Yet food-aversion learning has been demonstrated even when the x-rays were administered as much as 24 hours after the animals had eaten the food (Etscorn & Stephens, 1973). As another example, in typical cases of classical conditioning almost any kind of detectable stimulus can serve as the conditioned stimulus, but in food-aversion learning the stimulus must be a distinctive taste or smell (and taste works better than smell). Rats that become ill after eating a particular food subsequently avoid food that tastes or smells like what they had eaten, even if it looks different; but they do not avoid food that looks like what they had eaten if it tastes and smells different (Garcia & others, 1968; 1989).

The distinguishing characteristics of food-aversion learning make excellent sense in terms of the function of such learning in the natural environment. In general, poisons and spoiled foods do not make an individual ill immediately, but only after many minutes or hours. Moreover, it is the chemical quality of a food, detectable in its taste and smell, not the visual quality, that affects health. For example, a food that has begun to rot and makes an animal sick may look just like one that has not begun to rot, but its taste and smell are quite different. Thus, to be effective, a learning mechanism for food aversion must tolerate long delays and be tuned especially to those sensory qualities that correspond with the food's chemistry.

Food-Preference Learning

■ **37.** ***How might rats learn which food contains a needed vitamin?***

The other side of the coin from avoiding harmful foods is that of specifically choosing foods that satisfy a nutritional requirement. In a series of experiments on food-preference learning, researchers deprived rats of thiamine (one of the B vitamins, essential for health) for a period of time, and then offered them a choice of foods, only one of which contained thiamine (Overmann, 1976; Rozin & Kalat, 1971). Each food had a different flavor, and thiamine—which itself has no flavor—was added to a different food for different rats. The result was that, within a few days of experience with the foods, most rats strongly preferred the thiamine-containing food.

How did the rats "figure out" which food contained the thiamine? Close inspection of their eating patterns suggests a possible answer (Rozin & Kalat, 1971). When first presented with the choices, a rat usually did not eat all of them, but rather ate just one or two. Then, typically after several hours, the rat would switch to a different food or two. Such behavior—eating just one or two foods at a time—seems ideally suited for isolating particular foods that lead to an increase or decrease in health. If the rat had sampled all of the foods at once, it would have no basis for knowing which had affected its health. Thus, just as rats can learn to associate the taste of a food with subsequent illness and thereafter avoid that food, they may also (to a lesser extent) be able to associate a taste with a subsequent improvement in health, and thereafter prefer that food (Rozin & Schull, 1988).

A Food-Selection Experiment with Human Infants

■ **38.** ***How are Davis's observations with human babies similar to results of food-selection experiments with rats? Why should we be cautious in interpreting Davis's study?***

In the 1920s, before food-selection experiments with rats had been performed, a pediatrician named Clara Davis performed a bold experiment on food selection with human infants—so bold, in fact, that it would probably not pass the ethics review board of a modern research institution (which helps explain why the experiment has never been repeated). The subjects were newly weaned baby boys whose mothers consented to their participation, and the object was to determine whether the babies would feed themselves a nutritionally balanced diet if they could choose their own foods (Davis, 1928). For 6 months or longer, beginning at the age of 35 weeks, the babies lived in the children's ward of a hospital. At each meal a tray containing about a dozen different foods was placed before each infant. The choices were all natural, wholesome foods—including cereals, fruits, ground meats, fish, eggs, and vegetables—but no single food contained all of the needed nutrients. To remain healthy, the infants would have to select a variety. At first a nurse had to help the babies eat, but she was allowed to feed a baby only the food that he had chosen through reaching or pointing. Within a few weeks, all of the babies had learned to feed themselves, usually with their fingers, and the nurse's assistance was no longer needed.

The results of the experiment can be summarized as follows: The babies all developed clear food preferences, but the preferences varied from time to time such that over the long run each infant ate a nutritionally balanced diet. An infant would usually eat just two or three foods in quantity at any given meal and might stick to those for as long as a week, but then would switch to other foods and stick with them for a similar period. One baby, who had rickets (due to lack of vitamin D) at the beginning of the experiment actually self-selected cod-liver oil until his rickets was cured, and stopped selecting it after that. All in all, the babies' behavior was rather similar to that of rats in food-selection experiments. It was as if they were following a logic that goes like this: Eat only a few foods at a given time; if you feel well later, stick with those foods, but if you begin to feel less well, switch. Of course, if the babies could talk, they would probably tell us a different logic, something like: "Last week I loved the applesauce, but this week it tastes awful and the mashed eggs are great."

Observational learning has its limits

Children acquire the food preferences of their culture through observing their elders, but sometimes it takes a while. This young boy may enjoy most of the dishes at this family celebration, but he holds his nose to the gefilte fish—a fish preparation that has a very fishy smell.

We should be cautious, however, in interpreting these results. The observation that the boy with rickets self-selected cod liver oil is made less surprising by evidence that (contrary to popular opinion) some young children like the taste of cod liver oil, whether they have a vitamin D deficiency or not (Richter, 1942–1943). It is also possible that the changes in the infants' food preferences arose not from associating tastes with changes in their health, but simply from their becoming bored with a food they had eaten for several days (Galef, 1991). Moreover, the experiment probably would not have worked had unnaturally sweet foods, like fudge bars or sweetened cereals, been included among the choices. Even rats have great difficulty learning which food is good for them if one or more of the deficient foods is laced with sugar (Beck & Galef, 1989). From an ecological perspective, that is not surprising. The food-learning systems in rats and humans evolved long before refined sugar and fudge bars were invented.

The Role of Social Learning in Food Selection

■ ***39. What evidence, with rats and people, points to the importance of social learning in food selection?***

In addition to the individual trial-and-error mechanisms described above, rats learn what to eat from each other. Newly weaned wild rats do not go out on their own to forage, but rather follow older rats in the colony around and eat what they eat, until their own food habits are well established (Galef, 1985). Through this means, they can avoid even tasting a food that older animals have already learned is poisonous (Galef & Clark, 1971) and can choose, from the beginning, a nutritious food that older animals have already learned to prefer (Beck & Galef, 1989). Adult rats are also strongly influenced by each other's food choices. Bennett Galef (1990) has found that rats in a colony sniff around the mouth of a rat that has recently eaten, and, when subsequently presented with a choice of foods, strongly prefer the food they had smelled in the demonstrator rat's breath.

We humans, presumably, don't learn food preferences by smelling each other's breath, but we are certainly influenced by other kinds of observations about what those around us eat. In one experiment, children between 1 and 4 years old were more willing to taste a new food if they saw an adult eat it first than if they had never seen anyone eat it (Harper & Sanders, 1975). Cross-culturally, foods treated as a delicacy by one group are often considered by other groups to be disgusting.

Summary of Rules for Learning What to Eat

■ **40.** ***In sum, what has natural selection imparted to young omnivores about food selection?***

Suppose you were a wise teacher of young omnivorous animals and wanted to equip your charges with a few rules for food selection that could be applied in any environment, no matter what potential food materials were available. Two that you would probably come up with are: (1) When possible, eat what your elders eat. Such food is probably safe, as evidenced by the fact that your elders have most likely been eating it for some time and are still alive. (2) When you eat a new food, remember its taste and smell. If you don't feel sick within a few hours, continue choosing foods of that taste and smell, but if you do feel sick, avoid such foods.

Notice that these rules don't specify just what to eat, but rather specify *how to learn* what to eat. The first rule specifies a variety of observational learning, and the second specifies a particular kind of associative learning in which the stimuli to pay attention to are spelled out in a way that makes the learning most efficient. As you have just seen, rats in fact do behave in accordance with these rules, and young humans may also. Of course, we assume that these rules have been imparted not by a wise teacher of young omnivores, but by natural selection, which has shaped the brain to operate in accordance with the rules. Again, over evolution, animals have acquired instincts to learn about food in particular ways.

Other Examples of Selective Learning Abilities

Food selection is by no means the only functional area in which special learning abilities have apparently come about through evolution. Here are some other well-studied examples.

Innate Biases in Fear-Related Learning

■ **41.** ***What is some evidence that people and monkeys are biologically predisposed to learn to fear some things more easily than other things?***

Do you remember the demonstration by Watson and Rayner, in which little Albert was conditioned to fear a white rat through pairing the rat with a loud noise? Several years later, Elsie Bregman (1934), a graduate student working with Thorndike, tried to repeat that demonstration with one important modification. Instead of using a rat as the conditioned stimulus, she used various inanimate objects, including wooden blocks and pieces of cloth. Despite numerous attempts, with fifteen different infants as subjects, she found no evidence of conditioning. What are we to make of this apparent discrepancy? One possibility, suggested by Martin Seligman (1971), is that people are biologically predisposed to classify certain kinds of objects—rats among them—as potentially dangerous, and to associate those objects, but not others, with fear-provoking events that they experience.

More recently, Susan Mineka and her colleagues have shown that rhesus monkeys are not afraid of snakes when first exposed to them, but apparently have an innate bias to learn to fear them very easily. In one experiment, monkeys raised in the laboratory did not react fearfully to snakes until they saw another monkey (one raised in the wild) do so. After that, they showed strong fear reactions themselves (Mineka & others, 1984). In subsequent experiments, Michael Cook and Mineka (1989, 1990) used splicing to produce videotapes in which a monkey was shown reacting fearfully in the presence of various different objects, including toy snakes, flowers, and a toy rabbit. Through observing the tapes, monkeys who previously feared none of these objects developed a fear of toy snakes (and real snakes), but not of flowers or toy rabbits.

From an ecological perspective, this learning bias makes a good deal of sense. In some regions (depending on the kinds of snakes that are present) snakes are dangerous and in other regions they are not. In places where snakes are harmless, an inflexible instinctive fear of them would be maladaptive. Thus, the learning mechanism may have evolved because it allows monkeys who are exposed to dangerous snakes to learn quickly, by watching others, to fear and avoid them, while at the same time it allows other monkeys to go about their business relatively oblivious to snakes. We humans also vary greatly in the degree to which we fear snakes, and research suggests that we too learn to fear them more easily than other objects (Öhman, 1986).

Imprinting in Precocial Birds

42. ***What aspect of a young fowl's ability to follow its mother depends on learning, and how is that learning guided by inborn biases?***

Some of the earliest evidence for specialized learning abilities came from studies of young precocial birds. Precocial birds are those species—such as chickens, geese, and ducks—in which the young can walk almost as soon as they hatch. Because they can walk, they can get separated from their mother, and because of that they have acquired, in the course of evolution, an efficient means to recognize their mother and remain near her. In the nineteenth century, Douglas Spalding (1873/1954) observed that when newly hatched chicks saw him, rather than their mother, move past their nest shortly after they hatched, they followed him as if he were their mother. They continued to follow him for weeks thereafter, and once attached in this way they would not switch to following the mother hen. Some 60 years later, Konrad Lorenz (1935) made essentially the same discovery with newly hatched goslings. He labeled the phenomenon ***imprinting***, a term that emphasizes the very sudden and apparently irreversible nature of the learning process involved.

When imprinting studies go awry . . .

One interesting feature of imprinting is the rather restricted ***critical period*** during which it can occur. Spalding (1873/1954) found that if chicks were prevented from seeing any moving object during their first 5 days after hatching, and then he walked past them, they did not follow him but rather showed "great terror" and ran away. In more detailed studies, Eckhard Hess (1958, 1972) found that the optimal time for imprinting mallard ducklings is within the first 18 hours after hatching, and that by 30 hours after hatching most ducklings cannot be imprinted at all.

Although early studies suggested that young birds could be imprinted on humans or other moving objects as easily as on their own mothers, later studies proved otherwise. Given a choice between a female of their species and some other object, newly hatched birds invariably choose to follow the female of their species. Experiments with chicks indicate that this initial preference centers on visual features of the head. Newly hatched chicks will follow a box with a chicken head attached to it, as readily as they will a complete stuffed chicken, and more readily than any object without a chicken head (Johnson & Horn, 1988). The experience of following the object brings the imprinting mechanism into play, and this mechanism causes the chicks to be attracted thereafter to all the features of the moving object. Under normal conditions, of course, the moving object is their mother, so imprinting leads them to distinguish their mother from any other hen. Once again, we see an adaptive learning mechanism in which the effects of experience are guided and constrained by heredity.

Place Learning Revisited

Earlier we looked at Tolman's classic research on place learning as support for a cognitive view of learning. Subsequent studies of place learning have provided many examples of special learning abilities that can be understood in relation to the

■ **43.** ***How might the ecological perspective help us predict which place-learning tasks an animal will find easy or difficult to master?***

animal's natural ecology. Consider the behavior of a rat in a simple T-shaped maze. If a rat has, on one trial, found food in the right arm of the maze, what should the rat do on the next trial—turn right or turn left? A straightforward application of operant conditioning theory would have the rat turn right, because it was rewarded for that response on the previous trial. But if you think of this behavior in relation to normal foraging, turning right does *not* make the most sense. The rat has just cleaned out all the food hidden in the right compartment, and in nature food doesn't magically replenish itself in a given place within seconds or minutes after it has been removed. After removing food from one place, it makes sense for the rat to look anywhere other than that place to find more food. How do rats actually behave in such situations? In general, early in training, they behave in accordance with the ecological prediction, not the operant prediction. They tend to avoid the arm in which they have already been, whether they found food there or not, and to choose the other arm (Gaffan & others, 1983). Only after many trials in the maze do they learn to go always to the same arm if the reward is always in that arm.

Some research on maze learning employs conditions more in keeping with natural foraging conditions. David Olton uses a radial maze in which each arm leads away from a center platform like the spokes on a wheel and food is hidden at the end of each arm. When the food is found and eaten in a particular arm it is not replaced, so efficient behavior in this case involves avoiding those arms in which food has already been found. Rats quickly learn to behave very efficiently in this task, rarely returning to an arm from which they have already taken food until all of the other arms have been explored, even when there are as many as seventeen arms to remember (Olton, 1979). Olton and his colleagues have shown that the rats achieve this efficient behavior not by smelling or in some other way directly sensing the location of food, nor by a motor strategy such as taking one arm at a time in order, but by remembering the location of each place that they have been and using visual cues to avoid that location.

In other species, even more dramatic evidence of specialized learning abilities has been discovered. As one example, Clark's nutcrackers (a species of bird inhabiting the southwest United States) bury food in literally thousands of different sites, to which they return during the winter when the food is needed (Kamil & Balda, 1990). Experiments have shown that the birds' ability to find each site depends on their memory of visual landmarks, such as stones, near the site (Kamil & Balda, 1985; Shettleworth, 1983). Quite a different example is the extraordinary ability of Pacific salmon to find their hatching place. Salmon that hatch in small streams in the northwest United States migrate into the Pacific Ocean, where they swim around for 5 years or more carrying with them a memory of the exact smell of the water in which they hatched. Then, when they are ready to spawn, they use their sense of smell to find their way hundreds of miles back to the same stream from which they had come (Hasler & Larsen, 1955).

While the cognitive perspective often emphasizes the general intelligence of an animal (its ability to bring sophisticated cognitive processes to bear on a learning problem), the ecological perspective reminds us that animals appear much more intelligent when faced with problems similar to those posed by their natural environment than when faced with other problems. The intelligence does not come from a general ability to reason, but from specialized learning abilities that have evolved over thousands of generations in the wild. This will be an interesting point to keep in mind when reading about human intelligence in Chapters 11 and 12. Might it be that we humans, too, have not one general intelligence, but various specialized intelligences that came about to solve different kinds of problems in the environment in which we evolved?

Concluding Thoughts

You have read about learning from three different perspectives. What is a *perspective*? It is a point of view, a framework, a set of ground rules and assumptions, that scientists bring to the topic studied. The perspective helps determine the kinds of questions asked, the kinds of evidence regarded as important, the kinds of studies conducted, and the vocabulary used to describe observations. Perspectives are neither right nor wrong, but they may be more useful or less. As you review the chapter, think about how each boldfaced term and guide question is related to the larger perspective within which it falls. Here are some further thoughts about each perspective on learning:

1. **The behavioral perspective** As we have seen, behaviorists such as Watson and Skinner began with the assumption that learning is best described in terms of observable stimuli and responses. Although they acknowledged that inner processes are involved in learning, they assumed (a) that such processes are too obscure to study scientifically and (b) that lawful relations between stimuli and responses can be identified without worrying about the inner events that mediate them. Borrowing from Pavlov's lexicon to describe classical conditioning, and adding a parallel set of terms for operant conditioning, the behaviorists brought to psychology a rich, objective vocabulary for talking about learning and many learning-related phenomena. That vocabulary is still very much a part of psychology. As you review the terms and concepts in the behavioral section, try to avoid the temptation to translate them into mental terms. Try instead to define each in terms of relationships between responses and stimuli, including reinforcers.

2. **The cognitive perspective** This perspective grew out of the behavioral perspective by way of psychologists, like Tolman, who called themselves *S-O-R* behaviorists and began doing experiments to understand the *O*. These psychologists argued that you can go just so far without talking about inner processes. You can set out very general principles, but you can't predict how they will apply in a given situation. For example, you can set out the principle of stimulus generalization in classical conditioning, but you can't predict to what degree an individual will generalize from one stimulus to the next unless you understand something about the individual's mental concepts, which can lead the individual to perceive one stimulus as like another even if they aren't physically alike. Other cognitive constructs—such as expectancies, predictions, means-end relationships, and cognitive maps—can also be inferred from subjects' behavior and can be used successfully to help predict their future behavior. As you think about these constructs, try to imagine them not as conscious thoughts but as the kinds of rules for guiding behavior that one might program into a computer. That is how modern cognitive psychologists try to think of them.

3. **The ecological perspective** This, of course, is the perspective that most closely unites the two chapters on adaptation—the preceding one on evolution and the present one on learning. While behaviorism and cognitivism have roots in empiricist philosophy, which attempts to understand human behavior and the human mind in terms of general principles (such as the law of association by contiguity), the ecological perspective grew out of biology, which recognizes the diversity of life processes. The view that learning mechanisms are a product of natural selection implies that they should be especially designed to solve biologically important problems, related to survival and reproduction. Different animal species, whose ecological niches pose different problems, may have evolved different species-

specific learning mechanisms to solve those problems. This idea may seem more applicable to nonhuman animals than to humans, but psychologists are looking increasingly for special learning mechanisms to characterize various aspects of human learning. Humans may have relatively separate learning mechanisms for such domains as language, spatial relations, motor skills, and emotionality, just as they do for food selection. The future, I think, will bring closer ties between the cognitive and ecological perspectives in all realms of psychology.

Further Reading

B. F. Skinner (1978). *Reflections on behaviorism and society.* Englewood Cliffs, NJ: Prentice-Hall.

Skinner—who wanted to be a novelist before he went into psychology—is always fun to read, and there is no better place to begin than with this collection of some of his essays. The titles include: "Human behavior and democracy," "Why I am not a cognitive psychologist," "The free and happy student," "The force of coincidence," and "Freedom and dignity revisited." You will find here Skinner's basic philosophy about psychology and his suggestions for using behavioral learning principles to improve society.

Garry Martin & Joseph Pear (1992). *Behavior modification: What it is and how to do it.* Englewood Cliffs, NJ: Prentice Hall.

This is an easy-to-read introduction to the basic principles of conditioning and their application in modifying behavior in schools, hospitals, the home, and other settings. The book includes many self-modification exercises, through which readers can use conditioning principles to analyze and modify aspects of their own behavior.

Stephen B. Klein & Robert R. Mowrer (Eds.) (1989). *Contemporary learning theories.* Hillsdale, NJ: Erlbaum.

This is a sophisticated upper-level text, but many of its chapters—each by a different expert—are written clearly enough to be readable by first-year students. The book comes in two volumes and deals at length with most of the ideas that you read about in this chapter, plus many others. The first volume is about classical conditioning and learning theory in general, and the second is about operant conditioning and biological constraints on learning.

Robert C. Bolles & Michael Beecher (Eds.) (1988). *Evolution and learning.* Hillsdale, NJ: Erlbaum.

This collection of chapters, each authored by different specialists, shows how the traditions of behaviorism and ethology have merged in recent years and begun to provide rich detail about species-specific learning processes. The book begins with historical chapters about the relationship of learning theory to evolutionary theory, and then turns to contemporary research on learning in such biologically important domains as feeding, defending against predators, and sexual behavior.

Looking Ahead

In the three-chapter unit just completed, we have discussed the genetic basis of behavior and the ways in which evolution and learning adapt behavior to the environment. But genes affect behavior only through their role in building the body. The body, particularly its nervous system, contains the basic mechanisms for learning and all other processes studied by psychologists. In the next unit, we will look at the nervous system.

PHYSIOLOGICAL MECHANISMS OF BEHAVIOR

PART 3

Behavior is a product of the body's machinery, especially the nervous system. The nervous system receives information about the internal and external environments, integrates that information, and controls the body's movements. This unit consists of three chapters. The first examines the overall structure of the nervous system and its principles of operation. The second is concerned with the neural and hormonal mechanisms underlying motivation, sleep, and emotion. The third deals with the neural processes that allow us to see, hear, and in other ways sense the world around us.

THE NERVOUS SYSTEM

CHAPTER 6

A human brain is, I must admit, somewhat disappointing to look at. It is about the size and shape of a cantaloupe, but more gnarled in appearance. To the eye it seems quite dormant, even when viewed in a living person. Aristotle and many of the other ancient Greeks—who were among the first to try to figure out what the various parts of the body are for—were not much impressed by the brain. Noticing that the blood vessels leading into it are much larger than those entering other organs its size, they suggested that the brain's main function might be to cool the blood. They were much more impressed by the heart, an obviously dynamic organ, and proposed that the heart and blood are the source of feelings, thoughts, and all else that today we call "psychological."

But not all of the ancients agreed with the heart theory of psychology. One who didn't was Galen, a physician of the second century. Galen worked at the royal court in Rome, treating gladiators, among others, and perhaps he noticed that head injuries can create peculiar disturbances in people's behavior. He also is known to have practiced his surgical skills on animals, and in one experiment he found that when he cut a particular structure (which we would now call a *nerve*) that ran from a pig's brain to its vocal cords, the pig no longer produced vocal sounds (Robinson & Uttal, 1983). Perhaps because of observations such as these, Galen maintained that the brain is the organ of thought and feelings, and that it controls behavior through a system of connections to the various other organs. Galen was right, of course, and that is why essentially every introductory psychology text ever written, from William James's (1890) classic on, contains a chapter about the nervous system.

This chapter begins with the overall layout of the nervous system and the functions of each of its main parts. It then turns to the workings of individual neurons and how they can be modified by experience. The final section discusses how drugs and hormones act on the nervous system and influence behavior.

Functional Organization of the Nervous System

Well before Galen, in the fourth century B.C., the Greek physician Hippocrates (1923) wrote: ". . . from the brain, and from the brain only, arise our pleasures, joys, laughter and jests, as well as our sorrows, pains, griefs and tears. Through it, in particular, we think, see, hear. . . . Eyes, ears, tongue, hands and feet act in accordance with the discernment of the brain."

■ **1.** ***What are four basic tasks of the nervous system?***

To accomplish such wonders, the brain along with the rest of the nervous system must do four things: It must (1) receive sensory messages that provide information about the external environment; (2) organize that information and

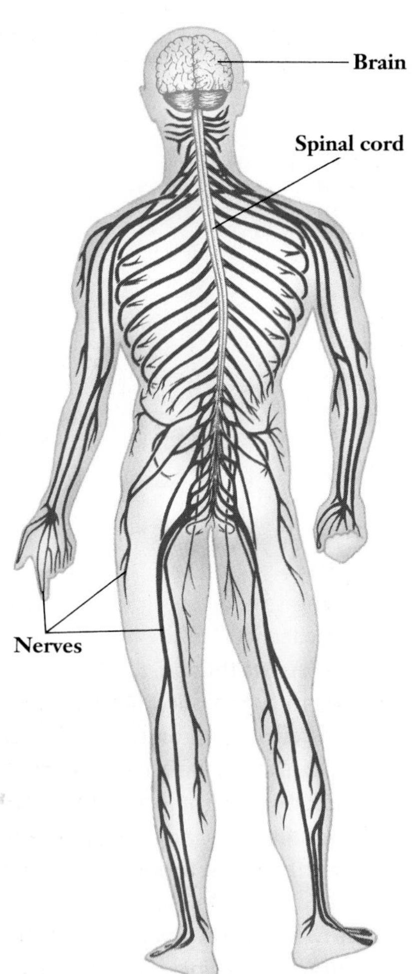

Figure 6.1 *The human nervous system*

The central nervous system consists of the brain and the spinal cord, which runs through the bones of the spinal column down the center of the back. The peripheral nervous system consists of the entire set of nerves, which connect the brain and spinal cord to the sensory organs, muscles, and glands.

integrate it with other, already-stored information in useful ways; and (3) use that integrated information to send out messages to the muscles and glands, thereby producing organized movements and adaptive secretions. In addition, and most wondrous of all, the nervous system must (4) somehow provide the basis for what we call conscious experience—the stream of perceptions, thoughts, and feelings that make up our mental life.

The nervous system, which does all this, is sketched in Figure 6.1. The brain and spinal cord (which extends from the brain down through the bones of the spinal column) together make up the ***central nervous system***. Extensions from the central nervous system, called *nerves*, make up the ***peripheral nervous system***. We will examine the various structures of the nervous system and their functions using a bottom-up approach. We will start with just a little about the basic cells of the nervous system and then look at the peripheral nervous system, the spinal cord, and progressively higher parts of the brain.

The Basic Functions and Structures of Neurons

2. *What are the three types of neurons and the function of each?*

The elementary units of the nervous system are ***neurons***, or nerve cells. Neurons are cells that have become specialized to carry information rapidly from one place to another and integrate information from various sources. They can be classified by function into three types that relate, respectively, to the first three tasks of the nervous system listed above (see Figure 6.2). (1) ***Sensory neurons*** carry information from sensory organs, through nerves, into the central nervous system. (2) ***Interneurons*** exist entirely within the central nervous system and carry messages from one set of neurons to another. By bringing messages from various sources together, they organize and integrate information. (3) ***Motor neurons*** carry messages out from the central nervous system, through nerves, to operate muscles and glands. The task of the interneurons is by far the most complex, and interneurons greatly outnumber the other two types. The human nervous system contains a few million sensory neurons and motor neurons and something like *100 billion* interneurons (Nauta & Feirtag, 1986).

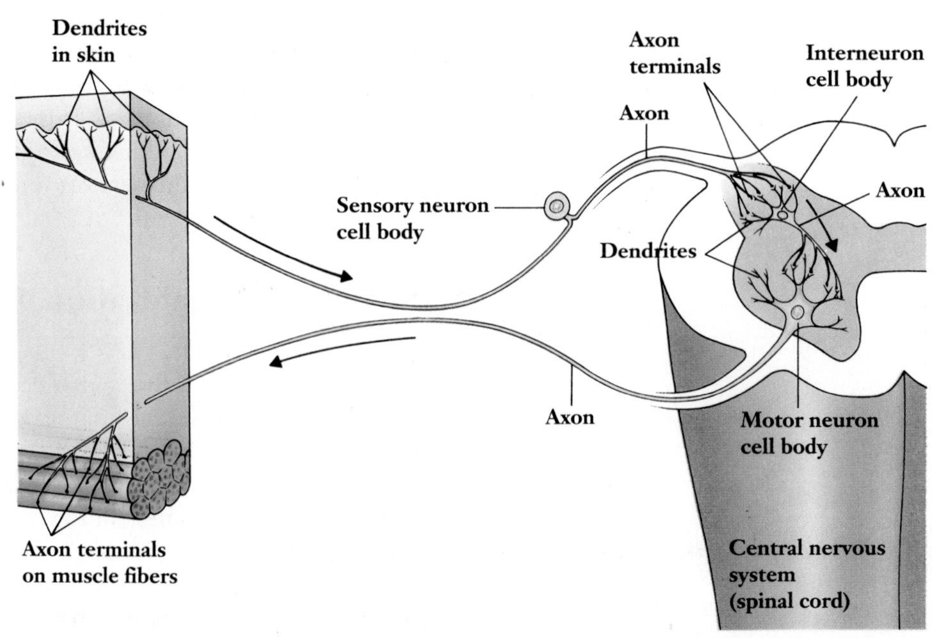

Figure 6.2 *Three classes of neurons*

This diagram shows the positions in the nervous system of the three classes of neurons. On the right is the central nervous system, and on the left are muscles and skin in the periphery. *Motor neurons* send messages from the central nervous system to muscles and glands. *Sensory neurons* send messages into the central nervous system from sensory organs, such as the skin. And *interneurons*, located entirely within the central nervous system, carry messages between neurons.

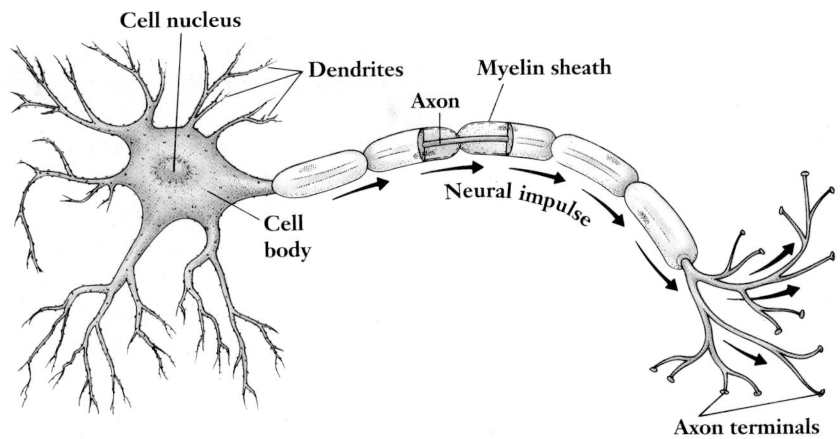

Figure 6.3 ***A motor neuron***

The parts common to many neurons can be seen in this diagram of a motor neuron. The neuron receives input from other neurons on its dendrites and cell body, and sends its own output down the axon to the axon terminals. The myelin sheath is not part of the neuron; it is formed of separate cells that are wrapped around the axon.

■ **3.** ***What are the main parts of a motor neuron, and what is the function of each part?***

Figure 6.3 shows the main part of a typical motor neuron. The ***cell body*** is the widest part and contains the cell nucleus and other basic machinery common to all cells. The ***dendrites*** are thin, tubelike extensions, which typically branch repeatedly near the cell body, forming a bushlike structure. Their function is to increase the surface area of the cell to allow for receipt of signals from many other neurons. The ***axon*** is another thin, tubelike extension. Its function is to carry electrical impulses, called *action potentials*, away from the cell body to other cells. Although microscopically thin, the axon is in some cases extraordinarily long. You have axons extending all the way from your spine down to the muscles of your big toe—a distance of over a meter. The axons of some neurons are surrounded by a casing called the ***myelin sheath***, made of fatty cells that are wrapped tightly around the axon. The axon usually branches some distance away from the cell body, and each branch ends with a small swelling called the ***axon terminal***.

The action potentials travel along the axon to the axon terminals. As each action potential reaches a terminal, it causes the terminal to release a chemical substance called a ***neurotransmitter***, or *transmitter*, onto a receiving cell. Interneurons and sensory neurons, which communicate only with other neurons, pass transmitter molecules to the dendrites of other neurons, as shown in Figure 6.2. Motor neurons, such as the one shown in Figure 6.3, pass transmitter molecules to muscle cells or gland cells. The place at which an axon terminal passes transmitter mole-

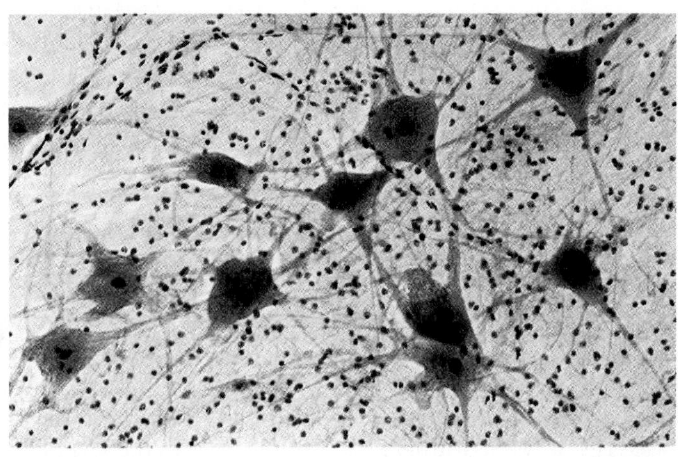

Motor neurons in the spinal cord

In this photograph taken through a microscope, you can see the cell bodies and some of the branching dendrites for several motor neurons.

cules to a receiving cell is called a ***synapse***. At the synapse, the transmitter molecules diffuse across a small cleft, or gap, and act on the membrane of the receiving cell.

The molecular mechanisms of action potentials and synapses will be described later in this chapter, in the section on how neurons work. For now it is enough to know that a neuron's message lies in the number of action potentials that move down the axon per second and cause the release of transmitter molecules from each axon terminal. In the case of an interneuron or sensory neuron, the transmitter acts on another neuron to either *excite* it (increase its rate of action potentials) or *inhibit* it (decrease its rate of action potentials). In the case of a motor neuron, the transmitter acts on a muscle cell or gland to alter the activity of that cell.

■ **4. *How do interneurons and sensory neurons differ anatomically from motor neurons?***

To compare the parts of a typical interneuron and sensory neuron with the motor neuron, look again at Figure 6.2 and read the labels. Interneurons come in an enormous variety of shapes and sizes, but the largest and most well studied are similar to motor neurons in their overall layout. The main difference is that the interneuron's axon does not leave the central nervous system and its terminals form synapses on other neurons rather than on muscle cells. Sensory neurons, in contrast, have a quite different layout from the other two types. The sensory neuron shown in Figure 6.2 carries information about touch or pressure to the skin (you will read about other kinds of sensory neurons in Chapter 8). Its cell body (unlike that of the motor neuron or interneuron) lies outside of the central nervous system, its axon extends out in both directions from the cell body, and its dendrites are branches at one end of the axon (the end in the skin) rather than direct protrusions from the cell body. In this cell, the tips of the dendrites are specialized to respond to physical stimulation of the skin, and the axon is designed to carry the action potentials initiated by that stimulation past the cell body and into the central nervous system.

Although neurons carry out the main function of the nervous system, the most numerous cells in that system are not neurons but ***glial cells***, or *glia*. In the central nervous system glia outnumber neurons by about 10 to 1 (Steward, 1989). Different varieties of glia serve different purposes. Some form the myelin sheaths around neuron axons (as shown in Figure 6.3). Others form barriers around blood vessels in the brain to help protect the nerve cells in the brain from poisons that could otherwise reach them from the blood. Still others help clean up waste products in the nervous system or help supply nutrients to neurons.

The amazing abilities of the nervous system reside not so much in the individual neuron as in the organization of the billions of neurons that make up the nervous system. The following paragraphs and accompanying figures paint a picture of that organization. We will begin with the peripheral nervous system (cranial and spinal nerves) and then turn to the central nervous system (spinal cord and brain), working upward from the more primitive lower parts to the more recently evolved higher parts. As you read about each part, pay particular attention to its main functions in the control of behavior and try to think about it in relation to other structures already described.

The Peripheral Nervous System

As mentioned earlier, the peripheral nervous system consists of the entire set of *nerves*. A ***nerve*** is a bundle of axons of sensory or motor neurons existing anywhere outside the central nervous system. By connecting the central nervous system with sensory organs and with muscles and glands, nerves serve as the vehicle through which the central nervous system receives information from and sends instructions to the rest of the body.

Cranial and Spinal Nerves

Cranial nerves come directly from the brain, and ***spinal nerves*** come directly from the spinal cord. Like most other structures in the body, nerves exist in pairs; there is a right and left member in each pair. Humans have twelve pairs of cranial nerves and thirty-one pairs of spinal nerves. With their various branches, these nerves form an enormous network extending to all portions of the body (look back at Figure 6.1).

Some pairs of cranial nerves are highly specialized. Three pairs are purely sensory—one pair conveys input just from the nose, another just before the eyes, and a third just from the ears. Five other pairs are purely motor—three pairs are involved exclusively in controlling eye movements, another controls tongue movements, and another controls the neck muscles that move the head. The remaining cranial nerves and all of the spinal nerves, however, contain axons of both sensory and motor neurons. The spinal nerves convey motor output to muscles and glands below the neck, and they convey sensory input from below the neck for the set of senses collectively referred to as *somatosensation*. *Soma* means body, and somatosensation is the set of senses that derive from the whole body—such as from the skin, muscles, and tendons—as opposed to those that come from the special sensory organs of the head.

The Autonomic Compared with the Skeletal Motor System

5. How do the autonomic and skeletal motor systems differ from each other?

Motor neurons act on two broad classes of structures. One class is the ***skeletal muscles***, the muscles attached to bones, which produce externally observable movements of the body when contracted. The other class consists of the ***visceral muscles*** and ***glands***. Visceral muscles include such internal muscular structures as the heart, arteries, and gastrointestinal tract. Glands include such structures as salivary glands and sweat glands. Neurons that act on skeletal muscles make up the ***skeletal*** portion of the peripheral motor system, and those that act on visceral muscles and glands make up the ***autonomic*** portion.

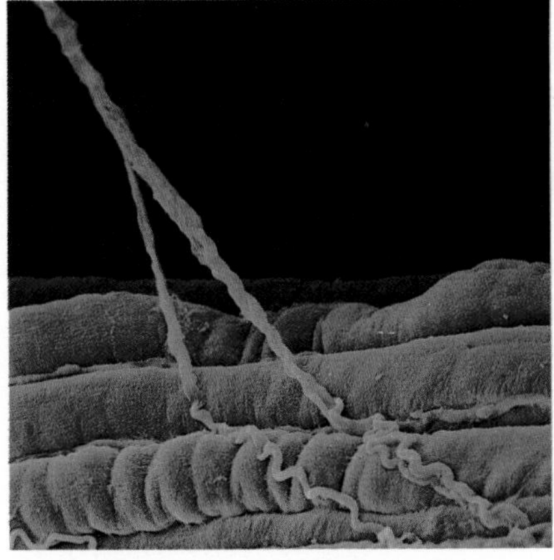

The axon of a motor neuron

This electron micrograph shows an axon and three skeletal muscle fibers.

The skeletal and autonomic motor systems differ anatomically. The motor neuron diagrammed in Figures 6.2 and 6.3 is a skeletal motor neuron; its cell body is in the central nervous system, and its axon extends all the way out to the muscle cells it operates. In the autonomic system, motor connections are not as direct. Autonomic motor neurons with cell bodies in the central nervous system send their axons not directly to a muscle or gland, but rather to a *ganglion* (a group of neural cell bodies that exists outside of the central nervous system), where they form synapses with a second set of neurons. The second set then send their axons to the muscle or gland.

An important functional difference between the skeletal and autonomic systems is that the autonomic *modulates* (modifies) rather than initiates activity in the muscles that it acts on. Skeletal muscles are completely inactive in the absence of neural input, but visceral muscles have built-in, non-neural mechanisms for generating activity. The heart continues to beat, and the muscular walls of such structures as the intestines and arteries continue to contract in response to local influences, even if all the nerves to these organs are destroyed. Significantly, most visceral muscles and glands receive two sets of neurons, which produce opposite effects and come from two distinct divisions of the autonomic system—the sympathetic and parasympathetic (see Figure 6.4 on page 168).

6. How do the sympathetic and parasympathetic portions of the autonomic system differ from each other?

The ***sympathetic division*** mediates many of the body's immediate responses to stressful stimulation by preparing the body for possible "fight or flight." Among its effects are (a) increased heart rate and blood pressure, (b) the release of energy molecules (sugars and fats) from storage deposits to permit high energy expenditure, (c) increased blood flow to the skeletal muscles, and (d) inhibition of digestive

Figure 6.4 ***The autonomic nervous system***

The autonomic nervous system modulates the activity of visceral muscles and glands. Its sympathetic and parasympathetic divisions commonly have opposite effects on any given organ. As a rule, the sympathetic division promotes bodily arousal and the parasympathetic division promotes relaxation, digestion, and bodily restoration.

processes (which helps explain why a heated argument at the dinner table can lead to a stomachache). Conversely, the ***parasympathetic division*** serves regenerative, growth-promoting, and energy-conserving functions. Its effects are generally the opposite of those just listed for the sympathetic division. If you are relaxed as you are reading this book, your parasympathetic activity probably predominates over your sympathetic, so your heart is beating at a slow, normal rate and your digestion is working fine. If, however, you are engaged in last-minute cramming for an important midterm exam, your sympathetic system may be going full blast, and perhaps you can feel its consequences in your gut and pounding heart. The sympathetic response is not always adaptive in today's world, where stressful stimuli often call for a response quite different from fight or flight. (For a graphic presentation of the subdivisions of the peripheral motor nervous system, see Figure 6.5.)

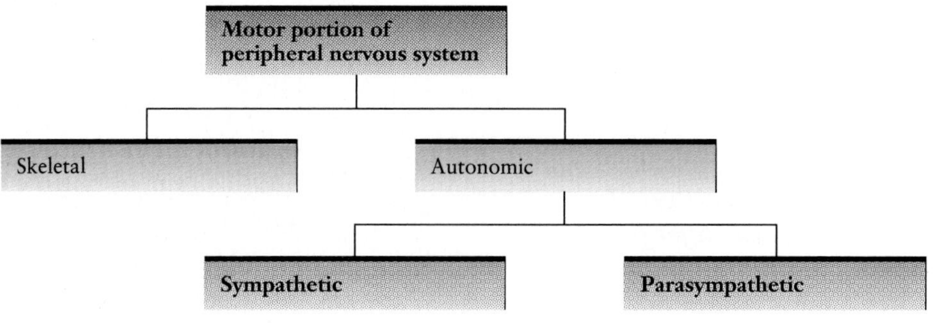

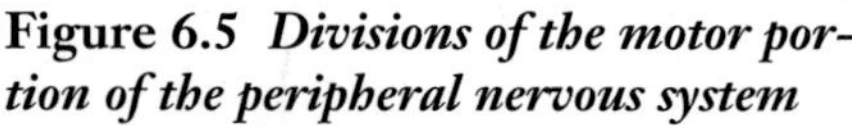

Figure 6.5 ***Divisions of the motor portion of the peripheral nervous system***

The motor portion of the peripheral nervous system consists of the skeletal and autonomic systems, and the autonomic system consists of the sympathetic and parasympathetic systems.

■ **7. *How does the existence of tracts and nuclei make brain science possible?***

Functional Approach to the Central Nervous System

The human central nervous system has been called the most complex living structure in the known universe (Bloom & Lazerson, 1988), though that might reflect a human-centered bias (the central nervous system of whales and dolphins are bigger than ours and may be equally complex). Our central nervous system contains billions of neurons and trillions of synaptic connections (a typical neuron has direct synaptic connections with thousands of other neurons). It would be hopeless to try to work out its complete wiring the way we might with a machine, such as a radio or even a computer. Fortunately, though, for those who wish to work out parts of it, patterns exist in the trillions of connections. Axons do not run willy-nilly; they usually run in bundles connecting one cluster of cell bodies with another. A bundle of axons coursing together in the central nervous system is called a ***tract*** (a tract in the central nervous system is analogous to a nerve in the peripheral system). A cluster of cell bodies in the central nervous system is called a ***nucleus*** (not to be confused with the cell nucleus within each cell). The myelin sheaths around axons cause tracts to appear relatively white, so tracts are referred to as *white matter*. Nuclei, which appear relatively darker, are referred to as *gray matter*. In general, neurons whose cell bodies occupy the same nucleus, and whose axons run along the same tract, have similar functions. Moreover, groups of nuclei that exist in the same area of the brain or spinal cord often have functions that are closely related to one another. Because of this we can talk about the functions of various relatively large anatomical structures within the central nervous system.

The following sections discuss the general functions of the largest subdivisions of the central nervous system—moving from the spinal cord up to the anatomically highest part of the brain, the cerebral cortex. The focus will be on the human central nervous system, but the same basic parts, serving the same basic functions, exist also in other mammals, such as rats and cats. In fact, as you will see, much of what we have learned about the human central nervous system comes from studies of other mammals.

The Spinal Cord

■ **8. *How does the spinal cord serve as (1) a conduit between spinal nerves and the brain, (2) an organizer of rhythmic locomotor movements, and (3) an organizer of certain reflexes?***

The spinal cord is, among other things, a conduit between the spinal nerves and the brain. Within the spinal cord are *ascending tracts*, which carry somatosensory information brought in by spinal nerves up to the brain, and *descending tracts*, which carry motor-control information down from the brain to be transmitted out by spinal nerves to muscles. A person who has an accident that completely severs the spinal cord at some point will be completely paralyzed, and without sensation, in those parts of the body that are innervated by spinal nerves that come from below the place of injury. As you can see by looking back at Figure 6.1 the closer the place of injury is to the neck or head, the greater is the number of spinal nerves cut off from the brain, and the greater, therefore, will be the extent of paralysis and insensitivity. Thus, if the spinal cord is completely cut through in the upper part of the neck, the paralysis and insensitivity will include the arms, trunk, and legs; but if the cut is farther down, it may include only the legs.

If you grew up on a farm and helped butcher chickens, you know that the spinal cord is more than just a pathway to and from the brain; it can also organize some behaviors on its own. The axe comes down, the head rolls off, and the wings begin flapping violently. If the flapping wings cause you to lose your grip on the chicken's feet, you then have the experience of chasing the headless bird across the yard. Such behaviors are often called "reflexes," but technically they are not. As defined in Chapter 5, a reflex is a direct, automatic response to a sensory stimulus. Research has shown that headless animals produce these organized movements even if all sensory neurons are cut, so they can't possibly be responding to stimuli (Gordon, 1991).

The spinal cord contains within it sets of interneurons called *pattern generators*, which produce bursts of action potentials that wax and wane in a rhythmic manner (Grillner & Wallen, 1985). These pattern generators act on the motor neurons in repeating bursts to produce the rhythmic sequence of muscle movements that results in flying or walking or running. In some animals, the pattern generators become active when released from the brain's control, and that is what produces the flying and running motions of the headless chicken. Normally, in animals that still have their heads, these pattern generators are controlled by neurons descending from the brain; they can be either inhibited, producing a motionless animal, or activated to varying degrees, producing varying rates of locomotion (Gordon, 1991). Thus, one function of the spinal cord is to provide the rhythmic organization of locomotor movements.

In addition, the spinal cord does organize many true reflexes. These are called *spinal reflexes*, and they are usually studied in animals whose spinal cords have been surgically separated from the brain. (Such experiments might seem cruel, but the knowledge gained from them has been extremely valuable in helping people who have spinal cord injuries.) Such animals, referred to as *spinal animals*, still have both a brain and a spinal cord, but neither of these can act on the other.

If the paw of a spinal cat is pricked with a pin, the animal does *not* hiss or show facial signs of pain as a normal cat would, because the stimulus input cannot reach the pain and vocalization centers of the brain. The animal cannot feel sensations from below the neck, because feeling is mediated by the brain. Nevertheless, the animal's paw quickly withdraws from the pin. This reflex is called the *flexion reflex*, because it involves contraction of the flexor muscles of the limb—the muscles that bend the limb at each joint, causing it to be pulled inward (flexed) toward the body. The adaptive advantage of the flexion reflex is obvious: It quickly and automatically moves the limb away from potentially damaging stimuli.

The mechanism of the flexion reflex (in simplified form) can be traced in Figure 6.2. A stimulus such as a pin prick triggers action potentials in a set of pain-sensitive sensory neurons in the skin, which in turn excite a set of interneurons in the spinal cord, which in their turn excite a set of motor neurons going to the flexor muscles of the same limb from which the sensory stimulus arose. In a normal cat, other interneurons would transmit a sensory message to the brain, and the animal would experience pain.

In sum, the spinal cord serves three important functions: (1) It carries messages upward and downward between spinal nerves and the brain. (2) It generates the rhythmic component of locomotor movements (walking, flying, and swimming) that are normally initiated or inhibited by the brain. And (3) it organizes certain reflexes, such as the flexion reflex.

Subcortical Structures of the Brain

Above the spinal cord are the *subcortical* structures of the brain, so called because of their position beneath the cerebral cortex, which is the topmost part of the brain. Working our way upward from the bottommost of the subcortical structures, we begin with the brainstem.

■ ***9. How is the brainstem similar to and different from the spinal cord? What role does the brainstem play in the control of behavior?***

The Brainstem and Thalamus

As it enters the head, the spinal cord enlarges and becomes the ***brainstem***. The parts of the brainstem, beginning closest to the spinal cord and going upward toward the top of the head, are the ***medulla***, ***pons***, and ***midbrain*** (see Figure 6.6).

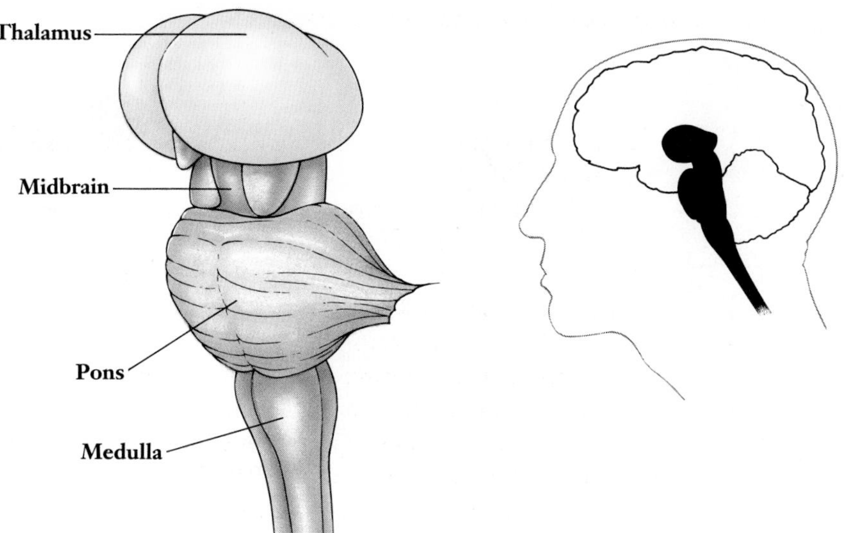

Figure 6.6 ***The brainstem and thalamus***

This figure makes it clear why the medulla, pons, and midbrain are collectively called the *brainstem*. They form a stem-like continuation from the spinal cord, to which other brian structures are attached. The thalamus is attached to the top of the brainstem.

The brainstem is functionally and anatomically quite similar to the spinal cord, but more elaborate. The spinal cord is the site of entry of spinal nerves, and the brainstem is the site of entry of most (ten of the twelve pairs) of the cranial nerves. The spinal cord contains ascending (sensory) and descending (motor) tracts connecting nerves to higher parts of the central nervous system, and so does the brainstem. Also like the spinal cord, the brainstem contains some neural centers that organize reflexes and other neural centers that help organize more complex behaviors that are governed by higher parts of the brain.

The medulla and pons organize reflexes that are more complex and sustained than those of the spinal cord. These include *postural reflexes*, which help the animal maintain balance while standing or moving, and certain so-called *vital reflexes*, such as those that regulate breathing rate and heart rate in response to input concerning the body's metabolic needs. The midbrain contains neural centers that help govern most of an animal's basic movement patterns, such as those involved in eating, drinking, attacking, or grooming (Klemm, 1990). The midbrain also contains the neurons that act on pattern generators in the spinal cord to increase or decrease the speed of locomotion (Skinner & Garcia-Rill, 1990). And together the midbrain and pons contain neural systems that help control sleep and level of arousal (to be discussed in Chapter 7).

An animal (such as a cat) whose central nervous system is cut completely through just above the midbrain can produce almost the entire set of behaviors that a normal animal can produce (Klemm, 1990; Schmidt, 1986). It can walk, run, jump, climb, groom, attack, produce copulatory movements, chew, swallow, and so on. However, it differs from a normal animal in that it makes these responses only when provoked by immediate stimuli; it does not behave in either a spontaneous or a goal-directed manner. If placed on a pole, for example, the animal climbs, but it does not itself *choose* to climb a pole that has food at the top or avoid one that doesn't. Such behavior indicates that the midbrain and the structures below it contain neural systems that organize movements, but do not contain neural systems that permit deliberate decisions to move or refrain from moving in accordance with the animal's long-term interests.

■ **10.** ***In what sense is the thalamus a relay station?***

Directly atop the brainstem is the ***thalamus*** (again see Figure 6.6). This structure, seated squarely in the middle of the brain, is most conveniently thought of as a relay station that connects various parts of the brain with each other. Most of the sensory tracts that ascend through the brainstem terminate in special nuclei in the thalamus, which in turn send their output to specific areas in the cerebral cortex. The thalamus also has centers that interconnect various higher parts of the brain, and other centers that relay messages from higher parts of the brain to movement-control centers in the brainstem.

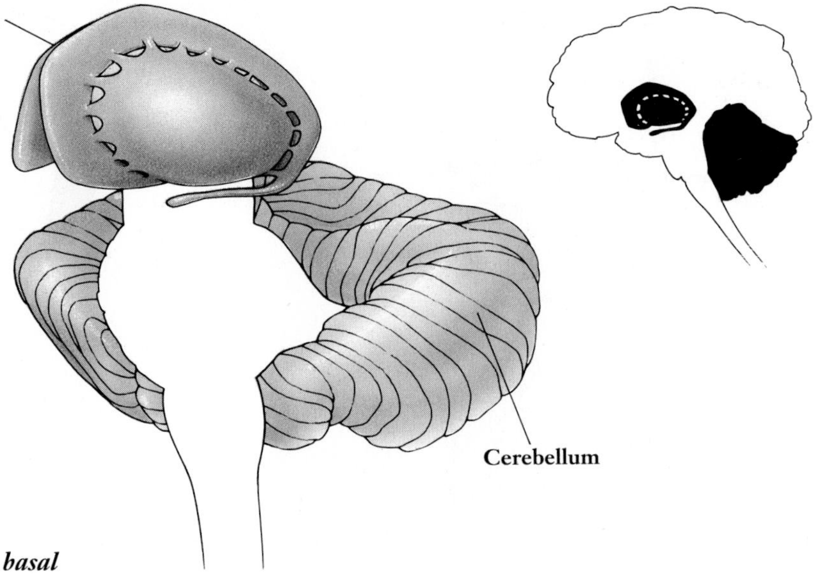

Basal ganglia

Cerebellum

Figure 6.7 ***The cerebellum and basal ganglia***

These two structures are critically involved in the initiation and coordination of movements.

■ **11. *What are the main functions of the cerebellum and basal ganglia? Why are these structures classed together even though they are anatomically distinct?***

The Cerebellum and Basal Ganglia

Cerebellum means little brain in Latin, and the ***cerebellum*** indeed looks something like a smaller version of the rest of the brain, riding piggyback on the rear of the brainstem (see Figure 6.7). Its most important function is to help initiate and control rapid movements of the limbs—movements that are too fast to be modified by sensory feedback once they are begun. Humans with damage in the cerebellum are often incapable of such rapid movements as kicking or throwing, but can still use their legs and arms for slower movements, such as walking or reaching (Kornhuber, 1974). It is noteworthy that both birds and monkeys have particularly large, well-developed cerebellums. Birds must continuously make rapid, well-timed movements in flying, and monkeys must do the same in leaping about in trees.

The cerebellum has been likened to a highly sophisticated computer. It receives and integrates information from all of the senses, including visual information about relevant objects in the external world and somatosensory information about the current positions of the limbs, and it makes rapid-fire calculations as to just what muscle groups must be activated, and by just how much, to leap over a hurdle, hit a baseball, or swing from branch to branch in the treetops.

The ***basal ganglia*** are large masses of gray matter lying on each side of the thalamus (see Figure 6.7). They are motor centers, playing a role that is complementary to that of the cerebellum. While the cerebellum is most involved in rapid movements, the basal ganglia are more involved in slower, deliberate movements, such as reaching for an object or walking (Kornhuber, 1974). Parkinson's disease, which is characterized by difficulty in starting and stopping deliberate movements and by involuntary muscle tremors, results from deterioration of certain neurons that run from the brainstem into the basal ganglia (Sourkes, 1989).

■ **12. *Why is the limbic system so named, and what functions does it perform?***

The Limbic System and Hypothalamus

The term *limbic* comes from the Latin word *limbus*, meaning border or edge. The ***limbic system*** can be thought of as the border dividing the evolutionarily older parts of the brain, below it, from the newest part (the cerebral cortex), above it. The limbic system consists of several distinct structures—including the *amygdala* and *hippocampus*—which interconnect with one another in a circuit wrapped around the thalamus and basal ganglia (see Figure 6.8). These structures are involved in the regulation of basic drives and emotions (to be discussed in Chapter 7). The limbic system is believed to have evolved originally as a system for the sophisticated analysis of olfactory input (Thompson, 1985), and its connections with the nose remain strong. This may help explain the special influence that smells—such

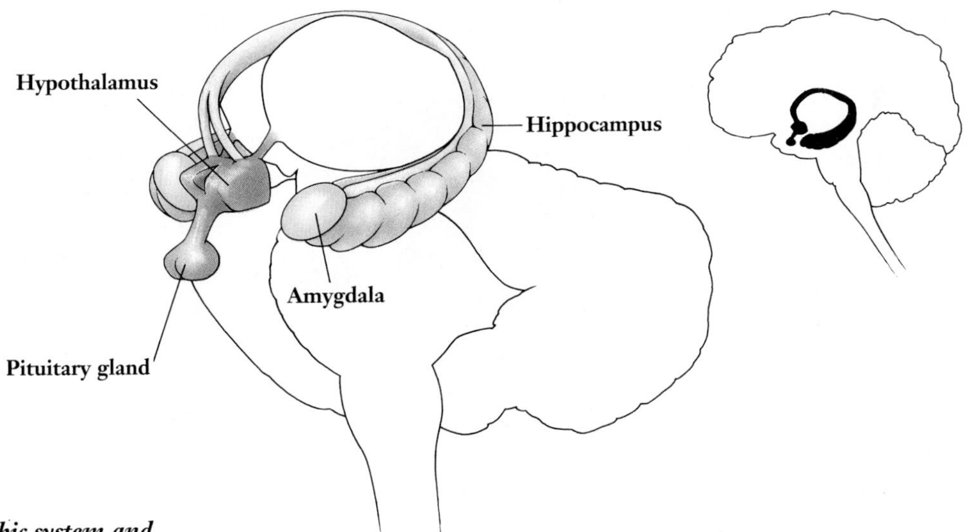

Figure 6.8 ***The limbic system and hypothalamus***

The most conspicuous structures of the limbic system are the hippocampus and amygdala, which have strong connections to the hypothalamus. The pituitary gland is not technically part of the brain, but it is strongly tied to the hypothalamus and is controlled by it.

as the aroma of good food or perfume, or the stench of vomit—can have on drives and emotions. But the limbic system also receives input from all of the other sensory systems. In addition, the limbic system is intimately connected to the basal ganglia, and those connections are believed to help translate emotions and drives into bodily movements.

At least one part of the limbic system, the hippocampus, is also critical to the formation of memories. People who have suffered a large amount of damage to the hippocampus on both sides of the brain are able to remember events that occurred before the damage but are unable to form new, long-term memories of events that occur after the damage. You will read in Chapter 10 of a man who sustained such damage and could read the same story day after day without realizing that he had read it before.

■ **13.** ***What are three ways by which the hypothalamus controls the body's internal environment?***

The ***hypothalamus*** is a small but extraordinarily important structure. Its name derives from its position directly underneath the thalamus (*hypo* in this case means underneath). The hypothalamus is intimately connected to all of the structures of the limbic system, and indeed it is sometimes classed as part of that system. The primary task of the hypothalamus is to help regulate the internal environment of the body. This it accomplishes by (a) influencing the activity of the autonomic nervous system, (b) controlling the release of certain hormones (to be described later), and (c) influencing certain drive states, such as hunger and thirst. In addition, through its connections with the limbic system, the hypothalamus helps regulate emotional states, such as fear and anger. You will read much more in Chapter 7 about the role of the hypothalamus in drives and emotions. If I had to give up a cubic millimeter (a tiny speck) of tissue from some part of my brain, the last place I would want it taken from is the hypothalamus. Depending on just which part was taken, I could be left without one or more of my basic drives, or without a normal cycle of sleep and wakefulness, or without the ability to regulate my body metabolism.

The Cerebral Cortex

We move now up to the anatomically topmost and evolutionarily newest part of the brain, the ***cerebral cortex***. *Cerebrum* is the Latin word for brain (the term is now sometimes used to refer to all parts of the brain other than the brainstem and cerebellum). *Cortex* is the Latin word for bark, and in anatomical usage it refers to the outside layer of any structure. The cerebral cortex, therefore, is the outermost layer—the bark—of the brain. It is by far the largest part of the human brain, accounting for approximately 80 percent of its total volume (Kolb & Whishaw,

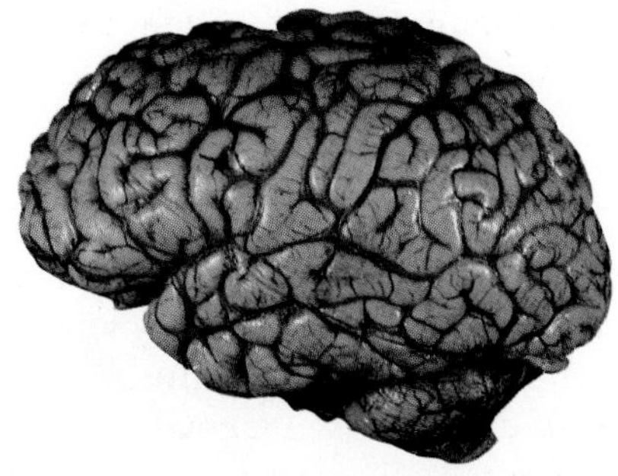

A cerebral cortex and cerebellum

What you can see here is only one-third of the cortex mass. The remaining two-thirds is hidden in the folds and fissures.

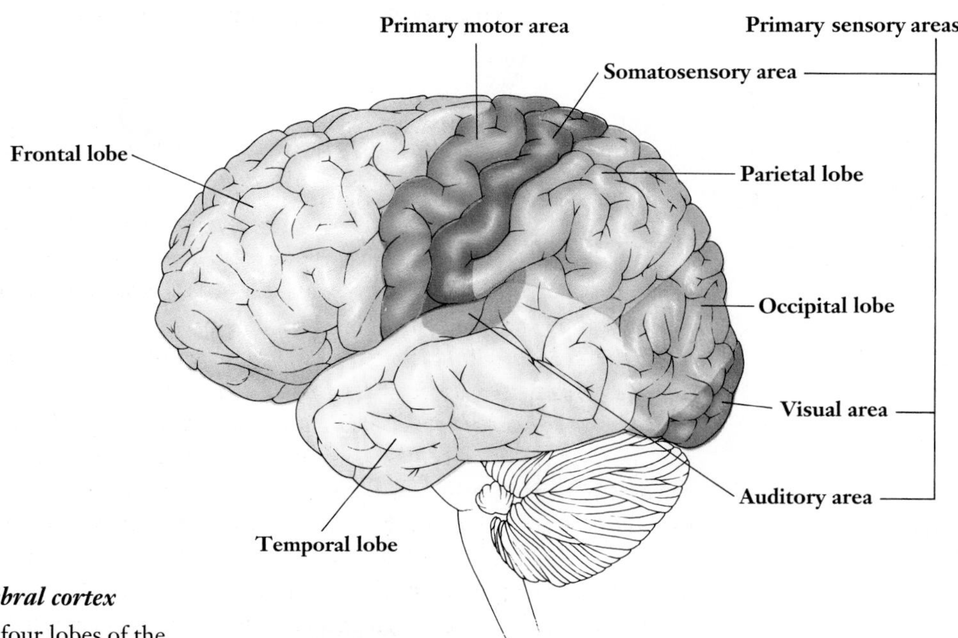

Figure 6.9 ***The cerebral cortex***

This figure shows the four lobes of the cortex, as well as the locations of the primary motor area and the primary sensory areas (visual, auditory, and somatosensory).

■ **14.** ***What are the four lobes of the cortex, and what are the three functional categories of areas that exist within these lobes?***

1990). Its surface area is much greater than it appears because it folds inward in many places. Approximately one-third of the surface of the human cortex is visible in a view of the undissected human brain, and the remaining two-thirds lies buried within the folds. The entire cerebral cortex is divided into left and right *hemispheres*, and each hemisphere is further divided into four lobes demarcated at least partly by rather prominent folds. The lobes, whose positions you can see in Figure 6.9 are, from back to front, the ***occipital***, ***temporal***, ***parietal***, and ***frontal lobes***.

Researchers who study the functions of the cortex divide it into three functional categories of regions, or areas. One category is the ***primary sensory areas***, which receive signals from sensory nerves and tracts by way of relay nuclei in the thalamus. As shown in Figure 6.9, primary sensory areas include the *visual area* in the occipital lobe, the *auditory area* in the temporal lobe, and the *somatosensory area* in the parietal lobe. A second category is the ***primary motor area***, which sends axons down to motor neurons in the brainstem and spinal cord. As shown in Figure 6.9, this area occupies the rear portion of the frontal lobe, directly in front of the somatosensory area. The third category consists of the remaining parts of the cortex which are called ***association areas***. These areas receive input from the sensory areas and lower parts of the brain and are involved in the complex processes that we call perception, thought, and decision making. As you can see in Figure 6.10, the amount of association cortex increases dramatically, relative to the other two categories, from simpler mammals such as the rat and the cat to more complex ones such as the monkey and the human.

Figure 6.10 ***Comparison of the brains of four mammals***

The brains all contain the same structures, but the monkey and human have much more cortical space devoted to association areas than do the rat and cat.

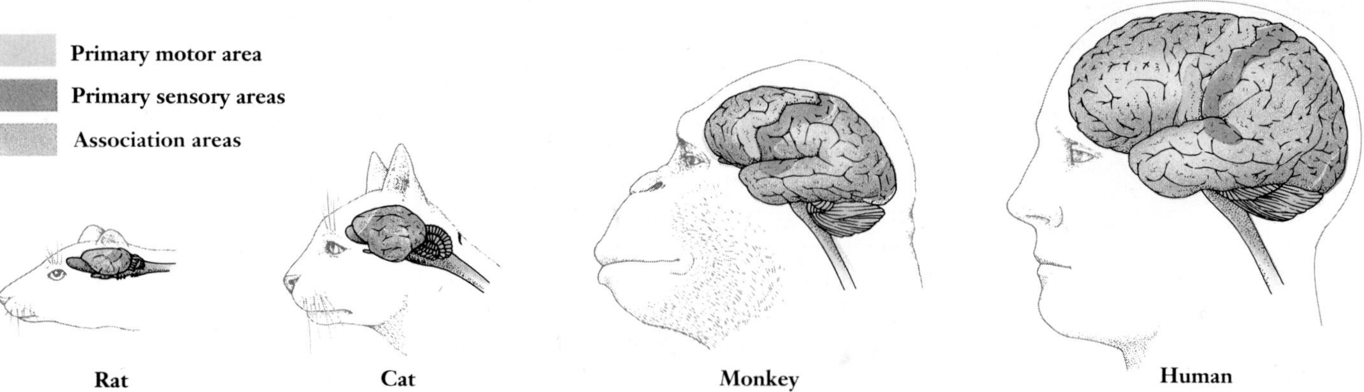

■ **15.** ***What does it mean to say that cortical sensory and motor areas are organized topographically? What is some evidence that these topographical maps can change with experience?***

Topographic Organization of the Primary Sensory and Motor Areas

The primary sensory and motor areas of the cortex are organized such that adjacent neurons receive signals from, or send signals to, adjacent portions of the sensory or muscular tissue to which they are ultimately connected. This fact is referred to as the *principle of topographic organization*. For example, neurons that are near one another in the visual cortex receive signals from receptor cells that are near one another in the retina of the eye. Similarly, neurons that are near one another in the somatosensory cortex receive signals from adjacent areas of the skin, and neurons near one another in the primary motor cortex send signals to adjacent sets of muscle fibers. It is possible to map onto the somatosensory cortex the part of the body from which each portion of the cortex receives its signals, or onto the motor cortex the part of the body to which each portion sends its signals (see Figure 6.11)

The maps in Figure 6.11 show a distorted view of the human body. This is because the amount of cortex devoted to each part of the body does not correspond to the size of the body part, but rather to the degree of sensitivity of that part (in the case of a sensory map) or the fineness of its movements (in the case of a motor map). As you can see in Figure 6.11, huge areas of the human primary motor cortex are devoted to control of the fingers and vocal apparatus, where fine control is needed. In other animals, other body parts have greater representation, depending on the range and delicacy of their movements. In cats, for example, large portions of the somatosensory and primary motor areas of the cortex are devoted to the whiskers, and in a spider monkey—a creature that uses its tail as a fifth arm and hand—large areas are devoted to the tail (Walker, 1973).

Figure 6.11 ***Organization of the somatosensory and primary motor areas***

As shown here, proportionately more cortical tissue is devoted to the more sensitive and delicately controlled body parts than to other parts.

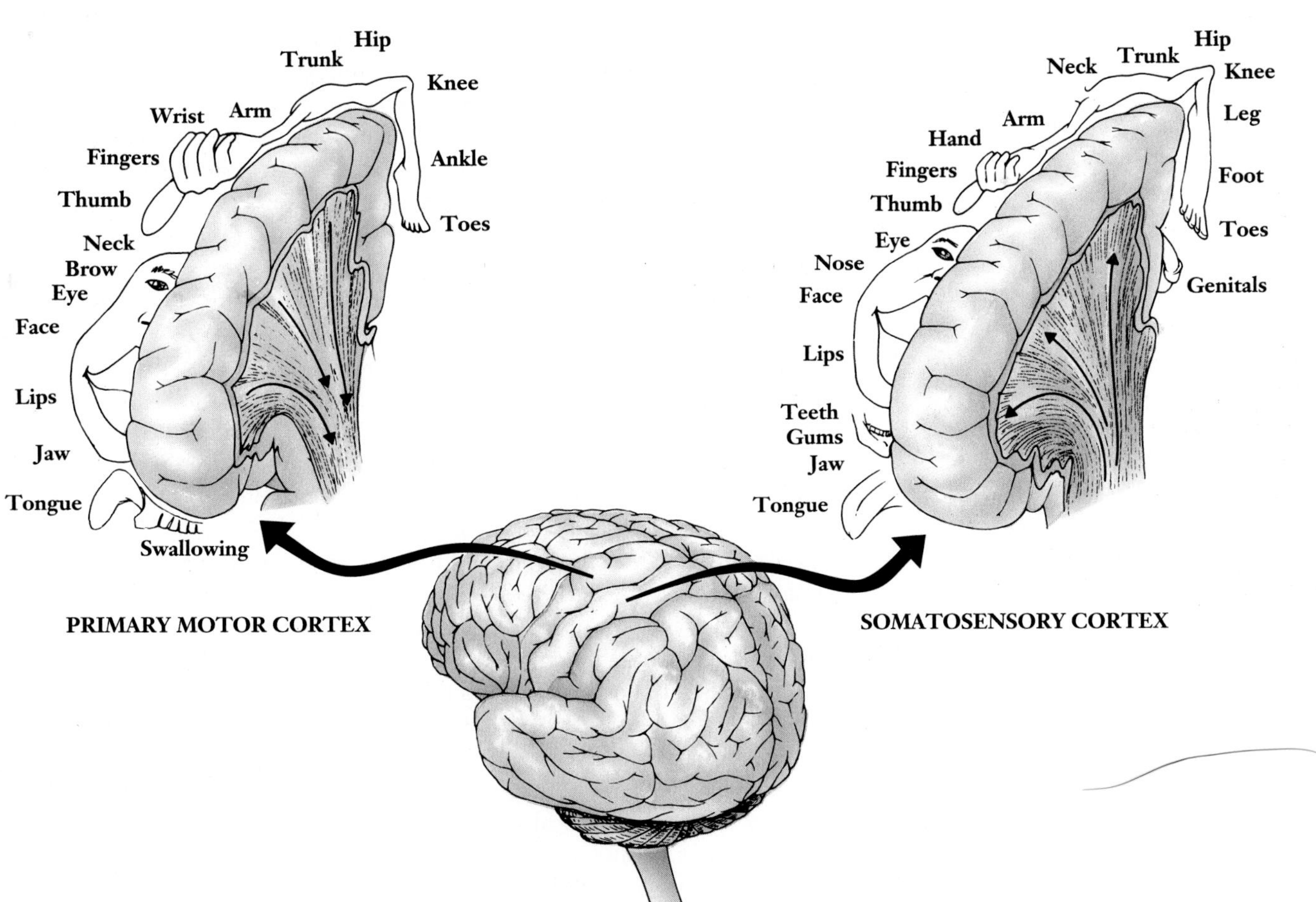

At one time scientists assumed that these maps in the cortex are permanently fixed by heredity. However, research in the 1960s showed that early experience with unusual stimuli can dramatically affect the maps in young animals, and recent research has shown that dramatic changes can occur even in adult animals. In one experiment, Gregg Recanzone, Michael Merzenich, and their colleagues (1992) trained adult owl monkeys over many sessions to discriminate a 20-cycle-per-second vibration applied to a particular spot of skin on one finger from a slightly higher rate of vibration applied to the same spot. (The monkeys received a banana flavored food pellet if they made a particular response each time the vibration rate increased above 20 cps.) The researchers then mapped the point-to-point connections from the monkeys' hands to the cortex by stimulating different points on the skin with a very thin probe while recording the activity of neurons in various parts of the hand area of the somatosensory cortex. They found by this means that the area of cortex that received inputs from the "trained" spot of skin was on average 2 to 3 times larger than the comparable area in untrained monkeys. Control monkeys, who experienced the same vibrations but received no rewards for discriminating one rate from another, did not show these changes. Apparently, the brain's ability to learn is mediated partly by its ability to reorganize patterns of connections within the cortex in order to give newly meaningful stimuli access to a greater number of brain cells than before (Edelman, 1987).

Cortical Control of Movement

■ 16. ***What is some evidence that the primary motor cortex comes relatively late in the chain of command preceding an action and that its function is to refine the more delicate parts of the action?***

As you know, the primary motor area of the cortex is involved in control of movement. This structure receives input from the basal ganglia and cerebellum and is specialized to fine-tune the signals going to the smaller muscles that must operate in a finely graded way. Experiments in which monkeys must make well-controlled hand movements to obtain a food reward have shown that each movement is preceded first by a burst of activity in the basal ganglia and then by a burst of activity in the motor cortex (Evarts, 1979; Kornhuber, 1974). This is part of the evidence that the primary motor cortex comes later than the basal ganglia and the cerebellum in the chain of command. Some of the output from the primary motor cortex occurs through extremely long neurons, whose cell bodies are in the primary motor cortex and whose axons terminate directly on motor neurons in the brainstem and spinal cord. These point-to-point connections, from cells in the primary motor cortex to small sets of motor neurons, help make delicate muscle movements possible.

Electrical stimulation of specific small areas of the primary motor cortex, through thin wires inserted into it, can produce twitches of single small muscles without activating nearby muscles (Asanuma & Sakata, 1967). It is through such experiments that motor maps like that in Figure 6.11 are produced. Other experiments have shown that monkeys whose primary motor cortex has been entirely destroyed behave normally in most respects, but are unable to make delicate hand movements, such as those needed to lift a small piece of food out of a narrow hole (Passingham & others, 1983).

■ 17. ***What is some evidence that the premotor and supplementary motor areas of the cortex help set up programs for skilled actions?***

Directly in front of the primary motor area lie two other cortical areas devoted to motor control—the *premotor area* and the *supplementary motor area* (see Figure 6.12). These are both involved in the initiation and coordination of learned, skilled movements (Ghez 1991b), and they exert their control partly by acting on neurons in the primary motor area. Experiments showing the functions of those areas in humans have taken advantage of techniques for monitoring the amount of neural activity in specific cortical regions by measuring changes in the flow of blood to those regions. Using such a technique, Per Roland and his colleagues (1980) in Denmark found that neural activity in the supplementary motor area precedes the

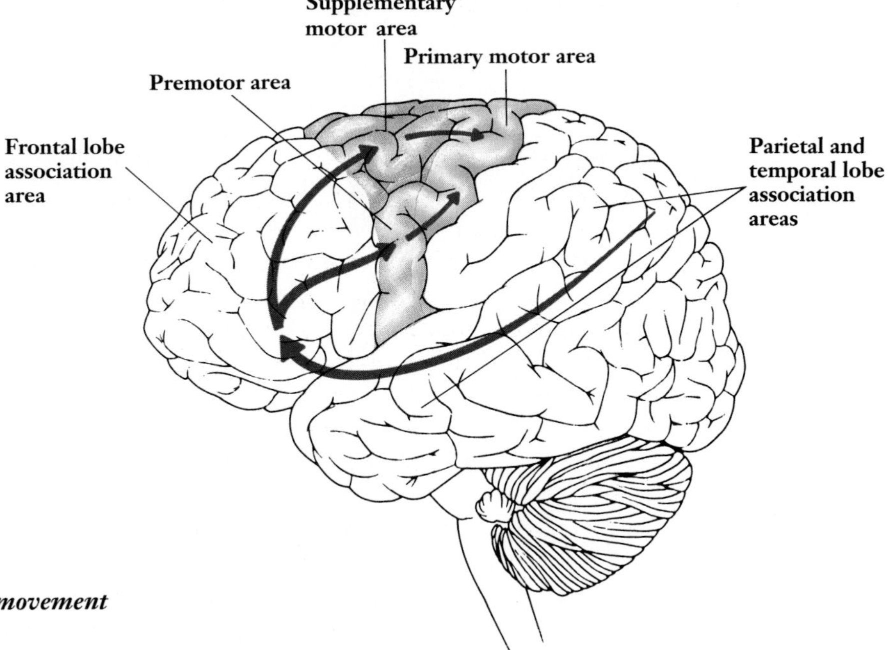

Figure 6.12 ***Control of movement by the cerebral cortex***

The frontal lobe association areas integrate information received from other brain areas and make a general plan for action. The premotor and supplementary motor areas convert this plan into neural programs for movement, which are then executed through connections to the primary motor cortex or through downward connections to the cerebellum and basal ganglia.

■ **18.** ***How do association areas in (a) the frontal lobe and (b) the parietal and temporal lobes contribute to movement control?***

performance of a skilled, learned motor task, and the more complex the task the greater is the degree of neural activity in that area. These researchers also found that when people were simply asked to rehearse a motor task mentally, without actually performing it, they again showed a large amount of activity in the supplementary motor area. Perhaps when skilled divers or gymnasts "visualize" their performance before they act, what they are doing, at least partly, is warming up the neurons in the supplementary motor area—in that way setting up the neural program that will eventuate in the perfect dive or vault.

Other areas of the cortex also contribute to the development of plans for action, in ways that are more complicated and less well understood than those just described. To get an idea of the general flow of information in the cortex in the control of movement, notice the arrows in Figure 6.12. Association areas in the rear parts of the cortex, especially the parietal and temporal lobes, are involved in the analysis of information that comes to them from sensory areas. These areas in turn send output to the association areas of the frontal lobe, which also receive information about the internal environment through strong connections with the limbic system. Combining all of this information, the frontal association areas set up general plans for action that can be put into effect through connections to the premotor and supplementary motor cortex, and also through downward connections to the basal ganglia.

Consistent with this interpretation, damage to the frontal lobes of the cortex does not, as a rule, harm one's ability to extract information from the environment, but it does harm one's ability to use that information effectively to control behavior. Depending on the location and extent of the damage, it can destroy either short-range planning, such as working out the series of movements needed to operate a lever, or long-range planning, such as organizing one's day, week, or life (Kolb & Whishaw, 1990).

Hierarchical Organization in the Control of Movement: A Summary

■ **19.** ***From an evolutionary perspective, why does it make sense to view the nervous system as a hierarchy of movement-control mechanisms?***

Thus far I have emphasized the role that each part of the nervous system plays in the control of movement. From an evolutionary perspective, control of movement is the overarching purpose of the nervous system. The nervous system integrates information to provide a basis for effective, life-preserving movement. The simplest nervous systems—found in the simplest invertebrate animals—control move-

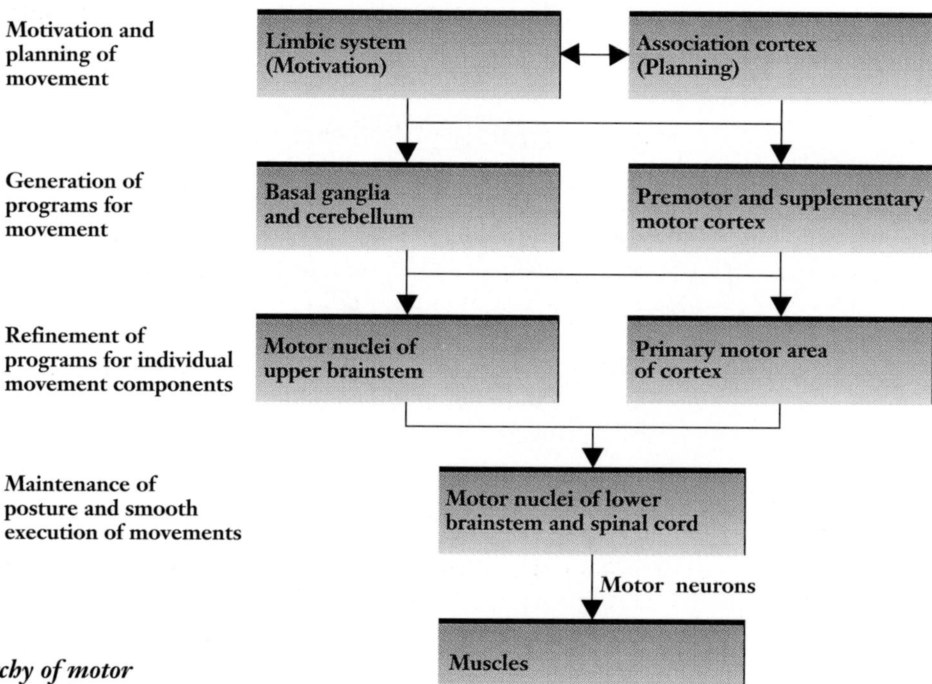

Figure 6.13 *A hierarchy of motor control*

This figure summarizes the broad functions of various structures of the nervous system in the control of movement. The structures shown higher up are involved in the more global aspects of an action, and those shown farther down are involved in the finer details of carrying it out. Notice that both subcortical and cortical structures exist at each of the top three levels of the hierarchy. Although there are flaws in this portrayal, it provides a useful way to think about the flow of information from the planning of an action to its execution.

■ **20.** ***How is the hierarchy of motor control illustrated by an imaginative tour through the nervous system of a person who decides to eat some peanuts?***

ment largely through means that are best described as reflexes. A stimulus produces a response, with relatively little intervening processing of the stimulus information. The evolution of more complex movement-control systems occurred not so much by replacing earlier systems as by building onto them. Thus, the human nervous system can be viewed as a *hierarchy* of systems, ranging from the most primitive, reflexive levels in the spinal cord up to the most complex, analytical levels involving association areas in the cerebral cortex. The higher and evolutionarily newer levels to a large degree exert their effects by controlling the activity of lower, older levels.

To review the functions of the various parts of the nervous system, and to visualize how they interact as a whole, look at the diagram shown in Figure 6.13 (based partly on Ghez, 1991a; and Schmidt, 1986). Structures are organized in this figure according to their general roles in controlling movement, not according to their anatomical position. At the top are structures involved in motivation and planning, and proceeding down are structures involved in refining and executing the plans, turning them into action. Notice that subcortical structures (shown on the left side of the diagram) and structures in the cortex (shown on the right side) are involved at each of the top three levels in the hierarchy.

To illustrate the hierarchy further, let's imagine events occurring in the nervous system of a person who hasn't eaten in a while and sees some peanuts. At the top of the hierarchy, the limbic system (which most directly monitors the internal state of the body) senses that food is needed and sends a message of "hunger" to the cortical association areas with which it is connected. These areas, which share the top of the hierarchy with the limbic system, analyze information coming to them from the visual cortex and determine that some peanuts lie in a bowl across the room. Other information is also considered by the association areas, including memories about the taste of peanuts, about how to eat them, and about the propriety of eating them in this room at this time. Such information, integrated by association areas in the frontal lobes, leads to a decision to cross the room, take a few peanuts, and eat them.

At the second level, the basal ganglia and cerebellum, as well as the premotor and supplementary motor areas of the cortex, receive the broad program from the limbic system and association cortex. They also receive direct somatosensory input concerning the exact position of parts of the body and visual input concerning the exact spatial location of the peanuts. They use this information to refine the motor program, working out the specific timing and patterning of the movements to be made.

At the third level, the motor program is conveyed through two pathways for further refinement. The program for larger movements, such as walking toward the peanuts, is sent directly down to a set of nuclei in the upper part of the brainstem. The program for delicate movements, such as removing the peanuts from their shells, is conveyed to the motor cortex, which in turn sends its output down to the brainstem and spinal cord. The motor cortex also receives sensory feedback from the fingers, through direct connections with the somatosensory cortex, which helps it make fine adjustments in the finger movements needed to shell the peanuts.

Finally, at the fourth level of the hierarchy are the motor neurons of the lower brainstem and spinal cord. In the words of the pioneering neurophysiologist Charles Sherrington, these neurons, which send their axons to muscles and glands, are the "final common path" of the nervous system. From an ultimate, evolutionary perspective, the whole function of all the billions of other neurons is to operate these few million motor neurons in a reasonable, life-promoting way.

A Word of Caution

■ **21.** ***What is the difference between knowing where a brain function occurs and knowing how it occurs?***

The hierarchy just described is useful as a first approach to understanding the nervous system, and it accurately reflects the kinds of behavioral deficits that occur when different parts of the nervous system are damaged. However, there is a possible danger in this portrayal: It can seduce us into believing that we know more than we actually do know. Specifically, the knowledge that certain parts of the brain are critical for certain aspects of behavioral control to occur can be mistaken for knowledge about *how* those processes are accomplished. But the discovery of "where" does not answer "how." In illustrating the hierarchy, I spoke of a "decision" made in association areas of the cortex, and of "programs for action" developed and refined by other brain areas. What do such statements mean? They only mean that individuals who suffer damage in one part of the brain lose the ability to make reasonable choices for action, and those who suffer damage in another part retain the ability to make reasonable choices but lose the ability to carry them out in a coordinated manner. Such statements don't address the far more difficult question of how the association cortex makes decisions, or how various other structures develop and refine programs for action.

In later chapters (Chapters 9–11) you will see theories about how information is analyzed and how decisions are made, but the theories will not deal with neural mechanisms. They will be general depictions, analogous to computer programs, of the stages through which information might be coded and interpreted. Detailed, explicit, neural-based theories cannot be presented—not for lack of space or interest, but because they have not yet been developed. Brain science has progressed a long way since the time of Galen, but it still has a long way to go before it can explain, in purely physiological terms, how you or I decide to eat some peanuts.

Asymmetry of Higher Functions of the Cerebral Cortex

Nearly every part of the brain exists in duplicate. We have a right and left member of each anatomical portion of the brainstem, thalamus, cerebellum, and so on. The part of the brain in which the right-left division is most evident, however, is the cerebral cortex. Each half of the cortex folds inward where it would abut the other half, forming a deep, fore-to-aft *midline fissure*, dividing the cortex into distinct

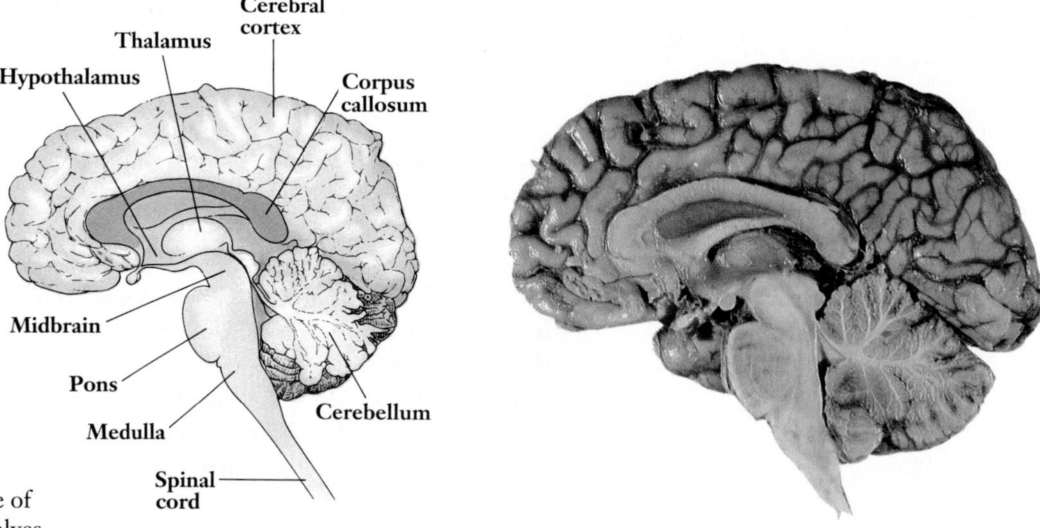

Figure 6.14 ***The corpus callosum***

The corpus callosum is a huge bundle of axons connecting the right and left halves of the cerebral cortex. You can see it here in an inside view of the right hemisphere of a human brain that has been cut in half. This photograph and matched diagram also allow you to see an inside view of other brain structures.

■ **22.** ***In what ways are the two hemispheres of the cortex functionally symmetrical and in what ways not?***

right and left *hemispheres*. The two hemispheres are connected, however, by a massive bundle of axons called the ***corpus callosum*** (see Figure 6.14).

Each hemisphere has the same four lobes, and the same primary sensory and motor areas, that were shown in Figure 6.9. Most of the neural paths between the primary sensory and motor areas and the parts of the body to which they connect are crossed, or *contralateral*. Thus, sensory neurons that arise from the skin on the right half of the body send their signals to the somatosensory area of the left hemisphere, and vice versa. Similarly, neurons in the primary motor cortex of the left hemisphere send their signals to muscles of the right half of the body, and vice versa. The two halves of the body function as a unified whole because the two hemispheres share their sensory information and coordinate their actions through the corpus callosum.

The two hemispheres are quite symmetrical in their basic sensory and motor functions. Each does the same job, but for a different half of the body. But the symmetry breaks down in association areas. The most obvious distinction, in humans, is that certain association areas in the left hemisphere are specialized for language and comparable areas in the right hemisphere are specialized for nonverbal, visual-spatial analysis of information.

Effects of Brain Damage in One Hemisphere or the Other

■ **23.** ***How do studies of people with brain damage contribute to our understanding of functional localization in the cortex?***

At the height of his career, the Russian composer V. G. Shebalin suffered a stroke (a rupturing of blood vessels in the brain) that damaged a portion of his left cerebral cortex. From then on he had great difficulty expressing himself in words and comprehending the words of others, but he continued to create great music. His *Fifth Symphony*, composed after the stroke, was described by the composer Dmitri Shostakovich as "a brilliant creative work, filled with highest emotions, optimistic and full of life" (Gardner, 1974).

We owe much of our understanding of functional localization in the human cortex to the misfortunes of people, such as Shebalin, who have suffered brain damage from strokes or other causes. In the nineteenth century, Paul Broca (1861) and others observed that people who suffer injuries to the left hemisphere are far more likely to lose their verbal abilities than are people with comparable injuries to the right hemisphere. Those with left-hemisphere damage are often unable to speak coherently or to understand what others are saying, even though their basic sensory and motor capacities remain intact. For decades, this observation was interpreted by the medical world to mean that the left hemisphere is "dominant" and that the right hemisphere is less important.

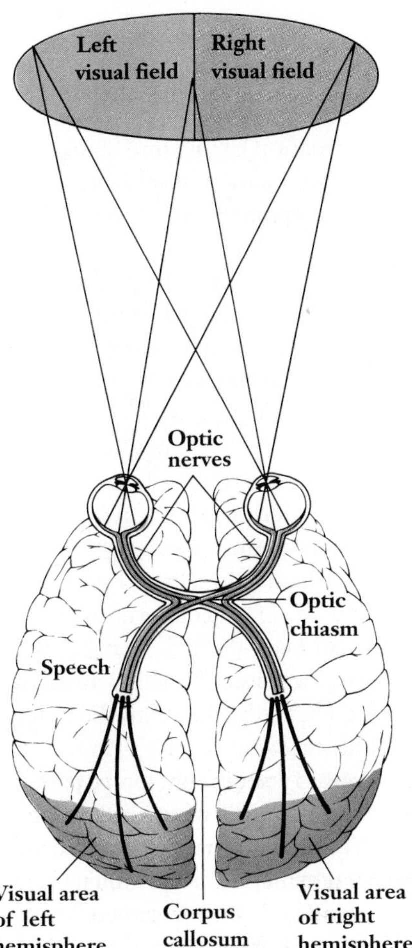

Figure 6.15 ***How visual information can be sent to one hemisphere or the other in a person whose corpus callosum has been cut***

Neurons of the optic nerves either cross or don't cross at the optic chiasm, as shown above, in such a way that those that receive input from the left visual field go to the right half of the brain, and vice versa. Thus, it is possible to present visual information to just one hemisphere in split-brain patients by having the patient focus on a dot on a screen and then quickly flashing the stimulus to one side or the other of the dot.

By the 1960s, however, evidence began to mount that the right hemisphere has special intellectual functions as well. In a study of soldiers who had suffered brain injuries in World War II, the Russian psychologist Alexander Luria (1966, 1970) found that people with right-hemisphere damage often have great difficulty with such tasks as recognizing faces, reading maps, or drawing geometric shapes. At about the same time, Brenda Milner (1974) and her colleagues in Montreal found that patients who had surgical destruction of part of the right hemisphere had specific deficits in the ability to recognize or remember pictures. Thus, the idea grew that the right hemisphere is specialized for understanding spatial relationships and the left is specialized for language.

The Split-Brain Syndrome

The most dramatic evidence for separate abilities of the two hemispheres appeared when Roger Sperry and Michael Gazzaniga began in the 1960s to study people who, as a last-resort treatment for epilepsy, had undergone an operation in which the corpus callosum had been entirely cut. Earlier, more casual observations had revealed no remarkable deficits in people who had had the operation. The operation was generally successful in reducing or eliminating epileptic seizures, and, after a period of recovery, there was usually no drop in measured IQ, in ability to carry on conversations, or even in ability to coordinate the two sides of the body in skilled tasks. But Sperry and Gazzaniga showed that under special test conditions in which information was provided just to one hemisphere or the other, these people behaved in some ways as if they had two separate minds with separate abilities.

The split-brain studies take advantage of the crossed sensory and motor connections of the brain. Recall that the right hemisphere most directly controls movement in, and receives somatosensory information from, the left half of the body, and the reverse is true for the left hemisphere. Connections from the eyes to the brain are such that input from the *right visual field* (the right-hand half of a person's field of view) goes first to the left hemisphere, and that from the *left visual field* goes first to the right hemisphere (see Figure 6.15). In the normal brain, information that goes first to one hemisphere subsequently travels to the other through the corpus callosum. But after the split-brain operation, such neural communication from one hemisphere to the other no longer occurs. Thus, with the testing apparatus shown in Figure 6.16, and with split-brain patients as subjects, it is possible to (a) send visual information to just one hemisphere by presenting the stimulus in the

Figure 6.16 ***Testing apparatus for split-brain subjects***

With this apparatus, it is possible to flash a stimulus to either visual field (or both at once) and to ask the person to identify objects by touch with either hand. With the image of a pencil flashed in his left visual field, this split-brain subject will be able to identify the pencil by touch with his left hand. Vocally, however, he will report having seen nothing on the screen. (Adapted from Gazzaniga, 1967.)

opposite half of the visual field, (b) send tactile information to just one hemisphere by having the subject feel an object with the opposite hand, and (c) obtain a response from just one hemisphere by having the subject point to an object with the opposite hand.

■ **24. *How is it possible to test each hemisphere separately in split-brain patients, and how do such tests confirm the view that the left hemisphere controls speech and the right hemisphere has superior spatial ability?***

In a typical experiment, pictures of common objects would be flashed in either the right or the left visual field. When flashed in the right field (to the left hemisphere), the split-brain patient could describe it as well as you or I might; but when flashed in the left field (to the right hemisphere), the patient would either claim that nothing had been flashed or would make a random guess. Then the researchers would ask the same person to reach under a barrier with one hand or the other and identify, by touch, the object that had been flashed. The fascinating result was that the person could reliably identify with the left hand (but not with the right) the same object that he or she had just vocally denied having seen (Gazzaniga, 1967). Thus, if the object flashed to the right hemisphere was a pencil, the subject's left hand would pick out the pencil from a set of objects even while the subject's voice was continuing to say that nothing had been flashed. In other tests, Sperry and Gazzaniga found that split-brain patients were much better at solving spatial puzzles or drawing geometric diagrams with their left hand than their right, indicating right-hemisphere superiority in spatial tasks.

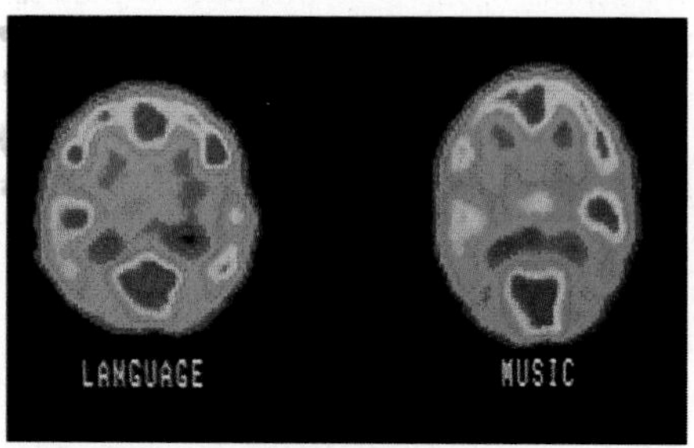

PET scans of person listening to language and music

Position emission tomography (PET) is a means of producing an image of the brain in which the varying rates of metabolic activity are depicted as colors of the spetrum. In the PET scans shown here, the front of the brain is at the top, and the areas of the greatest metabolic activity appear as red. These scans illustrate the typical finding that more activity occurs in the left temporal lobe than the right when a person listens to language, and more occurs in the right than the left when the person listens to music.

Researchers have found large individual differences among split-brain patients in the degree to which the right hemisphere can comprehend speech. Some show essentially no right-hemisphere comprehension. They cannot participate in experiments such as that just described, because their right hemispheres don't understand such instructions as, "Pick up the object that you saw on the screen." At the other extreme, some patients have right-hemisphere comprehension that is nearly as good as their left (though their right hemisphere is still unable to facilitate speech); and a few patients show a reversal, with the right hemisphere superior to the left in language comprehension and production. Other tests, on people without the corpus callosum cut, indicate that about 4 percent of right-handed individuals and 15 percent of left-handed individuals have their speech centers located in the right hemisphere rather than the left (Rasmussen & Milner, 1977).

Perhaps you are wondering how people who have had the split-brain operation get along in the world as well as they do. What keeps their two hemispheres from going off in opposite directions and creating conflict between the two halves of the body? In some instances, especially shortly after the surgery, conflict does occur. One man described a situation in which, while dressing in the morning, his right hand was trying to pull his pants on while his left hand was trying to pull them back off (Gazzaniga, 1970); apparently his right hemisphere wanted to go back to bed. But such conflicts are rare, and when they do occur the left hemisphere (right hand) usually wins.

The patient's ability to coordinate the two hemispheres probably involves several mechanisms. First, only the cerebral cortex and some parts of the limbic system are divided when the corpus callosum is cut. Motor centers that control whole-body movements such as walking lie in the lower, undivided parts, and some sensory information may also pass from one hemisphere to the other by way of those lower routes (Springer & Deutsch, 1989). In addition, under normal conditions, when the eyes can move around and things can be felt with both hands, the two hemispheres can receive the same or similar information through their separate channels. Finally, the hemispheres apparently learn to communicate indirectly with each other by observing the behavior that each other produces, a process that Gazzaniga (1967) labeled *cross-cuing*. For example, the right hemisphere may perceive something unpleasant and precipitate a frown, and the left may feel the frown and say, "I'm sad."

How Neurons Work and Influence Each Other

Thus far our concern has been with the functions of various parts of the nervous system in controlling behavior. We began by looking briefly at the three types of neurons (sensory neurons, interneurons, and motor neurons), and then we examined the functions of the various parts of the peripheral nervous system, the spinal cord, and (especially) the brain. Now let's look in more detail at the individual neuron. All the seeming magic of the nervous system is carried out at the cellular level by processes that in themselves are no more mysterious than any of the other processes of life. Knowledge of how individual neurons work can help us understand how neurons work together to provide the basis for all psychological processes. It can also help us understand how drugs and hormones act on the nervous system to influence mood and behavior.

Molecular Basis of the Action Potential

The Resting Potential and the Action Potential

The message that a neuron sends lies in the frequency of all-or-none ***action potentials***—electrical impulses that move down its axon and influence the activity of other cells. Action potentials are described as "all or none" for two reasons: (a) each action potential produced by a given neuron is the same strength as any other action potential produced by that neuron, and (b) the action potential retains its full strength all the way down the axon.

To understand action potentials, you need to know something about the functioning of the ***cell membrane***. The membrane is a porous "skin" that permits certain chemicals to flow into and out of the cell and blocks the passage of others. You can think of the neuron as a membrane-encased tube filled with a water solution called *intracellular fluid*, and bathed on the outside by another water solution called *extracellular fluid*.

■ **25. *How does the resting potential arise from the distribution of ions across the cell membrane?***

Among the various chemicals dissolved in the intracellular and extracellular fluids are some with electrical charges. These chemicals include: *soluble protein molecules*, which have negative charges and exist only in the intracellular fluid; *potassium ions* (K^+), which are more concentrated in the intracellular than the extracellular fluid; and *sodium ions* (Na^+) and *chloride ions* (Cl^-), which are more concentrated in the extracellular than the intracellular fluid. For the reason described in Figure 6.17,

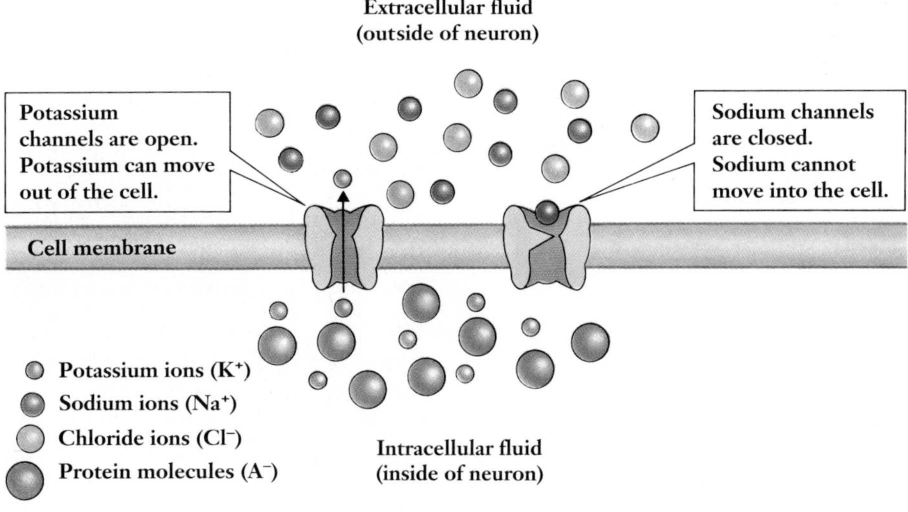

Figure 6.17 ***The resting potential***

Illustrated here is a portion of a neuron's cell membrane with ions dissolved on each side. Negatively charged protein molecules, or chains of amino acids (A^-), exist only inside the cell. Potassium ions (K^+) exist mostly inside the cell. Sodium ions (Na^+) and chloride ions (Cl^-) exist mostly outside the cell. Because channels in the membrane that are permeable to potassium remain open, some potassium ions diffuse out, resulting in a surplus of positive charges outside the cell and a deficit of positive charges inside. For this reason, the resting membrane has an electrical charge across it of about 70 mV, with the inside negative compared to the outside. (Adapted from: John Koester, "Membrane Potential," in *Principles of Neural Science*, 3E. Elsevier: New York, 1991, p. 85.)

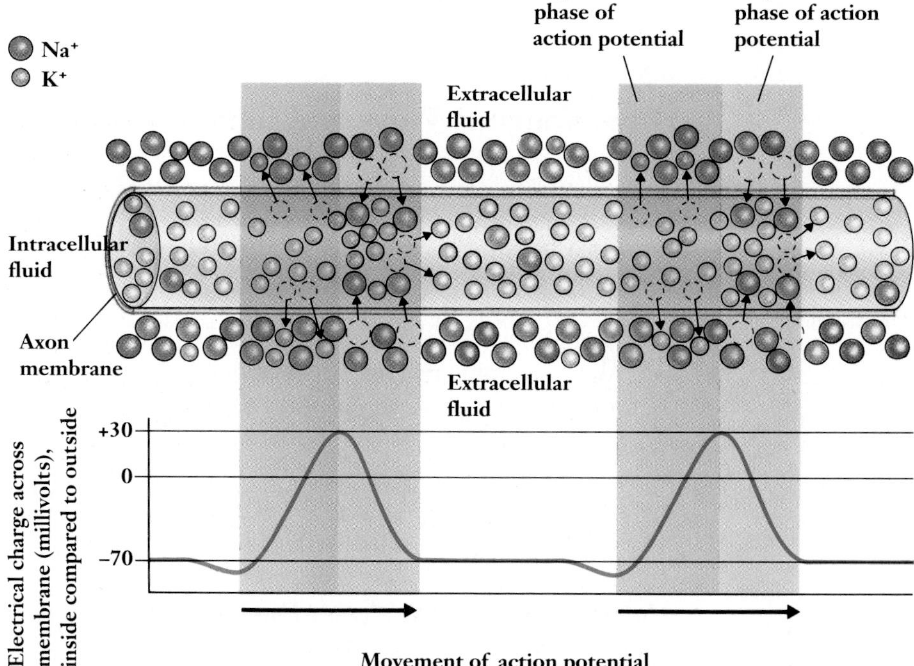

Figure 6.18 ***The action potential***

When an action potential is triggered, channels that allow Na^+ to pass through open their gates for a fraction of a millisecond, and enough Na^+ enters the axon to make it temporarily positive inside—the depolarization phase of the action potential. This depolarization triggers sodium channels to open in the part of the axon just ahead, causing the action potential to move like a wave down the axon. In the wake of depolarization, other channels open, which allow K^+ to move out of the axon, restoring the membrane potential to its original resting value—the repolarization phase. The bottom portion of the illustration shows two such electrical waves spread out along the axon. The front of each wave is on the right and the rear is on the left.

26. ***How do the two phases of the action potential (depolarization and repolarization) result from the successive opening and closing of two kinds of channels through the membrane?***

more negatively charged particles exist inside the cell than outside. This imbalance results in an electrical charge across the membrane, with the inside typically about –70 millivolts (a millivolt is a thousandth of a volt) relative to the outside. This charge across the membrane of the inactive neuron is called the ***resting potential***. Just as the charge between the negative and positive poles of a battery is the source of electrical energy in a flashlight, so the resting potential is the source of electrical energy that makes an action potential possible.

An action potential is initiated at one end of the axon and moves along the axon through a chain reaction that is sometimes likened to a row of dominoes falling after the first is tipped. As the action potential occurs at any given place on the axon (akin to the falling of one domino), thousands of tiny channels in the axon's membrane that are permeable to sodium open up, allowing some of the positively charged sodium ions in the extracellular fluid to pass into the intracellular fluid (see Figure 6.18). Two forces tend to drive sodium into the cell when the channels are open: (1) a concentration force, which occurs simply because more sodium ions exist outside the cell than inside; and (2) an electrical force, which occurs because like charges repel each other, so the positive electrical environment outside the cell pushes the positive sodium ions inward. As a result of these two forces, enough sodium moves inward to cause the electrical charge across the membrane to reverse itself and become momentarily *positive* inside relative to outside. This sudden shift constitutes the *depolarization phase* of the action potential.

As soon as this shift occurs, the channels that permitted sodium to pass through close up, and channels that permit only potassium to pass through open (Stevens, 1979). Because potassium ions are more concentrated inside the cell than outside, and because they are repelled by the temporarily positive environment inside the cell, they are pushed outward. In this process, enough positively charged potassium ions move out to reestablish the original resting potential. This constitutes the *repolarization phase* of the action potential. The entire action potential, from depolarization to repolarization, takes less than a millisecond (a thousandth of a second) to occur at any given point on the axon.

Knowing that some sodium moves into the cell and some potassium moves out each time an action potential occurs, you might wonder why a neuron doesn't eventually lose so much potassium and gain so much sodium that it can no longer produce action potentials. Actually, only a small amount of sodium and potassium moves with every action potential. (It takes only a tiny change in the balance of ions to reverse the electrical polarity.) But the question is still a good one, because neurons often produce several hundred action potentials per second, and eventually so much sodium could move in, and potassium out, that no more action potentials could occur. The answer is that the cell membrane continuously reestablishes the original balance of sodium and potassium with a *sodium-potassium pump*. The pump is actually a chemical mechanism, built into each part of the cell membrane, which moves sodium out and potassium in whenever the original balance is disrupted. One can think of it as the neuron's battery recharger. Like any recharger, it requires energy; to keep the pump going the neuron constantly needs food and oxygen, which come from the blood. (Remember the ancient Greeks' observation that the brain has particularly large blood vessels entering it? You now know a reason why.)

■ **27.** ***How does the neuron keep recharging itself?***

The Movement of Action Potentials Down the Axon

Action potentials are triggered at one end of the axon by any influences that tend to reduce the electrical charge across the membrane at that point. The axon's membrane is constructed in such a way that *depolarization*, or reduction in charge, to some critical value causes the sodium channels to open, thereby triggering an action potential. This critical value (for example, to –60 millivolts inside, compared with a resting potential of –70 millivolts inside), is referred to as the cell's *threshold*. Once an action potential occurs at one end of the axon, it depolarizes the area of the axon just ahead of where it is occurring, thus triggering the sodium channels to open up there. In this way the action potential keeps renewing itself and moves continuously down the axon. When an axon branches, the action potential follows each branch and thus reaches each of the possibly thousands of axon terminals.

■ **28.** ***How is an axon's conduction speed related to its diameter and the presence or absence of a myelin sheath?***

The speed at which an action potential moves down an axon is affected by the axon's diameter. Large-diameter axons present less resistance to the spread of electric currents and therefore conduct action potentials faster than thin ones. Another feature that helps speed up the rate of conduction in many axons is the presence of a myelin sheath. The cells that form the sheath insulate the axon's membrane, so ions can move through only at spaces (nodes) between adjacent cells. Each action potential skips down the axon, from one node to the next, faster than it could move as a continuous wave. The thickest and most thoroughly myelinated axons in the nervous system can conduct action potentials at a velocity of about 100 meters per second (that translates into about 250 miles per hour). Thus, it takes about one-hundredth of a second for an action potential to run along such an axon from the central nervous system to a muscle about a meter away (a toe or finger muscle, for example). Very thin axons without a myelin sheath, on the other hand, may conduct at rates as slow as 1 or 2 meters per second. When you poke your finger with a pin, you feel the pressure of the pin before you feel the pain. That is partly because the sensory neurons for pressure are large and myelinated, and those for pain are thin and mostly unmyelinated.

Molecular Basis of Neural Communication

■ **29.** ***How do neurotransmitters at excitatory and inhibitory synapses affect the rate at which action potentials are produced in the postsynaptic neuron?***

Synaptic Transmission

Neurons, as you learned earlier, exert their influence on other neurons or muscle cells at synapses. Although there are many kinds of synapses (including synapses of dendrites upon dendrites and axons upon axons), the best-understood synapses are those between an axon terminal and either a muscle cell or the dendrite or cell

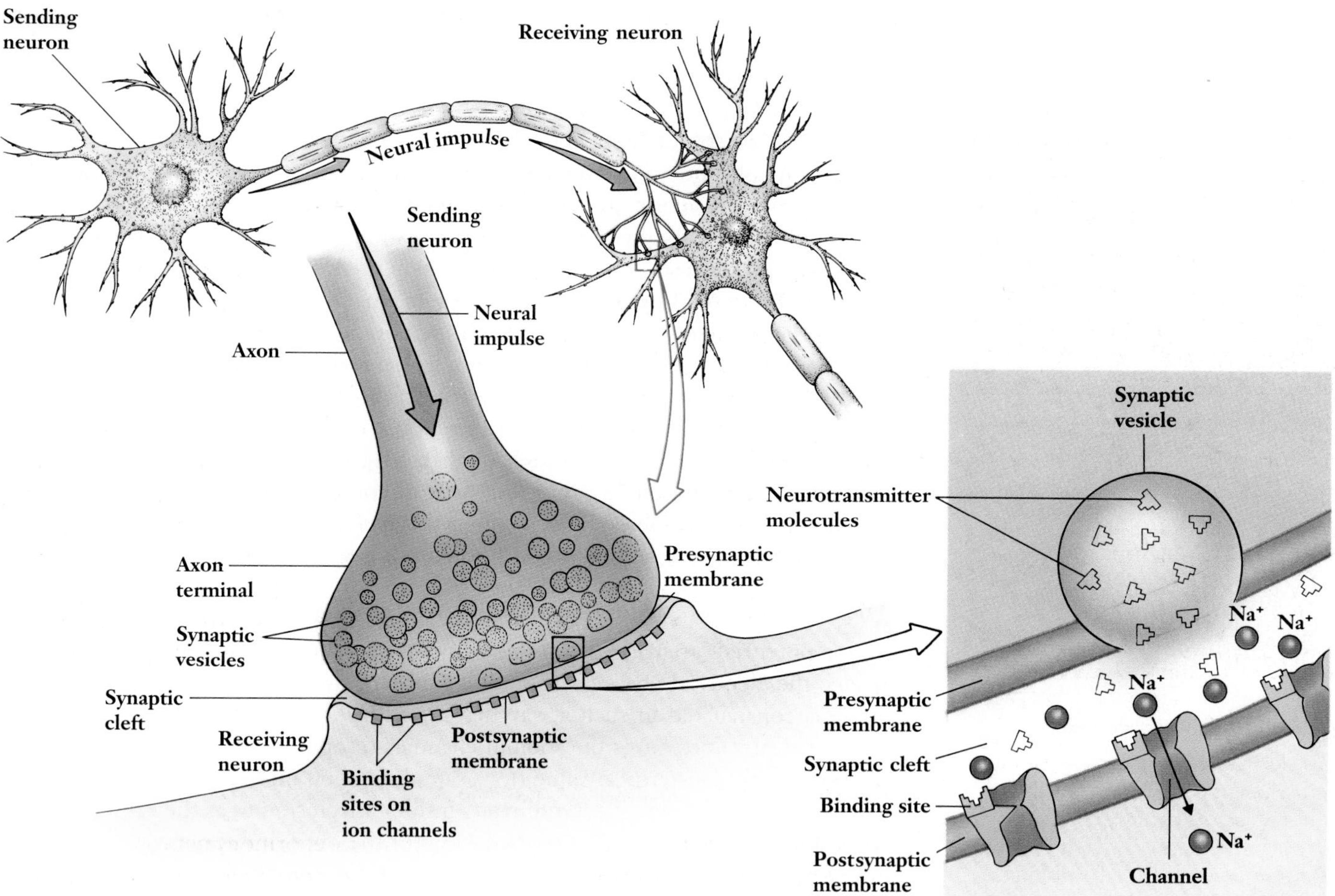

Figure 6.19 ***Transmission across the synapse***

When an action potential reaches an axon terminal, it causes some of the synaptic vesicles to spill their transmitter molecules into the synaptic cleft. Some of the molecules diffuse across the cleft and bind at special binding sites on the postsynaptic membrane, where they open channels that permit ions to flow through the membrane. In this example (an excitatory synapse), channels permeable to sodium ions (Na^+) open, causing an influx of positive charges into the receiving neuron. At an inhibitory synapse, channels permeable to chloride ions (Cl^-) would open, allowing an influx of negative charges.

body of another neuron. The axon terminal is separated from the membrane of the cell that it influences by a very narrow gap, the *synaptic cleft*. The membrane of the axon terminal that abuts the cleft is the *presynaptic membrane*, and that of the cell on the other side of the cleft is the *postsynaptic membrane*. Within the axon terminal are hundreds of tiny globe-like *vesicles*, each of which contains several thousand molecules of a chemical neurotransmitter (Stevens, 1979). These structures are all depicted in Figure 6.19.

When an action potential reaches the axon terminal, it causes some of the vesicles to spill their neurotransmitter molecules into the cleft. The molecules then diffuse through the fluid within the cleft, and some become attached to special binding sites on the postsynaptic membrane (the membrane of the receiving cell). Each molecule of transmitter can be thought of as a key, and the binding sites can be thought of as locks. A molecule key entering a binding-site lock opens a gate in the channel, allowing ions to pass through. If the postsynaptic cell is a muscle cell, this flow of ions triggers a biochemical process that causes it to contract. If the postsynaptic cell is a neuron, one of two opposite effects occurs, depending on the type of synapse. At an ***excitatory synapse*** (as shown in Figure 6.19), the transmitter opens sodium (Na^+) channels. The movement of the positively charged sodium ions into the cell causes a slight depolarization of the receiving neuron (the neuron becomes less negative inside),which tends to increase the rate of action potentials triggered by that neuron. At an ***inhibitory synapse***, the transmitter opens chloride (Cl^-) channels. The movement of negatively charged chloride ions into the cell causes a slight hyperpolarization of the receiving neuron (the neuron becomes even more negative inside than it was before), which tends to decrease the rate of action potentials triggered by that neuron.

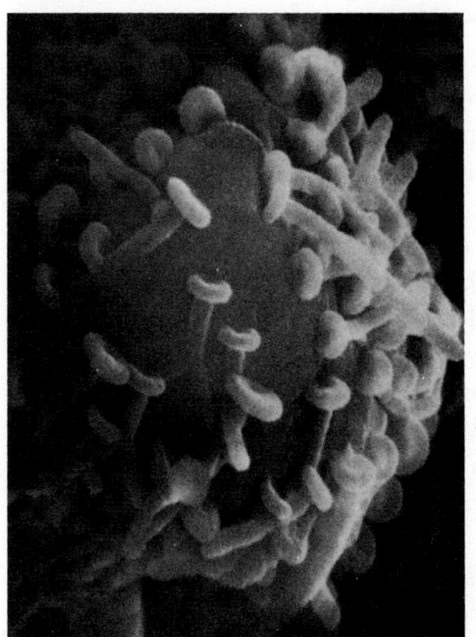

Figure 6.20 ***Axon terminals***

In this electron micrograph you can see the terminals of many axons forming synapses on the cell body of a single neuron. Synaptic vesicles, filled with neurotransmitter molecules, reside within the button-like swelling of each axon terminal. In the central nervous system, the cell bodies and dendrites of motor neurons and some interneurons are blanketed with thousands of such terminals.

Integration of Excitatory and Inhibitory Inputs

Any given neuron receives input via many synapses. In fact, the cell body and dendrites of some neurons are completely blanketed with axon terminals from thousands of other neurons (see Figure 6.20). Some of these synapses are excitatory and some inhibitory, and at any given moment transmission is occurring at some but not all of them (see Figure 6.21). At each excitatory synapse, the transmitter causes a slight depolarization, and at each inhibitory synapse the transmitter (which is a different substance from that at excitatory synapses) causes a slight hyperpolarization. These effects spread passively through the cell body and affect the electrical charge across the membrane of the axon at its junction with the cell body. Recall that whenever the axonal membrane is depolarized below the critical value, action potentials are triggered. The greater the degree of depolarization below that value, the greater will be the number of action potentials triggered per second. Thus, the rate of action potentials generated by the postsynaptic neuron's axon depends on the relative amount of activity at the excitatory as opposed to inhibitory synapses on that neuron. In this way the neuron integrates the total amount of excitatory and inhibitory signals to it and sends a message (in its rate of action potentials) reflective of that integration.

Modification of Neural Connections as a Basis for Learning

As you have seen, the nervous system consists of an enormous network of neurons connected with each other at synapses. Researchers sometimes refer to these connections as "wiring," but that analogy has limits. The nervous system is not *hard wired* like a computer or other human-made electrical device. Neurons are soft, pliable, living cells. They can change their sizes, shapes, excitabilities, and patterns of connections in ways that help adapt their possessor to life's circumstances. You don't grow new neurons after birth, but you do grow new synapses (and lose old ones) throughout your life.

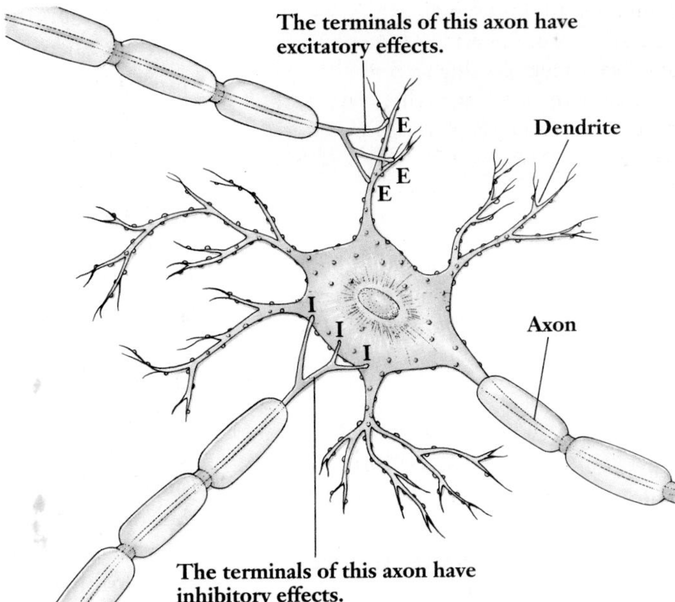

Figure 6.21 ***Excitatory and inhibitory synapses***

Neurons in the central nervous system receive many synaptic connections from other neurons, some excitatory and some inhibitory. All synapses from any single neuron are either excitatory or inhibitory, as shown here.

Effects of Enriched and Deprived Environments

■ **30.** ***What brain changes occurred when rats were raised in enriched compared to deprived environments?***

Evidence for the modifiability of neurons arose in the 1960s in research by Mark Rosenzweig and his colleagues (1972) on the effects of *enriched* and *deprived* environments on the brains of rats. The enriched environments were large group cages, with many objects to explore, and the deprived environments were small cages, where rats lived isolated from other rats and with no objects except food and a water bottle. The researchers found thicker cerebral cortexes, more acetylcholine (a prominent neurotransmitter in the cortex), and larger neurons in the brains of the enriched-environment rats. Subsequently, other researchers found that the cortexes of enriched-environment rats contained neurons with more, and more fully developed (strongly transmitting), synapses than did the cortexes of deprived-environment rats (Turner & Greenough, 1985). These changes attributable to living conditions could be produced not just in young rats but in old ones too, and were subsequently replicated in other mammalian species (Greenough & Black, 1992; Rosenzweig, 1984).

So neurons do change as a result of one's experience. But how, exactly, might changes in particular neurons and their connections provide the physiological basis for specific instances of learning? That question cannot be answered with the methods developed by Rosenzweig and his colleagues. Their enriched-environment rats had numerous experiences that differentiated them from deprived-environment rats. Moreover, the rat brain (or any other mammalian brain) is so complex that researchers have difficulty relating particular neurons to particular behaviors. For that reason, many researchers interested in the neuronal mechanisms of learning study invertebrate animals that have far simpler nervous systems.

Aplysia
Because of its relatively simple nervous system, this sea-dwelling mollusk has become a favorite subject for studies of the neuronal basis of learning.

How a Mollusk Learns

For more than 20 years, Eric Kandel (1991) and his colleagues have been studying the neural mechanisms of behavior in a shell-less, sea-dwelling mollusk commonly called a sea slug, or sea hare, and known to scientists by the genus name *Aplysia.* The advantage of using this invertebrate is the simplicity of its nervous system. Even the simplest of vertebrates has millions of neurons, but *Aplysia* has only about 20,000, some quite large and easy to identify. Several of *Aplysia's* natural behaviors can be modified by learning, and they involve as few as 100 neurons (Bailey & Chen, 1991).

One such behavior is the gill-withdrawal reflex. When touched with sufficient force anywhere on its skin, *Aplysia* reflexively pulls its gill into its body as protection against attack. Kandel and his colleagues have found that this reflex can be *sensitized* (made to occur to a weaker stimulus than it normally would) and *classically conditioned*, and have studied the neural bases of these changes.

To sensitize the gill-withdrawal reflex of *Aplysia* in the laboratory, a strong stimulus such as an electric shock is applied to the animal's skin. For some time afterwards, even a very light touch anywhere on the skin, which normally has no effect, elicits a gill-withdrawal response. If the shock is applied only once, this increased sensitivity lasts an hour at most—a change referred to as *short-term sensitization*. However, if the shock is applied several times, *long-term sensitization* ensues; the heightened response to touch may now last as long as two or three weeks (Bailey & Chen, 1991).

■ **31.** ***What is the neural mechanism of (a) short-term sensitization, (b) long-term sensitization, and (c) classical conditioning of the gill-withdrawal reflex in* Aplysia*?***

The mechanism of sensitization is diagrammed in Figure 6.22. (Try tracing the reflex as you continue to read.) The gill-withdrawal reflex is mediated by sensory neurons that come from various places on the animal's skin and terminate at synapses on motor neurons going to the animal's gill. These same sensory neurons also terminate on special interneurons called *modulatory neurons*, and these provide

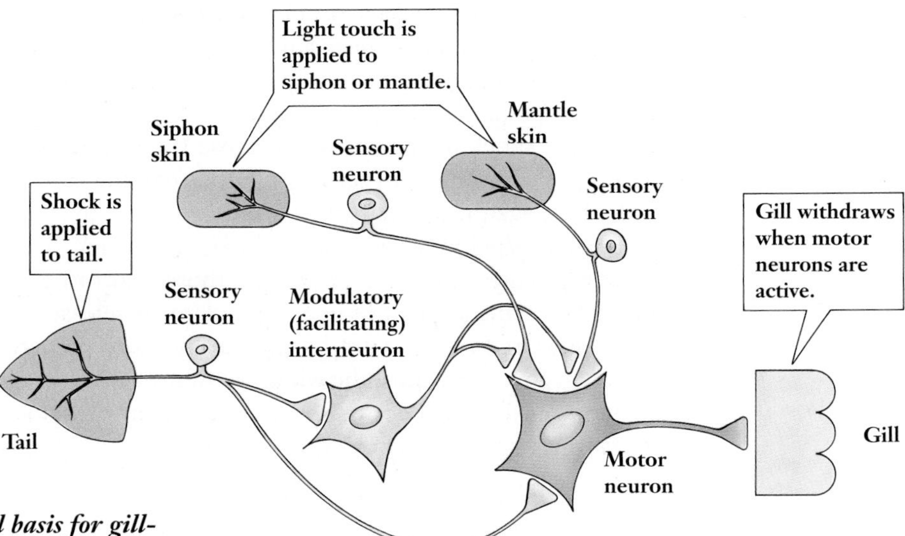

Figure 6.22 ***Neuronal basis for gill-withdrawal learning in*** **Aplysia**

In this diagram, each neuron stands for a set of neurons that operate in parallel. Sensory neurons from various parts of the animal's body (the tail, siphon, and mantle) all have synapses on motor neurons that act to withdraw the gill. Strong stimulation at any of these areas produces the gill-withdrawal reflex. Strong stimulation at any of these areas also sensitizes the reflex, though in the diagram this is shown only for a stimulus at the tail. Sensitization is reflected in this example by a heightened gill-withdrawal response to weak stimuli presented to either the siphon or the mantle. Sensitization can be either short-term or long-term, depending on the number of times the strong stimulus to the tail is presented, and in either case it occurs through the facilitating effect of modulatory interneurons on the synaptic terminals of sensory neurons that come from the siphon and mantle. This sensitizing effect is stronger on sensory neurons that have just been active than on other sensory neurons, and that provides the basis for classical conditioning of the reflex.

the basis for sensitization. The modulatory neurons are activated only when the sensory neurons are unusually active, as in response to an electric shock or (in natural conditions) a bite from a predator. When activated, the modulatory neurons release their transmitter, called a *modulatory transmitter* or ***neuromodulator***, directly on the synaptic terminals of sensory neurons.

The neuromodulator molecules act on the cell membrane of the sensory neurons, near and at the axon terminals, to block some of the potassium channels. Recall that the repolarization process that terminates action potentials involves the flow of potassium through the potassium channels (look back at Figure 6.18). With some of the channels blocked, each action potential that reaches the synaptic terminal lasts longer than it otherwise would and causes more neurotransmitter to be released onto the motor neuron. This is the basis for short-term sensitization (Kandel, 1991). When the shock or other strong stimulus occurs several times, the repeated action of the neuromodulator initiates an additional set of effects: It stimulates a chain of biochemical processes that strengthens existing synapses from the sensory neurons to the motor neurons and produces new ones. These changes are the basis for long-term sensitization (Bailey & Chen, 1991).

In further research, Kandel and his colleagues uncovered the neural mechanism of classical conditioning in *Aplysia*. As was described in Chapter 5, classical conditioning occurs when an *unconditioned stimulus*, which elicits a reflexive response, is paired with a *conditioned stimulus* often enough for the latter alone to call forth the reflex. In *Aplysia*, shock to the tail can serve as the unconditioned stimulus to elicit the gill-withdrawal reflex, and a light touch anywhere else on the animal's skin, such as on the siphon (see Figure 6.22), can serve as the conditioned stimulus. (Notice that in conditioning the shock is presented together with the conditioned stimulus during training, but in sensitization the shock is presented alone.) The conditioned gill-withdrawal reflex in *Aplysia* differs from the sensitized reflex in two ways: It is stronger, and it is specific to the area of the skin where the conditioned stimulus was applied during training. Thus, the conditioning process in which light touch to the siphon was paired with shock to the tail would *sensitize* sensory neurons from both the siphon and the mantle (Figure 6.22), but would *condition* only those from the siphon. The animal would now show a more pronounced gill-withdrawal response to a touch on the siphon than to a touch on the mantle.

At the molecular level, Kandel and his colleagues found that conditioning takes place exactly as short-term and long-term sensitization do, but with one addition: The neuromodulator has a greater effect on sensory neurons that have just fired action potentials than on those that haven't (Byrne, 1990). With reference to Figure 6.22, shock to the tail would cause the release of neuromodulatory molecules upon the terminals of sensory neurons coming from the siphon and from the mantle. However, if the sensory neurons from the siphon had just fired because of light touch applied to the siphon just before the shock, the effect of the neuromodulatory molecules would be greater on those neurons than on neurons from the mantle. The same amount of neuromodulator is released on both sets of neurons, but the just-fired neurons are biochemically more prepared to receive it and respond to it. In other words, the whole set of processes that produce short-term and long-term sensitization occurs to a greater extent on active neurons than on inactive neurons—and that is how *Aplysia* learns.

Relevance to Theories About the Human Brain

As you have seen, in *Aplysia* successively more complex forms of learning build upon each other, using the same underlying mechanism. Some researchers speculate that similar neuronal mechanisms—compounded a million-fold by the sheer number of connections—may provide the foundation for even the most complex forms of learning in humans. Long ago, the Canadian psychologist Donald Hebb (1949) proposed that the brain's ability to change with experience lies, at the cellular level, in the ability of neurons to form new connections with each other, or strengthen old ones, as a result of patterns of neural activity that occur in them. Kandel's work with *Aplysia* shows that neurons indeed can behave as Hebb proposed. Using artificial means to stimulate specific neurons and combinations of them, other researchers have shown that synaptic connections in mammals' brains also can change in ways similar to those proposed by Hebb and identified by Kandel (Lynch & others, 1991).

■ 32. ***How do Hebb's theory and Kandel's* Aplysia *research pertain to network models of the brain?***

Hebbs' idea and the research supporting it, coupled with progress in computer technology, has helped inspire an approach to studying learning and other psychological processes called ***neural network modeling*** (Rumelhart & McClelland, 1986; Sejnowski & Tesauro, 1990). The essence of this approach is to construct large networks of interconnected units (referred to metaphorically as "neurons") and provide the units with simple rules for increasing or decreasing the strength of their connections based on patterns of activity in them and their neighbors. The networks are also provided with input mechanisms, analogous to sensory receptors and output mechanisms, analogous to muscles (see Figure 6.23). The researchers do not actually build these networks with real electrical parts, but model them on computer software to see how they would behave if they were built. According to some reports, such network models often respond in ways that are remarkably similar to learning and perceptual phenomena that have been identified in research with humans and other mammals.

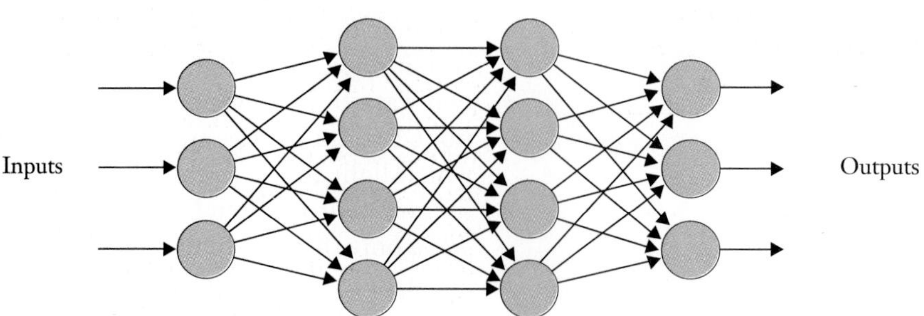

Figure 6.23 ***A neural net***

This type of network model is called a layered model. Each unit of each layer is connected to each unit of the next layer. With appropriate rules for increasing or decreasing the strength of individual connections, the pattern of response to a given pattern of inputs in such a net will change as a result of experience in a manner analogous to learning in a real nervous system. More complex models have feedback loops so that units can affect connections to their left as well as their right.

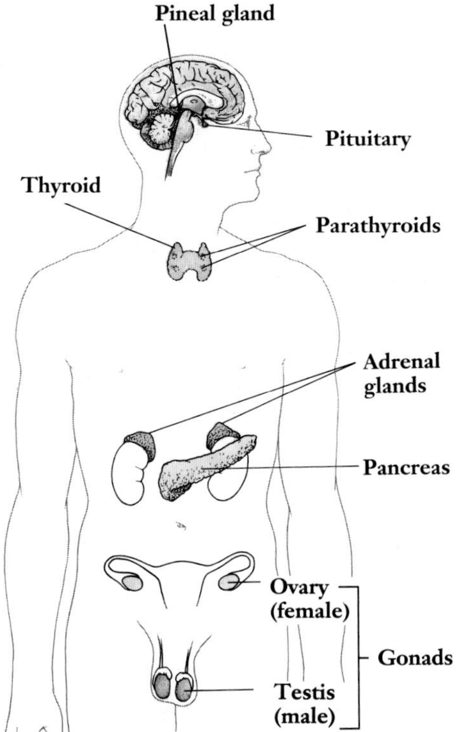

Figure 6.24 ***Endocrine glands***
These are some of the glands that secrete hormones into the bloodstream. The pituitary, which is controlled by the brain, secretes hormones that in turn control the production of hormones by the thyroids, adrenals, and ovaries or testes.

How Hormones and Drugs Interact with the Nervous System

When the ancient Greeks argued that the heart is the seat of thought, feeling, and behavioral control, they were not entirely without reason. Like the brain, the heart is an organ that has long protrusions from it (blood vessels, in this case), connecting it with other parts of the body. Blood vessels are easier to see than nerves, and because they can be found in all of the sense organs and muscles, as well as in other tissues, early theorists believed blood vessels to be the conduits of sensory and motor messages. Today we know that the circulatory system does indeed play a vital communicative role in the body. A slower messenger system than the nervous system, it carries chemicals that affect both physical growth and behavior. Among these chemicals are hormones, which are secreted naturally into the bloodstream, and drugs, which may enter the blood artificially through various routes.

Hormones

Hormones are chemical messengers that are secreted into the blood. They are carried by the blood to all parts of the body, where they act on specific *target tissues*. Dozens of hormones have been identified. The classic hormones—the first to be identified and the best understood—are secreted by special ***endocrine glands*** (see Figure 6.24). But many other hormones are secreted by organs not usually classified as endocrine glands, such as the stomach, intestines, kidneys, and brain.

33. ***How are hormones similar to, and different from, neurotransmitters?***

Comparison of Hormones to Neurotransmitters

Hormones and neurotransmitters probably have a common origin in evolution (Snyder, 1985). The earliest multicellular animals evolved a system of chemical messengers that allowed the cells to communicate and coordinate their actions so the animal could behave as a unit. As organisms grew more complex, the chemical communication system differentiated along two distinct routes. One route involved the nervous system and was designed for rapid, specific, point-to-point communication. In these cells the primitive chemical messengers evolved into neurotransmitters. The other route involved the circulatory system and was designed for relatively slow, diffuse, widespread communication. Here the primitive chemical messengers evolved into hormones.

The main difference between a hormone and a neurotransmitter is the distance that each must travel through fluid between its site of release and its site of action. Neurotransmitter molecules released from an axon terminal must diffuse across the synaptic cleft—a distance of about 20 nanometers (20 billionths of a meter)—in order to affect the postsynaptic cell. In contrast, hormone molecules often must travel through the entire circulatory system before they bind to their target cells and exert their effects.

34. ***What are two arguments supporting the idea that hormones and neurotransmitters have a common evolutionary origin?***

One argument for a common origin of hormones and neurotransmitters is their chemical similarity. In fact, some hormones are chemically identical to some neurotransmitters. The chemical *norepinephrine*, for example, is a hormone when secreted into the blood by the adrenal gland (shown in Figure 6.24), but is a neurotransmitter when released by sympathetic motor neurons of the peripheral nervous system upon visceral muscles and glands. It is also a neurotransmitter in certain pathways in the brain. In each of these roles norepinephrine helps arouse and alert the body. As a hormone and as a sympathetic transmitter it has such effects as increasing the heart rate, and as a brain transmitter it helps produce a state that we experience psychologically as high arousal or alertness.

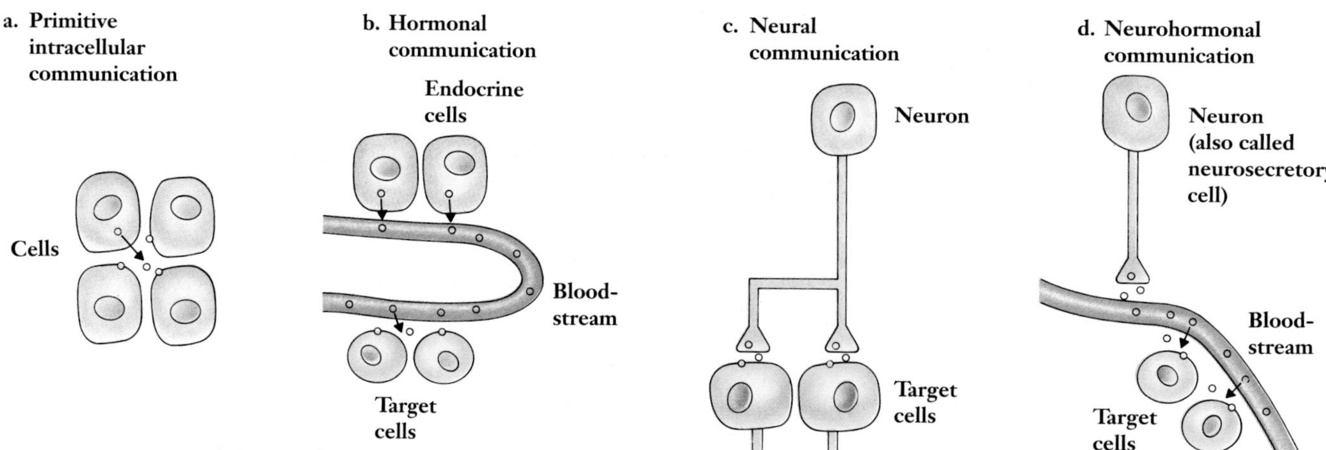

Figure 6.25 ***Four modes of chemical communication between cells***

Evolutionarily, the (a) primitive mode of intracellular communication differentiated to form (b) a slow, hormonal mode of communication and (c) a fast, *neural* mode of communication. The link between these two differentiated types is maintained by (d) neurohormonal communication. (Based on figure in Snyder, 1985.)

Another example of chemical sameness between hormones and transmitters can be found in the *endorphins.* These are a set of closely related chemicals that serve both as hormones, released by the pituitary and adrenal glands into the blood, and as neurotransmitters, released by neurons in certain parts of the brain and spinal cord (Snyder, 1985). Both as hormones and as transmitters, these substances help to reduce the sensation of pain (Henry, 1986). You will read more about endorphins in Chapter 8.

Another argument for a common origin of hormones and neurotransmitters is the existence of ***neurohormones***. Like neurotransmitters, these chemicals are produced by neurons and released from axon terminals in response to action potentials. But they are classed as hormones because they are released not into a synaptic cleft, but rather into a bed of capillaries (tiny blood vessels) where they are absorbed into the bloodstream. As you will see later, some neurohormones promote the secretion of other hormones, and in that way they provide a means by which the nervous system controls the activity of the endocrine system. (To compare the four modes of chemical communication just discussed, see Figure 6.25.)

How Hormones Affect Behavior

If you tried to imagine all the ways by which a chemical carried by the blood might act on the body to influence behavior, your list would probably be quite similar to the set of ways by which hormones actually do influence behavior. Hormones affect the growth of peripheral bodily structures, including muscles and bones, and in that way influence behavioral capacity. Hormones also affect metabolic processes throughout the body, and in that way influence the amount of energy one has for action. Of greatest interest to psychologists, hormones also act in the brain in ways that influence drives and moods.

35. ***What are examples of long-term and short-term effects of hormones?***

Some effects of hormones are long-term or irreversible, and some of these occur before birth. For example, essentially all of the anatomical differences between newborn boys and girls are caused by the hormone testosterone, which is produced by the male fetus but not the female. These anatomical differences include differences in the brain as well as the genitals (Feder, 1984). The brain differences provide a basis for sex differences in the adult sexual behavior of nonhuman animals and may for humans as well (discussed in Chapter 7). At puberty, an increased production of sex hormones—especially testosterone in the male and estrogen in the female—stimulates a new set of growth processes that further differentiate males and females anatomically and thus affects their behavior.

The shorter-term effects of hormones range in duration from a few minutes to many days. In response to stressful stimulation, for example, the adrenal cortex (the external layer of the adrenal gland) secretes a number of hormones, including cortisol, which act on tissues throughout the body to help prepare it to expend energy and withstand wounds. These hormones promote the release of sugar and fat mol-

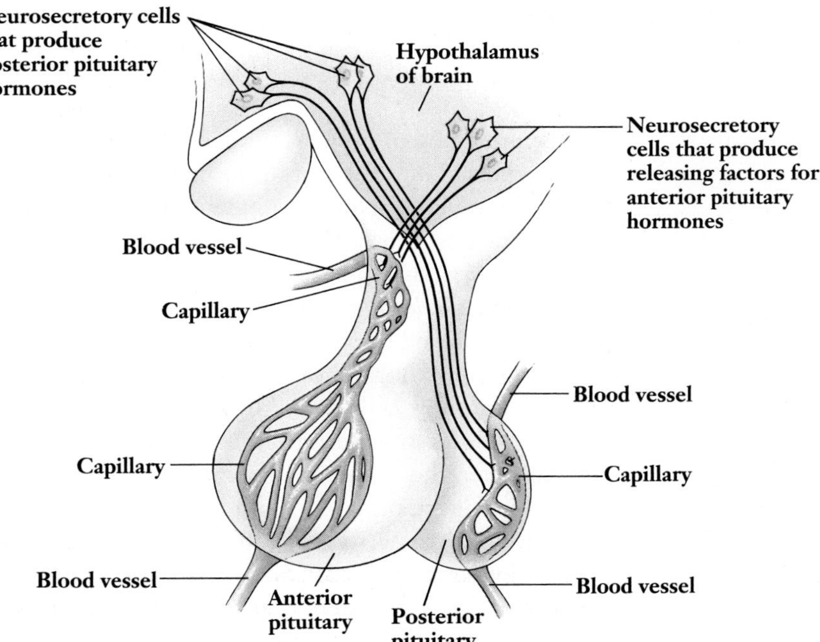

Figure 6.26 ***How the hypothalamus controls pituitary hormones***

Neurosecretory cells, specialized neurons in the hypothalamus, control the activity of the pituitary gland. Some neurosecretory cells secrete hormones directly into capillaries in the posterior pituitary, where they enter the general bloodstream. Others secrete hormones called *releasing factors* into a special capillary system that carries them to the anterior pituitary, where they stimulate the release of hormones manufactured there.

ecules into the blood to supply energy and help suppress inflammation at a wound site. Experiments with rats and other animals show that these same hormones are taken up by neurons in the limbic system, especially in the hippocampus (McEwen & others, 1986). Just what role they play there is not yet certain, but some evidence suggests that they help the animal calm down after a period of stress and help promote the formation of long-term memories related to the stressful experience (McEwen, 1989).

■ **36.** ***At a molecular level, how do hormones exert their effects?***

At the molecular level, hormones can work on cells in a variety of ways. Most hormones fall into one of two chemical classes: *peptides*, which are short-chain protein molecules, and *steroids*, which are chemically related to cholesterol. Neurohormones and all hormones produced by the pituitary gland are peptides; hormones produced by the adrenal cortex and the gonads (ovaries in the female and testes in the male) are steroids. Peptides do not easily pass through cell membranes, so they usually exert their effects at receptor sites on the outside of the cell membrane. In the nervous system, peptides can act like neurotransmitters. By causing channels to open up in cell membranes, they change the electrical charge across the membrane and alter the rate of neural activity. They can also stimulate more sustained changes in the neuron by activating other messenger systems that work inside the neuron. Steroids, in contrast, pass through cell membranes easily, and commonly exert their effects within the cell nucleus. There they may activate or inhibit specific genes, and in that way increase or decrease the production of specific protein molecules, which in turn can alter the neuron's activity in either a short-term or long-term manner (McEwen, 1989).

How Hormones Are Controlled by the Brain

■ **37.** ***How does the brain control the release of hormones from the two lobes of the pituitary and thereby control the release of other hormones as well?***

The pituitary, which sits at the base of the brain (see Figure 6.26), is sometimes called the "master endocrine gland" because it produces hormones that in turn stimulate the production of other hormones. In particular, its hormones control hormone production in the thyroids, adrenal cortex, and gonads. But we might more accurately say that the brain is the master endocrine gland, because through neurohormones it controls the pituitary.

To visualize the intimate relationship between the brain and the pituitary, look at Figure 6.26. The rear part of the pituitary, the *posterior lobe*, is in fact a part of the brain. The posterior lobe consists mainly of modified neurons, referred to as *neurosecretory cells*, which extend down from the hypothalamus and secrete neurohor-

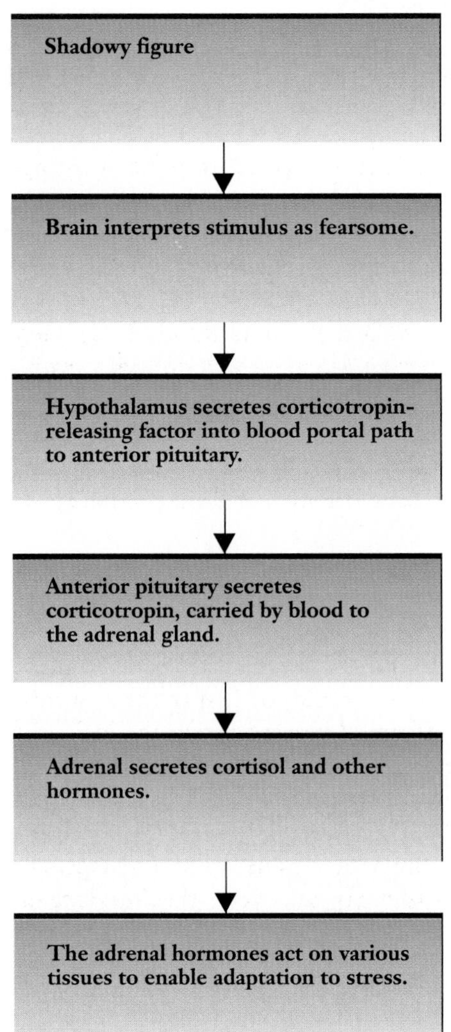

Figure 6.27 ***Brain-pituitary-adrenal response to a fearful stimulus***

This is one example of a brain-mediated hormonal response to sensory stimulation.

mones into a bed of capillaries. Once these hormones get into the capillaries they are transported into the rest of the circulatory system to affect various parts of the body. The remainder of the pituitary, the *anterior lobe*, is not actually part of the brain as the posterior lobe is, but it is intimately connected to it by a specialized set of capillaries, as shown in Figure 6.26. Neurosecretory cells in the brain's hypothalamus produce *releasing factors*, neurohormones that are secreted into the capillary system and carried to the anterior pituitary, where they cause the synthesis and release of pituitary hormones. Different releasing factors, produced by different sets of neurosecretory cells in the hypothalamus, act selectively to stimulate the production of different anterior pituitary hormones.

Consider the sequence of hormonal events triggered by the brain, as diagramed in Figure 6.27: (1) A shadowy figure is seen at night and the brain interprets it as fearsome. (2) The association cortex sends a neural message to the viewer's hypothalamus that causes it to secrete *corticotropin-releasing factor*. (3) The specialized capillary system transports this releasing factor to the anterior pituitary, where it stimulates the release of another hormone, *corticotropin*, into the bloodstream. (4) From the bloodstream, corticotropin enters the adrenal cortex, where it causes the release of a number of adrenal cortical hormones, including *cortisol*. (5) These adrenal hormones are carried throughout the body to help prepare it for a possible emergency. At the same time, of course, many other brain-controlled effects are also occurring to deal with the possible emergency suggested by the sight of the shadowy figure. These effects range from the activation of the sympathetic portion of the autonomic nervous system to the development of plans to escape.

Drugs

The main difference between a hormone and a drug is that the former is produced within the body and the latter is taken in from the outside. Like hormones, drugs are carried by the blood and taken up in target tissues in various parts of the body.

How Drugs Get to Neurons in the Brain

To be carried to potential sites of action, a drug must first get into an individual's blood. Sometimes drugs are introduced directly into the blood by intravenous injection, but more commonly they are administered by routes that bring them into contact with capillaries, where they are gradually absorbed into the blood. Drugs are absorbed by capillaries in the intestines if taken orally, by capillaries in the lungs if taken by inhalation, by capillaries in the rectum if taken by rectal suppository, and by capillaries under the skin or in the muscles if taken by subcutaneous or intramuscular injection. The preferred route of administration depends largely on the properties of the drug and the desired time-course of action. A drug that is destroyed by digestive juices in the stomach, for example, cannot be taken orally. A drug injected intravenously will act more quickly than one administered by any other route.

If a drug is going to act in the brain, it must pass from the blood into the extracellular fluid that surrounds neurons in the brain. The capillaries in the brain are much less porous than those in other tissues. In addition, they are tightly surrounded by the fatty membranes of a certain variety of glial cells. The tight capillary walls and the surrounding glial cells form a ***blood-brain barrier***, which helps protect the brain from poisons. To act in the brain, a drug (or hormone) must be able to pass through this barrier. In general, fat-soluble substances pass through easily, and other substances may or may not pass through, depending on other characteristics of their chemistry.

How Drugs Can Alter Synaptic Transmission

Many different drugs are used in psychiatry and neurology to alter a person's mood or behavioral capacities. Nearly all such drugs work by enhancing or blocking synaptic transmission somewhere in the nervous system (Snyder, 1985). In normal synaptic transmission, neurotransmitter molecules are released from the presynaptic neuron, diffuse across a narrow synaptic cleft, and then bind to the membrane of the postsynaptic cell and alter its activity (to review this, look back at Figure 6.19). Three ways that drugs can influence activity at a synapse are the following: (1) They can act on the presynaptic neuron to either facilitate or inhibit release of the transmitter, thereby affecting the amount of it that enters the cleft. (2) They can act in the cleft to either facilitate or inhibit the processes that normally terminate the action of the transmitter once it has been released, either prolonging or shortening the amount of time that the transmitter remains in the cleft and exerts its effects. (3) They can act directly on postsynaptic binding sites, either producing the same effect as the transmitter or blocking the transmitter from producing its normal effect.

■ **38.** ***What are three ways in which drugs can alter activity at a synapse?***

Of the three, the postsynaptic effect is best understood. To visualize how the postsynaptic effect occurs, recall the comparison of neurotransmitter molecules to keys and binding sites on postsynaptic membrane channels to locks (and look at Figure 6.28). A drug molecule that diffuses into a synapse may act as a substitute key, producing the same effect as the transmitter would, or it may act as a misshapen key, filling the keyhole for a period of time but not turning the lock, and thereby preventing the transmitter from having its normal effect. Many different neurotransmitters exist in the nervous system, and a particular drug may produce one or more of the above effects for just one or for several different transmitters. Thus, drugs can be more or less specific, affecting either a small class of synapses or a large class, and hence can be more or less specific in the effects they produce on behavior.

How Drugs May Act at Different Levels of the Behavior-Control Hierarchy

One way to imagine the many kinds of effects that drugs can have on behavior is to think of them in relation to the hierarchy of behavioral control depicted in Figure 6.13 (turn back to page 178). Drugs may act at any level of that hierarchy and have the effects the hierarchy predicts.

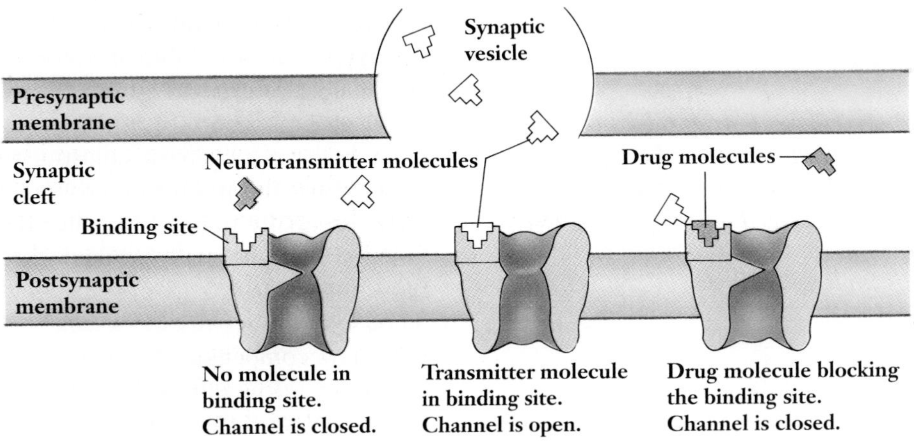

Figure 6.28 ***Lock-and-key view of drug effects in a synapse***

Each binding site on the membrane of the postsynaptic cell can be thought of as a keyhole, and each neurotransmitter molecule as a key that fits into it and opens the lock, causing the ion channel to open up in the cell membrane. A drug molecule can serve as a substitute key and produce the same effect as the neurotransmitter, or it can serve as a misshapen key (as shown here) that occupies the keyhole without activating the lock and thus prevents the neurotransmitter from acting.

■ **39.** ***How can the effects of curare, L-dopa, and psychoactive drugs be interpreted in terms of the hierarchical model of movement control?***

Curare is an example of a drug that acts at the lowest level, at synapses between motor neurons and skeletal muscle cells. This poison, long used by certain South American Indians on the tips of their arrows for hunting, paralyzes the animal that is hit. Curare produces paralysis by blocking the postsynaptic binding sites for *acetylcholine*, which is the transmitter released by skeletal motor neurons onto muscle cells. Because the muscle cells can no longer respond to acetylcholine, they can no longer contract, and the animal is unable to move. Acetylcholine is also a transmitter at many places within the central nervous system, but curare does not act in those places because it cannot pass the blood-brain barrier.

An example of a drug that acts somewhat higher in the movement-control hierarchy is *L-dopa*, which is used to treat victims of Parkinson's disease. As you may recall, Parkinson's disease is caused by the degeneration of certain neurons whose axons originate in the brainstem and terminate in the basal ganglia. The disease is characterized by muscle tremors and severe difficulty in initiating movements. These symptoms are manifested when the degenerating neurons fail to release a sufficient quantity of the neurotransmitter *dopamine*. It might seem logical to treat these symptoms by introducing additional dopamine into the body, but dopamine cannot cross the blood-brain barrier. However, L-dopa, a precursor in the synthesis of dopamine, can cross the barrier. Once in the brain, L-dopa is converted to dopamine.

Drugs that work still farther up in the behavior-control hierarchy may alter mood or general arousal, or affect one's thoughts and perceptions. These drugs are called *psychoactive drugs*, because they influence processes that we think of as psychological. In Chapter 18 you will read about some of the clinical uses of psychoactive drugs—in the treatment of anxiety, depression, schizophrenia, and other emotional or thought disorders. Meanwhile, Table 6.1 shows one way of categorizing psychoactive drugs and what is known about the action mechanism of some of them, including such everyday examples as caffeine and nicotine.

Tolerance, Withdrawal Symptoms, and Addiction

Some drugs produce progressively smaller physiological and behavioral effects if taken repeatedly, a phenomenon known as ***drug tolerance***. Because of tolerance, people who regularly take a drug may need to increase their dose over time to continue to achieve the original effect. In addition, repeated use of some drugs can produce *withdrawal symptoms* when their use is stopped, which can be very disturbing and in some cases life-threatening. Withdrawal symptoms are commonly opposite in direction to the initial direct effects of the drug. Thus, drugs taken to treat some symptom—such as constipation, headaches, sleeplessness, or anxiety—can have counterproductive effects in the long run. Upon withdrawal, the symptom may return to a higher level than before the drug regimen was begun. As a rule (though not an inviolable one), the same drugs that produce tolerance when taken repeatedly also produce withdrawal symptoms when stopped (Julien, 1988).

■ **40.** ***How can drug tolerance and withdrawal symptoms be explained in terms of physiological adaptation to a drugged state? For amphetamines, how might this adaptation occur at the molecular level?***

A general theory to explain both tolerance and withdrawal symptoms relates them both to long-term adjustments that the body makes to adapt itself to a drugged condition. During prolonged drug use, physiological changes occur that serve essentially to *counteract* the effects of the drug, permitting the individual to function more normally while in the drugged state. These changes may involve a reduction in the activity of physiological systems that are excited by the drug, or an increase in the activity of systems that are depressed by the drug. Because of these long-term compensatory changes, a continuously higher dose is needed to achieve the original drug effect, and absence of the drug results in an unbalanced state in which the long-term compensatory changes are not counteracted by the drug.

Table 6.1 ***Categories of psychoactive drugs based on their main behavioral effects***

1. **Behavioral stimulants and antidepressants**
   Drugs that increase alertness and activity level and elevate mood. Some examples are:
   - *Amphetamines and cocaine* Often abused because of the psychological "high" they produce, these drugs increase the release of *norepinephrine* and *dopamine* into synapses and prolong their action there.
   - *Clinical antidepressants* These counteract depression but do not produce the sleeplessness or euphoria that amphetamines and cocaine produce. These also increase activity at *norepinephrine* synapses. (See Chapters 17 and 18.)
   - *Caffeine* Found in coffee, tea, and cocoa beans, this drug increases neural activity throughout the brain. It does this partly by inhibiting the process that normally closes ion channels in postsynaptic membranes, thereby prolonging the effect of neurotransmitters.
   - *Nicotine* Found in tobacco, this drug increases neural activity by stimulating neurons where *acetylcholine* is the transmitter, including in the cerebral cortex (which may increase mental alertness) and in the sympathetic ganglia of the autonomic nervous system (producing such effects as increased heart rate).
2. **Tranquilizers and central-nervous-system depressants**
   Drugs that counteract anxiety and/or decrease alertness and activity level. Included in this category (and further described in Chapter 18) are:
   - *Benzodiazepines* Prescribed to counteract anxiety, these drugs (including diazepam, sold as Valium) act on postsynaptic receptors to make them more responsive to *GABA*, which is an inhibitory transmitter. Increased responsiveness to GABA causes a decrease in neural activity in those parts of the brain where it is present.
   - *Alcohol and barbiturates* These often-abused drugs depress neural activity throughout the brain by a variety of means that are not well understood. Low doses may produce relief from anxiety, and higher doses produce sedation, sleep, unconsciousness, coma, and death, in that order. Their antianxiety effects are believed to work in the same way as that of benzodiazepines.
3. **Opiates**
   These include *opium*, a crude extract from the opium plant; *morphine*, the most active ingredient in opium; *codeine*, an extract from opium that is chemically similar to morphine but less active; and *heroin*, which is synthesized by chemical modification of morphine. All are potent pain reducers and can also produce feelings of euphoria. They produce at least some of their effects by activating neurons that normally respond to *endorphins*, a class of slow-acting transmitters that are part of the body's natural system for relieving pain. (See Chapter 8.)
4. **Antipsychotic drugs**
   Prescribed mostly to treat schizophrenia, these drugs (including chlorpromazine and haloperidol) are believed to work by decreasing activity at synapses where *dopamine* is the transmitter. (See Chapters 17 and 18.)
5. **Hallucinogenic drugs**
   These induce hallucinations and other sensory distortions. Some, such as *mescaline* and *psilocybin*, exist naturally in plants and have a long history of use among various peoples, including Native Americans, in religious rites. Others, such as LSD (lysergic acid diethylamide), are synthetic compounds. Most are structurally similar to neurotransmitters, and they are believed to act either by mimicking or blocking transmitters that they resemble. Both LSD and psilocybin resemble the transmitter *serotonin*.

Source: Adapted from *A primer of drug action* (5th ed.) by R. M. Julien, 1988, San Francisco: Freeman.

To illustrate how tolerance and withdrawal symptoms may develop, consider *amphetamines*, a class of drugs that is often used (and abused) to sustain wakefulness or to produce a psychological feeling of elation (a drug "high"). Amphetamines promote the release of the neurotransmitter *norepinephrine* into synapses in the brain, and this provides at least part of the physiological basis for the arousal and mood elevation. Prolonged use of an amphetamine results in tolerance, and subsequent abstinence results in withdrawal symptoms, including extreme fatigue and psychological depression, which of course are opposite to the direct effects of the drug (McKim, 1991). Research suggests that both the tolerance and the withdrawal symptoms come about at least partly because the brain, reacting to the repeated, drug-induced oversupply of norepinephrine, begins to produce a specific chemical that blocks the postsynaptic binding sites for norepinephrine, by the misshapen-key method illustrated in Figure 6.28 (Caldwell & others, 1980). Because many of the binding sites are blocked, a larger than normal amount of norepinephrine is needed in the synapse to activate the postsynaptic neurons. Thus, a higher dose of amphetamine is needed to achieve the effect that was once achieved by a low dose, and, when no amphetamine is taken, the postsynaptic neurons are unusually inactive, accounting for the fatigue and depression. After a sufficient period of drug abstinence, however, the brain stops making the blocking chemical, and the person can once again achieve a normal mood and alertness without the amphetamine.

Thus far I have avoided the term *addiction*. People are said to be addicted to a drug if, despite contrary intentions, they cannot refrain from continuing to take it. Physiological withdrawal symptoms can certainly provide part of the basis for addiction. In some cases a person may continue to take a drug almost entirely to alleviate the withdrawal symptoms that emerge when the drug is not taken. But addiction may be present even without physiological withdrawal symptoms. Crack—the cocaine preparation that produces an extraordinarily rapid high and is currently ruining many people's lives—seems to induce addiction well before it produces long-term changes of the sort that cause tolerance or withdrawal symptoms.

In Chapter 17 you will read more about addiction, including evidence that it is a product not just of the direct biological effects of a drug, but also of the learned expectancies and values concerning the drug, which people acquire from their social experience. In Chapter 5 evidence was presented that classical conditioning can also affect the way a person reacts to a drug, so that the same drug dose can have different effects, depending on the environment in which it is taken. Whether we are talking about drugs or any other class of influences on human behavior, the effect can be fully understood only by considering it in the context of a great deal of other information about the person and the setting.

Concluding Thoughts

Hippocrates and Galen were right: The brain is the organ of the mind. The mind is a set of processes (feeling, thinking, initiating action, and so on), carried out by physical activities in the brain and interfered with by lesions in the brain. The brain, of course, does not work in isolation from the rest of the body or the environment. It needs input from sensory nerves, it is affected by chemicals carried in the blood, and it acts through motor nerves and (to a smaller degree) hormones. Yet the brain is the center of all that we call the mind: It contains the mechanisms needed to analyze all inputs and organize all outputs.

In reviewing this chapter, so full of terms and details, you may find it useful to keep the following broad points in mind:

1. The value of a functional perspective As you list the structures described in this chapter—ranging from the little ones, such as *synaptic vesicles* and *neuromodulators* up to the big ones, such as the *limbic system* and *autonomic nervous system*—ask yourself, for each: What is it for? That is, what role does it play in the larger machine that is the human being? How is it related to other parts of the machine, and how can variations in it affect human behavior? The structures are a lot easier to remember, and certainly more interesting, if you think of them in terms of their role in a larger system rather than as isolated entities.

2. Uses of the hierarchical model The hierarchical model described in this chapter (summarized in Figure 6.13) provides a way to organize thinking about the nervous system. It is a useful memory scheme, because it allows us to see each part in relation to the whole. It summarizes, in a very general way, the effects of damage to different parts of the nervous system. It also summarizes, again in a general way, the effects of drugs that act in different parts of the nervous system. As you review the discussion of the central nervous system, and the later discussion of drugs, tie the bits and pieces together into the hierarchical model.

3. **Brain science in relation to the rest of psychology** As more is learned about the brain, knowledge about it becomes relevant to broader areas of psychology. In later chapters you will be reading about the brain in relation to psychology's attempt to understand basic processes of motivation, sensation, memory, and thought. Still later, you will read of brain-based theories of mental disorders and of drugs that are believed to alleviate specific mental disorders through their interactions with neurotransmitters. Your review of the present chapter may be more interesting, and more effective, if you try to anticipate the ways that each topic discussed here might be relevant later. Ask yourself: Why might a *psychologist* want to know about this structure or process? You may surprise yourself with the frequency with which you come up with a good answer.

Further Reading

Floyd Bloom & Arlyne Lazerson (1988). *Brain, mind, and behavior* (2nd ed.). New York: Freeman.

Beautifully illustrated and clearly written, this book begins with chapters on basic neural mechanisms and proceeds to chapters on the brain's involvement in sensation and movement, motivation, behavioral rhythms, emotions, learning, thought, and psychopathology.

Richard Thompson (1985). *The brain: An introduction to neuroscience*. New York: Freeman.

This is a thoughtful introduction to the nervous system and ways of learning about it, written by an eminent physiological psychologist. It covers basic neural mechanisms, sensory and motor systems, and developmental changes that occur in the brain over the life cycle.

Gerald Edelman (1992). *Bright air, brilliant fire: On the matter of the mind.* New York: Basic Books.

After receiving a Nobel Prize for work on immunology, Edelman turned to neuroscience, which he believes is now in the midst of a major revolution. In this witty and thought-provoking book, written for the intelligent nonscientist, Edelman takes on the long-standing philosophical question of how the conscious mind emerges from matter (the brain) and brings to that question the insights of modern research on the brain.

Sally Springer & Georg Deutsch (1989). *Left brain, right brain* (3rd ed.). New York: Freeman.

Research on right- and left-hemisphere differences, including the split-brain studies, is always interesting. This book provides a well-documented account of such research in a form that can be understood by the beginning student.

Looking Ahead

You now have—stored somehow in that gnarled, cantaloupe-sized knot of protoplasm under your skull—a little knowledge about the extraordinary organization that exists within that knot, and how hormones and drugs can act upon it. Hold onto that knowledge. At least some of it will be useful in the next chapter, as we examine the physiological underpinnings of some psychological states: hunger, sexual drive, sleep, arousal, and emotionality.

Motivation and Reward

The Physiological Approach to the Study of Drives

Hunger

The Sex Drive

Reward Mechanisms and Their Relationship to Drives

Sleeping and Dreaming

The Electroencephalographic Description of Sleep

Functions of Slow-Wave Sleep

Dreams and REM Sleep

Brain Mechanisms Controlling Sleep

Emotion

High Arousal

Theories of Emotion That Emphasize Peripheral Feedback

A Brain-Based Theory of Emotion

MECHANISMS OF MOTIVATION, SLEEP, AND EMOTION

CHAPTER 7

The kaleidoscope that makes a day or a year of mental life has both fast-moving and slow-moving components. The fast-moving parts are the sensations, perceptions, thoughts, and actions that flit continuously across our consciousness and behavior. The slow-moving parts are the sustained phases, called *behavioral states*, that help modulate and direct the fast-moving parts. Behavioral states are those of motivation, sleep and arousal, and emotion. This chapter is primarily about their physiological base.

Changing metaphors from a kaleidoscope to a television set, you might think of the fast-moving components as the sounds and sights that a TV produces as it responds to signals in the air, and the slow-moving components, the states, as those produced when you change the channel, volume, or hue. A channel change causes the set to become attuned to different signals in the air, somewhat as you and I become attuned to different signals when hungry than when not. A change in volume is a bit like the change you and I undergo as we become more alert or sleepy. And a change in hue is somewhat akin to a change in emotional state, which colors our daily experience. This chapter begins with a section on the channel changer (motivation), then turns to the volume control (sleep and wakefulness), and finally moves to those hue knobs that seem so hard to keep set on any TV (emotion). The main questions throughout are: What physiological changes within the individual coincide with, and help bring on, specific changes in one's behavioral state? How do the channel changer, volume control, and hue knobs work in the living being?

Motivation and Reward

To *motivate*, in the most general sense of the term, is to set in motion. In psychology, the term ***motivation*** is often used to refer to the entire constellation of factors, some inside the organism and some outside, that cause an individual to behave in a particular way at a particular time. Motivation defined this way is a very broad concept, almost as broad as all of psychology. Every chapter in this book deals with one or another facet of motivation. Genes, learning, physiological variables, perceptual and thought processes, developmental variables, social experiences, and personality characteristics are all constructs that psychologists describe as contributors to motivation.

A more precise label for the specific topic of our present discussion is ***motivational state*** or ***drive***. These terms are used interchangeably to denote an internal condition, which can change over time in a reversible way, that orients an individual toward a specific category of goals. Different drives have different goals.

Hunger drives one toward food, *sex* toward sexual gratification, *curiosity* toward novel stimuli, and so on. For the most part, drives are thought of in psychology as hypothetical constructs. The psychologist does not observe a state of hunger, thirst, or curiosity inside the animal, but rather infers that state from the animal's behavior. An animal is said to be hungry if it behaves in ways that bring it closer to food, to have a sex drive if it behaves in ways that bring it into contact with a sexual partner, to be curious if it seeks out and explores new environments. To say that the drive varies over time is to say that the animal will work harder, or accept more discomfort, to attain the goal at some times than at others. The assumption is that something inside the animal changes, causing the animal to behave differently in the same environment.

■ **1.** ***How do drives and incentives (a) complement one another and (b) influence one another in the broad process of motivation?***

But the inside interacts constantly with the outside. Motivated behavior is directed toward ***incentives***, the sought-after objects or ends that exist in the external environment. Incentives are also called *reinforcers* (the term used in Chapter 5), *rewards*, or *goals*. The motivational state that leads you to stand in line at the cafeteria is presumably hunger, but the incentive for doing so is the hamburger you intend to purchase. Drives and incentives complement one another in the control of behavior; if one is weak, the other must be strong to motivate the goal-directed action. Thus, if you know that the cafeteria's hamburger tastes like cardboard (weak incentive) you are likely to wait in line for it only if your hunger drive is strong, but if they serve a really great hamburger (strong incentive) you are likely to wait even if your hunger drive is weak.

Drives and incentives not only complement one another, but also influence each other's strength. A strong drive can enhance the attractiveness (incentive value) of a particular object, and, conversely, a strong incentive can strengthen a drive. As an example of the first, if you are very hungry, even the hamburger that tastes like cardboard might seem quite attractive. As an example of the second, the savory aroma of a broiling hamburger wafting your way as you wait in line might increase your hunger drive, which might in turn induce you to eat something that previously wouldn't have interested you, if, by the time you get to the grill, all the hamburgers are gone.

In the following pages we will look first at physiological theories and methods in the study of basic drives, then at hunger and sex as two examples of drives, and finally at the neural basis of reward. I have chosen to focus on hunger and sex partly because they are the drives that have been most fully studied physiologically, and partly because of their obvious importance in the lives of humans as well as other species. Please do not assume from this that I or other psychologists believe that drives like hunger and sex are all that motivate human behavior. Later chapters, particularly those dealing with social psychology and personality theories, discuss drives that are more specific to humans, such as drives for achievement and self-esteem.

Even hunger and sex in humans always occur in a context of social influences, values, and beliefs that goes far beyond the basic biological influences discussed in this chapter. People don't just eat, they *dine*, which connotes all sorts of social and cognitive influences. And people don't just copulate; they fall in love, compose romantic sonnets, promise to be faithful, have affairs, suffer guilt, and engage in long, intimate discussions with their beloved. Moreover, human beings have enormous powers of conscious control over even their most basic drives, as witnessed in those who voluntarily undergo starvation to protest political repression or in those who choose a life of chastity, whether from religious conviction or prudence (especially in this era of AIDS). We will not discuss these social and cognitive influences in this chapter, but we should not forget them either.

A matter of time and place

Victorians were probably somewhat less concerned with propriety, and contemporary couples are probably somewhat more ambivalent about freedom, than these illustrations suggest. Nevertheless, permissible sexual behavior has changed dramatically over the past century, and the differences underscore the socially constructed nature of human sexuality.

The Physiological Approach to the Study of Drives

The very notion of drives, as defined above, almost begs us to look inside the organism to see what has happened there to cause a change in behavior. The goal of the physiological approach to the study of drives is to give substance to the hypothetical inner state, to make it no longer hypothetical. What really happens inside to make a person hungry, or driven in some other way? Historically, to answer such questions, some researchers have focused on the body's tissue needs, and others have focused on states of the brain.

Drives as Tissue Needs: The Concept of Homeostasis

■ **2. *How is the concept of homeostasis related to that of drive, and how is this demonstrated in the case of a little boy who craved salt?***

In an influential book entitled *The Wisdom of the Body* (1932), the physiologist Walter B. Cannon described simply and elegantly the requirements of the tissues of the human body. For life to be sustained, certain substances and characteristics within the body must be kept within a restricted range, going neither too high nor too low. These include body temperature, oxygen, minerals, water, and energy-producing food molecules. Physiological processes, such as digestion and respiration, must continually work toward achieving what Cannon termed ***homeostasis***, the constancy of internal conditions that the body must actively maintain. Most important, Cannon pointed out that maintenance of homeostasis involves the organism's outward behavior as well as its internal processes. To stay alive, individuals must find and consume foods, salts, and water and must maintain their body temperature through such means as finding shelter. Cannon theorized that the basic physiological underpinning for some drives is an upset in homeostatic balance, which induces behavior designed to correct the imbalance.

Following Cannon, psychologists and physiologists performed experiments showing that animals indeed do behave in accordance with their tissue needs. For example, if the caloric (energy) content of its food is increased or decreased, an animal will compensate by eating less or more of it, keeping the daily intake of calories relatively constant. As another example, removal of the adrenal glands causes an animal to lose too much salt in its urine (because one of the adrenal hormones is essential for conserving salt). This loss of salt dramatically increases the animal's drive to seek out and eat extra salt, which keeps the animal alive as long as salt is available (Richter & Eckert, 1938; Stricker, 1973).

The force of homeostasis in human behavior was dramatically and poignantly illustrated by the clinical case of a boy, referred to as D. W., who when 1 year old developed a great craving for salt (Wilkins & Richter, 1940). His favorite foods were salted crackers, pretzels, potato chips, olives, and pickles; he would also take salt directly from the shaker. When salt was denied him he would cry until his parents gave in, and when he learned to speak, "salt" was one of his first and favorite words. D. W. survived until the age of 3½, when he was hospitalized for other symptoms and placed on a standard hospital diet. The hospital staff would not yield to his demands for salt, and he died within a few days. An autopsy subsequently revealed that his adrenal glands were deficient; only then did D. W.'s doctors realize that his salt craving came from physiological need. His strong drive for salt and his ability to manipulate his parents into supplying it, even though they were unaware that he needed it, had kept D. W. alive for 2½ years—powerful evidence for "the wisdom of the body."

Limitations of Homeostasis: Regulatory and Nonregulatory Drives

■ 3. ***What is the difference between regulatory and nonregulatory drives, and why is "need" not useful in explaining the latter?***

Homeostasis is a useful concept for understanding thirst, hunger, and the drives for salt, oxygen, and temperature control, but not for understanding certain other drives. Consider sex, for example. People are highly motivated to engage in sex, but there is no tissue need for it. No vital bodily substance is affected by engaging in sexual behavior; nobody can die from lack of sex (despite what an overly amorous someone may have told you). In their desire to develop a unitary theory of drives, some psychologists proposed hypothetical needs for sex and other drives for which no tissue need can be found. But by doing so they were destroying the original advantage of the homeostatic theory. If needs cannot be identified in the body, independently of the behaviors they are believed to motivate, then the concept of need is not an objective explanation. In fact, it is no explanation at all, as the term "need" in that case is simply a substitute for the term "drive." Psychologists today find it useful to distinguish between regulatory drives and nonregulatory drives. A ***regulatory drive*** is one, like hunger, that helps preserve homeostasis, and a ***nonregulatory drive*** is one, like sex, that serves some other purpose.

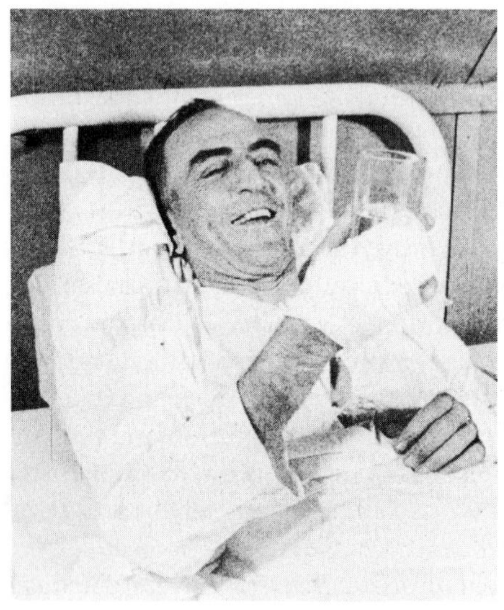

Consuming thirst

Twenty-one days on a life raft in the Pacific is enough to drive a man to drink. And, in fact, once World War II Captain Eddie Rickenbacker was rescued, he said, "Water was the only thing on my mind." Like hunger, thirst is a regulatory drive involving an elaborate interplay of neural and hormonal mechanisms.

Drives as States of the Brain

If drives are inner states, how can they best be described physiologically? Early theories, based on the concept of homeostasis, attempted to define drives as tissue needs. But such definitions were never fully satisfactory, even when applied to regulatory drives. For example, under certain conditions hunger can be high when the tissue need for more food is low, or low when the need for food is high. Most physiological psychologists today think of drives not as states of peripheral tissue, but rather as states of the brain. According to most versions of this ***central-state theory of drives***, different drives correspond to neural activity in different sets of neurons in the brain (Stellar & Stellar, 1985). The set of neurons in which activity constitutes a drive is called a ***central drive system***. Although the central drive systems for different drives must be at least partly different from one another, they may have overlapping components. For example, because hunger and sex are different drives, the neural circuits for them cannot be identical, yet they may share components that keep the animal alert and increase its general level of motor activity, which are behavioral aspects of both drives.

■ 4. ***In theory, what characteristics must a set of neurons have to function as a central drive system? What characteristics of the hypothalamus seem to suit it to be a hub of such systems?***

What characteristics must a set of neurons have to serve as a central drive system? First, concerning input, it must receive and integrate all of the various signals that can raise or lower the drive state. For hunger, these signals include chemicals in the blood, the presence or absence of food in the stomach, and the sight and smell of food in the environment. Second, concerning output, a central drive system must act on all of the neural processes that would be involved in carrying out the motivated behavior. It must direct perceptual mechanisms toward stimuli related to the goal, cognitive (thought) mechanisms to work out strategies to achieve the goal, and motor centers of the brainstem and spinal cord to produce the appropriate movements. Look back at Figure 6.13, which depicts a hierarchical model of the control of action, with mechanisms involved in motivation and planning at the

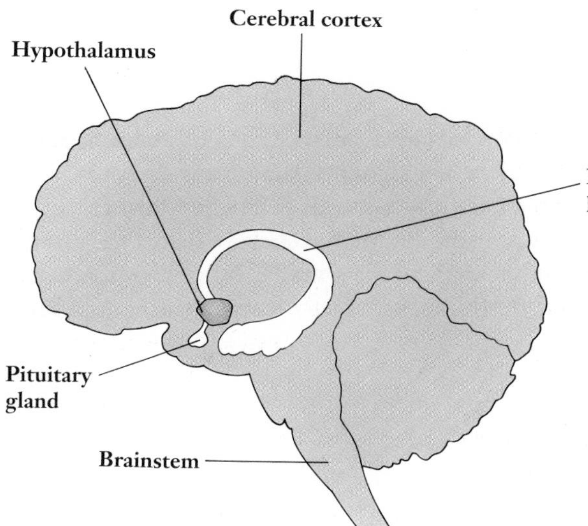

Figure 7.1 ***Location of the hypothalamus***

The hypothalamus is ideally situated to serve as a hub for central drive systems. It has strong connections to the brainstem below, the limbic system and cerebral cortex above, and the endocrine system (by way of its tie to the pituitary gland).

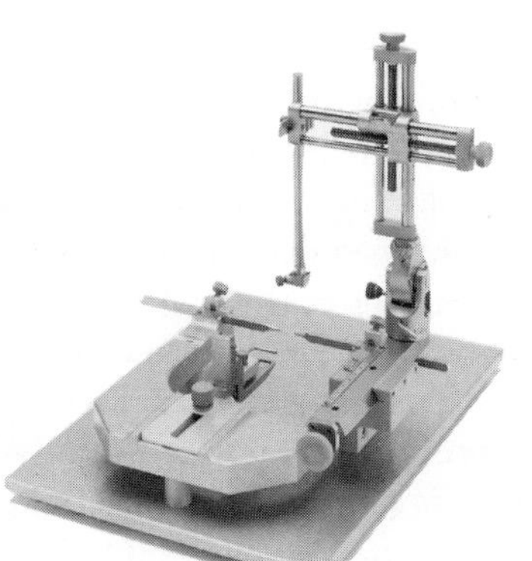

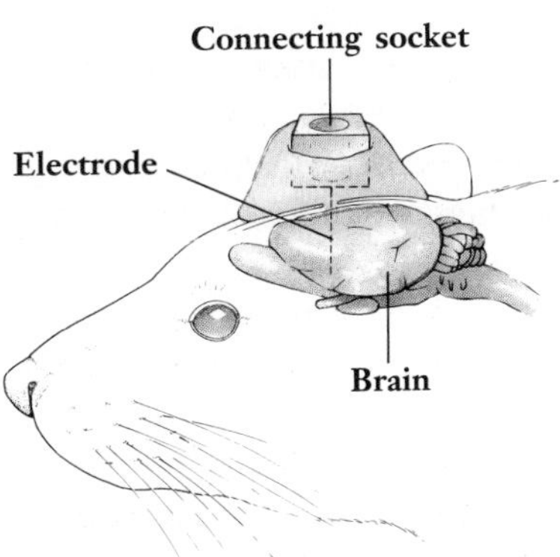

Figure 7.2 ***Method for making lesions in or stimulating a rat's brain***

A stereotaxic instrument, depicted above, is used to insert an electrode into a precise location in the anesthetized (unconscious) animal's brain. To produce a lesion, an electric current that is strong enough to destroy neurons near the electrode tip is sent through the electrode, and then the electrode is removed. To prepare the animal for electrical brain stimulation the electrode is cemented in place, as shown in the drawing, so that it can be stimulated through wire leads during behavioral tests after the animal has recovered from surgery.

top. The central drive systems are part of that top level of the hierarchy. To affect behavior (for example, to cause a hungry person to cross a room for some peanuts), they must influence the activity of motor systems at lower levels of the hierarchy.

Researchers have sound reasons to believe that a hub of many central drive systems lies in the hypothalamus. Anatomically, this brain structure is ideally located to play such a role (see Figure 7.1). It is centered at the base of the brain, just above the brainstem, and contains tracts that interconnect many areas of the brain. It also has direct connections to nerves that carry input from, and autonomic motor output to, the body's internal organs. It has many capillaries and is more sensitive to hormones and other substances carried by the blood than are other brain areas. Finally, through its connections to the pituitary gland, it controls the release of many hormones (as described in Chapter 6). Thus, the hypothalamus has all of the inputs and outputs that central drive systems would be expected to have. And, as you will soon see, small disruptions in particular parts of the hypothalamus can have dramatic effects on an animal's drives.

Brain Lesions and Stimulation as Ways to Locate Central Drive Systems

To identify the functions of specific nuclei (groups of neural cell bodies) or tracts (groups of axons running together) in the brain, researchers may either damage or stimulate them and assess the effect on the animal's behavior.

Specific brain areas can be damaged either through electrical or chemical means. To produce an area of damage, or ***lesion***, electrically, a thin wire called an *electrode* is lowered into the brain with the help of a *stereotaxic instrument* (see Figure 7.2), and enough current is sent through the electrode to destroy the neurons adjacent to its tip (the rest of the electrode is electrically insulated). To produce a lesion chemically, a tiny tube called a *cannula* is lowered into the brain, again using a stereotaxic instrument, and a small amount of a chemical is injected through the cannula, destroying neurons whose cell bodies are located near the cannula's tip. Lesions usually are made *bilaterally*, in the same area in both the right and left halves of the brain, because the right and left halves of such structures as the hypothalamus and limbic system usually serve identical functions; to eliminate a function, the same part of the structure must be destroyed on both sides. If, after a bilateral lesion, an animal no longer shows a particular drive (for example, no longer responds to food but does respond to other incentives), a researcher would infer that the destroyed area is a critical part of the central system for that drive.

Stimulation of specific areas of the brain can also be accomplished either electrically or chemically. To stimulate neurons electrically, an electrode is permanently implanted in the brain, as shown in Figure 7.2. The electrode can be activated at any time after surgery, through either a wire connection or radio waves. The electrical current used for stimulation is much weaker than that for producing a lesion—it is strong enough to activate, but not strong enough to destroy, neurons

5. *How and why are localized areas of the brain damaged or stimulated in research on drives?*

near the electrode's tip. To stimulate neurons chemically, a cannula is permanently implanted in the brain, and shortly before behavioral testing a tiny amount of a transmitter or other chemical known to activate neurons is injected through it. If electrical or chemical stimulation of a specific brain area elicits a drive (for example, if a previously nonhungry animal responds to the stimulus by seeking food and eating), a researcher would infer that the stimulated area is part of the central system for the drive elicited.

Hunger

No drive has been more fully studied physiologically than hunger. In fact, a major impetus for the initial development of the central-state theory of drives, about 50 years ago, was the demonstration that lesions or electrical stimulation applied to specific areas of the hypothalamus can drastically alter an animal's tendency to seek food and eat (Morgan, 1943). By the early 1950's, Eliot Stellar (1954) was able to spell out a simple and elegant theory about the brain's control of hunger.

6. *What theory was proposed in the 1950's to explain the brain's control of hunger, and what evidence supported that theory?*

The essence of Stellar's theory was that eating is controlled by two interacting centers in the hypothalamus, one for hunger and the other for satiety. The *hunger center*, located in the *lateral area* of the hypothalamus, induces food seeking and eating when its neurons are active. Support for that lay in the observations that (a) animals with bilateral lesions in the lateral area ignored food and would starve to death if not tube fed, and (b) animals receiving electrical stimulation in this area ate in direct response to the stimulation. The *satiety center*, located in the *ventromedial area* of the hypothalamus, reduces food seeking and eating when its neurons are active. Support for that lay in the observations that (c) animals with bilateral lesions of the ventromedial area ate voraciously and became obese (see Figure 7.3), and (d) previously hungry animals receiving electrical stimulation in this area would stop eating in direct response to the stimulus. (To see the relative locations of the lateral and ventromedial areas of the hypothalamus, look at Figure 7.4.) Stellar proposed further that the ventromedial area exerts its effect through inhibitory connections to the lateral area, such that neural activity in the satiety center would directly reduce neural activity in the hunger center.

Figure 7.3 ***Effect of a lesion in the ventromedial area of the hypothalamus***

After receiving a bilateral lesion, this rat overate and gained weight to the point where it tipped the scale at 1080 grams—about three times what a normal rat weighs.

Unfortunately for those who prefer simplicity and elegance, the many hundreds of experiments on the control of hunger conducted since 1954 have complicated the picture immensely, though they have by no means fully destroyed the original theory. The research illustrates wonderfully the adage that the more we learn, the more we become aware of how little we know. Let us look now at a few of the main ideas that have emerged from this research and then turn to some practical issues having to do with human obesity and dieting.

Roles of the Lateral Hypothalamus

7. *What is the evidence that the lateral hypothalamus plays two different roles in the control of hunger—one nonspecific (affecting many drives) and the other specific?*

One set of complications to Stellar's theory arose when researchers began to test animals in the presence of other incentives, not just food. Animals with lesions in the lateral hypothalamus not only failed to eat, but also failed to drink, copulate, build nests, care for young, hoard objects, or attack enemies. They would still move around in non-goal oriented ways and would effectively move away from painful stimuli. But they lacked the whole set of behaviors that involve goal-directed movement *toward* objects in the environment. Moreover, electrical stimulation in the lateral hypothalamus could produce any of those behaviors, depending upon what incentives were available (Stricker, 1982). Thus, if only food was available, the animal would eat in response to the stimulus, but if water and a sexual partner were also available, the animal might drink or copulate instead.

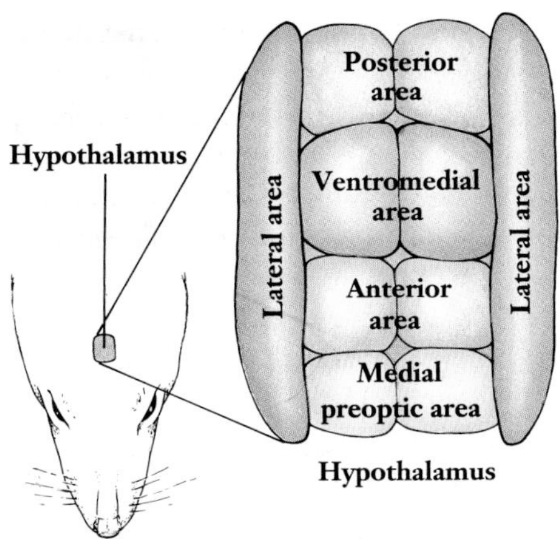

Figure 7.4 ***Diagram of some parts of the hypothalamus***

This schematic diagram shows the relative location of some of the parts of the hypothalamus where lesions or electrical stimulation produce dramatic effects on behavior. To interpret the diagram, imagine that you are looking straight down through the top of the animal's head and can see an x-ray view of the lower part of the hypothalamus, at the very bottom of the brain. The paired central structures lie along the midline of the brain, and the paired lateral areas lie to their right and left. For a bilateral lesion, both the right and left structures must be damaged.

Other experiments revealed that the most critical neurons for producing these effects of lesions and stimulation are not those with cell bodies in the lateral hypothalamus, as had previously been believed, but rather those whose cell bodies exist elsewhere and whose axons form a tract through the hypothalamus, connecting parts of the brainstem (below the hypothalamus) with the basal ganglia (above the hypothalamus). Lesions or electrical stimulation anywhere along this tract, including in the brainstem or at its entrance to the basal ganglia, were as effective as those in the lateral hypothalamus in abolishing or stimulating drives (Grossman, 1979). Researchers now believe that this tract through the lateral hypothalamus is part of a general motor-activation system, which prepares the basal ganglia to initiate deliberate movements regardless of the specific drive (Mogenson & Yim, 1991). Electrical stimulation of this tract seems to give the message, "Do something," leaving the animal to respond to whatever incentives are present in the environment.

But all is not lost for the theory that some lateral hypothalamic neurons are specifically involved in hunger. Using chemical rather than electrical means to produce lesions in the lateral hypothalamus, researchers can destroy neurons whose cell bodies are located there without destroying neurons whose axons pass through the area (the chemical must contact the cell body in order to destroy the neuron). Such lesions greatly reduce hunger (though they do not abolish it), but have a much smaller effect on other drives (Stellar & Stellar, 1985). Other evidence comes from another way to explore the brain, that of *recording* activity in single neurons, through permanently implanted microelectrodes (very tiny electrodes). Using this method, Edmond Rolls (1982) found a set of neurons in the lateral hypothalamus in monkeys that produced bursts of action potentials only when the monkey was both hungry (from having been deprived of food) and exposed to food-related stimuli. The cells would become active when the hungry monkey saw or smelled food, or saw a conditioned stimulus that had previously been used to signal the delivery of food, but not when exposed to stimuli that had never been associated with food. Moreover, if the monkey was fed its fill of one food (for example, bananas), the cells would stop responding when that food was present, but would continue to respond to other foods (peanuts and oranges) with which the animal was not yet satiated (Rolls & others, 1986).

Rolls's discovery is especially interesting because it provides a clue concerning the physiological basis for the interaction of drives and incentives. The motivational state of hunger apparently includes, as one of its components, the sensitization of certain neurons in the lateral hypothalamus, such that they respond to an incentive (food signals) to which they would not respond otherwise. Researchers have found that these same neurons both receive axons from and send axons to the association areas in the frontal lobes of the cerebral cortex, which are known to be important for planning and organizing goal-directed movements (Karadi & others, 1990; Rolls, 1982). Such findings help validate the theory that motivational mechanisms in the hypothalamus and limbic system work closely with planning mechanisms in the cerebral cortex when an individual chooses a course of deliberate action (such as moving toward and consuming food). Look back at Figure 6.13.

Role of the Ventromedial Hypothalamus

■ **8.** ***Why do animals with lesions in the ventromedial hypothalamus overeat and become obese?***

Stellar's original theory posited that the ventromedial hypothalamus contains a satiety center that influences hunger through direct inhibitory connections to the lateral hypothalamus. Research has since shown that the most potent effects of the ventromedial hypothalamus on hunger occur not by direct action within the brain, but rather by action within the autonomic nervous system. Bilateral lesions of the ventromedial hypothalamus cause the parasympathetic nerves involved in digestion and metabolism to become overactive. This causes food to be digested more rapidly than normal (Duggan & Booth, 1986) and food molecules in the blood to be converted very quickly to fat, leaving less for use as fuel for other tissues in the body (King & others, 1984). The result is that messages are sent from the body's tissues to the brain signaling that more food is needed. In other words, the lesioned animals are hungry and overeat because they are converting most of their food to fat rather than to the energy molecules needed to fuel the body. Occasionally a tumor at the base of the brain causes damage to the ventromedial hypothalamus in humans, and in such cases the person becomes obese, apparently for the same reasons that experimental animals do (Bray & Gallagher, 1975).

Stimuli That Act on the Brain to Increase or Decrease Hunger

■ ***9. What are some ways by which receptors sensitive to food materials in the stomach, blood, fat cells, and exterior environment can signal the brain and thereby induce satiety or hunger?***

In the early days of hunger research, many researchers hoped to find *the* signal to the brain that turns hunger on or off. Some thought it might be glucose (a sugar molecule that is the main source of energy for the brain) or some other type of food molecule carried by the blood. Others thought it might be signals from the stomach. Today, researchers know that the central nervous system is responsive to a wide variety of influences, none of which has full control. Among these influences are the following:

- ***Satiety signals from the stomach*** Some of the signals that indicate when to *stop* a meal come from the stomach. In fact, the stomach apparently sends two different types of satiety-producing signals to the brain (Deutsch, 1990). One type has to do with the sheer bulk of material in the stomach. Receptors in the stomach walls respond to pressure exerted on them when the stomach is full and send their message to the brain by way of a cranial nerve. If the branch of this nerve from the stomach is cut, animals will eat larger than normal meals and gain weight (Gonzalez & Deutsch, 1981); and if the receptors are artificially stimulated by a water-filled balloon in the stomach, animals will eat smaller meals and lose weight (Geliebter & others, 1987). The second type of signal has to do with the chemical content of the material in the stomach. Researchers have found that animals stop eating more quickly if the stomach contains nutrient-rich foods than if the same bulk in the stomach has few or no nutrients, but researchers do not yet know where these nutrient-responsive receptors are located or how they signal the brain (Deutsch, 1990).
- ***Signals indicating the amount of food molecules in the blood*** After being partially digested in the stomach, food passes into the small intestine for further digestion down to its molecular components, and then the molecules enter the bloodstream and are carried to all of the body's tissues. Receptors in various tissues may be sensitive to the level of food molecules in the blood, but one area of special sensitivity appears to be the liver. Food molecules (such as glucose) injected directly into the liver cause a previously hungry dog or rat to eat much less than it otherwise would. This effect is apparently mediated by sensory neurons that run from the liver to the brain by way of a cranial nerve (Novin & others, 1983; Russek, 1971). Other research shows that some neurons in the brain contain receptors for glucose and that glucose acts directly on them to modulate their activity. In fact, many of the same neurons in the lateral hypothalamus that respond to food-related cues in the environment are also sensitive to glucose (Karadi & others, 1990). When glucose carried to these neurons by the blood is high, the neurons become *less* active (thereby, presumably, decreasing hunger), and when glucose is low they become more active.
- ***Signals indicating the amount of fat in the body*** Hunger regulates not only the short-term supply of energy molecules, but also body weight. In both rats

and humans, weight tends to remain relatively stable throughout adult life (except for a gradual upward drift, in both species, from youth through middle age). Individuals find a particular weight, referred to as the ***set point***, easiest to maintain (Keesey, 1986). Rats that have been slimmed down below their set point by food deprivation, or fattened up above it by forced feeding through a tube, subsequently eat more or less than normal until their weight returns to the set point. Most weight changes over time are due to increased or decreased fat, stored in special fat cells. The amount of fat in such cells apparently contributes to hunger and satiety in a way that tends to return weight to the set point. During the period between meals, as the food molecules from the previous meal are used up, fat molecules enter the blood from fat cells and supply most of the energy needed to keep the body going until the next meal. When one's weight is below the set point, fat cells become less likely to give up their stored fat, so receptors (such as those in the liver) sensitive to blood levels of food send hunger messages to the brain sooner after a meal than they otherwise would.

■ ***The appetizer effect*** The signals described so far all come from inside the body and have to do with the actual need or lack of need for food. Food in the stomach, blood, and fat cells decreases hunger, and lack of food in those places increases hunger. But hunger is also affected by external stimuli. Any stimulus that reminds one of good food can increase the hunger drive—a phenomenon known as the *appetizer effect*. This effect may be mediated partly by the direct action of association areas of the cortex, which analyze the food-related stimuli, upon neurons in the lateral hypothalamus (consistent with the findings of Karadi & others, 1990, and Rolls, 1982). But it may also be mediated partly through reflexes involving peripheral digestive and metabolic processes (Powley, 1977). For example, one reflexive response to external cues is the secretion of insulin, a hormone that stimulates the transfer of glucose and other food molecules from the blood to storage cells in various parts of the body. The rapid drop in glucose that insulin secretions can produce has been found an especially effective stimulator of hunger in animals (Campfield & Smith, 1990).

Theories About Human Obesity

Magazines, self-help books, and various entrepreneurs are constantly peddling new ways to lose weight. In one survey in the United States, 46 percent of women and 24 percent of men were trying to lose weight at the time of the survey (National Center for Health Statistics, 1985). In part, the desire to be thin is related more to current societal notions of beauty than to health needs. Still, many of us *do* weigh more than is healthy, sometimes considerably more. Why is it that many people can't seem to lose excess weight and keep it off, despite their fervent desire to do so? Studies comparing obese people (usually defined as those whose weight is more than 20 percent above average for their sex, height, and bone structure) and nonobese people have revealed no consistent differences in willpower or other general personality characteristics (Rodin & others, 1989).

■ **10.** ***What is some evidence for the (a) cue-sensitivity and (b) stress-eating theories of obesity? What alternative explanation has been offered for that evidence?***

Many years ago, Stanley Schachter (1970) proposed that a basic difference between obese and nonobese people lies in their responsiveness specifically to food-related cues. In laboratory experiments he found that obese college students ate about the same amount of a snack (crackers or peanuts) regardless of whether or not they had just eaten prior to the experimental session, but ate more if the snack food was illuminated by a bright lamp than if it was less conspicuous. In contrast, nonobese students were unaffected by the degree of illumination of the food, but ate much less if they had eaten just before the session than if they hadn't. From

A cultural paradox

Members of our affluent society are constantly bombarded with food-related cues. And, no matter how "relaxed" the jeans, our culture conspires to make the wearer feel uptight about excess weight.

such evidence, Schachter proposed that people who become obese in our culture are those who are unusually responsive to external food-related cues (the appetizer effect is particularly strong in them) and unusually insensitive to internal cues signaling the need or lack of need for food. These tendencies, and the omnipresence of food-related cues in the environment, would cause overeating and obesity.

Another theory, developed at about the same time as Schachter's, proposed that obese people are obese at least partly because they use food as a means of coping with strong emotions, the so-called *stress-eating syndrome*. This theory was supported by experiments similar to those conducted by Schachter (McKenna, 1972). Subjects in the *stress* group were told (falsely) that they would have to give a large amount of blood at the end of the experimental session, while those in the *nonstress* group were given no such misinformation. Consistent with the theory, obese subjects in the stress group ate more cookies than obese subjects in the nonstress group, whereas the opposite was true for nonobese subjects.

More recently, a degree of doubt has been cast on Schachter's theory and the stress-eating theory by experiments suggesting that high sensitivity to external food cues and stress eating may be more a *consequence* of obesity than a cause. One consistent difference between obese and nonobese people—in our culture, at least—is that at any given time more obese people are likely to be on a diet, consciously trying to lose weight by restricting their food intake. Experiments similar in design to McKenna's and Schachter's have shown that dieters, *whether or not they are obese*, are more likely to eat in response to emotion-provoking and strong external cues than are nondieters, and less likely to eat in response to internal signals (Herman, 1980; Spitzer & Rodin, 1983). Dieters may learn to resist their internal hunger cues, but in emotional situations, or in the presence of really strong external cues for eating, this resistance may break down accounting for the well-known "binge" (Rodin & others, 1989). Thus, the findings of McKenna and Schachter could have resulted from there being more dieters among the obese subjects than among the nonobese.

■ **11.** ***How do the number of fat cells and the ratchet effect influence body weight?***

Heredity plays a large role in who becomes obese and who doesn't, as indicated by studies showing that adopted children are more similar to their biological parents than to their adoptive parents in weight (Price & others, 1987). Other research suggests that the number of fat-storage cells (fat cells) in the body is an important determinant of body weight, establishing the set point mentioned earlier (Faust, 1984). Obese rats and humans have more fat cells than do nonobese individuals; when they lose weight they do not lose these cells, but rather each cell becomes abnormally thin, which in turn may stimulate hunger (as described earlier). The number of fat cells seems to be determined mainly by heredity, but it may also be affected—in one direction only—by the amount of food intake. The number of

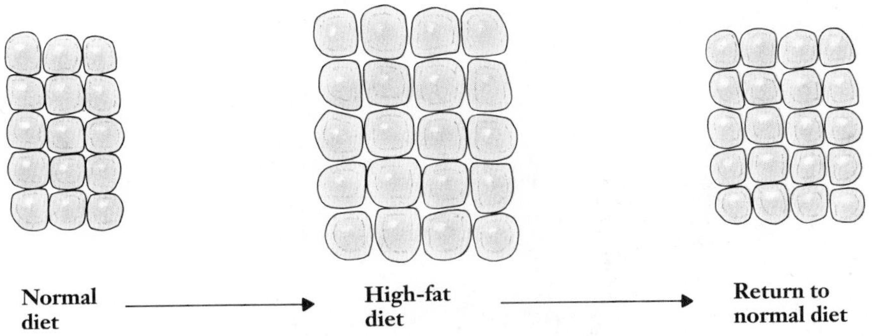

Figure 7.5 ***Effect of a high-fat diet on fat cells***

As illustrated by this schematic diagram, when rats were placed on a high-fat diet their fat cells increased in both number and size. When they were subsequently returned to a normal diet, their fat cells returned to normal size but did not decrease in number. The result was that the rats remained heavier than they would have been had they never been on the high-fat diet.

fat cells apparently does not decrease when one diets, but it does, alas, increase when one overeats for a prolonged period. This effect on fat cells may help explain why the set point does not go down when one eats less than usual for a period of time, but does go up when one overeats for a period of time—a phenomenon known as the *ratchet effect*. In one experiment, rats placed on a high-fat diet gained weight, and examination of their fat cells showed that the gain was due partly to an increase in the size of each cell and partly to an increase in number (Faust, 1984). When the rats were subsequently returned to a normal diet they lost some of the weight they had gained, but not all of it. The amount that they lost was accounted for by the return of their fat cells to normal size, and the amount *not* lost was accounted for by the increased number of fat cells (see Figure 7.5).

Some Problems with Dieting

Despite the promises of sales pitches, most diets fail in the long run. In one long-term study of people who lost weight in a behavior therapy program, fewer than 3 percent kept the weight off for a period of 4 or 5 years (Kramer & others, 1989).

People who lose lots of weight not only feel chronically hungry, but may find that they begin to gain weight even while staying on what for others would be a losing diet. When weight is reduced well below the set point, *basal metabolism* (the rate at which calories are burned up while the individual is at rest) slows down, so food is converted more efficiently to fat (Keesey & Corbett, 1984). In one extreme case, described by Judith Rodin and her colleagues (1989), a woman managed to reduce her weight from 312 pounds to a still-obese 192 pounds through diet. For at least 18 months after that she maintained her new weight, without losing any more, by eating a total of 1000 to 1200 calories a day—less than half the amount that most women would have to eat to maintain that weight.

■ **12.** ***What is some evidence that yo-yo dieting can reduce basal metabolism and thereby ultimately increase one's weight? Why might exercise be a better way to lose weight than diet?***

Other research indicates that repeated dieting followed by weight gain—commonly called *yo-yo dieting*—can permanently reduce basal metabolism, making each bout of dieting more difficult than the previous one. In one experiment, Kelly Brownell and his colleagues (1986) fed a group of rats with a low-fat food for a series of days, then switched them to a high-fat food for a series of days, then back to the low-fat food, and then back to the high-fat food again—two complete cycles of the yo-yo. The rats lost weight much more slowly, and gained it much more quickly, on the second cycle than on the first. This change was due partly to an increase in their food intake during the second cycle (they ate more of both foods), and partly to a decline in basal metabolism (they were about 50 percent more efficient in turning food into body weight at the end of the experiment than at the beginning). Control groups, who were on either the high-fat diet or the low-fat diet throughout the experiment, did not show these shifts. Comparable experiments have not been done with humans, but correlational research and clinical reports suggest that the same may occur with humans (Steen & others, 1988).

Brownell and his colleagues (1986) suggest that the effect of weight loss and regain on metabolism might have come about in evolution as an adaptation to periods of famine. An individual living where food is sometimes plentiful and other times absent would benefit from permanent bodily changes that make food use more efficient. A decline in basal metabolism during a famine would minimize weight loss, and continued low metabolism when the famine ended would maximize weight gain and build stores of fat for the body to draw on during the next famine.

Weight loss through exercise does not have the same effect as weight loss through diet. In an experiment with mice, animals that lost weight through forced exercise on a treadmill subsequently regained weight much more slowly than did animals who lost the same amount of weight by dietary restriction (Wainwright & others, 1991). Whereas weight loss by diet is due partly to loss in lean body mass (muscle) and partly to loss in fat, weight loss by exercise is due entirely to loss in fat (sometimes accompanied by gain in muscle). An increase in the ratio of muscle to fat leads generally to an increase in basal metabolism (VanItallie & Kissileff, 1990). Thus, a person who exercises can eat more without weight gain, not just because of the calories burned during exercise, but also because of heightened basal metabolism, which burns calories even when the person is not exercising.

Researchers who study metabolism and diet often have a few sensible words of advice for people who want to lose weight. The advice typically goes something like this: Don't try to lose weight rapidly. Don't go on a diet that you can't stay on for the rest of your life; it would probably be better in the long run to keep your present weight than to yo-yo. Instead of trying to reduce food intake to a level that leaves you hungry, try shifting the kind of food you eat—away from sweet or fatty foods (such as ice cream, red meat, butter, and fried foods) toward complex carbohydrates (breads, cereals, and vegetables), which are less readily turned into body fat. And, if you have a sedentary job or are a student, try to develop some pleasurable hobbies that involve exercise. (I, for one, can't stand jogging or weight lifting, but I love bicycling, walks in the woods, and ice skating.) Through changed food choices and increased exercise, many people find that they can lose a fair amount of weight and keep it off, without restricting the total amount they eat at all.

The Sex Drive

■ **13.** ***Why is caution especially necessary in extending findings about sexual mechanisms in nonhuman animals to humans?***

Just as hunger is the most thoroughly studied regulatory drive, the sex drive is the most thoroughly studied nonregulatory drive. As with hunger, most research on the physiological basis of the sex drive has been conducted with laboratory animals. In the case of the sex drive, however, more than in that of hunger, we must be wary about extending findings from other animals to ourselves. We appear to differ from other mammals even in some of the most basic biological aspects of sexuality.

One basic difference between humans and other species lies in the role of hormones in female sexual behavior. The females of nearly all other mammals are sexually motivated only during a specific time in their hormonal cycle. This is not true for human females. Another difference lies in the nature of sexual behavior itself. In other animals, including most other primates, copulation occurs in a stereotyped way, with one set of postures and movements for the female and a different set for the male (see Figure 7.6). In humans, by contrast, the variety of ways to copulate is limited only by imagination.

Figure 7.6 ***Copulation in rats***
Rats, like other nonhuman mammals, have a stereotyped (unvarying) pattern of copulation, with clearly different postures for the female and the male.

Despite our unique sexual characteristics, we humans certainly have not lost all traces of the biological determinants of sexual behavior found in other species, and studies of other species provide clues to such determinants in humans. As you read the following paragraphs, consider whether or not the mechanisms described have been observed in humans, and keep in mind the preliminary and tentative nature of the human research discussed.

Brain Mechanisms and Early Developmental Effects of Hormones

■ **14.** ***What is some evidence that different parts of the hypothalamus are involved in the male and female sex drives in nonhuman mammals?***

Numerous experiments, with rats and various other mammals, have shown that separate neural systems are involved in the control of male and female sex drives. An especially critical brain region for the male sex drive lies in the *medial preoptic area* of the hypothalamus (look back at Figure 7.4). Lesions there abolish, and electrical stimulation there increases, the male but not the female sex drive (Heimer & Larsson, 1967; Van Dis & Larsson, 1971). The same procedures show that the brain area most critical to the female sex drive is the *ventromedial area* of the hypothalamus (Pfaff & Sakuma, 1979; Powers & Valenstein, 1972). Such brain manipulations truly affect drive, not simply reflexive copulation, in that they influence the tendency to seek out and approach a member of the opposite sex, not just the tendency to copulate when presented with a sexual partner (Clark & others, 1981).

■ **15.** ***What are some effects of the presence or absence of testosterone before birth on development of the genitals, the brain, and behavior?***

Other research, mostly with rats, shows that the male-female brain differences responsible for the different adult sexual behaviors are determined by the presence or absence of the hormone *testosterone* during a critical period of development that begins before birth. As described in Chapter 3, the only *genetic* difference between the two sexes is that females have two X chromosomes, whereas males have one X and one Y. A specific gene on the Y chromosome causes the growth of testes (the male gonads) from structures that would otherwise grow into ovaries (the female gonads) (Page & others, 1987). Before birth the testes begin to produce testosterone. This hormone has a masculinizing effect on the brain and other body structures. Thus, rudimentary external genitals differentiate into the penis and other male structures if testosterone is present, or into the clitoris and other female structures if testosterone is absent. Within the brain, testosterone produced before birth acts on the hypothalamus to promote the development of neural systems involved in the male sex drive and to inhibit the development of those involved in the female sex drive (Feder, 1984). Thus, genetically female rats treated with testosterone during this period grow up predisposed to show male sexual behavior, and genetically male rats deprived of testosterone during this period grow up predisposed to show female sexual behavior.

One brain structure that is very much affected by testosterone during early development is a nucleus (cluster of neural cell bodies) called the *sexually dimorphic nucleus*, which lies within the medial preoptic area of the hypothalamus. It is typically about five times as large in the male rat as in the female rat, and the difference is due entirely to the early presence or absence of testosterone (Gorski & others, 1980). Female rats artificially treated with testosterone shortly before or immediately after birth develop a large sexually dimorphic nucleus, like males, and male rats artificially deprived of testosterone during this period develop a small sexually dimorphic nucleus, like females. This is just one of many areas of the brain that differ structurally between males and females, and research suggests that it contributes to male sexual drive (DeJonge & others, 1989).

Nobody knows just how testosterone causes sexual differentiation in the central nervous system, but some evidence suggests that it works by promoting or preventing the death of preexisting neurons (Arnold & Jordan, 1988). In other words, both male and female fetuses may first grow a full set of neurons in all brain areas. Then testosterone may promote the death of neurons in structures important for female behavior and prevent the death of neurons in those important for male behavior. However it works, the hormone must act within a critical period. In rats, this period runs from a few days before birth to a day or so after birth. In many other species, the critical period ends before birth. The critical period for testosterone's effect on the brain is later than that for its effect on the genitals. Thus, manipulation of hormones at the appropriate time can produce animals that have the genitals of one sex but the brain structures and behavior of the other (Feder, 1984).

■ **16. *How can prenatal stress affect the sexual development of male rats?***

In a fascinating series of experiments, Ingeborg Ward and her colleagues (1985) showed that stressful events experienced by pregnant rats can influence the future sexual behavior of their male offspring, apparently by reducing the level of prenatal testosterone. When the researchers subjected pregnant rats, late in pregnancy, to bright lights and physical restraint, the rats' male offspring manifested less male sexual behavior and more female sexual behavior in adulthood than did the male offspring of unstressed mothers. These researchers also found that males born to stressed mothers had unusually low levels of testosterone in their blood at the time of birth. Other researchers subsequently found that prenatal stress also reduced the size of the sexually dimorphic nucleus in the hypothalamus, and those rats with the smallest nuclei showed the least male sexual behavior (Anderson & others, 1986). Apparently, in response to stress the mother secretes hormones that inhibit the production of testosterone in male fetuses, which in turn causes their brains to be less masculinized, and more feminized, than they would be otherwise.

Perhaps you are wondering why a male hormone, rather than a female hormone, plays the key role in early sexual differentiation. The answer is that the female hormones progesterone and estrogen are produced by the mother and get into the tissues of all mammals during the prenatal period. If female hormones promoted growth of female structures during fetal development, all mammalian infants would be born looking like females. In birds and reptiles—which develop in eggs outside the mother's body—early sexual differentiation is determined by the presence or absence of estrogen, not testosterone (Adkins-Regan, 1981).

Prenatal Brain Development and Sexual Orientation in Humans

On behavioral grounds alone, one might doubt that the sharp distinction between male and female brain mechanisms for sexual behavior found in other mammals would exist in humans. Male and female sexual behaviors are not as different in us as in other species. Moreover, men and women show similar patterns of physiological changes during sexual arousal and climax (Masters & others, 1992) and describe their subjective feelings during sex in similar ways (Vance & Wagner, 1976). But one clear way in which most men and women do differ sexually is in the object of the sex drive: Most men are attracted to women, and most women are attracted to men. Might this difference result at least partly from a prenatal effect on the brain caused by the presence or absence of testosterone?

Of course not all of us are sexually most attracted to the opposite sex. About 4 percent of men and 2 percent of women are almost exclusively homosexual, and a larger percentage (harder to pin down) are strongly and consistently bisexual, attracted to both sexes (Bell & others, 1981; Kinsey & others, 1948, 1953). Many theories about the origin of homosexuality have focused on effects of family and other social experiences during childhood, but none of those theories has thus far been validated by evidence. The largest and most sophisticated study of sexual orientation to date, involving interviews with hundreds of homosexual and heterosexual men and women about their childhood and adolescent experiences, found no significant support for theories about social causes (Bell & others, 1981). No evidence was found that style of parenting, absence of a male or female parent, early seduction or rape by someone of the same or opposite sex, or degree of opportunity for one or another type of sexual experience in adolescence contributes significantly to the development of sexual orientation. The study did show, however, that whatever its cause or causes, sexual orientation is a deeply ingrained and early-emerging part of one's being. Homosexuals and heterosexuals alike reported that their sexual orientation was present, though not necessarily understood or accepted, in their childhood thoughts and fantasies; the *feeling* of stronger attraction to one sex or the other often existed for years before it was expressed. Sexual orientation apparently is not something that one can choose or change through willpower or therapy; it is rather something that one must discover about oneself.

■ **17. *What is some evidence that prenatal influences in humans may alter the brain in ways that affect sexual orientations?***

Recently, neurobiologist Simon LeVay (1991) found evidence of an anatomical brain difference between homosexual and heterosexual men. LeVay compared the brains of a group of homosexual men who had died of AIDS with the brains of two other groups: heterosexual men, some dead of AIDS and some of other causes; and heterosexual women, all dead of other causes. He focused on a nucleus in the hypothalamus that is believed to be homologous (evolutionarily related) to the sexually dimorphic nucleus found in rats and other nonhuman mammals. Other researchers had already shown that this nucleus is larger in heterosexual men than in heterosexual women, and LeVay confirmed that finding. In addition, however, LeVay found that this nucleus was on average less than half as large in the homosexuals' brains he studied as in the male heterosexuals' brains he studied. The difference was not due to AIDS; the nucleus was no smaller in the heterosexual men dead of AIDS than in the other heterosexual men and was significantly smaller in the homosexual men even when the comparison was restricted just to victims of AIDS.

For many people, anything having to do with homosexuality is emotionally charged. Not surprisingly, LeVay's report was quickly picked up by the popular press. Members of the gay community had two distinct reactions (Gelman & others, 1992). Some worried that it would strengthen prejudice against homosexuals by making their orientation appear to result from a "biological defect." A larger number, however, found the report consistent with their own view that sexual orientation is not subject to choice and were hopeful that the report would reduce prejudice. LeVay himself is homosexual, and he has frequently expressed the hope that his finding will foster greater acceptance of homosexuality as a normal biological condition that, like left-handedness, is much better to accept than try to change.

Keep in mind that LeVay's study is correlational, not experimental. It cannot tell us for sure what is cause and what is effect. However, assuming that his finding is repeatable, it does suggest that sexual orientation in men results at least partly from *something* that happens prenatally. And, unless the human brain is more different from other mammalian brains than most neuroscientists believe it to be, that something probably has to do with prenatal testosterone levels or with chemicals that interfere with testosterone's effects. Even before LeVay's study, other correlational research suggested that prenatal hormones and events affecting hormones are correlated with sexual orientation in humans (Ellis & Ames, 1987). Several studies found that men whose mothers experienced an unusual amount of stress during pregnancy are somewhat more likely than other men to be homosexual (Ellis & Ames, 1987; Ellis & others, 1988). This finding suggests that an effect similar to what Ward found in rats might occur in people. Genes may also play a role, either by affecting the timing of prenatal testosterone or through some other means. A recent study of identical and fraternal twins showed a rather high heritability for male homosexuality (Bailey & Pillard, 1991).

Nevertheless, LeVay's study remains to be replicated, and the correlational studies reviewed by Ellis and Ames all have possible alternative interpretations. The idea that sexual orientation in men is affected by prenatal development can still be disputed by reasonable people; and thus far almost no data exist concerning the development of sexual orientation in women.

Hormonal Effects on Sex Drive After Puberty in Males

In both humans and other mammals, the production of sex hormones greatly increases at puberty. In men, increased testosterone at this time stimulates such changes as beard growth and the male pattern of muscle development; in women, increased estrogen stimulates such changes as breast growth. These peripheral changes affect the way that other people react to the individual, and in that way change the developing person's self-concept and behavior (discussed in Chapter 13). But our concern now is with the possibility that the increase in hormones also affects behavior more directly by acting on brain mechanisms for the sex drive. We will look at this phenomenon first in the male and then in the female.

■ **18. *What is some evidence that testosterone is needed to maintain the male's sex drive, and that, at least in some species, it does so by direct action in the hypothalamus?***

In male animals, castration (removal of the testes and hence the main supply of testosterone) causes a marked decline in sex drive—not all at once, but gradually over time (it takes days to occur in rats, weeks in dogs, sometimes months in monkeys) (Feder, 1984). But the injection of testosterone into the bloodstream of castrated animals fully restores their drive. Sex drive can also be restored by implanting a tiny crystal of testosterone in the medial preoptic area of the hypothalamus, whereas the same amount of testosterone placed anywhere else does not produce this effect (Davidson, 1980). Thus, testosterone apparently augments and maintains the sex drive in males by acting directly on cells in the medial preoptic area, the same area where brain lesions destroy the drive. Other experiments have shown that neurons in this area contain testosterone receptors, where the hormone acts to modify neural activity (Pfaff & Modianos, 1985).

Testosterone is also critical for maintaining the sex drive in human males. Men castrated in an accident or for medical reasons almost always experience a decline (though often not a complete loss) in sex drive and behavior, but their drive is usually fully restored if they take injections of testosterone (Money & Erhardt, 1972). In other studies, testosterone injections administered to noncastrated men whose testes were producing abnormally low amounts of the hormone sharply increased their sexual behavior (Davidson & Myers, 1988; Davidson & others, 1979). This effect was more on drive than on sexual capability. Men with abnormally low levels of testosterone were fully capable of the mechanics of sexual behavior—including erection and ejaculation—but had little desire for it until injected with testosterone. The subjects in this research did not know when they were receiving testosterone and when they were not, so the results must have been due to the effects of the hormone and not to their expectations.

I should emphasize that this effect of injected testosterone has been documented only in men whose original testosterone level was very low. There is little evidence that variation in testosterone level within the range produced by gonadally normal men affects sex drive (Feder, 1984). Apparently, some minimal level of the hormone is needed for full sex drive, and testosterone beyond that level has little if any further effect.

Hormonal Effects on Sex Drive After Puberty in Females

■ **19. *What role does the ovarian hormone cycle play in the regulation of sex drive in rodents? How do nonhuman primates and humans differ from each other, and from rodents, in this regard?***

After puberty, a female's ovaries begin to secrete estrogen and progesterone in a cyclic pattern over time, producing the cycle of physiological changes referred to as the *menstrual cycle* in humans and the *estrous cycle* in other mammals. In both humans and nonhumans, this cycle controls ovulation (the release of one or more eggs so that pregnancy can occur). In rodents and many other mammals, it also tightly controls the sex drive—which ranges from very strong at the time of ovulation to nonexistent at other times. Removal of the ovaries completely abolishes sexual behavior in female rodents, and injection of hormones can fully restore it. For some species an injection of estrogen alone is most effective, and for others (including the rat) a sequence of estrogen followed 2 or 3 days later by progesterone is most effective. Just as testosterone increases the male sex drive in rodents by direct action in the medial preoptic area, estrogen and progesterone increase the female sex drive in rodents by direct action in the ventromedial area of the hypothalamus (Schwartz-Giblin & others, 1989). A tiny amount of hormone inserted into this area renews the sexual behavior of females whose ovaries have been removed.

Female monkeys and apes depend less on hormones for sexual behavior than do female rodents. Most primate females can, and sometimes will, copulate with a sexually active male at any time in their hormone cycle. In a review of such research, Kim Wallen (1990) concluded that ovarian hormones do not affect the sexual *capability* of female primates, but do affect their sexual *drive*. That is, female primates can and will copulate without such hormones, but are much more likely to seek out a male and initiate sexual behavior when the hormones are high than when they are low. In contrast, female rodents are unable to copulate without the hormones, because the hormones not only prime drive centers in their hypothalamus, but also prime motor centers in their spinal cord that are needed for reflexive aspects of their sexual behavior (Schwartz-Giblin & others, 1989).

Human females show still greater liberation of sexual behavior from hormones than do other primates. Women can experience a high or low sex drive at any time in their hormone cycle. In fact, debate exists as to whether women's sex drive is affected in a consistent way at all by the hormone cycle. A few studies in which women kept records of their daily sexual activities or thoughts showed a somewhat enhanced sex drive around the time of ovulation (Adams & others, 1978), but other studies showed mixed results (Davidson & Myers, 1988; Hill, 1988).

Other research suggests that if a hormone is involved in women's sex drive, that hormone may be testosterone, not estrogen or progesterone. In women, testosterone is produced in small amounts by the adrenal glands, and its production is stimulated by the ovarian hormones, so it cycles along with estrogen and progesterone. A study in which women kept records of their self-initiated sexual activity showed a correlation between the peak level of testosterone, occurring around the time of ovulation, and sexual activity throughout their cycle (Morris & others, 1987). That is, women with the highest testosterone levels around the time of ovulation tended to have the highest sex drive at all times in the cycle. One possible interpretation is that the testosterone peak produces a prolonged effect on the sex drive, which persists at least until the next peak. In clinical studies, women whose adrenal glands have been removed often report a decline in sex drive while women whose ovaries have been removed generally do not, and injection of testosterone reliably increases the sex drive reported by low-sex-drive women (Bancroft, 1978; Feder, 1984).

Evidence that testosterone is a critical hormone for sex drive in women leads to some interesting speculation. Perhaps, in the course of human evolution, part of the brain system previously devoted only to the male sex drive became incorporated into the control system for the female sex drive. That would help to explain why in many ways male and female sexual behaviors are less differentiated in humans than in other species. You might also find it interesting to speculate on why the capacity to experience high sex drive at any time in the cycle, with a resultant uncoupling of sex drive from ovulation and pregnancy, may have been an evolutionary advantage to females in the history of our species. One of several possibilities suggested by evolutionary theorists is that this capacity helps promote long-term pair bonding; a male may be more likely to remain with a partner who is potentially interested in sex at any time than with one who isn't.

The Role of External Stimuli

Brain structures primed with hormones provide the physiological *potential* for the sex drive. But the actual induction of the drive at any given time requires, in addition, sensory stimulation—usually some aspect of the sight, sound, smell, or touch of a potential sexual partner (or, in humans, the fantasy of such stimulation). The interplay between a drive (an inner, motivational state) and an incentive (an outer stimulus) is even stronger in the case of sex than in the case of hunger. Most ani-

More than skin deep

Physical attractiveness plays a major role in the initiation of romantic relationships, although standards of beauty vary across cultures. These men reside in (left to right) central India, North America, and eastern Africa.

mals have anatomical structures and behaviors that distinguish one sex from the other and serve innately to stimulate sexual interest. The huge tail feathers of the male peacock, fanned out to excite the female, and the female chimpanzee's display of the red swelling of her rump when she is in heat are examples. Concerning humans, we do not know to what degree biological distinctions between men and women (such as genital differences, or the woman's rounder form compared to the man's more angular form) innately serve as sexual stimuli, and to what degree such cues depend on learning. The fact that standards of sexual beauty vary across cultures, and even from individual to individual within a culture, shows at least that human biology permits a great deal of flexibility in the kinds of stimuli that can become cues for sexual attraction.

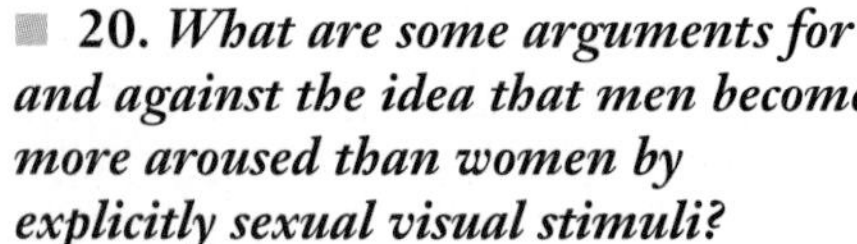

20. *What are some arguments for and against the idea that men become more aroused than women by explicitly sexual visual stimuli?*

A long-standing controversy centers on whether men are more easily sexually aroused than women by visual cues, such as the sight of a nude member of the opposite sex. In support of this sex difference, Donald Symons (1979) points out that men in our culture are by far the chief consumers of visual pornography, and he argues from cross-cultural research that men and boys throughout the world are more interested than women and girls in the nude body of the opposite sex. Even if Symons's cross-cultural analysis is correct, however, we cannot be sure that this sex difference isn't culturally produced. An argument can be made that throughout the world women and girls are punished more than men and boys for explicit expression of sexual interest (Small, 1992). Moreover, because women are everywhere more often the victims of sexual violence than are men (Smuts, 1992), and because pornography is often associated with sexual violence, women may reject pornography for reasons quite separate from its potential to arouse them sexually.

Reward Mechanisms and Their Relationship to Drives

We are endowed with a wonderful capacity to experience pleasure, which must have come about in evolution because it helped promote survival and reproduction. The pleasure brought by good food when hungry, water when thirsty, or drifting off to sleep when tired; the pleasure of sex; the pleasure of the company of good friends, or praise, or our own assessment of a job well done—it is easy to see how pleasures such as these can promote survival and reproduction. Of course, some activities that people find pleasurable, such as taking cocaine, threaten rather than promote survival and reproduction. But cocaine and other such drugs, as you will see, act directly on brain mechanisms that are normally stimulated by less direct means—such as by eating when hungry or by copulating when sexually motivated.

■ **21.** ***How are reward areas of the brain discovered by the self-stimulation technique?***

Rewards from Electrical Stimulation of the Brain

In the early 1950s, James Olds and Peter Milner made a remarkable discovery. They observed, by accident at first, that rats that received electrical stimulation in certain brain areas behaved as if they were trying to get more of it. For example, if a rat happened to receive the stimulation while exploring a particular corner of the cage, the animal would return repeatedly to that corner. To determine systematically if the brain stimulation would serve as a reward, Olds and Milner tested rats to see if they would stimulate their own brains by pressing a lever (see Figure 7.7). With certain electrode placements, rats learned very quickly to press the lever and would continue to press at high rates, sometimes for many hours without stopping (Olds & Milner, 1954).

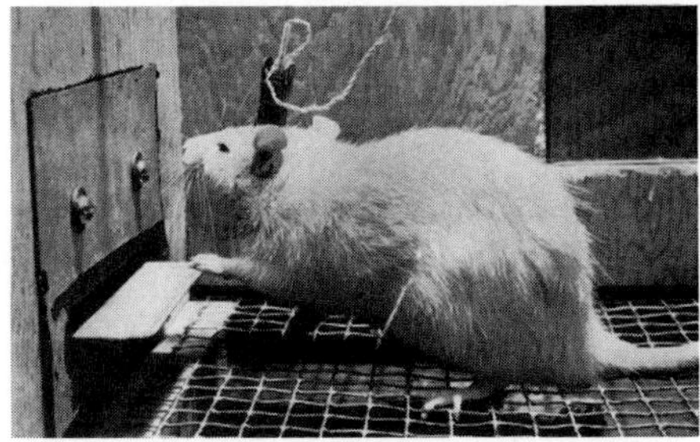

Figure 7.7 ***Lever pressing for electrical stimulation to the brain***

Each time this rat presses the lever it receives a brief pulse of electrical current through an electrode implanted in its brain. Some rats continued to press the lever for 24 hours without rest, as often as 5000 times per hour. (From Olds, 1956.)

Although Olds and Milner's rats behaved as if they liked the electrical stimulation, we can't know for sure what they were actually feeling. Very shortly after the initial discovery with animals, some researchers tried electrical stimulation in the brains of human patients as a possible treatment for various disorders, including epilepsy and severe schizophrenia (reviewed by Valenstein, 1973). With some electrode placements (mostly in the limbic system), patients reported intense pleasure, sometimes equating it with the feeling experienced during sexual orgasm (Heath, 1972). Other patients spoke vaguely of warm, glowing feelings. Patients who had electrodes in more than one brain area described the feeling differently depending on which electrode was stimulated. In no case did this procedure produce compulsive self-stimulation. Patients would stimulate their own brains when given the chance, and they liked it, but they had no difficulty stopping when they wished or were asked to stop. However, none of the electrodes were in the brain areas known to be most effective in rats for self-stimulation. Today such research with humans has been discontinued, apparently because the procedure is not sufficiently useful therapeutically to justify the risks involved.

■ **22.** ***What is some evidence that a particular neural tract that releases the neurotransmitter dopamine is critical for the rewarding effects of electrical brain stimulation and certain abused drugs?***

Subsequent research has shown that rats will work hardest and longest to stimulate a specific tract in the brain, called the *medial forebrain bundle*, which runs from the midbrain up through the lateral area of the hypothalamus, into a particular nucleus in the basal ganglia called the *nucleus accumbens*. The neurons of this tract secrete the neurotransmitter dopamine into the nucleus accumbens. Chemicals that selectively block the release of dopamine reduce or abolish animals' self-stimulation of this tract, and various manipulations that enhance the release of dopamine increase the rate of self-stimulation (Milner, 1991; Wise & Rompre, 1989).

Research with rats has also suggested that drugs such as amphetamines, cocaine, and opiates produce their pleasurable effects through action in the nucleus accumbens. All such drugs apparently promote the release of dopamine into the nucleus accumbens, and much if not all of their rewarding effect is lost, in rats, if the nucleus accumbens is chemically blocked (Roberts & Zitto, 1987; White & Milner, 1992; Wise, 1989). Moreover, rats have been shown to respond in the same way to tiny amounts of amphetamine or cocaine injected directly into the nucleus accumbens as they do to larger amounts injected into the bloodstream (Hoebel & others, 1983; Wood & Emmett-Oglesby, 1989). Thus, the nucleus accumbens appears to be a critical part of the neural pathway for two different artificial sources of pleasure—electrical and chemical stimulation of the brain.

■ **23.** ***What is some evidence that the neural systems involved in reward from electrical stimulation are also involved in reward related to natural drives such as hunger and sex?***

Brain-Stimulation Reward and Natural Drives

The neural circuitry underlying the reward effects just described surely did not come about in evolution to respond to drugs or to stimulation through wire electrodes. It must have evolved as part of the brain's mechanism for motivating behaviors that promote survival and reproduction, such as eating and copulating. Early research consistent with this view showed that, with some electrode placements, rats would stimulate their brains faster if a particular natural drive was strong than if it was weak. Thus, in several experiments, rats self-stimulated their brains faster if they were deprived of food than if they were not (Olds & Fobes, 1981). In another experiment, male rats self-stimulated their brains more slowly when their sex drive was reduced through castration and faster again when injected with testosterone (Caggiula & Hoebel, 1966). Food tastes better when one is hungry than when one is sated; sex is more pleasurable when the sex drive is strong than when it is weak. Perhaps the mechanism for such effects involves sensitization of the same neural pathways that provide the rewarding effect of electrical brain stimulation.

More recently, researchers have found that dopamine is released naturally from axon terminals in the nucleus accumbens when hungry rats eat or when sexually motivated rats copulate (Damsma & others, 1992; Phillips & others, 1991). Moreover, blockade of dopamine receptors may block the rewarding effect of food or sexual contact (Wise & Rompre, 1989). In one experiment, Roy Wise and his colleagues (1978) trained rats to press a lever for food pellets. Then, at a time when the rats were hungry, the researchers injected some with a dopamine-blocking drug and tested their rate of lever pressing. The drugged rats started off by pressing the lever and consuming pellets at the same high rate as did the undrugged rats, indicating that they were motivated for food. But within a few minutes their rate of pressing and eating slowed down and eventually fell nearly to zero. Apparently, the drug deprived the rats not of hunger but of the rewarding experience that normally comes from eating when hungry. Hence, their lever pressing underwent extinction, similar to that of undrugged, hungry rats whose lever presses brought no food.

Much remains to be learned about the roles of the brain's pleasure systems in motivation and learning. Presumably, these brain systems provide part of the basis for all forms of positive reinforcement in operant conditioning (the learning process discussed in Chapter 5), but little is known about how this may occur. Researchers also do not yet know to what degree different drives have their own associated sets of reward neurons or to what degree they share a common set. Are the neurons underlying the pleasure associated with eating different from those that underlie the pleasure associated with sex? Such questions are important in relation to the larger question, discussed in Chapter 5, of whether the brain contains many separate learning mechanisms, each associated with a different drive, or whether a common mechanism underlies learning motivated by many different drives. In the future, research on the brain's reward systems will no doubt bring psychological theories of motivation and of learning closer together.

Sleeping and Dreaming

Sleepiness can be thought of as a drive. A sleepy person is motivated to go to sleep and will expend some effort to reach a safe, comfortable place to do so—preferably one where the sheets are clean. Achieving this goal and drifting off to sleep provide a sense of pleasure analogous to that which comes from eating when hungry. But sleep is more than the end state of a drive: It is an altered state of consciousness, in which the brain for a time gives up some of its functions, leaving the person in a condition of reduced activity and responsiveness to the environment. Most of us spend about a third of our lives in this behavioral state. How, more precisely, can sleep be described? What is its function? What causes it physiologically? During sleep we dream. What are the function and cause of dreams? These are the questions we turn to now.

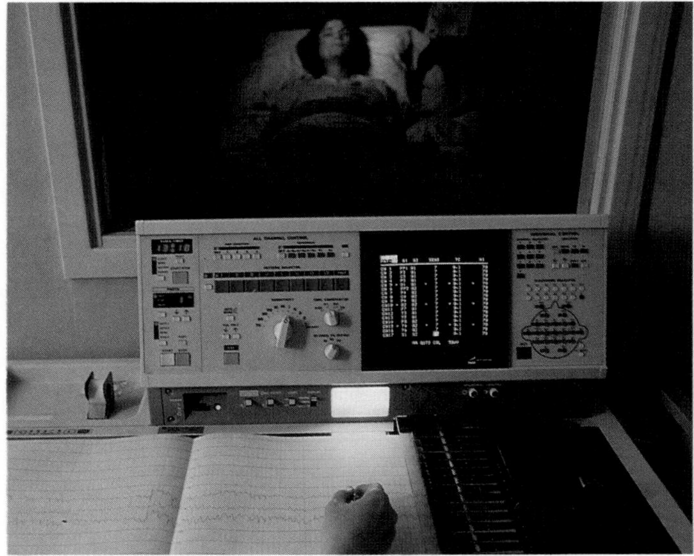

Figure 7.8 ***Recording an EEG in a sleep laboratory***

Electrodes pasted to this woman's scalp pick up weak electrical signals from her brain, which are then amplified and used to produce an EEG (ink tracings on the continuously moving roll of graph paper in the foreground). Other physiological changes, such as eye movements, can also be electrically recorded in this way.

The Electroencephalographic Description of Sleep

Because sleep is a state in which people show little overt behavior and cannot answer questions, scientists who study it must focus on subtle behavioral and physiological changes. The most valuable index of sleep is based on a recording of brain activity called the ***electroencephalogram*** (abbreviated ***EEG***).

■ **24.** ***What does the EEG actually measure?***

As you know (from Chapter 6), neural activity is electrochemical activity and can be measured as electrical change. The brain, with its billions of neurons, produces constant electrical "chatter," which to some degree penetrates the overlying skull and scalp. By placing electrodes on a subject's scalp, researchers can detect and amplify these signals. When the amplified signals are sent to an electroencephalogram recorder, they move pens up and down on a roll of paper that moves continuously under the pens, resulting in a permanent record of the signals. This record is the EEG (see Figure 7.8).

The EEG is a gross record of the electrical activity of the brain, representing a sort of average of activity of billions of neurons, with the greatest weight given to those lying closest to the recording site. As one group of electroencephalographers put it, "We are like blind men trying to understand the workings of a factory by listening outside its walls" (Hassett, 1978). You can't tell how the machines inside a factory work by listening outside the walls, but you can get some idea of the total amount of activity. You can tell, for example, when things have partly shut down and when they are going full steam ahead. If you listen long and hard enough you may begin to make finer distinctions than that, and if you also observe the factory's outputs you may be able to determine which sounds correspond with which outputs. Similarly, by correlating the types of ink squiggles recorded in the EEG with subjects' overt behavior or reported moods, researchers have developed a basis for using the EEG as a rough index of psychological states.

EEG Waves Accompanying Wakefulness and Stages of Sleep

■ **25.** ***How does a person's EEG change as the person goes from alert, to relaxed, to various stages of sleep?***

When a person is relaxed but awake, with eyes closed, and not thinking of anything in particular, the EEG typically consists of large, regular waves called *alpha waves*, which occur at a frequency of about 8 to 13 cycles per second (see Figure 7.9b on page 222). These relatively slow waves are believed to stem from a spontaneous, synchronized pulsing of neurons that occurs in the absence of focused mental activity or emotional excitement. When a person concentrates on an external stimulus, or tries to solve a problem, or becomes excited, the EEG pattern changes to low-amplitude, fast, irregular waves called *beta waves* (see Figure 7.9a). The low

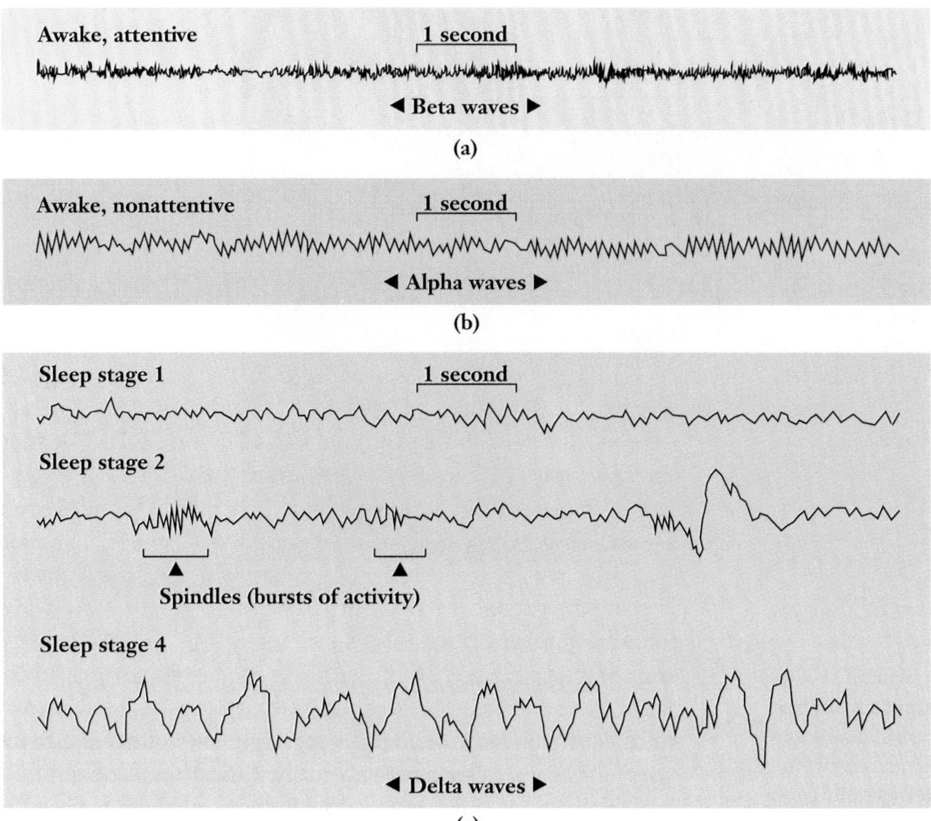

Figure 7.9 ***EEG waves of waking and sleep stages***

In general, as one goes from an alert to a relaxed state, and then to ever deeper stages of sleep, the EEG waves become slower in frequency and higher in amplitude. The brief bursts of rapid waves called sleep spindles that appear in stage 2 are the most distinctive markers of the onset of sleep. Sleep stage 3 is not shown here; it is arbitrarily defined as the period when 10 to 50 percent of the EEG consists of delta waves. (From Snyder & Scott, 1972.)

amplitude of these waves indicates that neurons are firing in an unsynchronized manner, such that their contributions to the EEG tend to cancel one another out. Whereas alpha waves are analogous to the large, regular waves that occur on a pond undisturbed by anything but the wind, beta waves are more akin to the effect of a million pebbles tossed suddenly onto the surface of the pond. The crests of the ripples created by some pebbles would cancel out the troughs created by others, resulting in a chaotic, high-frequency, low-amplitude pattern of ripples.

When a person falls asleep, the EEG goes through a fairly regular sequence of changes, which are used by researchers to divide sleep into four stages, illustrated in Figure 7.9c. *Stage 1* is a brief transition stage, when the person is first falling asleep, and *stages 2* through *4* are successively deeper stages of true sleep. They are characterized by an increasing percentage of EEG devoted to slow, irregular, high-amplitude waves called *delta waves*. Corresponding with this EEG change, muscle tension, heart rate, and breathing rate decline, and the person becomes increasingly hard to awaken.

Sleep Cycles

■ **26.** ***How do REM and slow-wave sleep differ, and how do they cycle through the night?***

Having reached stage 4 a person does not remain there for the rest of the night. Instead, after about 80 to 100 minutes of total sleep time, sleep rapidly lightens, returning through stages 3 and 2, and then a new, quite fascinating stage of sleep appears for a period of about 10 minutes or more. During this new stage the EEG is unsynchronized, looking much like the beta waves of alert wakefulness. Based on the EEG alone, one might think that the person had awakened, but direct observation shows that the person is sound asleep, and the record of muscle tension shows that the muscles are more relaxed than at any other sleep stage. Yet, consistent with the unsynchronized EEG, other indices of high arousal exist: Breathing and the heart rate become more rapid and less regular; penile erection occurs in males (even in infants and young boys); twitching movements occur in the small muscles of the fingers and face; and, most indicative of all, the eyes move rapidly back and forth and up and down under the eyelids. These eye movements, which can be

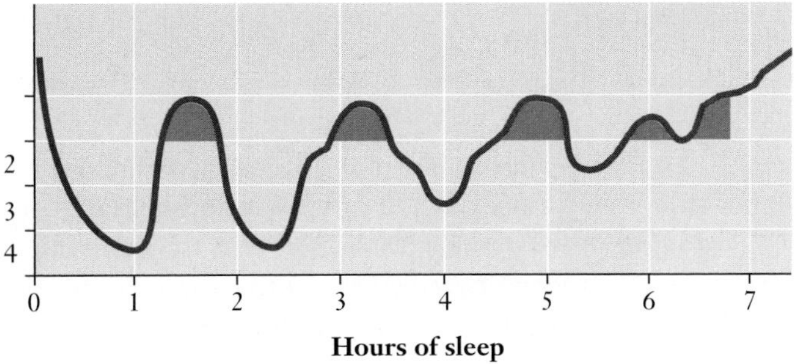

Figure 7.10 ***The cycle of sleep stages through a night***

People usually go through four or five sleep cycles per night, each ending with a period of REM sleep. With successive cycles the depth of slow-wave sleep becomes less, and the amount of time spent in REM sleep increases. (Adapted from Snyder & Scott, 1972.)

recorded electrically along with the EEG, give this stage of sleep its name, ***REM sleep*** (rapid eye movement sleep). As you may have guessed, REM sleep is when dreams occur—a topic to which we will return. REM sleep is also sometimes called *emergent stage 1*, because, even though it is different from the original stage 1, it marks the onset of a new sleep cycle. Stages 2, 3, and 4 are referred to collectively as ***slow-wave sleep***, because of the slow EEG waves that characterize those stages.

In a typical night's sleep, a person goes through four or five sleep cycles, each involving gradual descent into deeper stages of slow-wave sleep, followed by a rapid lightening of slow-wave sleep, followed by REM sleep (Hobson, 1987). Each complete cycle takes about 90 minutes. As you can see in Figure 7.10, the deepest slow-wave sleep occurs in the first cycle or two. With each successive cycle, less time is spent in the deeper stages of slow-wave sleep (stages 3 and 4) and more is spent in light slow-wave sleep (stage 2) and REM sleep.

■ ***27. What are two theories about the function of sleep, and what is some evidence supporting each?***

Functions of Slow-Wave Sleep

Why must we sleep? Countless children have asked that question to protest their parents' putting them to bed, and many scientists have asked it, too. Researchers have proposed two different theories to explain why a tendency to sleep came about in evolution, both of which probably contain more than a grain of truth.

The Restoration Theory

The *restoration theory* is the one that most people intuitively believe. It is the theory that your parents probably repeated to you as their reason for requiring you to go to bed at a certain hour. According to this view, the body wears out during the day and sleep is necessary to put it back in shape. Scientific support for this theory includes the observation that sleep *is* a time to rest. The muscles are relaxed, the metabolic rate is down, and the rate of neural activity in the brain is reduced (though only by about 10 percent, according to recordings from individual neurons in various brain structures [Hobson, 1987]). Moreover, extreme physical exercise, which would be expected to increase the need for restoration, is generally followed by increased depth and length of sleep (see Figure 7.11).

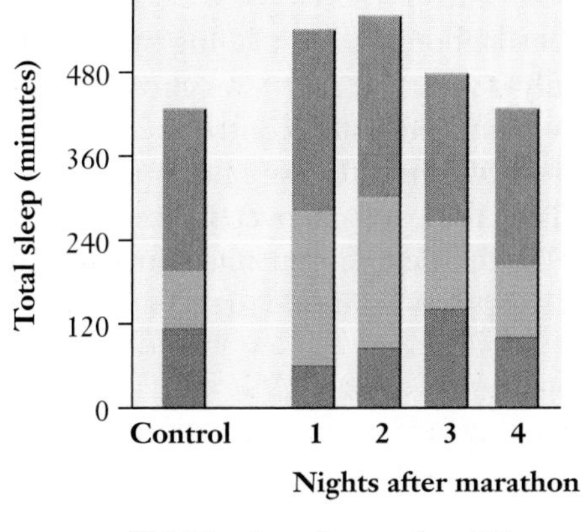

Figure 7.11 ***Effect on sleep of running a marathon***

Shown here is the average time spent in each sleep stage by athletes on each of 4 nights following a 92-kilometer marathon, compared to control nights (2 weeks before and 2 weeks after the marathon). Notice that the main effects were an increase in the time spent in deep slow-wave sleep (stages 3 and 4) and a decrease in REM sleep on the first 2 nights after the marathon. (From Shapiro & others, 1981.)

The Preservation and Protection Theory

The *preservation and protection theory* is less intuitive than the restoration theory and is based primarily on comparisons of sleep patterns in different species of animals. It posits that sleep came about in evolution to preserve energy and protect the individual during that portion of each 24-hour day when there is relatively little value and considerable danger in moving about. An animal needs only a certain number of hours per day to do those things that are necessary or useful for survival, and the rest of the time, according to this theory, it is better off asleep—quiet, hidden, and protected from predators and other possible dangers.

Support for this theory comes from evidence that variations in sleep time among different species do not correspond with differences in physical exertion while awake, but do correspond with feeding habits and ways of achieving safety (Allison & Cicchetti, 1976; Webb, 1982). At one extreme, large grazing animals such as bison and horses average only 2 or 3 hours of sleep per 24-hour day. Because of their large size and because they eat grass and other vegetation, which are extremely low in calories, they must spend most of their time eating, and therefore they have little time to sleep. Moreover, because of their size and the fact that they cannot burrow or climb trees, such animals are not adept at finding safe nooks in which to sleep. Thus, they are safer awake. (The fact that such animals sleep at all might be taken as evidence that some minimal amount of sleep is necessary for restorative functions.) At the other extreme, opossums and bats spend an average of 20 hours or more asleep each 24-hour day. These two species need only a couple of hours per day to obtain food (such as high-calorie insects), and they are adapted to hide in out-of-the-way places. Presumably, they sleep so much because they have no need to be awake for long and are protected from predators while asleep.

In addition to explaining species differences in total amount of sleep, the preservation and protection theory also helps explain differences in the time of day at which different species sleep. Animals that rely heavily on vision generally forage during the day and sleep at night. Conversely, animals such as mice and rats that rely more on other senses, and are preyed upon by animals that use vision, generally sleep during the day and forage at night. The theory also offers an explanation for the fact that infants in most species of mammals sleep much more than adults. Infants who are being cared for by adults do not need to spend time foraging, and sleep protects them from wandering away into danger. Their sleep also gives their caregivers an opportunity to rest or attend to other needs.

It is interesting to speculate, in this vein, about the evolutionary conditions that may have led to the 8-hour nighttime sleep pattern that characterizes adult humans throughout the world. Humans are highly visual creatures who need light to find food and do other things necessary for survival. At night it may have been best, throughout most of our evolution, for us to be asleep, tucked away in a cave or other hiding place, so as not to be tempted to walk about and risk falling over a cliff or being attacked by a nocturnal predator. Only during the past few centuries—an insignificant speck of evolutionary time—have lights and other contrivances of civilization made the night relatively safe for us. According to this line of thinking, our pattern of sleep might be in part a vestigial trait, a carryover from a period when the night was a time of great danger. To the degree that nighttime is still more dangerous than daytime, our pattern of sleep may continue to serve an adaptive function.

Sleep as a Biological Rhythm

One approach to understanding sleep is to view it in relation to other biologically based changes that accompany the 24-hour cycle of day and night. The day-night cycle has been a stable feature of our planet since its beginning, and all plants and animals have mechanisms that accommodate it. Among the physiological changes in humans that follow a daily rhythm are body temperature, which falls at night and rises during the day, and secretion of the adrenal hormone cortisol, which follows an opposite pattern.

■ **28.** ***What is some evidence that sleepiness is affected by an internal clock that can operate even without external time cues, but is continuously reset by daily changes in light?***

Experiments with animals have shown that cyclic changes in temperature, hormones, and behavioral activity (indicative of sleep or wakefulness) continue even when the animals are maintained in a time-free environment, that is, an environment in which there is no regular change in lighting or other cues that could indicate the time of day. In such an environment the cycle length is typically somewhat longer or shorter than 24 hours, and it varies from individual to individual but is remarkably constant within a given individual (Takahashi & Zatz, 1982). Similar experiments with human volunteers—who agreed to live for days or weeks in rooms with no windows, clocks, or other time cues—have produced results quite

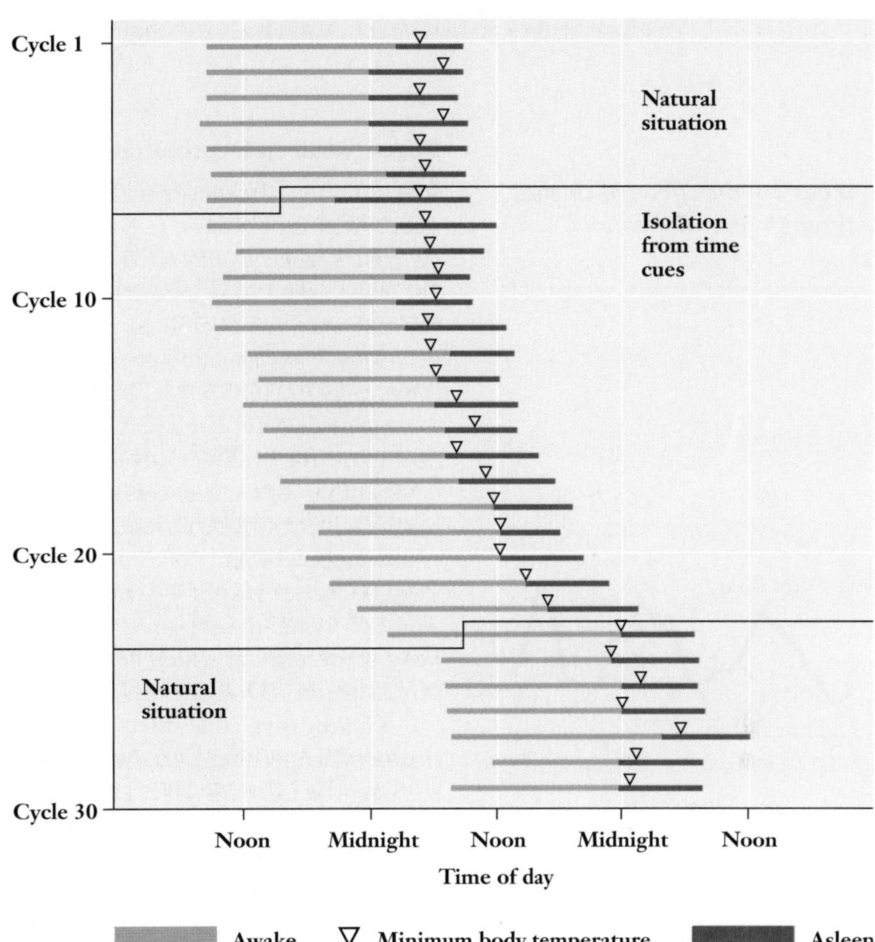

Figure 7.12 ***Human circadian rhythm in a time-free environment***

These data are from a single male subject. Each horizontal bar represents one circadian period of wakefulness followed by sleep, with successive periods drawn below each other. The triangles indicate the time of minimal body temperature in each period. Notice that during the period of isolation from time cues, the cycle period became somewhat longer than 24 hours, so the man fell asleep and woke up later each day. (Adapted from Aschoff, 1969.)

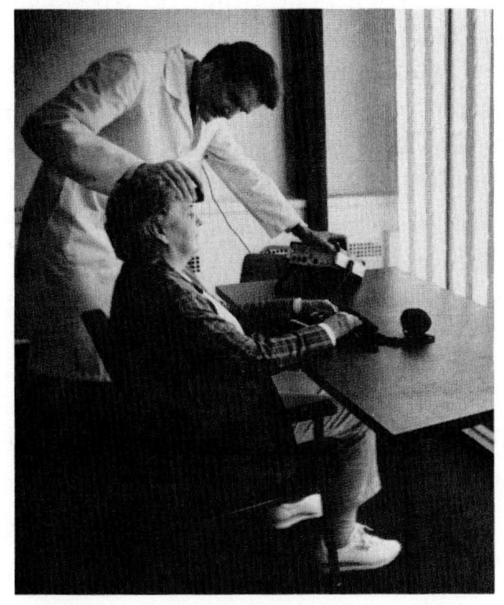

Figure 7.13 ***Resetting the circadian clock***

The woman shown here is being treated by Charles Czeisler for a sleep problem. Before treatment, she would routinely drop off to sleep at about 9 P.M. and awaken at about 4 A.M. After treatment—3 evenings of bright lights—she would fall asleep at about 11 P.M. and awaken at about 7 A.M., her preferred schedule. If her circadian clock were to drift back, it could be reset with another evening or two of lights. Other research by Czeisler and his colleagues suggests that even normal room lights can influence the circadian clock, but the very bright lights shown here are more effective.

similar to those found with other species. Temperature, cortisol production, and sleepiness continue to oscillate at close to a 24-hour period (see Figure 7.12).

The technical term for any rhythmic change that continues at close to a 24-hour cycle in the absence of external 24-hour cues is ***circadian rhythm*** (from the Latin words *circa*, meaning about, and *dien*, meaning day). Such rhythms are governed by cyclic changes in activity in the nervous system that can occur independently of external cues.

The environmental day-night cue that normally resets the circadian clock each day, so that rhythms occur in periods of exactly rather than approximately 24 hours, is daylight. Experiments with animals show that the cycle can be shortened or stretched somewhat, say, to a 22-hour or 26-hour period, by artificially changing the period of light and dark. And experiments with humans as well as other animals show that the cycle can be reset through carefully timed exposure to bright fluorescent lights.

In experiments with humans, Charles Czeisler and his colleagues (1989) found that just a few hours of bright fluorescent lighting at night, coupled with avoidance of daylight, over 3 successive days is enough to reverse a person's circadian clock so that he or she becomes sleepy during the day and alert at night. One practical application of this technique is to help night workers adapt their bodily rhythms to their work hours. In an experiment, subjects simulating night work for a week were more alert at work, slept better during the day, and showed a more complete shift in their body temperature cycle if their work environment was very brightly illuminated and their daytime sleep room was completely darkened than they did under more typical lighting conditions (Czeisler & others, 1990). Czeisler has also used lighting to help people with unusual sleep cycles modify their cycle to a more normal one (see Figure 7.13).

■ **29.** ***What are the effects of staying awake through several days and nights?***

Effects of Sleep Deprivation

In a number of experiments, people have voluntarily gone several days without sleep. After 3 or 4 days, they sometimes began to experience rather dramatic mental upsets, such as distorted perceptions and extreme irritability (Borbély, 1986). Yet when asked to work at tasks requiring physical skill or mental judgment, their abilities were remarkably unaffected by sleep deprivation. As a rule, sleep deprivation hurts performance on simple, boring tasks more than on challenging ones (Horne, 1979, 1988); this observation led sleep researcher William Dement (1979) to suggest that impaired performance, when it occurs, is caused mainly by subjects' dozing off for brief periods during boring tasks. Evidence that even extreme sleep deprivation does not necessarily impair physical coordination or judgment comes from Dement's observation of the world-record-setting vigil of a young college student named Randy Gardner. During the final hours of an 11-day period without sleep, Gardner played a penny arcade baseball game 100 times with Dement and won every one. Before going to bed, after 264 hours without sleep, Gardner held a news conference at which he was "very coherent and conducted himself in impeccable fashion" (Dement, 1972).

The most reliable effect of sleep deprivation is sleepiness itself. (This is also the most dangerous effect, because it can cause one to fall asleep at the wrong time, such as when driving.) Yet even this effect is not simply related to the amount of time that one has gone without sleep. During sleep deprivation the circadian rhythm maintains its 24-hour cycle, so subjects who manage to remain awake all night usually find it much easier to remain awake after daybreak than before (see Figure 7.14).

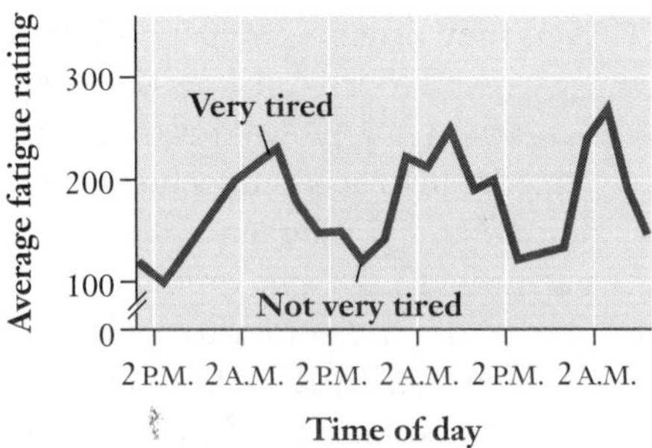

Figure 7.14 ***Rhythm of fatigue during 72 hours of sleep deprivation***

In this experiment, fifteen women went for 72 hours without sleep. Every 3 hours they rated their subjective feeling of tiredness on a scale on which 100 meant "normal fatigue" and 200 meant "twice as fatigued as normal." Notice that in each successive 24-hour period, the maximal fatigue ratings occurred around 2 to 6 A.M. and minimal ratings occurred around 2 to 8 P.M. (From Akerstedt and Fröberg, 1977.)

Other research on variations in sleep patterns has focused on *nonsomniacs*, people who naturally sleep very little. Ray Meddis (1977) identified a number of individuals who slept much less than the typical 8 hours per day and rarely felt tired. If 8 hours of sleep were essential for physical restoration, we would expect nonsomniacs to be extremely inactive during the day or to suffer in some way from their lack of sleep. But according to Meddis, the opposite seems to be true. Nonsomniacs as a group appear to be unusually vigorous and healthy. One such individual was a nurse who reported that for most of her life she had slept about 50 minutes per night. She was very active during the day and would usually spend the night in quiet activities, such as reading or painting. To verify her nonsomnia, Meddis tested her in the sleep lab. She slept not at all the first three nights in the lab, remaining cheerful and talkative throughout. Finally, on the fourth night, she slept a total of 99 minutes and awoke feeling fully rested.

■ **30.** ***What is the difference between a nonsomniac and an insomniac?***

Lest you gain the impression that the usual 8 or so hours that most people sleep per night is not necessary, I hasten to add that for most of us it *is* necessary. It is important to distinguish nonsomniacs from *insomniacs*. An insomniac is someone who has a normal desire for sleep but who, for some reason (such as worry), is unable to sleep at night. Unlike a nonsomniac, an insomniac feels tired all day as a result of not sleeping. And so do most people who voluntarily reduce their sleep. Again, the desire to sleep can be thought of as a drive, similar in some but not all ways to hunger. To oversimplify somewhat, we sleep because we have a mechanism in the brain that makes us *want* to sleep at certain periodic intervals. If we yield to this want, we experience pleasure as we drift off, and if we resist it we experience discomfort and an increased craving to sleep until we finally give in. The sleep drive varies from person to person. Most of us have a drive that can be satisfied by about 8 hours per night; but some have a drive that requires more, and others have a drive that requires less.

Dreams and REM Sleep

Dreams have always been a great mystery to people. In sleep one travels to distant places, speaks with friends long dead, and performs impossible feats as if they were commonplace. People at various times and places have believed that dreams foretell the future or are instructions from the spiritual world. Others (notably Sigmund Freud, as you will see in Chapter 16), less mystically inclined, have held that dreams express deep, hidden wishes and can be used to unlock the secrets of the unconscious mind. Today our knowledge of dreams has been advanced by studies in sleep laboratories, where sleep stages are monitored physiologically and people are periodically awakened and asked to report what was on their mind just before awakening.

■ **31.** ***How do researchers know that true dreams accompany REM sleep and that other forms of sleep thought can occur in other sleep stages?***

When people are awakened during REM sleep they usually (in about 90 percent of the cases) report a mental experience that researchers call a ***true dream*** (Foulkes, 1985). A true dream is experienced as if it were a real event rather than something merely imagined or thought about. The dreamer has the feeling of actually seeing or in other ways sensing various objects and people, and of actually moving and behaving in the dream environment. Moreover, the true dream usually involves a progression of such experiences, woven together in a somewhat coherent though often bizarre story. The longer the sleeper engages in REM sleep before awakening, the longer and more elaborate is the reported dream. Studies show that essentially everyone dreams several times a night. People who believe that they rarely dream, or who can recall only fragments of dreams upon normal awakening in the morning, describe vivid, detailed dreams if awakened during REM periods. Dreams are fleeting experiences, quickly lost from memory unless we catch them and think about them immediately upon awakening.

When people are awakened during slow-wave sleep, they report some sort of mental activity just before awakening in roughly 60 percent of the cases (Foulkes, 1985). Such reports are usually not of true dreams but of ***sleep thought***, which lacks the vivid sensory and motor hallucinations of true dreams and is more akin to daytime thinking. Often the subject of sleep thought is some problem that had been of concern during the day. For example, a student who had been cramming for a math exam might report working on a calculus problem while sleeping. The main difference between sleep thought and daytime thought is that the former is usually ineffective. Although the sleeper may feel that he or she is solving a calculus problem, questions upon awakening indicate that no real progress was made (Hobson, 1987).

■ **32.** ***According to one theory, what is the function of REM sleep, and how might dreams be a side effect? How is this theory supported by the high rate of REM sleep in fetuses and infants?***

Thus far, research has not answered the question: What are true dreams for? Theories about this that have emerged from the sleep labs are more mundane than those that others have sometimes proposed. One view prevalent today is that dreams don't serve any special purpose at all, but are side effects of physiological changes in REM sleep that do serve a purpose (Foulkes, 1985; Hobson, 1988). According to one version of this view, the purpose of REM sleep is to provide regular exercise to groups of neurons in the brain. Synapses can degenerate if they go too long without being active (Edelman, 1987), so neural activity during REM sleep may help preserve important circuits. Some of the neurons are in perceptual and motor circuits, and perceptual and movement hallucinations may be inevitable consequences of their activity. In research done many years ago, electrical stimulation in portions of the cerebral cortex produced dreamlike hallucinations in people who were awake (Penfield & Perot, 1963). A similar phenomenon may well occur in REM sleep. In addition to producing hallucinations, the brain continues in REM sleep to engage in some degree of thought, just as it does in slow-wave sleep. But now the thought becomes wrapped up in trying to make sense of the hallucina-

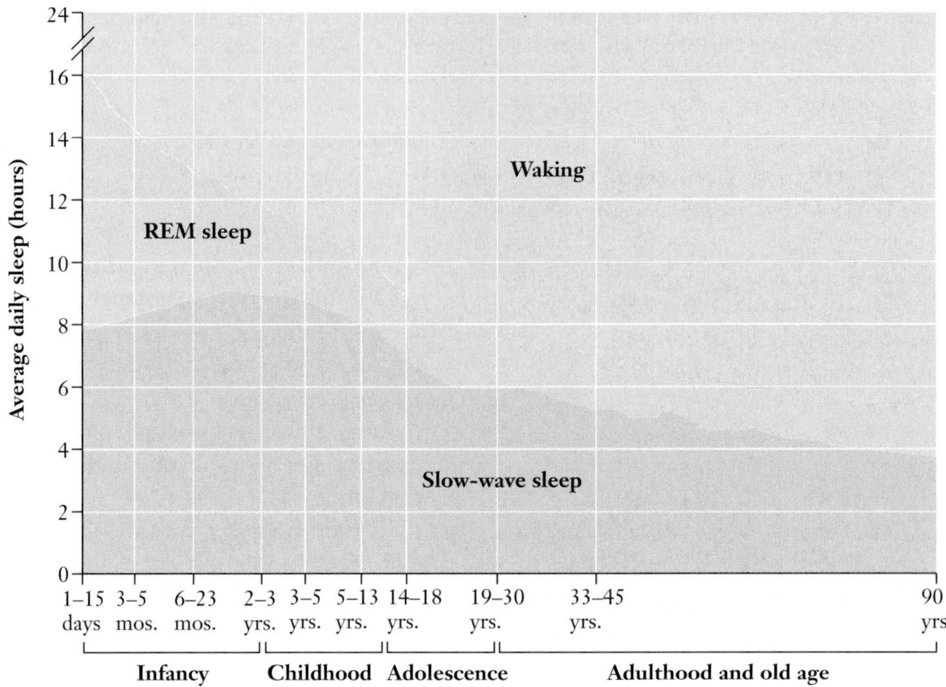

Figure 7.15 ***Changes in sleep over the course of life***

As shown here, both the total daily sleep time and the percentage of sleep time spent in REM sleep decrease as a person gets older. If the curves were extended to the left, they would show that prior to birth REM sleep occupies most of each 24-hour day. (Adapted from Snyder & Scott, 1972.)

tions. The result is the weaving of a story, of sorts, connecting one hallucination to the next—hence, the dream. Because of reduced mental capacity during sleep, the story is less logical than one the awake brain would develop, but it still contains some degree of logic.

Consistent with the view that the purpose of REM sleep is to exercise brain pathways, with dreams as a side effect, is the observation that REM sleep occurs in mammals besides humans, and to a much greater degree in fetuses and infants of all species than in adults (see Figure 7.15). In fact, the peak of REM sleep in the human occurs in the 30-day-old fetus, who spends almost 24 hours a day in this state (Parmelee & others, 1967). Why should fetuses spend so much time in REM sleep? Perhaps as their brains are developing in the relative isolation of the womb they need to exercise sensory and motor pathways, and REM sleep is their means for doing that (Hobson, 1988). In the fetus, REM sleep is accompanied by body movements such as kicking and twisting, which are apparently triggered by the bursts of activity in motor areas of the brain. By the time of birth a neural inhibitory system matures, which inhibits most motor neurons during REM sleep and thus prevents most movements that would otherwise occur. The motor neurons to the eyes, however, remain uninhibited, so eye movements remain as a visible effect of the brain's activity.

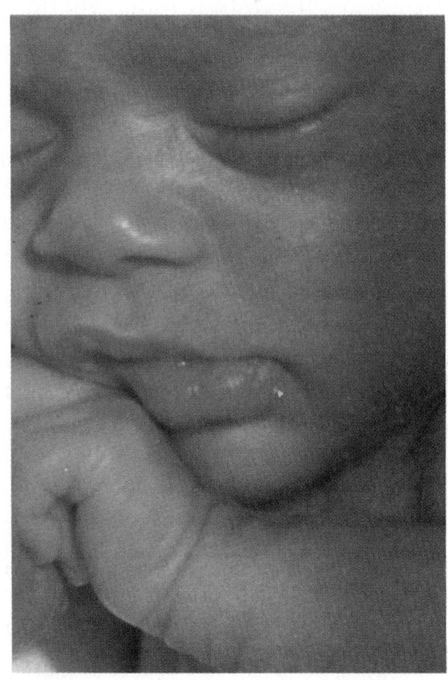

Sweet dreams?

We have no idea whether human fetuses, such as this one of 7 months, experience dream sensations or not, but we do know that they spend most of their time in REM sleep.

Sometimes the side-effect theory just described is interpreted as an argument against the psychoanalytic view that dream analysis can be useful for understanding the mind. But that interpretation seems unjustified. Even if dreams are triggered by random events in the brain, the actual images, emotions, and story lines that constitute the dream are not random. They certainly contain elements based on the dreamer's previous experience, and, because they occur at a time of reduced mental capacity, ideas or feelings that are normally suppressed by higher mental processes could emerge and perhaps be useful in psychoanalysis (Reiser, 1991). Evidence for or against this view would have to come from studies in which dream experiences are correlated in meaningful ways with other aspects of a person's life.

Brain Mechanisms Controlling Sleep

Are there special neural systems for inducing sleep, analogous to those for inducing drives such as hunger? In the early days of sleep research, some researchers believed that sleep is the natural state that the brain slips into when not aroused by external stimulation, so they saw no need to posit special sleep-inducing mechanisms. But such a view is inconsistent with the observation that sleepiness sometimes overwhelms us even when external stimulation is high, and other times we can't sleep no matter how quiet, dark, and unstimulating the environment. We now know that the early theory was mistaken and that sleep is actively promoted by special neurons in the brain. In fact, based on experiments with animals, researchers have identified three separate but interacting brain systems involved in sleep. These are:

33. ***What is some evidence that the circadian clock is in the hypothalamus and that specific centers for slow-wave and REM sleep are in the brainstem?***

- ***Circadian rhythm generators in the hypothalamus*** The circadian clock is located in a specific nucleus of the hypothalamus, called the *suprachiasmatic nucleus*. If this nucleus is damaged, animals lose their regular rhythms and fall asleep or wake up at rather random times over the 24-hour day. The same is true of human patients (Cohen & Albers, 1991). This nucleus contains rhythm-generating neurons, which gradually increase and decrease their rate of action potentials over a cycle of approximately 24 hours, even when surgically isolated from other parts of the brain (Takahashi & Zatz, 1982). This neural rhythm accounts for the circadian rhythm of sleep and wakefulness that occurs in a time-free environment. The same nucleus also receives direct input from the eyes by way of a special set of neurons in the optic nerve, through which the daily changes in sunlight synchronize the circadian clock to the 24-hour pattern of the earth's rotation (Takahashi & Zatz, 1982).
- ***A neural center for slow-wave sleep in the brainstem*** The brain area that most directly brings on slow-wave sleep is an interconnected set of nuclei (collectively called the *raphé nuclei*) in the medulla and pons of the brainstem. Neurons with cell bodies in these nuclei send their axons to all parts of the cerebral cortex and release the transmitter *serotonin*, which has an inhibitory effect, causing the reduced cortical activity that characterizes slow-wave sleep (Lindsley, 1983). Damage to these brainstem nuclei, or drug-induced depletion of serotonin in the brain, reduces or abolishes sleep in animals (Jouvet, 1967; Lindsley, 1983). These nuclei receive input directly from the rhythm generators in the hypothalamus, which accounts for the circadian change in sleepiness; and they also receive input from other brain areas, which may help explain why sleepiness can come and go at times that are out of sync with the circadian cycle, depending upon one's experiences during the day or night.
- ***Neural centers for REM sleep in the brainstem*** The shift from slow-wave to REM sleep seems to involve two interconnected sets of neurons in the pons. One set generates the increased brain activity that occurs in REM sleep, and the other set inhibits motor neurons and thereby produces the extreme loss of muscle tension that occurs in REM sleep. Cats with lesions in these inhibitory neurons begin to move about every time they fall into REM sleep and wake themselves by their own movements (Jouvet, 1972). People who have brain damage to this area produce, in fact, the movements that they dream they are producing—sometimes with quite harmful consequences (Culebras & Moore, 1989). Fortunately, this disorder can be treated with a drug. Some other people suffer from an opposite disorder, called *cataplexy*, in which the inhibitory brainstem center becomes active at unpredictable times during the day, with the result that their skeletal muscles become limp and they collapse, unable to move for several seconds or minutes, although they are otherwise awake (Chase & Morales, 1987). Perhaps you have experienced something akin to a cataplectic attack yourself when, while you were trying to sleep, your brain shifted into a REM mode while you were still half awake and you could sense the condition of being temporarily paralyzed.

Emotion

Enough sleep; wake up and face the challenges of the day. Midterm exams are just around the corner, your family is after you to get your life in order, your lover has just left you for another, the surgeon says your nose and left ear will have to go, and a hungry tiger is crouched behind you about to pounce. Are you awake? All of these events have something in common: All are likely to be psychologically disturbing, and all may—in some people at least—produce a pattern of physiological reactions referred to as *high arousal.* In this section we will look first briefly at the arousal response and its effects, and then at the psychological experience called *emotion.* (By the way, I was only kidding about your left ear.)

High Arousal

34. ***How does the arousal response help prepare the body for fight, flight, and possible wounds?***

The ***arousal response*** is a pattern of measurable physiological changes that helps prepare the body for "fight or flight" (to use Walter Cannon's famous phrase). The pattern varies from person to person and situation to situation, but commonly includes the following elements: (1) Skeletal muscles become tense, and blood is diverted from other parts of the body to muscles, preparing them to spring into action. (2) The heart rate, blood pressure, and breathing rate increase, and sugar and fat molecules are released into the blood from storage deposits—all of which help prepare the body metabolically for a possibly prolonged expenditure of energy. (3) Changes occur in the blood that enable it to clot more easily, and pain-relieving hormones called *endorphins* (discussed in Chapter 8) are released—both of which help prepare the body for possible injury. (4) Alerting mechanisms of the brain are strongly activated, and cognitive processes are narrowly focused on the arousing stimulus or thought. This pattern seems nicely designed to cope with the proverbial tiger about to attack, or with a bully at the neighborhood playground. But it can also occur in response to such challenges as taking midterm exams or asking someone out on a date, where neither fight nor flight is called for, and in these cases it may do more harm than good.

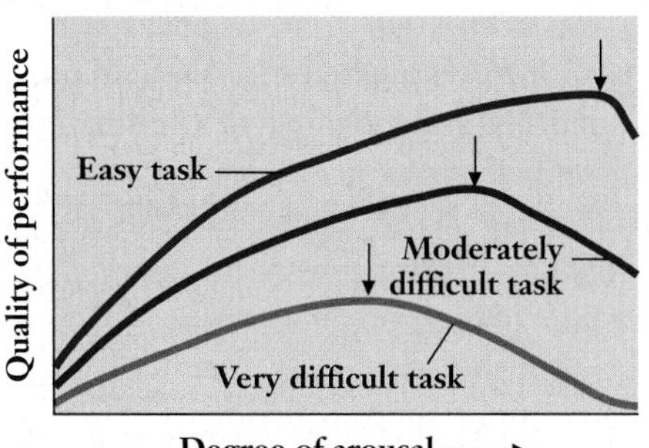

Figure 7.16 ***The relationship between degree of arousal and quality of performance for three different tasks***

For any given task, quality of performance increases as arousal increases, up to some peak, and then declines as arousal increases still further. In this illustration, peak performance for each task is indicated by the arrow. As shown, peak performance occurs at a lower arousal level for cognitively difficult tasks than for cognitively easy tasks. This relationship is referred to as the *Yerkes-Dodson law.*

In the short run, as shown by many experiments with both humans and other animals, the arousal response can be either helpful or harmful, depending on the task at hand. In general, high arousal is beneficial for tasks that require a good deal of physical energy, or when performance of the task is instinctive or very well practiced, but is harmful for tasks that call for novel (unpracticed) movements, creativity, or careful judgment. In other words, for any given task some level of arousal is optimal, and this optimal level is lower for intellectually difficult tasks than for those defined more by endurance, persistence, or ability to stay alert (see Figure 7.16).

35. ***What is the relationship between degree of arousal and task performance? In what way does that relationship depend upon the kind of task?***

This relationship between optimal arousal and type of task is called the ***Yerkes-Dodson law***, because a version of it was first proposed by Robert Yerkes and John Dodson (1908). These researchers performed experiments in which mice could avoid electric shocks by entering the brighter of two compartments. They varied the arousal level in the mice by varying the intensity of the shocks used, and they varied the task difficulty by varying the contrast in brightness between the two compartments. When the task was easy (a big difference between the two compartments), the mice did best with high arousal (from a strong shock). But when the task was difficult (little difference between the compartments), the mice performed best with lower arousal (from a weak shock). Chapter 15 discusses experiments showing a comparable effect in people—where arousal was manipulated not by shocks but by the presence or absence of an audience. An audience, as the Yerkes-Dodson law would predict, typically improves performance on routine tasks and worsens it on tasks requiring calm judgment or creativity.

If the arousal response is too strong and prolonged, and occurs too often, it can have harmful effects on the body. Prolonged overactivity of the sympathetic portion of the autonomic nervous system can produce ulcers, keep blood pressure too high, and increase the risk of heart attack; and prolonged oversecretion of cortisol and other hormones of the adrenal cortex can suppress the immune system and increase the risk of infectious diseases (Solomon & others, 1985). People differ in the degree and type of arousal response they show in similar situations, and these differences correlate with their likelihood of developing particular physical ailments—an idea discussed more fully in Chapter 16.

Theories of Emotion That Emphasize Peripheral Feedback

Stimuli that produce high physiological arousal also produce strong emotional feelings, such as terror, rage, and passion. An ***emotion***, as the term is used by most psychologists who study it, refers to a particular kind of subjective feeling. This feeling is elicited by objects or events, real or imagined, that have high significance to the individual. The significance may have to do with perceived threat or benefit. Thus, I might be terrified by a real or imagined tiger behind me or elated by my real or imagined winning of a sought-after prize. Emotions tend to come on rapidly and automatically and may be based on an unreasoned evaluation of the event or object that can run counter to rational thought. Thus, for a person afraid of snakes, even a harmless garter snake might elicit fear, despite the person's rational knowledge that the snake is harmless. Finally, strong emotions are typically accompanied by high physiological arousal.

There is no end to the possible number of different human emotions. The number depends on how finely graded a taxonomy we wish to create. You may recall from Chapter 4 that Ekman and Friesen identified six basic emotions—surprise, fear, disgust, anger, happiness, and sadness—each expressed by a unique set of muscle contractions in the face, and suggested that most other emotions are blends or variations of those six. Another way to classify emotions is illustrated in Figure 7.17, which portrays various emotions in a two-dimensional array. One dimension is the degree to which the emotion is associated with approach or avoidance, and the other the degree of bodily arousal associated with it.

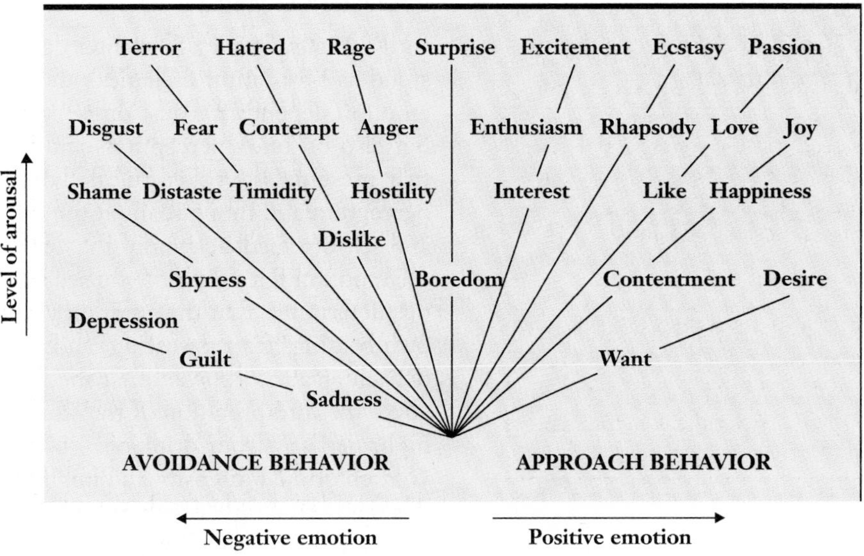

Figure 7.17 ***Spectrum of positive and negative emotions***

Shown here is an attempt to arrange emotions along two dimensions: the degree to which the emotion is experienced as positive or negative and the level of bodily arousal involved. Because emotional feelings are subjective, no such classification will be completely agreed upon by all observers. (From Kissin, 1986.)

Because emotions are associated with peripheral changes in the body, psychologists have long wondered if those changes contribute to, or are essential for, emotional feelings. By peripheral changes, I mean all bodily changes that occur outside the central nervous system, including changes in heart rate, breathing rate, muscle tension, body posture, and facial expressions.

James's Peripheral Feedback Theory

■ **36.** ***What was James's theory of emotion, and what evidence did he supply for it?***

In his famous textbook, *The Principles of Psychology*, William James (1890) argued that bodily arousal causes emotion. More specifically, he argued that arousal occurs immediately in response to the perception of certain kinds of environmental events, and that emotions are one's sense of arousal. In James's words,

> Our natural way of thinking . . . is that the mental perception of some fact excites the mental affection called the emotion, and that this latter state of mind gives rise to the bodily expression. My theory, on the contrary, is that *the bodily changes follow directly the perception of the exciting fact, and that our feeling of the same changes as they occur IS the emotion.* Common sense says, we lose our fortune, are sorry, and weep; we meet a bear, are frightened, and run; we are insulted by a rival, are angry, and strike. The hypothesis here to be defended says that this order of sequence is incorrect . . . and that the more rational statement is that we feel sorry because we cry, angry because we strike, afraid because we tremble, and not that we cry, strike, or tremble, because we are sorry, angry, or fearful. . . . Without the bodily states following on the perception, the latter would be purely cognitive in form, pale, colorless, destitute of emotional warmth. We might then see the bear, and judge it best to run, receive the insult, and deem it right to strike, but we should not actually feel afraid or angry.

James's evidence came not from experiments, but from introspection—looking inward at his own emotions. From his attempt to analyze his own emotional feelings, James concluded the feelings were really sensations stemming from bodily changes. Thus, his feeling of fear was really his feeling of a quickened heart, shallow breathing, goose-bumpy flesh, and trembly limbs. Similarly, his feeling of anger was his feeling of a seething chest, flushed face, dilated nostrils, and clenched teeth. James believed that he could identify a different constellation of bodily changes for each emotion, and that if he could not feel these changes he would not feel the emotion. In line with James's view, researchers have found that people throughout the world describe their emotions in terms of bodily changes and are quite consistent in the kinds of changes they associate with each emotion (Cacioppo & others, 1992; Rime & others, 1990).

Schachter's Cognition-Plus-Feedback Theory

■ **37.** ***How does Schachter's theory differ from James's?***

In the 1960s, Stanley Schachter developed a theory of emotion that can be understood as a variation of James's theory. According to Schachter, the feeling of an emotion depends not just on sensory feedback pertaining to the body's response, but also on one's perceptions and thoughts concerning the environmental event that presumably evoked the body's response. More specifically, he proposed that perception and thought about the environment influences the *type* of emotion felt, and sensory feedback about the degree of bodily arousal influences the *intensity* of the emotion felt. Thus, if you see a tiger, your perception that the tiger is dangerous determines that the emotion you feel will be fear, and your perception of your own beating heart, sweating, and so on determines how much fear you will feel. Schachter also proposed that the intensity of the emotional feeling in turn influences the interpretation of the stimulus. Thus, if your bodily arousal were already high, perhaps from drinking too much coffee, that arousal would contribute to your emotional intensity and might lead you to perceive the tiger as more dangerous than you would otherwise. (To compare Schachter's theory with James's and to compare both with what James called the "common sense theory," see Figure 7.18).

Common Sense Theory

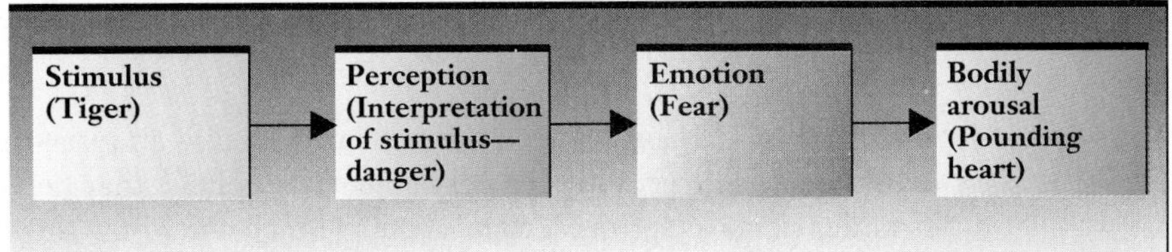

James's Theory

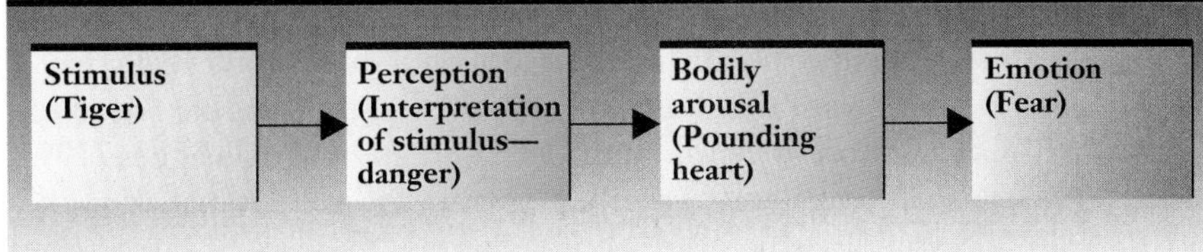

Schachter's Theory

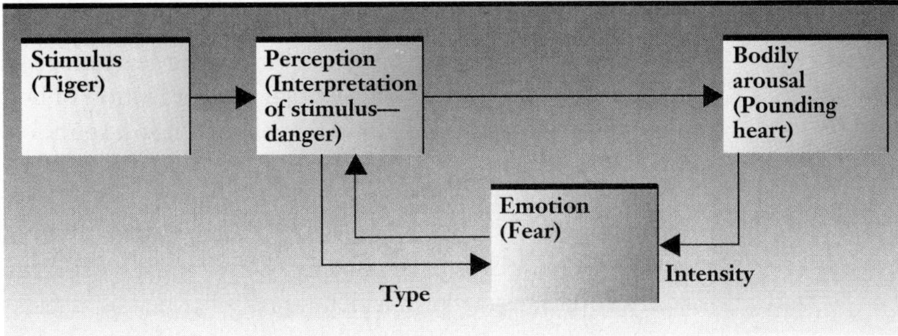

Figure 7.18 ***Three theories of emotion***
Each theory proposes a different set of causal relationships among perception of the stimulus, bodily arousal, and emotional feeling.

■ **38.** ***How did Schachter support his theory in laboratory experiments?***

In experiments testing his theory, Schachter (1971) injected people with either epinephrine (which raises heart rate and produces other effects associated with high arousal) or a placebo (an inactive substance) and then exposed them to various emotion-eliciting conditions. He found that epinephrine by itself did not produce any particular emotion (the subjects just said they felt jumpy), but when it was combined with an emotion-inducing environment it increased the intensity of the subject's emotion. As predicted by his theory, the kind of emotion subjects felt depended on the environment, but the intensity was heightened by epinephrine. The epinephrine-injected subjects manifested and reported more anger when insulted, more fear when watching a frightening film, and more hilarity when watching a slapstick comedy than did placebo-injected subjects. This emotion-enhancing effect only occurred if the subjects had *not* previously been informed of the physiological effects of epinephrine. Thus, according to Schachter, high physiological arousal increases emotion only when people believe that the arousal is caused by the external situation.

Emotion After Spinal Injury, and a Problem of Semantics

■ **39.** ***How did an early study of paralyzed men support James's and Schachter's theories? How did a subsequent study reveal a semantic problem, which also exists in other studies of subjective experiences?***

As further evidence that feedback from peripheral arousal contributes to emotional intensity, Schachter (1971) cited an interview study conducted by George Hohmann (1966) of men who had suffered spinal cord injuries. Because of their injuries, the men were insensitive and paralyzed in portions of their body below the neck and, therefore, could not feel bodily arousal stemming from those areas. Consistent with Schachter's theory (and James's), these men reported that their emotional feelings were, in general, less intense after their injury than before. Moreover, the closer the damage in the spinal cord was to the brain (and hence the greater the paralysis and loss of sensation), the greater was the decline in reported emotional intensity.

A problem with Hohmann's study, however, and indeed a problem with many studies in which people are asked to assess their emotional feelings, has to do with semantics. People may not have a fixed idea of what an emotion actually is, and their idea may be influenced by the words used in an interview or questionnaire. If Hohmann inadvertently led his subjects to believe that he equated emotions with feelings of bodily arousal, then of course they would say they felt less emotion after the injury (when they could no longer feel as much arousal) than before. That this may have happened is suggested by quotations in Hohmann's report. For example, Hohmann (1966) quoted one subject as saying: "I say I am afraid, like when I'm going into a real stiff exam at school, but I don't really feel afraid, not all tense and shaky, with that hollow feeling in my stomach like I used to."

More recently, Bob Bermond and his colleagues (1991) repeated Hohmann's study with another group of patients with spinal cord injuries, but used a more carefully structured set of questions. They asked subjects to rate separately the *bodily* experience and the *mental* experience of emotions. As predicted, subjects said they felt fewer bodily signs of emotion after their injury than before, but they did not report any reduction in the mental experience of emotions. In fact, they reported experiencing some emotions (including fear) more strongly after the injury than before. These results suggest that the perception of bodily responses—at least of bodily responses from below the neck—is not essential to the experience of intense emotions.

40. ***What is some evidence that molding the face into an emotional expression can affect mood, and that it may do so partly by producing changes elsewhere in the body?***

This issue of semantics is more than simply a technical problem pertaining to a particular study. It is a fundamental problem facing all psychologists who develop theories or conduct research having to do with subjective experiences. A term like *fear*, after all, is just a word, which we have learned to associate with certain kinds of thoughts, feelings, situations, and bodily conditions. Do I feel fear when placed in situation X? Well, maybe so, maybe not, depending on what you mean by fear. If I am the subject and you are the experimenter, I will try to figure out what you mean by fear before I answer. Schachter's and Hohmann's research, along with James's introspections, suggest that people indeed can perceive aspects of their own bodily arousal and can use those perceptions in their assessment of whether or not they feel a strong emotion. But Bermond's study suggests that people can also identify strong emotions independently of their perceptions of bodily states.

A Facial Feedback Theory

Paul Ekman (1984) has proposed a theory of emotions that is similar to James's peripheral feedback theory, but focuses particularly on the role of the face. As discussed in Chapter 4, Ekman and others have found that each basic emotion is associated with a unique facial expression. Ekman believes that those expressions are produced rapidly and automatically (though they can be inhibited), and that sensory feedback from the expression contributes to the emotional feeling. If Ekman is right, then people should be able to augment their own feeling of an emotion by mimicking the facial expression of that emotion.

If you form your face into a smile, will you feel happier? A Polyannaish suggestion, perhaps, but several experiments have suggested that there may be some truth to it. In one experiment, subjects were induced to move certain facial muscles in such a way as to mimic either a smile or a frown (Laird, 1974). They were not told that the purpose was to produce a smile or frown, nor that the study had anything to do with emotions, but rather that the study had to do with the relationship between muscles and perception. (Researchers pasted electrodes on each subject's face, as if recording muscle activity were indeed the main purpose.) The subjects were asked to examine a picture while holding the induced facial position. Then, as if it were incidental to the experiment, they were asked to fill out a questionnaire designed to assess their mood. The kind of picture they saw had the greatest effect on their mood, but the artificially induced facial expression also had an effect, as you can see in Figure 7.19. Those whose face had formed a smile were happier, and

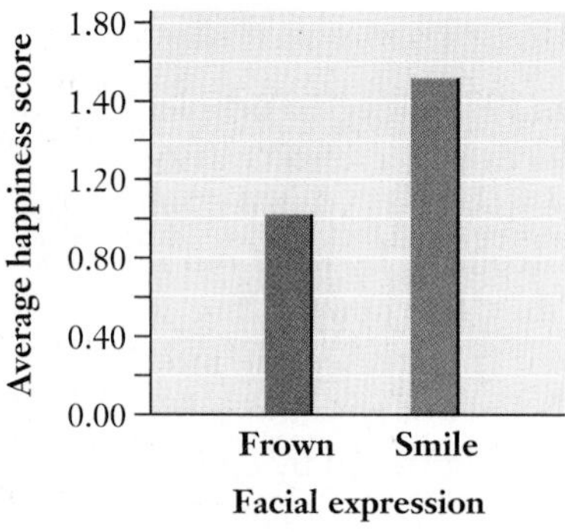

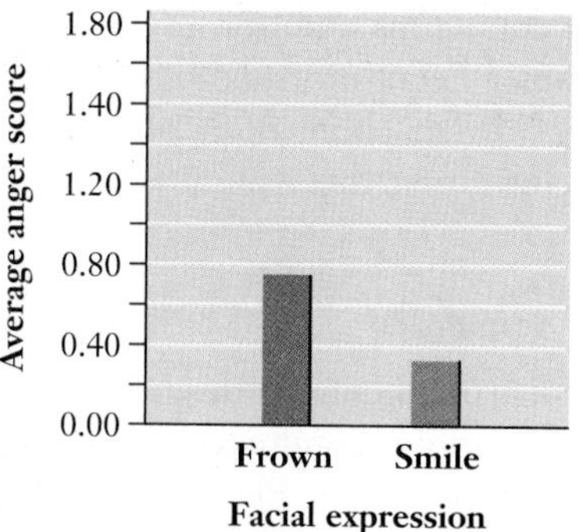

Figure 7.19 ***Effect of facial molding on self-reported happiness and anger***

Adult subjects were asked to contract certain facial muscles, which effectively molded their faces into either a smile or frown, while viewing a picture of children at play. The smile increased self-reported happiness and the frown increased self-reported anger. (Data from Laird, 1974.)

(a)

(b)

(c)

Figure 7.20 ***Inducing an expression of fear***

Shown here are frames from a videotape of a man following the instructions used by Ekman and his colleagues (1983) to induce an expression of fear: (a) "Raise your brows and pull them together," (b) "now raise your upper eyelids," and (c) "now stretch your lips horizontally, back toward your ears." Other instructions were used to induce other emotional expressions, producing the results shown in Figure 7.21.

those whose face had formed a frown were angrier, as measured by the mood questionnaire. In another experiment, people reported themselves to be happier after repeating the vowel sound of a long *e*, which forces the face into a smile, than after repeating other vowel sounds (Zajonc & others, 1989).

Research has also shown that forming the face into an emotional expression can produce effects on the rest of the body that are similar to those produced when the emotion is felt. Ekman and his colleagues (1983) asked subjects to move specific facial muscles in ways designed to mimic each of the six basic emotional expressions (see Figure 4.12 and Figure 7.20). For comparison, they asked other subjects to feel each emotion, by mentally reliving an event in which that emotion had been strong. While the subjects performed these tasks, the researchers assessed each subject's pattern of physiological arousal. The main finding was that different emotions coincided with somewhat different patterns of arousal, and the pattern for a given emotion was the same whether the subject had been asked to relive the emotion or simply to move certain facial muscles. In particular, skin temperatures increased more when the face mimicked the expression of anger than when it mimicked that of fear (consistent with other evidence that blood tends to flow into the skin in anger and away from it in fear), and the heart rate increased more when the face mimicked either anger or fear than when it mimicked other emotions (see Figure 7.21). Researchers have since replicated these findings with a wide variety of people and various experimental conditions (Levenson, 1992; Levenson & others, 1990). The results are consistent with Ekman's view that sensory feedback from the face influences both the feeling and the bodily state associated with the emotion.

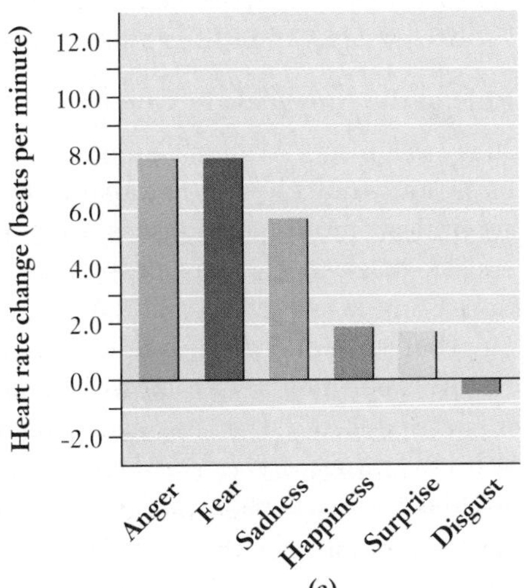

(a)

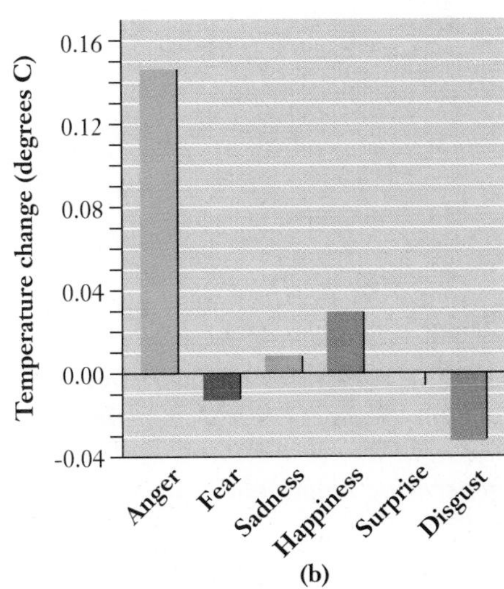

(b)

Figure 7.21 ***Effect of induced emotional expressions on the heart rate and skin temperature***

Ekman and his colleagues (1983) found that (a) the heart rate increased most when the induced facial expression was of anger, fear, or sadness, and (b) the skin temperature increased most when the induced expression was of anger. (From Ekman & others, 1983.)

A Theory of Primitive Emotional Contagion

41. ***How does the facial feedback theory, coupled with evidence that we tend to mimic others' facial expressions, lead to a theory of emotional contagion?***

Emotions are contagious. Everyday observations and laboratory experiments alike have shown repeatedly that people tend to take on the emotions of others around them (Hatfield & others, 1992). The idea that sensory feedback from one's own facial expression can influence one's emotional feeling suggests a possible mechanism through which emotional contagion can occur: Perhaps we automatically mimic the facial expressions of others, and then, perhaps, feedback from our own body alters our emotions to coincide with the expressions we are mimicking. Elaine Hatfield, John Cacioppo, and Richard Rapson (1992) have recently proposed this theory and reviewed evidence supporting it. They refer to it as a theory of *primitive* emotional contagion, because the mimicry does not involve higher thought processes.

Catching an emotion

The inborn tendency to mimic other people's facial expressions, coupled with the abilitiy of one's own facial expression to influence one's own mood, may be part of the mechanism of emotional contagion.

Much research shows that people do automatically mimic the emotional expressions of others. People laugh in response to a sound track of laughter, even if nothing funny was said (Provine, 1992). Very young babies mimic the facial expressions of their caregivers (Meltzoff & Moore, 1977; Reissland, 1988), and caregivers mimic the facial expressions of babies, unaware that they are doing so (O'Toole & Dubin, 1968). College students, in face-to-face interactions, mimic each other's facial expressions so rapidly (within about 20 milliseconds) that the mimicry could not possibly occur through deliberate, conscious thought; it must be reflexive (Condon & Ogston, 1966; Davis, 1985). The ability to synchronize emotions quickly with other people may have been an advantage in our evolution, and may still be today, by helping to promote our acceptance by those around us. Perhaps overt facial expressions of emotion, coupled with an automatic tendency to mimic those expressions, came about in evolution partly to facilitate social acceptance.

A Brain-Based Theory of Emotion

Thus far I have focused on the role of the peripheral bodily changes in emotion and have said nothing about the brain. But of course the brain is the center both for producing the bodily changes and for experiencing emotions. Research on the brain's emotional systems has focused especially on two structures: (1) the ***amygdala***, a portion of the limbic system, and (2) the ***frontal lobe*** of the cerebral cortex. Such research has led to the brain-based theory of emotion diagrammed and described in Figure 7.22 (LeDoux, 1989, 1992). According to this theory, the amygdala plays a central role in assessing the emotional significance of stimuli and generating some of the body's immediate responses; and the frontal lobe is crucial for the conscious experience of emotion and initiation of the more deliberate, controlled aspects of emotional behavior.

Role of the Amygdala in Computing the Emotional Significance of Stimuli

Many years ago, Walter Cannon (1927) proposed that some neural system in the brain must quickly and automatically assess stimulus input to determine if some survival-promoting response is needed. He argued that this system, not the peripheral feedback mechanism postulated by James, is the key to understanding emotion. Cannon suggested that the center for this neural system lies in the hypothalamus, but subsequent research led others to focus on the amygdala.

42. ***What is some evidence that the amygdala is critical in evaluating the significance of stimuli and generating emotional reactions?***

In experiments with monkeys, removal of the amygdala on both sides of the brain produced a dramatic set of changes in behavior described as *psychic blindness* (Klüver & Bucy, 1937; Weiskrantz, 1956). The monkeys could still see objects and could move in a coordinated fashion, but they seemed indifferent to the psychological significance of objects. They no longer responded fearfully to objects that pre-

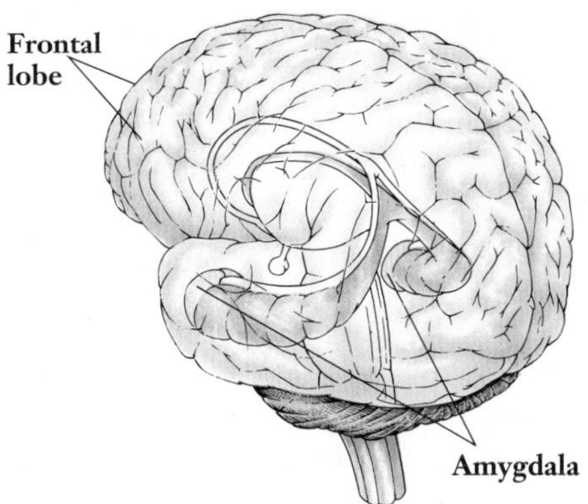

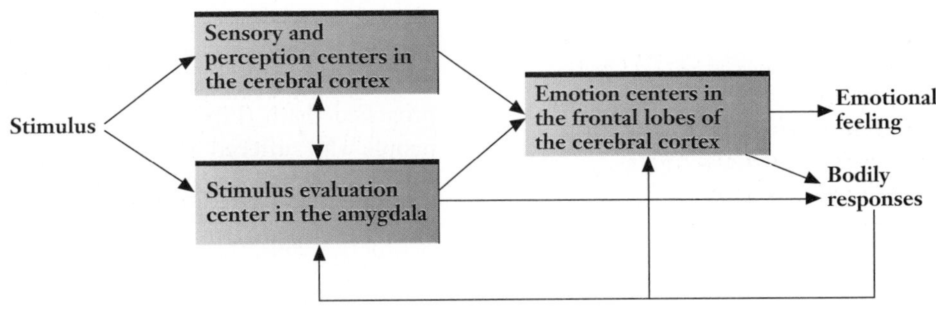

Figure 7.22 ***A brain-based theory of emotion***

According to this theory, the amygdala and the frontal lobes are essential to the generation and experience of emotion. As the flowchart shows, the amygdala receives sensory information about the external environment by both a subcortical route and a route that involves the sensory and perception areas of the cerebral cortex. The amygdala is critical in evaluating the emotional significance of that sensory input and generating immediate bodily reactions. It also sends output to the frontal lobes of the cortex, which are critical in experiencing the emotion consciously and developing the more deliberate behavioral responses. The model also shows that feedback from the bodily responses might act both in the amygdala and in the frontal lobe of the cortex to modify the emotion, in line with James's, Schachter's, and Ekman's feedback theories.

■ **43.** ***What is some evidence that the frontal lobes are important for conscious feelings of emotions and that the right and left frontal lobes may be involved with different emotions?***

viously frightened them, or aggressively to objects that previously angered them. They attempted to eat just about anything, showing little discrimination between what they previously would have considered good food or not food; and some also attempted to copulate with just about anything, animate or inanimate. Remarkably similar observations were subsequently made of human beings whose amygdalas, along with surrounding portions of the temporal lobes of the cortex, had been destroyed by disease (Kolb & Whishaw, 1990; Marlowe & others, 1975).

Extensive research, mostly with rats, has led to other conclusions about the amygdala that are consistent with the roles depicted for it in Figure 7.22. Neural activity in the amygdala indeed can, through connections to the hypothalamus, generate the hormonal secretions and autonomic responses (such as change in heart rate) that typically accompany strong emotions (Davis, 1992). Moreover, rats with lesions in a particular part of the amygdala fail to react fearfully to sights or sounds that had previously been paired with painful shock, whereas rats with lesions destroying the entire visual or auditory cortex without damage to the amygdala still do show such reactions (LeDoux & others, 1989; LeDoux, 1992). The latter finding is particularly interesting because it suggests that the amygdala can evaluate the emotional significance of stimuli through a route that, in humans, does not involve conscious perception. At least since Freud's time, many psychologists have argued that emotional reactions to a stimulus can occur without conscious perception of the stimulus, and research on the amygdala suggests a route through which this might occur (LeDoux, 1989).

Role of the Frontal Lobes in Emotional Experience

The amygdala also has strong connections to the frontal lobe of the cerebral cortex, and through these it apparently influences people's conscious emotional feelings. Many years ago, an altogether-too-common treatment for people with severe emotional disorders was *prefrontal lobotomy*—an operation that cut off the frontmost portion of the frontal lobes from the rest of the brain (discussed further in Chapter 18). The operation usually relieved people of their crippling emotions, but it also left them unable to plan and organize their lives effectively. Partly for that reason, and partly because effective drugs now exist for treating emotional disorders, lobotomies are no longer performed.

Recently, evidence has mounted that the left frontal lobe may be most involved in positive emotions and the right may be most involved in negative emotions (Davidson, 1992). Some of the evidence comes from experiments in which people were presented with emotion-eliciting stimuli while the overall rate of neural activity in each frontal lobe was recorded by means of an electroencephalograph. In one such experiment, the left frontal lobes of adult subjects became most active in response to happy films of a puppy playing with flowers or a gorilla taking a bath, and the right frontal lobes became most active in response to medical films showing third-degree burns or a leg amputation (Davidson & others, 1990). In a similar experiment, 10-month-old babies showed more activity in the left frontal lobe when their mothers approached them, and more activity in the right when a stranger approached them (Fox & Davidson, 1988). Other evidence comes from studies of people who suffered damage in one or the other frontal lobe due to a stroke. Damage in the left frontal lobe commonly produced a decline in positive emotions, and damage in the right more often produced a decline in negative emotions (Robinson & others, 1984).

Concluding Thoughts

This chapter has focused on the physiological bases for hunger, sexual drive, reward, sleep, and emotions. You might find the following two points useful in developing a strategy to review the chapter:

1. The goal of physiological psychology in the study of behavioral states Hunger, sexual drive, sleep, and emotions are all examples of *behavioral states*. That is, they all involve somewhat sustained but reversible changes in the way an animal or person behaves in a given environment. The goal of physiological psychology in the study of behavioral states is to equate them with *physiological states*. In other words, the goal is to identify the somewhat sustained but reversible physiological changes that modify the behavior-producing mechanisms and thereby create the behavioral changes. This goal is both fascinating and difficult to achieve because the machine being studied is so extraordinarily complicated. As you think about each behaviorial state discussed in this chapter, ask yourself: What have researchers discovered about the physiological changes that correspond with, and may help produce, the behavioral changes?

2. Two categories of methods in the physiological study of states Like every chapter in the book, this chapter is also about the methods that psychologists use to answer certain kinds of questions. If you think about the methods described in the chapter, you will find that they fall into two broad categories. One category involves *intervention* in ongoing physiological processes to see what happens to the behaviorally measured state. What happens to hunger, or the sex drive, or sleep, or an emotion if a particular part of the brain is destroyed or stimulated, or if the supply of a particular hormone is cut off or increased? As you review the chapter, notice how often such methods were mentioned. Intervention is a powerful way to identify causal relationships between physiology and behavior. But most intervention procedures are harmful or at least risky to the subject, so they are used more often in studies of other animals than of humans. The intervention approach is approximated, however, in studies of people whose natural physiology has been disrupted through accident or disease. Quite a few studies of that sort were described in the chapter.

The other category involves the *measurement* of physiological processes and the *correlation* of those measures with changes in behavioral state. Do natural changes in hormones, brain waves, and heart rate, or other physiological variables accompany natural changes in the behavioral state? Most measurement procedures are safe and can be used with humans. Notice, as you review the chapter, how often this correlational method was used in the human studies described. This method helps identify reliable relationships, but does not, by itself, tell us about cause and effect. The observation that brain waves slow down during sleep, or that skin temperature goes up during anger, does not tell us that slow brain waves *cause* sleep, or that high skin temperature *causes* anger. Do you see why scientists look for some way to intervene, to test cause-and-effect hypotheses in animals once they have found a correlation?

Further Reading

Alexandra Logue (1986). *The psychology of eating and drinking.* New York: Freeman.

This is an interesting introduction to the variables, both inside and outside the body, that affect hunger, thirst, and the ways they are expressed. The last unit is devoted to malfunctions of these processes, including anorexia and bulimia, overeating, and alcohol abuse.

J. Allen Hobson (1989). *Sleep.* New York: Scientific American Library.

Fun to read and beautifully illustrated, this nontechnical book on sleep and dreaming was written by one of the world's foremost experts on these topics.

Neil McNaughton (1989). *Biology and emotion.* Cambridge: Cambridge University Press.

This is a thoughtful, highly readable, up-to-date integration of evolutionary and physiological approaches to the understanding of emotion.

James Stellar & Eliot Stellar (1985). *The neurobiology of motivation and reward.* New York: Springer-Verlag.

For the student who wants to go beyond an introduction and see how contemporary physiological psychologists study motivation and reward, this is an excellent source. Though technically oriented, it is written with such clarity that the nonexpert who has some familiarity with the brain can read it profitably.

Looking Ahead

Many issues concerning drives and emotions that are hinted at in this chapter are discussed more fully in chapters to come. The role of social factors in human sexuality is discussed in Chapter 13. Freud's idea that the sex drive underlies behaviors that are not explicitly sexual, and his theory of dreams, are discussed in Chapter 16. Human motives having to do with affiliation, achievement, and self-esteem are important themes running through the chapters on social psychology and personality (Chapters 14–16). Emotional problems and treatments for them are the subjects of Chapters 17 and 18.

Now we turn from the slower-moving components of the kaleidoscope of mental life to the fast-moving components. The next chapter is on sensation.

SENSATION

CHAPTER 8

What would mental life be like if you had no senses? What if, from birth, you could not hear, see, touch, taste, smell, or in any other way sense the world around you? You would not be able to react to anything, because reactions require sensory input. You would not be able to learn anything, because learning begins with sensory input. Would you be able to think? What could you think about with no knowledge gained from the senses? Philosophers, from Aristotle on, have pondered these questions and have usually concluded that without sensation there would be no mental life. It is no wonder that the study of the senses has always been a fundamental part of the science of psychology.

This chapter is on sensation, and the next is on perception. ***Sensation*** refers both to the experience associated with a sound, a light, or some other simple stimulus and to the initial steps by which the sense organs and neural pathways take in stimulus information. ***Perception*** refers to the subsequent organizing of that information and to the meaningful interpretation (such as "That object before me is a coffee cup") extracted from it. This distinction between sensation and perception is convenient as a basis for organizing chapters, but, as you will discover, it is somewhat arbitrary. The organization of stimulus information in ways useful for extracting meaning actually begins during the early steps of taking it in.

Sensation is the area of psychological study that has enjoyed the longest and happiest marriage with physiology. In the mid-nineteenth century, around the time when psychology was just beginning to emerge as a recognized science, an esteemed German physiologist, Hermann von Helmholtz, became intrigued with certain elementary *psychological* questions about sensation. How is it that we can hear sounds as having different pitches? How is it that we can see objects as having different colors? Why do we see certain mixtures of colored lights as having a color entirely different from that produced by the original lights alone? Helmholtz went on to develop theories about how structures in the ears, eyes, and nervous system might respond differently to different aspects of sound and light stimuli in ways that would permit different psychological experiences to occur. Subsequent research confirmed and extended his early theories.

Sensation is easier to study physiologically than are other psychological processes. Many of the processes that control sensations occur in the sense organs themselves—in the ears, eyes, skin, tongue, and nose—and it is much easier to study sense organs than to study the brain. In the sense organs, information about the world is coded into neural messages that are sent to the brain for decoding and analysis. As you will discover in this chapter, much has been learned about the coding and relatively little has been learned about the decoding and analysis.

This chapter is divided into five main sections. The first provides an overview of basic questions, approaches, and processes pertinent to the study of sensation.

The second and third are devoted to hearing and vision, respectively, which are the two most studied senses. The fourth is on pain, which can be thought of as both a sense and a motivating force. And the fifth is concerned with psychophysics, a nonphysiological approach to describing relationships between physical stimuli and the sensory experiences they produce.

Overview

Most broadly, the process to which this chapter is devoted can be diagrammed as follows:

physical stimulus → physiological response → sensory experience

1. ***How can the process of sensation be depicted as a chain of three different kinds of events, and how can each class of event be measured?***

We have here three classes of events: (1) The *physical stimulus* is the matter or energy that impinges on sense organs; (2) the *physiological response* is the pattern of electrical activity that occurs in sense organs, nerves, and the brain as a result of the stimulus; and (3) the *sensory experience* is the subjective, psychological sensation—the sound, sight, taste, or whatever—experienced by the individual whose sense organs have been stimulated.

To be studied scientifically, events must be measurable. The first two classes of events in this chain can be measured by direct physical means, using such tools as light meters and recording electrodes. The third class cannot be measured directly—there are no meters that can be plugged into the head to read out sensory experiences—but it can be measured indirectly through observations of behavior.

The most useful indices of human sensory experience are verbal answers to carefully worded questions about stimuli presented under controlled conditions. If we show two different patches of light to a person, and the person repeatedly says that Patch A is brighter than Patch B, we can conclude that the person experiences the difference between the two patches on a dimension that he or she had learned to call *brightness*. If other people make the same judgment, we can conclude that brightness is a sensory experience that is regularly affected, in people, by whatever the physical difference is between Patches A and B. In studies of nonhuman animals or human infants, we can obtain information about sensory experiences through nonverbal means. For example, we might train a pigeon to peck one key when one stimulus is present and a different key when another stimulus is present. Whether working with humans or other animals, it is not raw sensory experience

A sensational device

Modern technology has made it relatively easy to measure physical stimuli and some of the physiological responses to them. Here an electroencephalograph records a response of an infant's brain to sound. The technique is useful for testing hearing in infants, who cannot yet describe their subjective experiences.

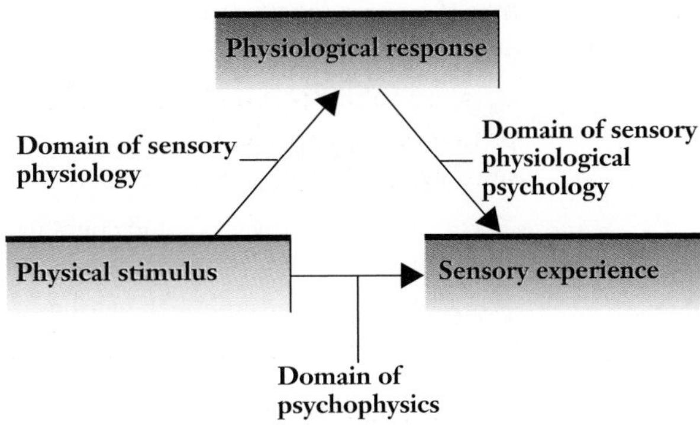

Figure 8.1 ***Three domains in the study of sensation***
Sensory physiology, sensory physiological psychology, and psychophysics are concerned with the relationship between different pairs of the three classes of events involved in sensation. (Adapted from Uttal, 1973.)

that is assessed, but the individual's ability to use that experience to guide a behavioral choice.

Questions Governing Three Domains of Research

■ **2. *What are the basic questions of (a) sensory physiology, (b) sensory physiological psychology, and (c) psychophysics?***

Another way to represent the three classes of events in the process of sensation is shown in Figure 8.1. Each arrow in the figure represents a different set of questions about sensation and, to some degree, a different domain of research.

Sensory physiology is the domain that investigates the relationship between the stimulus and the physiological response. The questions here are of the following general form: If stimulus X is present, what physiological response will occur in a sense organ, or in the nerve from that organ, or in neurons in the brain? Thus, a sensory physiologist interested in color vision might present lights that are seen as different colors and try to determine how cells in the eye or brain respond differently to them.

Sensory physiological psychology investigates the relationship between the physiological response and the sensory experience. The basic question of this domain is: What physiological occurrences are essential for a particular sensory experience (measured behaviorally) to occur? A common approach to answering this type of question in nonhuman animals is to destroy or temporarily inhibit the action of some specific part of the sensory system and assess the resultant deficits in sensory experience. A variant of this approach, common in human research, is to study individuals who are already missing some component of the normal sensory machinery. Thus, a scientist interested in color vision might identify people who, for genetic reasons, are missing a particular set of light receptors in the eye and then test them to see just which colors they can and cannot distinguish from each other.

Psychophysics investigates the relationship between the stimulus and the sensory experience, ignoring the physiological response that mediates that relationship. (You can remember *psychophysics* by recalling that it relates the *psychological* sensory experience to *physical* characteristics of the stimulus.) Questions in psychophysics take the following form: If the physical stimulus is changed in such-and-such a way, how will the sensory experience change? Thus, a psychophysicist studying color vision might present lights that vary physically in known ways. The researcher might then have people state the color they see, or match each light's color to another stimulus, to determine what sorts of physical changes produce changes in one's experience of color.

The Basic Anatomy of the Human Senses

Ever since Aristotle, people have spoken of the *five senses*, counting them as hearing, vision, touch, taste, and smell. Actually humans have more than five senses, and any attempt to tally them up to an exact number is arbitrary, because what one

Table 8.1 *Stimuli, receptors, and the pathways to the brain for various senses*

Sense	Stimulus	Receptors	Pathway to the brain
Hearing	Sound waves	Pressure-sensitive hair cells in cochlea of inner ear	Auditory nerve (8th cranial nerve)
Vision	Light waves	Light-sensitive rods and cones in retina of eye	Optic nerve (2nd cranial nerve)
Touch	Pressure on the skin	Sensitive ends of touch neurons in skin	Trigeminal nerve (5th cranial nerve) for touch above the neck. Spinal nerves for touch elsewhere.
Pain	Wide variety of potentially harmful stimuli	Sensitive ends of pain neurons in skin and other tissues	Trigeminal nerve (5th cranial nerve) for pain above the neck. Spinal nerves for pain elsewhere.
Taste	Molecules dissolved in fluid on the tongue	Taste cells in taste buds on the tongue	Portions of facial, glossopharyngeal, and vagus nerves (7th, 9th, and 10th cranial nerves)
Smell	Molecules dissolved in fluid on mucous membranes in the nose	Sensitive ends of olfactory neurons in the mucous membranes	Olfactory nerve (1st cranial nerve)

person thinks of as one sense may be thought of as two or more by another. For example, our skin is sensitive not just to touch but also to temperature and pain, neither of which is included in Aristotle's five senses. Other senses omitted by Aristotle have to do with body position and the body's internal environment. We have a sense of balance mediated by a mechanism in the inner ear, a sense of limb position and movement mediated by receptors in muscles and joints, and senses pertaining to homeostatic needs (such as sensitivity to the inner supply of food molecules, discussed in Chapter 7).

■ **3.** ***What are the common anatomical elements of all of our senses?***

Each sense has its own set of ***receptors***, specialized structures that respond to the physical stimulus by producing electrical changes that can initiate neural impulses, and its own set of ***sensory neurons***, which carry neural impulses from the receptors to the central nervous system (the structure of sensory neurons was described in Chapter 6). For some senses the receptors are simply the sensitive ends of sensory neurons, and for others they are separate cells, which form synapses upon sensory neurons. For some senses the receptors all exist in a specific, localized sensory organ, such as the ear, eye, or nose, and for others they exist in a wide variety of locations. Pain receptors, for example, exist not just in the skin, but also in muscles, tendons, joints, and many other places. The stimuli, receptors, and peripheral nerves involved in the most thoroughly studied senses are identified in Table 8.1. Regardless of whether they come from one location or many, the neurons for any given sense lead to sensory-specific pathways in the central nervous system. For most senses, these pathways in turn lead to specific ***sensory areas*** in the cerebral cortex (depicted in Figure 6.9 on page 174), which receive and analyze the neural input.

Transduction and Coding

■ **4.** ***How do receptors respond to stimulus energy and code information about the amount and kind of energy?***

The process by which a receptor cell produces an electrical change in response to a physical stimulus is called ***transduction***. It is the process by which receptors in the eye respond to light, receptors in the ear respond to sound, receptors on the tongue respond to chemicals dissolved there, and so on. Although the details of transduction are different for different senses, basic similarities exist across the

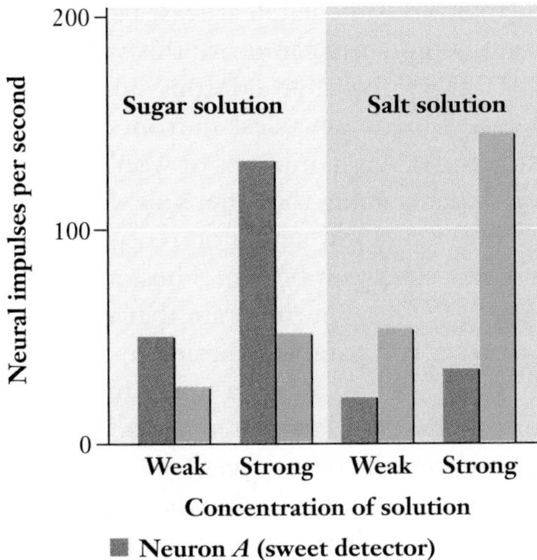

Figure 8.2 ***Quantitative and qualitative coding of taste***

Shown here are the rates of action potentials in two different taste neurons when a weak or strong solution of sugar or salt is placed on the tongue. Notice that each neuron responds at a faster rate to a strong solution of a given substance than to a weak one (quantitative coding), but that Neuron *A* always responds at a faster rate than Neuron *B* when the stimulus is sugar, and the reverse is true when the stimulus is salt (qualitative coding). (Data are hypothetical, but are based on findings, such as those of Nowlis & Frank, 1977, with laboratory animals.)

senses. In every case, the membrane of the receptor cell becomes more permeable to certain electrically charged particles, such as sodium or potassium ions, when the appropriate type of stimulus energy acts upon the receptor cell. These charged particles then flow through the membrane, either from outside the cell to inside, or vice versa, and change the electrical charge across the membrane. This electrical change is called the ***receptor potential***, and it is analogous to the postsynaptic potential produced on neurons by the action of synaptic transmitters (described in Chapter 6). Receptor potentials in turn trigger events that lead to the production of action potentials (also described in Chapter 6) in the axons of sensory neurons.

For senses to be useful they must not only respond to a particular class of stimulus energy (such as sound or light), but must also respond differently to variations in the energy. Every form of energy varies along at least two dimensions, a *quantitative* and a *qualitative* dimension. The quantitative variation has to do with the amount or intensity of energy present. A sound or light can be weak or strong; molecules stimulating taste or smell can be dilute or highly concentrated. The qualitative variation has to do with the precise kind of energy present. Lights of different wavelengths (which we perceive as different colors) are considered to be qualitatively different, as are sounds of different frequencies (which we perceive as different pitches), as are different chemicals (which we perceive as different smells or tastes). In every sense, transduction occurs in such a way that information about the quantity and quality of the stimulus is preserved in the pattern of action potentials sent to the brain. That preservation of information is referred to as ***coding***.

Coding of stimulus *quantity* results from the fact that stronger stimuli produce larger receptor potentials, which in turn produce faster rates of action potentials in sensory neurons. The brain interprets a fast rate of action potentials as a strong stimulus and a slow rate as a weak stimulus. Coding of stimulus *quality* occurs because different receptors within any given sensory tissue are tuned to respond best to somewhat different forms of energy. In the eye, for example, three different kinds of receptor cells, each most sensitive to a different range of wavelengths of light, provide the basis for color vision. In the ear, different receptors are most sensitive to different sound frequencies. And in the nose and tongue, different receptors are most sensitive to different molecules. Thus, in general, qualitative variations are coded as different *ratios* of activity in sensory neurons coming from different sets of receptors. For an illustration of qualitative and quantitative coding for the sense of taste, see Figure 8.2. You will see illustrations for hearing and vision later in the chapter.

Sensory Adaptation

When you first put on your wristwatch, you feel the pressure on your skin, but later you don't. When you first turn on the lights, after sitting in the dark, the room seems very bright, but later not so bright. When you first wade into a lake, the water may seem terribly cold, but later only slightly cool. When you first enter a chemistry lab, the odor may seem overwhelming, but later you hardly notice it. The change in sensitivity that occurs when a sensory system is either stimulated or not stimulated for a length of time is called ***sensory adaptation***. In general, in the absence of stimulation a sensory system becomes temporarily more sensitive (it will respond to weaker stimuli), and in the presence of stimulation it becomes temporarily less sensitive (it requires stronger stimuli to produce a response). Sensory adaptation is useful because it leads us to notice most the changes in, and to be relatively oblivious to the stable aspects of, our environment.

5. What is the value of sensory adaptation? How can you demonstrate that adaptation can occur in neurons in the brain, not just in receptors?

In many cases, sensory adaptation is mediated by the receptor cells themselves. If a stimulus remains for a period of time, the receptor potential and rate of action potentials are at first great, but over time they are much reduced, resulting in a re-

It's a nice place to work, but I wouldn't want to visit

Can you imagine the pungent smell you would experience if you walked into this cave full of Roquefort cheese? Yet, as suggested by this worker's equable expression, one adapts after a while. In general, our senses are designed to register changes in the environment, not steady states.

duced sensation. In other cases, however, adaptation is mediated at least partly by changes farther inward, in the central nervous system. You can prove this yourself for the sense of smell (Matlin & Foley, 1992). If you place an odorous substance (such as an open bottle of nail polish remover or cologne) on a desk in front of you, with one nostril plugged, you will adapt to it within about 5 minutes (it won't smell as strong). Then, if you unplug that nostril and quickly plug the other you will find that you are still adapted to the odor, even though it is now acting on receptors in the other nostril, different from those that it was acting on before. Thus, adaptation for smell must be due in part to changes in neurons in the brain that receive input from both nostrils. (You might wish to try a comparable experiment for vision. Keeping one eye covered, move from a dimly lit area into a much brighter area, and sit there for 2 or 3 minutes until the light no longer seems so bright. Then remove the cover and place it immediately over the other eye. Does the light suddenly look brighter? If adaptation is mediated by receptors in the eye, it should. On the other hand, if adaptation is mediated only by cells in the brain that receive input from both eyes, it should not.)

Now, having reviewed some of the general issues and approaches in the study of sensory systems, let us look in more detail at three specific senses: hearing, vision, and pain.

Hearing

If a tree falls in the forest where no one hears it, does it make a sound? This old riddle plays upon the fact that the term *sound* refers both to a type of physical stimulus and to the sensation produced by that stimulus. As a physical stimulus, sound is the vibration of air or some other medium produced by an object such as a tuning fork, one's vocal cords, or a falling tree. The vibration moves outward from the sound source in a manner that can be described as a wave (see Figure 8.3). The height of the wave indicates the total pressure exerted by the molecules of air (or another medium) as they move back and forth, which is referred to as the sound's ***amplitude*** or intensity and corresponds to what we hear as the sound's ***loudness***. Sound amplitude is usually measured in logarithmic units of pressure called *decibels* (abbreviated *dB*). (See Table 8.2, which further defines decibels and contains the decibel ratings for a number of common sounds.)

In addition to varying in amplitude, sound waves vary in ***frequency***, which we hear as the sound's ***pitch***. The frequency of a sound is the rate at which the molecules of air or another medium move back and forth. Frequency is measured in *hertz* (abbreviated *Hz*), which is the number of complete waves (or cycles) that occur at any given point per second. Sounds that are audible to humans have frequencies ranging from about 20 to 20,000 Hz. To give you an idea of the relationship between frequency and pitch, the dominant (most audible) frequency of the lowest note on a piano is about 27 Hz, that of middle C is about 262 Hz, and that of the highest piano note is about 4186 Hz (Matlin & Foley, 1992). The simplest kind of sound is a *pure tone*, which is a constant-frequency wave of vibration that can be described as a sine wave (see Figure 8.3). Pure tones, which are useful in auditory experiments, can be produced in the laboratory, but they rarely occur in other contexts. Natural sound sources, including even musical instruments and tuning forks, vibrate at several frequencies at once and thus produce more complex waves than that shown in Figure 8.3. Natural sounds can be thought of as consisting of many different tones at once.

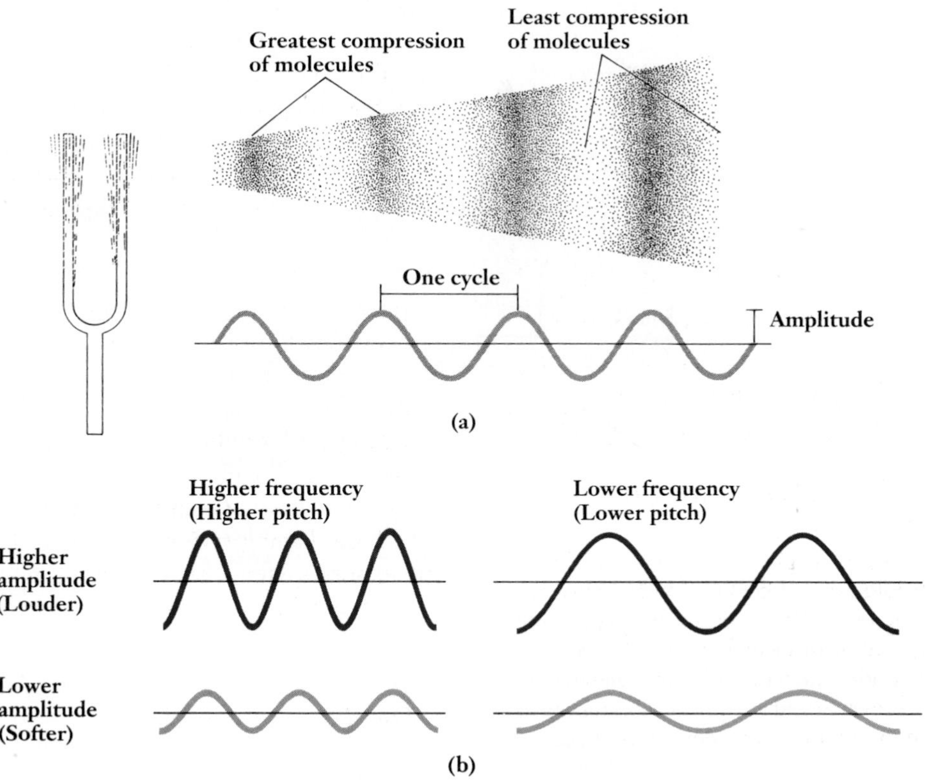

Figure 8.3 ***Characteristics of sound***
The oscillating tuning fork (a) causes air molecules to vibrate in a manner that can be represented as a wave of pressure. Each wave contains an area where the air molecules are more compressed (the dark regions in the upper diagram) and an area where they are less compressed (the light regions) than normal. The peak pressure (the highest compression) of each wave defines the amplitude of the sound, and the number of waves that pass a given point per second defines the frequency. The higher the amplitude, the louder the sound; and the higher the frequency, the higher the pitch (b). All of the wave drawings in this figure are idealized sine waves indicative of a pure tone. (Adapted from Klinke, 1986.)

Table 8.2 ***Sound-pressure amplitudes of various sounds, and conversion to decibels****

Example	*P* (in sound-pressure units)	Log *P*	Decibels
Softest detectable sound	1	0	0
Soft whisper	10	1	20
Quiet neighborhood	100	2	40
Average conversation	1000	3	60
Loud music from a radio	10,000	4	80
Heavy automobile traffic	100,000	5	100
Very loud thunder	1,000,000	6	120
Jet airplane taking off	10,000,000	7	140
Loudest rock band on record	100,000,000	8	160
Spacecraft launch (from 150 ft.)	1,000,000,000	9	180

*One sound-pressure unit (*P*) is defined as 2×10^{-5} newtons/square meter (Klinke, 1986). When measured in sound-pressure units, the amplitude range of human hearing is enormous. A reason for converting to logarithmic units is to produce a smaller range of numbers. The logarithm (log) of a number is the power to which 10 must be raised to produce that number. For example, the log of 10,000 is 4, because $10^4 = 10,000$. A decibel (dB) is defined as 20 log *P*. Thus, 4 log units = 80 dB.

Sources: *Human information processing*, 2nd ed. (p. 161) by P. H. Lindsay & D. A. Norman, 1977, New York: Academic Press. *Sensation and perception*, 3rd ed. (p. 250) by M. W. Matlin & H. J. Foley, 1992, Boston: Allyn and Bacon.

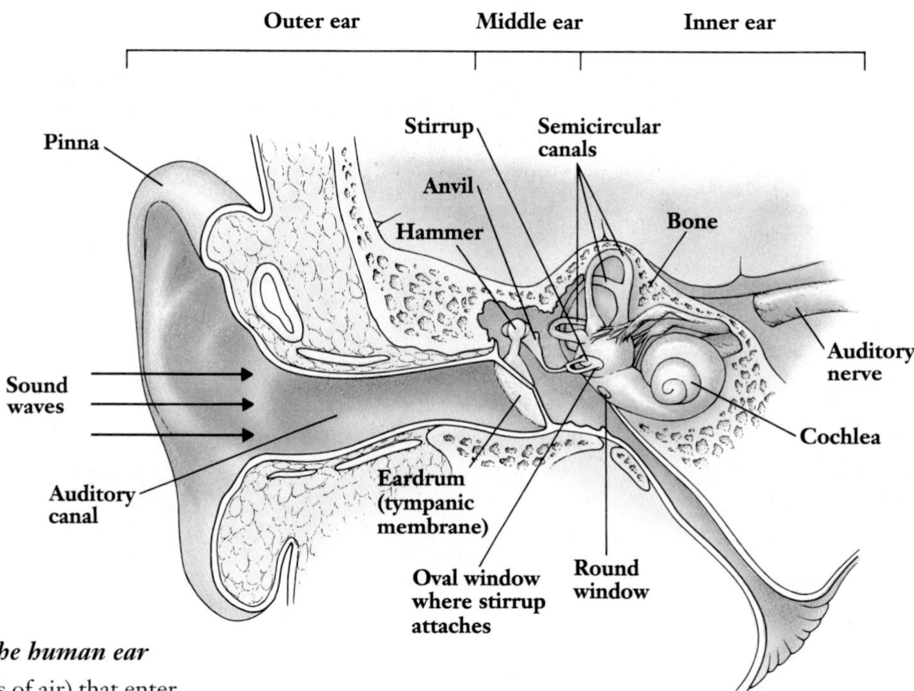

Figure 8.4 ***Parts of the human ear***

Sound waves (vibrations of air) that enter the auditory canal cause the eardrum to vibrate, which causes the ossicles (hammer, anvil, and stirrup) to vibrate, which causes the oval window to vibrate, setting up waves of motion in the fluid inside the cochlea. The semicircular canals are involved in the sense of balance, not hearing.

The Functional Organization of the Ear

Evolutionarily, hearing is a variation of touch. Touch is sensitivity to pressure on the skin, and hearing is sensitivity to pressure on a special sensory tissue in the ear. In some animals, such as moths, sound is sensed through modified touch receptors located on flexible patches of skin that vibrate in response to sound waves. In humans and other mammals the special patches of skin for hearing have migrated to a location inside the head, and special organs, the ears, have developed to magnify the pressure exerted by sound waves as they are transported inward. A diagram of the human ear is shown in Figure 8.4. To review its structures and their functions, we will begin from the outside and work inward.

Parts of the Ear and Their Role in Transduction

6. *What are the functions of the outer ear, middle ear, and inner ear?*

The ***outer ear*** consists of the *pinna*, which is the flap of skin and cartilage forming the visible portion of the ear, and the *auditory canal*, which is the opening into the head that ends at the *eardrum* (or tympanic membrane). It can be thought of as an air-filled funnel for receiving sound waves and transporting them inward. The vibration of air outside the head (the physical sound) causes air in the auditory canal to vibrate, which in turn causes the tympanic membrane to vibrate.

The ***middle ear*** is an air-filled cavity, separated from the outer ear by the eardrum. Its main structures are three tiny bones called ***ossicles*** (also called the *hammer, anvil,* and *stirrup*, because of their respective shapes), which are linked to the eardrum at one end and to the *oval window*, a membrane of the cochlea, at the other end. When sound causes the eardrum to vibrate, the ossicles vibrate and push against the oval window. Because the oval window has only about one-thirtieth the area of the tympanic membrane, the pressure (force per unit area) that is funneled to it by the ossicles is about thirty times greater than the pressure on the eardrum. Thus, the main function of the middle ear is to increase the amount of pressure that sound waves exert upon the inner ear so that transduction can occur.

The coiled ***cochlea***, in the ***inner ear***, is where transduction finally takes place. As depicted in the uncoiled view in Figure 8.5, the cochlea contains a fluid-filled *outer duct* that begins at the oval window, runs to the tip of the cochlea, and then runs back again to another membrane, the *round window*, located near the oval win-

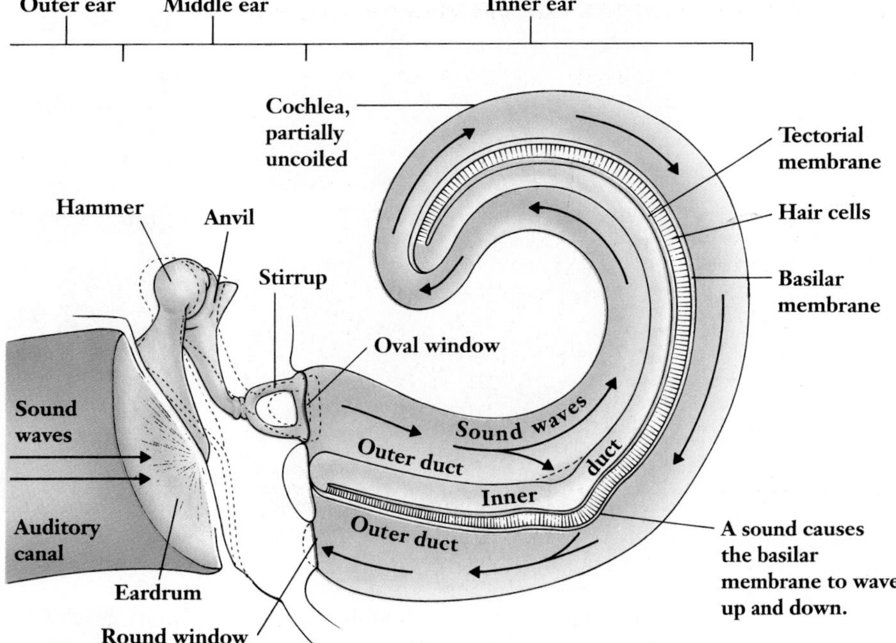

Figure 8.5 ***Transduction mechanism in the inner ear***

This diagram depicts a longitudinal section of the cochlea (partially uncoiled), showing the outer and inner ducts. Sound waves in the fluid of the outer duct cause the basilar membrane to wave up and down. When the basilar membrane moves upward, its hairs bend against the tectorial membrane, initiating receptor potentials in the hair cells.

■ ***7. How does transduction occur in the inner ear?***

dow. Sandwiched between the outgoing and incoming portions of the outer duct is another fluid-filled tube, the *inner duct*. The membrane forming the floor of the inner duct is the ***basilar membrane***, on which are located the receptor cells for hearing, called ***hair cells***. There are four rows of hair cells (three outer rows and one inner row), each row running the length of the basilar membrane. Tiny hairs (called *cilia*) protrude from each hair cell into the inner duct and abut against another membrane called the *tectorial membrane*. At its other end, within the basilar membrane, each hair cell forms synapses with several ***auditory neurons***, whose axons form the ***auditory nerve***, which runs to the brain.

The process of transduction in the cochlea can be summarized as follows: The sound-induced vibration of the ossicles against the oval window initiates vibration in the fluid in the outer duct of the cochlea, which produces an up-and-down waving motion of the very flexible basilar membrane. The tectorial membrane above the basilar membrane is less flexible and does not move when the basilar membrane moves, so the hairs issuing from the hair cells in the basilar membrane bend against the tectorial membrane each time the basilar membrane moves upward. This bending causes a physical change in the hair cell's membrane, which leads to an electrical change across the membrane (the receptor potential). This in turn causes each hair cell to release neurotransmitter molecules at its synapses upon auditory neurons, thereby increasing the rate of action potentials in those neurons (Hudspeth, 1983; Pickles, 1988).

Two Kinds of Deafness

■ ***8. How do two kinds of deafness differ from each other in their physiological bases and in possible treatment?***

With this knowledge of the ear it is possible to understand the physiological bases for two varieties of deafness. ***Conduction deafness*** occurs when the ossicles of the middle ear become rigid and cannot carry sounds inward from the tympanic membrane to the cochlea. People with conduction deafness can hear vibrations that reach the cochlea by routes other than the middle ear. A conventional hearing aid is helpful for such people, because it magnifies the sound pressure sufficiently to be conducted by other bones of the face into the cochlea.

Sensorineural deafness occurs from damage to the cochlea, the hair cells, or the auditory neurons. People with complete sensorineural deafness are not helped by a conventional hearing aid, but might be helped by a new form of hearing aid called a ***cochlear implant***. In essence, this device performs the task normally done

Figure 8.6 ***Warning: Noise can be dangerous***

These electron micrographs show hair cells and the basilar membrane of a guinea pig (a) before and (b) after exposure to 24 hours of sound loud enough to be comparable to a rock concert. Note that on some cells the tiny hairs are disarranged, and on others the hairs are destroyed.

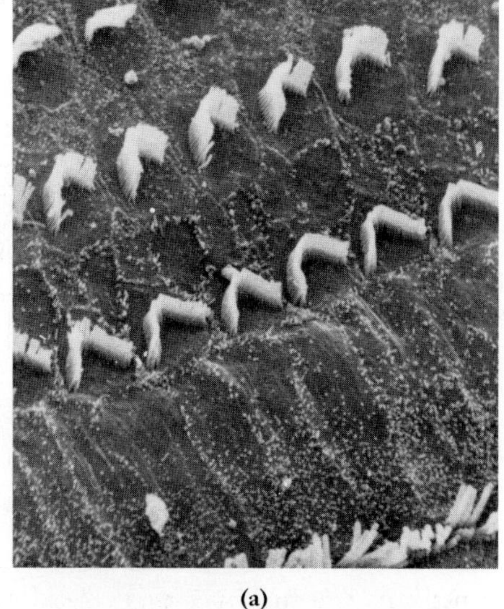

(a)

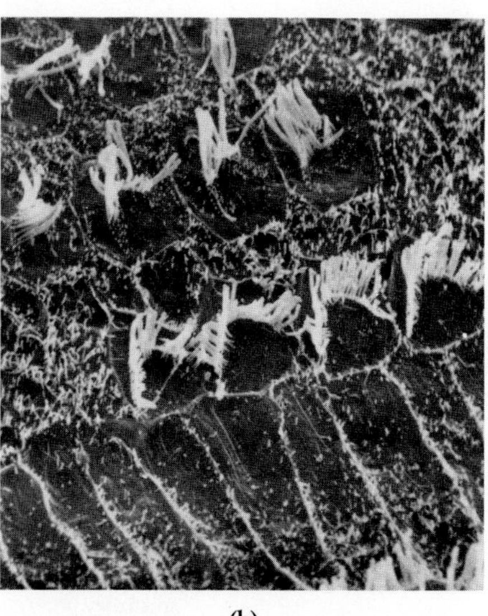

(b)

by the ear's hair cells (though not nearly as well). It transforms sounds into electrical impulses and sends the impulses through thin wires permanently implanted into the cochlea, where they stimulate the terminals of auditory neurons directly (Loeb, 1986). It can be used when deafness is due to the destruction of hair cells (see Figure 8.6), but not when the auditory nerve has been destroyed. Although still in the experimental stage, cochlear implants are currently used by thousands of people worldwide, and in some cases they permit sufficient sound resolution to enable the recipient to understand speech (Dorman & others, 1989, 1990).

The Coding of Sounds

How do receptors on the basilar membrane code the differences in sound frequency that permit pitch detection?

The Traveling-Wave Theory of Frequency Coding

In the nineteenth century, Hermann von Helmholtz suggested a possible analogy between the basilar membrane and the strings of a harp. A harp's strings vibrate not only when plucked, but also when sound waves strike them, and different strings vibrate best to different frequencies. Helmholtz proposed that the basilar membrane may contain separate fibers that, like a harp's strings, resonate to different tonal frequencies and activate different neurons in the auditory nerve (Zwislocki, 1981).

■ **9.** ***How does the basilar membrane of the inner ear operate to ensure that different neurons are maximally stimulated by sounds of different frequencies?***

Considerably later, in work begun in the 1920s that eventuated in a Nobel prize, Georg von Békésy showed that Helmholtz's general idea—that different frequencies activate different receptors—was correct, but that his details were wrong. Békésy developed a way to observe directly the action of the basilar membrane, and he discovered that it does not behave like a harp with separate strings, but rather like a bed sheet when someone shakes it at one end. Sound waves entering the cochlea set up *traveling waves* on the basilar membrane, which move from the proximal end (closest to the oval window) toward the distal end (the tip farthest away from the oval window). As each wave moves, it gradually increases in amplitude up to a certain maximum and then rapidly dissipates, as illustrated in Figure 8.7. Of most importance, Békésy found that the position on the membrane at which the waves reach their peak depends on the frequency of the tone. High frequencies produce waves that travel only a short distance, peaking near the proximal end, and low frequencies produce waves that travel farther, peaking nearer the distal end. From this observation, Békésy hypothesized that (a) rapid firing in neurons that come from the proximal end of the membrane, accompanied by little or no firing

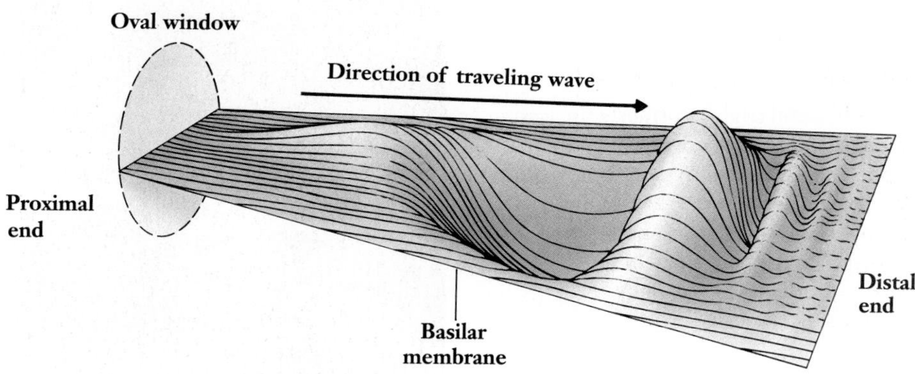

Figure 8.7 ***Diagram of a sound wave traveling on the basilar membrane***

The wave shown here, peaking near the distal end of the membrane (far from the oval window), is from a relatively low-frequency sound. A wave from a higher-frequency sound would peak closer to the proximal end (near the oval window).

in neurons coming from more distal parts, is interpreted by the brain as a high-pitched sound; and (b) rapid firing in neurons coming from a more distal portion is interpreted as a lower-pitched sound. Since then, other studies have confirmed the general validity of Békésy's hypothesis (Pickles, 1988).

Two Observations Consistent with the Traveling-Wave Theory

■ **10.** ***How does the traveling-wave theory explain (a) an asymmetry in auditory masking and (b) the pattern of hearing loss that occurs as we get older?***

One sensory phenomenon that is consistent with, and partly explained by, Békésy's traveling-wave theory is asymmetry in ***auditory masking***, a phenomenon that is important in the production of music. If two tones occur simultaneously, the more intense tone tends to mask (prevent the hearing of) the less intense tone. Auditory masking is asymmetrical in that low-frequency tones mask high-frequency tones much more effectively than the reverse (Scharf, 1964). Thus, a bassoon can drown out a piccolo; but a piccolo will not drown out a bassoon, even if it is played at a much higher amplitude than the bassoon. To see how Békésy's theory helps explain this phenomenon, look at Figure 8.8. The wave produced by a low-frequency bassoon note encompasses the entire portion of the basilar membrane that is encompassed by the piccolo note (and more). Thus, if the bassoon note is high enough in amplitude, it can interfere with the effect of the piccolo note; but the piccolo note, even at very high amplitude, cannot interfere with the effect that the bassoon note has on the more distal part of the membrane, because the wave produced by the piccolo note never travels that far down the membrane.

Another observation that can be accounted for by Békésy's theory concerns the pattern of hearing loss that occurs as we get older. We lose our sensitivity to high frequencies to a much greater degree than to low frequencies. Thus, young children can hear frequencies as high as 30,000 Hz, and young adults can hear frequencies as high as 20,000 Hz, but a typical 60-year-old cannot hear frequencies above about 15,000 Hz (to see a graph of this, you may want to look ahead to Figure 8.33). This decline is greatest for people who live or work in noisy environ-

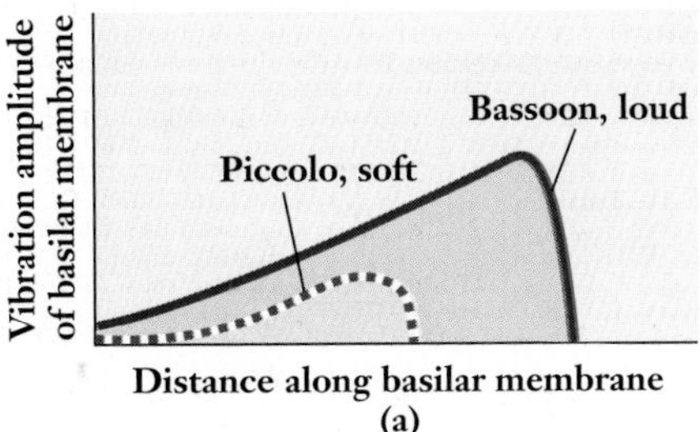

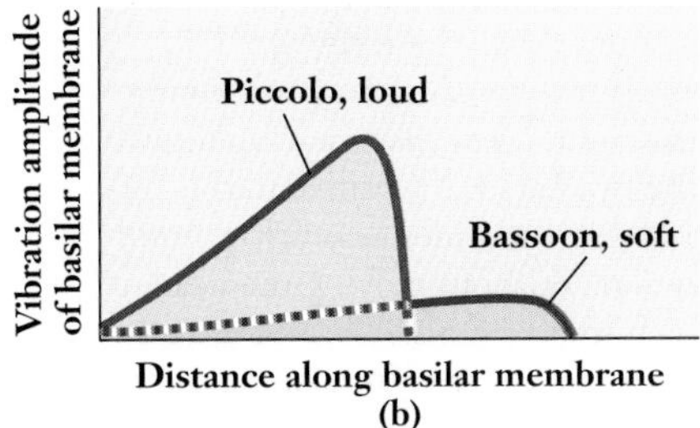

Figure 8.8 ***Why a low-frequency tone masks a high-frequency tone better than the reverse***

(a) When a low-frequency tone (such as that from a bassoon) and a high-frequency tone (such as that from a piccolo) are played simultaneously, the bassoon can mask the piccolo because the bassoon's action on the basilar membrane encompasses the entire portion on which the piccolo acts. (b) But the piccolo cannot mask the bassoon because, even when played at high amplitude, the piccolo does not affect the distal part of the membrane to which the bassoon's waves extend. (Adapted from Scharf, 1964.)

Unsafe sound

Pete Townshend (right), formerly the lead guitarist of The Who, can no longer play with the group because of severe damage to his hearing. Townshend has publicized his ailment to warn musicians and concert-goers of the dangers of loud music.

ments and is apparently caused by the wearing out of hair cells with repeated use (Kryter, 1985). But why should cells responsible for coding high frequencies wear out faster than those for coding low frequencies? The answer may lie in the fact that the former are acted upon by all sounds (as shown in Figure 8.8), while the latter respond only to low-frequency sounds.

Another Code for Frequency

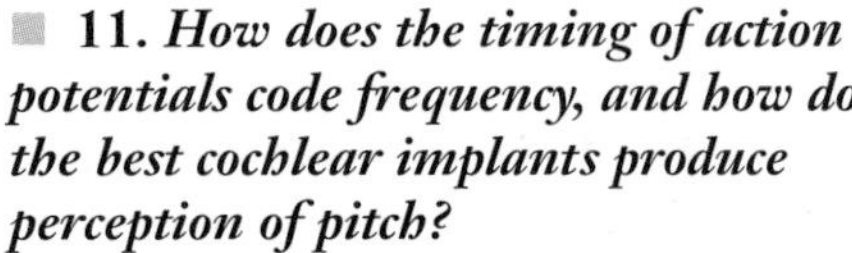

11. ***How does the timing of action potentials code frequency, and how do the best cochlear implants produce perception of pitch?***

Although the traveling-wave theory has been well validated, it is not the whole story. For frequencies below about 4000 Hz (which includes the entire range of human speech), perceived pitch depends not just on which part of the basilar membrane is maximally active, but also on the *timing* of that activity (Pickles, 1988). The action potentials triggered in sets of auditory neurons tend to be locked in phase with sound waves, such that a separate burst of action potentials occurs each time a sound wave peaks; this contributes to the perception of pitch. Interestingly, the most sophisticated cochlear implants use both place and timing to produce some degree of pitch perception in people with sensorineural deafness (Pickles, 1988; B. Townshend & others, 1987). These devices break a sound signal into separate frequency ranges and send electrical pulses from each frequency range through a thin wire to a different portion of the basilar membrane. The best pitch perception (still not very good) occurs when the electrical signal sent to a given locus of the membrane is pulsed at a frequency similar to that of the sound wave that would normally act at that location.

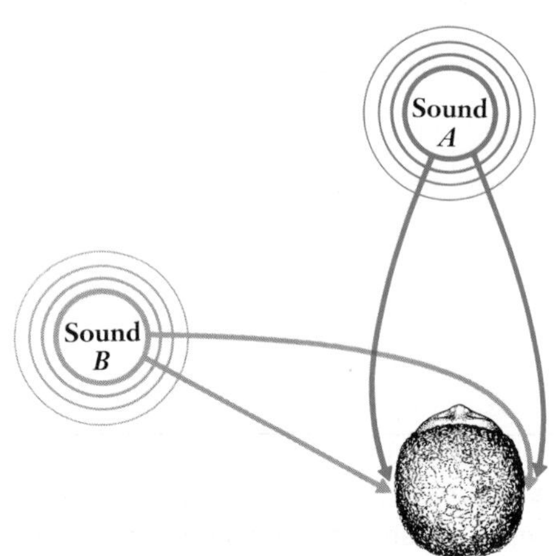

Figure 8.9 ***Locating a sound***

Waves coming from Sound *B* reach the left ear sooner than the right ear. The converse is true for sound waves coming from the right. Neurons receiving input from the two ears are sensitive to this difference, which provides a code for sound localization. Without moving the head, it is difficult to distinguish a sound directly in front (Sound *A*) from one directly behind the head, because in both cases the sound waves reach both ears simultaneously.

Further Processing by the Brain

The experience of a sound includes not only its loudness and pitch, but also its *location in space* (see Figure 8.9), its *timbre* (the quality, based on the exact form of the sound wave, that distinguishes a natural sound from a pure tone), its time of *onset* and *offset*, and its *inflection* (the rise and fall of the dominant pitch). Most sounds, such as spoken words, consist of simultaneous waves of many frequencies, which change continuously in both frequency and amplitude from the beginning of the sound to the end. All of the information that allows you to distinguish one such sound from another must be extracted by the brain from the pattern of action potentials in the auditory nerves. Studies based on single-cell recordings have shown that many neurons in the auditory cortex are highly specific in the pattern of sound to which they respond. Some respond only to a narrow range of frequencies, others only to certain combinations of frequencies, others only to rising or falling pitch, and still others only to brief clicks or bursts of sound (Phillips, 1989). In the end, activity in some combination of these cells must provide the basis for the auditory experience that occurs when you hear a canary singing or your professor enunciating the sweet word *psychology*.

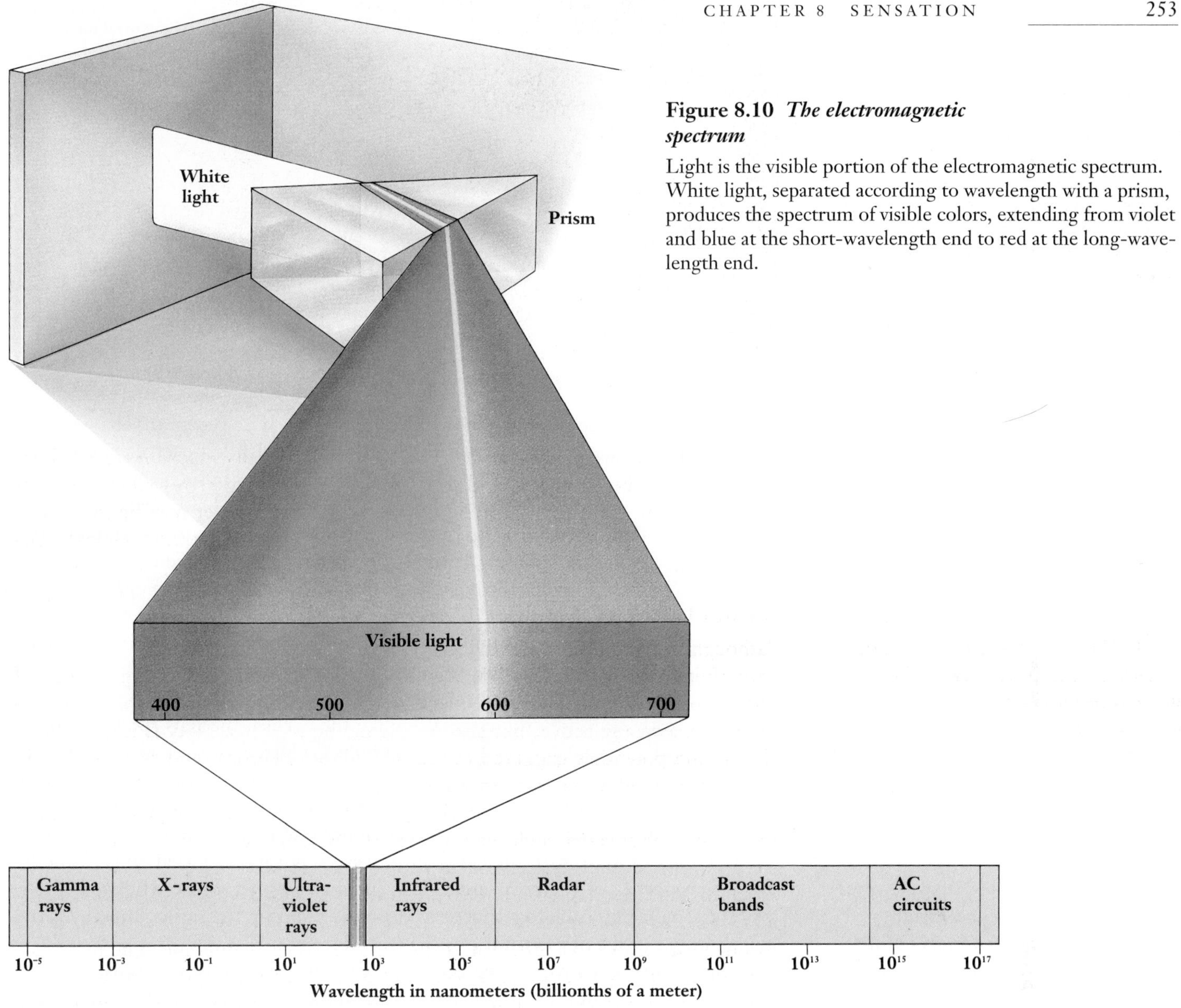

Figure 8.10 ***The electromagnetic spectrum***

Light is the visible portion of the electromagnetic spectrum. White light, separated according to wavelength with a prism, produces the spectrum of visible colors, extending from violet and blue at the short-wavelength end to red at the long-wavelength end.

Vision

■ **12.** ***How can light be described physically, and what is the relationship of its wavelength to its perceived color?***

Unlike sound, light can travel through empty space, as it does in going from the sun and stars to the earth. Partly for that reason, scientists assume that it consists of particles, called *photons*. For our purposes, however, it is more useful to emphasize light's wavelike properties. The particles pulse in a wavelike way. Light waves are usually described in terms of their amplitude (or intensity) and their ***wavelength*** (the physical length of one complete cycle of the wave). The wavelengths of visible light range from about 400 to 700 nm (one nm, or nanometer, is a billionth of a meter). White light, such as that from the sun, consists of all visible wavelengths combined. When the wavelengths in white light are separated (with a prism, for example), the visual effect is an array of colors like that of the rainbow, because different wavelengths are seen as different colors (see Figure 8.10). [The term for the entire spectrum of energy that includes light is *electromagnetic energy*. Shorter waves of electromagnetic energy, below the visible range, include ultraviolet rays, x-rays, and gamma rays; and longer waves, above the visible range, include infrared rays, radar rays, and radio waves.]

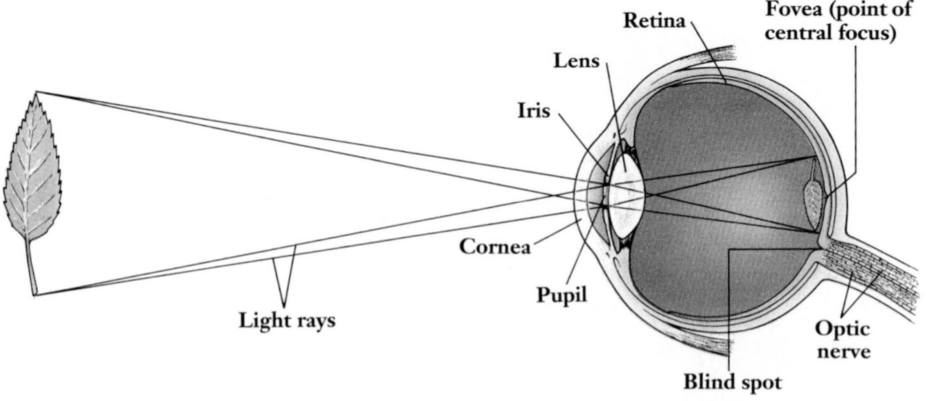

Figure 8.11 ***Cross section of the eye, depicting the retinal image***

The light rays that diverge from any given point on the surface of an object are brought back together (focused) at a distinct point on the retina, to create an image of the object on the retina. This drawing shows light rays diverging and being brought together for just two points on the leaf, but the same process is occurring for light rays coming from every point.

The Functional Organization of the Eye

■ **13.** ***How do the cornea, iris, and lens help form images on the retina?***

The main parts of the eye are shown in Figure 8.11. The receptor cells lie in the ***retina***, a membrane lining the rear interior of the fluid-filled eyeball. The rest of the eye is a device for focusing light reflected from objects, in such a way as to form an image on the retina. The front of the eyeball is covered by the ***cornea***, a transparent tissue that, because of its outward curvature, helps to focus the light that passes through it. Immediately behind the cornea is the pigmented, doughnut-shaped ***iris***, which provides the color (usually brown or blue) of the eye. The iris is opaque, so the only light that can enter the interior of the eye is that which passes through the ***pupil***, which is simply the hole in the center of the iris. The iris contains muscle fibers that can increase or decrease the diameter of the pupil to allow more or less light to enter. Behind the iris is the ***lens***, which adds to the focusing process already begun by the cornea. Unlike the cornea, the lens is adjustable—it becomes more spherical when focusing on objects close to the eye and flatter when focusing on those farther away. As people get older, the lens commonly loses some of its adjustability, which is why some of us wear bifocals (glasses that contain two lenses, a lower one for close vision and an upper one for far vision). Light rays diverge as they move toward the eye from any given point on a visual object. The focusing properties of the cornea and lens (plus glasses, for those who wear them) bring the light rays back together at a particular point on the retina, thereby forming an image of the object on the retina (see Figure 8.11).

■ **14.** ***How are cones and rods distributed in different parts of the retina, and how do they respond to light?***

The retina contains, among other things, millions of receptor cells, arranged mosaic-like in a single retinal layer. The receptor cells are of two types: ***cones***, which permit sharply focused color vision in bright light, and ***rods***, which permit vision in dim light. These cells are so named for their shape (see Figure 8.12). Cones are most concentrated in the ***fovea***, the pinhead-sized area of the retina that is in the most direct line of sight (look again at Figure 8.11), which is specialized for high visual *acuity* (the ability to distinguish minute details). The concentration of cones decreases sharply with increasing distance from the fovea. Rods, in contrast, exist everywhere in the retina except the fovea and are most concentrated in a ring about 20 degrees away from the fovea (see Figure 8.13). Each human retina contains about 6 million cones and 120 million rods (Wade & Swanston, 1991).

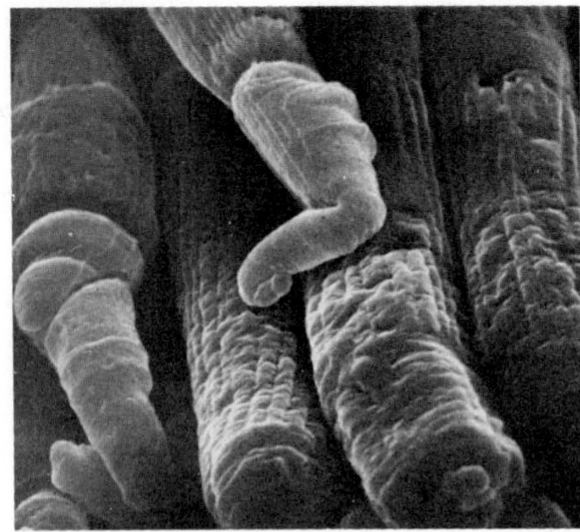

Figure 8.12 ***Rods and cones***

This electron micrograph shows that the photoreceptors are aptly named. Rods are responsible for vision in dim light, and cones for vision in bright light.

The outer segment of each receptor cell contains a *photochemical*—a chemical that reacts to light. In the rod this photochemical is ***rhodopsin***. When hit by light, the rhodopsin molecules undergo a structural change that triggers a series of chemical reactions in the rod's membrane, which in turn causes an electrical change across the membrane (Nathans, 1987; Schnapf & Baylor, 1987). The transduction process for cones is similar to that for rods, but (as you will see later) three different kinds of cones exist and each contains a different photochemical. The electrical change in rods and cones causes electrical responses in other cells in the retina. These responses lead to the production of action potentials in neurons that form the ***optic nerve***, which runs to the brain. At the place on the retina where the axons of these neurons come together to form the optic nerve there is a ***blind spot***,

Figure 8.13 ***Distribution of cones and rods in the retina***
Cones are most concentrated in the fovea. Rods are absent in the fovea and most concentrated in a ring 20 degrees away from it. No receptors at all exist in the blind spot.

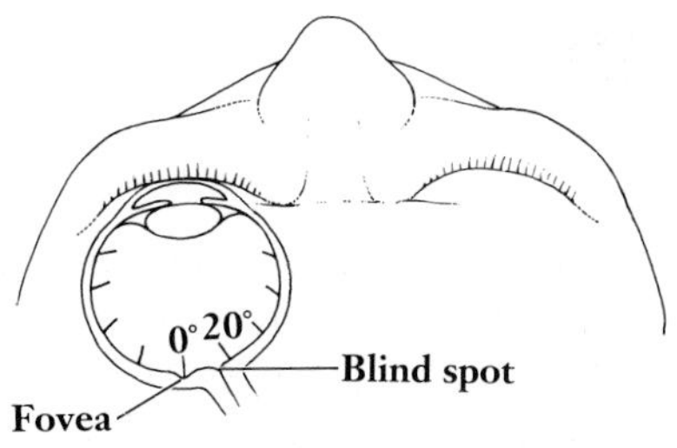

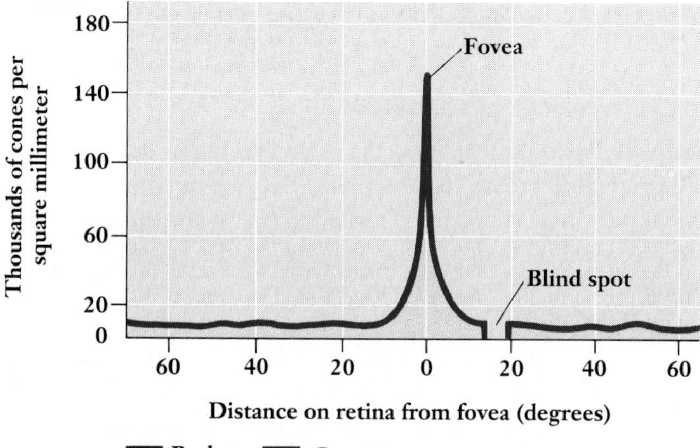

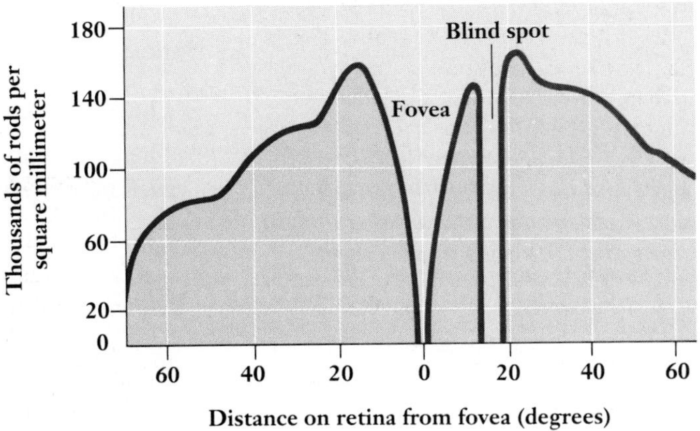

due to the absence of receptor cells (shown in Figure 8.13). We normally do not notice the blind spot, but you can demonstrate its existence by following the instructions in Figure 8.14.

Distinctions Between Cone and Rod Vision

■ **15.** ***How do cone vision and rod vision differ?***

Cones and rods provide the starting point for what can be thought of as two separate but interacting visual systems within the human eye. ***Cone vision*** (also called photopic vision or bright-light vision) is specialized for high acuity and for the perception of color. ***Rod vision*** (also called scotopic vision or dim-light vision) is specialized for sensitivity (the ability to see in very dim light). It lacks acuity (the edges of objects appear fuzzy) and the ability to distinguish colors. Rod vision is so sensitive that, based on calculations from laboratory studies, it should be possible on a clear night to see a single candle flame 30 miles away if no other lights are present (Galanter, 1962).

In very dim light, too dim to activate cones, you see only with rod vision; you can make out the general shapes of objects, but not their details and colors. In such light you can see dim objects best when not looking directly at them—because, as noted before, the fovea (the part of the retina in the direct line of sight) contains no

Figure 8.14 ***Demonstration of the blind spot***
Close your left eye, and focus on the X with your right eye. Start with the page a little more than a foot from your eye and move it gradually closer, still focusing on the X. At about 10 inches, the bird will disappear. At that location, the image of the bird falls on the blind spot of the retina, shown in Figure 8.13. Yet you will probably still see the bars of the cage running across the area where the bird was located, and the background color may fill the space previously occupied by the bird. The bars and color are perceptually filled in by a process of interpolation, which is discussed later in the chapter.

rods. Sometime on a starry but moonless night, when you are out in the country where there are no streetlights, stay in the dark for a good 20 minutes (so your eyes become fully adapted to the dark), and then find the dimmest star that you can see. The star will disappear when you look straight at it, but reappear when you look just a little away. You can see it best when looking 20 degrees away, because this angle allows the light from the star to strike the part of the retina where rods are most concentrated.

The Separate Adaptation Curves of Cones and Rods

■ **16.** ***What is the chemical basis for light and dark adaptation, and why do we see mostly with cones in bright light and with rods in dim light?***

The gradual increase in sensitivity to light that occurs as you sit in the dark is called ***dark adaptation***, and the gradual decrease in sensitivity that occurs after you turn on a bright lamp or step out into sunlight is called ***light adaptation***. These processes are mediated to a considerable degree by a change in the photochemicals of cones and rods. If you performed the experiment suggested earlier in this chapter, adapting one eye to the light while covering the other, you should have found an increase in brightness when you changed the cover to the other eye. That is because the cones and rods in the covered eye were still dark adapted. In bright light, the photochemical molecules tend to break down to two inactive substances, and in dim light or darkness they gradually reform. For rhodopsin, the process can be summarized as follows:

$$\text{rhodopsin} \underset{\text{dark}}{\overset{\text{light}}{\rightleftarrows}} \text{opsin} + \text{retinal}$$

Cone photochemicals also break down in the light, but not as extensively as in the case of rhodopsin. Because more of their photochemical molecules remain intact, cones are more responsive than rods in normal to bright light. Cones are also more responsive than rods when you first go from normal light into a dark room. In addition to enabling you to see a little immediately, they are responsible for the improvement in your vision during the first 5 to 10 minutes—the period during which their chemicals regenerate. Further improvement after that, however, is due to rods, as rhodopsin continues to regenerate for another 15 to 20 minutes after cones have fully adapted. This two-part process of dark adaptation is graphed in Figure 8.15. The two-part (lower) curve in the graph is typical of people with nor-

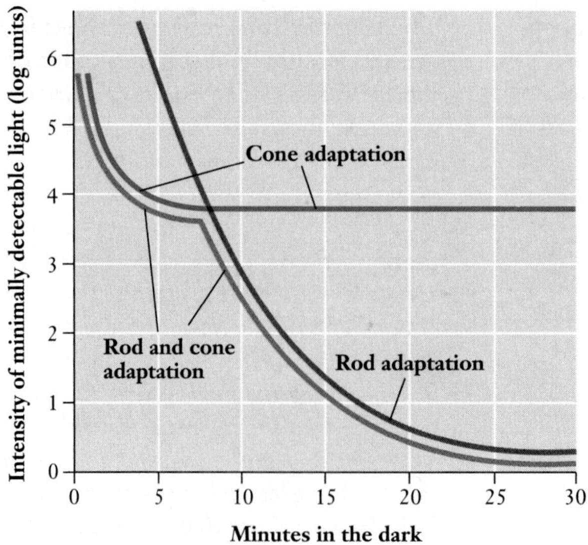

Figure 8.15 ***Dark-adaptation curves***
The brown curve shows the minimal intensity of a spot of light that a person with normal vision can see after varying amounts of time in the dark. The lower the curve, the greater the sensitivity to light. For the first 8 minutes or so, the cones are more sensitive than the rods, but after that the rods are more sensitive. The two-part nature of the curve can be understood by comparing it to the dark-adaptation curve obtained for a person who has only rods (the green curve) and to that obtained if the light is presented in such a way that it strikes only the fovea, where only cones exist (the red curve). (From Grüsser & Grüsser-Cornehls, 1986.)

mal vision. People who are completely color blind show the rods-only curve because they have no cone photochemicals (Grüsser & Grüsser-Cornehls, 1986), and people who have no rhodopsin (due to a temporary lack of vitamin A) show the cones-only curve (Hecht & Mandelbaum, 1938).

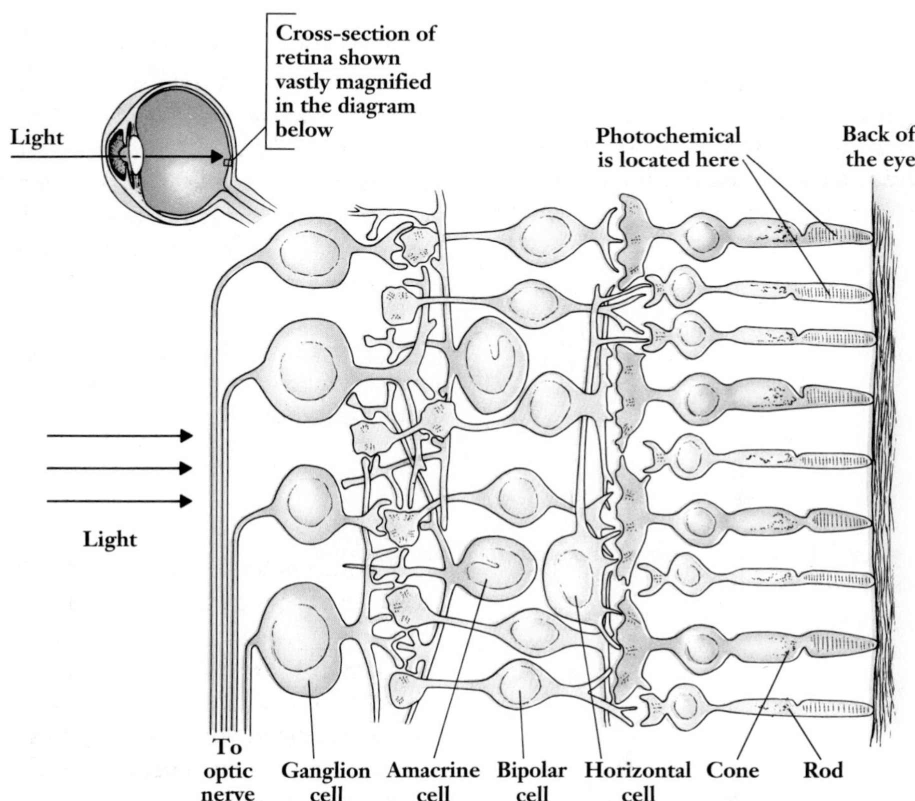

Figure 8.16 ***Diagram of cells in a cross-section of the retina***

Light that reaches the retina must pass through its relatively transparent inner layers of cells before reaching the sensitive ends of the rods and cones in the outermost layer, at the back of the eye.

Neural Convergence as a Basis for Differences Between Cone and Rod Vision

■ **17.** ***How does the pattern of neural connections within the retina help account for the greater sensitivity and reduced acuity of rod vision compared to cone vision?***

The superiority of rods over cones in detecting dim light stems not just from the greater sensitivity of the rods' photochemical, but also from a difference between the two classes of receptors in their pattern of connections to neurons of the optic nerve. As shown in Figure 8.16, both rods and cones form synapses on short neurons called ***bipolar cells***, which in turn form synapses on larger neurons called ***ganglion cells***. The ganglion cells have their cell bodies in the retina and have long axons that leave the eye at the blind spot to form the optic nerve. Other neurons (horizontal cells and amacrine cells) within the retina interconnect adjacent bipolar and ganglion cells, creating a good deal of complexity in the connections within the retina. The net effect of these connections is that each ganglion cell receives input from a set of rods and/or cones, which are located adjacent to one another and define the ***receptive field*** of that cell. The receptive field of a ganglion cell (or of any other neuron in the visual system) is the localized area on the retina from which that cell receives neural input. The connections are such that the size of the receptive field is greater for ganglion cells that receive input primarily or wholly from rods than for those that receive input primarily or wholly from cones.

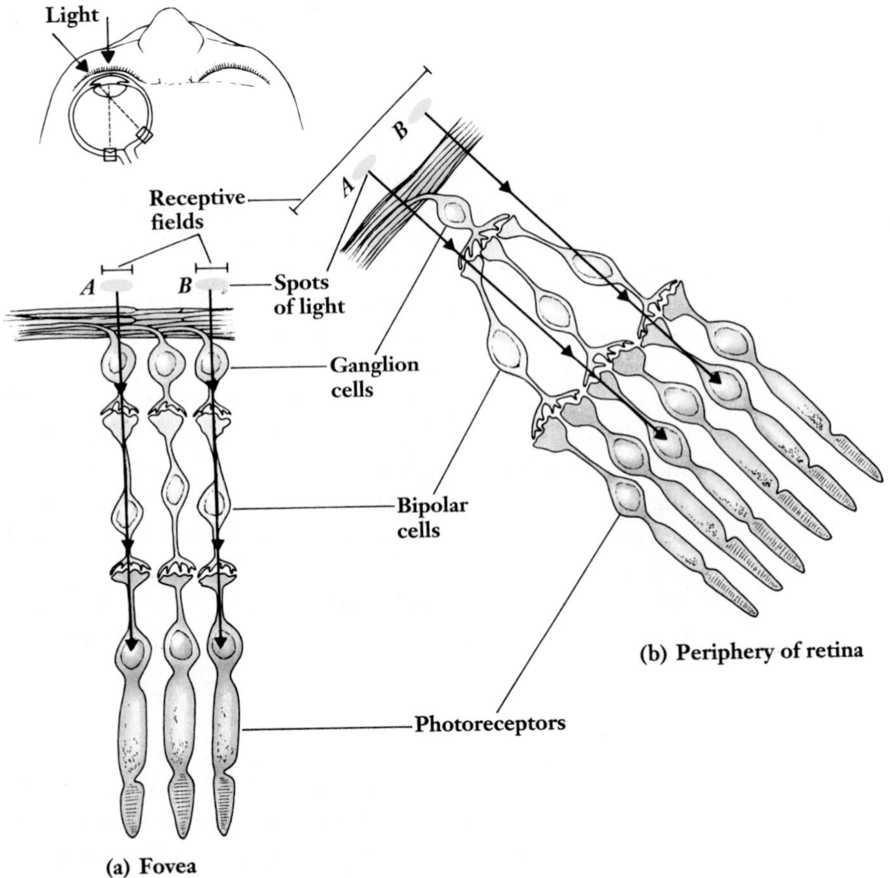

Figure 8.17 ***Relationship of receptive-field size to visual acuity and sensitivity***

Ganglion cells in the fovea have smaller receptive fields than do ganglion cells in the periphery; in other words, they receive input from fewer receptor cells. This difference accounts for high acuity in the fovea and high sensitivity (but low acuity) in the periphery. Spots *A* and *B* of light on the fovea [diagram (a)] will activate two different ganglion cells, and hence maintain their distinctiveness (high acuity). The same two spots in the periphery [diagram (b)] will activate the same ganglion cell and lose their distinctiveness (low acuity), but each spot will add to the total activity of that cell (high sensitivity). [Note: For the sake of simplicity, this figure omits the horizontal and amacrine cells and also underestimates the actual amount of convergence that occurs in both the fovea and periphery.]

To visualize this difference and how it bears on acuity and sensitivity, look at Figure 8.17. As depicted in the left-hand portion of the figure, each ganglion cell in the fovea receives input from a small number of cones, which means that its receptive field is small. Consequently, two spots of light very close to one another will act on separate ganglion cells, resulting in two distinct messages to the brain—a condition that permits them to be seen as separate spots (high acuity). The right-hand portion of the figure illustrates peripheral portions of the retina, where rods predominate. Here each ganglion cell receives input from a large number of receptor cells (thousands, in some cases), spread out over a relatively large area, which means that its receptive field is large. Two spots of light very close to one another will therefore act on the same ganglion cell, and thus lose their distinctiveness, causing them to blur into one spot in the person's perception (low acuity). For the same reason that acuity is decreased, however, sensitivity is increased. A small amount of electrical activity coming from each receptor cell, when stimulated by dim light, can add up to produce a relatively large amount of electrical activity in the ganglion cell. The funneling of the activity of many receptor cells to fewer sensory neurons is called ***neural convergence***; in general, in other sensory systems as well as vision, high neural convergence increases sensitivity at the expense of acuity.

Color Vision

18. ***How do pigments affect the perceived color of an object in white light? How does the mixing of pigments affect color by subtracting from the light that is reflected to the eye?***

As noted earlier, our experience of color depends on the wavelengths of light that reach our eyes, much as our experience of pitch depends on the frequencies of sound that reach our ears. The shortest visible waves are seen as violet, and as waves become longer the perceived color progresses through shades of blue, blue-green, green, green-yellow, yellow, orange, and red (look back at Figure 8.10). The colors of objects are determined by *pigments*, chemicals on their surface that absorb some wavelengths of light and thereby prevent them from being reflected. Different pigments allow different wavelengths to be reflected. A pigment that absorbs short and medium-length waves, for example, appears red, because only long (red-appearing) waves are reflected. Similarly, a pigment that allows only short waves to be reflected appears violet or blue, and one that allows only medium-length waves to be reflected appears yellow or green. A pigment that allows all wavelengths to be reflected about equally will appear white, gray, or black, depending on whether the relative amount of light reflected is high (white), moderate (gray), or low (black).

Subtractive Color Mixing

Because pigments create the perception of color by *subtracting* (absorbing) some of the light waves that would otherwise be reflected to the eye, the mixing of pigments is called ***subtractive color mixing***. As illustrated in Figure 8.18, if a blue pigment, which absorbs long waves, is mixed with a yellow pigment, which absorbs short waves, only medium-length waves will be reflected, and the mixture will be seen as green. When you were a child playing with watercolors you probably proved the basic facts of subtractive color mixing many times. You may remember being disappointed when your attempt to produce a brilliant reddish-yellowish-greenish-blue, by mixing all of the paints together, resulted in something pretty close to black. In that experiment you subtracted out all of the wavelengths by mixing all of the pigments together.

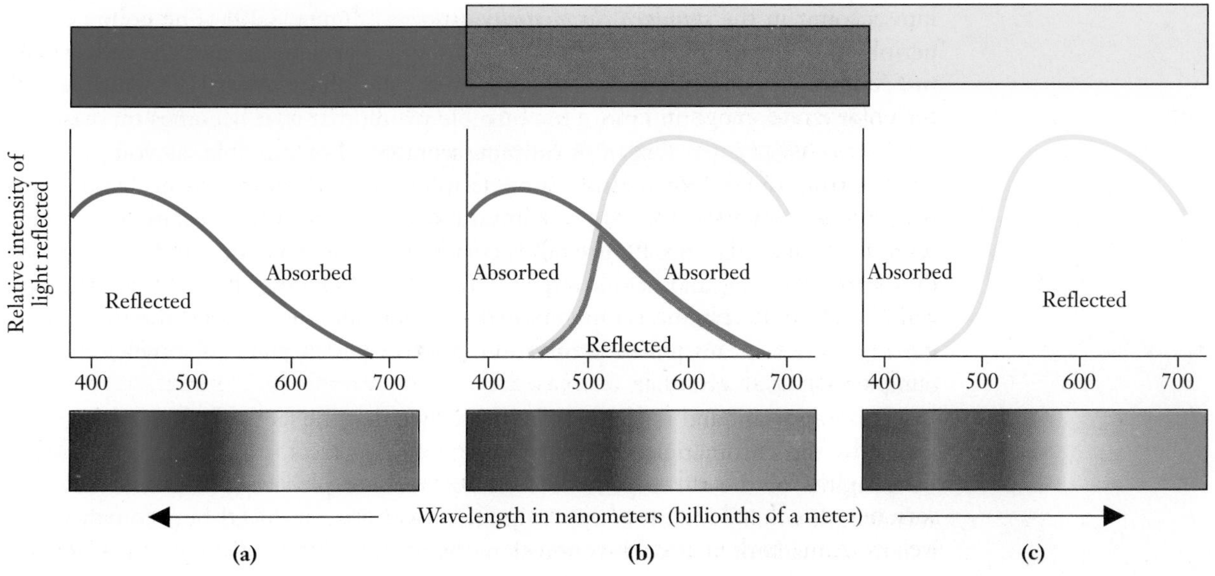

Figure 8.18 *Subtractive color mixing*
In this example, the blue pigment (a) absorbs most of the light that has wavelengths above 550 nm, and the yellow pigment (c) absorbs most of the light that has wavelengths below 500 nm. When the two pigments are mixed (b), the only light that is not strongly absorbed is that with wavelengths lying between 500 and 550 nm. This is the light that will be reflected, causing the mixture to appear green.

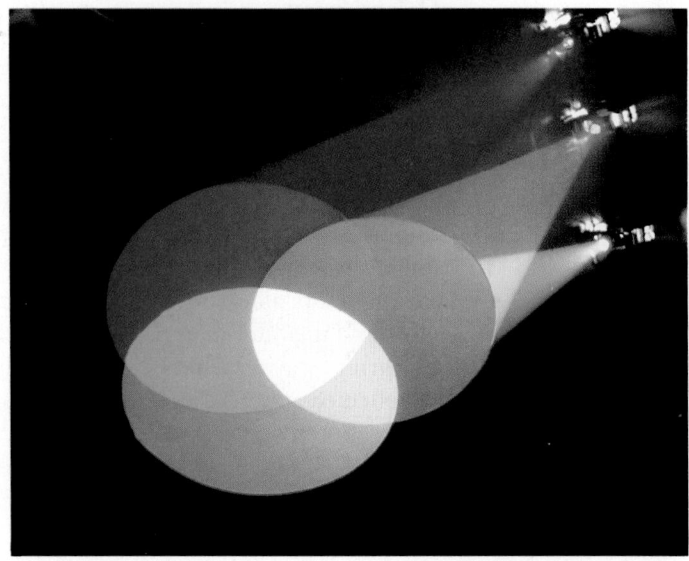

Figure 8.19 *Additive color mixing*

Additive color mixing occurs when lights of different wavelengths are mixed by shining them together on a surface that reflects all wavelengths. By varying the intensity of the three lights shown here it would be possible to match all of the colors that the eye can see.

19. ***How does additive color mixing differ from subtractive color mixing? What are the two laws of additive color mixing, and how is each illustrated in the standard chromaticity diagram?***

Two Laws of Additive Color Mixing

The opposite of subtractive color mixing is ***additive color mixing***, which occurs when colored lights rather than pigments are mixed. Additive color mixing can be demonstrated by shining two or more beams of light of different wavelengths at the same spot on a white screen; the screen then reflects them back mixed together (see Figure 8.19). By the early eighteenth century, experiments had led to two general laws of additive color mixing. According to the ***three-primaries law***, three different wavelengths of light (called *primaries*) can be used to match any color that the eye can see, if they are mixed in the appropriate proportions. The primaries can be any three wavelengths as long as one is taken from the long-wave end of the spectrum (red), one from the short-wave end (blue or violet), and one from the middle (green or green-yellow). According to the ***law of complementarity***, pairs of wavelengths can be found that, when added together, produce the visual sensation of white. Such a pair are referred to as *complements* of each other.

All of the facts associated with the two laws of additive color mixing are taken into account in the *standard chromaticity diagram* (Figure 8.20). The colors in the periphery of the diagram are produced by single wavelengths and are called *saturated* colors. As you move from any point on the periphery toward the white center, the color comes more and more to resemble white; that is, it becomes increasingly *unsaturated* (white is regarded as fully unsaturated). For example, as you go along the line from the 620 nm point on the periphery to the center, you go from red to progressively whiter shades of pink (unsaturated red) to white. [Because of the limitations of color printing, Figure 8.20 actually does not show this gradual change in saturation, but you can imagine it.] The figure's caption describes how the diagram can be used to determine (a) the color that will result from mixing the three standard primaries in any given proportion, and (b) which pairs of wavelengths are complements of each other.

It is important and rather exciting to realize that the facts of color mixing portrayed by the chromaticity diagram are *psychological* facts, not physical facts. The wavelengths of the three primaries do *not* become physically blended into one wavelength when added together to match the color produced by a fourth wavelength. A machine that detects wavelengths would have no difficulty distinguish-

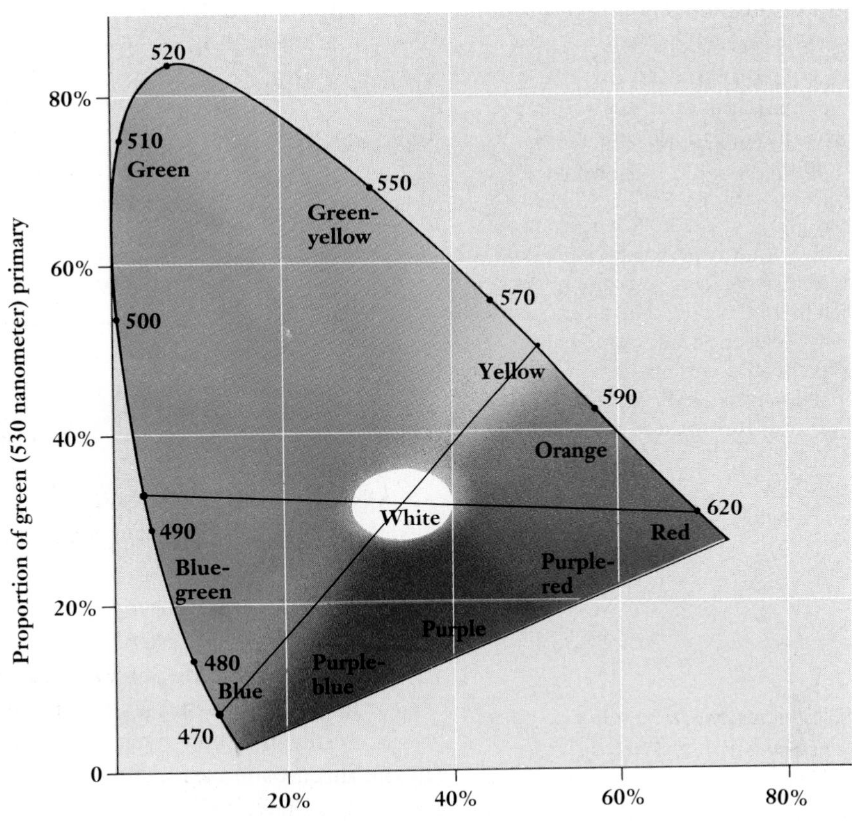

Figure 8.20 ***The standard chromaticity diagram***

All of the facts of additive color mixing—related to both the three-primaries law and the law of complementarity—are summarized in this diagram. The three primaries here are lights of 460 nm (blue), 530 nm (green), and 650 nm (red). The proportions of red and green primaries that must be added to the blue primary to match any given color on the diagram are shown, respectively, on the horizontal and vertical axes. The proportion of blue can be calculated by subtracting the other two proportions from 100%. For example, if you wish to match the blue-green produced by a 490 nm light, the figure indicates that your mixture must contain about 5% red primary, 30% green primary, and 65% blue primary (100% – 5% – 30% = 65%). As another example, the figure shows that the best white is produced by approximately equal (33.3%) proportions of the three primaries.

The chromaticity diagram can also be used to find all possible pairs of complementary colors. Two colors are complementary if their additive mixture produces white. In the diagram, the possible colors produced by mixing any two wavelengths lie along the straight line connecting the points representing the two wavelengths on the diagram. Thus, the two ends of any straight line passing through the white center of the diagram represent complementary colors. Two such lines are drawn on the figure for purposes of illustration. Notice that wavelengths in the red to orange part of the spectrum have their complements in the green to blue-green part, and that wavelengths in the yellow part of the spectrum have their complements in the blue part.

ing, say, a 550 nm light from the mixture of three primaries that would exactly match its greenish-yellow color. Similarly, when two complementary wavelengths are mixed to produce the sensation of white, they do not physically produce white light (which contains all the wavelengths). Such color matches, in which physically distinct stimuli look identical, must occur because of processes in the eye or in the brain. Indeed, the matches just described provided the insight that led, in the nineteenth century, to the development of two physiological theories of color vision—the trichromatic and opponent-process theories.

20. ***How does the trichromatic theory explain the three-primaries law? How was the theory validated by the discovery of three cone types?***

The Trichromatic Theory of Color Vision

According to the ***trichromatic theory***, color vision is mediated by three different types of receptors, each most sensitive to a different range of wavelengths. This idea was proposed first (in 1802) by Thomas Young, and later by Hermann Helmholtz (1852), as an attempt to explain the three-primaries law of color vision. Young and Helmholtz reasoned that if every color that we see is the result of a unique proportion, or ratio, of activity among three types of receptors, then it would be possible to match any visible color by varying the relative intensities of three primary lights, each of which acts maximally on a different type of receptor. Young and Helmholtz developed their theory purely from behavioral data, on perceptual effects of color mixing, at a time when nothing was known about receptor cells in the retina. We now know from physiological studies that their theory was correct. Three types of cones indeed exist in the human retina, each with a different photochemical that makes it most sensitive to the light within a particular band

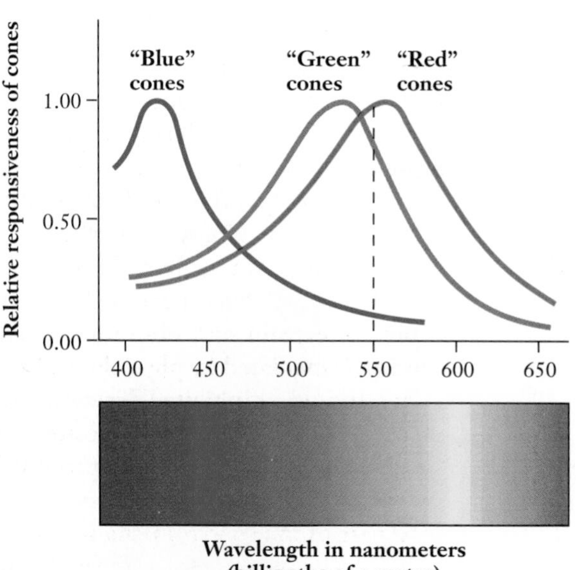

Figure 8.21 ***How the three types of cones respond to different wavelengths of light***

Any given wavelength produces a unique ratio of activity in the three cone types, and that ratio provides the initial code that permits us to see different wavelengths as different colors. For example, a 550 nm light, which is seen as greenish-yellow, produces a slightly larger response in red cones than in green cones, and a very low response in blue cones. Any combination of lights that would produce that same ratio of responses would be seen as greenish-yellow. (For precise data see Bowmaker & Dartnall, 1980; or Merbs & Nathans, 1992).

of wavelengths. In Figure 8.21 you can see an approximation of the actual sensitivity curves for each type of cone. The cones are labeled *blue*, *green*, and *red*, after the color that is experienced when that type of cone is much more active than the other types. Notice that any given wavelength of light produces a unique ratio of activity in the three cone types. For example, a 550 nm light, which is seen as greenish-yellow, produces a slightly larger response in red cones than in green cones, and a very low response in blue cones. That same ratio of response in the three cone types could be produced by shining into the eye a mixture of red, green, and blue primaries, with the first two much more intense than the last.

■ **21.** ***Why does vision in some people obey a two-primaries law rather than the three-primaries law, and why are they not good at picking cherries?***

Some people, referred to as *dichromats*, have only two types of cones rather than three. All of the colors that they can see are due to different proportions of activity in their two types of cones, so their visual system obeys a *two-primaries law* of color mixing. These people can match any color they can see by varying the proportion of just two different wavelengths rather than the usual three. The most common forms of dichromia involve the absence of either red or green cones (usually the green) due to a defect in the gene that normally produces the photochemical for that cone type (Nathans & others, 1986). Because the defective gene is recessive, and the genes for both the red and green photochemicals are located on the X chromosome, this trait is sex-linked and shows up much more often in men than in women (see Chapter 3).

People who lack either red or green cones are ***red-green color blind***, meaning that they have difficulty distinguishing colors ranging from green through the red end of the spectrum. If you look again at Figure 8.21 you will see why this would be the case. The normal ability to distinguish colors in this range (from about 520 to 700 nm) is mediated almost entirely by differential activity in the red and green cones, because blue cones are almost completely inactive in this range. If either the red or the green cones are missing, the person will have only one type of cone that responds in this range, and will have no physiological basis for distinguishing one wavelength from another. Many people with red-green color blindness don't know it and may wonder why certain perceptual tasks that are hard for them are easy for others. One man's red-green color blindness was not discovered until he told his family how much he admired the perceptual skill of cherry pickers: "After all," he said, "the only thing that tells 'em it's a cherry is . . . that it's round and the leaves aren't. I just don't see how they find 'em in those trees!" (Coren & Ward, 1989).

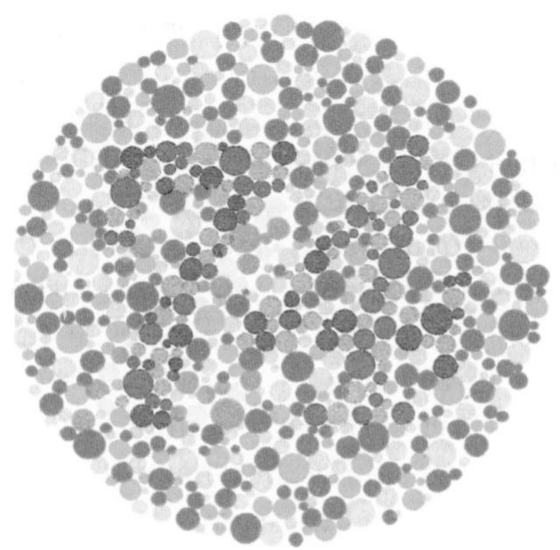

Test for color blindness

In this test people with normal vision will see the number, and people with red-green color blindness will not.

The Opponent-Process Theory of Color Vision

The trichromatic theory accounts nicely for the three-primaries law, and for certain types of color blindness, but it does not explain the law of complementarity. To explain that, Ewald Hering, another nineteenth-century scientist, developed the ***opponent-process theory***. Hering was most impressed by the observation that complementary colors (blue and yellow, or green and red) seem to swallow each other up, erasing each other's color, when added together. For example, if you begin with blue light and gradually add more of its complement (yellow), the result is not "bluish-yellow," but an ever paler (more unsaturated) blue, which finally becomes white. To explain such observations, Hering (1878/1964) proposed that color perception is mediated by physiological elements (which we now call cells) that can be either excited or inhibited depending on the wavelength of light, and that complementary wavelengths have opposite effects on these mediators.

■ **22. *How does the opponent-process theory explain (a) the law of complementarity in color mixing and (b) the complementarity of afterimages?***

More specifically, Hering proposed that the ability to see blues and yellows is mediated by blue-yellow opponent cells, which are excited by wavelengths in the blue part of the spectrum and inhibited by those in the yellow part, or vice versa. Similarly, he proposed that the ability to see greens and reds is mediated by green-red opponent cells, which are excited by wavelengths in the green part of the spectrum and inhibited by those in the red part, or vice versa. In addition, he proposed that the ability to distinguish bright from dim light, independent of wavelength, is mediated by a third set of cells (brightness detectors), which are excited by lights of any wavelength. This theory nicely accounts for the facts of complementary colors. A mixture of wavelengths from the blue and yellow parts of the spectrum, or from the green and red parts, would appear white (colorless but bright) because the two sets of wavelengths would have opposite effects on the opponent cells that promote color detection. Thus, they would cancel each other out, while at the same time acting in concert to excite the brightness detectors.

The opponent-process theory also accounts wonderfully for another psychological phenomenon, that of *complementarity of afterimages*. To demonstrate this phenomenon to yourself, follow the directions in Figure 8.22. You will see that the colors in the afterimage are the complements of those in the original: What was green becomes red; what was yellow becomes blue; and what was black becomes white. How does the opponent-process theory explain this phenomenon? Consider the example of green in the original resulting in red in the afterimage. The units in the retina that receive the green-appearing (middle-wavelength) light as you stare at the picture become fatigued. Therefore, when you shift your eyes to the white paper (which reflects all wavelengths), those units don't respond as strongly as they normally would, but other units, including those that respond to red-appearing (long-wavelength light) do respond strongly. Thus, opponent-process cells that are normally excited by red-appearing light and inhibited by green-appearing light in that part of the retina become active, resulting in the perception of red.

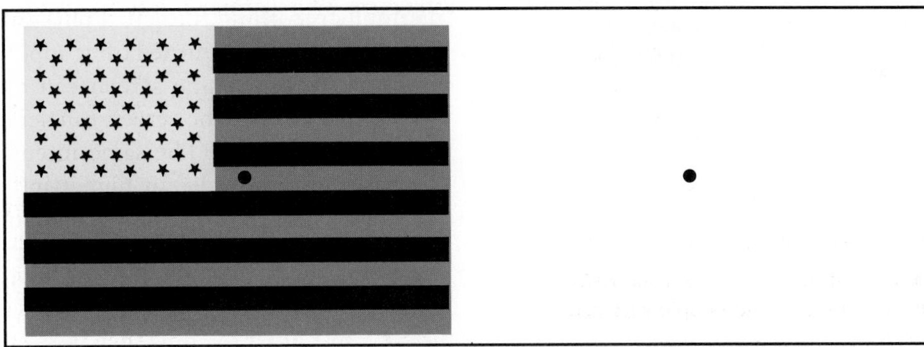

Figure 8.22 ***Complementarity of afterimages***

Stare at the dot in the middle of the flag for at least half a minute. Then look at the dot on the white space beside the flag. What do you see?

■ **23.** ***How has the opponent-process theory been validated in studies of the electrical activity of neurons that receive input from cones?***

A Physiological Reconciliation of the Two Theories

At one time the trichromatic and opponent-process theories were thought to be contradictory, but we now know that both are fundamentally correct. The retina contains three types of cones, and these code wavelength in accordance with Young and Helmholtz's trichromatic theory. But the cones feed into neurons in the brain through a pattern of connections that translates the trichromatic code into an opponent-process code, conforming to Hering's theory. By recording the activity in individual neurons while stimulating the eye with different wavelengths, scientists have found ganglion cells, and cells in the thalamus and the visual cortex, that behave in the manner predicted by Hering (De Valois & others, 1966; Jameson & Hurvich, 1989).

As you think back about the history of research and theories on color vision just presented, you will perhaps agree with me that it is a lovely illustration of the interplay of behavioral and physiological studies. The trichromatic and opponent-process theories were developed, in the nineteenth century, from behavioral evidence having to do with the perceptual effects of additive color mixing, before anything was known about the physiology of receptors and neurons. Later, both theories were confirmed physiologically, and today physiologists and psychologists are continuing to work out the finer details of the neural mechanisms through which they operate.

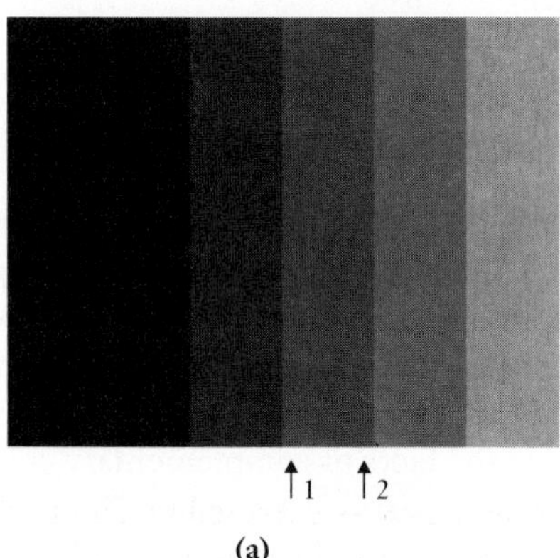

(a)

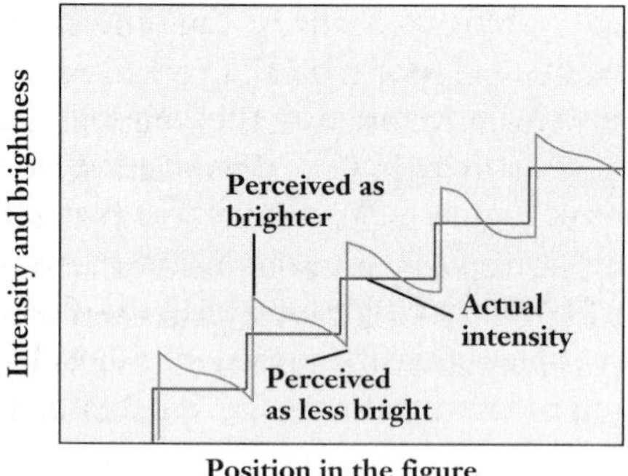

(b)

Figure 8.23 ***Enhancement of contrast***

(a) Each solid gray band appears lighter near its boundary with a darker band, and darker near its boundary with a lighter band. Compare the perceived brightness just above arrow 1 with that just above arrow 2, for example. The graph (b) shows how the perceived brightness changes across the figure, compared with the actual physical intensity of the reflected light. (Adapted from Matlin, 1988.)

The Coding of Light Intensity Patterns

The ultimate purpose of vision, in humans at least, is not to detect the simple presence or absence of light or differing wavelengths, but rather to identify objects. Color vision helps us in this task, because different objects have different pigments and therefore appear as different colors. But other aspects of our vision also contribute to object identification. The main cue besides wavelength and resultant color is *intensity* (amount of light reflected) and resultant brightness. The pencil on my desk not only reflects different wavelengths of light compared to its background (the desk), but also reflects a different intensity of light, which would allow me to see it as lighter or darker than the desk even in a black-and-white photograph. How does the visual system organize information about variations in light intensity in a way that helps us identify objects?

■ **24.** ***How can the visual system's ability to exaggerate contrast be demonstrated, and how does that ability help us to identify objects?***

Enhancement of Contrast

Objects are defined principally by their *contours* (their edges or borders). Visually (ignoring color), contours are lines of contrast created when one degree of brightness is juxtaposed against another. The visual system exaggerates that contrast, thereby increasing the clarity of our visual perceptions.

Stated differently, a greater difference in brightness between adjacent visual stimuli is registered by the visual system than would be registered by a machine faithfully recording the actual physical difference in the light. If you look at a television screen that is turned off it appears a relatively light shade of gray. Yet when it is turned on the same screen can create the impression of black objects, even though no part of the screen can send less light to the eye when the screen is on than when it is off. The same intensity of light that formerly looked gray looks black when surrounded by higher-intensity light. This is an example of heightened contrast. Another example which shows that contrast enhancement occurs maximally at borders, can be seen in Figure 8.23.

A clue to the mechanism by which the nervous system enhances contrast came from work by Stephen Kuffler (1953), who recorded the activity of individual gan-

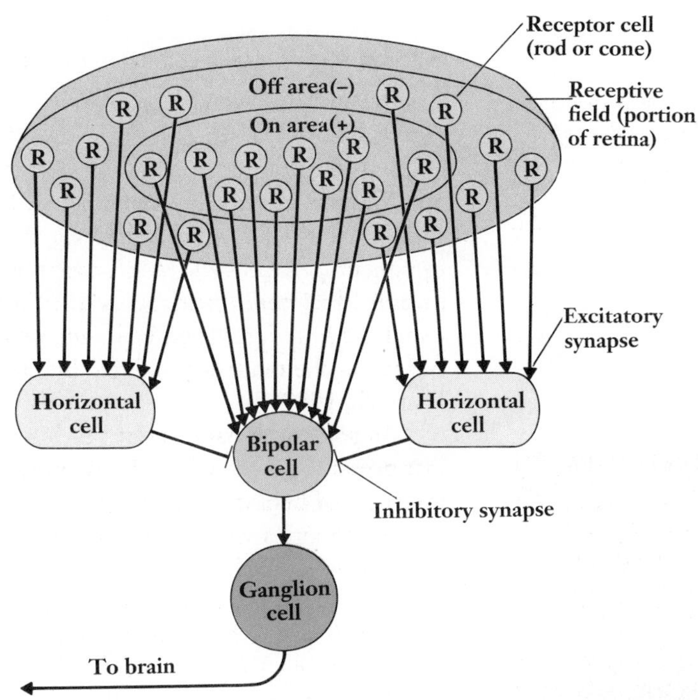

Figure 8.24 ***Neural explanation of* on *and* off *receptive-field areas for bipolar and ganglion cells***

The simplified diagram traces the neural connections between light receptors (rods and cones) and a ganglion cell into which their impulses feed. Receptors in the *on* area of the receptive field directly excite the bipolar cell. Receptors in the *off* area excite horizontal cells, which then inhibit the bipolar cell. The resulting activity in the bipolar cell is then transmitted to the ganglion cell. (Adapted from De Valois & De Valois, 1988).

■ **25.** ***How do connections from receptor cells to ganglion cells produce* on *and* off *receptive field areas and provide a basis for the coding of contrast?***

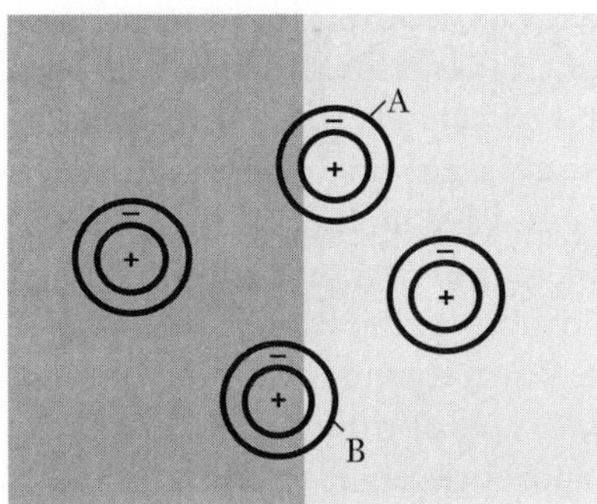

Figure 8.25 ***Neural explanation of contrast heightening***

Depicted here are the receptive fields of four ganglion cells that fall within adjacent rectangles of light striking the retina. For simplicity, only receptive fields with *on* centers (+) and *off* surrounds (–) are shown. Cells whose receptive fields lie entirely within either rectangle will be relatively unaffected because their *on* and *off* areas will be equally stimulated, but cells whose receptive fields overlap the edge will be affected. The cell whose receptive field is marked A will show increased activity, and the cell whose receptive field is marked B will show decreased activity.

glion cells (the cells whose axons form the optic nerve, as depicted in Figure 8.16) in anesthetized cats while stimulating various parts of the retina with small spots of light. He found that any given ganglion cell produces a relatively steady baseline rate of action potentials when not stimulated, and that its activity could be either increased or decreased by stimulation in different parts of the cell's retinal receptive field. That is, he found that the receptive fields for most ganglion cells contain two portions, an *on* portion where light increases activity in the cell, and an *off* portion where light decreases activity. These fields are circular in shape, with the *on* and *off* regions arranged concentrically, such that a given receptive field has either an *on* or *off* center and an opposite surround. Figure 8.24 shows the pattern of connections from receptors to the ganglion cell that could create such receptive fields. An important consequence is that ganglion cells are more sensitive to contrast than to uniform areas of illumination.

With the help of Figure 8.25 you can understand how Kuffler's discovery can explain contrast heightening at edges. When you look at the figure, the areas of light from the two gray rectangles strike adjacent patches on your retina. Ganglion cells whose receptive fields lie entirely within one patch or the other will be relatively unaffected, because the light acts uniformly on the *on* and *off* areas of their receptive fields (indicated by + and – signs in the figure), which tend to cancel one another out. But ganglion cells whose receptive fields overlap the two patches will be strongly affected. For example, the ganglion cell whose receptive field is marked A in the figure will show increased activity because its *on* area receives more total light than does its *off* area (its entire *on* area is on the lighter side but part of its *off* area is on the darker side). Similarly, the ganglion cell whose receptive field is marked B will show decreased activity, because its *off* area receives more total light than does its *on* area. Similarly, in your eyes the whole set of ganglion cells whose receptive field centers lie just to the right of the edge will signal the relative presence of light, and the whole set whose receptive field centers lie just to the left will signal the relative absence of light, thereby causing the edge to stand out in your visual experience.

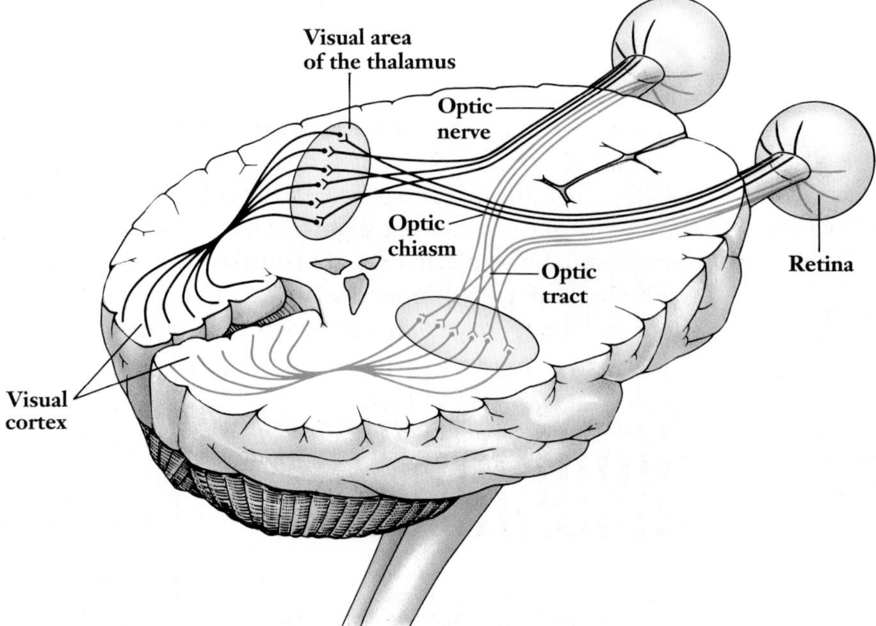

Figure 8.26 ***Pathway from the eyes to the visual cortex***

Neurons in the optic nerves come together at the optic chiasm at the base of the brain and form the optic tracts, which run to nuclei in the thalamus, where they synapse on neurons that run to the visual cortex.

Coding the Orientation of Contrasting Elements

To identify objects, we must detect not only contrast, but also the orientation, or slant, of contrasting areas. The contours that define the sharpened point of my pencil have a different slant than do the long, parallel contours that define most of the pencil's boundary. A few years after Kuffler's pioneering work, David Hubel and Torsten Wiesel (1962, 1979) performed similar studies with cats and monkeys, which led to their winning a Nobel prize in 1981. Rather than recording from ganglion cells, they recorded the electrical activity of individual neurons in the primary visual area of the cortex, which receive input from the eyes (see Figure 8.26).

Hubel and Wiesel found that the receptive fields for neurons in the visual cortex are not circular areas on the retina, as Kuffler had found for ganglion cells, but rather are oblong areas on the retina, with *on* and *off* regions that run parallel to each other along the length of the oblong. For some cells, one whole side of the field is an *on* area and the other side is an *off* area (see Example a in Figure 8.27). These cells respond best when the edge between an area of dark and light is aligned precisely along the line separating the *on* and *off* portions of the receptive field. For other cells, either an *on* or *off* area runs lengthwise down the middle of the oblong, with its opposite on either side (see Examples b, c, and d in Figure 8.27). These cells respond best to narrow bars of light or dark appropriately placed in the receptive field.

Unlike ganglion cells, cells in the visual cortex are sensitive to the orientation of the edges or bars that stimulate them. The cells respond maximally when the edge or bar of light is slanted at the same orientation as the long axis of the oblong visual field (again see Figure 8.27). Hubel and Wiesel found that as they went from

Figure 8.27 ***Retinal receptive fields for four cells of the visual cortex***

In each example, the whole oval represents the area on the retina where a change in lighting can affect the rate of action potentials in the cortical cell. Areas with plus signs (*on* areas) are places where a spot of light increases activity in the cell, and areas with minus signs (*off* areas) are places where a spot of light decreases activity in the cell. The best stimulus for eliciting a high rate of response in the cell is shown to the right of each receptive field.

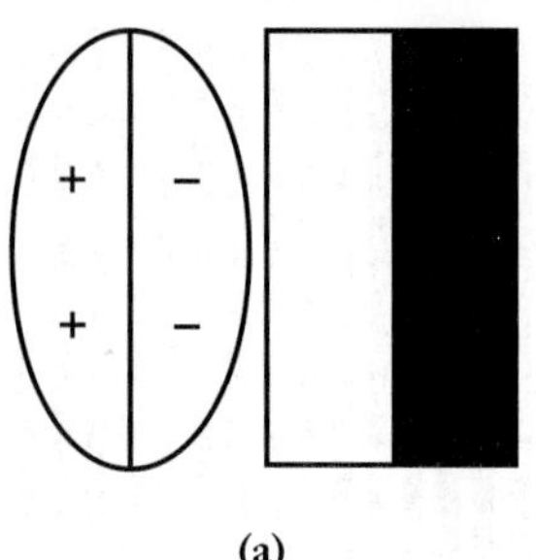

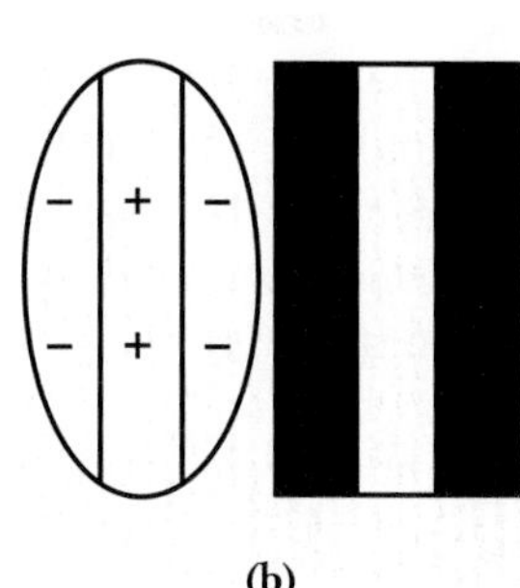

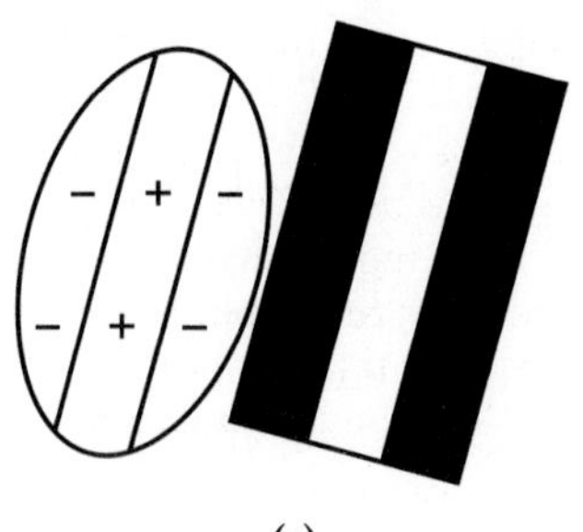

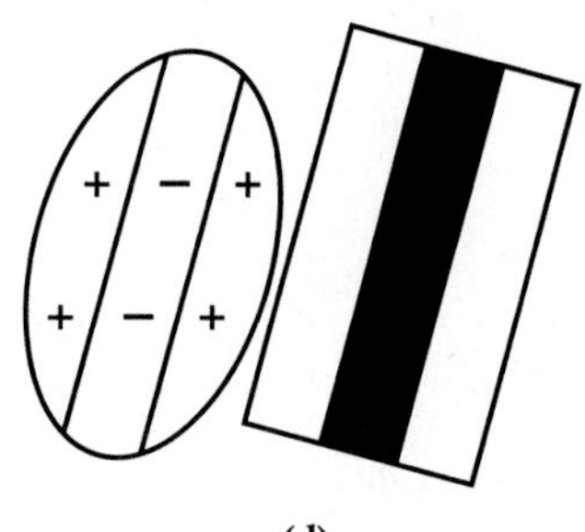

column to column of cells in the visual cortex, a systematic change occurred in the orientation to which the cells were most responsive. For example, in one column all cells might be most responsive to a vertical bar, in the next column they might be most responsive to a bar slightly rotated clockwise, and so on. Thus, these neurons, taken as a whole, have the potential to keep track of the relative orientation of each contrasting area in a visual scene. They are believed to provide the neural basis for an early stage in the detection of patterns and the identification of objects.

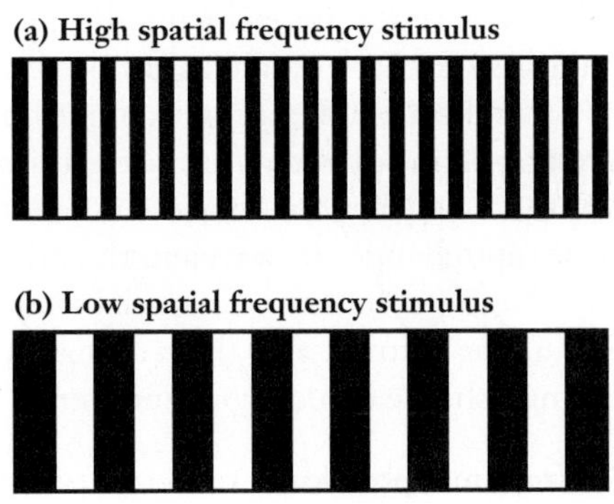

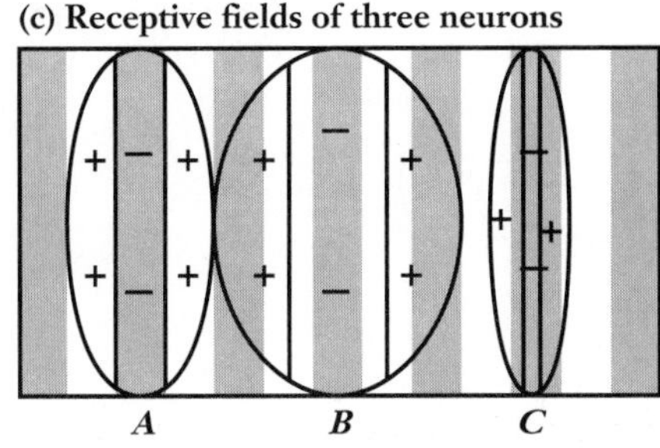

Figure 8.28 ***Spatial frequency***
A stimulus of higher spatial frequency (a) produces an image on the retina that contains more repeating elements per unit of distance than a stimulus of lower spatial frequency (b). Some visual neurons respond more strongly to higher spatial frequencies, others to lower spatial frequencies, depending on the nature of the neuron's receptive field. Depicted in (c) are the receptive fields of three cortical neurons superimposed on the retinal image of a gridlike stimulus. This stimulus evokes the strongest response from the neuron with receptive field *A* because its *on* and *off* areas are the same width as the bars of the image. The neuron with receptive field *B* does not respond strongly because its *on* and *off* areas are too wide for the grid; this neuron would respond better to a lower spatial frequency. The neuron with receptive field *C* does not respond strongly because its *on* and *off* areas are too narrow; this neuron would respond better to a higher spatial frequency.

Spatial Frequency Coding

The neurons studied by Hubel and Wiesel are sensitive not only to the orientation of bars and edges, but also to a characteristic called ***spatial frequency*** (De Valois & De Valois, 1988). In a pattern of repeating elements, spatial frequency is the number of repetitions per unit distance in the pattern's image on the retina. Figure 8.28 shows two stimuli with different spatial frequencies, and it also shows how the width of *on* and *off* receptive-field regions can provide the basis for distinguishing one spatial frequency from another. To demonstrate that your own visual system contains units that are sensitive to spatial frequency, follow the directions in Figure 8.29.

■ **26. *How can cortical neurons code the spatial frequency of repeated pattern elements, and why might such coding be valuable in identifying objects?***

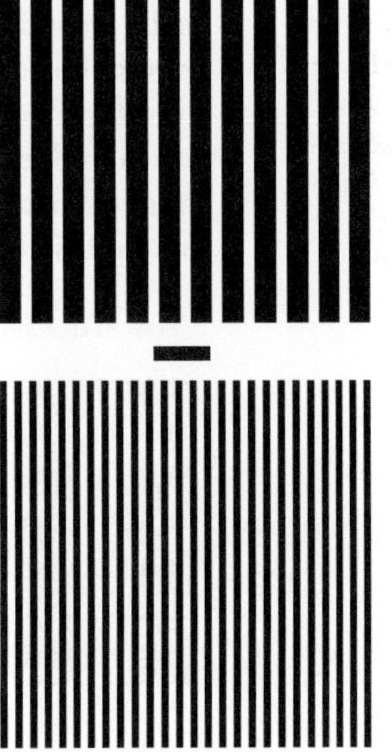

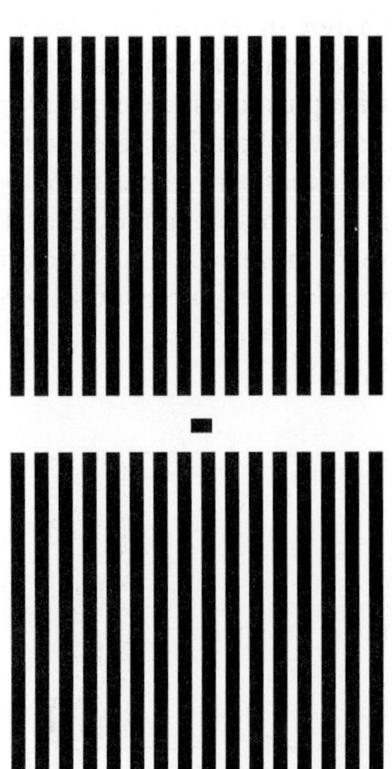

Figure 8.29 ***An adaptation effect based on spatial frequency***
Look at the two left-hand gratings by moving your eyes back and forth along the horizontal line between them for a full minute. Then shift your focus to the dot between the two right-hand gratings. The bars of the upper grating will temporarily appear more closely spaced (higher in frequency) than those in the lower grating, even though the two gratings are physically identical. This illusion can be explained physiologically as follows: When you looked at the left-hand grids, neurons sensitive to lower spatial frequencies in the upper part of your visual field (above the bar) became fatigued, as did neurons sensitive to higher spatial frequencies in the lower part of your visual field. This fatigue tipped the balance of response, so that when you looked at the grids of intermediate spatial frequency in the right part of the figure, the upper grid activated fewer lower-frequency neurons than it normally would, causing it to appear higher in spatial frequency; and the opposite was true for the lower grid. Notice how the reasoning here is similar to that for the color afterimage demonstration in Figure 8.22. (Based on Blakemore & Sutton, 1969.)

Vision researchers today are very interested in spatial frequency primarily because of its relation to a procedure, called Fourier analysis, by which any possible pattern of intensity changes in a visual scene can be described in terms of multiple, overlapping, regular, wavelike patterns. Fourier analysis is the most efficient means that mathematicians have been able to devise for describing all possible visual patterns, and some researchers suggest that the nervous system may use this same efficient code. For our purposes, however, an easier-to-understand rationale for interest in spatial frequency lies in the observation that the visual world in fact contains many repeating elements. Ripples on a pond, blades of grass in a field, leaves along a stem, bark on a tree trunk, scales on a fish, spots on a leopard—one could go on and on enumerating examples of repeating visual patterns found in nature. Such repeating elements are sometimes referred to as the *visual texture* of an object. Contours between one object and another in our visual world are defined not just by abrupt changes in wavelength and intensity, but also by abrupt changes in texture. Neurons sensitive to spatial frequency are ideally designed to code information about texture, and their doing so may be a crucial aspect of our capacity to distinguish one object from another.

Surface Interpolation

■ **27.** ***How can surface interpolation be demonstrated, and what might be the value of this process in normal vision?***

Our visual system seems to abide by the following rule: *In the absence of information to the contrary, assume that any given area in a visual scene has the same color, brightness, and texture as the immediately surrounding areas.* When researchers produce a gap in a visual scene by preventing their subjects' eyes from receiving any information at all from a specific area, the subjects do not detect a gap; the gap is filled in perceptually with a surface identical to that surrounding it (Ramachandran, 1992; Ramachandran & Gregory, 1991.) This filling-in process is called *surface interpolation.* If the blind-spot demonstration described in Figure 8.14 worked for you, then you experienced an effect of surface interpolation. The bird disappeared, but the area previously occupied by the bird did not—it probably looked yellow and had black bars running through it.

Surface interpolation may make normal vision more efficient than it otherwise would be. Because of surface interpolation, visual neurons do not have to keep constant track of every single spot in the visual field. By devoting fewer resources to the analysis of information within uniform surfaces, the visual system might devote more resources to areas where surfaces change, which typically define objects' boundaries. The neural mechanism of surface interpolation is not yet known, but a clue may lie in the recent discovery of neurons that run horizontally through the visual cortex and interconnect neurons that receive input from different parts of the retina (Gilbert & Wiesel, 1992). Perhaps, in the absence of direct input, neurons in the visual cortex that normally respond to vertical black bars at a particular retinal location are driven, through horizontal connections, by neurons that are responding to vertical black bars in adjacent parts of the visual field.

Toward a Brain-Based Model of Visual Perception

The cortical visual neurons that you have just been reading about lie in a relatively small area in the rear-most part of the occipital lobe. But this is only the first way station for visual information in the cortex, not the last. It sends outputs to many other visual-processing areas, some of which lie in adjacent parts of the occipital lobe and others of which lie in the temporal and parietal lobes. Researchers estimate that in humans somewhere between 25 and 40 percent of the entire cerebral cortex is devoted to analyzing visual information (Graham, 1992), and an even higher percentage may be so devoted in other primates (Van Essen & others, 1992).

28. *What happens to visual information at neural stations in the cortex beyond the primary receiving area?*

Research on the various visual areas of the brain has begun to produce a general brain-based model of visual perception (Graham, 1992; Van Essen & others, 1992). The first cortical way station, just described, contains neurons that are sensitive to all the important features of visual stimuli—their intensity, wavelength, orientation, spatial frequency, movement, and so on. But somehow, through the pattern of neural connections, these different features are separated from one another at subsequent stations. Thus, visual neurons in one area of the cortex are sensitive primarily to wavelength, those in another are sensitive primarily to spatial frequency, those in another primarily to movement, and so on. This separate processing of different features by different areas of the cortex explains why people who have had a stroke that damages part of the cortex can lose the ability to see colors without losing the ability to see contours, or lose the ability to see movements without losing the ability to see colors or contours (Kolb & Whishaw, 1990; Livingstone & Hubel, 1988). At later stages, neurons must somehow put all of that information back together so that we can see whole objects in which all of the features are combined.

In a fascinating essay entitled "The Man Who Mistook His Wife for a Hat," Oliver Sacks (1970), a neurologist, described the plight of a brain-damaged patient who could see all of the elementary features of objects (their color, contours, movements, and so on) and could recognize abstract geometric shapes (such as cubes and spheres), but could not recognize the more complex objects that make up the everyday visual world. When Sacks showed the man a rose and asked him to identify it, his response was, "About six inches in length. A convoluted red form with a linear green attachment. It lacks the simple symmetry of the Platonic solids, although it may have a higher symmetry of its own. . . ." After a period of such reasoning about its parts, he finally guessed, uncertainly, that it might be some kind of flower. Then Sacks asked him to smell it. "Beautiful!" he exclaimed. "An early rose. What a heavenly smell!" He could tell a rose by smell but not by sight, even though he could see every one of its features and could put some of them together, such as the greenness and the longness of the stem. How is it that in those of us with normal visual perception all of the features of a rose come effortlessly together, so that we see immediately that it is a rose, without consciously noticing the more abstract elements of which it is composed? That is the kind of question to which we do not yet know the answer physiologically. It will be addressed in a nonphysiological fashion in the next chapter.

Pain

From the beauty of a rose we move to the sensation you might get from its thorns. Pain is a body sense. When you hear, see, or touch something, you experience the sensation as coming from the external world; but when you feel pain, you experience it as coming from your own body. If you cut yourself with a knife, your feeling of pain is a sense not of the knife (that comes from your vision and touch), but of your own bodily state. Pain is not only a sense but also a drive. A person in pain is motivated both to reduce the pain and to avoid future behaviors like the one that produced it (such as careless handling of knives and rose bushes).

The value of pain—the reason, presumably, that it came about in evolution—is dramatically illustrated by those rare, unlucky people who are born with a genetic disorder that makes them insensitive to pain (Melzack & Wall, 1982). They can experience all other sensations, including touch and temperature, and they can even report increasing intensities of these feelings, but pain itself, with its motivating qualities, is missing. Children with this disorder are not motivated to remove their hand from a hot stove, or to refrain from chewing on their tongue as they eat, or to change their body position (as most of us do from minute to minute) to relieve the strain on muscles and joints. Even if they are constantly watched throughout their childhood, and even if they learn intellectually to avoid certain activities, people with this disorder usually die young from the tissue deterioration or infections that result from their wounds.

Neural Pathways for Pain

Anatomically, pain is closely related to the other cutaneous (skin) senses, touch and temperature. For all of these senses, the receptors are the sensory neurons themselves, which have receptive endings in the skin and long axons that enter the central nervous system by way of a spinal nerve or (in the case of neurons coming from the head) a cranial nerve. Pain neurons are thinner than other neurons from the skin, and their sensitive terminals, called ***free nerve endings***, are not encased in special capsules, or end organs, as are the endings of touch and temperature receptors (see Figure 8.30). Free nerve endings can be found in all body tissues from which pain is sensed, not just the skin but also the pulp of the teeth (from which comes the dreaded toothache), muscles (giving us the pain of cramps and muscle aches), membranes around bones and joints (from which we experience arthritis), and various visceral organs (giving us stomachaches and other inner pains).

■ **29. *What is the anatomical basis, in both the peripheral and central nervous systems, for a distinction between fast and slow pain?***

Two different types of peripheral neurons are involved in pain. In one category are the very thin, unmyelinated, slow-conducting neurons called C *fibers*, and in the other are thicker, myelinated, faster-conducting neurons called *A-delta fibers* (again see Figure 8.30). When your skin is bruised or burned you feel two different waves of pain—an initial *fast*, sharp, highly localized pain followed by a *slow*, dull, more diffuse, often burning pain. The fast pain is believed to be mediated by A-delta fibers, and the slow by C fibers (Jessell & Kelly, 1991). The terminals of A-delta fibers are activated by strong physical pressure or temperature extremes, and those of C fibers are believed to be activated by the chemical changes that occur in the tissue surrounding them when the tissue is physically damaged. Chemical changes in damaged tissue also sensitize the free nerve endings of both C fibers and A-delta fibers, such that they become more responsive to subsequent stimulation. That may help explain why even a light touch on a recently burned or wounded area of skin can be very painful (Jessell & Kelly, 1991).

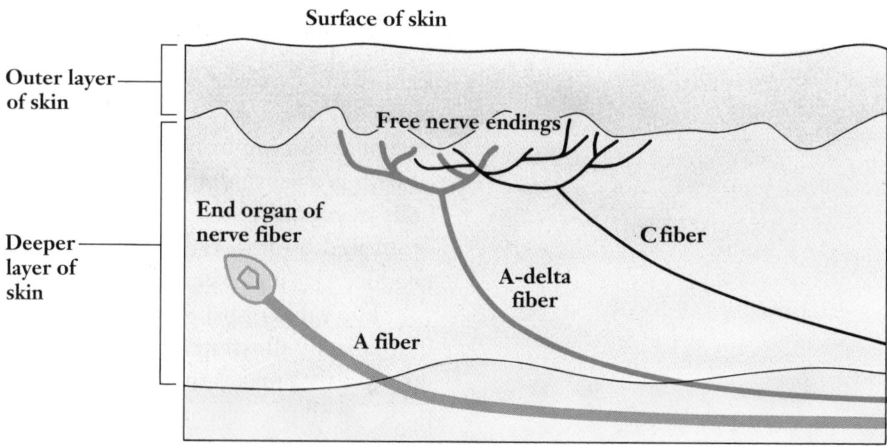

Figure 8.30 ***Pain receptors in the skin*** The pain receptors are the sensitive endings of sensory neurons, called *free nerve endings*. Slow, diffuse pain is carried by the very thin C fibers; fast, localized pain by the thicker A-delta fibers; and the sense of touch by still thicker (and faster) A fibers.

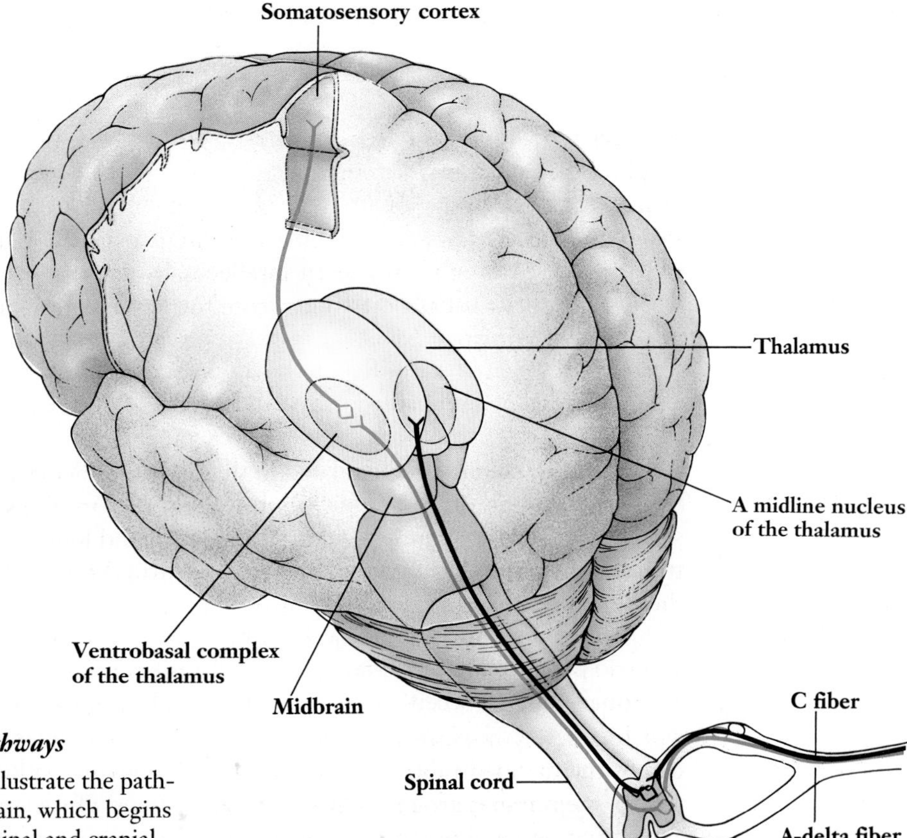

Figure 8.31 ***Pain pathways***

The red neurons here illustrate the pathway for fast, localized pain, which begins with A-delta fibers in spinal and cranial nerves and ends in the somatosensory cortex. The black neurons illustrate part of the pathway for slow, diffuse pain, which begins with C fibers in spinal and cranial nerves. Not shown are the slow-pain neurons that run from the midline nuclei of the thalamus to various areas of the cerebral cortex and limbic system.

The two systems of pain—fast and slow—maintain their distinctiveness in the central nervous system as well as peripherally, sending their input to different parts of the thalamus (see Figure 8.31). The A-delta fibers synapse on cells in the spinal cord that lead to an area of the thalamus called the *ventrobasal complex*. This area also receives neurons that mediate the sense of touch, and it sends its output to the somatosensory area of the cerebral cortex—the same area that receives input from all of the skin and muscle senses. The somatosensory cortex has localized areas that receive input from specific portions of the body (as was shown in Figure 6.11), and this point-to-point organization may underlie our ability to localize the place on the skin from which either touch or pain originates.

The C fibers, in contrast, synapse on neurons in the spinal cord that lead to a set of *midline nuclei* in the thalamus, which in turn send their output to many higher brain areas, including the frontal lobe of the cerebral cortex. Surgical studies aimed at relieving pain in late-stage cancer patients have shown that lesions placed in the midline nuclei successfully relieve (at least for a period of time) deep, chronic pain without abolishing the patient's sense of touch or the fast, acute pain that is mediated by A-delta fibers (Mark & others, 1963).

■ **30.** ***What is one line of evidence that the brain's pain mechanisms can become active without sensory input?***

The experience of pain, even of well-localized pain, does not always originate from stimulation of pain receptors. This fact is altogether too well known by those who have had a limb amputated. Such people often feel the missing limb as if it were still present, and often feel pain from that limb—an experience called *phantom-limb pain*. Such pain can persist even if all of the nerves from the limb's stump are destroyed, and even if the pain pathways entering the brain from the spinal cord are destroyed (Melzack, 1992). Apparently, in such cases the brain's mechanism for experiencing pain and assigning that experience to a particular body location can be activated even without sensory input from that part of the body. In fact, the *lack* of sensory input might help disinhibit that mechanism, accounting for the phantom-limb pain.

The Inhibition of Pain

Neural and Chemical Mechanisms of Pain Reduction

31. *How can pain input be inhibited at its entry into the central nervous system, and how might endorphins be involved in this process?*

In 1965, Ronald Melzack and Patrick Wall (1965, 1982) proposed a theory about pain and its inhibition called the ***gate-control theory***. In essence, the theory holds that the experience of pain will occur only if input from peripheral pain neurons passes through a "gate" located at the point where the neurons enter the spinal cord and lower brainstem. Research has since proven the theory to be correct and has identified a neural pathway involved in control of the gate. Neurons whose cell bodies lie in a portion of the midbrain called the *periaqueductal gray* (abbreviated PAG) have axons that descend to terminate on inhibitory neurons in the lower brainstem and spinal cord (Jessell & Kelly, 1991). When the PAG neurons are active they excite the inhibitory neurons, which in turn inhibit transmission from the peripheral neurons to neurons that would normally carry pain messages to the thalamus and cortex (see Figure 8.32).

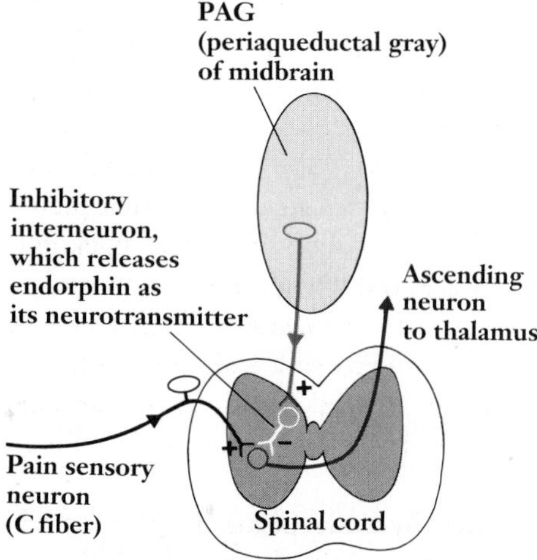

Figure 8.32 ***Pain-inhibiting system***

As illustrated here, activity in the midbrain's PAG inhibits pain input at its points of entry in the spinal cord and lower brainstem.

Electrical stimulation of the PAG has a powerful analgesic (pain-reducing) effect—so powerful, in fact, that abdominal surgery can be performed without drugs in animals that are receiving such stimulation (Reynolds, 1969). Electrical stimulation of this area has also been used successfully in humans to reduce or abolish chronic pain unrelievable by other means (Hosobuchi & others, 1979). The PAG is also believed to be the main site at which opiate drugs (derivatives of opium), such as *morphine*, have their pain-relieving effects. Morphine easily passes into the brain and is taken up at special binding sites on neurons in various parts of the brain, including the PAG. Research with animals has shown that morphine increases neural activity in the PAG, and that even a tiny amount of the drug, too small to have an effect if injected elsewhere, relieves pain if injected directly into the PAG (Basbaum & Fields, 1984).

Of course, the PAG and its pain-inhibiting system did not evolve to respond specifically to morphine or other substances foreign to the body. Its basic function is to mediate the body's *own* capacity to reduce pain. We now know that certain chemicals produced within the body act like morphine to relieve pain. These chemicals are collectively called ***endorphins***, a term that is short for *endogenous morphine-like substances* (*endogenous* means created within the body). Some endorphins are produced in the brain or spinal cord and serve as neurotransmitters. Others are secreted from the pituitary and adrenal glands, as hormones, into the blood, and have a variety of effects both peripherally and in the central nervous system (Henry, 1986). Endorphins are believed to inhibit pain by acting both in the PAG and at the point that pain-carrying neurons enter the spinal cord and lower brainstem (again see Figure 8.32).

Stress-Induced and Belief-Induced Analgesia

During his search for the source of the Nile, the famous explorer David Livingston was attacked by a lion. He survived the incident and later wrote that although the lion shook him "as a terrier does a rat" and crushed his shoulder, he had felt "no sense of pain nor feeling of terror, though quite conscious of all that was happening" (Livingston, 1857). Other people have had similar experiences. For example, soldiers severely wounded in battle often do not notice their wounds until the battle is over. We are apparently endowed with a mechanism that prevents us from feeling pain at times when, for survival purposes, it is best to ignore our wounds. An animal or person faced with a predator or similar threat cannot afford to nurse a wound or favor it by limping; all resources must be used to fight or flee. There is now good evidence that ***stress-induced analgesia***, as this phenomenon is called, occurs in response to many forms of stressful stimulation and is at least partly depen-

■ **32. *What is some evidence that stress-induced and placebo-induced analgesia are at least partly mediated by endorphins?***

dent on endorphins. Endorphins are secreted along with various other hormones by the pituitary and adrenal glands as part of the body's general response to stressful events (Terman & others, 1984).

In one study of stress-induced analgesia, rats that were subjected to a series of electric shocks to their feet (the source of stress) became relatively insensitive to pain for several minutes afterward, as indicated by their lack of response to normally painful heat that was applied to their tails (Lewis & others, 1980). Rats treated with either a drug that blocks the action of endorphins or one that blocks their release did not show this stress-induced analgesia, indicating that the effect must have been mediated by endorphins. In similar experiments, the mere presence of a cat produced analgesia in rats (Lichtman & Fanselow, 1990); a stressful math test produced analgesia in students (Bandura & others, 1988); and films depicting combat produced analgesia in veterans who had experienced the trauma of war (Pitman & others, 1990). In all of these cases the analgesic effect was shown to depend on endorphins.

In humans, dramatic reduction in pain can also, at times, be produced by the power of *belief* or faith. Some religious groups engage in practices that most of us would regard as torture, yet the participants appear to feel no pain. One group in India, for example, practices a hook-hanging ritual. A man who has been chosen to represent the power of the gods is secured to a rope by two steel hooks that pierce the skin and muscles on his back. He hangs from this rope, swinging back and forth, while he blesses the children and the crops of the village. He is honored to have been chosen, and apparently feels little or no pain (Melzack & Wall, 1982). A less dramatic example in our culture, where faith is more often placed in science and medicine, is the *placebo effect* on pain. In many cases a pill or injection that contains no active substance (the placebo) can reduce pain in a person who believes that the drug is a painkiller.

The placebo effect is at least partly mediated by endorphins. In one experiment, people who had undergone a tooth extraction reported less pain if given a placebo than if not, and this reduction in pain was abolished in subjects who were treated with a drug that inhibits the action of endorphins (Levine & others, 1979). Other experiments have shown that various cognitive techniques for relieving pain, such as meditating on the idea that the pain is disconnected from the rest of the body, also work at least partly through endorphins (Bandura & others, 1987). Might the man hanging from a hook in India also be secreting high endorphins? Much remains to be learned about the brain's ability to control pain, but the discovery of the endorphin system has provided a tremendous boost to that endeavor.

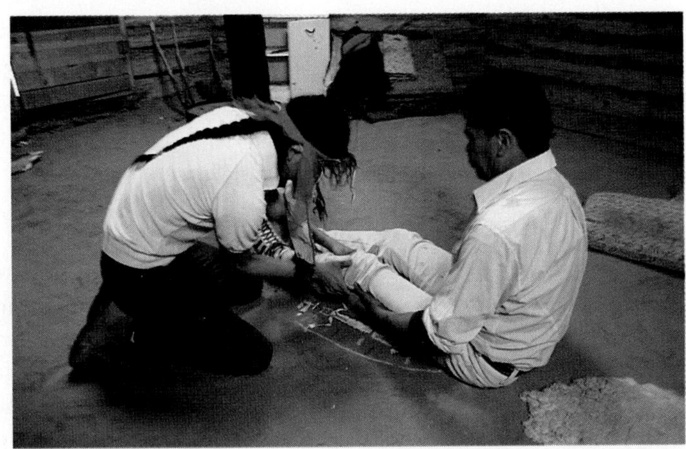

The power of faith

Ancient sand paintings and ancient belief systems are instruments of pain relief employed with apparent success by Native American healers.

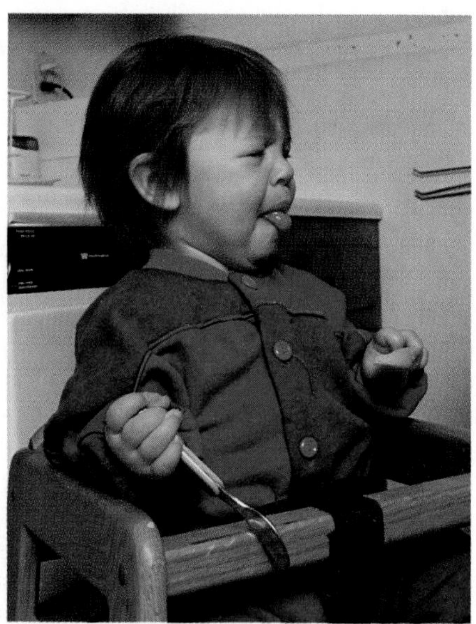

Yuck! Too sour

The sharp taste of a lemon may seem very sour to a young child and much less so to an adult. One of the many uses of psychophysical procedures is to track changes in sensitivity with age.

Psychophysics

Psychophysics, as you may recall, is the study of the relationship between the physical characteristics of a stimulus and the sensory experience that it produces (see Figure 8.1). The sensory experience is typically assessed by asking subjects to make some judgment about the stimulus, such as whether it is present or absent, or whether it is the same as or different from another stimulus. Many experiments already alluded to in this chapter were psychophysical, including the experiments on color mixing that led to the three-primaries law and the law of complementarity. Lights were shown in varying combinations, and people were asked to judge whether their color looked the same as or different from that of other lights.

This section describes some general psychophysical methods and findings concerning the detection of weak stimuli, the detection of small changes in stimuli, and the attempt to develop a general law relating the physical intensity of a stimulus to the intensity of the sensory experience it produces. As you will see, psychophysics is more mathematical than most other areas of psychology. That is one of the reasons why some psychologists find it exciting. Psychophysics is just the right cup of tea for those psychologists who like a degree of precision in their science, are drawn by the elegance of mathematics, and are fascinated by the idea that certain psychological phenomena can be described meaningfully with algebraic equations.

Detecting Weak Stimuli and Small Differences

The Absolute Threshold, and Why It Is Not Absolute

■ **33. *What are some variables that influence the absolute threshold, and why must it be arrived at by averaging?***

How sensitive are our senses? What is the faintest sound that we can hear or the faintest light that we can see? Psychophysicists refer to the faintest detectable stimulus, of any given type, as the ***absolute threshold*** for that type of stimulus. The absolute threshold within any sensory system—let's take hearing as our example—depends on a number of variables. It depends on who is tested (some people have more sensitive hearing than others), the precise kind of stimulus used as the signal (we are more sensitive to sounds at some frequencies than at others), the precise conditions in which the test is conducted (such as the amount of background noise), and the exact way in which the threshold is defined (for example, it might be defined as the weakest stimulus permitting 50 percent correct detection, or the weakest stimulus permitting 75 percent correct detection).

You can see the influence of two of these variables by looking at Figure 8.33, which shows an *audiogram* for a typical 60-year-old and a typical 20-year-old. An

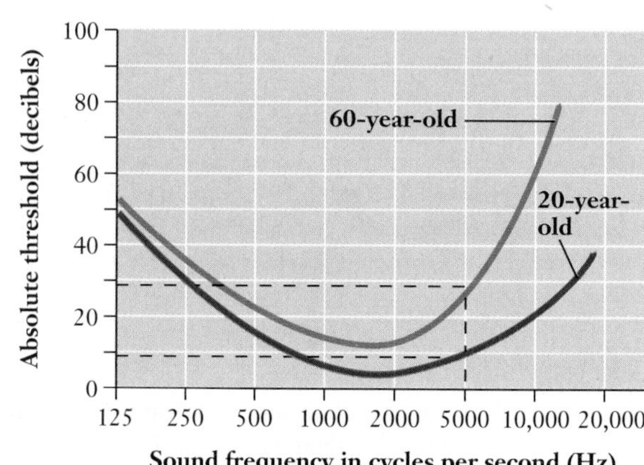

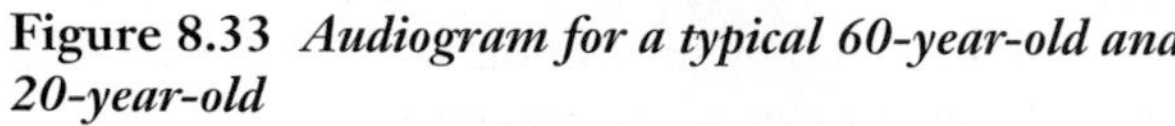

Figure 8.33 *Audiogram for a typical 60-year-old and 20-year-old*

The audiogram is a graph of the minimum intensity that the person can hear (the absolute threshold) for each tone frequency. Notice that the younger person has a lower threshold than the older person for each frequency, and the difference increases as the frequency rises. For example, the graph shows that for a 5000-Hz tone the 60-year-old's absolute threshold is about 30 dB and the 20-year-old's is about 10 dB.

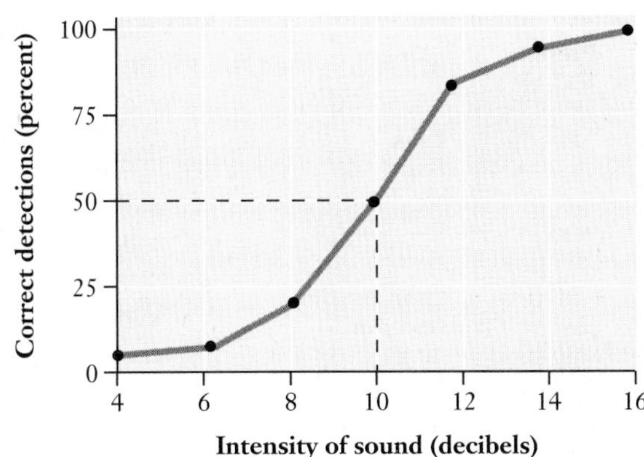

Figure 8.34 ***The absolute threshold is statistically derived*** If a stimulus—say, a 5000-Hz tone—is presented many times at each of several weak intensities, the proportion of times that the person correctly detects it increases as the intensity increases. Arbitrarily, the intensity at which correct detection occurs in 50 percent of the trials—in this case, 10 dB—is taken as the absolute threshold. (Data are hypothetical.)

audiogram is a graph depicting a person's absolute thresholds for tones of various frequencies. Notice that the 60-year-old has a higher absolute threshold than the 20-year-old at every frequency. That is, the tone must be more intense to be heard by the older person. The figure also shows how the absolute threshold varies with frequency. Both individuals are most sensitive (have the lowest thresholds) to tones in the range of 1000 to 3000 Hz. As the frequency becomes lower or higher than this, sensitivity decreases (the absolute threshold increases).

To determine a person's absolute threshold for a particular kind of stimulus (such as a 5000-Hz tone), a psychophysicist presents the stimulus many times, at various low intensities, each time asking the person if he or she detects it. The procedure sometimes also includes control trials in which the stimulus is not presented. When the stimulus is near the threshold level, it is sometimes detected and sometimes not, and sometimes the person believes the stimulus is present when it really isn't. Presumably, various random events—including outside noises and occurrences within the person's nervous system—may either mask the signal or mimic it. Thus, the absolute threshold is not truly "absolute," but rather is arrived at arbitrarily by statistical averaging. For a given study, it may be defined as that intensity of the stimulus that is detected on some specified percentage of the trials in which it is present (see Figure 8.34).

Signal Detection as a Decision-Making Task

■ **34.** ***How is the measure of absolute threshold affected by a liberal or conservative response bias, and how can the bias be assessed by a signal-detection experiment?***

A problem arising from the arbitrary nature of absolute thresholds is that reported stimulus detection depends not just on sensory ability, but also on *response bias*, the tendency to favor a particular response when uncertain about whether the stimulus is present or not. Some subjects might adopt a conservative response bias and say yes (present) only when certain that it is present. Others might adopt a liberal response bias and say yes when uncertain. Subjects who expect the stimulus to be present on most or all of the trials are more inclined to say yes on a given trial than those who expect that it will rarely be present. Also, those who are strongly motivated to detect the stimulus, even at the risk of sometimes saying that it is present when it isn't, will say yes more often than those who are less concerned about detecting it or more concerned about falsely reporting its presence.

Differences in subjective expectation and motivation take on great significance in signal-detection tasks in real-life settings. Consider, for example, a radiologist scanning x-ray images for faint signs of cancer. The likelihood of putting a particular set of x-rays in the possible-cancer pile versus the clean-bill-of-health pile may depend on (a) the radiologist's prior beliefs about the likelihood that the patient would have cancer, and (b) the balance between the radiologist's motivation, on the

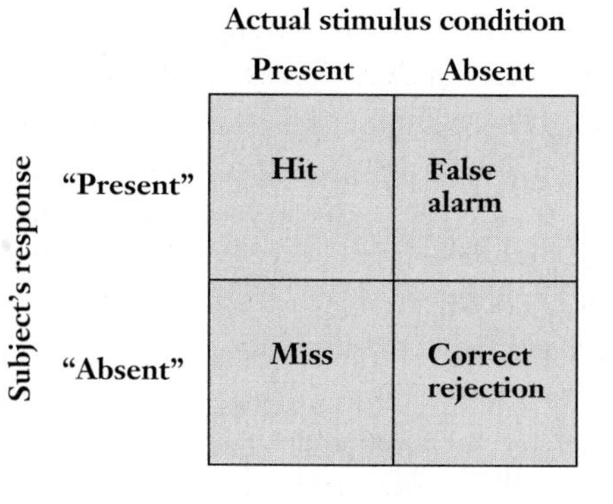

(a)
Possible outcomes
on each trial

Subject's response	Actual stimulus condition: Present	Actual stimulus condition: Absent
"Present"	Hit 90%	False alarm 30%
"Absent"	Miss 10%	Correct rejection 70%

(b)
Sample results with
liberal response bias

Subject's response	Actual stimulus condition: Present	Actual stimulus condition: Absent
"Present"	Hit 60%	False alarm 10%
"Absent"	Miss 40%	Correct rejection 90%

(c)
Sample results with
conservative response bias

Figure 8.35 ***Signal-detection outcomes***

Part (a) shows the definition of hits, misses, false alarms, and correct rejections. Parts (b) and (c) show hypothetical results for a person adopting a liberal or conservative response bias, with a signal near the absolute threshold. Notice that the liberal bias increases hits but also increases false alarms.

one hand, to detect cancer whenever it is present, and on the other hand, to avoid unduly frightening or inconveniencing patients when it is not present. Some radiologists are more liberal in their willingness to say "cancer may be present here," and others are more conservative.

To compare people's actual sensory ability, psychophysicists have developed ways to specify the degree to which a person responds according to a liberal or conservative bias and to correct for that bias. To do this, they include trials in which the stimulus is not present as well as trials in which it is, and then they separate the subject's responses into four categories: (1) *hits* (the stimulus is present and the subject reports sensing it); (2) *misses* (the stimulus is present and the subject reports not sensing it); (3) *false alarms* (the stimulus is absent and the subject reports sensing it); and (4) *correct rejections* (the stimulus is absent and the subject reports not sensing it). A liberal bias would increase the number of hits and false alarms and decrease the number of misses and correct rejections; and a conservative bias would have the opposite effect (see Figure 8.35). By comparing the proportion of hits to false alarms, psychophysicists can derive a measure of sensitivity that is independent of response bias, called *d prime* (written *d′*) (Green, 1964). The greater the ratio of hits to false alarms, the greater is the person's sensitivity to the stimulus. In real-life signal-detection tasks—such as radiologists looking at x-ray images, or airport guards scanning luggage with metal detectors—the hit and false-alarm rate, and hence the person's response bias and actual sensitivity to the signal, can be assessed by periodic tests with planted stimuli, which are known to contain or not contain the signal.

The Difference Threshold and Weber's Law

Whereas the absolute threshold is the minimum intensity of a stimulus that a person can detect, the ***difference threshold*** is the minimum difference that must exist between two stimuli for the person to detect them as different. To determine a difference threshold for sound intensity, a person is presented on each trial with a standard tone, always of the same intensity, and a comparison tone that is sometimes the same intensity as the standard tone and sometimes not, and is asked to report whether the two tones are the same or different. Like the absolute threshold, the difference threshold is a statistical concept. It is commonly defined as the amount of difference between the standard and comparison stimuli required for correct detection of the difference in 50 percent of the trials (although in some situations, where guessing would produce 50 percent correct, 75 percent is used as the criterion). Another name for the difference threshold is the ***just-noticeable difference***, abbreviated ***jnd***.

■ **35.** ***How did Weber derive a law from data on just-noticeable differences (jnd's)? How can Weber's law be used to predict the degree to which two stimuli must differ for a person to tell them apart?***

The first scientist to study the jnd systematically was the nineteenth century German physiologist Ernst Weber (1834). The question that interested Weber was this: What is the relationship between the jnd and the intensity (or magnitude) of the standard stimulus? That is, if the standard stimulus is increased in intensity, does the jnd stay the same, or does it change in some systematic way? In one series of experiments Weber applied this question to people's ability to judge differences between weights. On each trial he asked the subjects to pick up each of two weights (the standard weight and a comparison weight), one at a time, and judge which was heavier. Weber found that the jnd varied in direct proportion to the weight of the standard. Specifically, he found that for any standard weight that he used (within a certain range), the jnd was approximately 1/30 of the standard weight (Gescheider, 1976). Thus, a typical subject could just barely discriminate between a 15-gram and 15.5-gram weight, or between a 90-gram and 93-gram weight. In the first case the jnd was 0.5 gram, and in the second it was 3 grams, but in both cases it was 1/30 of the standard weight. In other experiments, Weber studied people's ability to discriminate between the lengths of two lines, one presented after the other, and again he found a constant proportionality between the standard stimulus and the difference threshold. For this task, however, the constant fraction was 1/100 rather than 1/30. Thus, a typical subject could just barely detect the difference between a 100- and a 101-millimeter line, or between a 1000- and a 1010-millimeter line.

Based on these and similar experiments, Weber formulated a general law, now called ***Weber's law***, stating that *the jnd for stimulus magnitude is a constant proportion of the magnitude of the standard stimulus.* The law can be abbreviated as

$$\text{jnd} = kM$$

in which M is the intensity or magnitude of the stimulus used as the standard and k is a proportionality constant referred to as the ***Weber fraction***, which is different for different sensory tasks (1/30 for weight judgment and 1/100 for length judgment in the examples above). Since Weber's time, psychophysical experiments have confirmed Weber's law for many different types of stimuli. The law holds rather well over a wide portion of the possible range of intensities or magnitudes for most types of stimuli, but not at the very low (near the absolute threshold) and very high ends of the range.

Relating the Psychological Amount of a Stimulus to the Physical Amount

When a physical stimulus increases, our sensory experience of it also increases. When a sound becomes more intense, we hear it as louder; when a light becomes more intense, we see it as brighter; and so on. Is it possible to specify in a mathematical equation the relationship between the magnitude of a stimulus and the magnitude of the sensory experience produced by it? Such an equation was proposed in the nineteenth century and tested experimentally and modified in the twentieth.

Fechner's Logarithmic Law

■ **36.** ***How did Fechner use Weber's law to derive a law relating sensory magnitude to the logarithm of stimulus magnitude?***

Gustav Fechner (1860/1966), like Weber a nineteenth-century German, used Weber's law to derive a mathematical relationship between stimulus magnitude and sensory magnitude. The jnd is measured in physical units (such as grams, or sound-pressure units), yet it reflects a sensory phenomenon, the just-noticeable difference between two sensations. Therefore, Fechner reasoned, the jnd could serve as a unit for relating physical and sensory magnitudes. His crucial assumption was that every jnd along a sensory dimension is equivalent to every other jnd along that dimension in the amount it adds to the sensory magnitude, and that jnd's can be added together. In other words, he assumed that a sound that is 100 jnd's above threshold would sound twice as loud as one that is 50 jnd's above threshold, or one-tenth as loud as one that is 1000 jnd's above threshold.

Fechner assumed that jnd's are subjectively equal, but he knew from Weber's work that they are not physically equal. As you just saw, the jnd is directly proportional to the magnitude of the original stimulus. Thus, Fechner assumed that the amount of physical change needed to create a constant sensory change is directly proportional to the magnitude of the stimulus, and he showed mathematically that this can be expressed as a logarithmic relationship (if you wish to see how he could prove this, turn to page A-9 of the Statistical Appendix at the back of the book). Thus, Fechner derived a general law, now called ***Fechner's law***, stating that *the magnitude of the sensory experience of a stimulus is directly proportional to the logarithm of the physical magnitude of the stimulus.* This law can be abbreviated as

$$S = c \log M$$

where S is the magnitude of the sensory experience, c is a proportionality constant, and M is the magnitude of the physical stimulus.

Table 8.3 ***Illustration of the relation between physical magnitude* (M) *and sensory magnitude* (S) *according to Fechner's law***

No. of light bulbs	M	S* (1 log M)	
1	100	2.00	+.30 (1→2)
2	200	2.30	
3	300	2.48	+.30 (2→4)
4	400	2.60	
5	500	2.70	
6	600	2.78	+.30 (4→8)
7	700	2.84	
8	800	2.90	

*In this hypothetical example, c in the formula $S = c \log M$ is 1. A change in c would change the values of S, but would not change the fact that each doubling of M adds a constant increment to S, which is the point that the table is designed to illustrate.

To gain a sense of the meaning of Fechner's law (if you are a bit foggy on logarithms), look at Table 8.3, which shows hypothetical data that are consistent with the law. Imagine a person judging the brightness of a room's illumination with 1 light bulb on, then 2 bulbs, then 3 bulbs, and so on. Although each successive bulb adds a constant amount (100 units) to the physical intensity (M) of the room's illumination, each bulb adds a progressively smaller amount to the perceived brightness (S). Thus, in the example, the second bulb adds 0.30 units to the brightness, the third adds another 0.18 units, the fourth adds 0.12, and so on. Notice too that every time the physical intensity (M) doubles, the sensed brightness (S) increases by a constant amount (0.30 units in the example). Stated differently, as the physical scale increases geometrically, the sensory scale increases arithmetically. That is the essence of a logarithmic relationship. Consequently, a huge intensity range on the physical scale is condensed to a much smaller range on the psychological scale.

Stevens's Power Law

■ **37.** ***How did Stevens test Fechner's law, and what did he find? How does Stevens's law differ from Fechner's?***

Although Fechner believed his law to be valid on theoretical grounds, he did not believe it could be tested experimentally. He wrote (in 1860), "A real measure of sensation would demand that we be able to call a given sensation twice, thrice, or so-and-so as many times as intense as another—but who would say such a thing?" (quoted by Stevens, 1975). The belief that people could not report the magnitudes of their sensations in a consistent way went relatively unchallenged until the early 1950s, when S. S. Stevens, a Harvard psychologist, began a series of experiments in which he asked people to do exactly that.

Stevens's technique, called the ***method of magnitude estimation***, was to ask subjects to assign numbers to the magnitudes of their sensations. For example, he would present a standard stimulus and call that a "10," and then he would present a comparison stimulus and ask the subject to give it a number that best approximated its sensory magnitude compared to that of the standard. Thus, a sensation that appeared to the subject to be twice that of the standard would be called "20," one that seemed half that of the standard would be called "5," and so on. Stevens found that people had little difficulty carrying out these instructions, and that their responses were remarkably consistent for any given set of stimuli.

If Fechner's law were correct, Stevens should have found that his subjects' magnitude estimates were directly proportional to the logarithms of the stimulus intensities he used. He found, however, that the logarithmic relationship was only roughly accurate for most senses, and very inaccurate for some senses, and that for every sense the results could be described better by a different mathematical relationship—a power relationship. Based on this, Stevens proposed a ***power law*** as an alternative to Fechner's logarithmic law. According to Stevens's power law, *the intensity of a sensation is directly proportional to the intensity of the physical stimulus raised by a constant power.* The law can be abbreviated as

$$S = cM^p$$

where S is the reported magnitude of the sensory experience, M is the physical magnitude of the stimulus, p is the power (or exponent) to which M must be raised (which differs from one sensory dimension to another), and c is a constant that depends on the size of the measurement units used.

How does Stevens's law compare to Fechner's? If you transform each side of the above equation logarithmically, the equation becomes:

$$\log S = \log (cM^p)$$

which can be rewritten as

$$\log S = \log c + p \log M$$

Because log c is simply a constant, the equation now shows that the logarithm of S is directly (linearly) related to the logarithm of M. In other words, whereas Fechner's law holds that the sensory magnitude is directly proportional to the logarithm of the physical magnitude, Stevens's law maintains that the *logarithm* of the sensory magnitude is directly proportional to the logarithm of the physical magnitude.

Stevens and his colleagues performed dozens of experiments, involving magnitude estimates for many different kinds of stimuli, and they almost always found that the results could be quite well represented by a power equation. For each kind of stimulus they could determine a unique exponent (p) to which the physical magnitude had to be raised to approximate the experienced magnitude. Table 8.4 shows the exponents that they compiled for several different kinds of stimuli. Notice that for most tasks shown in the table the exponent is less than 1, but for one task (estimating the length of a line) it is exactly 1, and for another (estimating the pain of an electric shock) it is greater than 1. In cases where p is less than 1, equal physical changes produce smaller sensory changes at the high end of the scale than at the low end, as was also true with Fechner's logarithmic law. When p is greater than 1, however, the opposite relationship holds. Thus, adding a certain amount of electric shock to a relatively strong shock produces a greater increase in pain than does adding the same amount to a relatively weak shock. Finally, when p is equal to 1,

Table 8.4 ***Power-law exponents for various stimuli***

Type of stimulus	Measured exponent (p)*
Brightness of a spot of light in the dark	0.33
Loudness of a 3000-cps tone	0.67
Smell of heptane	0.60
Taste of saccharine	0.80
Length of a line	1.00
Pain of an electrical shock on the fingers	3.50

*The exponent (p) is the power to which the stimulus magnitude must be raised to approximate the sensory magnitude.

Source: From *Psychophysics: Introduction to its perceptual, neural, and social prospects* (p.13) by S. S. Stevens, 1975, New York: Wiley.

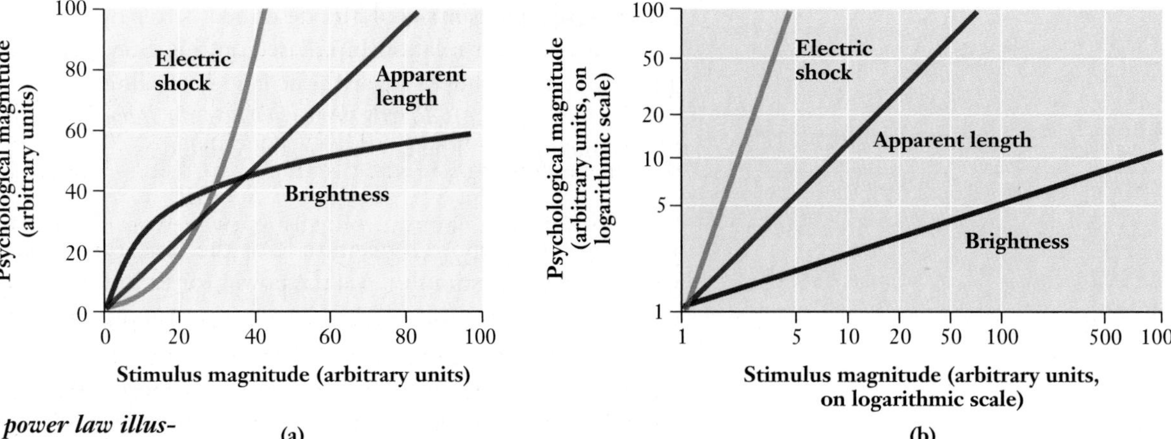

Figure 8.36 ***Stevens's power law illustrated for three sensory dimensions***

Graph (a) shows how subjects' estimates of the sensory magnitude that they experienced increased as the stimulus magnitude increased, separately for the pain of an electric shock, the length of a line, and the brightness of a spot of light. Notice that the curvature is upward or downward depending on whether the exponent, p, is greater or less than 1. Graph (b) depicts the same data (with different arbitrary units) after both scales have been converted to logarithms. Now all of the lines are straight. By definition, a power law specifies a relationship in which the logarithm of one variable is linearly related to the logarithm of the other. (Adapted from Stevens, 1962.)

38. ***What benefit of a power law over a logarithmic law might have led to the selection of a power law in the course of evolution?***

equal physical changes produce the same amount of sensory change whether one is starting with a strong or a weak stimulus. All of these relationships are graphically portrayed in Figure 8.36a. In Figure 8.36b, you can see that the results for each magnitude-estimation task fit a straight line when graphed on log-log coordinates—that is the proof of a power law. If Fechner's law had been correct, a straight line would have resulted from converting just the physical scale (the horizontal axis) to logarithms, without converting the sensory scale (the vertical axis) to logarithms.

Why a Power Law?

Why do our senses obey a power law for so many different kinds of stimuli? Is it just coincidence, or is there some advantage that would lead each sense, in the course of evolution, to operate in accordance with a power law? Stevens (1975) thought a good deal about that question, and the answer he suggested goes something like this:

Our world of stimuli is constantly changing. As we move closer to or farther from the sources of stimulation, or as day turns to dusk, the overall intensity of the energy reaching us from specific objects in the environment changes greatly. If we are to recognize the same scenes, sounds, and smells under such varying conditions, then we must extract those features of each stimulus constellation that remain constant. One such constancy is the ratio of the magnitudes of the stimulus elements with respect to each other.

As you move toward or away from a sound source, the ratio of the amplitudes of the various tones in the sound remains relatively constant, even though the overall amplitude increases or decreases greatly. Similarly, the ratio of light reflected from a darker compared to a lighter portion of a visual scene remains nearly constant as the overall intensity fades at dusk. A power law, and only a power law, preserves constant sensory ratios as the overall intensity waxes or wanes. (You can find a proof of this statement on page A-10 of the Statistical Appendix.) For example, in the case of the power function for brightness, with an exponent of 0.33, every eightfold change in light intensity results in a twofold change in apparent brightness, no matter where on the intensity continuum we start. Thus, if the light illuminating a visual scene decreases in physical intensity to one-eighth of what it was before, each part of the scene will appear half as bright as before, and the ratios of brightnesses among the parts will remain what they were before. The elegant feature of the power law, with p less than 1, is that it compresses large physical changes down to smaller sensory changes, as does the logarithmic law; but, unlike the logarithmic law, it does this while preserving the constancy of stimulus ratios.

Concluding Thoughts

Broad themes can easily get lost in a chapter that is full of details, such as the one that you have just read. As you review the chapter, you will find it useful to focus on the themes and organize the details around them. Here are four such themes:

1. The survival functions of sensory processes Our sensory systems, like all of the basic mechanisms underlying our behavior, evolved through natural selection based on their usefulness in promoting our ancestors' survival. They are not unbiased recorders of physical energies, but biological tools designed to pick out from the sea of energy around us the information that is potentially most useful. We are sensitive to some kinds of energies and not others, and, within the kinds to which we are sensitive, our senses extract and enhance some relationships and not others.

Here are some examples, described in the chapter, of how specific sensory processes might be understood in terms of their survival advantages: (a) Sensory adaptation (the decrease in sensitivity to prolonged, constant stimuli) helps us to ignore stimuli that remain unchanged and to attend most to changes in stimuli. (b) In vision, the heightening of contrast exaggerates the sensory effect of edges, so we see objects as standing out more sharply from their background than we would if our vision measured light intensities in an unbiased way. (c) Pain is a sensory system for warning us when our actions are damaging our tissues, and for motivating us to avoid such actions. But at times the necessity to respond to another threat overrides the advantage of favoring our wounds, and therefore we also evolved mechanisms for inhibiting pain. (d) The fact that our senses obey a power law in converting stimulus magnitude to sensory magnitude may have come about because the power law preserves the constancy of ratios, helping us recognize a pattern in sound or light as the same pattern when the overall intensity increases or decreases.

Had this chapter been about sensation in a species that inhabits a more confined niche than humans do, you would have read about sensory analyzers that respond specifically to prey, predators, or other important parts of that niche. For instance, the frog's retina contains "bug detectors," neurons that respond only to small, moving spots and that trigger tongue movements in the spot's direction; it also contains wavelength detectors ideally tuned to distinguish a blue pond from green grass and lily pads (Muntz, 1964).

2. Developing theories to explain behavior, and confirming the theories physiologically In essentially every subfield of psychology, researchers develop theories or models to explain what might happen inside the individual to produce or mediate the behavioral phenomena studied by that field. It is particularly exciting when the models are confirmed by discoveries about the nuts-and-bolts workings of the nervous system. In no other area of psychology has that form of excitement occurred as often as in the study of sensation. Here are some examples of the sequence from behavioral theory to physiological discovery that you read about in this chapter: (a) Helmholtz developed a theory to explain the fact that pitch perception is related to sound-wave frequencies, and Békésy later confirmed that theory (in modified form) through direct observations of the basilar membrane. (b) Young and Helmholtz developed the trichromatic theory to explain the three-primaries law of color mixing, and that theory was confirmed later by the discovery of three cone types. (c) Hering developed the opponent-process theory to explain the law of complementarity in color mixing, and that theory was confirmed later by the discovery of neurons that respond to wavelengths in opponent-process fashion. (d) Melzack and Wall developed the gate-control theory to explain the body's ability to shut off pain, and other researchers confirmed that theory (and elaborated on its details) through the discovery of a neural pathway that descends from the brain and inhibits pain input at its point of entry into the central nervous system.

3. The problem of objective assessment of subjective experience A problem running through all of psychology is that of assessing what is in people's minds through objective, behavioral means. In the study of sensation that problem can be confronted in a more straightforward way than in other areas of psychology because sensations are the aspects of mental life that are most reliably related to measurable aspects of the physical world. Psychophysics is the subfield that assesses these relationships most directly. Psychophysicists have developed means to assess the absolute threshold, the difference threshold, and the relative magnitude of one sensory experience compared to another, and they have tied these to measures of the physical stimulus. Psychologists in other fields sometimes borrow the methods of psychophysics to study subjective judgments that are far removed from raw sensations. The signal-detection procedure for assessing response bias has been applied in such tasks as the detection of guilt or innocence based on the kind of evidence that a jurist might hear; and Stevens's method of magnitude estimation has been used for such tasks as estimating the relative amount of pleasure that would be gained from winning various amounts of money.

4. Processes common to the various sensory systems Every sensory system has receptors, sensory neurons, and neural mechanisms in the brain. Thus, for every sensory system, certain basic questions can be asked: (a) What are the receptors, and how do they function to transduce some form of environmental energy in such a way as to change the rate of action potentials in sensory neurons? (b) How does the transduction process code the differing amounts and qualities of physical stimulation that we experience as different sensations? (c) How do neural mechanisms within the central nervous system modify sensory information as it goes from one way station to another, in ways that correspond with our sensory experiences? These questions might help guide your review of the physiology of hearing, vision, and pain.

Further Reading

James O. Pickles (1988). *An introduction to the physiology of hearing* (2nd ed.). San Diego: Academic Press.

This is an exceptionally clear, yet sophisticated and well-documented account of the mechanisms by which the ear and brain code auditory stimuli.

Nicholas J. Wade & Michael Swanston (1991). *Visual perception: An introduction.* London: Routledge.

This book spells out very clearly the basic problems that the visual system must solve to permit us to identify objects and their locations. The chapter entitled "Heritage" is especially interesting as it shows the central role that ideas about vision have played in the larger history of psychology.

Ronald Melzack & Patrick D. Wall (1982). *The challenge of pain.* New York: Basic Books.

Written by the men who developed the gate-control theory, this classic book on the psychology and physiology of pain is not a bit painful to read. In fact, it is delightful. Keep in mind, though, that the rapid rate of discoveries in this area has made the book's physiological account somewhat out of date.

S. S. Stevens (1975). *Psychophysics: Introduction to its perceptual, neural, and social prospects*. New York: Wiley.

A brilliant description of the research leading to the power law and the implications of that law, this slender book is quite readable by the beginning student who is not intimidated by exponents or algebraic equations. Stevens also shows how the power law applies to higher-order judgments, beyond sensory judgments, such as those about the seriousness of crimes.

Looking Ahead

Sensation can be thought of as the first step in the processing of information that we receive from the environment. It is the step that we have the best understanding of physiologically. But think of all that we subsequently do with the information we receive from our senses. We form meaningful *perceptions* from it, which guide our behavior. We form *memories* from it, which allow us to recall events long after they have happened. We use those perceptions and memories to *think* about our experiences and to make plans for future action. These things that we do with sensory experiences constitute a core part of the subject matter of psychology. They also constitute the topics of the next three chapters: perception, memory, and the human intellect.

Jacob Lawrence 60

COGNITIVE MECHANISMS OF BEHAVIOR

PART 4

Our behavior is governed by our knowledge. We respond not so much to physical reality as to our understanding of it. This three-chapter unit is about the processes by which we understand the world and use that understanding to guide our actions. The first chapter examines the basic processes of perception—how we recognize objects and scenes in our environment. The second deals with memory—how we store and organize information gained from experience. The third is concerned with the measurement and description of intelligence, and with the mental processes of reasoning and language.

PERCEPTION

CHAPTER 9

As I look at the top of my desk, what strikes my retinas is a continuous field of light, varying from point to point in amplitude and wavelength. But I see the scene neither as a continuous field nor as a collection of points, and I certainly do not see it as existing on my retinas. Instead, I see objects: a word processor, a pencil, a stapler, and a pile of books. The objects look solid, and they appear to occupy definite positions in the three-dimensional space atop my desk.

My experience is no illusion. The objects I see on my desk really exist and are located precisely where I see them. I can prove that: With vision as my only guide, I can reach out directly to the pencil and pick it up, without fumbling around at all, and then use it to write a note. If you were here now, you could do the same, even though you had never experienced my desk before.

Sensation entails the registration and coding of light, sound, and other energies that impinge on the sense organs. Through natural selection, our sensory systems have been designed to exploit these energies for information about objects and events in our environment. The ability to interpret this information, to extract from it meaningful and useful representations of our world, is called ***perception***. In essence, perception is the ultimate purpose of sensation.

Perception is as much a product of the nervous system as sensation is, and in theory is explainable in terms of the activity of neurons. But perception is much harder to study physiologically than is sensation. Its neural mechanisms are far more complicated and exist entirely within the brain, which is less accessible to physiological study than are the sense organs. Neuroscientists can offer fairly complete physiological accounts of many sensory processes, but have barely begun to explain perception physiologically. For this reason, we turn now from a primarily physiological approach to a primarily cognitive one. The cognitive approach involves the construction of hypothetical models that explain perception, memory, and other mental processes in terms of the manipulation of information, without reference to physiological mechanisms. You will see examples of such models in all three chapters of this unit.

All of the senses are involved in perception, and they often work together, as when you both see and smell the food on your plate or see and hear your dinner companion. This chapter, however, concentrates mainly on visual perception, which has long dominated the field of perceptual psychology. Auditory perception is covered only briefly; it has been studied far less, and the research has been concerned mostly with the perception of speech, a topic touched on in this chapter and again in the chapters on the human intellect and its development (Chapters 11 and 12).

The three main sections of this chapter deal respectively with the following three questions: (1) How do we perceive patterns and recognize objects? (2) How, from the vast array of stimuli that confront us, do we select the useful and ignore the irrelevant? (3) How do we perceive the spatial characteristics of objects and judge their distance, size, and motion in the three-dimensional world?

Perceiving Patterns and Recognizing Objects

■ **1. *What is the difference between bottom-up and top-down perceptual processes, and how are they assumed to interact in perceiving an object?***

How do I see the pencil on my desk? Most perceptual psychologists believe that the ability to perceive objects represents a form of problem solving that relies on two categories of mental processes: bottom-up and top-down. ***Bottom-up processes*** are those that register and integrate sensory information, and ***top-down processes*** are those that use preexisting knowledge to interpret that information.

The pencil on my desk is characterized by a point, a yellow color, two parallel lines that form most of its contour, and several other features. Bottom-up processes must somehow bring those features together, enabling me to see the pencil as a whole. But how does my perceptual system know which features to bring together? How does it know to combine the parallel lines with the yellow color and the point rather than, say, with the blue color and flat plane of the blotter on which the pencil rests? Scientists who have tried to build computers that can recognize objects have found that bottom-up processes cannot work alone (Watt, 1988). The computer must be provided with information that helps it decide which features to combine. For example, to recognize a pencil the computer must be programmed with some facts about what pencils look like, and with rules for distinguishing objects in general from their background. The top-down perceptual processes are those that use such knowledge.

My perception of the pencil requires an interplay of bottom-up and top-down processes. A simplified model might go something like this (see also Figure 9.1): (1) Bottom-up processes register a set of elementary features in the stimulus array before me—a set of lines, angles, colors, and so forth. (2) Top-down processes, using my knowledge of objects and my expectations about which objects are likely to be present, perform a preliminary analysis of the features and form the hypothesis that a pencil lies before me. (3) In response to the pencil hypothesis, bottom-up processes integrate the sensory features in such a way that the hypothesis can be tested. For example, bottom-up processes combine the parallel lines, the point, and the yellow color. (4) Top-down processes compare the integrated features to information in my memory about the appearance of pencils and confirm the pencil hypothesis. Amazingly, all this occurs almost instantly, with little or no conscious effort on my part.

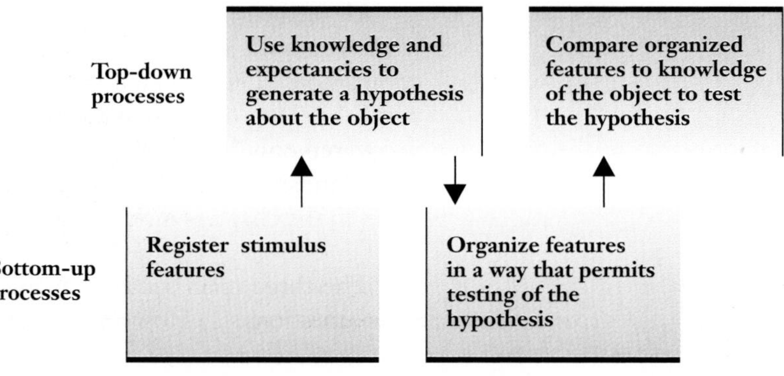

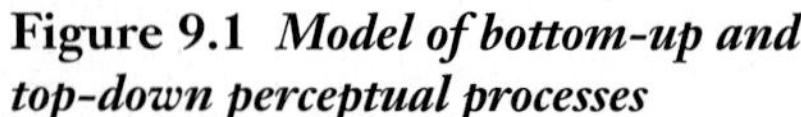

Figure 9.1 ***Model of bottom-up and top-down perceptual processes***

Bottom-up processes detect and organize the features of the sensory stimulus, and top-down processes use preexisting knowledge and expectancies to direct attention to relevant features and to recognize an object.

Holistic Perception and Top-Down Analysis of Stimulus Input

My *conscious* perception of the pencil begins with my seeing the whole pencil. The earlier registration and bringing together of features must occur at a level of my mind's activity that precedes conscious experience. Consciously, it seems easier for me to identify the whole object as a pencil than to identify its features (its parallel lines, point, and so on). Thus, conscious perception is holistic. ***Holistic perception*** refers to the primacy of the whole over the parts—the tendency to perceive whole patterns, objects, and scenes, and to ignore the smaller parts of which they are composed. The holistic perception of an object or scene in turn contributes, top-down, to identifying the individual parts of the object or scene. I can find the point on the object in front of me more easily if I recognize the object as a pencil than if I don't.

Gestalt Principles of Perceptual Grouping

Historically, the idea of holistic perception came largely from the ***Gestalt*** school of psychology. This movement arose in Germany during the early twentieth century in response to the then-dominant structuralist school (described in Chapter 1). The structuralists were interested in the basic elements of sensory experience. They believed that all perceptions could be understood as combinations of such elements. For example, Edward Titchener and his students attempted to count the number of brightnesses and hues that people could discriminate in visual stimuli. The Gestaltists, in contrast, argued that perception is not a matter of combining separate elements, but a matter of responding immediately to large, whole patterns. One of the leaders of the Gestalt movement, Max Wertheimer (1923/1938), argued against the structuralists as follows: "I stand at the window and see a house, trees, sky. Now on theoretical grounds I could try to count and say: 'here they are . . . 327 brightnesses and hues.' Do *I have* '327'? No, I see sky, house, trees. . . ."

The Gestalt point of view is characterized by the statement, *The whole is different from the sum of its parts.* The whole is different because it not only contains the parts, but contains them organized in a certain way. The meaningful information that is perceived lies in the organization. The German word *gestalt* translates roughly to "organized whole," and the Gestaltists believed that the gestalt, not the individual sensory elements, is the proper unit of study. To them, the structuralist approach was like trying to account for the beauty of the Mona Lisa by carefully weighing the amount of paint used to produce each part of the masterpiece.

Principle of similarity

Some sets of individuals in this crowd stand out as perceptual units because of the similarity in their clothing.

2. *What are some principles of grouping proposed by Gestalt psychologists, and how does each help explain our ability to see whole objects?*

The Gestaltists proposed that the nervous system is innately predisposed to group incoming sensory elements according to certain rules or *principles of grouping*. These principles include the following (Koffka, 1935; Wertheimer, 1923):

- ***Proximity*** We tend to see stimulus elements that are near each other as part of the same object, and those that are separated as part of different objects. This helps us segregate a large set of elements into a smaller set of objects (see Figure 9.2a).
- ***Similarity*** We tend to see stimulus elements that physically resemble each other as part of the same object, and those that don't resemble each other as part of different objects. This helps us distinguish between two adjacent or overlapping objects, based on a change in their texture elements (Texture elements are repeated visual features or patterns that cover the surface of a given object, as illustrated in Figure 9.2b).
- ***Closure*** We tend to see forms as completely enclosed by a border and to ignore gaps in the border. This helps us perceive complete forms even when they are partly occluded by other objects (see Figure 9.2c).
- ***Good continuation*** When lines intersect, we tend to group the line segments in such a way as to form continuous lines with minimal change in direction. This helps us decide which lines belong to which object when two or more objects overlap (see Figure 9.2d).

Proximity

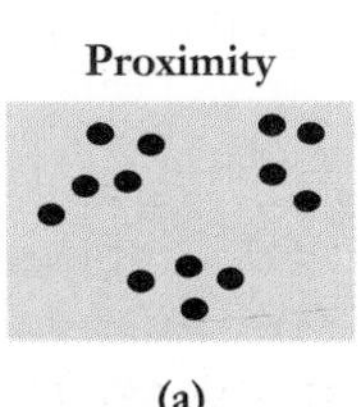

(a)

Similarity

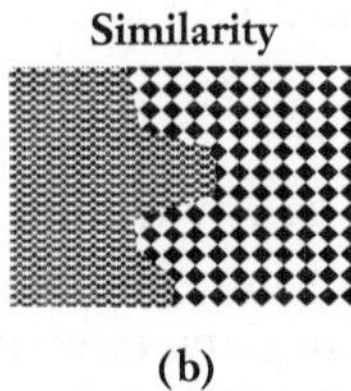

(b)

Closure

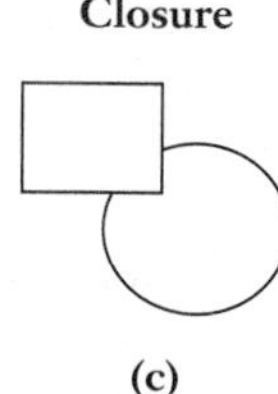

(c)

Good continuation

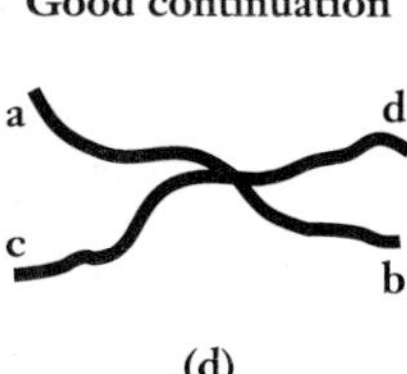

(d)

Common movement

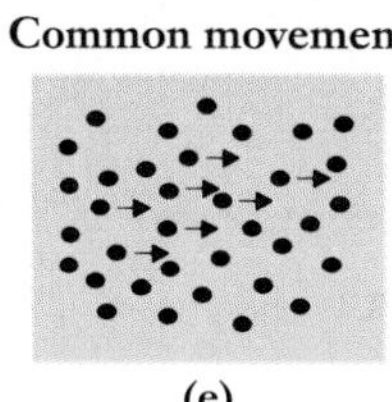

(e)

Good form

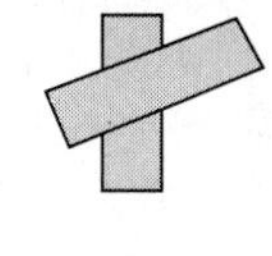

(f)

Figure 9.2 ***Gestalt principles of grouping***

(a) *Proximity*—we see three sets of dots rather than thirteen individual dots. (b) *Similarity*—because we group similar texture elements together, we see two separate forms here. (c) *Closure*—we assume that the boundary of the circle is complete, continuing behind the square. (d) *Good continuation*—we see two smooth lines here, a-b and c-d, rather than four shorter lines or two sharply bent lines such as a-c or b-d. (e) *Common movement*—if the set of dots with arrows were moving as a group, we would see the dots as a single object. (f) *Good form*—because of its symmetry, the left-hand figure is more likely than the middle figure to be seen as a single object. The middle figure is likely to be seen as two separate objects, like those depicted more clearly in the right-hand figure.

- ***Common movement*** When stimulus elements move in the same direction and at the same rate, we tend to see them as part of a single object. This helps us distinguish a moving object (such as a camouflaged animal) from the background. If the dots marked by arrows in Figure 9.2e were all moving as a group, you would see them as a single object.
- ***Good form*** This principle is less specific than the others. Essentially, it states that the perceptual system strives to produce percepts that are elegant—simple, uncluttered, symmetrical, and regular (Koffka, 1935). This principle encompasses the other principles listed above, but also includes more complex ways by which the perceptual system organizes stimuli into their most elegant arrangement. (Figures 9.2f and 9.6 both illustrate this.)

Figure and Ground

In addition to the six principles of grouping just listed, the Gestaltists called attention to our automatic tendency to divide any visual scene into ***figure*** (the object that attracts attention) and ***ground*** (background). As an example, look at Figure 9.3. The illustration could be described as two unfamiliar figures, one white and one black, whose borders coincide, but you probably do not see it that way. Most

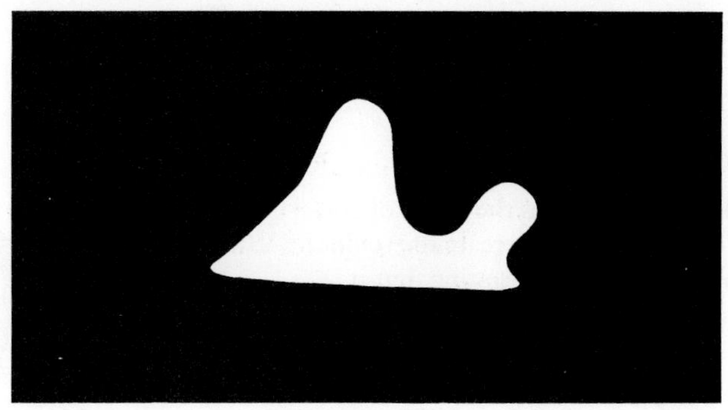

Figure 9.3 ***Figure and ground***

Because the white form is completely surrounded by the black form, we tend to see the white form as the figure and the black form as the ground.

people automatically see it as just one white figure against a black background. According to the Gestaltists, the division into figure and ground is not arbitrary, but is directed by certain stimulus characteristics. In the example in Figure 9.3, the most important characteristic is probably *circumscription*: Other things being equal, we see the more circumscribing form (the one that surrounds the other) as ground.

3. ***How do reversible figures illustrate the mind's strong tendency to separate figure and ground, even in the absence of sufficient cues for deciding which is which?***

The figure-ground relationship is not always completely determined by characteristics of the stimulus, however. With some effort, you can reverse the figure-ground relation in Figure 9.3 by imagining that the illustration is a black square with an oddly shaped hole cut out of it, sitting on a white background. When cues in the scene are sparse or ambiguous, the mind may vacillate in its choice of which shape to see as figure and which as ground. This is illustrated by the ***reversible figure*** in Figure 9.4, where you may see alternately either a white vase against a dark ground or two dark profiles against a white ground. At any given moment, you see one or the other, not both simultaneously. In line with the Gestalt figure-ground principle, the same part of the figure cannot simultaneously be both figure and ground, and thus at any instant you see either the vase or the faces, but not both at once.

Figure 9.4 ***Reversible figure***

Because it lacks strong cues as to which is figure and which is ground, this figure may be seen either as a white vase against a dark ground or as two dark profiles against a white ground. If you stare at it, your perception may alternate between the two.

Perceptual Set and Effects of Context on Object Recognition

If you had been mentally prepared to see a vase when you first looked at Figure 9.4—for example, if I had introduced it by calling it a vase—you would probably have seen the figure as a vase. Conversely, if you had been prepared to see people's profiles, that is what you would have seen. When the available stimuli offer a choice, what we see is affected by what we expect to see, that is, by our ***perceptual set***. The idea of perceptual set leads us from the Gestaltists' principles of grouping to the general role that context and mental concepts play in perception.

Typically, our perceptual set for what we will see in any given part of a scene is influenced by our global understanding of the whole scene, and this helps us recognize parts that otherwise we might not. For example, look at the set of features in Figure 9.5b. By themselves, they are unrecognizable curves and angles that might

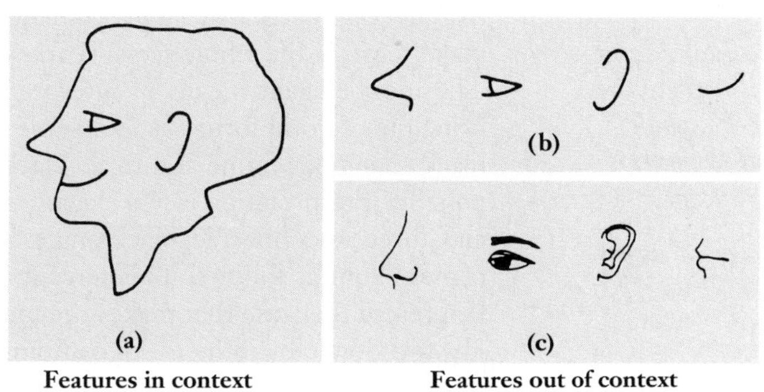

Figure 9.5 ***Role of context in feature recognition***

Very little detail is needed to recognize the nose, eye, ear, and mouth in the context of a face, but out of context more detail is needed. (From Palmer, 1975b.)

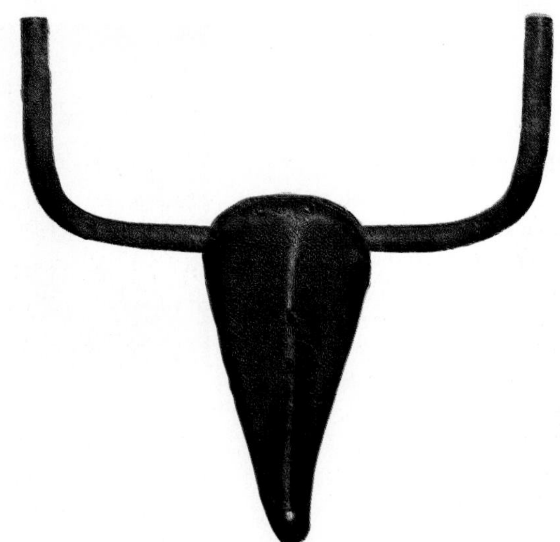

Death's head (Flayed head)

This sculpture by Pablo Picasso (1944) illustrates the effect of context on perception. The objects the artist used to create the sculpture would be immediately recognized in another setting, but it takes a moment to recognize them here as a bicycle seat and handlebars.

■ **4. *How does context affect the top-down processes involved in object recognition?***

be interpreted in any of a number of possible ways. When seen as features of a face, however, as in Figure 9.5a, they are unmistakably nose, eye, ear, and mouth. Notice, in Figure 9.5c, how much additional detail is required for the same features to be recognized out of context. In everyday life, practically every scene you look at contains elements that would be hard to recognize out of context. For example, when you look at a tree, you can find leaves or twigs that, because of their angle or distance from you, would be unrecognizable if seen away from the tree. Likewise, you probably recognize your psychology professor more easily in the classroom than you would at a shopping mall, and more easily at a shopping mall than at a Madonna concert. Numerous experiments have shown that people recognize objects more quickly and accurately in accustomed contexts than in unaccustomed contexts (for example, Palmer, 1975a).

Figure 9.6 ***Illusory contour***

In response to this stimulus, the perceptual system creates a white triangle, the borders of which appear to continue across the white page, such that the triangle seems whiter than the white page. (Adapted from Kanizsa, 1976.)

Illusions Deriving from Context

Most perceptual illusions derive from the context in which the illusory elements appear and can be described in terms of top-down processes. Most impressive are illusions in which the context not only affects perceived characteristics of an object (such as size), but causes us to see or hear something that isn't actually present in the stimulus at all. As an example, look at the *illusory contour* illustration in Figure 9.6. You probably see a solid white triangle sitting atop some other objects. The contour of the white triangle appears to continue across the white space between the other objects. This is not simply a misperception caused by a fleeting glance. The longer you look at the whole stimulus, the more convinced you may become that the contour (border) between the white triangle and the white background is really there; the triangle seems *whiter* than the background. But if you try to look at the contour isolated from the rest of the stimulus, by covering the black portions with your fingers or pieces of paper, you will see that the contour isn't really there. The white triangle and its border are illusions.

■ **5. *How do illusory contours and phonemic restoration illustrate the idea that perception of the whole influences perception of the parts?***

Debate exists about the exact cause of the illusion in Figure 9.6, but most researchers agree that it stems somehow from the perceptual system's attempt to make sense of the whole scene (Parks & Rock, 1990; Pomerantz & Kubovy, 1986). The most elegant means of interpreting the figure—consistent with the Gestalt principle of good form—is to assume that it contains a white triangle lying atop a black triangular frame and three black disks. Without the white triangle, the only possible interpretation is less elegant: three disks with wedges removed from them, and three unconnected black angles. From this view, then, the illusory contour comes about as follows: The perceptual system decides that a white triangle must be present (because that makes the most sense), and then it *creates* the white triangle, top-down, by influencing contour-detection processes in such a way as to produce a border where one does not actually exist in the stimulus.

Context can create illusions in auditory as well as visual perception. A well-studied example is *phonemic restoration*. ***Phonemes*** are the individual vowel and consonant sounds that make up words, and phonemic restoration refers to the finding that people hear phonemes that have been deleted from words or sentences as if they were still there. Richard Warren (1970) first demonstrated this illusion in an experiment in which he removed an *s* sound and spliced in a coughing sound of equal duration in the following tape-recorded sentence at the place marked by an asterisk: *The state governors met with their respective legi*latures convening in the capital city.* People listening to the doctored tape could hear the cough, but it did not seem to coincide with any specific portion of the sentence or block out any sound in the sentence. Even when they listened repeatedly, with instructions to determine what sound was missing, people were unable to detect that any sound was missing. After they were told which sound was missing, they still claimed to hear it each time they listened to the tape. In other experiments, thousands of practice trials failed to improve people's ability to judge which phoneme was missing (Samuel, 1991).

The context that provides the basis for phonemic restoration is the arrangement of the other phonemes and the meaningful words and phrases they produce. The restored sound is always one that turns a partial word into a whole word that is consistent in meaning with the rest of the sentence. Interestingly, even words that occur after the missing phoneme can influence which phoneme is heard. For example, people heard the stimulus sound **eel* (again, the * represents a coughlike sound) to be either *peel*, *heel*, or *wheel*, depending on whether it occurred in the phrase, *The *eel was on the orange*, *The *eel was on the shoe*, or *The *eel was on the axle* (Warren, 1984). Illusory restoration has also been demonstrated in music perception. People hear a missing note, in a familiar tune, as if it were present (DeWitt & Samuel, 1990).

Illusory contours, phonemic restoration, and music restoration are particularly powerful demonstrations of top-down processing. They show that our conception of the whole not only affects what parts of a stimulus array we notice, or what characteristics we ascribe to the parts, or how we label them, but also in certain conditions can cause us to see or hear parts that aren't present in the stimulus at all.

Feature Detection and Bottom-Up Analysis of Stimulus Input

Although perception of the whole influences the way we perceive the parts, the opposite is also true. Logic dictates that we base our perception of a whole at least partly on perception of its parts and their relative locations, even though we may not be conscious of doing so. To illustrate this point, think about your ability to read a word. When you read that last sentence you immediately and effortlessly perceived the last word in the sentence to be *word*. How did you do it? Top-down analysis, based on the context established by the rest of the sentence, certainly played a role. You would have taken longer to read a word there that didn't make sense. But top-down processes cannot be the whole story. The actual stimulus on the page had to play some role. If the stimulus had looked like this—poem—you would not have read it as *word*.

6. *What are the bottom-up processes in reading, and how do they illustrate the more general point that bottom-up perception can be described as features → components → object?*

Printed words consist of individual letters, and each letter consists of a set of straight or curved lines arranged in a certain way. As a skilled reader, when you perceived *word*, you probably did not consciously notice its individual letters, and you certainly did not consciously notice the individual lines that make up the letters. Yet at least some of these must have registered in your sensory system and contributed to your perception. In this example we can refer to the characteristics of the individual lines as features. Your perceptual system must have picked up at least some of the features, in order to pick up at least some of the letters, in order to perceive the word. Thus, the bottom-up processes in reading can be diagrammed as *features* → *letters* → *word*. For a skilled reader these processes are automatic and unconscious, but they still must occur. More generally, all visual objects are defined by a particular arrangement of components (analogous to letters), which in turn are defined by more primitive features. Thus, more generally, object perception can be diagrammed, bottom-up, as *features* → *components* → *object*. Research from a bottom-up perspective has focused on (a) the detection and integration of features, (b) the role of component recognition in object recognition, and (c) the role that learning plays in directing attention toward the most distinguishing features and components. Let us look at examples of each.

7. *What is the difference between parallel and serial processing, and what roles do these play in Treisman's feature-integration theory?*

Detection and Integration of Features

To explain the bottommost of bottom-up perceptual processes, Anne Treisman (1986; 1991) has developed a *feature-integration theory*. This theory holds that, in order to see an object, our perceptual apparatus must first pick up certain *primitive features* (such as the slant and curvature of individual lines) from the stimulus information, and then integrate those features into larger parts. These processes, according to Treisman, occur in two fundamentally different steps. The first step, *detection of features*, occurs automatically (it is not controllable by top-down mental processes) and involves ***parallel processing***. Parallel processing means that this step operates simultaneously on all parts of the stimulus array. That is, according to Treisman, we pick up at once the primitive features of all objects in our field of vision. The second step is the *integration of features*, which is less automatic (more controllable by top-down processes) and leads eventually to our conscious perception of whole, spatially organized patterns and objects. This step involves ***serial processing***, which occurs sequentially for the features at one spatial location at a time, rather than simultaneously over the entire array. To visualize Treisman's theory, and to read more about the distinction between parallel and serial processing, see Figure 9.7.

To understand the evidence on which Treisman's theory is based, look at the array of stimuli in Figure 9.8a. Notice that no effort is needed to find the single slanted line. You don't have to scan the whole array in serial fashion to find it; it just "pops out" at you. According to Treisman, this is because line slant is one of the primitive features that is processed automatically through parallel processing. Now

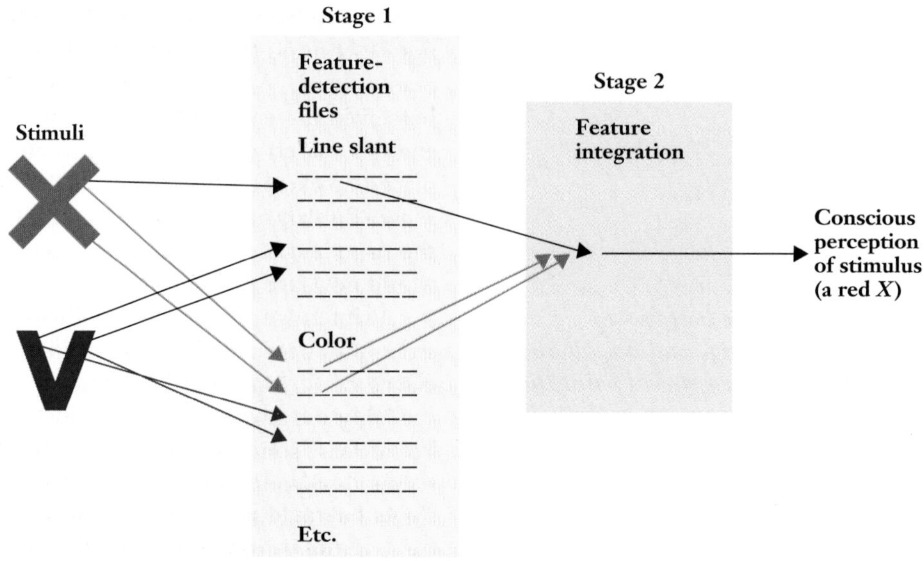

Figure 9.7 *Treisman's theory of feature detection and integration*

According to Treisman, stimulus features are detected and integrated in two separate stages of information processing. During Stage 1, the primitive features of all stimuli that reach the eyes are registered automatically and simultaneously. The parallel processing is illustrated here by showing that all of the features of both the X and V are detected at once (in different feature-detection files). Integration of features occurs at Stage 2, during which information is processed serially from one localized area of the visual field at a time. Serial processing is illustrated here by showing that only the information from one stimulus, the X, is being processed. An instant later, Stage 2 could operate on the V, but it cannot operate on the X and V at once.

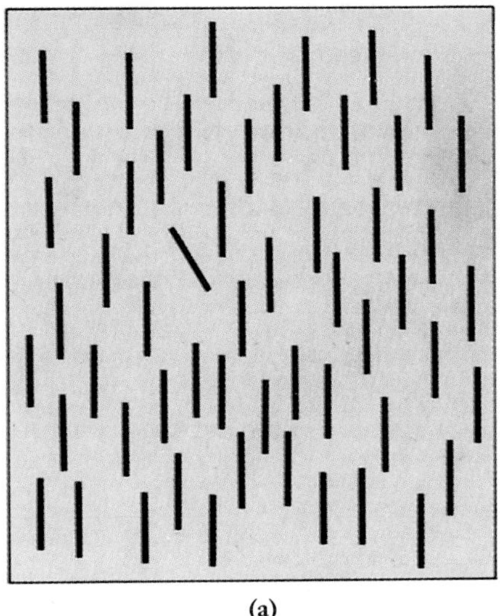
(a)

(b)

Figure 9.8 ***Stimuli that pop out or do not pop out***

These stimulus arrays are similar to those used by Treisman and Gormican (1988). In (a) the target stimulus (slanted line) differs from the other stimuli in a primitive feature, line slant. This target pops out at you; you immediately notice the slanted line even if you aren't looking for it. This is evidence that primitive features are identified by parallel processing. In (b) the target stimulus (crossed lines) does not differ from the other stimuli in a primitive feature—its two lines are the same as the many other vertical and horizontal lines in the figure. Rather, this target is distinct in its conjunction of two features (the crossing of two lines). This target does not pop out at you; you have to look for it to notice it. This is evidence that the perceptual integration of primitive features involves serial processing.

■ **8.** ***How do pop-out phenomena and mistakes in joining features provide evidence for Treisman's theory?***

look at Figure 9.8b and find the single set of crossed lines among the vertical and horizontal lines. In this case the target does not pop out; you have to scan through the items in serial fashion to find it (though you can still find it quite quickly).

In controlled experiments, Treisman and Stephen Gormican (1988) measured the time it took for people to locate specific target stimuli in arrays like those of Figure 9.8 but with varying numbers of distractors (defined as the nontarget stimuli). As long as the target differed from the distractors in one or more of Treisman's list of primitive features—such as slant, curvature, color, or movement—subjects detected it equally quickly no matter how many distractors were present. This lack of effect on detection time is indicative of parallel processing. But when the target combined two or more primitive features present in the distractors, as in Figure 9.8b, the amount of time subjects took to locate the target increased in direct proportion to the number of distractors. This increase in detection time is indicative of serial processing, the necessity to attend to each item separately until the target is found.

Treisman also found that subjects who saw simple stimuli flashed briefly on a screen easily identified which primitive features were present, but sometimes misperceived which features went together, a phenomenon that she calls *illusory conjunctions*. For example, when shown a straight red line and a green curved one, all subjects knew that they had seen a straight line and a curved line, and a red color and a green color, but were sometimes mistaken about which color belonged to which line. Such findings led Treisman to conclude that the first step (parallel processing) registers features independently of their spatial location, and that different features that coincide in space (such as the color and curvature of a given line) are joined perceptually only at the second step (serial processing), which requires separate attention to each location.

In early work related to her theory, Treisman (1986) reported that stimulus characteristics that are processed in parallel, and that thereby qualify as primitive features in her theory, correspond to features for which separate sets of feature-detecting neurons have been identified in the brain's visual cortex (described in Chapter 8). These included slant, curvature, line-length, brightness, color, and movement. However, research has since shown that some relatively complex stimulus characteristics, which depend on relations among spatially separate parts of the stimulus, can also "pop out" in tests for parallel processing (Wolfe, 1992). An

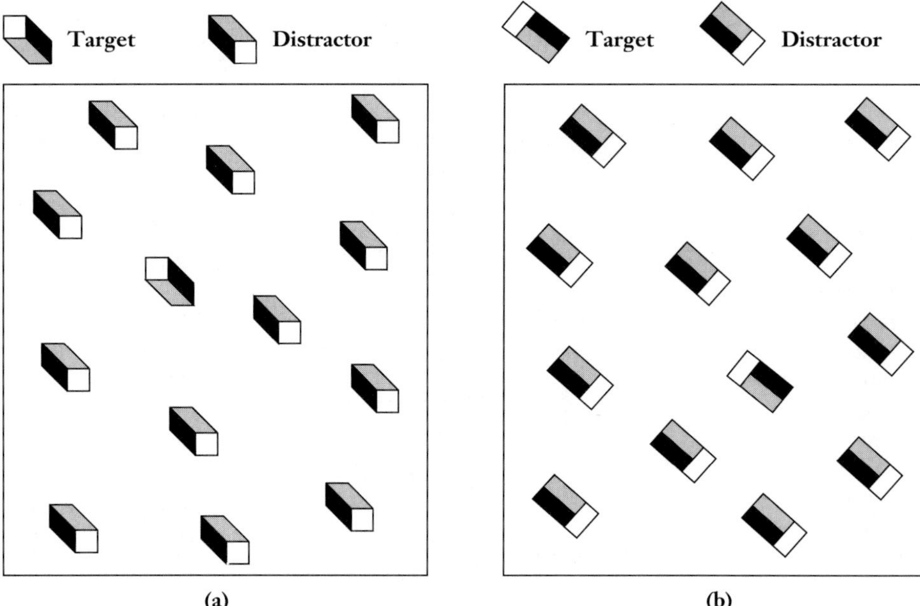

Figure 9.9 ***Evidence that 3-dimensionality is processed in Stage 1***

When the target differed from the distractors in a way that made it appear to take a different three-dimensional orientation (a), subjects identified the target equally quickly no matter how many distractors were present. But when the target differed from the distractors in a manner that was equally complex but did not signal three-dimensionality (b), the time subjects took to identify the target increased as the number of distractors increased. (Based on Enns & Rensink, 1990.)

example of that is shown in Figure 9.9. In consequence, Treisman (1991) has modified her original theory somewhat, to provide for a greater degree of stimulus analysis in Stage 1 than she had originally posited. Other research, to be discussed later, indicates that Stage 1 processing can be affected by learning. A stimulus that initially did not pop out may come to do so after extended practice.

Recognizing Objects Based on Components

While Treisman has been concerned with the initial pickup and integration of primitive stimulus features, other theorists, including Irving Biederman (1987; 1989), have been studying the later stages in the perception of whole, natural objects. From a bottom-up perspective, the integration of spatially congruent features postulated by Treisman's theory leads to further integration of spatially adjacent sets of features into components, which in turn leads to perception of the whole object. Biederman's *recognition-by-components theory* addresses the components that form the most immediate basis for perceiving natural objects.

9. How might a finite set of geometric forms (geons) provide the basis for perception of an infinite set of objects?

Biederman believes that our ability to recognize natural, three-dimensional objects is analogous to our ability to recognize printed words. There are only twenty-six different letters in the English alphabet, but these can be used to form hundreds of thousands of different words. Likewise, Biederman suggests, any object can be thought of as a particular arrangement of a small set of relatively simple geometric forms, such as blocks, cylinders, spheres, and cones. On the basis of certain fundamental properties of three-dimensional geometry, Biederman has suggested a list of thirty-six such forms, which he calls *geons*, some of which appear in Figure 9.10. By smoothing the edges and ignoring the details, all objects, according to the theory, can be seen as a set of geons organized in a certain way. You may already be familiar with this general idea from experience with learn-to-draw books that recommend sketching any object as a set of three-dimensional geometric shapes before fleshing it out with details. According to Biederman's recognition-by-components theory, perception of an object depends on recognizing at least some of its geons and their arrangement relative to one another.

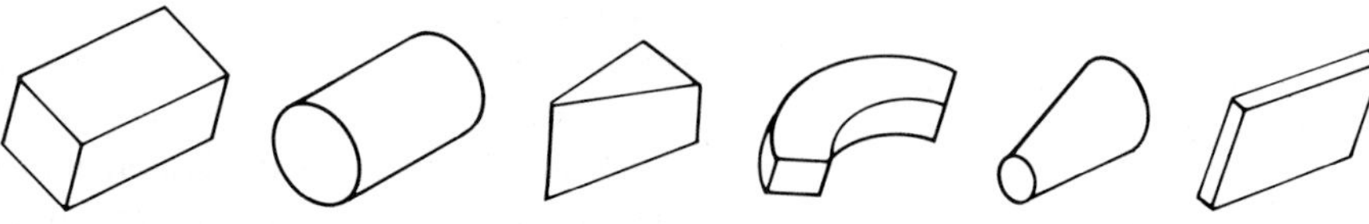

Figure 9.10 ***Some geons***

From principles of geometry, Biederman developed a list of thirty-six simple, three-dimensional forms or *geons*, which, he suggests, provide the basic perceptual components of more complex forms. Six sample geons are shown here. (Adapted from Biederman, 1987.)

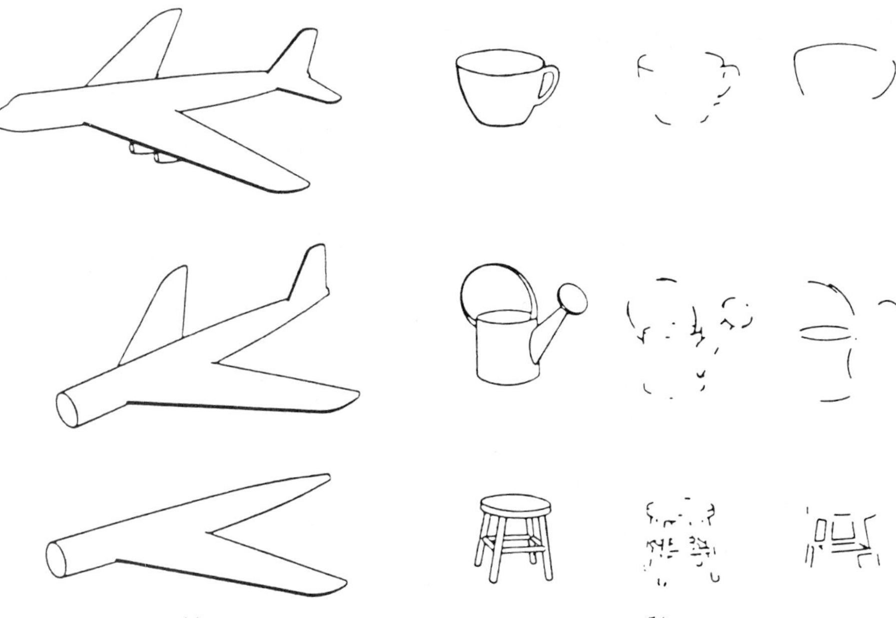

Figure 9.11 ***Support for Biederman's recognition-by-components theory***

Part (a) shows an airplane consisting of nine, four, or two components (geons). Even with just a few components present it is recognizable. Part (b) shows a set of line drawings of objects degraded in two different ways. The degradation in the middle column preserves the connections between adjacent components, and that in the right-hand column does not. When subjects saw the degraded figures alone, they recognized those in the middle column but not those in the right-hand column. (Adapted from Biederman, 1987.)

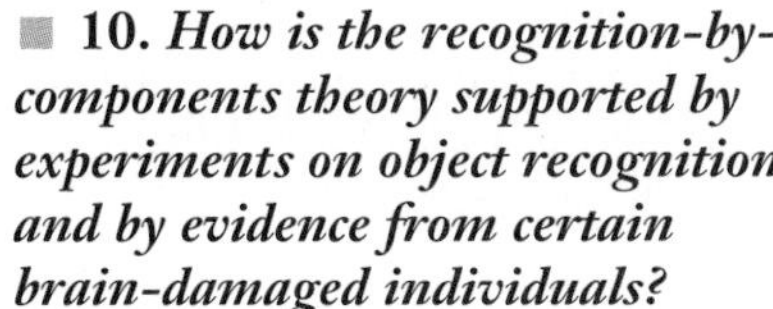

■ **10.** ***How is the recognition-by-components theory supported by experiments on object recognition and by evidence from certain brain-damaged individuals?***

Evidence for Biederman's theory comes from experiments in which he asked people to identify objects that were flashed briefly on a screen (Biederman, 1987). In these experiments, he found that the speed and accuracy of recognition depended very much on the intactness and arrangement of individual geons within the object, and very little on details within the geons themselves or on the outline of the object as a whole. Figure 9.11 illustrates some of the stimuli that Biederman used. The airplane in Figure 9.11a was recognized as an airplane even when most of its geons were removed (changing its overall outline), as long as the geons still present were intact and properly arranged. The various objects in Figure 9.11b were recognized when the lines were degraded in such a way as to preserve recognizability of individual geons and their connections to one another (middle column), but not when the same amount of line degradation occurred in such a way as to obscure the geons and their connections (right-hand column).

Biederman's theory is also supported by the presence of rare individuals who, because of damage to a specific part of the brain (in the occipital lobe of the cortex), suffer from a disorder called *visual-object agnosia*. The term *agnosia* (from the Greek *a*, meaning "not," and *gnosis*, meaning "perception") refers to any perceptual deficit, and visual-object agnosia refers to cases in which the person can perceive simple geometric forms (such as Biederman's geons), but not more complex objects (Kolb & Whishaw, 1990). One such individual was described in Chapter 8—the man who, when shown a rose, could describe its stem as "a long green attachment" and its petals as "convoluted red forms," but could not combine them to see the rose. Another patient with this disorder described a bicycle as a pole and two wheels, but could not identify it as a bicycle or guess its function (Hécaen & Albert, 1978). Apparently, the combining of components into recognizable whole objects is a separate step from the perception of components, and it is carried out by a unique set of neurons in the cortex.

Learning Which Parts to Attend To

■ **11.** ***According to Gibson, what do expert identifiers know that the rest of us do not know? What is some evidence that this knowledge can be unconscious?***

We may be able to recognize that an object is an airplane based on the arrangement of its component geons, but how do we distinguish between a Boeing 727 and a Boeing 747? Most perceptual psychologists agree that these finer distinctions don't come automatically, but must be learned through experience in which, for one reason or another, the distinction is important (see Biederman, 1988). Some years ago, Eleanor Gibson (1969) developed a *distinctive-feature theory* of that learning process. In essence, her theory is that we learn to notice the ***distinctive features*** of objects—those features that most clearly distinguish an object from others with which it might be confused—and to disregard other features. For example, Gibson proposed that we learn to recognize letters of the English alphabet efficiently by learning to attend to those features that distinguish each letter from other letters. In fact, she prepared a list of such distinctive features for each letter and found experimental evidence that skilled readers indeed do attend most to those features.

According to Gibson, the kinds of features that we learn to notice for any particular object depend on the kind of distinction that we need to make. Consider the problem (suggested by Gibson) of identifying goats. One level of identification involves distinguishing goats, as a category, from other barnyard animals such as pigs or sheep. That is the level with which most of us are concerned when we identify goats, and so we learn to pay attention to the properties that are common to all goats but not to other animals. We notice, for example, the beardlike tuft of hair on the chin and use that as one of the distinctive features—a feature that is exaggerated in cartoon drawings of goats to make for easy recognition. But a specialist in goats, someone who tends them or sells them, must not only distinguish goats from other animals, or one breed of goat from another, but must also distinguish individual goats within a breed. This is a difficult task for someone who is unfamiliar with goats, but easy for the goat expert because he or she has learned to notice the features that differ from goat to goat, such as the specific placement of spots of color, or the amount of separation between the eyes.

People often are not conscious of the features they use in making such distinctions, which explains why someone can be an expert identifier without necessarily being able to teach that skill to others. I remember, years ago, working on a maple sugar farm in Vermont and having to identify sugar maples without their leaves in late winter. The old hands teased me about tapping the wrong kinds of maple (they said I also tapped oaks, pines, and telephone poles, but they exaggerated). Yet, none of them—and I think they really tried—was able to tell me how to distinguish sugar maples from other maples. After several frustrated attempts, one expert concluded, "Well, you know, it just looks more *sugary* than other trees." Obviously he knew at some level of his mind what to look for, because he never made a mistake, but not at a level that was connected to his speaking ability.

Learning to look

For these birdwatchers, field guides may be as useful as field glasses. By highlighting the features that distinguish each species from the most similar other species, the guides help hobbyists identify species quickly and accurately. Field guides can also facilitate the identification of trees, even sugar maples in winter.

In a formal study, Irving Biederman and Margaret Shiffrar (1987) found that expert chicken sexers—people who could classify a newly hatched chick as male or female by glancing at the cloaca (the bird's genital opening)—typically could not explain just how the cloaca of the male and the female differed. Many claimed that this skill must be learned gradually through months or even years of experience. Yet Biederman and Shiffrar discovered that the difference, though subtle, could be described easily, and that a person who could describe it could, in just 15 seconds, train people who had no previous experience to make the discrimination as accurately as the experts (Biederman, 1988). (It is nice to know that in one realm, at least, 15 seconds with a good teacher is worth months of real-world experience.)

Attention: The Selectivity of Perception

In the discussion of the role of learning in object recognition, we saw that attention to distinctive features enables us to discriminate among similar objects. *Attention*, in its most general sense, refers to any focusing of mental activity along a specific track, whether that track consists purely of inner memories and knowledge (I am attending now to my knowledge of the meaning of *attention*) or of external stimuli (as when a chicken sexer attends to just the right features of the cloaca to distinguish male from female hatchling). Here we will use the term purely in the latter sense, as many perceptual psychologists do. We will define ***attention*** as the process or set of processes by which the mind chooses from among the various stimuli that strike the senses at any given moment, allowing only some to enter into higher stages of information processing.

The Ability to Focus Attention While Monitoring Unattended Stimuli

As I sit on my porch composing this paragraph, I can stop writing and attend to the chirping of a single bird. As I listen, I am vaguely aware of my neighbors arguing through the open window next door, of traffic on the street, and even of other birds chirping nearby, but these do not enter my consciousness in a clear and detailed way, as does the song to which I am attending. Everything to which I am not attending is part of the background. If I wish, however, I can shift my attention from the bird to any of the other sounds. I can choose to listen to the neighbors' argument, and when I do that, the bird becomes part of the background. I can do the same with sight as I do with hearing—shift my focus, say, from sight of the bird, to the twig that it is standing on, to anything else in my field of view.

There are two sides to our attentive ability. The one just described is the ability to focus on one source of information while ignoring others. The other is the ability to monitor in some way those stimuli to which we are *not* attending—those that do not reach consciousness or do so only dimly—and use them as a basis for shifting attention. As I watch and listen to the bird, my attention can be disrupted and drawn away by events that would otherwise be part of the background. Why do some stimuli but not others draw my attention? Simple intensity certainly plays a role. I cannot help but notice the motorcycle roaring down the street. In other cases, though, the ability of a stimulus to draw attention has more to do with its significance than intensity. I notice a mosquito about to land on my hand even though its sound and sight are slight. If one of the arguing neighbors were to use my name, I might notice that, even though I hadn't noticed any of their specific words before. Keep these two aspects of attention in mind as we turn to some experiments on selective listening and viewing.

■ **12. *What is some evidence that selective listening to a voice depends mainly on its physical qualities?***

Selective listening

Cocktail parties are not the only setting at which the ability to attend to one voice and ignore others is valuable.

Selective Listening

Most research on selective listening has focused on the so-called *cocktail-party phenomenon,* the ability to listen to and understand one person's voice while disregarding other voices nearby. (This ability is useful not only at parties, but also in such places as air-traffic control towers, where messages come in from many different speakers at once.) In the laboratory this ability is usually studied by playing two spoken, tape-recorded messages at once and asking the subject to *shadow* one message—that is, to repeat immediately each of its words as they are heard—while ignoring the other message.

Early experiments (reviewed by Hawkins & Presson, 1986) showed that successful shadowing depends primarily on physical differences between the two voices and differences in their spatial location. Shadowing is very poor if the two messages are read by the same voice and played through speakers that are near each other. It improves greatly if the messages are read by different voices (especially if one is a woman's and the other is a man's), or if the voices are altered electronically to make them different in pitch. It also improves greatly if the messages come through speakers located in different parts of the room, or if they are played through separate earphones, one into each ear—a procedure called *dichotic listening.* Differences in the meaning of words in the two messages have much less impact. When the two messages are read by the same voice, shadowing a passage of English prose is only slightly easier if the distracting message consists of nonsense words, or is in a foreign language, than if it is another passage of English prose.

■ **13. *What is some evidence that the meaning of the unattended voice is usually not consciously noticed, but may be registered unconsciously and affect subsequent behaviors?***

When people attend to one spoken message, what kinds of information, if any, do they notice in the other message? Early dichotic-listening studies showed that subjects usually could report such physical characteristics of the unattended message as the gender of the speaker or variation in tone, but usually were unaware of any of the message's meaning or even whether the speaker switched to a foreign language (Cherry, 1953; Cherry & Taylor, 1954). Subsequent research, however, showed that some degree of meaning can be picked up from the unattended message. In one experiment, subjects who failed to identify most words in the unattended message, including one that had been repeated thirty-five times, nevertheless noticed their own names in that message on about one-third of all occasions that it was presented (Moray, 1959). In another experiment, subjects shadowed sentences containing words with two possible meanings, such as *They threw stones at the bank* (MacKay, 1973). At the same time, the other ear was presented with a word that resolved the ambiguity (*river* or *money* in this example). After the shadowing task, the subjects were asked to choose from a pair of sentences the one that was most like the shadowed sentence. In the example just cited, the choice was between *They threw stones at the savings and loan association* and *They threw stones toward the side of the river.* Although the subjects could not report the nonshadowed word they usually chose the sentence that was consistent with the meaning of that word. Thus, the unattended word apparently influenced their interpretation of the shadowed message, even though they were unaware of having heard that word.

Selective Viewing

On the face of it, selective viewing seems to be a simpler task than selective listening; we can control what we see just by moving our eyes, whereas we have no easy control over what we hear. But we can also attend selectively to different, nearby parts of a visual scene without moving our eyes.

■ **14. *What is some evidence that people effectively screen out irrelevant visual stimuli that overlap relevant visual stimuli?***

An experiment by Irvin Rock and Daniel Gutman (1981) offers evidence for selective viewing without eye movement. The researchers presented, in rapid succession, a series of slides to viewers whose eyes were fixed on a spot at the center of the screen. Each slide contained two overlapping forms, one green and one red,

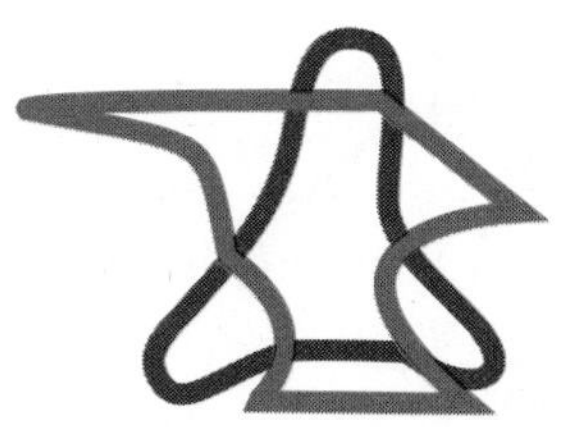

Figure 9.12 ***Overlapping forms used in an experiment on attention***

To assess the degree to which vision can be selective, Rock and Gutman (1981) directed subjects to pay attention to either just the red or just the green shape in slides such as this, and then tested their recognition of both shapes in each slide. (From Rock, 1984.)

and subjects were given a task that required them to attend to just one color (some to green, others to red). (See Figure 9.12.) Most of the forms were nonsense shapes, but some were shaped like a familiar object, such as a house or a tree. After viewing the sequence, subjects were tested for their ability to recognize which forms had been shown. The result was that they recognized most of the forms that had been presented in the attended color, but performed only at chance level on those that had been presented in the unattended color, regardless of whether the form was a nonsense shape or a familiar figure. Still, they did notice some of the physical characteristics of the unattended forms. For example, they were able to say whether a form was unusually large or small, or was composed of a dotted line rather than solid. As was typical in selective-listening studies, subjects frequently picked up basic physical features but not the meaning of unattended visual stimuli.

Robert Becklen and Daniel Cervone (1983) have described an even more dramatic example of selective viewing. These researchers made two separate videotapes of the same three men moving around a room, throwing a basketball to each other. In one tape the men wore black shirts, and in the other they wore white shirts. Then, with the aid of a mirror, the researchers showed the two tapes fully overlapping on the same screen, creating the effect of a television set showing two channels at once. A casual viewer would see six men moving around, throwing basketballs, with one man or a ball sometimes passing ghostlike through another. In the experiment, subjects were asked to attend just to the black-shirted players and to press a button each time one of them passed the ball, a task that they performed quite accurately. Midway through the 1-minute film an event occurred that, to a casual observer, was very noticeable. A woman carrying a large white umbrella sauntered across the playing area, spending a total of 5.5 seconds on screen, walking right through some of the players and the ball they were throwing (see Figure 9.13). Remarkably, when questioned immediately afterward, only eighteen of the eighty-five subjects in the experiment had any memory of seeing a woman carrying an umbrella. Apparently, people who focus intently on a visual task quite effectively screen out irrelevant information.

15. ***What is some evidence that unconscious processing for meaning may occur in vision, as it does in audition?***

As is true for auditory stimuli, however, evidence suggests that the meaning of an unattended visual stimulus can be registered in some way and affect the person's behavior, even when the person does not consciously notice the stimulus. In one experiment, Morris Eagle and his colleagues (1966) briefly showed students either

Figure 9.13 ***Overlapping videos***

Becklen and Cervone found that subjects attending to the black shirted players did not notice the woman with the umbrella crossing the screen. (Adapted from Becklen and Cervone, 1983.)

Figure 9.14 ***Tree with and without a duck***

When subjects were presented with the stimulus on the left (in three 1-second flashes on a screen), they were aware of seeing a tree but not a duck. Yet, when subsequently asked to draw a nature scene, they more frequently drew a scene having to do with ducks than did those who had been presented with the stimulus on the right. (From Eagle & others, 1966.)

of the two visual stimuli shown in Figure 9.14. The left-hand stimulus contains the outline of a duck, formed by the tree trunk and its branches. The researchers found that subjects who saw the duck-containing stimulus for a brief period did not consciously notice the duck. Yet when all subjects were subsequently asked to draw a nature scene, those who had been shown the duck-containing stimulus more frequently drew a scene containing a duck or other duck-related object (such as a pond) than did the other subjects.

The Ability to Divide Attention

Complementing our ability to focus narrowly on one source of information is our ability to divide attention, when necessary or desired, among more than one source of information. In everyday life we frequently engage in more than one complex perceptual task at a time. For example, to drive a car safely you must keep track simultaneously of other traffic, the road, pedestrians, your speedometer, and your own car's movement; if you are an experienced driver you can do all that *and* carry on an intelligent conversation.

Performing Two Tasks at Once

■ **16.** ***What is some evidence that practice at a task or set of tasks allows a person to attend to more than one source of information at once?***

Ulrich Neisser (1976) has argued that the ability to perceive and respond to more than one source of information at a time is best thought of as a *skill*, which, like any skill, improves with practice. He believes that attentional capacity has no fixed limits. Backing up this view, Neisser and his colleagues have shown that practice improves people's ability to divide attention. In one study (described in Becklen & Cervone, 1983), they found that subjects who had a lot of practice at viewing overlapping videos (like that depicted in Figure 9.13) were more likely than less practiced subjects to notice events that were irrelevant to the task at hand—including the woman with the umbrella in a replication of Becklen and Cervone's study. Apparently, once the task was well learned, and thus easier, people could devote more attention to other aspects of the incoming stimulation. In other experiments, Neisser and his colleagues studied the ability of college students to perform simultaneously two cognitively similar attention-demanding tasks, both involving verbal ability (Hirst & others, 1980; Spelke & others, 1976). One was to read an unfamiliar story or encyclopedia article, and the other was to write down words or sentences dictated by the experimenter. At first the requirement of taking dictation interfered greatly with reading, but after many hours of practice subjects could do both at once with no loss of reading speed or comprehension, compared to control trials in which they read without taking dictation.

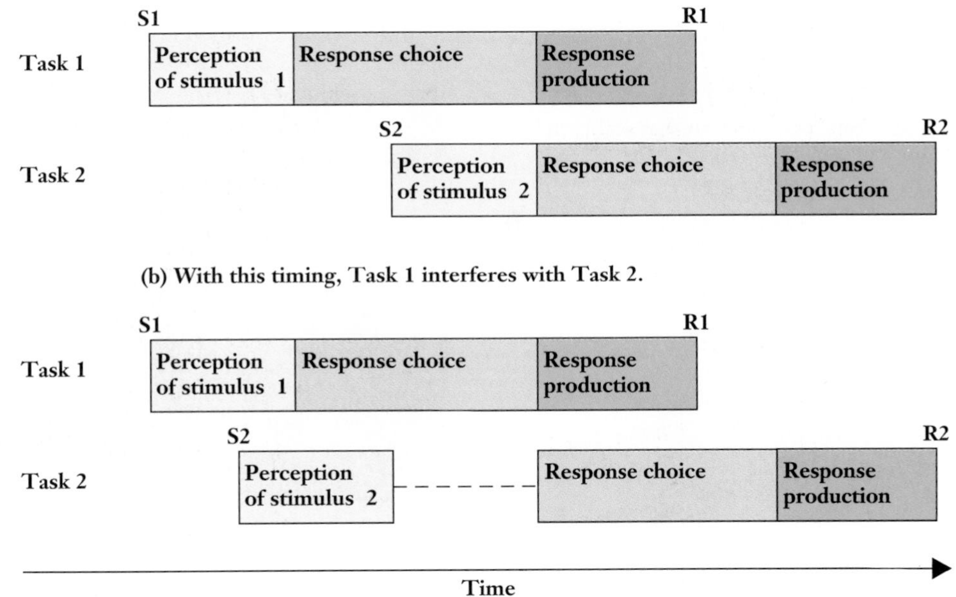

Figure 9.15 ***Response choice as a source of interference in dual-task performance***

When subjects had to make two different responses (R1 and R2) to two different stimuli (S1 and S2), the first task did not interfere with the second if S1 and S2 were sufficiently separated in time (Part a), but did interfere if S1 and S2 were closer together in time (Part b). Subjects apparently could perceive the second stimulus while choosing the first response and could choose the second response while producing the first response (Part a), but they could not choose the second response while choosing the first response (Part b). (Based on Pashler, 1992.)

■ **17.** ***What is the source of interference when a person must respond to each of two different stimuli presented simultaneously or one immediately after the other?***

Limits on Dual-Task Performance

Under what conditions will the performance of one task interfere with another? To answer that, researchers find it useful to distinguish among three different types of mental operations that occur one after the other in most tasks: (a) *perception* of the appropriate stimulus information (when driving, seeing that a traffic light has turned red); (b) *response choice* (deciding to depress the brake); and (c) *response production* (actually depressing the brake).

To learn which of these types of mental operations can or cannot occur simultaneously in more than one task, researchers typically use two-task problems that are much simpler than driving and carrying on a conversation. Harold Pashler (1990, 1992, 1993) conducted experiments in which, on each trial, the subject saw a letter (A, B, or C) and heard a tone (high or low in pitch). The two tasks were (1) to push one of three buttons depending on which letter appeared and (2) to say "high" or "low" depending on the tone's pitch. With sufficient practice subjects could perform both tasks extremely rapidly. However, when the interval between the letter and the tone was very brief, subjects could not complete the second task quite as fast as they could when it was the only task they were performing. By varying the time lapse between the two stimuli and by varying separately the difficulty of each of the three types of operation in each task (thereby varying the time required to complete the operation), Pashler found that the interference occurred in the response-choice stage of the two tasks. Subjects could perform either the perception or the response-production stage of one task while performing any of the three stages of the other task, but they could not perform the response-choice stages of the two tasks at once. Even though the tasks were very simple and so well practiced that they seemed reflexive, the choice of which response to make still took a fraction of a second, and subjects were unable to begin choosing the second response until they had finished choosing the first (see Figure 9.15). Apparently the human mind is constrained in decision-making capacity; we can make only one decision at a time about how to respond, no matter how simple the decisions are.

Other studies have shown that the first stage (perception) in the three-stage sequence just described may or may not be a source of interference in dual-task performance, depending on the nature of the stimuli. As you might expect, two stimuli that involve the same sensory system interfere with each other more than do two that involve different sensory systems (Allport & others, 1972). Thus, people find it

Headed for a fall?

People can divide attention between two tasks, but that ability may have limits.

easier to keep track of a visual signal and an auditory signal simultaneously than to keep track of two different visual signals, or two different auditory signals. Concerning vision, the difficulty lies not just in the need to move the eyes. Vision is very much object-based, and research suggests that people can attend visually to only one object at a time. Thus, subjects can make two judgments about a visual display faster if the judgments concern the same object than if they concern different objects, even if the two objects overlap in space so that the relevant parts are as close together in the two-object condition as they are in the one-object condition (Duncan, 1984; Kanwisher & Driver, 1992).

Given such sources of interference, how do people routinely become adept at performing two tasks at once in their everyday lives? One likely possibility is that they learn to time-share their mental resources efficiently between the two tasks so that mental operations that would interfere with each other are separated in time. For example, drivers who carry on conversations might learn to time the response-choice phases of their speaking in such a way that they do not overlap with the response-choice phases of their driving.

Automatization of Perception

■ **18. *What is some evidence that perceptual identification of a particular stimulus can become automatic with practice?***

In addition to improving the efficiency of mental time-sharing, extended practice might also improve dual-task performance by enabling a person to analyze an increasing amount of stimulus information automatically, without conscious attention. Walter Schneider and his colleagues (1984) have studied the automatization of perception in work that can be best understood by relating it to Treisman's work on feature detection. Treisman, you may recall, found that stimuli that are distinguished from others in certain primitive features, such as line orientation or color, can be detected at a glance, without a controlled search through the whole set of stimuli (shown in Figure 9.8). Schneider and his colleagues found that when subjects are given extended and consistent practice, stimulus differences that are more complex than those described by Treisman begin to pop out at them in a similar way. In their experiments, slides containing from one to four letters each were presented in rapid succession, and the subject's task was to press one button if any of a certain set of previously memorized target letters appeared on the slide, and another button if not. Accuracy and speed were influenced at first by the number of distractor letters on the slide. After much practice, however, subjects were able to notice a target letter immediately, no matter how many other letters also appeared on the slide. Similarly, a practiced driver might be able to perceive and respond to a red traffic signal, or a slight swerving of one of the many cars in view, without conscious attention.

■ **19. *Under what conditions might automatic processing interfere with task performance, and how is such interference illustrated by the Stroop effect?***

To say that a perceptual skill has become automatic is to say that certain information will be picked up whether the person consciously tries to pick it up or not. This has drawbacks as well as advantages. Schneider and his colleagues (1984) found that once subjects could automatically distinguish target letters from distractors, they had unusual difficulty with new tasks in which letters that had been targets were now among the distractors. Their attention continued to be drawn automatically to the previous targets, which slowed them down in finding the new targets. Similarly, if you are a skilled driver and are riding in the front passenger seat of a car, looking forward out the window, perhaps you can't help noticing that the car ahead of you is slowing down, and can't help pushing your foot down on an imaginary brake (the response, as well as the perception, may be automatic), even though you are trying to be a relaxed, trusting passenger. In other words, perception can become not only automatic but obligatory; even with conscious effort we have difficulty ignoring stimuli to which we have learned to respond automatically.

An often-cited example of the obligatory nature of automatic perception is the ***Stroop interference effect***, named after J. Ridley Stroop (1935), who was the first to describe it. Stroop presented words or shapes printed in colored ink to subjects and asked them to name the ink color of each as rapidly as possible. In some cases each word was the name of the color in which it was printed (for example, the word *red* printed in red ink); in others it was the name of a different color (for example, the word *blue* printed in red ink); and in still others it was not a color name. Stroop found that subjects were much slower at naming the ink colors of words that named a different color than they were at any of the other tasks, no matter how much they practiced. Apparently, when primed to report color names, people find it almost impossible *not* to read color names that appear before their eyes, and the reading interferes with the response of naming the ink color when the two are different. To demonstrate this effect yourself, follow the instructions in Figure 9.16. As you would expect, children who have not yet learned to read are not susceptible to the Stroop effect, and children who are just learning to read are only slightly susceptible to it (Gibson, 1971). In fact, the Stroop effect is sometimes used as an index of the extent to which reading has become automatic for a child.

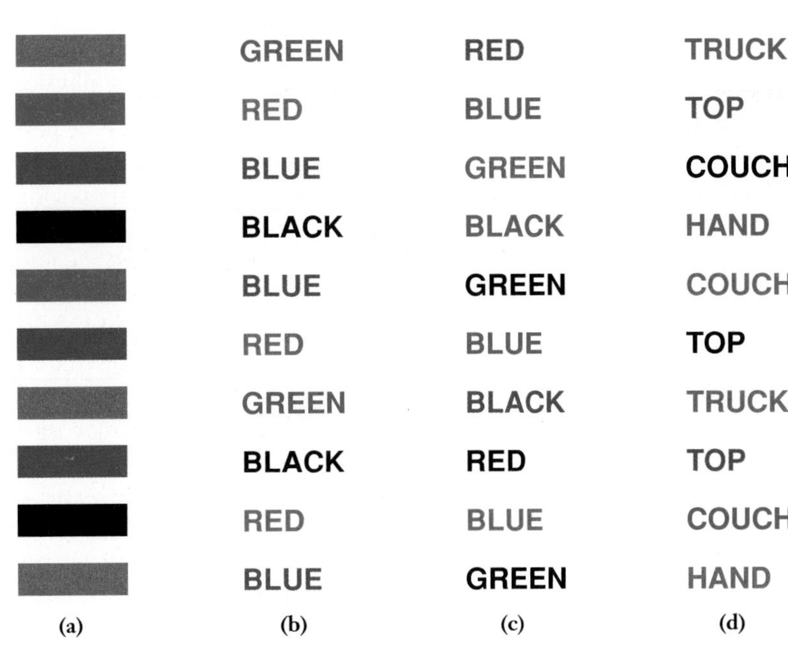

Figure 9.16 ***The Stroop interference effect***

Time yourself (or a friend) on each of the following tasks: (1) Name the colors in each box in column (a). (2) Name the ink colors used to print the words in columns (b), (c), and (d). (Time each of these separately.) Column (c) will take the longest, because the color words interfere with naming the ink colors—that is the Stroop interference effect. Column (d) may also take somewhat longer than either (a) or (b), because the noncolor words interfere somewhat with naming the ink colors. Column (b) should be quickest, because there the words facilitate naming the ink colors.

Theories of Attention

Suppose you were trying to design a machine that could select among sensory inputs in ways that were consistent with the research on attention that you have just been reading about. What would be the machine's main components, and what would each component do? That is the question perceptual psychologists tackle when they develop theories, or models, of attention.

A General Model and Broadbent's Filter Theory

■ **20. *What are the main components of most models of attention, and what is the function of each component?***

Figure 9.17 illustrates a simple model of attention containing only the components that are most commonly included in the various models developed by perceptual psychologists (Johnston & Dark, 1986). Notice that the model contains two main information-processing compartments. The first, called *automatic*, or *preattentive*, *processing*, receives input from the senses and performs some preliminary analysis of it. In most models, this compartment is assumed to be unselective and essentially unlimited in capacity, acting in parallel on all incoming information at once. The second compartment, called *controlled*, or *attentive*, *processing*, is assumed to be selective, limited in capacity, and to act serially on only a small portion of the available information. Information in the preattentive compartment is assumed to be unconscious, and information in the attentive compartment is assumed to be at least partly conscious. The *selector*, between the two compartments, determines what information enters the attentive compartment from the preattentive compartment.

Based on these components, various theories have differed in their description of (a) the amount or kind of processing that can occur preattentively, (b) the nature of the selector, and (c) the sources of influence that can modify the selector (so that it selects different kinds of information at different times).

The first version of the type of model depicted in Figure 9.17 was the *filter theory* developed by Donald Broadbent (1958). Broadbent likened the selector to a filter (or sieve), which completely blocks passage of most particles but allows through those that have a particular physical definition. He proposed that the preattentive stage analyzes only the physical features of sensory stimuli (such as colors and slants of lines, or pitches of sounds) and that the selector uses only that physical information, not information about the meaning of the stimuli, to determine what will enter the attentive stage. He proposed further that selection criteria can be varied, in top-down fashion, by mechanisms in the attentive compartment that choose the stimulus track to be attended based on physical features (say, a particular person's voice as defined by physical properties such as pitch range).

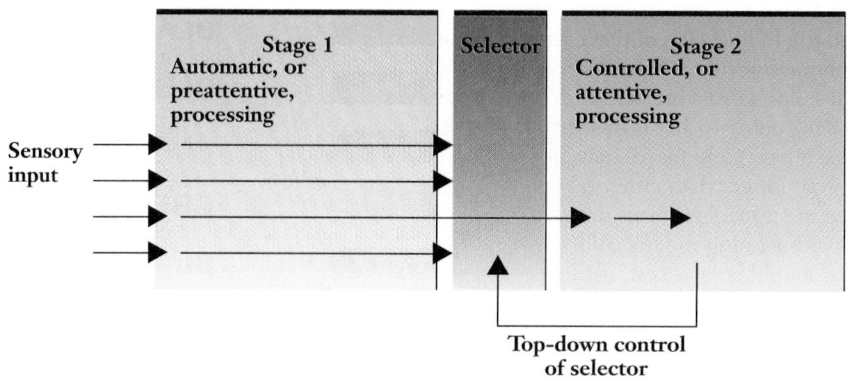

Figure 9.17 ***A generalized model of attention***

All sensory input is processed, in parallel, in the preattentive compartment, and then some of it is selected to enter the attentive compartment for further processing. The arrow going from the attentive compartment to the selector indicates top-down control of the selection criteria.

Late-Selection and Early-Selection Variations of the Model

Broadbent's filter model accounts for people's ability to hear or see selectively based on physical distinctions and for their failure to register the meanings of unattended stimuli, but it does not account for those occasions on which people do register the meanings of unattended stimuli. How might the model be modified to allow for people's ability to hear their own name in an unattended message or their ability to be influenced by the meaning of a stimulus that is not consciously perceived (such as the duck in Figure 9.14)?

■ **21.** ***How do late-selection and early-selection theories of attention differ from each other? How does each account for people's ability to respond to the meaning of a stimulus that they did not consciously perceive?***

One approach has been to expand the preattentive stage by proposing that people automatically and unconsciously analyze at least some incoming stimuli for meaning as well as for physical features. Theories of that sort are called ***late-selection theories***; they propose that selection occurs relatively late in the processing of stimulus information and is based at least partly on the meaning of the stimuli. Richard Shiffrin and Walter Schneider (1977) developed a late-selection theory based on their findings concerning the automatization of perception, discussed earlier. In their model, the preattentive stage can process very familiar stimuli for meaning, and based on this processing the selector can pass such stimuli into the attentive stage where they become conscious to the person.

Another approach has been to expand the attentive stage by proposing that not all information entering that stage reaches consciousness. Theories of this sort are called ***early-selection theories*** because they hold to Broadbent's original assumption that selection occurs early in the processing of stimulus information before it is analyzed for meaning. An example of such a theory is the *attenuation theory* developed by Anne Treisman (1969). Treisman proposed that the selector does not completely block unattended information, but rather attenuates (weakens) it, as if turning down the volume. Having entered the second stage, the attenuated information may or may not be analyzed for meaning. If the receiving mechanism in the second stage is highly sensitive to a certain stimulus (such as the person's own name), or has been prepared to receive a certain stimulus (because of the meaning of previous input), that stimulus will be analyzed for meaning even if it had entered in attenuated form.

How do early-selection theories, such as Treisman's, explain unconscious analysis of meaning? Essentially they do this by distinguishing between attention and consciousness (Kahneman & Treisman, 1984). These theories suggest that a great quantity of information passes into the attentive stage and is analyzed for meaning at any of various levels of consciousness. Only some of this information is analyzed at a level of consciousness that allows the person to describe it.

Perhaps it has already occurred to you that early-selection models of attention are very much like Treisman's feature-integration model of pattern recognition (depicted in Figure 9.7). In fact, Treisman's model of attention and her model of pattern recognition are essentially the same. Stages 1 and 2 of Figure 9.7 correspond with Stages 1 and 2 of Figure 9.17. In Treisman's view, attention is the process that brings the various physical features of an object together so that it can be recognized.

A Clinical Example of Perception Without Consciousness

I noted that some models of attention account for considerable stimulus analysis without the person's consciousness of the stimuli. That this can in fact occur is dramatically illustrated in people who have brain damage that separates some of their perceptual processing mechanisms from the mechanisms that permit consciousness.

■ **22.** ***How is the distinction between conscious and unconscious perception illustrated by a clinical example?***

Melvyn Goodale and his colleagues (1991) have described the case of a woman who, as a result of carbon monoxide poisoning, lost her conscious ability to see the shapes and orientations of objects in her environment. Despite that loss, she continued to behave appropriately toward objects in ways that depended on seeing those shapes and orientations. In one experiment, for example, when she was shown an upright disk with a slot cut through it, she claimed to be unable to see the orientation of the slot. Consistent with that claim, when she was asked to hold a card at the same angle as the slot, her accuracy (over several trials with the slot at varying orientations) was no better than chance. But when she was asked to slip the card into the slot as if posting a letter, she did so quickly and accurately on every trial, holding the card at just the right orientation before it reached the slot. Observations such as this add to the evidence that the mind can analyze stimuli and make complex, behavior-guiding judgments without conscious awareness of the information that underlies those judgments.

■ **23.** ***What is the distinction between an explicit and implicit test of perception?***

What was the essential difference between the task on which this woman failed and the one on which she succeeded? The first task was an *explicit* test of her perception of the slot's orientation, and the second was an *implicit* test of that perception. In other words, the first task made it clear that the job was to judge the orientation of the slot, but in the second task that judgment, though required, was not the stated problem. Similarly, all the evidence for a distinction between unconscious and conscious processes that you have read about in this chapter were based on failure at explicit tests coupled with success at implicit tests. For example, in Eagle's experiment (illustrated in Figure 9.14), subjects were unable to say that they had seen a duck when explicitly asked what was on the slide, but drew ducks or other duck-related objects when given a different problem. Thus, when psychologists say that a person perceives an item of information unconsciously but not consciously, they are really saying that the person cannot answer explicit questions about the item, but can use that item in solving other problems. In Chapter 10, you will read of research on memory that makes much use of this explicit-implicit distinction. Entirely different laws of memory seem to apply to the two.

Perceiving Depth, Size, and Motion

Our visual world is not flat like the retinas of our eyes, but is three-dimensional. Objects occupy and move in space that includes not only a vertical (up-down) and a horizontal (right-left) dimension in our field of view, but also a dimension of depth—objects can appear closer to or farther from our eyes. Historically, perceptual psychology grew out of early attempts to understand how people can perceive three-dimensional space and how that perception is involved in perceiving the size and motion of objects.

Hermann von Helmholtz

Considered by many to be the greatest of all nineteenth-century physiologists, Helmholtz was also a pioneer of what we now call cognitive psychology. His unconscious inference theory of perception posits that the mind constructs, through unconscious calculations, meaningful percepts from cues picked up by the senses.

A critical step in this history was the publication, in the mid-nineteenth century, of a treatise on visual perception by Hermann von Helmholtz (1867/1962), the German physiologist whose theories of pitch perception and color vision were discussed in Chapter 8. Helmholtz argued that visual perception is not a passive response of the visual system to the light that enters the eyes, but an active mental process. When we see a visual scene we do not see directly the light on our retinas, but rather we *use* that light to construct, in our mind, a mental representation of the scene. The light on our retinas is not the scene we see, but is simply a source of *cues* about the scene. As we look, our mind identifies the critical cues and uses them, detectivelike, to construct a mental representation of what must be out there in the world before us.

Seeing the light

How do we judge the size of the people and the objects in this photograph? This section is about our ability to see a three-dimensional world in a two-dimensional representation.

24. *Why did Helmholtz use the term* unconscious inference *to describe the mental processes that underlie perception?*

Thus, according to Helmholtz, visual perception is always a matter of *inference*. We infer the characteristics and positions of objects from cues in the reflected light, and those inferences are our perceptions. Helmholtz also pointed out that some of the steps in this inferential process can be expressed mathematically in equations relating the information in the reflected light to conclusions about characteristics of objects in the visual scene. He contended that the mind must perform such calculations in order to produce accurate perceptions. Of course Helmholtz realized people are not conscious of performing calculations as they look and perceive, and therefore he coined the term ***unconscious inference*** to refer to the mental processes that underlie perception. The top-down and bottom-up processes discussed earlier in the chapter are extensions of Helmholtz's concept of unconscious inference. Now, in the more direct tradition of Helmholtz, let us examine how unconscious inferences may provide the basis for our ability to perceive depth, size, and motion.

Cues for Depth Perception

What cues in the light on our retinas allow us to perceive three-dimensional space? It is relatively easy to understand how we can perceive the vertical and horizontal dimensions of space; those are represented directly on the two-dimensional surface of each retina (see Figure 8.11 in Chapter 8). But what cues enable us to perceive the third dimension, depth (distance from our eyes)? Helmholtz (1867/1962) was able to describe an impressive number of such cues based on work that preceded him, including all of those discussed below.

Binocular Cues

Depth perception works best when you use both eyes. You can prove that with a simple demonstration. Pick up two pencils and hold them in front of you, one in each hand, with their points toward each other. Now, with one eye closed, move the pencils toward each other to make the points touch at their tips. Chances are, you will miss by a little bit on your first attempt, and your subsequent adjustments will have something of a trial-and-error quality. Now repeat the task with both eyes open. Is it easier? Do you find that now you can see which adjustments to make to bring the points together and that you no longer need trial and error?

Research shows that two types of cues contribute to the binocular advantage. The less important of the two is *eye convergence*, the inward turning of the eyes that occurs when you look at an object that is close to you. The closer an object is, the more the two eyes must converge in order to look at it. To experience eye convergence consciously, try focusing both eyes on your finger as you hold it a few inches in front of your nose. In theory, the perceptual system could judge the distance of an object from the degree to which the eyes converge when looking at it. In practice, however, convergence is a poor cue for distance. Experiments in which convergence is the only cue available indicate that it is useful for objects that lie within a few inches of the eyes, but not for more distant objects (Hochberg, 1971).

■ **25.** ***How can binocular disparity serve as a cue for depth?***

The other, far more important cue requiring two eyes is ***binocular disparity***. Because the eyes are several centimeters apart, they view an object from slightly different directions, thus providing slightly different (disparate) views of it. The difference between the two eyes' views is called binocular disparity. To see how the degree of binocular disparity varies depending on an object's distance from your eyes, hold a closed book up vertically with its spine toward you, as shown in Figure 9.18. Notice that with both eyes open you can see not only the spine but also both the front and back covers of the book. You see the front cover with your right eye and the back cover with your left eye. (You can prove this by closing one eye and then the other. Notice also that the angle of the book appears to shift even though you are holding it stationary.) If you move the book farther away, you will find that the two eyes' views become less disparate than they were when the book was closer. The spine, which is the part of the view that the two eyes share, now takes up relatively more space and the covers take up relatively less space in either eye's view than they did before. Thus, the degree of disparity between the two eyes' views can serve as a cue to judge an object's distance from the eyes—the less the disparity, the

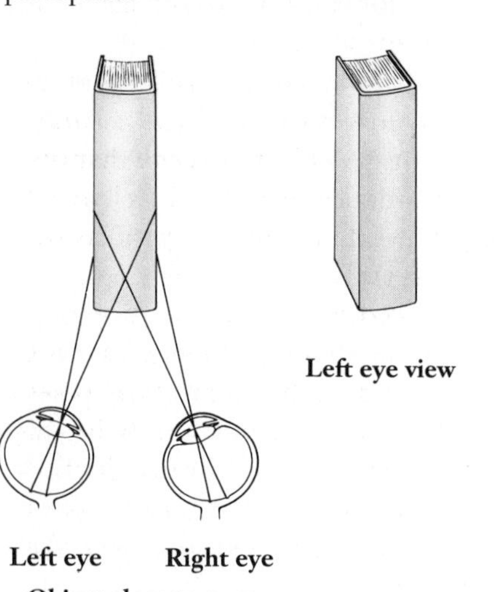

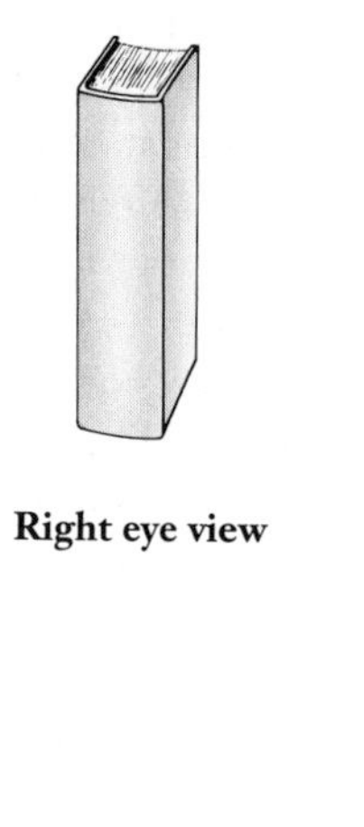

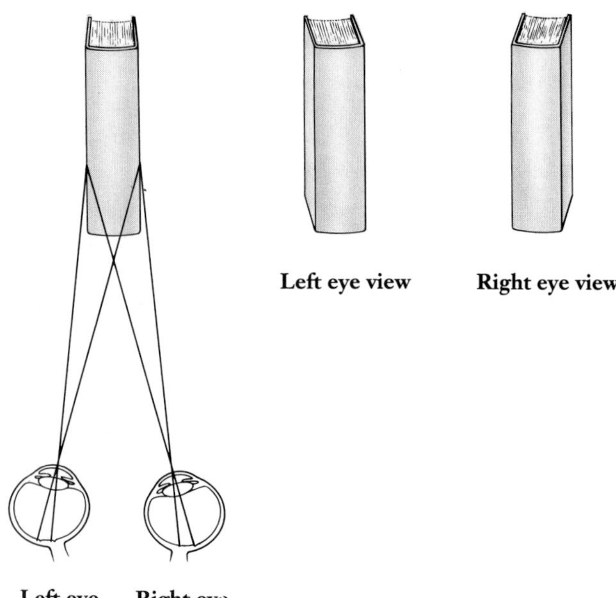

Figure 9.18 ***Demonstration of binocular disparity***

If you hold a book in front of you and view it first with one eye and then the other, you will see a different view with each eye, as shown here. You will also notice that the book shifts its position relative to background objects as you shift from one eye to the other. The farther away the book, the less difference you see. The amount of this difference (degree of binocular disparity) is a cue for depth perception.

greater the distance. Helmholtz (1867/1962) showed mathematically how the difference in distance of two objects from the eyes can be calculated from differences in the degree of binocular disparity.

26. *How did the invention of the stereoscope demonstrate the ability of binocular disparity to produce a vivid perception of depth?*

The ability to see depth when binocular disparity is the only depth cue available—called *stereopsis*—was first demonstrated in the early nineteenth century by Charles Wheatstone (described by Helmholtz, 1867/1962). Wheatstone wondered what would happen if he drew two slightly different pictures of the same object or scene, one as seen by the left eye and one as seen by the right, and then viewed them simultaneously, each with the appropriate eye. To permit such viewing, he invented a device called a *stereoscope*. The effect was dramatic. When viewed through the stereoscope, the two pictures were fused perceptually into a single image containing depth. Stereoscopes became a great fad in the late nineteenth century. People could see scenes such as Buckingham Palace or the Grand Canyon in full depth by placing cards that contained two photographs of the same scene, shot simultaneously from slightly different angles, into their stereoscope (The Viewmaster, a child's toy, is a type of a stereoscope in common use today.) Three-dimensional motion pictures and comic books employ the same general principle. In the simplest versions, each frame of the film or comic strip contains an overlapping pair of similar images, each in a different color, and the viewer wears colored glasses that allow only one image to enter each eye.

Entertainment in depth
The three-dimensionality of some movies is achieved by projecting an overlapping dual image on the screen and viewing it through special lenses that filter a different image to each eye, producing binocular disparity.

Monocular Cues

Although depth perception is optimal with two eyes, it is by no means absent with one. One important cue that does not depend on two eyes is ***motion parallax***, which refers to the changed view one has of a scene or object when one's head moves sideways to the scene or object. You can demonstrate motion parallax to yourself in a way very similar to the demonstration of binocular disparity. Hold a book up with the spine toward you again (as in Figure 9.18) and view it now with just one eye as you rock your head back and forth. As your head moves, you gain different views of the book, seeing first one cover and then the other. If you now move the book farther away, the same head movement produces a less-changed view. Thus, the degree of change in either eye's view at one moment compared to the next, as the head moves in space, can serve as a cue for assessing the object's distance from the eyes—the smaller the change, the greater the distance.

27. *How can motion parallax serve as a cue for depth, and how is it similar to binocular disparity?*

As you can see from this demonstration, motion parallax is very similar to binocular disparity. In fact, binocular disparity is sometimes called *binocular parallax*. The word *parallax* refers to the apparent change in an object or scene that occurs when it is viewed from a new vantage point. In motion parallax the changed vantage point comes from the movement of the head, and in binocular parallax (or disparity) it comes from the separation of the two eyes. Motion parallax also accounts for a phenomenon that you have probably noticed many times while staring out the side window of a moving train or car: Objects that are farther away cross your field of view more slowly than do those that are nearby. Signs or utility poles next to the road race past you, while trees off in the distance pass leisurely by. At the farthest extreme, the sun (which, for perceptual purposes, is infinitely distant) doesn't move past you at all, but seems to float through the sky at the same speed and direction as you and the train or car. Again, the closer the scene or object, the more sharply your view of it changes as your head moves sideways to it.

28. *What are some cues for depth that exist in pictures as well as in the actual, three-dimensional world?*

The cues discussed so far depend normally on the geometry of true three-dimensionality and cannot be used to depict depth in conventional two-dimensional pictures. All of the remaining monocular depth cues, however, can provide a sense of depth in pictures as well as in the real three-dimensional world, and thus are called ***pictorial cues***. You can identify the most important of these by examining

Figure 9.19 ***Pictorial cues for depth***

Occlusion, relative image size for familiar objects, linear perspective, texture gradient, and position relative to the horizon all serve as depth cues in this picture.

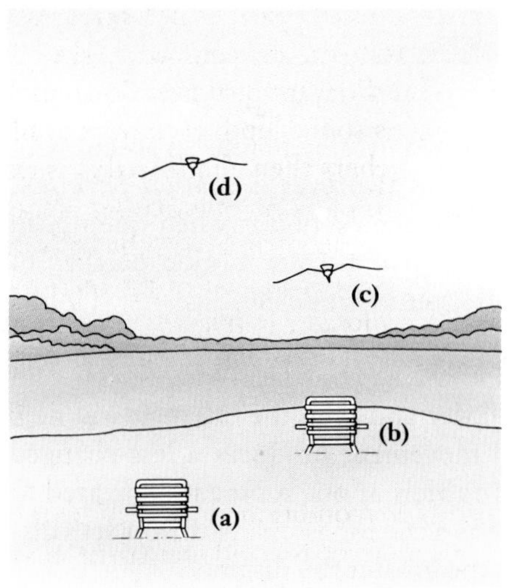

Figure 9.20 ***Proximity to the horizon as a depth cue***

In this picture, (b) and (c) are seen as farther away than (a) and (d), respectively, because they are closer to the horizon.

Figure 9.19 and thinking of all the reasons why you see the man as standing in the foreground and the house as more distant.

- ***Occlusion*** The man partially occludes (cuts off) the view of the house, which indicates that the man is closer to us than is the house. Near objects occlude more distant ones.
- ***Relative image size for familiar objects*** The image of the man (both in the picture and on the viewer's retina) is taller than that of the house. Because we know that people are not taller than houses, we take the man's larger image as a sign that he must be closer to us than is the house.
- ***Linear perspective*** The lines marking the sides of the driveway converge as they go from the man to the house, indicating that the house is farther away. Parallel lines appear to converge as they become more distant.
- ***Texture gradient*** Texture elements of the picture, such as the stones on the driveway and the grass blades on the lawn, become gradually smaller, more densely packed, and less defined moving from the man to the house.
- ***Position relative to the horizon*** The house is closer to the horizon than is the man. In outdoor scenes, objects nearer the horizon are usually seen as farther away than are those that are displaced from the horizon either up or down (see also Figure 9.20).

The Role of Depth Cues in Size Perception

The ability to judge the size of an object is tied intimately to the ability to judge its distance. As Figure 9.21 illustrates, the size of the retinal image of an object is inversely proportional to the object's distance from the retina. Thus, if an object is moved twice as far away, it produces a retinal image half the height and width it did before. But you don't see the object as smaller, just farther away. The ability to see an object as unchanged in size, despite change in the image size as it moves farther away or closer, is called ***size constancy***. For familiar objects, such as a pencil or a car, previous knowledge of the object's size probably contributes to size constancy. But size constancy also occurs for unfamiliar objects if cues for distance are available, and even familiar objects can appear to become larger or smaller if misleading distance cues are present.

Figure 9.21 ***Relationship of retinal image size to object size and distance***

If, as in the upper sketch, object B is twice as tall and wide as object A and also twice as far away from the eye, the retinal images that the two objects produce will be the same size. If, as in the lower sketch, object A is moved twice its former distance from the eye, the retinal image produced will be half its former height and width.

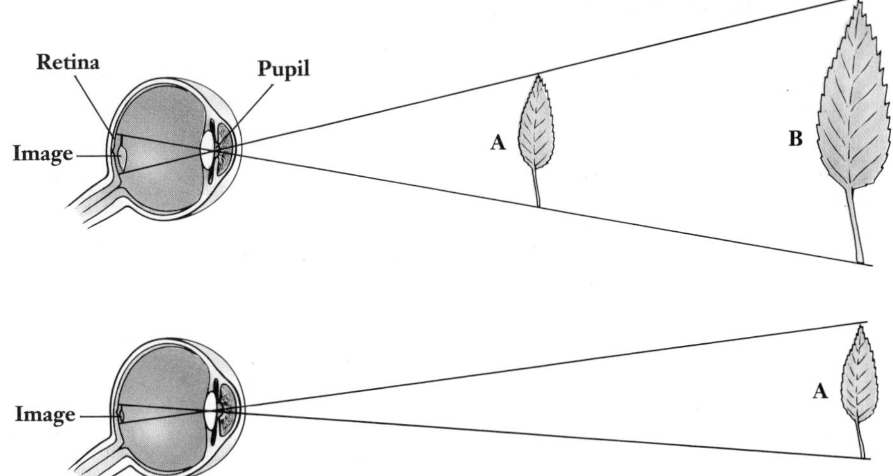

■ **29.** ***In theory, why should our ability to judge an unfamiliar object's size depend on our ability to judge its distance? What is some evidence that this dependence indeed exists?***

Psychologists have shown that people cannot judge the size of unfamiliar objects without cues about distance. In one such experiment, subjects were asked to judge the relative sizes of objects that were placed at different distances down each of two hallways (Holway & Boring, 1941). As long as some depth cues were available, the judgments were quite accurate. The researchers then eliminated all such cues by requiring the subjects to view each object with one eye (eliminating binocular cues), through a peephole (eliminating motion parallax), and with the hallway completely darkened except for the object being viewed (eliminating pictorial cues). Under these conditions the subjects could no longer judge size accurately. With no depth cues, an object that was twice as tall and wide, but also twice as far away, as a second object appeared to be the same size as the second object.

Depth Cues as a Basis for Size Illusions

Visual illusions are misperceptions that occur under conditions in which certain cues that would be present when viewing most normal, real-world scenes are missing. Perceptual psychologists usually study illusions not for their own sake (though they are interesting), but because such study can help isolate from the many cues available in normal scenes those that are most critical in producing a particular per-

A size-distance illusion

We know that these young women must be approximately the same size, so what explains this illusion? The back wall and both windows are actually trapezoidal in shape, and the wall is slanted, so that its left-hand edge is actually twice as tall and twice as far away from the viewer as its right-hand edge (see drawing at right). When we view this scene through a peephole (or the camera's eye), we automatically assume that the setting is normal, that the occupants are the same distance away, and therefore that their size is different. Rooms of this type are called *Ames Rooms*, after Adelbert Ames, who built the first one.

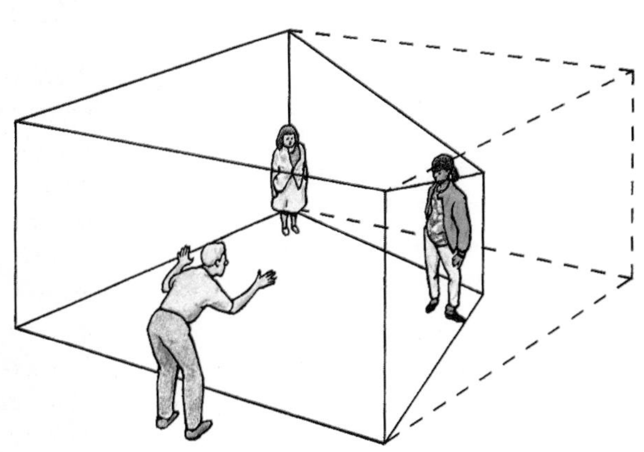

ceptual effect. Figure 9.22 illustrates two classic size illusions: the ***Müller-Lyer illusion*** (first described by F. C. Müller-Lyer in the mid-nineteenth century) and the ***Ponzo illusion*** (first described by Mario Ponzo in 1913). In each illusion two horizontal bars appear to be different in length, but if you measure them you will discover that they are identical.

30. *How might the unconscious assessment of depth provide a basis for the Ponzo and Müller-Lyer illusions?*

The most common explanation of size illusions is the *depth-processing theory* (Rock, 1984). This theory—consistent with everything said so far about the relation between size and distance—maintains that one object in each illusion appears larger than the other because of distance cues that, at some early stage of perceptual processing, lead it to be judged as farther away. If one object is judged to be farther away than the other, but the two produce the same-sized retinal image, then the object judged as farther away will be judged as larger. This theory applies most readily to the Ponzo illusion, in which the two converging lines provide the depth cue of linear perspective, causing (according to the theory) the upper bar to be judged as farther away and hence larger than the lower one. The photograph in Figure 9.23 makes this point clear.

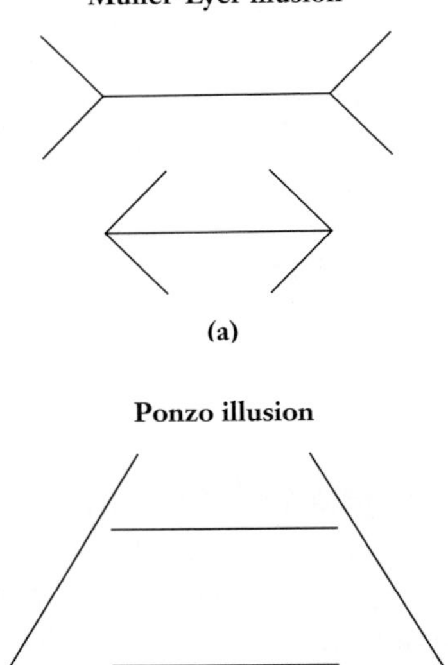

Figure 9.22 *The Müller-Lyer and Ponzo illusions*

In each case, the top horizontal bar looks longer than the bottom, although they are actually the same length.

The application of the depth-processing theory to the Müller-Lyer illusion is a bit more subtle. The assumption in this application is that people see the figures as three-dimensional objects, something like sawhorses viewed from above. The object with wings extending outward (top drawing in Figure 9.22a) may be seen as an upside-down sawhorse, with legs toward the viewer, and the one with inward wings (bottom drawing) may be seen as a right-side-up sawhorse, with its horizontal bar closer to the observer. If real sawhorses were viewed this way, the horizontal bar of the upside-down one would be farther from the observer than that of the right-side-up one, and if it produced the same-sized retinal image it would in fact be longer (see Figure 9.24).

The depth-processing theory seems to offer an elegant explanation of the Ponzo and Müller-Lyer illusions, but perhaps you have already thought of an objection to it. Most people, when they look at the Müller-Lyer figures, do *not* see them as three-dimensional objects, but rather as flat, arrowlike objects; yet they see the illusion. Even with the Ponzo illusion, many people do not notice depth in the picture; they do not see the top bar as farther away than the bottom one, yet they

Figure 9.23 *Depth-processing explanation of the Ponzo illusion*

If this were a real, three-dimensional scene, not a photograph, and the red bars really existed as shown, the one in the background would not only look larger but would *be* larger than the one in the foreground. (Adapted from Gregory, 1968.)

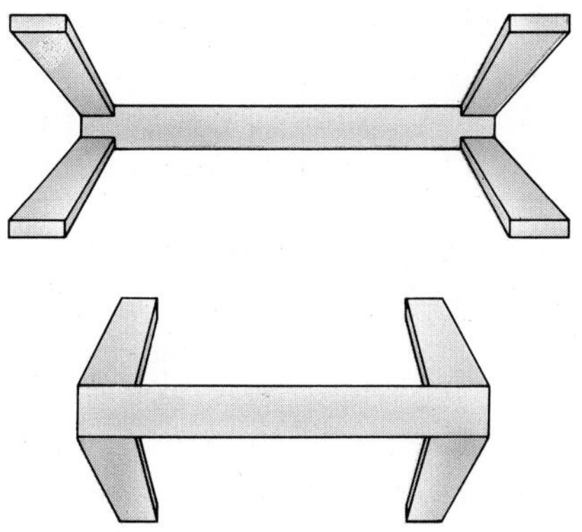

Figure 9.24 ***Depth-processing explanation of the Müller-Lyer illusion***

Compare these sawhorses to the Müller-Lyer drawings in Figure 9.22. If these were real sawhorses, viewed from above in the three-dimensional world, the upside-down one would be longer than the right-side-up one.

see the illusion. Researchers who support the depth-processing theory of these illusions are well aware of this objection, but it does not lead them to abandon the theory (Gregory, 1968; Rock, 1984). They remind the dissenters, as did Helmholtz, that the mental processes leading to perceptions are *unconscious*. The cues to depth in the Müller-Lyer and Ponzo figures may be too weak, or too ambiguous, to lead to a conscious perception of depth, yet they may still lead to an unconscious assessment of depth. That unconscious assessment may enter into the mental calculation that leads to a conscious perception of size differences even if it does not manifest itself in a conscious perception of depth.

The Moon Illusion

The oldest size illusion of all is the ***moon illusion***, which has provoked debate since ancient Greek and Roman times. Have you ever noticed how huge the moon looks when it is near the earth's horizon, just above the trees or buildings in the distance? The moon looks much smaller when it is closer to the zenith (straight up). This difference is truly an illusion. Objectively, the moon is the same size, and the same distance from us, whether it is located at the horizon or the zenith. If you view the horizon moon through a peephole, so that you see it in isolation from other objects such as trees and buildings, the illusion disappears; the moon looks no larger in that case at the horizon than it does at the zenith.

The moon illusion

Up against this tree, the moon at the horizon looks very large. Seen in isolation, with no other objects serving as size cues, the moon would appear to be the same size at the horizon as at the zenith.

■ **31.** ***How might the unconscious inference of depth provide a basis for the moon illusion?***

A depth-processing account of this illusion was first proposed by the Greek astronomer Ptolemy in the second century, was revived by Helmholtz (1867/1962) in the nineteenth century, and was supported through research by Lloyd Kaufman and Irvin Rock (1962, 1989) in recent times. The account can be summarized as follows: Most objects that we see near the earth's horizon are farther away than objects that we see near the zenith. For example, birds or clouds seen near the horizon are usually farther away than those seen straight up (look back at Figure 9.20). Thus, our perceptual system assumes that the moon is farther away at the horizon than at the zenith, even though in reality it is the same distance away from us in either position. As in the case of the Ponzo and Müller-Lyer illusion, when two objects produce the same-size retinal image and are judged to be of different distances away, that which is judged farther away is seen as larger than the other. (For more on this explanation, and some evidence supporting it, look at Figure 9.25 on page 316 and read the caption.)

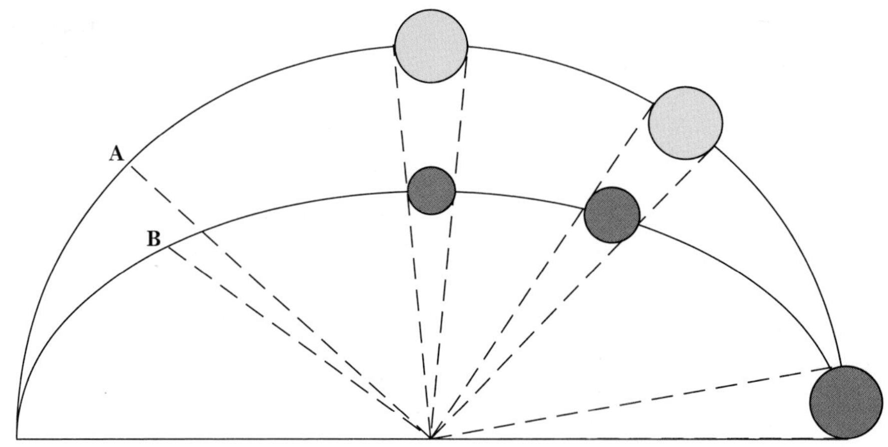

Figure 9.25 ***Depth-processing explanation of the moon illusion***

The upper curve shows the true positions of the moon as it pursues its circular orbit around the earth. If people unconsciously perceive the moon as moving across a sky shaped like a flattened dome (lower curve), the same-sized retinal image will appear smaller at the zenith than at the horizon, as indicated by the darker discs (compare this to the size-depth relation shown in Figure 9.21). In a test of whether people see the sky as a flattened dome consistent with the illusion, researchers asked subjects to direct a pointer midway between the horizon and the zenith. Line B shows the average direction in which they pointed. Notice that line B points to the midpoint appropriate for the flattened-dome view of the sky, and not that appropriate for the half-sphere view, which is indicated by line A. (Adapted from Kaufman & Rock, 1962.)

Even today, one of the leading objections to this explanation of the moon illusion is that people do not *consciously* see the horizon moon as farther away than the zenith moon (Hershenson, 1989). When people see the large-appearing horizon moon and are asked whether it seems farther away or closer than usual, they usually say closer. Again, however, as with the Ponzo and Müller-Lyer illusions, Kaufman and Rock (1989) counter that we must distinguish between unconscious and conscious assessments. From this perspective, the sequence of perceptual assessments about the horizon moon might be described as follows: (1) Unconscious processes judge that the moon is farther away than usual (because objects near the horizon are usually farthest away). (2) Unconscious processes judge that the moon is larger than usual (because if it is farther away but produces the same-sized retinal image, it must be larger). (3) The judgment that the moon looks larger than usual enters consciousness and leads to the conscious judgment that it must be closer than usual (because we know that the moon doesn't really change size, so its large apparent size must be due to closeness).

Assimilation as Another Explanation of Size Illusions

Not all researchers agree with the depth-processing explanation of size illusions, and few accept it as the only explanation. Of various alternatives offered, one that has drawn considerable research interest is the ***assimilation theory***, which maintains that the visual system tends to incorporate nearby elements into an object's boundaries when assessing its size (Rock, 1984). This explanation applies most readily to the ***frame illusion***, in which a frame surrounding an enclosed area makes the enclosed area seem larger (see Figure 9.26), but it may also partly explain the three illusions discussed above.

Regarding the Müller-Lyer illusion, you could imagine that at some unconscious level the perceptual system compromises between two alternative sets of boundaries in assessing the length of each bar; one set consists of the actual ends of

Figure 9.26 ***The frame illusion***

The shaded area is actually the same size in each of these drawings, but to most people it appears larger with an outside frame (b) and smaller with an inside frame(c). The shaded area also appears larger when any cues are added that would tend to draw the eyes from its border outward (d), and smaller when any cues are added that would tend to draw the eyes from its border inward (e). According to the assimilation theory of size illusions, stimuli near an object's boundary tend to be assimilated into the perception of the boundary, moving it outward or inward, depending on whether the stimuli are located outside the boundary or within it.

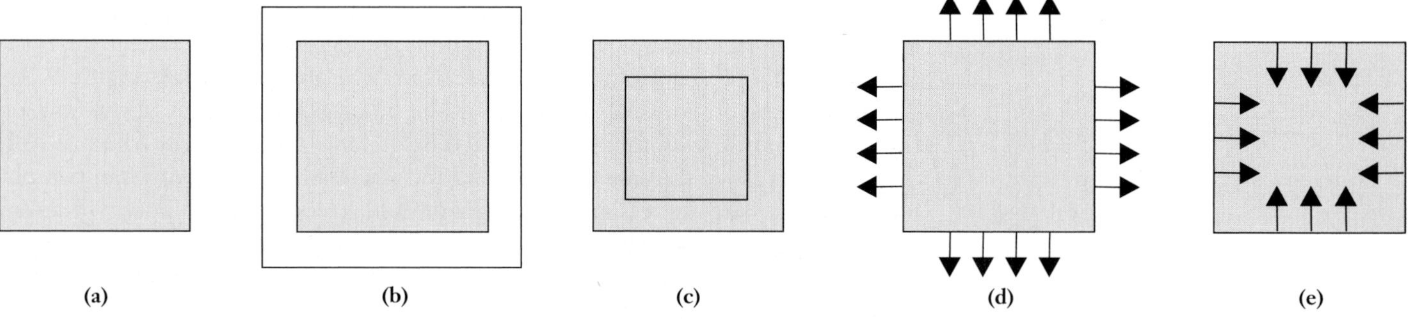

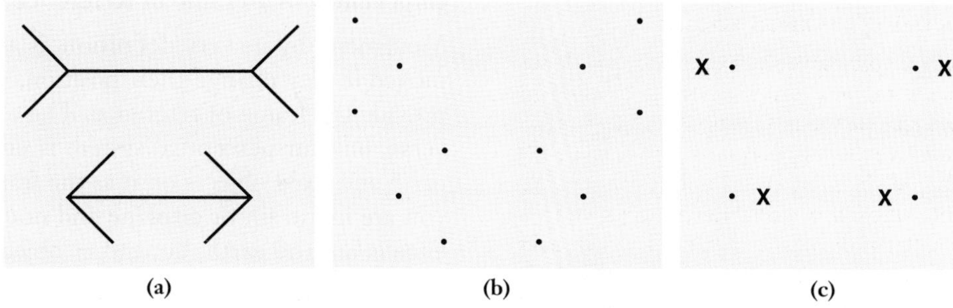

Figure 9.27 ***Müller-Lyer type illusions without depth cues***

In (b) the ends of each bar and tips of each wing are represented by dots, and in (c) the figure is simplified still further by replacing the wings with an x, either outside or inside the dots. In neither (b) nor (c) are there cues for depth, yet the illusion remains to some degree. In (b) and (c) most people see the two dots representing the ends of the bars as farther apart in the top figure than in the bottom figure. Such findings suggest that the illusion may be caused partly by a tendency for the nearby elements to be assimilated into the length that is being judged. (Adapted from Coren, 1986.)

■ **32.** ***How might the assimilation theory partly explain the Müller-Lyer, Ponzo, and moon illusions?***

the bar, and the other consists of the tips of the attached wings. When the wings extend outward the compromise increases the apparent length of the bar, and when they slant inward it decreases the apparent length. Experiments that support this explanation show that size illusions can occur to some degree in figures that are analogous to the Müller-Lyer figure but lack any suggestion of depth, as illustrated in Figure 9.27. The Ponzo illusion may also be partly explained in terms of assimilation—the bar whose ends are closer to the two outside lines may seem larger because the outside lines are assimilated into its perception, and the other bar may seem smaller because the outside lines are too far away to be assimilated (Jordan & Randall, 1987). Similarly for the moon illusion, the perceived horizon moon may assimilate into it other objects that appear near the moon at the horizon, whereas the perceived zenith moon has no objects near it that can be assimilated.

Perceiving Motion

■ **33.** ***Why can't the visual system use movement of an object's image across the retina as the only cue in assessing an object's movement?***

As mentioned in Chapter 8, the visual cortex contains neurons that respond to images moving across the retina in a particular direction and velocity. But the problem of movement perception is more complex than one of sensitivity to images moving across the retina. To convince yourself of this, imagine two different scenes. In the first, you are watching a car moving down the street. You keep your eyes fixed on the car, so its image remains stationary in the center of each fovea, yet you see the car as moving. All other objects in the scene, such as the lampposts that the car drives past, are moving across each retina as your eyes move to follow the car, yet you see them as stationary. In the second scene, you are sitting in the park admiring the flowers when a dog and squirrel dash across your line of sight. In this case, the objects that produce stationary retinal images are seen as stationary, and those that produce moving images are seen as moving. If you happen to have been moving your eyes at the same time, say from one flower to another, *all* of the objects would produce images that move across the retina, at different speeds; yet you would still see the flowers as stationary and the dog and squirrel as moving. Since both moving and stationary objects can produce images that move across the retina, how does the perceptual system decide what is moving?

In theory, there are two possible solutions to the problem just described. One is that the perceptual system keeps track of eye movements and factors them into an equation to assess objects' movement. If the eyes are moving at a certain speed and direction, and the image is moving across the retina at a certain speed and direction, then the object must be moving at a certain speed and direction. The other possibility is that the perceptual system establishes among the objects in any given scene a stable frame of reference and uses that, regardless of eye movements, to assess the movement of other objects. Research indicates that eye movements can contribute to the perception of movement, but generally the frame of reference is the primary determinant (Rock, 1984).

Importance of a Frame of Reference

Movement, by its very definition, is a relativistic concept. Objects are said to have moved if they change their position, over time, with respect to other objects that provide the frame of reference. The earth moves relative to other parts of the universe, but our perceptual system is unaware of this and most commonly takes the earth and fixed objects on it as the frame of reference. In some cases, such as when you are in a train or airplane and not looking out the window, the frame of reference is not the earth, but rather objects fixed to the inside of the compartment in which you are traveling. The person sleeping in the seat beside you is in such cases seen as stationary, and the person walking down the aisle is seen as moving.

34. *How do movement illusions provide evidence that the perceptual system establishes a frame of reference and judges movement relative to that frame?*

The importance of a frame of reference is demonstrated by movement illusions that are produced when information about which elements should be taken as the frame of reference is scant or ambiguous. If you are in a stationary train and a train right next to yours starts to move, you may experience your train as moving. That is because your visual system has established the other train, seen through the window, as the frame of reference. A more romantic example is the *moon-cloud illusion*. Have you ever gazed up at the sky on a cloudy evening and seen the moon sailing across gaps in the clouds? In reality the motion of the moon with respect to the earth is too slow to detect, but clouds drift across the sky at a perceptible rate. If nothing but the clouds and the moon are in your view, your perceptual system may take the clouds as the frame of reference and interpret the relative change in position of clouds and moon as movement of the moon. More systematic evidence of the importance of a frame of reference in motion perception can be found in experiments in which people view small spots of light or other illuminated objects in an otherwise completely dark room and are asked to judge which element or elements are moving. Figure 9.28 illustrates and describes some typical results.

Figure 9.28 ***Perceived motion of spots in a dark room***

(a) A single, slowly moving spot in an otherwise completely dark room may be seen as stationary, because it may be taken as the frame of reference. (b) When two dots are visible and one is moving slowly, either dot may be seen as moving while the other is seen as the (stationary) frame of reference. (c) When an illuminated moving frame surrounds a dot, movement of the frame is seen as movement of the dot, because the frame is taken as the frame of reference. This is analogous to the moon-cloud illusion.

Movement Within Movement: More Than One Frame of Reference

35. *How does our ability to establish different frames of reference allow us to see movement within movement, and how does that help us identify objects?*

If a bicycle with a reflector attached near the rim of one wheel were to cross your field of view, the reflector would move in a series of smooth hops, as shown in Figure 9.29a, a path that mathematicians refer to as a *cycloid curve*. If it were nighttime and the reflector were the only visible part of the bicycle, you would in fact see it moving in a cycloid curve and you might wonder what that strangely hopping object could be. But if you were to watch the same reflector during the day, you would not see it hop at all. Even if you consciously tried to see it moving in a cycloid path you would have difficulty doing so. Rather, you would see it as moving in a continuous circle around the center of the wheel, while the whole wheel was going forward. That is, you would see two different movements at once, each with a different frame of reference. The frame of reference for the forward movement would be the larger environment consisting of the road and stable elements along it, and that for the revolving movement would be the center of the wheel. The same applies to all instances in which elements within an object move relative to one another while the whole object moves relative to a larger frame.

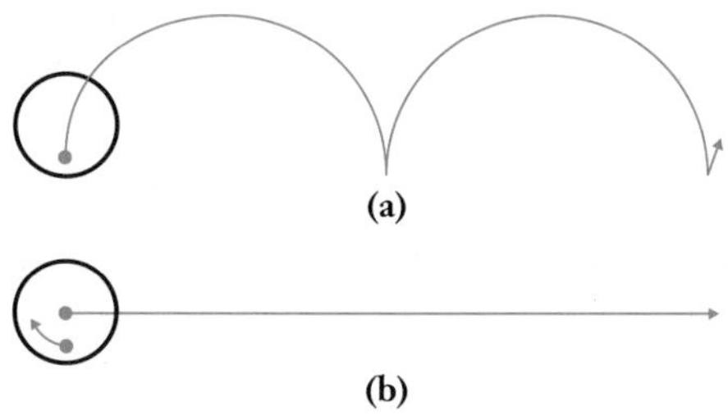

Figure 9.29 ***Perceived motion of spots on a rolling wheel***

Part (a) depicts the cycloid curve that is seen when only one spot is visible on the rim of a rolling wheel. Part (b) depicts what is typically seen when an additional spot is added to the center of the wheel. Now the cycloid curve is no longer seen, even though physically it is still present. Rather, the spot in the rim is seen as revolving around the center spot, which itself is seen as moving forward in a straight line.

Our perceptual system is remarkably adept at seeing movement within movement and can use that information to identify objects. People can often identify a wheel rolling forward on the basis of just two spots of light, one located at the wheel's center and the other located anywhere else on the wheel (see Figure 9.29b) (Cutting & Proffitt, 1982). Wheels, of course, have simple movement patterns compared to those of people and animals. Think, for example, of all of the movements within movements that you can observe while watching a person walk. The foot is moving with respect to the lower leg, the lower leg with respect to the upper leg, and so on. Every joint provides a separate frame of reference from which to observe a movement.

Gunner Johansson and his colleagues in Sweden attached a small light to each major joint of a person's body and then filmed the person in such a way that only the lights could be seen as the person engaged in various activities (see Figure 9.30). When observers saw a single still frame of the film, they had no idea what they were looking at; but as soon as the lights began to move, they recognized the object as a person performing a particular action. Just 1/10 second of viewing time, enough to go through two frames of the film, was sufficient for most viewers to see the lights as a human being walking (Johansson, 1975). Other experiments have shown that viewers can usually even judge the sex of the person in the film, based just on the way the tiny lights move as the person walks or jumps (Cutting & others, 1978; Runeson & Frykholm, 1986). Our ability to perceive subtle differences in movement patterns plays a more important role than we normally realize in identifying people and other animate objects.

Figure 9.30 ***Lights that are perceived as a person only when the person moves***

Lights attached to a person's major joints (a) are not perceived as a recognizable object in the dark when the person stands still. However, when the person begins to move (b), the lights are perceived immediately as a human form. (From Michaels & Carello, 1981.)

Two Perspectives on the Perception of Constancies

We have seen that the perceptual system uses information about *relationships* among different parts of a scene to perceive the distance, size, and movement of any given part. Thus, perception of the *distance* of an object depends on such relationships as whether the object occludes or is occluded by other objects; perception of *size* depends on the relationship between distance cues and the object's retinal image size; and perception of *movement* depends on changes, over time, in the spatial relationship between the object and other portions of the scene that serve as a frame of reference. For many years, psychologists have debated the merits of two ways of thinking about the ability of the perceptual system to use such relationships. One is the unconscious-inference theory and the other is the direct-perception theory.

To compare the two theories concretely, the following discussion focuses on how each theory explains three examples of ***visual constancies***. Visual constancies are those characteristics of objects that look constant despite retinal-image changes that occur when viewing conditions change. The three examples discussed are: (a) ***size constancy***, by which an object appears to remain the same size, even though its retinal image changes size when the object moves farther away or closer; (b) ***shape constancy***, by which an object appears to maintain the same shape, even though its retinal image changes shape when the object is rotated in space; and (c) ***lightness constancy*** (also called *whiteness constancy*), by which a white, gray, or black object appears constant in the degree to which it looks light or dark (white or black), even though the amount of light reflected from the object changes when the amount of light shining on it changes.

Helmholtz's Unconscious-Inference Perspective

You have already read of Helmholtz's theory that unconscious inference underlies perception and have seen applications of that idea in discussions of depth perception, size perception, and size illusions. The unconscious-inference perspective posits that perception involves problem solving, though at an unconscious level. The sensory input provides cues that the mind uses to figure out, or *infer*, the distance, size, movement, and other characteristics of an object.

36. ***How can constancies of size, shape, and brightness be explained by the unconscious-inference theory?***

To apply Helmholtz's theory to the problem of size constancy, look at Figure 9.31, which depicts a cylinder as it would appear at position A, close to the viewer, and at position B, farther away. The cylinder appears to be the same size at each position, despite the difference in size of the retinal image that it produces. (If this were a real, three-dimensional scene, this constancy would be even more apparent than it is in the picture.) Helmholtz would explain this constancy as follows: The mind first uses depth cues, such as the linear perspective and texture gradient provided by the brick wall, to judge how far away the cylinder is. Then the mind uses that distance information to calculate the object's size, and concludes that the object is the same size at each distance.

To see how the theory applies to shape constancy, look at Figure 9.32. A square sheet produces a trapezoidal retinal image when viewed at a slant, yet we see it as a

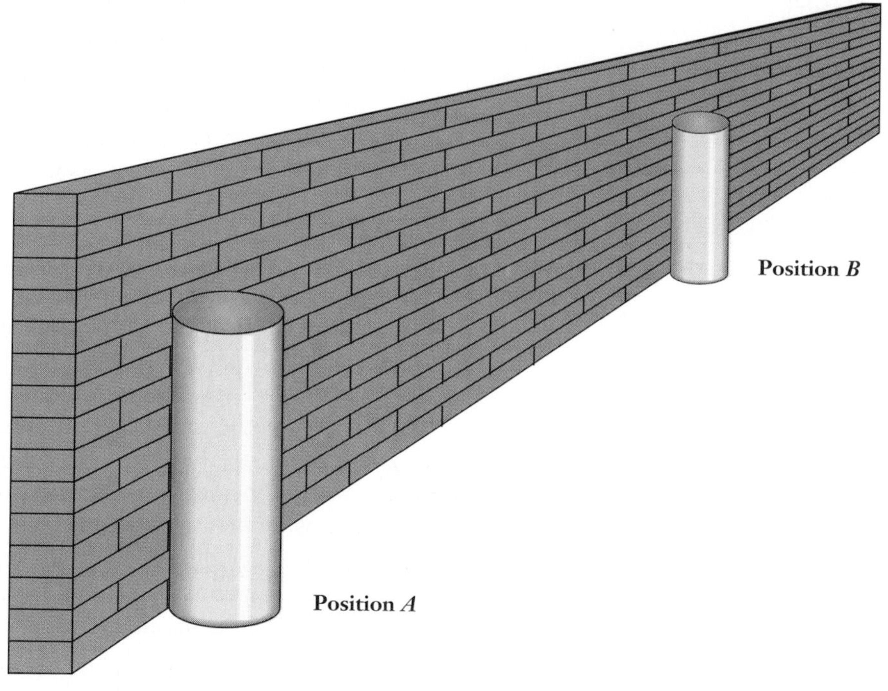

Figure 9.31 ***Size constancy explained by two theories***

This illustration shows the same cylinder as it would appear close to the viewer and farther away. According to the unconscious-inference theory, we use linear perspective to assess the distance of the object at both positions, and use that assessment, along with the retinal image size, to judge the stimulus as the same size in either position. According to Gibson's direct-perception theory, however, no such calculations are necessary. The size is seen directly in the higher-order stimulus, which includes the texture elements (bricks) of the adjacent wall. The cylinder is exactly ten bricks tall at either position.

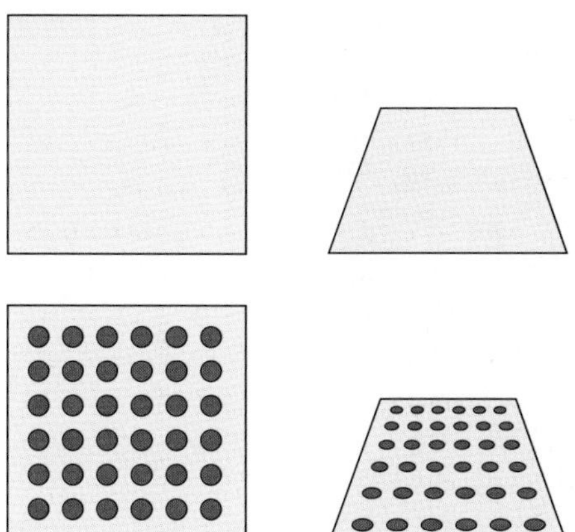

Figure 9.32 ***Shape constancy explained by two theories***

You cannot tell whether the upper right-hand object is a trapezoid or a tilted square because it contains no texture elements or other depth cues. You can tell that the bottom right-hand object is a tilted square because of the texture elements (shown here as dots). According to the unconscious-inference theory, we use the change in size and placement of texture elements as depth cues to judge the degree of tilt, and then use that to judge the true shape of the object. According to the direct-perception theory, however, we can see that this is a square without calculating depth, because each side spans the same number of texture elements.

37. *In what sense is the direct-perception theory an ecological theory, and how can it explain the constancies of size, shape, and brightness?*

square, not a trapezoid. (Again, this constancy is much stronger in a real, three-dimensional scene than in a picture.) According to the unconscious-inference theory, depth cues are used to assess shape in much the way they are used to assess size. The mind calculates the distance of various parts of the object from the eyes and then uses those calculations, along with the shape of the retinal image, to calculate the shape that the image would take if the object were viewed from any other angle (Rock, 1984). In this way, all retinal images that could be produced by the same object result in equivalent perceptions of the object's shape.

As an example of lightness constancy, look at a page of this book in normal reading light, and then move it to a place where illumination is much dimmer but not absent (maybe a closet with the door ajar). The page will look just about as white in the closet as it did in the brighter room, even though it now reflects much less light than it did before. An object that reflected so little light in the brighter conditions would have looked dark gray or maybe even black. By now you can probably guess how Helmholtz would explain this constancy. He would say that your perceptual system assessed the amount of light reflecting off objects other than the book's page in order to judge the total amount of illumination on the visual scene and then took total illumination into account, as well as the light reflected from the page, to infer the page's degree of whiteness or grayness.

Gibson's Direct-Perception Perspective

An alternative approach to the role of stimulus relationships in perception stems from a broad theoretical perspective called ***direct-perception theory***. This theory was developed by James Gibson in work that began in the 1940's. Gibson was influenced in his thinking by a modern understanding of biological evolution. We evolved through natural selection in the real, three-dimensional world, and that process eventuated in a perceptual system that is extremely efficient at picking up the kinds of information needed for survival in that world. An exquisite ability to perceive the distance, size, and motion of objects is essential to capture prey, avoid predators, and engage in other survival-promoting actions. Such perceptions are too important to be left to an inferential process, which would take time and effort and could result in errors. Evolution created a more efficient system attuned to the kinds of information that directly signal depth, size, and motion. Gibson (1966, 1979) referred to his theory as an *ecological theory* to emphasize the intrinsic, inseparable relationship between the perceptual system and the physical and biological environments in which it evolved.

Unlike the unconscious-inference theory, which assumes that the information in the stimuli that strike the sensory receptors is insufficient and must be supplemented with memories and calculations, the direct-perception theory assumes that the stimulus information is sufficient. According to Gibson, psychologists and philosophers had focused too much on mental processes and not enough on the stimulus array itself and the kinds of information it provides. Thus, Gibson shifted the emphasis from the study of the perceiver to the study of the external stimulus information that must be perceived.

Like the unconscious-inference theory, the direct-perception theory emphasizes the use of information about relationships; but while the former theory assumes that the relationships emerge from mental calculation, the latter assumes that they exist directly in the sensory stimuli. Gibson referred to the relational aspects of sensory stimuli as *higher-order stimuli* and argued that the perceptual system evolved to respond to these, not to the simpler, stimulus elements. Just as wavelengths of light are picked up and translated into color (without calculations), somewhat more complex stimulus information is picked up and translated directly into the depth, size, shape, and movement of objects.

A textured world

Texture elements—provided here by the plants in the field—allow us automatically to perceive the shapes and slants of surfaces and to perceive the junctions between surfaces, according to Gibson.

Concerning the size-constancy problems of Figure 9.31, Gibson would contend that the cylinder and the bricks are not separate stimuli to be analyzed separately and then compared. Rather, they are parts of the same higher-order stimulus. Nearly all natural scenes have texture elements within them, and we know innately that texture elements on a continuous surface are constant in size. The visual system automatically registers the object in relation to the texture elements surrounding it. Thus, we perceive the cylinder at position B as the same size as it is at position A because, in terms of the number of texture elements spanned, it *is* the same size (in both positions the cylinder is exactly ten bricks tall). Notice that in this account, size constancy is explained in terms of a constancy that actually exists in the stimulus. According to Gibson, the visual system evolved so as to ignore the size of the retinal image and automatically perceive an object's size in relation to other parts of the scene, especially texture elements.

Likewise, the direct-perception explanation of shape constancy involves no mental calculations. He argued that the visual system is attuned not just to the borders of objects, but also to surfaces, and surfaces normally have texture. According to Gibson, the surface in Figure 9.32 is seen as a square because, regardless of its slant, it remains a surface whose sides each have an equal number of texture units (represented by the dots in the figure). By defining a square in terms of a scale of texture units, the perceptual system makes its job much easier; it need not calculate the relative depth of each side in order to see an object as a square. Of course, the texture elements would be misleading if they varied in real size in a gradual way over the surface of the object, but this rarely happens in the real world. Most changes that do occur in texture are abrupt, and the perceptual system perceives them as borders between differently textured surfaces (an idea for which some physiological evidence was presented in Chapter 8).

By now you can probably guess how the direct-perception theory would explain the example of lightness constancy. From this perspective, separate assessment of the room illumination and the light reflecting from the book's page are not necessary and not performed. Rather, the page and its surrounding environment are all part of the same scene, and the visual system responds to the *ratios* of illumination in different parts of the scene (Wallach, 1948). Whether we view the page in bright light or dim light, it always reflects a high ratio of light compared to other objects near it, and that ratio is the higher-order stimulus from which we see the page as white. Chapter 8 described evidence that neurons in the optic nerve and visual cortex actually do respond to the ratio (or contrast) of light intensity in one part of their receptive field compared to another and are relatively insensitive to changes in the overall level of illumination. That evidence is very much in line with Gibson's theory.

The Complementarity of the Two Perspectives

Gibson offered his theory of direct perception as an alternative to Helmholtz's unconscious-inference theory nearly a century after Helmholtz had proposed his theory. In the interim, however, the unconscious-inference theory did not go unchallenged (Meyering, 1989). A contemporary of Helmholtz, Ewald Hering (whose theory of color vision was discussed in Chapter 8) developed an *intuition theory* of spatial perception that can be viewed as a precursor to Gibson's direct-perception theory. According to Hering's theory, we perceive depth and other spatial characteristics of objects automatically and innately with no need for complex mental operations. Hering maintained that Helmholtz's theory was implausible because perception occurs too quickly to be mediated by cumbersome calculations and inferences. In reply, Helmholtz (1867/1962) contended that Hering's theory simply avoided the real problems of spatial perception by failing to specify a mechanism, in the brain or mind, through which it can occur.

■ **38.** ***How can the two theories be understood as complements rather than mutually exclusive opposites, and what kinds of research does each theory motivate?***

Perceptual psychologists still debate occasionally along the same lines as Hering and Helmholtz. But the great majority now see the two theories as complementary to one another rather than mutually exclusive. The theories emphasize opposite sides of the same coin. Consistent with Gibson's direct-perception theory and Hering's intuition theory, the information needed to see depth, size, shape, motion, and so on does lie in relationships that exist in the stimulus input, and those relationships are registered quickly, efficiently, and effortlessly. Nevertheless, perception is also clearly a function of the brain. The brain somehow extracts the relevant relationships from the stimulus information, and the unconscious-inference theory calls our attention to that process.

Much of the attraction of the direct-perception theory lies in its assumption that the brain does not have to perform complex calculations to perceive the relevant stimulus relationships. But what does it mean to say that the brain directly "picks up" or is "attuned to" the correct relationships? How does the tuner work? Surely a complex neural system is involved. Any attempt to specify how neurons can pick up the relational information might lead to a model that is as complex—and perhaps not much different from—a model that specifies how neurons pick up elementary stimuli, integrate them, and perform the relevant calculations. By any account, the brain is an extraordinarily complex machine, vastly more sophisticated than our best computers. It is not unreasonable, therefore, to assume that the brain can perform with split-second timing the complex calculations that are required of it by the unconscious-inference theory.

The greatest value of the two perspectives lies in the research they have stimulated. While the unconscious-inference theory encourages psychologists to develop and test hypotheses about the sequence of mental steps involved in various aspects of perception, the direct-perception theory encourages them to focus more on the actual stimulus information available to the perceptual system. While the first theory encourages experiments involving simple, artificial stimuli, including those that produce illusions, the second reminds us that when viewing objects in the real world the perceptual apparatus may use varieties of information (higher-order stimuli) that are absent in such simple stimuli. Through emphasizing the kinds of information available in natural scenes, the direct-perception perspective encourages experiments involving new varieties of stimulus relationships and thus a better understanding of perception as it occurs in the natural environment.

Concluding Thoughts

One way to review this chapter is to reflect on the following three themes, which served as organizing principles for the chapter's three main sections:

1. The distinction between top-down and bottom-up processes The first section, on pattern perception and object recognition, was organized around a broad distinction between top-down and bottom-up mental processes. This distinction reflects the idea that any perceptual act requires some kind of matching of stimulus input with knowledge already in the mind. The processes that bring in the stimulus information are bottom-up, and those that bring preexisting knowledge to the interpretation are top-down. As you review the chapter, remind yourself of the experiments and demonstrations that support this broad distinction and have led to more specific ideas about the ways in which each class of processes operates.

If you think deeply about the top-down, bottom-up distinction, you will find that it is often fuzzy. For example, I presented the Gestalt principles of grouping in the section on top-down processes, but are those principles strictly top-down in their application? If you think of them as items of general knowledge applied to the analysis of stimuli, they are top-down. But if you think of them as automatic consequences of the way the brain registers and integrates stimulus input, they are bottom-up. As another example, I discussed the selective use of distinctive stimulus features in skilled, learned acts of recognition in the section on bottom-up processes. But are the skills involved in selecting distinctive features strictly bottom-up in nature? If you think of such skills as involving modification of the stimulus-input channels, so that certain features automatically are accented at the expense of others, then they are bottom-up. But if you think of such skills as learned knowledge applied to the stimulus input in order to recognize it, then they are top-down. Thus, depending on your point of view, you can often think of the same phenomenon as a demonstration of either bottom-up processing or top-down.

2. The distinction between preattentive and attentive processing The second section, on attention, centered on the idea that all (or at least much) stimulus input is analyzed to some degree, but only some of that input is analyzed in such a way as to contribute to the ongoing flow of conscious thought. This idea has led theorists to distinguish between two general compartments of the mind: a preattentive compartment, which can operate automatically, in parallel, on a vast amount of stimulus input at once; and an attentive compartment, which operates in a more controlled way, in series, on a limited amount of input selected from the preattentive compartment. As you review the discussions of selective listening, selective viewing, and the dividing of attention between two tasks, notice how the research supports this broad distinction between preattentive and attentive processes. Also note how different versions of the general model of attention account for a person's ability to extract meaning from stimulus information without conscious awareness of that meaning.

3. The idea of unconscious inference, and the role of illusions in perceptual research The final section began with a description of Helmholtz's unconscious-inference theory and then showed how that perspective underlies modern research on depth, size, and motion perception. Researchers in the Helmholtzian tradition think of stimuli that strike the senses as providing cues, which the mind uses to construct perceptions of the outside world. The steps in that construction are unconscious. To isolate and describe both the cues and the mental steps involved in acts of perception, these researchers perform experiments in which stimulus input is restricted in various ways to produce illusions or ambiguous perceptions. This approach coincides with the general approach in other areas of psychology—and in other sciences—of trying to understand how normal processes work by testing them in artificial conditions, where individual variables contributing to the processes can be separated and controlled. For example, if you want to describe mathematically the force of gravity, you will conduct your tests in a place with no air to interfere with falling objects, even though you know that in the real world falling objects are affected both by gravity and air. The same logic applies in trying to describe the cues and processes involved in various perceptual tasks, by assessing perceptions with some normal cues present and others absent.

The Helmholtzian theory was criticized by James Gibson as focusing too much attention on mental processes and not enough on the stimulus information itself. In his direct-perception theory, Gibson proposed that the perceptual system responds directly to the relational information present in higher-order stimuli to perceive depth, size, motion and so on, and does not have to piece cues together to do so. The difference between Helmholtz's and Gibson's approaches was illustrated by describing their differing views on size constancy, shape constancy, and brightness constancy. Many perceptual psychologists today see merit in both perspectives and view them as complementary.

Further Reading

Irvin Rock (1984). *Perception*. New York: Scientific American Books.

Written for the nonspecialist by a leading perceptual researcher, this richly illustrated introduction to visual perception emphasizes the unconscious-inference theory. It has chapters on visual constancies, spatial vision, pattern perception, motion perception, illusions, and perception in relation to art.

Claire F. Michaels & Claudia Carello (1981). *Direct perception.* Englewood Cliffs, NJ: Prentice Hall.

This is a thoughtful introduction to the philosophy behind the direct-perception theory. It situates the theory as part of a line of scientific inquiry that advocates the study of whole systems and not simply the parts. The perceiving animal and the perceived environment, according to these authors, are two parts of a single system.

Roger Shepard (1990). *Mind Sights*. New York: Freeman.

This is a book of playful drawings by a distinguished cognitive psychologist who is also a talented artist and humorist. The drawings use size illusions, figure-ground ambiguities, and other visual tricks to present jokes and puns. The author's commentary on his drawings explains what the various tricks tell us about perception and art.

Looking Ahead

Perception is the first step in cognition. The way we initially see or hear something influences the way we subsequently remember and think about it. Memory and thought are topics of the next two chapters, and many of the ideas that have just been discussed will be enlarged upon there. In particular, the distinction between bottom-up and top-down processes, the distinction between conscious and unconscious information, and the strategy of describing the mind in terms of compartments that serve differing information-processing functions will be applied to an analysis of memory.

MEMORY

CHAPTER 10

Repeatedly, while working on this book, I have lamented my seeming lack of memory. I can't remember who did that experiment. I forgot to bring home the articles I need for this section. I've looked up that word a thousand times but still don't remember how to spell it; now where did I put the dictionary?

Like digestion, memory is one of those abilities that we tend to take for granted except when it fails us. Usually we are more aware of forgetting than we are of remembering. But every waking moment is full of memories. Every thought, every learned response, every act of recognition is based on memory. It can reasonably be argued that memory *is* the mind. ***Memory***, defined most broadly, is an individual's entire mental store of information and the set of processes that allow the individual to recall and use that information when needed.

This chapter is the second of a trio on cognitive processes. The first, on perception, dealt with how information enters the mind from the environment; and this one, on memory, deals with how that information is stored by the mind and accessed to guide thought and action. We will begin with a general model of memory that cognitive psychologists use as a framework for talking and thinking about essentially all of mental activity and then discuss such issues as memory encoding, retrieval, organization, and distinctions between conscious and unconscious memories. Because memory is the core topic of cognitive psychology, this chapter, more than any of the others, will give you a strong flavor of the way that cognitive psychologists think and conduct research.

An Information-Processing Model of Memory

Memory is too large and multifaceted a topic to study or talk about all in one piece. Progress has been made in understanding memory by breaking it into components that can be described and studied separately. But any such breakdown implies a theory about memory—a theory that memory consists of the proposed components, that these can be studied relatively independently, and that an understanding of the components contributes to an understanding of the whole.

Theories in cognitive psychology are commonly called *models* and are often presented visually in diagrams that use boxes to represent the mind's components and arrows to represent interactions among components. Such models do not attempt to explain how mental tasks are accomplished at the level of neural activity. Rather, they attempt to describe the function and general characteristics of each task in a way that is useful in predicting how people will behave under particular conditions. The model that guides much of the discussion in this chapter (Figure 10.1 on page 328) has been so influential that it has come to be called the ***modal model of the mind***, where *modal* means "standard." Versions of this model were

■ **1. *What are the main components of the so-called modal model of the mind? What is the purpose of such a model?***

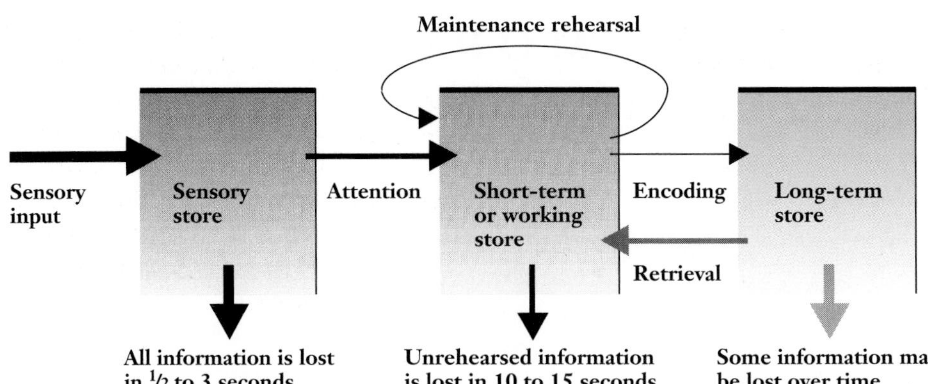

Figure 10.1 ***The modal model of the mind***

This model has long served as a framework for thinking about the human mind, and we will use it for that purpose throughout the chapter.

first proposed in the 1960s (by Waugh & Norman, 1965, and Atkinson & Shiffrin, 1968), and ever since it has served as a general framework for thinking and talking about the mind. As you use this model throughout this chapter, keep in mind that it is only a model. Like any general model in psychology, it is simply one way of trying to make sense of the data from many behavioral studies. And like any model, it can place blinders on thought and research if taken literally rather than as a metaphor. Not all of the data are consistent with the model, and eventually a new model, which makes sense of more data, may become the standard model for future cognitive psychologists.

The model portrays the mind as containing three ***memory stores*** (sensory, short-term, and long-term), conceived of as places where information is held. Each store is characterized by its *function* (the role it plays in the overall workings of the mind), its *capacity* (the amount of information it can hold at any given instant), and its *duration* (the length of time during which it can hold an item of information). In relation to the model, the term *memory* has two different meanings. It refers both to the mind's ability to hold information in a given store and to any individual item of information in that store. In addition to the stores, the model specifies a set of ***control processes***, such as rehearsal, encoding, and retrieval, which govern the processing of information within stores and the movement of information from one store to another. As long ago as the 1970s, some psychologists were reporting the death of the modal model, but their reports were premature (Raaijmakers, 1991). Even today the model is considered by most cognitive psychologists to be the most useful working model of the mind available. Let us now examine the characteristics of each memory store in this model and some of the evidence that led psychologists to divide the mind in this way.

Sensory Memory

When lightning flashes on a dark night you can still *see* the flash and the objects it had illuminated for a split second beyond its actual duration. Somewhat similarly, when a companion says, "You're not listening to me," you can still *hear* those words, and a few words of the previous sentence, for 2 or 3 seconds after their enunciation. Thus, you can answer (falsely), "I was too listening. You said . . ."—and then you can repeat your annoyed companion's last few words even though in truth you hadn't been listening when the words were uttered. These observations demonstrate that some trace of sensory input stays in your information-processing system for a brief period—less than 1 second for sights and up to 3 seconds for sounds—even when you are not paying attention to the input. This trace and the ability to hold it are called ***sensory memory***, and the ***sensory store*** is the hypothetical place in the mind where the trace is held.

2. *What is the function of sensory memory, and how do its characteristics suit it for that function?*

The sensory store is presumed to hold all incoming sensory information for a brief period so that it can be processed for physical characteristics. Consistent with that function, this store is of very high capacity (it can hold many items of information at once) but very short duration (information in it fades quickly). The sensory store is also called the *preattentive store*, and it coincides with the preattentive-processing stage of perception discussed in Chapter 9 (depicted in Figure 9.17). A separate sensory-memory store is believed to exist for each sensory system (vision, hearing, touch, smell, and taste), but only those for vision and hearing have been studied extensively.

Visual Sensory Memory: The Icon

Visual sensory memory is also called ***iconic memory***, and the brief memory trace for a specific visual stimulus is called the *icon*. The first psychologists to suggest the existence of iconic memory (or any form of sensory memory) was George Sperling (1960). In experiments on visual perception, Sperling found that when slides containing arrays of letters were flashed for only 1/20 of a second, people could read the letters, as if they were still physically present, for up to one-third of a second after the slide was turned off. This led him to propose that a memory store must hold a representation of the letters, in essentially their original sensory form, for about a third of a second.

Why don't we see this way?

If you're wondering why multiple representations of the icon don't distort your view of the visual world, the answer is that each new image from instant to instant blocks out the previous image.

3. *How did Eriksen and Collins demonstrate that seeing the icon is like seeing the original stimulus?*

More direct evidence that iconic memory holds information in its original sensory form was provided by Charles Eriksen and James Collins (1967), who found that superimposing two icons produces an effect comparable to that of superimposing two pictures. The researchers devised pairs of dot patterns that appeared random when shown separately but formed a three-letter syllable when superimposed (see Figure 10.2). When the two patterns of such a pair were flashed successively, with a very brief delay between them, most subjects saw the syllable, just as they did when the two patterns were flashed simultaneously. As the delay was increased (up to 0.3 second), the frequency with which the subjects saw the syllable dropped sharply.

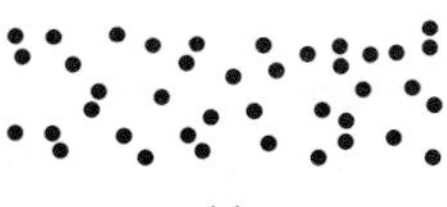

(a)

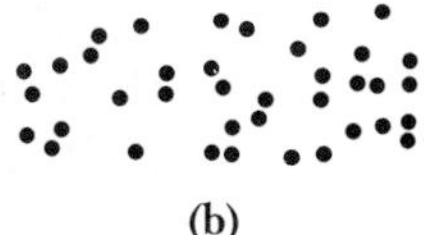

(b)

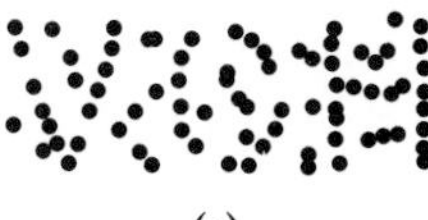

(c)

Figure 10.2 ***Sample stimuli used to show the picturelike nature of iconic memory***

When (a) and (b) are superimposed, the dot patterns form a visible syllable (c). The same effect occurs when (a) and (b) are flashed in rapid succession (less than 0.3 second apart) so that their icons are fused in sensory memory. (From Eriksen & Collins, 1967.)

Normally, we are not conscious of iconic memory. As our eyes move (in jumps called *saccades*) while scanning a visual scene, the image from each new fixation point blocks out our conscious perception of the icon from the previous fixation point, so we do not see two images superimposed. Research suggests that visual information is nevertheless retained in sensory memory from one fixation point to the next and helps us perceive an integrated view of the world rather than a succession of separate images, as we move our eyes from one point to another (Banks & Krajicek, 1991; Irwin & others, 1990).

Auditory Sensory Memory: The Echo

Auditory sensory memory is called ***echoic memory***, and the brief trace for a specific sound is called the *echo*. Early evidence for echoic memory came from experiments in which people heard two different sound tracks, each containing a short series of spoken words, played simultaneously from two different loudspeakers. These experiments showed that people could choose which track to report based on a signal presented *after* the physical sounds had ended. If the signal pointed to loud speaker A after the sounds ended, subjects could report the words that had come from A; and if the signal pointed to B, they could report the words that had come from B. Under no condition, however, could subjects report reliably the words that had come from *both* speakers. They could not consciously hear and report sounds from two simultaneous tracks (as discussed in Chapter 9), but they could choose which track to hear and report after the sounds were over. When the delay between the words and the signal was increased, the subjects' ability to choose correctly declined, reaching chance level at about 3 seconds' delay (Darwin & others, 1972). Such experiments showed that echoic memory lasts longer than iconic memory.

■ **4. *What is some evidence that echoes last longer than icons? What is some evidence that sounds can be modified in echoic memory before they are consciously heard?***

Why should an echo last longer than an icon? A possible functional answer is that hearing, by its nature, is a process requiring the accumulation of information over time. The elements of an auditory stimulus follow one another in time, while those of a visual stimulus can strike the eye all at once. To understand a spoken word or sentence, for example, we must accumulate over time a series of separate sounds; and a long echoic memory may help us do that.

Perhaps you recall the experiment on phonemic restoration (by Warren, 1984) described in Chapter 9, showing that the way people hear a word can depend on words that follow it. Subjects who were presented the sound **eel* (where * was a cough) heard it as *peel* when the subsequent words were *was on the orange*, and as *heel* when the subsequent words were *was on the shoe*. Their experience was not of inferring the first consonant, but of actually hearing it. For that to have happened, the sound **eel* must have remained in sensory memory while the rest of the phrase was spoken and must have been modified there before entering consciousness. This suggests that echoic memory is not an entirely passive store; some modification of sensory information apparently can occur within echoic memory in order to produce meaningful patterns.

Short-Term Memory

■ **5. *Why is* working memory *an apt synonym for short-term memory? How is the short-term store like the central processing unit of a computer?***

If you look again at Figure 10.1, you'll see that according to the modal model some of the information processed in the sensory store is passed to the second compartment, the ***short-term store***. Information in this store, and the mind's ability to hold it there, are referred to both as ***short-term memory*** and as ***working memory***. The latter term describes this store's function as the main workplace of the mind. Among other things, working memory is conceived of as the seat of conscious thought—the place where all conscious perceiving, feeling, comparing, computing, and reasoning takes place. As depicted by the arrows in Figure 10.1, information can enter the short-term store from both the sensory store (representing the pre-

The passing moment

The flow of thought through short-term memory is not unlike the flow of scenery past the window of a moving train.

sent environment) and the long-term store (representing knowledge gained from previous experiences). Both sources of input contribute to the continuous flow of thought that constitutes short-term or working memory. *Flow* is an apt metaphor here. The capacity of the short-term store is very small—only a few items of information can be perceived consciously or thought about at once. Yet the total amount of information that moves through the short-term store over a period of minutes or hours can be enormous, just as the amount of water flowing through a narrow channel over time can be enormous.

It may seem strange to conceive of thought as occurring within a memory store. But in order to think, you must have information to think about, and that information must be remembered while you are thinking about it. Cognitive psychologists frequently draw an analogy between the mind's short-term store and the central processing unit of a computer. Information can be transmitted directly into the computer's central processing unit from a keyboard (analogous to input from the mind's sensory store), or it can be entered from a floppy disk or other long-term storage device (analogous to input from the mind's long-term store). The real work of the computer—the computations and manipulations of the information—occurs within its central processing unit.

The Span and Duration of Short-Term Memory

■ **6. *What is the span of short-term memory and how is it measured?***

How many unrelated letters, or one-syllable words, or nonsense syllables, or single-digit numbers can you repeat after hearing or seeing them just once? That number is called the ***span of short-term memory***, and for most people it is about seven items. Telephone numbers without the area code are seven digits long. You can probably keep such a number in mind (in short-term memory) between the time you look it up and the time you dial it; but if the number includes the area code, you probably have to read the last few digits again as you dial.

Working memory

A seven-digit phone number can sometimes exceed one's short-term memory span. This sales executive's short-term memory may already be holding so much information about the person she's calling that there is no room to store the person's number.

One of the first people to measure the span of short-term memory (though he didn't call it that) was Hermann Ebbinghaus, a nineteenth-century German who was the foremost pioneer in memory research. Ebbinghaus (1885/1913) read lists of nonsense syllables (such as *rup, gox, pim*) and tried to repeat each list from memory immediately after reading it. He found that if a list contained seven or fewer syllables he could repeat it successfully after just one reading, as long as his mind was not distracted; but he could not remember the list the next day (or after any distraction) unless he had read it far more often. Using today's terms, we would say that the span of Ebbinghaus's short-term memory for nonsense syllables was seven. He could keep that many in mind without encoding them into long-term memory.

You can keep a set of pronounceable items in short-term memory by repeating them to yourself one after the other. Following each repetition of an item, its trace in short-term memory fades quickly and would be lost completely if not given new life by another repetition. The span of your short-term memory, therefore, is determined by the rate at which you can move mentally from item to item, repeating each as you go, and by the rate at which each trace fades when the item is not repeated. As you try to remember larger sets, it becomes harder to get through them all and back to the first before it disappears. Keeping a list of items in short-term memory is like a circus performer keeping a set of plates spinning on the ends of sticks. As the number of plates increases, the performer must work more frantically to get back to each and renew its spinning before it falls from the stick.

7. *How did the Petersons measure the rate of disappearance of unrehearsed short-term memories?*

Lloyd and Margaret Peterson (1959) developed a way to measure the rate at which items disappear from the short-term store when they are not rehearsed. The Petersons read meaningless sets of three consonants (such as *Q M B*) to their subjects, and the subjects were to recall these after intervals varying from 3 to 18 seconds. Normally this would be a very easy task; people would just repeat the three letters to themselves until the interval was over. But the Petersons prevented such rehearsal by adding a *distraction task*. Specifically, they required subjects to spend the interval counting backward by threes from a three-digit number. Under these conditions the three consonants were lost very quickly. Even after 3 seconds, the subjects' performance was less than perfect, and at 18 seconds the subjects seldom recalled any of the consonants (see Figure 10.3). This experiment not only shows how rapidly items fade when they are not rehearsed, but also confirms the assumption that concurrent tasks (mental arithmetic and repeating the syllables) compete with one another for the limited capacity of the short-term store. Think back to our frantic plate spinner. How much more difficult his task would be if, at the same time, he also had to build a tower of cups and saucers.

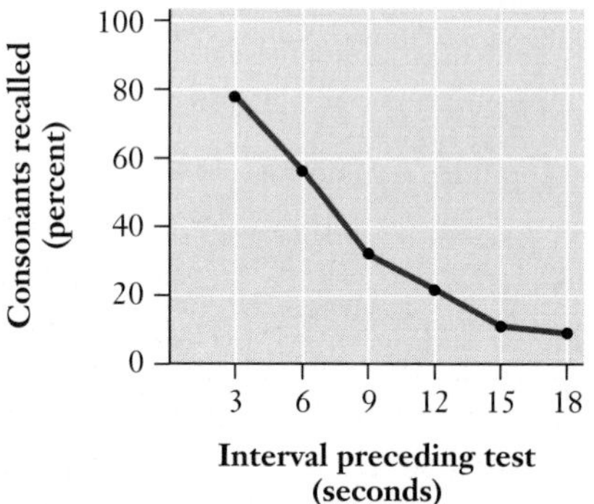

Figure 10.3 ***The duration of unrehearsed short-term memories***

In this experiment, the delay between reading three consonants and then recalling them was filled with a distraction task (mental arithmetic). Subjects' recall declined sharply as the delay increased, and was barely above chance level by the end of 15 seconds. (From Peterson & Peterson, 1959.)

Control Processes

In most versions of the modal model (for example, Baddeley, 1990), the short-term or working compartment is not only a memory store but also the hub of the mind's control processes. As noted earlier, control processes manipulate information within a store or move it from one store to another. Those that move information from one store to another, depicted as arrows in Figure 10.1, are attention, encoding, and retrieval. (Don't confuse *control processes* with *controlled processing*, which in Chapter 9 was contrasted with automatic processing. Control processes include all mental processes for controlling information, whether those processes are "controlled" or automatic.)

8. *In the modal model, what are the functions of attention, encoding, and retrieval?*

- ***Attention*** This process, which was discussed fully in Chapter 9, controls the flow of information from the sensory store into the short-term store. If you look back at Figure 9.17, you can equate preattentive processing with the sensory store and attentive processing with the short-term store, and you can visualize attention as the process that determines what information will flow from the first into the second. Information that is not selected by the attention process quickly fades and is lost from the information-processing system.

- ***Encoding*** This process controls movement from the short-term store into the long-term store. When you deliberately memorize a poem, or a list of names, you are consciously encoding it into long-term memory. Whatever rehearsal strategies you use, ranging from simple repetition to the most elaborate means, are part of the encoding process. But most encoding is not deliberate; rather, it occurs incidentally as a side effect of the special interest that you devote to certain items of information. One hypothesis, discussed later in the chapter, is that the likelihood of encoding information into the long-term store is related to the depth of thought that occurs concerning that information while it is in the short-term store. The deeper the thought, the greater the probability that the information thought about will be encoded.
- ***Retrieval*** This process controls the flow of information from the long-term store into the short-term store. Retrieval is what we commonly call remembering. Like both attention and encoding, retrieval can be either deliberate or automatic. Sometimes we actively search our long-term store for a particular piece of information. More often, however, information seems to float automatically into the short-term store from the long-term store. One image or thought in short-term memory seems to call forth the next in a stream that is sometimes logical, sometimes fanciful.

Other control processes have to do with the manipulation of information within the short-term store. For example, the mental processes that compare or organize items of information in various ways to solve problems—discussed in Chapter 11—can be thought of as control processes taking place in the short-term store.

Distinguishing Long-Term from Short-Term Memory

9. In the modal model, how is long-term memory different from short-term memory?

Once an item has passed from the sensory store into the short-term store, it may or may not pass to the ***long-term store*** and be encoded as ***long-term memory*** (again, see Figure 10.1). Long-term memory corresponds most closely to most people's everyday notion of memory. It is the stored representation of all that a person knows. As such, its capacity must be enormous, essentially unlimited. Long-term memory contains the information that enables us to recognize or recall the taste of an almond, the sound of a banjo, the face of a grade-school friend, the names of the foods eaten at last night's dinner, the words of a favorite sonnet, and the spelling of the word *sonnet*. Usually we are not aware of the millions of items of information in our long-term store. According to the model, the items lie dormant (or relatively so) like books on a library shelf or signals on a computer disk until they are called into the short-term store and put to use.

In the modal model, the long-term and short-term stores are sharply differentiated. The long-term store is passive (a repository of information) and the short-term store is active (a place where information is thought about). Long-term memory is of long duration (some of its items last a lifetime) and short-term is of short duration (items fade within seconds when no longer thought about). The long-term store has essentially unlimited capacity (all of your long-lasting knowledge is in it) and the short-term store has limited capacity (only your present thoughts are in it). Some of the early evidence for this sharp distinction came from list-learning experiments and from studies of people with memory impairments due to brain damage.

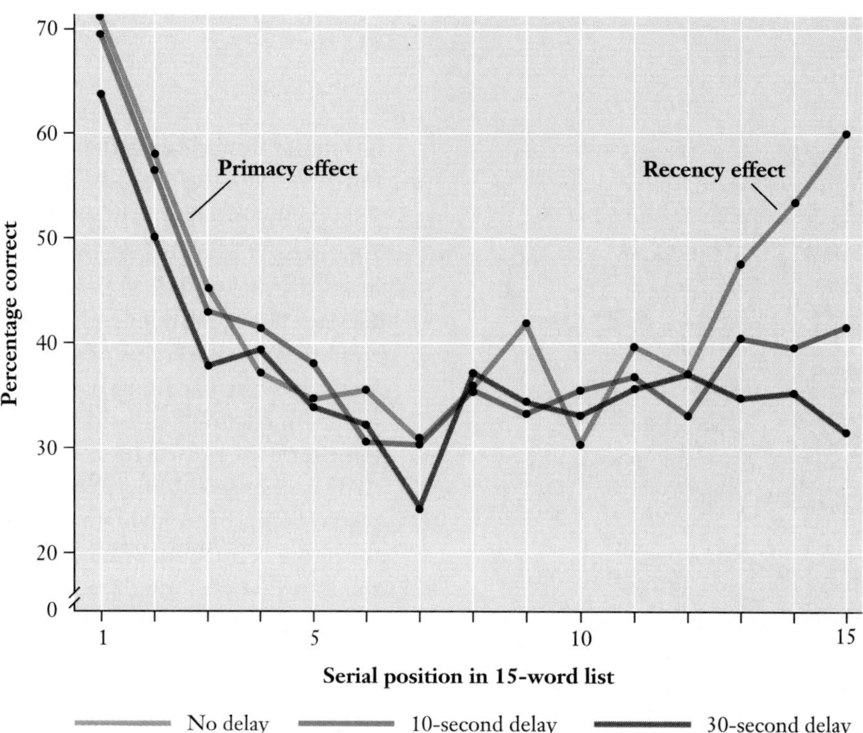

Figure 10.4 ***Primacy and recency effects, and evidence that the latter depends on short-term memory***

In this experiment, subjects rehearsed a list of fifteen words, one word at a time, and then wrote down as many words as they could remember in a free-recall test. When the free-recall test was conducted immediately after the subject rehearsed the last word (purple curve), both the primacy and recency effects were observed. When subjects spent either 10 seconds (red curve) or 30 seconds (green curve) doing mental arithmetic before the free-recall test, the recency effect was lost but the primacy effect remained. (Adapted from Glanzer & Cunitz, 1966.)

Primacy and Recency Effects in List-Learning

In many memory experiments, a series of words are presented one at a time for subjects to memorize, and after the last word the subjects are asked to recall and report all the words they can from the series in any order—a procedure called *free recall.* Subjects almost invariably recall more words from the beginning and end of the series than from the middle (see purple curve of Figure 10.4). The enhanced recall for items at the beginning of the list is called the ***primacy effect***, and that for items at the end is called the ***recency effect***.

■ **10.** ***How are the recency and primacy effects in list-learning explained in terms of the modal model? What experimental findings support those explanations?***

As Richard Atkinson and Richard Shiffrin (1968) pointed out in an early presentation of what we now call the modal model, one way to explain these effects is to invoke the concepts of short-term and long-term memory. The recency effect, by that account, occurs because the last few items in the list still reside in the short-term store when the test begins, where they can be accessed immediately. The primacy effect, in contrast, must be explained in terms of long-term memory. According to Atkinson and Shiffrin's account, the first few items in the list are recalled well because they are rehearsed more than later ones and, therefore, are more likely to be encoded into long-term memory, where they can be retrieved during the test. Early items are rehearsed more because they are the only items available to be rehearsed when they are first presented, whereas later items share rehearsal time with earlier ones. Items in the middle are not recalled as well because they were received too late to be rehearsed as fully as the early items and too soon to be in short-term memory at the time of the test. This two-part explanation, which attributes the recency effect to short-term memory and the primacy effect to long-term memory, finds support in a number of experiments.

If the recency effect results from short-term memory, then a distraction task that causes subjects to lose material from short-term memory should abolish that effect. Experiments have shown that this indeed happens. In one such experiment, Murray Glanzer and Anita Cunitz (1966) engaged subjects with mental arithmetic for a short time between the rehearsal period and the free-recall test and found that this distraction caused the recency effect, but not the primacy effect, to disappear. After distraction, subjects recalled items at the end of the list no better than items in the middle (see red and green curves in Figure 10.4).

Brenda Milner

The Canadian neuropsychologist is best known for her long-term studies of memory loss in a surgical patient (H. M.). The work of Milner and her colleagues has left little doubt that structures in the temporal lobe are directly associated with memory in humans.

By similar reasoning, if the primacy effect is caused by more frequent rehearsal of early items, then any manipulation that equalizes the rehearsal of early and later items should abolish the primacy effect. To see if that would happen, Atkinson and Shiffrin (1971) performed a list-learning experiment in which they instructed some subjects to recite aloud each item exactly three times when it was presented and not to go back and rehearse earlier items in the list. As predicted, this strategy abolished the primacy but not the recency effect.

Evidence from People with Brain Damage

In presenting their original version of the modal model, Atkinson and Shiffrin (1968) wrote that research on brain-damaged patients provides "perhaps the single most convincing demonstration for a dichotomy [between short-term and long-term memory] in the memory system." The most famous such patient is a man known as H. M., who was studied extensively first by Brenda Milner (1965, 1970) and then by many other researchers.

In 1953, at the age of 27, H. M. underwent surgery in which a portion of the temporal lobe of the cortex and underlying parts of the limbic system on each side of his brain were removed as treatment for severe epilepsy. The surgery was effective against the epilepsy, but it left H. M. with a severe, specific impairment in memory. He appeared to be unable to form new memories that would outlast his attention span. He could still remember events that had occurred before the operation. He could also converse, read, solve problems, and keep new information in mind as long as his attention remained focused on it. But the minute his attention was distracted he would lose the information that he had just been thinking about, and he would not be able to recall it later.

To hold information in his mind for a period of time, H. M. sometimes uses elaborate memory schemes. In one test, for example, he successfully kept the number *584* in mind for 15 minutes, and when asked how he did this, he replied, "It's easy. You just remember 8. You see, 5, 8, 4 add to 17. You remember 8; subtract from 17 and it leaves 9. Divide 9 by half and you get 5 and 4, and there you are—584. Easy." Yet, a few minutes later, after his attention had shifted to something else, he could not remember the number or the mnemonic scheme he had used, or even that he had been given a number to remember (Milner, 1970).

Of course, H. M.'s memory impairment has had an enormous impact on his life. His family moved shortly after his operation, and afterwards he was never able to find his way home. When asked where he lived, he would give the old address. For many years now he has lived in a nursing home (Squire, 1992). He must be accompanied wherever he goes and needs constant reminders of what he is doing. He is aware of his memory deficit and once described it in the following way (Milner, 1970): "Right now, I'm wondering, have I done or said anything amiss? You see, at this moment everything looks clear to me, but what happened just before? That's what worries me. It's like waking from a dream. I just don't remember."

■ **11.** ***How does the case of H. M. support the idea of a sharp distinction between short-term and long-term memory?***

As Atkinson and Shiffrin (1968) pointed out, the easiest way to explain H. M.'s memory loss is to posit a sharp distinction between short-term and long-term memory. Using the terms of the modal model, H. M.'s deficit can be described as an inability to encode new information into long-term memory. He can still retrieve information that had been encoded into long-term memory before the surgery. He can still bring new information into short-term memory and think about that information. But he cannot encode that information into long-term memory, so new experiences are lost to him as soon as his mind is distracted.

The case of H. M. suggests that short-term and long-term memories not only have different psychological characteristics, but involve different neural systems in the brain. When we return to H. M. later in this chapter, you will learn that he actually can form certain kinds of long-term memories and that studies of him and similar patients have provided a basis for new memory distinctions that are not described by the modal model.

Memorizing: Encoding into Long-Term Memory

Why does only some of the information that reaches short-term memory subsequently become encoded into long-term memory? Certainly repetition plays a role. At least under some conditions, the more often an item of information is repeated in short-term memory, the more likely it is to be encoded into long-term memory. Ebbinghaus (1885/1913) showed this long ago in his experiments on memorizing nonsense syllables. The more times he read a particular list of syllables, the more syllables he was able to recall the next day. But repetition does not always have this effect.

When Repetition Fails

I have looked up and dialed a certain telephone number dozens of times in the past few years, without ever memorizing it. Each time I looked it up it entered my short-term store until I dialed, and then it vanished. Yet my long-term store contains some other phone numbers that I have dialed far less often. Many years ago a psychologist named Edmund Sanford (1917/1982) tested his own memory for four short prayers that he had read aloud thousands of times over a 25-year period as part of his daily religious practice. He found that he could recite, on average, no more than three or four successive words of each prayer from memory before having to look at the printed text for prompting. Neither Sanford nor I had brain damage at the time of these observations (at least none that I know of). Apparently, repetition by itself does not ensure that information will be encoded into long-term memory.

■ **12. *How did an experiment demonstrate that increased time in short-term memory does not necessarily increase the likelihood of encoding into long-term memory?***

A lack of relation between amount of time in short-term memory and encoding into long-term memory has also been demonstrated in the laboratory. In one experiment, Fergus Craik and Michael Watkins (1973) asked subjects to listen to word lists of varying lengths and to write down, at the end of each list, the last word that began with a certain letter. To do this, subjects had to keep each word that began with the critical letter in mind (short-term memory) until the next word beginning with that letter occurred, or until the list ended. To vary the amount of time that each critical word remained in short-term memory, the researchers varied the number of words that intervened between one critical word and the next, and between the last critical word and the end of the list. Because the subjects believed that this was a test only of short-term memory, they had no motivation to try to encode the words into long-term memory. At the end of the session, however, after a distractor task involving mental arithmetic (to clear short-term memory of the most recent critical word), all subjects were given a surprise long-term memory test in which they were asked to recall as many of the critical words as possible.

Figure 10.5 shows the results. As you can see, the length of the interval during which a word was held in short-term memory bore no systematic relation to the likelihood of recall in the long-term test. In contrast, writing down a word *did* increase the likelihood of recall.

A weakness of the original modal model was its failure to distinguish between the rehearsal processes that maintain information in short-term memory and those that encode information into long-term memory. The model assumed that the

Figure 10.5 ***Words recalled from long-term memory after varying periods in short-term memory***

Subjects held each critical word in mind while other words were read and then either reported it in writing or did not. As the graph shows, the likelihood of recall in a subsequent test of long-term memory was not affected by the period that the word had been held in short-term memory, but was affected by reporting. The period measure (on the horizontal axis) is the number of other words (presented at a constant rate) between hearing the critical word and either reporting it or going on to the next critical word. (Data from Craik & Watkins, 1973.)

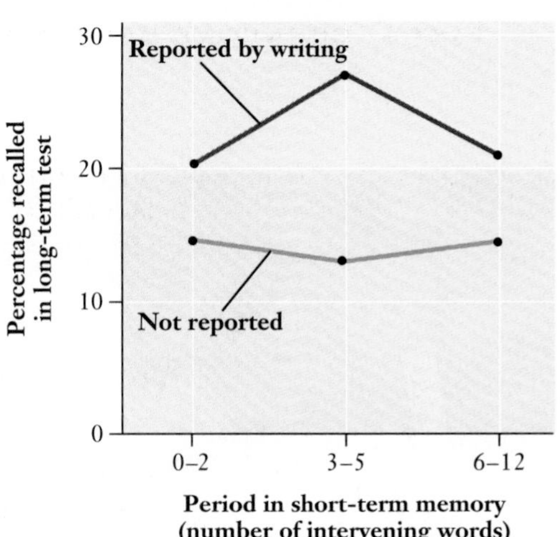

longer an item is held in short-term memory, the more likely it will be to enter long-term memory (Atkinson & Shiffrin, 1968; Waugh & Norman, 1965). Today, however, because of experiments such as Craik and Watkins's, psychologists distinguish between two kinds of rehearsal. ***Maintenance rehearsal*** is the process by which a person holds information in short-term memory for a period of time, and ***encoding rehearsal*** is the process by which a person encodes information into the long-term store. The activities that are effective for maintenance are not necessarily effective for encoding. What is effective for encoding?

Thinking through the lines

It is not exactly clear how performers commit long passages to memory, but, as suggested by the thoughtful expression on opera star Marilyn Horne's face, they apparently do much more than repeat the passages over and over.

Elaboration

Most of what we learn and remember in our everyday lives does not come from consciously trying to memorize. Rather, we remember things that capture our interest and stimulate our thought. The more deeply we think about something, the more likely we are to remember it later. To think deeply about an item is to do more than simply repeat it; it is to tie that item to a structure of information that already exists in long-term memory. This process is called ***elaboration***, or *elaborative rehearsal*, by psychologists who study its effect on memory. The immediate goal of elaboration is not to memorize but to *understand*; yet the attempt to understand is perhaps the most effective of all ways to memorize most material.

Memory techniques centering on elaborative rehearsal capitalize on the human tendency to remember things that conform to some sort of logic, even if the logic is fictional. There is no intrinsic logic to the fact that stone formations hanging down in a cave are called *stalactites* while those pointing up are called *stalagmites*. But you can invent a logic: A stalactite has a *c* in it, so it grows from the *c*eiling; a stalagmite has a *g*, so it grows from the *g*round. Memory of a person's name can be improved by thinking of a logical relation between the name and some characteristic of the person. Thus, you might remember Mr. Longfellow's name by noting that he is tall and thin, or, if he is actually short and stout, by recalling that he is definitely not a long fellow. I suspect that my students easily remember my name by relating it to the color of my hair.

Elaboration in School Learning

■ **13.** ***What is some evidence, from both the classroom and the laboratory, that the more deeply a person thinks about an item of information, the more likely it will be encoded into long-term memory?***

In a study of fifth graders, John Bransford and his colleagues (1982) found that students who received high marks in school were far more likely to use elaborative rehearsal than were those who received lower marks. The researchers gave the children written passages to study for a later test and asked them to explain what they did as they studied each passage. For example, one passage described two different kinds of boomerangs, a returning kind and a nonreturning kind, each used

A difference in elaboration

Flash cards and counting frames are both traditional ways to learn number facts. On the basis of what you have read, which method do you think is likely to be more effective?

for different purposes. Academically successful students often reported that they rehearsed the material by asking themselves questions about it. They might wonder what a nonreturning boomerang looked like, or why it would be called a boomerang if it didn't return, which caused them to think deeply about what a boomerang really was and about the information in the passage. Less successful students, in contrast, usually studied the passages simply by rereading them.

The study just described was correlational in nature, so it does not prove that elaborative study caused improved test performance, only that the two tended to go together. But research with college students suggests that elaborative study can improve students' grades. In one college learning program, developed by Marcia Heiman (1987), students are taught to write down questions about every textbook section that they read, as they read it, and about every set of lecture notes they take, as they take the notes. The process of generating these questions and thinking about the answers presumably produces deeper thinking about the information than would otherwise be achieved and thereby improves both understanding and memory. In a series of field experiments, Heiman found that students who were taught these techniques subsequently achieved higher grades in their college courses than did otherwise comparable students who received either subject-matter tutoring or no special help.

If I could offer a bit of advice about how to study this or any other textbook, it would be the following:

- Don't highlight or copy out passages as you read, but rather *question the text.*
- Constantly ask yourself such questions as: Do I understand the idea that the author is trying to convey here? Do I agree with it? Does it have relevance to my own life experiences? Has the author given evidence supporting it? Does the evidence seem reasonable? How is this idea relevant to the larger issues of the chapter? (In this textbook, the questions in the margins give you a start on this task.)
- As you ask such questions, jot down notes in the margins that bear on your answers, such as, "This idea seems similar to . . . ," or "I don't understand what he means by . . . ."

Through this active process, you will encode the material in a far richer and more lasting way than you could possibly encode it by simple rereading. You will also, in the process, generate questions that you might ask other students or your instructor.

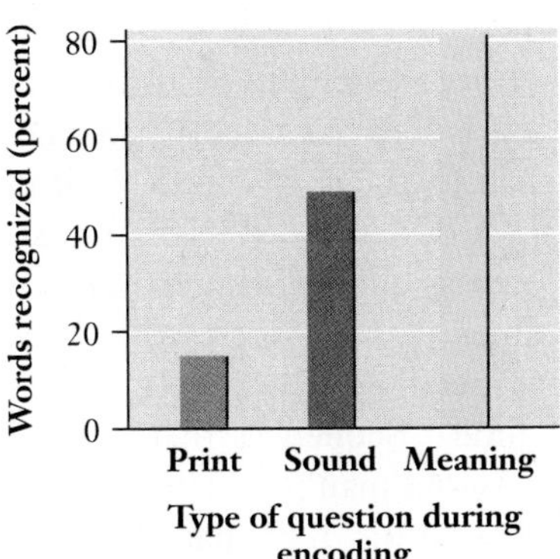

Figure 10.6 ***The method of elaboration used influences the likelihood of encoding into long-term memory.***

When subjects were shown a long sequence of words and were asked questions that required them to focus on the way the word was printed, or how it sounded, or what it meant, the type of question dramatically affected the subjects' later ability to recognize the word as one that had appeared in the sequence. (Adapted from Craik & Tulving, 1975)

Laboratory Evidence for the Value of Elaboration

Gary Bradshaw and John Anderson (1982) demonstrated that people can remember factual information better if it is presented in a relevant context, which presumably stimulates thought about it, than if presented alone or in an irrelevant context. These researchers presented college students with a set of unrelated core facts, such as "Newton became emotionally unstable and insecure as a child." Each fact was presented in one of four conditions. In the *single* condition, each core fact was presented alone. In the other three conditions, each core fact was presented along with other information that was described either as a *cause* of the core fact (for example, "Newton's father died when he was born"); or as a *consequence* of the core fact (for example, "Newton became irrationally paranoid when challenged by colleagues"); or as *unrelated* to the core fact (for example, "Newton went to Trinity College in Cambridge"). When tested for their memory of the core facts a week later, students remembered many more that had been presented in the cause or consequence conditions than in the other two conditions.

Elaboration improves memory even for sets of unrelated words. In a classic experiment demonstrating this, Fergus Craik and Endel Tulving (1975) showed subjects a long series of printed words, one at a time, and for each word asked a question that required a different form of thought about the word. In some cases the question was simply about the printing of the word ("Is it in capital letters?"). In other cases the question asked about the word's sound ("Does it rhyme with train?"). In still others, the question referred to the word's meaning ("Would it fit in the sentence, *The girl placed the ______ on the table*"?). As you can see by looking at Figure 10.6, subjects remembered many more words if they had been asked questions that focused on meaning than they did in the other conditions. Other experiments have shown that even better memory occurs when people are asked to relate each word's meaning to their own experiences or characteristics ("Does the word describe you?") (Rogers & others, 1977).

Organization

As a memory strategy, organization is closely tied to elaboration. Organizing items to be remembered is itself a means of elaboration; you must think about the items, not just repeat them, in order to organize them. Moreover, organization can improve memory by revealing or creating links among items that would otherwise be perceived as separate.

Chunking

14. ***How can chunking be used to increase the amount of information that can be maintained in short-term memory or encoded into long-term memory?***

One way to increase memory efficiency is to group adjacent items that are at first perceived as separate into single items. This procedure, known as ***chunking***, decreases the number of items to be remembered and increases the amount of information in each item (Miller, 1956). As a simple illustration, if you had to memorize the series *M D P H D U S A T W A*, your task would be made easier if you saw it not as a set of eleven independent letters but as a set of four common abbreviations—M.D., Ph.D., U.S.A., and TWA. You could make your task still easier if you then chunked these four abbreviations into one sentence: "The M.D. and Ph.D. left the U.S.A. on TWA." In developing such a story you would not only be chunking, but also elaborating—making the information more meaningful by adding some new information of your own to it.

Beginning music students find it easier to remember the notes on the lines of the treble clef as one sentence, *E*very *G*ood *B*oy *D*oes *F*ine, than as the senseless string of letters *E G B D F*. Similarly, physiology students can recall the seven physiological systems (skeletal, circulatory, respiratory, digestive, muscular, nervous,

A master of musical memory

The eminent conductor Arturo Toscanini was known during his lifetime for extraordinary feats of memory. He is said to have known every note of every instrument of 250 symphonic scores, 100 operas, and many other works. One famous story descibes him briefly visualizing the music for an entire concert, and then reassuring an agitated second bassoonist that he would not be using a broken bottom key during the concert.

and reproductive) by matching their first letters to the consonants in SACRED MANOR. Both devices involve chunking. In the first example, the five notes are chunked into one meaningful sentence, and in the second the seven systems are chunked into two meaningful words.

Chunking can enable a person with normal memory capacity to perform what seem to be miraculous memory feats. A dramatic case is that of a young man who, after many weeks of practice, increased his digit span (capacity to repeat a list of digits after hearing them just once) from the usual six or seven digits to approximately eighty (Ericsson & Chase, 1982). He was a cross-country runner, and his strategy was to chunk sets of digits into running times as they were read to him, and to elaborate on each chunk to give it additional meaning. Thus, 3–4–9–2 became "3 minutes 49.2 seconds, near record-mile time." Sequences that did not work well as running times became ages ("89.3, a very old man") or dates ("1944, near the end of World War II"). This strategy increased his digit span three- or four-fold, and to increase it still further he learned to combine these chunks into still larger ones (the three chunks just cited might become a single sentence, "3:49.2 by an 89.3-year-old in 1944"). In this way he gradually built up to the point where he could repeat strings of eighty randomly chosen digits that had been read to him just once. At the end of a session, he could still recall in the appropriate sequence over 90% of the 200 to 300 digits that had been presented to him in the session, showing that he had encoded them into long-term form. Yet, after all this, when given letters instead of digits to recall, his memory was no better than an average person's. His training had not increased his general memory capacity, but had enabled him to use it very efficiently for a certain kind of material.

15. ***Why can master chess players remember the arrangement of chess pieces after a single, brief look, whereas novices can't?***

Chunking helps explain why people who have had a good deal of experience with a certain kind of information are better at remembering a new set of items of that kind than are people with less experience. Master chess players, for example, can reproduce the arrangement of pieces on a chess board after looking at it for just a few seconds (de Groot, 1965). This is because games of chess normally progress in certain logical ways, so logical relationships exist among the pieces, which the expert can chunk together and remember as formations rather than as separate pieces. Because master players have those logical formations already stored in long-term memory, they can immediately organize the board into those meaningful chunks. If the pieces are arranged randomly rather than in ways that could occur in a real game, masters are no better than novices at remembering their location (Chase & Simon, 1973). Similarly, football coaches have excellent memories for logical football diagrams (Garland & Barry, 1991), and architects have excellent memories for logical floor plans (Atkin, 1980).

The Value of Hierarchical Organization

16. ***What is a hierarchical organization, and how can such an organization improve long-term memory?***

Perhaps the most useful format for organizing information is the hierarchy. In a hierarchy, related items are clustered together to form categories, and related categories are clustered to form larger categories, and so on.

In an experiment demonstrating the advantage of hierarchical organization for long-term memory, Andrea Halpern (1986) gave subjects a chart listing fifty-four well-known song titles to be memorized. In some cases the chart was organized in a hierarchical manner, with songs arranged according to meaningful categories and subcategories. In other cases a similar chart was used, but organized randomly, with no systematic relation among categories, subcategories, and song titles. When tested later for their memory of the song titles, subjects who had studied the organized chart recalled accurately many more titles than those who had studied the disorganized chart. During the test they would first recall a category name and then the songs that had been listed under that name.

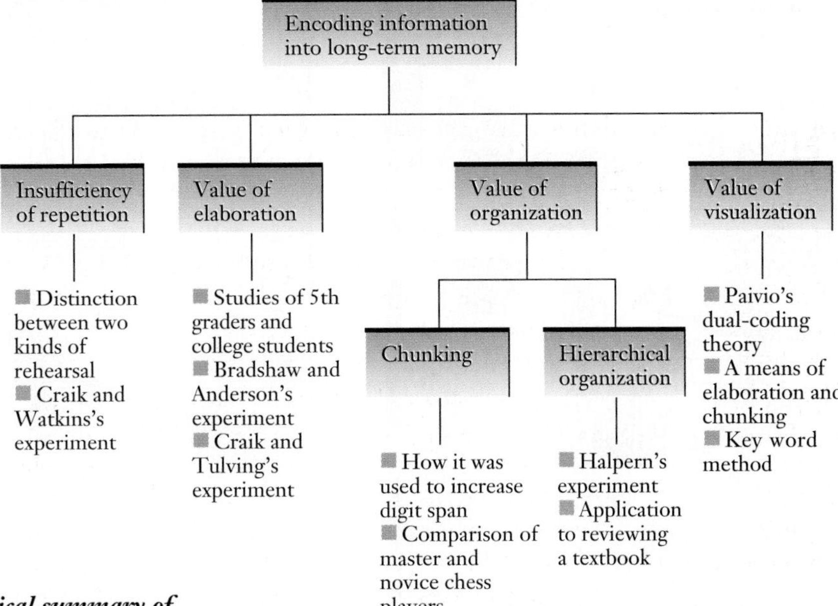

Figure 10.7 ***Hierarchical summary of a textbook section***

Summarized here are the ideas and evidence presented in this section (pp. 336–343) of the textbook. Such a chart is an aid to thought and memory because it reveals the logical connections among the items of information. Notice that the boxed items correspond to the headings within the section.

The information in the textbook that you are now reading (like that in nearly all textbooks) is hierarchically arranged: Each main heading refers to a large set of ideas, and each subheading refers to a smaller subset of ideas within the larger set. An efficient way to summarize the information in almost any textbook chapter is to sketch it out in a manner that preserves the author's hierarchical organization. As an illustration, a hierarchical sketch of the section you are now reading appears in Figure 10.7. Notice that the top node indicates in key words the theme of the section, the nodes subordinate to it indicate the main ideas pertaining to that theme, and the comments under them indicate the examples or evidence provided for each idea. You could summarize the whole chapter with five such sketches, one for each of the chapter's main sections. Such a summary would be a far more efficient aid in helping you commit the information to memory for a test than would a string of terms and names that does not preserve the connections of ideas to each other or of ideas to evidence.

Visualization

Most of our discussion thus far has concerned memory for verbal information—letters, syllables, words, sentences, prose passages, or verbally presented facts or ideas. But we can also remember pictures or visual scenes apparently in a nonverbal form. Our visual and verbal memories interact and supplement one another in our everyday experience. If you asked me to describe my living room, I would summon a pictorial memory of that room and then find the words to describe it.

17. ***How does Paivio's dual-coding theory explain the value of visualization in memory encoding? How does the key word method make use of both visualization and chunking?***

Some years ago, Allan Paivio (1971, 1986) developed a *dual-coding theory* of mental representation and memory. According to this view we have two separate but interacting forms of long-term memory—a linguistic form specialized for storing verbal information and a visual form specialized for encoding the spatial organization of scenes and objects that we see. Paivio's research suggests that in many cases we can improve our memory by encoding information into both of these memory systems at once. Thus, in memorizing a list of objects, picturing each object while thinking of its name may produce better memory than picturing or naming alone. The theory helps explain why, in list-learning experiments, people find concrete words, such as *accordion* or *dress*, easier to remember than abstract words, such as *satire* or *effort* (Paivio & others, 1968). The referents for concrete words are easier to visualize than are the referents for abstract words.

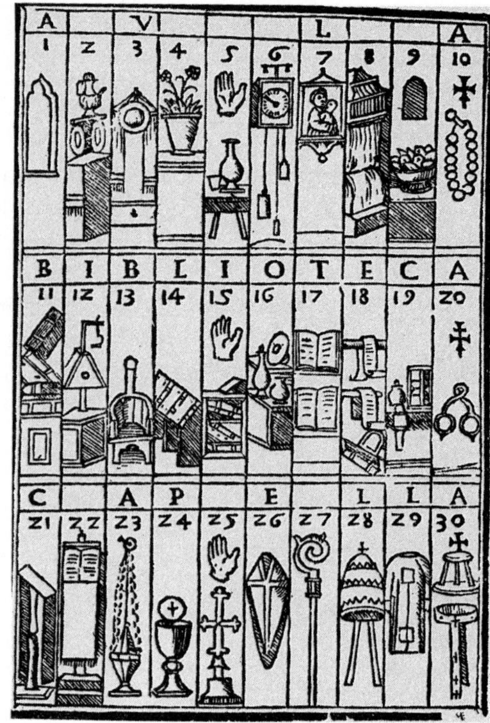

An ancient memory aid—the method of loci

These drawings from a sixteenth-century manual for Dominican friars illustrate a method used for memorizing a list of ideas by converting them into a concrete, organized visual image. The friars were instructed to associate each idea with one of the objects in the right-hand drawing and then to mentally place the object somewhere along the familiar route shown in the left-hand drawing of the abbey and its outbuildings. To recall the list, the friars had only to imagine themselves walking the route and seeing the objects—each object would remind them of the associated idea.

In addition to providing a second memory trace, the visualization of verbally presented information may improve memory by providing a means of elaboration and chunking. You have to think about (elaborate on) a word's meaning before you can form an image of it, and an image can chunk otherwise separate items of information together in a single scene. Consistent with the chunking interpretation, visualization is especially effective in *paired-associate learning*—in which people study pairs of words and then recite the second member of each pair after seeing or hearing the first member (Marschark & Hunt, 1989). To use visual imagery in such learning, a person forms for each pair of words a single image that ties the two together. To remember the association *accordion-dress*, for example, a person might form a mental image of an accordion wearing a dress.

One practical application of such research is the *key word method* of study developed by Richard Atkinson (1975) and his colleagues as an aid in learning foreign language vocabulary. With this method, the student learning a foreign word thinks of some easily visualized English word (the key word) that sounds like some portion of the target foreign word; then the student forms a visual image of that word interacting with the translated meaning of the foreign word. For example, suppose you want to remember that *pato* (pronounced "pot-o") is the Spanish word for duck. You might choose the English word *pot* as the key word and then imagine a duck with a pot over its head (see Figure 10.8). Later, in a vocabulary test on trans-

Figure 10.8 ***How mental images can be used to learn foreign vocabulary***

The Spanish word *pato*, meaning "duck," might be remembered by associating it with the English word *pot*, and then creating a mental picture associating *pot* with *duck*. The Spanish word *caballo* (pronounced *cob-eye-o*), meaning "horse," might be remembered by associating it with the English word *eye*, and then creating a mental picture associating *eye* with *horse*. (Adapted from Atkinson, 1975.)

Pato—pot—duck

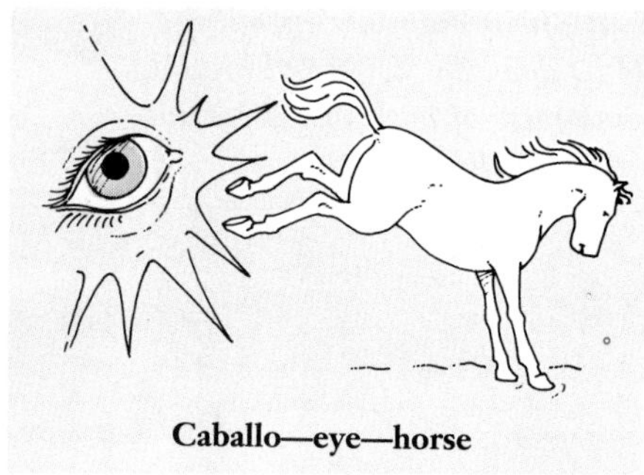

Caballo—eye—horse

lating from Spanish to English, you would associate *pato* with *pot* (because of the similarity in sound), and *pot* with *duck* (because of your mental image). In a test on translating from English to Spanish, this would be reversed—*duck* would remind you of *pot*, which would remind you of *pato*. The technique takes some effort to use, but research suggests that the effort may be worthwhile. In one experiment, students who studied a Spanish vocabulary list by the key word method got 88 percent correct on a subsequent test, contrasted to 28 percent correct for those who studied for the same length of time by the more common method of rote rehearsal (Raugh & Atkinson, 1975). The method has also been found useful for learning other types of vocabulary, such as medical terminology (Troutt-Ervin, 1990).

Representation and Organization in Long-Term Memory

Once information is encoded into a person's long-term memory, it becomes part of that person's store of knowledge. How is that store best characterized? To a cognitive psychologist, this question breaks down into two subsidiary questions: How is information *represented* in long-term memory, and how is information *organized* in long-term memory?

Representation of Verbal Information: The Meaning-Wording Issue

■ **18.** ***Under what conditions do people typically remember the meaning but not the wording of statements, and under what conditions do they remember the wording?***

Representation refers to the relationship between memory and the original sensory experience on which the memory is based. Much of the early research on representation had to do with memories for information presented through spoken or written words. When you hear or read a factual statement, what do you record in long-term memory? Do you record the exact words, like a tape recorder, or do you record the meaning without the exact words? Everyday experience, as well as laboratory evidence, suggests that the latter is most often the case. I doubt if you can tell me the exact words I used to define short-term memory earlier in this chapter, but you can probably convey quite well the meaning.

To test this assertion, Jacqueline Sachs (1967) asked people to listen to an informative prose passage and then state whether each of a set of test sentences was the same as or different from a sentence in the original passage. She found that people accurately identified new sentences as different if the meaning was changed, but not if only the wording was changed. For example, when the original sentence was *He sent a letter about it to Galileo*, most people identified *Galileo sent a letter about it* as different from the original, but did not identify *A letter about it was sent to Galileo* as different. The only condition in which subjects recognized changes in wording as accurately as changes in meaning was when the original sentence occurred at the end of the passage, so that it was still in short-term memory when the test occurred. This experiment and many others suggest that we usually encode the meaning of a statement but not its specific wording into long-term memory.

From a functionalist perspective, it makes sense that people would normally store the meaning and not the exact wording of verbal statements in long-term memory. It is the meaning rather than the wording that helps us deal more effectively with the world around us. It really doesn't matter if we remember *Close cover before striking* as *Close cover before lighting*. Either phrase is equally useful to prevent us from burning ourselves. On the other hand, sometimes we do remember statements verbatim (word for word). We may memorize poems whose sounds we enjoy, and actors memorize thousands of lines when their jobs require it. Even when not deliberately trying to memorize, we are likely to remember the exact wording of a statement if that wording was especially important to our original appreciation of the statement. Perhaps you can remember Rhett Butler's last line in the movie *Gone with the Wind* in exactly his words, because the same literal meaning stated differently would not have had the same impact.

In a study of memories from a natural conversation, Janice Keenan and her colleagues (1977) gave a surprise test to a group of psychology professors and graduate students 30 hours after they had held an informal luncheon seminar. They asked the subjects to select sentences that were identical to what had been uttered at the meeting from sets of sentences that had the same meaning but differed in wording. The main finding was that people quite accurately identified verbatim those sentences that were high in *interactional content*, that is, those in which speakers attempted to convey something about themselves or others present rather than simply factual information about the topic of the seminar. Such statements typically contained some degree of humor, sarcasm, or personal criticism, and their full meaning depended not just on the literal interpretation but on the exact words chosen. Rhett Butler could have said, simply, "I don't care" as he walked away from Scarlett. But instead he said, "Frankly, my dear, I don't give a damn," and that is what we remember.

Representation of Visual-Spatial Information: The Image Issue

If you remember what Rhett Butler said, do you remember what he looked like? Did he have a beard? Many people say that they try to answer such questions by calling up a visual image of the person and inspecting it for details.

Visual images appear to be involved in much of our thinking, especially that about the spatial layout of things. I can never remember which way is west when I am facing south unless I picture myself standing on a map of North America. Then I can see immediately that the West Coast is on my right. At a slightly higher level of thought, Einstein claimed that the concept of relativity came to him through visualizing what would happen if he chased a beam of light and caught up to it (Kosslyn, 1987). When you try to decide if a serving bowl you saw at the store would fit into a particular space in your cupboard, do you use a visual image? For a long time, psychologists avoided the concept of visual imagery because it seemed to imply the scientifically absurd notion of a picture actually existing in the head. But the study of such imagery eventually gained respectability through research such as that described below.

19. ***How do the propositional and analogue theories of visually acquired memories differ from each other, and what is some evidence favoring the analogue theory?***

Evidence That Visual Images Are in Some Ways Like Pictures

Are our memories for visual scenes fundamentally different from our memories for verbal information? According to the ***propositional theory*** they are not. This theory holds that visual memories and verbal memories alike are stored as sets of *propositions*, elementary units of meaningful information (Anderson, 1985). For example, if you look at the picture in Figure 10.9, you might store such propositions as: *It is a speedboat. It has an outboard motor at the stern, a small cabin with one porthole in the middle, and an anchor on the bow.* You would not necessarily store the propositions in those words, or in any words at all, but you could translate the propositions directly into words, just as if you had learned about the boat from a verbal description instead of a picture.

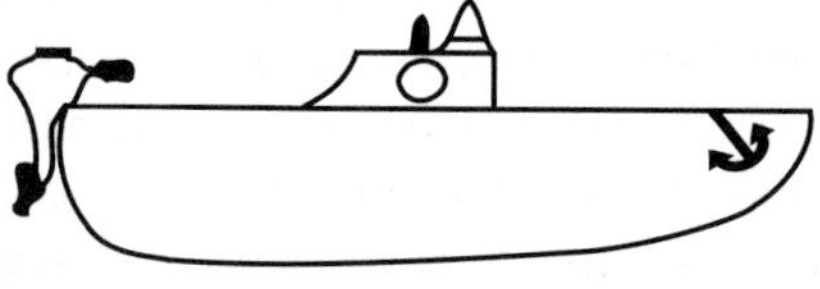

Figure 10.9 ***Sample stimulus used in a mental-imagery experiment***

Subjects saw line drawings such as this, and later, when answering questions based on their memory of the drawing, showed reaction times suggesting that they were scanning a mental image. (From Kosslyn, 1980)

According to the ***analogue theory***, however, visual memories are fundamentally different from verbal memories. The analogue theory maintains that visual information is stored in a way that preserves the spatial gradients of the original scene. The visual memory thus produced is functionally equivalent (analogous) to a picture. Of course, no one would claim that the memory really *is* a picture in the head or that it preserves all the information that a picture would preserve. Rather, the claim is that the memory is stored in a form that we must inspect mentally *as if it were a picture* in order to extract information from it. To grasp more fully the distinction between propositional and analogue representations of information, think of the difference between a digital clock, which gives you the time in terms of propositions (such as 1:32 P.M.), and the more traditional analogue clock, which indicates time by the position of its hands. With the digital clock you read the time directly, whereas with the analogue clock you must infer the time from the spatial arrangement of the hands. When we recall a visually acquired memory, is our task more like looking at a digital clock or an analogue clock?

Some researchers argue that the two theories underlying this question cannot be tested. Others contend that the theories can be tested because they lead to different predictions about how people should respond to questions about visually learned information. If the analogue theory is correct, people should respond as if they were looking at a picture. If the propositional theory is correct, they should respond as if they were looking up items in a dictionary. In one experiment, Stephen Kosslyn (1973) demonstrated that at least when people are instructed to form visual images, they do answer such questions as if looking at a picture.

Kosslyn showed people drawings, including that in Figure 10.9, and later asked them to visualize each drawing from memory. He asked them to focus, in their memory, on either the left or the right end of the drawing and then, as quickly as possible, to indicate (by pushing one of two buttons) whether or not a particular named component was present in the drawing. For example, referring to the boat drawing, he would say "motor" or "porthole" or "anchor" while the person was focusing at either the left or the right end of the boat in memory. He found that the farther away the named object was from the place of focus, the longer it took subjects to push the correct button. The time lag suggested that the subjects had to scan across the mental image to find the named component before they could respond. Kosslyn took the lags as evidence that the subjects' memory of the drawing indeed was organized spatially, like a picture.

Evidence That Visual Images Involve Visual Areas of the Brain

■ **20.** ***How have researchers shown that brain regions involved in visual perception are also involved in extracting information from visual memories?***

Perhaps the strongest evidence that some memories are fundamentally visual in nature comes from brain research. The same brain areas that are essential for normal visual perception also appear to be essential for extracting information from visually based memories.

In a series of neuropsychological studies, Martha Farah (1989a) found that people who lost certain aspects of visual perception because of brain damage showed visual memory deficits that were directly comparable to their perceptual deficits. For example, after an automobile accident damaged part of the visual area of his cerebral cortex, one man lost much of his ability to see the shapes of objects even though he could still see the relative locations of objects in a scene. In memory tests for information that he would have learned before the accident, he performed poorly on such shape-dependent questions as *Does a bear have a long tail or a short tail?* and *What does a cocker spaniel's ear look like?* Just as he was unable to see shapes in objects before his eyes, he was unable to "see" them in images recalled from memory. Yet he had no difficulty answering questions about the relative locations of objects. He could describe accurately, from memory, the layout of the furniture in his living room or the arrangement of buildings along a familiar street. Another man, with damage in a different part of the visual cortex, showed the opposite pattern of deficits. He could see, and describe from memory, the shapes of objects; but he could not see or describe from memory their locations. Such evidence led Farah and others to suggest that different brain regions are critical for

A bird and . . . well . . . two more birds
Some examples of birds, such as this North American goldfinch, immediately bring the bird concept to mind. Other examples, such as the two Australian cassowaries shown here, bring to mind the bird concept a bit more slowly. This is the kind of evidence that lies behind the prototype theory of concept representation.

seeing the shapes and locations of objects before a person's eyes, and that those same regions are also critical for identifying the shapes and locations of objects in visual memories.

In other research, people with intact brains were asked to engage in various mental tasks, or to answer questions from memory, while the activity of various parts of their brain was measured (Farah, 1989b; Goldenberg & others, 1988; Roland & Friberg, 1985). These studies, too, have shown that the same areas of the cortex that become active during visual perception—including the primary visual area in the occipital lobe (shown in Figure 6.9)—also become active when a person is asked to form a mental image of an object or to recall from memory the color, shape, or size of a familiar object. Those areas do not become active when the person engages in nonvisual mental tasks, such as mental arithmetic, or when the person answers questions about verbally acquired information, such as *When did Columbus discover America?*

Representation of Concepts: Schemas and Scripts

To understand a sentence such as *He sent a letter*, or to recognize the object in Figure 10.9 as a boat, a person must already have in long-term memory a mental representation of certain *concepts*—the concepts *he*, *sent*, *letter*, and *boat*. Concepts provide the basis for categorizing objects and events and can be considered the units of a person's general understanding of the world. Cognitive psychologists commonly use the term ***schema*** to refer to the mental representation of a concept. Whatever you have in long-term memory that allows you to classify some objects as boats and others as not boats is your schema for *boat*. How can schemas best be described? Psychologists have proposed two broad categories of answers to that question, which correspond at least roughly to the distinction between the propositional and analogue theories discussed previously.

■ ***21. How are concepts represented mentally, according to the feature theory and the prototype theory?***

According to the propositional theory, more often called the ***feature theory*** in this context, schemas are best understood as sets of *defining features*, which can be stated as propositions. For example, the concept *bird* might be defined by a set of features that includes the following: animate, feathery, beaked, stands on two legs, flies, sings. A problem with this theory lies in the difficulty or impossibility of creating a list of features that uniquely and fully defines the category. Penguins don't fly or sing, and a plucked bird (even a dead plucked bird) is still recognized as a bird. Conversely, other objects can be found that would not be called birds and that have one or more features from any list of bird features we could generate.

According to the analogue theory, called the ***prototype theory*** in this context, a schema is not a list of discrete features, but rather a holistic, picturelike representation of a typical or average member of the category. If you close your eyes and imagine what to you is a typical bird, that may be your *prototype* for the bird concept. When you recognize birds, you may do so by matching them to your prototype. You recognize more quickly and accurately those that are more similar to the prototype than you do those that are less similar. Likewise, when you use the word *bird* in a sentence without qualifying the word, your meaning is best represented not by all birds but by your bird prototype.

■ ***22. How did Rosch's experiments tend to support the prototype theory?***

The work of Eleanor Rosch is the best-known research used to support the prototype theory. In one experiment, Rosch (1973) asked people to rate various members of categories according to how typical each was of its category, and she found great consistency from person to person. For example, for the category *bird*, nearly everyone rated *robin* and *bluebird* as very typical and *chicken* and *penguin* as not very typical. In later experiments, Rosch (1975, 1977) showed that these ratings correlated positively with other behavioral measures that would presumably reflect people's concepts. When she asked people to use category labels in a sentence, she found that most people made up sentences that were sensible for typical members of the category but not for atypical members. For example, given the label *bird*, a person might say, *The bird sat twittering on the twig of a tree*, which works well if the bird is a robin or bluebird, but not if it is a chicken or penguin. When she asked people to say as quickly as possible whether specific pictured objects were or were not members of a certain category (such as *bird*), she found that they responded more quickly to typical members (such as robins) than atypical members (such as chickens). Recent research shows that this latter effect occurs even when the typical and atypical category members are equally familiar to the subjects (Casey, 1992).

The debate between feature and prototype theorists quickly enters into issues that are difficult if not impossible to resolve. Feature theorists point out that although people may take longer to say chickens are birds, their ability to do so at all means their schemas incorporate the whole category, not just typical members. Moreover, feature theories can be modified to account for Rosch's findings. One might posit that not all members of the category to which the concept refers need to have all of the features that define the concept. Typicality in this view is an index of the number of features that a given object has from the total set that makes up the concept (Smith & others, 1974). Theories have also been developed that incorporate characteristics of both feature and prototype theories to account, on the one hand, for people's ability to categorize according to defining principles and, on the other hand, for Rosch's findings regarding typicality (Greenberg & Kuczaj, 1982).

■ **23.** ***How are the terms* schema *and* script *used in reference to culture-specific representations of typical scenes and events?***

The term *schema* was used originally by the British psychologist Frederick Bartlett (1932) to refer not to concepts for specific objects such as birds, but to more complex concepts that may vary from culture to culture and have to do with the way objects or events are organized in a person's experience. For example, in our culture people might share a relatively common schema of a living room, perhaps including a couch, an easy chair, and a rocking chair, all oriented around a television set, with a coffee table in front of the couch. When we enter a new living room, we recognize it as a living room and assess its unique features by comparing it with our already existing schema. Schemas that involve the organization of events in time, rather than of objects in space, are commonly called ***scripts*** by today's cognitive psychologists (Schank & Abelson, 1977). The typical birthday party is a good example of a script in our culture: There are games, followed by the presentation of the cake, the blowing out of the candles, the singing of "Happy Birthday," the eating of the cake, the opening of the presents, and then more games. As you will see later, schemas and scripts do not just help us recognize familiar objects, scenes, or events that we encounter; they also affect the way that we remember those that we have previously encountered. We tend to distort our specific memories in directions that fit our schemas and scripts.

Organization of Knowledge

■ **24.** ***In what sense does our mind's store of information combine the features of a dictionary, supermarket, and innumerable other means of organizing items?***

To be retrievable, information must be organized. In a dictionary, information is retrievable because the entries are organized alphabetically. There it is easy to find every word that starts with *A*, but hard to find every word that is the name of a fruit. In a supermarket, items are organized in a different way: There it is easy to find the fruits, but hard to find all the items that start with *A*. We can draw an analogy here to our ability to find items in long-term memory. If I ask you to name things that start with *A*, you can easily read off a long string of such items from your memory. If I ask you to name different fruits, you can do that just as easily. Similarly, if I ask you to name things that are red, or that rhyme with cat, or that happened yesterday, or that taste sweet, you can use any of these categories to probe your memory and come up quickly with a number of items. In fact, it is difficult to think of any way of categorizing things that you cannot use to retrieve groups of items very quickly from long-term memory. The most remarkable aspect of human long-term memory is not the enormous number of items it contains, but the sophistication of its organization. The problem of how knowledge is organized in the mind has been a subject of speculation at least since the time of Aristotle.

The Traditional Associationist View

■ **25.** ***How can the principle of association by contiguity account for our ability to recall quickly the properties of an object when we are given the object's name?***

Aristotle described the organization of the mind in terms of the *association* of elementary ideas or concepts. He considered two concepts to be associated in a person's mind if the thought of one tends to evoke the thought of the other. According to his principle of ***association by contiguity*** (discussed in Chapter 5), some concepts are associated because their referents commonly occur together (contiguously) in a person's sensory experience. Thus, *napkin* and *plate* might be associated in a person's mind because the person has frequently seen napkins and plates together. This principle also accounts for our ability to bring quickly to mind the various properties of an object when we hear its name. If I hear *apple*, I can immediately think *red, round, sweet, tart, grows on trees, good in pies* because I have experienced all of those properties of apples contiguously with apples themselves and with the word *apple.*

Association by contiguity cannot, however, by itself account for our ability to generate quickly, from memory, a list of items that are red, or whose names start with *A*. To account for this ability, Aristotle proposed a second principle, ***association by similarity***. According to that principle, similar items are linked in memory whether they were ever experienced contiguously or not. Your thought *apple* might evoke the thought *fire engine* because both are red, even if you have never seen an apple and a fire engine together.

Aristotle's second principle is far more difficult to explain than the first in terms of a possible mechanism. Contiguity is based on just one variable, the time at which the items were experienced. But similarity can be based on any variable. Things can be similar in color, size, what they are used for, features of their names, and so on ad infinitum. To say that you can recall one red thing after another because of the principle of association by similarity is really no explanation at all. How did your mind ever group all red things together and at the same time preserve each item's groupings with other objects, based on other variables?

■ **26.** ***According to William James, how does association by similarity depend upon association by contiguity?***

One early psychologist to discuss the principle of association by similarity extensively was William James (1890). Although he did not suggest a mechanism for the principle, he highlighted its dependence on the more fundamental principle of association by contiguity. We initially learn the properties of objects and events through contiguity, and then we mentally reorganize them based on the similarity of their properties. For example, we learn through contiguity that apples have a certain color, shape, size, taste, name, and so on; and then we use those properties to link the apple concept in our minds with various other concepts. Any single property of an apple can link the apple concept to other concepts that share that property. The red color ties the apple to other red objects, the sweet taste to other sweet foods, the name to other things whose names start with *A*, and so on.

James (1890) believed that the ability to separate mentally the various properties of objects and events from their concrete referents, and to use those properties to link objects and events that were never experienced contiguously, represents the basic difference between the human mind and that of other animals. He expressed this idea when he wrote: "Thoughts [in dogs] will not be found to call up their similars, but only their habitual successors. Sunsets will not suggest heroes' deaths, but supper-time. This is why man is the only metaphysical animal."

A Network Model of Memory Organization

■ **27. *What sorts of experimental results was Collins and Loftus's spreading-activation model designed to portray? How does the model continue the tradition of associationism begun by Aristotle?***

Today, continuing the tradition begun by Aristotle, many cognitive psychologists depict the mind's storehouse of knowledge as a vast network of mental concepts (or schemas) linked by ties that could be called associations (but are more commonly given other names, such as *pointers*). Figure 10.10 illustrates one such model. Allan Collins and Elizabeth Loftus (1975) developed this model to explain the results of experiments regarding people's ability to recognize or recall specific words quickly after exposure to other words. For example, a person can recognize the word *apple* more quickly if the previous word was *pear* or *red* than if the previous word was *bus*. Collins and Loftus assumed that the degree to which one word speeds up the ability to recognize or recall another reflects the strength of the mental association between the two words or concepts.

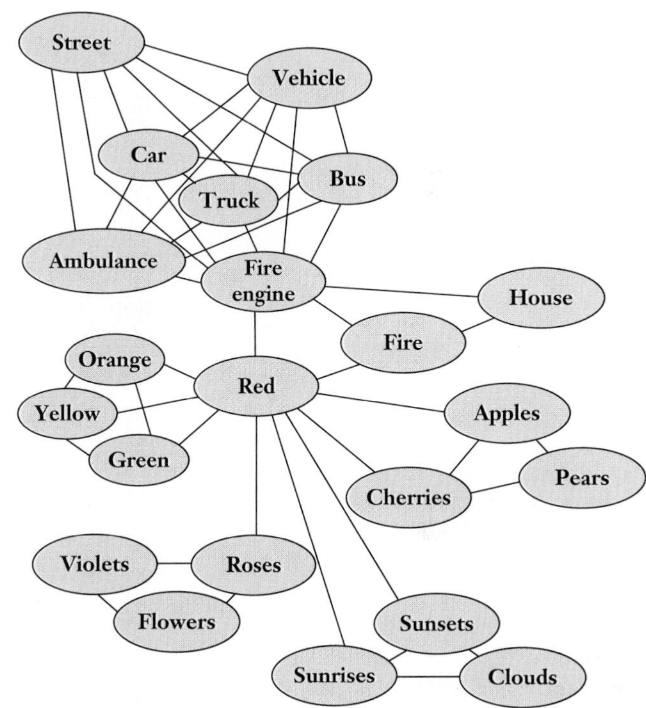

Figure 10.10 ***A spreading-activation model of memory organization***

This diagram depicts schematically some of the links, or associations, among a tiny fraction of the thousands of different concepts that are stored in a normal person's long-term memory. The shorter the path between two concepts, the more strongly they are linked in memory. (From Collins and Loftus, 1975.)

In Figure 10.10, the shorter the path between two concepts, the more strongly they are associated. Notice how the model incorporates the idea that common properties of objects often provide the basis for their link in memory. Thus, the model shows that *roses*, *cherries*, *apples*, and *fire engines* are all linked to the concept *red* and, in this way, are all linked to each other. The model is called a *spreading-activation model* because it proposes that the activation of any one concept initiates a decremental spread of activity to nearby concepts in the network. Your thought of red will temporarily activate most strongly those concepts that you associate most closely with red and make them more retrievable from long-term memory, more available to your ongoing flow of thought, than they normally would be. Such models are convenient ways to depict the results of many memory experiments, and they help us to visualize the patterns of associations that make up the mind.

Remembering and Forgetting: Problems of Retrieval from Long-Term Memory

What are the causes of forgetting? Why are we sometimes unable to remember a name or fact that we once knew well? Why do we other times remember a name or fact that we thought we had long since forgotten? Why, in some cases, do we remember an event differently each time we retell it? These are some of the questions that cognitive psychologists have addressed in theories concerning the retrieval of information from long-term memory.

The Role of Time

■ **28. *What is the decay theory of forgetting, and why is it not well accepted today?***

Clearly, time plays an important role in remembering and forgetting. Our ability to retrieve an item from long-term memory declines with time after original encoding, unless the item has been retrieved frequently in the interim. But the rate of decline varies tremendously, depending on the depth at which the information was encoded originally and on the circumstances under which we attempt to retrieve it. In Figure 10.11 you can see two very different *forgetting curves*. The first is from Ebbinghaus's classic research with lists of nonsense syllables. As you can see, most forgetting occurred within the first hour; then the rate of loss became increasingly gradual, with little difference between tests conducted 1 day or 1 month thereafter. The second is from a study by H. P. Bahrick and his colleagues (1975) on people's memories for names and faces of their former high-school classmates—information that would have been learned more solidly than Ebbinghaus's nonsense syllables. As you can see, in this study people who had graduated 34 years earlier were as good as recent graduates at matching names to faces in a recognition (multiple-choice) test. But a different test (recalling classmates' names from pictures with no other cues) revealed a considerable loss in memory since graduation.

What happens, over time, to cause forgetting? Is information lost *from* the long-term memory store, like a book that has disintegrated or been stolen from the library? Or is it lost *in* the long-term store, like a book that has been misnumbered or misshelved? One early theory held that memories simply fade away or decay gradually with disuse (Thorndike, 1913). This theory is not well accepted today. Its extreme form, that *all* memories fade away when not used, seems to be disproved by data such as those shown in Figure 10.11b. A milder form of the theory, that *some* memories are lost through decay, may be untestable because it is impossible to prove that loss of retrievability is not caused by something else. Alternatives to the decay theory are *interference theories*, which maintain that other memories may interfere with the ability to retrieve any given memory, and *retrieval-cue theories*, which maintain that the ability to retrieve information depends on the availability of appropriate cues (reminders).

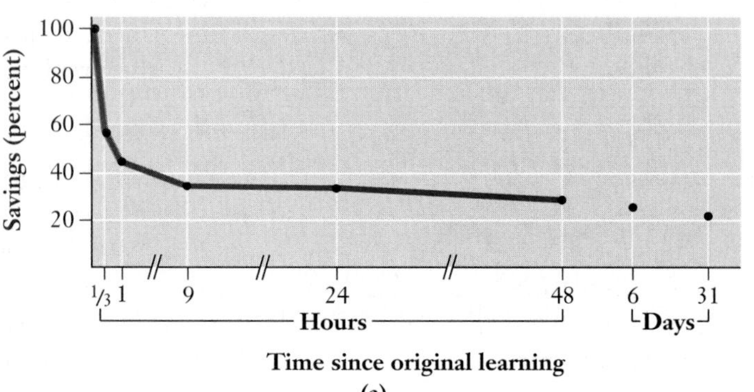

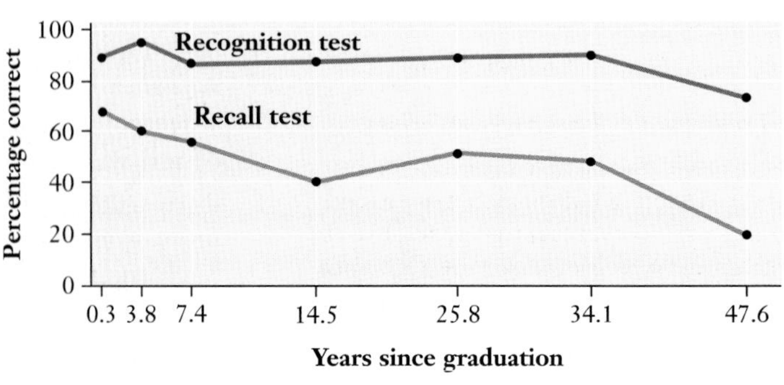

Figure 10.11 ***Forgetting curves for (a) nonsense syllables and (b) high-school classmates***

Graph (a) depicts the results of a classic experiment in which Hermann Ebbinghaus tested his own memory for lists of nonsense syllables (thirteen syllables per list) at various intervals after original learning. The measure of memory (percent saved) was the number of repetitions required to relearn the list as a percentage of the number required for original learning. (Based on Ebbinghaus, 1885/1913)

Graph (b) depicts the results of a more recent experiment in which memories for names and faces of high-school classmates were tested in people who had graduated from 3 months to nearly 50 years before testing. In the *recognition test*, subjects had to match each name to one out of a set of yearbook portraits. In the *recall test*, they were shown yearbook portraits and had to recall the names without any other cues. (Adapted from Bahrick & others, 1975.)

Interference as a Cause of Forgetting

In an experiment conducted many years ago (Jenkins & Dallenbach, 1924), some subjects memorized a list of nonsense syllables at night, slept for several hours, and then were tested for their memory of the syllables. Other subjects memorized the same list in the morning and then engaged in normal daytime activities for several hours before their test. The result was that those who slept between learning and test remembered more syllables than did the other group. This result suggested to the experimenters that memory loss is caused by interference from other learning and mental activity that occurs when awake, and not by the simple passage of time.

■ **29. *What is the difference between retroactive and proactive interference, and what are the conditions under which these effects are most likely to occur?***

Subsequent research has demonstrated two types of interference. ***Retroactive interference*** is the type that might have produced the greater forgetting by subjects who were awake compared to those who had slept in the experiment just described. This interference stems from material that is learned *after* the test material was learned. ***Proactive interference***, in contrast, stems from material learned *before* the test material was learned. Both types of interference are commonly studied in the laboratory by giving subjects lists of words or nonsense syllables to memorize. If two lists are learned, the inhibiting effect of the second on a person's memory of the first is retroactive interference; and the inhibiting effect of the first on a person's memory of the second is proactive interference (see Table 10.1).

Table 10.1 ***Experimental designs used to assess retroactive and proactive interference***

	Task 1	Task 2	Test
Retroactive interference			
Interference group	Learn *A*	Learn *B*	Test on *A*
Control group	Learn *A*	—	Test on *A*
Proactive interference			
Interference group	Learn *A*	Learn *B*	Test on *B*
Control group	—	Learn *B*	Test on *B*

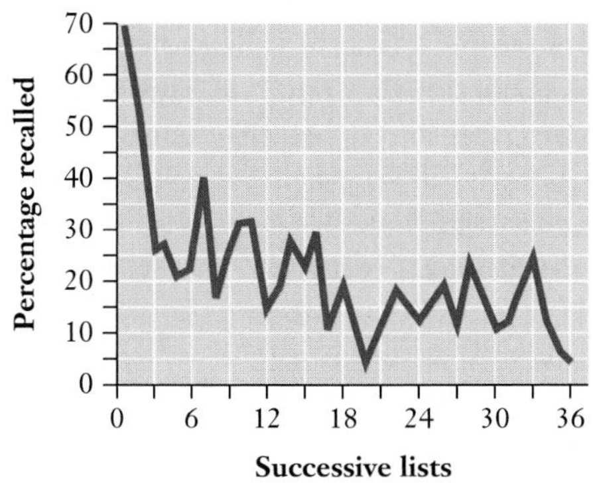

Figure 10.12 ***Proactive interference***
Subjects learned a new list every 2 days and were tested before each new session on only the most recently learned list. As the experiment progressed, performance deteriorated, indicating proactive interference. (Adapted from Keppel & others, 1968.)

A particularly striking example of proactive interference is shown in Figure 10.12. Subjects who learned thirty-six successive word lists, each separated by a 2-day interval, showed progressively poorer memory of the most recently learned list as the experiment continued. In the last 18 tests they remembered on average less than 15 percent of the words, compared to 70 percent in the first test. Proactive interference does not affect either the rate at which a new list is learned or the immediate memory for the list, but it leads to more rapid forgetting. The steep rate of forgetting shown by Ebbinghaus (look again at Figure 10.11a) is probably due to proactive interference, although he apparently was not aware of that phenomenon. Ebbinghaus learned hundreds of lists of nonsense syllables over the course of his experiments, so each new list would have been interfered with by the previous ones.

What causes retroactive and proactive interference? Nobody knows for sure, and the answer may be different for different situations. According to one theory, both forms of inhibition occur in list-learning experiments because the separately learned lists lose their distinctiveness with time and tend to merge, in memory, forming one large pool of information rather than two or more smaller ones (Ceraso 1967). It is harder to search through a large pool of information and find an appropriate item than to search through a smaller pool. Consistent with that

An artful solution

Classroom teachers, especially those who work with different groups of students each period, encounter serious interference effects in trying to learn their students' names. Name tags on each desk effectively solve this problem.

theory, many experiments have shown that interference is greatest when the different learning tasks involve similar items, which are presumably more likely than dissimilar items to merge into one pool (Wickens, 1972). Lists of nonsense syllables interfere with other lists of nonsense syllables, but not with lists of words; and lists of words drawn from the same category (say, *animals*) interfere with each other but not with those drawn from a different category (say, *household furniture*). I once heard a story about an absent-minded ichthyology professor (fish specialist) who refused to learn the names of his students. Asked why, he responded, "Every time I learn a student's name I forget the name of a fish." Had he studied cognitive psychology he would have known that learning the names of one group of students might have interfered with his memory for names of another group of students, but not with his memory for names of fish (that is, unless students and fish were similar entities in his mind).

Laboratory studies of interference are sometimes criticized for the unnatural memory items they employ. Rarely in everyday life do we memorize lists. Can interference be demonstrated in more natural conditions? Yes. An excellent example has to do with your memory for where you have parked your car. Parking each day at your place of work or study is the kind of situation that should lead to interference, since repeated instances of parking in the same lot fall within the same category of event. Alan Baddeley (1986) and his colleagues surreptitiously kept track of where scientists working at a research institute and visitors to the institute parked and then surprised these people with a test asking them to recall where they had parked on specific days. As would be predicted by interference theory, those who parked every day at the institute had poor memories of where they had parked several days earlier, whereas visitors who had parked there only once had excellent memories even when tested a month later. In addition, visitors who had parked twice at the institute showed poorer memories for either of their parking places than did those who had parked at the institute only once. Their poorer memory for the first parking place demonstrates retroactive interference, and their poorer memory for the second parking place demonstrates proactive interference.

Importance of Retrieval Cues

What is the capital of Vermont? Is Vermont's capital Brattleboro, Rutland, Montpelier, or Cabot? The first question is an example of a ***recall test***, a test in which the person must generate the answer from memory. The second is an example of a ***recognition test***, a test in which the person must use memory to decide which of several designated possibilities is the correct answer. Students familiar with both types of tests are not surprised to learn that people usually do much better on recognition tests than on recall tests for the same material. The difference is not just due to guessing, and it grows larger as the time between learning and testing increases. You already saw one example of that difference in Figure 10.11b: The ability to recall the names of classmates from yearbook photos declined with years since graduation, but the ability to recognize the correct names, when asked to match names with photos, did not decline at all over a 34-year period.

Why is recognition easier than recall? The difference must have to do with locating information in long-term memory. Seeing or hearing the correct answer in a recognition test apparently serves as an excellent ***retrieval cue***, a stimulus or hint, that helps the person find the same answer in memory. Other, less specific retrieval cues also aid memory. People are more likely to remember the capital of Vermont if told that it starts with *M*, or that it is a French name, than if they are given no cues. The power of retrieval cues to facilitate the retrieval of long-term memories has many ramifications for understanding memory and thought.

■ **30.** ***How does the encoding-specificity principle explain (a) good performance on recognition tests, (b) the value of elaborative encoding, and (c) the remarkable performance of some subjects on a recall test for 500 nouns?***

The Encoding-Specificity Principle

What kinds of stimuli are most helpful as retrieval cues? According to the ***encoding-specificity principle***, cues that were prominent during the original encoding of a long-term memory are most valuable for its retrieval (Tulving, 1974). In a recognition test, the correct answer is a powerful retrieval cue because it was necessarily prominent at the time of encoding. This principle helps explain the role of elaboration in encoding, discussed earlier in this chapter. To elaborate on a memory item is to associate it with many cues that can be used later for retrieval. Thus, if you had originally encoded Montpelier as the capital of Vermont by noticing that the syllable *mont* appears in both the capital name and the state name and then had thought about the fact that *mont* is French for *mountain*, that Vermont is known as the Green Mountain state, and that many of the early settlers were French, you would have provided yourself with many possible retrieval cues, any one of which might have reminded you of the name of the capital the next time you saw the word *Vermont*.

Consistent with the encoding-specificity principle, people have extraordinary recall ability if they make up their own retrieval cues at the time of encoding and are given those cues at the time of testing. In an experiment that verified this principle Timo Mäntylä (1986) presented 500 nouns to subjects, one by one, all in one very long session. He did not ask the subjects to memorize the nouns, but rather asked them to write down either one or three words that they regarded as properties of the object named by each noun. For example, for the word *barn* they might write *large, wooden, red.* He then surprised the subjects with a test of their ability to recall all 500 nouns. As cues, he gave them either their own self-generated properties or those produced by a different subject in the same experiment. Subjects who received three self-generated properties for each word were able to recall correctly more than 90 percent of the 500 nouns. When only one property was available or when the properties had been generated by someone else, recall was much poorer (see Figure 10.13).

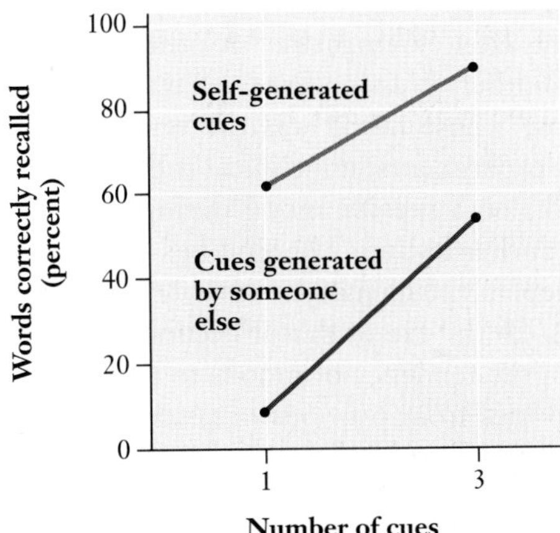

Figure 10.13 *Value of self-generated retrieval cues*

Subjects generated either 1 or 3 one-word properties related to each of 500 nouns. Later they were tested for their ability to recall each noun, using either their own self-generated properties or another subject's self-generated properties as retrieval cues. (Data from Mäntylä, 1986.)

31. *How can context-dependent memory be demonstrated, and how is it consistent with the encoding-specificity principle?*

Context-Dependent Memory

According to the encoding-specificity principle, memory retrieval is facilitated not just by cues that are properties of the learned material, but also by cues that are incidental to the learned material but happened to be present at the time of encoding. Have you ever returned to a former school, or a street where you once lived, and found that the sights and sounds, even the odors, evoked memories of people you knew or things you did—memories you thought were forgotten? The increment in memory that occurs when the test environment is similar to the encoding environment is called ***context-dependent memory***.

In one series of experiments demonstrating context-dependent memory, Frank Schab (1990) found that people who studied a list of words in a room that smelled of chocolate or cinnamon/apple or mothballs performed better on a recall test if the same smell was again present than they did if a different smell, or no smell, was present. Other experiments (for example, Metzger & others, 1979) have shown that, for students, a change in classroom can have a small but significant effect on recall: Students displayed slightly greater recall when tested in the room in which they had learned the material than when tested in a different room.

32. *How can state-dependent memory be demonstrated, and what significance might it have for understanding effects of mood on memory?*

State-Dependent Memory

Somewhat akin to context-dependent memory is ***state-dependent memory***, the increment in memory that occurs when a person's physiological condition or emotional state is the same in the test as it was during encoding. As an example, subjects who learned a list of words while under the influence of marijuana recalled more of the words when tested in the same drugged state than when tested undrugged, and subjects who learned the list undrugged recalled more when undrugged than when drugged (Eich, 1980). The usual explanation of state-dependent memory is that feelings evoked by the altered state serve as retrieval cues.

Several studies have explored the possibility that mood can provide a basis for state-dependent memory. In one, which capitalized on the dramatic mood shifts shown by manic-depressive psychiatric patients, patients learned a set of word associations on one day and were tested 4 days later (Weingartner & others, 1977). Those patients whose mood had shifted in either direction between training and testing showed poorer recall than did those whose mood was the same (either elated or depressed) on both days. In other experiments, nonclinical subjects have been induced through various means to take on a specific mood during learning and either the same or the opposite mood during testing. The findings have been mixed, some showing a degree of mood-dependent memory, others not (Blaney, 1986; Bower, 1981; Bower & Mayer, 1989). To the extent that it occurs naturally, mood-dependent memory may help explain the tendency of moods to perpetuate themselves. If a sad mood calls forth memories from previous occasions when a person was sad, the sadness will be enhanced and prolonged.

Memory Construction as a Source of Distortion

Remembering is not just a process of retrieving traces that were laid down during the original encoding; instead, it is an active, inferential process guided by a person's general knowledge about the world. When you hear a story or experience an event, your mind encodes into long-term memory only some parts of the available information. Later, when you try to recount the story or event, you retrieve the encoded fragments and fill in the gaps through your logic and knowledge, which tell you what must have happened even if you can't quite remember it. With repeated retelling, it becomes harder to distinguish what was present in the original encoding from what was added later. Thus, memory of the story or experience is not a

A memory or a fantasy?

People who travel to new places often come back with amazing stories of the sights they have seen. Their stories might be deliberately exaggerated to impress the audience or unconsciously exaggerated through the process of memory construction. This drawing from *Marco Polo's Book of Marvels* may represent a deliberately fantastic tale, a distorted memory construction, or a combination of the two.

simple readout of the original information, but a *construction* built and rebuilt from various sources of information. Our ability to construct the past is adaptive because it allows us to make sense of our incompletely encoded experiences. But the process can also lead to distortions.

Effects of Preexisting Schemas and Subsequent Information

■ **33.** ***How did Bartlett demonstrate that culture-specific schemas affect the way that people remember a story?***

One of the first psychologists to call attention to the role of general knowledge in our more specific memories was Frederick Bartlett, who originated the idea of culture-specific schemas as noted earlier. In one experiment, Bartlett (1932) asked British university students to listen to a Native American (Pima tribe) story entitled "The War of the Ghosts" and later asked them to retell the story from memory. He found that the story was often quite different in the retelling, and he noticed certain consistencies in the changes that occurred. Details not essential to the plot tended to drop out, and those that were essential were often exaggerated. Also, points in the story that were consistent with Native American beliefs but not with the students' beliefs were often changed to be more consistent with the latter. For example, the protagonist's obligation to certain spirits—an important part of the original story—tended to be transposed into an obligation to his parents. The changes were not deliberate; the students were trying to retell the story accurately, but they inevitably used their own ways of understanding things—their own schemas—to fill in the gaps in their memory.

■ **34.** ***How did Loftus demonstrate that information added after an event can affect people's apparent memory for the event?***

The manner in which a person constructs memories can also be affected by information acquired after the original experience. In one experiment demonstrating this, Elizabeth Loftus and J. C. Palmer (1974) had subjects view a film depicting a traffic accident. Later, the researchers asked some of the subjects how fast the cars were going when they *hit* each other, and others how fast they were going when they *smashed into* each other. The question with the word *smashed* elicited higher estimates of speed than did the question with the word *hit*. Moreover, when the subjects returned a week later and were asked to remember the film and say whether there was any broken glass in the accident, those who had heard the word *smashed* were more likely to say they saw broken glass (though actually there was none in the film) than those who had heard the word *hit*. In similar research, Loftus and others have shown that such memory distortion is especially likely if the original event occurred long ago and if the misinformation is introduced subtly in the context of recounting aspects of the event that really did occur (Loftus, 1992).

Loftus's findings have important implications for eyewitness testimony in court cases in which lawyers on both sides are trying to paint different pictures of what happened. A lawyer's account or question apparently can influence a witness's memory. The findings are perhaps especially relevant to cases based on recent memories of incidents that occurred long ago. If an adult begins to recall instances of childhood abuse, do the memories reflect the truth, or might they have been constructed from ideas planted by a therapist or a well-intentioned friend? In many such cases corroborating evidence has shown that the memories do reflect the truth. But if definite corroboration is lacking, to what degree should the memories themselves serve as evidence? This problem has been much discussed in both the psychological and legal worlds (Goleman, 1992).

Does Misleading Information Replace an Earlier Memory?

■ **35.** ***What evidence led McCloskey and Zaragoza to challenge Loftus's interpretation of her results?***

Aside from its practical implications, Loftus's research has provoked an interesting theoretical debate about the mutability of memories. Based on her experiments, Loftus suggested that the new, misleading information actually replaces or permanently distorts the original memory (Loftus & Loftus, 1980). Other researchers, including Michael McCloskey and Maria Zaragoza (1985), disagree, arguing that the new information merely supplements the original information and competes with it in subsequent tests. According to these researchers, misled subjects in Loftus's experiments must choose between their original memories and what they have been told by the experimenter and, in that case, are likely to believe the experimenter and assume that their own memories are wrong. The new information has not caused their original memories to vanish or become distorted, but rather has led the subjects to doubt their memories.

To test their hypothesis, McCloskey and Zaragoza (1985) conducted experiments similar to Loftus's but modified the procedure so that misled subjects could be tested either with or without competition from the misleading information. All subjects saw a series of slides; then some of them heard misleading information about one of the slides, and then all were tested in one of two ways for their memory of the critical slide. In one test the misleading information was one of the response options, and in the other test it wasn't. For example, in one experiment the critical slide contained a man holding a hammer, and the misled subjects were given information suggesting that he had been holding not a hammer but a screwdriver. Later, subjects were given one of two different tests. Half had to choose between a hammer and a screwdriver as the tool that the man was holding, and the other half had to choose between a hammer and a wrench.

Notice that one test required misled subjects to pit their original memory (hammer) against the misleading information (screwdriver). With that test, misled subjects performed more poorly than nonmisled subjects—they were more likely to choose the screwdriver. But the other test (hammer versus wrench) did not require subjects to pit the original information against the misleading information. With this test, the misled subjects performed just as well as the nonmisled subjects (see Table 10.2). Thus, the misleading information about the screwdriver apparently had not replaced the original information about the hammer, but had merely provided alternative information that competed with the original when it was one of the possible choices. Most, but not all, subsequent experiments have tended to confirm McCloskey and Zaragoza's conclusion that misleading information competes with original memory (Bonto & Payne, 1991; Chandler, 1991).

Even if McCloskey and Zaragoza's conclusion is valid, however, it by no means discounts the importance of Loftus's findings. Misinformation may not replace the original memory, but apparently it interferes strongly with the ability to retrieve it under test conditions similar to those found in a courtroom. Moreover, subjects in such experiments apparently believe that the new information is part of their original memory. In one experiment, subjects saw a series of slides and then some read a narrative that gave misinformation about some of the slides. Later, when tested for

Table 10.2 ***Procedure and results of experiments demonstrating that misleading information competes with, but does not replace, the original memory***

Group	Item on slide	Misleading information	Test	Results (percent correct)
Misled 1	Hammer	Screwdriver	Hammer vs. screwdriver	37
Misled 2	Hammer	Screwdriver	Hammer vs. wrench	72
Control 1	Hammer	—	Hammer vs. screwdriver	72
Control 2	Hammer	—	Hammer vs. wrench	75

Note: Results are averages from six experiments. The items shown are only illustrative of the various items used.

Source: "Misleading postevent information and memory for events: Arguments and evidence against memory impairment hypothesis" by M. McCloskey & M. Zaragoza, 1985, *Journal of Experimental Psychology: General, 114*, pp. 5 and 7.

their memory of the slides, the subjects were told that the information they had read was wrong and that they should answer the test questions based only on their memory for the original slides. Even in that case, many subjects claimed to have seen items in the slides that were suggested by the narrative but actually were not present (Lindsay, 1990).

Effects of Hypnosis on Memory

Perhaps you have read fantastic claims about the power of hypnosis to bring back long-lost memories. Are they true? And just what is hypnosis?

Hypnosis has been defined (by Kihlstrom, 1985) as "a social interaction in which one person, designated the subject, responds to suggestions offered by another person, designated the hypnotist, for experiences involving alterations in perception, memory, and voluntary action." The two most essential ingredients of the hypnotic state are: (1) a giving up of considerable control over one's own thoughts and actions, turning that control over to the hypnotist; and (2) a condition of highly selective perception, focused on the hypnotist's voice or on objects or scenes suggested by the hypnotist. The state can be induced by a variety of techniques, most of which include instructions to relax and to fix attention on a specific sight or sound over a period of time. In general, people who easily become engrossed in imaginative activity in the non-hypnotized state are more easily hypnotized than other people (Kihlstrom, 1985).

Does Hypnosis Improve Retrieval?

■ **36.** ***Why should hypnotized subjects' claims of vivid memories not be taken at face value?***

On theoretical grounds, the claim that hypnosis can help a person to retrieve lost memories seems plausible. The focusing of attention might relieve a person from distracting, interfering thoughts, and the hypnotist's suggestion to relive the incident might help revive context-dependent or mood-dependent memories. But despite common belief and theoretical plausibility, there is little evidence that hypnosis really does facilitate retrieval.

Laboratory experiments in which people learn specific material and then are tested with or without hypnosis have consistently produced negative results (Kihlstrom, 1985; Wagstaff, 1984). Hypnosis often increases the likelihood of saying yes in recognition tests to items that had actually been present, but it also increases the likelihood of doing so to items that had not been present. Other experiments have shown that hypnotized subjects are more susceptible than nonhypnotized subjects to misleading information presented in the examiners' questions (Sheehan & others, 1991; Zelig & Beidelman, 1981). That is, hypnotized subjects

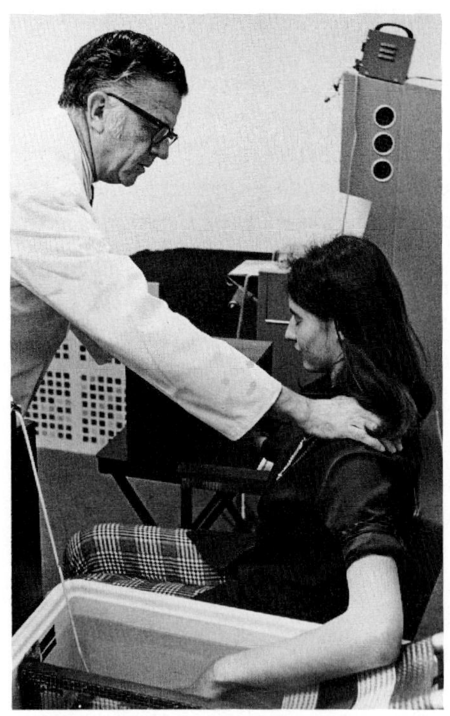

Hypnotic induction

To induce hypnosis, researcher Ernest Hilgard instructs the subject to relax, to focus attention on his words, and to give up conscious control of her own thoughts.

are more likely to claim to remember whatever the examiner seems to expect them to remember. This is not surprising because hypnosis, by definition, is a state of increased suggestibility. Another typical finding is that hypnotized subjects express more confidence in their memory than do nonhypnotized subjects, even though their memory is not objectively better (Krass & others, 1989).

Many police departments use hypnosis when interviewing witnesses, in the belief that it improves the witnesses' recall. Might hypnosis be useful in the situations in which police use it, even though it does not improve memory in laboratory studies? This possibility was tested in a field experiment involving the Los Angeles Police Department and witnesses to actual crimes (Sloane, 1981). Half of the witnesses were interviewed by techniques that included hypnosis by police hypnotists, the other half were interviewed only in a normal state of consciousness, and the information obtained from both groups was compared to objective facts turned up by subsequent police investigations. The results showed no effect of hypnosis at all, either on the amount of information recalled or its accuracy. Perhaps occasional cases exist in which hypnosis improves retrieval, but apparently as a rule it does not.

Post-Hypnotic Amnesia

Although hypnosis does not generally improve retrieval, it can have another effect on memory. When deeply hypnotized subjects are told that upon awakening they will not remember what happened while under hypnosis, they often (though not always) reveal the specified lack of memory when questioned later, a phenomenon called ***post-hypnotic amnesia***. (*Amnesia* means memory loss.) Their subjective experience is not one of pretending to forget, but of actual inability to remember. Post-hypnotic amnesia can be highly selective; subjects who are told to forget just one of several events that occurred during hypnosis will forget just that event. Such amnesia also can be combined with other post-hypnotic suggestions. For example, subjects may be told that they will not remember the hypnotist's words upon awakening, but will raise their hands when they hear a particular signal. Later, when the subjects are awake and find themselves raising their hands, they are unable to offer a reason for doing so.

A revealing feature of post-hypnotic amnesia is that it can always be reversed by a prearranged signal (Kihlstrom, 1985). If the subject is told, "You will forget everything that occurred under hypnosis until you hear this bell," the memories return when the bell is sounded. This shows that post-hypnotic amnesia does not involve actual loss of memories from the long-term store, but only a temporary interference with their retrievability. The memories must remain stored to be retrievable after the signal. Chapter 17 describes fugue states and states of multiple personality, which involve retrieval disruptions similar to post-hypnotic amnesia. Under certain conditions specific sets of memories apparently can be locked away for a period of time where they are not available for conscious recall, but can be unlocked and readily available at another time.

Multiple Memory Systems: Beyond the Modal Model

Look again at the illustration of the modal model in Figure 10.1. Its central feature is the box labeled short-term or working memory, which is equated with conscious perception and thought. According to the model, new information can be encoded into long-term memory only if it is first perceived consciously in short-term memory. To influence behavior at a future time, that information must be retrieved from long-term memory and brought back into short-term memory, where it again becomes part of the flow of conscious thought.

That model has proven to be an elegant framework for describing many memory phenomena. Essentially all the studies and ideas about memory discussed so far in this chapter can be described in terms of the model. But does the model work well for describing the entire range of phenomena that can reasonably be classed as memory? In its broadest sense, memory refers to all effects of prior experience on subsequent behavior. Do all such effects involve the conscious mind in the ways indicated by the model? Today most cognitive psychologists would answer *no*. The memories not well described by the model are called implicit memories.

The Distinction Between Explicit and Implicit Memory

Figure 10.14 shows a system of classifying memory that is becoming increasingly popular among cognitive psychologists (Schacter, 1992; Squire, 1992; Tulving & Schacter, 1990). The system identifies two broad classes of memory—explicit and implicit—and divides each into subclasses.

Explicit Memory

Encompassing essentially all the examples of memory discussed so far in this chapter, ***explicit memory*** is the type that enters a person's conscious thought. It is called *explicit* because it can be assessed directly (explicitly) in tests that ask the person to recall and report the remembered information. It is also called *declarative memory* because the remembered information can be declared—stated in words. As shown in Figure 10.14, explicit memory can be divided into two subclasses—episodic and semantic.

■ 37. ***How do the two subclasses of explicit memory differ from each other?***

Episodic memory is the explicit memory of one's own specific past experiences. Your memory of what you did and how you felt on your sixteenth birthday, or of what you ate for dinner last night, or of any other specific episode in your life, is episodic memory. The episodic subclass also includes the memories studied in list-learning experiments or in experiments asking people to remember what objects appeared on a slide. The task in such experiments is to remember the specific words or scenes experienced during the learning episode.

Semantic memory, by contrast, is explicit memory for information *not* tied mentally to a particular event or episode in one's own life. It includes knowledge of word meanings (which is one definition of *semantics*) plus all the myriad facts and ideas that constitute one's general understanding of the world. Your memory that

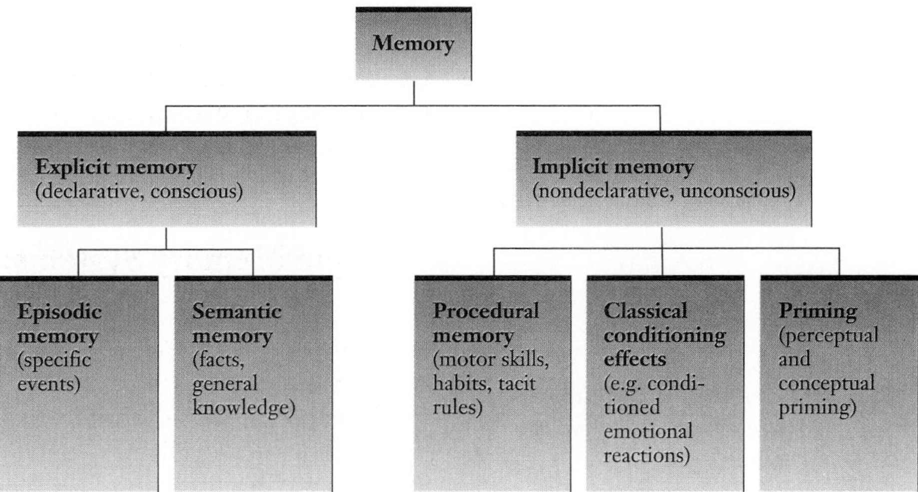

Figure 10.14 ***Types of long-term memory***

Experiments in which people must use a memory to solve a problem or complete a task, but need not recall the memory explicitly, suggest that implicit memory follows different rules than explicit memory and involves different neural systems in the brain. The implicit and explicit memory categories can be further subdivided into narrower categories that may also involve different neural systems. (Based on Tulving, 1985, and Squire, 1992.)

penguins are birds, that apples are red, and that psychology is the most interesting of all academic subjects are examples of semantic memory. Of course, all such information had to have been acquired through past events in your life, but your memory of them does not depend on remembering those events. To remember that penguins are birds, you do not have to remember anything about the circumstances in which you learned that fact. The discussion of concept representation (schemas and scripts) and the spreading-activation model of knowledge organization (Figure 10.10) had to do with semantic memory.

Implicit Memory

■ **38.** ***Why are implicit memories not well described in terms of the modal model? What are some examples of different kinds of implicit memories?***

The other broad class, ***implicit memory***, consists of all memories that are not explicit and is defined as the type of memory in which previously acquired information influences behavior or thought without itself entering the conscious mind. By definition, then, implicit memory does not operate through the means depicted by the modal model, in which the short-term or working store is equated with the conscious mind. Because people are unable to report the relevant information, implicit memory is also called *nondeclarative memory*. Among the subclasses of implicit memory are the memories produced by classical conditioning (discussed in Chapter 5), the memories that provide the basis for a phenomenon called priming (to be discussed later), and a large class called ***procedural memory***, which includes motor skills, habits, and unconsciously learned (tacit) rules.

With practice you improve at such motor skills as riding a bicycle, hammering nails, or weaving a rug. The improvement is retained (remembered) from one practice session to the next, even though you are unaware of the changes in muscle movements that make the difference. (For an operant-conditioning account of such improvement, see Chapter 5.) In other cases, a pattern of behavior that was learned through conscious means gradually becomes automatic or habitual with repetition; memories that were once explicit become implicit. When I first moved to my present house and job, I learned explicitly the names of the roads and the landmarks needed to find my way to work. Had you asked me then to describe the route, I could have done so easily. But now, having traveled the route thousands of times, I can no longer name all the roads and landmarks at critical corners where I turn. I don't think consciously about the route at all as I take it, but automatically turn my bicycle at the appropriate places while thinking about the lecture I am to give or the chapter I am writing. Thus, implicit memory guides me to work and leaves my conscious mind free for other tasks.

People can even learn to make decisions based on complex rules without ever becoming aware of the rules (Greenwald, 1992; Lewicki & others, 1992). Some of the experiments supporting this claim make use of what are called *artificial grammars* (Reber, 1989). The grammars consist of sets of rules as to which letters may and may not follow certain other letters in strings that are several letters long. For example, one rule might be that an X at the beginning of a string must be followed either by another X or a V, and another rule might be that a J anywhere in the middle of a string must be followed by a B, X, or T. Subjects are not told the rules. Instead, they are shown examples of grammatical and nongrammatical strings, labeled as such, and then are asked to categorize new examples as grammatical or not based on "gut feelings." The subjects typically do not learn any of the rules explicitly—they cannot state the rules—yet they learn to make correct categorizations at a rate better than chance. The memories that guide their correct choices are implicit.

■ **39.** ***In what sense are implicit memories more situation-dependent than explicit memories?***

An important characteristic of implicit memories is their extreme dependence on the immediate situation. An implicit memory is retrieved and used to guide behavior only at the moment when a specific set of stimuli call it forth. Thus, the implicit memory that I must make a right-hand turn at a particular intersection on my route to work is automatically called forth by the configuration of stimuli that make up that intersection and is not called forth at other times. Explicit memories, in contrast, can be retrieved in contexts other than those in which they were originally acquired and, therefore, can be used not just to guide repetitive behavior, but also to plan future behavior and to modify existing routines.

Priming as a Subclass of Implicit Memory

A variety of implicit memory much studied in recent years, ***priming*** can be defined as the activation of one or more existing memories by a stimulus (the priming stimulus). This activation is not experienced consciously, yet it influences subsequent conscious perception and thought and thus provides a link between implicit and explicit memory. The activated memories are more easily called into consciousness after the priming experience than before. A distinction can be made between two types of priming—perceptual and conceptual (Tulving & Schacter, 1990).

Perceptual Priming

The first class, ***perceptual priming***, refers to the effect of a priming stimulus on a person's subsequent ability to identify a test stimulus. A typical experiment consists of a training phase followed by a test. In the training phase, subjects are shown a sequence of familiar words or pictures of common objects, the priming stimuli. In the test, which may take place minutes or days later, the subjects are shown degraded forms of the same stimuli and asked to read or name them. The degraded stimuli may be fragments of the original stimuli (see Figure 10.15) or the original stimuli flashed on a screen so quickly that they are hard to identify. The subjects are deliberately not reminded about the training phase or told of any relation between it and the test. They are simply asked to read or name each degraded stimulus. Priming is demonstrated when the degraded forms of stimuli are more readily identified by subjects who had seen the nondegraded forms of those stimuli in training than by subjects who had not.

40. *What is some evidence that perceptual priming involves implicit memory and that the encoding process for it is different from that for explicit memory?*

Many experiments have shown that perceptual priming does not depend on explicit memory for the priming stimuli (Tulving & Schacter, 1990). In such experiments, people were given two tests after the training phase was completed: a test of priming, as just described, and an explicit recognition test, in which they were asked to state which words or pictures had or had not been shown during training. The experiments revealed no correlation between priming and explicit memory. Priming was just as strong for stimuli that subjects did not explicitly remember see-

Figure 10.15 ***Sample priming stimuli and fragmented test stimuli***

In some experiments on perceptual priming, complete words or pictures are used as the priming stimuli, and fragmented forms of the same words or pictures are used as the test stimuli. Exposure to the priming stimuli causes improved identification of the test stimuli, whether or not subjects explicitly remember the priming stimuli.

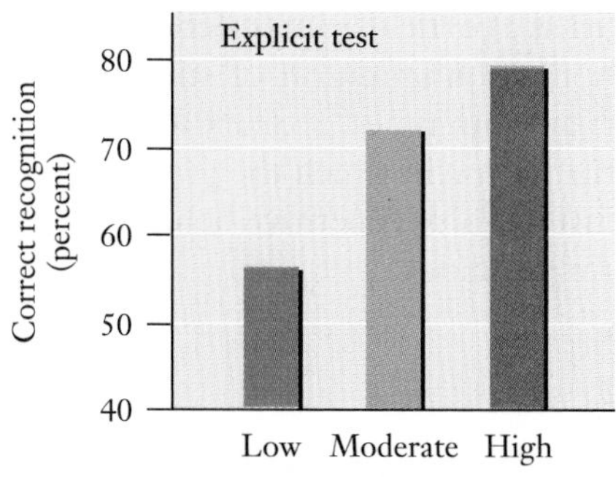

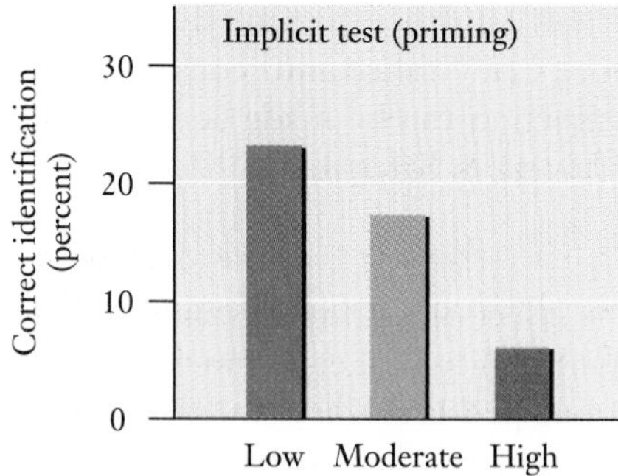

Figure 10.16 ***Effect of elaboration on explicit recognition and perceptual priming***

When subjects had to generate the critical words during training (high elaboration) or read them paired with their antonyms (moderate elaboration), they showed better explicit memory but poorer priming than when they simply read the words alone (low elaboration). (Adapted from Jacoby, 1983.)

ing, as it was for those that they did remember seeing. Since priming does not depend on explicit memory, then, by definition, the memory it depends on is implicit.

Other experiments have shown that elaborative rehearsal, which is known to improve explicit memory, does not improve perceptual priming and can even interfere with it. In one such experiment, Larry Jacoby (1983) exposed subjects to priming words in three different training conditions. In the *low elaboration* condition, each critical word (such as *COLD*) was simply presented for the subject to read. In the *moderate elaboration* condition, each critical word was presented along with its antonym (opposite) in order to draw attention to the word's meaning. For example, when cold was the critical word, the pair was *hot-COLD*. In the *high elaboration* condition, thought about meaning was insured by requiring subjects to generate each critical word from its antonym. Thus, when the cue *hot* was presented, the subjects said *cold*. Later, all subjects were tested for both explicit recognition memory (by asking them to state which words were or were not seen during training) and priming (by asking them to read the words when flashed quickly on a screen). As shown in Figure 10.16, elaborative rehearsal improved explicit memory, as expected, but had the opposite effect on priming. Apparently, perceptual priming, unlike explicit memory, depends on automatic perceptual registration of the stimulus during encoding and not upon conscious thought about its meaning.

Conceptual Priming

Priming can influence not only one's perceptual ability, but also the flow of one's thoughts. Priming of this sort is called ***conceptual priming*** and presumably involves the activation of concepts stored in semantic memory (Tulving & Schacter, 1990).

■ **41.** ***How can conceptual priming be demonstrated, and what function does it probably serve?***

In a typical experiment to test conceptual priming, subjects are first presented with a set of names or pictures of common objects. Later, they are tested with items for which an object in the priming list could be an appropriate answer. For example, the test might consist of a set of category names, such as *bird*, and subjects might be asked to name a member of each category. If the word *penguin* had been one of the priming words and if subjects who had seen that word proved more likely than other subjects to say "penguin" in response to the category *bird*, this result would exemplify conceptual priming. Like perceptual priming, conceptual priming occurs whether or not the person remembers the priming stimulus in an explicit memory test. Therefore, the memory on which conceptual priming depends is classed as implicit.

Unlike perceptual priming, conceptual priming is usually improved by elaborative encoding of the priming stimuli (Roediger, 1990; Tulving & Schacter, 1990). Still, conceptual priming can occur to some degree without elaborative encoding, and apparently it can even occur in the complete absence of conscious awareness of the priming stimulus. An example of the latter comes from an experiment described in Chapter 9. Subjects who had seen a slide containing a hidden figure of a duck (see Figure 9.14) did not consciously recognize the figure, but nevertheless proved more likely than other subjects to incorporate ducks or duck-related objects such as ponds into nature drawings that they were asked to produce (Eagle & others, 1966). This illustrates conceptual priming, because the priming stimulus activated the duck concept in subjects' minds, as manifested in their drawings.

Conceptual priming no doubt plays an important role in conscious, logical thought. When we see or think about an object, event, or idea, those elements of our semantic memory that are relevant to that perception or thought become activated (primed) for a period of time, more available than usual to conscious thought, more retrievable into short-term memory. This helps keep our thought running logically, rather than jumping randomly from one idea or image to another.

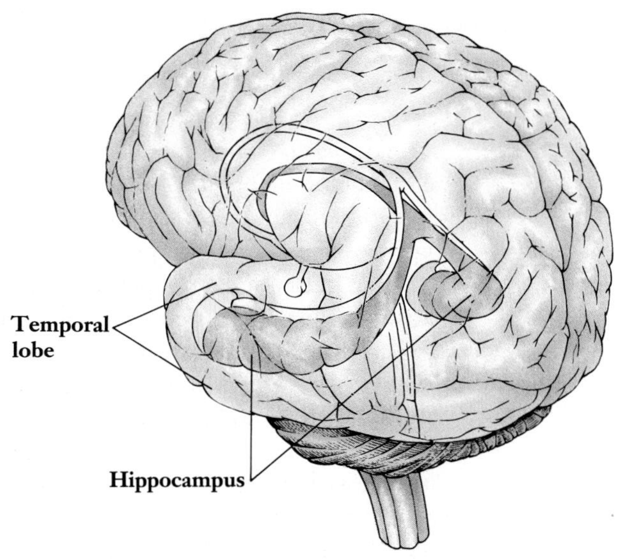

Figure 10.17 ***Brain area involved in temporal lobe amnesia***

As shown here, the hippocampus lies under the temporal lobe of the cerebral cortex. Destruction of this structure in both sides of the brain produces a profound inability to encode new explicit long-term memories, but has little effect on implicit memory.

Neuropsychological Evidence for Separate Memory Systems

We have just been examining evidence that implicit memory can occur even without explicit memory in normal, brain-intact people. Such evidence suggests that explicit and implicit memory might involve different neural systems in the brain. More direct evidence comes from research with people who have impaired memory (amnesia) due to brain damage.

Implicit Memory in Amnesic Patients

■ **42.** ***Based on studies of amnesic patients, what is some evidence that the encoding of explicit, but not implicit, memories involves the brain's hippocampus?***

In introducing the distinction between long-term and short-term explicit memory, I described the case of H. M., the man who, after destruction in both temporal lobes of his brain, could still perceive and think about new information, but apparently could not form new long-term memories of that information. Other patients have shown the same disorder (though usually not as strongly) after strokes or other sources of brain damage. The disorder is called ***temporal lobe amnesia***, and the critical area of destruction for memory loss to occur is the hippocampus, a limbic-system structure buried within the temporal lobe (see Figure 10.17) (Squire, 1992). The same kind of memory loss also occurs in long-term alcoholics suffering from a pattern of disorders called *Korsakoff's syndrome*, which stems from brain damage caused by a combination of alcohol and poor nutrition, specifically lack of vitamin B_1 (Parkin, 1987). In these patients the damage causing amnesia is apparently not in the hippocampus itself but in neural pathways that connect that structure with other parts of the brain (Squire, 1992).

Despite their deficit in explicit memory, temporal-lobe and Korsakoff's patients typically show normal memory in all sorts of implicit memory tests. If classically conditioned to blink their eyes in response to a conditioned stimulus, they show the conditioned response as strongly in subsequent tests as do nonamnesic subjects (Daum & others, 1989). If given practice with a new motor skill, such as tracing a pattern that can be seen only in its mirror image, they show normal improvement from session to session (Milner, 1965). Similarly, they can learn and retain artificial grammars and other tacit rules (Knowlton & others, 1992), and they manifest both perceptual and conceptual priming (Squire, 1992; Warrington & Weiskrantz, 1968, 1970). In all of these examples the implicit memory occurs even when the amnesic subjects cannot consciously remember anything at all about the original learning experience. In one experiment, a severely amnesic patient learned to program a microcomputer over a series of sessions. At each session his programming ability was better than in the previous session, even though he had no explicit memory of ever having programmed a computer before (Glisky & others, 1986).

Apparently, the hippocampus and its connections to the rest of the brain are essential for encoding new long-term explicit memories, but not for encoding new long-term implicit memories.

Evidence for Separable Memory Systems in Nonhuman Animals

■ **43.** ***How have studies of monkeys led to a distinction between habit and cognitive memory systems paralleling that between implicit and explicit systems in humans?***

A growing amount of research with monkeys and other nonhuman animals also supports the idea that different memory systems have different neural bases (Squire, 1992). Animals cannot report explicit memories in words, but can be tested by other means to distinguish between different memory types. In research with macaque monkeys, Mortimer Mishkin distinguishes between a *habit system* and a *cognitive memory system*, which seems to parallel the distinction between the implicit, procedural memory system and the explicit, episodic memory system in people (Mishkin & Appenzeller, 1987). To test the habit system, Mishkin uses straightforward operant-conditioning procedures in which monkeys are rewarded for consistently making particular responses to particular stimuli. For example, a monkey that receives a peanut each time it picks up the square object and ignores the round one in a two-object choice will demonstrate habit memory through its increased frequency of picking the square. To test the cognitive memory system, Mishkin combines operant conditioning with the requirement that the animal remember a new piece of information over a period of time on every trial. More specifically, one test he uses is *delayed nonmatching to sample*, in which on each trial the animal sees a specific object that it has never seen before (maybe a plastic square) and then, sometime later, is shown that object again along with a new object and must choose the new object to receive a reward.

Of greatest interest, Mishkin and his colleagues have found that destruction of the hippocampus along with some of the adjacent tissue in both temporal lobes completely abolishes the monkeys' abilities in cognitive memory tests, but has essentially no effect on their performance in habit tests. The animals can still be operantly conditioned, and they retain the effects of conditioning from one day to another. In addition, they can still perform a nonmatching-to-sample task if the delay between seeing the new object and the test is only a few seconds (within the span of short-term memory), but they cannot perform it if the delay is a minute or more. Based on this and other research, Mishkin suggests that cognitive encoding involves the hippocampus and associated parts of the temporal lobe, whereas habit encoding involves a more primitive neural system, most likely in the basal ganglia—structures buried deep in the brain and known to be involved in the control of deliberate movements (described in Chapter 6).

Separation of Episodic and Semantic Memories in Amnesic Patients

■ **44.** ***What is some evidence that episodic and semantic memory may involve different neural systems?***

Amnesic subjects are usually deficient in both classes of explicit memory—episodic and semantic. For example, H. M., the patient discusses earlier, not only fails to remember his own experiences that occurred after his brain surgery (in 1953), but also fails to remember factual information concerning developments after his surgery. He cannot name new world leaders or performers, and if asked to draw a car or a radio from memory, he persists in drawing the 1950's versions (Milner, 1984). Less severely impaired amnesic patients, however, commonly manifest a greater deficit in forming new episodic memories than in forming new semantic memories (Shimamura & Squire, 1991; Tulving & others, 1991).

In one experiment demonstrating this differential effect on the two explicit memory systems, patients with amnesia stemming from a variety of brain injuries (in areas not specified by the researchers) heard a series of fictitious statements, such as "Bob Hope's father was a fireman." When tested a few minutes later, many of the patients could answer questions based on the content of the fictitious statements, indicating that they had incorporated the information into their semantic memory (their general store of knowledge), but could not recall where or when they had learned the information, indicating lack of episodic memory (Schacter & others, 1984). Thus, if asked what Bob Hope's father did for a living, they said that he was a fireman; but if asked how they knew he was a fireman, they said they did not know.

How can a person encode information about the world without encoding whatever is needed to relate that information to an episode in his or her own life? Endel Tulving (1985) has argued that episodic memory is an evolutionarily new addition to our cognitive machinery, which may be relatively unique to human beings. This evolutionary add-on, which gives us each a sense of our own past, and thus a sense of ourselves as individuals, may be more fragile—more destructible by brain damage—than the more primitive semantic system or the still more primitive implicit memory system.

Concluding Thoughts

Memory indeed is the central topic of cognitive psychology. It is relevant to all aspects of both conscious and unconscious perception and thought. To help yourself organize, elaborate upon, and thereby encode the ideas in this chapter into your explicit long-term memory, you might find useful the following general thoughts:

1. The modal model as a functional representation of the mind Throughout this chapter, the modal model served as the organizing structure for our thinking about memory and about the mind in general. You have read of three memory stores, of control processes related to the stores, and of research aimed at characterizing the stores and processes. Your review and thoughts about all of this will be most effective, I think, if you adopt a functionalist perspective. From that perspective, each store and process represents not a different part (or structure) of the mind, but instead represents a different job that the mind performs in its overall task of acquiring and using information. What is the main job (the main function) of (a) sensory memory, (b) short-term memory, (c) long-term memory, (d) encoding, and (e) retrieval? Once you are clear on the main function of each, think about its properties in relation to its function. Think about the various stores, processes, and modes of representation in terms of their relevance to the normal, everyday functioning of the mind. Similarly, going beyond the model, think about the functions of the various types of implicit memory and consider why, in terms of those functions, implicit memory has different properties from explicit memory.

2. The modal model as an example of a schema To the degree that you and I have incorporated the modal model into our own minds, it has become our schema for understanding memory. Remember what Bartlett said about schemas: Schemas allow us to organize and make sense of the world around us, but in doing so they can also distort our perceptions and thoughts. The model is a valuable schema for organizing research and thought about an extraordinary complicated topic; but by encouraging us to fit all observations about memory into that model, it can constrict and bias the observations we make and the conclusions we draw. To some degree, I may have distorted the field of memory research in this chapter because I have written it with the model strongly in mind. To some degree, you may have distorted the research and findings even further to fit the model as you understand it. To some degree, cognitive psychology as a whole may have distorted the knowledge of memory by directing research toward aspects of memory that are most consistent with the model while ignoring other aspects that are equally important. The creative thinkers in this science, as in any other, are those who are not bound by current models or schemas, but find new ways to look at the topic and in that way open up new lines of research. Current research on implicit memory and its interaction with explicit memory may produce a new, improved schema of the human mind.

3. Standard laboratory and ecological approaches to memory A considerable amount of debate has arisen in cognitive psychology over the relative value of tightly controlled laboratory studies and more loosely controlled studies of memory in nonlaboratory contexts (Banaji & Crowder, 1989; Conway, 1991; Neisser, 1978). The laboratory approach to cognition stems directly from the work of the nineteenth-century German founders of experimental psychology, including Ebbinghaus and Wundt, who wished to isolate the separate processes of the mind and study them in relative independence of one another. Ebbinghaus invented the nonsense syllable in his effort to study memory independent of meaning, and that tradition has been continued by studies that use nonsense syllables or random strings of digits or unrelated words as memory items.

The contrasting approach, often called the ecological approach, emphasizes the value of studying memory in everyday life. Ecological theorists such as Ulrich Neisser (1982) argue that the standard laboratory procedures do not just isolate variables but often obliterate those that are most important to normal memory functions. Neisser and others point out that the purpose of memory is not to retain nonsense syllables or unrelated strings of words, but rather to retain knowledge, which implies meaning. Memories are useful precisely because they are meaningful; from this perspective, it is useless to study memory independent of meaning. The relation of memory to meaning was the main idea behind Bartlett's pioneering research on the role of schemas in people's memories for events in their lives or for stories they heard. Other studies described in this chapter that fall within the ecological purview are those of memories for school lessons, for the names and faces of former classmates, and for parking places.

But the two approaches are not incompatible. The role of meaning in memory, emphasized by the ecological theorists, can be studied in the laboratory. In fact, many of the experiments described in this chapter were of this type, including studies of (a) the effects of different forms of elaborative rehearsal on encoding, (b) the value of structuring the material to be remembered into a meaningful hierarchy, (c) the value of generating meaningful retrieval cues at the time of encoding, and (d) the effect that information provided after an original event can have on the constructed memory for that event.

Perhaps the theme of integrating ecological and laboratory approaches is becoming familiar to you. Chapter 5 described an ecological approach to learning, which originated with field studies but led to laboratory experiments on species-specific and domain-specific learning processes. Chapter 9 outlined an ecological perspective in perception, which began with an assumption that the entire array of stimuli, not the bits and pieces, must be considered to understand perception, but eventuated in new ways of breaking down the array of information and of studying that breakdown in the laboratory. In general, the ecological approach raises questions about psychological processes in relation to the real-life contexts in which they operate. Once the questions are identified in field studies, they often can be pursued most effectively in the more controlled conditions of the laboratory.

Further Reading

Allan Baddeley (1990). *Human memory: Theory and practice.* Boston: Allyn and Bacon.

This relatively brief textbook, by a leading memory researcher, is a thoughtful and interesting survey of current research and ideas about all aspects of human memory.

Ulrich Neisser (Ed.) (1982). *Memory observed: Remembering in natural contexts.* San Francisco: Freeman.

Edited by one of the leading advocates of an ecological perspective on memory, this collection of essays and research papers includes many interesting accounts of the strengths and failings of memory in everyday life. In one chapter, for example, Neisser analyzes John Dean's memory for meetings with President Nixon, as expressed in Dean's testimony to a Senate committee, for evidence of the role of schemas in memory construction and distortion.

Ronald A. Finke (1989). *Principles of mental imagery.* Cambridge, MA: MIT Press.

This in an interesting, nicely integrated summary of experimental research on the mental representation of visual-spatial information and the processes of encoding and retrieving such information.

Elizabeth Loftus & Katherine Ketcham (1991). *Witness for the defense: The accused, the eyewitness, and the expert who puts memory on trial.* New York: St. Martin's Press.

Memory researcher Elizabeth Loftus is frequently asked to testify in court on how memories introduced as evidence may have been distorted. This book is a collection of her more dramatic courtroom experiences. One chapter, for example, shows how a mother's well-intentioned but insistent questioning of her young daughter about her experiences at camp led the child to construct a memory that eventuated in a false accusation of sexual abuse.

Looking Ahead

In studying the topic of memory, we have entered the gate to the human intellect. Memories provide the basis for ideas, reasons, decisions, plans, and verbal utterances. Thinking and speaking are the abilities that appear to distinguish humans most from the other animals, and these are the central topics of the next two chapters, which deal with the human intellect and its development.

Conceptions of Intelligence

The Psychometric Approach I: Measuring Intelligence

The Psychometric Approach II: Statistically Inferring the Structure of Intelligence

The Information-Processing Approach: Identifying the Components of Intelligence

The Neuropsychological Approach: Relating Intelligence to Areas of the Brain

The Ecological Approach: Relating Intelligence to the Contexts of Life

Logical Reasoning and Problem Solving

Inductive Reasoning and Biases in It

The Concrete Nature of Deductive Reasoning

Some Strategies for Solving Problems: The Elements of Insight

Language and Its Relationship to Thought

Language as a Cognitive System

The Neuropsychological Approach to Language

The Relation of Language to Thought

THE HUMAN INTELLECT

CHAPTER 11

Compared with other species, we are not the most graceful, nor the strongest, nor the swiftest, nor the fiercest, nor the gentlest, nor the most long-lived, nor the most resistant to the poisons accumulating in our atmosphere. We do, however, fancy ourselves to be the most intelligent of animals; and, at least by our own definitions of intelligence, our fancy is apparently correct. We are the animals that know and reason; that classify and name the other animals; that try to understand all things, including even ourselves. We are also the animals that tell each other what we know, passing it along so that each generation starts off with more knowledge, if not more wisdom, than the previous one.

This chapter, the last of the trilogy introducing cognition, is about aspects of the human mind that most distinguish us from other animals. The first section is about four psychological approaches to describing and understanding the human intellect as a whole; the second is about mental processes involved in reasoning and problem solving; and the third is about language and its relationship to thought.

Conceptions of Intelligence

People sometimes argue about the true meaning of intelligence, but such arguments usually are pointless. *Intelligence* is just a word, and, like any word, it may be used by different people to refer to different concepts. To find out how psychologists and educators who specialize in intelligence define it, Mark Snyderman and Stanley Rothman (1987) asked more than 1000 such specialists to check off, on a list of human abilities, those they considered to be important elements of intelligence. Nearly all checked off abstract reasoning, problem solving, and capacity to acquire knowledge; more than half checked memory, adaptation to one's environment, mental speed, linguistic competence, mathematical competence, general knowledge, and creativity; and about one-fourth checked sensory acuity, goal directedness, and achievement motivation. Thus, some experts conceived of intelligence as specific to higher-order reasoning and knowing, while others conceived of it as a broad set of characteristics that help people deal with their environment.

A question that arises immediately when we think about the possible meanings of intelligence is: To what extent are various mental abilities interrelated or dependent on one another? More specifically, do good problem solvers also have good memories? Do people who have a large store of general knowledge also have keen senses or fast reaction times? Do people with excellent language abilities also have excellent abilities for solving spatial puzzles or understanding maps? To the extent that the answer to such questions is yes, we might think of intelligence as a single, general quality that affects performance on all sorts of mental tasks. To the extent that the answer is no, we must either choose which specific ability to call intelligence, or we must think of intelligence as a collection of separate qualities.

The following sections describe four different psychological approaches in the study of intelligence: (1) the *psychometric approach*, which attempts to characterize intelligence through the analysis of patterns of scores on mental tests; (2) the *information-processing approach*, which attempts to describe the steps involved in carrying out mental tasks; (3) the *neuropsychological approach*, which attempts to relate specific mental abilities to specific areas of the brain; and (4) the *ecological approach*, which attempts to relate intelligence to the environmental context within which it occurs. The question of whether intelligence is most usefully characterized as one entity or as a collection of entities is a theme that runs through each of these sections.

Francis Galton

A member of an intellectually gifted family, Galton's genius was wide ranging. In addition to his studies of individual differences and his development of the statistical concept of correlation, Galton invented a variety of mechanical devices, including a data-storage system and a periscope that enabled him to see over the heads of taller people.

The Psychometric Approach I: Measuring Intelligence

Psychometrics means psychological measurement. More fully, it refers to the measurement of psychological differences among people and to the statistical analysis of those differences as a way of learning about the structure of the human mind. Psychometrics encompasses personality measurement (discussed in Chapter 16) as well as intellectual measurement, but it began historically with the latter.

Galton and the Idea of Innate Mental Quickness and Acuity

One of the first to attempt to measure intelligence systematically was the English scientist Sir Francis Galton (1822–1911). Galton's interest in intelligence grew out of his interest in heredity. He greatly admired the ideas about heredity and evolution developed by his cousin, Charles Darwin, and wanted to extend them into the realm of human mental ability. In 1869, Galton published a book showing that people who were famous for their intellectual achievements often had similarly famous relatives, and contending that such similarity stems more from shared biological heredity than from shared environments (see Chapter 3). Subsequently, Galton began a research program aimed at identifying and measuring the biological differences that might allow some people to achieve much more than others. He viewed this not only as an academically interesting project that would advance understanding of the mind, but also as a practical endeavor. One of his goals was to develop a test that could screen people for their intellectual potential so that public funds for education could be reserved for those with high potential (Galton, 1865).

■ **1. *How did Galton attempt to measure intelligence? For what purpose did he invent a statistical method of correlation?***

Galton carried out this research in his Anthropometric Laboratory (*anthropometric* means human measurement), which he established in 1884 at the International Health Exhibition in London and later moved to a science museum. For a small fee, visitors could have various measures taken and receive a report of the results. Most of the measures were of basic motor and sensory abilities, such as the ability to react quickly to a signal or to detect slight differences between two sounds, lengths, or weights. Based on his assumption that intelligence is an inherited property of the nervous system, Galton (1885) hypothesized that it should be manifested in these simple measures. He hoped to show that the biological underpinning for intellectual differences among people lay in their neural quickness and acuity—the speed and accuracy with which they could respond to environmental stimuli.

As part of this research, Galton invented a statistical procedure to assess the degree of relationship between different measures. This procedure was subsequently refined by Karl Pearson (1920) to produce the correlational method still used today (discussed in Chapter 2). Galton hoped to demonstrate that his various measures of the mind were related to one another in such a way that a high score on one measure would predict high scores on the others. To his disappointment, Galton found only weak correlations. Research by other psychologists using Galton's measures proved even more disappointing. For example, an analysis of scores collected from 300 students at Columbia University and Barnard College showed no significant relationship between either reaction time or sensory acuity and academic grades (Wissler, 1901). Because Galton's measures seemed to be only moderately related to each other and unrelated to academic achievement, most researchers in the field of intelligence lost interest in them (Fancher, 1985). As you will see later, however, some psychologists have recently revived Galton's approach and produced evidence that some sensory and reaction-time measures do correlate with intellectual achievement.

Binet and the Idea of Intelligence as a Collection of Abilities

■ ***2. How did Binet's view of intelligence differ from Galton's? What was the purpose and form of Binet's intelligence test, and how did he develop it?***

Modern intelligence tests have their ancestry not in Galton's measures of sensory acuity and reaction time, but rather in a test called the *Binet-Simon Intelligence Scale*, which was developed in France in 1905 by Alfred Binet and his assistant Theophile Simon. From the outset, Binet's view of intelligence was quite different from Galton's. He argued against Galton's idea that intelligence is closely related to sensory acuity, citing as one line of evidence the example of Helen Keller, who had been blind and deaf since her early childhood but who was universally regarded as highly intelligent (Binet & Simon, 1916). Binet believed that intelligence is best understood as a collection of various higher-order mental abilities that might be only loosely related to one another (Binet & Henri, 1896). He also differed from Galton on the heredity question, arguing that intelligence is nurtured through interaction with the environment and that an important function of schooling is to increase intelligence. In fact, the purpose of Binet and Simon's test—developed at the request of the French Ministry of Education—was to identify children who were not profiting as much as they should from their schooling so that they might be given special attention.

Alfred Binet

Although he had a lasting influence on the appraisal of individual intelligence, Binet was not particularly appreciated by his contemporaries. He never obtained a university professorship, and his work with Theophile Simon was not publicly honored until 60 years after his death.

Binet and Simon's test was oriented explicitly toward the skills required for schoolwork. It consisted of questions and problems designed to test memory, vocabulary, common knowledge, use of numbers, understanding of time, ability to combine ideas, and so forth. The problems were selected by pretesting them with schoolchildren of various ages and comparing the results with teachers' ratings of each child's classroom performance (Binet & Simon, 1916). Items were kept in the test only if more of the high-rated than low-rated children answered them correctly; otherwise, they were dropped. Binet was aware of the circularity of this process: His test was supposed to measure intelligence better than existing measures, but to develop it he had to compare results with an existing measure (teachers' ratings). Yet, once developed, the test would presumably have advantages over teachers' ratings. Among other things, it would allow for comparison of children who had had different teachers or no formal schooling at all.

In 1908, Binet and Simon revised their test and introduced the concept of *mental age* to the scoring system (actually, they called it mental *level*, but others called it mental age and the latter term stuck). With this scoring system, a child received an intelligence score corresponding to the age group whose average score his or her performance best matched. Thus, a child of any age who performed as well as an average 10-year-old would be assigned a mental age of 10. For better or worse, this system probably did much to popularize the test. Mental age indicated directly whether a child was advanced or behind and played on the pride and anxiety of parents and teachers. Within a few years, English translations of the Binet-Simon Scale were available, and testing caught on in England and North America even more than it had in France.

How many objects can you name?

As part of the original Binet intelligence test, children were asked to name common household objects in this picture. Obviously, a child whose home contained such objects would do better than a child whose home did not.

Intelligence Tests After Binet

■ **3. *How was IQ calculated in the original Stanford-Binet procedure, and how was the procedure changed when tests for adults were developed?***

The first intelligence test commonly used in North America was the *Stanford-Binet Scale*, a modification of Binet and Simon's test that was developed in 1916 at Stanford University under the direction of Lewis Terman. By this time another refinement had been added to the scoring system: the *intelligence quotient*, or *IQ*, determined by dividing a child's mental age (MA) by his or her actual chronological age (CA) and multiplying by 100. Thus, IQ = (MA/CA) × 100. If a child's mental age as measured by the test was 11.5 and his or her chronological age was 10, then the child's IQ would be (11.5/10) × 100 = 115. An IQ of 100 would mean that a child was average for his or her age, and scores above or below 100 would mean that the child was above or below average.

Stanford-Binet test materials

These materials are from the current version of the test. In addition to an overall IQ score, separate scores are obtained for verbal reasoning, abstract/visual reasoning, quantitative reasoning, and short-term memory.

The Stanford-Binet Scale has been revised over the years and is still used quite widely, though the most common individually administered intelligence tests today are variations of a different test that was developed by David Wechsler in the 1930s. Wechsler's original purpose was to design an intelligence test for adults, because the Stanford-Binet Scale was designed for children. Later he modified his own adult test to produce a version for children (Aiken, 1991). The descendents of Wechsler's tests most used today are the *Wechsler Adult Intelligence Scale, Revised (WAIS-R)* and the *Wechsler Intelligence Scale for Children, Third Edition (WISC-III)*.

By the time Wechsler was developing his intelligence test for adults, the term IQ was so ingrained in public consciousness that he retained it in the scoring system even though its original meaning had to be abandoned. (It would be senseless to say that a 20-year-old who scores as well as an average 60-year-old has an IQ of 300.) The scoring system for the WAIS-R is based on results obtained from large samples of adults in nine different age groups, ranging from 16 to 75. Those whose performance is average for their age group receive an IQ score of 100, and those whose performance is above or below average receive a score above or below 100, assigned in such a way that the overall distribution of scores looks like that shown in Figure 11.1. Table 11.1 summarizes the various subtests of the WAIS-R. The WISC-R is similar to the WAIS-R, but contains simpler problems.

The Stanford-Binet and Wechsler scales must be administered one-on-one by a trained tester. To permit mass testing, many group-administered intelligence tests have been developed over the years. They usually are given in multiple-choice format and may serve purposes more specific than just the broad assessment of intelligence. For example, the mathematics and verbal *Scholastic Aptitude Tests (SATs)* are often considered to be intelligence tests, and their results correlate quite strongly with scores on individually administered intelligence tests (Brody, 1985).

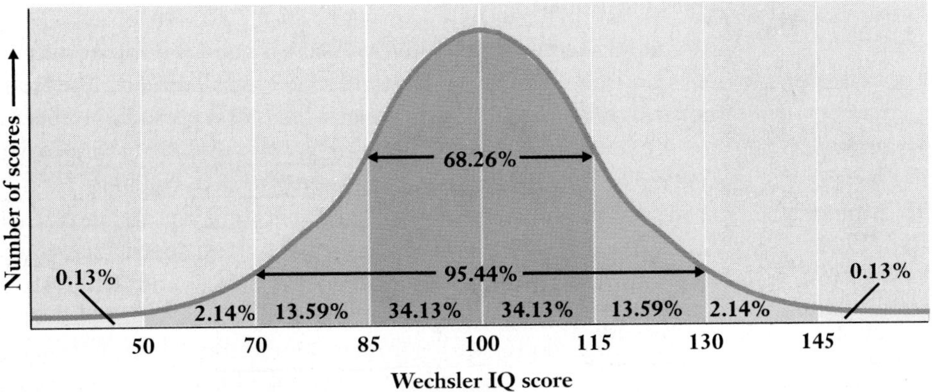

Figure 11.1 ***Standardized scoring of Wechsler IQ tests***

The scoring system for Wechsler IQ tests is based on the assumption that intelligence is distributed in the population according to a normal distribution (represented by the bell-shaped curve). Thus raw scores on the test are converted into IQ scores in such a way as to produce a normal distribution. Notice that with this system about 68 percent of IQ scores are between 85 and 115, and about 95 percent are between 70 and 130. (For more on normal distributions and the method for standardizing test scores, see the Statistical Appendix.)

Table 11.1 ***The eleven subtests of the WAIS-R***

Verbal subtests

Information General-information questions.

Digit Span The task is to recite a series of digits immediately after hearing them. The series is increased on each trial until the person fails twice in succession. A second phase is like the first except the digits are recited backwards. The purpose is to test short-term memory.

Vocabulary Words to be defined.

Arithmetic Arithmetic problems to be solved.

Comprehension Questions requiring rather detailed explanations are asked. The purpose is to test practical knowledge, social judgment, and ability to organize information.

Similarities Questions are asked that take the form, "In what way are A and B alike?" The purpose is to measure inductive-reasoning ability.

Performance subtests

Picture Completion Pictures with missing parts are presented and the task is to find the missing part. The purpose is to test visual alertness and attention to details.

Picture Arrangement The task is to arrange sets of pictures in a way that tells a story (similar to a comic strip). The purpose is to test sequencing ability and planning.

Block Design The task is to arrange sets of red and white blocks in such a way as to match a specific design. The purpose is to test ability to analyze visual patterns.

Object Assembly The task is to put puzzle pieces together to form a picture. The purpose is to test ability to visualize a final form from its parts.

Digit Symbol A key is provided relating symbols to single-digit numbers, and the task is to use the key in translating a series of single-digit numbers into symbols. The purpose is to test attentiveness, quickness, and persistence in a simple perceptual-motor task.

Note: The verbal subtests contribute to the *verbal IQ*, and the performance subtests contribute to the *performance IQ*. The average of the two is used as the basis for the overall IQ.

Source: Adapted from *Assessment of intellectual functioning* (pp. 163–164) by L. R. Aiken, 1991, Boston: Allyn & Bacon.

■ 4. ***How have psychologists attempted to assess the validity of IQ tests? What are the problems with Terman's study as an index of validity? What is the evidence that IQ tests are valid predictors of on-the-job performance?***

The Question of Validity

How valid are intelligence tests? A test is valid if it measures what it is supposed to measure (see Chapter 2). If intelligence tests measure intellectual ability, then IQ scores should correlate with other indices of a person's intellectual ability.

As you know, Binet deliberately constructed his original intelligence test in such a way that the scores would correlate with teachers' ratings of children's ability in school. Not surprisingly, given that modern intelligence tests are direct or indirect descendents of Binet's test, IQ scores do correlate moderately well with grades in school; the correlation coefficients found in various studies range from 0.30 to 0.70 (Jensen, 1980).

How well do IQ scores predict achievement outside of school? That is a more complicated question, and it has provoked enormous controversy over the years. One of the first to address the question was Lewis Terman, the psychologist who directed the development of the original Stanford-Binet Scale. Terman was particularly interested in the fate of highly intelligent children. Using the Stanford-Binet Scale, he identified about 1500 children in California who had IQs over 135—the upper 1% of their age group. He and his colleagues followed this group throughout their lives and found that, on average, they became very high achieving adults. A disproportionately high percentage of this group earned high incomes, published important writings, patented inventions, became business or political leaders, and made it into *Who's Who* (Terman, 1954).

But Terman's study—despite its large size, long duration, and the heroic devotion of Terman and his staff—was from today's perspective flawed in many ways (Ceci, 1990). The original subject selection was based not only on high IQ, but also on teachers' ratings of high motivation for success. Moreover, Terman limited his search for high IQ children to school districts in which students were predominantly white and in the higher range of socioeconomic status. In addition, he and his staff remained personally involved with the selected group (who referred to themselves as Termites), encouraging them and sometimes even helping them get into high-ranking universities and prestigious careers. Because Terman's selected group differed in many ways from the general public with whom he compared them, we have no way to judge the degree to which high IQ contributed to their success. Based on an informal comparison of Terman's group with a group comparable in social class but unselected for IQ, one early critic concluded that the Termites' success was attributable primarily to the high economic and social status of their parents (Sorokin, 1956).

Studies since Terman's time have shown that, even when parents' status is appropriately equated, people with high IQs are more likely to end up in high-status careers than are people with lower IQs (Brody, 1992). A problem with such studies, however, is that most high-status careers require higher education, and higher education is most available to people with high IQs (as indexed by SAT scores and grades in previous schooling). To get around this problem, a number of researchers have correlated IQ and actual on-the-job performance, as measured by supervisors' ratings or direct observation, for people already involved in a particular career. Most such studies reveal that, other things being equal, the higher a person's IQ the better his or her performance, especially in jobs that at face value would seem to require high intellectual ability (Hunter & Hunter, 1984; Ree & Earles, 1992; Schmidt & others, 1992). The correlation coefficients usually fall in the range of about 0.20 to 0.40. Some of the same studies show that, independent of IQ, work performance is positively correlated with high achievement motivation, on-the-job experience, and a personality trait labeled conscientiousness (Schmidt & Hunter, 1992). No surprise—if you ever find yourself in a position of employer, look for people who are smart, motivated, experienced, and conscientious!

Tests	2	3	4	5	6
1	0.35	0.62	0.40	0.59	0.45
2	–	0.41	0.55	0.39	0.64
3	–	–	0.28	0.63	0.30
4	–	–	–	0.34	0.60
5	–	–	–	–	0.38

Figure 11.2 ***Hypothetical correlations among scores on six tests***

Each correlation coefficient in the matrix is the correlation between the two tests indicated by its row and column. Thus, 0.35 is the correlation between Test 1 and Test 2. All the correlations are positive, which would be taken by Spearman as evidence that all are to some extent a measure of *general intelligence* (*g*). Notice, however, that the correlations among Tests 1, 3, and 5 (in gold) and among Tests 2, 4, and 6 (in purple) are higher than any of the other correlations. This pattern can be interpreted to mean that Tests 1, 3, and 5 measure one kind of ability (maybe verbal), and Tests 2, 4, and 6 measure a different kind of ability (maybe visual-spatial).

The Psychometric Approach II: Statistically Inferring the Structure of Intelligence

Having glimpsed some of the history and practical rationale behind intelligence testing, let us return to the theoretical issue of whether intelligence is a single entity or a collection of abilities. Galton believed it to be a single entity, perhaps best described as mental speed, which cuts across all intellectual tasks and should show up even in simple tests of reaction time and sensory acuity. Binet believed that intelligence is a collection of different abilities; yet, ironically, he founded the tradition of summarizing a person's intelligence with a single number.

Is it really possible to describe something as complex as the human intellect with a single number? By analogy, try to describe a person's physique with a single number. What number would you use—height? weight? arm length? girth of neck? some average of these plus others? No single measure nor any one-number average is adequate. To form a picture of what someone's body looks like, you would need a set of numbers measuring different parts of the body. Isn't the structure of intelligence at least as complex as that of the body?

Spearman, Factor Analysis, and the Concept of *g*

■ ***5. How did correlations among test scores lead Spearman to posit a general intelligence (g)?***

As you recall, Galton's approach to testing his idea that intelligence is a single entity was to look for correlations among scores on different mental tests. If people who did well on one test also tended to do well on all other tests, then intelligence could be defined as a single, underlying mental capacity that contributes to performance on all mental tasks. Galton's results were discouraging, but that may have been because both his tests and his statistical methods for analyzing correlations were crude. Charles Spearman (1904, 1927), an English psychologist and mathematician who was impressed by Galton's ideas, developed a more sophisticated battery of mental tests and a new statistical procedure, called ***factor analysis***, for analyzing sets of correlations. Factor analysis is still today the principal psychometric method for studying the structure of intelligence.

To get an idea of how factor analysis was used by Spearman, imagine that a set of six different mental tests had been given to a large number of individuals and that the correlation coefficient between each pair of tests had been calculated (using the correlational method described in Chapter 2). Imagine further that the results were as shown in Figure 11.2. Notice that each test correlates positively with each other test, meaning that people who tended to score high on one test also tended to score high on the others. According to the rationale developed by Spearman, such correlation implies that the tests measure some common, underlying mental ability, or *factor*. To Spearman, factor analysis was essentially a means of determining the degree to which different tests measure that single factor. Spearman referred to the common factor as *g*, for ***general intelligence***.

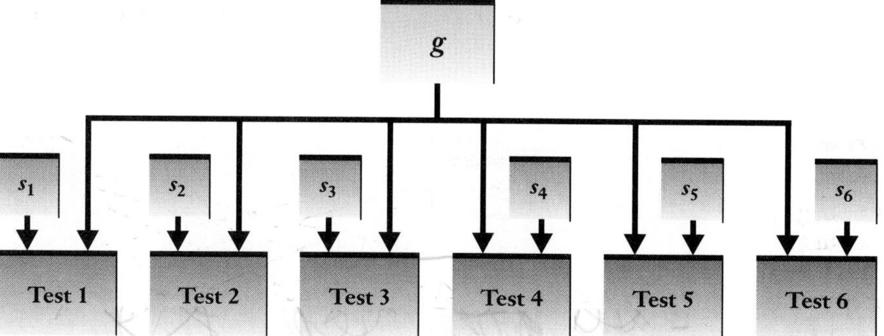

Figure 11.3 ***Spearman's theory of intelligence***

To explain why people who score high on one kind of mental test also tend to score high on other kinds of mental tests, Spearman hypothesized that people differ in general intelligence (g). To explain why the correlation among tests is not perfect, he hypothesized that each test score is also affected by a person's specific ability (s) related to that particular test. Thus, according to Spearman, a person's score on each test is affected by his or her amount of general intelligence plus his or her specific ability for that test.

Notice, however, that none of the tests in Figure 11.2 correlates perfectly with any other (all correlations are less than 1.00). Spearman took that kind of result as evidence that no test is a perfect measure of g, and that each test score is also affected by a more specific ability that he called s. Spearman believed that s varies from test to test and might stem from the person's previous experience with the specific information or method of thinking called for by a particular test. Spearman's theory of intelligence can be illustrated as in Figure 11.3. The mind contains a single general ability (g) that affects scores on all sorts of mental tests and a large set of specific abilities ($s_1, s_2, s_3, \ldots$) that affect scores on different tests differently.

In a long series of studies using an extraordinarily wide variety of tests, including tests of memory, visual perception, logic, and verbal fluency, Spearman found that essentially every kind of mental test correlates positively with every other kind of mental test. Stated differently, every test tends to rank people in the same way. This conclusion, which Spearman (1927) called *the indifference of the indicator*, is by no means trivial. You could imagine plausible theories that would predict a different result. For example, a theory might hold that we have only a certain amount of raw brain power, which, through development, can be channeled in one way or another. That theory would predict that people who are above average at one class of abilities (maybe verbal abilities) would be below average in another class (maybe visual-spatial abilities). But Spearman's results—and the many verifications of them since (Jensen, 1992)—prove such theories wrong.

Because any given test is influenced by a specific factor as well as by g, Spearman (1927) believed that the best measure of g comes from averaging the scores from a wide variety of tests. Thus, although he disagreed with Binet's idea that intelligence is a collection of separate abilities, he concluded that Binet's test provides an accurate assessment of intelligence when all the subtest scores are combined to produce a single IQ.

Thurstone and the Idea of Separate Primary Abilities

■ **6. *How did patterns of correlations among test scores lead Thurstone to posit the existence of separate primary mental abilities?***

All mental tests may correlate positively with one another, but the correlations among some of them are very small. In examining Spearman's results, the American psychologist Louis Thurstone (1938, 1947) was more impressed by how small some correlations were, compared to others, than by the fact that all were positive. He developed a different means of factor analysis, one that was more sensitive to differences among correlations, and with it provided evidence for a different model of intelligence—one more akin to Binet's view than to Galton's or Spearman's.

Thurstone used factor analysis to find clusters of tests that correlated more strongly with each other than with tests outside the cluster. For example, using the hypothetical correlations shown in Figure 11.2, Thurstone's method would detect the fact that Tests 1, 3, and 5 correlate more strongly with each other than with other tests, as do Tests 2, 4, and 6. From such a pattern, Thurstone would conclude that one subset of tests is a good measure of one mental ability (call it A) and another is a good measure of another ability (call it B). Thurstone assumed that the

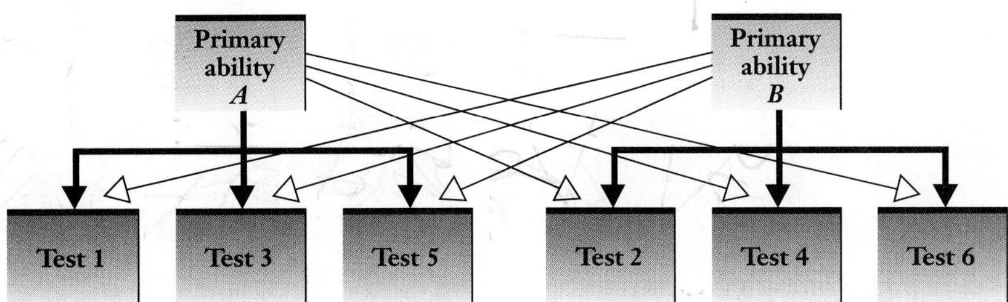

Figure 11.4 ***Thurstone's theory of intelligence***

To explain why the correlations among some mental tests are greater than those among others (as in Figure 11.2), Thurstone hypothesized that the human mind contains a small set of different primary mental abilities. Tests that correlate most strongly with one another are measures of the same primary ability (as indicated by the heavy arrows). To explain why tests in different clusters also correlate (to a smaller degree) with one another, Thurstone hypothesized that no test is a pure measure of any given ability, but is also to some degree affected by other abilities (indicated by the thin arrows). In this example, Primary Ability *A* might be verbal comprehension, and Primary Ability *B* might be spatial visualization.

different abilities best measured by different sets of tests are independent of one another, and he called them *primary mental abilities*.

Thurstone's model of the mind can be diagrammed as in Figure 11.4. At the top is not one general intelligence, but rather a set of primary abilities. Each primary ability affects scores on some tests more than on others. Based on an analysis of correlations among fifty-six different mental tests, Thurstone (1938) identified what he considered to be seven distinct primary abilities: verbal comprehension, verbal fluency, number (computation), spatial visualization, associative memory, perceptual speed, and reasoning.

Hierarchical Theories: *g* Plus Separate Abilities

Following Thurstone, many psychologists performed similar studies using new batteries of tests and new factor analytic procedures, generating new theories of the structure of intelligence. Most of the recent theories combine Spearman's idea of *g* with Thurstone's idea of separate abilities. In these theories, the mind is depicted as a hierarchy; *g* is at the top, and underneath are abilities that are affected by *g* but that can also vary independently of one another. In Figure 11.5 you can see how this hierarchical approach could be applied to explain the pattern of correlations in Figure 11.2.

■ **7.** ***How are Spearman's and Thurstone's views combined in hierarchical theories of intelligence, such as Vernon's?***

Different hierarchical models of intelligence differ primarily in the number of abilities (intelligences) they identify at the second level and in the way those abilities are described. One model, developed by Philip E. Vernon (1961), identifies two such abilities: a *practical-mechanical intelligence*, which contributes most to solving the kinds of problems encountered in everyday life; and a *verbal-educational intelligence*, which pertains to verbal ability and abstract thinking and contributes most to academic work. The scoring system for Wechsler IQ tests, which provides separate scores for performance and verbal abilities as well as an overall IQ score, is based on a model similar to Vernon's (look back at Table 11.1).

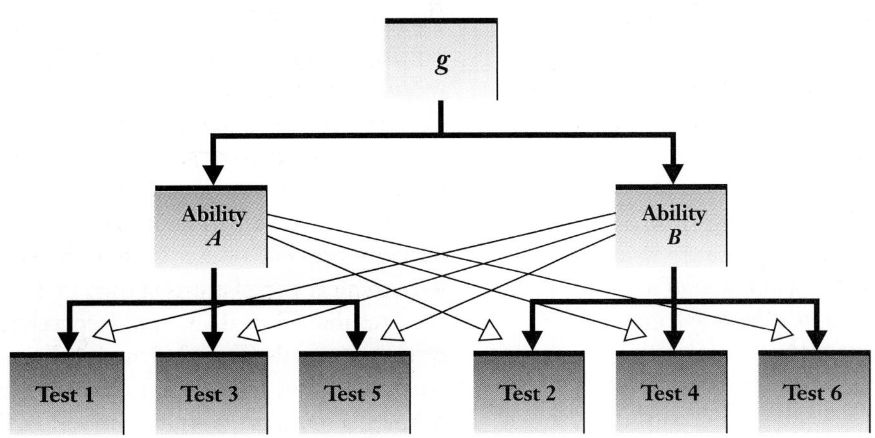

Figure 11.5 ***Hierarchical theory of intelligence***

Most modern psychometric theories of intelligence incorporate the basic elements of both Thurstone's and Spearman's positions. In these theories, different sets of tests are differentially affected by different mental abilities, but the mental abilities are not entirely independent of one another. They are all affected by a general intelligence (*g*).

Models of mental ability

What constitutes intelligence? Is it separate abilities or a single entity? As you think about these questions, ask yourself what may underlie the brilliant leadership and oratory of someone like Martin Luther King, Jr., shown here addressing a civil rights rally. And what may be the basis for the scientific ability and inventiveness of people like U.S. astronauts Kathryn D. Sullivan (left) and Sally L. Ride, shown displaying a device they created to hold them in place while sleeping in zero gravity?

The Information-Processing Approach: Identifying the Components of Intelligence

As you have seen, psychometricians attempt to understand the structure of intelligence by analyzing patterns of correlations among different tests given to a large number of people. With this method they identify different kinds of intelligence and determine the degree to which the kinds are independent of one another or are influenced by a common factor (*g*). The ***information-processing approach***, to which we now turn, is in some ways a complement to the psychometric approach (Sternberg, 1985b). The overall goal of the information-processing approach is to describe the specific mental steps, or cognitive processes, that give rise to any given act of intelligence. Advocates of this approach describe intelligence not in terms of abstract factors based on test scores, but rather in terms of the inner workings of the mind. Their descriptions are often based on the standard information-processing model of the mind described in Chapter 10 (depicted in Figure 10.1), which identifies various memory stores and processes that move information from one store to another. Differences among people in solving problems on intelligence tests might in theory arise from differences among them in any or all of the mental processes described by that model.

■ **8. *How does the information-processing approach to intelligence differ from the psychometric approach?***

Speed of Processing as a Correlate of Intelligence

One research strategy, which closely links the information-processing and psychometric approaches, is to look for correlations between people's IQ scores and their speed or accuracy in very simple tests—tests that require only a minimum of thought or judgment and yet engage one or more of the mind's information-processing steps. In one such test, a subject must hold a finger on a home button until one of a set of stimulus buttons lights up and then must move the finger as quickly as possible to that button. Using this test, Arthur Jensen (1987) and his colleagues found moderate correlations (coefficients from 0.3 to 0.5) between reaction speed and general IQ when subjects had a relatively large number of choices (eight or more buttons), but much weaker correlations when subjects had only a few choices. Based on these results, Jensen inferred that the component of the reaction-time task that correlates with IQ is not so much speed of muscle movement as speed in judging which stimulus has lit up and should be pressed.

■ **9. *What findings from information-processing studies have revived Galton's idea of mental quickness as a basis for general intelligence?***

Another test assesses *inspection time*—the minimal time that subjects need to look at, or listen to, a pair of stimuli to judge the difference between them. In one such test, two parallel lines, one 1.4 times as long as the other, are flashed on a screen, and subjects must say which line is longer. The duration of the stimulus varies from trial to trial, and inspection time is the shortest duration at which a sub-

High-speed information processing
Regardless of whether mental quickness is the basis for general intelligence, it is certainly important in many human endeavors. These air-traffic controllers must routinely make crucial decisions under extreme time pressure.

ject can respond correctly most of the time. A review of the results of many such studies concluded that the correlation between fast inspection time and scores on standard intelligence tests is about 0.3 to 0.5 (Kranzler & Jensen, 1989).

Based on such evidence, Jensen and others have revived the Galtonian notion of mental quickness (Vernon, 1987). They suggest that general intelligence may be strongly linked to what they call *speed of information processing*. Their view is strengthened by the further finding that the correlation between reaction time and IQ is equally strong when untimed IQ tests are used as when timed IQ tests are used (Vernon & Kantor, 1986), so the correlation is not simply a result of the fact that many standard IQ tests require the test taker to react quickly. Recently Jensen and his colleagues have even provided some physiological evidence that neural conduction in certain pathways in the brain may be faster in people with high IQs than in people with lower IQs (Reed & Jensen, 1991, 1992).

Short-Term Memory Capacity as a Correlate of Intelligence

In the information-processing model described in Chapter 10, short-term memory is the center of conscious thought (look back at Figure 10.1). Information enters the short-term store by way of the senses (through the sensory memory store) and by way of retrieval from long-term memory (one's store of previously acquired knowledge). According to this model, to solve a problem on an intelligence test you must bring the appropriate sensory information and the appropriate knowledge into the short-term store and combine them to come up with a solution. But short-term memory can hold only a limited amount of information at any given time. While it is the center of conscious thought, it is also a bottleneck that limits the amount of information one can bring together to solve a problem.

■ **10.** ***Logically, how might short-term memory capacity provide a basis for individual differences in intelligence, and how might speed of processing affect that capacity? What is some evidence supporting this logical possibility?***

Philip A. Vernon (1987), the son of the Philip E. Vernon mentioned earlier, has suggested that speed of information processing may contribute to intelligence by allowing people to make optimal use of their limited-capacity short-term memories. Information fades quickly from short-term memory when it is not being acted upon, so the faster a person can process information, the more items he or she can bring together to make a mental calculation or to arrive at a reasoned decision. Perhaps you recall the analogy suggested in Chapter 10 between holding material in short-term memory and a circus performer's task of spinning pie plates on sticks. The faster the performer could move from one stick to another, the more plates he or she could spin before one of them fell. Similarly, in performing a task such as mental long division, the faster you can move from one calculating step to the next, the more likely you are to complete the task before you lose track of what you accomplished in the previous steps.

Consistent with Vernon's suggestion, many studies have found significant positive correlations between scores on tests of complex reasoning and scores on simple tests of short-term memory capacity, in which people must report back a sequence of digits, letters, or words that they have just heard or seen (Carpenter & others, 1990; Kyllonen & Christal, 1990). In one recent study, Linda Miller and Vernon (1992) gave people separate tests of (a) short-term memory capacity, (b) speed of mental processing (using reaction-time tests), and (c) intelligence (as measured by a standard test emphasizing reasoning). They found that short-term memory correlated more strongly with the intelligence score than did speed of processing (the correlation coefficients were 0.46 and 0.26, respectively). Moreover, when they used statistical means to equate their subjects on the short-term memory score, they found that the remaining correlation between speed of processing and intelligence was reduced almost to zero and was not statistically significant. These findings support Vernon's view that short-term memory capacity is directly related to intelligence and that speed of processing influences intelligence through its effects on short-term memory.

■ **11. *In theory, how might the correlations of intelligence scores with scores on simpler tasks represent causal effects that are opposite those proposed by Jensen and Vernon?***

Researchers such as Jensen and Vernon, who study the correlation between intelligence scores and reaction-time or short-term memory capacity, usually interpret their results in a particular causal direction. They usually assume that mental speed, or high capacity short-term memory, is a cause of good reasoning ability. However, as was emphasized in Chapter 2, correlations do not by themselves identify cause and effect. Jensen's and Vernon's interpretations seem reasonable, but critics argue that the cause-effect relationship could be the other way around (Brody, 1992). Maybe intelligent people do well on reaction-time and short-term memory tests because they figure out better strategies for performing even those simple tasks. They might, for example, find ways to concentrate on the stimuli (and avoid boredom) or, in memory tasks, to chunk the items and improve their scores. One cognitive psychologist who had suggested this possibility is Robert Sternberg (Marr & Sternberg, 1987).

■ **12. *In Sternberg's theory, what are the roles of metacomponents and performance components in solving a problem?***

Sternberg's Theory of Intelligence: Regulating the Components

Sternberg (1986b) has described intelligence as "mental self-government." By this he means that intelligence is the ability to regulate and coordinate the various lower-level processes (components) of the mind in ways that increase the chance of solving problems. Sternberg (1985a) ascribes this regulating ability to a special set of mental processes that he calls ***metacomponents***. The prefix *meta-* in this context means beyond, or transcending. In Sternberg's theory, the metacomponents transcend the other components. They can be thought of as the executive officers of the mind, dealing with the overall goals and strategies of behavior and exerting their effects by controlling the lower components. Metacomponents define the problem, decide whether or not it is worth solving, select the lower components needed to solve it, control the order in which those components are activated, monitor the progress toward solution, and decide when the problem is solved.

Opponent components

Prosecution and defense in a courtroom bring into play many of the intellectual abilities that Robert Sternberg calls metacomponents, including defining the legal problem, choosing strategies to solve it, and selecting the subsidiary skills needed to bring the case to a successful conclusion.

Sternberg divides the lower components into two groups. One group consists of *knowledge-acquisition components*, which are involved in learning and are not directly applicable to our present discussion. The other group consists of ***performance components***, defined as the mental processes that act most directly on information when one solves a problem or chooses a course of action. Performance components are involved in encoding stimulus information, retrieving information from long-term memory, comparing different sources of information, and producing behavioral responses. These are the processes most commonly studied by cognitive psychologists. In fact, many of the performance components are part of the general model of the mind presented in Chapter 10 (Figure 10.1).

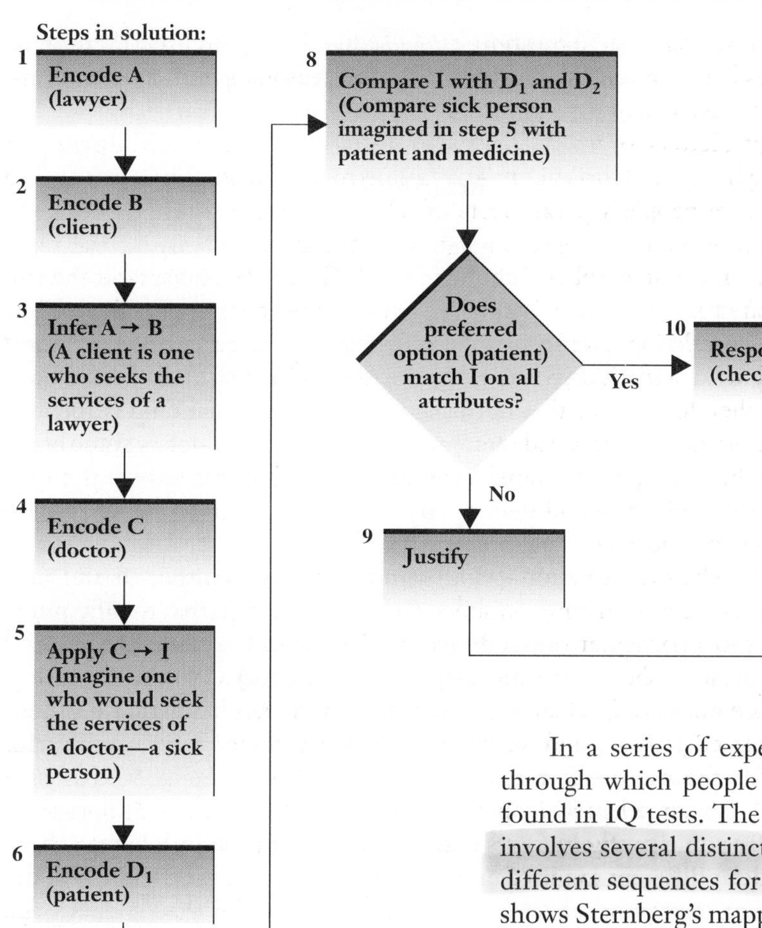

Figure 11.6 ***Steps in solving an analogy problem***

This chart depicts the sequence of steps involved in solving analogy problems, according to Sternberg. To make the steps clear, a specific problem is used, but the chart is meant to characterize the steps in solving any problem of the general form, A is to B as C is to ______ (choose either D_1 or D_2). Each of the steps in the chart is a performance component in Sternberg's broader theory, but the choice to use these steps and the decision as to how much time to devote to each is a task of the metacomponents. (Adapted from Sternberg & Gardner, 1983.)

■ **13.** ***According to Sternberg's research, what is one difference between successful and unsuccessful solvers of analogy problems? How does his theory account for general intelligence (g)?***

In a series of experiments, Sternberg and his colleagues mapped the steps through which people solve various logical-reasoning problems similar to those found in IQ tests. The results led Sternberg to hypothesize that logical reasoning involves several distinct performance components, which are brought into play in different sequences for different kinds of problems. The flowchart in Figure 11.6 shows Sternberg's mapping of this sequence for the type of problem called an *analogy problem* (Sternberg & Gardner, 1983). Among the components shown on the chart are (a) *encoding*, which means reading or hearing the words of the problem and forming a mental representation of their meaning; (b) *inference*, which means making a guess about the general rule that provides the basis for solving the problem; (c) *application*, which means using the general rule to imagine a possible solution to the problem; and (d) *comparison*, which means contrasting the imagined solution with the possible answers given in the problem statement to see if they are similar.

Sternberg (1985a) developed a way to measure the amount of time that people devote to the separate steps in solving various logic problems and found that people who perform well typically spend more time on the encoding steps and less time on other steps than do people who perform poorly. If you think about it, this is not a terribly surprising result. Encoding the available information carefully before moving to subsequent steps is important in solving any problem. How many times have you lost points on a test because you didn't read the question carefully or take the time to figure out exactly what was being asked before you started to work out the answer? In Sternberg's theory of intelligence, deciding how much time to devote to each step in solving a problem is a task of the metacomponents.

Sternberg (1985a, 1985b) has compared his information-processing theory of intelligence with the hierarchical theories of intelligence developed within the psychometric tradition. Like most of the psychometricians, he believes that a general intelligence, *g*, accounts for the correlations among scores on different tests. He explains *g* primarily—though not entirely—in terms of the metacomponents. People who are good at directing their mental resources toward a problem and developing a general strategy for solving it (the tasks of the metacomponents) are likely to do well on a wide variety of tests, from simple reaction-time tests to those involving complex calculations. Sternberg contends that people can increase their intelligence by improving their metacomponents and has developed a set of exercises to help them do so (Sternberg, 1986a).

The Neuropsychological Approach: Relating Intelligence to Areas of the Brain

As described in Chapter 1, neuropsychology is the attempt to understand the role of specific brain areas in human mental functioning. Neuropsychologists study people who have suffered strokes or other injuries to the brain in order to determine which cognitive abilities are lost or spared after particular parts of the brain are damaged. Examples of the value of this approach in understanding perception and memory were presented in Chapters 9 and 10. Here we will look at some broad ideas about intelligence that have come from neuropsychology.

Hemisphere-Specialization Theories of Intelligence

The most obvious physical division of the brain is that between the left and right hemispheres of the cerebral cortex. Chapter 6 offered evidence that the left hemisphere is specialized for language and the right is specialized for various nonverbal functions, including the analysis of visual-spatial information. Other research suggests that the left hemisphere may be specialized for mental tasks that require a step-by-step, sequential analysis of information and that the right may be specialized for the more holistic, intuitive aspects of perception and thought (Kosslyn & others, 1989; Springer & Deutsch, 1989).

■ **14.** ***What are two problems with the idea that people can be classified into left-brained and right-brained types?***

In the 1970s, some psychologists suggested that the two hemispheres are not only specialized for different kinds of tasks, but are differentially developed in different people. For example, Robert Ornstein (1977) suggested that Western culture's emphasis on verbal argument and abstract reasoning leads Westerners to develop their left brain more than their right, while people of other cultures develop their right brains to a greater degree. The popular press was quick to pick up ideas like this, and many people began to speak of themselves or their friends as left-brained or right-brained.

A problem with this dichotomy is its implication that people who are good at "left-brained" tasks are usually poor at "right-brained" tasks, and vice versa. Numerous studies have proven this implication untrue. As noted before, essentially every kind of mental ability correlates positively with every other kind. People who are above average in logical reasoning also tend to be above average in spatial and artistic abilities. Another problem with the dichotomy is that no direct means exists for assessing left- versus right-hemisphere development. If I declare myself left-brained because I am good at logical reasoning but not at aesthetics and intuition, I am really referring only to my abilities, and not to my neuroanatomy. I have no direct evidence that my left brain is anatomically or physiologically more developed than my right.

■ **15.** ***What is some evidence supporting the idea that the two hemispheres are specialized for different aspects of intelligence?***

Nevertheless, a certain logic does exist for the idea that the left and right hemispheres contain the machinery underlying different aspects of intelligence (Kaufman, 1990). Factor analysis of people's subtest scores on the WAIS-R (or other standard intelligence tests) shows that the subtests tend to cluster into two main factors—the same two that represent the second level in P. E. Vernon's hierarchical theory of intelligence. One factor seems to represent verbal reasoning and verbal knowledge; it is best measured by the Comprehension, Similarities, Vocabulary, and Information subtests (to review the WAIS-R subtests, look at Table 11.1). These subtests, it turns out, show the greatest decline in score among people who have suffered damage to the left hemisphere. The other factor seems to represent visual-spatial ability and is best measured by Block Design, Object Assembly, and

Picture Completion. These subtests show the greatest decline in people who have suffered damage to the right hemisphere. Thus, to some degree at least, it may be reasonable to say that the two main abilities (below *g*) in Vernon's theory of intelligence have their neural machineries primarily in one hemisphere or the other.

Neuropsychological Evidence That Some Abilities Are Independent of Each Other

■ **16. *Why are psychologists interested in the fact that brain damage can destroy some intellectual abilities while sparing others?***

In studying people who have suffered brain damage, one is struck by the uniqueness of each case and, often, by the remarkable specificity of the cognitive deficit. Contrary to what might be expected from the theory of general intelligence, people after brain damage are often as intelligent as they were before in some intellectual realms and very deficient in others.

Consider, for example, the case of a 54-year-old woman who, after a stroke, recovered most of her intellectual abilities outside the realm of arithmetic. She could converse intelligently and registered a normal IQ, but she was completely unable to deal with any numbers greater than 4. She could not add, subtract, multiply, divide, or even count if any of the numbers involved amounted to more than four (Sutherland, 1991). A very different example is that of the Russian composer V. G. Shebalin, mentioned in Chapter 6. After a stroke that destroyed part of his left cerebral cortex, Shebalin lost most of his ability to use or understand language, yet he continued to create great music (Gardner, 1974). Such cases are interesting because they tell us something about the structure of the mind. If ability *A* can be lost while sparing ability *B*, then we know that *B* does not depend upon *A*. Thus, Shebalin's ability to compose music apparently did not depend upon his ability to put ideas into words.

Figure 11.7 ***Drawing produced by a child who is deficient in other intellectual areas***

This remarkable drawing was produced by a 5-year-old girl, Nadia, afflicted with an inherited condition (autism) that includes severe retardation in development of speech and social interaction. Her artistic skill emerged from her own efforts, without any training. (From Gardner, 1985.)

Gardner's Case-History Approach and His Multiple Intelligences Theory

Neuropsychologist Howard Gardner (1985) has argued that the patterns of preserved and lost abilities across different cases of brain damage, along with other evidence, can be used to construct what he calls a *multiple intelligences theory*. Among the other evidence used by Gardner are case histories of other special individuals. One group of interest to Gardner are those rare individuals referred to as *idiots savants*, who are born with a condition that retards their development in most intellectual realms, but who—often with no special training—develop normal or even superior ability in one area such as math or art. In Figure 11.7 you can see an example of the remarkable artistic skill of one such individual. Less rare are *prodigies*, who show normal or above-normal abilities in most areas but extraordinary ability in one area, sometimes despite adverse environmental forces. Still another source of evidence used by Gardner is the difference in the age at which various abilities emerge in the developing child. For example, language and musical ability show their greatest spurt of development during the preschool years, but mathematical ability rarely begins to surge before the age of 10 or 11.

■ **17. *How did Gardner use case histories of special people to identify separate intelligences, and what criticisms have been made of his theory?***

On the basis of such evidence, Gardner has argued against the concept of a general intelligence that cuts across all mental tasks and has resurrected the Thurstonian notion of separate intelligences that may vary independently of one another. In a book that has had some impact on educational theory and practice, Gardner (1985) tentatively identified a set of seven such intelligences described briefly in Table 11.2, page 384. Notice that three of these (linguistic, logical-mathematical, and spatial) fall within the category of abilities usually tested in standard IQ tests, but the other four (musical, bodily-kinesthetic, interpersonal, and intrapersonal) involve skills not usually considered as part of intelligence in the psychometric tradition. Some psychologists contend that Gardner has stretched the meaning of intelligence too far and that the latter set of abilities should be called *talents* rather than intelligences. Gardner (1985) counters that he would be

Table 11.2 ***The seven intelligences of Gardner's multiple intelligences theory***

Type of intelligence	Description
1. *Linguistic*	Verbal ability in general, but especially the ability to understand subtle shades of meaning
2. *Logical-mathematical*	Reasoning
3. *Spatial*	The ability to perceive and draw spatial relationships
4. *Musical*	Singing, playing an instrument, composing music
5. *Bodily-kinesthetic*	The ability to control one's muscle movements in graceful and skillful ways, as in dance, athletics, and tool use
6. *Interpersonal*	Social skills, including the ability to understand and respond appropriately to others' nonverbal messages
7. *Intrapersonal*	The ability to understand oneself, including one's own emotions and wishes, and to use that understanding effectively in guiding behavior

glad to call them talents if people would also refer to linguistic, spatial, and logical abilities as talents. Part of his message is that psychologists have overemphasized certain abilities that can be tested easily with paper and pencil or puzzles—glorifying them with the term *intelligence*—at the expense of other abilities that, to the world at large, are just as valuable. Each of the abilities that Gardner refers to as an intelligence requires complex brain mechanisms, is valued by human beings everywhere (though cultures vary with regard to which they value most), and is more or less uniquely developed in humans as compared to other species.

A more damaging criticism of Gardner's theory is that, to date, relatively little statistical or other objective evidence exists that the seven intelligences he proposes are each functionally unitary and independent of each other (Brody, 1992). Certainly case histories can be found that fit Garner's theory quite well, but many others can be found that don't. Moreover, even the cases described by Gardner often involve more narrowly defined abilities or deficits than would be implied by his theory. For example, some idiots savants who perform remarkable feats of mental arithmetic nevertheless display little or no comprehension of mathematical theory. We cannot accurately describe them as high in logical-mathematical intelligence. Still, Gardner's work represents an interesting, pioneering attempt to make some sense of the remarkably diverse and unsystematic case-history literature.

An educational experiment

At the Key School in Indianapolis, Indiana, the curriculum is based on Howard Gardner's theory of multiple intelligences. Performing music they composed themselves is believed to develop musical intelligence, and building architectural models is believed to develop spatial intelligence. Equal time is devoted to English, computers, art, movement, and various other subjects.

The Ecological Approach: Relating Intelligence to the Contexts of Life

Most definitions of intelligence include the idea that its function is to help a person adapt to his or her environment. Yet psychologists most often study intelligence using tests, tasks, and environmental settings quite different from those that most people encounter in everyday life. The ***ecological approach*** to intelligence focuses on the relationship between intelligence and the environmental context within which it normally operates. How does intelligence manifest itself on the streets of the inner city, in solving problems at the factory, in raising children and running a household, or in the life of Eskimo seal hunters above the Arctic Circle?

Intelligence at Work

■ **18.** ***What is some evidence that intelligence in the work environment is not always reflected by scores on tests?***

One strategy of the ecological approach is to observe people solving problems in their usual employment settings and to ask questions or conduct tests designed to understand how they solve their problems. Sylvia Scribner (1986) and her colleagues used this approach to study such groups as dairy workers, bartenders, salespeople, and waitresses as they went about their jobs. They found that people in such settings regularly solve complex problems, frequently in more efficient and flexible ways than their scores on standard tests predict. For example, Scribner found that wholesale-delivery drivers who had to calculate the prices of different numbers of quarts of milk would vary their strategy depending on the number of quarts ordered. Thus, when milk was selling for 68¢ per quart, or $10.88 per case (16 quarts), and a customer ordered 17 quarts, the driver quickly converted the calculation from a cumbersome multiplication problem (17 multiplied by 68¢) to an easy addition problem (1 case at $10.88, plus 1 quart at 68¢). Interestingly, Scribner found no correlation between drivers' abilities to solve these pricing problems quickly and correctly and their high-school math grades or their performance on a conventional arithmetic test that she gave them.

Cross-Cultural Differences in Reasoning Style

Another strategy of the ecological approach is to compare standard test results of people from different cultures to see how culture affects mental development. One general conclusion from such research is that the way people approach intelligence tests—their understanding of what is expected of them—is culturally dependent. People of non-Western cultures often find it absurd or presumptuous to respond to questions outside their realm of concrete experiences (Cole & Means, 1981; Scribner, 1977). Thus, the logic question, "If John is taller than Carl, and Carl is taller than Henry, is John taller than Henry?" is likely to elicit the polite response, "I'm sorry, but I have never met these men." Yet the same person has no difficulty solving similar logic problems that present themselves in the course of everyday experience.

■ **19.** ***How do unschooled members of non-Western cultures typically perform on classification problems? What is some evidence that this may have more to do with preference than ability?***

Research also suggests that non-Westerners who have not received Western style schooling are more likely than Westerners to answer intelligence-test questions in practical, functional terms, and less likely to answer in terms of abstract properties (Hamill, 1990). An example can be found in classification problems, in which people are asked to sort pictures of common objects into separate categories or to state which of several objects doesn't belong with the others. Western researchers consider it more intelligent to sort by taxonomic category (such as putting animals in one group and plants in another) than according to function (such as putting things that people eat into one group and things they don't eat into another), and in the West intelligent people usually do sort by taxonomy. But in non-Western societies nearly everyone is more likely to sort by function than by taxonomy (Hamill, 1990).

The psychologist Alexander Luria (1971), of the former Soviet Union, asked unschooled Uzbekh peasants to indicate which of the following objects did not belong with the others: *ax*, *log*, *shovel*, *saw*. The correct answer in the eyes of those who made up the test was *log*, because it is the only object that is not a tool. But the Uzbekhi's consistently chose the shovel and explained their choice in functional terms: "Look, the saw and the ax, what could you do with them if you didn't have a log? And the shovel? You just don't need that here."

This difference in reasoning may be more of preference than ability. Michael Cole and his colleagues (1971) described an attempt to test a group of Kpelle people in Nigeria for their ability to sort pictures of common objects into taxonomic groups. No matter what instructions they were given, the Kpelle persisted in sorting the pictures by function until, in frustration, the researchers asked them to sort the way stupid people do. Then they sorted by taxonomy!

Cross-Cultural Differences in Spatial Ability

■ **20. *What is one line of evidence that a culture's means of existence affect the mental abilities its people develop?***

Other cross-cultural studies have demonstrated that the specific abilities tested by the subtests of standard IQ tests may be affected by cultural variation. People who survive by hunting and fishing, for example, commonly perform better on visual-spatial tests (such as Block Design and Object Assembly, described in Table 11.1) than do people who survive by other means such as farming (Berry, 1971). The likely explanation is that the long distances traveled in hunting and fishing require people to keep track of landmarks and make mental maps of their routes, activities that strengthen visual-spatial intelligence. The Eskimos living north of the Arctic Circle seem to have particularly well-developed abilities in this area (McShane & Berry, 1988). The Arctic environment provides very few cues telling hunting parties which way is home, so to find their way back from an excursion they must constantly construct mental maps based on the turns they make and the estimated distances between turns. Even Galton once remarked on the amazing spatial memories of Eskimo explorers (Werner, 1948). He had heard from a captain in the British Admiralty of an Eskimo who had explored 6000 miles of coastline just once in his kayak and had subsequently drawn from memory a map of the coast that was later found to be extraordinarily accurate.

Another cultural context

The ecological approach emphasizes the importance of the context in which intelligent behavior occurs. Micronesians' skill at navigating long distances using information from the stars and from ocean currents reflects a kind of intelligence that is well adapted to their environment.

Logical Reasoning and Problem Solving

Thus far we have been concerned with the broad problem of describing the human intellect as a whole. You have read of psychometric, information-processing, neuropsychological, and ecological approaches to that task. We now shift our focus to a narrower task, the attempt to understand how people solve problems that entail logical reasoning.

Perhaps because it is the main part of their own job description, philosophers have always placed reasoning at the pinnacle of human activity and been most interested in understanding it. Descartes's famous "I think, therefore I am" could have been "I move things, therefore I am"; or "I feel emotions, therefore I am"; but it wasn't. Psychology, in its more than 100 years of existence, has gone back and forth on the issue. When psychology first emerged from philosophy as a distinct discipline, reasoning was at the top of the list of phenomena to be studied by the new science. But two trends of the early twentieth century led psychologists away from it. One was behaviorism, which argued that observable action, not unobservable thought, is the proper subject matter for psychology; and the other was Freud's psychoanalytic approach, which emphasized the role of instinct and emotion and argued that what we call reason is often a rationalization for, rather than a cause of, what we do. With the rise of cognitive psychology during the second half of the twentieth century, however, the study of reasoning was revived and became again an important part of psychology.

■ **21. *How does the psychological approach to understanding reasoning differ from the philosophical approach?***

Logicians (philosophers interested in reason or logic) look at reasoning differently from the way psychologists do. Logicians are most interested in the ideal case, that is, in the laws that describe reasoning as it is most efficiently and effectively performed. Cognitive psychologists, in contrast, are more interested in reasoning as it is *typically* performed; hence, their theories are messier than those of the logicians. A theme running through this section is that human beings are not abstract thinking machines. Our thought is grounded in our concrete experiences and in the routines that make up our daily lives. Natural selection endowed us with a brain designed to help us survive, not necessarily designed to analyze information objectively and establish logical truths. Yet, to some degree, we can think logically; that is the amazing thing.

Inductive Reasoning and Biases in It

■ **22. *What is inductive reasoning, and why is it also called hypothesis construction?***

Philosophers and psychologists alike distinguish between two general classes of logical reasoning—deductive and inductive. Whereas deductive reasoning (to be discussed later) is reasoning from the general to the specific, ***inductive reasoning***, or *induction*, is reasoning from the specific to the general. In an inductive task, a person is presented with specific items, or facts, and is asked to use them to infer some more general conclusion. Inductive reasoning is also called *hypothesis construction* because the inferred conclusion is at best an educated guess, not a logical necessity. Scientists engage in inductive reasoning all the time as they try to infer general rules of nature from their observations of specific events in the world. Cognitive psychologists use inductive reasoning when they make guesses about the general workings of the human mind based on observations of many instances of human behavior under varied conditions.

As an example of an inductive reasoning task, consider the following series completion problem:

1 2 4 ___ ___

What numbers did you place in the two blanks? You might have constructed the

Gathering the evidence

Arthur Conan Doyle conveyed the thrill of inductive reasoning in his stories of Sherlock Holmes, who could form a plausible hypothesis as to who committed the murder and how from the subtlest of clues.

hypothesis that each number in this series is double the previous number, which would have led you to complete the series with 8 and 16. But suppose I now inform you that the first blank should be filled with a 7. With that, you would know that your original hypothesis was incorrect and you might generate a new hypothesis—that each number is the sum of the previous two numbers plus 1. With this hypothesis, you would place a 12 in the final blank. Notice that the more information you are given, the more certain you can be that your hypothesis is correct, as long as all of the numbers are consistent with it. But you can never be absolutely certain. No matter how many numbers you have seen, the next number might prove your hypothesis wrong.

As another, quite different inductive reasoning task, consider the following (modified from Tversky & Kahneman, 1974):

> Steve is meek, tidy, has a passion for detail, is helpful to people, but has little real interest in people or real-world issues. Is Steve more likely to be a librarian or a salesperson?

Notice that in this question you are asked to combine some information in the problem with ideas and information that you have already acquired from life, in order to make a reasonable guess. Psychologists who study inductive reasoning are interested in the kinds of information that people are most likely to use, or ignore, in answering inductive questions. Based on such studies, psychologists have proposed that certain systematic biases exist in people's inductive-reasoning strategies, which sometimes lead to less than optimal guesses. Let's examine some of these biases.

The Overuse of Representativeness and Underuse of Base Rates

What answer did you give to the question about Steve? More important, what information did you consider in making your choice? Did you compare the description of Steve's personality with your beliefs about the personalities of typical librarians and typical salespeople? If so, you used the kind of information that Amos Tversky and Daniel Kahneman (1974) call *representativeness*, which refers to the extent to which the item to be classified (Steve, in this case) has characteristics that are typical or representative of the possible classes into which the item might be placed (librarian or salesperson, in this case). Another kind of information that you might have used is *base rate*, which in this case refers to the likelihood that any randomly chosen man would be a librarian or a salesperson. If you know that salespeople vastly outnumber librarians and if you thought to consider this information, you might reasonably conclude that, even though Steve's personality is typical of a librarian's, he is more likely to be a salesperson.

■ **23.** ***How did Tversky and Kahneman demonstrate that, under some conditions, people ignore base rates in making inferences?***

Tversky and Kahneman (1974) found that people often ignore base rates in answering such questions, even if those rates are made explicit in the statement of the problem. In one experiment, they asked people to estimate the likelihood that a particular individual was either an engineer or a lawyer. One group of subjects was told that the individual had been randomly selected from a set of seventy engineers and thirty lawyers, and another group was told that the set consisted of thirty engineers and seventy lawyers. When subjects were asked to make the judgment with no other information, they used the 70:30 ratios effectively: Most in the first group said there was a 70 percent likelihood that the person was an engineer, and most in the second group said this likelihood was 30 percent. But when a personality description was added, most people ignored stated proportions (base rates), even when the personality description provided no useful information. For example, a man described as "30 years old, married with no children, and high in ability and motivation" was judged as 50 percent likely to be an engineer regardless of whether the stated proportion of engineers in the set was 70 percent or 30 percent.

The Availability Bias

■ **24.** ***What kinds of false inferences is the availability bias likely to produce?***

One of the least surprising biases identified by Tversky and Kahneman (1973, 1974) is *availability*: In making inferences, people are more likely to use information prominent in their senses or memory at the time of the test than information that is more difficult to summon. For example, when asked whether the letter *d* is more likely to occur in the first position or third position of a word, most people said first. In reality, *d* is more likely to be in the third position; but, of course, people find it much harder to think of words with *d* in the third position than to think of words that begin with *d*. As another example, when asked to estimate the percentage of people who die from various causes, most people overestimate causes that have recently been emphasized in the media (such as traffic accidents, fires, or murders) and underestimate less publicized but still well-known causes (such as heart disease).

The Confirmation Bias

Textbooks on scientific method routinely explain that scientists should design studies aimed at *disconfirming* their currently held hypotheses. In principle, one can never prove absolutely that a hypothesis is correct, but one can prove absolutely that a hypothesis is incorrect. The best hypotheses are those that survive the strongest attempts to disprove them. Nevertheless, research suggests that people's natural tendency is to try to confirm rather than disconfirm their current hypotheses.

■ **25.** ***How has a confirmation bias been demonstrated in research in which subjects are asked to discover a sequence rule or test a hypothesis about someone's personality?***

In an early demonstration of this *confirmation bias*, Peter Wason (1960) engaged subjects in a game in which the aim was to discover the experimenter's rule for sequencing numbers. On the first trial the experimenter gave the subject a sequence of three numbers, such as 6 - 8 - 10, and asked the subject to guess the rule. On each subsequent trial, the subject's task was to propose a new sequence of three numbers to which the experimenter would respond *yes* or *no*, depending on whether or not the sequence fit the rule. Wason found that subjects overwhelmingly chose to generate sequences consistent with, rather than inconsistent with, their current hypothesis and quickly became confident that their incorrect rule was correct. For example, after hypothesizing that the rule is *even numbers increasing by twos*, a subject would, on several trials, propose sequences consistent with that rule—such as *2 - 4 - 6* or *14 - 16 - 18*—and, after getting a *yes* on each trial, announce confidently that his or her initial hypothesis was correct. Such subjects never discovered that the experimenter's actual rule was *any increasing sequence of numbers*.

In contrast, the few subjects who discovered the experimenter's rule proposed, on at least some of their trials, sequences that contradicted their current hypothesis. Thus, a successful subject who initially guessed that the rule is *even numbers increasing by twos* might offer the counterexample *5 - 7 - 9*. The experimenter's *yes* to that would prove the initial hypothesis wrong. Then the subject might hypothesize that the rule is *any sequence of numbers increasing by twos* and test that with a counterexample, such as *4 - 7 - 32*. Eventually, the subject might hypothesize that the rule is *any increasing sequence of numbers* and, after testing that with counterexamples, such as *5 - 6 - 4*, and consistently getting *no* responses, announce confidence in that hypothesis.

Many research studies have since corroborated Wason's initial finding of a confirmation bias (Mayer, 1992). Such studies have also shown, however, that in games such as Wason's the confirmation strategy, while far from ideal, does not always fail. It failed in Wason's experiment because he deliberately chose a rule that was broader than the rules subjects were likely to guess on the first trial. If he had chosen a rule that was narrower than subjects were likely to guess on the first trial (such as *single-digit even numbers increasing by twos*), then some of the subjects' attempts at confirming their broader hypothesis (*even numbers increasing by twos*) would have produced *no* answers, and this would have led them to discover the rule (Klayman & Ha, 1987, 1989). The point is that, to be successful, a strategy in this game must produce at least some *no* answers from the experimenter, unless the subject happens to be lucky on the initial guess.

In other experiments demonstrating a confirmation bias, subjects were asked to interview another person to discover something about that individual's personality (Skov & Sherman, 1986; Snyder, 1981). In a typical experiment, some subjects were asked to assess the hypothesis that the person is an *extrovert* (socially outgoing), and others were asked to assess the hypothesis that the person is an *introvert* (socially withdrawn). The main finding was that subjects usually asked questions for which a *yes* answer would be consistent with the hypothesis they were testing. Given the extrovert hypothesis they tended to ask such questions as *"Do you like to meet new people?"* And given the introvert hypothesis they tended to ask such questions as *"Are you shy about meeting new people?"* This bias, coupled with the natural tendency of interviewees to respond to all such questions in the affirmative, gave most subjects confidence in the initial hypothesis, regardless of which hypothesis that was or whom they had interviewed.

■ **26.** ***How might a confirmation bias be adaptive (useful) in everyday life? What is some evidence from studies with syllogisms that most people do not use formal logic to solve deductive problems?***

Why do people show the confirmation bias? One possibility is that, in everyday life, the goal of gathering information for the long term often conflicts with the goal of behaving correctly or being rewarded at any given moment (Klayman & Ha, 1987). In my daily life, as long as my current hypotheses seem to be working and aren't costing me much, I might as well stay with them. My goal, after all, is not truth but survival. I don't honestly know that wearing my orange vest while bicycling helps keep motorists from hitting me; but I wear it each time I ride, and so far I haven't been hit. If my primary goal were knowledge rather than survival, I might perform an experiment: Wear the vest some days and not others and tally the number of times I get hit in either condition.

Similarly, if less dramatically, subjects in laboratory studies may feel more rewarded by getting *yes* responses from the experimenter or interviewer than by getting *no* responses. In everyday life people find it advantageous to get along with others, and *yes* is part of getting along. Moreover, people like to feel smart and therefore may feel more rewarded when their hypotheses are confirmed than when they are disconfirmed. This may be even more true of scientists than of most subjects in psychological experiments. In the process of writing this book, I have read thousands of research studies in psychology and have run across precious few in which a researcher actually disconfirmed his or her own hypothesis! Fortunately for the science, however, researchers seem to have no problem disconfirming other researchers' hypotheses. That is accepted as part of the game, and we usually get along well in person despite our feuds in the journals.

The Concrete Nature of Deductive Reasoning

■ **27.** ***What is the difference between deductive and inductive reasoning? What is some evidence from studies with syllogisms that most people do not use formal logic to solve deductive problems?***

Deductive reasoning, or *deduction*, is reasoning from the general to the specific. In a deductive-reasoning task, you are asked to accept the truth of one or more general premises or axioms and to assert, based on that acceptance, whether a specific conclusion is true, false, or indeterminate. If you studied plane geometry, you exercised deductive reasoning when you tried to prove or disprove various correlates based on axioms that you were told were true. You have also almost certainly seen deductive-reasoning problems in the form of ***syllogisms***—problems that contain two premises which the reasoner must combine in order to test a specific conclusion. Here is an example:

All chefs are violinists (*major premise*)

John is a chef (*minor premise*).

Is John a violinist?

Notice that in this problem you are asked to accept the truth of the two premises whether or not they fit with your real-world experience. The internal consistency of the argument is the point at issue. Syllogisms commonly appear on intelligence tests and are often used in experiments on deductive reasoning.

Psychological research on people's ability to solve such problems has shown that most people throughout the world who are not used to the game of syllogisms perform poorly unless the premises coincide with their concrete experiences and that even highly educated people who are familiar with the game do much better if the premises coincide with their experiences than if they don't (Johnson-Laird, 1985). Such findings contradict the idea that people use formal rules of logic to solve syllogisms. If they did, it would not matter whether the major premise of the syllogism fits with common experience (*All chefs are humans*), doesn't fit with common experience (*All chefs are violinists*), or is a bit of nonsense (*All quilogogs are boomjams*). All that would matter is the abstract form of the problem and the relationship expressed by the words, "All ______ are _______." Based on such considerations, Phillip Johnson-Laird and his colleagues (1992; Johnson-Laird, 1985; G. Kaufmann, 1990) have concluded that people typically solve syllogisms not through formal rules of logic but by building in their minds models that represent the literal content of the premises and can be consulted to find the answer. The easiest such models to understand are those that take the form of visual images.

Figure 11.8 ***An image that can be used to solve a specific set of syllogisms***

A person attempting to solve syllogisms based on the major premise *All chefs are violinists* might represent the premise with a mental image (or a drawing) that looks like this. The image can then be inspected to answer such questions as, If John is not a chef, is he a violinist?

The Role of Visual Imagery in Deductive Reasoning

Consider the following four syllogisms, all based on the same major premise but with different minor premises:

All chefs are violinists (*major premise*).

1. John is a chef (*minor premise*). Is he a violinist?
2. John is a violinist (*minor premise*). Is he a chef?
3. John is not a chef (*minor premise*). Is he a violinist?
4. John is not a violinist (*minor premise*). Is he a chef?

One way to solve all of these syllogisms would be to visualize a group of people. Some (the violinists) are holding violins and some (the chefs) are wearing chef's hats. The major premise says that all chefs are violinists, so you will have to put violins in the hands of all the chefs. But the major premise does *not* say that all violinists are chefs, so you will have to provide for the possibility that some are not chefs by including some violinists without chef's hats. In addition, of course, there may be some people who are neither chefs nor violinists. The resulting picture might look like the one in Figure 11.8.

Now, to answer the four questions, you need only examine the picture. The answer to question 1 must be yes, because everyone wearing a chef's hat is also holding a violin. The answer to question 2 must be indeterminate, because some of the people with violins are wearing chef's hats and some are not. The answer to question 3 must also be indeterminate, because some of the people without chef's hats have violins and some do not. And the answer to question 4 must be no, because none of the people without violins has a chef's hat.

If people really do use visual images to solve syllogisms, then the main constraint in solving them lies in the problem of generating a correct initial picture and

■ **28. *What is some evidence that people use visual imagery to solve syllogisms?***

holding it in mind while answering the questions. Consistent with the visual image hypothesis, the ability to solve syllogisms correlates more strongly with visual-spatial ability than with verbal ability, as measured by standard intelligence tests (Frandsen & Holder, 1969; Guyote & Sternberg, 1981). Also, other researchers have found that people solve syllogisms more quickly and accurately if the major premise is easy to visualize than if it isn't. In one such experiment, Catherine Clement and Rachel Falmagne (1986) presented college students with syllogisms such as these:

- If the man wants plain doughnuts, then he walks to the bakery across the intersection (*major premise*). The man walked to the bakery across the intersection (*minor premise*). Did he want plain doughnuts?
- If the woman reorganizes the company structure, then she makes a profit for the year (*major premise*). The woman made a profit for the year (*minor premise*). Did she reorganize the company structure?

Notice that these syllogisms are identical in form and similar in linguistic complexity and the degree to which the premises seem sensible. But most people can more easily form a mental picture of someone crossing an intersection than of someone reorganizing the company structure. Consistent with Johnson-Laird's hypothesis, Clement and Falmagne found that syllogisms whose premises had been rated as easy to visualize were solved correctly by a higher percentage of students than those whose premises had been rated as hard to visualize. (Incidentally, the correct answer to both of these syllogisms is indeterminate.)

All *A*'s are *B*'s

A's *B*'s — *A*'s *B*'s

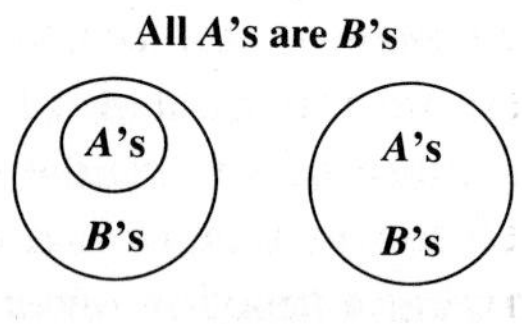

Figure 11.9 ***Euler circles***

Euler circles provide a means to turn the major premise of any syllogism into a concrete visual representation. One first converts the items of the premise (such as chefs and violinists) into *A*'s and *B*'s, and then represents the set of all possible *A*'s and *B*'s with circles that express the stipulated relationship. Notice that two possible representations are consistent with the premise that all *A*'s are *B*'s. In one, *A*'s are a subset of *B*'s, and in the other, *A*'s and *B*'s are identical sets. Now, if given the minor premise, *C is a B*, and asked, *Is C an A*, all you need do is imagine a *C* in each possible portion of the *B* circles. Because some of those *C*'s will fall in an *A* circle and some won't, the answer is indeterminate.

Most people who can solve any syllogism easily, regardless of content, have mastered a little trick that allows them to turn any syllogistic premise into a picture. One version of this trick, illustrated in Figure 11.9, involves *Euler circles*, named after Leonard Euler, who used them in teaching logic to a German princess (Johnson-Laird, 1983). But, of course, the main point here goes beyond the game of solving syllogisms on tests. Johnson-Laird and others contend that many important scientific and philosophical innovations have come about because the innovator discovered a new way to visualize the problem. As mentioned in Chapter 10, Einstein claimed that he first developed the idea of relativity by imagining himself catching up to a beam of light; in that image he could see some of the consequences.

Some Strategies for Solving Problems: The Elements of Insight

A *problem* exists whenever you are trying to reach some goal and are not sure how to get there. Any problem—whether it is a puzzle, a mathematical equation to be solved, or a real-life question such as how to improve your relationship with your family—has an *initial state* (the disarranged puzzle pieces, the unsolved equation, or the present state of your family relationships); a *goal state* to be achieved; and a set of possible moves or *operations* for achieving the goal. To solve a problem you normally must (a) understand the problem, (b) identify the operations that could lead to a solution, (c) carry out the operations, (d) check the results, and (e) return to some earlier point in this chain if the results are not correct. The first two steps (understanding the problem and identifying a possible route to a solution) are the most critical for solving many problems. They are the steps in which processes collectively called *insight* or *creative ingenuity* are often required.

How do people find a possible solution to a problem that at first seems unsolvable? A fair amount of research and thought have been directed at this question, and the following paragraphs describe four general ideas that have emerged (based on Chi & Glaser, 1985; Mayer, 1992; and Sternberg, 1986a).

Breaking out of a Mental Set

■ ***29. How is the concept of a mental set illustrated by the nine dot problem and the candle problem?***

Some problems are difficult because their solutions depend on breaking a well-established habit of perception or thought referred to as a ***mental set***. Two problems often used to illustrate mental sets are the *nine dot problem* and the *candle problem*, described respectively in Figures 11.10 and 11.11. You might look at these problems and try to solve them before reading further. When you have solved the problems or spent as much time on them as you wish, turn to Figure 11.18 at the end of the chapter for solutions.

Figure 11.10 ***The nine dot problem***

Without ever lifting your pencil from the page or retracing any line, draw four straight lines, no more and no less, that connect all nine dots shown above.

If you solved one or both problems, congratulations; if you didn't, join the crowd. Most people fail to solve the nine dot problem because they approach it from the mental set that each straight line must begin and end on a dot. Perhaps this mental set comes partly from connect-the-dots drawings done in childhood. Most people fail to solve the candle problem because they see the box as nothing but a container for the tacks; it never occurs to them that it could also serve as a shelf and candle holder. Karl Duncker (1945), who invented the candle problem and performed the first experiments with it, referred to this type of mental set as *functional fixedness*, the inability to see an object as having a function other than its usual one. The candle problem is easier for most people if the box and tacks are presented separately rather than with the tacks inside the box (Adamson, 1952). Apparently, alternative functions for an object are easier to see if the object is not currently being used for its more common function.

What allows people to overcome a mental set at some times but not others? Earlier in this century, Gestalt psychologists argued that problems such as those just described are a bit like reversible figures (such as the one shown in Figure 9.20) and that finding a solution is a matter of *perceptual reorganization*. You look at the problem from different angles, turn away from it for a while, look back again, try a few different manipulations of the objects, and then suddenly you see it differently from the way you did before, and the solution becomes obvious. Any procedures, therefore, that would allow your thought and perceptual processes to run more freely might help.

■ ***30. What is some evidence that a lighthearted mood can help a person transcend a mental set?***

Consistent with this view, experimental conditions that increase subjects' anxiety, such as the presence of a judge, tend to inhibit the solution of insight problems, and conditions that promote lightheartedness tend to facilitate their solution. Alice Isen and her colleagues (1987) found that college students who

Figure 11.11 ***The candle problem***

Using only the objects depicted at right—a candle, a book of matches, and a box of tacks—attach the candle to the bulletin board in such a way that the candle can be lit and will burn properly.

had just watched a comedy film were far more successful in solving the candle problem than college students who had seen either a serious film or no film.

Finding a Useful Analogy

Of course, insight is not *simply* a matter of overcoming a prior mental set. If it were, empty-headed people would be the best problem solvers. To solve an insight problem, you must not only set aside an approach that doesn't work, but also find a new one that does. The new approach, like the old one, must be grounded in past experience. As William James (1890) pointed out long ago, problem solving is often a matter of finding a useful analogy (similarity) between the new situation and some other situation with which you are more familiar. A creative genius, according to James, is a person who finds useful analogies where others would not think to look for them. For example, Charles Darwin solved the problem of the mechanism of evolution (with the concept of natural selection) in part because he could see the similarity between selective breeding by horticulturalists and conditions that limit breeding in nature.

31. *How can the deliberate search for an analogy help a person solve a problem that at first seems unsolvable?*

A useful analogy in solving the candle problem likens the tack box to a shelf; both can be attached to a wall and can provide a horizontal surface on which to mount a candle. Your reasoning in solving that problem might go something like this: *I know that I could set the candle upright on the wall if I had a shelf. Is anything in the picture like a shelf? Aha, the box—it has a flat surface and can be attached to the wall with tacks so the surface sticks out horizontally!* Thus, you may have solved the problem in a less mysterious way than that implied by the Gestalt psychologists' notion of perceptual reorganization. You may have solved it through a deliberate search for a useful analogy.

Representing the Information Efficiently and Finding Shortcuts

Many problems are difficult because of the sheer quantity of information that must be considered. Efficient representation of the information is often the key to the solution. You already saw one example of this in the use of Euler circles to represent the information in a syllogism. One reason experts in any given domain out-

Knocking off a novice?

Age holds no advantage when your chess opponent is an expert, because an expert of any age can represent mentally the possible arrangements of chess pieces more efficiently than can a novice.

perform novices is that they have learned to distinguish relevant from irrelevant information and to visualize the former in chunks, larger units made up of organized sets of smaller units (discussed in Chapter 10). Experts in such areas as chess, electronics, and architecture have all been found more able than novices to represent the arrangement of pieces (chess pieces, portions of electrical circuits, or parts of a building) in meaningful chunks that can be manipulated mentally into alternative arrangements without overtaxing the capacity of short-term memory (Chi & Glaser, 1985).

■ **32.** ***How can a problem sometimes be simplified by stating it differently?***

Sometimes, restating a problem in different terms can lead to a more efficient way to organize the information. Look at the *stick-configuration problem* in Figure 11.12 and see if you can solve it before reading on. The original problem statement (in the figure caption) leads many people to focus on the sticks and to remove different sets of five sticks, in trial-and-error fashion, in the hope of finding the solutions. The difficulty with this approach is that more than 6000 combinations of five sticks exist in the seventeen sticks available, so most people give up or lose track of which combinations they have already tried long before solving the problem (Fischler & Firschein, 1987). Success is more likely if you think in terms of squares rather than sticks. Thus, you might restate the problem, "Find three squares, out of the six available, which, if preserved, would allow for the removal of exactly five sticks." There are only twenty combinations of three squares out of six, so trying all possible combinations of the squares would not be too taxing. Focusing on squares reduces the number of trials needed for a trial-and-error solution by a factor of 1/300. But focusing on squares can also lead to a more elegant solution, involving deductive reasoning rather than trial and error. A square has four sides, so the only way that twelve sticks (the number remaining after five are removed) can form three squares with no sticks left is if they share no sides in common. Inspection of the figure reveals immediately that only two three-square sets have that characteristic: (1) upper left, middle right, lower left; and (2) upper right, middle left, lower right.

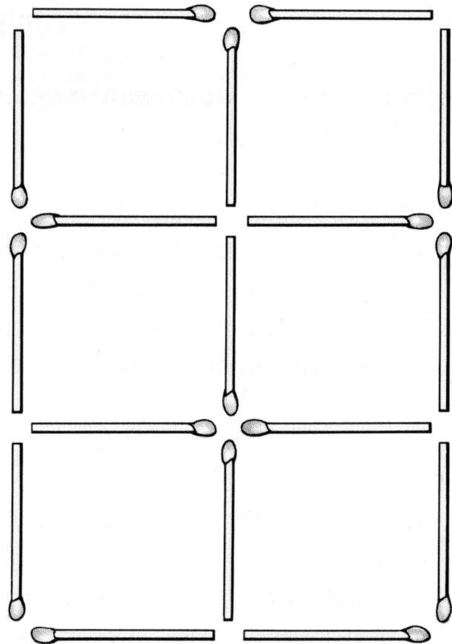

Figure 11.12 ***Stick-configuration problem***

Find all possible ways to remove exactly five sticks from the pattern so that only three squares are left, with no sticks left over.

The stick-configuration problem provides a nice example for distinguishing between two general classes of rules for solving problems—algorithms and heuristics. An ***algorithm*** is any rule that, if followed correctly, will eventually solve the problem. For many problems, an algorithm may simply specify that the problem solver produce the entire set of available moves (as defined by the problem), one at a time, until the correct solution occurs. Algorithmic reasoning might in such cases be called the brute-force approach to problem solving; it succeeds not by cleverness, but by tireless persistence. Computers use such algorithms well because they can perform simple manipulations very rapidly, have perfect memories, and don't run out of patience. An algorithmic approach to the stick-configuration problem is to remove every possible combination of five sticks out of the seventeen available—about 6000 trials in all—and to note which trials leave just three squares. A computer could solve this problem almost instantly with such an algorithm, whereas a human might spend hours trying to solve it this way before flinging the sticks aside in frustration.

■ **33.** ***What is the difference between an algorithm and a heuristic, and why are heuristics needed more by humans than by computers?***

A ***heuristic*** is any rule that allows one to reduce the number of operations that are tried in solving a problem. In colloquial terms, a heuristic is a shortcut. In the stick-configuration problem, one heuristic would be to focus on squares rather than sticks and to try to find three squares in the configuration whose boundaries are made up of twelve different sticks. In general, human problem solvers are successful to the extent that they can come up with useful heuristics. Computers can use heuristics, too, if they are programmed to do so, but they are not yet good at inventing their own. They also have less need for them.

34. ***What is the value of subgoals and clear definitions in solving a problem? How can fixation on a subgoal sometimes interfere with successful problem solving?***

Establishing Subgoals and Turning Ill-Defined Problems into Well-Defined Ones

In games such as chess that involve a sequence of moves, and in most long-range problems of real life, it is not possible to map out a solution from beginning to end before making the first move. Each move in chess elicits a countermove, which must be taken into account in choosing the next move. Similarly, each step you take to reach your chosen career has some effect, not fully predictable, which you must take into account when you decide on the next step. In chess and in life, plans must usually center on shorter-term subgoals that bring one closer to the ultimate goal of capturing the king or obtaining a desired life position. Experiments have shown that people who succeed in solving problems involving a series of choices typically establish explicit subgoals that lead ever closer to the final goal (Chi & Glaser, 1985).

A distinction between problems commonly studied in the laboratory and those confronted in real life lies in the extent to which they are well or ill defined. A *well-defined problem* is one in which the initial state, goal, and permissible operations for reaching the goal are all clearly stated; an *ill-defined problem* is one in which one or more of these is not clear (Voss & Post, 1988). Suppose you want to be happier. That is a problem worth tackling; everyone, I assume, wants to be happier. But it is an ill-defined problem; where does one begin to solve it? Counselors and therapists hired to help people solve such problems emphasize the value of restating the problem in more explicit, well-defined terms. What would bring happiness—more friends? more money? a more fulfilling job? more time to relax? Once that can be established, the problem has become better defined; some subgoals can be established and steps laid out to achieve them.

A difficulty with subgoals, or with any attempt to turn a general goal into a more explicit one, however, is that one may lose sight of the original purpose. Fixation on the subgoal itself can become a mental set that may blind a person to alternative routes to the larger goal. A chess player who focuses solely on trying to maneuver the bishop into a better position may overlook a shortcut to checkmate that was opened up by the opponent's last move. A person who focuses on more money as a path to happiness may lose sight of the original aim and devote his or her life to obtaining money for its own sake, overlooking other means to happiness that arise along the way. A successful problem solver establishes subgoals, but keeps them subordinated to their original purpose.

Language and Its Relationship to Thought

We take pride in ourselves as the thinking animal; but if a being from outer space were to characterize us compared to other earthly creatures, we might instead be classed as the linguistic animal. Other species can learn and use what they have learned to solve problems (discussed in Chapter 5), and they share with us a highly evolved capacity for nonverbal communication (discussed in Chapter 4). But only humans have a very flexible, abstract, symbol-based mode of communication—*verbal language* (hereafter just called *language*)—that permits the conveyance of every conceivable kind of information. Language allows us to tell each other not just about the here and now, but also about the past, future, far away, and hypothetical. We are effective problem solvers largely because we know so much, and we know so much because we learn not only from our own experiences, but also from others' reports. By allowing the transmission of knowledge from generation to generation, language provides the vehicle for human cultures.

Human language at the United Nations

Because all human languages contain certain underlying similarities, it is possible to translate any statement in one language into a corresponding statement in any other language. Language is a universal human trait, which, according to the spirit of the U. N., can be used to help bring peace and unity to humankind.

Cognitive psychologists are interested in language for two reasons. First, language itself is a cognitive ability. The ability to produce and understand linguistic statements is a fundamental capacity of the human mind, and as such it falls within the purview of cognitive psychology. Second, language is interwoven with other cognitive abilities. The words that we acquire from our culture may affect the way we perceive, remember, and think.

Language as a Cognitive System

Some Universal Characteristics of Human Language

Linguists estimate that approximately 3000 distinct languages exist in the world today, all different enough that the speakers of one cannot understand those of another, yet all similar in many basic ways (Foss & Hakes, 1978; Pinker & Bloom, 1992). This similarity allows us to speak of *human language* in the singular.

■ **35.** ***What is the difference between a morpheme and a word? What are two classes of morphemes?***

Every language makes use of a system of *symbols*, defined as entities that stand for (refer to) other entities (the referents of the symbols). In all languages, except for the sign languages used by the deaf, these symbols take the form of pronounceable sounds called ***morphemes***. A morpheme is the smallest meaningful unit of a language, that is, the smallest unit that stands for some object, event, characteristic, or relationship. Often it is a word, but it can also be a prefix or suffix used in a consistent way to modify a word. Thus, in English, *dog* is both a word and a morpheme, *-s* is a morpheme but not a word, and *dogs* is a word consisting of two morphemes (*dog* and *-s*). The word *antidisestablishmentarianism* contains six morphemes (anti-dis-establish-ment-arian-ism), each of which has a separate entry in an English dictionary.

In any language we can distinguish two general classes of morphemes. One class, ***content words***, includes nouns, verbs, adjectives, and adverbs—the morphemes that carry the main meaning of a sentence. The other class, ***grammatical morphemes***, includes (in English) articles (*a*, *the*), conjunctions (such as *and*, *but*), prepositions (such as *in*, *of*), and some prefixes and suffixes (such as *-ing*, *-ed*). These serve primarily to fill out the grammatical structure of the sentence, though they also contribute to meaning.

■ **36.** ***What does it mean to say that morphemes are arbitrary and discrete? How do these characteristics differentiate verbal language from nonverbal communication?***

Morphemes in any language are both arbitrary and discrete. A morpheme is *arbitrary* in that no similarity need exist between its physical structure and that of the object or concept for which it stands. Nothing about the English morpheme *dog*, or the French morpheme *chien*, naturally links it to the four-legged, barking creature it represents. Because of this arbitrariness, new morphemes can be invented whenever they are needed to stand for newly discovered objects or ideas or to express newly important shades of meaning. This characteristic gives language great flexibility. A morpheme is *discrete* in that it cannot be changed in a graded way to express gradations in meaning. For example, you cannot say that one thing is

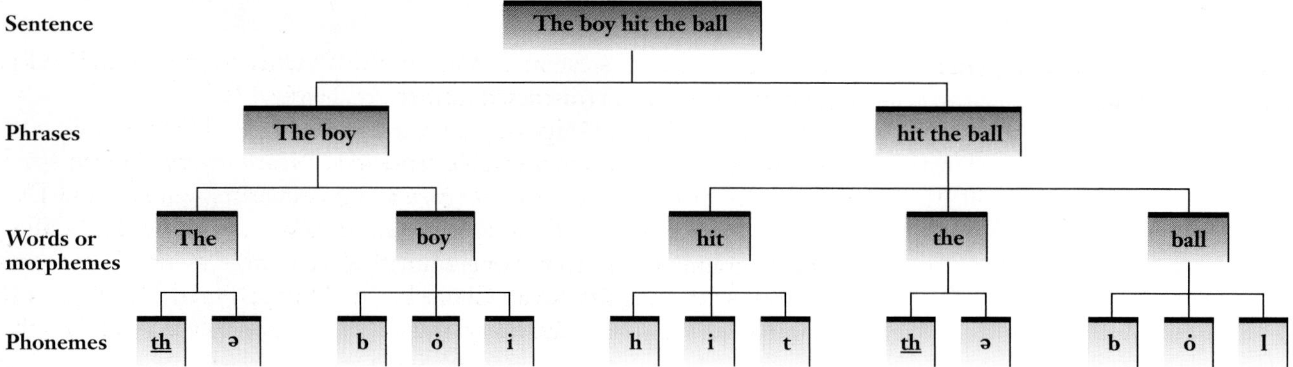

Figure 11.13 ***The hierarchical structure of language***

These four levels of organization characterize every spoken language.

bigger than another by changing the morpheme *big*. Rather, you must add a new morpheme to it (such as *-er*) or replace it with a different morpheme (such as *huge*).

Arbitrariness and discreteness distinguish language symbols from the types of signals used in nonverbal communication. As described in Chapter 4, nonverbal signals typically develop from and bear physical resemblance to the behavioral acts that they are designed to communicate, such as fleeing or fighting. Moreover, nonverbal signals can be presented gradationally. One expresses *more* surprise, anger, or whatever nonverbally by presenting the signal more vigorously or with greater amplitude of movement. In everyday speech, you might communicate that one thing is bigger than another by saying, "This one is big but that one is *big*," but the vocal emphasis placed on the second *big* is a nonverbal addition. In speech, we commonly mix nonverbal with verbal communication to get our point across (which is one reason why speaking is easier than writing).

■ **37.** ***How can any sentence be described as a four-level hierarchy?***

In addition to commonalities in their symbol systems, all languages share the same basic hierarchical structure. A sentence in any language can be broken down into at least four levels of units hierarchically organized (see Figure 11.13). At the top level is the sentence itself, which can be broken down into phrases, which can be broken down into words or morphemes, which can be broken down into elementary vowel and consonant sounds called ***phonemes***. The power of this organization lies in the fact that a relatively few different phonemes (anywhere from fifteen to eighty occur in any given language) can be arranged in different ways to produce an enormous number of different possible words, which themselves can be arranged in different ways to produce a limitless number of possible phrases and sentences.

Nonverbal supplements to verbal language

Many of the cues that give meaning to a conversation are nonverbal. Through gestures and tone of voice, people add graded, nonverbal modifiers to their morphemes.

Every language is also characterized by rules that specify permissible ways that units at one level can be arranged to produce the next higher level. Collectively, these rules are referred to as the ***grammar*** of the language. Grammar includes rules of ***morphology***, which specify how phonemes can be arranged to produce morphemes and words, and rules of ***syntax***, which specify how words can be arranged to produce phrases and sentences. These rules differ from language to language, but every language has them, and similarities exist across all languages in the fundamental nature of these rules (Pinker & Bloom, 1992).

The Tacit Nature of Grammar

People often think of grammar as something that they learned (or tried to learn) in elementary school (also known as *grammar* school, perhaps for this very reason). But grammar is learned tacitly long before formal schooling begins. The fact that 4-year-olds can carry on meaningful conversations with adults, producing and understanding new and unique sentences, implies that 4-year-olds have already acquired the essential grammar of their native language. Four-year-olds can't name or describe the rules of grammar (nor can most adults), yet they have somehow in-

■ **38.** ***What is meant by saying that grammar rules are tacit?***

corporated these rules mentally and use them tacitly to understand and produce grammatical sentences (discussed further in Chapter 12).

People's tacit knowledge of grammar is demonstrated in their ability to distinguish acceptable from unacceptable sentences. Nearly every English speaker can identify *The mouse crawled under the barn* as a grammatical sentence and *The crawled barn mouse the under* as not, though few can explain exactly why. The ability to distinguish grammatical from nongrammatical sentences is not based simply on meaning. As the linguist Noam Chomsky (1957) has pointed out, English speakers recognize *Colorless green ideas sleep furiously* as grammatically correct though absurd.

Chomsky's Approach to Grammar and Its Impact on Psychology

■ **39.** ***How did Chomsky link the study of grammar to psychology, and how did this help promote a shift from behaviorism to cognitive psychology?***

Noam Chomsky figures prominently in cognitive psychology, even though his own field is not psychology but linguistics. In 1957, he published a slender, enormously influential book entitled *Syntactic Structures*, the goal of which was to outline a model of grammar that could be applied in describing any language. His contention that such a model must have roots in the basic workings of the human mind explicitly linked grammar to psychology. At the same time, he attacked the then-dominant behavioral approach in psychology by arguing that any reasonable description of how people use language must go beyond behavioral observations to the mental rules underlying that behavior. Whereas behaviorists tended to emphasize the chainlike nature of sentences (one word following the next), Chomsky emphasized the hierarchical nature of sentences. Chomsky argued that a person must have some representation of the whole sentence in mind before uttering it and then must apply grammatical rules to that representation in order to produce the utterance. Similarly, he argued that when listening to a sentence a person must hear it as a whole (not a chain of separate words) and apply grammatical rules to understand it.

Noam Chomsky

In his 1957 book, *Syntactic Structures*, Chomsky called attention to the idea that producing a verbal statement is a creative act guided by implicit mental rules. This work, and the revolution in psycholinguistics that it inspired, have enriched research and theory in cognitive psychology.

To get an idea of the arguments that Chomsky employed, consider this sentence: *The boy who likes Mary hit the ball.* How do you know from the sentence that it was the boy and not Mary who hit the ball? *Mary* comes right before *hit the ball*, so a simple analysis in terms of adjacent pairs of words would tell you that Mary hit the ball. Apparently, you are able to view the sentence as more than a sequence of individual words or word pairs and use its whole structure to understand its meaning. Some rule you know about English syntax tells you that in this case *Mary* does not belong with *hit*, but rather is part of a set of words modifying *boy*. The rule tells you that the core sentence is *The boy hit the ball* and that *who likes Mary* has been inserted to clarify which boy.

Chomsky's main goal was to specify as efficiently as possible the relationship between the specific wording of a sentence, referred to as the ***surface structure***, and the meaning that the speaker wishes to convey or that the listener understands. He pointed out that sentences with very different surface structures can have similar or identical meanings. For example, *The boy hit the ball* and *The ball was hit by the boy* have similar meanings even though their surface structures are very different. Conversely, he also pointed out that sentences with similar surface structures can have very different meanings. Compare, for example, *The boy is eager to please* and *The boy is easy to please*. The change in one adjective turns the whole sentence around, such that the boy is the pleaser in one case and is the one who is pleased in the other.

As a framework for relating surface structure to meaning, Chomsky proposed that any given sentence exists in two forms: a surface structure, which is articulated and heard, and a ***deep structure***, which is not articulated, but exists only in the mind of the speaker or listener. The deep structure of a sentence is an abstract, mental representation of the meaning of the sentence organized in the simplest possible grammatical form consistent with that meaning. To produce a sentence,

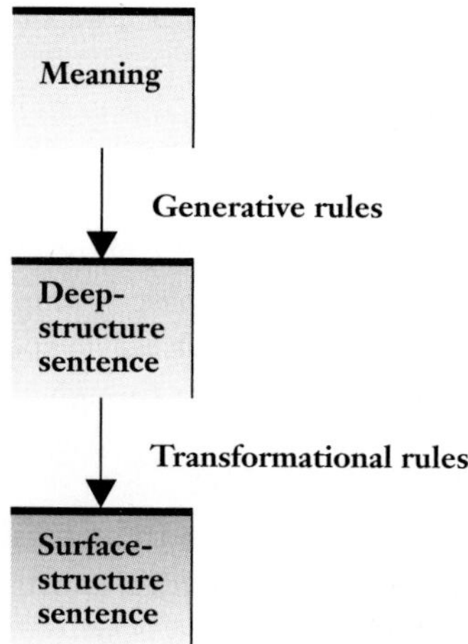

Figure 11.14 ***Chomsky's model of sentence production***

According to Chomsky, one first uses generative rules to turn the intended meaning into a deep-structure version of the sentence, and then uses transformational rules to produce the surface-structure version.

according to Chomsky (1968), a person begins with a mental representation of the idea to be conveyed, uses a set of grammatical rules called *generative rules* to generate the deep-structure representation of that sentence, and then uses another set of grammatical rules called *transformational rules* to transform the deep-structure sentence into one of the many possible surface-structure forms that it might take (see Figure 11.14). Conversely, to understand a sentence, a person uses the same set of rules in reverse, first producing a deep-structure representation and then extracting the meaning from it. Chomsky's theory is called the ***generative-transformational theory***, named after the two sets of rules.

Inspired by Chomsky's theory, many psychologists began to study language as a cognitive system. But while Chomsky's approach was theoretical, asking how an ideal language user *might* generate and understand sentences, the psychologists employed an empirical approach, asking how people actually *do* generate and understand sentences, and conducting research to try to find out.

Slips of the Tongue and Their Use in Understanding Speech Production

When you utter a sentence, you are rarely aware of any steps or rules by which you perform that act. It seems as if you have an idea to communicate, you open your mouth, and, *voilà*, out come the words. Yet, complex rule-abiding processes must mediate between the initial idea and its expression in words, and psycholinguists (psychologists who study language) have developed a variety of means to try to understand these processes. One fruitful tactic is to analyze the kinds of errors that people commonly make in speech production.

Of particular interest is the class of errors called ***spoonerisms***, named after William Spooner, an English clergyman and Oxford don who was famous for uttering them. A spoonerism is an error in which two elements in a sentence (phonemes, syllables, or morphemes) are mistakenly interchanged in position. Two of the most amusing spoonerisms attributed to Spooner himself were: "*Work* is the curse of the *drink*ing class," uttered when he meant to say, "*Drink* is the curse of the *work*ing class"; and "Our *q*ueer old *d*ean," when he meant to say, "Our *d*ear old *q*ueen." Some suspect that Spooner's legend is largely a creation of his students, but research shows that truly accidental spoonerisms are quite common and follow certain laws (Fromkin, 1973, 1980; Garrett, 1975, 1982).

■ **40.** ***How does an analysis of spoonerisms suggest that grammar is less destructible than meaning?***

Consistent with the idea that grammatical rules are firmly entrenched in the mind, slips of the tongue are far more likely to violate the meaning of a sentence than its grammar. In spoonerisms involving whole words or morphemes, those that switch places are usually in the same grammatical category. Nouns switch with nouns, verbs with verbs, adjectives with adjectives, and so on—in a way that preserves the grammatical structure. *The red pen is on the table* might be misstated as *The red table is on the pen*, but not as *The red on is pen the table*. Sometimes the switching of two words in a spoonerism requires an additional adjustment to keep the sentence grammatical, and in most cases that adjustment is in fact made. For example, the intended phrase *an aunt with money* might become *a money with aunt*. Here the article *an* changed to *a* to accommodate the switch from a noun starting with a vowel to one starting with a consonant.

A second generalization about spoonerisms is that swaps involving whole content words (nouns, verbs, adjectives, and adverbs) may occur across different phrases of a sentence, but those involving phonemes occur only within a phrase. *The red pen is on the table* might come out as *The red table is on the pen* (content words swapped across phrases) or *The ped ren is on the table* (phonemes swapped within the same phrase), but is not likely to come out as *The red ten is on the pable* (phenomes swapped across phrases). This reliable difference between content-word spoonerisms and phoneme spoonerisms suggests that the selection and sequencing of con-

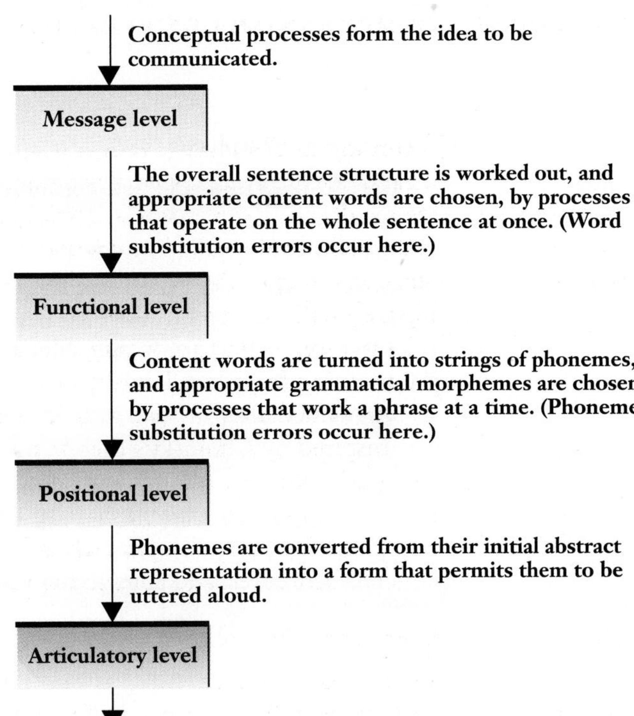

Figure 11.15 ***Garrett's model of speech production***

According to Garrett, a sentence is built mentally through a series of four stages or levels before it is uttered. The processes shown to the right of each arrow operate on what has already been built to produce the next level down. (Adapted from Smyth & others, 1987).

tent words, and the fleshing out of those words with appropriate phonemes, occur at two distinct stages of sentence production.

■ **41.** ***How is Garrett's distinction between functional and positional stages in sentence production supported by an analysis of spoonerisms?***

Based on such considerations, Merrill Garrett (1975,1990) has distinguished between a *functional* and a *positional* stage in the mental generation of a sentence. At the *functional* stage, a rough form of the whole sentence is held in mind and worked on at once. This is where content words, represented abstractly without their sounds, are selected and might accidentally switch places. At the subsequent *positional* stage, the sentence is refined one phrase at a time. This is where grammatical morphemes and phonemes are added into the sentence, phrase by phrase, and where phonemes might accidentally switch places. The existence of these two stages would explain why spoonerisms involving content words occur over the whole sentence, but those involving phonemes occur only within the same phrase.

Figure 11.15 depicts Garrett's complete model of sentence generation, which contains four stages in all, moving from the large and general to the small and specific. First, the whole meaning is represented in a nonverbal form (message level); then the overall sentence structure is roughed out (functional level); then the phonemes and grammatical morphemes are added in, phrase by phrase (positional level); and, finally, the sentence is further refined so it can be uttered aloud (articulatory level). In this model, building a sentence is analogous to building a house. First comes the overall plan; then the framework; and then the walls, floor, and roof; and finally the veneer (siding, roof shingles, and wallpaper) that you see when the product is complete. Other research using quite different methods has produced results consistent with this general model (Bock, 1990).

The Neuropsychological Approach to Language

For well over a hundred years, scientists have tried to relate aspects of language ability to specific areas of the brain. By far the most common approach to this task has been to study victims of strokes or other sources of brain damage and to correlate the type of language deficit such people experience with the location of the damage in their brain.

■ 42. *What are the differences between Broca's and Wernicke's aphasias in (a) language production, (b) language comprehension, and (c) area of brain destroyed?*

Two Classes of Aphasia

Any loss in language resulting from brain damage is called ***aphasia***. Aphasias can be classified into many different types, depending on the specific nature and degree of language loss (Garman, 1990). The two types most relevant to our discussion are ***Broca's aphasia***, also called *nonfluent aphasia*, and ***Wernicke's aphasia***, also called *fluent aphasia*. These disorders are named after the nineteenth-century neurologists Paul Broca and Carl Wernicke, who were among the first to describe them (Broca, 1861; Wernicke, 1874).

In Broca's aphasia, speech is labored and *telegraphic*—the minimum number of words is used to convey the message. The speech consists almost entirely of content words, devoid of grammatical morphemes, and a sentence is rarely more than three or four words long. If you ask a person with this disorder what he or she did today, the answer might be, "Buy bread store." Broca's aphasics show relatively good language comprehension, but often have difficulty understanding grammatically complex sentences. They become confused, for example, by sentence constructions in which the agent and object of an action are reversed from the usual word order, if the meaning is not obvious from the content words alone (Zurif, 1990). Thus, they easily understand *The boy pushed the girl* (a simple, active sentence), or *The apple was eaten by the boy* (which can be understood from the content words, because apples don't eat boys), but *The girl was pushed by the boy* leaves them unsure as to who pushed whom. The brain damage coinciding with Broca's aphasia usually encompasses a particular portion of the left frontal lobe, often called *Broca's area* (see Figure 11.16).

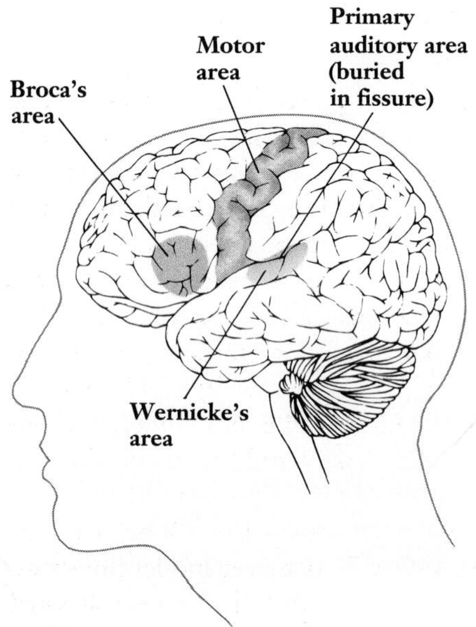

Figure 11.16 ***Left-hemisphere language areas***

Damage to Broca's area leads to loss of ability to generate grammatically complex sentences, but not to loss of ability to supply appropriate content words. Damage to Wernicke's area has the opposite effect on speech production, and it also greatly impairs speech comprehension.

Wernicke's aphasics, by contrast, are very deficient in language comprehension as well as production. Their most obvious symptom is a loss in ability to understand the meaning of content words and to produce appropriate content words in sentences. Their speech is almost the opposite of that of Broca's aphasics. It is rich in grammatical morphemes and superficially quite fluent, but it is deficient in content words and often contains nonsense words. Here is an example from one such patient, trying to describe a simple picture (Schwartz, 1987): "Nothing the keesereez the, these are davereez and these and this one and these are living. This one's right in and these are . . . uh . . . and that's nothing, that's nothing . . . ." The most apparent deficiency is that the person can't come up with the correct names of objects or actions, leading to a heavy use of pronouns and sometimes nonsense words as substitutes. The speech retains its grammatical structure but loses its meaning. The brain damage coinciding with Wernicke's aphasia usually encompasses a particular portion of the left temporal lobe, often called *Wernicke's area* (see Figure 11.16).

Brain-Based Models of Comprehension and Speaking

■ 43. *How does Wernicke's model account for speech comprehension and production, and what does the neo-Wernicke model add to the original account?*

One of the earliest researchers to develop a brain-based theory or model of language was Carl Wernicke himself. Based on the most obvious deficits in the two aphasias just described, Wernicke (1874) hypothesized that the brain area now named for him is critically involved in understanding speech (relating words to meaning) and the brain area now named for Broca is critically involved in producing speech (turning the mental representations of words into a form that can be spoken). According to this view, the poor language production of Wernicke's aphasics is secondary to their poor comprehension—you can't produce good speech if you don't understand what you are saying.

In Wernicke's model, comprehending a sentence is a two-step process: (1) Speech sounds are analyzed for their physical properties in the auditory sensory area of the temporal lobe; (2) the neural representations of the sounds are sent to

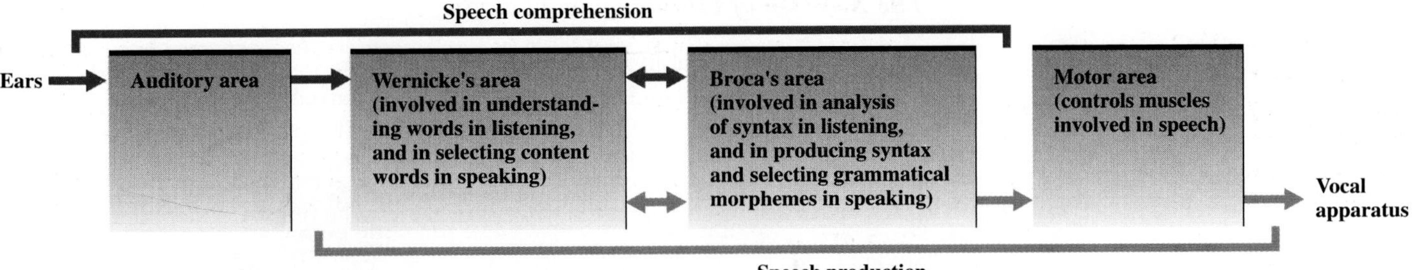

Figure 11.17 ***A brain-based model of speech comprehension and production (the neo-Wernicke model)***

In comprehension, speech information is transported from the auditory area to Wernicke's area for analysis of meaning of content words and to Broca's area for analysis of syntax. In speech production, content words are chosen by neural systems in Wernicke's area, grammatical refinements are added by neural systems in Broca's area, and then the information is sent to the motor cortex, which sets up the muscle movements for utterance.

Wernicke's area, where they are analyzed for meaning. Producing a sentence, according to the model, can be described as a three-step process: (1) The basic meaning to be conveyed is transformed into a neural representation of a sequence of words in Wernicke's area; (2) this representation is sent to Broca's area to be converted into a form that can be uttered; and (3) that, in turn, is sent to the primary motor area of the forebrain, which controls the muscles of speech. In addition to fitting the patterns of aphasia, Wernicke's model makes sense anatomically. Wernicke's area lies right next to the auditory area of the temporal lobe, and Broca's area lies very close to the primary motor cortex (look again at Figure 11.16). For a century, Wernicke's model, with minor elaborations, was the most widely accepted brain-based theory of language (Geschwind, 1972), and it still has many adherents (Mayeux & Kandel, 1991).

In recent years, however, a somewhat different model from Wernicke's has found support (Schwartz, 1987; Zurif, 1980, 1990). This newer model (illustrated in Figure 11.17) has no regularly accepted name, so I will call it the *neo-Wernicke* model. The main difference between the two is that, according to the newer model, Broca's area is important not just for turning sentences into forms that can be uttered, but also for comprehending and producing certain grammatical constructions. In comprehension, Wernicke's area remains critical for making sense of the content words, but Broca's area assumes the task of unraveling difficult grammatical constructions. In producing speech, Wernicke's area remains critical for generating appropriate content words, and Broca's area assumes the task of adding grammatical morphemes and refining the grammatical structure of the sentence. Notice that, with this model, the two brain areas can be related at least roughly to different stages in Garrett's model of speech production (in Figure 11.15). Wernicke's area is most involved in producing the functional-level sentence, and Broca's area is most involved in producing some aspects of the positional-level and articulatory-level sentence.

Cognitive psychologists are understandably pleased when two entirely different lines of evidence—such as that from slips of the tongue in brain-intact individuals and that from effects of brain damage—lead to similar models. But much disagreement remains among neuropsychologists about how to interpret different patterns of aphasia. Some researchers favor the theory outlined in Figure 11.17, but some favor other models. Research on aphasia is complicated because no two aphasic patients are alike either in the exact area of brain damage they have suffered or in the exact pattern of language loss they show. Most lesions are due to strokes (caused by ruptured blood vessels), which affect broad regions of the brain, not just Wernicke's or Broca's areas. Different researchers have found different ways to make sense of the innumerable patterns of aphasia that result.

The Relation of Language to Thought

In the history of psychology, a wide range of opinions has been expressed about the relationship between language and thought. One extreme view was that of behaviorist John B. Watson (1924), who wrote, "What the psychologists have hitherto called thought is nothing but talking to ourselves." Watson believed that we learn to talk in much the same way we learn other muscular skills (such as riding a bicycle) and that when we subsequently make the same muscular movements in a more hidden form (to ourselves rather than aloud), we call it thought. In a heroic experiment testing that hypothesis, a physician, Scott Smith, took a drug that temporarily paralyzed his muscles (he was on an artificial respirator during this period) and reported that the paralysis did not interfere with his ability to understand what was going on around him, nor with his ability to perform mental arithmetic or to reason in other ways (Smith & others, 1947). Thus, the extreme view that thought depends on the muscle movements of speech was proven wrong.

A more moderate theory of the dependence of thought on language was developed by the Russian psychologist Lev Vygotsky in the 1930s. Vygotsky (1934/1962) argued that thought and language are separate processes in very young children, but that as children become proficient at communicating with language, they gradually internalize it and use it for their private thought. At an early stage in this process, children's use of words for thought may require movement of speech muscles (you can see young children's lips move as they think), but with time children can use the words purely mentally, often in such abbreviated form that they are no longer recognized as words. Such thought, which uses symbols that were acquired originally in the form of words, is called *verbal thought*. According to Vygotsky, in the process of developing verbal thought the basic ideas of the culture—reflected in the culture's words—are incorporated into the minds of the individual members.

It's all relative

This hunter, clearing a path to open water, has many different words for the various kinds of snow around him. An important question in the study of the relationship between language and thought is whether the differences among the languages of people affect their perception of snow—or of any other phenomenon.

Vygotsky's theory is discussed in more detail in Chapter 12, along with the contrasting position of Jean Piaget, a Swiss developmental psychologist who argued that language plays very little role in the development of thought. Our focus for now will be on an idea closely related to Vygotsky's theory, but more often attributed to an American linguist, Benjamin Whorf—the idea of linguistic relativity.

The Idea of Linguistic Relativity

■ **44.** ***What is the theory of linguistic relativity, and in what sense is it obviously true?***

Benjamin Whorf, who was most active in the 1920s and '30s, was a specialist in Native American languages. He found that some of these languages differ greatly from each other and from European languages in the way they categorize various aspects of the physical world. For instance, some have many words for different types of snow, and others have only one. Some divide the spectrum of colors into just two or three categories, and others divide it into as many as twelve. In some languages verbs are clearly marked according to tense (present, past, and future), and in others they are not. Whorf (1956) came to believe that such differences affect the way people perceive and think about snow, color, time, and the like. He proposed from this the theory of ***linguistic relativity***: People who have different native languages perceive the world differently and think differently from each other because of their different languages.

Linguistic relativity (like most large theories in psychology) is not the kind of theory that will ever be proven completely right or wrong. Certainly, language differences affect people's thinking in some ways. Consider, for example, the realm of numerical reasoning. Our language, which contains a full set of number names conveniently organized in a base-ten system, certainly gives us an advantage in all sorts of numerical reasoning compared to Australian aborigines who speak

Worora. The Worora language has only three number words, which, translated to English, are *one*, *two*, and *more than two* (Greenberg, 1978). If you wanted to communicate any mathematical ideas to a group of Worora speakers, you would have to start by teaching them number names. The words, in this case, are essential tools.

Linguistic Relativity in the Realm of Colors

Much of the research on linguistic relativity has centered on the relationship between color perception and color labeling. In English (and in French, Spanish, and many other languages), we have simple, one-word labels for those colors that we perceive as focal (or pure) colors—blue, green, yellow, and red. We perceive and describe other colors (that lie between the focal colors on the physical wavelength spectrum) as if they were mixtures of focal colors, such as bluish-green and greenish-yellow. Do we see the colors in this way because of the words we use to describe them? That is, do we see blue and green as pure colors because, as children, we heard them labeled with single words (*blue* and *green*), and see bluish-green as a mixture because we heard it labeled as a mixture (*bluish-green*)? A number of studies have been performed to find out if people who speak languages in which the colors are labeled differently see colors differently from the way we do. The general conclusion, contrary to linguistic relativity, is that people everywhere see colors a similar way (Kay & Kempton, 1984).

■ **45.** ***What is some evidence that language does not affect basic sensory experiences of color, but does affect certain judgments concerning color?***

Eleanor Rosch (1973) conducted a set of studies of this type with native speakers of Dani, a New Guinea language that divides the color spectrum into just two categories. One category, *mili*, includes black, green, and blue (colors considered to be dark and cool); the other, *mola*, includes white, yellow, and red (considered to be light and warm). Rosch's evidence that Dani speakers see colors as Westerners do, even though they label them differently, includes the following findings: (a) When asked to select from a set of colors the best or most typical examples of *mili* or *mola*, they almost invariably chose one of our focal colors. Thus, for *mili*, different individuals chose black, green, or blue, but they did not choose bluish-green. (b) When taught new words for colors, they learned words for focal colors more easily than for nonfocal colors. (c) In a color-memory test, in which they had to pick a color that best matched one that they had previously been shown, Dani speakers performed better with focal than with nonfocal colors (as do English-speaking subjects). Rosch concluded that color perception is determined by universal characteristics of the visual system, not by language.

Nevertheless, language probably does affect subtler aspects of people's cognitive treatment of color. An illustration comes from an experiment by Paul Kay and Willett Kempton (1984), in which English-speaking and Tarahumara-speaking people were asked to judge the degree of similarity of various colored chips in the green to blue range (Kay & Kempton, 1984). Tarahumara, a Native American language spoken by a group living in Mexico, does not have separate labels for green and blue, but refers to both with one word, *siyóname*. In the experiment, some chips were on the side of the green-blue range that most English speakers call "green," and others were on the side that most call "blue." The result was that the English-speaking subjects judged colors that fell on the same side of the green-blue divide as more similar to each other and judged those that fell on opposite sides of the divide as more different from each other than would be predicted from purely physical and physiological considerations. No such distortion occurred for the Tarahumara speakers. From this and other evidence, Kay and Kempton concluded that language probably does not affect our direct sensory experience of color, but does affect some of the judgments we make about color similarities. These judgments may reflect a compromise between our direct sensations and the words we have available to categorize those sensations.

■ **46. *What is some evidence that bilingual speakers may think differently in different languages and that some mental schemas are specific to one language or another?***

Studies of Bilingual Speakers as Evidence for Linguistic Relativity

Many people who have lived in two cultures and are fluent in the language of each claim that they think differently in the two languages. Several studies have supported this claim.

Susan Ervin-Tripp (1964) studied women who had grown up in Japan, married American servicemen, and moved to the United States. These women continued to speak Japanese with their Japanese friends but spoke English with their families and co-workers. Ervin-Tripp tested the women psychologically in both Japanese and English. She found that the women often responded differently to the same questions depending on which language they were using and that the differences typically coincided with known differences between Japanese and American cultural patterns. For example, in a sentence-completion test, a woman tested in Japanese completed the stem *When my wishes conflict with my family . . . ,* with the words (in Japanese) . . . *it is a time of great unhappiness.* When the same stem was presented in English, she responded (in English) . . . *I do what I want.* Ervin-Tripp suggested that, for these women, Japanese words were tied to Japanese cultural values and ideas and English words were tied to American values and ideas. The Japanese and English words for *family* may have had the same dictionary meaning to the women, but the two words evoked quite different sets of thoughts and feelings.

More recently, Curt Hoffman and his colleagues (1986) found that bilingual speakers may develop different impressions of a person depending on which language they are using when forming an impression. In their experiment, Chinese students at the University of Alberta, in Canada, read descriptions of hypothetical individuals in either English or Chinese and then wrote essays about their impressions of the person described—using English when the original description was in English and Chinese when the original description was in Chinese. Two of the individuals described could easily be labeled by an English word but not by a Chinese word, and two were the reverse. For example, one description was designed to fit what in English is called an artist character—a person with artistic ability, a temperamental disposition, a tendency toward fantasy, and an unconventional lifestyle. Another description was designed to fit what in Chinese is called a *shi gu* individual—a person with much worldly experience, a strong family orientation, and good interpersonal skills. The labels were not used in the descriptions, but the descriptions were written so as to be consistent with those labels.

As predicted by the linguistic-relativity hypothesis, the students formed a firmer, more consistent impression of the artistic character when reading and thinking in English, and a firmer, more consistent impression of the *shi gu* character when reading and thinking in Chinese. Based on these results, Hoffman and his colleagues suggested that bilingual speakers have two different sets of schemas (mental representations of concepts), each tied to a different language. When the person thinks in one language, one set of schemas is evoked; in the other language, the other set is evoked.

Sexism and the Generic *Man*

If language shapes thought, then one way to change long-established ways of thinking is to modify the language. This reasoning lies behind the movement to rid English of constructions that tend to characterize males as more human than females. One such construction is use of the word *man* to stand for both human beings in general (the generic *man*) and human males in particular. Many writers have argued that because these two concepts have the same label, they become fused into the same mental schema and lead English-speaking people to think of males as more typical examples of human beings than are females. This form of labeling is no accident. Historically, and still among many people today, men have been considered quite explicitly to be the primary humans and women have been considered to be secondary.

What a difference a decade makes

When Richard Scarry's *Best Word Book Ever* was first published, few people thought about the effect of books on children's developing sense of their gender. Studies of children's literature in the early 1970s changed all that, and publishers began to replace stereotyped images and language with material that provides equal treatment, as these pages from the 1963 (left) and 1980 (right) editions of the book show.

47. *What is some evidence that the two traditional meanings of the word* man *are not distinct in many people's minds?*

To test the degree to which *man*, used in the generic sense, elicits a mental perception of humans in general versus males in particular, Joseph Schneider and Sally Hacker (1973) performed an experiment involving hypothetical titles for chapters of a sociology textbook. One set of titles used the generic *man* construction, which was still common in textbooks of that time: *Social Man, Urban Man, Economic Man*, and so on. Another set avoided that construction, with titles such as: *Society, Urban Life*, and *Economic Behavior*. The researchers gave one set of titles to one group of students and the other set to another group and asked each student to find pictures from newspapers and magazines that would be suitable for illustrating each chapter. The result was that about 65 percent of pictures brought back by students in the *man* group depicted males only (the rest contained either both genders or females only), compared to about 50 percent male-only pictures brought back by the other group. These percentages were about the same for female and male students. From this, the authors argued that the two meanings of *man* are in fact not distinct in people's minds. The students in this experiment surely knew, at one level, that *man* in those titles meant human beings in general, but their behavior suggested a mental compromise between that meaning and the male-only meaning.

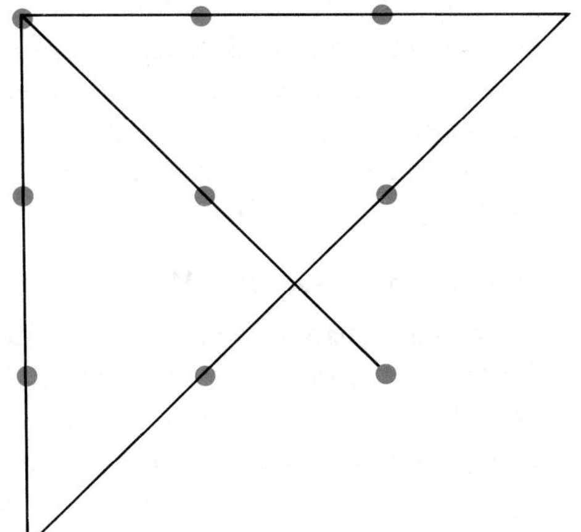

Figure 11.18 ***Solutions to the nine dot and candle problems***

These are the solutions to the problems in Figures 11.10 and 11.11.

Concluding Thoughts

The title of this chapter could have been the title of the book. Every approach in psychology contributes to an understanding of the human intellect, and all the psychological processes examined in previous chapters—learning, motivation, emotion, sensation, perception, and memory—are entwined with reasoning and language in forming the human intellect. In this chapter we have considered aspects of the mind that most distinguish us from other animals. As you review the chapter, you may want to pay particular attention to the following themes:

1. The issue of multiple intelligences One way to review the various theories of intelligence is to compare their stance on whether intelligence is one characteristic or many. Galton thought of intelligence as a single entity, best described as quickness and acuity of the nervous system, a view that finds some support in modern research correlating reaction-time measures with IQ scores. Binet thought of intelligence as a collection of school-related attributes, such as good memory and good vocabulary, and fluency with numbers. Spearman thought of intelligence as a single, hypothetical factor, *g*, that accounts for the statistical correlation found among different mental tests. Thurstone thought of intelligence as seven separate factors, based on his research showing that various kinds of mental tests can be grouped into seven clusters according to their patterns of intercorrelation.

P. E. Vernon and most other modern psychometric theorists think of intelligence as a hierarchy, with a single *g* at the top affecting two or more basic abilities that are partly independent of one another. Sternberg, from the information-processing perspective, also subscribes to a hierarchical theory; he thinks of intelligence as a hierarchy of mental components that are brought into play differently for different kinds of tests. Neuropsychological research has led some theorists to think of intelligence as an amalgam of two modes of thought: a discrete, propositional, left-hemisphere mode; and a holistic, graded, right-hemisphere mode. Based on case histories in which one ability flourishes in the relative absence of others, Gardner has resurrected Thurstone's idea of independent intelligences, at the same time broadening the concept of intelligence to include a wider range of abilities.

2. The concrete nature of human reasoning Logicians and psychologists alike have often distinguished between two types of reasoning—concrete and formal. Concrete reasoning is considered to be based heavily on one's memories of previous experiences that were similar or identical to the conditions posed by the present problem. Formal reasoning, in contrast, is described as involving abstract principles of logic, independent of familiarity with the specific contents of the problem. Research on how people actually reason, however, blurs this distinction and emphasizes concrete processes. That would be a good theme to keep in mind as you review the subsection on the ecological approach to intelligence and the entire section on reasoning and problem solving. Ecological research suggests that people everywhere seem far more intelligent when reasoning about things with which they are familiar than when reasoning about other things. Studies of logic suggest that people who are best at solving syllogisms and similar formal problems typically convert them to concrete images, such as Euler circles, before solving them. Other studies of problem solving suggest that people who reason well in new realms often do so by finding analogies between the new realm and one with which they have had concrete experience. In that way, the unfamiliar becomes familiar.

3. Two ways in which language is studied in cognitive psychology Language is studied by psychologists both as a human ability unto itself and as a vehicle for thought. In this chapter you saw samples of research pertaining to both of these ways of examining language. Chomsky's distinction between the deep structure and surface structure of sentences, Garrett's model of speech production based on slips of the tongue, and the neuropsychological model based on Broca's and Wernicke's aphasias are all part of the attempt to understand language as a human ability. The research on linguistic relativity pertains to the role of language in thought. Language holds increasing interest in psychology, and you will read more about it from a developmental perspective in the next chapter.

Further Reading

Nathan Brody (1992). *Intelligence* (2nd ed.). San Diego: Academic Press.

In clear and thoughtful prose, Brody discusses from the psychometric perspective such topics as the use of intelligence tests to understand the structure and nature of intelligence, the heritability of intelligence, and the continuity of intelligence over one's life span.

Stephen J. Ceci (1990). *On intelligence . . . more or less: A bio-ecological treatise on intellectual development.* Englewood Cliffs, NJ: Prentice Hall.

This book makes an interesting complement to Brody's. Ceci's thesis is that intelligence tests are not as valid as most psychometricians believe them to be and that intelligence is best understood in relation to the social-environmental contexts of everyday life.

Robert J. Sternberg (1986). *Intelligence applied: Understanding and increasing your intellectual skills.* San Diego: Harcourt Brace Jovanovich.

In this relatively slender paperback, Sternberg describes his information-processing theory of intelligence and presents numerous problems designed to exercise specific components of the reader's intelligence. I can't guarantee that the book will increase your IQ, but I do think you would enjoy it.

Richard E. Mayer (1992). *Thinking, problem solving, cognition* (2nd ed.). New York: Freeman.

This is a lively, informative textbook dealing with psychological research on such topics as inductive and deductive reasoning, computer simulation of human reasoning, the role of analogy in reasoning, and creativity training.

Daniel Osherson and Howard Lasnik (Eds.) (1990). *Language: An invitation to cognitive science, volume 1.* Cambridge, MA: MIT Press.

Each chapter of this introduction to the cognitive bases for language was written by a different expert. Included are a chapter by Merrill Garrett on sentence processing and one by Edgar Zurif on language and the brain.

Looking Ahead

In this chapter, you have read about several ways—psychometric, information-processing, and neuropsychological—of dissecting the abilities of the adult mind. Still another route to understanding mental abilities is to watch them as they are built—that is, to observe how they grow in the developing child. The next chapter is about cognitive development; it deals with many of the same issues that were raised in this chapter, but from a developmental perspective. What can we learn about thought and language by studying their development in children?

GROWTH OF THE MIND AND PERSON

PART 5

One way to understand any complex entity, be it a building under construction or a person growing, is to watch it develop over time. This is the approach taken by developmental psychologists, who study the changes through which human behavior becomes increasingly complex and sophisticated from infancy into adulthood. This unit consists of two chapters on developmental psychology. The first is about the development of perception, language, and thought. The second is about the development of social relationships and the roles they play in promoting other aspects of development.

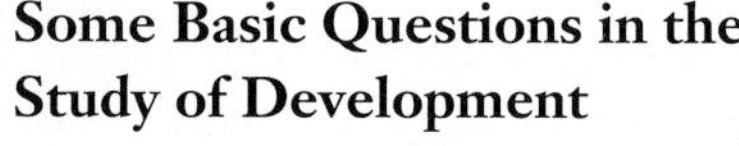

Some Basic Questions in the Study of Development

Development of Perception and Knowledge in Infancy

Perceptual Development

Early Knowledge About Physical Reality

Development of Language

The Course of Language Development

Internal and External Supports for Language Development

Can Chimpanzees Learn Human Language?

Development of Logical Thought

Piaget's Theory

The Information-Processing Perspective

Vygotsky and the Sociocultural Perspective

COGNITIVE DEVELOPMENT

CHAPTER 12

Nothing comes from nothing. Everything has a history, and the human mind is no exception. Actually, the human mind has more than one history. It has an *evolutionary history* (discussed in Chapter 3), which extends back through the millions of generations of our ancestors. It has a *cultural history*, the history of ideas and ways of thinking shared by people whose lives are intertwined. And it has a *developmental history*, which for each person begins at conception and continues throughout the person's life. Developmental history is not independent of the other two; it is affected by our genes (the embodiment of evolutionary history) and our social environment (the embodiment of cultural history).

Developmental psychology is the study of changes that occur in people's abilities and styles of behavior as they get older. It is the attempt to map such changes and to understand the forces that produce or influence them. Traditionally, developmental psychologists have focused on children, especially on young children. Changes early in life are more rapid and therefore easier to study than those that occur later on. Moreover, early changes may be especially important because they provide the foundation for subsequent development. Yet development continues throughout life, and in recent years adult development has become the focus of considerable research (discussed briefly in this chapter and more extensively in Chapter 13).

Our main concern in this chapter is with the development of cognition in infancy and childhood. After a brief introductory section listing some questions that are basic to all of developmental psychology, we will discuss the development of perception and knowledge in infancy, the development of language, and the development of logical thought.

Some Basic Questions in the Study of Development

Before exploring the development of specific abilities, let's consider some broad questions about ways of conceptualizing development in general—questions that will help guide the more specific discussions in this chapter and Chapter 13.

How Consistent Is Development from Person to Person?

1. ***What is the difference between normative and individual development? Why is the longitudinal method more useful than the cross-sectional method for studying individual development?***

Scientists in general seek orderliness in the phenomena they study, and developmental psychologists are no exception. Most developmental psychologists are interested primarily in developmental changes that occur in the same sequence in different people and are at least roughly linked to age. Finding such order contributes to an understanding of ***normative development***, the typical sequence of developmental changes for a group of people. For example, the typical sequence of motor abilities involved in the development of walking might include lifting up the head and chest from a prone position, crawling, pulling oneself up by grasping onto objects, and so on. A normative chart would list the average age at which each ability first occurs.

Developmental psychologists look for orderly developmental sequences partly because such sequences can provide a basis for theories about the nature of the more advanced (later-developing) abilities. Thus, if all children must learn certain other motor skills before they can walk, then those skills (or the basic abilities underlying them) may be part and parcel of the act of walking. Similarly, if all children can solve problems of type *A* before they can solve problems of type *B*, then whatever mental processes are required to solve the former problems may also be required to solve the latter. But development is not always as orderly as developmental psychologists might like it to be. Some developmentalists emphasize ***individual development***—the differences among individuals in developmental paths. They point out that individual development is obscured by the research method most commonly employed in developmental studies.

The easiest and most common method to chart changes with age is the ***cross-sectional method***, in which different groups of people, who vary in age, are tested and compared. In a cross-sectional study of reasoning ability, for example, the same test might be given to a group of 5-year-olds, a group of 8-year-olds, and a group of 12-year-olds. The average score or typical mode of behaving in each age group might then be taken as the norm for that age. This method is useful for detecting the average age at which new abilities emerge, but it tells us little about individual development because it does not track the sequence of changes that occur in any given person. To study individual development a researcher must follow a single set of people over a period of their lives, assessing each at different ages to see how he or she has changed. This method, called the ***longitudinal method***, often requires that both the researchers and the subjects remain involved with the study over many months or years. For that reason, it is not used as often as the cross-sectional method.

■ **2. *How do theories of development vary in their predictions concerning (a) the coherence of development across tasks and (b) the continuity of development across time?***

How Coherent Is Development Across Cognitive Domains?

To what degree does the mind develop as an integrated whole, and to what degree do different mental abilities develop independently of one another? The famous Swiss developmentalist Jean Piaget proposed that the mind develops as a whole. In his theory development entails fundamental changes in the mind, which affect thinking in all realms. At the other extreme, some theorists believe that mental development is principally a matter of learning the relatively specific information needed to perform specific tasks. From this view, a child might develop great skill

The sands of time

Age makes a difference in human behavior, and the research of developmental psychologists focuses on such change. Whether they are studying motor skills, creativity, or some other aspect of cognitive or social life, developmentalists are concerned with consistencies and differences across the life span.

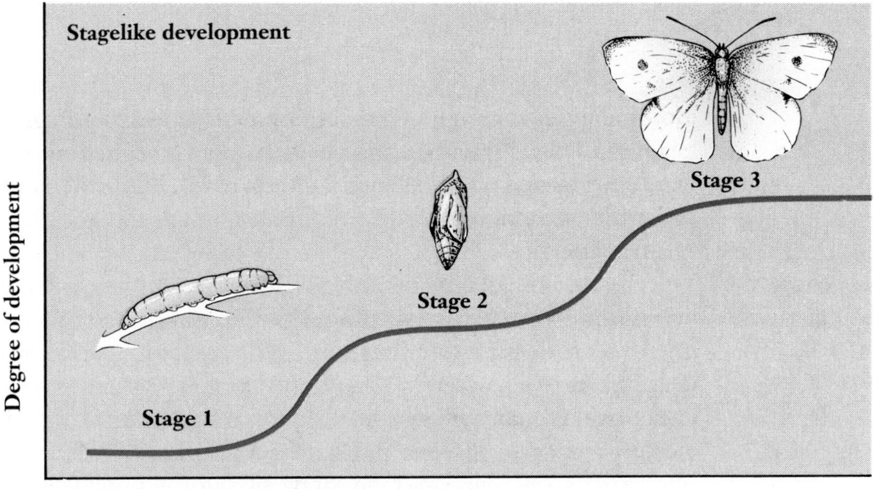

Figure 12.1 ***Stagelike compared to continuous development***

According to some theories, the human mind develops in a stagelike way, analogous to the changes in the different life stages of a butterfly. According to other theories, its development is gradual and continuous, analogous to the fish's increased size from year to year.

in, say, chess without advancing in other realms at all. An intermediate view is that the mind consists of a number of relatively separate compartments or *modules*, which can develop relatively independently of one another. Modular theorists believe that different classes of abilities—such as verbal, visual-spatial, and social abilities—can develop at different paces in different individuals because they are controlled by different modules.

Is Development Stagelike or Continuous?

"Oh, it's just a stage he's going through," is one of the most common (and optimistic) laments of parents. Used this way, *stage* refers simply to the parents' belief that the child's present way of behaving will change. As used by developmental psychologists, however, the term *stage* implies a particular view about the pattern of development. ***Stage theories*** maintain that development is discontinuous, characterized by plateaus (stages) of relatively stable behavior separated by transition periods during which behavior changes rapidly. Piaget's theory is a stage theory; he maintained that children go through a sequence of mental metamorphoses, each producing a distinct way of thinking that lasts for several years. In contrast, ***continuity theories*** maintain that change is gradual and continuous. (See Figure 12.1.)

What Are the Sources of Developmental Change?

The nature-nurture issue, a theme of Chapter 3, arises again now as we think about development. Traditionally, some developmental psychologists have emphasized the role of biological maturation in development (the nature side), and others have emphasized the role of learning (the nurture side). From a *maturationist perspective*, developmental change occurs because of genetically programmed growth, especially growth in the brain, that permits the individual to think in new ways or engage in new kinds of behaviors. From a *learning perspective*, in contrast, change occurs because of the acquisition of new habits and knowledge from experience in the world.

3. *What does it mean to say that most developmental psychologists today are interactionists? In what sense is each individual a force in his or her own development?*

Today, few developmental psychologists can be classed clearly in either camp. Most call themselves *interactionists* to emphasize their concern with how biological maturation and environmental experience combine to produce developmental change. As emphasized in Chapters 3 on genetics and 4 on evolution, genes never work in a vacuum, but instead require a certain environment for their effects to occur. And, as emphasized in Chapter 5's discussion of ecological views of learning, the capacity to learn specific kinds of information depends on genetically controlled, biological preparation. Thus, rather than ask, "Is this developmental change due to biological maturation or to experience?" developmental psychologists today are more likely to ask, "What kind of biological preparation and what kind of experience are needed for this change to occur?"

Ultimately, development emerges from the interaction of genes and environment. But the immediate and observable interaction is not between genes and the environment, but between the *whole person* and the environment. The person at any moment is a structure that has certain behavioral characteristics built into it. Genes and environment have played critical roles in building this structure, but the structure now must also be considered an active force in its own development. Even before birth, the fetus kicking and squirming in the womb is exercising its muscles in ways that help prepare it for life outside. And children in their self-motivated play are constantly developing skills that will help them in later life. Some developmental psychologists—most notably Piaget—have been most interested in understanding how the child's own, self-motivated activities at one stage of life promote growth to the next stage.

What do babies see?
In the early 1960s, the research of Robert Fantz and others undermined a commonly held belief that newborns see nothing but a blur of light and dark. Infants' visual acuity and their interest in looking at patterns are now so well established that parents can buy mobiles and other toys based on Fantz's test stimuli.

Development of Perception and Knowledge in Infancy

Infancy, roughly the first 18 to 24 months after birth, is the time of most rapid developmental change—change that lays the foundation for further development. Since infants (at least early in infancy) can't talk, psychologists can't ask them to describe what they perceive or know. But psychologists can observe infants' actions, and, through carefully designed experiments, can use those actions to draw inferences about infants' perceptual abilities and knowledge.

Perceptual Development

On the day they are born, infants can respond to sensory stimuli. They look toward moving, blinking, or high-contrast visual stimuli; turn toward sounds; turn toward anything that touches their face; turn away from unpleasant odors; and suck a nipple more readily for a sweet liquid than for a sour one. Although the senses are functional at birth, they are not yet fully developed. This is especially true of vision, which is by far the most studied sense and is our focus of attention here.

Visual Acuity

A common technique for measuring infants' visual acuity (ability to see detail) makes use of their natural preference for patterned rather than unpatterned stimuli (Fantz, 1961, 1963; Maurer & Maurer, 1988). In these studies, the patterns are

4. *How do researchers measure visual acuity in infants?*

black-and-white stripes, and the unpatterned stimuli are patches of gray that reflect the same amount of light as the stripes. When a striped patch and a gray patch are placed side by side, each 1 foot away from the infant's eyes, 1-day-old infants spend more time looking at the stripes than at the gray patch only if the stripes are at least 1/10 of an inch thick, suggesting that these infants cannot distinguish narrower stripes from gray. The same procedure reveals that 2-month-old infants can see stripes that are 1/20 of an inch thick and that 8-month-old infants can see stripes that are 1/80 of an inch thick. For comparison, both 6-year-olds and adults can typically see stripes that are about 1/300 of an inch thick. Improvement in visual acuity during infancy is at least partly due to continued maturation of the cones, the receptor cells in the retina that are most important for seeing detail (Yuodelis & Hendrickson, 1986).

Pattern Recognition

5. *What evidence suggests that newborns are predisposed to look at human faces and to learn quickly to recognize the face of their primary caregiver?*

Young infants show a preference not only for patterns over more homogeneous stimuli, but also for some patterns over others. One of the most effective patterns in eliciting attention from newborns is a human face or a schematic version of a face. In some studies, infants as young as a few minutes old were found to follow with their eyes a schematic human face more than other patterns of similar shape and visibility (Goren & others, 1975; Johnson & others, 1991). (See Figure 12.2.) In other studies, infants in their second or third day after birth looked longer at their mother's face than at another woman's face when both faces were present and had the same expressions. (Bushnell & others, 1989; Field & others, 1984). Although these findings are still controversial, they suggest that infants may come into the world predisposed to look at human faces and to learn, very quickly, to recognize and prefer the faces of their primary caregivers.

6. *How are infants' preferences for novelty used to assess their abilities to (a) see different stimuli as different, (b) remember what they have seen, and (c) categorize stimuli?*

In contrast to their preference for the familiar face of their mother, infants tested with other stimuli consistently prefer novelty over familiarity. When shown a new pattern, infants look at it intently at first, and then, over the course of minutes, look at it less and less—a phenomenon referred to as *habituation*. This decline in attention is not due to general fatigue; if a new pattern is substituted for the old one, the infants manifest renewed interest. Infants' preference for novelty can be used to assess their ability to remember what they have seen and their ability to distinguish one stimulus from another. In one experiment, for example, infants of one to three days old were shown a checkerboard for a series of 1-minute trials (Freidman, 1972). They looked less and less at the board each time it was presented, which indicates that they recognized it as the same checkerboard that they had seen before. When a new checkerboard (one with smaller checks) was presented, their looking time increased again, which indicates that they saw the new board as different from the old one.

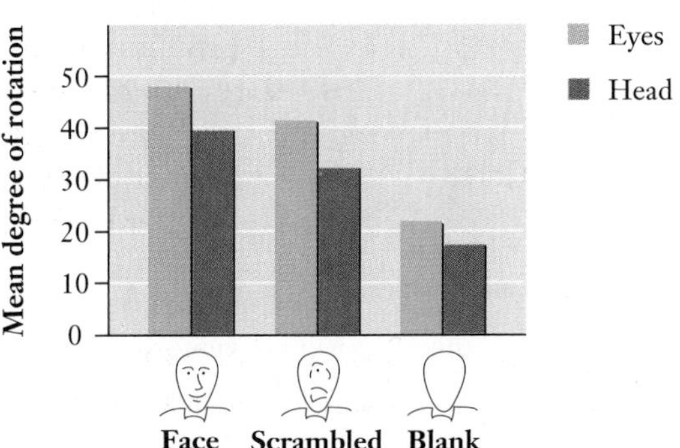

Figure 12.2 ***Newborns' preference to look at a schematic face***

Newborn infants, less than an hour old, were shown either a schematic face, a scrambled face, or a blank face-shaped stimulus. Each stimulus was moved slowly across the infant's field of view and the extent to which the infant rotated his or her head and eyes to follow the stimulus was measured. Although the face elicited only slightly more following than the scrambled face, the difference was statistically significant and has been observed in other experiments as well, using different examples of faces and scrambled faces. (Johnson & others, 1991.)

Experiments using the habituation procedure have shown that as infants mature they make increasingly fine distinctions among different patterns and remember familiar patterns over longer periods. Six-month-olds who were habituated to a set of photographs of faces looked less at those faces than at new ones even when tested two weeks later (Fagan, 1973). Infants also become more sensitive, with age, to the categories to which differing visual stimuli belong. Nine-month-olds who were shown a series of pictures of different varieties of birds subsequently looked more at a picture of a horse than at yet another type of bird (Roberts, 1988). This result implies that the infants had a mental concept of birds, which allowed them to distinguish birds in general from horses, and which itself could become habituated. The ability to form such mental concepts is, of course, a prerequisite for language. Before children can reliably name such objects as birds and horses, they must be able to distinguish them as perceptual classes.

Self-Produced Locomotion and Wariness of Perceived Heights

A good example of a stage shift in development is that which occurs when an infant begins crawling or moving about in other ways, typically between seven and nine months of age. A mobile infant is in many ways qualitatively different from a pre-mobile infant. The mobile infant obtains and explores objects that previously were out of reach, experiences new frustrations and triumphs in the attempt to move around barriers, and elicits new emotional reactions from proud but worried parents (to be discussed in Chapter 13). Research has shown that one rapid developmental consequence of mobility is a new understanding of heights and their potential danger.

■ 7. ***What is the evidence that self-produced locomotion leads to a wariness of heights and that the link is not produced by the experience of falling?***

Eleanor Gibson and Richard Walk (1960) conducted pioneering research on infants' reactions to height, using an apparatus called a *visual cliff* (similar to that shown in Figure 12.3). The apparatus consisted partly of a solid glass table top with a board running across the center. To produce an apparent cliff, a checkerboard-patterned material was placed directly underneath the glass on one side of the center board (the shallow side) and several feet below the glass on the other side of the board (the deep side). Gibson and Walk found that infants who could crawl would readily move off the center board onto the shallow side of the cliff, but would studiously avoid the deep side. Even if their mothers called them from the deep side, they would not crawl in that direction and often cried in apparent frustration.

In later experiments, Joseph Campos and Bennett Bertenthal tested younger infants on the visual cliff to understand how the fear develops. They found that

Courtesy of J. Campos, B. Bertenthal, and R. Kermoian

Figure 12.3 ***Visual cliff***
Although his mother is calling, this child will not venture over the deep side of the visual cliff.

nonmobile infants from 2 to 6 months old showed a decrease in heart rate on both sides of the cliff, but the decrease was greater on the deep side. In contrast, experienced crawlers showed an *increase* in heart rate only on the deep side (Campos & others, 1978). Based on other research, a decreased heart rate was taken to be a sign of interest and an increased heart rate to be a sign of fear. Apparently, the noncrawling infants could see the depth below them and were interested in it, but were not afraid of it. Subsequent experiments showed that this difference was not due simply to age. When crawling and noncrawling infants of the same age were placed on the cliff, the former again showed an increased heart rate and the latter a decreased heart rate (Bertenthal & Campos, 1990).

What is the connection between mobility and fear of the visual cliff? Most people would guess that mobile infants learn to fear drop-offs through experience with falling—for example, by crawling off the edge of a bed and falling onto the floor. But subsequent experiments have shown that this explanation is inadequate. Six- and seven-month-olds who had not yet learned to crawl were given approximately 40 hours of practice using a walker, which allowed them to move around on their own without falling. When subsequently placed on the deep side of the cliff, these infants, like those who could crawl, and unlike those who could not crawl and had not used the walker, showed an increased heart rate (Bertenthal & others, 1984; Campos & others, 1992). Apparently, self-produced locomotion promotes fear and avoidance of heights even without the experience of falling. The mechanism of this effect is not known, but Bertenthal and Campos (1990) propose that the effect stems from the new kinds of attention that the mobile infant must pay to sensory experiences. To move successfully, either alone or with a walker, infants must learn to adjust their movements to the changes they perceive in the environment as they move, and this ability may be a prerequisite for wariness of heights.

Regardless of the precise mechanism by which it comes about, the link between self-produced locomotion and wariness of heights is probably no coincidence. In the course of human evolution, infants who quickly developed a fear of heights when they began to move around on their own were surely more likely to survive than those who didn't. A fear of heights before the infant became mobile would provide little if any advantage and might cause the infant to become distressed when carried. According to this reasoning, natural selection may have provided us with (a) a tendency to fear heights, and (b) a triggering mechanism that causes this tendency to manifest itself when self-produced locomotion begins.

Early Knowledge About Physical Reality

You and I share certain assumptions about the nature of physical reality. We assume, for example, that objects continue to exist after they move out of view, that two objects cannot occupy the same space at the same time, and that when an object moves from one place to another it must do so along a continuous path. How did we acquire these assumptions, which serve us so well in our constant interactions with the physical world?

■ **8. *What are three differing views concerning the origin of fundamental concepts about physical reality, and how do infants' early behaviors tend to support Piaget's view?***

Empiricist philosophers such as Berkeley and Helmholtz argued that these assumptions are learned gradually in infancy through the same principles that apply to all other instances of learning. In contrast, nativist philosophers such as Descartes and Kant argued that at least some of these assumptions are innate and necessary to further mental development. An intermediate view—best represented by Piaget (1936)—is that we come into the world not with inborn assumptions about physical reality, but with inborn tendencies to manipulate objects in ways that inevitably teach us about that reality.

Infant Behavior Interpreted as Exploration

Consistent with Piaget's view, infants in many ways are little scientists, exploring and experimenting upon the world around them. Even newborns in their first day or two after birth look longer at new objects than at familiar ones. Later, they become especially interested in objects over which they can exert some control.

By two months of age, babies show more interest and delight in a mobile that moves in response to their own bodily movement than in an electrically propelled mobile that they do not control (Watson, 1972). Four-month-olds learned quickly to make a particular movement to turn on a small array of lights, but lost interest once they became proficient, and responded only occasionally. However, when the conditions were changed so that a different movement was needed to turn on the lights, the infants regained interest and made another burst of responses (Papousek, 1969). The renewed interest must have been generated by the new relationship between a response and the lights, because the lights themselves were unchanged. Apparently, the babies were interested not so much in the lights as in the ability to control them.

By five or six months of age, infants begin to explore objects with their hands and eyes together in a manner that researchers call *examining* (Ruff, 1986). They hold the object in front of their eyes, turn it from side to side, pass it from one hand to the other, squeeze it, mouth it, and in various other ways act as if they are deliberately testing its properties. Such behavior declines dramatically as the infant becomes familiar with a given object, but returns in full force when a new object, differing in shape or texture, is substituted for the old one (Ruff, 1986, 1989).

Piaget's View of Infant Cognitive Development

■ **9.** ***Why did Piaget refer to infancy as the* sensorimotor *stage? What did he see as the main developmental task during this stage? How did he test infants' progress in that development?***

Piaget was fascinated by the way infants manipulate objects. He observed such behavior closely in his own three children and mapped its increasing sophistication through the months of infancy. Partly from these observations, he developed the idea that, to infants, knowledge *is* action. Piaget (1936) argued that early in infancy children have no mental symbols, so their only way to think about things is to act on them, that is, to scan them with their eyes, suck on them, grasp them, and so on. He referred to infancy as the ***sensorimotor stage*** of intellectual development, because intelligence at that stage consists of motor actions toward objects and the immediate sensory feedback from those actions. Earliest actions are purely reflexive, but the infant is sensitive to their consequences and repeats those that deliver interesting consequences. Gradually, the infant's actions toward objects become more deliberate and varied.

Besides observing his children's spontaneous explorations of the physical world, Piaget formally tested their understanding of its principles. Piaget reasoned that to succeed at finding a hidden object, an infant must understand that the object exists even when it is out of view. Piaget referred to this understanding as ***object permanence***, and his test results suggested that it develops gradually during the first 18 months of life.

To chart the development of object permanence, Piaget invented three different kinds of search problems, which have since been used by other researchers, with hundreds of infants, and have produced results remarkably similar to Piaget's (see Figure 12.4). In the *simple hiding problem*, an attractive toy is shown to the infant and then is placed under a napkin directly in front of the infant. Infants younger than 6 months typically follow the toy with their eyes as it disappears under the napkin, but do not reach for it once it is there and quickly display a loss of interest. They do not lack the ability to reach; they consistently reach for the toy when it is placed on top of the napkin. What they lack, according to Piaget, is ob-

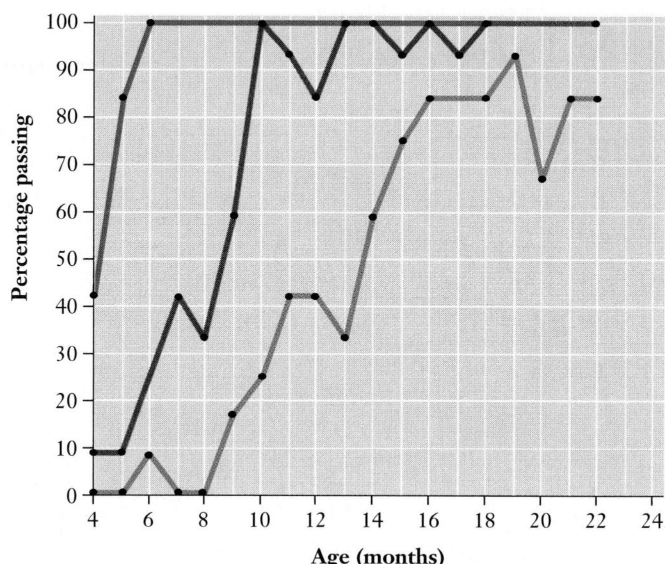

Figure 12.4 ***Improvement in finding hidden objects***
This graph shows the percentage of infants at various ages who succeeded at each of three kinds of hiding problems. The problems were as described in the text, except that objects were hidden under cups rather than under napkins. (Adapted from Wishart & Bower, 1984.)

ject permanence; they do not understand that an object continues to exist when out of sight.

By 8 months of age, most infants solve the simple hiding problem, but fail to solve the *changed hiding-place problem.* In this test, the toy is first hidden under one napkin for a series of trials and the infant retrieves it each time. Then the toy is hidden under another napkin, right next to the first. Despite having watched the object disappear under the new napkin, the child reaches to the original napkin. Piaget concluded that the 8-month-old's emerging object permanence is too fragile to prevail over a learned motor habit. The child's understanding of objects is still tightly bound to past actions.

By about 12 months, most infants solve the changed hiding-place problem, but fail the *invisible displacement problem.* In this test, the infant first watches as the researcher's hand closes around the toy, hiding it from view. In plain sight, the researcher's closed hand then moves under the napkin and deposits the toy. When the hand is brought back into view, the 12-month-old looks in and under it for the toy, but does not look under the napkin. According to Piaget, these actions reveal that the infant now understands that objects continue to exist when out of view and can be moved from one place to another when in view, but does not understand that objects can be moved from one place to another when out of view. Not until about 18 months do infants succeed at this problem, by which time, according to Piaget, their understanding of object permanence and the possible movements of objects is fairly complete.

Evidence of Early Understanding of Physical Principles

■ **10.** ***What evidence has led some researchers to believe that infants understand object permanence and other physical principles well before the age proposed by Piaget?***

Piaget's findings about the failures of young infants to retrieve hidden objects have been repeated many times, but his conclusion that they lack the concept of object permanence has been challenged. Recent studies suggest that infants as young as 3 months expect the continued existence of hidden objects and make the same basic assumptions about the physical properties and movement capabilities of those objects that you and I make.

Such studies capitalize on infants' tendencies to look longer at unexpected than at expected events. In one, conducted by Renée Baillargeon (1987) and described in Figure 12.5, infants behaved as if they were more surprised (looked

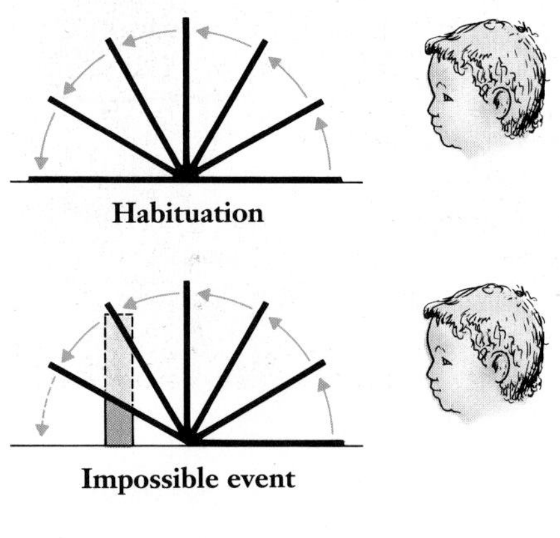

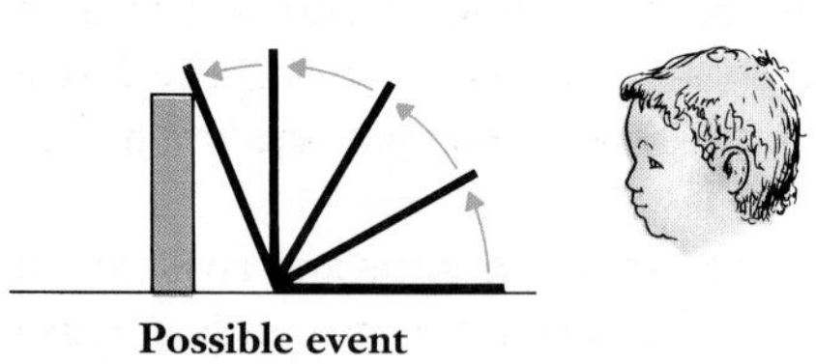

Figure 12.5 ***Evidence for object permanence in very young infants***
Baillargeon (1987) first showed infants a hinged screen rotating back and forth over a 180° arc until they were bored with it (habituation). Then, using mirrors, she created the illusion that a brightly colored object had been put just behind the place where the screen was hinged. Finally, she manipulated the screen to produce either of two events, one possible, the other impossible. In the impossible event, the screen rotated over the entire arc, as if the object behind it magically disappeared and then reappeared on each rotation. In the possible event, the screen stopped in each rotation at the place where it would have bumped into the object had it been physically present. Infants as young as 3½ months old looked longer at the impossible than at the possible event, suggesting that they were more surprised by it. (Adapted from Baillargeon, 1987.)

longer) when a rotating screen seemed to pass through and obliterate an object hidden behind it than when the screen seemed to stop at the point where it would bump into the object. In another, conducted by Elizabeth Spelke and her colleagues (1992), researchers showed 3- and 4-month-olds a solid shelf, then placed a screen in front of the shelf to block it from view, and then dropped an object so that the infants saw it fall behind the screen directly above the place where they had previously seen the shelf. When the screen was removed, infants who saw the object lying on the floor under the shelf looked longer than those who saw the object lying on top of the shelf. Apparently, infants as young as 3 months understand at some level that solid objects, whether in or out of view, cannot pass through other solid objects.

Based on such findings, Baillargeon and Spelke contend that infants know a great deal about the general properties of objects before they develop the motor capacity to manipulate them and that this knowledge may well be innate, as proposed by the nativist philosophers. If Baillargeon and Spelke are correct, manual examination helps infants to learn about the specific properties of specific objects, but is not needed for them to understand the general principles that apply to all objects. Why, then, do young infants fail at Piaget's search tasks? According to Spelke, young infants may not yet be able to coordinate their arm and hand movements with their mental understanding (Spelke & others, 1992). Their reaching may be guided only by their direct vision, not by their memory of a hidden object's location. At present, many researchers are pursuing the ideas about infants' abilities suggested by Baillargeon and Spelke, and such research may soon tell us whether those ideas or Piaget's are more correct.

Development of Language

At the same time that infants are interacting with and learning about the physical world, they are also interacting with people and beginning to learn language. Of all the things that people can do, none seems more complex than understanding and speaking a language. Thousands of words and countless subtle grammatical rules for modifying and combining words must be learned. Yet nearly all people master their native language by the time they grow up; in fact, most are well en route to this mastery by the time they are 3 or 4 years old. How can children too young to tie their shoes or understand that two plus two equals four succeed at such a complex task? Most developmentalists agree that language learning requires a combination of innate mechanisms that predispose children to it, coupled with an environment that provides adequate models and an opportunity to practice. In this section, we will first chart the normal course of language development; then examine innate and environmental prerequisites for language; and finally contrast the way humans learn language with attempts to teach language to chimpanzees.

The Course of Language Development

Early Perception of Speech Sounds

Infants seem to treat speech as something special as soon as they are born and maybe even when they are still in the womb. When allowed to choose between tape-recorded sounds by sucking in different ways on a nipple, 3-day-old infants chose to listen to human speech rather than to other sounds such as instrumental music (Butterfield & Siperstein, 1974) and chose their own mother's voice over that of another woman (DeCasper & Fifer, 1980). The mother's voice is audible in

(a)

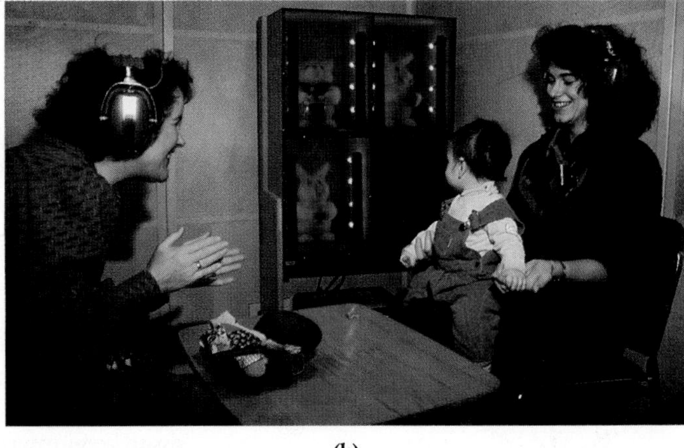

(b)

Figure 12.6 ***A procedure for testing infants' abilities to detect changes in a speech sound***

The infant sits on the mother's lap and attends to a toy held by the researcher while a speech sound is played repetitively through a loudspeaker (a). Occasionally the sound changes, and very shortly after each change an attractive toy to the infant's right is lit up and begins to move (b). Thus, the infant is rewarded by the sight of the toy for turning to the right when the speech sound changes. After the infant is well trained in this procedure, the head-turn response can serve as an index that the infant distinguishes the new sound from the old one. The mother and researcher wear headphones that prevent them from hearing the critical sound and inadvertently cuing the infant as to when to turn. (Werker & Tees, 1992.)

■ **11.** ***What is the evidence that as infants get older they lose the ability to distinguish between different sounds that belong to the same phoneme category in their native language?***

the womb, so humans may begin to recognize and prefer that sound even before they are born. Anthony DeCasper and Melanie Spence (1986) found that infants whose mothers had recited a particular prose passage each day during the last 6 weeks of pregnancy preferred listening to that passage over another one when they were tested shortly after birth.

Very young infants not only are attuned to the overall patterns and rhythms of speech, but also can distinguish the individual vowel and consonant sounds that are the *phonemes* of speech. One experimental technique is to allow the infant to suck on a pacifier that is wired to trigger the playing of a particular sound each time a sucking response occurs. When the infant becomes bored with a sound, as indicated by a reduced rate of sucking, the sound is changed (maybe from *pa* to *ba*). If the rate of sucking increases immediately thereafter, the assumption is that the infant hears the new sound as different from the previous one. Another method, which can be used with infants older than 5 months, is described in Figure 12.6.

Experiments using these techniques indicate that infants between about 1 and 6 months of age can hear the difference between very similar sounds, but that after 6 months they begin to *lose* the ability to hear the differences between different sounds that are classed as the same phoneme in their native language (Kuhl, 1987). Thus, children growing up in an English-speaking culture lose the ability to distinguish among different /t/ sounds, which belong to the same phoneme category in English but not in Hindi (Werker & others, 1981; Werker & Tees, 1992). Similarly, children growing up in a Japanese culture lose the ability to distinguish between the English /l/ and /r/, which belong to the same phoneme category in Japanese (Eimas, 1975).

Cooing and Babbling

From birth, infants can cry and produce various other vocal signs of distress, but at about 2 months they begin to produce a new, more speech-like category of sounds called *cooing*, which consists of repeated drawn out vowels (*oooh-oooh, eeeh-eeeh*). Between about 4 and 6 months, cooing changes gradually to *babbling*, which consists of repeated consonant-and-vowel sounds such as *paa-paa-paa* or *tooda-tooda*. Cooing and babbling occur most often when the infant is happy and seem to be forms of play that have evolved to exercise the infant's vocal apparatus in preparation for speech.

Coos and the earliest babbles are apparently not influenced by the spoken sounds that infants hear. Deaf infants coo and begin to babble at about the same age and in the same manner as hearing infants (Lenneberg, 1969), and early babbles are as likely to contain foreign language sounds as native-language sounds (Locke, 1983). By about 10 months of age, however, hearing infants begin to babble in ways that sound increasingly like their native language, and deaf infants who are exposed to a sign language begin to babble with their hands—repeating over and over some of the hand movements that are components of words in the language they see around them (Pettito & Marentette, 1991). Eventually, recognizable words appear in the hearing infant's vocal babbling and the deaf infant's manual babbling.

First Words

■ **12. *When is a word really a word?***

I can use examples from my own son's development to illustrate a general principle of early word acquisition. When Scott was about 10 months old, my wife and I noticed that some of his babblelike sounds were not random, but occurred reliably in specific contexts. He would say *ticka-ticka-ticka* while tickling things, *gooda-gooda-gooda* while playfully eating baby food, and *hewo* into the receiver of our telephone when we let him play with it. We excitedly recorded these as our son's "first words." But now I have to ask: Were they really words? A word is a *symbol* (see Chapter 11). A symbol is something that *refers* to something outside of itself—some object, action, event, characteristic, or abstract idea. Did Scott use *tickle*, *good*, or *hello* to refer to anything, or were the sounds simply part of his action of tickling things, eating, and playing with the telephone, which he had learned by imitating my wife and me? There is no way to answer this question with certainty, but systematic observations have shown that babies very commonly produce word-like sounds as components of other actions before they begin to produce them in a clearly referential way (Greenfield & Smith, 1976). Some developmental psychologists refer to these earliest wordlike sounds as *performatives* to distinguish them from words that serve true symbolizing functions. A performative can be defined as a wordlike sound that the child has learned to produce in a particular context (such as playing with the telephone) without knowing that the sound has meaning.

No sharp dividing line exists between performatives and true words. The vocalization that we recorded as our son's sixth "word" was *ba*. At first he would say *ba* only after he had already been given the bottle, so the sound may well have been a performative. He would say *ba-ba-ba-ba* as soon as he got the bottle, as part of the joyous act of taking it into his hands, and occasionally would repeat the sound between bouts of sucking. Eventually, however, he began to use the sound in different contexts. For example, one time he pointed to his bottle on the kitchen shelf and happily said *ba*. Now, at what may have been his first true use of a word, he seemed to be using the sound to label the object he saw. It is significant, too, that in this early use of *ba* as a label he was not hungry or asking for the bottle—he refused it when it was subsequently offered—but was simply pointing it out. A general rule, based on observations of many babies, is that early words are usually used first to name things that are present, and only later to ask for things (Bloom & Lahey, 1978).

First words

Naming objects is an important step in the mastery of language. It is also a source of great delight to infants and their caregivers. Here 1-year-old Genevieve uses her favorite word, *light*.

Mapping the World into Words

New words come slowly at first, but then the rate begins to accelerate. By the third birthday and for several years thereafter, the typical child is learning words at a phenomenal rate—an average of one or two every waking hour (Miller, 1981). Relatively few of these are explicitly taught to the child; most are learned contextually, through inferences drawn from the way others use the words. How does the child draw these inferences?

■ **13.** ***How do children link new words that they hear to appropriate referents in their environment?***

Of course a speaker's gestures, such as pointing, help children pick out the references to new words. In addition, by the time they are two years old, children understand enough words and grammar to extract meaning from linguistic context (Gleitman & Gleitman, 1992). Thus, if they are shown a videotaped scene and told that "The duck and bunny are biffing," two-year-olds—who understand *duck* and *bunny* and tacitly know that words ending in *-ing* refer to actions—can infer that *biffing* means whatever the duck and bunny are both doing.

Another aid in vocabulary learning seems to be a natural tendency for children to link new words with previously unnamed objects or events, rather than with objects or events for which the child already has a name (Clark, 1987; Golinkoff & others, 1992). In one experiment, for example, 3- and 4-year-olds were presented with toy animals for which they already had names (a pig, a sheep, and a cow) plus one for which they did not have a name (a tapir). When they heard the novel word *gombe* in the presence of these objects, all of the children applied it to the novel animal (Clark, 1987).

Extending Words to Fit Appropriate Categories

■ **14.** ***What do children's overextensions and underextensions of new words tell us about the meanings they ascribe to those words?***

In addition to linking new words to their immediate referents, children must learn how to *extend* each new word to new referents. Common nouns such as *ball* refer to categories of objects, and a full understanding is demonstrated when the child applies the word to all members of the category and not to nonmembers.

Often children *overextend* new words, using them more broadly than adult usage would allow. For a while, a child might use *ball* for anything round or spherical. My son overextended the word *dooda*, which was the name of a song on his favorite record. The only visible feature that distinguished the *dooda* record from the others in his set was its purple color, so he assumed that *dooda* must mean purple. For several months he referred to all purple things as *dooda*. Based on an analysis of a large collection of overextensions, Eve Clark (1973) proposed that young children implicitly define new words in terms of one or a few of the features of the objects that they have learned to label. Thus, a child who hears *ball* in association with a specific object might take the most prominent feature of the object—its roundness—as the defining characteristic and apply the word to all round objects.

Children also *underextend* new words, using them more narrowly than adults do (Anglin, 1977). In these cases, apparently the child first learns the new word as if it were a proper noun applying only to the original referent and then learns gradually to apply it also to other objects. Thus, a child might first use *dog* to refer only to a particular dog, then learn that the term also applies to another particular dog, and finally learn that the term can be applied to new animals that resemble the original referents in various ways.

In sum, children apparently understand some new nouns in terms of specific features, which leads to overextensions, and understand other new nouns in terms of overall similarity to the original referent, which leads to underextensions.

Putting Words Together and Using Grammatical Rules

All children go through a relatively prolonged period during which each of their utterances is only one word long. This one-word stage persists well beyond the age at which they can understand and respond appropriately to multiword sentences (Hirsh-Pasek & Golinkoff, 1991). Moreover, one-word utterances often express multiword ideas, which parents can interpret from the context and accompanying gestures (Greenfield & Smith, 1976). Thus, the statement *Ball* may mean "This is a ball," or "Billy is kicking the ball," or "Give me the ball." Only after several months of such one-word statements do children (typically at 18 to 24 months) begin to put two words together. From that point on, the average length of utterances increases gradually (Brown, 1973).

When children do begin to put words together, they typically use only content words (mostly nouns and verbs, with some adjectives and adverbs), avoiding non-content words such as articles (*a*, *the*) and prepositions (*in*, *under*), and arrange the content words in the grammatically correct sequence for simple, active sentences. For an English-speaking child, this means that subjects are placed before verbs, and verbs before objects. A child at the two-word stage will say "Billy kick" to mean that Billy is kicking the ball, and "Kick Billy" to mean that someone is kicking Billy. Upon reaching the three-word stage, the child will say "Billy kick ball," with the words in the correct order. Apparently, children learn the rules of word order for simple sentences in the active voice before they begin to produce such sentences. The ability to understand and produce passive-voiced sentences (such as "The ball was kicked by Billy") comes much later, typically at about age 5 (Bever, 1970).

15. ***What is some evidence that young children use grammatical rules and do not just mimic constructions that they hear?***

When children first acquire a new grammatical rule, such as adding *-ed* to the end of a verb to create the past tense, they almost invariably overgeneralize the rule at first. That is, they use it in a more consistent fashion than do adult users of the language (Bates & others, 1987; Kuczaj, 1977). The 3-year-old who says "kicked," "played," and "laughed," also says "goed," "thinked," and "swimmed." Similarly, children who have just learned to add *-s* to pluralize nouns will talk about many *mouses*, *sheeps*, and *childs*. This overgeneralization confirms that children really know the rule. If they followed the rule only when adults did, their usage might be attributed to simple imitation. As further evidence that their grammar is based on rules, young children have been shown to use the rules with made-up words that they had never heard before (see Figure 12.7).

This is a wug.

Now there is another one.
There are two of them.
There are two _____.

Figure 12.7 ***One wug and two _____?*** With this test, Jean Berko found that children who had just begun to use the rule of forming plurals by adding *-s* would use the rule correctly even for words they had never heard before. (From Berko, 1958.)

Children are not taught the rules of grammar explicitly; nobody sits a 2-year-old down and tries to explain how to create infinitives, possessives, or past-tense verbs. Some parents correct their children's grammar, but even this is rare (Brown & Hanlon, 1970), and long-term experiments in preschools have shown that a deliberate program of correcting grammar has little effect on rule acquisition (de Villiers & de Villiers, 1979). Through their own devices, children actively (and probably unconsciously) infer grammar rules from examples of rule-based language spoken around them and to them.

Internal and External Supports for Language Development

There is no doubt that we enter the world in many ways pre-equipped for language. We are born with (a) anatomical structures in our throat (the larynx and pharynx) that enable us to produce a broader range of sounds than any other mammal, (b) a preference to listen to speech and an ability to distinguish among the basic speech sounds, (c) mechanisms that cause us to go through a period of cooing and babbling, and (d) brain areas that apparently are biologically specialized for language (Broca's and Wernicke's areas, discussed in Chapter 11). There is also no doubt that most of us are born into a social world that provides rich opportunities for learning language. We are surrounded by language from birth on, and when we begin to use language we achieve many rewards through this extraordinarily effective means of communication.

Evidence for an Inborn Grammar-Learning Mechanism

The linguist Noam Chomsky (1965) has long argued that linguistic rules are too complex for young children to learn through their general intelligence alone. He contends that children must have an inborn understanding of elements common to all languages (universal grammar) and inborn guidelines for acquiring the unique rules of their culture's language. Chomsky refers to these innate grammar-learning aids as the ***language-acquisition device***, usually called by its acronym, ***LAD***.

■ **16. *How is the concept of a LAD supported by (a) cross-cultural studies of language acquisition, (b) a study of creole languages, and (c) observations concerning a particular genetic disorder?***

To learn about the characteristics of the LAD, Dan Slobin (1973, 1985) studied language development in various cultures and found some underlying regularities. For example, he found that grammatical rules involving word order are almost always learned earlier than rules involving suffixes or prefixes. Thus, children learning English acquire the rule that the subject of a sentence precedes the verb and the object comes after the verb (*Billy kick ball*) before they acquire the rule that past tense is created by adding the suffix *-ed*. In some other languages, subjects and objects are distinguished by suffixes added to the nouns, rather than by word order, and children learning those languages begin to mark subjects and objects later than do children learning English. From this, Slobin suggests that one innate guideline in acquiring grammar is *Pay attention to the order of words*. Other guidelines he proposed concern more sophisticated aspects of grammar, acquired after word order rules.

Another approach to learning about the innate basis for grammar acquisition is to study new languages that emerge when people with different native languages colonize the same region. The first generation of such colonists communicate with a primitive, grammarless collection of words taken from their various native languages, referred to as a ***pidgin language***. Subsequently, the pidgin develops into a true language, with a full range of grammatical rules, at which point it is called a ***creole language*** (not to be confused with Creole, a language spoken in Haiti and by some southern Louisianans, which is just one example of a creole language). Derek Bickerton (1984) has studied creole languages from around the world and has arrived at two quite startling and controversial conclusions. First, creole languages appear to become fully developed in one generation by the children of the original colonists. Apparently, the children impose grammatical rules on the pidgin they hear and use those rules consistently in their own speech—powerful evidence, in Bickerton's view, that children's minds are innately predisposed to grammar. Second, Bickerton concluded that creole languages that developed in different parts of the world from different combinations of parent languages, are more similar to one another in grammatical structure than are long-standing languages. Bickerton takes this, too, as evidence for innate grammar. Other languages have evolved away from the grammatical constructions that are most natural to the human mind, but creole languages have not existed long enough to undergo this transformation.

Further evidence for an innate grammar-learning mechanism comes from studies of a rare genetic disorder called *developmental dysphasia*, which at least in some family lines appears to be caused by a single dominant gene (Gopnik & Crago, 1991). Children with this disorder develop normal general intelligence, eventually acquire an adequate vocabulary, and manage to communicate effectively; but they never become fluent in the use of grammatical rules (Gopnik, 1990a & b). Most difficult for them are rules that involve suffixes or prefixes, such as adding *-s* to produce plural nouns or *-ed* to produce past-tense verbs. Even adults with this disorder have difficulty with the *wug* test, illustrated in Figure 12.7. When they do succeed on such tests, they appear to rely on conscious application of a memorized rule, not on the intuitive, automatic process that the rest of us would use (Gopnik & Crago, 1991). In contrast, people with other inherited forms of mental retardation are remarkably unimpaired in grammar acquisition (Bellugi & others, 1990; Curtiss, 1981). Apparently, the human brain contains special grammar-learning mechanisms that are distinct from the mechanisms that underlie other learning abilities.

The Critical-Period Hypothesis

■ **17.** ***How does the case of Genie and other evidence support the view that grammar, but not vocabulary, is learned more readily in early childhood than later in life?***

In 1970 a 13-year-old girl, referred to as Genie in the psychological literature, was rescued from the inhuman conditions in which her deranged father and dominated, partially blind mother had raised her. From shortly after birth until her rescue, Genie had been isolated in a small bedroom and had heard very little speech. She understood a few words, but could not string words together and had learned no language (Curtiss, 1977; Rymer, 1993). When finally discovered, she was placed in a foster home where she was exposed to English much as infants normally are and also received tutorial help. In this environment, she eventually acquired a large vocabulary and learned to produce meaningful, intelligent statements; but even after seven years of language practice, at age 20, her use and understanding of grammar lagged way behind other indices of her intelligence (Curtiss, 1977). A typical sentence she produced was "I hear music ice cream truck," and after hearing a sentence such as "The boy hit the girl" she would be unsure as to who had hit whom.

The case of Genie is one line of evidence supporting *the critical-period hypothesis*—the idea that the LAD functions more effectively in childhood than later in life (Lenneberg, 1969). This hypothesis, implicit in Bickerton's explanation of the origin of creole languages, is also supported by evidence that adults who move to a new language environment rarely become as grammatically fluent in the new language as children do (Johnson & Newport, 1989). Also, deaf people who have learned no other formal language become and remain much more fluent in the grammar of American Sign Language if they have the opportunity to learn it before age 12 than if they are first exposed to language after that age (Newport, 1991).

■ **18.** ***In what special ways do people speak to infants, and what evidence suggests that this helps their language development?***

The Language-Acquisition Support System

In contrast to Chomsky and others who focus on the role of inborn language-learning mechanisms, theorists within the social-learning tradition focus on the role of the social environment in linguistic development. Because humans have a strong desire to learn about and communicate with each other, parents and children pay close attention to each other's gestures and utterances and modify their own to get their point across. Whereas Chomsky assumes that infants must learn language by extracting principles from complex adult conversation, social learning theorists point out that adults speak much more simply and clearly to young children than they do to other adults (Snow, 1984). There may be a LAD, as Chomsky posits, but equally important from the social learning perspective is the ***LASS***—the ***language-acquisition support system***—provided by the social world into which the infant is born (Bruner, 1983).

Taking account of the listener
Most people automatically simplify their speech when talking to young children. Even 4-year-olds addressing a younger child will deliberately slow their rate of speech, choose simple words and grammatical structures, and gesture broadly.

Research in the social learning tradition has shown that when adults speak to a young child they often simplify their speech in ways that seem ideally suited to help the child learn word meanings and simple grammatical constructions. Typically, they speak in short sentences that focus on the here-and-now, repeat salient words, and use gestures to help convey their meaning (Snow, 1984). A 6-month-old playing with a ball might be told, "Oh, you have a *ball*. A nice *ball*. What a pretty *ball*." Such speech is often referred to as *motherese* (though it is not just mothers who speak this way to infants), and evidence suggests that it does help infants learn language. In one study, 2- to 3-year-olds whose mothers had spoken the simplest forms of motherese to them during the previous year spoke more maturely than did those whose mothers had used more complex language (Furrow & others, 1979). Another study revealed that the degree to which mothers commented to their 13-month-olds about aspects of the environment to which the infant was attending correlated positively with the infants' subsequent rate of vocabulary development (Dunham & Dunham, 1992). The correlation held only when the mother was the child's principle caregiver during the day, suggesting that the mother's behavior was indeed the causal factor in the correlation.

Other researchers, however, have argued that motherese, at least as we know it, is not universal, yet language acquisition is. Bambi Schieffelin and Elinor Ochs (1983) found that the Kalikuli people of the New Guinea rain forest believe there is no reason to speak to infants who cannot yet speak themselves. These infants hear no motherese, but they go everywhere with their mothers and constantly hear the speech of adults and children. Once Kalikuli children do begin to speak, adults help them not so much by simplifying their own speech as by explicitly pointing out the proper way to say things. Apparently, large variations can occur in the LASS without impairing children's ability to learn language.

Can Chimpanzees Learn Human Language?

As we have been using the term, language is a means of expression using a system of agreed-upon symbols that permits communication and facilitates thought. Is it, then, a uniquely human attainment, or can nonhuman animals acquire anything like it? Most attempts to teach language to nonhumans have used chimpanzees as subjects because they are the species most closely related to us. At first, researchers tried to teach chimps to speak, but chimpanzees lack the vocal apparatus to produce speech sounds (Kellogg, 1968). The supreme accomplishment in spoken language was that of a chimp named Viki, who could mouth barely recognizable renditions of four words: *Papa*, *Mama*, *cup*, and *up* (Hayes & Hayes, 1951).

■ **19. *Why did the Gardners succeed in training a chimp to use a language, whereas previous chimp language projects had failed? What questions were subsequently raised by Terrace?***

To circumvent the problem of vocalization, Allen and Beatrix Gardner (1978) began in 1966 to teach a chimp named Washoe to use American Sign Language (ASL). A system of hand signals used by deaf people to communicate, ASL has all the structural characteristics of language and none of the vocal requirements. Chimpanzees have flexible fingers and are expert mimics of movements, so ASL seemed ideally suited to their physical abilities. Indeed, Washoe learned to produce and respond to many signs, and researchers have since trained other chimpanzees, a gorilla, and an orangutan in ASL (Miles, 1983; Patterson & Linden, 1981). Early reports and films, shown on *Nova* and other television programs, seemed to suggest that the apes were saying all kinds of wonderful things. Some even suggested that a chimp might soon answer questions such as, "What is it like to be a chimpanzee?"

By 1980, however, the picture changed when Herbert Terrace, who had trained a chimp in ASL, began to question the chimp's abilities. Terrace argued that

Nim, Ernie, and Terrace

Although Terrace's chimp Nim learned no grammar, the animal did learn to make many signs appropriately. Here Nim signs "hug" while Terrace holds the puppet Ernie.

Figure 12.8 ***Kanzi using the lexigram keyboard***

Each symbol is a different word. When the chimpanzee (Kanzi, in this case) depresses a key, it is illuminated, both on the keyboard and on a larger screen that the trainer can see.

his chimp showed no evidence of grammar acquisition and seemed to use signs almost entirely as operant responses—that is, as tools to get immediate rewards—rather than as symbols to refer to objects or events (Terrace, 1985; Terrace & others, 1980). Terrace had named his chimp Neam Chimpsky (nicknamed Nim) to poke gentle fun at the linguist Noam Chomsky, the leading advocate of the view that only humans can learn language, which Terrace had hoped to disprove. In the end, ironically, Chimpsky convinced Terrace that Chomsky was more right than wrong. Terrace challenged other researchers to prove that their chimps had learned rules of grammar and used signs as symbols.

One researcher to take up the challenge was Sue Savage-Rumbaugh, who had been training chimps to communicate not with ASL but with an invented language in which the words were geometric figures called *lexigrams* arranged on a keyboard (see Figure 12.8). She conducted many experiments to understand the ways in which her chimps' use of lexigrams did or did not resemble human language. Also, in 1981 she began to work with a young pygmy chimpanzee named Kanzi, whose performance soon outstripped that of other language-using apes. Pygmy chimpanzees (*Pan paniscus*) have been reported to be better communicators in their natural environment than common chimpanzees (*Pan trolodytes*) (Susman, 1984), the species to which Washoe, Nim, and the other language-trained chimps before Kanzi belonged.

Let's now examine the training methods and results of the chimp language projects and compare the chimps' accomplishments to those of human children.

Conditions for Learning

Children learn language eagerly and easily while interacting with language users who haven't given a shred of thought to how to teach it. In contrast, the language training experienced by chimps has been more systematic and deliberate.

■ **20.** ***What were the differences among the training methods used with Washoe, Nim, and Kanzi? How did each compare with the conditions in which children learn language?***

Washoe was surrounded constantly by people who used ASL with each other and with her, much as a child is surrounded by language users, but she also received systematic training (Gardner & Gardner, 1989). Using operant conditioning procedures, her trainers rewarded her with treats and affection for appropriate uses of and responses to ASL signs, and they showed her new signs by molding her hand into the proper positions. Terrace (1985), who had been a student of Skinner's and was well known for his previous research on operant conditioning, made even more use of operant conditioning with Nim than the Gardners did with Washoe. The Gardners contend that Nim's relatively poor language learning compared with Washoe's might be attributed to Nim's more formal training and the relative lack of spontaneous ASL use with and around him (Gardner & Gardner, 1989).

Savage-Rumbaugh used systematic operant conditioning to teach her lexigram language to several common chimps, before she hit upon a very different method with the pygmy chimp Kanzi. As an infant, Kanzi was allowed to run free in the lab while his mother was being trained at the lexigram keyboard. Quite unexpectedly he learned about 30 lexigrams simply by watching her. When he was finally allowed to use the keyboard himself, he was not deliberately trained as other chimps had been (Savage-Rumbaugh & others, 1986, 1990). His hand was never guided to a particular lexigram, and he was never systematically rewarded for naming objects or for selecting objects named to him. Rather, he was constantly free but not forced to communicate with his caretakers, using the stationary keyboard in the lab and a portable one outdoors. Kanzi's caretakers used both spoken English and lexigrams with and around him, and responded to his lexigrams and gestures as parents might to those of their children. Their task was not to *teach* Kanzi language, but rather to communicate with him as best they could as he went about his daily activities. Still, my inference from the reports on Kanzi is that he received much more linguistic attention than a typical child receives.

Vocabulary and Functions of Language

All language-trained chimps have learned to use and respond appropriately to many signs or lexigrams. After about 4 years of training, Washoe's vocabulary consisted of at least 132 signs (Gardner & Gardner, 1989). Because the number of lexigrams that can be placed on a keyboard is limited, Kanzi's production vocabulary is smaller than that, but through his exposure to spoken English Kanzi has apparently learned to understand at least 200 English words (Savage-Rumbaugh & others, 1993).

■ **21.** ***What is the evidence that Washoe and Kanzi used their words as symbols and not simply as operant responses?***

More critical than the size of their vocabulary is how the chimps use their vocabulary. Children do often use words to ask for what they want, but even more often they use words to describe their experiences. A 3-year-old who out of the blue says, "Yesterday Mrs. Webster showed me the hugest and most beautiful apple," is not asking for anything, but is sharing an experience. Based on Nim's signs and those recorded in films of Washoe, Terrace and his colleagues (1980) argued that chimpanzees use signs almost exclusively as operant responses to obtain rewards, and rarely if ever to comment on their world. When chimps talk about apples, they usually say in one way or another, "Gimme apple."

If chimps use signs simply to obtain immediate rewards, then maybe they are not using the signs as words at all. A word is a symbol for some object, action, or characteristic in the environment. Perhaps the chimp who makes the *gimme apple* signs and receives an apple knows only that a particular combination of hand movements will result in an apple, just as a rat trained in a Skinner box knows that a lever-press response will result in a food pellet.

In response to Terrace's argument, Savage-Rumbaugh (1984) showed that her common chimps could use appropriate lexigrams to refer to out-of-view objects even when reward was not contingent upon that use. For example, they would specify which of several absent foods they wanted before going to another room and selecting that food. Later, Savage-Rumbaugh reported that many of Kanzi's spontaneous uses of lexigrams could not be explained in operant terms (Savage-Rumbaugh & others, 1985, 1986). Kanzi would use the lexigram for apple *after* he had received an apple. He would also routinely announce his intentions before acting. For example, before taking a trip to the tree house he would press the lexigram for *tree house*.

Further evidence that chimps treat signs or lexigrams as symbols comes from the chimps' appropriate use of these in novel situations. For example, Washoe once dropped a favorite toy into a hole in the inner wall of her house trailer when nobody was around. When Allen Gardner returned to the trailer, Washoe pointed to the wall under the hole, near the floor, and signed, "Open, open." From this, Gardner figured out what had happened and managed to fish out the toy (Gardner & Gardner, 1989). Washoe had learned the sign for *open* in such contexts as opening refrigerator doors for food, but now she used it in a completely new context that was consistent with the sign's meaning. Chimps can also understand novel requests. When Kanzi was 8 years old, he was tested for his ability to carry out spoken requests that he had never heard before, such as, "Put the egg in the noodles," and "Hammer the ball." The requests were made by a caretaker who was out of view so that nonverbal cues could not guide his behavior. Kanzi met most of the requests successfully—performing at a rate similar to that of a 2-year-old human girl who was given the same requests (Savage-Rumbaugh & others, 1993).

Statement Lengths and Grammar

Even after chimps have had many years of language practice, most of their statements are only one word long, and very few are more than three words in length. The longer statements they occasionally make are highly redundant strings. For example, Nim's longest statement was translated as, "Give orange me eat orange me eat orange give me eat orange give me you" (Brown, 1986). In contrast, as children gain linguistic competence, their sentences grow longer, and the additional words usually provide additional meaning. Their sentences also show grammatical structure.

■ **22. *What can we conclude about chimps' use of grammar compared to that of children?***

As discussed earlier, young children seem uniquely primed to acquire and even invent grammar rules. They master most of the subtleties of their native language's grammar by their fourth year. In contrast, chimps' grammatical capacities appear to be slight. To date no chimp has acquired or invented a rule for distinguishing plural from singular nouns, for marking the tense of verbs, or for marking words by grammatical class. Kanzi does show a statistically significant word-order preference in some of his two- and three-word constructions (Greenfield & Savage-Rumbaugh, 1991), and he uses word order to understand English statements (Savage-Rumbaugh & others, 1993). When as an 8-year-old he was tested for his ability to carry out spoken requests, he responded appropriately to about 80% of those that depended on word order, such as "Make the doggie bite the snake" and "Make the snake bite the doggie" (using a toy dog and toy snake as props). Apparently, some aspects of grammar are not impossible for a nonhuman ape to master; still, even Kanzi's grammatical skills do not approach those of a typical four-year-old child.

In sum, chimpanzees, especially pygmy chimpanzees, seem capable of acquiring an ability to communicate with symbols that bears resemblance to human language. Whether we call it language or not is arbitrary. It will be fun to see what future chimps will say, but my guess is that we will remain alone on earth as the only animals who can carry on a really interesting conversation.

Development of Logical Thought

As children grow, their thinking becomes ever more logical, ever more effective in solving problems. How can these changes in thinking be characterized, and what are the processes through which they develop? In considering these questions, Piaget's theory on the growth of logical thought is the logical place to begin. Then we will turn to two other perspectives on the same issue—the information-processing and sociocultural perspectives.

Piaget's Theory

If asked who has had the greatest influence on the study of cognitive development, nearly all psychologists would name Jean Piaget. In his long career at the University of Geneva (from the 1920s until his death in 1980), Piaget wrote more than fifty books and hundreds of articles on children's reasoning. He referred to himself as a *genetic epistemologist* (Piaget, 1970). *Epistemology* is the study of the structure of human knowledge, and *genetic,* in this context, refers to the origin and development of something. Thus, genetic epistemology is the study of the origin and development of the structure of knowledge that comprises the human mind. Piaget's goal was to understand how the adult mind, particularly its capacity for objective reasoning, develops from the child's more primitive abilities. His basic method was to ask children to solve specific problems and to question them about the reasons for the solutions they offered. From this work, Piaget developed an elaborate, comprehensive theory of cognitive development.

Piaget conceived of mental development as an adaptive process that has its origins in the child's own actions on the environment. At first, according to Piaget, in-

■ **23.** ***How does Piaget's concept of a scheme embody his idea that mental development stems from the child's actions?***

fants react only reflexively toward objects. As they gain voluntary control of their movements, however, they begin to develop internal, mental representations of the kinds of actions they can perform on particular categories of objects. Piaget called these internal representations ***schemes***. A scheme can be defined as a mental blueprint for a class of actions that can be performed upon entities in the environment. The earliest schemes are closely tied to the actual actions that an infant makes. Thus, a young infant might have a sucking scheme most applicable to nipples, a grasping and shaking scheme most applicable to rattles, and a smiling scheme most applicable to human faces. As a child grows older, new, more sophisticated, more abstract schemes develop, which are less closely tied to actual objects in the immediate environment or to actual actions.

Piaget divided the span of cognitive development into four major stages, each characterized by a qualitatively different kind of thinking that is made possible by the emergence of a new kind of scheme built from the child's experiences in the preceding stage. A person cannot enter one stage without having gone through the previous one, so the order of the stages is invariant. Piaget was not much concerned with the precise age at which people enter each stage (the ages given below are only approximations), but he was much concerned with the kind of thinking that characterizes each stage and the processes through which schemes change and lead to a new stage.

Jean Piaget

Because of his interest in the influence of the environment on children's cognitive development, Piaget preferred to observe children in natural settings. Here he is shown during a visit to a nursery school.

The Sensorimotor Stage (*Birth to about 2 years*)

This stage was discussed earlier in the chapter in connection with the infant's knowledge of the environment. It is the period during which the child understands objects mainly through his or her direct actions on them. The major task of this stage is to internalize schemes of action, so the actions can be thought of without actual muscle movements. As schemes are increasingly internalized, infants develop the ability to think of objects that are not in sight and to act in purposeful ways toward goals that are not in sight. That is, their schemes begin to provide them with symbols for thought. The development of language in infancy also reflects this change in schemes. Earliest words are part of the infant's actions toward objects that are present, but gradually the child comes to use words as symbols to represent absent objects.

■ **24.** ***What abilities or deficits distinguish the preoperational stage from the earlier sensorimotor stage and the later concrete-operational stage?***

The Preoperational Stage (*About 2 to 7 years*)

As their thinking becomes free from strict control by the here-and-now, children enter the preoperational stage, which is characterized by a well-developed ability to symbolize the static qualities of objects and events. Now the child can easily think about absent objects, and delights in developing new symbols to represent them (Piaget, 1962). Put a saucepan into the hands of a preschooler and it is magically transformed into a ray gun or a guitar—the saucepan becomes a symbol in the child's play.

Yet, according to Piaget, severe limits remain on the ways in which preoperational children can think. Preoperational children can fully appreciate the stable, identifying features of objects, but they cannot yet think *operationally*. That is, they cannot imagine the logical outcome of certain kinds of actions (operations) on objects. If you roll a ball of clay into a sausage shape, preoperational children do not understand that this operation changes the object's shape but not its substance. They are not aware that the new shape must contain the same amount of clay as the old one. Noting that the sausage is longer than the ball was, one preoperational child might say that the sausage has more clay than the ball had. Another child, noting that the sausage is thinner than the ball, might say that the sausage has less clay. Both children have based their judgment on appearance rather than logic. In

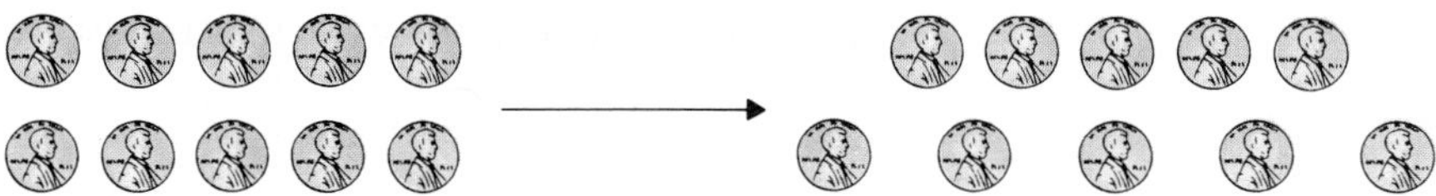

In conservation of number tests, two equivalent rows of coins are placed side by side and the child says that there is the same number in each row. Then one row is spread apart and the child is again asked if there is the same number in each.

In conservation of length tests, two same-length sticks are placed side by side and the child says that they are the same length. Then one is moved and the child is again asked if they are the same length.

In conservation of substance tests, two identical amounts of clay are rolled into similar-appearing balls and the child says that they both have the same amount of clay. Then one ball is rolled out and the child is again asked if they have the same amount.

Figure 12.9 ***Tests of children's understanding of conservation***

The transition from the preoperational to the concrete-operational stage, in Piaget's theory, is marked by success on tests such as these. Children usually succeed on conservation of number and length tests before they succeed on conservation of substance tests.

this case, they have failed to apply the principle of *conservation of substance*—the understanding that the amount of a substance doesn't change when the substance changes shape. Figure 12.9 explains how Piaget tested children's understanding of this principle and two others, *conservation of number* and *conservation of length*.

Piaget (1926, 1927) also contended that preoperational children lack a true understanding of cause and effect. When he asked them about causal mechanisms, they usually couldn't answer and often failed to see the relevance of the question. For example, when he asked children younger than 7 or 8 whether or not a bicycle would still work if the chain were removed, they often said yes, and those who said no commonly responded in the same way when asked about an inessential part such as the fender. According to Piaget, 6-year-olds can make things work, but they do not think about mechanisms. A 6-year-old might ask *how* to make a particular light come on, but is not likely to ask *why* the light comes on when the switch is pushed. A 9-year-old, in contrast, will ask why and expect an answer in terms of some mechanism connecting the switch to the light.

Although (or perhaps because) preoperational children do not fully understand principles of change, they actively and continuously produce changes in the environment—pushing, pulling, squeezing, mixing, and in other ways manipulating objects to see what happens. Through this process they gradually develop schemes that include an understanding of change, and this development brings them to the next stage.

The preoperational stage

Sarah, here aged 5¾, does not pass Piaget's test of conservation. Even though she knows the short glasses contain the same amount of milk and carefully watches the milk being poured into the tall glass, she still points to the tall glass when asked, "Which has more?"

25. ***In Piaget's theory, what is meant by an operation? What are concrete-operational schemes and what new abilities do they permit?***

The Concrete-Operational Stage (*About 7 to 12 years*)

According to Piaget, true logic begins when children can think about and understand ***operations***. As defined by Piaget, an operation is a *reversible action*, that is, an action that can be undone by another action. Rolling a ball of clay into a sausage is an operation because it can be reversed by rolling the clay back into a ball. Turning a light on by pushing a switch up is an operation because it can be reversed by pushing the switch back down. Children in the preoperational stage perform such operations all the time, but they cannot yet represent them mentally. When they can, they are said to have *concrete-operational schemes*, and a whole battery of new reasoning abilities emerges. Such schemes are mental representations of the operations that can be performed on actual (concrete) objects in the world.

According to Piaget, the power of operational schemes lies in their reversibility. Because concrete-operational children can imagine rolling the clay sausage back into the same ball that it was before, they know that the sausage must contain the same amount of clay as did the ball. Thus, they are prepared to understand, at least as applied to the clay, the principle of conservation. Similarly, reversibility permits an understanding of physical causation. The child who can imagine that pushing a light switch back down will restore the whole physical set-up to its previous state has the basis for understanding the cause-effect relationship between the switch and the light. The reversibility of operational schemes allows a person to manipulate knowledge mentally without losing track of its original form, which to Piaget is a prerequisite for all logical reasoning.

Although concrete-operational children have come a long way in the development of logic, their cognitive development is not yet complete. Piaget used the term *concrete* to describe the schemes of this stage because he believed that they are still tied closely to the child's experiences in the real world. The transition from understanding the actual to recognizing the possible has yet to be made.

The concrete-operational stage

According to Piaget, thought is increasingly logical during middle childhood, but it still depends on the presence of real objects. Puzzles, like the one these 9- to 12-year-olds are solving, offer concrete opportunities for thinking through alternatives and tracing the steps to a solution. From such activities, formal-operational thinking eventually emerges.

26. ***How does formal-operational reasoning differ from concrete-operational reasoning?***

The Formal-Operational Stage (*About 12 years through adulthood*)

The last stage in Piaget's theory, the formal operational stage, begins near the onset of adolescence. Now schemes are independent of specific, concrete experiences. Now the reasoner can apply operational thinking even to actions that are not reversible in actuality but are in theory. You cannot really unbeat an egg, but as a formal-operational reasoner you can understand the theoretical principle that an egg can be unbeaten and restored to its original form. Thus, you can answer correctly conservation questions about a beaten egg as well as about a rolled-out piece of clay: "Is the amount of egg more, less, or the same after it has been beaten?"

The formal-operational stage

These young people are part of a recent campaign to fight drug and alcohol abuse. The idealism that attracts adolescents to social and political movements depends in part on their ability to imagine hypothetical possibilities, which is part of formal-operational thought.

Piaget referred to formal-operational thinking as *hypothetico-deductive reasoning*. Formal-operational schemes enable a person to formulate hypotheses through inductive logic and to test them through deductive logic (discussed in Chapter 11). In one of his tests of such reasoning, Piaget gave children and adolescents four flasks containing colorless liquids and a fifth flask containing an indicator liquid (Inhelder & Piaget, 1958). After explaining that a combination of one or more of the four liquids with the indicator would yield a yellow color, he asked the subjects to try to produce that color. Those under about age 12 usually failed, because their trials were unsystematic. Older subjects usually succeeded by trying each combination in a logical, exhaustive sequence until they produced the yellow color. Their formal-operational schemes allowed them to think of the logical possibilities and to test them systematically.

According to Piaget, the formal-operational thinker can reason based on what is *possible*, while the concrete-operational thinker is limited to what *is*. Formal mathematics and theoretical science can now be understood, whereas only arithmetic and empirical (fact-based) science could be understood before. The concrete-operational child can attend only to the substance of an argument, but the formal-operational adolescent can attend also to the *form*. Consider this syllogism: *If all animals can fly, and if all rhinoceroses are animals, then all rhinoceroses can fly.* Concrete-operational reasoners will test this statement against their personal experience with rhinoceroses and conclude at once that it is false. Formal-operational reasoners, realizing that this is a question about logic, not about rhinoceroses, will accept the empirically false initial premise as a given, note the internal validity of the argument, and conclude that the statement is true.

How Schemes Develop: Assimilation and Accommodation

■ **27. *In Piaget's theory, how do assimilation and accommodation work together to produce mental development? In what sense is the mind more like a spider's web than a brick wall?***

In Piaget's theory, the child's own activities and thoughts within each stage serve constantly to expand the schemes that predominate at that stage, resulting eventually in a qualitative change in the schemes and hence transition into the next stage. This growth of schemes involves two complementary processes: assimilation and accommodation.

Assimilation is the process by which experiences are incorporated into existing schemes. If you encounter a new object and match it to an existing scheme, you have assimilated that object into the scheme. For example, if right now you were to see an Australian terrier, you would in some way recognize it even if you had never seen one before, because it would fit at least roughly with one or more of your schemes for small dogs. Just how you assimilated this new object, however, would depend on the kinds of schemes you have already developed. If you are a dog lover, you might assimilate the terrier as a friendly pet, a companion for play; otherwise, you might assimilate it as a barking, biting beast to be avoided. Piaget was a biologist by training, and he considered the assimilation of experiences to be analogous to the assimilation of food. Two people may eat the same type of food, but the food

Accommodation

This 11-month-old may be accommodating her "stacking scheme" in order to assimilate the experience of one block fitting inside another. From such experiences, a new "fits inside" scheme may develop.

will be assimilated into the tissues differently depending on the inner structures involved in digestion and building the body. Just as nondigestible foods will not result in body growth, new experiences that are too different from existing schemes will not result in mental growth. A hand calculator given to a very young child will not contribute to the child's arithmetic skills, because the young child has no calculating scheme into which to assimilate the calculator's functions.

Few new stimuli fit perfectly an existing scheme. Assimilation usually requires that existing schemes expand or change somewhat to accommodate the new object or event. Appropriately, this process is called ***accommodation***. The mind and its schemes are not like a brick wall, which only grows bigger as each new brick (unit of knowledge) is added; they are more like a spider's web, which changes its entire shape somewhat as each new thread is added. The web accommodates to the thread while the thread is assimilated into the web. The addition of new information to the mind changes somewhat the structure of schemes that are already present. Consider an infant who in play discovers that an object placed on top of an open box will fall inside the box. Perhaps the child already had a scheme for stacking objects, which included the notion that one object placed on top of another will remain on top. But now that scheme must be modified to accommodate this new experience—to include the notion that if one object is hollow and open-topped, another object placed upon it may fall inside. At the same time, other schemes that include the notion that two objects cannot occupy the same place at the same time may also undergo accommodation; mental growth has occurred. In Piaget's view, children are most fascinated by those experiences that can be assimilated into existing schemes, but not too easily, so that accommodation is required. This natural tendency leads children to direct their own activities in ways that maximize their mental growth.

Criticisms of Piaget's Theory

■ **28.** ***What criticisms have been raised concerning (a) Piaget's theory of stages, (b) his theory of the process of change, and (c) his emphasis on the physical rather than social environment?***

To accept anyone's findings and theories as dogma runs counter to the nature of science: Findings are to be replicated, theories challenged. Like Freud, Skinner, and others who have attempted to build strong, explicit, wide-ranging theories in psychology, Piaget has been challenged on many counts. Here are some of the most common criticisms of his theory:

- ***Lack of evidence for qualitatively different stages*** The most dramatic and interesting claim of Piaget's theory is that children develop through stages in which they think in qualitatively different ways from the ways they think in other stages. If that claim is true, mental development should be characterized by periods of rapid change, when whole new constellations of abilities emerge more or less at once, followed by periods of relative stability (look back at Figure 12.1). But the bulk of evidence seems to contradict this prediction. The ability to solve conservation problems, for example, does not appear suddenly, but rather develops gradually over several years. Most children can solve conservation-of-number problems by age 5 but can't solve conservation-of-substance problems until about age 8 (Gross, 1985).

  Piaget was aware that children succeed at some tasks sooner than at other tasks in any given problem area—he even gave this phenomenon a name: *horizontal décalage*. He understood that the stage transitions are not sharp, the new abilities that depend on the new kind of schemes do not emerge all at once. But Piaget's critics argue that the changes occur over such a long span, with each stage blurring so completely into the next, that the stage concept loses its meaning.

  Other research challenges the idea that people's ways of thinking at different ages are as qualitatively different as Piaget maintained. Earlier in this chapter, you read of recent research suggesting that infants as young as three months can, at some level of their mind, comprehend the physical reality of absent objects. At the other end of the developmental scale, research with adults challenges the distinction between concrete and formal reasoning. Such research (discussed in Chapter 11) suggests that people who are good at solving abstract problems usually do so by thinking of analogies to more familiar problems, or by turning the problem statement into a familiar visual image so as to convert a formal task into a concrete one.

- ***Vagueness about the process of change*** Some critics argue that Piaget's theory of the process by which the mind develops is too vague, too general, too distanced from the behavioral data. What precisely is a scheme? What information must a scheme have in order, say, to permit a child to succeed in the conservation-of-clay problem? What exactly changes when assimilation and accommodation occur? Theorists in the information-processing tradition (to be described shortly) believe that theories of mental development should be more explicit than Piaget's in describing the links between observed behavioral changes and the posited changes occurring in the mind.

  Piaget's belief that action is essential to mental growth has also generated criticism. Piaget maintains that the child acquires new knowledge by physically manipulating things in the physical environment. Yet babies born without arms and legs, or with an inability to move them, develop normal cognition despite their relative lack of ability to act physically on the environment (Jordan, 1972). Also, as Kagan (1984) has pointed out, the theory doesn't explain how a 2-year-old can understand terms such as *you*, *is*, *like*, and *why* that refer to abstract concepts unrelated to specific actions.

- ***Underestimation of the role of the social environment*** The children Piaget studied were growing up in Geneva in a Western culture where particular ways of thinking are valued and are taught in schools. Yet Piaget attributed the children's mental development primarily to their individual interactions with the physical world, not to their culture or schooling. He tended to conceive of each child as a lone scientist discovering anew the laws of nature. But cross-cultural research has shown that success on Piaget's tests of formal-operational reasoning, and even on some of his tests of concrete-operational reasoning, depends very much on experience with Western culture and schooling (Dasen & Heron, 1981; Segall & others, 1990). As you will see, theorists in the sociocultural tradition argue that mental development occurs largely through interaction with other people, not through solo interaction with nature.

■ **29. *What are some of the lasting contributions of Piaget's work and theory?***

Despite the criticisms, Piaget's work is still greatly admired by most developmental psychologists. His pioneering methods of learning about children's thought stimulated other scientists to conduct new research and develop new ideas about the mind's growth. He outlined a sequence of mental change that, if not fully stage-like, nevertheless describes accurately the order in which a child's ability to reason seems to develop. By theorizing that mental growth stems from the child's actions in the environment and leads to increasingly effective ways of dealing with the environment, he emphasized the adaptive nature of development. Perhaps the most admired of Piaget's contributions is his contention that children actively promote their own mental development. Given the opportunity, children select from their environments those stimuli and problems that sufficiently challenge their present ways of thinking—that is, whose assimilation requires just enough accommodation—to help advance their thought to new levels. This comes not from a conscious concern to educate themselves, but from a natural tendency to enjoy an attainable challenge.

The Information-Processing Perspective

■ **30.** ***What is the information-processing perspective on cognitive development, and how does it differ from Piaget's perspective?***

Piaget treated the mind as a single entity. Cognitive developmentalists who adopt the information-processing perspective, in contrast, treat the mind as a set of interacting components. Their general goal is to relate specific changes in children's problem-solving abilities to specific changes in one or another of these components. Their method is to describe explicitly the logical requirements of the task, on the one hand, and the change that has occurred in the child's mind, on the other.

As described in Chapters 10 and 11, the information-processing approach to cognition begins with the assumption that the mind is a system, analogous to a computer, for analyzing information from the environment. The components that make up the mind's basic machinery are analogous to the all-purpose operating systems that are built into a computer. In the standard information-processing model (shown in Figure 10.1, page 328), these operating systems consist of three memory stores (sensory, short-term, and long-term stores) and the processes that enable information to move from one store to another. The strategies and rules for analyzing particular types of information or solving particular types of problems are analogous to the more specific programs, such as a word-processing program or a statistical package that you would insert into a computer. Cognitive development can stem from changes in the mind's general operating systems, or in its specific programs, or both.

Increased Capacity of Short-Term Memory

In the standard model of the mind, the component called *short-term memory*, or *working memory*, is the center of all conscious thought. Analogous to the central processing unit of a computer, it is the place where information is combined and manipulated to solve problems. As discussed in Chapters 10 and 11, the short-term store is limited in the amount of information it can hold at any given time, and this limitation constrains a person's problem-solving ability.

■ **31.** ***How might a continuous increase in the capacity of short-term memory produce stagelike development in problem-solving ability? From what sources does improved short-term memory appear to derive?***

Some years ago, a mathematically oriented psychologist, Juan Pascual-Leone (1970), proposed that the most fundamental change underlying cognitive development is a gradual, maturational increase in the capacity of short-term memory, which he referred to as *M space* (mental space). Pascual-Leone and others working with this theory showed mathematically how the stages posited by Piaget could be accounted for by a gradual (not stagelike) change in *M* space (Case & others, 1982). Certain kinds of intellectual tasks require a particular amount of *M* space just as certain computer programs require a particular amount of computer memory, and children can perform such tasks only when they have developed enough *M* space.

The growth of cognitive strategies

Schooling promotes the development of many cognitive strategies, such as those involved in attending to relevant information and committing it to memory.

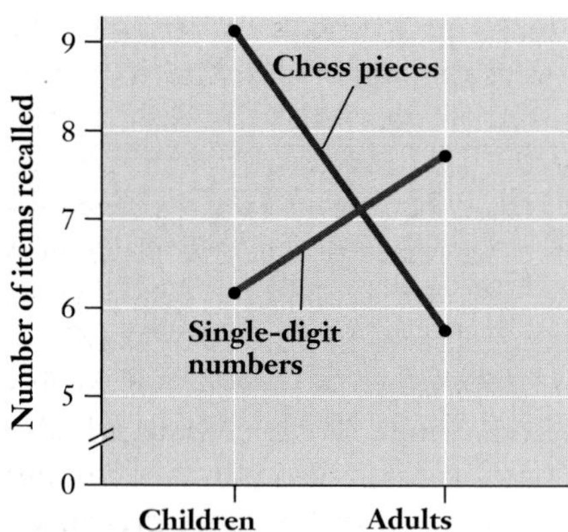

Figure 12.10 ***Short-term memory in 10-year-old chess experts and in adult novices***

When tested for their short-term memory of the location of chess pieces on a chess board, the 10-year-old experts performed better than adults who were novices at chess. When the same groups were tested for their short-term memory of single-digit numbers, the adults performed better than the children. (Adapted from Chi, 1978.)

Pascual-Leone and his colleagues devised ways to estimate the amount of *M* space required for various Piagetian tasks and suggested that the tasks used to mark the onset of Piaget's concrete-operational stage all require about the same amount.

In line with Pascual-Leone's theory, measures of short-term memory capacity do increase with age throughout childhood. When asked to repeat after a brief delay a string of digits or letters that was presented just once, a typical 5-year-old can repeat about four, an 11-year-old can repeat about six, and an adult can repeat seven or eight (Chi, 1978). In theory, the improvement in memory capacity could be attributed to learned strategies and the greater familiarity that older subjects have with the memory items. One bit of evidence for this view comes from an experiment by Michelene Chi (1978) that compared memory abilities of 10-year-old chess experts with those of adults who were novices at chess. The children outperformed the adults in memory for the locations of chess pieces on a chess board that they had briefly examined, and the adults outperformed the children in memory tests unrelated to chess (see Figure 12.10). Presumably, the children's superior chess memory came from their greater experience with the game, which allowed them to acquire efficient ways to represent chess pieces mentally. By the same token, the adults might have acquired their superior memory in other realms through their greater experience in those realms.

Domain-specific experiences are a significant source of memory improvement, but probably not the only source. When the difference in experience is less extreme than in Chi's experiment, adults or older children outperform younger subjects in short-term memory tests even if the latter are more experienced with the memory items (Kail, 1991). Research suggests that much of the improvement in short-term memory stems from a change in the underlying cognitive apparatus—specifically, an increase in *speed of processing*, the speed at which elementary information-processing tasks can be carried out. Tests that assess the speed at which one can make very simple judgments, such as whether two letters or shapes flashed on a screen are the same or different, consistently reveal age-related improvement up to the age of about 15 to 20 (Case, 1992; Kail, 1991).

As discussed in Chapter 11, faster processing means faster mental movement from one item of information to another, which can increase short-term memory capacity and general problem-solving ability. Robbie Case (1992) and Robert Kail (1991) contend that improvement in speed of processing derives from biological maturation of the brain independent of specific kinds of experiences. Consistent with their view, similar increases in speed of processing have been observed in people growing up in widely different cultures, with or without schooling (Dasen & de Ribaupierre, 1988).

Acquiring Rules to Solve Specific Classes of Problems

As children get older they acquire, through experience, many general strategies for dealing with information and solving problems. They become better at attending to relevant information and ignoring irrelevant information (Pick & others, 1972), and they develop increasingly sophisticated ways of committing information to memory (Kail, 1984). They also learn specific rules for dealing with specific classes of problems (Siegler & Jenkins, 1989).

Consider, for example, the task of judging which side of a balance beam will tilt down when different numbers of equally heavy weights are placed at varying distances on the two sides of the fulcrum (see Figure 12.11). This was one of the tasks that Piaget commonly used to test formal-operational thinking. More recently, from an information-processing perspective, Robert Siegler (1983) has described performance on this task in terms of rules that are specific just to this class of problem.

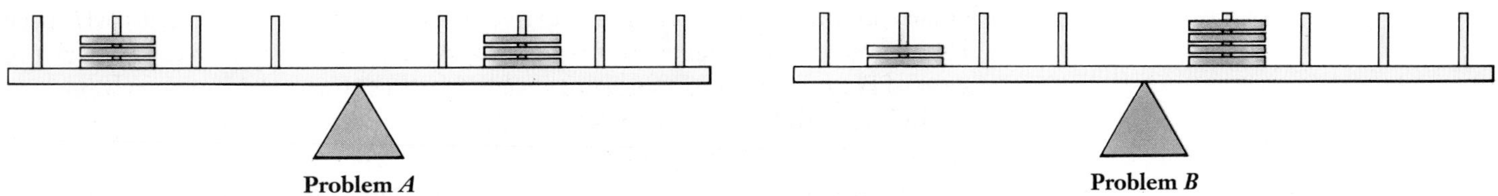

Figure 12.11 ***Sample balance-beam problems used by Siegler***
Children and adolescents were told that each ring was the same weight and that the pegs were spaced equally on each side of the fulcrum. The task was to predict which side would tilt down when the beam was released. (Adapted from Siegler, 1983.)

32. *How does Siegler's explanation of improvement in solving balance-beam problems differ from the kind of explanation that Piaget would offer?*

The ultimate rule for solving balance-beam problems is to multiply the amount of weight on each side by its distance from the fulcrum; the side for which this product is greater is the side that will go down. Siegler found that even among adults only a small minority understood this rule and that most people responded in accordance with more primitive rules that could be ranked in a sequence directed toward the ultimate rule. Specifically, Siegler found that people performed in accordance with one of four rules. In rule 1, the most primitive, weight alone is taken into account; the person predicts that the end with the most weight will go down. In rule 2, weight alone is used unless the weights on the two sides of the fulcrum are the same (as in Problem *A* of Figure 12.11), in which case distance is also taken into account. In rule 3, both weight and distance are taken into account, but when these conflict—when weight is greater on one side and distance greater on the other (as in problem *B* of Figure 12.11)—the person just guesses at which end will go down. Finally, in rule 4, the ultimate rule, judgment is based on weight multiplied by distance. Based on their performance on problem sets that would be solved either correctly or incorrectly by a given rule, nearly everyone whom Siegler tested showed consistent rule use from problem to problem. The errors were not random; rather, they were predictable based on use of one of the four rules. Developmentally, Siegler found that most 5-year-olds behaved according to rule 1; that most 9-year-olds behaved according to rule 2; and that most people aged 13 and up behaved according to either rule 2 or 3, in about equal numbers (Siegler, 1983).

In other experiments, Siegler (1983) allowed children to gain feedback on each trial by releasing the beam (so it could tip freely on its fulcrum) after their response to show them which end would go down. He found that the effect of feedback depended on the type of problem for which it was given. Children who behaved according to rule 1 profited from feedback on problems that disconfirmed rule 1 and confirmed rule 2 (such as problem *A* in Figure 12.11), but did not profit from feedback on problems that disconfirmed both rules 1 and 2 (such as Problem *B* in Figure 12.11). From such data, Siegler suggests that children at one level of rule use may be prepared to use information needed to acquire the next rule in the sequence, but they cannot fathom information that would require them to skip the next rule and go directly to a more advanced one.

Notice that Siegler's account differs from Piaget's not only in its explicitness regarding the mental change, but also in its narrowness regarding the kinds of behaviors that change together. Moving to a higher rule to solve a balance-beam problem would not necessarily move the child to a higher level on conservation problems. Information-processing theorists adopt a less holistic view of mental development than Piaget's. They believe that one can become an expert in certain areas of reasoning and remain a novice in others.

The Lifelong Nature of Cognitive Development

33. *How can cognitive changes during adulthood be described and explained from an information-processing perspective?*

From the information-processing perspective, cognitive development does not end at adolescence. Throughout life, people who involve themselves in new mental activities acquire new strategies and rules for thinking. Longitudinal research has shown that scores on standard intelligence tests can increase or decrease at any time in adult life depending on one's experiences (Schaie, 1984). Increases in IQ often follow mind-challenging life changes, such as getting an intellectually stimulating job, traveling, or marrying a highly intelligent person. Conversely, lack of new experiences can result in IQ decline. The intellect is a bit like a muscle; it can grow with use or atrophy with disuse.

For intellectually active people, development in adulthood often entails an increased ability to see both sides of an argument and to understand that some questions do not have absolute answers. For example, in a discussion of education, more older adults than young adults claimed that the purpose and best form of education are not fixed, but are relative to the larger needs and goals of society, which can differ from place to place and time to time (Basseches, 1986). In another study, adolescents and adults were asked to describe their views about certain emotion-laden conflicts, such as one between a man and woman over whether to abort an unplanned pregnancy (Blanchard-Fields, 1986). Adolescents typically believed that one side was right and the other wrong; adults in their early twenties more often saw validity to both sides but still believed that an objectively best solution could be found; and adults in their thirties and forties more often saw the two sides as embedded within different frames of reference, each valid within its frame, and concluded that there is no objectively best solution for both parties.

Developmental change of this sort is sometimes referred to as increased wisdom. Others call it a shift toward more *dialectical thinking*, a form of thinking that takes into account more than one side of an argument at once (Basseches, 1984). Information-processing theorists suggest that such development may reflect both an increased knowledge base and an increased ability to integrate disparate kinds of knowledge in the quest for workable solutions (Case, 1992). Of course, wisdom, or dialectical thinking, is by no means entirely a function of age. We all have met many obstinate older people and wise young ones.

In old age, general intellectual ability may decline for biological reasons. Speed of mental processing, as measured by reaction-time tests, typically begins to decline in mid-adulthood, and this decline may account for eventual declines in capacity of short-term memory, in ability to retrieve information from long-term memory, and in some aspects of logical reasoning (Salthouse, 1991; Schaie, 1989). Great variability exists from person to person in the timing and extent of such changes, however, and many older people minimize the negative consequences through such strategies as writing notes to compensate for poor memory (Lovelace & Twohig, 1990).

Vygotsky and the Sociocultural Perspective

34. ***How does the sociocultural perspective on cognitive development differ from Piaget's?***

As its label implies, the sociocultural perspective on cognitive development highlights the role of culture and social interaction. The person most often credited with originating this perspective is Lev Vygotsky, a Russian scholar who died in 1934 at age 38, after devoting just 10 years to formal research and writing in psychology. Vygotsky was well aware of Piaget's research and theory, and agreed with much of it. He agreed that cognitive development can be described in terms of the child's internalization of experiences and that the main force for development is the child's active interaction with the environment. But he disagreed with Piaget's conception of the relevant environment. Whereas Piaget emphasized the child's interaction with the physical world, Vygotsky emphasized the child's interaction with the social world. Vygotsky argued that children learn even about the physical world through verbal descriptions from other people and through involvement in activities that are guided and interpreted by other people. In Vygotsky's view, cognitive development is largely a matter of internalizing the symbols, ideas, and modes of reasoning that have evolved over the course of history and constitute the culture into which the child is born.

Contrasting Interpretations of Noncommunicative Speech

■ **35.** ***How did Vygotsky's explanation of children's noncommunicative speech differ from Piaget's?***

The distinction between Vygotsky and Piaget is typified by their divergent interpretations of a kind of speech that both observed in young children. In listening to children's "conversations" in a kindergarten and in various other settings, Piaget (1923) was struck by the degree to which the children seemed not to be communicating. While working at separate projects, one child might say, "I'll make it green" (not indicating what would be made green), and another might respond, "Horses like sugar and oats."

Piaget referred to such noncommunicative speech as *egocentric speech* and argued that it is part of a more general *egocentrism* that characterizes the preoperational child. By egocentrism he did not mean selfishness, but rather an inability to take another person's perspective and understand what that person does or does not see or know. Because they have little conception of what is or is not in others' minds, argued Piaget, young children commonly fail to include enough information in their statements to make them comprehensible.

Vygotsky (1934/1962) interpreted such noncommunicative speech very differently. He claimed that young children are not egocentric and do communicate even with their earliest use of words, and that at about age 4 they begin to use speech not just to communicate, but also to aid their own thinking. At first this new use of speech occurs in a conversational format, because it is not yet fully separated from communicative speech. The result, according to Vygotsky, is the pseudo-conversations that Piaget had observed and labeled *egocentric*. When Vygotsky observed young children in various settings, he found that they were most likely to use egocentric speech in exactly the kind of setting in which Piaget had observed it—one in which children were physically together but working on separate projects. When children were just sitting and talking, or working on the same project, their speech was genuinely communicative.

Consistent with Vygotsky's interpretation, much recent research indicates that 4-year-olds indeed can make reasonable inferences about what others know and don't know, and that they modify their speech accordingly (Wellman, 1990; Whiten, 1991). Piaget's view that young children are egocentric is today one of his least accepted ideas.

The Internalization of Speech as a Force in Cognitive Development

■ **36.** ***In Vygotsky's view, how does the internalization of speech promote cognitive development?***

According to Vygotsky, noncommunicative speech declines at around age 7 because by then the child can think in words without saying them aloud. Noncommunicative speech has become *inner speech* (Vygotsky's term) or *verbal thought*. With experience, inner speech becomes increasingly abbreviated, and in older children and adults the words are no longer pronounced to the self but are purely mental symbols. According to Vygotsky, this new form of thought is far more powerful than the child's earlier forms. Words are symbols developed through hundreds of generations of language use. In internalizing words, children internalize a far richer set of symbols than they could develop on their own.

Vygotsky agreed with Piaget that a qualitative change in thinking occurs at about age 6 or 7; but while Piaget attributed that change to concrete operational schemes, Vygotsky attributed it to the internalization of speech. Early in this process, the child can think better by using words aloud than by using them silently. Consistent with this view, Vygotsky (1934/1962) found that 5- and 6-year-olds were more likely to talk about what they were doing when working on difficult tasks than when working on easy tasks, and other researchers later found that talking aloud does improve children's performance (Kendler, 1972; Kohlberg & others, 1968).

To see how a word might promote cognitive development, consider the word *because.* Both Vygotsky (1934/1962) and Piaget (1927) noted that children begin to use this word (or rather its Russian or French equivalent) before they fully understand its meaning. Children under age 6 or 7 commonly reverse cause and effect, saying such things as "Billy fell off the porch because he broke his arm." To Piaget the word is incidental to cognitive development; its use or misuse only reflects the child's level of understanding. But to Vygotsky the word is critical to cognitive development. Using the word in a communicative, social context induces the child to think about its meaning, which leads the child toward a more advanced understanding of cause and effect relationships. *Because* becomes not only a tool for communication, but a tool for thought about events in the physical world.

The Child as Apprentice

■ **37. *In what sense can a child's daily activities and discussions be understood as an apprenticeship? How does age mixing promote development?***

While Piaget's child can be characterized as a little scientist performing experiments on the world and discovering its nature, Vygotsky's child can be characterized as an apprentice (Rogoff, 1990). The child is born into a social world in which people routinely engage in activities that range from setting the table to discussing the nature of the universe. Children are attracted to these activities and seek to participate. At first the child's role is small, but it grows as the child gains skill and understanding. From this view, cognitive development is less a progression from simple tasks to more complex ones and more a progression from small roles to larger roles in the activities of the social world.

Barbara Rogoff (1990) has documented the many ways in which children in various cultures involve themselves in family and community activities. Parents and others appreciate any actual help the child provides (in grinding grain, carrying napkins to the table, or adding a bit of information to a family discussion) and also enjoy observing the child's improvement. Moreover, they are as interested in communicating with the child as the child is in communicating with them. In a series of experiments, Rogoff (1990) and her colleagues showed that children learn new problem-solving strategies more efficiently and fully if they work at the problems with their parents or with older children than if they work at them alone or with their peers.

To understand how a typical conversation might promote development, imagine a 4-year-old girl who begins to play with crayons and paper while her mother is in the room. The mother, simply out of curiosity, asks, "What are you going to draw?" The child had perhaps not thought of that question before, but to keep the conversation going she answers, "A horse." Now she has a plan, and further conversation with her mother helps her keep that plan in mind as she continues to draw. The result is a more purposeful drawing than she would have produced alone. The mother's intention may not have been educational, but education has occurred nevertheless.

I have for years been involved with a school (the Sudbury Valley School, described more fully in Chapter 13) that in some ways exemplifies Vygotsky's apprenticeship view. This school, with students of age four through young adulthood, has facilities for a wide variety of activities, including cooking facilities, art and craft facilities, a photography lab, sports equipment, desktop computers, and an extensive library. Students are given no assignments, but are free to use or not use the facilities and staff as they choose. The school's founder, Daniel Greenberg (1992) has

Apprenticeship
Vygotsky pointed out that children are attracted to activities that involve them in family and community life. The Balinese boy finishing a stone sculpture and the Peruvian girl knitting alongside her mother are preparing themselves for full adult participation in their respective cultures.

long maintained that the school's success as an educational institution lies in the free mixing of people of different ages and abilities. Younger children are often drawn to activities in which older children are involved, and older children often help the younger ones in order to keep the action or dialogue going. In such exchanges, the younger child learns something from the elder, and the elder child consolidates his or her own understanding through the process of demonstration or explanation. Segregating children into classrooms by age and ability negates this powerful force for learning.

Of course, one prediction of the apprenticeship analogy is that people growing up in different cultures will acquire different cognitive abilities. A child surrounded by people who drive cars, use computers, and read books will not learn the same mental skills as a child surrounded by people who hunt game, weave blankets, and tell stories far into the night. The apprenticeship analogy also reminds us that logic itself is not the goal of mental development. The goal is to function effectively as an adult in one's society. Achieving that goal entails learning to get along with people and to perform economically valuable tasks. In our society, such ends may for many people entail the linear, abstract thinking that Piaget labeled formal operational, but (as discussed in Chapter 11) in another society they may not.

Concluding Thoughts

In concluding this chapter, it might be interesting to think about two different but not mutually exclusive philosophical perspectives on the developing child. One perspective emphasizes the role of the child's own activities and the other emphasizes the role of the social environment.

1. Development as a product of the child's own activities Children actively promote their own development. They arrive in the world not as blank tablets to be written on by experience, but as active beings who produce their own experiences.

They come with reflexes, some of which develop through maturation and exercise into voluntary behaviors such as walking and manipulating objects. They come also with a natural tendency to be bored by what is too familiar and to look for what is new—a tendency that makes almost every moment a time of learning. You have seen how researchers have capitalized on infants' preference for the new in experiments aimed at learning about infants' perceptual abilities and knowledge.

Infants also enter the world with a special interest in language and a biological predisposition to go through a period of vocal play that moves them along a path toward the utterance of words. Language—maybe the most cognitively complex body of information that anyone learns in a lifetime—is acquired by young children through their day-to-day interactions with people around them, regardless of whether or not anyone tries to teach it to them. Children who grow up hearing grammarless pidgin languages apparently even invent their own grammar and turn the pidgin into a real language. Piaget's theory of cognitive development centers on the active role of the child. Assimilation—the incorporation of new information into the mind—is, according to Piaget, a process that is necessarily governed by the child. Children direct their attention at any given time to those elements of the environment for which their minds are prepared, and they incorporate the information in whatever way they can understand it at the time.

2. The dependence of development on the social environment Although children are active beings who promote their own development, they are at the same time absolutely dependent on the environment into which they are born. All of their innate behavioral drives and abilities are useless without a responsive environment. They need solid surfaces against which to exercise their muscles if they are going to walk, and they need other people with whom to exercise their vocal play if they are going to talk. Infants and children may select what to assimilate from the smorgasbord of information around them, but adults to a large extent provide the smorgasbord. Whereas Piaget emphasized the importance of children's own activities, Vygotsky and the sociocultural tradition emphasize the role of the social environment. Through acquiring the words, skills, and reasoning processes of the social world, children grow mentally toward adulthood.

Further Reading

Daphne Maurer & Charles Maurer (1988). *The world of the newborn.* New York: Basic Books.

This excellent description of the abilities of very young infants and the research methods used to learn about them is written for the nonspecialist, but is well documented. Topics include life in the womb, the process of birth, sensory abilities, motor abilities, and early acquisition of knowledge.

Jerome Bruner (1983). *Child's talk: Learning to use language.* New York: Norton.

In this slender book, Bruner introduces the concept of the LASS (Language-acquisition support system) to complement Chomsky's LAD (Language-acquisition device). The book emphasizes the social nature of the child and the communicative role of language. In Bruner's view, the child's desire to understand and be understood, complemented by the same on the part of his or her adult caregivers, is the driving force behind language acquisition.

Jean Piaget (1929) *The child's conception of the world.* London: Routledge & Kegan Paul.

Many of Piaget's books are difficult to read, but this one, written early in his career, is an exception. In the introduction he spells out his method of learning about children's minds through interviewing them about their ideas. The data for this book are children's thoughts on such issues as where the names of things come from, how the sun and moon originated, where rain comes from, and what it means to think. The ideas expressed here provided a basis for much of Piaget's subsequent research.

John McShane (1991). *Cognitive development: An information-processing approach.* Cambridge, MA: Basil Blackwell.

This is a thoughtful introduction to contemporary theory and research on cognitive development from the information-processing perspective. It deals with the development of perception, concepts, memory, quantitative reasoning, and grammar.

Barbara Rogoff (1990). *Apprenticeship in thinking: Cognitive development in social context.* Oxford: Oxford University Press.

Based on observational studies in various cultures and on laboratory research, Rogoff expands upon Vygotsky's view that cognitive development occurs through children's guided participation in the work, play, and dialogue of their social world.

Looking Ahead

This chapter has been about the development of perception, language, and thought; but you have already seen evidence that such development depends on the child's social experiences. The next chapter, about the development of social relationships, responsibility, and personal identity from birth through old age, extends more fully the idea that development is a social process.

SOCIAL DEVELOPMENT

CHAPTER 13

Each of us is born into a social world to which we must adapt. Throughout life we are involved in relationships with other people. During *infancy* we depend physically and emotionally on adult caregivers. During *childhood* we learn to get along with others and to abide by the rules and norms of society. During *adolescence* we begin to explore romantic relationships, and we may also work out a conscious set of values and life plans. During *adulthood* we assume responsibility for the care and support of others and contribute through work to the broader society.

Social development refers to the changing nature of a person's social relationships over the life span. How can these relationships at each phase of life best be characterized? What forces promote the changes? How does social development in one phase influence development in the next? How variable is social development from culture to culture? To answer such questions, let's begin by looking briefly at some broad theories of development, and then let's examine specific ideas and findings concerning each phase of development, from infancy through old age.

Perspectives on Social Development

Theories of social development can be divided roughly into three classes. The first emphasizes inborn drives, biological maturation, and the idea that human development everywhere follows certain common patterns. The second emphasizes differences from culture to culture and describes development as adaptation to the surrounding social structure. The third emphasizes the role that cognitive development plays in one's ways of thinking about and acting in the social environment.

Theories Emphasizing Inborn Drives, Maturation, and Universal Sequences

The best-known pioneer in thinking about social development was Sigmund Freud (1856–1939). His theory centered on the role of universal human drives, particularly the sexual and aggressive drives, which are most likely to bring a person into conflict with other people. According to Freud, social development is at base a matter of learning to channel these drives in socially acceptable ways. The most crucial aspects of this learning occur in the first 5 to 6 years, through the child's interactions with parents. Events such as weaning from the breast and toilet training conflict with the child's drives, and the manner in which such conflicts are resolved provides the basis for the child's future interactions with others. Freud's *psychoanalytic theory* of personality, including its developmental aspect, is described more fully in Chapter 16. You will find there that Freud divided the life span into five stages, each involving a different manifestation of the sexual drive.

■ 1. ***What kinds of conflicts form the basis for Erikson's stages, and what are the consequences of successful or unsuccessful resolution of a given conflict?***

Erikson's Theory of Life Stages

A stage theory that is more accepted than Freud's by modern developmental psychologists is that developed by Erik Erikson (1902–). Erikson was trained in psychoanalysis by Anna Freud, Sigmund Freud's daughter, and has always considered himself to be a Freudian. His theory emphasizes inner drives and conflicts, as does Freud's; but instead of centering on sexual and aggressive drives, it centers on a set of *social drives*, which motivate people to develop social ties and to establish themselves as useful members of society. Erikson believes that these drives are biologically based and are not simply acquired from social experience. The inborn social drives are what make the human being a fundamentally social animal.

Whereas Freud thought that the course of a person's development is almost fully determined by experiences during the first 5 or 6 years of life, Erikson (1963) argued that development can be influenced by experiences throughout life. Erikson divided the life span into eight *psychosocial stages* (as opposed to Freud's five psychosexual stages), each associated with a different problem or crisis to be resolved. A new dimension of personality is added at each stage, as described in Table 13.1.

As you study the table, notice that the outcome of each stage can vary along a continuum between two opposite poles. One pole is positive, strengthening the

Table 13.1 *Erikson's stages of psychosocial development*

Stage 1: Basic trust versus mistrust (birth to 1 year)

The baby enters the world completely at the mercy of others. If the first caregiver (usually the mother) meets the baby's needs dependably, the baby learns to trust that person, and this generalizes into a trust of others and the self.

Stage 2: Autonomy versus shame and doubt (1 to 3 years)

As they gain voluntary control of their actions—learn to walk, talk, feed themselves, and so on—children become increasingly willful, and this runs counter to their parents' desires to control them. The resulting battle of wills is resolved in the direction of *autonomy* if the child acquires a positive sense of self-control. It is resolved in the direction of *shame and doubt* if the child acquires a sense that whatever he or she does is inadequate or bad.

Stage 3: Initiative versus guilt (3 to 5 years)

Having gained control of their own actions, children now begin to plan their actions in advance, which leads to a crisis about ability to plan. A positive resolution entails a sense of *initiative* (the ability to plan and initiate new actions), and a negative resolution entails a sense of *guilt* about one's plans and a sense of inability to guide one's own future.

Stage 4: Industry versus inferiority (5 to 12 years)

Children become increasingly involved with tasks such as school assignments, chores at home, and self-chosen games and hobbies. The lesson to be learned now is "the pleasure of work completion by steady attention and persevering diligence" (Erikson, 1963), which will promote a sense of competence, or *industry*. Unsuccessful resolution leaves the child with a sense of *inferiority*.

Stage 5: Identity versus identity confusion (adolescence)

Identity is the sense of who one is and where one is going in life (Erikson, 1959). Adolescents must establish an identity appropriate for adult life. Successful resolution leaves the person with a *positive identity* and a consequent ability to function in ways that are beneficial to self and society. Unsuccessful resolution leaves the person with either *identity confusion* (lack of a stable identity) or a *negative identity* (one that is unhealthy or antisocial).

Stage 6: Intimacy versus isolation (young adulthood)

Intimacy is "the capacity to commit to concrete affiliation and partnership and to develop the ethical strength to abide by such commitments, even though they may call for significant sacrifices and compromises" (Erikson, 1963). Young adulthood is a time for learning to share oneself with another person. A person who fails at this will go through life with a sense of isolation, even if surrounded by other people.

Stage 7: Generativity versus stagnation (middle adulthood)

The crisis of this longest stage, from about 25 to 65 years, has to do with *generativity*, a sense of contributing to the next generation, which may be met through caring for children, teaching, or work that benefits the community at large. Those who fail at this will fall into *stagnation*, a sense of boredom and meaninglessness.

Stage 8: Integrity versus despair (late adulthood to death)

Those who successfully resolve the previous conflicts will have a sense of completeness, or *integrity*. The key trait of the integrated person is *wisdom*, an ability to look objectively at life and see broad truths and offer counsel to those in earlier stages. Failure to resolve the earlier crises may lead to *despair*, a sense of helplessness and bitterness that comes from feeling that life has been incomplete and will end incomplete.

Erik H. Erikson

Erikson is an intellectual nonconformist whose formal academic training ended with high school. His novel views have had a major impact on the study of children's development, and his clear and graceful literary style has made his books accessible to the general public.

person and fostering further healthy development, and the other is negative, weakening the person and hindering further healthy development. Most often, the person resolves the conflict somewhere between the two extremes. An infant, for example, usually emerges from the first stage somewhere between the extremes of *basic trust* and *basic mistrust*. Notice also how each stage builds on the stage preceding it. To a considerable degree, successful resolution at one stage is a prerequisite for successful resolution at the next. However, Erikson does not believe that all is lost if a person fails to achieve a positive resolution at any given stage. With an appropriate social environment, the person can reverse the outcomes of previous stages, though such reversals are difficult.

The Influence of Ethology

■ ***2. How did Bowlby help bring Darwin's insights to bear in the understanding of human development?***

Freud, Erickson, and other psychodynamic theorists were influenced by Darwin in their emphasis on instincts, but stopped short of analyzing particular instincts or behaviors in terms of their contribution to survival and reproduction. As noted in Chapter 4, in the 1930s ethologists in Europe began to analyze animal behavior in explicitly Darwinian terms. They observed that many behavior patterns are universal to a species and can be understood as evolved adaptations that help individuals to survive and reproduce. These patterns include certain social interactions that occur at particular life stages—including behaviors that help bond an infant with its parents during the period when it needs care and behaviors that help bond an adult male and female for the purposes of mating and rearing young.

One of the first developmental psychologists to be influenced by ethology was John Bowlby (1907–1990), a British child psychiatrist. Bowlby had been trained in Freud's psychoanalytic theory, but found it in some ways inadequate. He read extensively the works of Konrad Lorenz and other ethologists and began to apply ethological ideas to an understanding of children. He argued, for example, that the bonding between human infant and adult caregiver is promoted by a set of instinctive tendencies in both partners (Bowlby, 1982). These include the infant's crying to signal discomfort, the adult's distress and urge to help upon hearing the crying, the infant's smiling and cooing when comforted, and the adult's pleasure at receiving those signals. Bowlby also discussed certain universal childhood fears, such as fear of the dark and of strangers, in terms of their role in promoting survival.

Theories Emphasizing Cross-Cultural Differences

Where biologically oriented theories emphasize cross-cultural universals, other theories emphasize cross-cultural differences. From the *sociocultural perspective*, human development is a process of adapting to the social customs and economic conditions of the society into which one is born. From this view, understanding a person's development requires that we look not just at the person, or just at the person and family, but also at the entire social structure of which the person and family are a part.

Bronfenbrenner's Social Ecology Theory

One of the leaders in the attempt to account for cross-cultural differences in development is Urie Bronfenbrenner (1979, 1986), with his *social ecology theory*. In biology, the term *ecology* refers to the entire network of interactions among different plants and animals and the environments to which they must adapt. In Bronfenbrenner's usage, ***social ecology*** refers to the entire network of other people and the social setting to which the developing person must adapt psychologically, which varies from culture to culture.

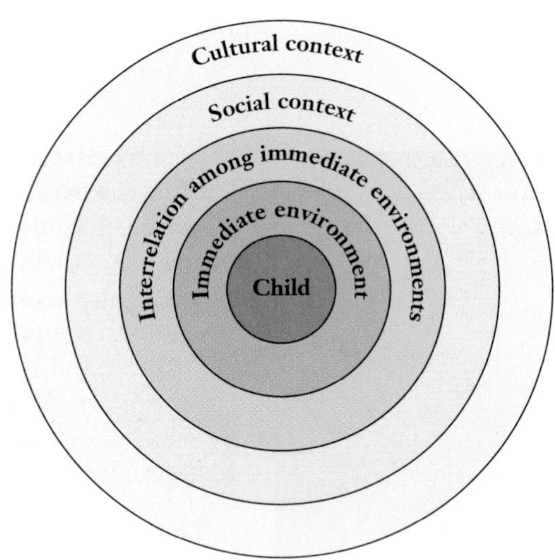

Figure 13.1 ***Bronfenbrenner's theory of the contexts of development***

Urie Bronfenbrenner conceives of the child as developing within a set of social contexts, which can be arranged (as they are here) according to the degree to which they pertain specifically to the child or to the broader society and culture of which the child is a part. (Adapted from Bronfenbrenner, 1979.)

3. ***How does the social ecology theory explain why any specific aspect of the immediate environment can produce different effects on children in different cultures?***

Bronfenbrenner finds it useful to depict a person's social ecology as a set of concentric rings, illustrated in Figure 13.1. He gave technical names to the rings, but I have chosen to substitute the more descriptive labels shown in the figure. At the center is the child himself or herself. Surrounding the child is the *immediate environment*, consisting of the people and things with which the child is in contact at any given moment. The next level, the *relationships among immediate environments*, refers to the relationships that exist among those parts of the world that serve as the child's immediate environment at different times. For example, home and school are two immediate environments of a child. According to Bronfenbrenner (1986), the relationship between home and school is as important to the child's development as are the separate qualities of home and school. Thus, a child's ability to learn at school depends not only on how he or she is taught there, but also on the parents' attitudes toward the school, which in turn affect the child's attitudes. The next ring in Bronfenbrenner's theory is the *social context*, which refers to aspects of society that affect the child even though the child does not come into direct contact with them. In our culture the parents' places of work, the school board, the local government, the producers of television programming, and so on, all influence development through their effects on the child's environment.

The outermost ring in Bronfenbrenner's theory is the *cultural context*, the entire set of beliefs, values, and accepted ways of behaving that characterize the historically connected group of people of which the child and his or her family are a part. As an extreme example of the power of the cultural context, consider the act of *scarification*—the creation of decorative scars through knife cuts or burning. In our culture, scarifying a child would be considered abuse; it would be interpreted that way not only by neighbors and the law, but by the child, too, and hence the scars would be more than physical. But where it is part of a long-established puberty ritual, scarification is regarded by everyone, including the child, as a sign of respect and acceptance into a new stage of life. In such a culture, a child who was *not* scarified at the appropriate time might feel neglected and ill-used.

The Concept of a Social Clock

Every culture has its expectations of what people normally do at various ages. People internalize that ***social clock*** and judge their lives by it. "How am I doing for my age?" asks the 10-year-old, the 20-year-old, the 40-year-old, and the 70-year-old. In our society, the social clock for children is timed to a considerable degree by school, and for adults is timed to a considerable degree by societal expectations concerning family and career. The idea of a social clock, as described by Bernice Neugarten, is not a formal theory, but it is a useful tool for thinking about social development (Hagestad & Neugarten, 1985; Neugarten, 1979).

■ **4. *How might the concept of a social clock provide an alternative explanation of Erikson's stages?***

Look back at Erikson's eight stages with the social clock in mind. Notice that the onset of Stage 4, *industry*, coincides with the age at which children in our society start school; Stage 5, *identity*, coincides with the age at which people in our society are trying to decide on a career; Stage 6, *intimacy*, with the age at which people are expected to get engaged or married; Stage 7, *generativity*, with the age at which people are expected to be raising children and working hard at their careers; and Stage 8, *integrity*, with retirement and the expectation of a more contemplative style of life. Do the stages stem from a biologically ingrained set of human needs, which must play themselves out in that order, or do they stem from the traditional expectations of our society, which have come down to us through cultural history? If Erikson had been raised in a non-Western, agrarian (agriculture-based) society, in which people live in extended families and children work alongside their elders in the fields at a very early age, would he have come up with the same eight stages? This is the kind of question that the social-clock concept begs us to ask.

Theories That Relate Social Development to Cognitive Development

■ **5. *How did Piaget's work on cognitive development influence theories of social development? How does Vygotsky's theory integrate the cognitive, sociocultural, and biological perspectives?***

Most developmental psychologists today consider the child to be an active contributor to his or her own development, an idea most strongly emphasized in Piaget's theory of cognitive development (discussed in Chapter 12). Piaget (1932) argued that changes in children's social behavior reflect changes in their more general understanding of the world. For example, as children become more cognizant of cause-effect relationships in the physical world, they also become more cognizant of cause-effect relationships in the social world, and this understanding influences their views of right and wrong and their modes of interacting with others. You will read later of Lawrence Kohlberg's theory of moral development, which was inspired by Piaget's work.

Lev Vygotsky (1986–1934), the Russian psychologist discussed in Chapters 11 and 12, outlined a theory of development that integrates the cognitive perspective with the sociocultural. In Vygotsky's view, children actively build mental models of appropriate behavior from examples in the social environment. Concepts such as right, wrong, female, male, friend, enemy, privilege, and responsibility lie in the social environment and are symbolized in the words that children learn. From these examples and symbols children construct their own understanding and then use that understanding to guide their behavior. Vygotsky's theory can be extended to link the cultural and cognitive perspectives to the biological. Children may be biologically primed to attend to those facets of their social environment that are most relevant to their own acceptance and future roles, and thus most relevant to their survival and reproduction. Later you will read about Vygotsky's theory that imaginative play is a universal vehicle through which children consolidate their understanding of social roles, rules, and responsibilities.

Infancy

Infants come into the world as social and emotional beings, biologically prepared to learn who their caregivers are and elicit from them the help they need. Researchers have found that newborns show a preference for their own mother's voice within minutes after birth (discussed in Chapter 12) and for their mother's smell and (more debatably) sight within a few days after birth (Bushnell & others, 1989; Macfarlane, 1975). Newborns, of course, can express distress through fussing or crying, and, according to some reports, they can also manifest elements of seven

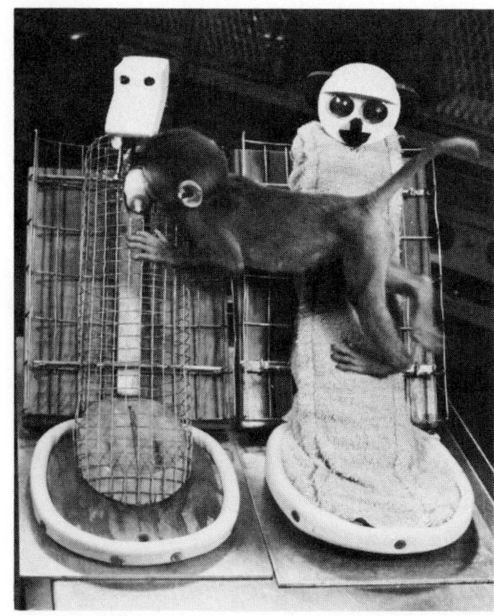

Figure 13.2 ***Harlow's motherless monkeys***

Harlow found that infant monkeys isolated from other monkeys and raised with two surrogate (substitute) mothers, one wire and one cloth, treated the cloth surrogate in many ways as they would their real mother. The monkey shown here received its nourishment from a bottle attached to the wire surrogate, but went to the cloth surrogate for comfort, affection, and reassurance.

universal facial expressions of emotion—happy, sad, surprised, interested, disgusted, angry, and fearful (Field & others, 1984). By the time they are two to four months old, infants express each of these emotions quite fully and reliably, in response to appropriate stimuli, and can recognize and respond to at least some of these expressions in others (Field, 1990). With these beginnings, infants help build an emotional bond between themselves and their mothers or other consistent caregivers.

Attachment to Caregivers

In 1950, John Bowlby, the child psychiatrist mentioned earlier who was influenced by ethology, undertook a massive study of the effects on children of separation from their parents. World War II had made orphans of many thousands of children, and Bowlby found in them serious, long-lasting emotional scars that went beyond whatever physical suffering they had endured. He also observed grief in infants and young children who were separated from their mothers for relatively short periods such as hospital stays. To explain these and other observations, Bowlby (1958, 1982) outlined a theory of early development that centered on the young child's emotional bond, or ***attachment***, to the principal caregiver, most commonly the mother. Before we examine some of the specifics of Bowlby's theory, let's look at some related research conducted with monkeys.

Harlow's Monkeys

At about the same time that Bowlby began to develop his theory of attachment, Harry Harlow began a program of research on the effects of maternal deprivation in rhesus monkeys. Harlow's work was inspired by René Spitz's research with infants in many orphanages in Canada and the United States in the 1940s. Spitz observed that, despite adequate food and cleanliness, about one-third of such infants died before their first birthday, and many others were severely retarded both physically and psychologically. Spitz concluded that the infants withered away from lack of handling and emotional stimulation (Gardner, 1972). To study the conditions that might lead to such effects in children, Harlow raised monkeys in isolation from their mothers and other monkeys. He found that these monkeys behaved as if extraordinarily depressed and fearful and were unable to gain acceptance when finally placed with other monkeys. Most relevant to an understanding of attachment are experiments in which Harlow raised infant monkeys with inanimate surrogate (substitute) mothers.

■ **6.** ***How did Harlow assess infant monkeys' attachment to surrogate mothers, and what did he find?***

In one experiment, Harlow (1959) raised infant monkeys in individual, isolated cages containing two surrogate mothers—one made of bare wire and the other covered with soft terry cloth (see Figure 13.2). The infants could feed themselves by sucking milk from a nipple that for half of them was attached to the wire surrogate and for the other half was attached to the cloth surrogate. Harlow's purpose was to determine if the infants would become attached to either of these surrogate mothers, as they would to a real mother, and to determine which characteristic—the milk-providing nipple or the soft cloth exterior—would be more effective in inducing attachment.

Harlow's main finding was that regardless of which surrogate contained the nutritive nipple, all infants treated the cloth-covered surrogate, not the wire one, as a mother. They clung to it much of the day and ran to it when threatened by a strange object (see Figure 13.3). They also were braver in exploring an unfamiliar room when it was present than when it was absent and would press a lever repeatedly to look at it through a window in preference to other objects. Harlow con-

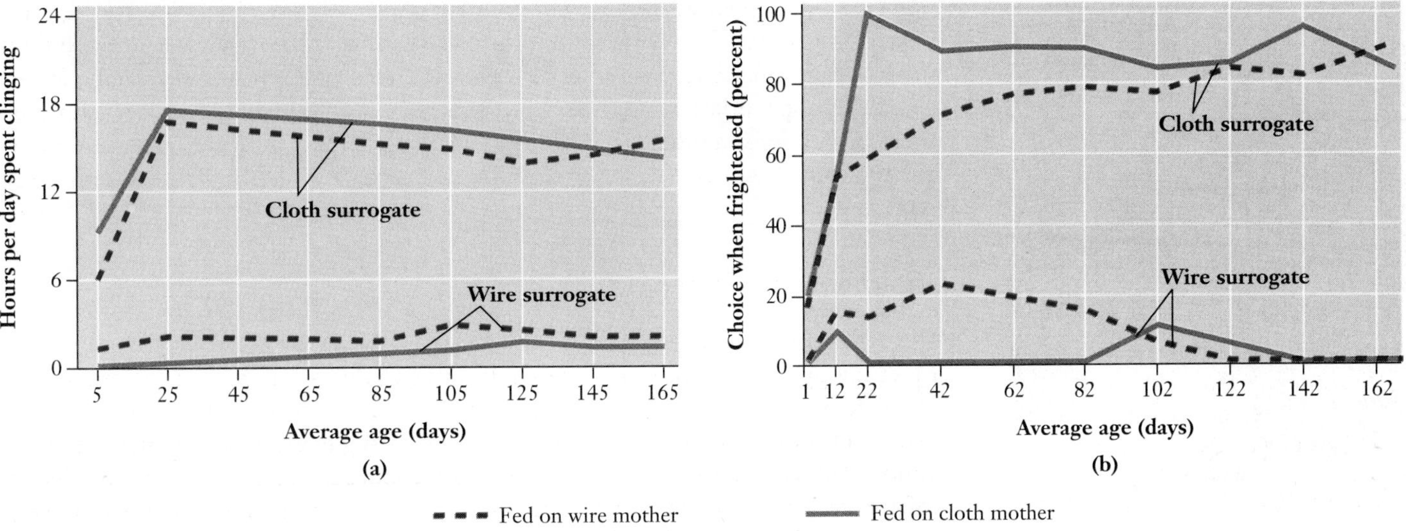

Figure 13.3 ***Evidence of infant monkeys' preference for the cloth surrogate*** These graphs show (a) the average number of hours that Harlow's monkeys spent on each of the surrogate mothers and (b) the percentage of time that they ran to each when they were frightened by a strange object. Notice that the preference for the cloth surrogate was as strong for the monkeys that were fed on the wire surrogate as for those fed on the cloth surrogate. (Adapted from Harlow, 1959.)

cluded that, in the formation of an infant monkey's attachment to its mother, *contact comfort* is more important than feeding.

The Form and Function of Human Infant Attachment

■ **7.** ***According to Bowlby, what infant behaviors indicate strong attachment, and why would these have come about through natural selection?***

According to Bowlby (1982), children manifest the strongest attachment to their mother (or another consistent caregiver) between about 8 months and 3 years of age. During this period they (a) exhibit distress when the object of their attachment leaves them; (b) exhibit pleasure when reunited with that person; (c) exhibit distress when approached by a stranger, especially if the object of their attachment is not present; and (d) are more likely to explore an unfamiliar environment if the object of their attachment is present than if she (or he) is absent.

According to Bowlby's theory, these behaviors are universal, and the biological basis for them derives from natural selection. Infants are potentially in danger when out of sight of a reliable caregiver. During our evolutionary history, the infants most likely to survive were those who successfully scrambled after their mother, or protested her departure and thus secured her return, and avoided unfamiliar objects when their mother was absent. In this way, genes promoting attachment behaviors were selected. Evidence that similar behaviors occur in other mammals (such as Harlow's monkeys) and in all human cultures that have been studied (Kagan, 1976) corroborates this evolutionary interpretation.

The fact that these attachment behaviors become strongest at about the time that the infant becomes mobile is also consistent with Bowlby's evolutionary theory. An infant who can crawl or walk can get into more danger than an immobile infant. From an evolutionary perspective, the value to the infant of exploring and learning must be balanced by appropriate fears. Exploration is much safer if the caregiver is present than if she (or he) is not. Research has shown that beginning when they can first crawl or walk, infants show a high degree of ***social referencing*** as they explore; that is, they frequently look to their mother or another familiar adult for cues to guide their behavior (Walden, 1991). In an experiment with 12-month-olds, not one crawled over a slight visual cliff (an apparent 30-cm drop-off under a glass surface) if the mother showed facial signs of fear, but most did crawl over if she showed facial signs of joy or interest (Sorce & others, 1985). In another experiment, 12-month-olds avoided a new toy if the mother showed a facial sign of disgust toward it, but played readily with it otherwise (Hornik & others, 1987).

(a)

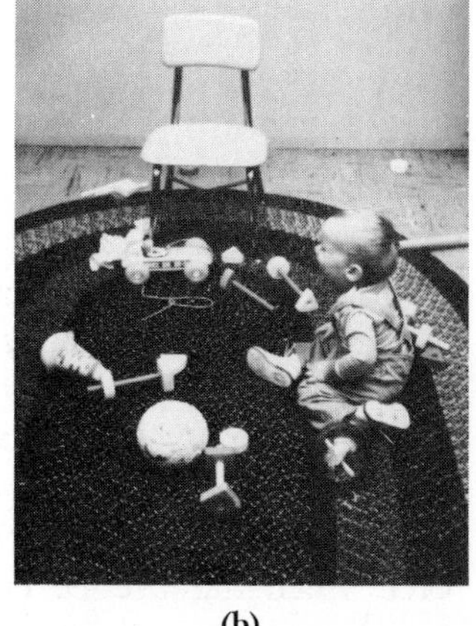

(b)

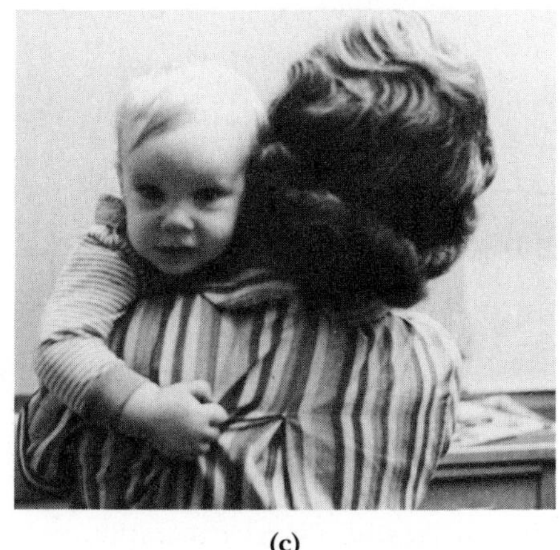

(c)

Figure 13.4 ***The strange-situation test***

In this test of attachment, the mother (or other person to whom the infant is attached) moves in and out of an unfamiliar room, leaving the infant either with a stranger or alone. Here we see one infant, Brian, at different stages in the test: In (a) he plays confidently when his mother is present, in (b) he cries when she leaves, and in (c) he is comforted when she returns. Brian's behavior indicates that he is securely attached to his mother.

The Strange-Situation Test

In order to assess attachment systematically, Mary Ainsworth—who originally worked with Bowlby—developed the ***strange-situation test***. In this test the infant and mother (or other possible object of attachment) are brought into an unfamiliar room that contains toys with which the infant can play. The infant remains in the room while the mother and an unfamiliar adult move out of and into the room according to a prescribed sequence. The infant is sometimes with the mother, sometimes with the stranger, and sometimes alone. Infants are classed as *securely attached* if they explore the room confidently when the mother is present, become mildly upset and explore less when the mother is not present, and show pleasure when reunited with the mother (see Figure 13.4). Other patterns of responses—such as showing distress even when the mother is present, or no distress when she leaves, or no pleasure upon her return—result in a classification of insecure attachment. By these criteria, Ainsworth and other researchers have found that about 70 percent of middle-class North American infants 12 to 24 months old are securely attached to their mothers (Ainsworth & others, 1978; Lamb & others, 1992).

■ **8. *How does the strange-situation test assess the security of attachment? What are some limitations of this measure?***

Like most measures of psychological attributes, the strange-situation test has limitations (Goldsmith & others, 1986). The test is designed to assess the infant's reactions to the caregiver in a *mildly* fearful situation, but in some infants the situation might induce either too much or too little fear to provide a valid measure. Infants vary in the degree to which they fear new situations for reasons of heredity as well as experience (Kagan & others, 1992). A temperamentally fearful infant may be distressed by the strange situation even when the mother is present, and a temperamentally confident infant may explore the room even when the mother is absent and may be oblivious to her return. Neither infant would be classed as securely attached, but observations of the same infants in other settings might tell a different story.

Cultural differences may also affect the results. In some cultures the test shows a considerably lower rate of secure attachment than it does in North America, and the difference may be due not to attachment but to the meaning the test has to the infants (Sagi & others, 1991). In Japan, for example, where infants are seldom separated even briefly from their mothers, an infant may become so distressed by the mother's departure as to be inconsolable on her return. The resulting classification of insecure attachment could be misleading (Miyake & others, 1985).

Mary Ainsworth

Ainsworth's pioneering studies have explored the qualitative differences in the emotional bonds between infants and their caregivers.

Correlation Between Caregiver Behavior and Secure Attachment

In her early research with the strange-situation test, Ainsworth wished to discover the conditions of care that lead to secure attachment. She and Bowlby had theorized that infants will become securely attached to a caregiver who provides regular contact comfort, who interacts in an emotionally synchronous manner with the infant (see Figure 13.5), and who responds promptly and reliably in a comforting and

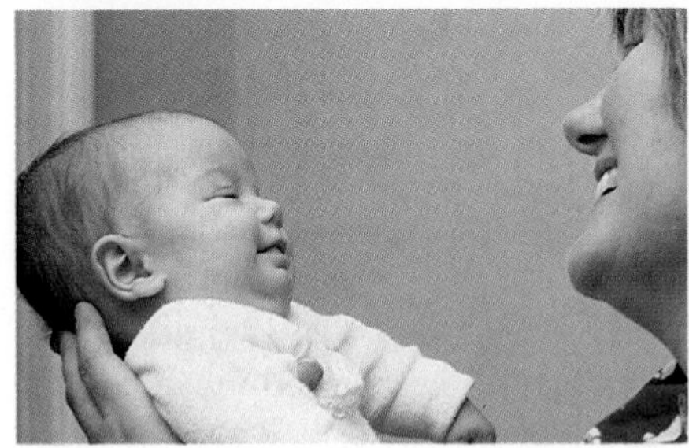

Figure 13.5 ***Interactional synchrony***
Researchers have found that interactions such as this during the first 3 months of life correlate with secure attachment measured several months later.

need-fulfilling way to the infant's crying and other signals of distress. To test this theory, Ainsworth and her followers assessed various aspects of mothers' responsiveness to their infants, either at home or in the laboratory, and correlated those measures with the infant's attachment rating in the strange-situation test.

Consistent with Ainsworth and Bowlby's theory, such research has produced positive correlations; the more comforting and responsive the mother, the more likely is the infant to show secure attachment (Ainsworth, 1979; Cox & others, 1992; Sroufe & Fleeson, 1986). The correlations are usually not very strong, however, which might reflect error in measurement or might indicate that considerable variation can occur in maternal behavior without seriously undermining the chance of secure attachment. Moreover, since all of this research is correlational, alternative cause-effect interpretations are possible (as discussed in Chapter 2). For example, some infants may for genetic reasons be more inclined than others to respond positively to the mother's attention. Such behavior would both lead to a secure attachment rating and reward the mother for comforting the infant, leading to the observed correlation. Most researchers today would agree that the infant and mother must both be considered as active forces in the development of attachment.

■ **9.** ***What early caregiver behaviors are predictive of secure attachment? How do Bowlby and Ainsworth interpret the correlations, and how else might they be interpreted?***

Multiple Attachments and Effects of Day-Care

Goslings become imprinted on only one mother or mother-substitute (described in Chapter 5), but human infants can become attached to more than one person—including the father, siblings, grandparents, and other caregivers (Ainsworth, 1982). When infants are tested with their mother and father in the strange situation, most can be comforted by either parent but prefer the mother (Cox & others, 1992; Lamb, 1986). This is true even for families in which the mother works outside the home and the father is the principal caregiver (Lamb & Oppenheim, 1989). The difference apparently lies in the quality of care, not the quantity. Mothers in all cultures that have been studied are on average more gentle and affectionate toward infants than are fathers (Lamb & Oppenheim, 1989). Such research of course does not tell us the causes of these differences; they may or may not lie entirely in the fact that in every culture females are expected to be the primary caregivers, and therefore they receive more early training and encouragement for that role.

■ **10.** ***What are the general findings of research comparing attachment to fathers with that to mothers and attachment in day-care infants with that in home-care infants?***

In many families in our culture, both parents work outside the home and infants spend their days at a day-care center. Does this affect the infant's attachment to his or her parents? Studies using the strange-situation test to address this question have produced mixed results. Some indicate that secure attachment to a parent

Having a good day
Researchers may argue about the long-term effects of day-care on children's social and emotional development, but there is little disagreement that high-quality settings like the one shown here offer the best opportunity for growth. Such centers offer toddlers a safe environment, with opportunities for exploration, and responsive, consistent, nurturing care.

is less frequent in day-care children than in children cared for by a parent at home, and some do not (Belsky & Rovine, 1988; Lamb & others, 1992). Over all studies combined, the effects of day-care on attachment are quite small. The difference from study to study may reflect the quality of the day-care center and the quality of the parents' interactions with the child when they are at home. It is also possible that the appearance of insecure attachment in day-care children simply reflects the fact that they are used to being left by their parents in environments away from home; the strange situation may be insufficiently frightening to them to elicit attachment behavior (Field, 1990).

Possible Developmental Effects of Quality of Attachment

■ **11.** ***What evidence supports the theory that infant attachment affects subsequent emotional and social development, and what are the limitations of that evidence?***

Many psychologists have theorized that the quality of an infant's early attachment to the mother or another caregiver strongly influences the child's later development. For instance, Erik Erikson proposed that secure attachment in infancy results in "basic trust," which permits the infant to enter subsequent life stages in a confident, growth-promoting manner (see Table 13.1). Bowlby (1973) and Ainsworth (1989) postulated that infants develop an internal "working model," or cognitive representation of their first attachment relationship, which influences the relationships they develop throughout life.

Many research findings are consistent with such theories. Infants judged as securely attached in the strange-situation test have been found to be on average more confident, better problem solvers, emotionally healthier, and more sociable in later childhood than those who were judged as insecurely attached (Ainsworth, 1989; Frankel & Bates, 1990; Jacobson & Wille, 1986). Moreover, studies of young adults have revealed that the warmth and security of their attachments in romantic relationships correlate positively with the degree to which they remember their early relationships with their parents as warm and secure (Feeney & Noller, 1990; Hazen & Shaver, 1987).

Secure attachment in infancy clearly helps predict positive development in later life. Again, however, correlation does not tell us about the direction of causality. While it seems logical that the security of infant attachment would help cause the positive later effects, other explanations of the correlation are possible. Perhaps some people are temperamentally predisposed to close relationships throughout life. Their temperament might independently promote secure attachment in infancy and success in social interactions later on. Another explanation may lie in the continuity of parental behavior. Parents who are affectionate toward their children typically remain so even into their children's adulthood (Levitt, 1991), and the continuing emotional support may be more influential than the infant attachment in producing positive development. Consistent with this view is evidence that children who were emotionally deprived during infancy but were adopted later into affectionate homes usually developed warm relationships with their adoptive parents and adjusted positively to life's subsequent challenges (Tizard & Hodges, 1978).

Cross-Cultural Differences in Infant Care

Beliefs and practices regarding infant care vary considerably from culture to culture. Our Western, Euro-American culture is in many ways less indulgent of infants' desires than are other cultures.

Infants' Sleeping Arrangements

Our culture is unusual in the expectation that infants and young children should sleep alone. A survey of ninety other cultures revealed that, in every one, infants

■ **12.** ***How do sleeping arrangements for infants and toddlers differ across cultures, and how might this help explain cross-cultural differences in attachments to blankets?***

and toddlers slept in the same room with their mother or another closely related adult, usually in the same bed (Barry & Paxson, 1971).

Interviews of Mayan mothers in rural Guatemala and middle-class mothers in the United States revealed that sleeping practices in these two cultures are supported by different sets of beliefs (Morelli & others, 1992). The Mayan mothers, who all slept with their infants and toddlers, emphasized the comforting value of physical closeness. When told that young children in the United States often sleep alone, in separate rooms, they expressed dismay and pity at what seemed to them a heartless practice. In contrast, the United States mothers, none of whom slept regularly with their youngsters, expressed concern that to do so would establish a hard-to-break habit, would foster dependency, and might even be physically dangerous in that the infant could be smothered. Moreover, the United States mothers saw bedtime as a time for intimate relations with their husbands, whereas the Mayan mothers saw it as a time for family togetherness. Not surprisingly, the task of putting young children to bed was much easier for the Mayan mothers than the United States mothers, who commonly engaged in elaborate bedtime rituals.

Other research indicates that infants in other cultures, who sleep with an adult, are much less likely to develop attachments to an inanimate object—the so-called security blanket or the special doll or teddy bear—than are infants in the United States (Honig & Townes, 1976). This suggests that attachments to inanimate objects may derive at least partly from sleeping alone. Perhaps, to relieve their fear at night, infants in our culture—much like Harlow's monkeys—attach themselves to the softest, most comforting mother substitute available. Unlike Harlow's monkeys, of course, the human infants are in contact with their mother and other caregivers during the day, so the attachment to the inanimate object is in addition to other attachments. Nevertheless, security blankets apparently do increase the child's sense of security. In a test similar to the strange-situation test, blanket-attached infants were as calmed by their blankets as either they or other infants were by their own mothers (Passman & Weisberg, 1975). With the blanket present, they explored the room; without it, they cried or showed other signs of distress.

Infant Care in Hunter-Gatherer Societies

During the great bulk of our species' history, our ancestors lived in small groups made up mainly of close relatives, who survived by gathering and hunting food cooperatively in the forest or savannah. The biological underpinnings of infants' and caregivers' behaviors evolved in the context of that way of life. Partly for that reason, an examination of infant care in the few hunter-gatherer cultures that remain is of special interest.

■ **13.** ***How is infant care managed differently by the !Kung and the Efe? In what ways are both cultures highly indulgent toward infants?***

Melvin Konner (1976, 1982) studied the !Kung people who live in Africa's Kalahari Desert (the *!K* in *!Kung* stands for a clicklike sound that is different from our *K*). He observed that !Kung infants spend most of their time during their first year in direct contact with their mothers' bodies. During the day the mother carries the infant constantly in a sling at her side. The sling is situated in such a way that the infant has constant access to the mothers' breast and can nurse at will—which, according to Konner, occurs on average every 15 minutes. The infant's position also enables the infant to see what the mother sees and in that way to be involved in her activities. At night the mother sleeps with the infant at her side. Nursing typically continues until the child is about 3 years old. When not being held by the mother, the infant is passed around among others who cuddle, fondle, kiss, and enjoy the baby. According to Konner, the !Kung never leave an infant to cry alone, and usually they detect the distress and begin to comfort the infant before crying even begins.

Efe girl and her infant brother

In hunter-gatherer cultures, infants are in direct physical contact with a caregiver almost constantly. Among the Efe, the principal caregiver is the mother. The infant spends about half of each day with her and the rest of the day with other members of the group, most of whom are close relatives.

■ **14. *What evidence suggests that indulgence of infants does not spoil them? How might infant indulgence be related to interdependence and to the degree to which people live in extended families?***

Studies in other hunter-gatherer cultures have shown a similarly high degree of indulgence toward infants, but patterns of who provides the care can vary. Gilda Morelli and her colleagues have studied the Efe (more commonly known as Pygmies, a term they consider derogatory), who live as hunters and gatherers in the Ituri forest of Zaïre (Morelli & Tronick, 1991; Tronick & others, 1992). These researchers found that infants are in physical contact with their mothers only about half the day and during the other half are in direct contact with other caregivers, including siblings, aunts, and unrelated women of the group. Efe infants nurse at will, not just from their mother but also from other lactating women in the group. At about 8 to 12 months of age—the age at which research in many cultures has shown that attachment begins to grow strong—Efe infants begin to show an increased preference for their own mother. They are less readily comforted by other people and will often reject the breast of another woman and seek their mother's.

Issues of Indulgence and Dependence

Books on infant care in our culture (for example, Spock & Rothenberg, 1985) commonly advise parents that offering infants immediate comfort whenever they cry could lead them to become ever more demanding and would prevent them from learning to cope with frustration. Similarly, the U.S. mothers in the cross-cultural study of sleeping arrangements felt that their children would become overly dependent if permitted to sleep with them (Morelli & others, 1992).

Konner (1982, 1976), however, has argued that such indulgence does not produce overly demanding and dependent children, at least not among the !Kung. In a cross-cultural test, !Kung children over the age of 4 explored more and sought their mothers less in a novel environment than did their British counterparts (Blurton-Jones & Konner, 1973). By the time they are teenagers, !Kung children must do their share of providing food and other necessities in an environment that is full of danger (including wild animals) and hardship (such as prolonged periods of drought). If their child-rearing practices had produced uncooperative or incompetent adults, the !Kung would not have survived in their harsh environment.

Some researchers speculate that high indulgence of infants' desires, coupled with the complete integration of infants and children into the community's social life, may foster long-lasting emotional bonds that are stronger than those developed by our Western practices (Tronick & others, 1992; Rogoff, 1990). The result is apparently not dependence, in the sense of fear when alone or inability to function autonomously, but *interdependence*, in the sense of strong loyalties or feelings of obligation to a particular set of people. In cultures such as the !Kung and the Efe, where people depend economically throughout their lives on the cooperative efforts of their relatives and other members of their tribe, such bonds may be more important to each person's well-being than they are in our mobile society, where the people with whom we interact change as we go from home, to school, to work, or move from one part of the country to another.

Regardless of what one's beliefs may be about appropriate infant care, the range of possible practices is limited by other aspects of the culture. In our culture, where nuclear families live in relative isolation from one another, most parents could not possibly indulge their infants to the degree seen in other cultures. !Kung mothers are constantly in contact with their young infants, but they are also constantly surrounded by other adults who provide social stimulation and emotional and material support (Konner, 1976). A survey of infant care in 55 cultures in various parts of the world revealed a direct correlation between the degree of indulgence and the number of adults who live communally with the infant (Whiting, 1971). Indulgence is greatest for infants who live in large extended families, and least for those who live just with one or both parents.

Childhood

Childhood, for the purposes of this discussion, is the period of life that begins at about age 3 and ends at puberty. After infancy the strong drive to remain physically close to adult caregivers begins to fade and is replaced by a desire to move in increasingly wider circles from the home and interact with people outside the family. Childhood is a time when, given the opportunity, play with peers is a dominant activity. It is also a time to learn the knowledge, skills, and values of the larger culture and to adapt oneself to its concepts of appropriate male or female roles.

The Continuing Role of Parents

■ **15. *What are some universal goals of parenting, and why might the best means of achieving those goals be more ambiguous to parents in our culture than to parents in traditional, preindustrial cultures?***

Parents in all cultures share certain broad goals for their children beyond the satisfaction of immediate physical and emotional needs (LeVine, 1980; Whiting & Edwards, 1988). Parents everywhere want their children to acquire the habits of hygiene needed for long-term health and survival, the moral values and rules of etiquette needed for social acceptance, and the skills and work habits needed for self-support. The specifics of what the children must learn toward these ends and how the parents figure into the process, however, vary greatly from culture to culture.

In non-Western, preindustrial cultures, parents impart habits, rules, skills, and knowledge by involving their children directly in the full range of the culture's activities (Rogoff, 1990). Even very young children take part in family or community tasks such as gardening, hunting, weaving, and caring for infants. As children grow older they assume increasingly responsible and skilled roles, in a kind of natural apprenticeship. Children are also present at adult social functions and by observation learn the rules and norms of their community.

Our culture, in contrast, offers many more options for conducting and supporting ourselves and fewer immediate adult models. The adult's work and social world is largely separated from the child's world. Appropriate skills, knowledge, and values for living successfully in our culture are more varied and less certain than in traditional cultures. Living in isolated homes, parents have less direct support from relatives and neighbors. All this makes the task of parenting especially difficult in our culture. Perhaps that is why issues about how to be a good parent are frequently debated in our culture and are a common topic of psychological investigation. Much of that debate and research focuses on *discipline*—defined narrowly in this context as the attempts of parents to stop or correct their children's misbehavior.

Hoffman's Theory of Discipline

■ **16. *What are Hoffman's three categories of discipline, and why does he favor the category called induction?***

Martin Hoffman (1983) has proposed that the discipline techniques commonly used by parents in our culture can be divided into three categories. One category is *power assertion*—the use of rewards and (more commonly) actual or threatened punishments to control a child's behavior. The second category is *love withdrawal*, which occurs when parents—often unwittingly—express disapproval of the *child*, rather than just of the child's specific action. This may take the form of verbal statements such as, "You are worthless," or nonverbal actions such as coldly ignoring the child. Like many other psychologists, Hoffman points to harmful effects of power assertion and love withdrawal. He argues that power assertion focuses attention on the punishments and rewards rather than on reasons why an action is wrong or right. A child so disciplined may continue the undesirable behavior when there is little chance of being caught and may behave well only when someone is sure to notice and provide a reward. Moreover, both punishment and love withdrawal elicit negative emotions in the child (anger in the case of punishment, anxiety in the case of love withdrawal) that may weaken the parent-child relationship and promote further misbehavior.

Hoffman's third category of discipline is ***induction***, a form of verbal reasoning in which the parent induces the child to think about his or her actions and the consequences they may have for other people. This technique, which Hoffman strongly favors, uses and nourishes the child's capacity for empathy (feeling what another person feels). For example, a parent may say to a young child, "When you hit Billy, it hurts him and makes him cry"; or to a somewhat older child, "When you tease Susan and call her names, it makes her feel that nobody likes her." Stating the case this way helps make the child aware of the negative consequences of an action and demonstrates respect for the child's desire to act responsibly. Being the decision-maker allows the child to attribute a change in behavior to his or her own moral standards ("I don't want to hurt someone") rather than to an external and not always present source of reward or punishment.

Although Hoffman favors induction, he believes that power assertion is sometimes necessary to get a child to stop engaging in a seriously wrong action. In such cases, he contends, induction combined with power assertion helps reduce the potentially negative consequences of the latter. If the child who has been deprived of the privilege of going to the park because he persists in hitting Billy understands that the parents have a moral reason behind their punitive action, that it is not arbitrary or motivated by spite or loss of love, then the child is less likely to react with anger or anxiety and more likely to think about and possibly internalize the parents' moral reasoning.

Notice that Hoffman's theory is highly cognitive in nature. The goal of discipline is to induce the child to think in moral terms about his or her actions, not to elicit automatic compliance. This goal may be particularly appropriate for our culture, where people regularly face new situations and moral dilemmas to which learned habits and precepts may not readily apply.

Correlations Between Discipline Style and Children's Behavior

Many research studies, mostly of middle-class, North American families, have shown correlations between parental styles of discipline and children's behavior that are at least consistent with Hoffman's theory. In one study, for example, seventh graders were assessed through ratings by teachers and peers for their tendency to behave morally, and the children's parents were assessed through interviews for the extent to which they used power-assertive and inductive discipline techniques (Hoffman & Saltzstein, 1967). The measures of moral behavior correlated positively with parental use of induction and negatively with power assertion.

■ **17.** ***How did Baumrind classify parents' discipline styles into three types, and how do her and others' results support Hoffman's theory?***

In another study, Diana Baumrind (1967, 1971a) assessed the behavior of young children by observing them at nursery school and in their homes, and assessed the discipline styles of their parents through interviews and home observations. Based on the discipline styles, she classed parents into three groups. (1) *Authoritarian* parents valued obedience for its own sake and used a high degree of power assertion to control their children. (2) *Authoritative* parents were less concerned with obedience for its own sake and more concerned that their children learn and abide by basic principles of right and wrong. In Hoffman's terms, they preferred inductive discipline, but coupled it with power assertion when they felt it was needed. (3) *Permissive* parents were most tolerant of their children's disruptive actions and least likely to discipline at all. What responses they did show to their children's misbehavior seemed to be manifestations of their own frustration more than reasoned attempts at correction.

Baumrind found that children of authoritative parents showed the most positive qualities. Among other things, they were friendlier, more cooperative and less likely to disrupt others' activities than children of the other groups. A follow-up study of the same children showed that the advantages for those with authoritative parents were still present at age 9 (Baumrind, 1986). From the perspective of Hoffman's theory, the authoritarian parents may have used too much power assertion, the permissive parents may have used too little discipline of any kind, and the authoritative parents may have balanced a principally inductive discipline style with just enough power assertion to ensure attention to the message.

A few of the parents in Baumrind's study did not fit any of the three categories. Instead they showed a discipline style that Baumrind (1971b) labeled *harmonious.* These parents were like permissive parents in their lack of power assertion and apparent lack of concern about controlling their children, but they had unusually great respect for their children's ideas and capacity for self-control. Their interactions with their children involved a great deal of two-way communication, which seemed to help the children internalize values very early, so that direct parental control was rarely necessary. Although too few families were found in this group for statistical significance, these children seemed to be as sociable and competent as those in the authoritative group.

■ **18.** ***Why is caution needed in interpreting correlational results as evidence of parents' effects on children?***

Many other correlational studies have produced results comparable to Baumrind's (Devocic & Janssens, 1992; Lamborn & others, 1991; Maccoby, 1992). In general, children of authoritarian parents comply with adult wishes when an adult is present, but they are less likely to behave ethically when no adult is present, and they are less popular with peers than are children of authoritative parents. Moreover, when parents are warm and interested in their children's views, the children are themselves warmer and more self-confident than others.

All such studies are certainly suggestive in relation to the question of how to be a good parent in our culture. Still, we should be careful not to assume that children's behavior is a simple product of parents' discipline. Though positive and significant, the correlations are not very strong. Many children from authoritarian homes are well adjusted and many from authoritative homes are not. Moreover, as you by now well know, correlation does not necessarily imply causation. Researchers in this area tend to assume that a correlation between parental style and behavioral traits in children implies that the parental style is the cause of the children's traits. But in doing so they may be underestimating the extent to which children influence their parents (Bell & Harper, 1977). You can probably think of many reasons, completely independent of parenting style, why some children

"Sam, neither your father nor I consider your response appropriate."

might misbehave more than others; such misbehavior may alter their parents' discipline style in the direction of greater power assertion and less warmth, contributing to the observed correlation.

Play with a purpose
In their self-initiated play, children in all cultures exhibit their fascination with the tools and actions they see their elders use. This 11-month-old Efe boy is trying to cut a papaya with a huge, sharp knife.

The Developmental Functions of Play

Children learn to control their behavior not only through their interactions with parents and other adults, but also through their interactions with each other, particularly in play. Cross-cultural research indicates that similar forms of play exist throughout the world, though the details and the amount of time that children are free to play vary greatly (Johnson & others, 1987; Schwartzman, 1978). The forms include *rough-and-tumble play* (play fighting and chasing), *constructive play* (building or making things for fun), *sociodramatic play* (acting out imaginary roles), and *formal games* (games and sports with prescribed rules, usually competitive in nature).

The first scholar to write extensively about play in terms of Darwin's theory of evolution was the philosopher Karl Groos (1898, 1901). Groos contended that play stems from instinctive drives that evolved because they serve educative functions. He argued that play is a vehicle through which young mammals in general, and young humans in particular, acquire the skills they will need as adults. For example, lion cubs acquire through their playful fighting, stalking, and chasing the skills they will need to compete and hunt as adults. Groos noted that human children incorporate skills important to their culture into their play, and cross-cultural research since his time has confirmed this observation (Johnson & others, 1987). Boys in hunter-gatherer cultures play endlessly at hunting; my son played with computers.

■ **19.** ***How did Groos explain play in evolutionary terms?***

Learning About Rules and Roles

Psychologists contend that play promotes not just physical and technical competence, but other aspects of social and cognitive development as well. In his book *The Moral Judgment of the Child*, Piaget (1932) argued that social play helps the child gain a more advanced understanding of rules and morality. Parents—at least the Genevan parents of the 1920s and 1930s that Piaget knew—establish rules for their children in black-and-white terms, with little room for discussion. In contrast, during play with peers when no all-powerful authority is present, children learn to argue out their disputes. In the process, they develop an understanding of right and wrong based at least partly on reason rather than on authority.

■ **20.** ***In Vygotsky's view, how does play help children acquire a conscious understanding of rules and social roles and help them learn to control their own behavior?***

Lev Vygotsky was another cognitive theorist who wrote about play. Vygotsky, as described in Chapter 12, contended that social interaction is central to all aspects of mental development, so it is not surprising that he ascribed great importance to social play. He argued that, contrary to popular opinion, social play is not free and spontaneous, but is always governed by rules that define the range of permissible actions for each participant (Vygotsky, 1933/1978). In real life, young children behave spontaneously—they cry when they are hurt, laugh when they are happy, and express their wants. But in social play they must suppress their spontaneous urges and behave in accordance with the rules of the game or the role that they have agreed upon. Consider, for example, children playing "house," in which one child is the mommy, another is the baby, and another is the dog. To play this game, each child must keep in mind a conscious conception of what it means to be a mommy, a baby, or a dog, and must govern his or her actions in accordance with that conception. Thus, Vygotsky argued, social play fosters an ability critical to socialization—an ability to behave according to a conscious understanding of roles and rules. As children grow older, they transfer this ability to nonplay situations: At school they take the role of student, at work the role of worker.

Let's pretend

In sociodramatic play, children plan out situations and abide by the rules and roles they invent.

Consistent with Vygotsky's view, Catherine Garvey (1990) has found that young children put great effort into planning and enforcing rules in their sociodramatic play. Children who break the rules—who start acting like themselves rather than the role they have agreed to play—are sharply reminded by the others of what they are supposed to be doing: "Dogs don't sit at the table; you have to get under the table." Other recent research supports Vygotsky's view of the benefits of such play. Positive correlations have been found between the amount of sociodramatic play children engage in and subsequent ratings of their social competence (Connolly & Doyle 1984; Howes & Matheson, 1992).

Coping with Trauma

Psychoanalytic theorists such as Erikson (1963) maintain that children use play to help themselves cope with emotional crises. Consistent with this view are reports that children who have experienced emotionally traumatic events often center their play on issues pertaining to the event. For example, a group of nursery-school children who saw a man fall 20 feet to the ground and suffer serious injury were very disturbed by the incident, and for months afterward their play centered on such themes as falling, injury, hospitals, and death (Brown & others, 1971).

■ **21.** ***According to Eisen, how did children's play in concentration camps help them survive?***

Children's self-directed play may also help them harden themselves and develop skills to cope with prolonged misery. The most dramatic evidence can be found in George Eisen's (1988) book, *Childhood and Play in the Holocaust*. Through an analysis of diaries and interviews with survivors, Eisen found that even in the Nazi death camps during World War II, children played. Adult inmates used games and fantasies to avoid thinking about their situation, but the children invented games to confront the horrors head on. They played at war and murder. They even played "gas chamber," a game in which they would imitate the screams of dying people. At Birkenau, children invented a game that was modeled after the camp's daily roll calls. One child would be hit hard on the face while blindfolded and then with the blindfold removed would try to guess from facial expressions which other child had done the hitting. The game was called *klepsie-klepsie*, based on the German word for stealing. At Birkenau, the ability to mask one's facial expressions when questioned about such issues as stealing food was probably a survival skill.

Schools as Social Environments

In our culture and many others, children spend much of their lives in school. Schools are designed to teach skills and knowledge for living in the larger society, but they are also social settings in their own right to which children must adapt.

The Traditional School Environment

■ **22.** ***What are some of the unique features of traditional schools as social settings, and how might children's ability to adapt to school depend on values outside of school?***

An educational psychologist (Weinstein, 1991) described some of the paradoxes presented to children by the typical school: "Assigned to classes that may contain strangers, perhaps even adversaries, students are expected to interact harmoniously. Crowded together, they are required to ignore the presence of others. Urged to cooperate, they usually work in competition. Pressed to take responsibility for their own learning, they must follow the dictates of a dominant individual—the teacher."

One of the most striking characteristics of school compared to other social settings is its intensely competitive nature. At school children are confined to a room filled with many others of their age and made to engage in the same activities, a condition that by itself promotes competition. In addition, children's performance in the classroom is constantly evaluated and compared; children are ranked, and they know their standing and others'. Even "play" in school is usually competitive and evaluated by adults. At school, children must follow a strict schedule and subordinate their own curiosity and interest to the activities set by the teacher—activities that, unlike chores at home, seem to serve no immediate purpose.

Studies throughout the world suggest that in most cultures children do not adjust readily to this set of conditions (Whiting & Edwards, 1988). Horseplay and fighting are common, especially among boys, and a great deal of time and teacher energy goes into maintaining order. The degree to which children adjust to school may depend in part on cultural values and practices outside of school. The high value that North Americans place on individuality and independence may contribute to ambivalence in children and adults alike concerning the school's pressure for conformity and submission. In contrast, Japanese and Chinese cultures place relatively greater value on duty to family and obedience to authority. Classroom observations suggest that the transition from home to school in Japan and China is much smoother than in North America, and teachers in those Asian cultures spend far less time keeping order than do American teachers (Stigler & Perry, 1990).

In Western cultures, unease about strict control of children's activities has, from time to time, prompted experiments in alternative modes of education. In the 1970s, for example, many public schools in the United States developed *open classrooms*, which offer children more freedom of movement and more choices than traditional classrooms, but still have a teacher firmly in charge. Far more radical than open classrooms are schools that allow children complete freedom in matters pertaining to their education. One such school that has been much written about is Summerhill, an English boarding school run for half a century by A. S. Neill (1960). A more recent example is the Sudbury Valley School.

The Sudbury Valley School

Sudbury Valley is a day school for people of kindergarten through high-school age. It has been operating for more than 25 years in Massachusetts, and I have had the opportunity to observe it for many years. Recently this school has drawn a good deal of national and international attention, and a number of new schools have been modeled after it.

■ **23.** ***How was the Sudbury Valley School designed to be consistent with American cultural ideals, and how might free age mixing contribute to its educational success?***

The founders and staff at Sudbury Valley are committed to democratic ideals. They believe that institutions, including schools, work best when governed by the people they serve. They also believe that the sense of personal responsibility essential to a democracy develops best when children experience democracy first hand. Sudbury Valley is, first and foremost, a participatory democracy. All school rules and other important decisions—even the hiring and firing of staff—are made by students and staff through a one-person, one-vote procedure, and infractions of rules are tried through a judicial system involving school members of all ages. The weekly School Meeting is run in accordance with strict parliamentary procedure; it is not for "airing one's feelings," but rather for engaging in reasoned debate and decision making. The students in this setting know that their arguments and votes have real consequences for themselves and other school members. Staff members do not patronize students by holding back their own views, but rather argue as forcefully as they can.

How does education take place in this setting? If you were to walk onto the school's grounds or into its buildings at any time of day, you would assume that it must be recess time. You would see lots of socializing and playing, and very little of what looks like school. The school imposes no academic requirements, tests, grades, or other evaluations, and formal classes are rare. Daniel Greenberg (1992), one of the school's founders, believes that the secret of the school's educational suc-

Sharing an interest

These three members of the Sudbury Valley School appear to be equally intent on completing their project correctly. Free age mixing is one of the key elements of the educational philosophy of this nontraditional school.

cess is that it brings together people of different ages and allows them to mix freely. Younger children seem to be naturally drawn to the activities and discussions of older children and adults, who in turn often enjoy the chance to share their knowledge and ideas with younger children. Thus, as people become engaged in various activities—in the art room, computer room, kitchen, library, playground, or any number of other places—they are reciprocally involved as students and as teachers. Of course not everyone in this setting learns the same things; but in our culture, with so much diversity in employment, there seems little purpose in uniform learning. Those who decide they want to go to college usually sit down and deliberately study algebra and geometry so they can do well on the math SAT; they usually have read enough by then to do well on the verbal SAT with little extra preparation.

Extensive follow-up studies have shown that as a group the school's graduates have done remarkably well, even by the most traditional standards (Gray & Chanoff, 1986; Greenberg & Sadofsky, 1992). They have had no particular difficulty getting into and graduating from reputable colleges, and they have become successful in a wide variety of careers. In interviews and questionnaires, most of the graduates maintain that their unique schooling has made them more self-disciplined and socially responsible than they otherwise would be.

More than any other long-lived school I know of, Sudbury Valley challenges our thinking about the purposes and nature of formal education. The school's success suggests that, even in our complex technological culture, children can acquire the skills and knowledge they need for adulthood without coercion, through their own curiosity and concern for their own future. But for those drives to work, children must come into close contact with a variety of successful and caring adult members of the culture and must have the opportunity to observe and become directly involved with culturally valued activities. In a sense, Sudbury Valley provides—in a manner appropriate for our culture—the same opportunities for age-mixed, self-initiated learning that throughout most of our evolutionary history served as the foundation for education.

The Sociocultural Basis of Gender Role Development

Life is not the same for boys and girls. That is true not just in our culture, but in every culture that has been studied (Maccoby & Jacklin, 1987). To some degree, differences are biological in origin, mediated by hormones (see Chapters 4 and 7). But hormones don't explain why the differences vary from culture to culture, as

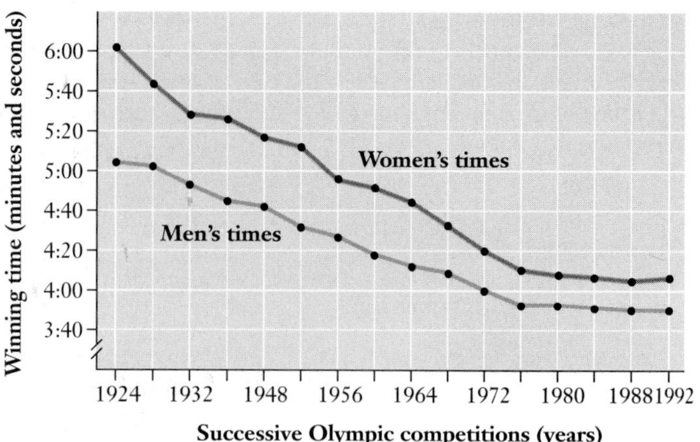

Figure 13.6 ***Example of a gender difference changing over time***

In competitions that require strength, the difference between the best male and female athletes at any time in history is due partly to biological-based sex differences, but cultural expectations also play a role. As women's athletics became more accepted and popular, the difference between men's and women's records declined,as shown here for 400-meter freestyle Olympic swimming competitions. Every female gold medalist from 1976 on swam faster than did the male gold medalist of 1964 or any previous years. (Data from the 1993 *World Almanac.*)

shown by Margaret Mead (1935) and many other anthropologists, or why in Western culture the differences have changed over the course of history (for an example of one such change, see Figure 13.6).

Although *sex* and *gender* are synonyms in most dictionaries, psychologists tend to use the former term when referring to the clear-cut biological bases for categorizing people as male or female, and the latter term when referring to the entire set of differences attributed to males and females, which may be partly or wholly socially determined (Deaux, 1985). You were born one sex or the other, but from the moment of birth—from the moment that someone announced, "It's a girl!" or "It's a boy!"—you also had a gender. Immediately, in the minds of all who heard the announcement, you were tied through a web of mental associations to all kinds of "girlish" or "boyish" traits, activities, and material belongings.

24. ***In what ways are girls and boys treated differently by parents, teachers, and other community members? How do these differences relate to adult female and male roles?***

Differential Treatment by Adults

Research in North America indicates that people view and handle even very young infants differently depending on their gender. Fathers who were asked to rate their infants on the day after birth were more likely to rate the newborn as soft, small, and beautiful if it was a girl, and as firm, strong, and well coordinated if it was a boy (Rubin & others, 1974). Fathers also play more gently with infant girls than with infant boys (Maccoby & Jacklin, 1974). Mothers, too, tend to handle baby boys and girls differently, though the difference is more subtle. In one study, mothers were asked to hold a 6-month-old female infant, who in some cases was dressed as a girl and introduced as Beth, and in other cases was dressed as a boy and introduced as Adam (Culp & others, 1983). The mothers talked to Beth more than to Adam, and gave Adam more direct gazes unaccompanied by talk. Parents also furnish infants' rooms differently depending on gender. Boys are more likely to have toy vehicles, toy animals, and live animals, and girls are more likely to have dolls and lace fabrics (Rheingold & Cook, 1975). These early differences in treatment cannot be due to differences stemming from the infants themselves, since objective studies show that girls and boys younger than 18 months do not differ perceptibly in size, physical strength, temperament (Plomin & DeFries, 1985), and preferences for various toys (Maccoby & Jacklin, 1974; Rheingold & Cook, 1975).

Eleanor E. Maccoby

In her long and distinguished career, Maccoby has immeasurably increased our understanding of the processes by which children acquire the habits, values, goals, and knowledge of their societies.

Cross-cultural research indicates that as girls and boys grow beyond infancy they are expected, by their parents and other community members, to behave in ways that are consistent with the culture's conception of female and male roles. In all cultures that have been studied, girls are more likely than boys to be asked to help care for younger children and to perform domestic chores such as cooking, and boys are allowed to explore farther from home and are more encouraged to be independent (Huston & others, 1986; Whiting & Edwards, 1988). But the magnitude of this difference varies from culture to culture, depending on the degree to which the adult gender roles are different. Consider two cultures in Zaïre. The Lese are a farming community in which women and men are sharply segregated during the day, and men essentially never engage in child care or other domestic chores. The Efe are a hunter-gatherer community in which women and men have different roles away from camp (women gather and men hunt), but often work together at cooking and other chores within the camp. Predictably, the gender difference in task assignment to young children is much greater among the Lese than among the Efe (Morelli, 1993, in press).

In our society school is supposed to be the great homogenizer. Boys and girls usually attend the same classes and study the same subjects. But a number of studies indicate that teachers often expect different results from boys than from girls and that such expectations may become self-fulfilling prophesies. In one study, observations in many classrooms revealed that second-grade teachers spent more time with boys on math and more time with girls on reading (Leinhardt & others, 1979). Such differential treatment may help explain why, on average, boys become better than girls at math and girls become better than boys at reading (Good & Findley, 1985). Other studies have shown that teachers criticize boys and girls differently for poor academic performance, especially in math (Dweck & Bush, 1976; Dweck & others, 1978). Criticism of boys more often contains the implication that poor performance comes from not trying hard enough, whereas that of girls is more muted and has the implication that poor performance is due to lack of ability. Carol Dweck and her colleagues suggest that this difference may help explain why girls tend to be less confident than boys in their own competence. When asked to describe their academic abilities, girls usually underestimate theirs, especially in math, and boys usually overestimate theirs (Eccles, 1985).

Mastering the machine

As computers have become increasingly common in North American classrooms, considerable disagreement about their impact has arisen. Some critics fear that their presence will accentuate gender differences if boys are encouraged to become competent users of the machines and girls are not.

■ **25. *How does children's knowledge of gender roles and of their own gender identity affect their behavior?***

Children's Active Assertion of Gender Identity

Children are not just molded by adults to behave according to the culture's conception of male and female; they actively mold themselves. By the age of 4 or 5, they have learned quite clearly their culture's stereotypes of male and female roles

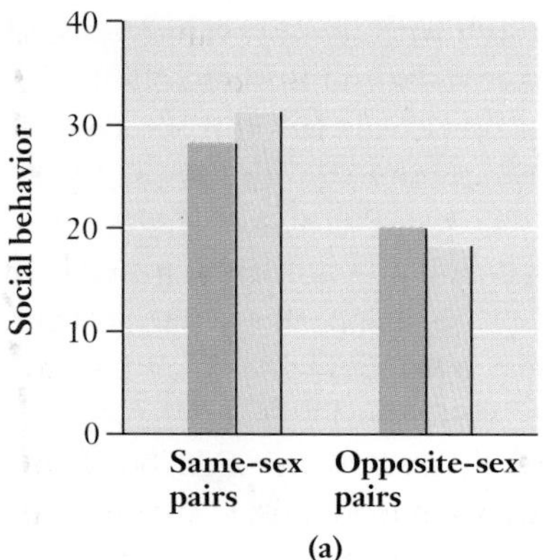

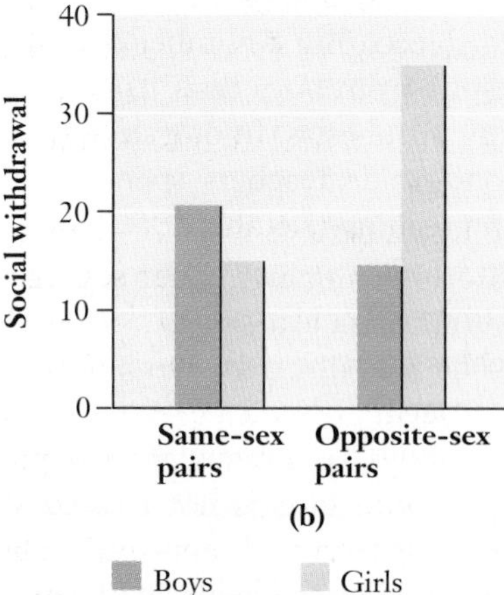

Figure 13.7 ***Effects of gender on social interactions between 33-month-olds***

(a) Jacklin and Maccoby found that the total amount of social behavior exhibited by 33-month-old children, paired together in a playroom, was greater for same-gender pairs than it was for opposite-gender pairs. (b) This difference was accounted for mostly by the strong tendency for girls to withdraw from interaction with male partners. The scores shown on both graphs reflect the average number of 10-second observation intervals, out of a maximum of 156, during which the indicated category of behavior occurred. (Adapted from Jacklin & Maccoby, 1978.)

26. ***How did Jacklin and Maccoby study gender segregation in 33-month-olds, and what did they find?***

(Williams & Best, 1990) and recognize that they themselves are either male or female and always will be, an understanding referred to as *gender identity* (Kohlberg, 1966; Whiting & Edwards, 1988). Once they have this understanding, children in all cultures that have been studied seem to become concerned about projecting themselves as clearly male or female. They attend most closely to people of their own gender and model their own behavior accordingly, often in ways that exaggerate the male-female differences they see. When required to carry out a chore that they regard as gender inappropriate, they often carry it out in a style that clearly distinguishes them from the other gender. For example, in a culture where fetching water is considered women's work, young boys who are asked to fetch water carry it in a different manner from that employed by women and girls (Whiting & Edwards, 1988).

That children everywhere assert their gender identity is probably no coincidence. From an evolutionary perspective, gender is not an arbitrary concept but an expression of one's sex, which must be plainly identifiable for the purpose of reproduction. Children may well have a biologically based need to establish, in their own minds and in the minds of others, that they are clearly one gender or the other. In our culture, over the past thirty years or so, gender distinctions in adult roles have in many ways diminished. This is due in part to economic conditions and in part to an active attempt to create greater equality of opportunities for women and men. It would be interesting to learn whether the degree to which girls and boys differentiate themselves in their self-chosen activities has likewise diminished in our culture over the past thirty years, but I know of no research that directly addresses this question.

Gender Segregation

That girls and boys commonly play separately is, I am sure, no news to you. Some degree of self-imposed gender segregation is observed in our culture even in three-year-olds, who presumably do not yet have a clear conception of gender identity (Maccoby & Jacklin, 1987). Among very young children, the tendency of girls to avoid boys is stronger than the tendency of boys to avoid girls (LaFreniere & others, 1984), and research suggests that this difference may stem at least partly from a difference in mode of communication.

Carolyn Jacklin and Eleanor Maccoby (1978) placed pairs of unacquainted 33-month-olds in the same room, with their mothers present, and recorded their behavior as each pair was given one interesting toy after another. As Figure 13.7 shows, same-gender pairs interacted with each other considerably more than did mixed pairs. In mixed pairs, the girl tended to withdraw after a brief period and stand near her mother while the boy continued to play with the toy. This occurred despite the fact that the children were dressed in similar clothing and were not referred to by name or other gender-identifying terms, and despite the fact that boys in this setting were not noticeably rougher than girls. Analysis of the children's behavior suggested that the girls may have withdrawn because they found themselves unable to exert an equal share of influence in the interaction when the partner was a boy (Maccoby & Jacklin, 1987). Boys responded less often to girls' requests and suggestions than did either boys or girls to boys' requests and suggestions. Consistent with the finding, other studies of preschoolers have shown that girls are more likely than boys to produce and respond to polite suggestions and that boys are more likely to produce and respond to direct commands (Maccoby & Jacklin, 1987; Serbin & others, 1984).

As children grow older, their tendency to play in gender-segregated groups grows stronger (Maccoby & Jacklin, 1987). Some social scientists consider boys'

■ **27.** ***What are some reported differences between boys' and girls' play in peer groups?***

and girls' peer groups to be separate subcultures, each with its own values, directing its members along different developmental lines (Maltz and Borker, 1982). The *world of boys* has been characterized as consisting of relatively large, hierarchically organized groups in which individuals or coalitions attempt to prove their superiority or dominance through competitive games, teasing, and boasting. The *world of girls* has been characterized as consisting of smaller, more intimate groups, in which cooperative forms of play predominate and competition, though not absent, is more subtle. These general differences between boys' and girls' groups have been observed in many cultures (Whiting & Edwards, 1988).

But such characterizations may overstate the differences between boys' and girls' typical social experiences. Most of the research supporting the "two worlds" concept was conducted in school playgrounds and summer camps, where there are large numbers of same-age children. At home or in their neighborhoods, children are more likely to play in small, mixed-age and mixed-gender groups, and under those conditions the difference between boys' and girls' styles of play is less extreme (Thorne, 1990). Quite often young boys and girls who play together in their neighborhood avoid each other like the plague at school.

■ **28.** ***How do children maintain gender segregation at school, and how might teachers influence the degree of segregation?***

Based on systematic observations at recess and lunch periods in U. S. elementary schools, Barrie Thorne (1986) found that children maintain gender segregation by ridiculing those who cross gender lines. But this ridicule is not symmetrical. Boys who play with girls are much more likely to be teased and taunted by both gender groups than are girls who play with boys. Indeed, girls who prefer to play with boys are often referred to with approval as "tomboys" and retain their popularity with both genders. A boy who prefers to play with girls is not treated so benignly. The terms "sissy" and "sallygirl" are never spoken with approval. The implication, according to Thorne, is that it is worse for a boy to like or be like girls than it is for a girl to like or be like boys. Thorne, like many other psychologists, is concerned that the sharp degree of gender segregation and differentiation in play at school may be harmful. Among other things, it may prevent boys from exercising the tenderer side of their nature and girls from exercising more self-assertion.

Some research suggests that the simple act of labeling girls and boys as different groups at school may increase their self-imposed segregation, presumably by reinforcing the group distinction. Gender segregation on school playgrounds was found to decline when teachers consciously avoided calling attention to gender in the classroom—for example, when they refrained from lining boys and girls up separately or using such phrases as, "I see the girls are ready and the boys aren't" (Maccoby & Jacklin, 1987). In recent years, teacher training has included increased sensitization to such issues. I don't know whether gender segregation in schools has, as a consequence, declined or not.

Adolescence

Adolescence is the transition period from childhood to adulthood. It begins with the first signs of puberty (the physical changes leading to reproductive capacity), and it ends when the person is viewed by himself or herself, and by others, as a full member of the adult community. In traditional societies, in which adult roles are clearly defined and are learned through direct involvement with the adult world, the child's transition to adulthood may coincide with the physical changes of puberty and be officially marked by puberty rites or other celebrations. But in our society the transition to adulthood has no clear-cut marker. Laws, for example, commonly grant different adult privileges at different ages—in my home state you can drive a car at 16, vote at 18, and purchase alcohol at 21. More important, the age at which people begin careers or families in our society—often seen as marks of entry into adulthood—varies greatly. It is not uncommon to hear people in their late twenties, especially those in graduate school, refer to themselves as "kids," a tacit acknowledgment of their sense that they are still adolescents.

■ **29.** ***How have psychologists' theories of adolescence changed historically, depending upon the prevailing economic conditions?***

In North America, psychologists' views about adolescence have changed markedly over time. In an analysis of articles on adolescent psychology published during various historical eras, Robert Enright and his colleagues (1987) found that the changes in theories coincided with changes in social and economic conditions. During World Wars I and II, when young people were needed to fight and to work in factories, adolescence was typically described as a brief period, essentially over by age 16, and teenagers in general were portrayed as competent and adultlike. In contrast, during the economic depressions of the 1890s and 1930s, when work was scarce, adolescence was described as a lengthy developmental period, and teenagers were portrayed as immature, unstable, and incompetent to enter the work force without prolonged education. Enright and his colleagues argue convincingly that the changes in theories reflect psychologists' biases that were in tune with the economic needs of the time. But the changing theories may also to some degree reflect real changes in adolescents' behavior resulting from the changing social and economic conditions.

In this section we will examine some of the relatively recent psychological research and ideas concerning social relationships, self-concept, and moral reasoning in adolescence. Some of these findings and ideas may well be specific to our culture and time in history.

Relationships in Adolescence

Adolescence is typically a time when parental influence fades, peer influence intensifies, and sexuality becomes a major concern.

Breaking Away, or Establishing New Relationships with Parents

"I said, 'Have a nice day' to my teenage daughter as she left the house, and she responded, 'Will you *please* stop telling me what to do!'" This joke, long popular among parents of adolescents, could be matched by the following, told by an adolescent: "Yesterday, I tried to really communicate with my mother. I told her how important it is that she trust me and not try to govern everything I do. She responded, 'Oh, sweetie, I'm so glad we have the kind of relationship in which you can be honest and tell me how you really feel. Now please if you are going out, wear your warmest coat and be back by 10:30.'"

■ **30.** ***What is the nature of the so-called adolescent rebellion?***

Adolescence is often characterized as a time of rebellion against parents. But the rebellion, if we call it that, is rarely out-and-out rejection. Surveys taken at various times and places over the past several decades have shown consistently that most adolescents admire their parents, accept their parents' religious and political convictions, and claim to be more or less at peace with them (Adelson, 1986; Offer & Schonert-Reichl, 1992). Rather, the typical rebellion is aimed specifically at the immediate controls that parents hold over the child's behavior. At the same time that adolescents are asking to be treated more like adults, parents may fear new dangers that can accompany this period of life—such as those associated with sex, alcohol, drugs, and automobiles—and try to tighten controls instead of loosen them. So adolescence is often marked by conflicts centering on parental authority.

Using questionnaires and analyzing family discussions held in the laboratory,

31. ***How does parent-adolescent conflict involve sons differently from daughters, and mothers differently from fathers?***

psychologists have identified a number of reliable patterns related to the conflicts that emerge in middle-class North American families as children enter adolescence (Galambos, 1992, Steinberg, 1981, 1989): (a) For both sons and daughters, increased conflict with parents is linked more closely to the physical changes of puberty than to chronological age. If puberty comes earlier or later than usual, so does the increase in conflict. (b) For both sons and daughters, conflict typically involves the mother more than the father. For sons, such conflict increases in early adolescence and then decreases, primarily because mothers begin to defer to their sons as their sons get older. Mothers are less inclined to defer to their daughters, however, so mother-daughter conflicts tend to remain intense throughout adolescence. (c) Fathers are typically less emotionally involved with their offspring than are mothers, and during adolescence that emotional distance increases. The reason may have more to do with the parent's role in the family than with gender. In families where both parents work outside the home, or where the mother is the only parent and works outside the home, the relationship between adolescents and mothers typically involves less conflict and more emotional distancing than in two-parent families where the mother does not work outside the home (Galambos, 1992; Smetana & others, 1991).

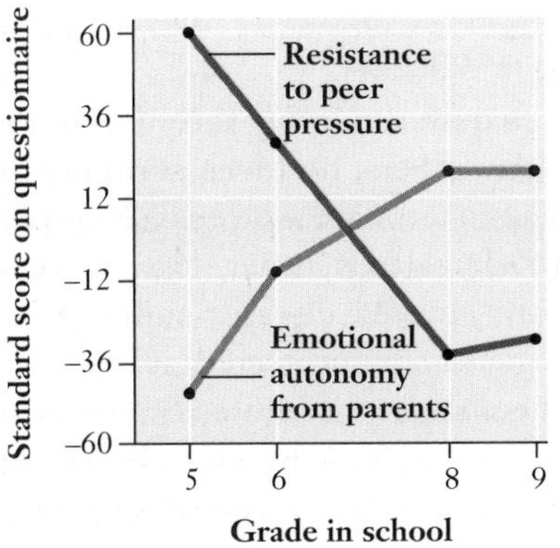

Figure 13.8 ***Changes in perceived dependence on parents and peers during adolescence***

Based on responses to questionnaire items, the sense of *emotional autonomy from parents* (including feeling independent from parents and no longer idealizing them) increased, and *resistance to peer pressure* decreased, from fifth through eighth grade. The latter change was assessed with questions that asked the young person to choose between two hypothetical courses of action, one suggested by the youngster's best friends and the other representing what the youngster really thinks he or she should do. (Adapted from Steinberg & Silverberg, 1986.)

Importance of the Peer Group

As young people in our culture gain a feeling of independence from their parents, they look increasingly to their peers, both for clues as to how to behave and for emotional support. A number of studies, such as that described in Figure 13.8, suggest that conformity to peers increases during the same years that the sense of dependence on parents decreases. Other studies indicate that both boys and girls begin to spend much more time talking with peers than they did before, often in close and caring ways (Kelly & Hansen, 1987), though, as noted earlier, girls have a head start in this. When asked to describe the meaning of their friendships, adolescents of both genders talk about the sharing of thoughts, feelings, and secrets, whereas younger children are more likely to talk about playing together and sharing of material things (Berndt, 1992; Damon & Hart, 1992).

32. ***According to Dunphy's study, how do cliques and crowds help break down the gender barrier?***

Adolescent peer groups help break down the gender barriers that were erected in childhood. This is one of the main conclusions of a classic study conducted by Dexter Dunphy (1963) in Sydney, Australia. By gaining the confidence of a large number of adolescents, Dunphy was able to chart the membership of many peer groups and study them both by direct observation and questionnaires given to group members. He found two varieties of such groups, which he labeled *cliques* and *crowds*. A clique was a close-knit group, ranging from three to nine individuals, who saw themselves as best friends and who spent great amounts of time together throughout the week. A crowd was a larger group consisting of several cliques who go together for parties or other planned occasions, usually on weekends.

Younger adolescents' cliques were exclusively one sex or the other, but their crowds usually consisted of a mix of girls' and boys' cliques. The clique leaders were usually the earliest to begin dating, and crowds were often made up of the cliques to which dating couples belonged. In the crowd, boys and girls could interact in a setting made more secure by the presence of their best same-sex friends. Between crowd gatherings, the members of cliques would spend hours analyzing the events of the last gathering and encouraging each other toward further interaction with members of the opposite sex. In later adolescence, as more individuals began to date regularly, single-sex cliques tended to break apart, and new, more loosely associated groups, consisting usually of two or more pairs of dating couples, would take their place.

Dunphy's study shows one route—perhaps most common in middle-class, urban settings—by which adolescents break down the gender barrier and begin dating. Once dating has begun there is much to be learned. Girls and boys—who have to some degree been members of different worlds—must overcome awkward stages of fear and embarrassment, adjust their styles of communication, and somehow match their idealized images of a romantic relationship with the realities of the person they are getting to know. This process may be further confounded by ambiguities and fears surrounding sexuality.

Problems Associated with Emerging Sexual Relationships

33. ***How might lack of sex education, the persistent double standard for males and females, and cultural prejudices contribute to problems in adolescents' sexual relationships?***

Some young people in our culture may progress quite smoothly into dating relationships and increased sexual intimacy. For many others, however, serious problems occur. The majority of American youth begin to engage in sexual intercourse sometime in their teenage years (Smith, 1989; Zelnick & Kantner, 1980). Even in this era of AIDS, and despite other sexually-transmitted diseases and the well-known problems associated with teenage pregnancy, unprotected sexual intercourse is common among teenagers. One result is that, in the United States, nearly one-third of all sexually active females become pregnant at least once during their teenage years, a rate far higher than in other industrialized countries, such as Canada, England, Sweden, and the Netherlands, where teenage sex is discussed more openly and sex education is more available (Gordon & Gilgun, 1987; Jones & others, 1985; Zelnick & others, 1981).

Numerous studies have shown that the double standard for adolescent boys and girls concerning sexual behavior is still very much alive in our culture (Gordon & Gilgun, 1987). Boys are more likely to be encouraged in their sexual adventures and to feel proud of them, whereas girls are more likely to be discouraged and to feel ashamed. Boys are more likely than girls to say that they are eager to have sex for the sheer pleasure of it; and girls are more likely to equate sex with love or to say they would have sex only with someone whom they would marry.

Adolescents still expect the male to take the lead in a romantic relationship, and this aspect of the double standard can create problems on both sides. A sensitive boy, especially if he fears rejection or feels inept, may lack the courage to pursue a sexual relationship. A girl, especially if she is dating an older, more experienced boy, may be overly trusting and vulnerable to exploitation. Perhaps most problematic is the chance that romantic leadership will blur into sexual aggression.

In a survey on date rape conducted several years ago in the U. S., 25 percent of college men admitted that they had attempted to force intercourse on a woman to the point where she screamed, pleaded, or cried for him to stop; and in another survey a similar percentage of college women said they had been the subject of that kind of experience (Gordon & Gilgun, 1987). To some degree, such behavior may be attributable to social pressures that young males feel to have sexual intercourse. They may also have heard from peers, and from society at large, that the girl's resistance is a natural part of the process, or even that she wants to be forced—a notion belied by studies showing that all forms of sexual coercion, whether they involve intercourse or not, are extremely negative if not traumatic experiences for the victim (Gordon & Gilgun, 1987).

Adolescence is also a time when those whose sexual orientation is not the culture's ideal may face an extraordinary personal crisis. The reasons why some people are heterosexual and others homosexual are not yet known, but research shows that, for most people, sexual orientation is discovered, not chosen (see Chapter 7). Approximately 4 percent of males and 2 percent of females discover that they are almost exclusively homosexual in orientation (Bell & others, 1981).

Gay pride

Houston Area Teen Coalition of Homosexuals is one of a large number of social and support groups set up by and for members of gay and lesbian communities. These groups offer opportunities for education, empowerment, comfort, and recreation to homosexual men and women of all ages, races, and cultures.

At other times and places, homosexuality has been a culturally accepted and even valued practice (Ford & Beach, 1951). But in our culture, despite a politically influential gay and lesbian movement and despite growing acknowledgment by psychologists and physicians that homosexuality is compatible with a normal, healthy life, young people who find that they are sexually oriented toward members of their own sex risk rejection by parents, friends, employers, and society at large. To help people come to terms with a homosexual orientation, the gay and lesbian community has developed a variety of services, including support and social groups and counseling centers.

Self-Concept and Identity

"I yam what I yam," says Popeye to Olive Oyl. "Who am I? Who do I want to be? Who *should* I be?" says the less certain adolescent to himself or herself. One's physical body, one's relationship to family and friends, and one's sexuality are part of one's identity. Here let us consider studies having to do specifically with the development of people's ways of thinking about themselves.

Changes in Ways of Describing the Self

34. *How do self-descriptions change as one progresses from early childhood into young adulthood?*

William Damon and Daniel Hart (1992) have studied the self-concepts of middle-class children and adolescents in the United States by asking them to describe themselves. Preschoolers describe themselves almost exclusively in physical terms. An articulate 4-year-old might say, "I have curly hair, I can run fast, and I have blue sneakers." By about ages 6 to 8, children begin to describe themselves in psychological as well as physical terms, with such phrases as "I'm pretty smart," or "I feel sad quite a bit," and as they get older the frequency and sophistication of such descriptions increases.

As young people enter adolescence, according to Damon and Hart, their self-descriptions begin to be organized around social relationships. Thirteen-year-olds frequently comment on personal characteristics that have to do with getting along with others, such as "I am shy," or "I have many good friends," or "I get along well with my parents." Later in adolescence, the focus on social relationships declines, and people begin to describe themselves more in terms of their personal beliefs and plans, with statements such as "I am a devout Christian," or "I hope to become a doctor." At each step in this sequence the earlier understanding of the self is not lost, but is incorporated into the newer understanding. Thus, the girl who commented on her curly hair at age 4 might, at age 13, comment on how it affects her popularity, and at age 18 she might add to that a deep concern about overcoming vanity. We are complex creatures, indeed, and the development of the self-concept is a process of understanding ever more of our own complexity.

Research on Identity Formation

In Erik Erikson's life-span theory of development (shown in Table 13.1), adolescence is the stage of *identity crisis*, when the main task is to give up one's childhood identity and establish a new identity—including a sense of purpose, a career orientation, and a set of values—appropriate for entry into adulthood (Erikson, 1968). Erikson and other psychoanalytic theorists posited that this process necessarily entails a great deal of emotional turmoil. But systematic surveys show that most people in our culture do not experience noticeably more turmoil during adolescence than during other periods of life (Offer & Schonert-Reichl, 1992).

35. ***How do researchers identify four categories of identity status? In what ways does such research support and fail to support Erikson's theory of an identity crisis?***

Much research on identity formation has been based on a method of assessment and categorization developed by James Marcia (1966, 1980). Marcia defined identity in terms of two dimensions that are key aspects of Erikson's notion of identity—*occupational commitment* (commitment to a specific career or other long-term activity) and *ideological commitment* (commitment to a definable set of religious, ethical, or political values). He developed a set of interview questions to measure these commitments, and the degree of psychological struggle involved in achieving them, and devised a way to sort the combined results of the commitment and struggle measures into four possible categories of identity status.

Historic note: Until his life's destiny was further clarified, Robin Hood spent several years robbing from the rich and giving to the porcupines.

Three of Marcia's categories can be arranged to match what Erikson believed to be a normal developmental sequence. The first is *identity diffusion*, in which a person lacks commitments and is not concerned about them. The second is *moratorium*, in which the person is actively thinking about and questioning various occupational paths and values. The third is *identity achieved*, in which the person has gone beyond the moratorium and has established firm commitments. As would be predicted by Erikson's theory, research using Marcia's system indicates that young people typically shift from identity diffusion to moratorium to identity achieved as they go from early adolescence into adulthood (Waterman, 1982, 1985). The research also indicates that the prime time for experiencing the moratorium (or identity crisis), at least for middle-class males in our society, is between 18 and 21.

But not everyone goes through the predicted sequence. Marcia's fourth category is *foreclosure*, the unquestioning acceptance of ideological and career commitments from parents or other authority figures. Research using Marcia's interview method indicates that many people with the foreclosed status retain that status; they go into adulthood without experiencing an identity crisis (Archer & Waterman, 1990; Marcia, 1980). Also, some people in the identity diffusion category never go through an identity crisis and show little concern about career or ideology as they enter adulthood.

Erikson's theory predicts that people who go through the moratorium (or crisis) will be better off than those who don't, and at least some research supports that prediction. Marcia (1980) found that college students in the identity-achieved and moratorium categories had higher self-esteem, a stronger sense of independence, and a greater capacity for intimacy than did those in the diffusion or foreclosure categories. Still, as Marcia pointed out, the two noncrisis categories have a healthy side as well. Identity-diffused individuals can be seen as careless and irresponsible, or as carefree and open-minded. Foreclosed individuals can be seen as rigid, dogmatic, and conformist, or as steadfast, loyal, and cooperative. One researcher found that college students in the foreclosed category studied diligently, kept regular hours, seemed happy, and described their families as loving and affectionate (Donovan, 1975).

36. ***How might identity formation depend upon gender and culture?***

Identity formation may not be the same for women as it is for men. Carol Gilligan has argued that Erikson's concept of identity (and, by implication, Marcia's measurement of it) is biased toward males (Gilligan, 1982; Gilligan & others, 1990). Even though most women in our society are gainfully employed and are as likely as men to have chosen a set of values, they are less likely than men to define themselves in terms of their occupation or ideology and more likely to define themselves in terms of personal relationships and responsibilities. Gilligan suggests that Erikson's fifth life stage (the identity crisis) is more closely intertwined with the sixth stage (the crisis of intimacy) for women than it is for men. Consistent with Gilligan's view, fewer correlations are found between identity achievement (measured by Marcia's method) and self-esteem for women than for men (Waterman, 1982). In other research, Susan Archer (1985) found that young women in our culture regularly go through a crisis about how to balance commitment to family against commitment to career, a crisis that is rarely experienced by young men and is not addressed by Marcia's standard assessment method.

The self-concept and adult identity also vary greatly across cultures. In cultures where fewer choices or actual changes in one's life occur as one enters adulthood, the kind of questioning that constitutes an identity crisis is probably less likely to occur than in our culture. Moreover, in cultures that emphasize people's relationships and obligations to one another more than our culture does, and that place less emphasis on individuality, the self-concept and sense of identity are, throughout life, more closely tied to one's family and friends than they are in our culture (Markus & Kitayama, 1991). More about this will be discussed in Chapter 14.

Moral Reasoning

The importance of empathy

Although most research on moral reasoning focuses on thinking processes, such thought does not take place in an emotional vacuum. It depends in part on the capacity to feel what other people are feeling, even if that means sharing another's distress.

Even young children show a concern for others. Preschool children (ages 3 to 5) who were paired with their younger brothers and sisters in the strange-situation test were observed trying to comfort their younger siblings (Stewart & Marvin, 1984). Infants less than 2 years of age have been observed to hug, kiss, or give toys or food to persons who were showing signs of distress, apparently to cheer them up (Radke-Yarrow & others, 1983; Zahn-Waxler & others, 1992). Martin Hoffman (1975, 1987) has argued that the origins of morality lie in an innate capacity for *empathy*, that is, a capacity to feel what another person is feeling. Because we can feel the sadness or pain of another person, we strive to help that person overcome that sadness and pain. As you recall, Hoffman's theory of discipline emphasizes the parent's role in calling forth the child's empathy when the child has hurt or failed to help another person.

Another line of research on moral development focuses on the development of logical reasoning about moral dilemmas. Piaget pioneered this approach; but the psychologist who pursued it most fully, and most strongly emphasized changes that occur in adolescence, is Lawrence Kohlberg.

Kohlberg's Theory: Stages of Moral Reasoning

Kohlberg's basic approach—in research that he began in the 1950s and has been carried on by others since his death in 1987—is to present people with dilemmas that embody conflicting claims for justice, ask them what the story's protagonist should do and why, and analyze their answers for evidence of different types of moral reasoning. Consider Kohlberg's best-known dilemma (slightly modified from Colby & others, 1983):

> In Europe a woman was near death from a special kind of cancer. A druggist in her town had recently discovered a drug that doctors thought might save her, but he was charging $2000 for a small dose—ten times what the drug cost him to make. The sick woman's husband, Heinz, went to everyone he knew to borrow the money, trying every legal means to obtain it, but he could only get about $1000, which was half of what he needed to buy the drug. He told the druggist that his wife was dying, and asked him to sell it cheaper or allow him to pay the rest later. But the druggist said, "No, I discovered

the drug and I'm going to make money from it." Heinz became desperate and considered breaking into the drugstore to steal the drug for his wife. Should Heinz steal the drug? Why or why not?

■ **37. *What is Kohlberg's method of assessing moral reasoning, and how can his stages be described as the successive broadening of one's social perspective?***

Before proceeding further, you might find it interesting to think about how you would respond to this dilemma. Why do you think Heinz should or shouldn't steal the drug? Give as complete a response as possible. Or, better yet, raise the dilemma with a friend or two to see how they explain their answers. This will give you a feeling for the reasoning processes by which people form or defend moral judgments. Kohlberg was interested in the method of thinking rather than the actual moral decision in these dilemmas. Kohlberg developed a system for classifying people's reasoning into five different categories, which he believed represent successive stages in the development of moral reasoning. The stages, along with examples of responses to the Heinz dilemma that illustrate each, are described in Table 13.2 (based on Kohlberg, 1984; Rest, 1986).

As you study the table, notice that each stage takes into account a broader portion of the social world than does the previous one. The sequence begins with thought of oneself alone (Stage 1), and then progresses to encompass other individuals directly involved in the questioned action (Stage 2), others who will hear about and evaluate the action (Stage 3), society at large (Stage 4), and, finally, universal principles concerning all of humankind (Stage 5). According to Kohlberg, the stages represent a true developmental progression in the sense that to reach any given stage a person must first pass through the preceding ones. Thinking within one stage, and discovering the limitations of that way of thinking, provides the motivating force for progression to the next. Kohlberg did not claim that everyone

Table 13.2 *Kohlberg's stages of moral reasoning*

Stage 1: Obedience and punishment orientation

Reasoners in this stage focus on direct consequences to themselves. An action is bad if it will result in punishment, not bad if it will not. *Pro* (reason for stealing the drug): "If he lets his wife die, he will get in trouble." *Con* (reason for not stealing the drug): "He shouldn't steal it because he'll be caught and sent to jail."

Stage 2: Self-interested exchanges

Reasoners here understand that different people have different self-interests, which sometimes come into conflict. To get what you want you have to make a bargain, giving up something in return. *Pro*: "It won't bother him much to serve a little jail term, if he still has his wife when he gets out." *Con*: "His wife will probably die anyway before he gets out of jail, so it won't do him much good."

Stage 3: Interpersonal accord and conformity

Reasoners here try to live up to the expectations of others who are important to them. An action is good if it will improve a person's relationships with significant others, bad if it will harm those relationships. *Pro*: "Your family will think you're an inhuman husband if you don't." *Con*: "Everyone will think you are a criminal. You won't be able to face anyone again."

Stage 4: Law-and-order morality

Reasoners here argue that, to maintain social order, each person should resist personal pressures and feel duty-bound to follow the laws and conventions of the larger society. *Pro*: "It's a husband's duty to save his wife." *Con*: "It's always wrong to steal. What if everyone stole? Then there would be no law."

Stage 5: Human-rights and social-welfare morality

Reasoners here still have a strong respect for laws, but balance that with ethical principles that may transcend specific laws. Laws that fail to promote the general welfare or that violate basic ethical principles can be changed, reinterpreted, or in some cases deliberately flouted as a form of protest. The goal is justice within the law. *Pro*: "The law isn't really set up for these circumstances. Taking the drug in this situation isn't really right, but it's justified." *Con*: "You can't completely blame Heinz for stealing in this case, but he shouldn't get carried away by his own emotions and forget the long-range point of view. He has to consider the value of respect for law and the value of all of the lives involved."

Note: Under each stage description are examples of pro and con responses on the Heinz dilemma (based on examples in Kohlberg, 1984, and Rest, 1986). Earlier versions of the theory included a sixth stage, which emphasized universal ethical principles almost to the exclusion of other considerations. Stage 6 has been dropped in current versions, however, because of failure to find people who reason in accordance with it.

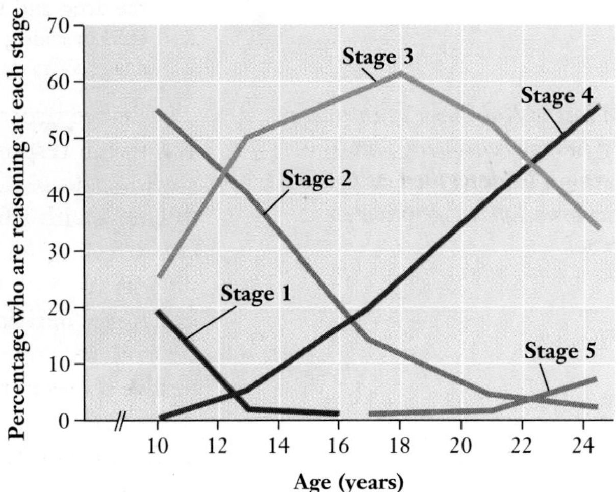

Figure 13.9 ***Results of a longitudinal study of moral reasoning***

This graph, based on a longitudinal study of males from a relatively high socioeconomic background, shows the percentage of subjects at each age who were reasoning at each of Kohlberg's stages. Notice the sharp drop in the two most primitive stages of reasoning (Stages 1 and 2) through early adolescence, the rise and fall in Stage 3, and the consistent rise in Stage 4 reasoning over the adolescent and young adult years. Very little Stage 5 reasoning was found, but it, too, increased with age. (Adapted from Colby & others, 1983.)

goes through the entire sequence; in fact, his research suggested that few go beyond Stage 4, and many don't go past Stage 2 or Stage 3. Nor did he link his stages to specific ages, though he believed that adolescence and young adulthood are the times when advancement into the higher stages is most likely to occur. The higher stages require formal-operational thinking (ability to think abstractly and hypothetically), which Kohlberg, like Piaget (discussed in Chapter 12), saw as emerging in adolescence. Figure 13.9 illustrates the results of one long-term study supporting Kohlberg's theory about the sequence of stages.

■ **38.** ***What are some limitations and criticisms of Kohlberg's theory?***

Kohlberg's theory concerns moral *reasoning*, which may or may not be related to moral *behavior*. A high-caliber moral philosopher, great at coming up with reasons for one choice or another in hypothetical dilemmas, is not necessarily a moral person. Still, Kohlberg expected to find a positive correlation between stage of moral reasoning and moral behavior, and some of the research on this issue has borne him out (Blasi, 1980). Students who reason at Stages 3 and 4 (which emphasize interpersonal agreements and rules) have been found to cheat less on tests than those who reason at lower stages (Kohlberg, 1975). Also, as one might expect, people who reason at Stage 5 have been found more likely to participate in public protests on moral issues than people who reason at other stages (Haan & others, 1968). Also, in one study, people who reasoned at Stage 5 were more likely than others to refuse an experimenter's demand that they give what appeared to be painful electrical shocks to another person (Kohlberg & Candee, 1984).

Some researchers have challenged Kohlberg's claim that the sequence of stages is invariant and have cited evidence that people sometimes go from a higher-numbered stage to a lower one as they grow older (Liebert, 1984). Others have argued that Kohlberg's theory does not adequately explain why a person progresses from stage to stage; it places too much emphasis on thought alone and not enough on social learning (Gibbs & Schnell, 1985).

Cultural Differences in Moral Reasoning

■ **39.** ***What limitation in Kohlberg's theory has been revealed by cross-cultural research?***

The most fundamental criticism of Kohlberg's theory, however, is that it fails to represent all possible moral perspectives. Specifically, critics contend that the theory is biased toward a Western tradition of codified laws and abstract principles of justice and that it has no category that adequately captures non-Western traditions in which moral thought is embedded in an understanding of personal relationships, responsibilities, and communal needs (Boyes & Walker, 1988; Simpson, 1974).

Non-Westerners tested by Kohlberg's method—including Tibetan monks and village leaders in Kenya and New Guinea selected for their ethical leadership—rarely score beyond Stage 3, primarily because they frame their answers in terms of people's obligations to relatives, friends, and other close associates (Snarey, 1985). But Stage 3, according to Kohlberg's critics, does not do justice to the sophisticated and principled nature of their reasoning. In at least some non-Western cultures, a person's obligation to favor people with whom one has social ties is seen not simply as a matter of personal preference but as a matter of high moral principle (Miller & Bersoff, 1992). Their view is not without logic: In non-Western societies, people are usually economically dependent on their relatives and friends. If people broke their obligations to family and friends and behaved toward everyone in the same way (the extreme of Kohlberg's Stage 5), their society would fall apart. Again, we see a recurring psychological principle: The way people think about themselves, others, and obligations is influenced by the economic conditions in which they live.

Gilligan's "Two Voices" Dichotomy

■ **40.** ***What are the "two voices" in Gilligan's theory of moral reasoning? What is the status of her view that one voice is stronger in men and the other is stronger in women?***

Kohlberg's original studies of moral reasoning were of males only, and Carol Gilligan (1982, 1987) has argued that his stages fail to capture the mode of moral reasoning that is most prevalent in our culture among females. Consistent with Gilligan's view, some (but not all) subsequent studies have indicated that women in our culture are more likely to be placed at Stage 3 by Kohlberg's system, and less likely to be placed at higher stages, than are men (Bussey & Maughan, 1982; Haan & others, 1968; Walker, 1984). According to Gilligan, women often are placed at Stage 3 for essentially the same reason that Tibetan monks are—they frame their answers more in terms of personal relationships than in terms of abstract principles of justice.

Gilligan studies moral reasoning by asking people to describe, in extended interviews, moral dilemmas that they have actually faced, not hypothetical dilemmas. She then analyzes the transcripts of these descriptions for the presence of two "voices" or moral perspectives—one she calls *justice* and the other *caring*. The justice voice speaks of principles of right and wrong. The caring voice speaks of specific people's feelings and the consequences that an action will have for them. For example, when a 12-year-old girl discussed her decision to confront a camp director about an unfair rule, the justice voice described why the rule was unfair, and the caring voice described how the rule was upsetting her younger brother and how the camp director might feel if his rule were challenged (Gilligan & others, 1990).

In studies comparing the two genders for the extent to which each voice was present in such interviews, Gilligan (1987) found that the justice voice was stronger in boys and men and the caring voice was stronger in girls and women. Other researchers, however, using somewhat different methods of measuring the two voices, have failed to find consistent gender differences (Ford & Lowery, 1986; Walker & others, 1987). Researchers agree that the caring voice becomes relatively stronger and the justice voice relatively weaker when the dilemma is personal and real rather than hypothetical, but at present they do not agree that one voice is stronger in females and the other is stronger in males.

Adulthood

Sigmund Freud (1935) defined emotional maturity as the capacity to love and work. Erik Erikson, in his life-span theory, proposed that establishing intimate, caring relationships and finding fulfillment in work are the main tasks of early and

Resetting the social clock
Bernice Neugarten believes that social expectations about what people should be doing at particular stages of life are becoming increasingly flexible. One exemplar of such change is Bill Gates, who became president of a major computer software company at age 32.

middle adulthood (Stages 6 and 7 in Table 13.1). In essentially every psychological theory of adult development, caring and working are the two threads that weave the fabric of adult life.

Some psychologists have proposed that adult development follows a certain inevitable sequence (Erikson, 1963; Levinson, 1986; Vaillant, 1977). Others, including Bernice Neugarten, have argued that it does not. Recall Neugarten's concept of a social clock, the social expectations about what people should be doing at particular times in life. Neugarten (1979, 1984) has pointed out that our society has entered an era of relative "clocklessness" for adults; we are becoming accustomed to such images as the 28-year-old college president, the 50-year-old grandmother who has just completed medical school, and the 65-year-old father of a preschooler who takes care of the child while his wife works. Adult lives in our culture follow many different patterns, but nearly all of these patterns involve some combination of love and work.

Love and Family

In the fairy tale, love allows the frog prince and child princess to transform each other into fully human adults who marry and live happily ever after. Reality is not always like that. Why do some marriages work and not others? Why do some couples seem to grow continuously happier together, while others fall into boredom or strife? What is the nature of adult love?

Characteristics of Romantic Love

■ ***41. What evidence has been offered for a relationship between infant attachment and adult romantic love?***

Based on questionnaires assessing people's love experiences, Phillip Shaver and his colleagues (1988) have argued that adult romantic love is similar in form, and perhaps in underlying mechanism, to infants' attachments to their parents. Close physical contact and caressing are critical to both, and cooing and babytalk are common. The partners feel more secure and confident in the presence of each other and experience distress upon separation and delight upon reunion. A sense of fusion with the other reigns when all is well, and a feeling of exclusivity—that the other person could not be replaced by someone else—prevails. Like infant attachments, adult romantic attachments can be classed as secure or insecure, and some evidence suggests continuity between one's attachment style in infancy and in romantic love. Whether people describe their childhood relationship with their parents as secure, anxious, or ambivalent, they tend to describe their adult romantic relationships in the same way (Feeney & Noller, 1990; Hazen & Shaver, 1987).

■ ***42. In Sternberg's triangular theory, how are the three components used to describe different types of love? How do the components differ in their time course of development?***

Another way to characterize love is offered by the *triangular model*, developed by Robert Sternberg (1986c, 1988). Through statistical analysis of questionnaires in which people described their feelings in various love and friendship relationships, Sternberg found three distinct components: passion, intimacy, and commitment. *Passion* (the *hot* side of love) includes sexual desire and other emotional feelings of need to be with the beloved. *Intimacy* (the *warm* side of love) includes a sense of closeness, mutual understanding, and the sharing of thoughts and feelings. *Commitment* (the *cool*, rational side of love) is the person's conscious decision to promote and maintain the relationship.

In this model, passion is critical to romance, intimacy is critical to friendship, and commitment is critical to the long-term maintenance of any relationship. The model can be used to describe an infinite variety of relationships, each differing from others in the relative proportions of the three components. To illustrate its range, Sternberg (1986c) used the model to describe eight *limiting types* of relationships, which can occur if each component is either entirely present or entirely absent. These are shown in Figure 13.10 on page 482.

Figure 13.10 ***Sternberg's typology of love***

These types of relationships represent hypothetical extremes based on Sternberg's triangular theory. Most actual relationships will fit between these types, because the various components are not all-or-none, but exist as a matter of degree. (Adapted from Sternberg, 1986c.)

Type of relationship	Component: Passion	Intimacy	Decision/ commitment
Nonlove	Absent	Absent	Absent
Liking	Absent	Present	Absent
Infatuated love	Present	Absent	Absent
Empty love	Absent	Absent	Present
Romantic love	Present	Present	Absent
Companionate love	Absent	Present	Present
Fatuous love	Present	Absent	Present
Consummate love	Present	Present	Present

■ Present
■ Absent

Endless love

In Western society, romantic love can be found across the age span.

■ **43.** ***What is Gottman's evidence that a husband's responsiveness to his wife's nonverbal signals is an ingredient of marital success?***

The triangular theory can also be used to describe the development of relationships over time (Sternberg, 1986c). Passion is usually the fastest-rising of the three components, which fits with research showing that at the very beginning of a dating relationship physical attractiveness of the partner is the main determinant of a person's desire to continue the relationship (Hatfield & Sprecher, 1986; Walster & others, 1966). Intimacy develops more slowly; people may feel passion in an instant, but it takes time to become friends. The third component, commitment, may develop gradually, as the partners' lives intertwine; or it may develop in quantum leaps, tied to such events as a decision to marry or to have children.

Ingredients of Marital Success

Interviews of people in our culture who are happily married consistently reveal the importance of intimacy and commitment (Buehlman & others, 1992; Lauer & Lauer, 1985). Happily married partners *like* one another; they think of each other not just as husband and wife but also as best friends and confidants. They use the term "we" more than "I" as they describe their activities, and they tend to value their interdependence more than their independence. They also talk about their individual commitment to the marriage, their willingness to go more than half way to carry the relationship through hard times. Happily married couples apparently argue as much as unhappily married couples, but they argue more constructively (Gottman & Krokoff, 1989). They stick to the issue of disagreement, avoid bringing in past hurts or grievances that are irrelevant to the current issue, and genuinely listen to one another.

In other research, John Gottman and his colleagues have found that the husband's ability and willingness to understand and respond to his wife's nonverbal signals may be a key ingredient to marital success in our culture. In one study, Gottman (1979) analyzed videotapes of married couples engaged in conversations about marital problems. He found that in unhappy marriages the wife responded to the unspoken emotional needs of her husband, but the husband did not respond to the unspoken needs of his wife; in happy marriages, by contrast, the two were equal in understanding and responding to each other's needs. In another study, Gottman and Albert Porterfield (1981) asked each partner to try to communicate to his or her spouse a particular meaning using words that could be interpreted in more than one way. For example, the words, "I'm cold, aren't you?" might be used to communicate any of three possible messages: (1) I wonder if you are cold. (2) Please warm me with physical affection. (3) Please turn the thermostat up. Each person's attempt to communicate such messages was videotaped and then was "read" both by that person's spouse and by a stranger (another married man or woman). In unhappy marriages the husband was worse, on average, at reading his wife's signals

Cultural connections

Research on successful marriage may misrepresent the lives of couples in traditional societies. Contrast the two couples shown here, and think about what might constitute success for people living outside of modern industrial societies.

than was the stranger; and in happy marriages the husband was better. No such relationship was found for wives—they seemed equally good at reading their husband's messages whether the marriage was happy or not.

Gottman's work brings us back to a theme developed earlier in the chapter. Remember those 33-month-old girl-boy pairs in Jacklin and Maccoby's experiment who couldn't play well together because the boy didn't respond to the girl's signals for change, which were more subtle than the boy's? Apparently the same thing can happen at 33 *years* old. Clearly, one of the prerequisites of a good marriage is that two people of different genders—who grew up in somewhat different worlds, with different patterns of communication—learn to understand one another.

Parenthood

■ **44.** ***What are some effects of parenthood on adults' activities and social relationships?***

When more than 2000 married men and women were asked what event was most important in making them feel that they were really an adult, the most common response for both genders was, "Becoming a parent" (Hoffman & Manis, 1979). Based on studies in several cultures, David Gutmann (1975) has argued that certain universal changes occur in men and women when they become parents. Men become less reckless, more authoritative, and more preoccupied with making a living for their family; and women become more nurturant, more gentle, and more preoccupied with direct care of the child. In our society, parenthood leads a couple into new ties with the larger community. Parents are naturally more concerned than nonparents about such issues as schools, parks, and safety on the streets; they vote more often than nonparents (Adelson & Hall, 1987); and they are more likely to join a religious organization. Parenthood promotes new friendships with other couples who have children and a drifting away from old friends who don't. It also strengthens the couple's ties with their own parents, the child's grandparents, who now may be looked to for guidance, emotional support, and help with child-care.

The obligations associated with parenting can strain the marriage. Several studies have shown that couples' satisfaction with their marriage tends to decrease during the childrearing years and increase again when the children leave home (Cavanaugh, 1990; Nock, 1982). With children there is less opportunity for husband and wife to be alone—less dialogue, intimacy, and sex. Many couples experience what seems like a second honeymoon when their children leave home and they have the opportunity to rediscover each other, perhaps with a bit less passion but with more wisdom and tenderness.

Employment

A job in our culture is more than a source of income. For many adults, it also provides social support and the opportunity to take pride in one's accomplishments.

Job Satisfaction

■ **45.** ***What are some possible explanations of the finding that job satisfaction increases with age?***

People whose jobs require self-direction and decision making are usually happier with their employment than are those whose jobs are more regulated, even when the jobs are equal in the amount of education required and the income they produce (Kohn, 1980; Kohn & Schooler, 1983). For some people, advancement to higher status within the career is a high priority and for others it is not. A longitudinal study of men in managerial positions at AT&T revealed that many refused promotion when it meant moving and disrupting their families (Bray & Howard, 1983). Over all, those men who did not move up the career ladder had a different set of priorities from those who did; they were less aggressive, less selfish, more nurturant, more family oriented, and more religious.

Large-scale statistical studies show that most people—in most lines of work, both blue collar and white collar—experience a continuous increase in job satisfaction as they grow older, at least from age 20 through 60 (Rhodes, 1983). Older people not only *say* that they like their jobs better, but they demonstrate it through such evidence as fewer avoidable absences from work (Rhodes, 1983). Increasing satisfaction during the first couple of work decades may result from changing jobs until a more satisfying one is found, advancement to more interesting positions within a given job, and acquisition of greater skill and competence. The continued rise in satisfaction after that may be due to the increased job security that accompanies seniority and a changed attitude toward work (Cavanaugh, 1990; Levinson, 1978). With age, many workers become less concerned with further advancement and enjoy the day-to-day work more for its own sake and the social relationships associated with it.

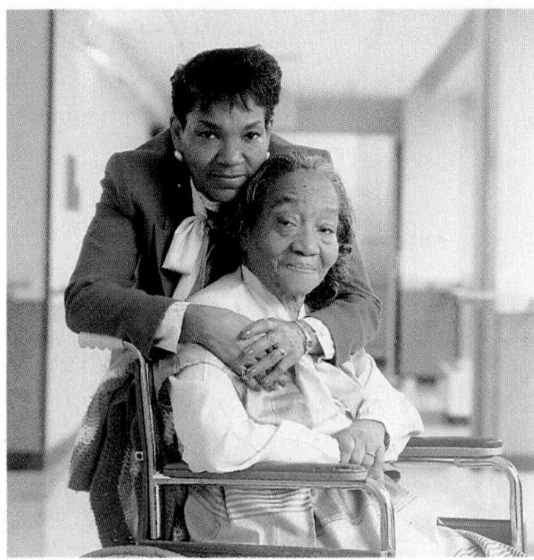

The daughter track

Most women, whether employed or not, accept the social identity of caregiver. For Charlas Rhodes, 51, shown with her 71-year-old mother, Arena Whytus, this has meant leaving a job and moving to another city so that her mother would not have to live in a nursing home. Although she gets little sleep and has virtually no social life, Rhodes says she has no regrets and feels blessed by the opportunity to care for her mother.

Women today are more likely than men to hold two jobs—one outside the home and the other inside. In families in which the husband and wife work an equal number of hours outside the home, the wife still usually does most of the childcare, grocery shopping, cooking, and house cleaning (Biernat & Wortman, 1991; Hochschild, 1989). Women in careers are more likely than men to feel torn between the obligations of career and family. One study found that female business executives and college professors were much more likely than their husbands to rate themselves negatively on their performance as parents, despite having assumed more of the parenting role than their husbands (Biernat & Wortman, 1991).

■ **46.** ***What are the psychological effects of out-of-home employment for women with families?***

Despite such strains, numerous studies have shown that women today who work outside the home are better off psychologically than those who don't, whether they have families or not (Baruch & others, 1987; Rodin & Ickovics, 1990). The job at the office or plant, hectic as it may sometimes be, may be more ordered and predictable than the job at home and provide relief. Also, in a world where the role of housewife is afforded little esteem, where social relationships frequently originate at the workplace, and where "money talks," the out-of-home job gives a woman respect, friends, and power that she might not have otherwise. Only when a low-prestige job is added on top of a particularly heavy family load has out-of-home work been shown statistically to increase the stress experienced by women (Baruch & others, 1987).

Effects of Unemployment

■ **47.** ***What are some psychological consequences of job loss for men?***

Researchers have found that job loss can have devastating effects on people, which extend beyond the loss of income (Price, 1992). Almost all such research has focused on loss of men's jobs. In one study, based on a series of interviews of eighty-two families in which the husband had lost his job due to general layoffs, job loss was found to produce anxiety, depression, and self-blame in most men (Liem & Liem, 1988; Liem, 1987). This occurred for both white-collar and blue-collar workers, whether the family had extra economic resources to carry them through the period of unemployment or not. The men talked about their sense of not fulfilling expectations; of losing the personal friendships that they had at work; and of losing the pleasures and sense of achievement associated with the work itself. Wives also suffered when the husbands were unemployed, even when the wives were employed. According to Ramsay Liem (1987), the husband's emotional state—not the wife's reaction to his loss of job—was the main source of tension in the marriage. Husbands often turned their frustration against their wives, thereby alienating the one person who could provide them the most comfort and support during a hard time.

Growing Old

Beyond age 65 or 70, most people in our culture are retired from their jobs and are finished with the direct care of children. What happens then? Based on current projections of life expectancy, and taking into account the greater longevity of college graduates compared to the rest of the population, the majority of you who are reading this book will live past your eightieth birthday. Many of you will live more years in retirement than you have lived so far. If your health and pension are good, retirement will allow you greater freedom than you ever had before.

■ **48.** ***What are some possible reasons why women live longer than men?***

Women in the United States live an average of 7 years longer than men (Hoffman, 1992). Some people have attempted to explain this difference by arguing that women's occupations are less stressful than men's, but that explanation is contradicted by evidence that the advantage for women persists regardless of occupation (Rodin & Ickovics, 1990). Part of the difference undoubtedly stems from the fact that women take better care of their health than do men. They smoke less, drink less, drive more carefully, have better diets (especially in old age), and consult doctors more readily when something is wrong (Botwinick, 1984). The difference in smoking may be a major factor. Smoking dramatically increases the risk of heart disease (the single leading killer today) and lung cancer, both of which occur at higher rates in men (Peto & others, 1992). To the degree that the gender gap in longevity is due to smoking, we should find it narrowing over the next couple of decades, as fewer men and more women smoke today than in times past.

The joys of aging

For many people, interacting with grandchildren is one of the pleasures of old age. Contrary to the stereotype of aged people as lonely and isolated, most live within visiting distance of relatives and see a good deal of them.

Some people fear old age. There is no denying that aging entails loss. We lose gradually our youthful looks and some of our physical strength, agility, sensory acuity, and mental quickness. We lose some of our social roles (especially those related to employment) and some of our authority (as people take us less seriously). We lose loved ones who die before us, and of course with each year we lose one more year from our own life expectancy. Yet, if you ask the elderly, old age is not so bad as it seems to the young. In one study, in which younger adults were asked to project themselves into the future and rate their expected life satisfaction in late adulthood, their ratings were much lower than the life-satisfaction scores obtained from people who had already reached that age (Borges & Dutton, 1976). Researchers have found that ratings of life satisfaction and self-esteem are on average as high in old age as at any other time in adulthood (Bengston & others, 1985; Costa & others, 1987). As we age, priorities and expectations change to match realities, and along with losses there are gains. With greater free time and fewer responsibilities comes the opportunity to spend more time at hobbies, community service, travel, reading, contemplation, and enjoying friends and relatives.

The Value of Continued Engagement and Control

■ **49. *What is some evidence against the view that disengagement and giving up of control is a natural part of aging?***

The psychoanalytic theorist Carl Jung (1969) contended that as people grow older, past middle age, their personality shifts gradually from *extroversion*, defined as orientation to the outer world, to *introversion*, defined as orientation to the inner, subjective world of thoughts and dreams. Some researchers, observing a decline in the social activity of elderly people, have proposed that gradual disengagement is a natural and healthy part of aging (Cumming & Henry, 1961). Most psychologists who write about aging today, however, dispute such views. Researchers have found that personality, as measured by standard tests (to be described in Chapter 16), changes very little as people grow past middle age; those who were extroverts when younger remain so when old (Costa & McCrae, 1980). Disengagement, when it occurs, stems not so much from choice as from illness, loss of friends, and other imposed constraints. In general, those elderly people who are most socially active and engaged are also most likely to describe themselves as happy (Botwinick, 1984).

Neugarten (1974) distinguishes between two groups of older adults, the *young-old* and the *old-old*. The young-old, which includes the vast majority of older people, are those whose health allows them to be self-sufficient. Most of the young-old live in their own homes, cook their own meals, and choose their own activities. The old-old are those who cannot fully take care of themselves and are cared for by

Engaged with life

Many elderly people use their skills, experience, and energy to enrich not only their own lives but those of others. This woman, tutoring a prison inmate, is a volunteer in the Retired Senior Volunteer Program of New York City.

their adult children or in nursing homes or other institutions. Research on the old-old indicates that their happiness and even their ability to stay alive depend to a considerable degree on retaining some control over their lives despite their dependent status. In one experiment conducted in convalescent homes, residents who were given some degree of control—such as the ability to choose what they ate and how the furniture in their room was arranged—showed an improved mood and a higher survival rate compared to other residents of the same homes (Rodin, 1986).

The Value of a Confidant

50. *What is some evidence that having someone with whom to share thoughts and feelings contributes to happiness and health in old age?*

In an experiment that was concerned primarily with memory abilities in old age, researchers visited a nursing home and interviewed the residents four times during a 6-week period (Langer & others, 1979). In one condition, the interviewers simply asked a lot of questions about the resident's daily activities and past experiences. In the other condition, called *reciprocal self-disclosure*, the interviewers also told the interviewees about themselves, disclosing details about their own activities and experiences. This simple intervention had a remarkable effect. The reciprocal self-disclosure group not only showed greater improvement in memory on the formal tests used in the experiment, but also, according to the ratings of nurses who did not know which residents were in which group, showed improved mood, alertness, and sociability compared to the other group.

These results are consistent with other evidence that one of the principal requirements for a happy and healthy old age is someone to confide in. For most elderly people who are not in nursing homes, the spouse is the main confidant, and loss of a spouse can be tragic to the surviving person if he or she has no other confidant. Death of a spouse has repeatedly been shown to produce depression, anxiety, and reduced satisfaction with life (Lieberman & Borman, 1981). Death rates from practically all causes—including heart disease, stroke, hypertension, cancer, accidents, suicide, pneumonia, diabetes, and tuberculosis—are dramatically higher among widowed or divorced older people than among those of the same age who are still living with a spouse (Lynch, 1977). All these effects occur for both genders, but are greater for men than for women.

Why do women seem to cope better with the loss of a spouse than do men? The statistical finding may stem partly from a selection effect. Men are much more likely than women to remarry following the death of a spouse (partly because there are so many more elderly women than elderly men). Those men who remarry are not counted among the widowers, and those who don't remarry may have been the ones who were at greater risk of death to begin with. But selection aside, there is reason to believe that widows adapt to the single life better than do widowers. Women know better how to take care of themselves, and they keep closer social ties to relatives and friends than do men.

Approaching Death

The one certainty of life is that it ends in death. Surveys have shown that fear of death typically peaks in the person's fifties, which is when adults first begin to find a significant number of their age-mates dying from such causes as heart attack and cancer (Karp, 1988; Riley, 1970). Older people have less fear of death. They are more likely to accept it as inevitable; and death in old age, when a person has lived a full life, seems less unfair than it did earlier on.

Various theories have been proposed regarding the stages or mental tasks involved in preparing for death. Based on her experience with caring for dying patients, Elisabeth Kübler-Ross (1969) proposed that people go through five stages when they hear that they are incurably ill and will soon die: (1) *denial*—"The diagnosis can't be right," or "I'll lick it"; (2) *anger*—"Why me?"; (3) *bargaining*—"If I do this, can I live longer?"; (4) *depression*—"All is lost"; and (5) *acceptance*—"I am prepared to die." Another theory is that preparation for death consists of reviewing one's life and trying to make sense of it (Butler, 1975).

As useful as such theories may be in understanding individual cases, research shows that there is no universal approach to death. Each person does it differently. One person may review his or her life, another may not. One person may go through one or several of Kübler-Ross's stages but not all of them, and others may go through them in different sequences (Kastenbaum, 1985). The people who I have seen die all did it in pretty much the way they did other things in life. When my mother discovered that she would soon die—at the too-young age of 62—it was very important to her to have her four sons around, not so we could comfort her as much as so she could tell us some of the things she had learned about life that we might want to know. She spent her time talking about what, from her present perspective, seemed important and what seemed not. She reviewed her life not to justify it, but to tell us why some things she did worked out and others didn't. She had been a teacher all her life, and she died one.

Concluding Thoughts

There are many ways to think about the course of human life. Biographers, who write about specific individuals, usually focus on those aspects of their subjects' lives that made them unique. A unique temperament, set of family expectations, hometown, set of friends, and set of meaningful chance experiences might all be described as part of the stew that produced a particular scientist, artist, or diplomat. Developmental psychologists, in contrast, are usually more interested in the life course of people in general than that of a particular individual, which means that they usually study the recurring similarities rather than the differences in development. To conclude this chapter (and this two-chapter unit on development), you might find it worthwhile to think about three possible sources of regularity in development from person to person:

1. Biological maturation Psychoanalytic theories and theories originating in ethology or sociobiology tend to emphasize that the body changes in certain obvious and predictable ways from infancy through childhood, adolescence, and adulthood—and those changes certainly influence behavior. The degree to which more subtle biological changes in drive and temperament may also occur and contribute to the regularity in behavioral development is more debatable. Erikson's theory of the eight stages of life is a good example of an attempt to link psychological development to biologically based capacities and drives (though Erikson does not ignore the role of experience).

2. Logical inevitability Cognitive theories of development tend to emphasize that the understanding of certain concepts necessarily depends on the prior understanding of one or more simpler concepts. Inevitably, the simpler concepts and the behaviors they produce will always precede the more complex concepts and the behaviors they produce. Kohlberg's theory of the development of moral reasoning is a good example of this idea. Kohlberg argued that people progress through the stages in a specific order because each stage logically builds on the ones before it; it is not possible to reason at Stage 3, for example, without being able to reason at Stage 2, because Stage 3 logically encompasses Stage 2. Presumably any kind of being capable of moral thought, or even a computer programmed to learn ways of thinking morally, would have to go through the stages in that order.

3. Social constraints and expectations The source of regularity most emphasized in this chapter is the social environment. Bronfenbrenner's social ecology theory and Neugarten's concept of a social clock both emphasize this source. People who develop in the same culture, in which laws, customs, and social expectations are based on a shared set of assumptions about what people can or should do at certain ages, will as a result share a similar life course. In our culture, people usually learn algebra at about age 14 not because of biological or logical inevitability, but because that is the age at which they are required to study it in school. Similarly, laws and social expectations affect the age at which people in our culture get jobs, become independent of their parents, start families of their own, and retire.

One way to review this chapter (and the previous one, too) would be to look back at each theory or finding that had to do with predictable change over the life course or some portion of it and to think about it in relation to the three sources of regularity. How might biological maturation, logical inevitability, and/or social constraints account for the development change described?

Further Reading

William Crain (1992). *Theories of development*, 3rd edition. Englewood Cliffs, NJ: Prentice-Hall.

This brief text describes clearly most of the major theories of cognitive and social development. Among the theorists who receive chapter-length treatment and whose names you will recognize are Bowlby, Piaget, Kohlberg, Chomsky, Vygotsky, and Erikson.

Melvin Konner (1991). *Childhood*. Boston: Little, Brown, & Co.

Konner is a biological anthropologist interested in the underlying similarities of children's development across cultures. In this engrossing and beautifully illustrated book, with examples from around the world and with extensive use of psychological as well as anthropological research, he tells the tale of human development from birth to adolescence.

Jean Piaget (1932/1965). *The moral judgment of the child*. New York: Free Press.

For the beginning student, this is perhaps the most readable and interesting of Piaget's books. It is also the only book in which Piaget places great emphasis on the role of social relationships in development. Especially interesting is his description of the manner by which children's unsupervised play in games, such as marbles, leads them to a higher understanding of rules and democratic processes.

Erik H. Erikson (1968). *Identity: Youth and crisis*. New York: Norton.

For students who wish to learn about Erikson's psychoanalytic view of development, this is perhaps the best place to begin. In the first half of the book, Erikson describes his clinical approach to understanding the life cycle and his overall view of the various life stages, centering on the role of each stage in the development of one's personal identity. In the second half, Erikson discusses the identity crisis of adolescence and young adulthood, illustrating it with the case history of the famous psychologist William James.

Looking Ahead

One theme of the chapter you have just read is that psychological development is in part a product of the social setting within which the person develops. We turn now to a two-chapter unit on social psychology, which focuses even more explicitly on the social environment. It deals with the processes through which people perceive, understand, and are influenced by each other.

u. Sohn
Butter - Eier - Käse
FAHRRADHAUS
J. MIKUS
BOCHUM
Campagnolo

THE PERSON IN A WORLD OF PEOPLE

PART 6

We are social beings through and through. We are motivated to understand others; we are concerned about what others think of us; and our understanding of ourselves is strongly affected by our perception of what others think of us. This two-chapter unit is on social psychology—the attempt to understand human thought and behavior in relation to the social contexts in which they occur. The first chapter is about the mental processes involved in understanding others, ourselves, and the social world in general. The second is about some of the ways in which the presence or activities of other people, real or imagined, influence our behavior.

Perceiving Others

First Impressions

Making Attributions from Behavior

Some Psychological Bases of Prejudice

Perceiving and Presenting the Self

The Self as a Social Product

The Self as a Cognitive Construct

The Social Presentation of the Self

Attitudes

Functions and Origins of Attitudes

Cognitive Dissonance as a Force for Attitude Consistency and Change

Why Don't People Always Behave According to Their Attitudes?

SOCIAL COGNITION

CHAPTER 14

As Aristotle pointed out 23 centuries ago, we are by nature social animals. We are born completely dependent on other humans and we remain largely so throughout life. We need others as much for our emotional welfare as our material welfare. If alone too much, we feel lonely; and loneliness is a drive, not unlike hunger, that impels us to behave in such ways as to remove the aversive state. We are motivated not only to be with others, but to be approved of by them, and that motive plays an enormous role in how we think and act.

Social psychology, which will occupy us for this chapter and the next, is the area of psychology most directly concerned with the influence that other people have on an individual's thought and behavior. Gordon Allport (1968) once defined social psychology as "an attempt to understand and explain how the thought, feeling, and behavior of individuals are influenced by the actual, imagined, or implied presence of others." Notice that this definition includes the study of *thought* and *feeling* as well as behavior, and that these are viewed as functions of the *imagined* or *implied* presence of others as well as their actual presence.

One long-standing theme in social psychology is that our perceptions and thoughts about specific other people, about ourselves, and about the larger social world do not necessarily reflect reality but nevertheless help to create reality. Our actions, which have real effects in the world, are guided by our beliefs about others and ourselves, whether or not those beliefs are accurate. From this perspective, one of the greatest contributions psychology can make to human welfare is to reveal the processes and systematic biases that underlie our social beliefs. The study of those processes and biases is called ***social cognition***.

How do we perceive other people? How do we perceive ourselves? How do we influence the way others perceive us? How do we form general attitudes about our social world, and how do those attitudes influence our behavior? These are the major questions of social cognition, and they form the framework of this chapter.

Perceiving Others

We are amazingly quick to form impressions of other people, often based on little information. When we see a painting or photograph of a person we may use the two-dimensional cues there to size up the whole person—we may assign the person a past, a personality, a set of feelings. Artists and photographers play on our tendency to do that. Similarly, when we hear a description of a single utterance or action produced by a total stranger, we tend to build a mental picture of the whole person from that shred of information. And when we have actually met someone, no matter how briefly, we are inclined to say, "I *know* that person," and to half believe that we do. Let us examine some processes and biases involved in forming first impressions.

First Impressions

Nearly 50 years ago, Solomon Asch (1946) outlined a perspective on person perception that was closely tied to the Gestalt view of object perception. The basic premise of the Gestalt view (discussed in Chapter 9) is that we naturally see objects as wholes, not as separate parts. When only a portion of an object is present, we automatically fill in the gaps to create, in our minds, a representation of the whole object. In applying this view to person perception, Asch argued that we use whatever information we have about a person to build a mental picture of the whole person.

In modern cognitive terminology, the organized set of information or beliefs that we have about any entity or event is called a schema (discussed in Chapter 10), and the organized set of information or beliefs that we have about a person is called a ***person schema***. A schema can be either sketchy or detailed. Suppose you are going to meet a person about whom you know nothing specific. Immediately you activate your general person schema, a sketch containing the qualities common to most people. As you get more information about the person, you begin filling in the details of the schema, making it more distinctive, more representative of that specific person. Generalities such as *two arms* and *some degree of friendliness* are supplemented, often very quickly, by specifics, such as *long arms with delicate fingers* and *quiet but friendly once you get to know her*. This way of organizing information is extraordinarily efficient. It makes use, at every moment, of information that you already have about a person to enable you to understand and incorporate new information.

Using a Schema to Interpret New Information About a Person

■ **1. *How might your schema for a particular person influence your interpretation of new information about that person?***

Person perception, like perception in general, involves both bottom-up and top-down processing of information. As discussed for perception in general in Chapter 9, bottom-up processing refers to the detection and integration of parts of an object to build a conception of the whole object, and top-down processing refers to the use of one's current conception of the whole to identify or interpret the parts. In person perception as in object perception, various illusions or perceptual errors can arise from top-down processing. One's current schema of a person, whether it is accurate or not, can guide the detection and interpretation of new information about that person in a way that seems to confirm the current schema.

As an example, suppose you have been led to believe that a particular person, Paul, has a tendency toward sadism, and later you learn that he is training to join the police force. Because you already see him as a cruel person, you are likely to attribute his career choice not to courage, respect for social order, or other positive qualities, but to his cruelty. Images of police brutality may come to mind, and these may even serve as further evidence of Paul's basic cruelty: "It figures that Paul would become a cop. It gives him the opportunity to beat up on poor people and minorities. He must be even more sadistic than I thought." But suppose you had initially been led to believe that Paul is a warm and caring person. Now if you hear that he is training to join the police, you are likely to conjure up heartwarming images of police officers rescuing kittens and babies, helping children cross the street, and gently convincing young delinquents to reform: "It figures that Paul would become a police officer. He wants to serve humanity and is willing to risk his life to do so. What a fine man!" Thus, the very same information can be used as evidence for Paul's cruelty or his kindness, depending on the initial schema.

Early evidence that this kind of effect can occur was found in an experiment by Harold Kelley (1950) involving perception of a guest lecturer by students in a course at MIT. Before the guest arrived, half the students received a written biographical sketch of him that included the statement, "People who know him consider him to be a very warm person, industrious, critical, practical, and determined," and the other half received the same sketch except that the words "very warm" were replaced by "rather cold." After the guest had appeared and led a 20-minute discussion, the students were asked to fill out a form evaluating his performance. The main results were that the students who had received the sketch containing the description "very warm" took greater part in the discussion and rated the guest and his performance more positively than did the students who had received the sketch containing the description "rather cold." Thus, the two groups responded differently to the same lecture and made different attributions about the lecturer's performance depending on the initial schema set up for them.

The Disproportionate Influence of Early Information

■ **2. *What is some evidence that early information weighs more heavily than later information in our impression of a person?***

Information received early tends to carry more weight in one's assessment of a person than information received later, a phenomenon referred to as the ***primacy effect***. The existence of this tendency suggests that people develop a schema of the person as soon as any information becomes available and then use that schema to interpret (and possibly distort) subsequent information. In an early demonstration of the primacy effect, Asch (1946) showed that people who hear someone described first as *intelligent* and *industrious*, then as *impulsive* and *critical*, and finally as *stubborn* and *envious* develop a more positive final impression of the person than do those who hear the same descriptors in the opposite order. Apparently, hearing the positive adjectives first leads people to interpret the subsequent neutral and negative adjectives in a positive light—being impulsive, critical, and stubborn could be understood as aspects of being intelligent and industrious. Conversely, hearing the negative adjectives first may cast a negative light on the other adjectives—being critical, impulsive, and industrious could be understood as aspects of being envious and stubborn.

Asch's demonstration is somewhat artificial and could be explained as resulting from subjects' intuitive assumption that someone describing another person would list the most prominent traits first. But experiments using other methods have generally confirmed the primacy effect. In one experiment subjects were given two paragraphs about a young man named Jim. Paragraph *A* described him in activities that would lead to an inference that Jim was quite sociable, and paragraph *B* described him in activities that would lead to an inference that he was a loner. The result was that subjects who read the paragraphs in the order *A-B* most often described Jim in the end as sociable, and those who had read them in the reverse order most often described him as a loner (Luchins, 1957).

The Undue Influence of Surface Characteristics

■ **3. *What are some ways in which a person's facial features may influence people's judgments of that person?***

Some aspects of a person are noticeable immediately, even before the person has said or done anything. You can immediately see a person's facial features and clothing, and these may influence your initial schema and hence the way you interpret subsequent information. Consistent with all those children's stories in which the good people (the princesses and princes) are beautiful and the bad people (the witches and ogres) are ugly, many experiments have shown that we in our culture tend to judge physically attractive people as more intelligent, competent, sociable, and moral than less attractive people (Dion, 1986; Eagly & others, 1991). In one experiment, fifth-grade teachers were given report cards and photographs of children whom they did not otherwise know and were asked to rate each child's intelli-

Figure 14.1 ***Who would deceive you?***
Adults whose faces are babyish (left) are commonly seen as more naive, honest, helpless, kind, and warm than are mature-faced adults (right). The characteristics of a baby face include a round head, large forehead, large eyes, short nose, and small chin.

gence and achievement. The teachers rated physically attractive children as brighter and more successful than unattractive children with identical report cards (Clifford & Walster, 1973). In a similar experiment, adults more frequently attributed a child's misbehavior to environmental circumstances if the child was physically attractive and to the child's personality if the child was not physically attractive (Dion, 1972).

Another surface characteristic that can affect judgments is the degree to which a person's facial features resemble those of a baby (see Figure 14.1). In a series of experiments conducted in both the United States and Korea, researchers found that baby-faced adults are perceived as more naive, honest, helpless, kind, and warm than are mature-faced adults of the same age, even though the perceivers could tell that the baby-faced person was not really younger (Berry & McArthur, 1985; McArthur & Berry, 1987). Recently, Leslie Zebrowitz and Susan McDonald (1991) have shown that this bias can affect real court cases. These researchers had observers rate the baby-facedness, as well as various other attributes, of defendants and plaintiffs at 506 small-claims court cases tried by 25 different judges in Massachusetts. The main finding is graphed in Figure 14.2. When the defendant was accused of a deliberate attempt to harm or deceive the plaintiff (such as refusing to return a security deposit to a tenant), baby-faced defendants were judged innocent far more often than were mature-faced defendants. This effect was highly significant even when statistical means were used to equate baby-faced and mature-faced defendants for age, sex, physical attractiveness, amount of damages requested, type of evidence offered, and various other legal and extralegal factors that could affect

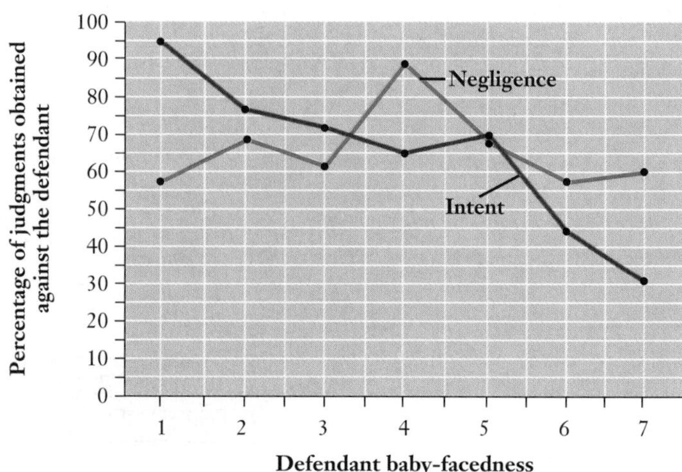

Figure 14.2 ***Evidence that a face can influence a verdict***
Defendants in small-claims cases were rated on a 7-point scale for degree of baby-facedness. Those given a 1 had the most mature faces and those given a 7 had the most babyish faces. The decline in judgments against the defendant as baby-facedness increased, in cases involving intentional action, was highly significant statistically. In contrast, no significant trend occurred in cases involving negligence. (The apparent increase in negligence judgments against defendants at the midpoint on the baby-facedness scale is intriguing, but was not statistically significant.) (Adapted from Zebrowitz & McDonald, 1991.)

the judge's decision. In contrast to cases involving intent, baby-facedness had no significant effect in cases involving negligence (such as performing a contracted job in an incompetent manner). Apparently, judges find it hard to think of baby-faced persons as deliberately causing harm, but do not find it hard to think of them as incompetent or forgetful.

Making Attributions from Behavior

Of course our judgments about people are based not just on what they look like or what we have heard about them, but also on what they do. Any such judgment involves an inference, or attribution, about the causes of their actions. In its most general sense, an attribution is any claim about the cause of something. In the field of social cognition, ***attribution*** is the process of ascribing a person's behavior to a specific cause, and *an attribution* is the ascribed cause itself.

■ **4. *According to Heider, in what way are all people "naive psychologists"? Under what conditions, according to Heider, should people make external rather than internal attributions about a person's behavior?***

The study of how people make attributions was initiated by Fritz Heider, who, like Asch, was one of the pioneers in the field of social cognition. Heider (1958) suggested that all people are "naive psychologists" in that they try to explain the behavior of others by attributing it to stable, internal characteristics of the person. For example, if you see a man smile, you may attribute the smile to his friendliness or to his guile, depending on other information that you have about him and the circumstances under which the smile occurred. What you carry away from the encounter is not so much a memory that the man smiled as a memory that he was friendly or deceitful; and that memory is added to your schema of that person.

Heider also noted that under some circumstances people attribute another person's behavior not to characteristics of the behaving person (*internal causes*) but rather to characteristics of the environment (*external causes*). If you saw a man running and screaming in fear and then saw that a tiger was chasing him, you would probably attribute his fear not to timidity but to the situation—almost anyone would be afraid of a loose tiger. To use behavioral observations to build a picture of a person, one must first judge whether the behavior implies anything unique about the person or is the sort of action to be expected of anyone under the circumstances.

Kelley's Model of the Logic of Attributions

Following Heider's ideas about attributions, Harold Kelley (1967, 1973) developed a model of the logic that people might use to judge whether a particular behavior should be attributed to some characteristic of the person or to something about the immediate environment. The model, illustrated in a modified version in Figure 14.3, is most easily understood if applied to a concrete example.

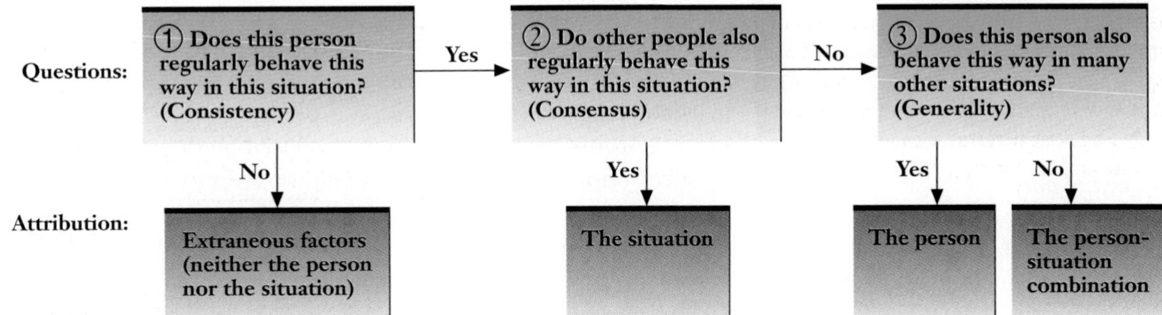

Figure 14.3 ***The logic behind an attribution***

According to Kelley, our decision to attribute an observed behavior to internal causes (the person) or external causes (the situation) depends ideally upon our answers to three questions. Although Kelley did not specify a sequence for asking the questions, this flow chart depicts the most efficient sequence and the attribution that would follow each combination of yes and no answers.

■ ***5. According to Kelley's model, when should a person's behavior lead to an attribution about (a) the situation, (b) the person, and (c) the person-situation combination?***

Suppose you observe Susan getting angry while she is caught in a traffic jam. You might attribute her anger to her *personality* (say, her irritability), to the *situation* (being caught in a traffic jam), to some *extraneous factor* distinct from either the traffic jam or her personality (perhaps she had just had a bad day at work), or to some combination of these. According to Kelley's model, before making the attribution you would ideally ask three questions about the behavior: (1) Is it *consistent*? Does Susan regularly get angry when caught in traffic jams? (2) Does it represent *consensus*? Do most other people who get caught in traffic jams get angry? (3) Does it reflect a *general* aspect of her behavior? Does Susan get angry in many other situations besides traffic jams? If the answer to the first question is no (she does not usually get angry in traffic jams), you will probably attribute her anger on this occasion to an extraneous factor. However, if the answer is yes, you will probably attribute her anger to either the traffic jam, her personality, or a combination of both, depending on the answers to the next two questions.

Kelley's model is a model of common sense in making attributions. To convince yourself of that, trace out the various paths in Figure 14.3 and think about the logic. If Susan regularly gets angry in traffic jams and so do many other people (*yes* to questions 1 and 2), you are likely to attribute her anger to the situation (the traffic jam). If Susan regularly gets angry in traffic jams and other people do not, and if she gets angry in many other situations (*yes-no-yes*), you are likely to attribute her anger to her personality. Finally, if Susan regularly gets angry in traffic jams and other people do not, and if she does not get angry in many other situations (*yes-no-no*), you are likely to attribute her anger to the combination of her personality and the situation, and to conclude that she is not in general an angry person but is unusually reactive to traffic jams. Not surprisingly, a number of research studies have shown that when people are given sufficient information to answer the three questions about a particular behavior and are asked to explain the behavior logically, they usually do make attributions that accord with Kelley's model (McArthur, 1972). But in real life people frequently lack the information, the time, or the motivation to make a logical attribution. Instead, they often take shortcuts in their reasoning, which can result in certain consistent errors or biases.

■ ***6. What is some evidence that the fundamental attribution error is at least sometimes truly an error and that, in at least one sense, it is truly fundamental?***

The Fundamental Attribution Error

In his original writings on the process of attribution, Heider (1958) argued that people tend to ignore the circumstances (external causes) that give rise to a particular behavior and too often attribute the behavior solely or mainly to the person's character (internal causes). Later, Lee Ross (1977) referred to this bias as the ***fundamental attribution error***, and, for better or worse, that label has stuck.

A victim of bias?

Leonard Nimoy called his autobiography *I Am Not Spock*. He has apparently often encountered the fundamental attribution error.

Often there is no objective way to judge whether a particular behavior reflects the person's character more than the situation or the other way around. Attributing a behavior to character, however, would clearly be an error if the observer knew that the behavior was staged. In one experiment, male college students listened to a fellow student read an assigned political statement that was written by someone else (Gilbert & Jones, 1986). Even when the assignment was made by the subjects themselves, so that they knew the reader had not chosen it, subjects tended to rate him as liberal when the assigned statement was liberal and as conservative when the statement was conservative.

According to a hypothesis proposed by Daniel Gilbert (1989), the fundamental attribution error reflects the natural operation of the mind. Along with many other cognitive psychologists (see Chapters 9 and 10), Gilbert distinguishes between two classes of mental processes—*automatic* and *controlled*. The former are rapid, effortless, and unconscious, and the latter are slow, deliberate, and conscious. Gilbert's hypothesis, which we might call the *automaticity hypothesis*, is that attributions to internal characteristics are automatic and attributions to the situation are, by comparison, more controlled. If Gilbert is correct, your automatic impulse upon seeing Susan get angry in a traffic jam is to assume that she is the kind of person who is easily angered. Only through conscious effort might you counter that impulse by considering that many people are angered by traffic jams and that Susan is not easily angered in other situations. In support of this hypothesis, Gilbert and his colleagues have shown that the fundamental attribution error is greater for subjects whose conscious mental attention is occupied with other tasks (such as reciting lists of words) than for subjects who can devote their full attention to the attributional process (Gilbert, 1989).

■ ***7. What is some evidence that the fundamental attribution error may be partly a product of Western culture?***

Another hypothesis, not necessarily incompatible with the automaticity hypothesis, is that the fundamental attribution error is at least partly learned from the larger culture (Jellison & Green, 1981). According to this *cultural-norm hypothesis*, Western philosophies and religions emphasize the idea that people are in charge of their own destinies, so people growing up in Western cultures learn to attribute behavior more to character than to environment. If so, then in a culture such as India's—in which philosophies and religions emphasize the role of fate or circumstances in controlling one's destiny—people might not show the fundamental attribution error. To test this theory, Joan Miller (1984) asked middle-class children and adults in the United States and in India's Hindu community to think of an action by someone they knew and then to explain why the person had acted in that way. Consistent with the cultural-norm theory, the Indians made fewer attributions to personality and more to the situation than did the Americans. This difference was greater for adults—who would presumably have incorporated the cultural norms more strongly—than it was for children (see Figure 14.4).

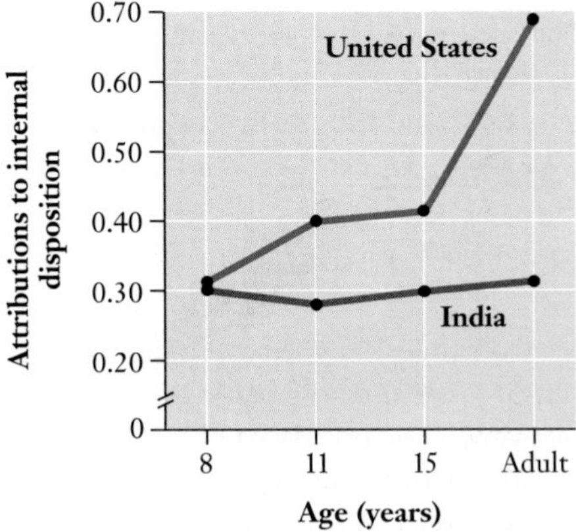

Figure 14.4 ***Cultural differences in making attributions***

When asked to explain a particular behavior produced by a particular person, the proportion of attributions to internal disposition (personality or attitude) was greater among people in the United States than it was among Hindus in India, and this difference was greater for adults than for children. (Data from Miller, 1984. The proportions were determined by dividing the number of internal attributions by the total number of internal plus external attributions for each group, ignoring attributions that were neither clearly internal nor external.)

The Actor-Observer Discrepancy

The fundamental attribution error is less likely to occur when people make attributions about their own behavior than when they make attributions about someone else's. This difference is referred to as the ***actor-observer discrepancy*** (Nisbett & others, 1973). The person who performs an action (the actor) commonly attributes the action to the situation—"I am whistling because it is a beautiful day," or "I read those statements because I was asked to read them." In contrast, another person who sees the same action (the observer) is more likely to attribute it to the actor's internal characteristics—"She is whistling because she is a cheerful person," or "He read those statements because he is a political liberal."

■ ***8. What are two theories to explain why people are more likely to make internal attributions about others' behavior than about their own, and what is some evidence for each?***

What causes the actor-observer discrepancy? One hypothesis, which we can call the *knowledge-across-situations hypothesis*, is that because people have seen themselves in many more situations than they have seen others, they have become sensitized to the variations in their own behavior from setting to setting. You know that your own behavior varies to suit the situation, but you are less likely to know that about someone else's behavior. For example, you may assume that your psychology professor's calm demeanor in the classroom is indicative of his or her behavior everywhere and thus attribute it to personality, but this may be only because you haven't seen your professor at home, in traffic court, or on the softball diamond. Consistent with this interpretation, people usually judge the behavior of their close friends as more flexible—more determined by the situation and less by unvarying personality traits—than that of people whom they don't know as well (Nisbett & others, 1973; Sande & others, 1988).

Another hypothesis is the *visual-orientation hypothesis*, which holds that the actor-observer discrepancy stems from a basic characteristic of visual perception: Our eyes point outward and are drawn toward other people. When we watch someone *else* perform an action, our eyes are fixed on that person, so we are most aware of the person and attribute causal properties to him or her. But when we perform an action ourselves, we see the surrounding environment, not ourselves, and attribute causal properties to that.

Support for the visual-orientation hypothesis can be found in an experiment conducted by Michael Storms (1973) in which some male college students (the actors) engaged in 5-minute get-acquainted sessions while others (the observers) watched. After the session, each observer was asked to evaluate the degree to which the behavior of the actor whom he had been assigned to watch was the result of the actor's personality or aspects of the situation (such as being in an experiment and meeting someone for the first time), and each actor was asked to make the same evaluation of his own behavior. In one condition of the experiment, the subjects (actors and observers) made these evaluations after watching a videotaped replay of the session that reversed their original visual perspectives: The actors saw themselves, and the observers saw the environment from the actors' vantage points. This condition tended to reverse the actor-observer discrepancy. The actors made relatively more attributions to their own personality, and the observers made relatively more attributions to the situation.

Some Psychological Bases of Prejudice

In its broadest sense, prejudice refers to any influence that our preconceptions, whether conscious or unconscious, reasonable or unreasonable, may have on the way we evaluate any specific person, object, or event. The effects of prior information or a person's facial features on the attributions we make about that person's behavior—which we have already discussed—are examples of prejudice in this broad sense. In the more common and specific use of the term, however, prejudice refers to negative views that large numbers of people hold toward members of particular groups. Prejudice of this sort is an enormous social problem worldwide and has attracted the attention of many social psychologists.

Stereotypes and Their Role in Attributions

■ ***9. What is some evidence that stereotypes can bias our perceptions of individuals?***

We all carry around in our heads schemas not just for individual persons, and persons in general, but also for particular groups of persons. You may have schemas for men, women, Asians, Californians, blacks, Catholics, and college professors. Such schemas are called ***stereotypes***. The first person to use the term *stereotype* in this way was the journalist Walter Lippmann (1922), who defined it as "the picture in the head" that a person may have of a particular group or category of people. Lippmann pointed out that stereotypes can distort our perceptions of individuals and provide a basis for prejudice.

Plenty of evidence, from experiments and real-world observations, bears Lippmann out. Consistent with the cultural stereotype of women as less competent than men at certain tasks, experiments have shown that both men and women are more likely to attribute successful performance to luck if the performer is a woman and to ability if the performer is a man (Deaux, 1984). Consistent with a stereotype that black men are violent, white viewers who saw one man lightly shove another during a heated discussion more often interpreted the shove as aggressive if the shover was black and as playful or theatrical if he was white (Duncan, 1976).

Experiments have shown that college students are more likely to use stereotypes in making attributions if they are tired or mentally preoccupied than if they are mentally refreshed and focused on the attributional task (Bodenhausen, 1990; Gilbert & Hixon, 1991; Pratto & Bargh, 1991). Such findings corroborate the view that stereotypes provide shortcuts to judgment in situations where we lack the time, mental resources, or motivation to evaluate the facts of the individual case.

A Dual-Processes Theory of Prejudice

■ **10.** ***In Devine's theory, what are the roles of automatic and controlled mental processes in prejudice and the attempt to overcome prejudice? What is some evidence for her theory?***

Patricia Devine (1989) has developed a theory of prejudice based on the distinction between automatic and controlled mental processes. According to her theory, stereotypes pervade the culture and exert an automatic, and unconscious, influence on our perceptions of and behavior toward members of stereotyped groups. All people automatically apply a stereotype on first seeing or hearing about a member of a stereotyped group. The difference between *prejudiced* people and *unprejudiced* people, in Devine's terminology, is that the former consciously accept the stereotype while the latter consciously reject it and censor its influence on their behavior when they can.

In experiments testing her model, Devine used a questionnaire to identify white college students who were either relatively prejudiced or unprejudiced toward blacks. She found that both groups were equally knowledgeable about the culture's stereotype of blacks, but that when asked to describe anonymously their own attitudes the prejudiced group tended to agree with the stereotype and the unprejudiced group disagreed. Then, to test the most unique prediction of her model—that both groups would be equally affected by the stereotype when they weren't conscious of it—Devine (1989) performed an experiment in which the stereotypes were mentally activated without awareness.

To do this she involved the subjects in a perceptual task that seemed to have nothing to do with stereotypes. Both prejudiced and unprejudiced subjects were asked to look at a spot at the center of a screen and to identify the location of words flashed at various positions off center. The words were flashed too quickly to be read consciously and remembered, but, in line with other experiments on unconscious perception (discussed in Chapter 9), Devine assumed that the words would nevertheless be perceived unconsciously and affect the conscious interpretation of later information. For subjects in the *stereotype-activation* condition, the words were designed to call forth the stereotype of a black person. They included such words as *Negro*, *black*, *ghetto*, *Africa*, *blues*, and *basketball*. For subjects in the *nonactivation condition*, words were used that are not especially associated with black people. Neither set contained words connoting hostility, which was the element of the black stereotype that was to be tested in this study.

Immediately after the perceptual task, subjects heard a description of some behaviors that had been performed by a man named Donald, and they were asked to form an impression of his character. Among Donald's behaviors were some that might or might not be interpreted as hostile, such as refusing to pay his rent until his apartment was painted. No mention was made of Donald's race, but Devine assumed that those who had been exposed to the black-associated words in the perceptual task would unconsciously have in mind the stereotype of a black man as they heard the paragraph and would interpret ambiguous information about Donald in terms of that stereotype. Consistent with Devine's prediction, subjects in the stereotype-activation condition rated Donald higher in hostility and unfriendliness than did those in the nonactivation condition, and this was as true for unprejudiced subjects as it was for prejudiced subjects.

Surmounting a stereotype
Mountain climber Hulda Crooks, shown here at age 91 atop Mount Fujiama, is helping to dispel the stereotyped view that older people are incapable of vigorous, disciplined physical activity.

One implication of Devine's work is that overcoming prejudice is like resisting any well-learned habit. In recent research, Devine and her colleagues have found that unprejudiced people are aware that their reactions sometimes reflect cultural stereotyping and that they experience discomfort or guilt when they catch themselves behaving in ways that violate their beliefs (Devine & others, 1991; Monteith & others, 1993). Devine suggests that this discomfort is a motivating force that may lead unprejudiced people to work hard at countering the automatic, stereotype-driven reactions until such reactions disappear. When and if that happens, prejudice is defeated at the unconscious as well as the conscious level.

■ **11.** ***What is some evidence that people perceive outgroups as (a) more homogeneous and (b) less virtuous than their ingroup?***

Ingroup-Outgroup Biases

Stereotyping and prejudice are based on people's tendency to develop schemas for whole groups of individuals. Not surprisingly, the kinds of schemas that people develop for ***ingroups***, groups to which they themselves belong, differ in certain systematic ways from the kinds of schemas they develop for ***outgroups***, groups to which they themselves do not belong. One difference, called the ***outgroup homogeneity effect***, is that people typically perceive members of an outgroup as very similar to each other (homogeneous), but do not perceive members of an ingroup that way. This effect has been demonstrated with many different kinds of groups (Mullen & Hu, 1989). In one study, for example, business majors exaggerated the similarity of engineering majors but not of themselves, and engineering majors did the same for business majors (Judd & others, 1991). In another, college students described the behavior of students at another college as more uniform and predictable than that of students at their own college (Quattrone & Jones, 1980). In still another, men perceived women as more similar to each other than men are, and women perceived the opposite (Park & Rothbart, 1982). Such findings probably stem at least partly from the fact that people know more individuals in their ingroups than in their outgroups and thus are more aware of the differences that exist among those in their own group. In addition, people may react negatively to the idea that they themselves are "just like" others of their group, and this may lead them to see their own group as more diverse than other groups.

Not surprisingly, people typically view members of their ingroups more favorably than they view members of outgroups. This favoritism is often labeled ***ethnocentrism***, though it occurs for all kinds of groups, not just ethnic groups (Mullen & others, 1992). It can occur even when there is no realistic basis at all for assuming that two groups differ. For example, in one laboratory experiment, people who knew that they had been assigned to separate groups by a purely random process—a coin toss—nevertheless rated members of their own group more positively than they did members of the other group (Locksley & others, 1980).

Henri Tajfel (1982) has argued that this tendency to exaggerate the virtues of one's own group at the expense of others is part of a more general drive to build one's self-esteem. According to Tajfel, people define themselves partly in terms of the groups to which they belong and, therefore, bias their perceptions of those groups positively, just as they bias their perceptions of themselves. Other research (examined in Chapter 15) emphasizes the role that competition among different groups plays in the development of positive ingroup and negative outgroup biases. In the real world, groups are more likely to hold negative attitudes toward one another if they are competing for jobs or other resources than if they see their interests as compatible.

Blaming the Victim

Another bias in person perception that contributes to prejudice is ***blaming the victim***, a tendency to seek out flaws in the behavior or character of people who have suffered some misfortune. Numerous studies have shown that victims of rape, robbery, terrorism, accidents, illnesses, and social injustice often suffer doubly: once from the misfortune itself, and again from the subtle or not-so-subtle blame that they receive from others for "causing" or "allowing" the misfortune to happen (Lerner & Miller, 1978; McDuff, 1988). The behaviors or traits that were previously praised ("He is a friendly person") may now be seen as negative and the cause of the person's suffering ("He is the kind of man who lets strangers into his home, so of course he was robbed"). In one laboratory demonstration of victim blaming, college students evaluated another student's character less favorably if they be-

12. *How might the irrational blaming of victims be explained as a defense against one's own fear or anxiety?*

lieved she was going to receive a prolonged series of painful electric shocks as part of the experiment than if they believed she wasn't (Lerner & Simmons, 1966).

Victim blaming on a massive scale occurs when groups of people who are discriminated against or persecuted by the larger society are themselves blamed for the results. For example, when the horrors of the Nazi Holocaust became well known, some people reacted by blaming the Jews for not resisting more strenuously. William Ryan (1971) has argued that negative views toward blacks in the United States are instances of victim blaming. On the one hand, blacks have been blamed for passively accepting their condition and, on the other, they have been blamed for trying to change things too fast. Today, negative reactions to people with AIDS, particularly those who are homosexuals, can be described as victim blaming (Anderson, 1992). In some quarters, AIDS has reinforced a negative view of homosexuals; in one newspaper poll, 25 percent of respondents agreed with the statement that AIDS is God's punishment to homosexuals (Herek & Glunt, 1988).

Is life fair?

Our tendency to blame the victims of misfortune may stem partly from an implicit assumption that life is fair—an assumption called the just-world bias.

Why does victim blaming occur? To some degree it may simply be another manifestation of the fundamental attribution error—the general tendency to attribute a person's behavior or condition to inner characteristics and to ignore the role of chance or circumstance. But that hypothesis alone may not explain the full extent of victim blaming. Melvin Lerner (1980) has proposed that victim blaming is part of what he calls the ***just-world bias***, a general tendency to believe that life is fair. If life is fair, then people who suffer must for some reason deserve to suffer. Why do people believe that life is fair? One possible answer is that people have a psychological need to defend themselves from the fear that bad things could happen to them: "If life is *not* fair, then no matter how I behave, or how good a person I am, something terrible could happen to me."

Some support for the self-defensive view stems from research showing that victim blaming increases when subjects can see their own image in a mirror as they hear about a victim (Thornton, 1984). Apparently, the self-awareness induced by the mirror increases the likelihood that the listeners, at some level of their consciousness, will consider the idea that the same thing might happen to them. To defend against that thought, the listeners look for differences between the victim and themselves, negative characteristics that could have brought about the victim's fate.

Perceiving and Presenting the Self

Philosophers and psychologists have long contended that self-awareness is a hallmark of our species. My dog surely has some sort of mental conception of me. She recognizes me, expects certain behaviors from me, correctly anticipates many of my actions, and treats me differently than she treats the mail carrier. But does she have any conception of herself? Most researchers who have studied the question would answer no.

13. *What is one line of evidence that most nonhuman animals do not develop a self-concept?*

One line of evidence for this difference comes from research with mirrors. At about 15 months of age, human infants stop treating their image in a mirror as if it were another child and begin to treat it as a reflection of themselves. If a researcher surreptitiously places a bright red spot of rouge on the child's nose before placing the child in front of the mirror, the 15-month-old responds by touching his or her *own* nose to feel or rub off the rouge; a younger child, by contrast, touches the mirror or tries to look behind the mirror to find the red-nosed child (Lewis & Brooks-Gunn, 1979). The only other animals besides ourselves who have passed the rouge test of self-recognition are chimpanzees and orangutans (Gallup, 1970; Lethmate

& Dücker, 1973). Other animals, including monkeys, continue to treat the mirror image as another animal—a creature to threaten and try to chase away—no matter what their age or how much experience they have had with mirrors.

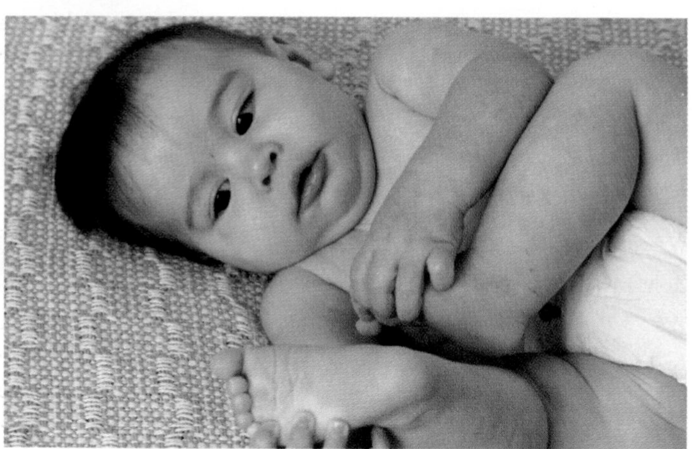

Is this me?

Self-discovery begins in early infancy, but not until 15 months of age do infants recognize their image in a mirror as themselves.

An experiment with chimpanzees suggests that for them social interaction is critical for self-recognition. Chimps raised in isolation from others of their kind did not learn to make self-directed responses to their mirror images, while those raised with other chimps did (Gallup & others, 1971). Many psychologists and sociologists have argued that the self-concept—for human children as well as chimpanzees—is always fundamentally a *social* product. To become aware of yourself as a person, you must first become aware of other people and then become aware that they treat you as if you are something like them; you, indeed, are one of them.

The Self as a Social Product

Who are you? Before reading further, try to answer that question by writing twenty brief statements that begin, *I am* ______. After you have completed your list, examine it to find ways that your self-understanding has derived from your social world. Some of your statements may link you to socially defined groups: *I am a student . . . a Roman Catholic . . . an adult*. Other statements may refer to the nature of your interactions with other people or with society at large: *I am socially outgoing . . . a family-oriented person . . . a political activist.* Still other statements may refer to traits that you attribute to yourself either because other people have attributed them to you or because you have seen that you stand out in those ways in comparison to other people: *I am short . . . conscientious . . . good at math*.

You probably won't find any self-statement in your list that does *not* stem in one way or another from your social environment. Many years ago, in making this point, the sociologist Charles Cooley (1902) coined the term the *looking-glass self* to refer to the idea that we learn about ourselves by looking at others around us. Our social world is the looking glass in which we see ourselves. We see ourselves in others' reactions to us, and we use our perceptions of others' traits and abilities as the yardsticks to measure our own. Research on expectancy effects, social roles, and social comparison all support the idea of the looking-glass self; these are the topics to which we now turn.

One true self

Some people seem more driven than others to present a public self. As you consider this collection of bumper stickers, ask yourself which way the influence flows. Are the labels emblematic of the person's influence on society, or of society's influence on the person?

Effects of Others' Expectations

In George Bernard Shaw's play *Pygmalion* (upon which the musical *My Fair Lady* was based), Eliza Doolittle, who has been transformed by a language professor from an impoverished cockney flower girl to a fine lady, remarks pointedly to the professor's friend: "You see, really and truly . . . the difference between a lady and a flower girl is not how she behaves, but how she's treated. I shall always be a flower girl to Professor Higgins, because he always treats me as a flower girl, and always will; but I know I can be a lady to you, because you always treat me as a lady, and always will."

■ **14. *What is some evidence that others' expectations can so affect a person's behavior and self-concept that the expectations become self-fulfilling prophesies?***

To some degree, we are what others expect or assume us to be. Others' beliefs affect the way they behave toward us, which in turn affects our own behavior and self-concept. Experiments have shown that when person *A* is deliberately misled about the characteristics of person *B*, *A*'s behavior toward *B* tends to cause *B* to behave in accordance with the originally misleading expectation. In one such experiment, young men were asked to engage in 10-minute phone conversations with young women whom they had not met. If the man was led to believe that the woman was especially attractive, bright, and warm, he opened the conversation in a brighter and warmer manner than if he was led to believe the opposite. The woman at the other end, not knowing that the man's view of her had been biased, responded in kind—brightly and warmly if she was believed to be that, more dully otherwise (Snyder & others, 1977). In another experiment, the same result occurred in reverse—the woman was misled about the man with whom she was speaking, and he responded in kind (Anderson & Bem, 1981). In these and similar experiments, an initially arbitrary designation, determined by a random procedure, became for a short period a self-fulfilling prophecy.

What might happen if a person were treated in accordance with an arbitrary set of expectations over a longer period of time? To find out, Robert Rosenthal and Lenore Jacobson (1968) led elementary-school teachers to believe that certain students would show a spurt in intellectual growth during the next few months, as indicated by a special test that all students had taken. In reality, the students labeled as *spurters* had been selected not on the basis of a test score, but at random. Yet, when they were tested 8 months later, the selected students showed significantly greater gains in IQ and academic performance than did their classmates.

What caused the "spurters" to spurt? Many studies since Rosenthal and Jacobson's have shown that teachers who expect some children to perform particularly well in fact treat those children quite differently from the rest. They are more likely to engage the high-expectations children in conversations, praise them for work well done, give them adequate time to answer difficult questions, give them challenging assignments, and notice and reinforce their self-initiated efforts (Cooper & Good, 1983; Harris & Rosenthal, 1985). In response, the children apparently develop a better self-concept of their scholastic ability, and they work harder (Jussim, 1986; 1991).

Other experiments have shown that when schoolchildren learn that a certain positive trait has been attributed to them, their behavior begins to reflect the trait. In one experiment, some children were told in the course of classroom activity that they *are* neat and tidy (*attribution condition*); others were told that they *should be* neat and tidy (*persuasion condition*); and still others were given no special message about neatness and tidiness (*control condition*). The result was that those in the attribution condition showed significantly greater gains in neatness, as measured by the absence of littering, than did those in either of the other conditions (Miller & others, 1975). In a similar experiment, children who were told that they are good at math

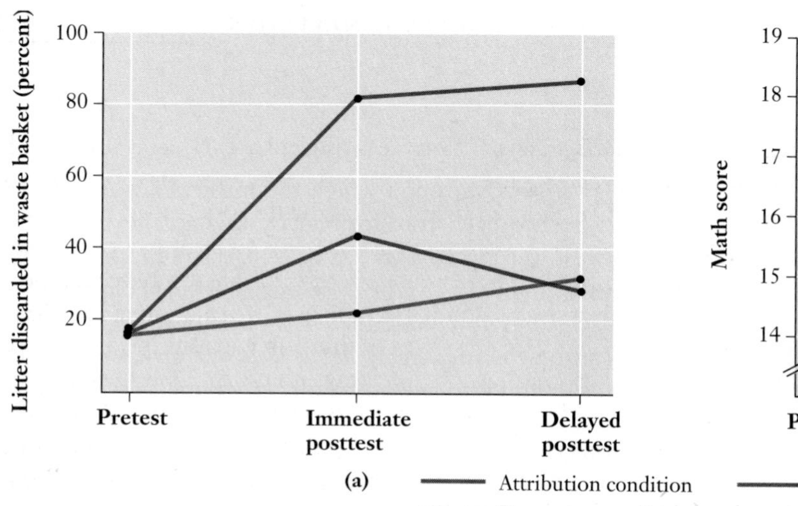

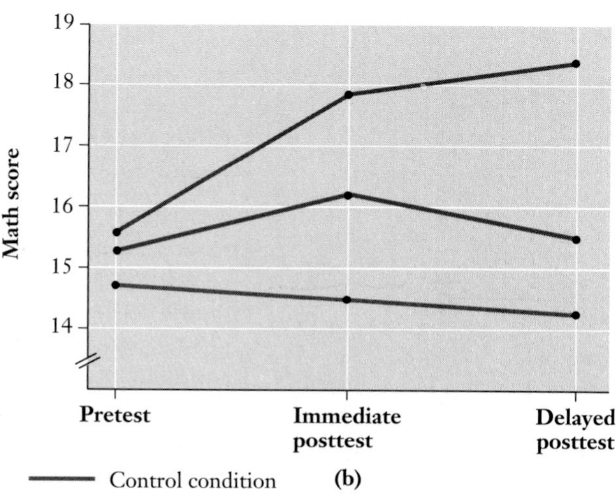

Figure 14.5 ***Effect of attribution compared to persuasion***

(a) Fifth graders who were repeatedly told that they were neat and tidy (attribution condition) showed greater gain in use of the wastebasket than did those in the other conditions. (b) Second graders who were repeatedly told that they were good at math (attribution condition) showed greater improvement in math scores than did those in the other conditions. In each case, the students were tested three times: once right before (pretest), once immediately after (immediate posttest), and once a few weeks after (delayed posttest) the experimental conditions were in effect. (Adapted from Miller & others, 1975.)

showed greater improvements in math scores than children who were told that they should try to become good at math (see Figure 14.5). Apparently, when children are given a positive label, it can become part of their self-concept, and they tend to live up to it.

Social Roles and Multiple Selves

Long ago, William James (1890) argued that each person has not just one self, but many, each corresponding to his or her relationship with a different person or set of people. Psychologists who emphasize the relationship between self-concept and *social role* have expanded upon this idea. Each of us plays a number of different roles in society, and we have a somewhat different concept of ourselves associated with each. I am a *father*, *husband*, *son*, *neighbor*, and *college professor* to different people. When I think of myself in each role, different sets of traits and abilities come to mind. My understanding of myself in each role is mediated partly by the larger society's stereotype of what fathers, husbands, sons, neighbors, and college professors are like, and partly by the more specific expectations of the individuals to whom I am those things.

■ **15. *What might lead us to develop multiple self-concepts, and why might they be useful?***

Research has shown that people typically describe themselves differently when one of their social roles is mentally activated than when another is. Such work has led to weblike models of the self-concept, in which some self-perceived traits are attached to specific roles (the nodes in the web), while others are attached to several or all roles, tying the nodes together (Hoelter, 1985; Rosenberg, 1988). For example, a person might see herself or himself as *authoritative* in the role of employer, *submissive* in the role of daughter or son, *companionable* in the role of wife or husband, and *caring* in all of these roles—so here the trait of being caring cuts across roles and is a source of consistency in the self-concept (see Figure 14.6).

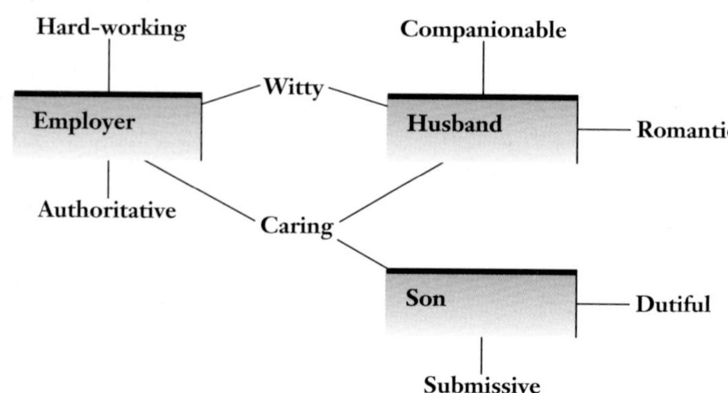

Figure 14.6 ***The multiple nature of the self-concept***

The self-concept can be represented as a web with different nodes for different social roles. Some self-perceived traits may be tied to just one role (such as husband or employer), and others may be tied to several or all roles.

You might expect that having multiple self-concepts, each associated with a different role, would be psychologically stressful, but research suggests that the opposite is more often true (Dance & Kuiper, 1987; Linville, 1985, 1987). The sense of having multiple roles and a wide variety of traits seems to protect a person from depression when one role is lost or diminished in importance—as might happen in a divorce, or when children grow up and leave home, or when a job is lost. Moreover, the sense of having many roles and traits to draw on apparently adds to a person's confidence in his or her ability to handle new situations. The flexibility that characterizes people's self-attributions compared to their attributions about others (the actor-observer discrepancy) may stem at least partly from their belief that they have many different, even contradictory, personality traits that they can call on in different situations (Sande & others, 1988).

Walking a line between two cultures Masako Owada was born in Japan, attended a public high school in Massachusetts, graduated from Harvard in 1985, distinguished herself as a brilliant executive in Japanese foreign trade, and then—after much hesitation—accepted the marriage proposal of Japanese Crown Prince Naruhito. She realizes that her new role requires that she give up much of her Western independence, but she intends to push for greater women's rights in Japan. The Japanese press has criticized her for answering questions too directly and expressing her own ideas. As one news executive put it, "[She must] give up her endeavor to build up her own character . . . and find a way to express herself simply with her smile."

■ **16. *How has the Twenty Statements Test provided evidence that American students have a relatively independent sense of self and Japanese students have a relatively interdependent sense of self?***

The Independent and the Interdependent Self: A Cultural Difference

In a review of cross-cultural research on people's self-concepts, Hazel Markus and Shinobu Kitayama (1991) identified two distinct views of the self. The *independent view*, which is predominant in North America and parts of Western Europe, emphasizes the separateness of the self from the rest of the social world. Although people in the West do describe themselves as manifesting different characteristics in different contexts, they have a strong sense of an immutable core, a "real me," that cuts across contexts and establishes the self as a unique entity separate from the environment. This independent sense of self is consistent with a long tradition of Western philosophy that emphasizes personal freedom, self-determination, and competition.

In contrast, the *interdependent view* of the self, which is predominant in Asia, Africa, Latin America, and parts of Southern Europe, emphasizes the inherent connectedness of the self with specific other people and various social roles. Consistent with religions and philosophies that focus on the communal nature of human existence and the obligations of individuals to specific others, the self is seen not as a bounded entity that remains constant from setting to setting, but as an entity that changes in accord with social needs and expectations. This view is captured in the Japanese word for self, *jibun*, which can be translated as "one's share of the shared life space" (Hamaguchi, 1985).

Several studies supporting the independent-interdependent distinction used the *Twenty Statements Test*—the same test I asked you to administer to yourself—in which people describe themselves in twenty brief statements. In one such study by Steven Cousins (1989), college students in Japan and the United States were each given four different versions of the test. One was the *noncontextualized format*, the standard version that simply asks for twenty statements addressing the question, "Who am I?" In the other three versions, the *contextualized formats*, context was provided by adding the words "at home," "at school," or "with close friends," to the "Who am I" question. After filling out each form, the students were asked to circle the five statements that were most important in defining themselves.

To analyze the results, a count was made of how many circled statements fell into each of several categories, including personal attributes and social identifiers. The *personal attributes* category consisted of statements in which the subjects described some aspect of their personality (for example, *I am easygoing* or *I am ambitious*) in a manner that added no social context beyond that provided by the test format. As you can see in Figure 14.7 on page 508, in the noncontextualized format the Americans were far more likely to describe themselves with personal attributes than were the Japanese. In the contextualized format, however, the Japanese used more personal attributes than did the Americans. In keeping with the idea that they have an interdependent view of themselves, the Japanese students apparently saw themselves not as having consistent characteristics across all social contexts, but as having consistent characteristics within a given context.

The *social identifiers* category, also graphed in Figure 14.7, consists of statements in which people described themselves in terms of a group they belong to, their social role, or some other socially defined status (for example, *I am a student*, or *I am the eldest daughter in my family*). As you can see in the figure, in the noncontextualized format the Japanese students described themselves more often than the American students in terms of social identifiers. These results, too, corroborate the idea that Japanese people are more likely than Americans to define themselves in terms of their various social identities and responsibilities, and less likely to define themselves in terms of traits that cut across all situations.

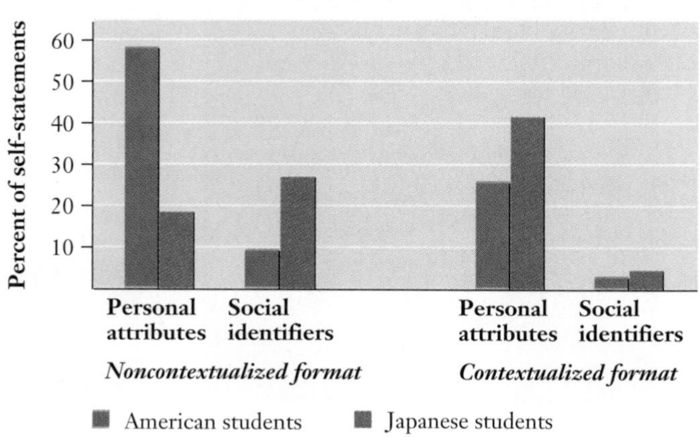

Figure 14.7 ***Differences between American and Japanese self-concepts***

American and Japanese students were asked to take the Twenty Statements Test of self-concept in four formats. The noncontextualized format asked, "Who am I?" The three contextualized formats asked, respectively, "Who am I at home? . . . at school? . . . with close friends?" In each format the students circled the five self-statements that they considered most revealing of themselves. The graph shows the proportion of these statements, in each type of test format for each nationality, that were coded as personal attributes and as social identifiers. (The percentages for a given nationality and test format do not total 100 because some statements were coded as neither personal attributes nor social identifiers.) (Data from Cousins, 1989.)

The Self as a Cognitive Construct

Although our self-concepts are to some degree sketched out for us by the expectations of others and the values of the culture, we do not passively accrete these sketches. Rather, we actively draw our own self-concepts, using the sketches provided by the social environment as models, but selecting from among them and modifying them in our own unique way to suit our unique needs and understanding. However, even these active processes are inherently social.

Comparing Ourselves to Others

17. *What is some evidence that people construct a self-concept by comparing themselves with a reference group?*

To understand ourselves, to identify our unique characteristics and measure our abilities, we actively compare ourselves to other people, a process called ***social comparison***. In perception everything is relative to some frame of reference, and in self-perception the frame of reference is other people. To see oneself as short, conscientious, or good at math is to see oneself as those things *compared to other people*. A direct consequence of social comparison is that the self-concept varies depending on the ***reference group***, the group with whom the comparison is made. If the reference group against which I evaluated my height were professional basketball players, I would see myself as short; if they were jockeys, I would see myself as tall.

In studies of children's self-concepts, children who were asked to describe themselves tended to focus on those traits that most distinguished them from others in their group (McGuire & McGuire, 1988). Thus, children in racially homogeneous classrooms rarely mentioned their race, but those in racially mixed classrooms quite commonly did, especially if their race was in the minority. Children who were unusually tall or short compared to others in their group more frequently mentioned height, and children with opposite-gender siblings more frequently mentioned gender than did other children in their self-descriptions (see Figure 14.8).

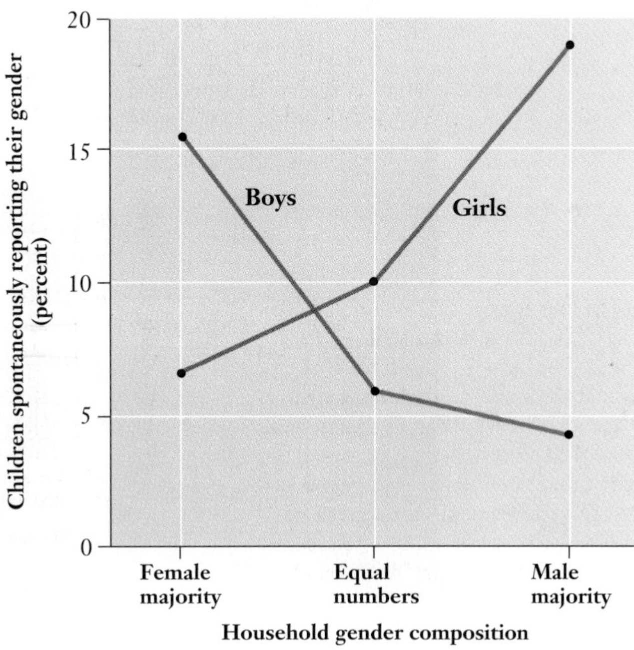

Figure 14.8 ***Evidence that children define themselves in terms of differences from their reference group***
As shown here, children were more likely to mention their gender when describing themselves if their gender was in the minority in their household than if it was in the majority. (Adapted from McGuire & McGuire, 1988.)

People compare themselves to others not simply to identify or describe themselves, but also to evaluate themselves, a process that can be charged with emotion. Since one's relative standing in any comparison depends as much on the reference group as on one's own characteristics or abilities, the choice of reference group can dramatically affect one's self-esteem. Many first-year college students who received outstanding grades in high school feel crushed when their marks are only average compared to their new reference group of college classmates. William James (1890), reflecting on extreme instances of these kinds of comparisons wrote: "So we have the paradox of the man shamed to death because he is only the second pugilist or second oarsman in the world. That he is able to beat the whole population of the globe minus one is nothing; he has 'pitted' himself to beat that one and as long as he doesn't do that nothing else counts."

Self-Enhancing and Self-Effacing Biases: Another Cultural Difference

■ **18.** ***What is some evidence that people in North America and Japan show opposite biases in evaluating themselves?***

Research in North America and Western Europe has produced abundant evidence for a general ***self-enhancing bias***: People see themselves as better than they really are in comparison to others. In surveys asking people to rate their abilities against their peers, most respondents rate themselves as above average on most abilities. Furthermore, research on attributions shows that people tend to attribute their successes to inner qualities and their failures to external circumstances. In one study, students who performed well on an examination attributed their high grades to their own hard work and ability, while those who performed poorly attributed their low grades to luck, the unfairness of the test, or other factors beyond their control (Bernstein & others, 1979). Essentially the same result was found for college professors who were asked to explain why a paper they had submitted to a journal was either accepted or rejected (Wiley & others, 1979). So consistent is the self-enhancing bias in the United States that some psychologists see a failure to manifest it as a sign of depression. Depressed people, according to some reports, evaluate themselves more accurately than do nondepressed people; if they are average at some task, they tend to see themselves as average (Peterson & Seligman, 1984).

But what is true in the West is not necessarily true everywhere. Sometimes what Western psychologists report to be human nature is not *human* nature, but Western nature. Markus and Kitayama (1991) asked university students in the United States and Japan to estimate the percentage of their classmates who had higher intellectual abilities than their own. The average response for the Americans was 30%, consistent with the self-enhancing bias, but the average for the Japanese was 50%, which of course is what the average would have to be for both groups if they were estimating accurately.

In another study, Michael Bond and Tak-Sing Cheung (1983) gave the Twenty Statements Test to university students in the United States, Hong Kong, and Japan and analyzed each statement for its evaluative content. They found that the ratio of positive to negative self-statements was nearly two to one for the American students, one to one for the Hong Kong students, and one to two for the Japanese students. In other words, the Japanese students showed a ***self-effacing bias*** that was as strong as the Americans' self-enhancing bias. This result is consistent with much that has been written about the Japanese culture's preference for modesty over self-aggrandizement (Markus & Kitayama, 1991).

The Social Presentation of the Self

As self-conscious social beings, we know that other people form impressions of us just as we form impressions of them, and we care about those impressions. So, when among other people, we control our behavior to influence what they will think. We present ourselves: Here I am, this is the way I want you to perceive me. Social psychologists use the term ***impression management*** to refer to the set of ways by which people either consciously or unconsciously attempt to influence others' impressions of them (Schlenker, 1980).

19. ***What is the theater analogy to impression management, and how might that analogy be misleading?***

The sociologist Erving Goffman was a pioneer in the study of impression management. In a book entitled *The Presentation of Self in Everyday Life* (1959), he elaborated extensively on the Shakespearean metaphor, "All the world's a stage, and all the men and women merely players." Goffman portrayed us as actors, playing at different times on different stages to different audiences, always trying to convince our current audience that we are the character we are playing. The members of each of our audiences in this play of life are also actors trying to convince *us* that they are the characters they are playing. As the play goes on we may see through each other's costumes, lines, and pantomimes, but we rarely let on that we do. An unspoken social rule—which is part of politeness or tact—is to act toward others as if they are the characters they are playing, as long as they remain reasonably believable. To break this rule would be to upset the smoothness of social life and run the risk of having ourselves exposed as well.

Although the theater analogy is useful, it can also be misleading. It may suggest more duplicity, more conscious deception, than is warranted by what is known about impression management. There need not be a division in our minds between the images we are trying to project to others and our sincere, though sometimes

Managing an impression

Even more than the rest of us, politicians must constantly be on guard about the impression they are making. The impression of a sincere listener and problem solver that U.S. president Bill Clinton conveyed during his campaign helped him to win the election.

deluded, beliefs about ourselves. If the self-concept has multiple nodes corresponding to different social roles, then behavior that varies with context is not mere posturing but an expression of selected aspects of one's true self.

Looking Good

The foremost goal of impression management is to make ourselves look good to other people. Most of us want to project *friendliness* (so others will be friendly to us), *honesty* (so others will trust us), and *competence* (so others will admire us). Few of us are above putting on a friendly smile for show, hiding our transgressions and weaknesses, or subtly exaggerating our virtues and abilities when we think we can get away with it.

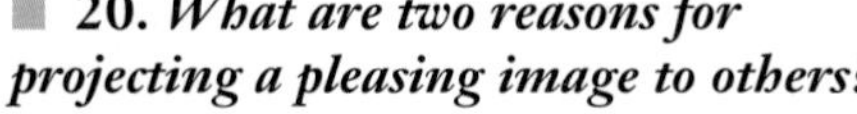

■ **20.** ***What are two reasons for projecting a pleasing image to others?***

Psychologists have described two relatively distinct motives for wanting to look good to others (Leary & Kowalski, 1990). The first is to elicit favors or rewards from other people. In general, people are more likely to treat us well if they like us than if they don't. The second is to enhance our self-esteem. If others' reactions to us are our looking glass, we will want to project toward that glass the most pleasing image we can. The image we project for either of these purposes will depend upon our understanding of what will please or displease our audience, and that will vary with the audience and the culture. Behavior that elicits rewards and esteem in the United States might not in Japan.

Asserting and Validating the Self-Concept

William Swann (1987, 1992) has argued that people manage impressions not just to look good but also to validate their self-concepts, which may or may not be favorable. According to Swann, we are motivated to maintain a stable view of ourselves, partly to give order to our lives, and to do so we must get others to accept that view. If I think of myself as a Rambo-like character but cannot convince you, my faith in that image will be shaken. I must eventually arrive at a self-image that you and others accept; then, to maintain that image, I must continue to play the part. Swann (1985) contends that the drive to maintain a consistent self-image can even lead people who have a negative self-image to portray themselves to others in negative ways. As an illustration, he described the case of a battered child who, to maintain a self-image as deserving to be beaten, consistently avoided people who liked him, sought out those who disliked him, and responded to praise by increasing his negative behavior and self-derogation.

■ **21.** ***How might people's drive to maintain a consistent self-concept lead to behavior that is opposite to the typical expectancy effects?***

In a series of experiments, Swann found that when people discover that another person's concept of them is different from their own, they often respond by projecting their own more strongly. For example, in one experiment, people who perceived themselves as dominant became all the more dominant if their conversation partner initially thought they were submissive, and people who perceived themselves as submissive became all the more submissive if their partner initially thought they were dominant (Swann & Hill, 1982). Notice that this is the opposite of the expectancy effects discussed earlier, in which people behaved in accordance with others' expectations. Swann's research suggests that conformity to others' expectations occurs when the person's self-concept is relatively neutral concerning the trait in question, but that active resistance occurs when those expectations run counter to the person's firmly held self-concept (Swann & Ely, 1984).

Self-Handicapping

One impression-management strategy that has attracted a good deal of research is ***self-handicapping***, giving oneself an obvious disadvantage in order to provide an excuse for anticipated poor performance (Berglas & Jones, 1978). This tactic seems to be employed most often by people, particularly men, who have a high reputation that they are afraid they can't live up to. Fearing defeat to a young upstart in chess, the old master may surrender a few playing pieces at the beginning so that a loss will be attributed to graciousness rather than less ability. Fearing a poor grade on a test, the student whom everyone calls brilliant may stay out all night beforehand, flaunting the lack of study, to set up an excuse in case he fails.

■ **22.** ***How did an experiment demonstrate that an undeserved high reputation can promote self-handicapping?***

In a laboratory study showing that an undeserved high reputation can lead to self-handicapping, male college students were given a set of problems to solve, and then some were told they had done well and others were told they had done poorly (Tucker & others, 1981). Actually, the problems were unsolvable, so those who were told they had done well could only assume that they had been lucky. Then, on the pretext that this was a study of the effects of alcohol on thought, the students—all of whom were drinkers and of legal drinking age—were given a choice of how much alcohol they would like to drink before taking a second test with similar problems. The result was that those who were told they had done well chose to drink more alcohol than those who were told they had done poorly. Apparently, the "successful" group did not want to risk the reputation that they had just established; so to invalidate the second test as a measure of their ability, they chose to drink a lot. The "unsuccessful" group, however, with little to lose and the possibility of gain from a second test, did not want to invalidate the test, and chose to drink little.

Experiments comparing the two genders in self-handicapping suggest that it occurs rarely if at all in women (Rhodewalt, 1990). Women, like men, will offer excuses after the fact for poor performance, if excuses are available, but apparently are not inclined to create excuses in advance (Rhodewalt, 1990). Researchers are unsure how to explain this consistent gender difference, but one guess is that it stems from the generally higher motivation that men in our culture have to prove their competence in the types of tasks used in most self-handicapping studies (Ross, 1992). It would be interesting to know if women would self-handicap more than men at a task that is clearly a stereotypical female task in our culture.

Individual Differences in Impression Management: Self-Monitoring

The two general goals of impression management—looking good to different audiences and asserting a consistent self-concept—can run into conflict with one another. Some years ago, Mark Snyder (1974) developed a test for a personality characteristic that he labeled ***self-monitoring***, which seems to distinguish between people who favor one or the other of these two goals. Snyder defines self-monitoring as sensitivity to other people's immediate reactions to oneself, combined with a desire and ability to control those reactions. *High self-monitors* are those people who will most dramatically modify their behavior to please their current audience,

Table 14.1 ***Sample questions from the self-monitoring scale***

1. I can make impromptu speeches even on topics about which I have almost no information. (*T*)*
2. When I am uncertain how to act in a situation, I look to the behavior of others for cues. (*T*)
3. I rarely need the advice of my friends to choose movies, books, or music. (*F*)
4. Even if I am not enjoying myself, I often pretend to be having a good time. (*T*)
5. I would not change my opinions (or the way I do things) in order to please someone else or win their favor. (*F*)
6. I never have been good at games like charades or improvisational acting. (*F*)

*The *T* or *F* in parentheses is the response (True or False) that indicates high self-monitoring.
Source: From "Self-monitoring of expressive behavior" by M. Snyder, 1974, *Journal of Personality and Social Psychology*, *30*, pp. 526–537.

and *low self-monitors* are those who maintain greater consistency in behavior from one audience to another. Table 14.1 shows some sample questions from Snyder's self-monitoring scale.

In a series of studies, Snyder and others have found that high scorers on the self-monitoring scale differ from low scorers in the following ways: (a) High self-monitors are the better actors. When asked to convey specific emotions while reading lines, highs conveyed the emotions better than lows (Snyder, 1974). (b) High self-monitors care more about social norms and conformity. While filling out a personality test, highs more often than lows glanced at a sheet indicating how others had answered before they themselves answered the questions (Snyder, 1974); in discussions, highs more often than lows accommodated their opinions to those of their audience (Snyder & Monston, 1975); and in a social situation where an expression of joy might be deemed inappropriate, highs more often than lows suppressed that expression (Friedman & Miller-Harringer, 1991). (c) High self-monitors have more friends, but their friendships are usually less intimate (Snyder & Smith, 1986). Moreover, highs tend to choose friends who appear attractive or competent or who share some specific activity with them, whereas lows tend to choose friends who share their values and attitudes (Jamiesen & others, 1987).

Other research suggests that high self-monitors, based on Snyder's test, actually have two separate characteristics. One is a strong concern about other people's impressions of them and the other is the self-confidence and acting ability needed to manipulate those impressions (Briggs & Cheek, 1986). People who have the first characteristic but not the second are not considered to be high self-monitors, but fall into the category commonly called shy (Buss, 1980). Because they care strongly about others' reactions and doubt their ability to obtain favorable reactions, they become anxious and tend to withdraw from social situations.

Self-monitoring, like any other personality measure, varies in degree. Most people score neither extremely high nor extremely low on the scale, but somewhere near the middle (Snyder, 1979). They are consistent enough to carry a sense of an integrated self from one situation to another, but at the same time adaptable enough to get along reasonably well with a wide variety of people in a wide variety of situations.

The self-monitoring scale has apparently not been used in cultures such as Japan where the interdependent sense of self prevails. I suspect that the scale would be less valid, less useful as a predictor, in such cultures than in ours. The scale is based on an assumption, which is apparently reasonably valid in North America, that acting and modification of behavior to fit the social context correlate positively with one another. In Japan, however, the modification of behavior to fit the social context is experienced not as acting but as a genuine expression of the interdependent self (Dio, 1986; Markus & Kitayama, 1991).

Attitudes

Thus far we have been discussing social cognition as applied to the perception of other individuals and the self. Now we turn to a broader application, one that ties the individual to the entire social world.

An ***attitude*** is any belief or opinion that has an evaluative component—a belief that something is good or bad, likable or unlikable, moral or immoral, attractive or repulsive. Attitudes express positive or negative emotions toward particular objects, people, events, or ideas; they range from one's feelings about a specific brand of toothpaste to one's feelings about democracy or religion. Attitudes are a key topic in social cognition, because they link the individual and society at large; they arise from the individual's experience in the social environment and help guide that person's behavior in that environment. The study of attitudes and how they are formed or changed also has a practical side. An enormous amount of effort in our society goes into the attempt to modify people's attitudes. Advertising, political campaigning, and the democratic process itself (in which people speak freely in support of their views) can be thought of as attempts to change other people's attitudes.

Functions and Origins of Attitudes

■ **23.** ***What are four different functions that attitudes might serve?***

What are attitudes for? That is perhaps the most basic question one can ask about attitudes. Ideas about the functions of attitudes carry implications concerning all other questions we might ask about attitudes, such as how they are acquired or how they influence behavior. Several theorists (Herek, 1986; Katz, 1960; Smith & others, 1956) have proposed that attitudes serve four types of purposes:

1. ***Utilitarian function*** The most obvious function a given attitude might serve is *utilitarian*—that of guiding one's behavior toward or away from the object of the attitude. The utilitarian function is typically strongest for attitudes that are acquired through direct experience with the object of the attitude. If you have a positive attitude toward strawberry ice cream and French literature, and a negative attitude toward freezing weather and calculus, those attitudes are serving a utilitarian function to the degree that they actually lead you to seek out the former and avoid the latter.

2. ***Defensive function*** Attitudes can serve to quiet one's anxiety or boost one's self-esteem. A person who loves to play hockey but is cut from the hockey team may develop a negative attitude toward hockey as a psychological defense against the feeling of loss or failure. Similarly, a negative attitude toward someone who is suffering might be a defense against the fear that the same thing could happen to oneself (as discussed in the section on blaming the victim). A person duped into paying too much for a new car might develop an unrealistically positive attitude toward the car in defense against the thought that he or she made a big mistake.

3. ***Social-adjustive function*** People sometimes remake their attitudes for purposes of impression management. Adopting the attitudes of a new group one

A social-adjustive appeal

This ad obviously plays on people's social-adjustive needs in its attempt to persuade. Can you think of ways in which it appeals to any of the other classes of attitude functions?

has joined, for example, may (unconsciously or consciously) be a bid for acceptance or esteem within the group. Conversely, adopting attitudes that differ pointedly from the group's may be a bid for admiration as a unique or strong-minded person. In either case the attitudes expressed serve a social-adjustive purpose.

4. ***Value-expressive function*** Some attitudes—such as belief in freedom, or worship, or the value of hard work—may reflect deeply felt values that help to define the self and make life meaningful. To assert them is to assert one's self and one's sense of purpose in life. Such attitudes may be ingrained through early training or may arise later in thoughtful reflection or in sudden experiences of insight or revelation.

These functions are not mutually exclusive. A single attitude may serve all four relatively equally, or it may serve almost entirely just one or another. My attitude toward strawberry ice cream is purely utilitarian; but if my parents had owned a strawberry ice-cream factory, my attitude might encompass any of the other functions as well. Notice that the latter three functions are served by the *expression* of the attitude, either to the self or to others, whether the attitude helps guide one's behavior in relation to the attitude object or not.

■ **24.** ***What is some evidence that a particular positive or negative attitude can serve different functions for different people?***

In an analysis of essays written by heterosexuals about homosexuality, Gregory Herek (1986, 1987) demonstrated how the expressed attitudes could be evaluated in terms of the degree to which they appeared to serve each of the four functions. Some essays focused on practical considerations and the author's experiences with homosexuals, which would lead the author either to approach or avoid homosexuals in the future (utilitarian function). Other essays seemed to be grounded in the author's anxiety about his or her own sexuality (defensive function). Others centered either implicitly or explicitly on the relation between the author's view and what other people think about homosexuals (social-adjustive function). And still others expressed humanitarian values or religious principles that seemed dear to the author (value-expressive function).

Other research has indicated that people with different personality styles are differentially affected by persuasive messages or commercials that appeal to one or another of the four attitude functions (Snyder & DeBono, 1987; 1989). As you might expect, people who score high on Snyder's self-monitoring test are most influenced by messages that emphasize how others feel about the issue (social-adjustive function), and people low in self-monitoring are most influenced by messages that appeal to their personal values (value-expressive function) or give practical information (utilitarian function).

Role of a Reference Group in Influencing Attitude: The Bennington College Study

People who live with or interact with each other typically have similar attitudes. Children have similar attitudes to their parents, and people of all ages have similar attitudes to the peer groups with whom they most commonly interact (McGuire, 1985). It is not hard to think of possible reasons for this: People living with or communicating with each other are exposed to similar information, are subject to the same persuasive messages, may have come together partly because of preexisting similar attitudes, and may have modified their own attitudes to accommodate each other's for social-adjustive purposes. The process of social comparison, discussed earlier in relation to evaluating one's own traits and abilities, also applies to attitudes (Festinger, 1954). People tend to validate their attitudes by comparing them to those of a reference group either of peers or of superiors (upward comparison) and are uncomfortable with attitudes that are out of step with those of the reference group. One of the most thorough, long-term studies of the role of a reference group in attitude change and persistence was initiated in 1934 by Theodore Newcomb (1943) at Bennington College, a women's college in Vermont.

■ **25.** ***How did a long-term study at Bennington College and a followup study of Bennington graduates illustrate the social-adjustive function of attitudes?***

At the time of Newcomb's study, Bennington College had a politically liberal faculty, but drew most of its students from wealthy, politically conservative families. Most first-year students shared their parents' conservative views, but with each year at Bennington they became more liberal. In the 1936 presidential election, for example, 62 percent of the first-year students, 43 percent of the sophomores, and only 15 percent of the juniors and seniors favored Alf Landon, the conservative Republican, over the liberal Democrat, Franklin Roosevelt. By the time the first-year students became juniors and seniors, they too had become politically liberal.

What produced this change in attitude? The specific classroom lessons to which students were exposed may have played some role, but other social forces were also at work. People who occupied the most prestigious positions—the faculty, older students, and leaders of various campus organizations—were politically liberal, and adopting their views helped one fit in with the community. In interviews, many women said that they adopted and expressed new attitudes at least partly to make friends and gain prestige. The relatively few who remained conservative throughout their 4 years at Bennington were far more likely than the others to be socially isolated, to feel that they were not really part of the college community.

What happened to these women's political attitudes after they left Bennington? Without the Bennington College community to support their new-found liberalism, did they slip back to their original conservatism? To answer this question, 20 years after the initial study Newcomb located and reinterviewed most of the graduates whom he had previously studied (Newcomb, 1963; Newcomb & others, 1967). Most of these women had remained liberal compared to others of comparable wealth and station in life, and the interviews suggested that they retained their liberalism at least partly because they continued to associate with people whose views were like theirs. The staunchest liberals were those who had married liberal husbands and who belonged to political and social groups with liberal attitudes.

The Bennington study offers an opportunity to think about the relationship between attitudes and some of the ideas discussed earlier about the self. Your attitudes, at least some of them, influence the concept that others form of you and contribute to your own self-concept. If your attitudes run sharply counter to those of admired others around you, you may fear a loss of their esteem, which could reduce your self-esteem. To avoid this, you might seek a more compatible group, or you might gradually modify your attitudes so that you can remain comfortable with the present group. An expression of new attitudes might at first seem to you like deliberate impression management and make you uncomfortable. But the more often you express a new attitude and find acceptance for it, the more it will become part of your self-concept and not just something you are professing for the sake of approval.

Of course, this social-adjustment account of your attitude change is not the whole story. You are also concerned for the truth. But how do you decide what is true? If others consistently invalidate your old attitudes and support your new ones, the new ones might begin to seem true. Religious cults have long known that the most certain way to win a convert is to isolate the person from all who disagree with the cult and surround the person for at least several months with "true believers" only.

Two Routes to Attitude Construction

Thus far we have considered four functions of attitudes and the role that reference groups can play in attitude change. Now let's turn to a more cognitive question: What sorts of mental processes do people bring to bear in evaluating the persuasive messages they hear? Researchers have found it useful to distinguish between two general routes by which the mind can engage the information in a persuasive message—a ***central route***, which entails logical analysis of the message content, and a ***peripheral route***, which includes all of the other ways of processing the information (Petty & Cacioppo, 1986).

■ **26. *What are some examples of the decision rules that make up part of the peripheral route to attitude change?***

The peripheral route includes simple association and respondent conditioning (discussed in Chapter 5), in which the mere pairing of an object or idea with a positive or negative event leads to a positive or negative attitude toward the object or idea. Presumably, this is the basis for all those television ads that pair a product (beer, car, shirt, or whatever) with beautiful people, happy scenes, and lovely music. Beyond simple association, the peripheral route may also involve certain *decision rules*, also called *heuristics*, which are shortcuts to a full, logical elaboration of information in the message (Chaiken, 1986). People use decision rules implicitly, unaware that they are doing so. Examples of these rules include the following: (a) If there are a lot of numbers and big words in the message, then it must be well documented. (b) Famous or high-status people are more likely to be correct than unknown or low-status people. (c) If many other people believe this, then it must be true. (d) If the message is phrased in terms of values that I believe in, it is probably right. In one series of experiments, high self-monitors relied most heavily on rule (c) in the above list, consistent with a social-adjustive use of the attitude, and low self-monitors relied most heavily on rule (d), consistent with a value-expressive use of the attitude (Snyder & DeBono, 1987).

In a theory of persuasion called the *elaboration likelihood model*, Richard Petty and John Cacioppo (1986) proposed that a major determinant of whether a message will be processed by the central or the peripheral route is the personal relevance of the message. According to Petty and Cacioppo, we tend to be *cognitive misers*; we reserve our elaborative reasoning powers (central route) for messages that seem most relevant to us and rely on mental short-cuts to evaluate messages that seem less relevant to us. Petty and Cacioppo also proposed that attitudes formed through the more effortful central route last longer than those formed through the peripheral route. A good deal of research supports both of these propositions, especially the former (Eagly & Chaiken, 1993).

■ **27. *How did an experiment support the idea that people are most likely to process a personally relevant message by the central route and a personally less relevant message by the peripheral route?***

In one experiment on the role of personal relevance in persuasion, Richard Petty and his colleagues (1981) presented college students with messages in favor of requiring students to pass a set of comprehensive examinations in order to graduate. Groups of students received different messages, which varied in (a) the *strength* of the arguments (a central factor), (b) the alleged *source* of the arguments (a peripheral factor), and (c) the *personal relevance* of the message. The weak-argument message consisted of slightly relevant quotations, personal opinions, and anecdotal observations, and the strong-argument message contained well-structured statistical evidence that the proposed policy would improve the reputation of the university and its graduates. The source was varied by stating in some cases that the arguments had been prepared by high school students and in other cases that the arguments had been prepared by the Carnegie Commission on Higher Education. Finally, the personal relevance was varied by stating in the high-relevance condition that the proposed policy would begin next year, so current students would be subject to it, and in the low-relevance condition that it would begin in 10 years. After hearing the message, students in each condition were asked to rate the extent to which they agreed or disagreed with the proposal.

Figure 14.9 shows the results. As you can see, in the high-relevance condition the quality of the arguments was most important. Students in that condition tended to be persuaded by strong arguments, and not persuaded by weak arguments, regardless of the alleged source. Thus, in that condition, students were processing the message by the central route. In the low-relevance condition, the quality of the arguments had much less impact, and the source of the arguments had much more. Apparently, when the policy was not going to affect them, students did not attend carefully to the arguments, but instead used the peripheral route, invoking the decision rule that experts (members of the Carnegie Commission) are more likely to be right than are nonexperts (high-school students). There is no real surprise here. The idea that people will think more logically about issues

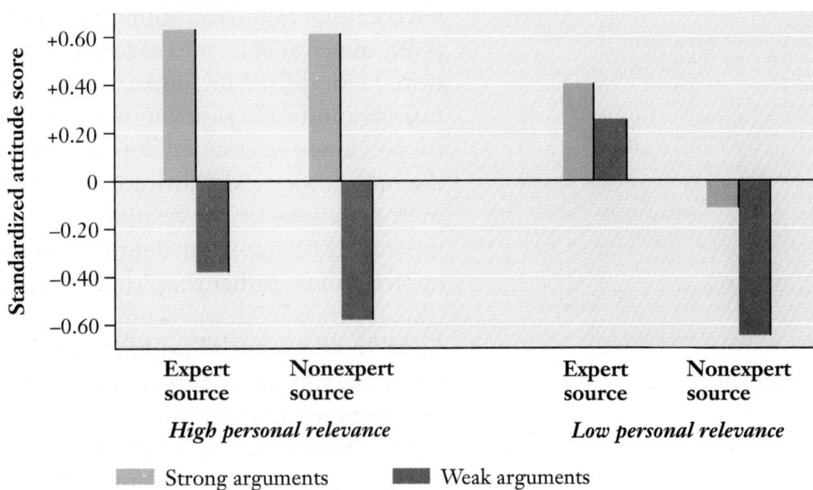

Figure 14.9 ***Effect of persuasive arguments on attitude under various experimental conditions***

In this graph, movement above the horizontal axis indicates agreement with the persuasive message, and movement below the axis indicates disagreement. When the issue was of high personal relevance (left half of graph), the strength or weakness of the arguments had more impact than did the source of the arguments, but when the issue was of low personal relevance (right half of graph), the reverse was true. (Adapted from Petty & others, 1981.)

that directly affect them than about those that don't was a basic premise of philosophers who laid the foundations for democratic forms of government.

Cognitive Dissonance as a Force for Attitude Consistency and Change

An attitude may enter the mind from the social environment by either a peripheral or central route, but once there it joins the other attitudes, beliefs, and bits of knowledge that make up the person's whole mind. What happens if two of those elements are contradictory? Many years ago, Leon Festinger (1957) proposed that the awareness of contradiction or lack of harmony among two or more elements of one's mind creates a feeling of disturbance or discomfort, which he called ***cognitive dissonance***. Festinger proposed, in his *cognitive dissonance theory*, that people are motivated to avoid or alleviate this uncomfortable state. In other words, they are motivated to behave and think in ways that reduce disharmony (dissonance), or maintain harmony (consonance), among their various attitudes, beliefs, and bits of knowledge. Here we will consider some implications of this theory, as applied to the maintenance and change of attitudes.

Avoiding Dissonant Information

28. ***How does the cognitive dissonance theory explain people's attraction to some information and avoidance of other information?***

I once heard a person cut off a political discussion with the words, "I'm sorry, but I refuse to listen to something that I disagree with." People don't usually come right out and say that, but have you noticed how often they seem to behave that way? Given a choice of books or articles to read, lectures to attend, or documentaries to watch, people most often seem to choose those that they have reason to believe are consistent with their preexisting views. That observation is consistent with the theory of cognitive dissonance. One way to avoid dissonance is to avoid situations in which we might discover facts or ideas that run counter to our current views. People certainly don't always behave that way, but a considerable body of research indicates that they very often do (Eagly & Chaiken, 1993; Frey, 1986).

Paul Sweeney and Kathy Gruber (1984) conducted a study during the 1973 Senate Watergate Hearings that provides a real-world illustration of this phenomenon. (The hearings uncovered illegal activities associated with then President Richard Nixon's reelection campaign against George McGovern.) By interviewing the same voters before, during, and after the hearings, Sweeney and Gruber discovered that (a) Nixon supporters avoided news about the hearings (but not other political news) and were as strongly supportive of Nixon after the hearings as they were before; (b) McGovern supporters eagerly sought out information about the hearings and were as strongly opposed to Nixon afterward as they were before; and (c) previously undecided voters paid moderate attention to the hearings and were the only group whose attitude toward Nixon was significantly influenced (in a negative direction) by the hearings. So, consistent with the dissonance theory, all but the undecideds approached the hearings in a way that seemed designed to protect or strengthen, rather than challenge, their previous view.

Firming up an Attitude to Be Consistent with an Action

■ ***29. How does the cognitive dissonance theory explain why people are more confident about a choice just after they have made it than just before?***

We make most of our choices in life with less than absolute certainty. We vote for a candidate without certainty that he or she is best, buy one car even though some of the evidence favors another, or choose to major in psychology even though some other fields have their attractions. After we have irrevocably made one choice or the other—after we have cast our ballot, made our down payment, or registered for courses and drop-add is past—any lingering doubts would be discordant with our knowledge of what we have done, so, according to the cognitive dissonance theory, we should be motivated to set them aside.

A number of studies have shown that people do tend to set their doubts aside after making a decision. Even in the absence of new information, people suddenly become more confident of their choice after acting on it than they were just before. For example, in one study, bettors at a horse race were more confident that their horse would win if they were asked immediately after they had placed their bet than if they were asked immediately before (Knox & Inkster, 1968). In another study, voters who were leaving the polling place spoke more positively about their favored candidate than did those who were entering (Frenkel & Doob, 1976).

Changing an Attitude to Justify an Action

■ ***30. How does the cognitive dissonance theory explain why people who behave in a manner contrary to their attitude are likely to change their attitude?***

Sometimes people do behave in ways that run counter to their attitude and then are faced with the dissonant cognitions, "I believe *this*, but I did *that*." They can't undo their deed, but they can relieve dissonance by modifying—maybe even reversing—their attitude. More than 200 years ago, the great inventor, statesman, and master of practical psychology Benjamin Franklin recognized this phenomenon and used it to his advantage. Franklin (1818) (1949) describes in his autobiography how he changed the attitude of a political opponent who was trying to block his appointment to a high office:

> I did not like the opposition of this new member, who was a gentleman of fortune and education with talents that were likely to give him in time great influence. . . . I did not, however, aim at gaining his favour by paying any servile respect to him, but after some time took this other method. Having heard that he had in his library a certain very scarce and curious book, I wrote a note to him expressing my desire of perusing that book and requesting he do me the favour of lending it to me for a few days. He sent it immediately; and I returned it in about a week with another note expressing strongly my sense of the favour. When we next met in the House, he spoke to me (which he had never done before), and with great civility. And he ever afterwards manifested a readiness to serve me on all occasions, so that we became great friends, and our friendship continued to his death. This is another instance of the truth of an old maxim I had learned, which says, "He that has once done you a kindness will be more ready to do you another than he whom you yourself have obliged."

According to the cognitive dissonance theory, what might have happened in the former opponent's mind to change his attitude toward Franklin? He received Franklin's request to borrow the book, and for reasons of which he may not have been fully aware, such as the simple habit of courtesy, he did not turn it down. But once he sent the book to Franklin he was thrown into a state of cognitive dissonance. One belief, *I do not like Ben Franklin*, was discordant with another, *I have just lent Franklin a very valuable book*. The second of these beliefs could not be denied, since that was objective fact, so dissonance could best be relieved by changing the first: *Ben Franklin isn't really a bad sort. At least I know he's honest. If he weren't honest, I certainly wouldn't have lent him the book.* Such thinking reduced or erased the dissonance and set the stage for new, friendlier behaviors toward Franklin in the future.

Notice that, according to this analysis, the man changed his attitude toward Franklin because he saw the decision to lend the book as his own choice and he saw no good reason why he should have made that choice if he didn't like Franklin. If Franklin had paid him or threatened him to get him to lend the book, the lending of it would not have created dissonance with the belief that he disliked Franklin. He would say, "I lent the book to Franklin only because he paid me," or ". . . only because he threatened me." Since either of these would have been sufficient justification, no dissonance would have resulted, and no attitude change would have been necessary.

The effect illustrated by this analysis of Franklin's story is an instance of what is now called the ***insufficient-justification effect***, defined as a change in attitude that occurs because, without the change, the person cannot justify his or her already completed action. During the last few decades many dozens of experiments have demonstrated this effect and have helped identify the conditions under which it occurs.

Conditions That Optimize the Insufficient-Justification Effect

■ **31.** ***How have researchers identified four conditions that increase the likelihood that the insufficient-justification effect will occur?***

One requirement for the insufficient-justification effect to occur is that there must be no obvious, high incentive for performing the counter-attitudinal action. In an early demonstration of this, Leon Festinger and James Carlsmith (1959) gave college students a boring task (loading spools into trays and turning pegs in a pegboard) and then offered to "hire" them to tell another student that the task was exciting and enjoyable. Some students were told they would receive $1 for telling this lie, and others were told they would receive $20. The result was that those in the $1 condition changed their attitude toward the task and saw it as enjoyable, while those in the $20 condition continued to see it as boring. Presumably, subjects in the $1 condition could not justify their lie on the basis of the little they were promised, so they convinced themselves that they were not lying. Those in the $20 condition, in contrast, could justify their lie: "I said the task was enjoyable when it was actually boring, but who wouldn't tell such a small lie for $20?"

Another essential condition for the insufficient-justification effect is that subjects must perceive their action as stemming from their own free choice. Otherwise, they could justify the action simply by saying, "I was forced to do it." In one experiment demonstrating the role of free choice, students were asked to write essays strongly supporting a bill in the state legislature that most students opposed (Linder & others, 1967) Students in the *free-choice condition* were clearly told that they didn't have to write the essays, but were encouraged to do so (and none refused). Students in the *no-choice condition* were simply told to write the essays, as if by volunteering to be in an experiment they were now obliged to do what the experimenter directed them to do. After writing the essays, all students were asked to describe their own attitude toward the bill; only those in the free-choice condition showed a significant shift in the direction of favoring it compared to a control group who had not written counter-attitudinal essays.

Research also indicates that the insufficient-justification effect is strongest when the action to be justified not only runs counter to the original attitude, but also would be expected to cause harm if the original attitude were correct. In this case, the cognition underlying the attitude change might be, "I would not deliberately do something harmful. Therefore, I must believe that what I did is helpful." Consistent with this interpretation, subjects in most studies that have demonstrated the insufficient-justification effect were led to believe that their actions could have real consequences. In the experiment just described, for example, the subjects were told that their essays would be read by people who had power to influence the policy (Linder & others, 1967). In a subsequent experiment, some subjects were led to believe that their essays could influence policy while others were led to believe that theirs couldn't, and only the former group changed their attitude (Scher & Cooper, 1989).

Still other research suggests that at least sometimes the insufficient-justification effect has more to do with impression management than with a drive for real cognitive consistency. People changed their attitude after performing a counter-attitudinal action only if they believed that others knew how they had acted (Baumeister & Tice, 1984). Thus, in some conditions at least, the attitude change may serve to convince others, not the self, that no discrepancy exists between one's attitude and behavior.

Taking all of this research into account, modern-day Ben Franklins who want to get someone to adopt a new attitude by inducing the person to behave in a way that is consistent with that attitude are most likely to succeed if they (a) minimize any obvious incentive for the behavior, (b) maximize the appearance of free choice, (c) choose a behavior that would seem harmful if viewed from the perspective of the old attitude, and (d) maximize the public nature of the behavior so that the person would have to justify it to others.

Why Don't People Always Behave According to Their Attitudes?

Social scientists first became interested in attitudes mainly because they conceived of them as mental guides of behavior (Allport, 1935). The premise, consistent with common sense, was that by knowing a person's attitudes you could predict how that person would behave. Thus, someone with a positive attitude toward the environmental movement should be more likely to recycle newspapers than someone with a negative attitude toward it, and someone with a strong attitude favoring honesty should behave more honestly than someone with a weaker pro-honesty attitude. It may seem surprising that this common-sense assumption has often been challenged, both on theoretical grounds and on the basis of research.

■ **32.** ***How did some behaviorists account for attitude-behavior inconsistency?***

The strongest theoretical challenge came from strict behaviorists such as B. F. Skinner (1957), who argued that attitudes are simply *verbal habits* that play a role in what people say but are irrelevant to what they do. According to this view, people learn to say things like, "Honesty is the best policy," because they are rewarded for such verbalizations by their social group. But when confronted by an inducement to lie, their behavior may be controlled by a new set of rewards and punishments that can lead to an action completely contrary to the attitude they profess.

All the insufficient-justification studies just described demonstrate that people's behavior often contradicts their attitudes. Those studies in fact reverse the common-sense view of the attitude-behavior relation. Instead of attitudes determining behavior, behavior determined attitudes—people modified their attitudes to justify their actions.

One of the earliest studies to question the predictability of behavior from atti-

■ **33.** ***How did two early studies demonstrate attitude-behavior inconsistency?***

tudes was conducted by Richard LaPiere (1934). During the early 1930s, when attitude surveys showed rampant prejudice against Asians in the United States, LaPiere traveled back and forth across the country with a young Chinese couple. Together they checked into 67 different hotels, auto camps, and tourist homes, and entered 184 different restaurants and cafes. Only one of these establishments refused them service, and in nearly all they were treated with at least an acceptable degree of courtesy. Yet, when LaPiere subsequently surveyed the proprietors of these same establishments by questionnaire as to whether they would house or serve Chinese customers, a resounding 92 percent of those who responded said no.

Another early demonstration of non-correlation between attitude and behavior occurred in a study of cheating in a college course (Corey, 1937). Early in the semester, students filled out a questionnaire measuring their attitude toward cheating, and later they were given what appeared to be an easy opportunity to cheat while grading their own true-false tests. Actually, the tests had been graded previously by the instructor, so cheating could be detected by comparing the score determined by the instructor with that reported by the student. A good deal of cheating occurred, and no correlation at all was found between the attitude measure and actual cheating. Those who had expressed a very strong anticheating attitude were just as likely to cheat as were those who had expressed a weaker anticheating attitude. A strong correlation was found, however, between cheating and the student's true score on the test. The lower the true score, the more likely the student was to try to raise it by cheating.

By the end of the 1960s, based on studies like those just described, some psychologists had concluded that attitudes play almost no role in guiding behavior (Wicker, 1969, 1971). But others responded with evidence that under some conditions a strong relationship between attitudes and behavior is found. The question soon turned from, "*Do* attitudes predict behavior?" to "*When*, or under what conditions, do they predict behavior?" Let's examine some of the answers to the latter question.

Attitudes Must Be Retrieved from Memory to Affect Behavior

From an information-processing perspective, attitudes, like any other beliefs, are stored in memory and can influence a person's decision to behave in a certain way only if recalled at the time the decision is made. Behavior occurs in a continuous flow, and we rarely stop to think about all of our relevant attitudes before we act. Perhaps, in LaPiere's study, the hotel and restaurant proprietors who had a negative attitude toward Asians were simply not reminded of that attitude upon seeing a friendly, clean-cut Asian couple, and therefore the attitude did not manifest itself. Or perhaps, in Corey's study, the stress of seeing how badly they had done on the test so overwhelmed the students that they simply failed to recall their attitudes about cheating.

■ **34.** ***How can the presence of a mirror increase attitude-behavior consistency?***

This line of reasoning suggests that cues reminding a person of his or her attitudes at the time of action would increase the attitude-behavior correlation. Consistent with this view, experiments have shown that if people are presented with a task that requires them to think about their attitude on an issue shortly before they must act on it, the correlation between the attitude and behavior increases markedly (Aronson, 1992; Snyder & Swann, 1976). Other experiments have shown that the presence of a mirror, apparently by reminding people of all aspects of their self-concept, including their attitudes, can promote attitude-behavior consistency (Wicklund & Frey, 1980). In one experiment, for example, trick-or-treaters who were told to help themselves to a certain amount of candy, under conditions in which they believed nobody could see them, more often took extra candy if no mirror was present than if a mirror was placed behind the candy bowl (Beaman & others, 1979).

Russell Fazio (1986; 1990) has argued that the strongest attitude-behavior correlation occurs when the attitude was formed through direct, repeated experience with its object, because then the object automatically reminds the person of the attitude. If you have a negative attitude toward bacon because on several occasions you ate it and got sick, then the sight and smell of bacon will automatically elicit your negative attitude and you won't eat it. However, if you have a negative attitude toward bacon only because you read that it is high in nitrates and nitrates are bad for you, your attitude will not be elicited automatically by bacon's sight and smell. In that case you will need some other cue, extrinsic to the bacon, to remind you of the attitude, or you will need to rely on a habit of checking your set of food-related attitudes whenever you eat. Only after repeated rehearsal would your intellectually derived attitude about bacon come automatically to mind when you saw or smelled it.

People May Perceive Barriers to Behaving According to Their Attitudes

■ **35.** ***According to the theory of planned behavior, what kinds of cognitions might inhibit people from behaving according to their attitudes?***

The decision to behave in a certain way involves other cognitions as well as attitudes. In what he calls a ***theory of planned behavior,*** Icek Ajzen (1985, 1991) has proposed that the conscious intention to behave in a particular way depends on one's (a) *attitude*, defined as one's own desire to act in that way or not; (b) *subjective norm*, defined as one's beliefs about what others who are important at the moment would think about the action; and (c) *perceived control*, defined as one's sense of his or her ability to carry out the action (see Figure 14.10). Applying Ajzen's model to LaPiere's study, the proprietors may have wanted to turn the Chinese couple away (consistent with their attitude), but decided against it either because they perceived that others who were present, including LaPiere and the Chinese couple themselves, would have disapproved (subjective norm), or because they perceived that they lacked any gracious means to carry out the action (low perceived control).

Research supporting Ajzen's model has shown that, depending on various factors, any of the three inputs to behavioral intention may predominate. For example, in a study of dieting and weight loss based on Ajzen's model, perceived control (confidence in the ability to stay on a diet) was a better predictor of weight loss than was either attitude (desire to lose weight) or subjective norm (belief about whether others thought one should lose weight) (Schifter & Ajzen, 1985). In another study, students who scored high on a personality measure of self-monitoring were most influenced by the subjective norm in determining how much time they devoted to their studies, whereas students who were low in self-monitoring were most influenced by their own attitude (Miller & Grush, 1986).

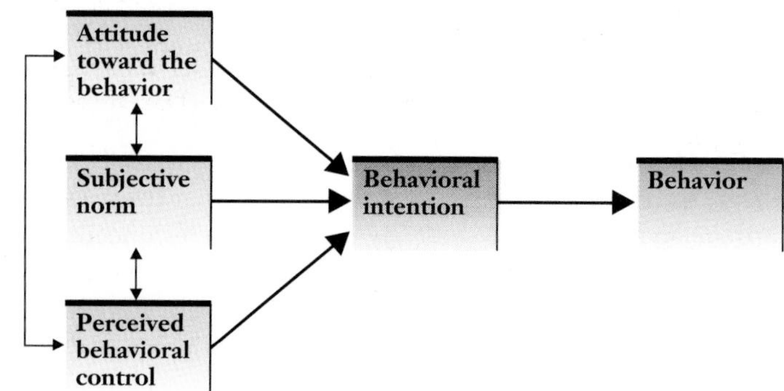

Figure 14.10 ***A theory of planned behavior***

According to Ajzen's theory, the decision to behave in a certain way is a product of three categories of cognitions. (Adapted from Ajzen, 1987.)

Attitude Assessments May Be Biased

Sometimes an apparent lack of congruence between attitudes and behavior is due to bias in the procedure used to assess the attitude. The way people respond to attitude questions can be strongly influenced by the specific wording of the question and the context in which it is asked. In a survey of attitudes in the United States about public assistance, two different versions of the same question were asked of different people (Rasinski, 1989). One version asked, "Are we spending too much, too little, or the right amount on assistance to the poor?" The other version was identical to the first, except the word *welfare* replaced *assistance to the poor*. The result was that 64 percent of respondents to the first version said "too little," but only 23 percent of respondents to the second version said "too little." "Assistance to the poor" and "welfare" may literally mean the same thing, but they apparently evoke quite different images in the minds of many U.S. citizens.

■ **36.** ***How can the lack of congruence between pre-election polls and the actual election results in a gubernatorial election in Virginia be explained?***

Responding to an attitude questionnaire or interview is itself a social act, subject to social influences. People want to look good to other people, including interviewers. In the 1989 gubernatorial election in Virginia, in which the Democrat Douglas Wilder became the first black governor of a U.S. state, the polls predicted that Wilder would win by a wide margin. But the actual election was extremely close—50.3 percent for Wilder to 49.7 percent for his white Republican opponent, Marshall Coleman. Why the discrepancy between the polls and the actual votes? According to Steven Finkel and his colleagues (1991), the discrepancy came largely from the reluctance of many white voters to admit to black interviewers that they planned to vote for Coleman. These researchers compiled the results obtained in a large pre-election telephone poll, in which the respondents apparently could tell if the interviewers were black or white by their voices or their names, which were announced when the interviewers introduced themselves.

As you can see in Figure 14.11, white Democrats and Independents, but not white Republicans, were much more likely to say they were going to vote for Wilder if the interviewer was black than if he or she was white. Why was the effect limited to Democrats and Independents? Perhaps the respondents intuitively felt that their party affiliation would influence the attribution the interviewer would make from their vote preference. A Republican vote for the Republican candidate requires no special justification, but a Democratic or Independent vote for a white Republican over a black Democrat might be interpreted as an act of racism. To avoid appearing racist to a black interviewer, many white Democrats and Independents may have said they were going to vote for Wilder even if they weren't. An alternative possibility, favored by Finkel and his colleagues, is that more Democrats

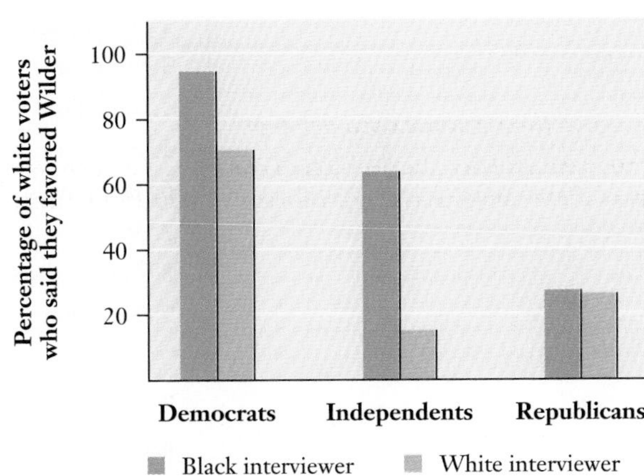

Figure 14.11 ***A race-of-interviewer effect in a pre-election poll***

In a pre-election telephone survey in Virginia, white Democrats and Independents more often expressed preference for the black Democratic gubernatorial candidate, Douglas Wilder, if the interviewer was black than if the interviewer was white. (Data from Finkel & others, 1991.)

and Independents than Republicans were uncertain of whom they would vote for, and being uncertain they were more likely to be influenced by the race of the interviewer.

Attitudes May Conflict with One Another

■ **37.** ***How can the presence of conflicting attitudes create the appearance of attitude-behavior inconsistency?***

A limitation of many attitude-behavior studies is that they measure only one attitude, when in fact behavior can be affected by a whole set of attitudes, some of which may conflict with one another concerning the behavior in question. In LaPiere's study, the couple who approached the proprietors were not only Chinese, but also clean-cut, friendly, articulate, married, and accompanied by a white sociology professor; the proprietors' negative attitude toward Asians may have been outweighed by a positive attitude toward these other factors. Similarly, in Corey's study, students' negative attitude toward cheating may have been outweighed by a stronger negative attitude toward failing a test.

A number of studies have shown that if attitude questions are phrased in specific terms, identifying the conditions that would be present in the behavioral test, the attitude-behavior correlation increases greatly (Ajzen & Fishbein, 1980; Cooper & Croyle, 1984). Perhaps if LaPiere's questionnaire had asked, "Would you accept a clean-cut, friendly, articulate, married Chinese couple accompanied by a white sociology professor as guests in your establishment?" he would have found a stronger correlation between the questionnaire response and the behavior measured.

■ **38.** ***How can a procedure involving the ranking of attitudes or values increase the ability to predict behavior?***

Another approach to the problem of conflicting attitudes is to try to develop a fuller picture of a person's whole set of attitudes and to see how that picture relates to specific behaviors. In experiments using this approach, Milton Rokeach focused on central attitudes, or *values*—such as the importance one ascribes to freedom, equality, or personal happiness—which he views as basic axioms that underlie one's decisions about appropriate ways to behave. Instead of asking people about their attitude on one specific issue, Rokeach asked them to rank a set of values according to the importance they attach to each (see Table 14.2). This procedure forces respondents to pit commonly accepted values against one another, which should increase the likelihood of making accurate predictions of behavior in situations in

Table 14.2 ***Values studied by Rokeach***

Values in rank order	
1. A world at peace	10. True friendship
2. Family security	11. A sense of accomplishment
3. Freedom	12. Inner harmony
4. Equality	13. A comfortable life
5. Self-respect	14. Mature love
6. Happiness	15. A world of beauty
7. Wisdom	16. Pleasure
8. National security	17. Social recognition
9. Salvation	18. An exciting life

Note: The values are listed, top to bottom, in the order in which they were ranked by a cross-sectional sample of U.S. citizens.

Source: Adapted from "Change and stability in American value systems, 1968–1971" by M. Rokeach, in M. Rokeach (Ed.), *Understanding human values*, 1979, New York: Free Press.

which values conflict. In a series of studies, Rokeach found high correlations between the relative ranking of particular values on his questionnaire and quite specific, real-world behaviors. For example, he found that white college students who ranked equality especially high were more likely than other students to (a) make eye contact when speaking with a black person, (b) join a political group supporting equal rights, and (c) participate in a rally for equal rights (Rokeach, 1980).

■ **39.** ***How can political positions be analyzed in terms of two sometimes conflicting values—freedom and equality?***

Rokeach's research on values has helped inspire some attempts to understand the complexities of political thought. For example, based partly on a model developed by Rokeach, Phillip Tetlock (1984) analyzed the political reasoning of members of the British House of Commons in terms of the relative weight that each individual placed on the sometimes conflicting values of freedom and equality. According to Tetlock's analysis, extreme liberals and extreme conservatives develop simple, straightforward policy arguments because they rely heavily on just one of those two values. For conservatives that value is freedom, and for liberals it is equality. Moderates, by contrast, develop more complex, multifaceted arguments because they weigh freedom and equality more equally. Thus, conservatives oppose a more steeply graded income tax because it infringes on people's freedom to do what they want with their money, liberals favor it because it promotes a more equitable distribution of wealth, and moderates see merit on both sides and look for a compromise solution.

As you have seen, the study of attitudes is a huge domain. It spans the distance from your reaction to bacon on your plate to your beliefs about how it should be distributed across society.

Concluding Thoughts

In this chapter you have read of many different findings about people's perceptions of others, themselves, and their social world, and you have seen how such perceptions can affect behavior. To help you think elaboratively about the various effects and findings and integrate them mentally as you review, you might find the following three thoughts useful.

1. Automatic versus controlled processes in social cognition In the terminology of modern cognitive psychology, automatic processes are those mental activities that occur without conscious attention, and controlled processes are those that require conscious attention. One way to review this chapter would be to go through it, section by section, thinking about the relative roles of automatic and controlled processes in each of the phenomena described. That distinction was discussed explicitly in relation to Gilbert's explanation of the fundamental attribution error, Devine's theory of prejudice, and the research on peripheral versus central routes of attitude change. But it can be found implicitly in many other parts of the chapter as well.

The biases in people's thinking that have been the focus of much social-psychological research can be attributed largely to automatic processes; and people's deliberate attempts to counteract such biases can be attributed to controlled processes. Many other phenomena described in the chapter might stem from either automatic or controlled processes or a combination of the two, depending on the situation. Some examples are the use of social comparison to construct self-concepts and attitudes, the use of impression-management strategies to preserve or build a reputation, and the use of various behavioral and mental strategies to reduce cognitive dissonance.

2. The value of a functionalist perspective A theme emphasized throughout this book is that behavior usually serves some purpose for the behaving individual. This is as true of automatic and irrational behaviors as it is of controlled and rational behaviors. Even self-harmful behaviors may stem from processes that originated (through evolution or learning or both) to serve some beneficial function. As social animals, one of our most basic needs is to be accepted and approved of by those other members of our species who constitute our close community. Our ability to survive and reproduce depends on that. We also seem to need to think well of ourselves, perhaps because such thoughts encourage our belief that we can surmount various obstacles to our survival. Thus, another way to review this chapter is to go through it, section by section, thinking about ways in which each phenomenon might be related to one or both of these twin needs—getting along with others and thinking well of ourselves. In cases where these needs do not apply, you might think about other functions that the phenomenon might serve or about how it could be a side effect of some aspect of our mental construction that is useful in a different context.

3. Theory in social psychology Social psychologists commonly divide their field into theories. Some examples discussed in this chapter are attribution theory, social comparison theory, impression-management theory, and cognitive dissonance theory. The term *theory* has different meanings in different contexts, and in this context it obviously does not refer to a specific hypothesis that is to be proven correct or incorrect. All of the just-listed theories are clearly correct in the sense that they refer to phenomena that really occur. People certainly make attributions about others' behavior, compare themselves to others as a way of evaluating themselves and their attitudes, attempt to control the impressions that others develop of them, and are sometimes upset when they become aware of contradictions in their own cognitions. The issue for social psychologists working on any of these theories is not whether or not the characteristic named by the theory exists, but rather is the extent to which the characteristic adequately explains specific behaviors that could, in principle, stem from other causes. Thus, impression management obviously occurs, but it is not obvious that the specific category of behavior called self-handicapping is best explained in terms of impression management. Similarly, cognitive dissonance obviously occurs and affects behavior, but it is not obvious that this is the best explanation of the observation that people often change their attitude after performing a counter-attitudinal action. As you review each research study described in this chapter, think about how the findings might be explained by one or another broad social-psychological theory.

Further Reading

Edward E. Jones (1990). *Interpersonal perception*. New York: Freeman.

For students interested in how people attempt to understand each other in everyday life, I know of no better place to begin than this book by a leading researcher in the study of person perception. In a personal and thoughtful manner, Jones discusses such topics as attributions, the formation of stereotypes, and interpersonal expectancy effects.

Alan O. Ross (1992). *The sense of self: Research and theory*. New York: Springer.

This is a concise, highly readable summary of social psychology's major ideas and research findings concerning the sense of self. It includes chapters on the origins and structure of the self-concept, self-awareness and self-consciousness, self-assessment and self-esteem, self-handicapping, self-regulation, and self-monitoring.

Erving Goffman (1959). *The presentation of self in everyday life*. Garden City, NY: Doubleday.

This classic work, based on Goffman's insightful observations of people at work and leisure, helped inspire research and theory in the area of impression management. It is fun to read.

Alice H. Eagly & Shelly Chaiken (1993). *The psychology of attitudes*. Orlando, FL: Harcourt Brace Jovanovich.

The major models of attitude structure, function, and origin—and the evidence for and against each model—are discussed fully and clearly in this scholarly text.

Looking Ahead

Because we are concerned about what others think of us, other people greatly influence our behavior. The next chapter is about that influence. It deals with such topics as compliance, conformity, audience effects, and group decision making.

A Perspective: The Person in a Field of Social Forces

Influence of Others' Requests

Some Principles of Compliance

Obedience: Milgram's Experiments and Beyond

Influence of Others' Presence or Examples

Effects of Being Observed

Conformity

Group Discussion and Decision Making

Social Interdependence: Forces for Conflict and Harmony

Social Dilemmas

Group Versus Group and Harmony Through Shared Goals

SOCIAL INFLUENCES ON BEHAVIOR

CHAPTER 15

As thinking, social beings, we are sensitive to the pressures of our social world—the demands, requests, expectations, judgments, and examples, real and imagined, that seem to flow constantly toward us from other people. This chapter is about such pressures, or ***social forces***. After a brief general discussion of the influence of social forces, we will examine, respectively, three classes of social forces: (a) those resulting from direct requests (the pressure to comply or obey); (b) those resulting from the mere presence of others or the examples they provide (including performance anxiety and the pressure to conform); and (c) those resulting from other people's capacity to help or hinder us in achieving our goals (the forces of cooperation and competition). Throughout the chapter we will be concerned with characterizing social forces, understanding the psychological mechanisms through which they work, and understanding the conditions that strengthen or weaken them.

A Perspective: The Person in a Field of Social Forces

The perspective of this chapter is rooted in the thinking of Kurt Lewin (1890–1947) who, as noted in Chapter 1, emigrated to the United States from Hitler's Germany in 1933. Throughout his career, Lewin was concerned with real-world social problems. He understood that people's thought and behavior are influenced, toward good and for ill, by their social environment, and his goal was to understand the psychological principles that underlie those influences. Lewin saw no conflict between practical psychology and theoretical psychology. He was fond of saying to his students, "Nothing is more practical than a good theory." He was also a strong advocate of laboratory, experimental methodology. Lewin would identify problems and formulate hypotheses from observations in the real world and then test the hypotheses under controlled conditions in the laboratory. Among Lewin's many students who went on to help shape modern social psychology was Leon Festinger, whose theory of cognitive dissonance is discussed in Chapter 14.

Lewin's Field Theory

■ **1.** ***What was the basic premise of Lewin's field theory?***

Having been trained in Gestalt psychology in Germany, Lewin rejected the stimulus-response perspective that characterized much of North American psychology at his time. His own perspective, which he called ***field theory***, was grounded in the premise that each person exists in a field of forces that act simultaneously to push or pull the person in various directions (Lewin, 1951). Some of these forces come from within—they are the person's own desires, goals, and abilities. Interacting with these are forces that stem from the social environment but must be interpreted by the person in order to exert their influence. Consider the forces that

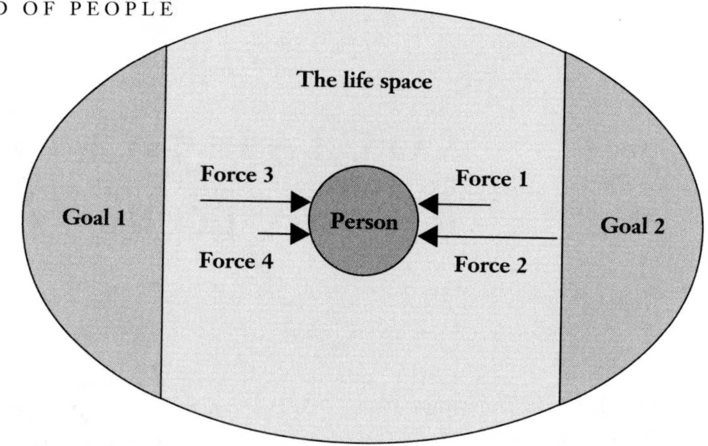

Figure 15.1 ***Lewinian diagram of the life space***

Lewin viewed the person as subject to a field of forces that push him or her toward or away from various goals. In this simplified diagram, Goal 1 might be going to a party this evening, and Goal 2 might be spending the evening studying; Force 1 might be the person's own wish; and Forces 2, 3, and 4 might be the person's perceptions of the desires of friends, family, and professors, respectively.

Kurt Lewin

A pioneer in social psychology, Lewin was known for his ability to identify problems in the social environment and study them within a theoretical framework.

2. *What are the propositions of social impact theory? Why must they be understood in psychological rather than physical terms?*

might come into play as you decide whether to spend this evening at a party (Goal 1) or studying (Goal 2). Your decision might depend partly on your own beliefs about what would be most enjoyable or prudent (Force 1) and partly on your perceptions of what your friends (Force 2), family (Force 3), and professors (Force 4) want or expect you to do (see Figure 15.1). Of course, Lewin did not believe it was possible to produce a picture of all of the forces acting on any given person at any given time. Rather, he wanted to understand the various *kinds* of forces and the conditions that affect their strength so as to predict in a general way the effects that particular social changes would have on behavior. To do this, he and his students would conduct experiments in which one social force would be varied at a time. You will encounter many examples of such experiments in this chapter.

Social Impact Theory

More recently, the concept of social force has been elaborated upon by Bibb Latané, in what he calls ***social impact theory***. Latané (1981) defines *social impact* as "any of the great variety of changes in physiological state and subjective feelings, motives and emotions, cognitions and beliefs, values and behavior, that occur in an individual . . . as a result of the real, implied, or imagined presence or action of other individuals." In short, social impact is any detectable effect that occurs in a person as a result of a social force. Social impact theory is concerned with variables that strengthen or weaken the impact of any social force. In this theory, a *source* is a person who exerts a social force, and a *target* is a person who experiences its impact. Latané formulated three general propositions, two suggesting how the impact of a social force accrues from its various sources, and one suggesting how the impact of the force disperses among its various targets:

- ***Accretion of impact:*** Latanés first proposition is that the impact of any social force increases as the *strength*, *immediacy*, and *number* of sources increase. To illustrate, Latané (1981) drew an analogy between social impact and the effect of light bulbs illuminating a solid surface. Impact (illumination) increases as the sources (light bulbs) increase in strength (wattage), immediacy (closeness to the surface), and number (see Figure 15.2a). In social relations, of course, these variables must be understood in psychological terms. The *strength* of a source depends on the extent to which the target respects, admires, needs, or fears that source. You are not affected by people whom you do not care about. The *immediacy* of a source is in some cases measurable in physical distance from the target, in inches or miles, but in other cases it is not. If you live separately from your parents, they may become more immediate as sources of impact if you have just been reminded of them, even though they are still the same number of miles away. The *number* of sources is in some cases a simple count of the people who are physically present and exerting a specific influence on the target, but in other cases it is the number of people whom the target imagines or

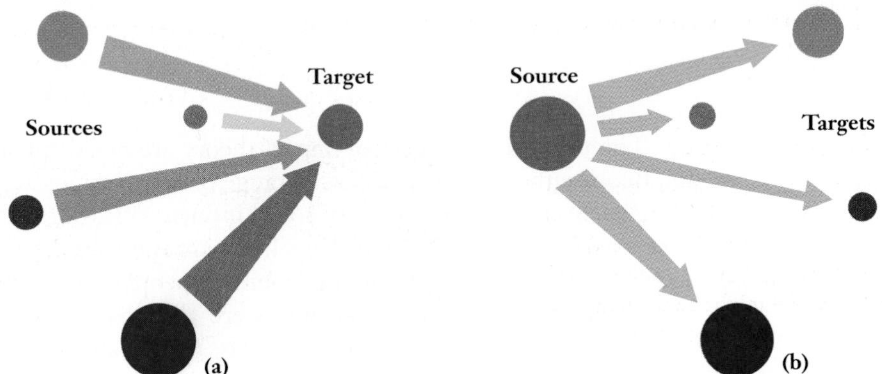

Figure 15.2 ***Multiplication and division of social impact***

(a) The total impact of a social force on an individual target increases as the strength, immediacy, and number of sources increases. (b) The total impact of a social force is divided among the targets, so the impact on any one target decreases as the number of targets increases. (From Latané, 1981.)

believes to be exerting an influence. Your belief that your parents want you to behave in a certain way makes them sources of social force for you to do so, regardless of their actual wishes.

Extending further the analogy to light bulbs, Latané noted in a second proposition that the increased impact of each additional source diminishes as the number of sources becomes larger. Lighting a single additional bulb has a big effect if only one bulb is already lit, but a small effect if ten bulbs are already lit. Similarly, two people who want you to do something will have considerably more impact on you than one person, but eleven people will have barely more impact than ten.

- ***Dissipation of impact:*** Latané's third proposition is that the impact of a social force on a given target is inversely related to the number of targets. In other words, the impact is divided among targets; so, as the number of targets increases, the impact on any one target decreases (see Figure 15.2b). Latané's light-bulb analogy doesn't work for this proposition. Imagine instead a power source that can divide a fixed amount of wattage among any number of separate spotlights, each directed at a different target. As the number of spotlights increases, the amount of light that hits each target decreases. Similarly, children scolded in a group will feel less impact of the scolding, per child, than will one child who receives the same scolding alone.

3. ***How are social impact theory's principles of accretion and dissipation illustrated by experiments on stage fright?***

To illustrate the principles of social impact theory, Latané used the results of various experiments on stage fright. Consistent with the accretion principles, stage fright increases as the status (strength) and number of people in the audience increases (see Figure 15.3a), and the slope of the curve describing the increase in stage fright diminishes as the size of the audience gets larger (again see Figure 15.3a). Consistent with the dissipation principle, stage fright decreases as the number of performers who share the stage increases (see Figure 15.3b).

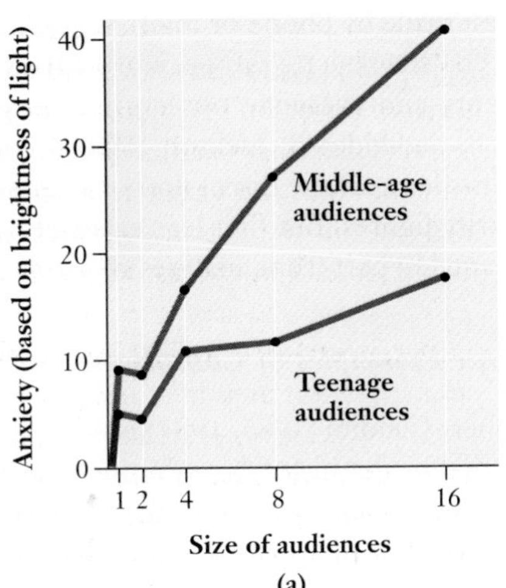

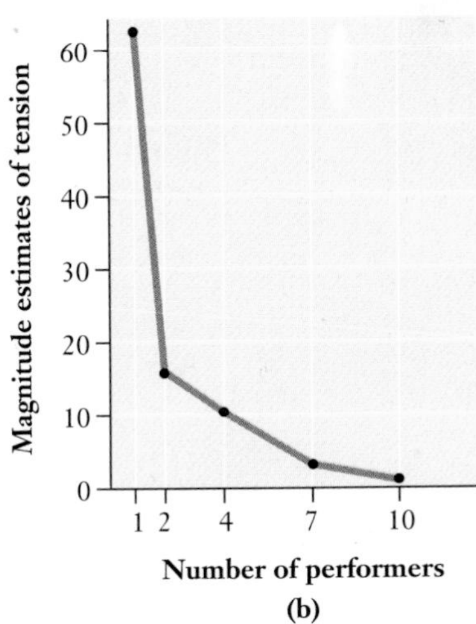

Figure 15.3 ***Effects of audience status, audience size, and number of performers on stage fright***

These results come from two different studies. The results in (a) are from an experiment in which subjects imagined themselves reciting a poem in front of various audiences and then adjusted the brightness of a light to match their anticipated anxiety. Those in (b) are from a study in which college students who performed either alone or in groups of various sizes in an actual talent show estimated—using Stevens's method of magnitude estimation, described in Chapter 8—the degree of anxiety they had felt while on stage. [Graph (a) is adapted from Latané, 1981; graph (b) is adapted from Jackson & Latané, 1981.]

The propositions of social impact theory are not surprising, but they are useful. Because they summarize a wide range of observations about social forces, they bring some unity to the study of social influence. Regardless of the kind of influence—be it stage fright stemming from an audience, shame stemming from a scolding, sales pressure stemming from salespeople, or pressure to conform stemming from the perception that others are all behaving in a particular way—the amount of influence on the person increases as the strength, immediacy, and number of individuals perceived as exerting the influence increases, and decreases as the number of perceived other targets of that influence increases.

As you progress through the rest of the chapter, you will find many examples of relationships that conform to social impact theory. But the focus will be more on questions that are not directly addressed by the theory—questions about the differing kinds of social influences that exist and the psychological mechanisms through which they operate.

Influence of Others' Requests

One of the most obvious and potent forms of social influence is the direct request. If the request is small and made politely, we tend to comply automatically (Langer & others, 1978), and this tendency increases when our attention is otherwise occupied (Cialdini, 1988). But even if the request is onerous or offensive, most people find it hard to look a requester in the eye and say no. In one experiment demonstrating this, researchers who did not look physically intimidating walked up to strangers in Grand Central Terminal in New York City and asked them to empty their pockets to prove that they had not just taken a dime from a phone booth (Moriarty, 1975b). Only 20 percent refused. It was as if people were primed to comply and needed some reason or excuse to say no. Lacking an excuse that would seem acceptable to the requester, people will very often do or give what they would rather not.

In polite society, the tendency to comply usually serves us well. Most requests are reasonable, and we know that in the long run doing things for others pays off, as others in turn do things for us. But not all of society is polite. There are people who, out of selfishness, or because their jobs demand it, or because they are working for causes in which they sincerely believe, will exploit our tendency to comply.

Social impact theory predicts that you should be more likely to comply with a request if (a) the person making the request is high rather than low in status, (b) the person making the request is right in front of you rather than far away (as in a request made by phone or mail), (c) more than one person is making the request, and (d) you stand alone rather than with others as the target of the request. Both experiments and everyday observations suggest that all of these hold true (Cialdini, 1988; Sedikides & Jackson, 1990). You will see some evidence supporting these points later, in the discussion of a classic series of experiments on obedience to authority figures. But first let's examine some other general principles of compliance, gleaned in part from analyses of sales techniques.

Some Principles of Compliance

Robert Cialdini (1985, 1987) is a social psychologist who has devoted more than lip service to the idea of combining real-world observations with laboratory studies. To learn about compliance from the real-world experts, he took training in how to sell encyclopedias, automobiles, and insurance; infiltrated advertising agencies and fundraising organizations; and talked to recruiters, public-relations specialists, and political lobbyists. He learned their techniques, extracted what seemed to be basic principles, and showed those principles in operation under the controlled conditions of experimental research. The following paragraphs describe a set of compliance principles taken primarily from Cialdini's work, but also much studied by other social psychologists. As you read each principle, think about it from both the scientific viewpoint (what evidence supports it) and the practical (in what real situations, beyond those mentioned, might this principle apply).

Congnitive Dissonance as a Compliance Principle: The Four-Walls and Low-Ball Techniques

Chapter 14 contains an extensive discussion of the theory of cognitive dissonance. The basic idea of the theory is that people are discomforted by contradictions among their beliefs, or between their beliefs and actions, and thus are motivated to change their beliefs or actions to maintain consistency. According to Cialdini's analysis, a number of standard sales tricks make use of cognitive dissonance to elicit compliance.

■ **4.** ***How can the four-walls and low-ball sales tricks be explained in terms of cognitive dissonance?***

The objective of one such trick, called the ***four-walls technique***, is to induce the potential customer to make statements that are consistent with the idea that owning the product would be a good thing. The customer's own statements set up cognitive walls, which more or less box the customer in to agreeing to the deal when it is finally proposed. This is the technique of door-to-door salespeople who begin, as if conducting a survey, with questions such as the following (from Cialdini, 1987): (a) "Do you feel that a good education is important for your children?" (b) "Do you think that children who do their homework will get a better education?" (c) "Do you believe that a good set of reference books can help children do their homework?" (d) "Well, then, it sounds like you'll want to hear about this fine set of encyclopedias I have to offer at an excellent price. May I come in?" After expressing a favorable attitude toward education and reference books in response to the first three questions, most people find it hard to say no to the fourth.

Perhaps the most underhanded sales trick involving cognitive dissonance is the ***low-ball technique***, or *throwing the low ball*, reported to be used quite often in automobile dealerships. The salesperson works out a very attractive deal (the low ball) on a particular car, and the customer verbally agrees to the deal. Then the salesperson draws up the papers, takes them into the manager's office ostensibly for his or her signature, and comes out apologizing because the manager won't allow the car to be sold at such a low price. Meanwhile—while the salesperson has been enjoying a cup of coffee in the manager's office—the customer has become more strongly committed to the car than before. Thinking that the purchase is all but made, the customer sets aside lingering doubts and mentally exaggerates the car's advantages to reduce cognitive dissonance; and this in turn prepares the customer to agree in the end to a higher price than he or she would have accepted before.

In controlled experiments, Cialdini and his colleagues (1978) showed that this technique is indeed effective in getting people to accept a less favorable deal than they would have accepted otherwise. The basis of the technique is that people who think they have just bought something exaggerate its worth, presumably to reduce dissonance about buying it; then, when they discover that they haven't bought it after all, they are willing to pay a higher price than they were before.

More Dissonance: The Foot-in-the-Door Technique

Another common sales trick that may operate through cognitive dissonance relies on getting the potential customer to grant a small initial request made by the salesperson. Let me show you how this ***foot-in-the-door-technique*** works by giving you an example in which I was outwitted by a clever gang of driveway sealers. One day while I was raking leaves in front of my house, these men pulled up in their truck and asked if they could have a drink of water. I, of course, said yes; how could I say no to a request like that? Then they got out of the truck and one said, "Oh, if you have some lemonade or soda, that would even be better; we'd really appreciate that." Well, all right, I did have some lemonade. As I brought it to them, one of the men pointed to the cracks in my driveway and commented that they had just enough sealing material and time to do my driveway that afternoon, and they could give me a special deal. Normally, I would never have agreed to a bargain like that on the spot; but having given them the lemonade, I found myself unable to say no. I ended up paying far more than I should have, and they did a very poor job. I had been taken in by what I now see clearly to be a novel twist on the foot-in-the-door sales technique.

■ **5. *How can the foot-in-the-door technique be explained in terms of cognitive dissonance?***

The basis of the foot-in-the-door technique is that people are more likely to agree to a large request if they have already agreed to a small one. The driveway sealers got me twice on that: Their request for water primed me to agree to their request for lemonade, and their request for lemonade primed me to agree to their deal about sealing my driveway. Cialdini (1987) has argued that the foot-in-the-door technique works largely through the principle of cognitive dissonance. Having agreed, apparently of my own free will, to give the men lemonade, I must have justified that action to myself by thinking, *These are a pretty good bunch of guys*, and that thought was dissonant with any temptation I might have had a few moments later, when they proposed the sealing deal, to think, *These people may be cheating me*. So I pushed the latter thought out of my mind before it fully registered.

■ **6. *How, according to an experiment, might the foot-in-the-door technique be used to increase a person's general tendency to support good causes?***

In cases like my encounter with the driveway sealers, the foot-in-the-door technique may work because compliance to the first request induces a sense of trust, commitment, or compassion toward the person making the request. In other cases it may work by inducing a sense of commitment toward a specific cause, or toward causes in general, as demonstrated in one of the first experiments on the foot-in-the-door technique (Freedman & Fraser, 1966). A researcher approached homeowners in California with one of four different small requests regarding a specific cause. For some the cause was safe driving and for others it was keeping California beautiful. Within each of these groups, some homeowners were asked to support the cause by placing a small placard in their window and others were asked to support it by signing a petition. Nearly all the homeowners complied. Then, two weeks later, a different researcher approached the same individuals, as well as a new group of homeowners, with a much larger request—to place a large, ugly sign saying "Drive carefully" on their front lawn.

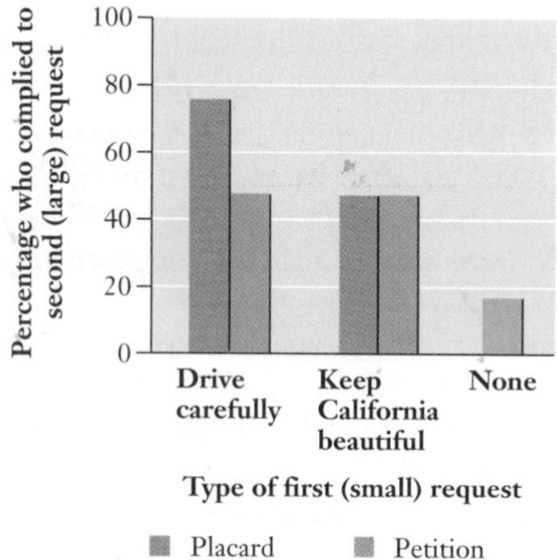

Figure 15.4 ***Results of a foot-in-the-door experiment***

Shown here are the percentages of people who agreed to put a large "Drive carefully" sign on their front lawn, when asked 2 weeks after receiving one of four smaller requests or no request. (Data from Freedman & Fraser, 1966.)

Figure 15.4 shows the results. As you can see, the highest rate of compliance to the second request occurred when the first request had involved the same cause (driving safely) and type of action (putting up a placard) as the second. But the other groups who had received an initial request also complied more than those who had received none, even when the first request involved a different cause (keeping California beautiful) and action (signing a petition). As suggested by the experimenters, compliance to the first request may have solidified in people's minds the idea that they were public-spirited individuals who in general would do things for good causes—an idea that would be consistent with agreeing to the second request and dissonant with refusing.

The Reciprocity Principle and Downward Negotiation

Anthropologists and sociologists have found that people all over the world abide by a ***reciprocity norm*** (Gouldner, 1960). That is, people everywhere feel obliged to return favors. This norm is so ingrained that people may even feel driven to reciprocate favors that they didn't want in the first place. Cialdini (1985) suggests that this is why such techniques as pinning a flower on the lapel of an unwary stranger before asking for a donation or giving a free bottle of furniture polish to a potential

■ 7. ***How can the door-in-the-face technique be explained by the reciprocity norm? Why should this technique backfire if a delay occurs between the first and second requests?***

vacuum-cleaner customer are so effective. Having received the gift, the victim finds it hard to turn away without giving something in return.

Another common sales and solicitation method that may work partly through the reciprocity principle is to start with a very large request or high price and quickly negotiate down to a smaller one (Cialdini, 1985; Reeves & others, 1991). This method is commonly called the ***door-in-the-face technique***, because the first request usually elicits a clear no. You may have experienced this technique in telephone solicitations. The caller describes some good cause and then mentions an astronomically high figure as a suggested donation. Then, after giving you just a moment to gasp and explain that the suggested amount is way out of your range, the caller very politely suggests a much lower amount, which would also be valued. According to Cialdini (1985), this method probably raises your likelihood of agreeing to the second request for two reasons: (1) Reducing the request seems like a concession, an attempt to accommodate your personal needs, so you feel compelled to reciprocate through the only means available in that interaction—complying with the smaller request. (2) Contrasted with the first request, the second seems much smaller than if it had stood alone.

The door-in-the-face method is the opposite of the foot-in-the-door method, and this suggests a possible problem. If people who comply with an initial low request feel *more* committed to the cause (the rationale of foot-in-the-door), then shouldn't people who refuse an initial high request feel *less* committed to the cause? Based on the cognitive dissonance principle, turning down the request to donate a huge amount of money to my alma mater should make me think of many reasons not to donate to the college, and this in turn should reduce the likelihood of my complying with the second request. Maybe that is why the caller moves so quickly to the smaller request—in doing so, he or she doesn't give me time to summon up the negative thoughts that would reduce cognitive dissonance. Perhaps if more time elapsed between the first and second request, the door-in-the-face method would boomerang, reducing the likelihood of compliance to the second request. Research has shown that such a reversal can indeed occur (Cann & others, 1975).

Obedience: Milgram's Experiments and Beyond

Obedience refers to those cases of compliance in which the person making the request is perceived as an authority figure or leader and the request is perceived as an order or command. Most often we think of obedience as a good thing. Obedience to parents and teachers is part of everyone's social training. Running an army, an orchestra, a hospital, or any enterprise involving large numbers of people would be almost impossible if people did not routinely carry out the instructions given to them by their leaders or bosses.

But obedience has its dark side. Most tragic are those cases in which people obey a leader who is evil, unreasonable, or sadly mistaken. As the novelist and social critic C. P. Snow (1961) once wrote, "When you think of the long and gloomy history of [humankind], you will find more hideous crimes have been committed in the name of obedience than have ever been committed in the name of rebellion." In the Holocaust of World War II, millions of Jews, gypsies, homosexuals, mentally ill people, and other men, women, and children deemed worthless by the Nazi government were systematically slaughtered through a chain of command in which many of the participants viewed themselves as simply following orders. In the My Lai massacre of 1968, U.S. soldiers obeyed orders from their platoon leader, who claimed to be obeying orders from higher up, to murder the defenseless women, children, babies, and old men of the village of My Lai in Vietnam. Some of the soldiers objected to the order, and some wept as they carried it out, but none rebelled (Kelman & Hamilton, 1989).

The horrifying aspect of obedience led Stanley Milgram to carry out a series of experiments at Yale University in the early 1960s that are now perhaps the best-known of all experiments in social psychology.

Milgram's Basic Procedure and Finding

■ **8.** ***How did Milgram demonstrate that a remarkably high percentage of people would follow a series of orders to hurt another person?***

Let us suppose that you are a volunteer who has answered Milgram's ad to participate in a psychological experiment. You enter the laboratory and meet the experimenter and another person who is introduced to you as a volunteer subject like yourself. The experimenter, a stern and expressionless man of 31, explains that this is a study of the effects of punishment on learning and that one of you will serve as teacher and the other as learner. You draw slips of paper to see who will play which role and find that your slip says "teacher." The other subject, a pleasant man of 47, will be the learner. You watch while his arms are strapped into a chair and electrodes are taped to his wrist (see Figure 15.5). The experimenter explains that the straps will prevent excessive movement while the learner is shocked and that the electrode paste on the skin has been applied "to avoid blisters and burns." While he is being strapped in, the learner expresses some apprehension, saying that he is concerned because he has a heart condition. The experimenter explains, "Although the shocks can be extremely painful, they cause no permanent tissue damage."

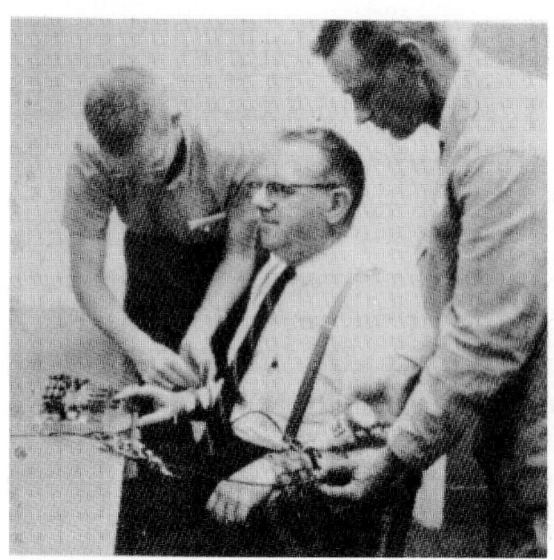

Figure 15.5 ***The victim in Milgram's obedience experiments***

While being strapped into a chair and fitted with electrodes, this pleasant man—the "learner"—mentioned that he had a heart condition.

After observing this part of the procedure, you—the teacher—are taken to an adjoining room, from which you can communicate with the learner through an intercom. Your job is to read off the questions of a verbal-memory test and to give the learner an electric shock whenever he gives a wrong answer. The shock generator in front of you is an impressive instrument with thirty switches, each labeled with a voltage designation from 15 up to 450 volts. In addition, verbal descriptions are written on the box for successive sets of switches, ranging from "Slight shock" up to "Danger, severe shock," followed by two switches labeled "XXX."

As the experiment progresses, the learner makes frequent mistakes, and at each mistake you give him a stronger shock than you had given before. The learner receives the early shocks silently, but when you get to 75 volts he responds with an audible "unghh," and at stronger shocks his protests become more extreme. At 150 volts he cries out, "Experimenter, get me out of here! I won't be in the experiment any more! I refuse to go on!" At 180 volts he hollers, "I can't stand the pain!" By 270 volts his response to each shock is an agonized scream, and at 300 volts he shouts in desperation that he will no longer provide answers in the memory test. The experimenter instructs you to continue anyway and to treat each nonresponse as a wrong answer. At 315 and 330 volts the learner screams violently, and then, most frightening of all, from 345 volts on, the learner makes no sound at all. He does not respond to your questions, and he does not react to the shock.

What do you do in this situation? At various points you look to the experimenter and ask if he should check on the learner or if the experiment should be terminated. You might even plead with the experimenter to let you quit giving shocks. At each of these junctures, the experimenter responds firmly with well-rehearsed prompts. First he says, "Please continue." If you still protest, he responds, "The experiment requires that you continue." This is followed, if necessary, by "It is absolutely essential that you continue," and "You have no other choice; you must go on." These prompts are always used in sequence. If you still refuse to go on after the last one, the experiment is discontinued. In reality—as you, sitting comfortably and reading this book, have probably figured out—the learner receives no shocks. He is a confederate of the experimenter, trained to play his role. But you, as a subject in the experiment, do not know that. You believe that the learner is suffering, and at some point you begin to think that his life may be in danger. What do you do? If you are like most people, you will go on with the experiment to the very end and eventually give the learner the strongest shock on the board—450 volts,

"XXX." In a typical rendition of this experiment, 65 percent (twenty-six out of forty) of the subjects continued to the very end of the series. They did not find this easy to do. Many pleaded with the experimenter to let them stop, and almost all of them showed signs of great tension, such as sweating and nervous tics, yet they went on.

Why didn't they quit? There was no reason to fear retribution for halting the experiment. The experimenter, although stern, did not look physically aggressive. He did not make any threats. The $5 pay for participating was so small as to be irrelevant; and all subjects had been told that the $5 was theirs just for showing up. So why didn't they quit?

Explaining the Finding

■ ***9. Why does Milgram's finding call for an explanation in terms of the social situation rather than in terms of unique personality characteristics of the subjects?***

Upon first hearing about the results of Milgram's experiment, people are tempted to suggest that the volunteers must have been in some way abnormal to give painful, perhaps deadly shocks to a middle-aged man with a heart condition. But that explanation—which, incidentally, is in line with the fundamental attribution error described in Chapter 14 (the tendency to attribute behavior too much to internal characteristics of the person and not enough to the environmental situation)—doesn't hold up. The volunteers were demonstrably normal, and the experiment was replicated dozens of times, using many different groups of subjects, with essentially the same results each time. Milgram (1974) himself found the same results for women as for men, and the same results for college students, professionals, and workers of a wide range of ages and backgrounds. Others repeated the experiment outside the United States, and the consistency from group to group was far more striking than the differences (Miller, 1986). No category of person has been found immune from the tendency to obey at a high rate in the Milgram experiment.

■ ***10. How might the high rate of obedience in Milgram's experiments be explained in terms of subjects' preexisting beliefs, the experimenter's demeanor, the proximity of the experimenter, and the sequential nature of the task?***

Another temptation is to interpret the results as evidence that people in general are sadistic. But nobody who has seen Milgram's film of subjects actually giving the shocks would conclude that. The subjects showed no pleasure in what they were doing, and they were obviously upset by their belief that the learner was in pain. How, then, can the results be explained? Milgram (1974) and other social psychologists (Miller, 1986) have identified some facilitating factors, including:

- ***Preexisting beliefs about authority and the value of science*** The subject comes to the laboratory as a product of a social world that effectively, and usually for beneficent reasons, trains people to obey legitimate authorities. An experimenter, especially one at such a reputable institution as Yale University, must surely be a legitimate authority in the context of the laboratory. In addition, the subject arrives with a degree of faith in the value of scientific research, which Milgram referred to as an *overarching ideology*, analogous to the overarching political or religious ideologies that motivate people to make much greater voluntary sacrifices when, for example, they join an army. Thus, the person enters the laboratory highly prepared to do what the experimenter asks.

  Consistent with the idea that subjects' prior beliefs about the legitimacy of the experiment contributed to this obedience, Milgram found that when he moved the experiment from Yale to a downtown office building, under the auspices of a fictitious organization, Research Associates of Bridgeport, the percentage who were fully obedient dropped somewhat—from 65 percent to 48 percent.

- ***The experimenter's self-assurance and acceptance of responsibility*** Obedience is predicated on the assumption that the person giving orders is in control and responsible and that your role is essentially that of a cog in a wheel. The preexisting beliefs mentioned above helped prepare subjects to accept the cog's role, but the experimenter's unruffled self-confidence during what seemed to be a time of crisis no doubt helped subjects to continue accepting that role as the experiment progressed. To reassure themselves, they often asked the experimenter questions like, "Who is responsible if that man is hurt?" and the experimenter routinely answered that he was responsible for anything that might happen. The importance of the subjects' attribution of responsibility to the experimenter was shown directly in an experiment conducted by another researcher (Tilker, 1970), patterned after Milgram's, in which obedience dropped sharply when subjects were told beforehand that they were responsible for the learner's well-being.

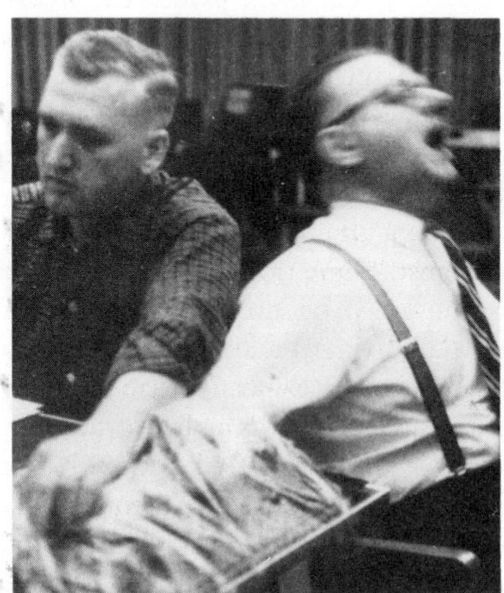

Figure 15.6 ***Giving a shock while in close proximity to the victim***
In one of Milgram's experiments, subjects were required to hold the victim's arm on the shock plate each time a shock was given. Fewer obeyed in this condition than when the victim received shocks in another room.

- ***The immediacy of the experimenter and the distance of the learner*** If you think of Milgram's subjects in relation to social impact theory, you can picture them as caught between two conflicting social forces. On one side was the experimenter demanding that the experiment be continued, and on the other was the learner asking that it be stopped. Not only did the experimenter have the greater initial authority (higher strength), but he was also physically closer and perceptually more salient (higher immediacy). He was standing in the same room with the subject while the learner was in another room, out of sight. To test the importance of immediacy, Milgram (1974) varied the placement of the experimenter or the learner in some replications of the experiment. In one variation, the experimenter left the room when the experiment began and communicated with the subject by telephone, using the same verbal prompts as in the original study; in this case, only 23 percent obeyed to the end, compared to 65 percent in the original condition. In another variation, the experimenter remained in the room with the subject, but the learner was also brought into that room; in this case, 40 percent obeyed to the end. In still another variation, the subject was required to hold the learner's arm on the shock plate while the shock was administered (see Figure 15.6), with the result that 30 percent obeyed to the end. Thus, any change that moved the experimenter farther away from the subject, or the learner closer, tended to tip the balance away from obedience.
- ***The sequential nature of the task*** At the very beginning of the experiment, Milgram's subjects had no compelling reason to quit. After all, the first few shocks were very weak, and subjects had no way to know how many errors the learner would make or how strong the shocks would become before the experiment ended. Although Milgram did not use this term, we might think of his method as a very effective version of the foot-in-the-door technique. Having complied with earlier, smaller requests (giving weaker shocks), subjects found it hard to refuse new, larger requests (giving stronger shocks). The technique was especially effective in this case because each shock was only a little stronger than the previous one. At no point were subjects asked to do something radically different from what they had already done. To refuse to give the next shock would be to admit that it was probably also wrong to have given the previous shocks—a thought that would be dissonant with subjects' knowledge that they indeed had given those shocks.

The Ethics and Validity of Milgram's Experiments

11. ***How has Milgram's research been criticized on grounds of ethics and scientific validity, and how has the research been defended?***

Because of their dramatic results, Milgram's experiments immediately attracted much attention and criticism from psychologists and other scholars. Some critics focused on ethics (for example, Baumrind, 1964). They were disturbed by such statements as this one made in Milgram's (1963) initial report: "I observed a mature and initially poised businessman enter the laboratory smiling and confident. Within 20 minutes he was reduced to a twitching, stuttering wreck, who was rapidly approaching a point of nervous collapse." Was the study of sufficient scientific merit to warrant inflicting such stress on subjects, leading some to believe that they might have killed a man? To this day disagreement persists, but in a survey made a year later, 84 percent of Milgram's subjects said they were glad to have participated, and fewer than 2 percent said they were sorry (Milgram, 1964).

Milgram took great care to protect his subjects from psychological harm. Before leaving the lab, subjects were fully informed of the real nature and purpose of the experiment; they were informed that most people in this situation obey the orders to the end; they were reminded of how reluctant they had been to give shocks; and they were reintroduced to the learner, who offered further reassurance that he was fine and felt very well disposed toward them. A year later, psychiatric interviews were held with forty of the former subjects, and no evidence of harm was found (Errera, 1972). Still, the question of whether the results justified even the temporary psychological anguish that these people experienced is a valid one for which no easy answer exists. Today such research would not be approved by the ethics review boards at most research institutions.

Other critics challenged Milgram's view that experiments of this type can help elucidate such real atrocities as the Nazi Holocaust. Some (for example, Orne & Holland, 1968) argued that Milgram's subjects must have believed, at some level of their consciousness, that they could not really be hurting the learner, because no sane experimenter would allow that to happen. From that perspective, the subjects' real conflict may have been between the belief that they weren't really hurting the learner and the possibility that they were. Unlike subjects in Milgram's study, Nazis who were gassing people could have had no doubt about the effects of their actions. They had far less cause to believe that they were following a benevolent authority, and far more to believe that they were following a dangerous one. Their motive could not have been based on a belief that the authority was actually kindly disposed toward the victim of the order; it was more likely to have been based either on their fear of the authority, who might harm them or their families, or on their own acceptance of the evil cause. Milgram's study offers no shortcut to understanding the Holocaust or the many other atrocities involving obedience that have occurred both before and since. To understand them we must understand the historical context in which they occurred—the fears, prejudices, economic conditions, and propaganda of the time.

Accepting its limitations, I personally am persuaded that Milgram's work was worthwhile for two reasons. First, science aside, the experiments provide a moral allegory for our time. People all over the world have heard of the research, and hearing about it has caused many to think about obedience in ways that they might not have before. Precisely because the experiments involved a less complicated situation and had no real victims, they are easier to grasp than the Holocaust, and knowing about them may help people like you and me resist the temptation to surrender moral authority. Second, from a scientific position, Milgram's studies are part of a larger body of research that has helped identify some of the principles of compliance and obedience. Preexisting beliefs about the importance of obedience, the authority's confident manner, the immediacy of the authority, and the sequential nature of tasks may contribute to real atrocities in much the same way that they contributed to obedience in Milgram's studies, even though the motives and specific conditions are very different.

Other Obedience Studies: The Role of Social Support for Rebellion

■ **12.** ***What is some evidence that the presence of others who question an order can decrease the likelihood of obedience?***

In most of Milgram's experiments subjects were alone in their predicament. In two variations, however, the task of teacher was divided between the subject and another ostensible subject who was actually a confederate of the experimenter (Milgram, 1974). When the confederate refused to continue at a specific point and the experimenter asked the real subject to take over the whole job, only 10% of real subjects obeyed to the end. When the confederate continued to the end, 93% of the real subjects did too. In an unfamiliar and stressful situation, having a model to follow has a potent effect. What would have happened if the other "teacher" had been a second real subject, hearing the experimenter's orders and genuinely trying to decide how to respond? Milgram's experiment has never been run with more than one real subject at a time (Brown, 1986), but some research suggests that if it were, in most cases the two subjects would hear each other's protests, begin to share their concern through dialogue, and join forces in rebelling.

Of special interest here are two separate but similar experiments performed in hospitals. In both, hospital nurses on regular duty were telephoned by a man who identified himself as a doctor and asked them to administer immediately a particular drug, to a particular patient, at a dose that the nurses knew to be dangerously high. In the first experiment, the nurses were called at a time when they were likely to be alone on the ward, and the result was that 95 percent would have given the drug had they not been stopped by the experimenter's accomplice who was secretly watching and had the drug not been replaced with a harmless placebo (Hofling & others, 1966). In the second experiment, the nurses were called at a time when other medical professionals were present, and in this case only 11 percent would have given the drug (Rank & Jacobson, 1977). In the second experiment, most nurses immediately said something about the unusual order to another nurse or doctor, who encouraged them in their belief that it was strange, which in turn led them to check with other hospital authorities. Although other differences between the two experiments could have contributed to the different results, the presence of other medical professionals with whom to consult seemed to be the major factor.

Influence of Others' Presence or Examples

You have seen that the way a person responds to an order can vary depending on whether other people are present or not and how they react to the order. Now let us look more broadly at how the presence of others and the examples they set can affect a person's behavior.

A victim of pressure?

It is hard to imagine the social pressure that young gymnasts who reach the status of favorite—such as Kim Zmeskal shown here toppling in Barcelona—must feel in Olympic competition. They are children, yet they are made to feel that the hopes of a nation ride on their shoulders.

Effects of Being Observed

The first published experiment in social psychology (according to Hendrick, 1977) was conducted near the end of the nineteenth century by Norman Triplett (1898), who had observed that bicycle racers usually perform better when they race with each other than when they race alone against the clock. To test the generality of this phenomenon, he asked children to wind fishing reels as rapidly as possible and found that they worked faster in pairs than when each worked alone.

Triplett's experiment did not distinguish between the competitive effect that might be engendered when two individuals perform the same task together and other energizing effects that might stem from the presence of another individual. Subsequent experiments showed that improvement often occurs even when others are present just to watch. In one, college students who had achieved skill at a particular motor task (following a moving target with a hand-held pointer) subsequently performed it more accurately when observed by a group of graduate students than when tested alone (Travis, 1925). Similar effects were also demonstrated with nonhuman animals, including insects. In one experiment, individual ants built tunnels faster with one or two other ants present than alone (Chen, 1937). The tendency to perform a task better in front of others than when alone was soon accepted as a general law of behavior and was given a name—***social facilitation***.

Although many experiments confirmed the phenomenon of social facilitation, others showed the opposite effect—***social interference***, a decline in performance when observers are present. For example, students who were asked to develop arguments opposing the views of certain classical philosophers developed better arguments when they worked alone than when they worked in the presence of either coperformers or observers (Allport, 1920). The presence of observers also reduced performance in solving math problems (Moore, 1917), learning a finger maze (Husband, 1931), and memorizing lists of nonsense syllables (Pressin, 1933). In animal studies, too, the presence of others inhibited the learning of new responses (Rasmussen, 1939).

A Theory of Social Facilitation and Interference

13. ***How does Zajonc's theory use the effect of arousal to explain why social facilitation occurs for some tasks and social interference occurs for others?***

Why did social facilitation occur in some experiments and social interference in others? Surprisingly, not until the 1960s was a coherent theory developed to answer this question. Robert Zajonc (1965), in reviewing the experiments, noticed that social facilitation usually occurred with relatively simple or well-learned tasks (such as winding fishing reels or, for ants, digging tunnels) and that social interference usually occurred with tasks that were more complex or involved learning something new (such as constructing logical arguments or learning a route through a maze). From this observation, Zajonc proposed the following generalization: *The presence of others facilitates performance of dominant (habitual, simple, or instinctive) responses and interferes with performance of nondominant (nonhabitual, complex, or unnatural) responses.*

Zajonc explained both effects by linking them to a more general phenomenon—the effect of high arousal or drive on performance. As discussed in Chapter 7, high arousal—no matter how it is produced—typically improves performance of simple or well-learned tasks and worsens performance of complex or poorly learned tasks in both humans and other animals. According to Zajonc, the primary effect of the presence of others is to increase arousal or drive, after which easy responses become easier and hard responses become harder (see Figure 15.7). Evidence for the theory comes from studies showing that (a) the presence of observers does often increase arousal in a person performing a task (Cacioppo & others, 1990; Zajonc, 1980) and (b) either facilitation or interference can occur in the same task, depending on the performer's skill. As an example of the latter, in one experiment expert pool players performed better when they were watched conspicuously by a group of four observers than when they thought they were not being observed, and the opposite was true for novice pool players (Michaels & others, 1982).

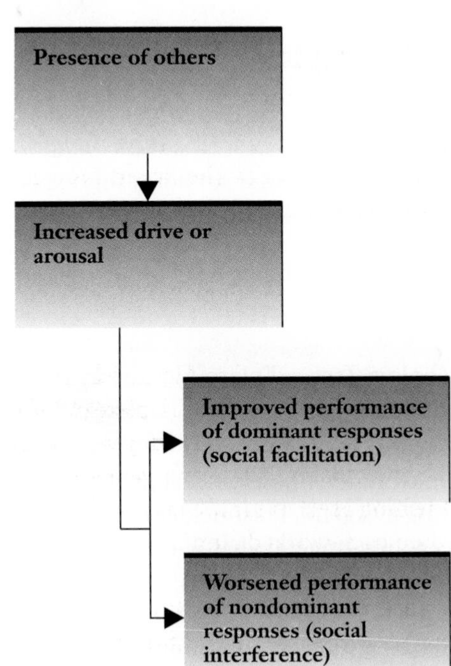

Figure 15.7 ***Zajonc's theory of social facilitation and interference***

This theory relates social facilitation and interference to a more general effect of high arousal or drive on dominant (habitual) and nondominant (nonhabitual) responses.

The presence of others may enhance arousal in various ways. Zajonc (1965) suggested that humans and other animals are innately aroused by other members of their species. But other theorists, focusing on humans, have placed greater emphasis on learned effects such as evaluation anxiety. The role of evaluation anxiety has been demonstrated in experiments showing that both social facilitation and social interference decline if the audience is blindfolded or not paying attention (Cottrell & others, 1968), and that both increase if the audience is high in status or expertise and is there explicitly for the purpose of evaluation (Geen, 1980; 1991). Other research suggests that social facilitation or interference may depend more on the performers' perception of their skill than on their actual skill at the task (Sanna, 1992). In one experiment, subjects who were misled into believing they were unusually good at a memory task performed the task better in front of an evaluator than alone, and subjects who were misled into believing they were unusually poor at the task performed worse in front of an evaluator than alone (Sanna & Shotland, 1990).

The Home-Audience Disadvantage in Championship Games

■ **14.** ***How might home-team collapse in championship games be explained by Zajonc's theory or by an alternative theory centering on self-consciousness?***

A remarkable audience effect in professional sports has been uncovered that might be explainable through an extension of Zajonc's theory. In examining the records of World Series baseball games over a 59-year period, Roy Baumeister and Andrew Steinhilber (1984) discovered that, contrary to the usual home-field advantage, the home team usually *lost* the final and decisive championship game. Specifically, home teams won 60 percent of the first two games in the World Series, but won only 41 percent of final, decisive games. Baumeister and Steinhilber (1984) found a comparable home-court disadvantage for the decisive game of championship tournaments in professional basketball, and other researchers found a home-course disadvantage in the decisive round of championship golf tournaments (Wright & others, 1991). What could be causing players to collapse in decisive championship games at home?

That the home players did indeed collapse is evidenced by another of Baumeister and Steinhilber's findings: In final World Series games, the number of fielding errors made by the home team doubled in comparison with their previous games. One possible explanation, consistent with Zajonc's arousal theory, is that the potentially decisive championship game, coupled with the strong desire to perform well in front of the home audience, leads to a level of arousal so great that it interferes with performance even in these highly skilled professionals. The optimal level of arousal for a task increases with skill, but even the optimum for the most skilled person can be exceeded (look back at Figure 7.16).

Although their findings can be interpreted as support for Zajonc's arousal theory, Baumeister and Steinhilber favor a different explanation. They suggest that the combination of a potentially decisive game and a supportive audience increases the players' *self-consciousness* (rather than general arousal). As their attention becomes focused more on themselves than on external stimuli associated with the game, their automatic responses become less automatic, with the result that errors become more common. Their situation may become a bit like that of the centipede who, when asked, "Which leg do you move first when you start to walk," found itself no longer able to walk. A considerable amount of research supports this explanation of "choking" under pressure (Baumeister & Showers, 1986).

Watching While Others Watch: The Unresponsive Bystander

In a normally quiet neighborhood in New York City in 1964, a young woman named Catherine Genovese was brutally attacked for a period of 30 minutes outside her apartment building. Her screams drew the attention of at least thirty-eight people, who watched through their apartment windows while she was repeatedly stabbed and finally murdered. Not one of the bystanders came to her aid or even called the police. The incident stirred a national outcry: Have we become so inured to horror that we simply watch it without lifting a finger? This incident, and others like it, also stirred many social psychologists to investigate what is now called the ***unresponsive-bystander phenomenon***.

Most people who hear of such an incident try to explain it in terms of personality characteristics of the bystanders—they are "uncaring," or "numb," or "New Yorkers," or whatever. But, to repeat what must by now be a familiar refrain, social psychologists are more likely to explain such an incident in terms of the social context in which the incident occurred. What social forces operating on normal, ordinary people might inhibit them from helping? In the years since Genovese's death, social psychologists have staged hundreds of emergencies—in laboratories, in subway cars, on the street—to identify conditions that affect the likelihood that bystanders will help. One of the most influential variables uncovered in such research, and the one most relevant to our present discussion, is the presence or absence of other bystanders.

Is help on the way?

Research suggests that this disabled motorist would be more likely to receive help if fewer motorists were on the road. Why?

Many experiments have shown that a lone witness to an emergency is more likely to help than is one witness among others (Latané & Nida, 1981). For example, in one experiment, college students filling out a questionnaire were interrupted by the sound of the researcher, behind a screen, falling and crying out, "Oh . . . my foot . . . I . . . can't move it; oh . . . my ankle . . . I can't get this thing off me" (Latané & Rodin, 1969). In some cases the student was alone, and in other cases two students sat together filling out questionnaires. The remarkable result was that 70 percent of those who were alone went to the aid of the researcher, and only 20 percent of those who were in pairs did so. What a strange finding. Apparently an accident victim is better off with just one potential helper present than with two! Why? Researchers have suggested three interrelated explanations, each of which has received experimental support (Latané & Nida, 1981; Dovidio, 1984):

■ **15. *What are three possible explanations of the inhibiting effect of other bystanders on each bystander's likelihood of helping?***

1. ***Informational influence*** If you are the only witness to an incident, you decide whether it is an emergency or not and whether you can help or not based on information from the victim. But if other bystanders are present, you look to them, as well, to help you interpret the situation. You wait just a bit to see what they are going to do, and chances are you find that they do nothing (because they are waiting to see what you are going to do). Their inaction is a source of information that may lead you to question your initial judgment: Maybe this is not an emergency, or, if it is, maybe nothing can be done. Consistent with this explanation, experiments have shown that if other bystanders indicate, by voice or facial expressions, that they *do* interpret the situation as an emergency, then their presence has a much smaller or no inhibiting influence on the target person's action (Bickman, 1972). In general, social psychologists use the term ***informational influence*** to refer to the effect that other's behavior has on the target person's reasoned judgments about the objective nature of an event or situation.

2. ***Normative influence*** If you are alone, your attention is focused on the victim and how you can help. But if others are present, your attention is split between the victim and your concern about how others may evaluate you. Since the others aren't acting, you would be violating what seems to be a norm if you were to spring into action, and you might look foolish to them. In general, social psychologists use the term ***normative influence*** to refer to all social influences that are mediated by people's concerns for how others will judge them. In this case, the normative influence may involve *evaluation anxiety*, which interferes with your ability to develop a plan of action, or your willingness to carry it out, or both. From this perspective, the unresponsive-bystander phenomenon can be interpreted as a special case of social interference. Studies show that if the bystanders know each other well—and presumably realize they share a norm of helping, which would reduce their anxiety about each other's

evaluation—they are more likely to help than if they don't know each other well (Rutkowski & others, 1983; Schwartz & Gottlieb, 1980).

3. ***Diffusion of responsibility*** If you are alone when an emergency occurs, the responsibility to help rests entirely with you. But if others are present, the responsibility is divided—each person feels less responsible than he or she would alone (Schwartz & Gottlieb, 1980). Depending on the situation, the sense of personal responsibility may be reduced below the threshold needed to induce action in any one of the bystanders. Experiments show that the presence of other bystanders does not keep an individual from helping if that individual is clearly in the best position to help (because of location or special ability) or had been previously designated as the one who should help if something goes wrong (Bickman, 1972; Moriarty, 1975a).

In sum, the presence of other bystanders is most likely to reduce the chance that any one of them will respond if (a) none of the bystanders acts as if the situation demands action, (b) the bystanders don't know each other and have no idea what the others would think about their action, and (c) no particular bystander is obviously better able to help than any of the others.

Caught up in the Crowd: Deindividuation

■ **16. *What is some evidence that reduced accountability and highly arousing stimulation can promote aggressive behaviors that violate one's personal standards?***

People sometimes do things in crowds or mobs that they wouldn't do alone—sometimes horrible things. At My Lai, for example, once the slaughter began, some of the soldiers went beyond their orders and got caught up in a frenzied spree of rape and torture before murdering their victims (Kelman & Hamilton, 1989). Many years ago, the French sociologist Gustave LeBon (1896) argued that people in a crowd may lose their sense of personal responsibility and behave as if governed by a primitive, irrational, hedonistic mind that seems to belong more to the group as a whole than to any one individual. Psychologists today refer to this state of reduced personal responsibility as ***deindividuation***. It seems to be brought on by a combination of *reduced accountability* that comes from being a relatively anonymous member of a crowd and *shifted attention* away from the self and toward the highly arousing external stimulation associated with the mob's actions (Diener, 1977; Prentice-Dunn & Rogers, 1983).

The role of anonymity in crowd-induced deindividuation is supported by a study of *suicide baitings*, incidents in which crowds gather to egg on a person who is threatening suicide (such as shouting "jump" to a distraught person perched on the ledge of a tall building). Based on news reports, the study showed that suicide baiting occurs most often in large cities, at night, when a large crowd has gathered (Mann, 1981)—all of which are factors that would promote anonymity. Other evidence for the role of anonymity comes from anthropological studies showing that in general the more brutal a group's customs are, the more likely they are to wear uniforms or paint their faces (Watson, 1973). By wearing uniforms or war paint they erase their personal identities and merge themselves with the group. It is not Billy who murders the villagers—it is the army that does, and the uniform helps Billy and those who know him make the distinction.

A number of researchers have attempted to produce states approximating deindividuation in the laboratory. In one experiment showing the role of anonymity, groups of students were asked to take part in giving electric shocks to another student (who was actually a confederate of the researcher). The students could choose the shock intensity, and the main result was that they chose to give stronger shocks if they wore hooded costumes and were not identified by name than if they wore their normal clothes and name tags (Zimbardo, 1970). In an experiment showing the role of intense stimulation, students who had just completed a set of invigorat-

Potential for violence?

In the excitement of sporting events, crowds sometimes lose control—a phenomenon that researchers studying deindividuation have tried to explain. Although this crowd of soccer fans did not riot, the ingredients for such violence are present: anonymity (due to the size of the crowd and their similar costumes) and highly arousing external stimulation.

ing group activities while rock music blared in the background chose to give stronger shocks than did students who hadn't been exposed to these conditions (Prentice-Dunn & Spivey, 1986). A self-report questionnaire in the latter experiment also revealed that students in the deindividuating condition experienced reduced self-awareness, a greater sense of being part of the group, and more euphoria than did those in the control condition.

By weakening self-awareness and inhibitions, deindividuating conditions can increase the frequency of all sorts of non-normative behaviors, not just those related to violence. In one experiment, deindividuation made subjects more willing to finger paint with their nose and suck on baby bottles (Diener, 1980), and in another it increased subjects' participation in and enjoyment of a discussion of pornographic literature (Singer & others, 1965).

Conformity

17. *How did Asch demonstrate that a tendency to conform could lead people to disclaim the evidence of their own eyes?*

Have you ever been in a situation in which something seemed obvious to you, but others around you all held a different opinion—the same different opinion—from yours? If so, what effect did their unanimity have on you? Did you honestly change your opinion to match theirs, either because you assumed that they must be right or because their opinion led you to reexamine the issue and see it differently? Or did you pretend to agree, to get along or to avoid seeming odd or like a troublemaker, even though you continued to hold your original view privately? Or did you—like the fabled child who announced that the Emperor was wearing no clothes—continue to assert your original opinion publicly as well as privately, despite what everyone else said? During the 1950s, Solomon Asch performed a series of experiments in which people were placed in this kind of dilemma, but in a starker way than most of us experience in everyday life.

Asch's Experiments: Basic Procedure and Finding

Asch's original purpose was to show *absence* of conformity (Asch, 1952). He expected to demonstrate that people will not be swayed from opinions based on their direct perceptual experience. But the results of his experiments surprised Asch and changed the direction of his research.

Asch's (1956) procedure was as follows: A college student was brought into the lab and seated with six to eight other students who also appeared to be subjects, and the group was told that their task was to judge the lengths of lines. On each trial they were shown one standard line and three comparison lines and were asked to judge which comparison line was identical in length to the standard (see Figure 15.8). As a perceptual task, this was almost absurdly easy; in previous tests, subjects performing the task alone almost never made mistakes. But, of course, this was not really a perceptual task; it was a test of conformity. Unbeknownst to the real subject, the others in the group were confederates of the experimenter who had been

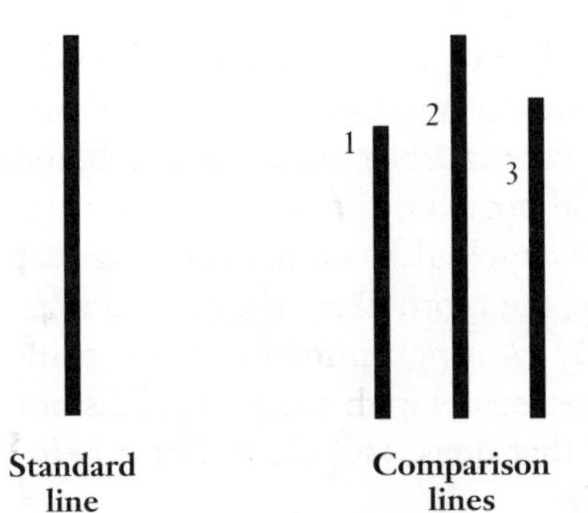

Figure 15.8 ***Sample stimuli used by Asch to study conformity***

The task on each trial was to select the comparison line that was identical in length to the standard. On critical trials, the confederates unanimously made a specific wrong choice (either 1 or 3, in this example). (Adapted from Asch, 1956.)

Figure 15.9 ***A perplexed subject in Asch's experiment***

It is not hard to tell who the real subject is in this photograph taken on a critical trial in one of Asch's experiments.

instructed to give a specific *wrong* answer on certain prearranged "critical" trials. Choices were stated out loud by the group members, one at a time in the order of seating, and seating had been arranged so that the real subject was always the next to last to respond (see Figure 15.9). The question of interest was this: On the critical trials, would subjects be swayed by the confederates' wrong answers?

Of more than 100 subjects tested, 75 percent were swayed by the confederates on at least one of the twelve critical trials in the experiment. Some of the subjects conformed on every trial, others on only one or two. On average, subjects conformed in 37 percent of the critical trials. That is, in about one-third of trials on which the confederates gave a wrong answer, the subject also gave a wrong answer, usually the same wrong answer as the confederates had given.

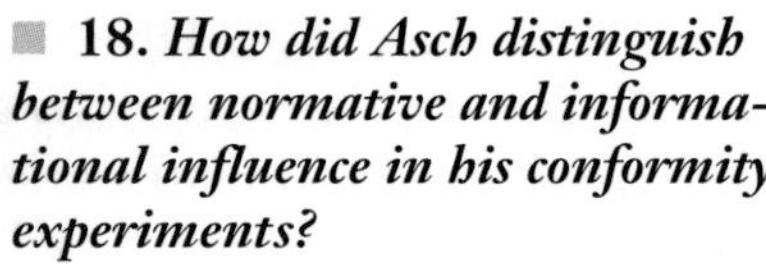

18. ***How did Asch distinguish between normative and informational influence in his conformity experiments?***

Conforming to Be Right, or to Be Liked?

Why did Asch's subjects yield to the majority? To use the terms introduced a few pages back, was the influence on the subjects *informational* or *normative*? That is, did they use the majority response as evidence regarding the objective lengths of the lines, or did they conform with the majority out of fear of looking different or non-normative to the others present? When Asch (1956) questioned the subjects after the experiment, very few said that they had actually seen the lines as the confederates had seemed to see them, but many indicated that they had been led to doubt their own perceptual ability. They made such comments as: "I thought that maybe because I wore glasses there was some defect"; "At first I thought I had the wrong instructions, then that something was wrong with my eyes and my head"; and "There's a greater probability of eight being right [than one]." Such statements suggest that to some degree the subjects did yield because of informational influence; they really believed that the majority was right.

But maybe these comments were rationalizations. Maybe the real reason for conformity had more to do with a desire to be liked or accepted by the others (normative influence) than with a desire to be right. To test this possibility, Asch (1956) repeated the experiment under conditions in which the confederates responded out loud as before, but the subjects responded privately in writing. To accomplish this, Asch arranged to have the real subjects arrive "late" to the experiment and be told that although no more subjects were needed, they might participate in a different way by listening to the others and then writing down, rather than repeating aloud, the answer they believed to be correct. In this condition, the amount of conformity dropped to about one-third of that in the earlier experiments. Apparently, the primary influence on Asch's subjects was normative. Their conformity was motivated more by the desire to be liked or accepted by the group than by the desire to give an objectively correct answer. When subjects did not have to respond publicly, their answers in the critical trials rarely reflected conformity.

More recent experiments indicate that the relative amounts of normative and informational influence of unanimous confederates vary with the difficulty of the perceptual task (Campbell & others, 1986; Campbell & Fairey, 1989). Conformity is motivated primarily by normative influence when the task is easy (as in Asch's original experiments) and primarily by informational influence when the task is difficult.

■ **19. *In Asch's conformity experiments and later experiments modeled after Asch's, how did a minority opinion influence subjects' responses?***

Influence of a Minority

Thus far we have examined conformity only in tests in which a single subject was faced by a group of others who *unanimously* favored a response that was objectively incorrect. What would happen if the others were not unanimous? Asch (1956) found that if a single confederate disagreed with the others, regardless of how many others there were (from two to fourteen), the amount of conformity on the line-judging task dropped dramatically—to about one-fourth of that in the unanimous condition. This effect occurred even if the dissenting confederate gave a wrong answer. Any response that differed from the majority response encouraged subjects to resist the majority's influence and to give the correct answer.

Subsequently, the French psychologist Serge Moscovici and his colleagues (1969) turned Asch's question around and asked: What effect can an incorrect *minority* have on the responses of a majority? Their experiments involved groups containing four real subjects and two confederates. In each critical trial, the group was shown a sky-blue patch and its members were asked to name the color. When the two confederates called the blue patch green on every trial, about a third of the subjects also called it green on one or more trials. But when they called it green on most but not all trials, the confederates had essentially no effect on the subjects' response. According to Moscovici and Gabriel Mugny (1983), minority influence operates through a different mechanism than majority influence does in such tasks. If people conform to a minority, they do so not to be liked or accepted, but because they genuinely believe the minority may be correct. That is, their motive is informational rather than normative. To convince subjects that they knew something the others didn't know, the minority in Moscovici's experiments had to be unwavering in their claim that the blue patch was green.

Other experiments, using more difficult tasks, have shown that a minority opinion, even if wrong, can improve subjects' performance by at least two means: (a) it provides a model of nonconformity, which frees people to resist social pressure and say what they think; and (b) it shakes people from complacency, which leads them to reexamine their original response and find a better one (Nemeth, 1986).

Group Discussion and Decision Making

All of the conformity experiments just described were conducted under artificial conditions in which the judgment to be made was all or none and no discussion was permitted. We turn now to some studies conducted under more natural conditions in which the judgments were more complex or subjective and in which people could argue out their disagreements.

Group Discussion as a Way of Changing a Norm: Lewin's Experiment

■ **20. *How did Lewin explain meat-buying habits in terms of a perceived group norm, and how did he show that group discussion could change those habits by changing the perceived norm?***

A useful place to begin our examination of group discussion is with a classic experiment conducted by Kurt Lewin (1947) during World War II. Among the many practical problems occasioned by the war was a shortage of meat. To ease the shortage, the U.S. government tried to persuade people to buy visceral meats such as heart, kidney, and sweetbread (thymus), which, although nutritious and regarded as delicacies in other cultures, were viewed with distaste in the United States. Propaganda had failed. What else could be done?

Lewin hypothesized that people's refusal to consume visceral meats was motivated by their sense that to do so would be considered abnormal. An individual might become convinced privately that sweetbread would be good for the family, but would be inhibited from buying and serving it through fear of deviating from the norm. This reasoning suggested to Lewin that people would buy visceral meats if they could be persuaded that others would not think worse of them for doing so, and he hypothesized that group discussion would be an effective way to accomplish this.

To test his hypothesis, he compared two different approaches—lecture and group discussion—for persuading female Red Cross volunteers to begin preparing visceral meats at home. Some volunteers attended a lecture at which the advantages of using visceral meats were explained clearly, and others attended a group discussion at which the same information was presented in a setting in which they were encouraged to present their own views. As expected, early in the discussion the volunteers were reluctant to express an interest in trying visceral meats, but after one or two broke the ice many others were emboldened to say that they, too, were convinced that the use of such meats would be good for their pocketbooks, their family's health, and their country's security. By the end of the discussion, all of the participants indicated, by a show of hands, that they would be willing to serve such meats at home. A follow-up survey several weeks later showed that about 30 percent of the people in the discussion group had actually bought and prepared visceral meats, whereas only 3 percent in the lecture group had done so.

According to Lewin's analysis, the discussion succeeded and the lecture failed because only the discussion had permitted a shift in perceived norms to occur. Sitting at the lecture, people had no way to know what others in the audience were thinking. The discussion, on the other hand, allowed them to learn that others also favored the idea of using visceral meats, so the idea no longer seemed so abnormal. To state the case more generally, when people favor a form of behavior but don't carry through with it for fear of what others would think, a discussion that clarifies what others do think may lead to changed behavior.

Group Polarization of Attitudes

In Lewin's experiment, people learned through group discussion that a certain social norm was not as deeply ingrained as they had thought it was, and this emboldened them to shift their publicly expressed attitude and their behavior. Since Lewin's time, social psychologists have conducted countless experiments on the varying effects that group discussion can have on people's attitudes, depending on such factors as the mix of people involved in the discussion, the particular issue under discussion, and the format of the discussion. One of the most robust, repeatable findings to come from such research is a phenomenon called ***group polarization***. The general rule of group polarization can be stated as follows: *If people who lean toward a particular view on some issue get together to discuss it with others similarly inclined, most will eventually adopt a more extreme view in the same direction as their initial tendency.*

■ **21. *How has group polarization been demonstrated, and what are some natural social circumstances in which it is likely to occur?***

Group polarization has since been demonstrated with a wide variety of problems or issues for discussion. In one experiment, for example, mock juries evaluated traffic-violation cases that had been set up to produce either high or low initial judgments of guilt. After group discussion, jurors rated the high-guilt cases at even higher levels of guilt, and the low-guilt cases at even lower levels, than they had before the discussion (Myers & Kaplan, 1976). In other experiments, researchers divided people into groups based on their initial view on a controversial issue and found that discussions held separately by each group widened the gap between groups. Group discussion caused racial prejudice to increase in initially prejudiced groups and to decrease in initially unprejudiced groups (Myers & Bishop, 1970). Similarly, advocacy of a strong military increased in groups initially favoring a strong military and decreased in groups initially favoring a weaker military (Minix, 1976; Semmel, 1976). (See Figure 15.10.)

Group polarization can have socially important consequences. For example, when students whose political views are barely right of center get together to form

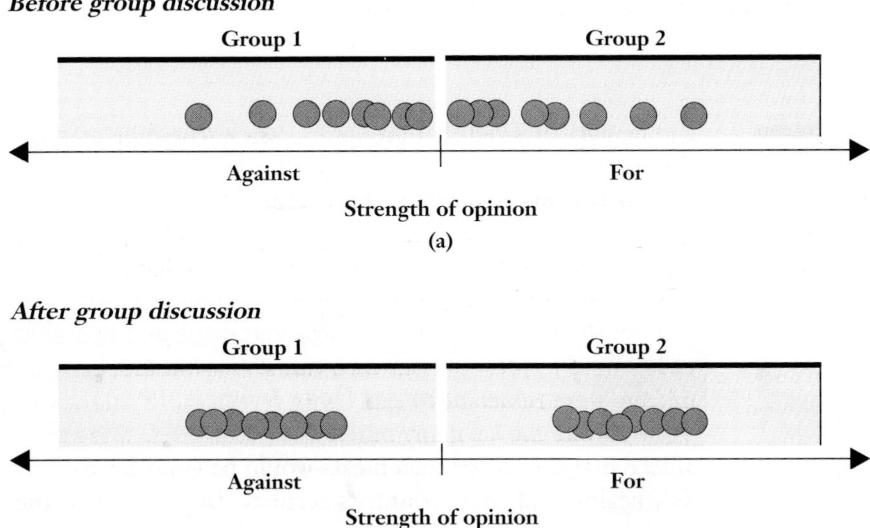

Figure 15.10 ***Schematic illustration of group polarization***

Each circle represents the opinion of one individual. When the individuals are divided into two groups based on the direction of their initial position (a), and then discuss the issue with other members of their group, the majority move toward a more extreme position than they held before (b).

■ **22.** ***How might group polarization be explained in terms of informational influence?***

■ **23.** ***What are three ways to explain group polarization in terms of normative influences?***

a young-conservatives club, their views are likely to shift farther toward the right; similarly, a shift to the left is likely to occur in a young-liberals club. Prisoners who enter jail with little respect for the law and spend their time talking with other prisoners who share that view are likely to leave prison with even less respect for the law than they had before. Professors who believe that students are getting lazier each year are likely to become even more convinced of that after having lunch with other professors who also hold that view. Everyday observations suggest that such shifts indeed do occur.

What causes group polarization? Several hypotheses have been proposed, which, as you might by now guess, can be divided roughly into two types—informational and normative. *Informational hypotheses* propose that polarization stems from the cumulative effect of the logic and evidence presented in the group discussion (Kaplan, 1987; Vinokur & Burnstein, 1974). People vigorously put forth arguments favoring the side to which they lean and tend to withhold arguments they can think of favoring the other side. Therefore, each group member hears, in the course of discussion, a disproportionate number of arguments on the side of their initial leaning, which may persuade them to lean further in that direction.

Normative hypotheses attribute group polarization to people's concerns about group norms and the approval of group members. One might expect normative influences to cause people within a group to become more similar to one another in their opinions, but not more extreme. In fact, as illustrated in Figure 15.10, they do become more similar as well as, on average, more extreme. Several variations of normative hypotheses have been offered to explain why people within a like-minded group become more extreme.

One of these, which I will call the *group-stereotyping hypothesis*, is based on evidence that people stereotype groups, including those to which they belong, by mentally exaggerating the group's point of view (Mackie, 1986). According to this hypothesis, people perceive the group's opinion as more extreme than it actually is, and then, to fit in, they shift their own view toward that more extreme position.

Another normative hypothesis, the *one-upmanship hypothesis*, maintains that when the group as a whole favors the same general position, each member tries to come across as a more vigorous supporter of that position than the others, which pushes the group toward an increasingly extreme position. This hypothesis originated partly from evidence that people indeed do admire points of view that are more extreme but in the same direction as their own (Levinger & Schneider, 1969; Myers, 1982). Thus, by adopting increasingly extreme positions, group members might enhance their standing in the group.

Save the forest

Any group who initially shares an opinion is likely to hold that opinion even more strongly after they have met and discussed it than they did before.

A third normative hypothesis, the *ingroup-outgroup hypothesis*, maintains that group polarization is part of a general tendency to identify with the ingroup and distinguish oneself from the outgroup (Turner, 1985). According to this view, people in a group either implicitly or explicitly contrast their group's opinions with the opinions of outsiders. To identify themselves clearly as members of the ingroup, they exaggerate their own opinions in a direction away from those of the outgroup. Consistent with this hypothesis, researchers have found that the direction of group polarization can be varied by giving subjects fictitious information about the views of one or more other groups (Hogg & others, 1990). When the outgroup was presented as more conservative than the ingroup on the issue under discussion, the ingroup polarized in the liberal direction. When the outgroup was presented as more liberal, the ingroup polarized in the conservative direction. And when two outgroups were presented, one more liberal and one more conservative than the ingroup, polarization did not occur.

Conditions That Lead to Good or Bad Group Decisions

Decisions made by groups are sometimes better and sometimes worse than decisions made by individuals working alone. To the degree that the group decision arises from the sharing of the best available evidence and logic, it is likely to be better. To the degree that it arises from collective ignorance, selective withholding of arguments on the less-favored side, false perceptions of others' views, and participants' attempts to outdo each other or to distinguish themselves from an outgroup, the group decision may be worse than the decision most group members would make alone.

■ **24.** ***How did Janis explain some White House policy blunders with his groupthink theory?***

In a book entitled *Groupthink*, Irving Janis (1982) analyzed some of the most ill-fated policy decisions made in the United States White House in recent decades. Among them is the decision to invade Cuba in 1961 (the Bay of Pigs invasion), to escalate the Vietnam War during the late 1960s, and to cover up the Watergate burglary in the early 1970s. Janis contends that each of these decisions came about because a tightly knit clique of presidential advisors, whose principal concerns were group unity and pleasing their leader (Presidents Kennedy, Johnson, and Nixon, respectively), failed to examine critically the choice that their leader seemed to favor and instead devoted their energy to defending that choice and suppressing criticisms of it. To refer to such processes, Janis coined the term ***groupthink***, which he defined as "a mode of thinking that people engage in when they are deeply involved in a cohesive ingroup, when the members' striving for unanimity overrides their motivation to realistically appraise alternative courses of action." More recently, many other ill-fated decisions, including the decision to launch the U.S. space shuttle *Challenger* in below-freezing weather, have been attributed to groupthink (Moorhead & others, 1991; 't Hart, 1990).

■ **25.** ***How can the tendency toward groupthink be countered?***

A number of experiments, conducted both before and after Janis developed his groupthink model, have examined the effects of group composition and leadership on groups' abilities to solve problems. In one such experiment, actual bomber crews—each consisting of a pilot, a navigator, and a gunner who were used to working together—were given problems to solve individually or as a group. As individuals the navigators were best at solving the problems, but working in a group they were relatively ineffective because both they and the gunners deferred to the pilots, who held the highest status in the crew (Torrance, 1954). Consistent with Janis's theory, other experiments have shown that the ability of groups to arrive at effective decisions or correct solutions to problems is improved if (a) the leaders are instructed not to advocate a view themselves but to encourage group members to present their own views and challenge each other (Leana, 1985; Maier & Solem, 1952) and if (b) the groups focus on the problem to be solved rather than on developing group cohesion (Callaway & Esser, 1984).

The* Challenger *incident

The flawed decision making that Irving Janis called *groupthink* has been implicated in the 1986 explosion of the U.S. space shuttle *Challenger*. In striving for unanimity in the decision to launch, managers ignored engineers' warnings about the dangers posed by subfreezing temperatures.

■ **26. *What is the distinction between positive and negative interdependence?***

Social Interdependence: Forces for Conflict and Harmony

We turn our attention now from the influence people have on each other through their presence and opinions to the influence that stems from their striving for shared or differing goals. People everywhere live interdependent lives. What one does affects the welfare of others, and what others do affects the welfare of the one. Interdependence can be positive or negative (Johnson & Johnson, 1989). ***Positive interdependence*** is the condition in which each person's real or perceived success depends on others' success, and ***negative interdependence*** is the condition in which each person's real or perceived success depends on others' failure. In sports and games, teammates are positively interdependent. One can win only if the other wins, so they support each other in their efforts. Members of opposing teams, in contrast, are negatively interdependent. One can win only if the other loses, so they do what they can within the rules of the game to hinder each other's efforts.

A pair or set of people can simultaneously be both positively and negatively interdependent. Teammates are interdependent positively in their shared goal of winning, but negatively in jockeying for favored positions on the team. Members of opposing teams are interdependent negatively in their games against each other, but positively in promoting the sport they all enjoy. The proprietors of the three video rental establishments in my neighborhood are interdependent negatively in their attempt to attract each other's customers, but positively in lobbying for lower taxes on video rentals.

Social Dilemmas

In many cases an interdependent relationship can be interpreted in either negative or positive terms, and then a dilemma arises. I imagine that the three video rental proprietors in my neighborhood are each faced regularly with a dilemma about pricing. Each knows that if she reduces her rental rate a little and the others don't, then she will attract customers away from the others and make more money. Each also knows, however, that she will be worse off if either or both of the other proprietors reduce their rates and that all will be worse off if they all reduce their rates because none will attract enough new customers to offset the lower profit margin.

Each of these proprietors, I imagine, is also something of a psychologist. Each knows that her interdependence with the other can be perceived by the other, as well as by herself, in either negative or positive terms. From the perspective emphasizing negative interdependence, each can say, "Business is business. I want more customers, and if I have to lower my prices to get them I will." From the perspective emphasizing positive interdependence, each can say, "We're colleagues. We all know we have to keep our rates up or we'll go bankrupt. None of us can afford a price war."

■ **27. *What are the defining characteristics of a social dilemma, and why are such dilemmas critical to human survival?***

The three proprietors are in what social scientists call a ***social dilemma***—a situation in which a particular action will (a) benefit the individual who takes it; (b) harm the individuals who don't; and (c) cause more harm than benefit to everyone if everyone takes the action. We all become involved in social dilemmas, some minor, some far reaching. If I hold a noisy party late at night, I might gain from the fun involved while my neighbors suffer. But if everyone in my neighborhood did that routinely, none of us would sleep.

The ecologist Garrett Hardin (1968) dramatically illustrated the relevance of social dilemmas to human survival in a now classic article entitled "The Tragedy of the Commons." He pointed out that our whole planet is analogous to the common grazing land that used to lie at the center of New England towns. All of the town's farmers would graze their cattle on the common pasture, and that was fine until the number of cattle began to reach the pasture's carrying capacity. Then, each farmer was faced with a dilemma: "Should I add another cow to my herd? One more cow will only slightly hurt the pasture and my neighbors, and it will significantly increase my profits. But if everyone adds a cow, the pasture will fail and my cattle, like everyone else's, will die." The tragedy comes because a typical next line to the logic is this: "It is not my increase in cattle, but everyone else's, that will determine the fate of the commons. I will lose if everyone increases their herd, but I will lose even more if everyone except me increases their herd." Everyone uses that logic, they all add a cow, the pasture gives out, and the cattle die.

We are rapidly approaching the carrying capacity of the planet. Sound logic tells me that the pollution I personally add to the atmosphere by driving a gasoline-burning car does not seriously damage the air or deplete the ozone layer. But because everyone thinks that way, the pollution keeps getting worse and the ozone layer upon which our survival depends is vanishing. Social dilemmas involving this many people, I suspect, can be resolved only with tough, enforceable laws. But social dilemmas involving fewer people can often be resolved in a positive direction through interpersonal understanding and negotiation.

Social Dilemma Games

■ **28. *What are the features of prisoner's dilemma games, and why are they of interest to social psychologists?***

To study the conditions that lead people to one choice or the other in social dilemmas, psychologists have invented games that put people into such dilemmas in the laboratory. One class of these is called ***prisoner's dilemma games***, because they were based originally on a hypothetical dilemma in which each of two prisoners must choose between remaining silent or confessing. If both remain silent, both will get a short prison sentence based on other charges. If both confess, they will both get a moderately long sentence. If only one confesses, that one will get no sentence, but the partner will get a very long sentence. They can neither communicate nor learn the other's choice until both have chosen.

In variations played in the psychology laboratory, the consequence for one choice or the other is not a reduced or increased prison sentence, but an increased or reduced monetary reward. Figure 15.11 shows a typical payoff matrix. On each trial, each player can make either a cooperative response or a competitive response. Neither learns the other's choice until both have responded, and the payoff to each player depends on the combination of the two responses. As in all prisoner's dilemma games, the payoff matrix has the following characteristics: (a) the *highest*

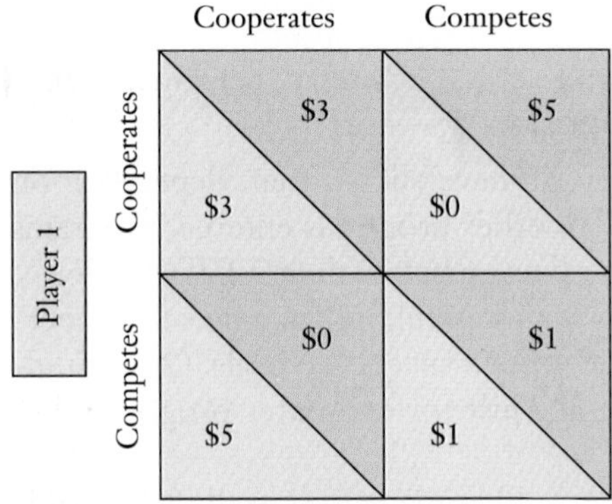

Figure 15.11 ***Sample payoff matrix for a prisoner's dilemma game***

On each trial, each player must decide whether to cooperate or compete, without knowing in advance what the other player will do. The payoff to each depends on the combination of that player's decision and the decision of the other player. In this example, the possible payoffs to Player 1 are shown in the yellow portions of the matrix, and the possible payoffs to Player 2 are shown in the green portions.

total payoff to the two players combined occurs if both cooperate ($3 + $3 = $6 in the example); (b) the *lowest total payoff* occurs if they compete ($1 + $1 = $2 in the example); (c) the *highest individual payoff* goes to a player who competes while the other cooperates ($5 in the example); and (d) the *lowest individual payoff* goes to a player who cooperates while the other competes ($0 in the example).

When the players are anonymous to each other, are not allowed to discuss their play, and know they will play it only once, they usually compete. Each player reasons as follows: "If the other player cooperates, then I will get $5 for competing compared with $3 for cooperating. If the other player competes, then I will get $1 for competing compared with $0 for cooperating. Either way, I do best by competing." Since both players are logical, they both compete and get $1. What a shame they are so logical. If they were not, they might both cooperate and receive $3 each.

Reciprocity as a Basis for Cooperating

■ **29.** ***Why are players more likely to cooperate in an iterative (repeated) prisoner's dilemma game than in a one-trial game?***

Imagine now an *iterative* prisoner's dilemma game—one in which the two players play over a succession of trials rather than just once. Now the logic changes, because each player's choice on one trial has the potential to influence the other's choices on future trials. Each player might reason: "If I cooperate on this trial, maybe that will convince the other player to cooperate on the next. We'll both do a lot better over time if we cooperate and get $3 each per trial than if we compete and get $1 each per trial." In other words, logic, which led players to interpret the one-shot game as a situation of negative interdependence, can lead them to interpret the iterative games as one of positive interdependence. The goal is no longer to beat the other player, but to cooperate with the other player to beat the system—to get the most combined money that the game allows.

What, in the long run, is the best strategy to employ in an iterative prisoner's dilemma game? To find out, Robert Axelrod (1984) held two round-robin tournaments played by computer programs submitted by social scientists, mathematicians, teenaged computer hacks, and others knowledgeable about game strategy. Each program was made to play a series of trials with each other program in a round-robin tournament. The objective was to see which program would accumulate the most total points in the tournament. Some of the programs were very complicated, able to remember all of the opponent's previous plays and take them into account in deciding on the next play. But in the end, it was the simplest program that won the most points.

■ **30.** ***Why was Rapoport's TFT program so successful in Axelrod's prisoner's dilemma tournaments?***

The winning program, sent in by the psychologist Anatol Rapoport, was called TIT-FOR-TAT (or TFT). It consisted of just two rules: (1) The first time you meet a new program, cooperate with it. (2) After that, do on each trial what the other program did on its previous trial with you.

Notice that TFT is incapable of "beating" any other program in head-to-head competition. It never cooperates less often than the other program does, and therefore it can never win more points in play with another program than that program wins in play with it. The TFT program won the tournament not by beating other programs in individual encounters, but by getting them to cooperate with it. Other programs earned as many points as TFT in their games with TFT, but they did not do so well in their games with each other, and that is why TFT earned the most points in the end. Why is TFT so effective in eliciting cooperation? According to Axelrod's analysis, there are four reasons: (1) TFT is *nice*. By cooperating from the start, it encourages the other player to cooperate. (2) TFT is *not exploitable*. By reciprocating every failure to cooperate with its own failure to cooperate on the next turn it discourages the other from competing. (3) TFT is *forgiving*. It resumes cooperating with any program as soon as that program begins to cooperate with it. (4)

TFT is *transparent*. It is so simple that other programs quickly figure out its strategy and learn that they are best off cooperating with it.

Computer tournaments held since Axelrod's have shown that, depending on the specific payoff matrix and the assortment of other programs entered, programs a little more generous than TFT can do as well as or better than TFT (Bendor & others, 1991; Godfray, 1992). For example, one successful program fails to cooperate only after the other has failed to cooperate on two successive trials. Other studies have shown that TFT is highly effective not just for computer programs, but also for people.

When naive human subjects play prisoner's dilemma games in the laboratory, they learn most quickly to cooperate if the other player uses the TFT strategy (Komorita & others, 1991). Evolutionary theorists have argued that people don't have to reason logically to adopt a strategy of reciprocity or to learn to cooperate in response to one in everyday life (Cosmides & Tooby, 1992; Trivers, 1971; also see the discussion of helping in Chapter 4). Because this strategy is so effective, they contend, we have evolved a tendency to behave reciprocally: We are naturally inclined to help those who help us, and disinclined to help those who fail to help us. We keep our eyes open for cheaters and punish or avoid them when we can. Yet we also forgive past cheaters who repent and begin to cooperate.

Group Identity as a Basis for Cooperating

31. ***What is some evidence that group identity can lead to helping others even in the absence of reciprocity?***

Thus far I have focused on material gain as the motive for one choice or the other in social dilemmas, but in some conditions a high percentage of people will choose the response that helps others even when no personal material gain can result from that choice. In particular, they will do so if they perceive the other players to be members of their own group. As discussed in Chapter 14, people tend to categorize others as either *ingroup members* or *outgroup members* and to favor the former. The sense of who is in one's ingroup and who is not is a matter of perception and can be manipulated in experiments. In one experiment, for example, subjects cooperated more often in a social dilemma if they were led to think of each other as citizens of the same town, and competed more often if they were led to think of each other as members of different age groups (Kramer & Brewer, 1984).

In another set of experiments, groups of subjects were involved in one-shot social dilemma games, structured so that nobody could know who cooperated and who didn't (Dawes, 1991). The subjects did not know one another before coming into the lab and had nothing particularly in common with one another. After the rules of the game were explained to them, they were assigned to one of two groups. In some cases they were then asked to discuss the game within their own group before playing it, and in other cases they weren't. The result was that subjects who had held a discussion cooperated at a high rate with members of their own group but not with members of the other group, and subjects who had not held a discussion did not cooperate at a high rate with anyone. According to Robyn Dawes's (1991) analysis, the group discussions promoted cooperation by leading group members to develop a sense of group identity, which in turn led them to care about each other's welfare, not just their own. Apparently, when people see others as ingroup members, they can move beyond tit-for-tat to something a bit closer to the Golden Rule.

Group Versus Group and Harmony Through Shared Goals

Identification with a group increases people's willingness to help ingroup members, but *decreases* their willingness to help outgroup members. In the laboratory, people play prisoner's dilemma games much differently in a group that is playing with an-

Rattlers versus Eagles
What at first were friendly competitions, such as the tug-of-war shown here, degenerated into serious hostility and aggression between the two groups of boys in Sherif's field study at Robbers Cave.

other group than as individuals. They are far more competitive and less cooperative as groups than as individuals, even though the payoffs are the same in both conditions (Insko & others, 1987; Schopler & others, 1991). Sadly, groups in real life are also more likely than individuals to interpret their interdependence negatively, and such interpretations frequently move beyond healthy competition to spiteful hostility. The history of humankind can be read as a record of intergroup conflict.

Conflict Among Boys at Robbers Cave

In order to learn about intergroup conflict and possible ways to resolve it under natural conditions, Muzafer Sherif and his colleagues (1961, 1966) conducted a now famous study of 11- and 12-year-old boys at a 3-week camping program in Oklahoma's Robbers Cave Park (an area once used as a hideout by Jesse James). To establish two groups, the researchers assigned the boys to two separate cabins at a considerable distance from each other and assigned them tasks, such as setting up camping equipment and improving the swimming area, designed to build group cohesiveness. In a few days, with little adult intervention, each cabin of boys acquired the characteristics of a distinct social group. Each group had its own leaders, its own rules and norms of behavior, and its own name—the Eagles and the Rattlers.

■ **32.** ***How did Sherif and his colleagues demonstrate that negative interdependence promotes intergroup hostility and positive interdependence promotes intergroup friendship?***

When the groups were well established, the researchers proposed a series of competitions—an idea that the boys eagerly accepted. They would compete for valued prizes in such games as baseball, touch football, and tug-of-war. As Sherif had predicted from previous research, the competitions had three effects: (1) They promoted *ingroup solidarity*. As the boys worked on plans to defeat the other group, they set aside their internal squabbles and differences, and their loyalty to their own group became stronger. (2) The competitions promoted *negative outgroup stereotyping*. Even though the boys had all come from the same background (white, Protestant, and middle class) and had been assigned to the groups on a purely random basis, they began to see members of the other group as very different from themselves and as very similar to each other in negative ways. For example, the Eagles began to see the Rattlers as dirty and rough, and in order to distinguish themselves from that group they adopted a "goodness" norm and a "holier-than-thou" attitude. (3) Most noteworthy, the competitions promoted *hostile intergroup actions*. Initial good sportsmanship collapsed. The boys began to call their rivals names, accuse them of cheating, and cheat in retaliation. After being defeated in one game, the Eagles burned one of the Rattlers' banners, which led to an escalating series of raids and other hostilities. What at first was a peaceful camping experience turned gradually into something verging on intertribal warfare.

In the final phase of the experiment, the researchers tried to reduce hostility between the two groups—a much harder task than provoking it. In two previous experiments similar to the one at Robbers Cave, Sherif had tried a number of procedures to reduce hostility, all of which had failed. *Peace meetings* between leaders had failed because those who agreed to meet lost status within their own group for conceding to the enemy. *Individual competitions* (similar to the Olympic games) had failed because the boys turned them into between-group competitions by keeping track of total victories by members of each group (just as we find with the International Olympics). *Sunday sermons* on brotherly love and forgiveness had failed because, while claiming to agree with the messages, the boys simply did not apply them to their actions.

At Robbers Cave, Sherif tried two new strategies. The first was *joint participation in pleasant activities*. Hoping that mutual enjoyment of noncompetitive activities would lead them to forget their hostility, Sherif arranged for the two groups to eat their meals together and share in other enjoyable activities such as watching movies and shooting firecrackers. This didn't work either. It merely provided opportunities for further hostilities. For example, meals were transformed into what the boys called "garbage wars."

The second new strategy, however, was successful. This involved the establishment of *superordinate goals*, defined as goals that were highly desirable and could be achieved best through cooperation between the two groups. The researchers created one such goal by staging a breakdown in the camp's water supply. In response to this crisis, boys in both groups volunteered to explore the 1-mile-long water line to find the break and on their own initiative worked out a strategy to divide their efforts in doing so. Two other staged events similarly elicited cooperation. By the end of this series of cooperative adventures, hostilities had nearly ceased, and the two groups were arranging friendly encounters on their own initiative, including a campfire meeting at which they took turns presenting skits and singing songs. On their way home, one group treated the other to milkshakes with money left from its prizes.

In sum, Sherif and his colleagues demonstrated that negative interdependence, established in this case by competitive games, can induce hostility between groups beyond that structured by the formal competition and positive interdependence, established in this case by superordinate goals, can reduce hostility and promote intergroup friendship that extends beyond the achievement of the original shared goals. Research since Sherif's suggests that the intergroup harmony brought on by superordinate goals is mediated by the fading of group boundaries (Bodenhausen, 1991; Gaertner & others, 1990). The groups merge into one, and each person's group identity expands to encompass the former outgroup members.

Jigsaw Classrooms

■ **33.** ***How were the beneficial effects of positive interdependence demonstrated in Aronson's jigsaw classrooms?***

In the early 1970s, the city of Austin, Texas, was required by a court order to desegregate its schools. To help find ways to reduce or prevent racial conflict within classrooms—where white, black, and Mexican-American students were to be brought together for the first time—the school board hired Elliot Aronson, a social psychologist. As part of this project, Aronson and his colleagues (1978) developed and implemented a method of instruction they called the *jigsaw classroom*. The

Fun for all

At work and at play, positive goal interdependence has been found to be extremely effective in breaking down barriers between groups.

essence of this method was to divide children in each classroom into mixed-racial groups of five or six and to establish positive interdependence both within and among groups so that children of different races would have to cooperate with each other to achieve their desired goals.

In one fifth-grade lesson, for example, each of the six children in each group received a different portion of a biography of Joseph Pulitzer to study and teach to the others in preparation for a test. To do well on the test, the children had to cooperate with each other. They had to ask the right questions to learn what the others knew and, in turn, answer the questions that others asked of them. Grading on the test was not competitive; everyone could get an A if everyone learned the lesson. To prepare, the children first read the part of the biography they were given. Next, they met with children from other groups, who had been given the same part, to share and consolidate what they had learned. Then they returned to their own group to teach their part to, and learn the other parts from, the other group members. Controlled comparisons to children in traditional classrooms in the same school showed that children of all races in the jigsaw classrooms liked each other more, developed higher self-esteem, and learned more. Other experiments on cooperative learning have since produced similar results (Slavin & others, 1985).

The World

As I write this I hear the TV news in the background, full of stories of "ethnic cleansing," race-motivated violence, wars over national boundaries, and other intergroup atrocities. Researchers have found that the degree of animosity between different ethnic or national groups correlates strongly with the degree to which they see each other as competing for the same resources (Struch & Schwartz, 1989; Vanneman & Pettigrew, 1972). The problems of the world are far, far more complex than the problems that social psychologists study experimentally. Yet the results of their experiments may provide insights for thinking about, and maybe even helping to solve, some of the world's problems.

As the world grows ever more interconnected and as more people acknowledge the interdependence of all upon all, perhaps some of our superordinate goals will become more binding. Just as the Eagles and Rattlers cooperated to stop the leak in the water line at Robbers Cave, perhaps nations will cooperate to stop the leak in the ozone layer—and the pollution of the oceans, and the international drug trade, and the worldwide threat of AIDS, and the famines that strike periodically, and. . . . Perhaps such goals will yet bring us together and lead us to think of all humankind as members of one tribe spinning together on a small and fragile planet.

Concluding Thoughts

Underlying the specifics in this chapter are some broad themes that may enrich your understanding as you reflect on what you have read:

1. The desire to be accepted by others as an underpinning of much of social influence In surveying the body of research and theory on social influence, one cannot help being struck by the frequent recurrence of a single, simple idea: Human beings have a remarkably strong desire to be approved of by other human beings nearby. This theme emerged in the discussion of impression management in Chapter 14 and has continued through much of this chapter.

Why do we find it hard to refuse a direct request? Why do we find it hard not to reciprocate a favor, even one that we did not want in the first place? Why did

Milgram's subjects find it hard to tell the experimenter that he was asking them to do a terrible thing and they would not go on? Why do people become aroused—leading to social inhibition or facilitation—when they know that their performance is being evaluated, even if the evaluator is a stranger and the evaluation doesn't count for anything? Why did subjects in Asch's experiment deny the clear evidence of their own two eyes when it ran counter to what others were saying? Why did the opinions of peers (expressed in group discussion) in Lewin's experiment have a greater impact on people's meat-buying behavior than the sound logic and expert advice presented by the lecturer? Why do group polarization and groupthink occur? Why do subjects in prisoner's dilemma games find it much easier to take a competitive stance if they have colleagues on their side than if they play alone?

I don't want to oversimplify. The desire to be accepted is surely not the *whole* answer to these questions, but it seems to be an important part of it. As you review each of the phenomena and experiments described in the chapter, you might ask yourself: To what extent (if at all) can this be explained by the desire for acceptance, and what additional explanatory principles seem to be needed?

2. Normative versus informational influences on behavior The dichotomy between normative and informational sources of social influence was discussed in three distinct places in the chapter. You read of normative versus informational theories of (a) the effect that other bystanders have on any one bystander's willingness to help a person in distress, (b) the tendency to conform in Asch's and similar experiments, and (c) the polarizing effect that group discussion has on people's opinions or attitudes. In reviewing these topics, think again about the basic difference between the two kinds of influences. Normative influences reflect people's concern to behave in a way that is like, or will be perceived as better than, the norm for their group. Informational influences reflect people's use of other's responses as information to be included in solving a problem. Normative influences stem from people's desire to be accepted or liked, and informational influences stem from people's desire to be right. You might also think about how this dichotomy could be applied to some of the other phenomena described in this chapter. For example, can any of the proposed explanations of Milgram's obedience findings be characterized as either normative or informational?

3. Social interdependence and human evolution The discussion of social interdependence brings us back to ideas about evolution introduced in Chapter 4. An individual's survival and reproduction depends on successful acquisition of essential resources, and members of the same species, inhabiting the same niche, are in some ways necessarily competitors for those resources. Yet, for social species, survival also depends on cooperation. The tension between competition and cooperation has probably been with us throughout the history of our species, and therein lies the basis for social dilemmas.

Therein, too, may lie the basis for the distinction we make between ingroups and outgroups. During the bulk of human evolution, survival of the individual depended on the survival of that person's tribe, so natural selection favored concern for the welfare of the members of one's tribe. But individual survival may have been more often threatened than benefitted by other tribes, so natural selection may have favored distrust of them. The effect of such evolution may contribute today to intergroup conflicts ranging from the trivial squabbles among cliques at work or school to ethnic clashes and international wars. It may or may not be wishful thinking to suggest that greater awareness of superordinate goals will help us to weaken group boundaries and make the world more peaceful.

Further Reading

Robert Cialdini (1985). *Influence: The new psychology of modern persuasion* (Rev. ed.). New York: Morrow.

Cialdini has combined field observations of sales techniques with laboratory research to identify basic principles of social influence. In this fun-to-read book, oriented toward the nonspecialist, he spells out these principles and provides numerous examples. After reading it, you will never be quite as susceptible to sales pressure as you were before.

Stanley Milgram (1974). *Obedience to authority: An experimental view.* New York: Harper & Row.

This is a fascinating, firsthand account of one of the most famous series of experiments in social psychology. Milgram describes here his reasons for initiating the research, his findings in many variations of the basic experiment, and his interpretations of and reactions to the findings.

Irving Janis (1982). *Groupthink: Psychological studies of policy decisions and fiascoes* (2nd ed.). Boston: Houghton Mifflin.

In this interesting book, Janis describes his theory of the causes and symptoms of groupthink and applies it to an analysis of a number of unsuccessful policies (and two successful policies) developed by advisors to U.S. presidents.

Robert Axelrod (1984). *The evolution of cooperation.* New York: Basic Books.

The first half of this brief, nontechnical book tells the story of Axelrod's computer tournaments of a prisoner's dilemma game and presents his analysis of the success of TIT-FOR-TAT. The second half presents examples of the reciprocity principle in evolution and modern-day life. One chapter tells how a "live-and-let-live" reciprocity norm emerged between opposing lines in trench warfare in World War I and operated against officers' commands to shoot.

Elliot Aronson (1992). *The social animal* (6th ed.). New York: Freeman.

Like many social psychologists, Aronson has a knack for relating social psychological theories to real-world problems. In this discursive, idea-oriented, unconventional textbook, Aronson does so through chapters on conformity, propaganda and persuasion, aggression, prejudice, loving and liking, and several other topics.

Looking Ahead

As you have seen, social psychologists attempt to explain human behavior in terms of the social environment within which the behavior occurs. Their goal usually is to identify general principles that characterize most people's responses to specific social situations, and they are relatively unconcerned with individual differences among people. In the next chapter, on theories of personality, we turn to the opposite approach—the attempt to explain behavior in terms of inner characteristics that differ from one person to the next.

PERSONALITY AND DISORDERS

PART 7

We do not all approach life in the same way. We differ in our emotions, motives, and styles of thinking and behaving, and these differences give each of us a unique personality. Although most of these differences are healthy and add spice to our lives, some create problems for the differing individual and are classed as mental disorders. This final unit has three chapters. The first is about broad theories that psychologists have developed to account for the differences among us. The second is about identifying mental disorders and understanding their origins. And the third is about methods that psychologists and psychiatrists have developed to help people overcome or live with their problems or disorders.

THEORIES OF PERSONALITY

CHAPTER 16

Personality is a word that was used a lot in my junior high school. A girl attempting to explain her latest infatuation would say, "It's not his looks, it's not his athletic ability, it's certainly not his intelligence—it's his *personality* that I like." All listening would nod their heads knowingly.

Personality, as the term is used in psychology, means pretty much the same thing it did in junior high. It refers to a person's general style of interacting with the world and especially with other people—to such things as whether a person is withdrawn or outgoing, excitable or placid, tidy or messy, generous or stingy. A basic assumption underlying the personality concept is that people do differ from one another in their general style of behavior, in ways that are at least relatively consistent across time and place.

■ **1. *What are the general purpose and main components of most personality theories?***

A ***personality theory*** is a formal attempt to describe and explain the ways in which people differ in their general style of behavior. Because personality theories are about the whole person, they are among the broadest, most sweeping theories in psychology. They are perhaps best thought of as philosophies of the person. Most personality theories include an opinion about each of the following four elements: (1) the motivating forces, or drives, that underlie behavior; (2) the mental structures, or components of the mind, that interpret the environment and make decisions that guide behavior; (3) the ways in which personalities can differ from one another, either in motivating force or mental structure; and (4) the ways in which such differences develop from birth to adulthood. Thus, a complete theory of personality is a theory of motivation, cognition, individual differences, and development—all rolled into one.

■ **2. *How can personality theories be categorized according to the kinds of evidence on which they are based?***

One useful way to categorize theories of personality is in accordance with the types of evidence used in their construction. *Clinically based theories* are those developed primarily by psychotherapists, who use their intimate knowledge of their clients as a basis for developing a theory of personality. The psychodynamic and humanistic theories, which make up more than half the discussion in this chapter, are clinically based. *Laboratory-based theories* are those developed primarily by research psychologists who study such traditional issues as learning, cognition, and social influence through experimental means, and who then extrapolate from such research to develop a theory of personality. The social cognitive theories in this chapter are laboratory based. Finally, *psychometrically based theories* are those developed by researchers whose main tools are paper-and-pencil questionnaires and statistical procedures for compiling and analyzing the results. The trait theories in this chapter are psychometrically based.

Now, let's examine the issue of personality more deeply—though perhaps no more passionately—than we did in junior high school. As you study each theory, think about the principal explanatory concepts that it invokes, the evidence upon which it is based, and whether or not it is useful in understanding the behavior of people you know. Personality theories are useful to the degree that they help us make sense of the real-life behavior of individuals or help us predict how they will behave in the future. Theories are detrimental to the degree that they sidetrack our thinking by causing us to focus too heavily on one set of motives or mental structures while ignoring others that may be more important.

Psychodynamic Theories

Before you began studying psychology, your image of a typical psychologist might have been a caricature of Sigmund Freud, stroking his beard and mumbling, "I wonder what he really meant by that." Freud more or less founded psychotherapy and the clinical approach to the development of personality theories. As a young physician in late nineteenth-century Vienna, Freud came to believe that many of his patients' complaints were rooted not in organic disease but in mental conflicts of which they themselves were unaware. Based on this insight, he developed an approach to psychotherapy and a theory of personality, both of which he referred to as ***psychoanalysis***. Freud's theory is the prime example of what today are called ***psychodynamic theories***—personality theories that emphasize the interplay of mental forces (the word *dynamic* refers to energy or force). Let's examine Freud's theory in some detail and then contrast it with some alternative psychodynamic theories that evolved from it.

Freud's Model of the Mind

The Idea of Unconscious Motivation

The most basic idea in Freud's theory is that the main causes of behavior lie deeply buried in the unconscious mind, that is, in the part of the mind that affects the individual's conscious thought and action but is not itself open to conscious inspection. The reasons people give one another and themselves to explain their behavior are not the true motivating causes of their behavior. To illustrate this idea, Freud often drew an analogy between everyday behavior and the phenomenon of posthypnotic suggestion.

■ **3.** ***How is the concept of unconscious motivation illustrated by the phenomenon of posthypnotic suggestion?***

In a demonstration of posthypnotic suggestion, a person is hypnotized and then given an instruction such as, "When you awake, you will not remember what happened during hypnosis. However, 10 minutes from now you will walk to the back of the room, pick up the umbrella lying there, and open it." Then the subject is awakened and appears to behave in a perfectly normal, self-directed way until the prearranged moment arrives, at which point he or she is overcome by an irresistible impulse to perform the commanded action. The person consciously senses the impulse and consciously performs the behavior, but has no conscious memory of the origin of the impulse (the hypnotist's command). If asked why he or she is opening the umbrella, the subject may come up with a plausible though clearly false reason, such as, "I thought I should test it, because it may rain later." According to Freud (1912/1932), this illustrates artificially the relationship between unconscious and conscious reasons that underlie everyday actions. The real reasons lie in our unconscious minds, and the conscious reasons that we give are cover-ups, plausible but false rationalizations designed to justify our actions to ourselves and others. They are not false in the sense of conscious lies, however; consciously, we believe them to be true.

Oh, my racing heart!
Freud described a number of mechanisms by which drives become redirected into other forms of behavior. If monster truck racing had existed in his day, he might have interpreted it as a relatively undisguised manifestation of both sex and aggression.

Sex and Aggression as Motivating Forces

■ **4. *What is the significance of sex and aggression in Freud's theory?***

The normal source of unconscious motivation in Freud's theory is of course not the voice of a hypnotist, but rather the person's own inner, unconscious, instinctive drives. Freud was particularly interested in the sex drive, which he interpreted broadly as the main pleasure-seeking and life-seeking drive. The most direct ways of expressing this drive (and thereby obtaining pleasure) often run counter to the dictates of society. Therefore, the instinctive force, called ***libido***, that underlies this drive becomes redirected and provides the mental energy that motivates a wide range of thoughts and actions that at the surface do not appear to be sexual. Freud was also interested in the drive of aggression. Like sex, aggression must be controlled if people are to live peaceably in society, and Freud postulated that this drive too becomes redirected. Thus, in Freud's view, much of human behavior consists of disguised manifestations of sex and aggression.

Routes to the Unconscious: Free Association, Dreams, and Mistakes

Freud believed that to understand his patients' actions and problems he had to learn about the content of their unconscious minds. But how could he do that if by definition the unconscious consists only of information that the patient cannot talk about? He could do it by *analyzing* certain aspects of their speech and other observable behavior. This is where the term *psychoanalysis* comes from. His technique was to treat the patient's behavior as clues to the unconscious. In detectivelike fashion he collected clues and tried to piece them together into a coherent story about the unconscious causes of the person's conscious thought and behavior.

What sorts of clues would be most useful? Since the conscious mind always attempts to act in ways that are consistent with conventional logic, Freud reasoned that those elements of thought and behavior that are *least* logical would provide the best clues to the unconscious. They would represent elements of the unconscious mind that leaked out relatively unmodified by consciousness.

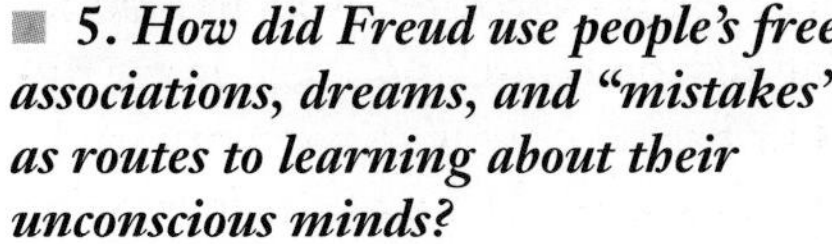
■ **5. *How did Freud use people's free associations, dreams, and "mistakes" as routes to learning about their unconscious minds?***

To encourage a flow of such clues, Freud developed the technique of ***free association***. He instructed patients to sit back (or lie down on a couch), relax, free their minds from the constraints of conventional logic, and report every image and idea that entered their awareness, no matter how absurd it might seem. As an exercise, you might try this technique on yourself, recording your session on tape or writing down each idea that comes to you. When you review the associations you produce, you may find them fascinating; you might feel that you can infer from them certain wishes, fears, or thoughts that you would not otherwise admit to yourself.

Freud also used the technique of asking patients to describe their dreams to him. According to Freud's theory, a dream is the purest exercise of free association. During sleep, conventional logic is largely absent, and the forces that normally hold down unconscious ideas are weakened. Still, even in dreams the unconscious

Figure 16.1 ***Freudian symbols in a work of art painted 4 centuries before Freud***

This is a detail from *The Garden of Earthly Delights*, painted in the late fifteenth century by the Dutch artist Hieronymus Bosch. It is believed to represent Bosch's conception of decadence or hell. Notice the dreamlike (nightmarish) quality and the numerous Freudian symbols.

is partially disguised. Freud distinguished the underlying, unconscious meaning of the dream (the *latent content*) from the dream as it is consciously experienced and remembered by the dreamer (the *manifest content*). The analyst's task in interpreting a dream is the same as that in interpreting any other form of free association—to see through the disguises and uncover the latent content from the manifest content. The disguises in dreams come in many forms. Some are unique to a particular person, but some are universal (which, according to Freud, makes the analyst's job much easier). These universal disguises have become known as ***Freudian symbols***, some of which were described by Freud (1900/1953) as follows (also see Figure 16.1):

> The Emperor and Empress (or King and Queen) as a rule really represent the dreamer's parents; and a Prince or Princess represents the dreamer himself or herself. . . . All elongated objects, such as sticks, tree-trunks, and umbrellas (the opening of these last being comparable to an erection) may stand for the male organ—as well as all long, sharp weapons, such as knives, daggers, and pikes. . . . Boxes, cases, chests, cupboards, and ovens represent the uterus, and also hollow objects, ships, and vessels of all kinds. Rooms in dreams are usually women; if the various ways in and out of them are represented, this interpretation is scarcely open to doubt. In this connection interest in whether the room is open or locked is easily intelligible. There is no need to name explicitly the key that unlocks the room.

Still another route to the unconscious for Freud was to analyze mistakes, especially slips of the tongue, that occur in everyday behavior. In Freud's view, mistakes are never simply random accidents, but are expressions of unconscious wishes. In one of his most popular books, *The Psychopathology of Everyday Life*, Freud (1901/1960) backed up this claim with numerous examples of such errors, along with his interpretation. For example, he reported an incident in which a young woman, complaining about the disadvantages of being a woman, stated, "A woman must be pretty if she is to please the men. A man is much better off. As long as he has his *five straight limbs* he needs no more." According to Freud, this slip involved a fusion of two separate clichés, *four straight limbs* and *five senses*, which would not have occurred had it not expressed an idea that was on the woman's mind (either unconscious or conscious) that she consciously would have preferred to conceal. In another context the same statement could have been a deliberate, slightly off-color joke; but Freud claims that in this case it was an honest slip of the tongue, as evidenced by the woman's embarrassment upon realizing what she had said.

Just as he believed that slips of the tongue are meaningful, Freud also believed that instances of forgetting are meaningful. For example, when a person forgets a previously well-known word or phrase, the unconscious motive is to protect the conscious mind from some idea associated with that word or phrase. To illustrate this point, Freud (1901/1960) described an incident in which a young man he met on vacation was unable to recall the Latin word *aliquis* while trying to quote a line from Virgil's *Aeneid*. As a challenge, the young man, aware of Freud's theories, asked Freud to explain why he had been unable to think of that particular word. Taking up the challenge, Freud said that he could answer the question only if the man would undergo the procedure of free association and say aloud, uncensored, every idea that came to his mind after first saying the word *aliquis*. In the ensuing chain of associations, *aliquis* brought forth the idea of *liquid*, which brought forth the idea of *blood*, which brought forth a number of other ideas, including two saints—St. Januarius and St. Augustine—the first of whom was involved in the "miracle of the blood" and both of whom have names that are associated with months of the calendar. Putting together the ideas of month, blood, and certain other notions that had come from the man's associations, Freud announced that he had solved the mystery. He asked the young man if it were not true that a lady friend of his had recently failed to show her monthly menstrual period! Amazed, the young man confessed that this was true and that indeed he had reason to fear she might be pregnant. According to Freud, the man's unconscious mind had caused him to forget the word *aliquis* to protect his conscious mind from being reminded of a possibility that he greatly feared.

Divisions of the Mind: Id, Ego, Superego

■ ***6. In Freud's theory, what are the functions of the id, ego, and superego? How do those functions conflict with one another?***

To explain the kinds of conflicts that seemed to reside in the minds of his patients and others he knew, Freud (1933/1964) postulated that the mind consists of three often conflicting components: the id, the ego, and the superego.

The ***id*** is the basic source of mental energy in Freud's theory. It is the entire set of drives with which a person is born, and its only goal is the gratification of those drives. It operates in strict accordance with the *pleasure principle*: Find pleasure (through the gratification of drives) and avoid pain. It has no concern for right or wrong, no respect for constraints imposed by the environment, and, for that matter, no appreciation of reality. If the id generates a wish for which there is no available object of gratification, it can satisfy itself simply through imagination. This kind of thinking, in which reality and fantasy are not differentiated, is referred to by Freud as the ***primary process***. The closest we come to experiencing such thought consciously is in dreams, in which primary-process thought emerges into consciousness in least-disguised form.

The ***ego***, which develops in infancy as an outgrowth of the id, is the part of the mind that permits a person to function reasonably in the environment. It operates according to the *reality principle*: A wish can be gratified only if a means for gratification is available in the environment. The ego includes, among other things, a person's understanding of reality and capacity for logic. Freud referred to the ego's mode of thinking, which involves conscious perception of the environment and logical thought, as the ***secondary process***. In accordance with the reality principle, the ego prevents the individual from being satisfied completely by fantasies. Your ego tells you that if you want to become a famous psychologist, you must study and work hard in the real world, not simply daydream about being a famous psychologist. The ego is also the great arbiter of the mind. It works out compromises among the demands of the id, the superego, and external reality.

The ***superego*** develops in early childhood as another outgrowth of the id. It is the internalized representation of society's moral rules, which the child acquires primarily through interaction with his or her parents. Its purpose is to oppose the gratification of drives when the means to gratification would violate morality. Its main weapon toward that end is its ability to create the painful feeling of guilt, which the pleasure-seeking id and the peace-seeking ego strive to avoid. Perhaps you could become a famous psychologist by fabricating data—pretending you had done experiments that you really hadn't. Your id would approve of that, and so would your ego if it thought you could get away with it. But your superego would create such a strong sense of guilt that your ego, constantly striving for tranquility, would shut the thought off before it was acted upon.

Look at Figure 16.2 to see the relationship between each of these three components and the unconscious-conscious distinction discussed earlier. Notice that the id is entirely unconscious and that the superego and ego are each partly conscious and partly unconscious. The superego includes not only one's conscious, declarable moral premises, but also one's deep-seated, unconscious, unreasoned moral forces. The ego includes not only one's conscious knowledge of the world, but also one's *repressed memories*, that is, memories so anxiety provoking that they have been pushed into the unconscious and can't be recalled through normal retrieval procedures. In addition, the processes by which the ego interacts with the id and superego are unconscious.

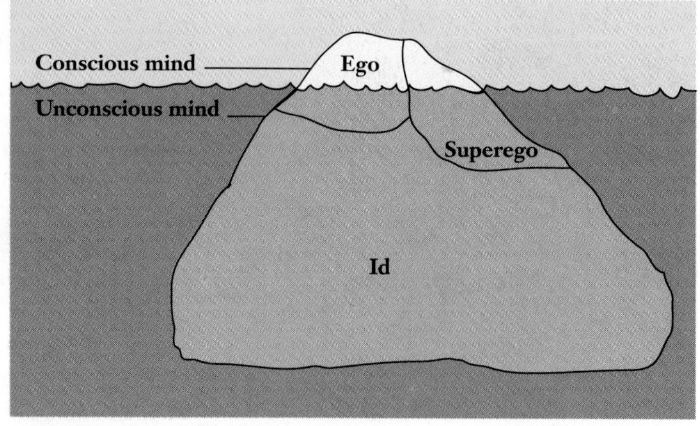

Figure 16.2 ***Freud's divisions of the mind***
The conscious mind is depicted here as the visible tip of an iceberg, and the unconscious mind as the much larger mass that is submerged. Notice that the id is entirely unconscious and that the ego and superego are partly conscious and partly unconscious. (Adapted from Freud, 1933/1964.)

Anxiety and the Ego's Defense Mechanisms

■ ***7. What are three sources of anxiety in Freud's theory, and how do various defense mechanisms reduce the ego's conscious experience of anxiety?***

In Freud's model, the ego has the most direct control of conscious thought and behavior. It attempts to exert that control in such a way as to meet the demands of three different forces that act on it: the real world, the id, and the superego. These forces exert their demands by producing *anxiety*, defined by Freud (1926/1964) as the unpleasant feeling that accompanies the ego's sense of impending danger. The real world contains real dangers, such as a snake about to bite or a threatened loss of job and income. The id contains dangers in the form of its strong drives and desires, which, if not controlled, could cause a person to behave in self-destructive ways (such as jumping off a cliff to experience the pleasure of flight). The superego poses the danger of crippling the ego with guilt if it recognizes an action as violating a moral stricture. Freud gave separate names to the anxieties stemming from each of these three sources: *Reality anxiety* is the ego's fear of threats in the real world, *neurotic anxiety* is the ego's fear of the id's irrational wishes, and *moral anxiety* is the ego's fear of the guilt that the superego can produce.

How does the ego reduce anxiety? It may do so in some cases through realistic problem solving. For example, it may reduce the threat of job loss by causing the person to look for a more secure job. In other cases, however, the ego may reduce anxiety through means of self-deception, which are referred to as ***defense mechanisms***. The theory of defense mechanisms was most thoroughly developed by Anna Freud (1936/1946), Sigmund's daughter, who herself became a psychoanalyst. Among the most common defense mechanisms are repression, displacement, reaction formation, projection, and rationalization.

Repression is the process by which the ego keeps anxiety-provoking wishes or memories out of the conscious mind. Repression holds the id's fearsome wishes down in the unconscious id, preventing them from entering and threatening the ego. A person who is afraid of sexual wishes may repress them so they do not enter consciousness. Repression also pushes anxiety-provoking memories out of consciousness, into the unconscious portion of the ego. For example, at age 5 a young friend of mine witnessed a person with a knife attack his father. A day later, when his father tried to talk to him about the incident, the boy appeared to have no memory of it at all; he didn't know what his father was talking about. Given the circumstances, it seems unlikely that he was pretending not to remember. The thought that his father (who was his only parent) might be killed was apparently so threatening that he had repressed the entire incident.

Defense!!!

The rerouting of aggression into sports—an example of Freud's construct *sublimation*—offers rewards to players and fans alike. Although Freud based his notion of defenses on observations of disordered behavior, he recognized their adaptive functions in everyday life.

According to Freud, some degree of repression is essential to normal functioning, but too much is harmful. In Freud's theory, a person has only a certain allotment of mental energy, so if too much is bound up in the active process of repression there will be little left for other activities. People who are highly repressed have so little energy left that they behave in stilted, wooden, nonspontaneous ways. Also, repression of the id's wishes reduces the opportunity to gratify those wishes consciously, and hence reduces a person's experience of pleasure. With little energy and little pleasure, the repressed person is at risk of becoming depressed.

Repression provides the basis for most of the other defense mechanisms. Freud visualized repression as a damming up of a pool of mental energy. Just as water will leak through any crack in a dam, repressed wishes and memories will leak through the walls of repression, into the conscious part of the ego, wherever the barrier is not perfect. When such material leaks through, however, the ego can still defend itself by distorting the ideas in ways that make them less threatening. The other defense mechanisms are the means to such distortion.

Displacement occurs when a drive that was directed toward one activity by the id is redirected by the ego toward a safer activity that is symbolically equivalent to the original. For example, a child long past infancy may still have a desire, in the id, to suck at the mother's breast—a desire that is now threatening and repressed, because it violates the superego's assessment of what is proper and the ego's assessment of what is possible. When this desire enters the ego it may be displaced, say, toward sucking a lollipop—an action that is both realistic and morally acceptable. In some cases, displacement may direct the id's energies toward activities that are particularly valued by society, such as artistic, scientific, or humanitarian endeavors. These displacements, which are most in line with the ideals of the superego, are referred to as ***sublimations***. A highly aggressive person, for example, may perform valuable service in a competitive profession as sublimation of the drive to beat others. In a book on the life of Leonardo da Vinci, Freud (1910/1947) suggested that da Vinci's fascination with painting Madonnas was a sublimation of his desire for his mother, which had been frustrated by his separation from her.

Reaction formation is the turning of a frightening wish into its safer opposite. For example, a young woman who unconsciously hates her mother and wishes her dead may consciously experience these feelings as intense love for her mother and strong concern for her safety.

Projection occurs when a person consciously experiences his or her own unconscious emotion or wish as though it were someone else's. A person with intense, unconscious anger may project that anger onto her friend—that is, she may feel that it is her friend, not she, who is angry.

Rationalization is the use of conscious reasoning to explain away anxiety-provoking thoughts or feelings. A man who cannot face his own sadistic tendencies may rationalize the beatings he gives his children by convincing himself that children need to be beaten and that he is only carrying out his fatherly duty. Freud's theory encourages us to be wary of conscious logic, since it often serves to mask true feelings and wishes.

Freud's View of Personality Development

Personality, as defined earlier, refers to the more or less consistent differences among people in their behavioral styles. In Freud's theory, personality is composed of the characteristic ways that individuals channel their inborn mental energy, especially their libido. These characteristics emerge from an interaction between the child's wish-fulfilling behaviors and the way that others, especially parents, react to those behaviors early in childhood. Freud conceived of personality development as a progression through five stages, now referred to as ***psychosexual stages***: the *oral, anal, phallic, latency,* and *genital* stages. The most important are the first three, which occur within the first 5 years of life. Freud believed that by the end of the phallic stage a person's basic personality is fixed. Behavior continues to change after age 5 as a result of such factors as bodily maturation and new learning, but those changes simply represent new ways of expressing one's personality, not changes in the personality itself.

The names of the first three stages refer to different parts of the body that Freud considered to be *erogenous zones*—the areas where sexual pleasure is experienced. Thus, each of these stages is associated with a particular type of sexual pleasure and a particular orientation toward the world for gaining pleasure. As a person passes through each stage, some portion of the total libido may become *fixated* at that stage. ***Fixation*** at any stage means that to some degree the person will, throughout life, attempt to achieve pleasure in ways that are symbolically equivalent to the ways that pleasure was achieved at that stage in childhood. Fixation can occur because of either too little gratification at a given stage (the person goes through life trying to find what was missed) or too much gratification (the person has no motivation to move beyond that stage). Let us examine briefly each stage and the contribution it can make to adult personality.

The Oral and Anal Stages and Styles

■ **8.** ***According to Freud, what are the effects of fixation at (a) the oral stage and (b) the anal stage?***

During the *oral stage*—roughly the first year of life—pleasure comes from taking things into the mouth and sucking on them, especially the mother's breast. The infant at this stage is a relatively passive receiver of pleasure, which is given by another person more or less at the infant's demand. Fixation at this stage can have a number of possible consequences for adult personality. At the most direct behavioral level, it may lead to continued oral activities, such as gum chewing, smoking, or overeating. More important, the oral drive can be displaced toward symbolic

Too much pleasure?

Freud believed that gratification as well as deprivation can cause fixation at a developmental stage. If he could have seen this infant's unrestrained enjoyment, he might have predicted future resistance to toilet training.

■ **9. *In Freud's theory, what is the oedipal crisis, and how does its incomplete resolution influence personality in men and women?***

ways of taking in. Orally fixated individuals may go through life trying to take in such things as knowledge, love, or money—often in demanding ways, expecting others to feed them whatever it is that they want.

During the *anal stage*—roughly the second year—the focus of pleasure is the anus, which is stimulated most directly through the passing of feces. The most significant activity now is toilet training, in which the child is for the first time subjected to parental demands. The demands produce mental conflict in the child. On the one hand, the child wishes to gain immediate pleasure by expelling feces whenever there is an urge to do so. On the other hand, the child wishes to gain the parental praise that would come from holding feces in and expelling them only in the toilet. Fixation at the anal stage implies continued conflict between the drive to hold feces in and the drive to expel them. Through displacement, the holding in may take the form of stinginess, excessive neatness, and rigidity of behavior; and the expelling may take the form of generosity, messiness, and creativity or looseness of behavior. Some anally fixated people are at one end of this spectrum, others are at the other end, and still others are at different ends in different realms of their life (one may keep a messy kitchen but a neat notebook).

The Phallic Stage and Oedipal Crisis

During the *phallic stage*—from about age 3 to 5—the penis becomes the focus of pleasure for the boy, and the lack of a penis becomes the critical issue in the girl's development. The boy's discovery of the pleasure of masturbation is mixed with love of his mother, who has satisfied all his needs so far. His id becomes filled with sexual fantasies directed toward his mother and aggressive fantasies directed toward his father, whom he fears and hates as the main rival for his mother's attention. Freud referred to this set of wishes and emotions as the ***oedipal crisis***, named for the tragic hero of Sophocles' play *Oedipus Rex* (who unknowingly killed his father and married his mother). In Freud's theory, the boy eventually resolves the oedipal crisis by identifying with his father, that is, by thinking of himself in some sense as his father. In this way he can stop hating and fearing his father, and he can indirectly (through his father) satisfy his sexual desire for his mother. If a satisfactory identification with the father does not take place, the boy will fail to resolve completely the oedipal crisis. Fixated at the phallic stage, he may be compelled to go through life trying to prove that he is a man, constantly putting on a show of toughness and repressing the gentler side of his nature.

The girl's phallic stage centers on her discovery that boys have a penis and she doesn't. Her sense of deprivation, referred to as *penis envy* (not one of Freud's more popular concepts today), causes her to turn against her mother, who also lacks a penis and whom the girl blames for her own lack, and to develop a sexual longing for her father, who possesses the organ that she would like to have. Eventually, the girl resolves her oedipal crisis (sometimes called the *electra crisis* for Electra, the Greek tragic heroine who conspired to murder her mother) by identifying with her mother and symbolically possessing her father through her mother. Fixation at the phallic stage for a woman implies failure to form a successful identification with the mother, and therefore failure to overcome penis envy. The fixated woman will go through life feeling inferior to men. Consequently, she may attempt to satisfy her needs through men (especially older men, who are father figures), using seductive and flirtatious behaviors to keep their attention. Or she may attempt to dominate men, symbolically castrating them, to overcome her sense of inferiority.

In both sexes, fixation at the phallic stage also implies failure to overcome the incestuous desire for the opposite-sex parent. Sexuality in such individuals is therefore tinged with the fear and guilt associated with incest. Both the male and the female may appear highly sexual, but deep down they are afraid of sex.

Beyond Age Five

The remaining two stages occupy the bulk of life, during which the already-formed personality plays itself out in various kinds of interaction with the world. The *latency stage*—from age 5 or 6 to the onset of puberty—is a time of repressed sexuality, during which libido is displaced into such midchildhood activities as hobbies, athletics, school learning, and making friends. At puberty, sexuality reappears in a new form, oriented in a more realistic way toward other people and less toward the person's own body, marking the onset of the *genital stage*, which lasts to the end of life. Libido is now invested in activities that lead to the *generation* of new life, such as falling in love, marrying, raising children, and caring for other people. (The term *genital* is misleading as the name for this stage, since now, unlike in the phallic stage, sexuality goes beyond sensations in the genitals. It is unfortunate that Freud's translators didn't call it the *generative stage*, since that better expresses Freud's meaning.) Of course, the way a person meets the tasks of the genital stage depends on how crises were met and resolved in the first three stages. If too much libido is fixated at earlier stages, little will be left for the adult tasks. As Freud (1935/1960) once put it, the healthy adult finds pleasure in love and work, which are the central generative tasks. The unhealthy adult doesn't, because energy is tied up in infantile wishes and fears.

A distinguished gathering

In 1909, Freud and several disciples journeyed to Clark University in Massachusetts, where he gave a series of lectures on psychoanalysis. The invitation was arranged by psychologist G. Stanley Hall, seated between Freud (left) and Jung (right) in the front row.

Post-Freudian Psychodynamic Theories

Freud's work inspired many clinicians throughout Europe to learn his theory and approach to therapy, and some subsequently developed theories of their own that differed substantially from Freud's. Four of the most prominent of these post-Freudian psychodynamic theorists are Alfred Adler (1870–1937), Carl Jung (1875–1961), Karen Horney (1885–1952), and Erik Erikson (1902–).

Adler lived in Vienna and was a close associate of Freud's from 1902 to 1911, but then split with Freud and developed a theory centering on people's sense of competence or incompetence. Jung was a Swiss psychoanalyst who exchanged hundreds of letters with Freud between 1906 and 1913, but then split with him and developed a complex, somewhat mystical theory focusing on the need to achieve a balance among various contrary inner forces that make up the personality. Horney, who began a psychoanalytic practice in Berlin in 1918, was one of the first female psychoanalysts. She opposed some of Freud's male-centered ideas, including his view that women suffer from penis envy, and developed a theory centering on the need for security. Erikson studied under Anna Freud (Sigmund's daughter) in Vienna and then went on to enjoy a long career in the United States as a researcher and child psychoanalyst. His theory of the stages of personality development was discussed in Chapter 13. All four of these theorists placed less emphasis on the sex drive, and more emphasis on other social needs, than did Freud.

■ **10.** ***How do most post-Freudian psychodynamic theories resemble Freud's theory and differ from it?***

Although each of these theories (and others that could be listed) differ substantially from Freud's, they retain certain core Freudian ideas that mark them as psychodynamic theories. Among these ideas are that (a) unconscious mental forces underlie and help determine a person's conscious thought and behavior; (b) these unconscious forces work largely by producing anxiety, which the person strives to reduce through his or her modes of thought and action (personality style); and (c) early childhood experiences are especially influential in shaping one's personality. In addition to sharing characteristics acquired from Freud's theory, most post-Freudian psychodynamic theories share with each other certain characteristics that tend to differentiate them as a group from Freud's theory. Among these are their strong emphases on (a) social needs, (b) the need for self-esteem, and (c) the value of psychological wholeness.

Social Needs

■ **11.** ***How are ego-social needs exemplified in Horney's and Erikson's theories?***

Freud viewed people as basically asocial, forced into society more by necessity than desire, and interacting principally in terms of sex, aggression, and displaced forms of these. In contrast, most post-Freudian theorists have viewed people as inherently social beings whose needs for others extend well beyond sex and aggression. These needs are generally seen as belonging to the ego rather than to the id, and therefore are referred to as *ego-social needs*. Among them are the needs for the security and favorable evaluation that others can provide and the need to sense that one is contributing to others.

Karen Horney
One of the first psychoanalysts to offer a rebuttal to Freud's ideas about women, Horney argued that psychoanalysis must consider facts about women's social circumstances as well as their anatomy.

Different theories emphasize different ego-social needs. Horney's theory focuses on *security* as an inborn human need that can be filled only by other people. A central concept in her theory is that of *basic anxiety*, which she defined as "the feeling a child has of being isolated and helpless in a potentially hostile world" (Horney, 1945). In her theory, parents influence a child's lifelong personality through the ways in which they succeed or fail in helping the child feel secure. A child who finds security in relating to parents will continue to find security in other relationships throughout life. A child who fails to find security in relating to parents will grow up feeling insecure and distrustful of others (Horney, 1937). This distrust may manifest itself in any of three unhappy personality styles: avoiding others, consistently giving in to others, or dominating others.

Erikson's theory identifies a variety of ego-social needs and proposes that different ones predominate at different stages of development. Infants most need security, children most need support and encouragement for their independence and skills, adolescents most need models to help them form adult identities, young adults most need intimacy, and older adults most need to care for others. At each stage, the manner in which these needs are met influences the personality that enters the next stage. (A more complete summary of Erikson's theory can be found in Table 13.1 in Chapter 13.)

The Need for Self-Esteem

The need for self-esteem can be thought of as one of the social needs, since a person's sense of self-esteem depends very much on feedback from other people (an idea discussed in Chapter 14). This need and the anxiety it produces was especially emphasized by Alfred Adler (1930), who argued that everyone begins life with a feeling of inferiority that stems from the helpless and dependent nature of early childhood. In Adler's theory, the manner in which people learn to cope with or to overcome this feeling provides the basis for their lifelong personality. Some people are overwhelmed by their sense of inferiority and develop an *inferiority complex*, meaning that they go through life feeling inadequate and dependent. Others develop a *superiority complex*, which is really a mask for their sense of inferiority; their attempt to overcome inferiority centers on trying to prove that they are better than other people. The psychologically healthy person has neither of these complexes, but rather has a mature sense of his or her own abilities and worth (high self-esteem) and can direct those abilities toward socially useful achievements.

■ **12.** ***How does the need for self-esteem figure into Adler's and Horney's theories?***

Self-esteem is also a crucial idea in Horney's theory. Horney (1950) proposed that people have two self-images—an *ideal self* and a *real self*—and that to relieve anxiety people strive to make the real more like the ideal. Those whose ideal self is unrealistic, overly discrepant from their real self, go through life with low self-esteem and suffer from the *tyranny of the should*, the constant, anxious feeling that they *should* be doing things differently or better than they currently are. Psychologically healthy individuals, in contrast, have a close enough fit between their ideal and real selves to feel good about themselves and their activities.

The Value of Psychological Wholeness

In Freud's theory, the mind contains separate, often conflicting components, and the ego must work out compromises among them. Theorists since Freud have often viewed the ego as not just an arbiter but an integrator, a device to produce cohesion and harmony among the mind's potentially conflicting forces. This idea is most prominent in Carl Jung's theory of personality.

■ **13.** ***In Jung's theory, what is meant by psychological wholeness?***

Jung's (1968) very complex theory includes the idea that the mind contains various forces, which, for optimal mental health, must be brought into balance by an integrating force called the *Self* (a concept roughly analogous to Freud's *ego*). Many of these forces are polar opposites of one another. Each person has a *persona* (a mask, or outer person, presented to others) and a *shadow* (a dark, deep, passionate inner person capable of evil). Each person also has an *anima* (the female side of the person) and an *animus* (the male side). In addition, each person has two opposing orientations to the world: *introversion* (orientation toward the inner world of thoughts and feelings) and *extroversion* (orientation toward the external world of things and people). These forces, when integrated, do not have to conflict; they can complement one another to produce a sense of wholeness and an ability to deal with life's challenges. In Jung's view, a psychologically healthy person is one who can accept and use constructively all sides of his or her human nature rather than allow any one side to dominate at the expense of its opposite.

Research into Defensive Styles

Perhaps the most central idea unifying all psychodynamic theories is this: People differ in their characteristic ways of defending themselves against anxiety, and those differences affect all aspects of their lives. Not surprisingly, much of the research on personality that has been inspired by psychodynamic theories is concerned with defense mechanisms. Can people be reliably categorized according to the kinds of defenses they use, and does that categorization allow us to make meaningful predictions about other aspects of their lives?

Evidence for the Existence of Defensive Styles

■ **14.** ***How did Sears demonstrate the existence of projection as a defense mechanism?***

Many years ago, when the theory of defenses was still quite new, Robert Sears (1936) performed a study to see if one particular defense mechanism—projection—could be demonstrated to exist. Recall that projection is the unconscious attribution to others of characteristics that actually exist in oneself. Sears asked members of college fraternity houses to rate themselves and each of their housemates, confidentially, on such traits as *stinginess vs. generosity* and *obstinacy vs. agreeableness.* He found that some of the men were rated by their housemates as extreme on a given trait but rated themselves as either neutral on that trait or tending in the other direction. They apparently lacked conscious insight about their own trait. In keeping with the view that projection occurs in such cases, Sears found that these men rated their housemates as unusually high on the same traits that they failed to see in themselves, but not unusually high on other traits. In contrast, fraternity members who were rated high on a trait and had insight (that is, who also rated themselves high) did not show this tendency to rate others high on the trait.

■ **15.** ***How do people identified as* repressers *respond differently from others in laboratory studies?***

More recently, a group of researchers including Daniel Weinberger and Gary Schwartz performed a series of studies on repression. They identified with a questionnaire people who seemed to repress their emotional experiences and then studied these repressers to see if they differed from others in their responses to emotionally provocative situations. When asked to complete sentences that contained sexual or aggressive themes, repressers claimed not to feel stressed, yet by physiological indices (heart rate, muscle tension, and sweating) they manifested more stress than other subjects who claimed that they did feel stressed (Weinberger, 1990; Weinberger & others, 1979). In other tests, repressers recalled fewer childhood emotional experiences and were found less likely to report noticing or remembering emotion-arousing words or phrases in messages presented during the experiment than were nonrepressers (Bonanno & others, 1991; Davis & Schwartz, 1987).

Evidence That Some Defensive Styles Are Healthier Than Others

In the late 1930s, an ambitious longitudinal study was begun of men who at the time were sophomores at Harvard University. Each year until 1955, and less often after that, the men were asked to fill out an extensive questionnaire concerning such issues as their work, ambitions, social relationships, emotions, and health. Nearly thirty years after the study had begun, when the men were in their late 40s, a research team headed by George Vaillant (1977) interviewed in depth 95 of these men, selected by a random procedure. By systematically analyzing the content and the style of their responses in the interview and in the previous questionnaires, the researchers rated the extent to which each man used specific defense mechanisms.

■ **16.** ***What relationships did Vaillant find between defensive styles and measures of life satisfaction?***

Vaillant divided the various defense mechanisms into three categories according to his judgment of the degree to which they would promote either ineffective or effective behavior. *Immature defenses* were those presumed to distort reality the most and lead to the most ineffective behavior. Projection was included in this category. *Intermediate defenses*, including repression and reaction formation, were presumed to involve less distortion of reality and lead to somewhat more effective coping. *Mature defenses* were presumed to involve the least distortion of reality and lead to the most adaptive behaviors. One of the most common of the mature defenses was *suppression*, which involves the conscious avoidance of negative thinking. Suppression differs from repression in that the negative information remains available to the conscious mind and can be thought about constructively when the person chooses to do so. Another defense in the mature category was *humor*, which, according to Freud and other psychodynamic theorists, stems from fears that may be either conscious or unconscious (for a comparable view, see the discussion of the evolutionary basis of laughter, in Chapter 4).

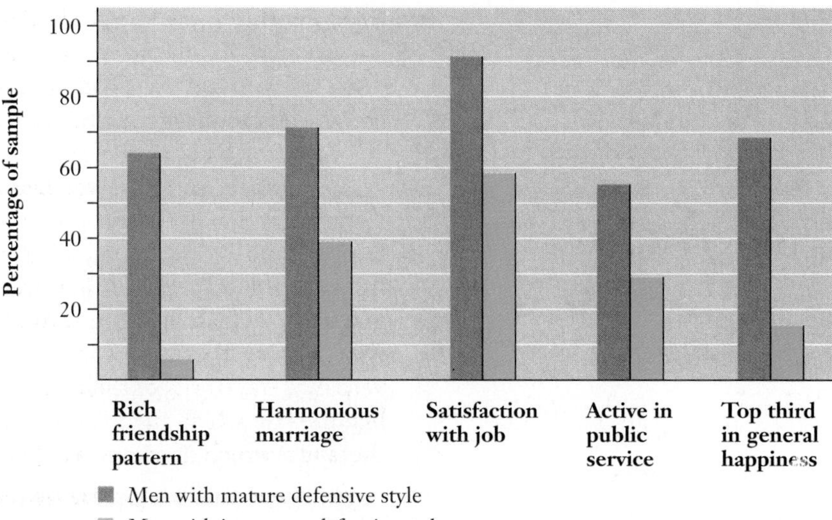

Figure 16.3 ***Love, work, and happiness in men with mature and immature defensive styles***
Harvard alumni who were classed as using primarily mature defenses were more frequently rated as having rich friendships, a good marriage, satisfaction with their work, active involvement in public service, and a high degree of happiness than those who were classed as using primarily immature defenses (data from Vaillant, 1977).

Consistent with Vaillant's expectations, those men who used the most mature defenses were the most successful at all measures of love and work (Freud's criteria for mature adulthood) and were also, by their own reports, the happiest. For comparisons of the 25 men classed as using mainly mature defenses with the 31 classed as using mainly immature defenses, see Figure 16.3. Subsequently, Vaillant found similar results with a group of men from a working-class background and a group of women who had been identified in childhood as unusually bright (Vaillant & Vaillant, 1992). Of course such correlations do not prove that mature defenses help *cause* successful coping, but they do show that mature defenses and such success tend to go together. Vaillant (1977) also found, not surprisingly, that as the Harvard men matured—from age 19 into their 40s—the average maturity of their defenses increased. Immature defenses such as projection declined, and mature defenses such as suppression and humor increased.

Critique of Psychodynamic Theories

17. ***How have psychodynamic theories, particularly Freud's, been criticized for the subjectiveness of the evidence and the vagueness of the terms and concepts?***

Freud's theory, which still reigns as the prototypical psychodynamic theory, has been described by both admirers and critics as creative (which is not always praise) and insightful (also, incite-full to some). Freud called himself a scientist, but psychologists engaged in scientific research have always been among his harshest critics. Many have argued that Freud's genius was not that of a scientist, but closer to that of a novelist or playwright. He gleaned insights from his patients and worked them into fascinating dramas, the main characters of which lay deep in the patient's mind. To appreciate this more fully, read one or more of his case histories, such as *The "Rat Man"* (described in Chapter 18) or *The Psychotic Doctor Schreber*. From the vantage point of modern scientific psychology, the most common criticisms of Freud's theory, and of psychodynamic theories in general, are the two summarized below:

- ***Limitations of the data*** All psychodynamic theories are based primarily on clinical evidence subjectively interpreted by the theorist, who is also usually a psychotherapist. Such evidence has inherent limitations. Clients who seek psychotherapy are not a representative sample of humanity. The great emphasis that psychodynamic theories place on the role of anxiety in personality processes may reflect the high anxiety levels that characterize people who seek psychotherapy. The clients treated by any given theorist may be narrowly defined in other respects as well. Freud's patients were mostly wealthy citizens of Vienna who had the leisure and inclination to reflect on their childhoods, subtleties of their sex lives, and other such topics that might have been of less concern to people struggling to put food on the table.

Another limitation of such clinically derived data is the lack of safeguards against subject and observer biasing effects (discussed in Chapter 2). Freud's clients, for example, were aware of his theories; they came to him because his theories appealed to them. This awareness and attraction surely must have influenced the contents of their free associations, dream reports, and childhood memories, which Freud in turn used to confirm his theory. Freud did not take notes during therapy sessions, and even today psychotherapists rarely record verbatim the words of their clients. Thus, anyone wishing to evaluate the case histories on which theories are built must rely upon the interpretations of the therapist, which of course would be influenced by that person's biases.

- ***Vague terms and untestable concepts*** Good science is different from good poetry. In poetry, a word or phrase may be valued precisely because it can inspire a multitude of interpretations. But scientists must take pains to state clearly and literally what they mean. Terms have to be defined in such a manner that all readers will get the same meaning. Flexibility of meaning poses a problem in Freud's writing and in that of many other psychodynamic theorists. For example, Freud attributes an enormous amount of human behavior to the sex drive, so it makes a difference how he defines that drive. Does he literally mean the drive to copulate, or does he mean the drive for any bodily pleasure? The theory loses much of its plausibility if the former is true, and much of its punch if the latter is true. By playing it both ways, Freud keeps some measure of plausibility while retaining the punch—good literature, but bad science.

  Partly because of the vagueness of terms and concepts, it is hard to imagine how some of Freud's central ideas could be tested scientifically. Take, for instance, his concept that all children experience an oedipal wish—to have sex with the opposite-sex parent. How could you ever prove that concept right or wrong if you added to it (as Freud did) that the wish may be entirely unconscious and expressed only in masked ways? If you begin with the assumption that Freud is right, you can easily explain almost anything a child does as an expression of the oedipal wish. For example, every instance in which a child crawls into bed with a parent could be interpreted as oedipal behavior. But if you begin with the assumption that Freud was not right, you could find a dozen other plausible ways of explaining the same behavior; for example, the child might be seeking warmth or security.

18. *How has Freud's work affected Western culture and the science of psychology?*

For better or worse (most likely both), Freud's work has had an enormous impact on twentieth-century Western culture. Think of all the Freudian terms that can be heard in everyday conversation—*projection, repression, id, superego, oral fixation, anal retentiveness*, and so on. In art, music, and literature courses, you may hear your instructor apply Freudian terms to the process of creation, alluding perhaps to libidinal desires welling up from the creator's unconscious and spilling out in the flow of paint, notes, or words. Moreover, despite the rejection of Freud's specific theory by most scientific psychologists, his work has affected the course of scientific psychology in ways that most would agree are positive. By calling attention to the unconscious, irrational, emotional aspects of human nature, Freud helped direct psychology away from its comparatively sterile attempts in the late nineteenth century to understand the mind purely in terms of conscious thought. Also, by portraying even infants as mentally active beings and by calling attention to the role of early experience in personality development, Freud sparked interest in developmental psychology.

Humanistic Theories

In the emphasis of post-Freudian psychodynamic theories on social needs and conscious (ego) processes, you saw a movement away from Freud's pessimistic view that the person is driven by sexual and aggressive instincts that are necessarily at odds with the goals of society. The culmination of this movement—toward a more optimistic view of humanity—resides in the personality theories labeled *humanistic*.

In their founding of an official organization and a journal (the *Journal of Humanistic Psychology*, first published in 1961), the early leaders of the humanistic movement—including Carl Rogers, Abraham Maslow, Charlotte Buhler, Rollo May, Victor Frankl, and Thomas Szasz—declared themselves to be a "Third Force" in the science of psychology. The other two forces, seen as the dominant schools of thought at the time, were behaviorism and Freudian psychoanalysis. Rogers, Maslow, and the others argued that both of those forces missed the essential characteristics of being human, and thus tended to dehumanize the person. Behaviorism focused on simple learning processes, and Freud's theory focused on basic drives (sex and aggression) that we share with other animals. The goal of humanistic psychology was to emphasize the uniquely human aspects of the person.

Basic Tenets of Humanistic Psychology

■ **19.** ***How are humanistic theories characterized by their emphasis on phenomenology, their resistance to reductionism, and their concept of a self-actualizing drive?***

All humanistic personality theories are grounded in three principles, referred to as phenomenology, holism, and self-actualization.

The Phenomenological Approach to the Mind

Phenomenology is the study of subjective mental experiences. Humanistic theorists argue that people do not simply react to the physical reality of the world around them, but instead behave according to their mental interpretation of that reality, that is, according to their *phenomenological reality*. For example, if you are approached on a deserted street by a stranger, you behave in accordance with your interpretation of what the stranger is doing, which may or may not coincide with what the stranger is actually doing. An especially influential aspect of phenomenological reality is the *self-concept* (an idea that was also important in post-Freudian psychodynamic theories), defined as the set of beliefs that one has about oneself. Whether it is accurate or not, a person's self-concept helps determine how that person will behave. For example, a person who believes, rightly or wrongly, that he or she is socially incompetent will avoid social experiences.

Phenomenological reality

Humanistic personality theorists point out that people's subjective understanding of themselves and their world—their phenomenological reality—influences their feelings and behavior even if that understanding is objectively inaccurate.

The emphasis on phenomenological reality stems directly from the humanists' view that people (unlike animals) control their own actions through conscious decision making. Over time, each person acquires a unique set of beliefs, which collectively constitute his or her self-concept and understanding of the world, and which provide the foundation for decisions about how to behave. To know the person you must learn about those beliefs.

The Holistic View of the Person

Humanistic psychology is in part a reaction against the reductionism of other approaches. *Reductionism* is the attempt to understand an entity by reducing it to a set of basic elements. The early behaviorists' attempt to understand the flow of behavior by breaking it down into separate, reflexive, stimulus-response connections is one form of reductionism. Freud's attempt to break down the structure of personality into id, ego, and superego—each with its various components and energies—is another. Most humanistic psychologists do not deny the value of reductionism for understanding specific mental processes such as sensation or memory, but they argue that reductionism should be avoided in a personality theory, because a person is a unified whole that is more than the sum of its parts. A person is not just memory plus emotion plus reason, or learning plus instinct, or id plus ego plus superego, but rather is a single, unified entity that works toward goals that apply to the whole person. This is the principle of ***holism***.

The argument for a holistic approach can perhaps be made clearer by considering what would happen if you suddenly lost some particular aspect of your functioning. Suppose you suddenly became blind. At one moment you would be a person who could see, and the next you would be a person who couldn't. But that would be only the beginning. Over time you would change in ways that would allow you to continue to exist and grow mentally without vision. You would replace old hobbies and old ways of interacting with people with new ones. You would learn to use your other senses more efficiently than before, and you would strengthen certain aspects of your memory to compensate for the loss of ability to use visual cues. In a less dramatic way, everything that happens to you as you go through each day of life reverberates through your entire being, and anyone wishing to understand those happenings must consider you as a whole, not as a collection of separate parts.

The Actualizing Tendency

In contrast to psychodynamic theories, which emphasize the tendency to protect the self against anxiety and return to a more quiescent state, humanistic theories emphasize the positive tendency of a person to grow psychologically. The overriding, holistic purpose of individuals is ***self-actualization***—that is, to become what they are capable of becoming. What this means specifically will vary from person to person and from time to time in one's life. But for each individual, the goals of this process must come from within, and the route to their achievements can be chosen only by the person himself or herself. If the environment places obstacles in the way of actualization, one's whole being becomes oriented toward overcoming those obstacles.

Self-actualization

Humanistic theorists draw an analogy between the self-actualization process in humans and the inner growth potential of all living things. This beech tree has long been using its environment to promote its own growth, and these children have for a much shorter time been doing the same.

Carl Rogers

Rogers's humanistic theory centers on the self-concept and the ways in which it can be distorted by socially imposed conditions of worth.

Rogers (1963, 1977) often compared psychological actualization in humans to physical growth in plants. A tree growing on a cliff by the sea must battle against the wind and salt water, and it does not grow as well as it would in a better setting; yet, its inner potential continues to operate and it grows as best as it can under the circumstances. Nobody can tell the tree how to grow—its growth potential lies within itself.

Humanistic theorists do not ignore the role of the environment. Full growth, full actualization, requires a fertile environment. But the direction of actualization and the ways of using the environment must come from within the organism. In the course of evolution, organisms have acquired the capacity to use the environment in ways that maximize growth. In humans, some of these ways are experienced phenomenologically as free, conscious choices. This inner ability to make choices that promote positive psychological development is the actualizing tendency. To grow best, individuals must be permitted to make those choices and must trust themselves to do so.

Rogers's Theory

Carl Rogers (1902–1987) was born in Illinois, raised in a devoutly Protestant family, studied theology, earned a Ph.D. in clinical psychology, and enjoyed a long career as a psychotherapist, university professor, writer, and founder of various self-improvement groups. His theory of personality is often referred to as *self theory*, because its central construct is the person's sense of self. Rogers (1959) claimed that at first he avoided this construct because it seemed unscientific, but was forced to consider it after listening to his clients in therapy sessions. Person after person would say, "I feel I am not being my real self"; "I wouldn't want anyone to know the real me"; "I wonder who I am." From such statements, Rogers gradually came to believe that a concept of self is an important part of a person's phenomenological world and that the most general goal that people have when they enter therapy is "to become their real selves."

Incongruence and Conditions of Worth

■ **20. *What does it mean not to be oneself, according to Rogers, and how is the ability to be oneself affected by childhood experiences?***

But how, you might ask, can one *not* be oneself? If we look at this question in terms of physical reality, then of course the notion of not being yourself is ridiculous. By definition, whatever you are is you. But if people *feel* that they are not always themselves, then the phenomenological experience of self must be different from the physical self and its behavior. Rogers concluded that when people sense that they are not themselves, they are sensing an *incongruence* (discrepancy) between their self-concept and their actual thoughts or behavior.

What is the source of this incongruence? According to Rogers, it arises from *conditions of worth* that distort the self-concept and make it incompatible with normal human experience. Conditions of worth stem originally from judgments made by other people. For example, a little girl who is told that she is bad when she is feeling angry may come to exclude anger from her self-concept. Yet, being human, she can't avoid feeling angry at times, and this feeling makes her anxious because it is incongruent with her self-concept. To reduce that anxiety, and to maintain her self-concept, she may deny or distort her experiences of anger, but in doing so she thwarts her opportunity to grow psychologically from those experiences. Anger, like any other emotion, is an aspect of the actualizing tendency, and one must accept all aspects of that tendency if healthy growth is to occur.

Rogers's Views of Therapy, Parenting, and Education

■ **21. *Why, according to Rogers, should therapists, parents, and educators avoid evaluating and directing their clients, children, or students?***

In Rogers's view the main goal of psychotherapy is to allow clients to lose some of their dependence on other people's judgments (their conditions of worth) so that their self-concept and behavior can be more consistent with their actualizing tendency. The therapist accomplishes this by listening to and accepting everything that the client says without judging it. By accepting, empathizing with, and reflecting back all the client's thoughts and feelings, the therapist helps the client accept those aspects of the self that were being denied.

Ideal parents, according to Rogers, are those who affirm and accept all of a child's experiences and do not impose conditions of worth. Parents may have to control a child's behavior, but in doing so they can still show that they accept the child's feelings and experiences. If the angry little girl begins to destroy valuable objects, the parents should not say, "Stop being angry." Instead, they should say something like, "I understand that you are angry. That's okay. I get angry, too. But you're going to have to express it in a different way—I'm not going to let you break these things."

Regarding education, Rogers (1969) argued that the drive to learn is an inherent aspect of the actualizing tendency and that learning occurs best when it is self-motivated, self-directed, and involves the whole person (emotions and intellect). Rogers suggested that the term *facilitator* (short for facilitator of education) be substituted for *teacher* and proposed that facilitators should provide an atmosphere conducive to learning, but should not direct or coerce the child's learning.

■ **22.** ***What is some evidence supporting Rogers's view of the conditions that promote creativity?***

A central aspect of self-actualization is creativity. In a paper on that topic, Rogers (1954) predicted that creativity would be maximized by child-rearing practices that included (a) unconditional love and acceptance (no conditions of worth) and (b) freedom to explore ideas and modes of expression without external criticism or evaluation. Years later, David Harrington and his colleagues (1987) tested this prediction by examining data they had collected over an 11-year period concerning more than 100 children and their parents. Using questionnaires and direct observations to rate parenting style, and using teachers' ratings and other means to rate creativity, they found a strong positive correlation between a Rogerian parenting style in the preschool years and creativity in adolescence. Another source of support for Rogers's theory comes from a study suggesting that graduates of the Sudbury Valley School (described in Chapter 13), which operates in ways consistent with Rogers's theory, have been particularly successful in music, art, and other fields that require high creativity (Gray & Chanoff, 1986).

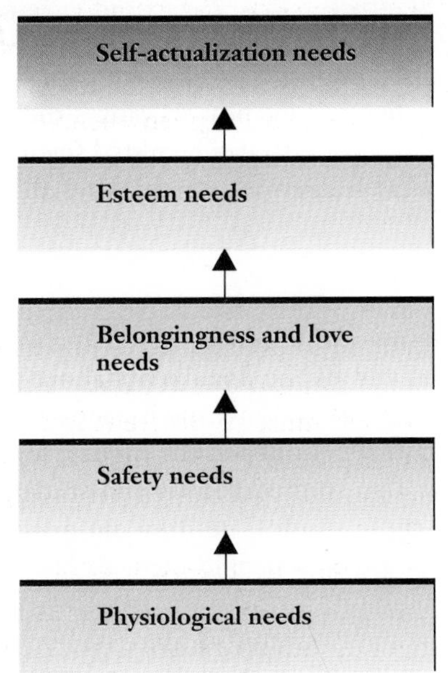

Figure 16.4 ***Maslow's hierarchy of human needs***

According to Maslow, needs at the lower portion of the hierarchy must be at least relatively satisfied before people can satisfy needs higher up. The most psychologically healthy people are those whose deficiency needs are sufficiently satisfied to free their energies for self-actualization.

Maslow's Theory

Abraham Maslow (1908–1970) was born in New York City of immigrant parents, received a Ph.D. in psychology studying dominance behavior in monkeys, left animal research to study human needs, and became one of the leaders of humanistic psychology. Unlike the other personality theorists discussed so far, Maslow was not a psychotherapist. Yet his method was basically the clinical one of attempting to understand people through getting to know them well. Unlike the therapists, however, Maslow focused on psychologically healthy people.

The Hierarchy of Needs

Maslow (1970) argued that to become a self-actualizing person, one must satisfy five sets of needs that can be arranged in a hierarchy of immediacy (see Figure 16.4). From bottom to top, they are (1) *physiological needs*, which include the minimal essentials for life, such as food and water; (2) *safety needs*, which have to do with protection from possible threats in the environment; (3) *belongingness and love needs*, the needs to establish bonds with other people; (4) *esteem needs*, the needs for competence, self-respect, and respect from others; and, finally, (5) *self-actualization needs*, the needs for self-expression, creativity, and in Maslow's words, "a sense of connectedness with the broader universe." Maslow argued that a person can focus on higher needs only if lower ones, which are more immediately linked to survival, are already relatively satisfied.

Notice that Maslow's deficiency needs (all levels below self-actualization) correspond closely with needs that play central roles in psychodynamic theories. Freud's theory centers on needs at Maslow's lowest level (assuming that sex and aggression are physiological needs, which is where Freud would have put them); Horney's theory of basic anxiety centers on Maslow's second and third levels (needs for safety and love); and Adler's theory of overcoming inferiority centers on Maslow's fourth level (esteem needs). Thus, Maslow's theory incorporates the needs of these previous theories and then adds to them the self-actualizing needs.

■ **23.** ***How does Maslow's hierarchy of needs combine the needs emphasized by psychodynamic theories and add to them?***

Also notice that Maslow's view of the prerequisites for creativity is different (almost opposite) from Freud's. According to Freud, people create because they *can't* satisfy a more basic need (usually the sexual need), and therefore they direct the energy from that need through sublimation into art, poetry, or whatever is their chosen means of expression. In contrast, Maslow posits that people can be truly creative only if they have satisfied their more basic needs sufficiently to be relatively free of them. Maslow's idea runs counter to the concept of the starving artist, the idea that great art is based on suffering.

But Maslow qualifies his theory by adding that lower needs do not have to be fully satisfied—only *relatively* satisfied—before the person can focus on higher needs, and that any one form of behavior might be motivated by more than one level of need at once. To a self-actualizing comedian, for example, humor might put food on the table (level 1), provide a psychological defense against real or imagined threats (level 2), serve as a vehicle for bonding with other people (level 3), bring praise and self-esteem (level 4), and, at the same time, be an aesthetic form of self-expression that brings the humorist into contact with an elevated form of consciousness (level 5). Given its ability to accommodate just about any relationship between lower needs and self-actualization, it is hard to see how Maslow's theory could be proven wrong; thus, it is not the kind of theory that can be tested scientifically. Still, many people find it useful as a general framework for thinking about human motives.

Table 16.1 ***Maslow's list of characteristics of self-actualizing individuals***

According to Maslow, self-actualizers:

- perceive reality accurately
- accept themselves, others, and nature
- are spontaneous and unpretentious
- are problem-centered rather than self-centered
- value solitude
- are self-directed
- react with awe to the mysteries of life
- have peak experiences
- identify with all of humanity
- seek relatively few friendships, but take them seriously
- have democratic values
- have a strong ethical sense
- have a philosophical, unhostile sense of humor
- are creative
- resist enculturation

Source: Adapted from *Motivation and personality* by A. H. Maslow, 1970, New York: Farrar, Straus & Giroux.

Characteristics of Self-Actualizing Individuals

One of Maslow's goals was to describe a prototype of the healthy, self-actualizing human being. To do this he studied biographies and public documents about the lives of famous people such as Abraham Lincoln, Albert Einstein, Eleanor Roosevelt, and Albert Schweitzer, who seemed to have functioned at the highest level. Using interviews and informal observations, he also studied friends and students whom he judged to be self-actualizing. From these studies, he drew up a list—shown in Table 16.1—of the characteristics that all such people seem to have in common.

■ **24.** ***How did Maslow study the characteristics of self-actualizers, and how is his study criticized on scientific grounds?***

Maslow's method in producing this list was not very scientific. Since he himself was the judge both of whom to include in the study and of their characteristics, it can be argued that he simply chose as subjects people who had certain characteristics of which he approved, and then studied those people and found that they indeed *did* have those characteristics—a circular process. Maslow (1970) argued that his method was not circular. He claimed that his criterion for choosing subjects was their proven ability to make full use of their talents and potentials, and that he was surprised to discover that they were also similar in so many other ways. But a more objective, systematic validation of Maslow's list is still wanting. At present it can be read as an inspiring statement of Maslow's personal values or as a set of hypotheses for possible future study, not as scientific evidence for a core set of characteristics of the most psychologically healthy people.

A peak experience

As they ecstatically celebrate their triumph over the Lobuche Peak in Nepal, these climbers exemplify the exploration, curiosity, and self-development that are basic to the human personality as seen by the humanists.

■ **25. *What are three common criticisms of humanistic theories?***

Critique of Humanistic Theories

Humanistic psychology, like Freud's theory before it, has had a strong impact on the culture at large. It is associated with what has come to be called the *human-potential movement*, which refers to the entire collection of means—including group encounters, meditation, and physical exercises—by which people consciously attempt to actualize their potentials. It has affected thinking about parenting and has helped inspire experiments in education, and it has provided the basis for effective means of psychotherapy (discussed in Chapter 18). The main criticisms of humanistic psychology can be summarized as follows:

- ***Concepts difficult to test scientifically*** Like clinically based theories in general, scientific support for humanistic theories is relatively weak. How can researchers test a concept such as self-actualization unless it is defined in such a way as to be objectively identifiable? Also, it is especially hard to know how to generate valid data for a theory that emphasizes phenomenology. How can anyone know for sure when people's statements about themselves represent what they really think about themselves? People may actually have a wide variety of self-concepts (as discussed in Chapter 14), each pertaining to a different social role or setting. The self-concept expressed in therapy may not be the same as the one expressed in other situations, and it may be strongly influenced by the client's perception of what the therapist expects to hear.
- ***Paucity of explanatory power*** To say that higher human actions are motivated by an actualizing tendency is to say little unless one can spell out the conditions under which the tendency arises. Maslow's idea that lower needs must be partly met doesn't help much, unless one can state in a clear, measurable fashion what is meant by "partly met." Rogers's ideas about the conditions of child rearing conducive to self-actualization are more testable and have generated some research that tends to support his view, but more is needed.
- ***Overly romantic view of human nature*** Humanistic theorists often seem to assume that everything good about a person stems from within the person and that everything bad stems from external social forces (such as conditions of worth) that act on the person. This is the opposite of Freud's view that the instincts of the id tend to lead us to behave in unacceptable ways and that morality (the superego) is imposed by society. The truth probably lies somewhere in between. Evolutionary theory and observations of people everywhere suggest that selfishness is as much a part of human nature as is cooperativeness and that society must operate to restrain the one and facilitate the other.

Social Cognitive Theories

Social cognitive theories of personality are also sometimes called *social learning theories* or even *social cognitive learning theories*. They derive from the long tradition in psychology of laboratory research on learning, cognition, and social influence—the types of research described in previous chapters of this text. The leading contributors to this perspective are not primarily therapists, but rather are laboratory scientists attempting to understand basic processes that control human behavior.

In general, social cognitive theorists are distrustful of the intuitive judgments of the clinically based psychodynamic and humanistic theorists. They also tend to distrust the questionnaire data of the psychometrically based trait theorists (to be described in the next section), unless the questionnaires have been well validated through direct behavioral observations. They argue that a useful personality theory must predict people's actual behavior, objectively measured, not just what people *say* about themselves in the clinician's office or on questionnaires.

If there is a principal founder of the social cognitive perspective on personality, it is Julian Rotter (1916–). While still in high school, he became fascinated by the writings of Alfred Adler and especially by Adler's idea that people's beliefs about their own abilities influence their efforts and achievements (Rotter, 1982). Rotter earned a Ph.D. in clinical psychology; enjoyed a long career conducting basic research on learning, cognition, and the relationship of these to personality; and wrote the first book explicitly describing a social cognitive approach to personality (Rotter, 1954). Two other well-known pioneers of this approach are Albert Bandura (1925–) and Walter Mischel (1930–), who also earned doctoral degrees in clinical psychology and went on to do university-based research. The careers of these three scholars are intertwined: Rotter was one of Mischel's main advisors in graduate school, and for a long time Mischel and Bandura worked together at Stanford University.

Basic Tenets of the Social Cognitive Approach

■ **26.** ***How are social learning theories characterized by their emphasis on cognitive constructs, social learning, and situational specificity of traits?***

In addition to its basis in laboratory methods and objective behavioral measures, the social cognitive approach is formed around three premises—that *cognitive constructs* provide the basis for personality, that these constructs are developed and modified through *learning in the social environment*, and that they are to varying degrees *situation-specific*:

- ***Cognitive constructs as the basis for personality*** From the social cognitive perspective, a person's behavior at any given moment results from an interaction between the environmental situation and the cognitive constructs (mental entities) that the person brings to the situation (Bandura, 1986; Rotter, 1954). These constructs include *goals and values* (beliefs about appropriate purposes or ends of behavior) and *expectancies* (beliefs about what will happen if one acts in a certain way). From this perspective, personality can be defined as the entire set of one's cognitive constructs. Because everyone has a unique set of constructs, everyone has a unique personality.
- ***Learning in the social environment*** The goals, values, expectancies, and other cognitive constructs that provide the basis for personality are, from the social cognitive perspective, learned primarily through interactions with other people (Bandura, 1986; Mischel, 1968). Social rewards such as praise and acceptance help motivate and reinforce such learning. People also learn simply by observing others. As discussed in Chapter 5, Bandura was a pioneer in the study of observational learning, or modeling. People continue to learn and

thereby modify their cognitive constructs throughout life as they interact with and observe others. Bandura (1986) has referred to the interaction between internal (cognitive) and external (environmental) variables as *reciprocal determinism*. The person acts on the environment, and the environment on the person, in a continuous, lifelong process. Personality is never completely fixed.

- ***Situational specificity of personality variables*** Learning always occurs within an environmental context, a situation. Therefore, according to social cognitive theorists, learned cognitive constructs, which provide the basis for personality, are more or less *situation-specific* (Mischel, 1968). For example, if you learned to be aggressive as an athlete, the effect of this learning might remain confined to the athletic field or it might generalize in varying degrees to other situations, depending on the degree to which you experience those situations as similar to athletics. Thus, from the social cognitive perspective, people cannot be described adequately in terms of global traits that apply to all situations, but can be described meaningfully in terms that include both the trait and the context in which it is manifested. One person might be aggressive on the athletic field but timid in the classroom, outgoing on the stage but socially withdrawn at parties, or scrupulously honest with neighbors but dishonest in calculating income taxes.

A Sample of Cognitive Personality Constructs

The cognitive constructs that have been most studied by personality researchers in the social cognitive tradition are all in the category of expectancies. These include expectancies about one's control over rewards, about one's ability to perform effectively, and about the brightness or bleakness of the future.

> 27. ***What experiments led Rotter to conclude that people's beliefs about their control over rewards affect their behavior? How did this lead to Rotter's concept of* locus of control, *and what correlational research supports that concept?***

Rotter's Concept of Locus of Control

In early research, Rotter found that people behaved differently at various tasks or games in the laboratory depending on whether they believed that success depended on skill or luck (Rotter & others, 1961). When they believed that success depended on skill (which it did), they worked hard and improved. When they believed that success depended solely on luck, they did not work hard and did not improve. Rotter found that he could manipulate the amount of improvement over trials by manipulating cues that influenced the subjects' beliefs about the degree to which success depended on skill or luck. Based partly on these observations, Rotter disputed the then-prominent view that people's behavior can be predicted simply from knowledge of the actual relationship between their responses and rewards. He argued that to predict behavior you must also know something of the beliefs that people acquire about the relationship between their responses and rewards.

Consistent with the general emphasis of social cognitive theories on the situation, Rotter (1966) argued that expectancies about the control of rewards are often situation-specific. That is, people learn that in some situations they can control what rewards they receive and in other situations they cannot. But in many situations the degree to which rewards depend on a person's own efforts is not apparent. Rotter suggested that in these situations people behave according to a generalized disposition (a personality trait), acquired from past experience, to believe that rewards either are or are not usually controllable by their own efforts. He referred to this disposition as ***locus of control***, and developed a questionnaire designed to measure it.

Table 16.2 on page 588 shows some sample questions from Rotter's locus-of-control questionnaire. People whose answers reflect a belief that individuals control their own rewards (and, by extension, their own fate) are said to have an *internal*

Table 16.2 ***Sample questions from Rotter's locus-of-control scale***

The task on each item is to decide which alternative (*a* or *b*) seems more true. The actual test consists of twenty-three items similar to those shown here.

Item:	a. In the long run, people get the respect they deserve in this world.
	b. Unfortunately, an individual's work often passes unrecognized, no matter how hard he or she tries.
Item:	a. I have often found that what is going to happen will happen.
	b. Trusting to fate has never turned out as well for me as making a decision to take a definite course of action.
Item:	a. In the case of the well-prepared student, there is rarely if ever such a thing as an unfair test.
	b. Many times exam questions tend to be so unrelated to course work that studying is really useless.

Note: For the items shown here, *internal* locus of control is indicated by choosing *a* for the first and third items and *b* for the second item.
Source: "Generalized expectancies for internal versus external locus of control of reinforcement" by J. B. Rotter, 1966, *Psychological Monographs: General and Applied, 80* (Whole no. 609), p. 11.

locus of control, and those whose answers reflect a belief that rewards (and fate) are controlled by factors outside the self are said to have an *external* locus of control.

Since its development, hundreds of studies have shown consistent, though usually not very high, correlations between scores on Rotter's locus-of-control scale and actual behavior in various situations. People who score toward the internal end of the scale are, on average, more likely than those who score toward the external end to try to control their own fate. They are more likely to take preventive health care measures (Phares, 1978); more likely to seek information on how to protect themselves during a tornado warning (Sims & Baumann, 1972); more likely to resist group pressures to conform in laboratory tests of conformity (Crowne & Liverant, 1963); and more likely to prefer games of skill over games of chance (Schneider, 1972).

Skill or luck?

People approach an activity—such as a game of cards—very differently depending on whether they believe its potential rewards are controlled by skill or luck. This insight lay behind Rotter's concept of locus of control. In this painting by Paul Cézanne, *The Card Players*, what can you infer about each player's locus of control?

Other research has indicated that people who score toward the internal end of the scale are, on average, less anxious and more content with life than those who score toward the external end (Phares, 1978, 1984). Of course, as with all correlational research, we cannot be sure what is cause and what is effect. Does a sense of control promote hard work, success, and happiness; or do hard work, success, and happiness promote a sense of control? Consistent with the concept of reciprocal determinism, most social cognitive theorists would contend that both causal hypotheses are correct.

Bandura's Concept of Self-Efficacy

■ **28.** ***How does self-efficacy differ from locus of control, and what is some evidence that high self-efficacy predicts high performance?***

Much of Bandura's recent research centers on people's beliefs about their own ability to perform specific tasks, which he refers to as ***self-efficacy***. People who expect that they can perform a certain task are said to have high self-efficacy about the task, and people who expect that they cannot perform the task are said to have low self-efficacy about it. Self-efficacy may sound similar to locus of control, but Bandura (1982, 1986) considers the two concepts to be distinct. Self-efficacy refers to the person's sense of his or her own ability, while locus of control refers to the person's sense of whether or not that ability will pay off. Although self-efficacy and an internal locus of control usually go together, they do not always. If you believe, for example, that you are skilled at math, but that the skill is worthless because it is unrecognized by your math professor or others in society, then you have high self-efficacy but an external locus of control in that area. Conversely, if you believe that skill at math would bring rewards, but that you don't have the skill, then you have low self-efficacy and an internal locus of control in that area.

Bandura and his colleagues have shown in many experiments that methods for improving subjects' performances on tasks are effective insofar as they convince people they *can* perform the task better. In other words, improvement techniques are helpful to the degree that they raise self-efficacy. In one study, various treatments were used to help people overcome their fear of snakes, and the result was that those subjects who claimed after treatment that they now *expected* to be able to pick up and handle a large snake were indeed most likely to succeed at the task (Bandura & others, 1977). Similar results have been found for such diverse tasks as arithmetic problems (Schunk & Hanson, 1985) and physical exertion on an exercise machine (Bandura & Cervone, 1983).

■ **29.** ***What is the cause-and-effect problem concerning self-efficacy, and what evidence suggests that self-efficacy may play a causal role?***

Bandura's self-efficacy concept implies that educational and child-rearing methods highlighting the person's abilities or successes will lead to greater success than methods highlighting inabilities or failures. But this implication is based on the assumption that self-efficacy helps *cause* improved performance and is not simply a by-product of it. Bandura (1989) believes this assumption to be true, but others have pointed out that most of the experiments purporting to show causal effects of self-efficacy can be interpreted in alternative ways (Brody, 1988). For example, in the snake-handling study, treatment may have resulted primarily in decreased fear of snakes, which in turn may have had two separate consequences: (1) increased real ability to handle them and (2) increased confidence in ability to handle them. By this analysis, the increased ability was not caused by increased self-efficacy; instead, increases in both were caused by the decreased fear. To carry this analysis one awful step further, perhaps *The Little Engine That Could*—in that classic children's story about self-efficacy—made it up the mountain *not* because it kept saying, "I think I can, I think I can," but rather because it was strong enough and had enough fuel; and perhaps it said, "I think I can" because it could tell that it was strong enough and had enough fuel. Self-efficacy may predict behavior accurately without helping to cause it.

Some experiments, however, do provide evidence that self-efficacy can play a

I think I can

Until the moment in 1954 at Oxford, England, when Roger Bannister crossed the finish line at 3 minutes 59.4 seconds, many people believed it physically impossible for a person to run a mile in less than 4 minutes. Consistent with Bandura's theory of self-efficacy, that belief may have provided a psychological barrier to faster performance.

causal role in improved performance. Perhaps the most compelling are those in which subjects who have been led to believe that they can solve problems that are actually unsolvable (and therefore have developed high self-efficacy concerning them) persist longer at trying to solve them than do subjects who have not been deceived in this way (Bandura, 1982; Schunk, 1984). Such studies provide a plausible chain through which self-efficacy may affect success on solvable problems:

High self-efficacy → increased effort or persistence → success

The Power of Positive Thinking

■ **30.** ***What is some evidence for the benefits of optimism, and what is the most plausible mechanism through which optimism can produce such effects?***

Much has been written, by psychologists and nonpsychologists alike, about the benefits of a positive, optimistic outlook on life (Cousins, 1977; Peale, 1956; Seligman, 1990). You have just read of research indicating that people who believe in their own abilities and that their abilities will be rewarded are on average more successful than people who don't have those beliefs.

A number of psychologists have developed questionnaires designed to assess people's general tendency to think positively or negatively. C. Rick Snyder and his colleagues (1991) developed a questionnaire to assess *hope*, which they construe as a belief in one's ability to solve solvable problems (generalized self-efficacy) combined with a belief that most problems in life are solvable. Martin Seligman (1990) and his colleagues developed a questionnaire to assess the degree to which people explain negative events in their lives in a pessimistic or optimistic manner (discussed in relation to theories of depression in Chapter 17). Michael Scheier and Charles Carver (1993) developed a questionnaire to assess *dispositional optimism*, the tendency to believe in a rosy future. On the questionnaire, people indicate the degree to which they agree or disagree with such statements as, "In uncertain times, I usually expect the best."

Correlational studies using all of these questionnaires have shown that, in general, people with an optimistic style of thought tend to cope more effectively with life's stressors than people who have a pessimistic style (Aspinwall & Taylor, 1992; Elliott & others, 1991; Peterson, 1991). In one such study, Scheier and his colleagues (1989) used their questionnaire to assess dispositional optimism in middle-aged men who were about to undergo coronary artery bypass surgery. They found that those who scored high on optimism before the surgery made quicker recoveries than those who scored low, even when the medical conditions that led to surgery were equivalent. The optimists were quicker to sit up on their own, to walk, to resume vigorous exercise, and to get back to work full-time than the pessimists. The most likely explanation for this and other positive correlations with optimism is that optimistic thinking leads people to devote attention and energy to solving their problems or recovering from their disabilities, which in turn leads to positive results. Pessimists are relatively more likely to say, "It won't work out anyway, so why try?" A more controversial idea is that optimistic thinking and psychological equanimity in general may facilitate physical health and recovery through direct effects on body chemistry (see Chapter 17).

Critique of Social Cognitive Theories

■ **31.** ***How is the social cognitive approach to personality limited by its lack of holism, its neglect of drives and emotions, and its general reliance on laboratory and short-term correlational research?***

The social cognitive approach to personality is valued for its use of objective methods and its attempt to relate behavior to specific cognitive constructs. Ironically, these characteristics are also the source of the most frequent criticisms of the approach:

- ***Lack of holism*** Some psychologists argue that social cognitive theories are not really personality theories, but rather are theories of specific cognitive processes. A theory of self-efficacy or locus of control may be very useful, but it is not the same thing as a theory of the person. Clinically based psychodynamic and humanistic theorists contend that to build a framework for understanding people as whole entities—which they take to be the goal of any personality theory—one must begin by knowing individual people well, and that can best be done through the hours of dialogue that occur in a clinical setting. You can't build a meaningful picture of individuals as wholes by patching together the pieces discovered in separate experiments or correlational studies, in which groups of subjects rather than individuals are the focus of study and only narrow aspects of behavior are assessed. One person's sense of self-efficacy or control may be understood as quite different from another's in the light of knowledge about the whole person.

- ***Underemphasis on drives and emotions*** In focusing on cognitive constructs or beliefs, the social cognitive approach tends to ignore drives and emotions as personality variables. This narrowness of focus may be due at least partly to the heavy reliance on laboratory and short-term correlational studies. Drives and emotions may be unconscious (not verbally stateable by subjects) and not easily detected in short-term research. Also, the laboratory setting tends to produce a certain uniformity of drive and emotion. People do not approach the laboratory as a place to enjoy a sexual adventure or to blow off steam; rather, they approach it as a scientific research facility where their job is to do as well as possible whatever task the researcher asks them to do. For this reason, personality constructs such as self-efficacy and locus of control, which influence success on assigned tasks when motivation is uniformly high and emotions are muted, may be more amenable to laboratory research than are drives and emotions.

In other words, the variables that account for differences among people in controlled behavioral studies may not be just the same as those that account for such differences in real life. Real life is not controlled. We choose our tasks and create our problems in the context of a rich web of drives, emotions, cognitions, and environmental events. Clinicians who spend long hours talking with people about their lives and problems are less likely than statistically oriented researchers to ignore such issues. Research such as that relating hope or optimism to real-life adjustment, however, helps bridge the gap between the social cognitive and clinical approaches.

Trait Theories and Psychometric Research

32. ***How do trait theories differ from other personality theories in their approach to identifying individual differences?***

Each of the personality theories discussed so far includes ways of describing differences among people. Freud differentiated among people according to how they channel sexual energy (such as in oral fixation or anal retentiveness); Horney according to their ways of dealing with the inborn sense of insecurity; Maslow according to their position on a hierarchy of needs that they are trying to fulfill (with self-actualizers at the top); and Rotter according to their beliefs about the link between behavior and rewards (locus of control). Yet the way each theory describes individual differences is secondary to its explanation of behavior in general. Psychodynamic, humanistic, and social-cognitive theories are first and foremost theories of human motives or cognitive constructs, with individual differences accounted for within the context of the motives or constructs emphasized by the theory (sex for Freud, security for Horney, self-actualization for Maslow, and locus of control for Rotter). Trait theories, in contrast, take the description of individual differences as their main purpose.

A ***trait theory*** can be defined as a formal system for describing and measuring the ways in which personalities differ. Whereas the theories discussed up until now were developed primarily through either the clinical or laboratory method, trait theories are developed primarily through the psychometric method. Psychometrics (introduced in relation to intelligence testing in Chapter 11) refers to the systematic attempt to measure psychological characteristics, usually with written questionnaires or tests. Trait theorists attempt to discover the most basic dimensions along which people differ, using quantitative, psychometric methods that (at least in principle) are unbiased by prior theoretical considerations.

Basic Tenets of the Trait Approach

As background to the discussion of specific theories to follow, let's first consider the meaning of *trait* (a concept used implicitly thus far in the chapter) and the general approach of trait theorists to studying traits.

The Trait Concept

A ***trait*** can be defined as a relatively stable predisposition to behave in a certain way. It is considered to be part of the person, not part of the environment. People carry their traits with them from one environment to another, though the actual manifestation of a trait in the form of behavior depends on an interaction between the trait and the environment. For example, aggressiveness as a trait might be narrowly defined as one's inner predisposition to fight. That predisposition is presumed to stay with the person in all environments, although the actual behavior of fighting depends on an interaction between that predisposition and provocations that exist in the environment. Aggressiveness or kindness or any other trait in a person is analogous to "meltability" in margarine: Margarine melts only when subjected to heat, but some brands take less heat to melt than do others, and that difference lies in the margarine, not the environment.

■ **33. *How do traits differ from states?***

It is useful also to distinguish the term *trait* from *state*. Chapter 7 is about states (of motivation and emotion), which, like traits, are defined as inner entities that can be inferred from overt behavior. The conceptual difference is that one is enduring and the other is temporary. A trait is the enduring attribute that influences the likelihood of a person's entering temporarily into a particular state. Thus, the trait of aggressiveness might influence the likelihood that a person will enter the state of anger. In the margarine analogy, the trait of meltability influences the likelihood that the margarine will enter the state of being melted.

Another point to keep in mind is that traits are not characteristics that people have or lack in all-or-none fashion, but rather are dimensions along which people differ in degree. If we measured aggressiveness or any other trait in a large number of people, our results would approximate the kind of curve referred to as a normal distribution (illustrated in Figure 3.10), in which the majority of people are near the middle of the range and few are at the extremes.

Surface Traits and Source Traits

■ **34. *How are surface traits inferred from behavior, and how are source traits inferred from surface traits?***

Traits cannot be observed directly, but are inferred from people's behaviors, including their responses to items on questionnaires. One way to depict the relationship between behaviors and traits is shown in Figure 16.5. Notice that the depiction is hierarchical. At the bottom are specific, observable behaviors. At the next level up are ***surface traits***, each of which is linked directly to a different class of behaviors. For instance, a person who argues a lot might be said to have the surface trait of high argumentativeness. At the highest level, linking more than one surface trait, are ***source traits***, the most basic personality dimensions, which are

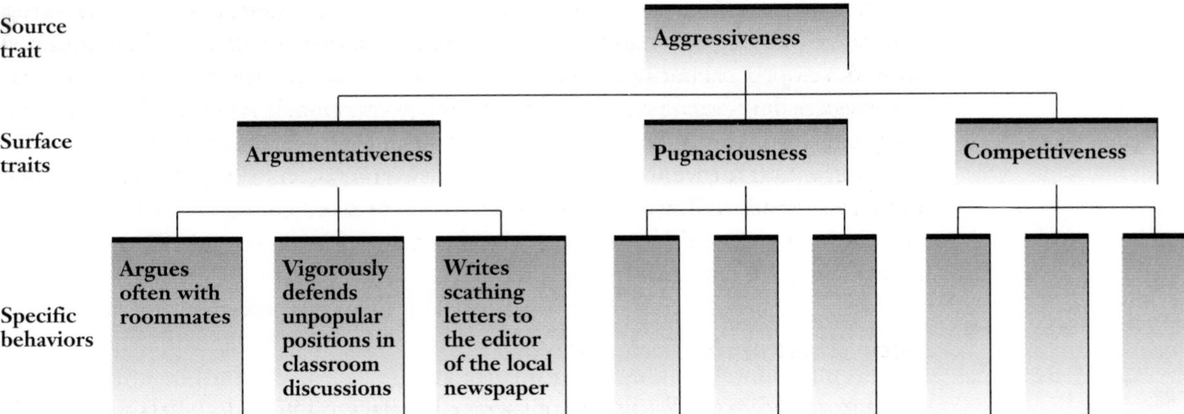

Figure 16.5 ***Hierarchical relationship among behaviors, surface traits, and a source trait***

In trait theories, surface traits are inferred from people's behaviors and source traits are inferred by identifying surface traits that correlate with one another. (Adapted from Eysenck, 1982.)

taken to be the source of the surface traits. To identify a source trait, one must first identify a number of surface traits that seem to go together. For instance, if the highly argumentative person also gets into a lot of physical fights, a source trait of aggressiveness might underlie the two kinds of behaviors. In contrast, if the argumentative person is one who also reads a lot, asks lots of questions, and rarely gets into physical fights, we might conclude that the source trait is not aggressiveness but intellectuality, with argument being the person's way of testing ideas.

The goal of most trait theorists is to identify a single set of trait dimensions that can be used to describe all people. To achieve this goal, trait theorists use statistical means to identify source traits that account for the greatest variation among people, and develop ways to measure those traits through written questionnaires.

A Sample of Trait Theories

Fundamentally, a trait theory is simply a statement of the source traits that account for the greatest statistically measured variation among people. Different theories differ in the number of source traits they identify and in the description of those traits. The trait theories that have inspired the most research and controversy are Cattell's theory, Eysenck's theory, and the more recent Big Five theory.

Cattell's Sixteen-Dimensional Theory

Raymond Cattell (1905–), a British-born psychologist who has spent most of his research career in the United States, is one of the pioneers of the attempt to describe personality in terms of measurable traits. His undergraduate degree was in chemistry, and his goal in psychology was to develop a sort of chemistry of personality. Just as an infinite number of different molecules can be described in terms of a finite number of atoms, Cattell wished to develop a system by which an infinite number of different personalities could be described in terms of a finite number of elemental trait dimensions. To do this, he needed to discover the source traits (or personality factors, as he called them) that most efficiently describe the differences among people and develop a way to measure them.

■ **35.** ***How did Cattell identify a set of sixteen source traits, and how did he develop a questionnaire to measure them?***

How can a researcher discover source traits? Cattell prided himself in making no prior assumptions about what these might be—he wanted to find them through objective, statistical means. In essence, his approach was to collect massive amounts of data concerning as many surface traits as possible in a large sample of people, and then to use statistical means to determine which surface traits correlated most strongly with one another and were thus indicative of a common source trait. He

Table 16.3 ***Cattell's sixteen source traits or personality factors***

A. Sociable–unsociable
B. Intelligent–unintelligent
C. Emotionally stable–unstable
E. Dominant–submissive
F. Cheerful–brooding
G. Conscientious–undependable
H. Bold–timid
I. Sensitive–insensitive
L. Suspicious–trusting
M. Imaginative–practical
N. Shrewd–naive
O. Guilt proclivity–guilt rejection
Q_1: Radicalism–conservatism
Q_2: Self-sufficiency–group adherence
Q_3: Self-disciplined–uncontrolled will
Q_4: Tense–relaxed

Note: In this table, descriptive terms have been substituted for the technical terms that Cattell coined for each trait.

Source: Adapted from *Personality and mood by questionnaire* (pp. 53–54) by R. B. Cattell, 1973, San Francisco: Jossey-Bass.

began with data about the lives of the people he was studying, which he called *L-data* (life data). Ideally, L-data would have come from objective observations of people's actual behavior, but in practice the data consisted mostly of ratings of each person on a long list of surface traits, made by individuals who knew that person well. The result for each person was a score on each of many different surface traits, such as talkativeness, patience, jealousy, and so on. The list used for these ratings was produced by condensing the 18,000 or so adjectives describing personality that can be found in an unabridged dictionary down to about 170 that seemed logically to be different from one another.

Cattell then subjected the L-data to factor analysis (described in Chapter 11) to determine which surface traits were most strongly correlated with one another. His assumption was that highly intercorrelated surface traits must be influenced by the same source trait. By finding clusters of surface traits that correlated strongly with one another within the cluster, but not across clusters, Cattell identified a preliminary set of source traits and gave each a name. His next step was to develop and administer questionnaires asking people about their own characteristics. The data from these he called *Q-data* (questionnaire data). He then subjected the Q-data to factor analysis to see if they would generate the same set of factors that had been obtained from the L-data. If this occurred, he could assume that the questionnaire was measuring the same source traits as had been revealed in the L-data, and thus that the traits measured by the questionnaire were valid in the sense of being related to the person's ways of behaving in daily life.

The upshot of this research, which spanned many years and involved dozens of separate studies, was the identification of sixteen different source traits and the development of a questionnaire called the *16 PF Questionnaire* to measure them (Cattell, 1950, 1973). (PF stands for *personality factors*, which was Cattell's term for source traits.) The questionnaire consists of nearly 200 statements about specific aspects of behavior, such as "I like to go to parties." To each statement, the respondent must select one of three possible answers—*yes*, *occasionally*, or *no*. The sixteen source traits that the questionnaire is designed to measure are listed in Table 16.3. Today, the 16 PF Questionnaire is used both as a clinical tool for assessing personality characteristics of clients in psychotherapy and as a research tool in studies of personality. As an example of the questionnaire's use in research, see Figure 16.6.

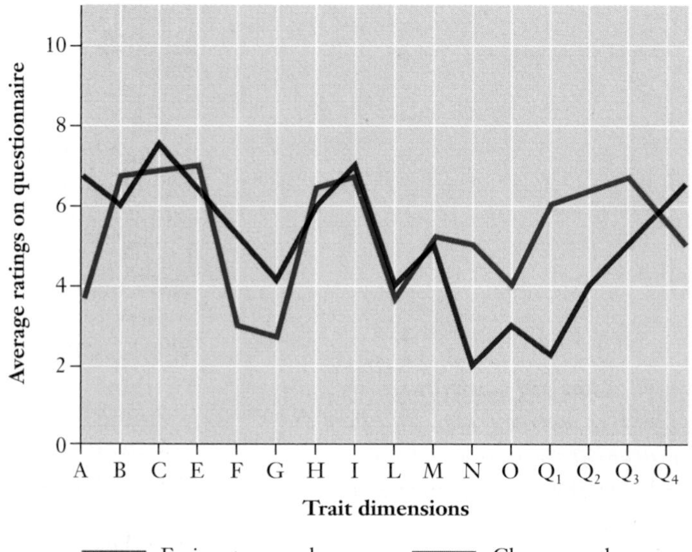

Figure 16.6 ***Personality profiles of scientists and clergy members***

Shown here are the average ratings on each of the source traits, or factors, in Cattell's 16 PF Questionnaire for a group of well-known scientists and a group of clergy members. The sixteen trait dimensions, indicated along the horizontal axis, are as described in Table 16.3. For each dimension, a high score indicates tendency toward the left-hand term in Table 16.3, and a low score indicates tendency toward the right-hand term. By comparing the two curves, you can find differences between the average personalities of the two groups. For example, the researchers are lower in sociability (Factor A) and higher in radicalism (Factor Q_1) than the clergy members. (Adapted from Cattell, 1965.)

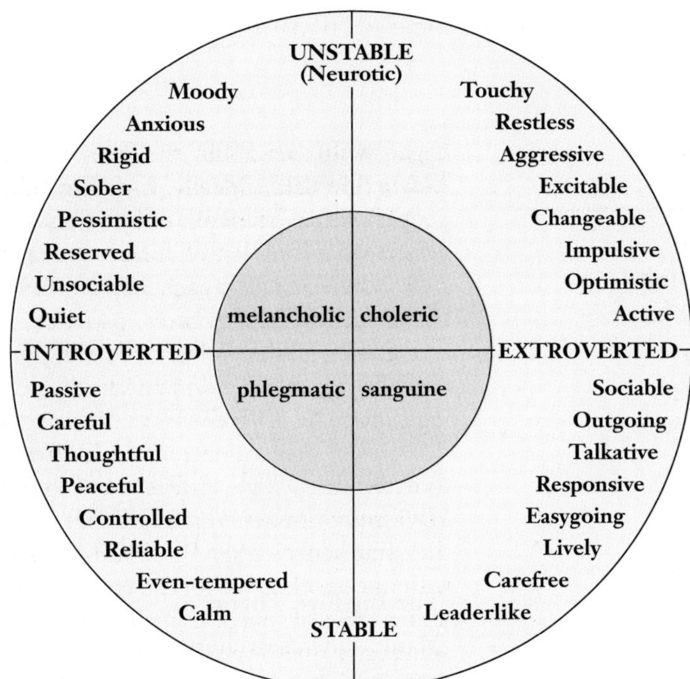

Figure 16.7 ***Eysenck's depiction of personality types***

The four quadrants of this circle represent the four possible combinations of introversion-extroversion and neuroticism-stability in Eysenck's theory. Some of the surface traits associated with each of these combinations are listed in the outer ring. The terms in the inner circle refer to an ancient Greek topology that divided people into four types that are similar to Eysenck's types: melancholic (moody and withdrawn), choleric (irritable and outgoing), sanguine (stable and outgoing), and phlegmatic (stable and withdrawn). (Adapted from Eysenck, 1982.)

Eysenck's Two-Dimensional Theory

Hans Eysenck (1916–) is a German-born, British psychologist whose basic approach to developing a trait theory was quite similar to Cattell's. In his early studies, Eysenck (1952) gathered large amounts of data, including objective life-history information and scores on psychological tests concerning men at a military hospital, and subjected the data to factor analysis. Eysenck used factor analysis somewhat differently than did Cattell, and his method resulted in a factor structure containing far fewer factors or source traits than Cattell's. In fact, his early studies revealed just two source-trait dimensions that seemed to account quite well for most of the consistent individual differences in the original data.

One dimension, which he labeled *introversion-extroversion* (using terms coined by Jung), seemed to be related to a person's tendency to avoid or seek excitement in the external environment. The surface traits associated with introversion included the tendencies to seek quiet, to be introspective, and to be relatively nonsociable; and the opposite were associated with extroversion. The other dimension, which he labeled *neuroticism-stability*, seemed to be related to a person's tendency to become emotionally upset. The surface traits associated with neuroticism included moodiness, anxiety, suggestibility, and low willpower; and the opposite were associated with stability.

To measure people's positions along these source trait dimensions, Eysenck developed a questionnaire called the *Eysenck Personality Inventory*. With scores from this inventory, people can be classified into four groups, depending on their position along each of the two dimensions: introverted-neurotic, introverted-stable, extroverted-neurotic, and extroverted-stable. Figure 16.7 illustrates Eysenck's two-dimensional system for classifying people and notes some of the surface traits of those who fall in different parts of the grid. (In later work, Eysenck identified a third dimension, having to do with concern or lack of concern for others' needs, which turned his two-dimensional theory into a three-dimensional one.)

■ **36.** ***How does Eysenck explain the difference between introverts and extroverts in terms of a basic property of the nervous system, and how has research supported his explanation?***

Eysenck contends that differences among people in the basic traits depicted by this theory are determined by inherited physiological characteristics of the nervous system (Eysenck & Eysenck, 1985). In particular, he contends that differences in introversion-extroversion stem from differences in how easily the central nervous system is aroused by sensory input. Eysenck postulates that all people seek a moderate level of central nervous system arousal, which is optimal for psychological functioning. He proposes further that introverts have central nervous systems that are more easily aroused by environmental stimulation than are those of extroverts. The result is that introverts seek a lower level of environmental stimulation than do extroverts. Put differently, an extrovert might need a roller-coaster ride or a rock concert to achieve the same arousal that an introvert can get from a merry-go-round ride or a sonata.

Supporting this theory is evidence that introverts (as identified by Eysenck's personality inventory) do react more strongly than extroverts to various stimuli. Introverts (a) show greater disruption in performance on a learning task when loud noise is present (Geen, 1984); (b) manifest a greater physiological arousal response to a sudden noise (Stelmack, 1990); (c) salivate more profusely when lemon juice is squirted into their mouth (Eysenck & Eysenck, 1967); and (d) are less tolerant of painful electric shock (Bartol & Costello, 1976).

The Big Five Theory

Many trait researchers today find that Cattell's theory, with sixteen different dimensions, is too complex and contains redundant factors and that Eysenck's theory is too simple, failing to capture meaningful differences among personalities. In recent years, a large number of factor-analytic studies have been conducted using more sophisticated versions of the methods pioneered by Cattell and Eysenck, and the results have been described by researchers in this area as remarkably consistent. To quote one pair of researchers (Digman & Inouye, 1986): "A series of research studies of personality traits has led to a finding consistent enough to approach the status of a law. The finding is this: If a large number of rating scales is used and if the scope of the scales is very broad (that is, if they cover a large number of behaviors or surface traits), the domain of personality descriptors is almost completely accounted for by five robust factors."

The five factors, often referred to by trait researchers as the *Big Five*, have turned up repeatedly in studies conducted in various countries, in several languages, and with children as well as adults (Digman, 1989; Goldberg; 1990, 1993; McCrae & John, 1992). They are described in Table 16.4. Notice that two of the dimensions are the same as Eysenck's original two (*extroversion* and *neuroticism*). The other three are *agreeableness*, *conscientiousness*, and *openness to experiences*. The contention of many trait researchers today is that, if you want to choose a convenient number of trait terms that will most efficiently summarize the measurable personality differences among people, these are the terms to choose. Nearly all of the hundreds of different adjectives commonly used to describe personalities correlate quite strongly, in factor-analytic studies, with one of these five dimensions.

Table 16.4 ***The "Big Five" personality factors***

Extroversion–introversion: Sociable–retiring; fun loving–sober; talkative–quiet; spontaneous–inhibited.

Neuroticism–stability: Worrying–calm; vulnerable–hardy; self-pitying–self-satisfied; impatient–patient.

Agreeableness–antagonism: Courteous–rude; selfless–selfish; trusting–suspicious; flexible–stubborn.

Conscientiousness–undirectedness: Careful–careless; reliable–undependable; fair–unfair; ambitious–aimless.

Openness–nonopenness: Imaginative–unimaginative; independent–conforming; curious–uncurious; daring–unadventurous.

Note: Next to each source trait are listed some of the surface traits whose intercorrelation provided the basis for inferring that source trait.

Source: Adapted from "Updating Norman's 'adequate taxonomy': Intelligence and personality dimensions in natural language and in questionnaires" by R. R. McCrae & P. T. Costa, 1985, *Journal of Personality and Social Psychology, 49*, p. 85.

Are traits consistent across situations?
Do people usually show the same traits in different contexts of their lives, as this woman seems to? After 25 years of controversy, researchers still disagree. Some emphasize sameness across situations; others focus on differences due to situation.

Questions About the Consistency and Heritability of Traits

You now have a general understanding of how trait theorists identify and measure personality traits. Now let's turn to some fundamental questions about traits: Are they consistent in a given person from situation to situation? Are they consistent over time? Are they passed on genetically from one generation to the next?

Are Traits Consistent Across Situations? The Challenge from Mischel

A basic premise of trait theory is that traits are inner characteristics of the person and are carried with the person from one environmental context (situation) to another. The strongest challenge to this premise has come from social cognitive theorists, especially Walter Mischel (1968, 1984). Recall that social cognitive theories in general maintain that people learn to behave in particular ways in particular situations, so the same person's behavioral style may vary greatly from one setting to another. Mischel has argued forcefully that trait theorists make the same error that people in general make when they try to explain other people's behavior. They overemphasize the role of personality characteristics and underemphasize the role of environmental provocation—an error referred to by social psychologists as the *fundamental attribution error* (discussed in Chapter 14). Mischel argues that real evidence for cross-situational consistency of traits would have to come from observations of people's actual behavior in a variety of situations, not from questionnaires or clinical inferences.

In his initial argument against the trait concept, Mischel (1968) referred to a classic study of morality conducted by Hugh Hartshorne and Mark May (1928), in which thousands of schoolchildren were provided with opportunities to be dishonest, in a wide variety of situations, under conditions in which they did not know that their dishonesty could be detected. The test included such forms of dishonesty as lying to parents, falsifying school records, cheating on a test at school, and stealing money at a club meeting. Of greatest relevance to Mischel's argument, Hartshorne and May found that correlations within any given situation were quite high, but correlations across situations were very low. That is, children who were dishonest in one situation (say, cheating on a test) were quite likely to be dishonest again in a similar situation (cheating on another test), but were not much more likely than average to be dishonest in a different situation (say, stealing money).

Later, Mischel and Philip Peake (1982) performed a similar study, though smaller in scope, in which they assessed repeatedly, by direct observation, nineteen different forms of behavior presumed to be related to a trait of conscientiousness in a group of students at Carleton College in Minnesota. Included were measures of regularity of class attendance, promptness in completing assignments, bed neatness, and neatness of class notes. Like Hartshorne and May, they found high consistency within any of these measures, but low consistency across different measures. From such evidence, Mischel argued that to describe people meaningfully you have to speak in terms that relate behavior to the situation—such as *honest on tests*, or *conscientious about keeping room clean*—not in such global terms as *honest* or *conscientious*, which would be at the level of source traits.

■ **37. *What evidence did Mischel provide for his contention that traits are not consistent across situations?***

Trait Theorists' Response to Mischel

Trait theorists have not taken Mischel's arguments lying down. They have responded, among other ways, by reexamining data from the studies that Mischel referred to and arguing that even they can be interpreted as support for the trait concept. Regarding Hartshorne and May's study, to say that people differ with respect to the situations in which they are most likely to manifest dishonesty is not the same thing as saying that they do not differ in overall dishonesty. Hartshorne and May themselves noted that, despite the situational differences, the differences

■ **38. *What did trait theorists find when they analyzed the data from studies that Mischel had used to refute the trait concept?***

that occurred among individual children in average dishonesty scores when all situations were combined were much larger than could be accounted for by chance. Similarly, when two separate averages were calculated for each child—by dividing the different situations randomly into two sets—a high correlation was found between the two averages (Epstein, 1979). That is, children who were unusually likely to be dishonest in one combined set of situations were also unusually likely to be dishonest in the other.

Concerning Mischel and Peake's study, Douglas Jackson and Sampo Paunonen (1985) have argued that it shows merely that conscientiousness—defined as Mischel and Peake defined it, to encompass such diverse activities as studying many hours and keeping one's bed neat—is not a meaningful source trait. (Conscientiousness is a source trait in the Big Five theory, but it is not defined as Mischel and Peake defined it.) These investigators subjected Mischel and Peake's original data to factor analysis and found that the measures clustered into several groups, each of which might be construed as a separate trait. For example, different measures of *neatness* (bed neatness, desk neatness, and neatness of class notes) correlated highly with one another, as did different measures of *academic diligence* (class-assignment punctuality, time spent studying, percentage of studies completed, and study-session attendance). The lack of correlation between neatness and academic diligence simply means that these are different traits and should not be lumped together.

■ **39.** ***How might the trait-situation debate represent a difference between the goals of different researchers?***

Today, more than 25 years after Mischel inaugurated the debate, the two sides seem to agree on the facts but to disagree—because of their different goals—about which facts are most relevant (Epstein & O'Brien, 1985; Funder, 1991; Mischel, 1984; Shoda & others, 1989). Clearly, traits can be found that yield a statistically significant degree of cross-situational generality, especially if generality is assessed by comparing one large set of situations with another large set. This fact is most important to trait theorists, whose goal is to develop convenient ways to describe overall differences among people—the types of differences that may not matter much for one specific action but may matter considerably over a person's lifetime. It is also clear, however, that traits show a considerable degree of situational specificity, and this fact is most important to social cognitive theorists, whose goal is to understand how people will behave in specific situations.

Are Traits Consistent Across Time? Evidence from Longitudinal Studies

If you ever have the opportunity to attend a twenty-fifth-anniversary reunion of your high-school class, don't miss it; it is a remarkable experience. Before you stands a person who claims to be your old friend Marty, whom you haven't seen for 25 years. The last time you saw Marty he was a skinny kid with lots of hair, wearing floppy sneakers and a sweatshirt. What you notice first are the differences: This Marty is not skinny, has very little hair, and isn't wearing sneakers. But within 10 minutes you have the almost eerie knowledge that you are talking with the same person you used to pitch pennies with behind the school. The voice is the same, the sparkle in the eyes, the quiet sense of humor, the way of walking. And when it is Marty's turn to stand up and speak to the group, he, who always was the most nervous about speaking before the class, is still most reluctant to do so. There's no doubt about it—this Marty, who now has two kids older than he was when you last saw him, is the same Marty you always knew.

But that is all impression. Is he really the same? Perhaps Marty is in some sense *your* construction, and it is your construction that has not changed over the years. Maybe if they put an imposter there and called him Marty and gave him some shared memories to talk about, you would still see him as the same old Marty. Or maybe it's just the situation. This, after all, is a high-school reunion held in your old school gymnasium, which hasn't changed a bit, and maybe you've all been transported back in your minds and are coming across much more like your old selves than you normally would. Maybe you're all trying to be the same kids you were 25 years ago, if only so people will recognize you. Clearly, if we really want to answer the question of how consistent personality is over long periods, we've got to be a bit more scientific.

■ **40.** ***How has research shown that certain traits are remarkably stable over the course of adult life?***

By now, a good many studies have been conducted in which people fill out personality questionnaires, or are rated by family or friends on a long list of characteristics, at widely separated times in their lives. In general, the results suggest a high degree of stability of central personality traits throughout adulthood. Among the most stable traits, interestingly, are extroversion-introversion and neuroticism-stability—the same two that Eysenck highlighted in his theory (Conley, 1984; West & Graziano, 1989). In one such study, women were rated for numerous personality traits at age 30 by one set of observers and at age 70 by a different set, with the finding that the degree of extroversion and neuroticism was especially consistent over this 40-year period (Mussen & others, 1980).

In another study, a large number of men filled out a personality inventory at various times over a 30-year period, with the finding that the 30-year test-retest correlation was highest on the items that measured degree of extroversion—a whopping 0.74 (Leon & others, 1979). (Keep in mind that +1.00 is a perfect correlation and that test-retest reliability on most personality tests is well below perfect even when one test is taken immediately after the other.) In still another study, self-ratings, ratings by others, life-history information, and scores on personality questionnaires were collected from several hundred men and women at three widely separated times, when the subjects were about 24, 42, and 68 years old. All of these data were then factor analyzed in such a way as to identify source traits that were most consistent over time, and the three that emerged as most consistent were the degree of extroversion, neuroticism, and impulse control (Conley, 1985).

In sum, the evidence is strong that in certain basic ways of relating to the world you are going to be pretty much the same person 20 or 40 years from now as you are today. Whether you are outgoing and sociable now or prefer a quiet evening at home, whether you are emotionally excitable now or generally stolid, you will probably continue to be so. This, of course, does not mean that you will not change in many significant ways, nor that you have no control over your future. But to a large extent those changes will be in the ways you work with your basic traits, not in the traits themselves. One introvert is happy in middle age because his job as a scientist offers ample opportunity for solitude and reflection, and another is miserable because he persists at politics.

How Heritable Are Traits?

■ **41.** ***How have the twin and adoption methods, described in Chapter 3, been used to assess the heritability of personality traits?***

Numerous research studies—using the quantitative behavior genetics methods described in Chapter 3—have shown that the traits identified by trait theories are strongly heritable. The most common approach in these studies has been to administer personality questionnaires, such as Cattell's 16 PF inventory or Eysenck's inventory, to pairs of genetically identical twins and fraternal twins (who are no more similar genetically than are ordinary siblings). The usual finding is that identical twins are much more similar than fraternal twins on every personality dimension measured, enough so as to lead to an average heritability estimate of about 0.50 for most traits (Eysenck, 1990; Loehlin, 1992). As explained in Chapter 3, a heritability of 0.50 means that about 50 percent of the variability among individuals is due to genetic differences and the remainder is due to a combination of environmental differences and measurement error.

Such findings have frequently been criticized on the grounds that parents and others may treat identical twins more similarly than fraternal twins, and similar treatment may lead to similar personality. To get around that possibility, re-

■ **42.** ***What is some evidence that the personality similarity of identical twins is due to their genes and not to their similar treatment?***

searchers at the University of Minnesota, led by David Lykken, have given personality tests to twins who were separated in infancy and raised in different homes, as well as to twins raised in the same home (Bouchard, 1991; Tellegen & others, 1988). Their results are consistent with the previous studies: The identical twins were more similar to one another than were the fraternal twins on essentially every trait, whether they had been raised in the same home or different homes, again leading to heritability scores averaging close to 0.50.

Identical twins

Research indicates that identical twins raised in different homes are nearly as similar to one another in personality as those raised in the same home.

Lykken and his colleagues were surprised to find high heritability even for traits that seem as if they should be heavily affected by learning. For example, the score on *traditionalism*—a measure of conservative values and respect for discipline and authority—was quite strongly heritable. This must mean that people who are born with a certain set of genetic predispositions are more likely to pick up traditional values from their environment than are those born with a different set.

Another finding from the Minnesota study that has surprised many psychologists is the remarkably small effect that being raised in the same home had on the personality measures. Twin pairs were about equally similar to one another on most traits whether they were raised in the same family or not. The Minnesota group concluded that the environmental differences that contribute to people's differing personalities must be nearly as great for people who live in the same family as for those who live in different families. Sandra Scarr and her colleagues (1981) earlier came to a similar conclusion through a different route. They compared nontwin, adopted children with both their biological and their adoptive siblings, and found much greater personality similarities to the biological than to the adoptive. In fact, for most personality measures, they found that children were no more similar to their adoptive siblings than any two randomly compared children were to each other. Such findings have recently encouraged psychologists to look for ways in which children living in the same home may be treated differently, or may, through their own activities, create effectively different environments (Dunn & Plomin, 1990).

Critique of Trait Theories

■ **43.** ***How have trait theories been criticized on the grounds of measurement validity, oversimplification, and overemphasis on biological determinants?***

Trait theories, associated as they are with the psychometric approach, are explicit attempts to bring statistical methods to the study of personality. As you have seen, repeated studies have produced similar results regarding such issues as the identification of a common set of source traits (the Big Five), consistency of traits over the life span, and genetic heritability of traits. Yet, this approach is not without its critics. Some of the main criticisms are as follows:

- ***The problem of measurement validity*** Although trait theorists pride themselves on their statistical procedures, their data come almost exclusively from questionnaires. People's descriptions of themselves or others on questionnaires are subjective and may not reflect actual behavior. Correlations among different questionnaire items, which provide the basis for factor analysis, may stem from the respondents' learned, and perhaps mistaken, views about what behaviors go together—that is, from their learned stereotypes about personality rather than from accurate observations (Shweder, 1982). Although some studies have shown significant correlations between trait scores and objectively measured behaviors, more such studies are needed to support the premise that trait scores truly measure the behavioral tendencies they are supposed to measure.
- ***Traits as oversimplifications*** Human beings may be too complex to sum up meaningfully through scores on two, five, or even sixteen trait dimensions. Trait theories are based implicitly on the assumption that a finite set of source traits exists, each of which controls a different set of observable behavioral

characteristics, and this assumption may be false. By averaging the responses to many different questionnaire items to produce each trait score, trait theorists may ignore differences in the meaning that any given score may have for different people. For example, two people who both score moderately high on introversion may do so for quite different reasons—one, perhaps, hates to give public lectures but enjoys parties, and the opposite may be true for another. This is the main point that Mischel and other social cognitive theorists make in their argument that the proper unit of personality is not the trait (something solely within the person) but the trait-situation interaction.

- ***Overemphasis on biological determinants*** The very concept of traits as internal constructs tends to promote the assumption that they are biologically determined. Both Cattell and Eysenck assumed that their differences are due largely to genetic differences. As you have seen, trait scores on psychometric tests are to a considerable extent influenced by heredity. But the degree of that influence may be partly dependent on the way that traits are measured. Any given trait score is based on answers to a large number of questions, which cut across a large set of environmental situations. Learned differences among people may be situation specific and may be lost in the averaging that occurs across situations when trait scores are compiled. Thus, personality tests may measure those aspects of personality that are most susceptible to genetic influence and ignore those that are most susceptible to environmental influence, thereby exaggerating the degree to which personality as a whole is genetically determined. At least one study showed far less heritability of personality traits, and much greater influence of the family, when traits were measured by objective behavioral observations, in specific contexts, rather than through questionnaires (Plomin & Foch, 1980).

Concluding Thoughts

One way to review this chapter would be to expand (either mentally or on paper) the summary of personality theories in Table 16.5. For each theory (or class of theory) described in the chapter, you might elaborate on (a) the drives, or motives, that it emphasizes; (b) the mental constructs that it identifies; (c) the kinds of differences among individuals that it focuses on; and (d) its explanation of the developmental origins of such differences. Another way to review the chapter would be to think about each theory or class of theory in relation to two questions:

1. What is the purpose of each personality theory? Each personality theory can be viewed as an effort by the theorist to solve a particular kind of intellectual or practical problem. Freud was a pioneer in the field of psychotherapy. In his private practice, he spent many hours with patients whose suffering was not caused by organic disease, poverty, or other externally observable causes, but instead seemed to stem from irrational forces in their minds. Freud's main purpose was to try to understand those forces. His theory, with its emphasis on instinctive drives and unconscious ways of directing them, makes most sense in relation to that purpose. Clinically based theories following Freud's were designed in part to correct what seemed an excessive emphasis on instinctive, unconscious drives and to account for the problems in social relationships and self-esteem that many people seeking psychotherapy presented. Thus, post-Freudian psychodynamic theorists began to emphasize social drives, the self-concept, and conscious thought patterns, and humanistic theorists went even farther in that direction.

Table 16.5 ***Summary of some personality theories***

Theory	Motivation	Mental Structure	Individual differences	Developmental source of individual differences
Freud's psychodynamic theory	Instinctive drives (especially sex and aggression)	Id (instincts), ego (realistic logic), and superego (morality)	Different ways of channeling the energy of instinctive drives	Interaction between inborn drives and responses of society (especially parents) in early childhood
Adler's psychodynamic theory	Socially acquired drives (especially that for personal achievement)	Beliefs about one's own abilities (organized by the ego)	Differences in feelings of inferiority or superiority	Interaction between the child's achievement attempts and the responses of society (especially parents)
Rogers's humanistic theory	Self-actualization (self-expression)	The self-concept (beliefs about the self)	Different conditions of worth associated with the self-concept	Value judgments made by parents and other authority figures
Rotter's social cognitive theory	To obtain rewards by completing tasks	Beliefs about the value of rewards and their dependence on behaviors	Different beliefs about one's ability to control rewards (locus of control)	Learning, based on rewards provided by the social environment, throughout life
Eysenck's trait theory	To find environments and tasks consistent with one's traits	Traits (hypothetical inner constructs inferred from observed behaviors)	People differ in degree on basic traits, such as introversion versus extroversion	Basic traits are inherited, but people learn ways of coping that are suitable to their traits and environments

The social cognitive theories and trait theories are not as tightly tied to clinical issues as are the other theories. Social cognitive theorists are primarily laboratory-based psychologists who share with other laboratory psychologists the general goal of predicting how people will behave in particular situations. They recognize that individuals often behave differently from one another in any given situation, and their goal is to understand such differences in terms of people's previous experiences. Thus, their explanatory principles usually center on learned cognitive constructs, such as self-efficacy. Trait theorists, in contrast, are less interested in predicting specific behaviors than in identifying differences among individuals that cut across situations and are relatively impervious to effects of learning. Thus, trait theories can be understood as attempts to identify the most stable and heritable ways in which people differ from one another.

2. On what sorts of evidence is each theory based? Related to their differing goals, personality theories also differ in the kinds of evidence used to support them. Psychodynamic and humanistic theories are based principally on the theorist's intimate knowledge of clients in therapy or on extensive case histories collected through interviews, biographies, or other means. Social cognitive theories are based primarily on laboratory research, conducted under objective conditions, usually with subjects the researcher does not know personally. Trait theories are based primarily on the statistical analysis of questionnaires, on which people have rated their own characteristics or have been rated by friends or family members who know them well. As you review the theories and the critiques of each, think about the ways in which each theory's source of evidence accounts for both its strengths and weaknesses.

Further Reading

Sigmund Freud (1901; reprinted 1960). *The psychopathology of everyday life* (J. Strachey, Ed.; A. Tyson, Trans.). New York: Norton.

This is one of Freud's most popular and fun-to-read books. It is full of anecdotes having to do with forgetting, slips of the tongue, and bungled actions. In each anecdote, Freud argues that an apparent mistake was really an expression of an unconscious wish.

George E. Vaillant (1977). *Adaptation to life*. Boston: Little, Brown, & Company.

With an engaging blend of case histories and statistical summaries, Vaillant describes how a group of Harvard graduates, followed for over 30 years, coped with the inevitable stresses of life. Written from a psychodynamic perspective, the book distinguishes between mature and immature ego defenses. [To see how Vaillant subsequently extended this work in other longitudinal studies, see his more technically oriented 1992 book, Ego mechanisms of defense *(Washington, DC: American Psychiatric Press).]*

C. William Tageson (1982). *Humanistic psychology: A synthesis.* Homewood, IL: Dorsey.

This is a cogent account of the major philosophical themes of humanistic psychology and their relationship to the more specific ideas developed by individual theorists.

Martin E. P. Seligman (1991). *Learned optimism.* New York: Knopf.

In this book for nonspecialists, Seligman, a leading social cognitive researcher, distinguishes between the pessimistic and optimistic explanatory styles, discusses the origins and life consequences of these styles, and suggests applications for child rearing and self improvement.

Barbara Krahé (1992). *Personality and social psychology: Towards a synthesis.* Newbury Park, CA: SAGE Publications.

In an even-handed manner, Krahé outlines the long-standing controversy between trait theorists and social cognitive theorists concerning the relative role of internal traits and external situations in controlling human behavior. Her synthesis is one that accepts the roles of both traits and situations and points to research aimed at understanding better how they interact.

John C. Loehlin (1992). *Genes and environment in personality development.* Newbury Park, CA: SAGE Publications.

This is a brief, clear, yet rather sophisticated summary of the evidence concerning the heritability of personality traits by one of the leading researchers in the field.

Looking Ahead

All of the personality theories that you have read about in this chapter were developed at least partly as a way of understanding people's psychological problems. The remaining two chapters focus directly on such problems. Chapter 17 deals with the issues of defining, categorizing, and explaining mental disorders—issues that are similar to those met by trait theorists in defining, categorizing, and explaining traits in general. Chapter 18 deals with the treatment of mental disorders, and there you will see how various theories of personality relate directly to different approaches to psychotherapy.

MENTAL DISORDERS

CHAPTER 17

A theme running through this book is that psychological processes are usually adaptive; that is, they usually promote survival and well-being. Drives and emotions motivate survival-enhancing actions; perceptions provide useful information to guide such actions; and thoughts produce effective plans for actions. But sometimes these processes break down: Drives become too strong, too weak, or misdirected; emotions become overwhelming; perceptions become inaccurate; thoughts become confused; and behavior becomes ineffective. All of us experience such disturbances occasionally to some degree and accept them as a normal part of life. But sometimes these disturbances are so strong, prolonged, or recurrent that they seriously interfere with a person's ability to live a satisfying life. Then the person is said to have a ***mental disorder***.

Basic Concepts and Perspectives

What is a mental disorder? How are mental disorders best described? What causes them? How are they categorized? Before we examine specific types of mental disorders, let's discuss these overarching questions.

What Is a Mental Disorder?

■ ***1. How is the concept of mental disorder defined by the American Psychiatric Association?***

Mental disorder is a fuzzy concept, impossible to define in a precise way. This should come as no surprise. Most concepts, if you think about them, are fuzzy. Try to define precisely, for example, such an everyday concept as a *chair*. Some things are clearly chairs, and others, like the rock you sometimes sit on in the park, are only "sort of" chairs. Every attempt to define *mental disorder* raises controversy. The most frequently used definition was developed by the American Psychiatric Association for its diagnostic manual, referred to as *DSM* and discussed extensively later in this chapter. This definition treats mental disorders as analogous to medical diseases and borrows from medicine the terms *symptom* and *syndrome*. A ***symptom*** is any characteristic of a person's actions, thoughts, or feelings that could be a potential indicator of a mental disorder; and a ***syndrome*** is a constellation of interrelated symptoms manifested by a given individual. According to the American Psychiatric Association (1987; 1993), a syndrome may be taken as evidence of a mental disorder if, and only if, it satisfies the following criteria:

- ***Clinically significant detriment*** The syndrome must involve *distress* (painful feelings) or *impairment of functioning* (interference with ability to work, play, or get along with people) or both, and it must be *clinically significant*, meaning that

Mental distress or mental disorder?

Feelings of sadness, pessimism, and low self-esteem are evident here, but is the source of the distress the situation or something inside the person? This question is central to defining the concept mental disorder.

the distress or impairment must be serious enough to warrant professional treatment.

- ***Internal source*** The source of distress or impairment must be located within the person, that is, in the person's biology, mental structure (ways of perceiving, thinking, or feeling), or learned habits, and not just in the person's immediate environment. The distress or impairment must not be simply a normal response to a specific event in the person's life, such as the death of a loved one. Although it may be triggered by such an event, it must go well beyond the usual reaction to such events.
- ***Involuntary manifestation*** The syndrome must not be explainable purely as an effect of poverty, prejudice, or other social forces that prevent or discourage a person from behaving adaptively, nor as a deliberate decision to act in a way contrary to the norms of society. Thus, a person who voluntarily undergoes starvation to protest a government policy is not considered to have a mental disorder.

■ **2. *Why does the determination of mental disorder always entail human judgment?***

Although this definition is useful as a guide for identifying mental disorder, it raises many questions. Just how "distressing" or "impairing" must a syndrome be to be considered "clinically significant"? What if it is distressing or impairing to other people, but not to the person whose behavior is presumably disordered? Since all behavior involves an interaction between the person and environment, how can we tell whether the source of impairment is really within the person, rather than just in the environment? How unusual must a response to a stressful situation be to be considered out of the range of normal? In the case of someone living in poverty or experiencing discrimination, how can we tell if the person's actions are normal responses to those conditions or represent something more? How can we distinguish deliberate acts of deviance from acts that result from mental disorder? Who has the right to decide that a person is mentally disordered: the person, the person's family, a psychiatrist or psychologist, a court of law? These are all tough questions that can never be answered strictly scientifically. The answers always represent human judgments, and they are always tinged by the social values of those doing the judging.

Perspectives on Mental Disorders

Clinicians, researchers, and scholars with a variety of backgrounds and interests have adopted different perspectives, different ways of describing and explaining mental disorders. The most prominent are the medical, the psychodynamic, the cognitive-behavioral, and the sociocultural. None of these perspectives has a monopoly on the truth; rather, each accounts for different aspects of a very complex phenomenon. Although each perspective can in principle be applied to all types of mental disorders, each seems to explain some types better than others.

■ **3. *How do the biological/medical, psychoanalytic, cognitive-behavioral, and sociocultural perspectives differ from each other in their accounts of the origins of mental disorders? What kinds of terms does each perspective bring to the task of describing disorders?***

The Biological/Medical Perspective

The biological/medical perspective, sometimes referred to as the ***medical model***, begins with the assumption that mental disorders are, or are like, physical diseases. The ancient Greeks are often credited with originating this perspective, and the physician Hippocrates recorded a system for identifying emotions and their disturbances with specific body fluids (see Figure 17.1). The medical model was revived in Europe near the end of the Middle Ages. By the nineteenth century, it was the dominant perspective in Europe and North America, and it remains so today.

Adherents of the medical model are most likely to speak of mental disorders as *illnesses* that have distinct *etiologies* (causes) and *prognoses* (expected outcomes) and to

Figure 17.1 ***The four temperaments***

The ancient Greek physician Hippocrates promulgated the belief that disturbed emotions and behavior are caused by an imbalance in the body's fluids. A melancholy (gloomy) temperament was attributed to an excess of black bile, a choleric (angry) temperament to an excess of yellow bile, a sanguine (cheerful) temperament to an excess of blood, and a phlegmatic (apathetic) temperament to an excess of phlegm.

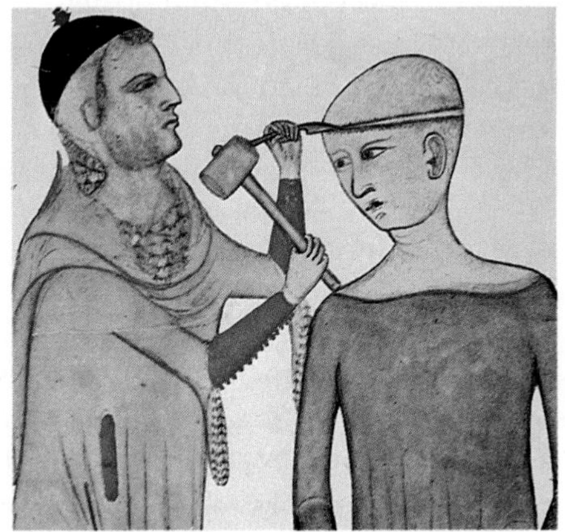

Madness as possession

This twelfth-century painting probably depicts trephination (piercing the skull to permit evil spirits to escape). With the revival of the medical model in the late Middle Ages, people gave up the use of trephination and other brutal treatments that were based on the belief that abnormal behavior indicates possession.

refer to persons receiving treatment as *patients*. The medical model is accepted most widely today among *psychiatrists*—mental health professionals who have undergone standard medical training and received an M.D. degree before specializing in mental problems. *Clinical psychologists*—who typically have a Ph.D. from a clinical psychology program—are somewhat less likely to accept the medical model. (Distinctions among various mental health professionals are described further in Chapter 18.)

Actually, there are two versions of the medical model. One is the literal version, which holds that mental disorders really *are* physical diseases—diseases of the brain or other physiological systems (such as the endocrine system) that act on the brain. The other, more figurative version, reflected in the diagnostic manual of the American Psychiatric Association, holds that mental disorders are *analogous* to physical diseases. From this view, disordered thoughts or emotions stem from disturbances that are not identifiable in concrete, anatomical or chemical terms, but are nevertheless considered to be located within the individual.

Freud's Psychodynamic Perspective

Freud's psychodynamic perspective, also called *psychoanalysis*, falls within the figurative mode of the medical-model tradition, but I have listed it separately because of its enormous influence. As discussed in Chapter 16, Freud described the mind in terms of divisions that are often in conflict with one another. The id (center of instincts), ego (center of reason, compromise, and self-protection), and superego (center of morality) are not physical parts of the brain, but are functional parts of the mind. They are products of the brain, to be sure, but are not something that one would expect to find in the anatomy.

In Freud's view, mental disorders occur when conflicts among these parts of the mind become extreme enough to cause severe anxiety, which the ego's defense mechanisms cannot control in an adaptive manner. The anxiety and maladaptive defenses can produce severe distortions of reality, obsessive thoughts or actions, physical manifestations such as paralysis of body parts, and other effects that impair the person's chance of surviving or finding happiness. The therapist's task is to discover through psychoanalysis the conflicts in the person's unconscious mind and to make the person aware of them so that the ego's conscious reasoning processes can begin to resolve them.

The Cognitive-Behavioral Perspective

The *behavioral perspective* in clinical psychology grew from the attempt to apply the findings of research on basic learning processes—particularly classical and operant conditioning—to the understanding and treatment of psychological problems. Similarly, the *cognitive perspective* grew from the attempt to apply the findings of research on cognitive processes to the understanding and treatment of psychological problems. These perspectives have merged to form what is often called the *cognitive-behavioral perspective.*

Clinical psychologists who adopt this perspective usually refer to the people they treat as *clients* who have *problems*, rather than as patients who have illnesses. The problems are seen as originating not in the client, but in the client's past or present environment. From this perspective, mental disorders are described as learned, maladaptive ways of acting and thinking that have been acquired through the person's interaction with the environment. Thus, irrational fears may have been learned through classical conditioning; such maladaptive behaviors as excessive drinking may have been learned through operant conditioning, and maladaptive thought patterns, such as "Nobody likes me," or "Anything I do will fail," may have been learned from demanding parents or through other social interactions. Various procedures for replacing such undesired habits with desired habits have been developed, and these are described in Chapter 18.

The Sociocultural Perspective

■ **4. *How do the examples of anorexia and bulimia illustrate the value of the sociocultural perspective?***

Mental disorders are products not only of the person and the person's immediate environment, but also of the larger culture within which the person develops. The kinds of psychological distress that people experience, the ways in which they express that distress, and the ways in which other people respond to a distressed person vary greatly from culture to culture and over any given culture's history. The *sociocultural perspective* brings insights from social psychology, sociology, and anthropology to the attempt to understand these variations.

The most striking evidence of cross-cultural variation in mental disorder can be found in *culture-bound syndromes*—expressions of mental distress that are almost completely limited to specific cultural groups. A syndrome called *koro*, for example, marked by an incapacitating fear that the penis will withdraw in the abdomen and cause death, is relatively common among men in Southeast Asia but almost nonexistent anywhere else (Tseng & others, 1992). Examples closer to home are *anorexia nervosa*, marked by an extraordinary preoccupation with thinness and a refusal to eat, sometimes to the point of death by starvation; and *bulimia nervosa*, marked by periods of extreme binge eating followed by self-induced vomiting, misuse of laxatives or other drugs, or other means to undo the effects of the binge.

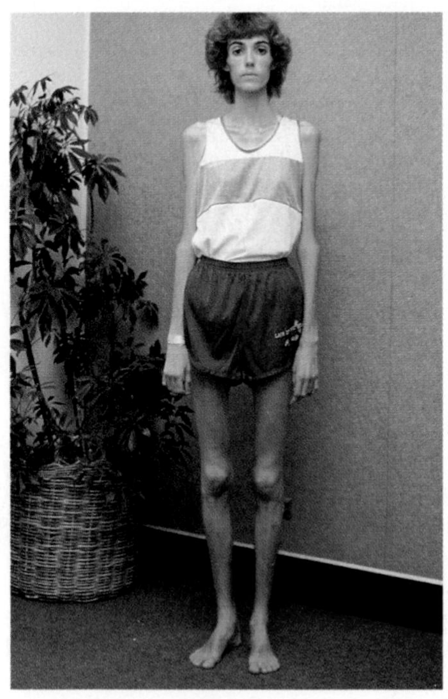

A syndrome of our times
Anorexia nervosa is increasingly prevalent among young women in our culture today, but was rare in the past and still is rare in non-Western cultures.

From the sociocultural perspective, it is no coincidence that these eating disorders first began to appear with some frequency in the 1970s in North America and Western Europe, primarily among adolescent girls and young women of the middle and upper social classes, and that their prevalence increased rapidly through the 1970s and 1980s (Gordon, 1990). During this period, Western culture became increasingly obsessed with dieting and the ideal of female thinness. Recent studies indicate that over half the college women in North America now suffer from some sort of eating problem and that somewhere between 2 percent and 18 percent meet the clinical criteria for a diagnosis of bulimia (Betz & Fitzgerald, 1993). Moreover, as would be predicted from the sociocultural perspective, the degree of disturbed eating among college women correlates strongly with the degree to which they believe that their worth, in the eyes of others, depends on their being attractive and thin (Mintz & Betz, 1988).

As you will see later in this chapter, the sociocultural perspective is concerned not just with culture-bound syndromes, but also with how the culture labels and reacts to manifestations of mental distress, and with how those labels and reactions affect the afflicted person.

A Framework for Thinking About Multiple Causation

■ **5. *How can the causes of mental disorders be categorized into three types?***

The four just-described perspectives emphasize different ways of thinking about the causes of mental disorders; but theorists of all perspectives recognize that any given disorder is likely to have multiple causes. A disorder typically arises from a preexisting susceptibility coupled with a triggering set of circumstances, and the consequences of the disorder may help to perpetuate it. Accordingly, a general framework for thinking about causes recognizes three main categories.

Predisposing causes are those that were in place well before the onset of the disorder and make the person susceptible to the disorder. Genetically inherited characteristics are most often mentioned in this category. But learned beliefs and habitual patterns of reacting to or thinking about stressful situations may also be included here, as may the sociocultural conditions under which one acquires such beliefs and habits. A young woman reared in upper-class, Western society is more likely to have acquired beliefs and values that predispose her to anorexia nervosa than is a young woman from a rural community in China.

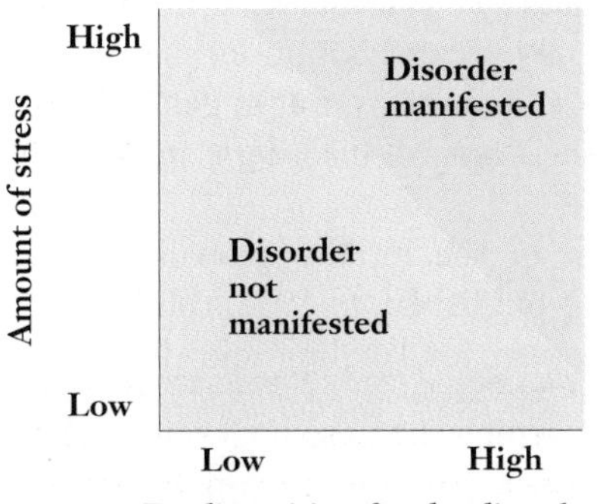

Figure 17.2 ***Inverse relationship between predisposition and stress in initiating a mental disorder***
The amount of stress needed to bring on a mental disorder decreases as the predisposition to the disorder increases.

Precipitating causes are the immediate events in a person's life that bring on the disorder. Any loss, such as the death of a loved one or the loss of a job; any real or perceived threat to one's well-being, such as physical disease; any new responsibilities, such as might occur as a result of marriage or job promotion; or any large change at all in the day-to-day course of life can, in the sufficiently predisposed person, bring on the mood or behavioral change that leads to diagnosis of a mental disorder. Precipitating causes are often talked about under the rubric of *stress*, a term that sometimes refers to the life event itself and sometimes to the worry, anxiety, hopelessness, or other negative experiences that accompany the life event (Lazarus, 1993). When the predisposition is very high, a seemingly trivial event can be sufficiently stressful to bring on a mental disorder. When the predisposition is very low, even an extraordinarily high degree of loss, threat, or change may fail to bring on a mental disorder. Figure 17.2 depicts this inverse relationship.

Maintaining causes are those consequences of a disorder that help keep it going once it begins. In some cases, a person may gain rewards, such as extra attention, which help to maintain the maladaptive behavior. But probably more often, the negative consequences of the disorder tend to maintain it. For example, a sufferer of depression may withdraw from friends, and lack of friends may perpetuate the depression. Expectations associated with a particular disorder may also play a maintaining role. In a culture that regards a particular disorder as incurable, a person diagnosed with that disorder may simply give up trying to change for the better.

Categorization and Diagnosis of Mental Disorders

We humans are inveterate categorizers. Rarely do we see an unfamiliar object as completely new and unique; instead, we see it as a member of some familiar category—a chair, a rose, a piece of quartz. Our world is more predictable and describable when we can relate each new object and event to a familiar category. This same response applies in the realm of mental disorders. Beginning long before the era of modern psychology and psychiatry, people everywhere have had systems for categorizing and labeling their psychological miseries. In keeping with the medical model long predominant in Western culture, the process of assigning a label to a person's mental disorder is referred to as *diagnosis*.

Classification and diagnosis are essential to any scientific study of mental disorders. Without a system to identify people whose disorders are similar to each other, the accumulation of knowledge about causes, effective treatments, and eventual outcomes would be impossible. But such a system is useful only to the degree that it is reliable and valid.

The Quest for Reliability: Development of *DSM-IV*

■ **6. *What does reliability mean with reference to a diagnostic system, and how did the developers of recent versions of the DSM strive to increase reliability?***

The *reliability* of a diagnostic system refers to the extent to which different diagnosticians, all trained in the use of the system, reach the same conclusion when they independently diagnose the same individuals. If you have ever gone to two different doctors with a physical complaint and been given two different, nonsynonymous labels for your disease, you know that, even in the realm of physical disorders, diagnosis is by no means completely reliable.

From the late nineteenth into the mid-twentieth century, various methods of categorizing and labeling mental disorders emerged in Europe and North America. One commonly used system divided mental disorders into two main categories: *neuroses*, in which anxiety is the underlying problem but the person is still in touch with reality; and *psychoses*, in which marked distortions in perception or thought render the person seriously out of touch with reality. Within these broad categories, certain terms for more specific disorders also became common, such as *phobia* as a type of neurosis and *schizophrenia* as a type of psychosis. But in general there was no agreed-upon way of defining these or other classes of disorders, and thus no agreed-upon diagnostic system.

To promote more effective communication in the rapidly growing mental health field, the American Psychiatric Association published, in 1952, the first version of what was meant to be a standardized system for labeling and diagnosing mental disorders. It was called the *Diagnostic and Statistical Manual of Mental Disorders*, abbreviated *DSM*. The first revision of the manual, *DSM-II*, appeared in 1968. Both editions were quite slim; diagnostic categories were defined briefly, in general terms, and much was left to the judgment of individual diagnosticians. Many of the classes were based on tenuous assumptions about the inner causes of the disorders, taken largely from Freud's theory. For example, some disorders within the general category of neuroses were defined in terms of unconscious anxiety and defenses against it, even though anxiety was not an observable symptom. The result was that studies aimed at assessing diagnostic reliability with those versions of the *DSM* revealed very little of it. For some categories, in fact, reliability was barely greater than would be expected if the labels had been assigned randomly (Matarazzo, 1983; Spitzer & Fleiss, 1974). Clearly, the manual needed major revision.

Hundreds of psychiatrists, clinical psychologists, and other mental health professionals worked in teams to create *DSM-III*, a much thicker volume published in 1980. Their goal was to define mental disorders as objectively as possible so as to remove as much guesswork as possible from the task of diagnosis and thereby increase diagnostic reliability. To do this, they dropped *DSM-II* categories that were based on unobservable symptoms or inferred causes (including the overriding categories of neuroses and psychoses) and formulated new categories in terms of symptoms that an unbiased clinician or researcher could observe in the subject or learn from the subject by asking appropriate questions. To test alternative ways of diagnosing each disorder, they conducted field studies in which subjects who might have a particular disorder were diagnosed independently by a number of clinicians or researchers using each of several alternative diagnostic systems. In general, those systems that produced the greatest reliability—that is, the greatest agreement among the diagnosticians as to who had or did not have a particular disorder—were retained. As a result, the diagnostic reliability of *DSM-III* was quite high—comparable in many cases to the levels achieved in diagnosing physical disorders (Grove, 1987; Matarazzo, 1983).

The manual was updated somewhat and reissued as *DSM-III-R* in 1987. A fourth edition, ***DSM-IV***, also a relatively minor revision but based on extensive research aimed at improving its reliability still further, is scheduled for publication in

1994. All references to *DSM-IV* in this chapter are to a near-final draft that was released in March, 1993.

As an example of diagnostic criteria arrived at by these methods, consider those used in *DSM-IV* for anorexia nervosa. The person must (a) have a body weight less than 85 percent of expected weight; (b) express an intense fear of gaining weight or becoming fat; (c) express a distorted body image, for example, by saying "I feel fat" even when emaciated; and (d) if a post-pubertal female, have lost her menstrual cycle for at least three successive periods (a condition brought on by a lack of body fat). If any of these criteria—which are spelled out in more detail in a set of diagnostic procedures for clinicians (Spitzer & others, 1987)—are not met, a diagnosis of anorexia nervosa would not be made. Notice that all of these criteria are based on observable characteristics or self-descriptions by the person being diagnosed; none rely on inferences about underlying causes or unconscious symptoms that could easily result in disagreement among diagnosticians who have different perspectives.

The Question of Validity

■ 7. ***How can the validity of the DSM be improved through research and further revisions?***

The *validity* of a diagnostic system is an index of the extent to which the categories it identifies are clinically meaningful (see Chapter 2 for a more general discussion of both validity and reliability). Do two people with the same diagnosis truly suffer in similar ways? Does their suffering stem from similar causes? Does the label help predict the future course of the disorder and help in deciding on a beneficial treatment? To the degree that questions like these can be answered in the affirmative, a diagnostic system is valid.

Some psychologists and psychiatrists argue that the creators of *DSM-III* and *-IV* sacrificed validity for the sake of reliability (Wakefield, 1992). They contend that the effort to attain agreement among different diagnosticians led to an overemphasis of superficial symptoms at the expense of more basic underlying symptoms or causes, which must be inferred through subjective clinical judgments. Others, however—especially those who are engaged in systematic research on mental disorders—counter that reliability is a prerequisite for validity (Wilson, 1993). In order to conduct the research needed to determine whether or not a diagnosis is valid, by the criteria listed above, one must first form a *tentative, reliable* diagnostic system. To determine whether people suffering from anorexia nervosa, for example, have similar histories, experience similar outcomes, and benefit from similar treatment, one must first have a consistent way of deciding who falls into the population to be studied. The results of such studies can lead to new means of diagnosis, or new subcategories that describe variations within the original category, leading to increased validity.

Robert Spitzer, who led the task force that created *DSM-III* and *DSM-III-R*, and who served as special advisor in the creation of *DSM-IV*, routinely refers to the diagnoses in the *DSM* as "hypotheses to be tested" (Wilson, 1993). The results of research based on each version of the manual led to the changes incorporated into the next, and future research will eventuate in further changes. Psychiatry has moved past its early tendency toward dogma and become increasingly amenable to science—an enterprise in which the presumption of ignorance, not knowledge, is the driving force. In the subsequent sections of this chapter, you will read about the results of research studies concerning causes and outcomes of various disorders that were diagnosed by *DSM-III* or *DSM-III-R* criteria; the results partly confirm and partly challenge the validity of those diagnostic systems.

The main categories of *DSM-IV*, most of which also existed in *DSM-III* and *-III-R*, are surveyed in Table 17.1 on page 612.

Table 17.1 ***Summary of DSM-IV categories of mental disorders***

Anxiety disorders[1] Disorders in which fear or anxiety is a prominent symptom. Examples: *generalized anxiety disorder, phobias, obsessive-compulsive disorder, panic disorder,* and *posttraumatic stress disorder.*

Mood disorders[1] Disorders marked by depression or mania. Examples: *major depression, dysthymia, bipolar disorder,* and *cyclothymia.*

Somatoform disorders[1] Disorders involving physical (somatic) symptoms arising from unconscious psychological processes. Examples: *conversion disorder, somatoform pain disorder, somatization disorder,* and *hypochondriasis.*

Psychological factors affecting medical condition[1, 2] Characteristic ways of behaving or thinking that exacerbate or can bring on adverse medical conditions. Example: the hostile, pressured behavior known as *Type A behavior,* which can promote cardiovascular disease.

Substance-related disorders[1] Disorders brought on by drugs such as alcohol, amphetamines, cocaine, or opiates. Examples: intoxicating effects, withdrawal effects, dependence (the intense craving for the drug), and effects of brain damage caused by prolonged use of the drug.

Dissociative disorders[1] Disorders in which a part of one's experience is separated off (dissociated) from one's conscious memory or identity. Examples: *psychogenic amnesia, fugue states,* and *multiple personality disorder.*

Schizophrenia and other psychotic disorders[1] *Schizophrenia* is a long-term disorder marked by delusions, hallucinations, disorganized thought and speech, and flattened or inappropriate affect. Another psychotic disorder is *delusional disorder,* which involves persistent delusions (usually of persecution) *not* accompanied by other disruptions of thought or mood that would lead to a diagnosis of schizophrenia.

Sexual and gender identity disorders *Sexual disorders* are those of sexual functioning, and include *paraphilias* (in which bizarre imagery or acts are necessary for sexual excitement, such as *fetishism, exhibitionism,* and *sexual sadism*), and *psychosexual dysfunctions* (inability to become sexually aroused or to complete intercourse in a satisfying way). *Gender identity disorders* involve a strong and persistent desire to be, or appear to be, a member of the other gender.

Eating disorders Disorders marked by extreme undereating, overeating, or purging, or by excessive concern about gaining weight. Examples: *anorexia nervosa* and *bulimia nervosa.*

Sleep disorders Disorders include *insomnia* (too little sleep), *hypersomnia* (too much sleep), *sleep-wake disorder* (inability to establish a sleep-wake cycle corresponding with the 24-hour day), and disorders involving sleepwalking, fear of sleep, or fear of nightmares.

Impulse control disorders not elsewhere specified Disorders characterized by impulsive behaviors that are harmful to the self or others. Examples: *intermittent explosive disorder* (outbursts of aggression resulting in assault or property destruction), *kleptomania* (impulsive stealing), *pyromania* (impulsive setting of fires), and *pathological gambling.*

Disorders usually first diagnosed in infancy, childhood, or adolescence A diverse group of disorders that always or almost always first appear before adulthood. Examples: various forms of mental retardation, learning disorders, and language development disorders.

Delirium, dementia, amnestic, and other cognitive disorders A diverse group of disorders of perception, memory, and thought that stem from known damage to the brain. Examples: disorders due to strokes, physical trauma to the brain, and degenerative brain diseases such as *Alzheimer's disease.*

Adjustment disorder Maladaptive, excessive emotional reaction to an identified stressful event that occurred within the previous six months.

Factitious disorders Made-up or self-induced syndromes designed to attract attention or care.

Personality disorders[3] Disorders involving inflexible, maladaptive personality traits. Examples: *antisocial personality disorder* (a history of antisocial acts and violation of others' rights, with no sense of guilt), *histrionic personality disorder* (excessively emotional, overly dramatic attention seeking), and *narcissistic personality disorder* (unwarranted sense of self importance and demand for constant attention or admiration).

[1]The first seven categories in the list correspond with major sections of this chapter.

[2]*Psychological factors affecting medical condition* is a subcategory of a larger, miscellaneous category called *other conditions that may be a focus of clinical attention,* which includes such diverse problems as movement disorders induced by medicines, marital problems, child neglect or abuse, and religious or spiritual problems.

[3]Because personality disorders involve a person's long-standing style of thinking and acting rather than a change in the person, they are categorized on a separate dimension, or *axis* (Axis II), from the other categories (which comprise Axis I).

Source: Developed from a preliminary draft of *DSM-IV* published in March, 1993 (American Psychiatric Association, 1993).

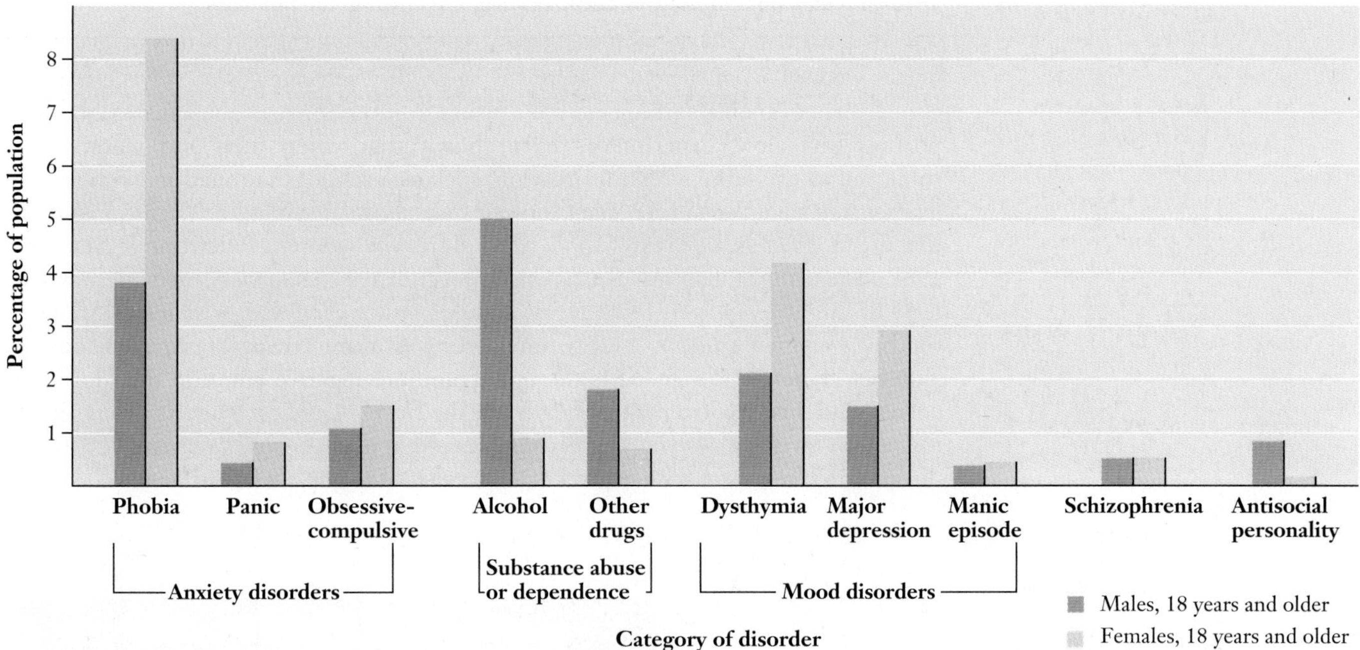

Figure 17.3 ***One-month prevalence of various mental disorders***

A mental-health survey conducted in five U.S. metropolitan areas revealed the percentages shown here of men and women diagnosed by *DSM-III* criteria as having manifested various mental disorders within the month preceding the survey. Only those disorders for which the 1-month prevalence was greater than 0.3 percent are shown in this graph. (Data from Regier & others, 1988.)

Prevalence of Mental Disorders

Shortly after the development of *DSM-III* (and before *DSM-III-R*), the National Institute of Mental Health initiated a massive survey to assess the prevalence of mental disorders in various locations in the United States. The data were collected by trained interviewers and analyzed by computers programmed to make diagnoses according to *DSM-III* criteria. The results for the most common disorders assessed in the study are summarized separately for men and women in Figure 17.3. The graph shows the percentage who manifested each disorder within the 1-month period prior to the interview (Regier & others, 1988). Most of these prevalences are about half as great as the lifetime prevalences—the percentage estimated to manifest the disorder at some point in their lives (Robins & others, 1984). You may wish to look back at this figure as you read about the various disorders later in the chapter.

What Accounts for Apparent Gender Differences in Prevalence?

■ **8.** ***From the sociocultural perspective, what are three ways to account for gender differences in the prevalence of specific mental disorders?***

Figure 17.3 reveals a pattern of gender differences that has also been found in other studies. Little difference between males and females occurs in the overall prevalence when all disorders are combined, but large differences are found for specific categories. In particular, women are more likely than men to be diagnosed with anxiety and mood disorders, and men are more likely than women to be diagnosed with alcohol and other drug-use disorders. In theory, such differences might arise directly from biological differences between men and women, or they might arise from the different roles and expectations that society ascribes to men and women. Within the sociocultural category of causes, specific explanations have centered on self-report biases, observer biases, and real experimental differences.

Differences in Reporting or Suppressing Psychological Distress

The diagnosis of anxiety and mood disorders necessarily depends to a great extent on self-report. Men, who are supposed to be the "stronger" sex, may be less inclined than women to admit mental distress in interviews or questionnaires. Supporting this view, experiments have shown that when men and women are subjected to the same stressful situation, such as a school examination, men report less anxiety than do women even though they show physiological signs of distress that are as great as, or greater than, those shown by women (Polefrone & Manuck, 1987). Men might also use alcohol and illegal drugs to suppress their mental distress or might express it in the form of anger rather than fear or sadness. Anger is the one negative emotion that in our society is more acceptable in men than in women (Hyde, 1986), and it is the only common negative emotion that does not correspond directly to a major category in the *DSM*. A person who expresses severe distress in terms of fear or sadness may receive a diagnosis of an anxiety or mood disorder, but a person who expresses it in terms of anger usually will not.

A substantial difference

Far more men than women are diagnosed with alcoholism. This may reflect both a difference in the actual prevalence of the disorder and a difference in the way it is manifested.

Bias in Diagnosis

Diagnosticians may, to some degree, find certain disorders more often in one gender or the other because they *expect* to find them there. To test this possibility, Maureen Ford and Thomas Widiger (1989) mailed a fictitious case history to several hundred clinical psychologists throughout the United States and asked them to make diagnoses using *DSM-III* criteria. For some the case was constructed to resemble the criteria for *antisocial personality*, a disorder found more often in men than women. For others the case was constructed to resemble the criteria for *histrionic personality*, a disorder found more often in women. (You can find a brief description of these disorders under Personality Disorders in Table 17.1.) Each of these case types was written in a separate, otherwise identical form applying to a male patient or a female patient. As you can see in Figure 17.4, the diagnoses were strongly affected by gender. Given the exact same case histories, the male patient was far more likely than the female to receive a diagnosis of antisocial personality, and the female was far more likely than the male to receive a diagnosis of histrionic personality.

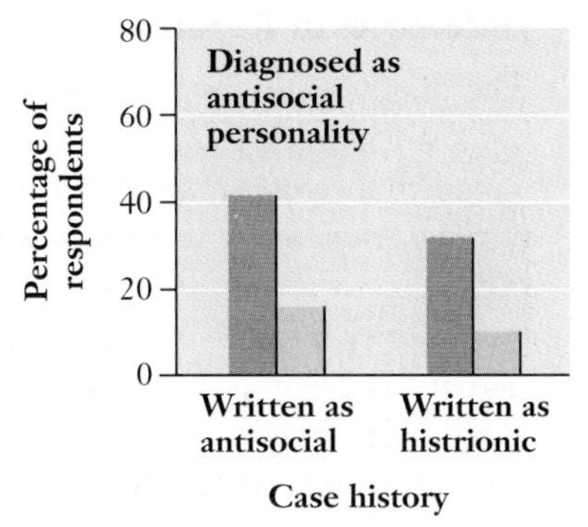

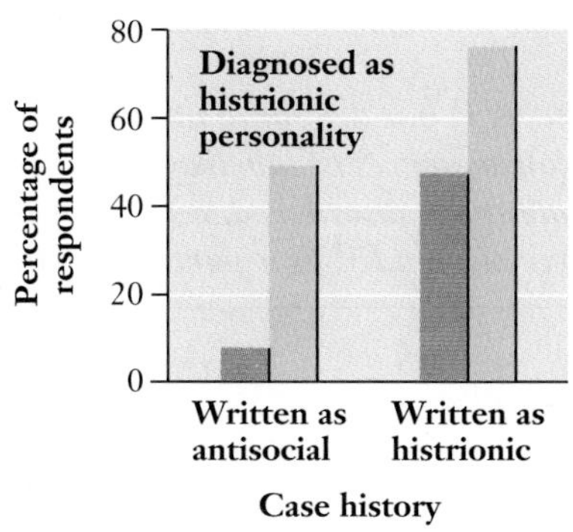

Male case
Female case

Figure 17.4 ***Evidence of a gender bias in diagnosis***

In this study, fictitious case histories were more likely to be diagnosed as antisocial personality if they described a fictitious male patient, and as histrionic personality if they described a fictitious female patient, regardless of which disorder the case history was designed to resemble. (Data from Ford & Widiger, 1989.)

Might a similar bias have operated in the survey of the prevalence of disorders, shown in Figure 17.3? That question is hard to answer. On the one hand, the interviewers were trained to ask questions and record data using a standard format, and diagnoses were then made from those data by a computer program, which presumably had no gender bias programmed into it. On the other hand, there is no way to rule out the possibility that interviewers unconsciously interpreted and recorded responses differently depending on the gender of the person they were interviewing.

Some critics have argued that the *DSM* contains inherent gender biases within the definitions of some of its disorders. For example, they argue that the diagnostic system is such that staying home during the day—an event more common among women than among men due to social roles in our society—can under some conditions be counted as a symptom of depression. Thus, if a woman whose job is caring for the home and children, and a man whose job is outside of the home, are the same in all other respects, the woman is more likely to receive a diagnosis of depression. (For both sides of the inherent-bias argument, see Kaplan, 1983, and Williams & Spitzer, 1983.)

Differences in Stressfulness of Men's and Women's Experiences

A third approach has been to assume that to some degree gender differences in mental disorders are real and to search for possible causes in the different social experiences of men and women. Women in our culture are more likely than men to live in poverty, to experience discrimination, to have been sexually or physically abused in childhood, and to be physically abused by their spouse—all of which can contribute to depression, anxiety, and various other disorders (Koss, 1990; Strickland, 1992). Moreover, some psychologists have argued that the traditional role of wife and mother in our society is more conducive to anxiety and depression than is the role of husband and father (Barnett & Baruch, 1987). The wife and mother spends more time in isolation from other adults and performs jobs that are accorded little prestige by society at large. She is often made to feel responsible for events over which she has little real control, such as her children's illnesses, accidents, or poor school performance. The combination of high demands, low real control, and low prestige is the ideal mix for creating both anxiety and depression. Consistent with this view, taking a job outside of the home (even when it is added to the at-home job) has been found to reduce psychological distress in women (Baruch & others, 1987). In addition, analysis of data collected between 1950 and 1980 suggests that over the course of those years, as employment for men and women became somewhat more similar, the gender gap in anxiety and mood disorders decreased (Kessler & McRae, 1981).

A Danger in Labeling

9. *What are some negative consequences of labeling a person as mentally disordered, and what is recommended as a partial solution?*

Diagnosing and labeling may be essential for the scientific study of mental disorders, but labels can be harmful. Controlled experiments have shown that a label implying mental disorder can blind clinicians and others to qualities of the person that are not captured by the label, can reduce the esteem accorded to the person by others, and can reduce the labeled person's self-esteem. For example, in one experiment psychotherapists who watched a videotape of a man talking about his personal problems rated the man's level of adjustment far more negatively if they were led to believe that he was a mental patient than if they believed he was not a patient (Langer & Abelson, 1974). In another experiment, former mental patients performed more poorly in a social interaction if they believed that the person with whom they were interacting knew about their former patient status than if they believed that the person was unaware of that status (Farina & others, 1971). Chapter 18 describes further evidence for harmful effects of labels, based on the personal experiences of hospitalized mental patients and of individuals who have feigned that status for research purposes.

Labeling the Disorder, Not the Person

What can be done to diminish the blinding effect of labels? As a partial solution to the problem (but certainly not a complete one), the American Psychiatric Association (1987, 1993) recommends that clinicians apply diagnostic labels only to people's disorders, not to people themselves. For example, a client or patient might be referred to as *a person who has schizophrenia*, or *who suffers from alcoholism*, but should not be referred to as *a schizophrenic* or *an alcoholic*. The distinction might at first seem subtle, but if you think about it you may agree that it is not so subtle in psychological impact. If we say "John has schizophrenia," we tend to be reminded that John is first and foremost a person, with qualities like those of other people, and that his having schizophrenia is just one of many things we could say about him. In contrast, the statement "John is a schizophrenic" tends to imply that everything about him is summed up by that label. As I talk about specific disorders in the remainder of this chapter and the next, I will attempt to follow this advice even though it produces some awkward wording at times. I also urge you to add, in your mind, yet another step of linguistic complexity. When I refer to "a person who has schizophrenia," you should read this statement as "a person who *has been diagnosed by someone* as having schizophrenia," keeping in mind that diagnostic systems are never completely reliable.

Medical Students' Disease

The ability of labels to cause psychological harm demonstrates the power of suggestion. The power of suggestion also lies behind *medical students' disease*. This disease, which could also be called *introductory psychology students' disease*, is characterized by a strong tendency to relate personally to, and find in oneself, the symptoms of any disease or disorder described in a textbook. Medical students' disease was described by the nineteenth century humorist Jerome K. Jerome (1889/1982) in an essay about his own discomfort upon reading a textbook of medical diagnoses. After explaining his discoveries that he must have typhoid fever, St. Vitus's Dance, and a multitude of diseases he had never heard of before, he wrote, "The only malady I concluded I had *not* got was housemaid's knee . . . I had walked into that reading-room a happy, healthy man. I crawled out a decrepit wreck." As you read the following pages, brace yourself against medical students' disease. Everyone has at least some of the symptoms, to some degree, of essentially every disorder that can be found in this chapter, *DSM-IV*, or any other compendium.

Anxiety Disorders

The rabbit crouches, frozen in the grass, minimizing its chance of being detected. Its sensory systems are at maximum alertness, all tuned to the approaching dog. With muscles tense, the rabbit is poised to leap away at the first sign that it has been detected; its heart races, and its adrenal glands secrete hormones that help prepare the body for extended flight if necessary. Here we see fear operating adaptively, as it was designed to operate by evolution.

We humans differ from the rabbit on two counts: Our biological evolution added a massive, thinking cerebral cortex atop the more primitive structures that organize fear; and our cultural evolution led us to develop a habitat far different from that of our ancestors. Our pattern of fear is not unlike the rabbit's, but it can be triggered by an enormously greater variety of both real and imagined stimuli, and in many cases the fear is not adaptive. Fear is not adaptive when it causes a job candidate to freeze at an interview, or overwhelms a student's mind during an examination, or confines a person who can vividly imagine the worst possible consequence of every change to chronic inaction and familiar paths.

Anxiety disorders are those in which fear or anxiety is the most prominent symptom. Although *fear* and *anxiety* can be used as synonyms, fear is more often used when the feared stimulus or event is specific and present, and *anxiety* is more often used when the stimulus or event is vague, not identifiable, or in the future. Cognitively, the anxious person seems to focus on his or her own lack of ability to cope with unpredictable future dangers (Barlow, 1991). The treatment of these and other disorders is discussed in Chapter 18; but it is worth noting here that anxiety disorders are, as a group, the easiest disorders to treat and have the best long-term prognosis (chance of recovery).

The *DSM* recognizes five subclasses of anxiety disorders, each of which is discussed briefly below.

Generalized Anxiety Disorder

Generalized anxiety is called *generalized* because it is not focused on any one specific threat; instead, it attaches itself to various threats, real and imagined. Sufferers of ***generalized anxiety disorder*** experience continuous muscle tension, irritability, difficulty in sleeping, and sometimes gastrointestinal upset due to overactivity of the autonomic nervous system. Their most common psychological complaint is worry. In one study conducted at an anxiety clinic, all patients who had been diagnosed with generalized anxiety disorder, but only about half of those diagnosed with other anxiety disorders, answered yes to the question, "Do you worry excessively about minor things?" (Barlow, 1988). They worried most about family members, money, work, and illness—as do other people—but to a far greater extent and with much less provocation.

Generalized anxiety disorder was not assessed in the prevalence study illustrated in Figure 17.3, but other research suggests that somewhere between 2% and 5% of the North American population suffer from the disorder, by *DSM-III* criteria, at some time in life (Barlow, 1988). These percentages probably underestimate the actual number who suffer from generalized anxiety, because the *DSM-III* diagnostic criteria are quite stringent: The generalized anxiety must seriously impair daily functioning for at least 6 months and occur independently of any other diagnosable mental disorder.

■ **10.** ***How can the onset of generalized anxiety disorder be explained in terms of predisposing and precipitating causes?***

Research suggests that generalized anxiety disorder is moderately heritable and that the genes promoting it may be the same as those promoting major depression. In one large-scale twin study, the identical twins of people suffering from either generalized anxiety disorder or major depression had equally elevated prevalences of both disorders (Kendler & others, 1992). Other studies have shown that people who suffer from one of these disorders frequently suffer at some point in their lives from the other (Hollandsworth, 1990).

On the environmental side, frequent, unpredictable traumatic experiences in childhood can apparently predispose a person to generalized anxiety disorder (Torgersen, 1986), and the disorder typically first occurs in adulthood following a major life change such as getting a new job or having a baby, or a disturbing event such as an accident or illness (Blazer & others, 1987). Researchers approaching the disorder from a cognitive perspective suggest that *hypervigilance*—a persistent tendency to scan the environment for signs of impending danger and to disregard cues indicative of safety—may provide the link between early trauma and generalized anxiety disorder (Beck & Emery, 1985; Eysenck, 1992). Consistent with this view, people who develop generalized anxiety disorder are apparently hypervigilant before the onset of the disorder and continue to be so when the disorder is in remission (Eysenck, 1992).

Taking all these findings into account, the typical etiology (description of causes) of generalized anxiety disorder might be summarized as follows:

> Genetic predisposition and/or early traumatic experiences → hypervigilance → generalized anxiety disorder following a life change or other disturbing event

From a sociocultural perspective, the uncertainties of modern life may help explain the high incidence of generalized anxiety. In a world of rapidly changing values and expectations, how do we judge right from wrong or safe from unsafe? Of the many unpredictable paths that seem open at any point in life, how do we decide which to take? Will today's skills meet tomorrow's demands? Such threats may be felt only dimly and lead not to conscious articulation of specific fears but to generalized anxiety. And, unlike the predator that scares the rabbit one minute and is gone the next, these threats are with us always.

Phobias

In contrast to generalized anxiety, a ***phobia*** is an intense, irrational fear that is very clearly related to a particular category of object or event. In the most common cases, referred to as ***simple phobias***, the fear is of something specific, such as a particular type of animal (such as snakes), substance (such as blood), or situation (such as heights, or being closed in). In other cases, referred to as ***social phobias***, the fear is of being scrutinized or evaluated by other people; included here are fears of public speaking, of eating in public places, and of meeting new people. Usually a phobia sufferer is aware that the fear is irrational but still cannot control it. The person knows full well that the neighbor's kitten won't claw anyone to death, that people don't ordinarily drown in ankle-deep water, or that the crowd of 10-year-olds at the corner won't attack. People with phobias suffer doubly—from the fear itself and from knowing how irrational they are to have such a fear.

■ **11.** ***What evidence links phobias to normal fears, and how might phobias be explained in terms of learning, evolution, and culture?***

Probably everyone has some irrational fears, and, as in all other anxiety disorders, the difference between the normal condition and the disorder is an arbitrary one of degree, not kind. Simple phobias are usually of things that many people fear to some extent, such as snakes, spiders, blood, darkness, or heights; and social phobias may simply be extreme forms of shyness. In line with this view, simple phobias usually originate in early to middle childhood, when fears of such things as animals and darkness are most common among people in general; and social phobias usually originate in adolescence, when normal shyness is most likely to be a problem (Marks, 1987). Simple phobias are much more often diagnosed in females than in males, whereas social phobias are diagnosed about equally often in both genders (Barlow, 1988), and these facts are also consistent with the idea that phobias lie on a continuum with normal fears. Men and boys in our society are much less likely

A dreadful view

Phobia comes from a Greek word meaning "flight," or "fear." If you experience such feelings when viewing this scene, you have some sense of what a person with a height phobia feels when looking out a one-story window.

than women and girls to admit to fears of such things as spiders and darkness, but are about equally likely to admit to shyness. The gender difference in simple phobias could stem from the fact that boys in our society are more strongly encouraged than are girls to overcome or to hide their childhood fears (Fodor, 1982).

As with most other mental disorders, little is known about how phobias usually arise. Behaviorists, from John B. Watson (1924) on, have argued that phobias are acquired by classical conditioning, through experiences in which the now-feared stimulus had been paired with some unconditionally fearful stimulus. A problem with this interpretation is that most people with phobias cannot recall any specific experiences with the feared stimulus or situation that could have provided the basis for such learning (McNally & Steketee, 1985; Murray & Foote, 1979). It also does not explain such findings as this: In Burlington, Vermont, where there are no dangerous snakes, the single most common simple phobia is of snakes (Agras & others, 1969). If phobias are acquired by conditioning, why aren't phobias of such things as automobiles or (in Burlington) icy sidewalks more common? Another theory, first proposed by Martin Seligman (1971), is that people are genetically prepared by evolution to fear certain classes of objects or events (discussed in Chapter 5). This idea is helpful in understanding why phobias of snakes, darkness, and heights are more common than are those of automobiles and electric outlets, but it does not explain why some people acquire phobias and others don't.

Consistent with the sociocultural perspective, phobias can take different forms in different cultures. For example, a social phobia common in Japan but almost nonexistent in the West is *taijin kyofusho*, an incapacitating fear of offending or harming others through one's own awkward social behavior or imagined physical defect (Kirmayer, 1991). The focus of cognition for a sufferer of this phobia is on the harm to others, not on embarrassment to the self as in social phobias in the West. *Taijin kyofusho* is described by Japanese psychiatrists as a pathological exaggeration of the modesty and sensitive regard for others that, at lower levels, is considered proper in Japan.

Obsessive-Compulsive Disorder

An *obsession* is a disturbing thought that intrudes repeatedly on a person's consciousness even though the person recognizes it as irrational. A *compulsion* is a repetitive action that is usually performed in response to an obsession. Most people experience moderate forms of these, especially in childhood. I remember a period in sixth grade when, while reading in school, the thought would repeatedly enter my mind that reading could make my eyes fall out. The only way I could banish this thought and go on reading was to close my eyelids down hard—a compulsive act that I fancied might push my eyes solidly back into their sockets. Of course, I knew that both the thought and the action were irrational, yet the thought kept intruding, and the only way I could abolish it for a while was to perform the action. Like most normal obsessions and compulsions, this one did not really disrupt my life, and it simply faded with time.

12. ***How is an obsessive-compulsive disorder similar to a phobia?***

People who are diagnosed with ***obsessive-compulsive disorder*** are those for whom such thoughts and actions don't fade, but worsen and seriously interfere with daily life. An obsessive-compulsive disorder is similar to a phobia in that it involves a specific irrational fear, and different primarily in that the fear is of something that exits only as a thought and can be reduced only by performing some ritual. People with obsessive-compulsive disorder, like those with phobias, suffer also from their knowledge of the irrationality of their actions and go to great lengths to hide them from other people.

Comparing the obsessions experienced by people who have this disorder with those experienced by people who don't has revealed no systematic differences in

Magnificent obsession

An obsession is a disorder only if it is harmful to the self or others. If it is not harmful, it may sometimes bring a measure of fame.

content, only in intensity (Rachman & DeSilva, 1978). The most common obsessions concern death, disease, or disfigurement, and the most common compulsions involve checking or cleaning. People with checking compulsions may spend hours each day repeatedly checking doors to be sure they are locked, the gas stove to be sure it is turned off, automobile wheels to be sure they are on tight, and so on (Rachman, 1985). People with cleaning compulsions may wash their hands every few minutes, scrub everything they eat, and sterilize their dishes and clothes in response to their obsessions about disease-producing germs and dirt. Some compulsions, however, bear no apparent logical relationship to the obsession that triggers them. For example, a woman obsessed by the thought that her husband would die in an automobile accident could in fantasy protect him by dressing and undressing in a specific pattern twenty times every day (Marks, 1987).

13. ***From the behavioral perspective, what is posited as a maintaining cause of obsessive-compulsive disorder, and from the cognitive and biological perspectives, what are posited as predisposing causes?***

As with other disorders, theorists with different perspectives focus on different possible causes of obsessive-compulsive disorder. Behavioral theorists point out that compulsive actions, regardless of how they are started, are reinforced each time they occur by the sharp reduction in anxiety that follows them (Foa & others, 1985). Cognitive theorists have supplied evidence that this disorder occurs most often in people who already have a general tendency to think in rigid ways and to expect the worst in new situations (Steketee & Foa, 1985). Biologically oriented theorists point to success in treating the disorder with drugs; to evidence that the disorder sometimes follows known damage to the basal ganglia of the brain; and to brain-scan studies showing an unusual pattern of metabolic activity in the basal ganglia of those with the disorder (Rapaport, 1989, 1991). One possibility is that a predisposing condition for the disorder is an abnormality in the basal ganglia—a brain structure (discussed in Chapter 6) that is known to be involved in the initiation and inhibition of learned, habitual actions (Rapaport, 1991).

Panic Disorder

Panic is a feeling of helpless terror, such as one might experience if cornered by a predator. For people who suffer from ***panic disorder***, this sense of terror comes at unpredictable times, unprovoked by any specific threat in the environment. Because the panic is unrelated to any specific situation or idea, the panic victim, unlike the victim of a phobia or obsessive-compulsion, cannot avoid it by avoiding certain situations or relieve it by engaging in certain rituals. Panic attacks usually last several minutes, and are usually accompanied by high physiological arousal (including rapid heart rate and shortness of breath) and a fear of losing control and behaving in some frantic, desperate way (Barlow & Craske, 1988). Between attacks the victim may experience almost constant anxiety about having another attack. The victim especially fears having an attack in a public place, where embarrassment or humiliation might follow a loss of control in front of others. About 90 percent of panic-attack victims develop *agoraphobia*, an intense fear of public places, sometime after their first panic attack (Breier & others, 1986).

14. ***What learned thought pattern might be a maintaining cause of panic disorder?***

Twin studies indicate that panic disorder is at least moderately heritable (Torgersen, 1990). On the environmental side, the panic victim commonly experiences the first attack shortly after some stressful event or life change (Breier & others, 1986). In the laboratory or clinic, panic attacks can be brought on in people with the disorder by lactic acid injection, high doses of caffeine, carbon dioxide inhalation, and other procedures that increase heart and breathing rate (Hecker & Thorpe, 1992). This has led to the view that a maintaining cause, if not a predisposing cause, of the disorder is a learned tendency to interpret physiological arousal as catastrophic (Clark, 1988). One treatment, used by cognitive therapists, is to help the person learn to interpret each attack as a temporary physiological condition rather than a sign of mental derangement or impending doom.

Post-Traumatic Stress Disorder

■ **15.** ***How does post-traumatic stress disorder differ from other anxiety disorders?***

Unlike the other anxiety disorders, ***post-traumatic stress disorder*** is directly and explicitly tied to a traumatic incident or set of incidents that the affected person has experienced. It is most common in torture victims, concentration camp survivors, people who have been violently assaulted, people who have survived a horrible accident, and soldiers who have experienced the horrors of battle. The disorder may begin immediately after the traumatic experience or later, sometimes many months later. It typically involves painful and uncontrollable reliving of the traumatic events, both in nightmares and daytime thoughts. Other common symptoms are sleeplessness, guilt (perhaps for surviving when others didn't), depression (perhaps from a sense of injustice in the world and lack of control over one's fate), and general irritability. In an effort to relieve such symptoms, post-traumatic stress victims may turn to alcohol or street drugs, which often compounds the problem.

Post-traumatic stress seems to be particularly likely to occur if a person cannot make sense of the trauma. This observation has been used by some to explain why U.S. veterans of the Vietnam War have experienced this disorder at a much higher rate than did U.S. veterans of World War II. U.S. citizens felt a sense of national unity about their purpose in World War II, but ambiguity and in many cases hostility concerning their purpose in Vietnam. According to one study, 20 percent of Vietnam veterans were still—15 years after their period of service—suffering from post-traumatic stress disorder by *DSM-III* criteria (Card, 1987).

Mood Disorders

Mood refers to a prolonged emotional state that colors many if not all aspects of a person's thought and behavior. It is useful (though somewhat oversimplified) to think of a single dimension of mood, running from depression at one end to elation at the other. Because we all have tasted both, we have an idea of what they are like. Both are normal experiences, but at times either of them can become so intense or prolonged as to promote harmful, even life-threatening actions. Severe depression can keep a person from working, lead to withdrawal from friends, or even provoke suicide. Severe elation, called *mania*, can lead to outrageous behaviors that turn other people away, or to dangerous acts that stem from a false sense of security and bravado. *DSM-IV* identifies two main categories of ***mood disorders***: These are ***depressive disorders***, characterized by prolonged or extreme depression; and ***bipolar disorders***, characterized by alternating episodes of depression and mania.

Table 17.2 *Comparison of anxious thoughts with depressive thoughts*

Anxious person
What if I get sick and become an invalid?
Something will happen to someone I care about.
Something might happen that will ruin my appearance.
I am going to have a heart attack.
Depressed person
I'm worthless.
I'm a social failure.
I have become physically unattractive.
Life isn't worth living.

Source: Adapted from "Differentiating anxiety and depression: A test of the cognitive content-specificity hypothesis" by A. T. Beck, G. Brown, J. I. Eidelson, R. A. Steer, & J. H. Riskind, 1987, *Journal of Abnormal Psychology*, *96*, p. 181.

Depression

■ **16.** ***How does depression differ from generalized anxiety?***

Much has been written about the differences and similarities between depression and generalized anxiety. You have already seen evidence that the two disorders often co-exist in the same people and seem to be predisposed by the same genes. Both also involve a shared cluster of negative feelings (Zinbarg & others, 1992). Two major distinctions between them are that (a) anxiety is more likely than depression to be accompanied by physiological arousal and hypervigilance, and (b) depression is more likely than anxiety to entail an absence of pleasure and a sense of hopelessness (Clark & Watson, 1991). Behaviorally, anxiety is associated with active engagement in life and depression is associated with disengagement (Barlow, 1991). Cognitively, the anxious person worries about what might happen in the future, while the depressed person feels that all is already lost (see Table 17.2). The sense of worthlessness and hopelessness typical of depressed thinking are captured

Depression

As expressed in this woodcut by Edvard Munch, the world looks bleak to a depressed person.

in the following quotation from Norman Endler (1982), a highly respected psychologist describing his own bout with depression:

> I honestly felt subhuman, lower than the lowest vermin ... I could not understand why anyone would want to associate with me, let alone love me . . . I was positive that I was a fraud and a phony . . . I couldn't understand how I had written the books and journal articles that I had and how they had been accepted for publication. I must have conned a lot of people.

Other symptoms of depression—beyond the main ones of sadness, self-blame, sense of worthlessness, and absence of pleasure—may include increased or decreased sleep, increased or decreased appetite, and either agitated or retarded motor symptoms. Agitated symptoms include repetitive, aimless movements such as hand wringing or pacing; and retarded symptoms include slowed speech and slowed body movements. To warrant a *DSM-IV* diagnosis of a depressive disorder, the symptoms must be either very severe or very prolonged and must not be attributable directly to a specific life experience. Two main classes of depressive disorders are distinguished. ***Major depression*** is characterized by very severe symptoms that last essentially without remission for at least 2 weeks. ***Dysthymia*** is characterized by less severe symptoms that last for at least 2 years. Quite often, bouts of major depression are superimposed over a more chronic state of dysthymia, in which case the person is said to have *double depression*. As was shown in Figure 17.3, both major depression and dysthymia are quite prevalent, and both are diagnosed more often in women than in men.

A Biological Theory: Reduced Action of Monoamines

■ **17. *What is some evidence for and against the monoamine theory of depression?***

In the 1950s researchers discovered that many sufferers from depression could be treated successfully with drugs, and subsequent studies showed that the most effective of these drugs act in the brain to increase the action of a group of neurotransmitters known as monoamines. In other research, drugs that reduce sharply the level of brain monoamines were found to induce feelings of depression in people who were not initially depressed. Such findings led to the ***monoamine theory of depression***, which holds that depression results from too little activity at brain synapses where monoamines are the neurotransmitters (Schildkraut, 1965).

The three main monoamine transmitters in the brain are norepinephrine, dopamine, and serotonin, all of which are known from animal research to be involved in neural mechanisms underlying motivation and arousal. Dopamine and norepinephrine are especially important in motivational and pleasure-enhancing mechanisms (discussed in Chapter 7), and serotonin is especially important in mechanisms that promote calmness, sleep, and relief from pain. Thus, a decline in norepinephrine or dopamine could be responsible for the loss of motivation and pleasure that accompanies any severe depression, and decline in serotonin could be responsible for the sleeplessness, irritability, and restless movements that occur specifically in agitated depression (Willner, 1985).

Despite the evidence and logic supporting the monoamine theory, its validity is still much in doubt (Mann, 1989). One problem is a lack of consistency between the known neurochemical effects of antidepressant drugs and their clinical effects. Drugs that selectively augment serotonin activity seem to produce the same effects on mood and behavior as drugs that selectively augment norepinephrine and dopamine activity, even though these different transmitters are known to act in anatomically and functionally different parts of the brain. Another problem is the time-course of the drugs' effects. The drugs increase neurotransmitter activity in the brain immediately, but do not begin to affect mood until after 2 to 3 weeks of continuous treatment. Researchers now are exploring the possibility that the drugs produce their antidepressant effects not directly through the elevation of monoamine activity, but rather through some long-term stabilizing effect they may have on the brain (Hollandsworth, 1990).

A Behavioral Theory: Learned Helplessness

■ **18. *What is some evidence that depression may stem from stressful events that one cannot control?***

Another line of research has related the onset of depression to stressful experiences in people's lives. In one such study, Andrew Billings and his colleagues (1983) interviewed more than 400 men and women who were beginning treatment for depression, and an equal number of nondepressed subjects selected from the same neighborhoods in which the depressed subjects resided, about their experiences over the previous year. Compared to the nondepressed group, the depressed group had experienced about twice as many losses, such as death of a loved one, loss of a job, decline in income, or divorce. The depressed group had also been subjected to relatively more sources of prolonged psychological pressure, including medical conditions, frequent family arguments, work pressures, and ambiguity about the expectations of employers or bosses. These findings did not simply represent a report bias on the part of the depressed individuals; they were confirmed in separate interviews of nondepressed family members (usually spouses).

One theory consistent with these findings is that depression is a psychological giving up of the attempt to control one's own fate, brought on by repeated negative experiences over which one has no control. This theory, called the ***learned helplessness theory of depression***, was originally proposed by Martin Seligman based on experiments with dogs (Seligman & others, 1968). Seligman found that dogs that had previously received a series of inescapable electric shocks failed, when tested later in a different apparatus, to learn to escape shocks by jumping over a hurdle. These dogs passively accepted the shocks without looking for a means of escape. In contrast, dogs that had either received no previous shocks or had received shocks that they could turn off by pressing against a panel learned quickly to jump over the hurdle.

Subsequent research, mostly with rats, revealed that the experience of inescapable shock or other such trauma not only produces behavioral changes indicative of learned helplessness, but also causes a long-lasting reduction in brain levels of norepinephrine and dopamine (Henn, 1989; Weiss & others, 1976). Such research suggests that uncontrollable stressful events might produce depression in a way that is consistent with the monoamine theory:

helpless situation → reduced monoamines → depressed mood and behavior

A Cognitive Theory: The Attribution of Hopelessness

Although stressful events can increase a person's chance of becoming depressed, not everyone who undergoes such experiences becomes depressed. In the study by Billings and his colleagues, some of the nondepressed subjects had experienced losses and pressures that were objectively more severe than the average of those for the depressed group. Observations of this sort provide the starting point for cognitive theories of depression, which hold that depression stems not so much from the objective events themselves as from the way they are interpreted.

One of the first to emphasize the role of cognition in depression was Aaron Beck (1967), a psychiatrist who observed that his depressed clients held consistently pessimistic views of themselves, their world, and the future and that they seemed to maintain these views by distorting their experiences in negative ways. They would mentally exaggerate bad experiences and minimize or overlook good ones. Beck developed a mode of therapy (discussed in Chapter 18) that centers on training depressed people to assess their experiences more optimistically.

■ **19.** ***How does the hopelessness theory of depression differ from the learned helplessness theory, and what is some evidence for and against the hopelessness theory?***

Following Beck, Lyn Abramson and Martin Seligman developed a more specific cognitive theory of depression, which has undergone a number of revisions and is now called the ***hopelessness theory of depression*** (Abramson & others, 1989). This theory originated from Seligman's earlier learned helplessness theory. It shares with the earlier theory the idea that depression involves a sense of helplessness, but adds to it the idea that in humans the sense comes not just from the objective events that happen, but from the *attributions* that people make about those events. As described in Chapter 14, an attribution is an inference about the cause of something. According to the hopelessness theory, people differ in their *attributional style*, and that is what determines who will or will not become depressed as a result of particular experiences. More specifically, the theory holds that people who are most prone to depression consistently attribute their negative experiences to causes that are *stable* (unlikely to change) and *global* (apply to a wide sphere of activities and experiences), and attribute their positive experiences to causes that are *unstable* (likely to change) and *specific* (apply to a narrow sphere of activities and experiences).

Consider some attributions that a college student might make for a poor grade on one test and a good grade on another. A student prone to depression might say, "I received the poor grade because I am incompetent; I received the good grade because the test just happened to be on the few things I remembered." Here the attribution for the poor grade is stable and global (incompetence is the kind of trait that stays with a person and affects all realms of life), and the attribution for the good grade is unstable and specific (it applies just to that one test). Another student—one least prone to depression—might make the opposite attributions: "I received the poor grade because that test just happened to be on those things I didn't know (unstable, specific); I received the good grade because I am bright and work hard (stable, global)."

Seligman and his colleagues have developed an *attributional style questionnaire* to assess people's routine ways of explaining their negative and positive experiences, and they and others have used it in research aimed at testing the hopelessness theory. Depressed people do clearly make attributions in a manner consistent with the theory (Seligman & others, 1988), but that observation by itself does not show that the attributional style is a cause of depression; it could simply be a symptom of depression. Some researchers have found that as depressed people wax and wane in their degree of depression, their attributional style follows suit, suggesting that a negative attributional style is more a symptom than a cause of depression (Gotlib, 1992). Two or three studies, however, have indicated that at least the subclinical levels of depression commonly found in college students depend on attributional style.

In one study, students first filled out the attributional styles questionnaire along with another questionnaire that was aimed at assessing their degree of depressed mood. Then, five weeks later, they filled out the depression questionnaire again along with a third questionnaire, designed to assess the number and severity of negative events that had happened to the respondents over the 5-week period. The main result was that depression increased only in those students who (a) had a negative attributional style for negative events (attributed them to stable, global causes) *and* (b) had a high score on the negative-events questionnaire. In other words, consistent with the hopelessness theory, neither negative events alone nor a negative style of attribution alone predicted a high depression score at the end of the 5-week period; but the two together did predict a high depression score (Matelsky & Joiner, 1992).

Depression Breeds Depression

■ **20. *How can depression be depicted as a vicious triangle, and how do different approaches to treating depression correspond with the triangle's corners?***

Most of us, when we are in a depressed mood, are able to relieve it through our own thoughts and actions. After a certain period of gloom, we grab our bootstraps and pull ourselves up, using such means as positive thinking, talking with friends, or engaging in activities that we especially enjoy. But severely depressed people—those who qualify for a diagnosis of major depression—typically don't do those things. Their patterns of thought and action continue to work against their recovery, rather than for it. Figure 17.5 depicts what might be called the *vicious triangle of severe depression*, in which a person's mood, thought, and action interact in such a way as to keep him or her in a depressed state. Depressed mood promotes negative thinking and withdrawal from enjoyable activities; negative thinking promotes withdrawal from enjoyable activities and depressed mood; and withdrawal from enjoyable activities promotes depressed mood and negative thinking. Each corner of the triangle supports the others.

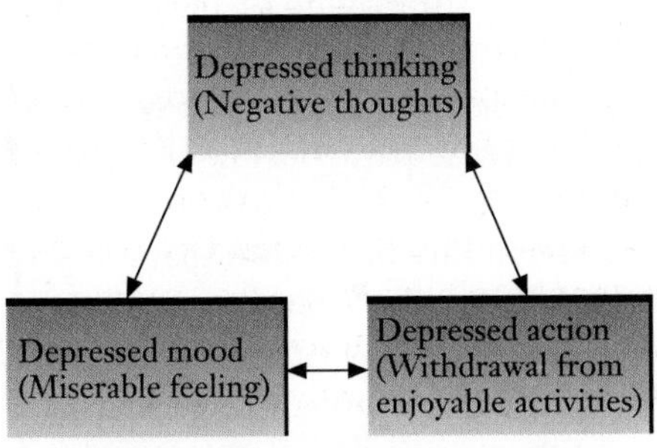

Figure 17.5 ***The vicious triangle of severe depression***

Mood, thought, and behavior feed on one another to maintain the depressed state.

Each corner of the triangle also corresponds to a different therapeutic approach to breaking the triangle of depression (described more fully in Chapter 18). Drug therapy attempts to elevate mood through direct action on the brain, which in turn should increase positive thinking and actions. Behavioral therapy attempts to get the person to act in ways that bring more pleasure and a greater sense of control, which in turn should improve mood and promote positive thoughts. Cognitive therapy attempts to change the person's way of thinking in a positive direction, which in turn should improve behavior and mood.

Bipolar Disorders

Major depression and dysthymia are sometimes called *unipolar disorders*, because they are characterized by mood changes in only one direction—downward from normal. Bipolar disorders (also called *manic-depression*) are characterized by mood swings in both directions: downward in *depressive episodes*, and upward in *manic episodes*. Such episodes may last anywhere from a few days to several months, and periods of normal mood may occur in between. *DSM-IV* identifies two main varieties of bipolar disorders, which differ in degree. ***Bipolar disorder*** (in the singular) is the more severe variety, and ***cyclothymia*** is the less severe variety, in which the mood changes are not as great. The manual also acknowledges the possibility of disorders characterized only by recurrent mania without depression, but notes that they are very rare.

Characteristics of Bipolar Disorder and Cyclothymia

■ **21.** ***How are manic states experienced, and what is some evidence that mild manic episodes can be accompanied by heightened creativity?***

The manic episodes in bipolar disorders typically involve inordinate feelings of power, confidence, and energy, as illustrated by the following quotation from a woman describing her own disorder (Fieve, 1975):

> When I start going into a high, I no longer feel like an ordinary housewife. Instead, I feel organized and accomplished, and I begin to feel I am my most creative self. I can write poetry easily. I can compose melodies without effort. I can paint . . . I have countless ideas about how the environmental problem could inspire a crusade for the health and betterment of everyone . . . I don't seem to need much sleep . . . I feel sexy and men stare at me. Maybe I'll have an affair, or perhaps several. I feel capable of speaking and doing good in politics.

The feeling of enhanced ability and creativity during mild to moderate manic episodes is probably not entirely an illusion. A number of studies have found a disproportionately high incidence of cyclothymia among eminently creative artists and writers and have shown that those individuals produced their best work during manic episodes (Andreasen, 1978, 1987; Hershman & Lieb, 1988). In another study, people with cyclothymia, selected only on the basis of their clinical diagnosis, were found to be more creative in their regular work and home life than were a control group with no diagnosed mental disorder (Richards & others, 1988). In the same study, however, people with the more serious bipolar disorder were not more creative than those in the control group. Apparently, the disorganization of thought and action that accompanied their more extreme bouts of mania offset any creative advantage that they may have enjoyed.

On the negative side, mania can result in actions that are highly disruptive to the lives of affected individuals and their families. Extreme mania may be accompanied by bizarre thoughts and dangerous behaviors, such as jumping off a building in the false belief that one can fly; and even milder states may be accompanied by spending sprees, absence from work, or sexual escapades that the affected person later regrets. Moreover, not all people with bipolar disorder experience the manic state as euphoric. Some experience it as a time of intense paranoia and destructive rage (Carroll, 1991).

Research with twins and adoptees to assess heritability has shown that the predisposition to bipolar disorder is strongly influenced by genes (Bertelsen, 1979). To date, neither the environmental nor the biological factors that may induce the mood swings in bipolar disorders have been identified. Although some evidence exists that stressful life events may help bring on manic and depressive episodes in people who are so predisposed (Ambelas, 1987), the evidence for such effects is not nearly as strong as it is for unipolar depression. As described in Chapter 18, bipolar disorder can often be controlled with the drug lithium, but how it works is as yet unknown.

Seasonal Affective Disorder

■ **22.** ***How does SAD differ from bipolar disorder and cyclothymia?***

Some people undergo severe depression every fall and winter, followed either by normal mood or mild mania in the spring. Their problem—called ***seasonal affective disorder***, or ***SAD*** (Rosenthal & others, 1984)—is more than simply doldrums stemming from cold weather and snow, and elation created by birds and flowers. The mood changes in SAD are apparently controlled by seasonal changes in sunlight, as the depression can be treated by extending the effective period of daily light with bright fluorescent lights during the evening or early morning hours in fall and winter (Terman & others, 1989). One highly successful treatment is lighting that becomes gradually more intense, simulating the natural dawn, applied daily during the last two hours of sleep (Avery & others, 1993). The light apparently passes through the eyelids, which are partly translucent, and stimulates visual receptors, setting off physiological processes yet unknown that reverse the depression. SAD is different from either bipolar disorder or cyclothymia; people with the latter disorders rarely show seasonal regularity to their mood changes and are not successfully treated with light.

Somatoform Disorders

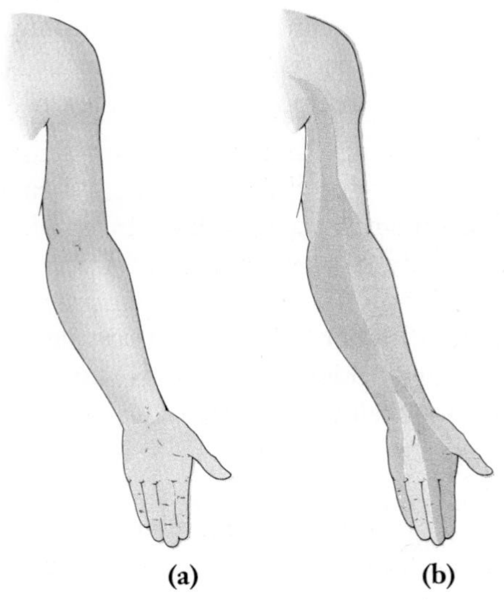

Figure 17.6 ***A conversion disorder***
Glove anesthesia—the experience of no sensation in the hand but continued sensation in all other parts of the arm, as shown in (a)—cannot result from nerve damage, because no nerves innervate the hand without innervating part of the arm. The actual areas of sensory loss that would occur if specific nerves were damaged are shown in (b). Thus, whenever glove anesthesia occurs, it is most likely a conversion disorder.

23. ***Why are somatoform disorders especially difficult to diagnose?***

Somatoform literally means "bodily form," and ***somatoform disorders*** are those in which the person experiences bodily ailments in the absence of any physical disease that could cause them. Four varieties of somatoform disorders are described in *DSM-IV*: (1) *conversion disorder*, in which the person temporarily loses some bodily function, perhaps (in the most dramatic cases) becoming blind, deaf, or partially paralyzed; (2) *somatoform pain disorder*, which is similar to conversion disorder except that the complaint is of pain in some part of the body rather than loss of a bodily function; (3) *somatization disorder*, which is characterized by a long history of dramatic complaints about many different medical conditions, most of which are vague and unverifiable, such as dizziness, heart palpitations, and nausea; and (4) *hypochondriasis*, which is characterized by a long-term, unwarranted preoccupation with physical health and the belief that every slight ailment is a symptom of some grave disease. Little reliable information exists about the prevalence of somatoform disorders. This is partly because people with such disorders usually go to physicians rather than to clinical psychologists or psychiatrists and partly because the diagnoses are inherently difficult to make.

In the past, somatoform disorders (especially conversion disorders) were referred to as *hysteria*, from the Greek word for uterus. The ancient Greeks believed that such disorders occur only in women and arise from a "wandering uterus," which could invade various parts of the woman's body and inflict pain, paralysis, or loss of sensations. For centuries, hysteria was diagnosed far more often in women than in men. Even today, somatoform disorders are diagnosed more often in women, although some studies suggest that their actual occurrence is equally high in both genders (Lipowski, 1988; Slavney & Teitelbaum, 1985).

The Problem of Diagnosis

How can a diagnostician tell if a patient's physical complaint represents a somatoform mental disorder or an actual physical disease? Occasionally, the mental origin can be inferred because the complained-of symptom could not logically come from a physical disease (see Figure 17.6 for an example). In other cases, it can be inferred because the problem came on suddenly after a psychologically stressful event, or disappeared suddenly after the resolution of a psychological problem. But in most cases no clear way exists for deciding to what degree the complaint stems from real bodily problems or from psychological causes. Many errors of diagnosis have been made in both directions. Sometimes needless surgery or other medical treatment occurs because a somatoform disorder is mistaken for a physical disease, and at other times needed medical treatment is withheld because a physical disease is mistakenly considered to be purely psychological. In one study of patients originally diagnosed as having a conversion disorder, about half were later found to have a physical disease that could have been the basis for their complaint (Slater, 1975).

Another problem in diagnosing somatization disorder is that of distinguishing it from a consciously faked physical disorder (Ford, 1983). Such faking might be done for material gain. The distinction between faking and not faking may be fuzzy even in the affected person's mind. Imagine a man who, after involvement in a traffic accident, hears his lawyer and relatives saying, "Are you *sure* your neck doesn't hurt? You know, if it does, you can collect $20,000." If he discovers a slight twinge of pain that later becomes so strong he has to miss work, is he (a) a liar, (b) a person whose vivid imagination has led to somatoform pain disorder, or (c) a legitimate victim of slowly developing whiplash? He himself may not know.

Defensive Functions of Conversion Disorder

Sigmund Freud, who saw many cases of conversion disorder, believed that the bodily symptoms were always generated by the unconscious mind to protect the person from anxiety related to a sexual conflict originating in childhood. For example, a man afraid of sex because of an unresolved oedipal conflict might, when confronted by sexual opportunities in adulthood, become ill or partially paralyzed to make himself and others believe that sexual activity would be impossible. Today, few psychiatrists and psychologists advocate the narrow version of Freud's theory, but many hold to a liberalized psychodynamic theory of conversion disorder—the theory that the symptoms are unconsciously generated to protect the person from any of a wide variety of real or imagined dangers or frightening feelings. Consider the following case (quoted from Rosenhan & Seligman, 1984):

> Baer, a burly, young construction worker, is paralyzed from the waist down. Since the problem does not seem to have a neurological basis, he is sent from Neurology to Psychiatry, where the following dialogue takes place:
>
> **Doctor:** *Do you know anyone else who is paralyzed?*
>
> **Baer:** (after thinking for a period of time and showing no emotion) *Yeah, come to think of it, Tom, a good friend of mine, is . . . Broke his neck.*
>
> **Doctor:** *How did it happen?*
>
> **Baer:** *It was really sad, and you know, I guess I was pretty much at fault . . . We were at a party about a month ago . . . I thought he should live a little, try some LSD . . . We downed a couple of tabs, and within a few minutes he was flying, seeing all sorts of weird things. He ran out of the apartment . . . Next thing I know, he jumped off the bridge . . . He was still alive when the rescue squad got him down from the high tension lines. They say he'll never walk, or anything, again.*
>
> **Doctor:** *Baer, tell me again when your problem started.*
>
> **Baer:** *Out of nowhere. I was at work, driving my forklift down at the station. As I crossed the tracks under the high tension lines, suddenly I was all dead down there . . . Oh, my God! Don't you see what I have done!*

Traumatic blindness

This woman is one of many Cambodian women whose acute vision problems have been tied to seeing atrocities committed by, and being tortured by, the Khmer Rouge. Because of cultural differences and problems with diagnosis, Western psychologists have just begun to develop ways of treating the disorder.

A psychodynamic interpretation of this incident might go as follows: Baer felt guilty about his involvement in the event that led to his friend's paralysis. Later, when he saw the high tension lines on which his friend had become paralyzed, his guilt was elevated to an unbearable level, and his unconscious mind responded by rendering him paralyzed—an act that relieved his guilt by placing him in the role of victim rather than perpetrator. The conversation with the psychiatrist made the relationship between his own paralysis and his friend's clear to him, and when that occurred his own paralysis could no longer function as a defense mechanism. Shortly thereafter he regained the use of his legs, and, one hopes, eventually found some less crippling and more productive way to deal with his feelings of guilt.

Some cases of conversion disorder seem to be aimed explicitly at threats in the real world. For example, a considerable number of pilots in World War II developed blindness conversions that prevented them from continuing dangerous missions, and often the blindness they experienced was specific to their duties: Night flyers lost the ability to see in dim light but not in daylight, and day flyers developed the opposite symptoms (Ironside & Batchelor, 1945).

Conversion disorder can also result from extraordinarily traumatic events, in which case it may serve to help the victim shut out cues that remind him or her of the trauma. An example of this is the high rate of psychologically based blindness discovered among Cambodian women who managed to emigrate to the United States after the Khmer Rouge reign of terror in Cambodia in the 1970s (Rozée & Van Boemel, 1989). All these women manifest post-traumatic stress syndrome brought on by the tortures they suffered and witnessed. Many of them had seen their own children being slowly tortured and murdered. One woman described the onset of her blindness in these words: "My family was killed in 1975 and I cried for 4 years. When I stopped crying I was blind." Another described becoming blind "from the smoke" as she was looking at the cooking pot in a forced labor camp where she was held—a pot that, she knew, often contained human flesh, rats, and worms, which the women were forced to cook for themselves and other inmates.

Sociocultural Perspective on Somatoform Disorders

■ **24.** ***What is the sociocultural perspective on somatoform disorders, and how might it be applied in explaining chronic fatigue syndrome in North America?***

From a sociocultural perspective, the incidence of somatoform disorders and the form they take are affected by cultural beliefs. Few people in North America or Europe today believe that a person can be stricken suddenly blind, deaf, or paralyzed; so those forms of somatoform disorders are much rarer in the West now than they were in the nineteenth century and earlier (Shorter, 1992). Moreover, as disorders purely of mood or emotion become more legitimized by a culture, the incidence of somatoform disorders tends to go down and that of anxiety and mood disorders tends to go up. Based on cross-cultural and historical research, Arthur Kleinman (1988) has argued that somatization and depression may be two ways of feeling and expressing the same underlying problem. According to Kleinman, a sense of hopelessness is usually experienced as depression in Western cultures today, but in the past was more often experienced as physical aches and pains, as it still is in China and many other parts of the world.

Within the last ten years, North America has seen an outbreak of an ailment called *chronic fatigue syndrome* (CFS), which for a while was called "yuppie flu" in the popular press because of its prevalence among fast-track professionals. The syndrome is described as including chronic tiredness, muscle weakness, and various aches and pains, which can last for months or even years. Sufferers insist adamantly that CFS is an organic disease and is not psychological, despite the lack of evidence one way or the other (Shorter, 1992). When the hypothesis that CFS is caused by a particular virus was disproved, organized patient groups renamed the disorder *chronic fatigue immune deficiency syndrome* (CFIDS) and claimed that it is similar to AIDS. An organic basis for CFS may yet be discovered, but currently many psychologists and psychiatrists believe it to be a somatization disorder (Abbey & Garfinkel, 1991; Shorter, 1992). They suggest that it is an expression of suffering by people who are disenchanted with their careers or other aspects of their lives, but who strongly resist that idea and seize upon currently well-publicized diseases (viral syndromes and AIDS) as models to explain their symptoms.

Psychological Factors Affecting Medical Condition

In the previous section you read of disorders in which bodily pain or disability is experienced in the absence of any medical explanation. We now turn to a different category of psychological effects on the body—cases in which one's behavior or emotions precipitate or influence the course of a disease that clearly does have a physical, medical basis. Although the harm-producing behavior or emotions do not necessarily constitute a mental disorder in the usual sense of the term, a category—called *psychological factors affecting medical condition*—is reserved for them in *DSM-IV*. These factors range from persistent refusal of prescribed medicines to chronic emotional states that may directly alter one's internal chemistry in a disease-promoting manner. The most extensively researched and still-controversial of these factors are emotional states that may affect the cardiovascular system and the immune system.

Psychological Factors and Cardiovascular Disease

25. ***How did two heart specialists find evidence for their hypothesis that a set of behaviors designated Type A promotes heart disease? How have subsequent studies altered our understanding of the psychological factors that promote heart disease?***

In the 1950s, two California cardiologists—Meyer Friedman and Ray Rosenman—observed that many of their heart-attack patients (most of whom were men) were similar to each other in personality. They seemed to be competitive, aggressive, easily irritated, impatient workaholics, constantly concerned with deadlines and getting ahead. Friedman and Rosenman coined the term *Type A* to refer to this constellation of behaviors, and *Type B* to refer to the opposite, relaxed constellation of behaviors that they believed would be associated with low risk for heart attack. After conducting several preliminary studies that yielded results consistent with their hypothesis, Friedman and Rosenman received a government grant to conduct a large-scale study.

As subjects for their study, they recruited 3,100 businessmen, none of whom had heart disease. Based on an interview procedure that took into account not just the subjects' literal answers to questions but also their manner of answering (such as irritation in their voices), Friedman and Rosenman's team of researchers classified the subjects as best they could into Type A and Type B groups, using criteria designed to produce groups of approximately equal size. Then they followed the subjects medically, for a period of 9 years, and found strong evidence supporting their hypothesis; 178 of the Type A subjects, but only 79 of the Type B subjects developed a cardiovascular disease. This difference was highly significant statistically and could not be accounted for by a difference between the two subject groups in any other known risk factor such as smoking, diet, weight, or cholesterol level. Friedman and Rosenman (1974) wrote a book on their findings, which became a best seller, and by the late 1970s *Type A* was a familiar term. In some corners, "I'm Type A" became a kind of boast, meaning "I'm so hard-working and competitive that I'm likely to get a heart attack."

Frantic but content?
This stockbroker's risk of heart attack is predicted better by the negative emotions he may feel than by the pace of his work.

Subsequent attempts to corroborate Friedman and Rosenman's finding produced mixed results. Some found a relation between Type A behavior and heart disease, some found none and some found that certain other characteristics predicted heart attack more reliably than the Type A constellation. A quantitative review of such studies concluded that (a) Type A is moderately but reliably predictive of heart disease in men and probably also in women (though relatively few studies have included women); (b) the hurried lifestyle and job involvement aspects of Type A are not predictive of heart disease, but the irritableness and hostility are; (c) depression and anxiety, which are not part of the definition of Type A, are also predictive of heart disease; and (d) these effects are not mediated by other known risk factors, such as smoking or high cholesterol (Booth-Kewley & H. Friedman, 1987).

In sum, the picture emerging today is that prolonged or frequent negative emotions in general can increase one's risk for heart disease, but that a hard-working, constantly rushed person who enjoys what he or she is doing is not at special risk (Dienstfrey, 1991; H. Friedman & Booth-Kewley, 1987; Williams, 1989). Nobody knows just how negative emotions promote heart disease, but most researchers assume that the effect is mediated somehow though the autonomic nervous system and endocrine system, both of which are altered during emotional states (discussed in Chapter 6).

Psychological Factors and the Immune System

Does emotional distress increase our likelihood of coming down with infectious diseases such as colds and flu? A number of studies suggest that the answer is yes (Cohen & Williamson, 1991).

■ **26. *What is some evidence that one's emotional state can alter the chance of catching a cold, and that this may be mediated by effects on the immune system?***

In one study, 394 healthy men and women agreed, for the sake of science, to have a fluid containing known respiratory viruses dribbled into their nostrils and then to remain quarantined for six days while researchers assessed their medical condition (Cohen & others, 1991). At the outset of the study, each volunteer filled out a set of questionnaires aimed at assessing the degree of psychological distress he or she had experienced recently. The result was that the more distress people reported at the outset of the study, the more likely they were to develop a cold within the 6-day period (see Figure 17.7). The colds were real, not imagined; they were assessed by direct viral counts as well as by external symptoms. Moreover, the relation between distress and the incidence of colds could not be accounted for by any other risk factors the researchers measured, including smoking, alcohol consumption, diet, and quality of sleep.

Because of the correlational nature of this study, we cannot be sure that increased emotional distress was a cause of the increased susceptibility to colds. Perhaps people who are prone to emotional distress are also constitutionally susceptible to colds. Other research, however, has shown that emotional distress can suppress the body's immune response. In one study, people given frustrating cognitive tasks (including difficult mental arithmetic) manifested a temporary decline in production of T-cells, a class of white blood cells known to be involved in fighting disease organisms (Manuck & others, 1991). This effect occurred only in those subjects who showed other physiological signs of distress in response to the tasks. In other studies, laboratory animals subjected to various long-term stressful conditions showed long-term declines in immune responses to infectious agents (Ader & Cohen, 1993; Cohen & others, 1992).

■ **27. *How did an experiment with breast cancer patients demonstrate an effect of psychological intervention on survival? Through what mechanisms could that effect have occurred?***

More controversial than the effects on colds and flu is the suggestion that emotional states can also influence the progression of cancer through their impact on the immune system. Despite much study, the evidence so far for such an effect is inconsistent and, over all, relatively weak (Levenson & Bemis, 1991). Perhaps the strongest evidence comes from an experiment in which women with breast cancer were randomly assigned either to routine care or to a special treatment group that received training in self-hypnosis to control pain and attended weekly group therapy for emotional support for one year (Spiegel & others, 1989). A 10-year follow-up showed that those in the special treatment group survived, on average, twice as

Figure 17.7 ***Relation between psychological distress and subsequent development of a cold***

The psychological distress score was based on a combination of recent stressful life events and negative emotions reported by volunteer subjects on questionnaires. As the degree of psychological distress increased, so did the percentage of subjects who developed a cold within 6 days of deliberate exposure to respiratory viruses. (From Cohen & others, 1991.)

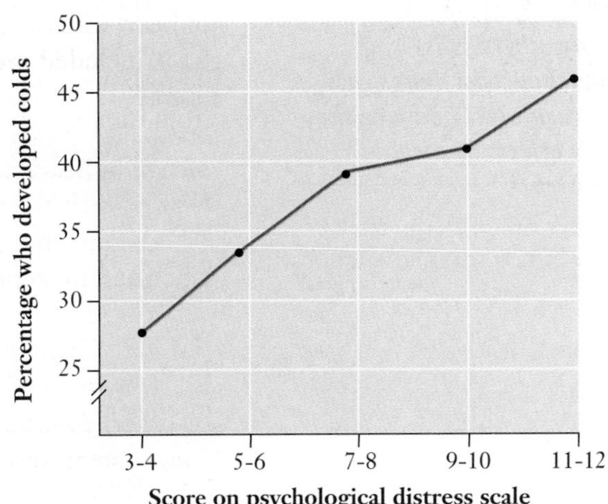

long as those in the other group (37 months compared to 19 months). As the authors of the study point out, this result does not necessarily imply that the effect occurred through the immune system or any other direct physiological route. Maybe those in the treatment group, because of their improved mood and reduced pain, took better physical care of themselves and complied better with the medical program prescribed by their physicians. Regardless of the mechanism, the results certainly add to the evidence that it is a good idea for people with a serious disease to try to keep their mood elevated.

Psychoactive Substance-Use Disorders

A psychoactive substance is a drug that acts on the brain and affects a person's emotions, perceptions, or thoughts. A ***psychoactive substance-use disorder*** involves the abuse of or dependence on such a drug. ***Drug abuse*** implies persistent use of the drug in a way that is harmful to the self or society. ***Drug dependence*** (which in *DSM-IV* is a synonym for *addiction*) implies that the person feels compelled—for physiological or psychological reasons or both—to take the drug on a regular basis, and feels severe distress without it. A person who repeatedly drives while drunk, or who drinks despite awareness that alcohol is exacerbating a stomach ulcer, or who periodically misses work because of a drinking spree, is said to abuse alcohol. A person who feels that he or she cannot get through the day without drinking is said to be dependent on alcohol. In *DSM-IV* separate abuse and dependence disorders are listed for alcohol, cocaine, opiates (such as heroin), and a variety of other drugs.

It would be hard to overestimate the problems that drugs cause for individuals and society. The most abused drug by far, today as well as in the past, is alcohol. In the United States, alcohol is implicated in about 55 percent of automobile fatalities, 50 percent of homicides, 30 percent of suicides, 65 percent of drownings, 50 percent of deaths by falling, 52 percent of fires leading to death, 60 percent of child-abuse cases, and 85 percent of home violence (FitzGerald, 1988; National Institute of Alcohol Abuse and Alcoholism, 1987). Drugs that cannot be obtained legally—especially cocaine and heroin—wreak additional havoc in the form of murders, robberies, and wasted lives.

The following paragraphs examine the causes of substance-use disorders from the biological, cognitive-behavioral, and sociocultural perspectives. The focus is on alcohol abuse and dependence, because that disorder is most common and has been most fully studied.

The Biological Perspective

■ **28. *What are three classes of effects that psychoactive drugs can have on the brain, and how are they exemplified by effects of alcohol?***

Psychoactive drugs alter mood, thought, or behavior by altering the biology of the brain. Such alterations may stem from intoxicating effects of the drug, withdrawal from the drug, or permanent damage caused by the drug.

Intoxicating effects are the short-term effects for which the drug is usually taken, and they may last for minutes or hours after a single dose. (For a summary of such effects and their physiological mechanisms for many drugs, see Table 6.1 in Chapter 6.) The intoxicating effects of alcohol include relief from anxiety, slowed thinking, poor judgment, slurred speech, and uncoordinated movements. Beyond reducing anxiety, alcohol can have varying, sometimes contrary effects on emotion: It can promote happiness or sadness, good will or pugnaciousness. Such extremes in emotion may be due to the dulling effect of alcohol on the ability to use logic and concern for the long run in order to modulate the influence of the immediate environment on thought and emotion, a condition called *alcohol myopia* (Steele &

Josephs, 1990). If cues in the environment promote happiness, the intoxicated person will feel extreme happiness; if they promote sadness, the person will feel extreme sadness.

Withdrawal effects occur after the drug is removed from the system. Usually such effects occur only after a long period of continuous or frequent drug use. These effects apparently result from adaptation to the drug such that the brain functions in some ways more normally with the drug than without it. (For a more complete discussion, see Chapter 6.) In a person who is physiologically addicted to alcohol, withdrawal effects begin to occur within 8 to 20 hours after alcohol has been cleared from the body. These symptoms—referred to as *delirium tremens* (or DTs)—are those of an extraordinarily overactive brain. They include hallucinations; feelings of panic; muscle tremors ("the shakes"); sweating, high heart rate, and other signs of autonomic arousal; and sometimes brain seizures. Delirium tremens is not only frightening, but truly dangerous. When not treated medically, it results in death in somewhere between 15 and 50 percent of instances (Light, 1986).

Permanent effects are irreversible forms of brain damage that can result from frequent drug use or that can occur in a developing fetus if the mother uses the drug during pregnancy. One permanent effect of long-term, heavy alcohol use is *alcohol amnesic disorder* (also called *Korsakoff's syndrome*), which entails severe memory impairment and difficulties with motor coordination associated with damage to certain areas of the brain's limbic system. Another permanent effect of alcohol is *fetal alcohol syndrome*, a condition of mental retardation and physical abnormalities in a child stemming from the mother's consumption of large amounts of alcohol during pregnancy.

Twin and adoption studies indicate that alcohol dependence is moderately heritable and is apparently more heritable in males than in females (Cloninger & others, 1981; Goodwin, 1976, 1979; Pickens & others, 1991). In other words, the incidence of alcohol dependence in women is apparently influenced relatively more by environmental factors and less by genetic factors than it is in men. Alcohol abuse without dependence is less heritable than dependence. Both run in families, but dependence does so primarily because of shared genes, and abuse does so primarily because of shared environment (Pickens & others, 1991). Behavioral genetic studies have also produced evidence that more than one type of alcohol dependence exists, and that different types have different degrees of heritability (Cloninger, 1990; Pickens & others, 1991).

Alcoholics Anonymous

In A.A. groups, people meet as equals to share their experiences and strengths and to help one another recover from alcohol misuse. The core of the recovery program is a series of twelve steps, the most basic of which is admitting that one suffers from alcoholism.

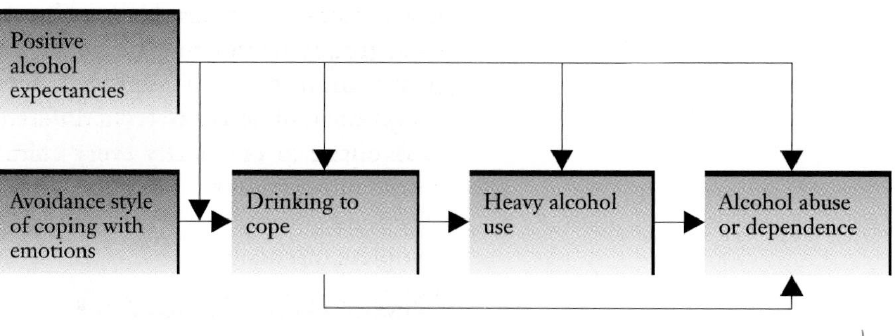

Figure 17.8 ***A cognitive model of alcoholism***

In this model, positive alcohol expectancies plus a tendency to avoid confronting one's own strong emotions are predisposing causes of alcohol abuse or dependence. (Adapted from Cooper & others, 1988.)

The Behavioral and Cognitive Perspectives

■ **29.** ***How do behavioral theorists describe addiction in terms of conditioning, and how do cognitive theorists describe it in terms of learned expectancies?***

Consuming alcohol or taking any drug is a learned, voluntary action. Behaviorists have long described addictive behavior in terms of operant conditioning. From this view, the short-term pleasure or relief caused by the drug is a powerful reinforcer for continued drug use. Classical conditioning may also come into play. As described in Chapter 5, cues associated with an environment in which a drug is frequently taken can become conditioned stimuli for physiological responses that tend to counteract the drug effect (Siegel & others, 1988). This phenomenon has been used to explain why a person who has been drug free and has felt no craving for it during a long stay in a treatment center may suddenly experience an intense craving upon returning to the environment in which he or she had habitually taken the drug. Cues in the drug-taking environment can trigger conditioned physiological responses that are opposite to those produced by the drug. The responses feel like withdrawal symptoms and thus induce the craving.

From a cognitive perspective, the act of taking a drug requires a decision to take it, and that decision is based in part on a person's beliefs or expectancies concerning the drug and its effects. In a longitudinal study, researchers found that they could predict which nondrinking teenagers would become alcohol abusers on the basis of their beliefs about alcohol (Roehling & others, 1987). Those who believed that alcohol has valued effects—such as making a person more sociable, powerful, or sexually vital—were more likely to be alcohol abusers 1 or 2 years later than were those who did not have such beliefs. Other studies have shown that a critical step in the development of alcoholism occurs when a person begins to use alcohol not just socially but as a way of coping with negative emotions (Cooper & others, 1988). Once the person thinks of alcohol as a general way of quieting negative emotions, its use increases and the person is well on the path to alcohol abuse or dependence. Based on such research, M. Lynne Cooper and her colleagues (1988) have proposed a cognitive model of alcoholism in which the predisposing causes are (a) positive expectancies about the effects of alcohol and (b) a learned fear of negative emotions or a tendency to avoid such emotions (see Figure 17.8).

The Sociocultural Perspective

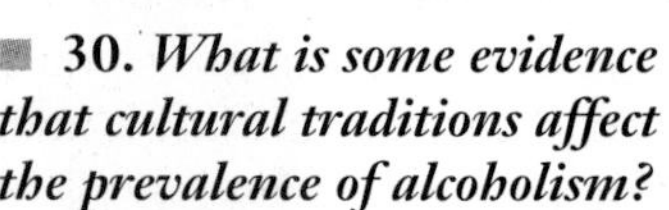

■ **30.** ***What is some evidence that cultural traditions affect the prevalence of alcoholism?***

If the likelihood of abusing alcohol or other drugs is related to a person's beliefs about the substance, where do these beliefs come from? They come from family, friends, and the entire social environment to which the person is exposed. Research has shown that most young people who abuse alcohol or other drugs were first encouraged to do so by their peers and that the ability to resist such peer pressure is directly related to the strength and cohesiveness of family ties (Oetting & Beauvais, 1988; Zucker & Gomberg, 1986). Other research has shown large cultural and subcultural differences in alcohol abuse that correspond to cultural traditions. In the United States, the lowest rates of alcoholism occur among ethnic Jews, Chinese, Japanese, Italians, and Greeks, all of whom have traditions of strong negative sanctions against heavy drinking or drunkenness (Vaillant, 1983; Peele, 1988). Among such groups alcohol may be used for religious purposes or as a beverage to accompany a meal, but drinking to get drunk is not accepted. Cultural beliefs probably also contribute to the fivefold difference between men and women in prevalence of alcoholism; in practically every culture, drunkenness is seen as less acceptable in women than in men.

Dissociative Disorders

Dissociation is the process by which a period of a person's life, ranging from a few minutes to years, becomes separated from the rest of one's conscious mind in such a way that it cannot be recalled or can be recalled only under special conditions. Dissociation can be produced in many people through hypnosis. Given an appropriate posthypnotic suggestion, the hypnotized person may not be able to recall any events that occurred during the hypnotic period, or may be able to recall them only when a prearranged signal occurs (Hilgard, 1977). Dissociative disorders are believed by many who study them to involve states that are similar to hypnosis (Bliss, 1986).

Varieties of ***dissociative disorders*** are distinguished in *DSM-IV* according to their complexity. In the simplest type, *dissociative amnesia*, memory loss is the only prominent symptom. The amnesia may be selective for a specific traumatic experience, or it may be more global and include loss of memory for all facts about the self, including one's own name and place of residence. A second level of complexity occurs in those rare cases diagnosed as *dissociative fugue*. Here the person not only loses memory of his or her previous identity, but wanders away from home and develops a new identity that is quite separate from the earlier one (the term *fugue* stems from the Latin word *fugere*, to flee). When the fugue ends, perhaps days or months later, the person regains his or her original identity, with all of its associated memories, and at the same time loses memory of everything that happened during the fugue. The most complex and intriguing variety of dissociative disorder is ***multiple personality disorder***, which is the focus of the rest of this section.

Identifying Multiple Personality Disorder

Let us assume that you are a clinical psychologist or psychiatrist interviewing a new client. Before you sits a demure, exhausted-looking young woman who speaks in earnest tones about her complete devotion to her husband and child and about the headaches that she has been experiencing lately. Then, at a difficult moment in the conversation, she closes her eyes, and when she opens them you see before you a new person. She sits differently, speaks differently, and the expression on her face is that of a different person. No longer demure and exhausted, she is vivacious and talkative. She looks you in the eye, speaks with confidence, and calls you "Doc." This woman has no headaches, and she claims to have no children or husband either. "I can't be bothered with that. Life is too short," she says, and gives you a wink. This woman calls herself by a different name from the other one. She knows the other, though, and speaks of her with a combination of contempt and pity as a person who has never learned how to live. She knows the husband and child, too, and doesn't like them at all. In later sessions, as you get to know both of these women better, you find that although the second woman knows about the first, the first woman knows nothing of the second. The first talks about "losing time" (discovering that time has passed without her knowing what happened); about finding herself in strange places such as hotel rooms; and about finding dresses that had mysteriously appeared in her closet—garish ones that she would never buy herself.

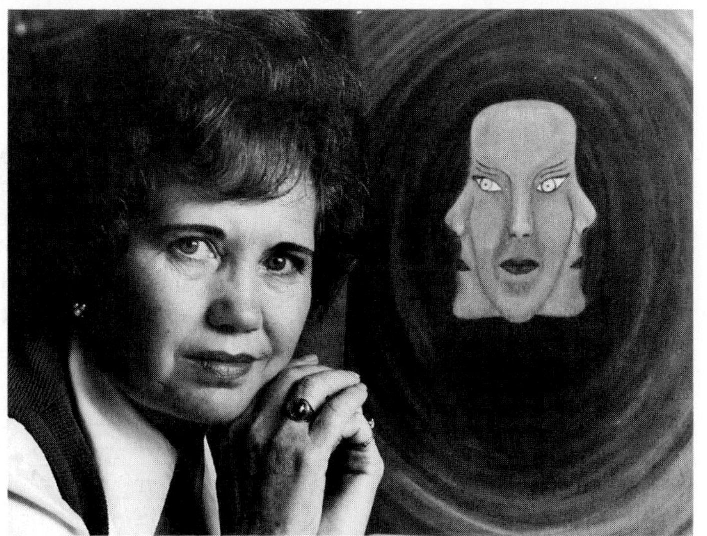

The integrated "Eve"

After many years of psychotherapy, Chris Sizemore—the real "Eve"—overcame her multiple personality disorder. Here she is shown with a painting she made to symbolize the three personalities that were apparent when she first entered therapy.

The account just described is based on the book *The Three Faces of Eve*, written by two psychiatrists, Corbett Thigpen and Hervey Cleckley (1957), about a woman they had treated for multiple personality disorder. The first personality is referred to as Eve White, the second as Eve Black. Later, a third, more mature and stable personality emerges, referred to as Jane. Still later, after the book was completed, new personalities continued to emerge—twenty-two in all—over a period of nearly 20 years (McKellar, 1979). Eventually, after many years of therapy, the woman overcame the disorder and since 1974 has been one person—the integrated person whom she considers to be her real self (Sizemore, 1989).

Multiple personality disorder is defined in *DSM-IV* as a disorder in which two or more distinct personalities or self-identities are manifested by the same person at different times. The switch from one identity to another apparently occurs automatically, usually in response to some environmental provocation. At the time of Thigpen and Cleckley's book, this disorder was believed to be extraordinarily rare. In fact, prior to 1970 only about 100 cases could be found in the psychiatric literature (Boor, 1982), but since then the number of reported cases has mushroomed. One specialist reported having known of 500 cases by 1979 and of over 5000 by 1985 (Braun, 1985).

In most reported cases, the personality change is not as obvious as that described for Eve, and individuals often go through years of psychotherapy before their multiple personalities are discovered. Skeptics have suggested that the popularization of this disorder over the past 2 decades has led patients to simulate its symptoms in therapy (either consciously or unconsciously) and has led therapists to see it where it doesn't exist (Spanos & others, 1985). Another suggestion is that multiple personalities are inadvertently created by the hypnotic procedures that therapists commonly use to identify them. In other words, a patient who has been hypnotized and asked to produce an alternative personality may unconsciously oblige the therapist and produce one, at the same time accepting the idea that this personality was always there and is just now being uncovered. Perhaps that occurs in many cases, but considerable evidence now exists that multiple personality is a legitimate disorder in a substantial number of people.

Causes of Multiple Personality Disorder

■ **31.** ***What evidence suggests that multiple personality exists as a real disorder and that it stems from childhood abuse coupled, perhaps, with an inborn ability to dissociate?***

One of the most carefully documented studies of multiple personality was conducted by Philip Coons and his colleagues (1988) in Indiana. Over a 13-year period they identified fifty cases at their clinic that satisfied *DSM-III* criteria, and they studied them through interviews and by searching out confirmatory evidence outside of the clinic. They found that of the 50 patients, 46 were women and 48 had been physically and/or sexually abused repeatedly and severely in childhood, most often by their parents. Of the two patients who were not abused as children, one was a man whose mother had been diagnosed with schizophrenia and the other was a woman whose disorder originated in her early twenties at a time when she was repeatedly beaten by her husband. Except for this woman, each patient had apparently begun a pattern of dissociation sometime before the age of 10. Large-scale studies in The Netherlands and Canada have likewise shown that the vast majority of people diagnosed with multiple personality disorder are women and that the vast majority (of either sex) were repeatedly tortured or sexually abused beginning in early childhood (Boon & Draijer, 1993; Ross & others, 1989).

Apparently, multiple personality typically begins in early childhood as a way of coping with repeated abuse. The child learns to go into a hypnotic-like trance that reduces pain or emotional feelings during the abuse and helps shut out the memory of it when it stops. With time these trances may become more elaborate, taking the form of distinct personalities. For example, a child being tortured might construct a personality who "enjoys" the torture, or a tough personality who "can take it." Having learned to produce new personalities to deal with these extreme conditions, the individual may use these same personalities or may develop new ones to deal with the more normal problems of life. Of course, not everyone who is abused repeatedly in childhood develops multiple personalities. Another prerequisite may be an inborn, biologically based capacity to dissociate. Consistent with this view, multiple personality patients are extremely easy to hypnotize compared to those who suffer from other mental disorders or have no disorder (Bliss, 1986).

Schizophrenia

John sits alone in his dismal room, surrounded by plastic garbage bags that he has hoarded during late-night excursions onto the street. He is unkempt and scrawny. He has no appetite and hasn't eaten a proper meal in weeks. He lost his job months ago. He is afraid to go out during the day because he sees in every passing face a spy who is trying to learn, by reading his mind, the secret that will destroy him. He hears voices telling him that he must stay away from the spies, and he hears his own thoughts as if they were broadcast aloud for all to hear. He sits still, trying to keep calm, trying to reduce the volume of his thoughts. John suffers from ***schizophrenia***.

Characteristics and Variations of the Disorder

Schizophrenia is a serious and relatively prevalent disorder. It is found in about 0.5 percent of the adult population at any given time (as shown in Figure 17.3) and in about 1 percent of people at some time in their lives (Robins & others, 1984). It accounts for a higher percentage of the inpatient population of mental hospitals than any other diagnostic category. The disorder seems to be equally prevalent in males and females, but, for unknown reasons, it typically strikes earlier in males; the most frequent age range for first symptoms is 18 to 25 for men and 26 to 45 for women (Straube & Oades, 1992). Sometimes people make a full recovery from schizophrenia, sometimes they make a partial recovery, and sometimes the disorder takes a deteriorating course throughout the person's life.

The label *schizophrenia* was first used by the Swiss psychiatrist Eugen Bleuler (1911/1950), whose writings are still a valuable source of information and insight about the disorder. The term comes from the Greek words *schizo*, which means split, and *phrenum*, which means mind, so it literally means "split mind." Bleuler believed, as do many theorists today, that schizophrenia entails a split among such mental processes as attention, perception, emotion, motivation, and thought, such that these processes operate in relative isolation from one another, leading to bizarre and disorganized thoughts and actions. Bleuler's term has caused many nonpsychologists to confuse schizophrenia with multiple personality. The mind of a person with schizophrenia is *not* split among more than one personality; dissociation is not a symptom of schizophrenia.

Symptoms

No two sufferers of schizophrenia have quite the same symptoms. But to receive the *DSM-IV* diagnosis of schizophrenia, the symptoms must include: (a) cognitive or perceptual distortion that renders the person in some ways seriously out of touch with reality; and (b) deterioration from a former level of functioning, usually including a sharp decline in ability to work and care for oneself. In addition, most cases are marked by social withdrawal. The person may be physically withdrawn from others, as is John, or psychologically withdrawn, as are those living within a family but not communicating with its members in a socially connected way. Disturbances in emotion are also common. The most common classes of symptoms, which need not all be present in any given case, are delusions, hallucinations, formal thought disturbances, and negative symptoms.

■ **32.** ***What are the main classes of symptoms of schizophrenia?***

Delusions are false beliefs held in the face of compelling evidence to the contrary. Common types of delusions in schizophrenia are *delusions of persecution*, which are beliefs that others are plotting against one; *delusions of grandeur*, which are beliefs in one's own extraordinary importance, for example, that one is the queen of England; and *delusions of being controlled*, such as believing one's thoughts or movements are being controlled by radio waves or by invisible wires in puppet-like fashion. Often several delusions occur together in a single delusional scenario.

Hallucinations are false sensory perceptions—seeing or hearing things that aren't there. The most common hallucinations are auditory, usually the hearing of voices. Hallucinations and delusions typically work together to support one another. For example, a man who has a delusion of persecution may repeatedly hear the voice of his persecutor insulting or threatening him. When asked to describe the source of the voices, people with schizophrenia typically say that they come from inside their own head, and some even say that the voices are produced (against their will) by their own vocal apparatus (Smith, 1992). Consistent with

Art by persons diagnosed with schizophrenia

These pieces by Adolf Wolfi (left) and Adolph Nesper (right) typify the unusual personal symbolism and eerie rhythmical forms that characterize the artwork of many patients with schizophrenia.

these reports, people with schizophrenia can usually stop the voices by such procedures as humming to themselves, counting, or holding their mouth wide open in a way that immobilizes the vocal apparatus (Bick & Kinsbourne, 1987). These same procedures also prevent people who don't have schizophrenia from vividly imagining the sound of a spoken word (Reisberg & others, 1989) and hearing hallucinated voices under hypnotic suggestion (Bick & Kinsbourne, 1987). Apparently, auditory hallucinations in schizophrenia occur through the same mechanism that produces vividly imagined speech sounds in everyone; the difference is that during a schizophrenic hallucination the person experiences the sound as truly audible and as a phenomenon separate from his or her own thoughts.

Figure 17.9 ***A person in a catatonic stupor***

People with schizophrenia withdraw from their environment in various ways. One of the most extreme forms of withdrawal is the *catatonic stupor*, in which the person may remain motionless for hours on end in an uncomfortable position.

Formal thought disturbances are breakdowns in the form or pattern of logical thinking. In some instances, the mind jumps wildly from one idea to another in a manner not guided by logic but by such factors as simple word associations—a pattern referred to as *overinclusion*. A classic example is this greeting to Bleuler (1911/1950) from one of his patients: "I wish you a happy, joyful, healthy, blessed and fruitful year, and many good wine-years to come as well as a healthy and good apple-year, and sauerkraut and cabbage and squash and seed year." Notice that, once the patient's mind hooked onto fruit (in "fruitful year"), it entered into a chain of associations involving fruit and vegetables that had little to do with the original intent of the statement. Another variety of formal thought disturbance is known as *paralogic*, in which reasoning is superficially based on rules of logic, but in fact is flawed in ways that are obvious to others. Paralogic may help support a delusion, as in the case of a woman who supported her claim to be the Virgin Mary this way: "The Virgin Mary is a virgin. I am a virgin. Therefore, I am the Virgin Mary" (Arieti, 1966).

Negative symptoms involve an absence of, or reduction in, expected behaviors, thoughts, feelings, and drives. They include a general slowing down of bodily movements, poverty of speech (slow, labored, unspontaneous speech), flattened affect (reduction in or absence of emotional expression), loss of basic drives such as hunger, and loss of the pleasure that normally comes from fulfilling drives. The majority of people with schizophrenia manifest negative symptoms to some degree, and for many these are the most prominent symptoms. I once asked a dear friend, who was suffering from schizophrenia and was starving himself, why he didn't eat. His answer, in labored but thoughtful speech, was this: "I have no appetite. I feel no pleasure from eating or anything else. I keep thinking that if I go long enough without eating, food will taste good again and life might be worth living."

Attempts to Divide Schizophrenia into Types

■ **33.** ***What are two systems for classifying types of schizophrenia, and what are the limitations of those systems?***

Ever since Bleuler's classic work, people who study schizophrenia have attempted to divide it into distinct types based on the predominant symptoms. *DSM-IV*, using a system similar to that first developed by Bleuler, identifies four main types: (1) *paranoid type*, characterized mainly by delusions of persecution and grandeur; (2) *catatonic type*, characterized mainly by nonreaction to the environment (see Figure 17.9); (3) *disorganized type*, characterized mainly by formal thought disorders, incoherence of speech, and either inappropriate or flattened affect; and (4) *undifferentiated type*, a sort of catch-all category for cases that do not meet the criteria of the other categories. These types are not discretely separate from one another, and probably do not represent truly different disorders, but are convenient labels to indicate which symptoms are most prominent in particular individuals.

Another system divides schizophrenia into two types: *Type 1*, or *positive schizophrenia*, characterized mainly by hallucinations, delusions, and bizarre thought and actions, and *Type 2*, or *negative schizophrenia*, characterized mainly by poverty of speech, flattened affect, and other negative symptoms (Crow, 1980). A problem with this system is that the great majority of people with schizophrenia show both positive and negative symptoms, so the distinction is at best one of degree, not type (Kay, S. R., 1992; Lenzenweger & others, 1989). Although some research has indicated a better prognosis (greater frequency of complete recovery) for people with primarily positive symptoms than for those with primarily negative symptoms, other research has failed to show this difference (Kay, S. R., 1992).

Behavioral genetics research aimed at identifying patterns of symptoms that run in families has also failed to produce evidence of clear subtypes of schizophrenia. Although particular symptoms do tend to run in families, they do not cluster into consistent patterns from family to family (Gottesman, 1991; Gottesman & others, 1987). So far, all attempts to develop a typology of schizophrenia point to one rather unsatisfying conclusion: The disorder comes in myriad forms (patterns of symptoms), probably stems from a wide variety of causes, and can vary greatly in long-term outcome; but the variations in form seem to defy classification in a way that relates them strongly to either causes or outcomes (Fowles, 1992; Heinrichs, 1993).

Ideas About the Causes of Schizophrenia

Twin and adoption studies indicate a strong genetic influence on the incidence of schizophrenia (look back at Table 3.3 in Chapter 3), but they have left many questions about the causes of schizophrenia unanswered. Through what physiological mechanisms do genes predispose people to schizophrenia? Before schizophrenia appears, are the people predisposed to it identifiably different from other people? What environmental experiences tend to bring on schizophrenia in those who are predisposed? Why does the disorder wax and wane over time once it develops, and why do some people make a full recovery while others do not? Let's look now at some research bearing on these questions from three perspectives—biological, cognitive, and sociocultural.

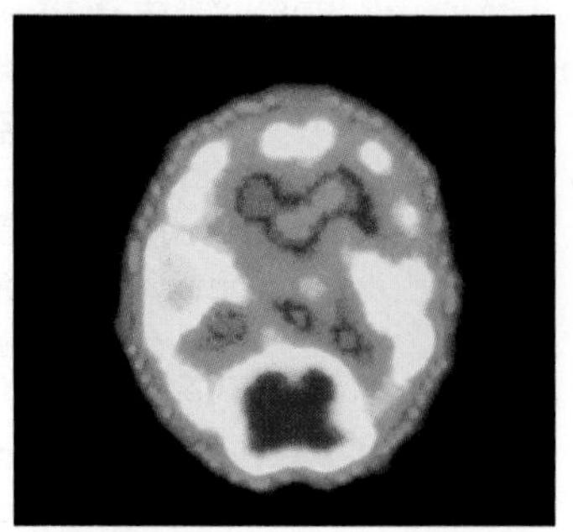
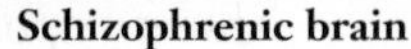

Schizophrenic brain

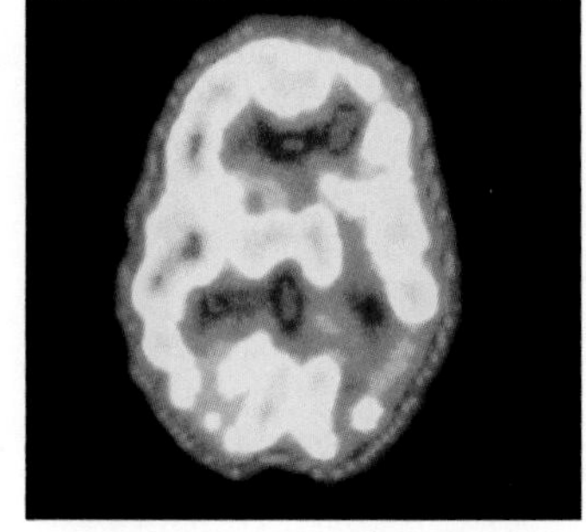

Normal brain

Disorder in the brain

In these PET scans, the blue areas are cerebral ventricles and the green represents relatively low levels of neural activity. The brains are oriented so that the front is at the top. Notice that the brain of the person with schizophrenia has less activity in the frontal lobes (more green) than the brain of the person without schizophrenia.

Biological Theories: Abnormalities in the Brain

■ **34.** ***What is some evidence for and against the dopamine theory of schizophrenia?***

The most long-standing physiological theory of schizophrenia is that it arises from overactivity at synapses where dopamine is the neurotransmitter. Support for the ***dopamine theory of schizophrenia*** comes mainly from the effects of drugs. Antipsychotic drugs reduce the symptoms of schizophrenia by blocking the release of dopamine from presynaptic terminals and by blocking postsynaptic receptor sites from receiving dopamine. Early studies comparing the clinical effectiveness of various antipsychotic drugs with their effectiveness in blocking dopamine release revealed a close correspondence (see Figure 17.10). Other support for the dopamine theory came from the finding that drugs such as cocaine and amphetamine, which

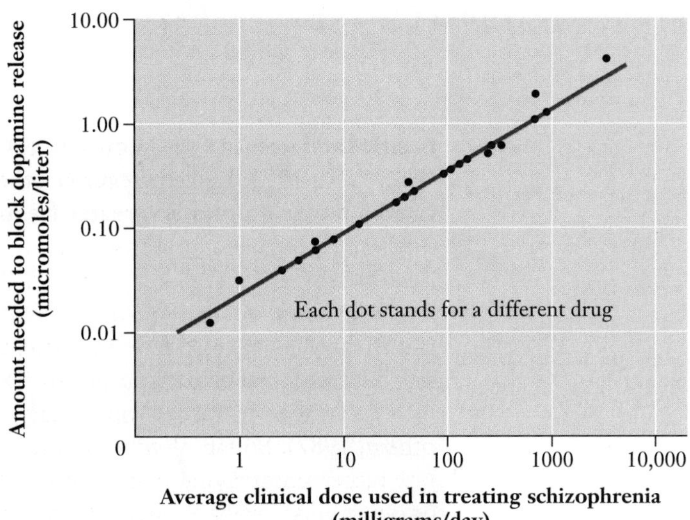

Figure 17.10 ***Correlation between the clinical and chemical potency of antipsychotic drugs***

Each dot in this graph represents a different antipsychotic drug. Its position on the horizontal axis depicts the average daily dose used to treat schizophrenia, and its position on the vertical axis depicts the amount needed to block the release of dopamine from synaptic terminals. The strong positive correlation between these two measures, shown here, is evidence that the clinical effectiveness of these drugs occurs through their dopamine-blocking action. (From Seeman & Lee, 1975.)

increase the action of dopamine in the brain, can greatly exacerbate the symptoms of schizophrenia in people with the disorder (Davis, 1974), and at higher doses can even induce such symptoms in people who do not have the disorder (Griffith & others, 1972).

Despite such support, the dopamine theory remains controversial. Studies aimed at assessing directly the amount of dopamine or the prevalence of dopamine receptors in the brains of people with schizophrenia have produced mixed results (Meltzer, 1992). A new antipsychotic drug, *clozapine*, which is at least as effective as the traditional antipsychotic drugs in reducing the symptoms of schizophrenia, has been found to have a smaller effect than the traditional drugs on dopamine and a relatively larger effect on various other transmitter systems (Tandon & Kane, 1993). Today a modified version of the dopamine theory seems most tenable: Unusual patterns of dopamine activity, perhaps including overactivity in some areas of the brain and underactivity in others, may provide at least part of the physiological basis for schizophrenia (Fowles, 1992). Antipsychotic drugs, including clozapine, may exert their action through a long-term stabilizing effect on dopamine-using synapses coupled, perhaps, with effects on other transmitter systems as well.

Other biological research has revealed that the brains of people with schizophrenia often have unusually large cerebral ventricles (fluid-filled spaces in the brain) that may be accompanied by loss of neural tissue bordering the ventricles (Raz & Raz, 1990) and often show reduced metabolic activity (indicative of reduced neural functioning) in the prefrontal lobes of the cortex (Buchsbaum, 1990). Studies vary greatly in the percentage of people with schizophrenia found to manifest these brain differences. Taking them all together, fewer than half of people with schizophrenia appear to manifest either one (Heinrichs, 1993). Some studies have shown a positive correlation between the degree of abnormal brain anatomy and the severity of negative symptoms, and other studies have failed to show such a correlation (Andreasen & others, 1990).

Prenatal or birth traumas may play a causal role in schizophrenia. Birth records of identical twins only one of whom developed schizophrenia reveal that in most cases the afflicted twin was born second and had a lower birth weight (indicative of a less favorable uterine position) than the co-twin (Wahl, 1976). Other studies have shown that people with schizophrenia are unusually likely to have had a difficult birth, involving oxygen deprivation or other trauma to the brain (Spohn & Patterson, 1980; DeLisi & others, 1988). Prenatal viral infection may also play a role (Torrey, 1988). In one long-term study, prenatal and birth traumas correlated positively with subsequent development of schizophrenia in people who were genetically at high risk for the disorder (whose mothers had schizophrenia), but not in people who were not genetically at risk (Mednick & others, 1987). Such research suggests that genes may predispose people to schizophrenia in part by increasing their vulnerability to the damaging effects of prenatal stress or difficult births.

A Cognitive Theory: Defective Attention

Regardless of possible biological causes, schizophrenia is manifested and diagnosed primarily as a set of cognitive symptoms. It is useful to distinguish two classes of cognitive symptoms. *Episode indicators,* such as delusions and hallucinations, wax when the disorder becomes active and wane when it goes into remission. *Vulnerability indicators* remain even during periods of remission and may predate the initial onset of the disorder (Green, 1993). Certain deficits in attention and concentration have been proposed as possible vulnerability indicators and possible predisposing causes.

Many years ago, Bleuler (1924/1951) hypothesized that a general characteristic of schizophrenia is that its sufferers are "incapable of holding a particular thought in a particular channel." Many people with schizophrenia describe their own early symptoms in terms of defective attention and concentration (Freedman & Chapman, 1973), as exemplified by the following quotations: "Every face in the windows of a passing streetcar would be engraved in my mind . . . A hodge-podge of unrelated stimuli were distracting me from things that should have my undivided attention" (MacDonald, 1960). "Nothing settles in my mind—not even for a second. . . . Too many things come into my head at once and I lose control" (Chapman, 1966).

■ **35.** ***What is some evidence that a deficit in attention may be a predisposing cause of schizophrenia?***

These gross effects on attention are episode indicators, because they wax and wane along with the other symptoms of schizophrenia. But laboratory studies have revealed more subtle deficits in attention in people who have recovered from all overt symptoms of schizophrenia (Green, 1993). In one such study, a group of people diagnosed with schizophrenia continued throughout periods of complete remission to perform poorly at a vigilance task, in which they were required to press a button whenever a specific two-digit sequence (such as 3–7) appeared in a series of digits flashed rapidly on a screen (Nuechterlein & others, 1992). In other research, an unusually high percentage of children who were genetically at risk for schizophrenia (because one of their parents had the disorder) were found to show attention deficits similar to those seen in adults with schizophrenia (Cornblatt & Erlenmeyer-Kimling, 1985; Green, 1993). Moreover, a longitudinal study of at-risk children produced compelling evidence of a correlation between attention deficits in childhood and social isolation in adolescence and suggestive evidence of a correlation between the attention deficits in childhood and schizophrenia in adulthood (Erlenmeyer-Kimling & others, 1993). Such findings are consistent with the idea that a deficit in selective attention may contribute to one's vulnerability to schizophrenia.

Other research suggests that people who are prone to schizophrenia first develop the overt symptoms of the disorder, or show a relapse of those symptoms, after disturbing life changes (Fowles, 1992; Nuechterlein & others, 1992). Perhaps a deficit in the ability to filter out irrelevant stimuli and to focus on what is relevant adds to the cognitive burden created by disturbing life events.

A Sociocultural Perspective on the Maintaining Causes of Schizophrenia

In the late 1970s, the World Health Organization initiated an ambitious cross-cultural study of schizophrenia involving locations in 10 countries (Jablensky & others, 1992). Three of the countries—Colombia, Nigeria, and India—were identified as relatively nonindustrialized, developing countries. The others were identified as developed countries—England, Ireland, Denmark, the United States, Japan, Czechoslovakia, and Russia (then part of the Soviet Union). Using agreed-upon criteria and cross-cultural reliability checks, the researchers diagnosed new cases of schizophrenia in each location, classed them according to symptom types and apparent severity, and reassessed each case through interviews conducted one year and two years later. In all, 1379 patients were included in the study.

The results showed remarkable evidence of cross-cultural consistency in the onset of schizophrenia. The prevalence of the various symptoms, the average age of onset of the disorder, and the sex difference in age of onset (later for women than for men) were strikingly similar from location to location despite wide variations in the ways that people lived. The study also revealed a remarkable cross-cultural difference, which had been more than hinted at by earlier, less systematic studies: The patients in developing countries showed *better* recovery during the two-year follow-up period than did those in developed countries. This was true of every category of schizophrenia identified in the study, for nearly every index of recovery that was used. When all categories were combined, 63 percent of patients in the developing countries, compared to only 37 percent in the developed countries, showed a full recovery by the end of the two year period (Jablensky & others, 1992).

Why should people in less industrialized countries fare better after developing schizophrenia than people in more industrialized countries? The cross-cultural study revealed some reliable differences in treatment between the two classes of countries. Patients in the less industrialized countries were more likely than those in the industrialized countries to receive non-Western folk or religious treatments, less likely to be hospitalized, and less likely to receive antipsychotic drugs over prolonged periods (Jablensky & others, 1992). Some controversial studies in Europe and the United States have suggested that prolonged use of the antipsychotic drugs, while dampening immediate symptoms, may impede full recovery (Warner, 1985). Most researchers interested in cross-cultural differences in schizophrenia outcome have, however, focused not on these differences but on differences in the prevailing attitude toward the disorder and those who have it.

■ **36.** ***How has the concept of expressed emotion been used to explain cross-cultural differences in recovering from schizophrenia?***

Much cross-cultural research on schizophrenia has centered on a concept referred to as *expressed emotion*, defined as criticisms and negative attitudes or feelings expressed about and toward a person with schizophrenia by family members with whom that person lives. Research within various cultures has indicated that, other things being equal, the greater the expressed emotion the lower is the chance of full recovery from schizophrenia, and research across cultures has shown that the average level of expressed emotion is greater in more industrialized countries than in less industrialized countries (Jenkins & Karno, 1992). Apparently, emotional acceptance by family members helps a person with schizophrenia to recover from the disorder, and lack of acceptance prolongs or exacerbates the disorder.

Why do people in less industrialized countries find it easier to accept a relative with schizophrenia than do people in more industrialized countries? Many plausible reasons have been suggested (Jenkins & Karno, 1992; Lin & Kleinman, 1988). People in less industrialized countries are less likely to call the disorder "schizophrenia" or to think of it as permanent, and more likely to refer to it with terms such as "a case of nerves," which sound more benign and tie it to experiences that everyone has had. They place relatively less value on personal independence, and more on interdependence and family ties, which may lead them to feel less resentful and more nurturing toward a family member who needs extra care. They are more likely to live in large, extended families, which means that more people share in providing the extra care. Finally, in a less industrialized country a person with schizophrenia is more able to play an economically useful role. The same person who could not hold a job at a factory or an office can perform useful chores on the family farm or at the family trade.

Concluding Thoughts

Here are three final ideas that may help you organize your thoughts as you reflect on what you have read in this chapter.

1. The continuum between normality and abnormality Although a diagnosis of a mental disorder is categorical (all or none), the symptoms on which diagnoses are made are not; they vary in degree throughout the population. Thus, any decision as to whether a particular person does or does not have a mental disorder is based on arbitrary criteria as to how severe or prolonged each symptom must be in order to call the syndrome a disorder.

As you review each disorder described in the chapter, think about its symptoms in relation to the moods, emotions, thoughts, and behaviors that all of us manifest to some degree. Doing so helps remove some of the mystique from the concept of mental disorder and helps us identify with people whose troubles are like ours, only stronger. Thinking of disorders in terms of extremes of normal processes has also helped scientists to understand them better. For example, in this chapter you read about evidence (a) relating the symptoms of phobias and obsessive-compulsive disorders to normal fears, thoughts, and actions; (b) relating the symptoms of depression and bipolar disorders to normal despondency and elation; and (c) relating the hallucinations experienced in schizophrenia to a normal capacity for vivid mental imagery.

2. The multiple causes of mental disorders By this time in your study of psychology, you are no doubt used to the idea that human feelings, thoughts, and actions emerge from the interaction of many causes. This idea also applies to the feelings, thoughts, and actions that lead to the diagnosis of a mental disorder. The differences among us that are considered disorders—no less than the differences that are considered normal—are caused by differences in our genes and in our past and present environments.

One way to review this chapter would be to think about each disorder in relation to the three classes of causes—predisposing, precipitating, and maintaining—that were introduced near the beginning of the chapter. How might genes operate through the person's physiology to predispose him or her to the disorder? How might learned ways of thinking or acting predispose a person to the disorder? How might specific stressful events in life interact with the predisposition to precipitate the disorder? How might the disordered behavior itself, or people's reactions to it, help maintain the disorder once it begins? For each disorder, think about the relationship between the research or ideas described and the possible answers to these questions.

3. Perspectives on mental disorders The various perspectives (biological, psychodynamic, behavioral, cognitive, and sociocultural) that were discussed in the chapter focus on different sets of causes of mental disorders. To a considerable degree, the perspectives exist because people who conduct research or therapy on mental disorders differ in their goals and training. Psychiatrists have medical degrees; they are trained to think in terms of diseases, and they are the only mental health professionals who can regularly prescribe drugs. Psychiatry also has a long tradition, stemming from Freud, of emphasis on unconscious mental processes. Thus, psychiatrists lean toward biological and psychodynamic perspectives. Clinical psychologists, in contrast, are trained heavily in psychology and little in biology or medicine. They are well versed in research on learning and cognition; thus, their perspective is frequently behavioral and cognitive. Sociologists, anthropologists, and social psychologists who study mental disorders are trained to focus on the social and cultural context of behavior. They tend to take the sociocultural perspective and to see the predisposing and maintaining causes of mental disorders as lying in the values, attitudes, and expectations that prevail in the culture.

Further Reading

Dale Peterson (Ed.) (1982). *A mad people's history of madness.* Pittsburgh: University of Pittsburgh Press.

In this fascinating collection of excerpts from autobiographies written over the past 500 years, people who either were, or were regarded as, seriously mentally disordered describe their suffering, the reactions of others, and their own efforts toward recovery. Some of the excerpts are from well-known books that have helped shape reforms in the understanding and treatment of people with mental disorders.

Peter Tyrer & Derek Steinberg (1987). *Models for mental disorder: Conceptual models in psychiatry.* Chichester, England: Wiley.

This is a concise, easy-to-read introduction to the medical, psychodynamic, behavioral, and sociocultural perspectives on mental disorders.

Robert Spitzer, Miriam Gibbon, Andrew Skodol, Janet Williams, & Michael First (1989). *DSM-III-R casebook.* Washington, DC: American Psychiatric Press.

Designed to help clinical students learn to use DSM-III-R, this book is free of jargon and can be read easily by the first-year psychology student. It consists of brief case descriptions of the problems suffered by real individuals, each followed by an explanation of how that case would be diagnosed. It is an excellent source from which to gain a more vivid understanding of mental disorders, even for the person who will never be required to diagnose one.

Richard Gordon (1990). *Anorexia and bulimia: Anatomy of a social epidemic.* Cambridge, MA: Basil Blackwell.

Not only a lucid discussion of anorexia and bulimia, this book is also a fine example of a sociocultural analysis of a class of mental disorder. The first chapter, on the notion of an ethnic disorder, is an excellent introduction to the sociocultural perspective.

Samuel Barondes (1993). *Molecules and mental illness.* New York: Scientific American Library.

This introduction to the genetic and neurochemical bases for schizophrenia, mood disorders, and anxiety disorders is brief, clearly written, and colorfully illustrated. It ends with a clever four-page poem that summarizes the history behind the attempt to understand the molecular bases for mental disorders.

Looking Ahead

I hope you didn't catch medical students' disease from this chapter, but in case you did, don't worry: The next chapter is on treatment. Of course, real mental disorders are serious problems, and effective means for treating them are among the most valuable contributions that psychology has made and is continuing to make to human welfare.

TREATMENT

CHAPTER 18

The worst thing about having a Ph.D. in psychology is that when I go to a party and am introduced as a psychologist, people either become embarrassed and quiet, or they start telling me their problems. I have learned to explain immediately that I am not *that* kind of psychologist—not a clinical psychologist who treats people, but a teacher and a researcher who studies certain aspects of learning and motivation. Apparently, many people think that psychology *is* clinical psychology. This chapter, then, is about that part of psychology with which most nonpsychologists have the greatest familiarity. You will read about (a) the social issue of care for the severely disturbed; (b) methods of clinical assessment (how clinical psychologists and psychiatrists try to determine what is wrong); (c) four major forms of psychotherapy (psychodynamic, humanistic, cognitive, and behavioral); and (d) biological approaches to treatment (especially drugs).

Care as a Social Issue

What To Do with the Severely Disturbed?

■ **1.** ***How has Western society's response to people with serious mental disorders changed since the Middle Ages?***

Prior to the last 2 centuries or so, society felt little obligation toward people with mental disorders. During the Middle Ages, and even into the seventeenth century, people with serious mental disorders—the kind called madness or lunacy (and today most commonly diagnosed as schizophrenia)—were often considered to be in league with the devil, and "treatment" commonly consisted of torture, hanging, burning at the stake, or being sent to sea in "ships of fools" to drown or be saved, depending upon divine Providence. By the eighteenth century, such "religious" views had waned somewhat and a more secular attitude began to prevail, which attributed mental disorders not to supernatural powers, but to the basic degeneracy and unworthiness of the disordered people themselves. Now the principal treatment for those who couldn't care for themselves was to put them out of the way of decent society in places that were called hospitals, but in reality were dark, damp, miserable dungeons, where inmates were frequently kept chained to the walls, alive but in a state that was perhaps worse than death (see Figure 18.1 on page 648).

Not until the beginning of the nineteenth century did humanitarian reform begin to occur in a significant way. The best-known leader of reform in Europe was Philippe Pinel (1745–1862) who, as director of a large mental hospital in Paris, unchained the inmates, transferred them to sunny and airy rooms, and gave them access to the hospital grounds for exercise. Under these conditions some inmates who had been deemed permanently and hopelessly deranged actually recovered sufficiently to be released from the hospital. In the United States, the leading re-

Figure 18.1 ***Life in a nineteenth-century mental hospital***

One source of pressure for mental hospital reform in early nineteenth-century England were portraits, such as this, drawn by George Cruikshank. The man shown here had been bound to the wall by foot-long chains for 12 years at the time of the portrait.

former was Dorothea Dix (1802–1887), a Boston schoolteacher who visited dozens of jails and almshouses where people with mental disorders were housed, and publicized the appalling conditions she found. As this *moral-treatment movement* grew, it spurred the building of large, state-supported asylums for the mentally disordered. The idea behind such institutions was high minded: to provide kindly care and protection for those unable to care for themselves. Unfortunately, public sympathy was rarely sustained at this high level, at least not in the tangible form of financial support. Almost invariably the asylums became overcrowded and understaffed, and reverted to conditions not unlike those that had appalled Pinel and Dix. As recently as the 1940s, the following report could be written about a state mental institution in Philadelphia (Deutsch, 1948):

> The male "incontinent ward" was like a scene out of Dante's Inferno. Three hundred nude men stood, squatted and sprawled in this bare room . . . Winter or summer, these creatures never were given any clothing at all . . . Many patients [in another ward] had to eat their meals with their hands . . . Four hundred patients were herded into a barn-like day room intended for only 80. There were only a few benches; most of the men had to stand all day or sit on the splintery floor . . . The hogs in a nearby pigpen were far better fed, in far greater comfort than these human beings.

By the mid-1950s, disenchantment with large state institutions led to a new kind of reform movement in the United States—a movement to *deinstitutionalize* people with mental disorders, to get them back into the community. This new movement was inspired partly by the development of effective antipsychotic drugs and partly by a general mood of optimism in the nation, a feeling that everyone could "make it" if given the chance. President John F. Kennedy gave the movement a boost in 1961, by encouraging the U.S. Congress to pass legislation to establish community-based mental health centers (Bassuk & Gerson, 1978). By the early 1970s, hundreds of such centers were in operation, offering transitional homes and outpatient care to patients capable of living in the community.

Unfortunately, the dream of the community mental health movement, like the earlier dream of asylums, has remained mostly unrealized. The number of chronic patients in state mental institutions has been greatly reduced, but it is debatable whether the quality of life for former patients has been improved. Today, they are often found in run-down rooming houses, shelters for the homeless, understaffed nursing homes, and, as in the days of Dorothea Dix, in jails (Abram & Teplin, 1991; Fischer & Breakey, 1991). They have generally not been integrated into the community, but are living on the fringes of the community. We still have a long way to go toward adequately funded, humanitarian care.

Continuing Problems with Mental Hospitals: Rosenhan's Study

Mental hospitals today are not the same horrors they once were. Some are quite decent places, with excellent staff and successful programs of therapy and rehabilitation. Yet, in many such institutions, especially those that depend on government support, enormous problems persist. Studies conducted within the past 15 years indicate that many state mental hospitals make no real attempts at therapy and often use drugs more as a means of keeping order than as part of a well-planned program of treatment (Okin, 1983).

■ **2.** ***How did Rosenhan study the experiences of patients in mental hospitals, and what did he find?***

To get a patient's-eye view of life in mental hospitals, David Rosenhan (1973), a psychologist at Stanford University, conducted a study in which he and seven other sane individuals feigned mental illness to gain admission to different psychiatric hospitals. After making an appointment, they appeared at the hospital admitting office and complained of a single symptom—hearing voices that said, "Empty, hollow, thud." They answered all other questions about their problems and history honestly. Once in the hospital, they behaved as normally as possible, and when asked about the voices they said that they no longer heard them. None of these

Dorothea Dix

This Boston schoolteacher's crusade resulted in new asylums for the mentally ill and improved conditions in existing institutions.

pseudopatients was ever detected as an imposter by hospital staff, though real patients often saw through the ruse and said things like, "You're not really mentally ill; you must be a reporter studying the hospital." Perhaps the main reason that they remained undetected is that the staff had very little contact with them; pseudopatients' total time with psychiatrists and psychologists averaged less than 7 minutes per day, including group meetings. Even in hospitals that were adequately funded and staffed, staff members who could have spent more time interacting with patients chose instead to stay inside the glass "cage" that separated them from patients.

Even more striking than the minuscule amount of interaction with staff was the dehumanizing nature of those interactions that did occur. When pseudopatients (or real patients) approached them to ask questions, staff members commonly averted their eyes and walked away, or gave a reply that was irrelevant to the question. In other ways as well, staff members communicated an attitude that patients were not to be taken seriously as thinking individuals. They talked about patients in front of them as if they were not there. A nurse unbuttoned her uniform and adjusted her brassiere before a ward of male patients, not to be seductive, but because she felt no need to show normal social decorum in front of patients. Some attendants beat or verbally abused patients in front of other patients, but stopped immediately when other staff members approached. As Rosenhan put it, "Staff are credible witnesses, patients are not." The pseudopatients' normal behaviors were frequently interpreted in terms of mental illness. For example, no staff member ever asked the pseudopatients why they were so often writing in notebooks (which they did to record their experiences), yet a subsequent inspection of the hospital records showed that their "writing behavior" was regularly described as part of their pathological symptomatology. All in all, staff members seemed unable to look through the label *mentally ill*, or through the bizarre symptoms that patients *sometimes* show, to see that patients are not always crazy and are usually capable of normal human interactions.

Bright Spots

Within the past 2 decades, a number of highly successful programs for helping seriously disordered individuals have been developed, both in and out of mental hospitals, which have served as models of improvement elsewhere.

3. ***How did Paul and Lentz show that people who had been long-term mental patients could profit from a therapeutic environment that was quite different from the standard hospital treatment?***

In a remarkable study within the state mental hospital system in Illinois, Gordon Paul and Robert Lentz (1977) selected eighty-four very dysfunctional patients who had been hospitalized for an average of 17 years, each with a diagnosis of schizophrenia, and assigned them randomly to different treatments. One group continued to receive *standard hospital treatment*, emphasizing custodial care and drug therapy. A second group was assigned to *milieu therapy*, which involved close interaction between staff and patients, increased respect for patients (who were referred to as residents), heightened expectations concerning the responsibilities of both staff and patients, a degree of democratic decision making in the ward, and reduction or elimination of antipsychotic drugs wherever possible.

A third group was assigned to *social learning therapy*, which involved most of the elements of milieu therapy plus a highly directed effort to teach patients the social skills they would need to live outside the hospital. Patients in this group were engaged in organized, skill-learning activities during 85 percent of their waking hours. In contrast, those in the standard ward spent only 5 percent of their waking hours in classes, therapy sessions, or other organized activities. The staff-to-patient ratio and the proportion of professional to nonprofessional staff were the same in all three wards. The study continued for 5 years, by which time 97 percent of the patients in the social learning ward, 71 percent in the milieu ward, and 46 percent in the standard ward had been able to leave the hospital and live in the community for at least 18 months. By other measures as well—including improved behavior in the ward and reduced total cost per patient—the social learning ward was far more successful than the standard ward.

Many communities have developed intensive intervention programs for seriously disturbed patients outside of mental hospitals, which go by the names *Assertive Community Intervention* and *Training Community Living*. Such programs actively reach out to the mentally disabled, offering them training in daily living and advocating for them as they attempt to secure housing, employment, and other necessities. Rather than wait for the disabled to come to them, they go to the disabled. Controlled studies have shown that such programs can be highly effective in preventing the need for hospitalization and in increasing the proportion who eventually recover from their disorder (Test & others, 1991). Although expensive, they are no more so than custodial care in a mental hospital (Levine & others, 1993).

Structure of the Mental Health System

Public concern about mental health generally centers on the most severely disordered individuals. But most people who seek mental health services have much milder problems. The most common reasons for seeking help are anxiety and depression (Shapiro & others, 1984). The mental health system is structured to provide help for every degree of mental distress and disorder.

Places of Treatment

■ **4. *Where and from whom can treatment for mental disorders be found?***

Mental health services can be found in a number of settings, which vary in the severity of the disorders they are designed to treat.

- *Mental hospitals* provide custodial care for patients who cannot care for themselves or be cared for by family members at home. In addition, they provide brief hospitalization (typically 2 to 4 weeks) to stabilize individuals who are suffering from acute psychotic attacks. The number of people in mental hospitals has greatly declined over the past 40 years.
- *General hospitals* have been admitting an increasing number of psychiatric inpatients, while the number in mental hospitals has declined. In fact, today the majority of psychiatric inpatients are in general hospitals, sometimes in special psychiatric wards but more often not (Kiesler 1993). A general hospital is usually preferable to a mental hospital for patients whose stay will be short. Among other things, less stigma is associated with hospitalization there, and its location near the patient's home makes visiting easier for family members and friends.
- *Nursing homes* now care for many older chronic mental patients who in former times would have been in mental hospitals. These homes usually do not employ special treatment personnel for such people (Kiesler & Sibulkin, 1987), and living conditions vary tremendously.
- *Halfway houses,* usually located in residential areas of cities, are places where people who have been discharged from a hospital reside during their transition back to the community. The halfway house (or *group home*, as it is often called) provides a place to sleep, eat, and socialize; and it may also provide help in finding employment and a permanent place to live. Residents are expected to leave the house during the day to work, look for work, or go to school. Such houses are usually run by nonprofessionals who consult regularly with government-employed psychiatrists, psychologists, and social workers.
- *Community mental health centers* offer free or low-cost services, including psychotherapy, support groups, and telephone crisis hotlines. In addition, such

centers often sponsor classes, initiate legislation, and engage in other activities aimed at preventing psychological problems, in the community.

- *Private offices* of psychiatrists, clinical psychologists, or psychiatric social workers are usually the preferred places of treatment for those who can afford such treatment and do not require hospitalization.

Providers of Treatment

Psychotherapy and other mental health services are provided by an array of professionals with various kinds of training.

- *Psychiatrists* have a medical degree, obtained through standard medical school training, followed by special training and residency in psychiatry. They can work in any of the settings above, but most often choose hospitals and private practice. They are the only mental health specialists who can prescribe drugs.
- *Clinical psychologists* have a doctoral degree in psychology with training in research and clinical practice. Many are employed by universities as teachers and researchers in addition to their clinical practice. As clinicians they may work in any of the settings described above.
- *Counseling psychologists* have a doctoral degree from a counseling program. Their training is similar to that of clinical psychologists, but usually entails less emphasis on research and more on practice. They may work in any of the settings described above. In general, counseling psychologists are more likely than are psychiatrists or clinical psychologists to work with people who have problems of living that do not warrant a diagnosis of mental disorder.
- *Counselors* have a master's degree from a counseling program. Though they may work in any of the settings above, they are more likely to work in a school or other institution, with people who are dealing with school- or job-related problems. They receive less training in research and psychological assessment procedures than do doctoral-level clinical or counseling psychologists.
- *Psychiatric social workers* have a master's degree in social work, followed by advanced training and experience working with people who have psychological problems. They may be employed in any of the settings above, but are most often employed by public social work agencies, and commonly visit people in their homes to offer support and guidance.
- *Psychiatric nurses* usually have a bachelor's or master's degree in nursing followed by advanced training in the care of mental patients. They usually work in hospitals and may conduct psychotherapy sessions as well as provide more typical nursing services.

Clinical Assessment

Assessment is the process by which a mental health professional gathers and compiles information about a patient or client for the purposes of developing a plan of treatment. Diagnosis—defined in Chapter 17 as the classifying and labeling of the disorder according to some standard set of guidelines, such as those in *DSM-IV*—is only one goal of assessment. In fact, some clinicians deliberately avoid such labeling except when required for bureaucratic purposes such as filing for insurance reimbursement. The more important goal is to understand the person as a unique individual with a unique set of life circumstances, ways of thinking, and ways of behaving. Assessment ideally occurs not only before treatment, but throughout it, to monitor changes and determine when treatment should be modified or discontinued. Assessment is far from an exact science. Despite clinicians' attempts to be objective, assessment is largely a matter of educated guessing and is subject to the biases and distortions that can affect anyone's judgments of another person.

Clinicians who have different theoretical orientations have different views as to what kinds of information are most useful in assessment. To a psychodynamically oriented clinician, what the client *doesn't* say (and thus may be repressing) may be at least as revealing as what he or she *does* say. To a humanistic clinician, the client's conscious perceptions and beliefs (his or her phenomenological world) are most useful whether they are objectively accurate or not. To a cognitively oriented clinician, the client's habitual patterns of thinking are crucial. And to a behaviorally oriented clinician, objective facts about the client's actual behaviors and the settings in which they occur are most important. Some of the assessment aids available to clinicians are described below.

Assessment Interviews and Objective Questionnaires

5. *What are the advantages of interviews and objective questionnaires for assessing a client's condition?*

George Kelly (1958), a clinical psychologist whose ideas helped to found the humanistic and cognitive traditions, once offered the following simple advice about clinical assessment: "If you want to know what is going on in a person's mind, ask him; he may tell you."

The ***assessment interview*** is by far the most common assessment procedure. It is basically a dialogue through which the clinician tries to learn about the client. The dialogue may be unstructured, leaving to the client the task of deciding what is important or unimportant; or it may be a highly structured set of questions asked by the clinician and answered by the client. The interview typically touches on the client's immediate symptoms, home and work environment, personal history, and other information that seems relevant to the client's problem. The client's nonverbal behaviors, such as long pauses, body tension, or emotional expressions may also be taken into account in interpreting his or her verbal responses.

To supplement interviews, ***objective questionnaires*** have been developed to help clients report their feelings, thoughts, and behaviors. Some of these are simply lists of adjectives or brief, descriptive statements; the client is asked to check off those that apply to himself or herself. Others use a multiple-choice format in which the client chooses from among several possible statements the one that most applies to himself or herself. Some cover a broad range of possible symptoms or characteristics. Others, such as the *Beck Depression Inventory* illustrated in Table 18.1, focus on a narrow range of symptoms associated with a particular class of disorder. Objective questionnaires offer a degree of standardization that is useful for clinical

Table 18.1 ***Sample items from the Beck Depression Inventory***

The client's task on each item is to pick out the one statement that best describes how he or she has been feeling for the past week.

Item (pessimism)
I am not particularly discouraged about the future.
I feel discouraged about the future.
I feel I have nothing to look forward to.
I feel that the future is hopeless and that things cannot improve.

Item (sense of failure)
I do not feel like a failure.
I feel I have failed more than the average person.
As I look back on my life, all I can see is a lot of failures.
I feel I am a complete failure as a person.

Source: BDI by Aron T. Beck, 1978, New York: Harcourt Brace Jovanovich.

research or for any comparison of one client with others. In addition, they are less subject to bias than are face-to-face interviews in which the clinician's way of asking the questions may influence the client's answers.

A Psychometric Personality Test: The *MMPI*

Psychometric personality tests are objective questionnaires that have been developed through psychometric methods (discussed in Chapter 16) to assess a wide range of personality characteristics. Two examples of such tests are Cattell's 16 PF Questionnaire and Eysenck's Personality Inventory (discussed in Chapter 16), both of which are sometimes used for clinical assessment. But by far the most commonly used psychometric personality test for clinical assessment is the *Minnesota Multiphasic Personality Inventory*, abbreviated ***MMPI***.

■ **6. *How was the* MMPI *developed, and why was it revised? What is the purpose of its clinical, content, and validity scales?***

The purpose of the *MMPI*—developed at the University of Minnesota in the late 1930s—was to provide an objective means to diagnose mental disorders, uncontaminated by the biases of any particular clinician (Hathaway & McKinley, 1943). In developing the test, all potential questions were pretested on groups of patients (criterion groups) who had already been diagnosed as having a specific mental disorder, and on a large control group with no diagnosed disorder (the so-called Minnesota normals). Questions that were commonly answered differently by a patient group than by the controls were kept, and others were thrown out. The goal was to identify questions that would distinguish different patient groups from each other and from the control group.

Despite its frequent use, or perhaps because of it, the original version of the *MMPI* was often criticized. One critic referred to it as a "psychometric nightmare," impossible to interpret in any objective way (Rodgers, 1972). Others argued that the test was culturally biased, producing false signs of disorder in people whose backgrounds were different from those of the mostly white, middle-class Minnesotans with whom the test was developed (Gynther, 1972). Consider the statement *People say insulting and vulgar things about me*. A response of *true* was scored as a sign of paranoia even in a member of a discriminated-against minority (Pervin, 1980). In the late 1980s the test was revised on the basis of results obtained from a large, representative sample of U.S. citizens (Butcher, 1990). The revision was designed to remedy the problems in the original version, and research currently under way will provide evidence concerning the test's usefulness.

Referred to as *MMPI-2*, the revised test contains 567 statements about the self, to which the person must reply *true* or *false*. Most statements contribute to a score on one or more of ten *clinical scales* and fifteen *content scales*. In some cases the relationship between a statement and the clinical scale to which it contributes is obvious. Thus, the response *true* to the statement *The future seems hopeless to me* adds a point to the clinical scale measuring depression. In other cases, the relationship is not obvious. For example, answering *false* to *At times I feel like swearing* also contributes to the clinical scale measuring depression. This is because in the research on which the scale was built, depressed people responded *false* to that item significantly more often than did nondepressed people. The content scales are similar to the clinical scales, but contain only statements that are obviously related to the characteristic being measured. Thus, the content scales assess most directly what people choose to say about their psychological condition.

In addition, the test has several *validity scales* designed to assess honesty and care in completing the test. The *L* scale was designed to assess lying (or lack of frankness) motivated by the attempt to make a good impression. For example, the response *true* to the statement *I never get angry* adds a point to the *L* scale, based on the assumption that everyone gets angry at times. The *F* scale was designed to assess the tendency to "fake bad," that is, to exaggerate problems or to claim nonexistent symptoms. The response *true* to *Everything smells the same* will add a point to the *F* scale, based on the assumption that true inability to discriminate among different odors is practically nonexistent. High scores on the *L*, *F*, and other validity scales can also reflect random responses, which might stem from carelessness or from insufficient reading or reasoning ability. Whatever their cause, high scores on the validity scales imply that the answers to other questions cannot be trusted and the results should be either thrown out or interpreted with caution.

Projective Tests

■ **7. *Why and how do clinicians use projective tests?***

The interviews and objective questionnaires just described rely on the person's conscious mind to supply accurate information about the self. But defense mechanisms, conscious or not, can cause the person to give misleading answers. For this reason, some clinicians supplement objective questioning techniques with ***projective tests***, which use the conscious mind to uncover the unconscious mind. Projective tests are an outgrowth of *free association* (Chapter 16), one of the methods that Freud devised to probe the unconscious mind. The client or subject is shown ambiguous visual stimuli and asked to say quickly, without logical explanation, what each one looks like or what ideas it brings to mind.

Taking a projective test is a bit like responding to a work of art. If you and a friend look at a painting or a piece of sculpture, you may see something quite different in it from what your friend sees. Your interpretation says something about yourself. In psychoanalytic terms, you are projecting some aspect of yourself onto the work of art. Unconscious thoughts that would never get past your defense mechanisms and into conscious expression if you were talking about yourself may be freely expressed in the guise of artistic interpretation.

The projective tests most commonly used are the *Rorschach* and the *Thematic Apperception Test (TAT)*. In the Rorschach test, the visual stimuli are symmetrical inkblots, and the task is to say what each inkblot looks like. In the TAT, the stimuli are pictures of ambiguous scenes that include one or more persons, and the task is to tell a story about what might be happening in the picture. These tests are used in research studies as a basis for statistical comparison between groups of people, but their primary application is in therapy.

Clinicians have developed standard procedures for scoring projective tests, in which rules are used to code the content of the client's responses (Groth-Marnat,

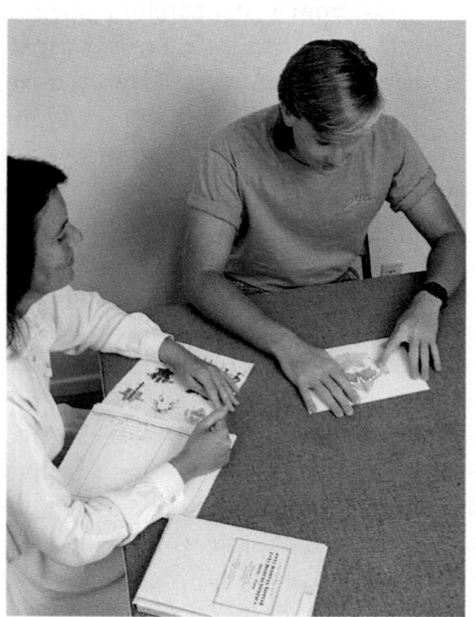

The Rorschach and TAT tests

In the Rorschach test, people say what they see in the inkblots. In the TAT, they tell a brief story for each picture. The rationale of both tests is that people project their unconscious wishes and memories into their perceptions or stories.

1990). For example, standard scoring for the Rorschach includes methods to rate the degree of morbidity (tendency to see death and decay) and aggressiveness (tendency to see conflict) in each response. But the validity of such systems is highly controversial. Many clinicians who use projective tests prefer to interpret them less formally, using their own experience coupled with other information they have about the client. In a sense, all of psychoanalysis is assessment, and the therapy process itself is much like projective testing. Everything that the client says and does—whether in response to inkblots or in response to requests to free-associate or describe dreams—contributes to the picture that the therapist develops of the client's unconscious mind. When they are used in this intuitive way, there is no statistical way to determine whether or not projective tests are valid.

Behavioral Monitoring

■ **8. *How does behavioral monitoring contribute to both assessment and treatment?***

The term ***behavioral monitoring*** refers to any system for counting or recording actual instances of desired or undesired behaviors. In Paul and Lentz's experiment comparing treatments for hospitalized patients, staff members charted each patient's progress by keeping daily counts of their positive and negative actions (defined according to their symptoms). In a less formal way, ward nurses or other observers in any mental hospital keep a daily log of patients' activities to assess improvement or deterioration. Behavior therapists who work with noninstitutionalized clients emphasize *self-monitoring*, in which clients keep written records of their own actions that they are trying to increase or decrease. Thus, a person trying to eliminate a hand-washing compulsion might keep a record of each instance of hand washing, or a person with an eating disorder might keep a record of each food eaten and the amount consumed. The very process of keeping records heightens awareness of the behavior, which in itself can sometimes solve the problem. In addition, the records and graphs can provide a strong incentive for change—everyone likes to see evidence of improvement.

Neuropsychological Assessment

■ **9. *What is the purpose of neuropsychological tests such as the Halstead-Reitan battery?***

If there is a reason to think that brain damage might underlie a patient's psychological difficulties, the patient may be sent to a neurologist or a neuropsychologist for a set of tests designed to find clues to such damage. The most commonly used set of neuropsychological tests, the *Halstead-Reitan battery*, includes tests of motor control (such as moving the index finger rapidly up and down), perception (such as identifying objects by touch), and cognition (items from a standard IQ test are used) (Reitan & Wolfson, 1985). If these or other neuropsychological tests suggest brain damage, more direct approaches for detecting such damage may be used, such as an EEG, a CAT scan, or an MRI scan.

The *EEG (electroencephalogram)* is a measure of the pattern of electrical activity of the brain, taken through electrodes attached to the scalp (see Chapter 7); it can be analyzed for abnormal patterns that indicate possible brain damage. The *CAT scan* (CAT stands for computerized axial tomography) is a newer, much more costly method, in which multiple x-rays of the brain are taken from various angles and analyzed by a computer to produce pictures of individual sections of the brain, which can be inspected to find anatomical abnormalities. The *MRI scan* (MRI stands for *magnetic resonance imaging*) is a still newer and more costly technique, by which pictures of brain sections are constructed based on electromagnetic radiation produced by specific molecules in the brain when the brain is subjected to a strong magnetic field. If any of these tests indicates brain damage, the patient may be given special training to compensate for the deficits. The damage may also be treated with medicine or even with surgery if such treatment is warranted (for example, in the case of a potentially lethal tumor).

Family therapy
A premise of this form of therapy is that disorder often lies not in the individual but in the interactions among family members.

Psychotherapies

Psychotherapy refers to any formal, theory-based, systematic treatment for mental problems or disorders that uses psychological rather than physiological means and is conducted by a trained therapist. Psychotherapy normally involves dialogue between the person in need and the therapist, and its aim is usually to restructure some aspect of the person's way of feeling, thinking, or behaving. If you have ever helped a child overcome a fear, encouraged a friend to give up a bad habit, or cheered up a despondent roommate, you have engaged in a process akin to psychotherapy, though less formal.

By one count, more than 400 nominally different forms of psychotherapy have appeared over the years (Karasu, 1986). Here we will limit ourselves to the approaches most often taught in clinical psychology and psychiatric programs and most often practiced by those trained in such programs. We will also limit ourselves to *individual therapies*, those in which a therapist works with one person at a time. Many psychotherapists work with groups (in *group therapy*), couples (in *couple therapy* or *marriage counseling*), or families (in *family therapy*), but generally the principals behind their work are extensions of the individual approaches described below. The main addition in group therapies is that they allow more opportunity to practice social skills and get feedback from people other than the psychotherapist. The main addition in couple and family therapies is that they allow couples and families to express their interpersonal difficulties in front of one another on neutral ground and to practice new ways of communicating with one another. Moreover, the problem is seen as residing in the dynamics of the family system, rather than any one individual.

Psychoanalysis and Other Psychodynamic Therapies

Psychoanalysis refers specifically to the approach developed by Sigmund Freud, and ***Psychodynamic therapy*** refers generally to any therapy approach that is based on the premise that psychological problems are manifestations of inner mental conflicts and that conscious awareness of those conflicts is a key to recovery.

Breuer's Treatment of Anna O.: A Precursor of Psychoanalysis

■ **10.** ***How did the case of Anna O. lead to the idea that unconscious memories and their associated unconscious emotions can cause neurotic symptoms?***

In describing the origin of psychoanalysis, Sigmund Freud often credited an older friend and colleague of his, Joseph Breuer, and specifically referred to Breuer's treatment of a patient known as Anna O. In turn, Breuer gave credit to Anna O. herself, who often took the lead in telling him how he could help her (Erdelyi, 1985). Anna was a brilliant, aristocratic Viennese woman who in 1880 at the age of 21, while caring for her dying father, developed a multitude of symptoms indicative of what was then called hysteria (and is now called conversion disorder, discussed in Chapter 17). Among her symptoms, which would come and go, were an inability to drink fluids (hydrophobia), a squint in both eyes that rendered her unable to see, and paralysis of her right arm. Breuer, a neurologist, was called in to treat Anna, but because her symptoms had no apparent neurological basis he at first just visited her regularly to check on her and try to comfort her.

Often when Breuer arrived to visit Anna, he found her in a hypnotic-like trance, and in that state she often talked in an animated, uninhibited fashion about herself and her past experiences. As she talked she sometimes recalled experiences that she had previously forgotten (or had repressed, to use Freud's later term), and her recollection of those experiences often brought her relief from one or more of her symptoms. For example, at a time when she felt revolted by the thought of drinking any fluids and could quench her thirst only by eating fruits, Anna recalled a scene in which she had observed her governess's dog drinking from a glass. The event had greatly disgusted her at the time, partly because she already felt contempt for both the dog and the governess, but out of politeness she had stifled her emotional reaction. After recalling this incident and reexperiencing her emotional reaction to it, she was immediately relieved of her dread of drinking. She asked for a glass of water and drank heartily for the first time in weeks.

These sessions were so productive that Breuer began to use hypnosis when Anna was not in one of her naturally-occurring trances. Under hypnosis, Anna traced the origins of her squint to an experience in which, while caring for her father, she had squinted to hold back tears so he would not see that she was crying. She traced the origin of her paralyzed arm to another experience in which, while sitting by her father's sickbed, she had a terrifying fantasy of a snake attacking him and found that she could not reach out to protect him because her arm, slung over the back of the chair, had (in reality) gone to sleep and was temporarily paralyzed. By tracing each of her symptoms back to an initial triggering event and experiencing the emotions related to that event, Anna overcame her symptoms one by one.

Why was the recollection of emotionally stressful events helpful? Anna herself referred to the technique as "chimney sweeping," an allusion to her idea that digging up and sweeping away unpleasant memories was helping her. Breuer called it the *cathartic technique*. *Catharsis* means purging (eliminating some foul substance), and in Breuer's view the technique purged the patient of the destructive effects of

An experiment in hypnosis

The hypnotic technique with which Breuer treated Anna O. was earlier used by the French neurologist Jean Charcot, who showed that people suffering from "hysterical" loss of motor or sensory function could be made to see or walk. Charcot is shown here demonstrating hypnosis.

bottled up, emotionally charged memories. Breuer suggested that when an emotional event occurs but the emotion is not consciously experienced, the unconscious memory of the event festers in the mind and can produce symptoms of the sort that Anna O. experienced (Breuer & Freud, 1895/1955). Only if the patient relives the event, and consciously feels the emotion, can the symptoms be alleviated.

Freudian Psychoanalysis

From Anna O. and several other early cases (described by Breuer & Freud, 1895/1955), Freud determined that (a) conscious memories can become unconscious, (b) emotionally charged unconscious memories can provide the basis for neurotic symptoms, and (c) these symptoms may disappear if the patient becomes conscious of the underlying memories and consciously experiences the emotions associated with them. These ideas provided the framework from which Freud began his work with neurotic patients and the ground upon which he based his theory and practice of psychoanalysis. Psychoanalysis as a theory of personality is described in Chapter 16. Here I will briefly summarize its main characteristics as an approach to psychotherapy:

11. ***What is the significance of childhood experience in Freudian psychoanalysis?***

- ***Importance of childhood sexual experiences*** The greatest difference between Freud's eventual psychoanalytic approach and the earlier one that emerged from Breuer's work with Anna O. concerns the role of infantile sexual conflicts (discussed in Chapter 16). In Freud's theory, all neuroses (emotional disorders) stem from an interaction between two categories of experiences. The first and most basic category consists of *predisposing experiences*, which occur in the first 5 to 6 years of life and relate to infantile sexual wishes and conflicts. The second category consists of *precipitating experiences*, which occur later and most immediately bring on the emotional breakdown. From this vantage point, all of the experiences identified in Breuer's treatment of Anna O. were in the precipitating category.

  Had Freud (after developing his full theory) been Anna O.'s therapist, he would have tried to uncover not only the events that immediately brought on her symptoms, but also her childhood memories and wishes that made those events so significant. *Why* was the sight of a dog drinking from a glass so traumatic? *Why* was it so important to hide her tears from her father? *Why* did she have the snake fantasy while watching over her ill father? Freud would have framed his answers in terms of Anna's childhood sexual feelings, probably involving her father, that must have been rearoused when she was caring for him.

12. ***In Freudian theory, how do free association and dreams, resistance, and transference contribute to the therapeutic process?***

- ***Free association and dreams as clues to the unconscious*** The term *analysis* in psychoanalysis comes from Freud's finding that patients rarely recall unconscious memories simply by talking (with or without hypnosis), as Anna O. did, so the psychoanalyst must infer them from clues in the patient's words and behavior. Freud's principal technique for obtaining such clues was free association, in which the patient would lie on a couch in a relaxed state and talk freely about whatever came to his or her mind in relation to certain symptoms or ideas. Freud also asked patients to describe their dreams. As explained in Chapter 17, he interpreted the seemingly illogical associations and ideas that came from these methods as symbolic expressions of the unconscious memories or wishes that were at the core of the person's psychological problems.

- ***Role of resistance*** Freud found that patients resist the therapist's attempt to bring their unconscious memories or wishes into consciousness. The ***resistance*** may manifest itself in such forms as refusing to talk about certain topics, "forgetting" to come to therapy sessions, or arguing incessantly in a way that diverts the therapeutic process. Freud assumed that resistance stems from the more general defensive processes (described in Chapter 16) by which people

The original therapeutic couch

This photograph of Freud's consulting room shows the couch on which patients reclined while he sat, out of their line of sight, listening to their free associations. Contemporary psychoanalysts have generally abandoned the couch in favor of a more egalitarian face-to-face encounter.

protect themselves from becoming conscious of anxiety-provoking thoughts. Resistance provides clues that therapy is going in the right direction, toward critical unconscious material; but it can also slow down the course of therapy or even bring it to a halt. To avoid too much resistance, the therapist must present interpretations gradually, when the patient is ready to accept them.

- ***Role of transference*** In psychotherapy a patient expresses strong emotional feelings—sometimes love, sometimes anger—toward the therapist. Freud believed that the true object of such feelings is usually not the therapist but some other significant person in the patient's life whom the therapist symbolizes. Thus, ***transference*** is the phenomenon by which the patient's unconscious feelings about a significant person in his or her life are experienced consciously as feelings about the therapist. Freud considered transference to be especially important to psychoanalysis because it provides an opportunity for the patient to become aware of his or her strong emotional feelings. With help from the analyst, the patient can gradually become aware of the origin of those feelings and their true target.

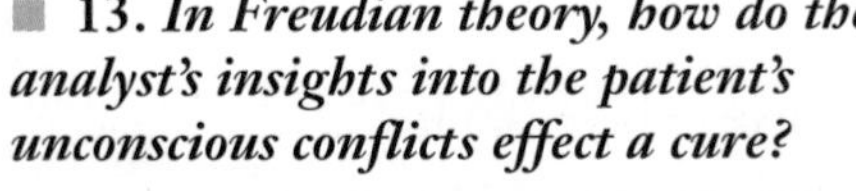

■ **13.** ***In Freudian theory, how do the analyst's insights into the patient's unconscious conflicts effect a cure?***

- ***Relationship between insight and cure*** Psychoanalysis is essentially a process in which the analyst makes inferences about the patient's unconscious conflicts and relays that information to the patient. How does such knowledge help? In Freud's theory, it helps by making conscious the disturbing wishes and memories that are the source of the neurotic symptoms. Once conscious, they can be expressed and experienced directly, or, if they are unrealistic, the conscious ego can modify them into healthier pursuits. At the same time, the patient is freed of the defenses that had kept that material repressed, and has more psychic energy for other activities. But for all of this to happen, the patient must truly accept the analyst's insights, viscerally as well as intellectually. The analyst

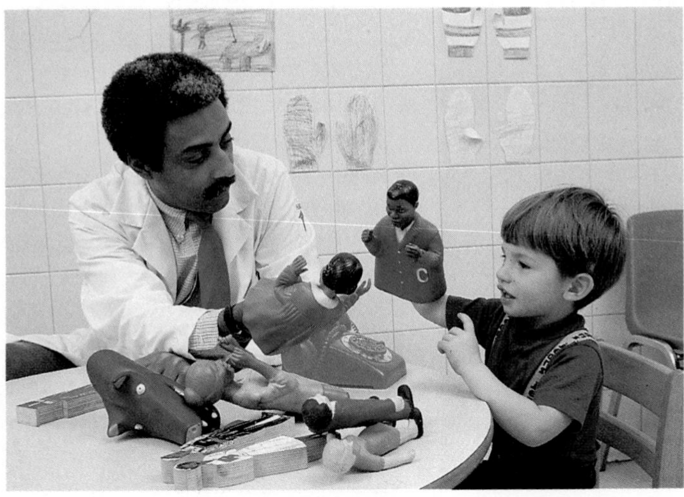

Play therapy

In this extension of psychodynamic therapy, children use dolls and other toys to express and gain insight into their feelings.

cannot just tell the patient about his or her unconscious conflicts, but must lead the patient gradually in such a way that he or she actually experiences the emotions.

Case Example: Freud's Analysis of the Rat Man

■ **14.** ***How does the case of the Rat Man exemplify Freud's concepts of precipitating and predisposing causes?***

One of Freud's most famous and illustrative cases is that of a 29-year-old man referred to in the case history as the Rat Man. This patient came to Freud complaining of various fears, obsessions, and compulsions that had begun 6 years earlier and had prevented him from completing his university studies and going on to a career. One of the most revealing symptoms was an obsessive fantasy of a horrible torture applied to both his father and the woman whom the Rat Man was courting, in which a pot of hungry rats strapped against the victims' buttocks would chew their way out through the only available opening. Freud used this fantasy along with many other clues to interpret the Rat Man's problems. Here I will sketch the outlines of Freud's interpretation and some of the evidence on which he based it. You can decide for yourself from the sketch, or better yet from Freud's original case history (see Further Reading), whether or not the interpretation seems plausible.

According to Freud (1909/1963), the *precipitating cause* of the Rat Man's disorder was his conflict over whether or not to marry the woman he had been courting since the age of 20. Unable to decide consciously, he had allowed his unconscious mind to resolve the conflict by making him too ill (producing his neurotic symptoms) to complete his studies and start a career (which were prerequisites for marriage). The *predisposing cause* was an unconscious oedipal conflict, originating in early childhood, between love and hatred for his father. These two causes were linked. The Rat Man's conflict about marrying the woman was a reenactment of his love-hate feelings about his father. To marry her would be an act of hatred against his father, and to spurn her would be an act of love toward him.

The connection between these two conflicts had been cemented by the death of his father shortly after the Rat Man had begun to court the woman in question. Knowing his father's oppositions, the Rat Man unconsciously and irrationally believed that he had caused the death by continuing the relationship with the woman against his father's wishes. Yet he also imagined unconsciously and irrationally that his father was still alive and that he could murder his father once more by following through with the marriage. Among the many converging lines of evidence that led Freud to these conclusions were these:

■ **15.** ***How did free association, dream analysis, and transference contribute to insight about the Rat Man's neurotic conflict?***

- At one point Freud asked the Rat Man to free associate to the concept *rats* (*ratten* in German), and the man immediately came up with *rates* (*raten* in German), meaning "installments" or "money." The Rat Man had previously mentioned that the woman had little money, and his father wanted him to marry a certain wealthy cousin. These facts suggested to Freud that the rat fantasy was related to the father's opposition to the woman.
- At another point the Rat Man described his mother's account of an event that took place when he was about 4 years old. His father had begun to beat him for having bitten his nurse. He responded with such a torrent of angry words that his father, shaken, stopped the beating and never beat him again. In Freud's analysis, this incident had great significance. Freud assumed that biting the nurse was a sexual act for the boy and that the beating contributed to the Rat Man's lifelong fear of his father's reactions to his sexual wishes. At that same time his apparent power over his father—his anger had made the father stop the beating—helped stamp into the Rat Man the unconscious fear that he could kill his father through anger. From that time until his psychoanalysis, the Rat Man never consciously experienced anger toward his father. In addition, Freud saw direct symbolic links between this early childhood incident and the

rat-torture obsession: Rats, biting into and destroying his woman friend and his father, symbolized another small, biting beast—the boy who had once bitten first his beloved nurse and then, with angry words, his father.

Transference also entered into the analysis. The Rat Man reported a fantasy in which Freud wanted him to marry his (Freud's) daughter, and a dream in which Freud's daughter had two spots of dung on her face instead of eyes. Freud interpreted the dung as symbolic of money, and he interpreted the fantasy and dream as a symbolic reconstruction of the man's conflict, with Freud replacing the Rat Man's father in urging him to marry a wealthy relative. At another point—which Freud regarded as the major breakthrough—the Rat Man became irrationally angry at Freud, jumping up from the couch and shouting abusive words at him. Reflecting on this incident later, the Rat Man recalled that his sudden anger was accompanied by a fear that Freud would beat him and that he had jumped up to defend himself. By this time in the analysis, it took little convincing for the Rat Man to share Freud's view that this was a reenactment of the incident in which his father had beaten him and he had responded so angrily.

This transference experience helped the Rat Man to overcome his resistance to the idea that he felt fear and anger toward his father. The Rat Man's conscious acceptance of those feelings led, according to Freud, to recovery from his neurotic symptoms. In a sad footnote to the case, Freud (1923/1963) added that after a short period as a healthy man, the Rat Man was killed as an officer in World War I.

Post-Freudian Psychodynamic Psychotherapies

16. *How do modern variations of psychodynamic psychotherapy differ from Freud's psychoanalysis?*

Since Freud's time many varieties of psychodynamic psychotherapy have been developed. All share certain aspects of Freud's approach, including the bringing of troublesome feelings into consciousness, the attribution of present troubles to mental conflicts stemming from past experiences, and the use of the therapist-client relationship as a model for understanding the client's relationships outside of therapy (Jones & Pulos, 1993). The most common modification today, motivated largely by economic considerations, is to reduce the number of sessions required for analysis by using methods that get more quickly at unconscious material. So-called *short-term psychodynamic psychotherapies* attempt to accomplish in ten to forty sessions the task that usually takes hundreds of sessions in classic psychoanalysis. The couch is dispensed with and the client and analyst sit face to face. The analyst more actively calls the client's attention to relevant material and ideas, and sometimes uses techniques such as role playing to facilitate transference and speed the therapeutic process.

Other variations differ from Freud's psychoanalysis in their theoretical underpinnings as well as their methods. *Ego-oriented psychodynamic therapies* pay less attention than did Freud to early childhood and the id's wishes, and more attention to the client's adult life and the ego's defense mechanisms (discussed in Chapter 16). These therapies aim to discover and expose ways in which defenses distort the client's experiences and relationships. By breaking down the defenses, even without uncovering their origins, the therapist helps the client develop a healthier range of responses. Still other variations, called *non-Freudian psychodynamic therapies*, are based on alternative psychodynamic personality theories such as Adler's, Jung's, or Horney's (discussed in Chapter 16) that emphasize mental conflicts different from those deemed important by Freud. In Adlerian therapy, for example, the client's feeling of inferiority, and the conflicts engendered by that feeling, are considered to be most significant.

Humanistic Therapy

■ **17.** ***What is the primary goal of humanistic psychotherapy?***

As described in Chapter 16, the humanistic view of the person emphasizes the inner potential for positive growth—the so-called actualizing potential. For this potential to exert its effects, people must be conscious of their inner feelings and desires, and not deny or distort them. Humanistic therapy is similar to psychodynamic therapy in that both attempt to help clients become more aware of their feelings and wishes. The humanistic view is that people often deny or distort their feelings and wishes in response to judgments imposed from outside. The main goal of humanistic therapy is to help clients become aware of their own feelings and wishes, so that they can gain control of their own lives rather than operate in accordance with their perceptions of what others expect. In one version of humanistic therapy, called *Gestalt therapy*, the therapist uses the client's facial expressions, body posture, and other nonverbal cues to judge whether the client's statements are consistent with what the client truly feels or believes, and actively challenges the client each time inconsistency is detected (Perls & others, 1951). But by far the most common humanistic therapy is that developed by Carl Rogers, which rarely involves a direct challenge to the client's statements.

Rogers's Client-Centered Therapy

■ **18.** ***How does the client's role in Rogers's humanistic therapy differ from that in other psychotherapies?***

When a random sample of psychotherapists were asked in the early 1980s to name the person who most strongly influenced their work, Carl Rogers (1902–1987) was cited more often than anyone else (Smith, 1982). Rogers called his therapeutic approach ***client-centered therapy***, because it focuses on the thoughts, abilities, and cleverness of the client rather than those of the therapist. The client, not the therapist, figures out what is wrong, makes plans for improvement, and decides when improvement has occurred. The therapist in this case is not an analyst, not a detective trying to infer things about the client that the client doesn't know, but instead is more like a sounding board, a compassionate yet professional sounding board for the client's ideas and emotions. How these ideas and emotions sound and feel to the client, not to the therapist, is most important.

From Rogers's perspective, psychological problems originate when people learn from their parents or other authorities to deny their own feelings and to distrust their own ability to make decisions. As a result of such learning, they look to others as guides to how to feel and act, and at the same time rebel inside or feel resentful about living according to others' preferences. The client-centered therapist tries to provide a context within which clients can become aware of and accept their own feelings and learn to trust their own decision-making abilities. To do so, the therapist must display empathy, positive regard, and genuineness (Rogers, 1951).

Carl Rogers

The inventor of client-centered therapy was a charismatic individual who personally embodied the empathy and genuineness that are the essence of his method of therapy.

■ **19. *Why are empathy, positive regard, and genuineness essential aspects of Rogers's approach to psychotherapy?***

Empathy refers to the therapist's attempt to comprehend what the client is saying or feeling at any given moment from the client's point of view rather than as an outside observer. As part of the attempt to achieve and manifest such empathy, the therapist frequently *reflects back* the ideas and feelings that the client expresses. A typical exchange might go like this:

Client: *My mother is a mean, horrible witch!*

Therapist: *I guess you're feeling a lot of anger toward your mother right now.*

To an outsider, the therapist's response here might seem silly, a statement of the obvious. But to the client and therapist fully immersed in the process, the response serves several purposes. First, it shows the client that the therapist is listening and trying to understand. Second, it distills and reflects back to the client the feeling that seems to lie behind the client's words—a feeling of which the client may or may not have been fully aware at the moment. Third, it offers the client a chance to correct the therapist's understanding. By clarifying things to the therapist, the client clarifies them to himself or herself.

Positive regard implies a belief on the therapist's part that the client is worthy and capable even when the client may not feel or act that way. Through experiencing the therapist's positive regard, clients begin to feel more positive about themselves, and this is essential if they are going to take charge of their lives. Positive regard does not imply approval of everything that the client does, but does suggest faith in the client's *capacity* to make appropriate decisions. Consider the following hypothetical exchange:

Client: *Last semester in college I cheated on every test.*

Therapist: *I guess what you're saying is that last semester you did something against your values.*

Notice that the therapist has said something positive about the client in relation to the misdeed without condoning the misdeed. The shift in focus from the negative act to the client's positive values affirms the client's inner worth and potential ability to make constructive decisions.

Genuineness reflects the belief that it is impossible to fake empathy and positive regard, that the therapist must really feel them. If the therapist's words don't match the therapist's feelings, the words will not be believable to the client. The capacity for genuine empathy and positive regard toward all clients might seem to be a rare quality, but Rogers suggests that it can be cultivated by deliberately trying to see things as the client sees them.

The humanistic approach is often described as nonscientific (see Chapter 16), but Rogers himself had great respect for science and urged clinical psychologists to test their theories with objective data. Beginning in 1940, Rogers and his colleagues recorded and transcribed complete sets of therapy sessions and compared clients' statements in later sessions with their statements in earlier ones (Rogers, 1951; Rogers & Dymond, 1954). Consistent with humanistic theory, they found that as time in therapy increased, clients made more comments about their own feelings, wishes, responsibilities, and ability to control their fate, and fewer comments about outside forces that controlled them. Statements such as, "My mother is a mean, horrible witch!" made in early sessions would later give way to statements such as, "I can see both good and bad qualities in my mother, and to some extent it is my own fear of being like her that has been a problem."

Of course, it is one thing to show changes in what clients *say* over the course of therapy, and another to demonstrate that these statements reflect real changes in their lives outside of therapy. The latter is harder to test objectively, and is an issue to which we will return later, for psychotherapy in general. Critics of the client-centered approach also argue that therapists may actually lead the client far more than they think. Therapists do not just mirror the client's thoughts and feelings; they reflect selectively, and their choices could condition the client to focus on matters that the therapist deems important. This unwitting direction may be more subtle than that which occurs in other therapies, but it is direction nonetheless.

Case Example: Rogers's Treatment of a Silent and Bitter Young Man

■ **20.** ***How did Rogers use empathy, positive regard, and genuineness to help a man who had been diagnosed with schizophrenia?***

Rogers's greatest challenge as a therapist came when, as part of a research study, he conducted client-centered therapy with severely withdrawn inpatients in a state mental hospital (Rogers, 1967). One of these individuals was Jim, a 28-year-old man who had been hospitalized for 2½ years with a diagnosis of schizophrenia. Prior to the two sessions excerpted below, Rogers had met with Jim once a week for months, and most of that time had been spent in silence. According to Rogers, these two sessions marked a turning point, because for the first time Jim began to express how he felt.

[At about 40 minutes into the session, marked mostly by silence.]

Jim: *I just ain't no good to nobody, never was and never will be.*

Rogers: *Feeling that now, hm? . . . Those really are lousy feelings. Just feel that you're no good at all, hm?*

Jim: *Yeah.* [Muttering in a low, discouraged voice.] *That's what this guy I went to town with just the other day told me.*

Rogers: *This guy that you went to town with really told you that you were no good? Is that what you're saying? Did I get that right?*

Jim: *M-hm.*

Rogers: *I guess the meaning of that, if I get it right, is that here's somebody that meant something to you and what does he think of you? Why, he's told you that he thinks you're no good at all. And that just really knocks the props out from under you.* [Jim weeps quietly.] *It just brings the tears.*
[Silence of 20 seconds.]

Jim: [Defiantly.] *I don't care though.*

Rogers: *You tell yourself you don't care at all, but somehow I guess some part of you cares because some part of you weeps over it.*
[This is followed by more silence, more weeping, and more reflection by Rogers on how it must hurt to feel that someone thinks you're no good. The next session begins again with lots of silence, punctuated by bitter statements in which Jim says that he wants to die. We pick up the conversation as Rogers breaks a long silence by asking whether the wish to die is related to the comment discussed in the previous session.]

Rogers: *Can't help but wonder whether it's still true that some things this friend said to you—are those still part of the thing that makes you feel so awful?*

Jim: *In general, yes.*

Rogers: *M-hm.*
[Silence of 47 seconds, interrupted by another comment from Rogers. Then:]

Jim: *I ain't no good to nobody, or I ain't no good for nothin', so what's the use of living?*

Rogers: *M-hm. I guess a part of that is—here I'm kind of guessing and you can set me straight, I guess a part of that is that you felt, "I tried to be good for something as far as he was concerned. I really tried. And now—If I'm no good to him, if he feels I'm no good, then that proves I'm just no good to anybody." Is that, uh—anywhere near it?*

Jim: *Oh, well, other people have told me that, too.*

Rogers: *Yeah, m-hm. I see. So you feel if, if you go by what others—what several others have said, then, you are no good. No good to anybody.*

[This is followed by more silence, interrupted by a few comments along the same track. Then:]

Jim: [Muttering in discouraged tone.] *That's why I want to go, cause I don't care what happens.*

Rogers: *M-hm, m-hm . . . You don't care what happens. And I guess I'd just like to say—I care about you. And, I care what happens.*
[Silence of 30 seconds, and then Jim bursts into tears.]

Rogers: [Tenderly.] *Somehow that just—makes the feelings pour out.* [Silence of 35 seconds.] *And you just weep and weep. And feel so badly.*

Commenting on the transaction above, Rogers (1967) wrote:

> Jim Brown, who sees himself as stubborn, bitter, mistreated, worthless, useless, hopeless, unloved, unlovable, *experiences* my caring. In that moment his defensive shell cracks wide open, and can never be quite the same. When someone *cares* for him, and when he feels and experiences this caring, he becomes a softer person whose years of stored up hurt come pouring out in anguished sobs. He is not the shell of hardness and bitterness, the stranger to tenderness. He is a person hurt beyond words, and aching for the love and caring which alone can make him human. This is evident in his sobs. It is evident too in his returning to my office [shortly after the session], partly for a cigarette, partly to say spontaneously that he will return.

After this session, according to Rogers, Jim gradually became more open, spontaneous, and optimistic at their meetings. After several months, he was able to leave the hospital and support himself with a job. Eight years later, on his own initiative, Jim called Rogers to tell him that he was still employed, had friends, was content with life, and that his feelings toward Rogers were still important, even though they had not been in touch during all that time (Meador & Rogers, 1973).

Cognitive Therapy

Cognitive therapy begins with the assumption that people disturb themselves through their own thoughts. Maladaptive thoughts make reality seem worse than it is and in that way produce anxiety or depression. The goal of cognitive therapy is to identify maladaptive ways of thinking and replace them with adaptive ways that provide a base for more effective coping with the real world.

■ **21.** ***How does cognitive therapy differ from Rogers's humanistic therapy?***

Cognitive therapy is similar to humanistic therapy in its focus on conscious mental experiences, but in other respects it is different. While humanistic therapy is client centered, cognitive therapy is *problem centered.* That is, whereas humanistic therapists try to help their clients understand themselves better as whole persons, cognitive therapists focus more directly on their clients' specific problems. Compared to either humanistic or psychodynamic therapists, cognitive therapists adopt more of a let's-get-down-to-business attitude. The cognitive therapist-client relationship is similar to a teacher-student relationship in that the therapist helps the client identify and correct his or her faulty reasoning. Most cognitive therapists even assign homework to be completed between one session and the next. The two best-known pioneers of cognitive therapy are Albert Ellis and Aaron Beck.

Ellis's Rational-Emotive Therapy

■ **22.** ***How does Ellis explain people's emotions in terms of their beliefs?***

After trying the psychodynamic and the humanistic approach to therapy and becoming disenchanted with both, Albert Ellis began in 1955 to develop his own approach, which he labeled ***rational-emotive therapy*** (RET) (Ellis, 1986, 1993). The basic premise of RET is that negative emotions arise from people's irrational interpretations of their experiences, not from the objective experiences themselves. Ellis gives humorous names to certain styles of irrational thinking. Thus, *musturbation* is the irrational belief that one *must* have some particular thing or *must* act in some particular way in order to be happy or worthwhile. If a client says, "I must get all *A*'s this semester in college," Ellis might respond, "You're musturbating again." *Awfulizing*, in Ellis's vocabulary, is the mental exaggeration of setbacks or inconveniences. A client who feels bad for a whole week because of a dent in her new car might be told, "Stop awfulizing." Ellis is notoriously direct in his approach to correcting what he sees as clients' irrational views, quite the opposite of Rogers.

The following dialogue between Ellis (1962) and a client not only illustrates Ellis's style, but also makes explicit his theory of the relationship between thoughts and emotions. The client has just complained that he was unhappy because some men with whom he played golf didn't like him.

Ellis: *You think you were unhappy because these men didn't like you?*

Client: *I certainly was!*

Ellis: *But you weren't unhappy for the reason you think you were.*

Client: *I wasn't? But I was!*

Ellis: *No, I insist: You only think you were unhappy for that reason.*

Client: *Well, why was I unhappy then?*

Ellis: *It's very simple—as simple as A, B, C, I might say. A in this case is the fact that these men didn't like you. Let's assume that you observed their attitude correctly and were not merely imagining they didn't like you.*

Client: *I assure you that they didn't. I could see that very clearly.*

Ellis: *Very well, let's assume they didn't like you and call that A. Now, C is your unhappiness—which we'll definitely have to assume is a fact, since you felt it.*

Client: *Damn right I did!*

Ellis: *All right, then: A is the fact that the men didn't like you, and C is your unhappiness. You see A and C and you assume that A, their not liking you, caused your unhappiness. But it didn't.*

Client: *It didn't? What did, then?*

Ellis: *B did.*

Client: *What's B?*

Ellis: *B is what you said to yourself while you were playing golf with those men.*

Client: *What I said to myself? But I didn't say anything.*

Ellis: *You did. You couldn't possibly be unhappy if you didn't. The only thing that could possibly make you unhappy that occurs from without is a brick falling on your head, or some such equivalent. But no brick fell. Obviously, therefore, you must have told yourself something to make you unhappy.*

In this dialogue, Ellis invokes his famous *ABC theory of emotions: A* is the *Activating event* in the environment, *B* is the *Belief* that is triggered in the client's mind when the event occurs, and *C* is the *emotional Consequence* of that belief. Therapy proceeds by changing *B*, the belief. In this particular example, the man suffers because he believes irrationally that he must be liked by everyone (an example of musturbation), so if someone doesn't like him he is unhappy. The first step will be to convince the man that it is irrational to expect everyone to like him and that there is little or no harm in not being liked by everyone. The next step, after the man admits to the belief's irrationality, will be to help him get rid of the belief, so that it doesn't recur in his thinking. That takes hard work. Long-held beliefs do not simply disappear once they are recognized as irrational. They have become habits that occur automatically unless they are actively resisted. Ellis gives his clients homework designed to train them to catch and correct themselves each time the habitual thought pattern appears.

Beck's Cognitive Therapy

Aaron Beck began to develop a cognitive approach to the treatment of depression in 1960, after observing that his depressed clients routinely distorted their experiences in ways that helped them maintain negative views of themselves, their world, and their future (Beck, 1976, 1991). He observed that they would *minimize* positive experiences, *maximize* negative experiences, and *misattribute* negative experiences to their own deficiencies when they were not really at fault. In later work, Beck and his associates also identified patterns of thinking that promote anxiety (such as exaggerating the likelihood of accidents or diseases occurring), and they expanded their cognitive therapy to include clients with anxiety disorders (Beck & Emery, 1985). In therapy sessions, Beck's approach is gentler than is Ellis's. Instead of telling his clients directly about their irrational thoughts, he leads them, with a Socratic style of questioning, to discover and correct the thoughts themselves. He prefers this approach, because it is less threatening than the direct approach and because it helps show clients that they can correct their own thoughts and need not always depend on the therapist. Beck's approach is illustrated by the following case summary.

Case Example: Beck's Treatment of a Depressed Young Woman

■ **23.** ***How does Beck's treatment of a depressed woman illustrate his approach to identifying and correcting maladaptive, automatic patterns of thought?***

The client in this case (from Beck & Young, 1985) was Irene, a 29-year-old married woman with two young children who was diagnosed with major depression. She had not been employed outside her home since marriage, and her husband, who had been in and out of drug-treatment centers, was also unemployed. She was socially isolated and felt that people looked down on her because of her poor control over her children and her husband's drug record. She was treated for three sessions by Beck and then was treated for a longer period by another cognitive therapist.

During the first session, Beck helped her to identify a number of her automatic (habitual) negative thoughts, including: *Things won't get better. Nobody cares for me. I am stupid.* By the end of the session, she accepted Beck's suggestion to try to invalidate the first of those thoughts by doing certain things for herself, before the next session, that might make life more fun. She agreed to take the children on an outing, visit her mother, go shopping, read a book, and find out about joining a tennis group—all things that she claimed she would like to do. Having completed that homework, she came to the second session feeling more hopeful. However, she began to feel depressed again when, during the session, she misunderstood a question that Beck asked her, which, she said, made her "look dumb." Beck responded with a questioning strategy that helped her to distinguish between the *fact* of what happened (not understanding a question) and her *belief* about it (looking dumb), and then to correct that belief:

Beck: *OK, what is a rational answer [to why you didn't answer the question]? A realistic answer?*

Irene: *I didn't hear the question right, that is why I didn't answer it right.*

Beck: *OK, so that is the fact situation. And so, is the fact situation that you look dumb or you just didn't hear the question right?*

Irene: *I didn't hear the question right.*

Beck: *Or is it possible that I didn't say the question in such a way that it was clear?*

Irene: *Possible.*

Beck: *Very possible. I'm not perfect so it's very possible that I didn't express the question properly.*

Irene: *But instead of saying you made a mistake, I would still say I made a mistake.*

Beck: *We'll have to watch the video to see. Whichever. Does it mean if I didn't express the question, if I made the mistake, does it make me dumb?*

Irene: *No.*

Beck: *And if you made the mistake, does it make you dumb?*

Irene: *No, not really.*

Beck: *But you felt dumb?*

Irene: *But I did, yeah.*

Beck: *Do you still feel dumb?*

Irene: *No. Right now I feel glad. I'm feeling a little better that at least somebody is pointing all these things out to me because I have never seen this before. I never knew that I thought that I was that dumb.*

As homework between the second and third sessions, Beck gave Irene the assignment of catching, writing down, and correcting her own dysfunctional thoughts using the form shown in Figure 18.2. Subsequent sessions were aimed at eradicating each of her depressive thoughts, one by one, and reinforcing the steps she was taking to improve her life. Progress was rapid. She felt increasingly better about herself, as measured by the Beck Depression Inventory (illustrated in Table 18.1). During the next several months, she (a) joined a tennis league, (b) got a job as a waitress, (c) took and performed well in a college course in sociology, and (d) left her husband after trying and failing to get him to develop a better attitude toward her or to join her in couple therapy. By this time, according to Beck, she was cured of her depression, had created for herself a healthy environment, and no longer needed therapy.

Figure 18.2 ***Homework sheet for cognitive therapy***

The purpose of this homework is to enable clients to become aware of and correct the automatic thoughts that contribute to their emotional difficulties. (Adapted from Beck & Young, 1985.)

DATE	SITUATION	EMOTION(S)	AUTOMATIC THOUGHT(S)	RATIONAL RESPONSE	OUTCOME
	Describe: 1. Actual event leading to unpleasant emotion, or 2. Stream of thoughts, daydream, or recollection, leading to unpleasant emotion.	1. Specify sad/anxious/angry, etc. 2. Rate degree of emotion, 1–100.	1. Write automatic thought(s) that preceded emotion(s). 2. Rate belief in automatic thought(s), 0–100%.	1. Write rational response to automatic thought(s). 2. Rate belief in rational response, 0–100%.	1. Rerate belief in automatic thought(s), 0–100%. 2. Specify and rate subsequent emotions, 0–100.
7/15	Store clerk didn't smile at me when I paid for purchase.	Sad - 60 Anxious - 40	Nobody likes me - 70% I look awful - 80%	Maybe the clerk was having a bad day or maybe she never smiles at customers – 70%	1. 20% 30% 2. Pleasure - 25

Explanation: When you experience an unpleasant emotion, note the situation that seemed to stimulate the emotion. (If the emotion occurred while you were thinking, daydreaming, etc., please note this.) Then note the automatic thought associated with the emotion. Record the degree to which you believe this thought: 0% = not at all, 100% = completely. In rating degree of emotion: 1 = a trace, 100 = the most intense possible.

Hanging in the balance
Confidence-building activities, such as this one, are sometimes recommended by behavior therapists to help clients increase their feelings of self-worth and self-efficacy.

■ **24. *How and why has behavior therapy become increasingly similar to cognitive therapy, and in what respects have the two always been similar?***

Behavior Therapy

Behavior therapy is the psychotherapy approach rooted in the laboratory research of such pioneers as Ivan Pavlov, John B. Watson, and B. F. Skinner, who formulated principles of classical and operant conditioning in terms of stimulus-response relationships (see Chapter 5).

In principle, and in line with their philosophical forebears, behavior therapists might prefer to ignore mental phenomena such as thoughts and emotions, and concentrate only on direct relationships between observable aspects of the environment (stimuli) and observable behaviors (responses); but in practice they cannot. After all, clients in behavior therapy, like those in any form of psychotherapy, complain about such mental phenomena as fears, anxiety, obsessive thoughts, and depressed feelings. To deal with these problems, within the theoretical framework of behaviorism, behavior therapists have traditionally spoken of mental events as *covert responses* (hidden responses) that follow the same laws of conditioning as overt responses.

Contemporary behavior therapists, however, increasingly use language similar to that of cognitive therapists in describing mental events. In fact, behavior and cognitive therapies have to a considerable degree merged to form what is often called ***cognitive-behavior therapy***. This merging parallels a similar progression in academic research laboratories, where studies of learning have shifted from a stimulus-response emphasis to one that focuses on mental processes as mediators between stimuli and responses (see Chapter 5).

Behavior and cognitive therapies have always shared certain central characteristics. Both commonly claim to be "problem centered" more than "client centered"; their focus is on helping the person overcome specific problems, not on treating the "whole person." Both usually characterize these problems as learned habits, and take the approach that what has been learned can be unlearned. Both monitor the patient's behavior closely over time and advocate the changing of techniques if improvement does not occur rather quickly. In the following sections we will look at some of the most common behavior therapy techniques, beginning with those most closely related to principles of classical and operant conditioning.

Exposure as Treatment for Unwanted Fears

Behavior therapy has proven especially successful in treating simple phobias, in which the fear is of something well defined such as high places or a specific type of animal (Marks, 1987). From a behavioral perspective, fear is a reflexive response, which through classical conditioning can come to be triggered by various nondangerous as well as dangerous stimuli. An unconditioned stimulus for fear is one that elicits the response even if the individual has had no previous experience with the stimulus, and a conditioned stimulus for fear is one that elicits the response only because the stimulus was previously paired with some fearful event in the person's experience (see Chapter 5). Opinions may differ as to whether a particular fear—such as a fear of snakes—is unconditioned or conditioned (see Chapter 17), but in practice this does not matter because the treatment is the same in either case.

A characteristic of the fear reflex, whether conditioned or unconditioned, is that it declines and gradually disappears if the eliciting stimulus is presented many times or over a prolonged period in a context where no harm comes to the person. In the case of an unconditioned fear reflex—such as the startle response to a sudden noise—the decline is called *habituation*. In the case of a conditioned fear reflex, the decline that occurs when the conditioned stimulus is presented repeatedly without the unconditioned stimulus is called *extinction* (discussed in Chapter 5). For example, if a person fears all dogs because of once having been bitten by a particular dog, then prolonged exposure to various dogs (the conditioned stimuli) in the absence of being bitten (the unconditioned stimulus) will result in loss of the fear.

Fear of flying

Airline pilot Tom Bunn (left) and a friend encourage a man who has chosen flooding as a means of overcoming his fear of flying. Through an organization called SOAR, Bunn offers his services to individuals with airplane phobias.

■ **25. *How are flooding, counter-conditioning, and systematic desensitization used to eliminate fears, and how can they all be described as exposure treatments?***

Any treatment for an unwanted fear or phobia that involves exposure to the feared stimulus in a safe context is referred to as an ***exposure treatment*** (Foa & Kozak, 1986). The simplest, most direct form of exposure treatment is ***flooding***, a procedure in which the person is "flooded" with the stimulus and the accompanying fear until it declines and disappears. For example, a person who is afraid of dogs might be induced to sit in the same room with several dogs until the fear is gone. In some cases, flooding is accomplished through imagination rather than actual exposure to the feared stimulus. The therapist teaches the client techniques for vivid imagining, and then the client imagines the feared object or event until it is no longer feared.

Variations on Exposure

Flooding is not always possible or desirable. Some clients refuse to expose themselves in that way to the feared situation, even in imagination, and others panic and have to leave the feared situation or terminate the imagined scene. The experience of panic can intensify the original fear. An alternative procedure, described long ago by John B. Watson (1924), is ***counter-conditioning***, in which the person is trained through classical conditioning to react to the feared stimulus with a response—such as pleasure, relaxation, or anger—that is incompatible with fear. To illustrate this procedure, Watson described a demonstration carried out by one of his associates, Mary Cover Jones, with a 3-year-old boy named Peter.

Peter was extremely frightened of rabbits, and Jones's goal was to counter-condition him to react to rabbits with pleasure rather than fear. Peter enjoyed his daily snack of milk and crackers, so Jones decided to make a live rabbit a conditioned stimulus for a pleasure response by pairing it with the snack. The most straightforward method would have been to place the rabbit directly in front of Peter simultaneously with the snack; but the rabbit would probably have been a stronger stimulus than the snack, and Peter, rather than lose his fear of rabbits, might have developed an unfortunate fear of milk and crackers. So Jones used a more cautious approach. On the first day, she put the rabbit in a cage at the other end of a long room in which Peter ate his snack. Peter noticed the rabbit, but it did not disturb his enjoyment of the snack. Then, each day Jones moved the rabbit a little closer, until eventually she could put it on Peter's lap without his showing any fear. Figure 18.3 illustrates the interpretation of this as classical conditioning. Notice that the rabbit is used as the conditioned stimulus, and the snack as the unconditioned stimulus, for a response (pleasure) that is incompatible with fear.

Before conditioning
Rabbit → fear
Snack → pleasure

Conditioning
Rabbit: Snack → pleasure
Rabbit: Snack → pleasure
Rabbit: Snack → pleasure
Rabbit: Snack → pleasure

After conditioning
Rabbit → pleasure

Figure 18.3 ***Outline of the counter-conditioning procedure used by Mary Cover Jones***

At first, the boy is afraid of the rabbit. During the conditioning phase, the rabbit is the conditioned stimulus, and the snack is the unconditioned stimulus for a pleasurable response incompatible with fear. After conditioning, the boy responds to the rabbit with pleasure rather than fear.

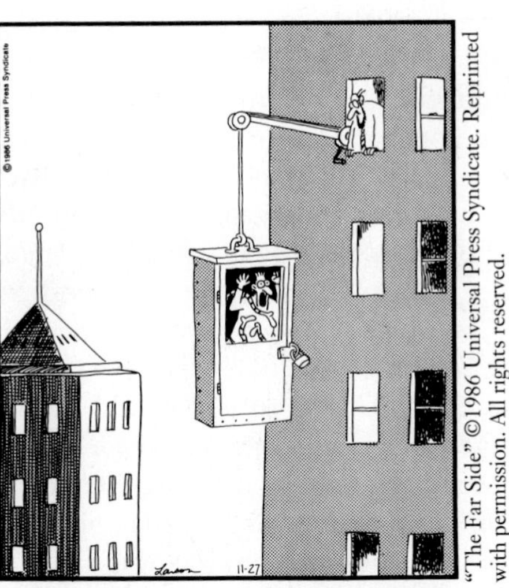

Professor Gallagher and his controversial technique of simultaneously confronting the fear of heights, snakes and the dark.

A version of counter-conditioning most often used today is ***systematic desensitization***, originated by Joseph Wolpe (1958). In this technique, clients are first trained in muscle relaxation until they can relax easily in response to a cue from the therapist. Then they are asked to imagine a scene that would normally elicit some degree of anxiety, and they are given the cue to relax while imagining that scene. When that is accomplished with ease, they gradually move on through increasingly frightening scenes, again imagining each while relaxing. For example, a woman afraid of heights might be asked to relax first while imagining that she is looking out a second-floor window, then a third-floor window, and so on, until she can relax while imagining that she is looking down from the top of a skyscraper.

Notice the similarity between this procedure and Jones's counter-conditioning procedure. The feared scene, paired in imagination with the cue to relax, presumably becomes a conditioned stimulus for relaxation, which is incompatible with fear. Just as Jones started with the rabbit far away and gradually brought it closer, systematic desensitization starts with a mildly fearful imagined scene and gradually works up to more fearful ones. An assumption here is that the ability to relax while imagining the previously feared situation will generalize, so that the person will be able to relax in the presence of the actual situation. Research involving long-term follow-up has shown that systematic desensitization and variations of it can be highly effective in treating simple phobias, and can often be accomplished in a single session (Öst, 1989; Zinbarg & others, 1992). Although counter-conditioning and systematic desensitization were not originally called exposure treatments, today they are commonly classed as such (Foa & Kozak, 1986). From this perspective, counter-conditioning and systematic desensitization are effective not because they teach the individual a new response (such as pleasure or relaxation) to the previously feared stimulus, but because they help induce the reluctant client to remain in the presence of the feared stimulus, without panicking, until habituation or extinction occurs.

■ **26. *How might the effect of catharsis in psychoanalysis be interpreted as an exposure treatment?***

It is interesting in this context to think back on the psychoanalytic treatment of fear-related conditions. Why did Anna O. lose the paralysis in her arm when she recalled, under Breuer's hypnosis, the fearful memory of the fantasized snake attacking her father? Why did the Rat Man lose his neurotic obsessions after he recalled, on Freud's couch, the fearful incident of being beaten by his father? If we assume that fear responses can occur without conscious awareness (an assumption compatible with both psychoanalytic and behavioral theory), and that Anna O.'s symptoms and the Rat Man's were manifestations of learned, unconscious fears, then we might assume that Breuer's and Freud's treatments were effective at least partly for the same reason that systematic desensitization is effective. The client vividly imagines and re-experiences, in the safe environment provided by the psychoanalyst, the stimuli associated with the original traumatic event, thereby permitting extinction of the conditioned fear response to those stimuli, and hence loss of symptoms. Too simple? Maybe. But Breuer himself noted that in the early stages of Anna O.'s disorder, her arm paralysis was brought on whenever she saw something (such as a tree branch) that resembled a snake (Breuer & Freud, 1895/1955)—a reaction akin to a conditioned response.

Aversion Treatment to Eliminate Bad Habits

■ **27. *How can maladaptive habits be interpreted in terms of operant conditioning and eliminated by use of aversive stimuli?***

From the behavioral perspective, much of what we do can be understood as *habit*. A habit is a learned action that has become so ingrained that the person performs it unconsciously and may even feel compelled to perform it. Most habits are good; they permit us to do automatically things that are beneficial. Stepping on the automobile brake in response to a red traffic light is a habit that saves many lives every day. But some habits—such as addictive drinking, compulsive gambling, or compulsive hand washing (in obsessive-compulsive disorder)—are harmful. No matter how such behaviors originated, they persist at least partly because they are followed immediately by pleasure or relief from discomfort. The person addicted to alcohol feels pleasure or relief from withdrawal symptoms after a drink, the compulsive gambler experiences a thrill when placing a bet, and the obsessive-compulsive hand washer experiences relief from the fear of germs after washing his or her hands. Thus, such behaviors can be understood at least partly in terms of operant conditioning, the process by which responses that are followed either by positive reinforcement (something pleasant) or by negative reinforcement (removal of something unpleasant) are likely to occur again in the future (see Chapter 5).

A behavioral analysis suggests that the basic obstacle to getting rid of bad habits is that operant responses are controlled more by their immediate effects than by their long-term effects. A person might know that drinking alcohol in quantity destroys the liver and brain, that gambling is in the end a losing proposition, and that repeated hand washing wastes time and may eat away the skin; yet the behaviors persist because knowledge of the long-term harm they bring is less effective in controlling the behaviors than is the short-term pleasure or relief they bring. To eliminate such harmful habits, the person must somehow change the reinforcement contingencies, and this is where aversion treatment comes in. Put simply, ***aversion treatment*** is the application of an aversive (painful or unpleasant) stimulus immediately after the person has made the unwanted habitual response, or immediately after the person has experienced cues that would normally elicit the response. Thus, a compulsive gambler might be given shocks to the fingers while reaching out onto a simulated gambling table to place a bet; or an alcohol addict might be given a drug to induce nausea after taking a drink (Clarke, 1988). Such treatment can be understood in terms of either operant or classical conditioning (see Chapter 5). In operant conditioning terms, the aversive stimulus is punishment for behaving in the objectionable way or for initiating such behavior. In classical conditioning terms, the aversive stimulus is an unconditioned stimulus for an avoidance reaction, which becomes conditioned to cues, such as the sight of the gambling table or the smell of alcohol, that previously elicited attraction.

■ ***28. How does the treatment of alcohol addiction with antabuse illustrate a general limitation of aversion treatment?***

Aversion treatment has always been controversial, partly because of ethical questions associated with deliberately hurting a person (even when the person agrees to the procedure), and partly because of its mixed results. Learned aversions often do not generalize beyond the specific conditions in which the learning occurs. This limitation may stem from the fact that conditioning depends more on cognition (the subject's knowledge of the conditions present) than the early behav-

Aversion treatment

In an attempt to eliminate this man's tobacco addiction, the therapist is trying to make him sick. Do you think the client will learn that smoking a cigarette produces nausea, or only that smoking two cigarettes does?

iorists believed. Clients may experience the learned aversion only as long as they know that they are connected to the shock generator or that they have taken the illness-inducing drug.

A well-documented illustration of this point involves the use of the drug *antabuse* to treat alcohol addiction. Antabuse reacts with alcohol in a person's body to induce severe flushing, dizziness, nausea, and headaches shortly after alcohol is consumed. In the early days of antabuse use, behavior therapists believed that people who drank alcohol after taking the drug would develop a conditioned aversion to alcohol, which they would retain even without further antabuse treatment. Unfortunately, however, experience has shown that most people suffering from long-term alcoholism avoid alcohol when on antabuse but go back to it quickly after they stop taking the drug (Forrest, 1985). Today, antabuse is recognized as an effective first-stage treatment for alcoholism, a means of helping the client keep sober while other treatments are begun. The drug is not recommended for long-term treatment because it induces some feelings of illness even when the person is sober (Littrell, 1991).

Some Other Behavioral Techniques

■ **29. *What are the therapeutic uses of token economies, contingency contracts, assertiveness training, and modeling?***

In addition to the exposure and aversion treatments described above, behavior therapists have developed an arsenal of other techniques to help people cultivate constructive behaviors and eradicate destructive ones. Among them are the following:

- ***Token economies*** A token economy is essentially a monetary-exchange system adapted for use in a mental hospital or other institution where patients are confined. Its purpose is to provide a direct incentive for patients to do things that are deemed good for them or others. Thus, patients may receive tokens for such activities as making their bed, helping out in the kitchen, or helping other patients in specified ways, and they can cash in the tokens for desired privileges, such as movies or treats at the hospital commissary. This technique helps combat the lethargy, boredom, and dependence that are so common in mental hospitals (Ayllon & Azrin, 1968), and it was an important part of the successful social learning program in the study by Paul and Lentz (1977) described earlier.

- ***Contingency contracts*** A contingency contract is a formal, usually written agreement between two or more people in which certain specified services or rewards provided by one party are made contingent upon the actions of the other. For example, a contingency contract between a therapist and a client might specify that the therapist will meet with the client each week only if the client completes the agreed-upon homework. As another example, a family therapist might help an embattled husband and wife work out a contract in which one party agrees to behave in certain ways toward the other (say, continue to live in the same house) only if the other behaves in certain ways (say, takes specific steps toward getting a job or overcoming a drug addition). To be effective, a contingency contract must clearly spell out the behaviors expected and the consequences for meeting or not meeting those expectations.

- ***Assertiveness and social skills training*** *Assertiveness* can be defined as the ability to express one's own desires and feelings and to maintain one's rights in interactions with others, while at the same time respecting the others' rights. A high percentage of people in therapy are there partly because they lack the assertiveness or social skills necessary for effective and comfortable social interaction. Because of this lack, they may either avoid other people or, when with others, fail to assert their own feelings, wishes, and opinions. In either case,

Assertiveness training

In this technique, widely used in business organizations, individuals learn the skills necessary for effective social interaction.

they feel lonely, because they have not made real emotional contact with others. Assertiveness and social skills training include all direct methods by which a therapist attempts to teach a client to be more assertive, effective, and comfortable in social interactions. At first the therapist may demonstrate social skills or methods of assertion, or may give the client phrases to memorize and practice—such as *Well, that's not a bad idea, but today I would really rather* ______________. Later, *role-playing* sessions might be introduced, in which the person plays out, with the therapist or with other clients in a group, various scenes requiring assertion (such as asking for a raise, refusing a sexual advance, or explaining to parents that one's mail is private) or social skills (such as asking for or accepting a date).

- ***Modeling*** As a therapy technique, modeling is the process of teaching a person to do something by having that person watch someone else do it (discussed more generally in Chapter 5). As part of assertiveness training a therapist might model (demonstrate) ways to be assertive. In the realm of fear reduction, Albert Bandura and his colleagues (1982) have shown in many experiments that people can overcome snake or spider phobias by watching others handle the feared creature during several sessions and then being asked to approach or handle it themselves.

Evaluating Psychotherapies

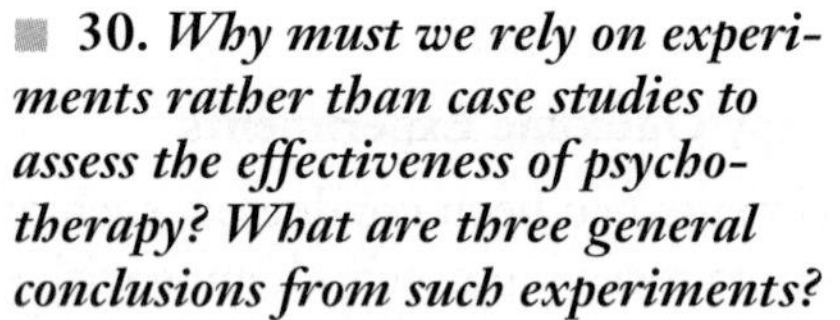

30. ***Why must we rely on experiments rather than case studies to assess the effectiveness of psychotherapy? What are three general conclusions from such experiments?***

You have just read about four major varieties of psychotherapy. Do they work? That might seem like a strange question at this point. After all, didn't Freud cure the Rat Man, didn't Rogers help the silent young man, didn't Beck and his associates cure the depressed young woman, and haven't behavior therapists cured many people of their fears and bad habits? But case studies—even thousands of them—showing that people are better off at the end of therapy than at the beginning cannot tell us for sure that therapy works. Maybe they would have improved anyway, without therapy. An adage about the common cold goes something like this: "Treat a cold with the latest remedy and you'll get rid of it in 7 days; leave it untreated and it'll hang on for a week." Maybe psychological problems or disorders are like colds in this respect. Everyone has peaks and valleys in life, and people are most likely to start therapy while in one of the valleys. Thus, even if therapy has no effect, most people will feel better at some point after entering it than they did when they began (see Figure 18.4). The natural tendency for both therapist and client is to attribute the improvement to the therapy.

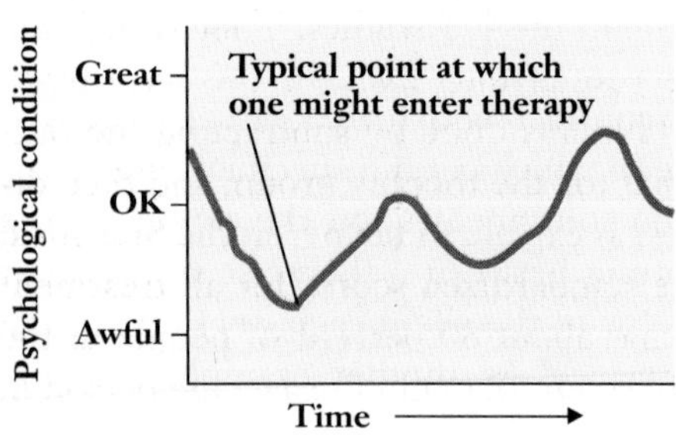

Figure 18.4 ***The peaks and valleys of life***

If a person enters psychotherapy while in a valley, he or she is likely to feel better after a time even if the therapy is ineffective.

The only way to know if psychotherapy really works is to perform controlled experiments, in which groups of people undergoing therapy are compared with otherwise similar control groups who are not undergoing therapy. Within the last 3 decades, hundreds of such experiments have been conducted, and reviews of them have led to the following general conclusions (Crits-Christoph, 1992; Smith & others, 1980; Stiles & others, 1986):

1. Psychotherapy works: On average, people in treatment improve more than do those not in treatment.
2. No single type of psychotherapy stands out as clearly better than any other type when all studies are combined, though some types may be better for specific kinds of problems.
3. Various *nonspecific factors*, which are common to all recognized types of psychotherapy, seem to contribute heavily to therapy outcome.

The following paragraphs summarize some of the evidence behind these conclusions.

■ **31. *How did an experiment in Philadelphia demonstrate the effectiveness of behavior therapy and psychoanalytic psychotherapy?***

Example of a Therapy Outcome Study: The Philadelphia Experiment

One of the best known and most highly esteemed experiments on therapy outcome was conducted at a psychiatric outpatient clinic in Philadelphia (Sloane & others, 1975). The subjects were ninety-four men and women, ages 18 to 45, who sought psychotherapy at the clinic. Most of these individuals suffered from anxiety disorders. They were assigned by a random procedure to one of three groups. One group received once-a-week sessions of *behavior therapy* for 4 months (including such procedures as systematic desensitization and assertiveness training) from one of three highly experienced behavior therapists. The second group received the same amount of *psychoanalytical psychotherapy* (including such procedures as probing into childhood memories, dream analysis, and interpretation of resistance) from one of three highly experienced psychoanalytically oriented therapists. The members of the third group, the *control group*, were placed on a waiting list and given no treatment during the 4-month period, but were called periodically to let them know that they would eventually be accepted for therapy.

To measure treatment effectiveness, all subjects, including those in the control group, were assessed both before and after the 4-month period by psychiatrists who were uninformed of the groups to which the subjects had been assigned. As illustrated in Figure 18.5, all three groups improved during the 4-month period, but the treatment groups improved significantly more than did the control group. Moreover, the two treatment groups did not differ significantly from each other in degree of improvement.

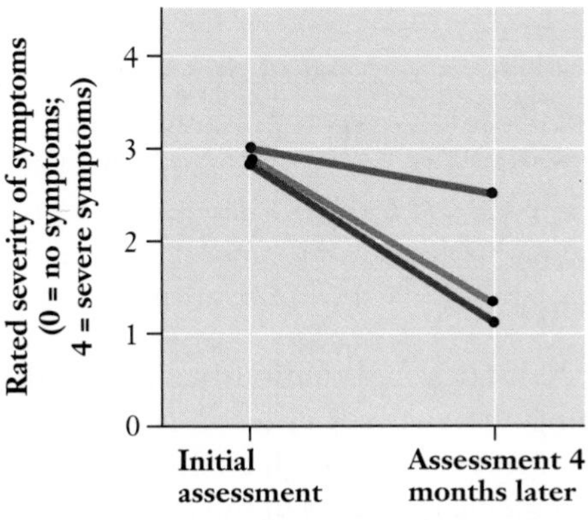

Figure 18.5 ***Results of the Philadelphia experiment***

Psychiatrists rated the severity of each subject's symptoms before and after a 4-month treatment period. As shown here, those in the two therapy groups improved more than did those who were placed on the waiting list. (Adapted from Sloane & others, 1975.)

■ **32. *How did an analysis of hundreds of therapy outcome experiments show that therapy works, that various therapies are about equally effective overall, and that particular therapies may be most effective for particular problems?***

An Analysis of the Combined Results of Therapy Outcome Experiments

By the late 1970s, 475 separate outcome experiments had been conducted, each of which had compared one or more groups of people receiving psychotherapy with a control group that did not receive therapy. Like the Philadelphia study, most showed therapy to be superior to no therapy. Unlike the Philadelphia study, many showed one kind of therapy to be superior to another, though in different studies different therapies came out on top. To digest the results of all of those experiments and arrive at some general conclusions, Mary Lee Smith and her colleagues (1980) performed what is called a *meta-analysis* of the 475 studies. They reanalyzed the data from every study, converting the results into *standard effect-size units*, which could be compared across studies. (This was done by subtracting the outcome measure for the control group from that for the therapy group, and then dividing by the standard deviation of the scores, as explained further in the Statistical Appendix.) When they averaged all of these standardized scores for all treatment groups in all studies, the results indicated that about 80 percent of people in the psychotherapy groups showed greater improvement than did the average person in a control group.

When Smith and her colleagues computed the average effect-size separately for different types of psychotherapy, they found that every type produced significant improvement and that little if any difference existed in the average improvement for different types. In another analysis, however, they calculated the effect-sizes for each type of therapy separately for different kinds of outcome measures, and that analysis suggested that some therapies may be better than others for treating certain kinds of problems. For example, as you can see in Table 18.2 on page 676, fear and anxiety seem to be treated more effectively by behavioral and cognitive therapies than by psychodynamic therapies, whereas the reverse seems true for achievement problems and addictions; and humanistic therapy seems best for raising self-esteem. More recent meta-analyses suggest that cognitive and cognitive-behavioral therapies are considerably more effective than psychodynamic psychotherapies in treating depression (Dobson, 1989; Svartberg & Stiles, 1991).

Table 18.2 *Average effectiveness of various therapy types in treating various problems*

	Type of Problem				
Type of therapy	*Fear or anxiety*	*Self-esteem*	*Addiction*	*Social behavior*	*Work or school achievement*
Psychodynamic	0.78	0.66	1.05	0.94	1.24
Humanistic	0.61	0.99	*	0.45	0.54
Cognitive	1.67	0.65	0.53	*	0.28
Cognitive-behavioral	1.78	0.73	*	1.23	0.60
Behavioral	1.12	0.23	0.75	0.42	0.45

Note: The measure of effectiveness shown here is a statistic called the standard effect size. Any score above zero on this scale indicates that the average person in the treatment groups improved more than did the average person in the control groups, and a score of 1.0 indicates that 84.13% of the people in the treatment groups improved more than did the average person in the control groups (see Statistical Appendix).
*Too few studies to warrant inclusion.

Source: Adapted from *The benefits of psychotherapy* (p. 97) by M. L. Smith, G. V. Glass, & T. I. Miller, 1980, Baltimore, MD: Johns Hopkins University Press.

The results of all such meta-analyses must be interpreted cautiously, because the experiments that are combined in performing the analyses differ in many more ways than just the type of therapy employed. Nevertheless, such analyses do offer interesting hypotheses to test in large-scale single experiments in the future.

The Role of Nonspecific Factors in Therapy Outcome

If psychotherapy works, the next logical question is: Why does it work? Although each therapy has its own set of principles to explain its effects, some people have argued that therapy works mostly because of so-called ***nonspecific factors***, which are common to many or all therapies and are unrelated to the specific principles on which the therapy is based. Many such factors have been proposed, but they fall into two general categories: support and hope (Stiles & others, 1986).

■ **33.** ***What is some evidence that the most important ingredients of psychotherapy may be the offering of support and hope?***

Support includes acceptance, empathy, encouragement, and guidance. By devoting time to the client, listening warmly and respectfully, and not being shocked at the client's statements or actions, any good psychotherapist communicates the attitude that the client is a worthwhile human being, and this may directly enhance the client's self-esteem and indirectly lead to other improvements as well. Moreover, almost any therapist, regardless of theoretical orientation, will start sessions by asking the client how things have gone since the last meeting; the anticipation of such reporting may encourage clients to work on self-improvement so they can give a better report. In addition, most therapists make at least some common-sense suggestions that have little to do with their theories, of the sort that anyone's wise friend or relative might make, but carrying more weight because they come from a recognized authority.

Many studies have demonstrated the value of such support. In a long-term study at the Menninger Clinic, Robert Wallerstein (1989) found that contemporary psychoanalysts, in fact, provided more support and less insight to their clients than would be expected from psychoanalytic theory, and that support even without insight seemed to produce stable therapeutic gains. In another study, the success rate of therapists was found to depend more on the degree to which their clients felt understood by them than on their theoretical orientation (Lafferty & others, 1989). And in still another study, college professors with no training in psychology or methods of therapy, but with reputations for good rapport with students proved able to help depressed college students in twice-a-week therapy sessions as effec-

Support and hope offered here

Regardless of whether this therapist employs psychodynamic, humanistic, cognitive, or behavioral techniques, the emotional support and hope she offers may contribute to the therapy's success.

tively as highly trained and experienced clinical psychologists (Strupp & Hadley, 1979). Such results have led one well-known psychodynamic therapist, Hans Strupp (1989), to conclude that "the first and foremost task for the therapist is to create an accepting and empathic context, which in itself has great therapeutic value because for many people it is a novel and deeply gratifying experience to be accepted and listened to respectfully."

Hope, the second category of nonspecific factors, may come partly from the sense of support, but may also come from other aspects of the therapeutic environment. Most psychotherapists believe in what they do. They speak with authority and confidence about their methods, and they offer scientific-sounding theories or even data to back up their confidence. Thus, clients also come to believe that the therapy will work. Many studies have shown that people who believe they will get better have an improved chance of getting better, even if the specific reason for the belief is false. This is the basis for the well-known ***placebo effect*** in studies of drugs. In these studies, patients given a pill that contains no active substance (the placebo) improve, compared to those given no pill, if the patient believes that the pill has curative powers. The term *placebo effect* is now used to refer to any improvement that comes from a person's belief in the treatment rather than from other therapeutic factors. The placebo effect is an element that all sought-after healing procedures have in common, whether provided by psychotherapists, medical doctors, faith healers, or folk healers.

How much of the improvement observed in psychotherapy is due to the person's belief in the process (hope)? That is hard to answer. In tests of drug treatments, the psychological effects of hope and the direct chemical effects of the drug are relatively easy to separate by using a placebo, but in psychotherapy—where the whole treatment is psychological—no clear distinction can be made between hope as a nonspecific side effect of psychotherapy and hope as a specific goal of psychotherapy. Some experiments on therapy outcome include a *placebo group* who receive pseudo-psychotherapy that is designed to provide the element of hope without providing the specific elements deemed important to the therapy being tested. For example, in one study systematic desensitization was compared to a made-up placebo treatment called *systematic ventilation*, in which people talked about their fears in systematic ways (Kirsch & others, 1983). In general, in such experiments the placebo group does better than nontreated controls, but not as well as those receiving the more standard form of psychotherapy being tested (Barker & others, 1988). But it is hard to interpret such results. On the one hand, hope may not be raised as fully in placebo groups as in therapy groups, and on the other, placebo treatments may include elements that could produce therapeutic effects through means other than hope. For example, talking about fears in systematic ventilation could have therapeutic value.

■ **34.** ***Why have many psychotherapists moved away from rigid adherence to specific schools?***

The Movement Toward Eclecticism

As more is understood about the common elements of different psychotherapies, and as evidence accrues that different procedures may be most effective for different problems, many psychotherapists are moving away from strict allegiance to a single approach and becoming *eclectic* in orientation. That is, they use techniques gleaned from various approaches, in accordance with the specific problems and characteristics of the client with whom they are working. In a survey conducted about a decade ago, 41 percent of psychotherapists identified themselves as eclectic (see Figure 18.6), and smaller surveys suggest that the percentage has increased since then (Lazarus & others, 1992). To borrow a phrase from Bernard Beitman and his colleagues (1989), the "dogma eat dogma" environment that has traditionally characterized debate about psychotherapy is giving way to discussion based more on research and less on rigid adherence to specific theories. If the trend continues, schools of thought in psychotherapy may be replaced before long by catalogues of alternative methods and principles, all described in a common language, available to any practitioner, and complete with citations to research indicating the disorders or problems for which each technique has proved most useful.

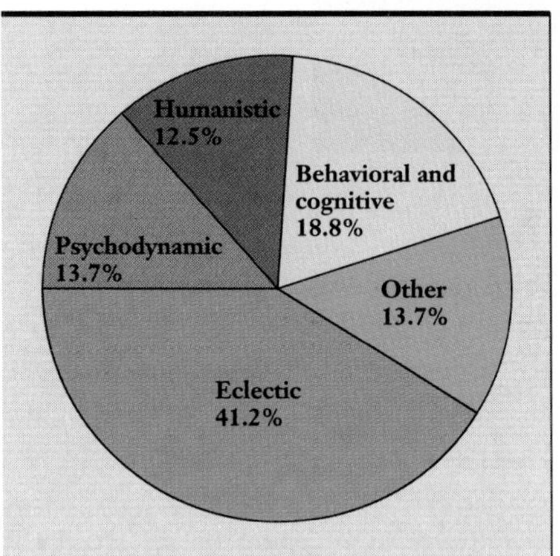

Figure 18.6 ***The theoretical orientations of a sample of psychotherapists***

Shown here are the results of a survey in which 422 practicing clinical and counseling psychologists were asked to identify their theoretical orientation. (Data from Smith, 1982.)

Biological Treatments

Biological treatments for mental disorders attempt to relieve the disorder by directly altering bodily processes. In the distant past, such treatments included drilling holes in the skull to let out bad spirits and blood-letting to drain diseased humors. Today, in decreasing order of extent of use, the three main types of biological treatments are drugs, electroconvulsive shock therapy, and psychosurgery.

Drugs

A new era in the treatment of mental disorders began in the early 1950s when two French psychiatrists, Jean Delay and Pierre Deniker (1952) reported that they had reduced or abolished the psychotic symptoms of schizophrenia with a drug called *chlorpromazine*. Today, a plethora of drugs is available for treating essentially all major varieties of mental disorders.

Drugs for mental disorders have been far from unmixed blessings, however—a point dramatically made by patients and clinicians who have organized anti-drug movements and written books (for example, Breggin, 1991) denouncing the overuse of such drugs. Like drugs used in general medicine, drugs that are effective in treating mental disorders nearly always produce at least some undesirable side effects; there are no magic bullets that zero in on and correct a disordered part of the mental machinery while leaving the rest of the machinery untouched. Some of the drugs are also addictive, and the attempt to withdraw from them sometimes produces symptoms worse than those for which the drug was prescribed. As you read of the various categories of drugs described below, notice their problems as well as their benefits.

■ **35.** ***What are the value and limitations of drugs used to treat schizophrenia, depression, bipolar disorder, and generalized anxiety?***

Antipsychotic Drugs

Antipsychotic drugs are used to treat schizophrenia and other disorders in which psychotic symptoms predominate. Chlorpromazine (sold as Thorazine), belonging to a chemical class called *phenothiazines*, was the first such drug, but now many others exist as well. As described in Chapter 17, most antipsychotic drugs seem to produce their effects by decreasing the activity of the neurotransmitter dopamine in

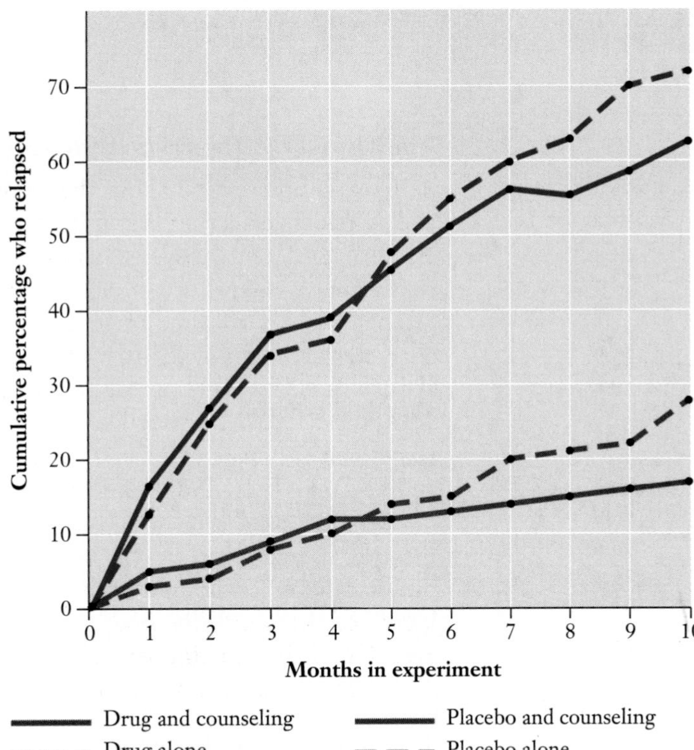

Figure 18.7 ***Effects of antipsychotic drug treatment and counseling on rate of relapse among people with schizophrenia***

In this experiment, 374 patients with schizophrenia were randomly assigned to treatment with either an antipsychotic drug (chlorpromazine) or a placebo, following a 2-month period during which all had received the drug. Within each of these two groups, half received regular counseling, which focused on their social and vocational roles, and half received no regular counseling. As shown here the rate of relapse (defined as worsening of symptoms enough to be rehospitalized) was much less for those receiving the antipsychotic drug than for those receiving the placebo. Counseling produced a smaller, but still significant, beneficial effect, beginning after the sixth month. (Adapted from Hogarty & Goldberg, 1973.)

the brain. Many well-designed experiments have shown that such drugs really do reduce or abolish the hallucinations, delusions, and bizarre actions that characterize the active phase of schizophrenia, and that they prevent or forestall the recurrence of such symptoms when they are taken continually (Ashton, 1987; Linden & others, 1984). For the results and methods of one such study, see Figure 18.7. Nevertheless, serious problems remain with such drugs.

One problem is that although the drugs relieve the positive symptoms of schizophrenia (hallucinations, delusions, and bizarre behavior) in many patients, they often fail to relieve the negative symptoms (flattened affect, poverty of speech and thought, and lack of motivation) and in some cases make them worse (Carpenter & others, 1985; Fowles, 1992). Thus, although the drugs help make it possible for someone with schizophrenia to live outside of the hospital, they usually do not restore the zest or pleasure that should come from doing so. Life becomes more normal but not necessarily happier. Moreover—and this is why many people with schizophrenia refuse to take them—the drugs can produce very unpleasant and potentially harmful side effects. Through direct action on the autonomic nervous system, they can produce dizziness, nausea, dry mouth, blurred vision, constipation, and (in men) sexual impotence. Through effects on motor control areas in the brain, they can produce symptoms akin to Parkinson's disease (shaking and difficulty in controlling voluntary movements) (Klein & others, 1980). In addition, about 40 percent of patients who take antipsychotic drugs for long periods of time eventually develop a serious and often irreversible motor disturbance called *tardive dyskinesia*, manifested as involuntary jerking of the tongue, face, and sometimes other muscles (Karon, 1989). A far more controversial problem is that antipsychotic drugs may, in some people, reduce the chance of eventual full recovery—an idea supported by a considerable amount of correlational research and at least one experimental study (Warner, 1985). Prolonged use of the drugs causes the brain to undergo a permanent biochemical adjustment that effectively increases its sensitivity to dopamine (Rupniak & others, 1984a, b). This change probably provides the basis for tardive dyskinesia (Lickey & Gordon, 1991) and some suggest that it might also provide a basis for the exacerbation of schizophrenia itself.

A relatively new drug, *clozapine*, operates through different chemical mechanisms than traditional antipsychotic drugs and does not produce the same permanent brain changes (LaHoste & others, 1991). This drug is at least as effective in reducing psychotic symptoms as traditional drugs and does not cause tardive dyskinesia or other motor problems (Kane, 1992). Clozapine is not often prescribed, however, because of its high cost (about $9,000 per year in 1992) and its ability in some cases to cause a potentially lethal blood disorder. Researchers have not yet addressed the question of whether the chance of eventual recovery from schizophrenia is better for people taking clozapine than for those taking traditional drugs.

Antidepressant Drugs

The drugs used most commonly to treat depression are members of a chemical class called *tricyclics*, of which *imipramine* (sold as Tofranil) and *amitriptyline* (sold as Elavil) are examples. In line with the monoamine theory of depression discussed in Chapter 17, these drugs are believed to reduce depression by increasing the availability of norepinephrine and other monoamine transmitters in synapses. In controlled experiments, about 70 percent of people on such drugs recovered from major depression over a period of several weeks, compared to about 30 percent of those who took a placebo (Lickey & Gordon, 1991). Therapy outcome experiments have revealed that antidepressant drugs are, on average, about as effective as psychotherapy in treating depression (Murphy & others, 1984; Robinson & others, 1990), and at least in some cases the two combined are better than either alone (see Figure 2.3 in Chapter 2). Antidepressants are not addictive, and their side effects—which can include fatigue, dry mouth, and blurred vision—are not as bad as those of antipsychotic drugs but are still a problem for many people. In recent years, a so-called new generation of antidepressants has emerged; these drugs have milder side effects and appear to be as effective as tricyclics (Lickey & Gordon, 1991).

Lithium for Bipolar Disorder

Lithium is a mineral element that, taken regularly in pill form, has long been the preferred treatment for bipolar disorder. Lithium helps control both the manic and the depressive phases of the disorder, but is especially effective against the manic phases (Klein & others, 1980). To date, no one knows just how lithium works, but consistent with the monoamine theory of mood disorder, the most prevalent view is that it stabilizes the level of monoamines in the brain, or it stabilizes the brain's sensitivity to monoamines (Leonard, 1992). The main problem with lithium is that it produces serious side effects at high doses, including dehydration, and an overdose can cause death.

Antianxiety Drugs

By far the most commonly prescribed psychoactive drugs are those used to treat anxiety, commonly referred to as *tranquilizers*. At one time, barbiturates such as phenobarbital were often prescribed as tranquilizers, and many people became seriously addicted to them. During the 1960s, barbiturates were replaced by a new, safer group of antianxiety drugs belonging to a chemical class called *benzodiazepines*, including *chlordiazepoxide* (sold as Librium) and *diazepam* (sold as Valium). According to some estimates, by 1975 more than 10 percent of adults in the United States and western Europe were taking these drugs on a regular basis (Lickey & Gordon, 1991; Lipman, 1989). Since then their use has declined, partly because of growing recognition that they are not as safe as they were once thought to be.

Benzodiazepines are most effective against generalized anxiety and are usually not effective against phobias, obsessive-compulsive disorder, and panic disorder (Lipman, 1989). Biochemically, the drugs appear to produce their tranquilizing effects by augmenting the action of the neurotransmitter GABA (gamma-aminobutyric acid) in the brain (Lickey & Gordon, 1991). GABA is an inhibitory transmitter, so its increased action decreases the excitability of neurons where it acts. Side effects of benzodiazepines at high doses include drowsiness and a decline in motor coordination. More important, the drugs potentiate the action of alcohol, so that an amount of alcohol that would otherwise be safe can produce a coma or death in people taking a benzodiazepine. (If you're taking such a drug, don't drink!) In addition, antianxiety drugs are now known to be at least moderately addictive, and very unpleasant withdrawal symptoms—sleeplessness, sweating, anxiety, and even panic—occur in those who stop taking them after having taken high doses for a long time (Petursson & Lader, 1986). These symptoms subside within about 2 weeks, but they drive many people back to the pills before the end of that period.

Other Biologically Based Treatments

The development of effective drugs, coupled with the increased understanding and acceptance of psychotherapy, has led to the abandonment of most non-drug biological therapies for mental disorders. The two such treatments still occasionally used are electroconvulsive shock therapy and, in very rare cases, psychosurgery.

Electroconvulsive Shock Therapy

■ **36.** ***What evidence indicates that ECT is effective in treating severe depression?***

Electroconvulsive shock therapy, or *ECT*, is used primarily in cases of severe depression that do not respond to psychotherapy or antidepressant drugs. To the general public this treatment often seems barbaric, a remnant of the days when victims of mental disorders were tortured to exorcise the demons, and indeed it once was a brutal treatment. The brain seizure induced by the shock would cause muscular contractions so violent that they sometimes broke bones. Today, however, ECT is administered in a way that is painless and quite safe. Before receiving the shock, the patient is given drugs that block nerve and muscle activity so that no pain will be felt and no damaging muscle contractions will occur. Then an electric current is passed through the patient's skull, which touches off a seizure in the brain that lasts a minute or so. Usually such treatments are given in a series, one every 2 or 3 days for about 2 weeks.

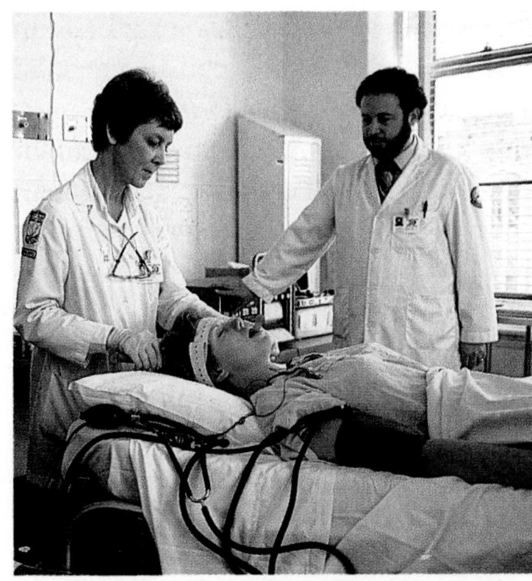

Electroconvulsive therapy
ECT is the treatment of choice for severe depression that does not respond to drug therapy. Although modern technology has rendered the treatment painless and physically safe, controversy remains over the question of whether it produces any lasting brain dysfunctions.

Overall, about 70 percent of people who are suffering from major depression and have not been helped by other treatments experience remission with ECT (Weiner & Coffey, 1988). In some cases, the remission is permanent; in others, depression recurs after a period of several months or more, and then another series of treatments may be given. Nobody knows how ECT produces its antidepressant effect. In animals, such shocks cause a massive, immediate release of monoamines and other neurotransmitters, followed by longer-lasting changes in transmitter production and in the sensitivity of postsynaptic receptors. Most theories of the effects of ECT focus on one or another of those long-term changes (Sackeim, 1988).

Clinicians and researchers have long been concerned about the possibility that ECT can produce permanent brain damage. This concern is fueled by evidence of brain damage in laboratory animals subjected to intense electroconvulsive shocks. To date there is no evidence that such damage occurs with the shock levels used in clinical treatment, but temporary disruptions in cognition, especially in memory, are known to occur (Lickey & Gordon, 1991). When ECT is applied in the traditional manner—*bilaterally*, with the current running across both of the brain's hemispheres—the patient typically loses memory for events that occurred a day or two before the treatment. With a series of treatments, some memories for earlier events may also be lost, but these usually return within two or three weeks after the last treatment.

■ **37. *Why is ECT now often given just to the brain's right hemisphere?***

Many clinicians today prefer to apply ECT *unilaterally* to the right hemisphere only, because that produces little apparent memory loss. Controversy exists as to whether the unilateral procedure is as effective against depression as the bilateral procedure; it seems to be so when moderately high shock levels are used, but not when low levels are used (Sackeim, 1989). Even at the relatively higher shock levels, the right-hemisphere treatment causes very little loss of conscious, verbal memories, although it may cause some loss of pictorial memories as measured by the recognition of geometric designs seen before the shocks (Sachs & Gelenberg, 1988). Unilateral left-hemisphere treatment—which is now almost never used—reduces verbal memories almost as much as bilateral treatment does and is substantially less effective in relieving depression (Sackeim, 1989). Such findings are consistent with other evidence (discussed in Chapters 6 and 11) that the left hemisphere is more involved in verbal processes and the right in visual-spatial processes and emotion.

Psychosurgery

■ **38. *Why are prefrontal lobotomies no longer performed, and why are less drastic forms of psychosurgery occasionally performed?***

The most controversial treatment for mental disorders is *psychosurgery*, the surgical cutting or production of lesions in portions of the brain to relieve a mental disorder. From the late 1930s into the early 1950s, tens of thousands of men and women were subjected to an operation called *prefrontal lobotomy*, in which the front portions of the brain's frontal lobes were surgically separated from the rest of the brain. Individuals with severe cases of schizophrenia, bipolar disorder, depression, obsessive-compulsive disorder, and pathological violence were subjected to the operation. Prefrontal lobotomy was so highly regarded that in 1949 the Portuguese neurologist who developed the technique, Egas Moniz, was awarded the Nobel Prize. By the mid-1950s, however, prefrontal lobotomies had gone out of style, partly because newly developed drug treatments offered an alternative, and partly because of mounting evidence that, although lobotomy relieved people of their incapacitating emotions, it left them incapacitated in new ways (Valenstein, 1986). The anterior portions of the prefrontal lobes are a critical part of the brain's circuit for integrating plans with action (see Chapter 6), and lobotomized patients showed lifelong deficits in the ability to make plans and behave according to them.

Beginning about 1960, a refined version of psychosurgery came into use, and it continues to be used in rare cases today. The new procedure involves destruction of small areas of the brain by applying radio-frequency current through fine wire electrodes implanted temporarily into the brain. In the most common such operation, called a *cingulotomy*, the cingulum (a small structure in the limbic system known to be important in emotionality) is partly destroyed. Follow-up studies of patients who have undergone these electrode operations—including two studies by U.S. government commissions to determine if the procedure should be banned—have led to the following general conclusions (reported in Valenstein, 1980): (a) After the operations, patients do not seem to be worse off than they were before; there is no obvious neurological, behavioral, or cognitive harm. (b) Cingulotomies have successfully relieved severe, chronic depression in some patients who had failed to respond to any other treatment. (c) Psychosurgical lesions in another limbic area (the amygdala) have successfully relieved repeated episodes of uncontrollable violence in some patients, especially those whose violent outbursts were initiated by abnormal neural activity. (d) Psychosurgery has not been successful in relieving thought disorders and flattened affect in people with schizophrenia.

For the foreseeable future, psychosurgery will probably continue to be used sparingly, as a treatment of last resort for a few people who are very severely and chronically incapacitated by strong emotions that have proven untreatable by any other means.

Concluding Thoughts

The best way to review this chapter is to think about the principles underlying each approach to treatment, about the potential problems of each, and about the evidence concerning the effectiveness of each. As a start in that review, the following ideas may be useful:

1. Self-knowledge and self-acceptance as goals of psychodynamic and humanistic therapies The psychodynamic and humanistic approaches to treatment focus less on the person's specific symptoms or problems and more on the person as a whole than do the other approaches. A psychoanalyst or other psychodynamic therapist who is asked to describe the purpose of therapy might well respond with the Socratic dictum: *Know thyself.* The goal of such therapies is to enable clients to learn about aspects of themselves that were previously unconscious, so that they can think and behave in ways that are more rational and integrated than they did before. Most humanistic therapists would agree with the Socratic dictum, but they would add, and place greater emphasis on, a second dictum: *Accept thyself.* Humanistic therapists argue that people often learn to dislike or deny important aspects of themselves, because of real or imagined criticism from other people. The task for the humanistic therapist is to help clients regain their self-esteem, so they can regain control of their lives.

2. Biological, behavioral, and cognitive therapies as derivatives of basic approaches to psychological research Biological, behavioral, and cognitive therapies focus more closely on clients' specific symptoms than do psychodynamic and humanistic therapies. These three approaches differ from each other, however, in that they emphasize different levels of causation of behavior. In that respect, they mirror the approaches taken by research psychologists who focus on (a) physiological mechanisms, (b) the role of environmental stimuli and learned habits, and (c) the role of cognitive mediators of behavior.

Biological treatments are founded on the knowledge that everything psychological is a product of the nervous system. Drugs, electroconvulsive therapy, and psychosurgery all involve attempts to help a person overcome psychological problems or disorders by altering the nervous system in some way. Behavioral treatments are founded on the knowledge that people acquire, through conditioning, habitual and sometimes maladaptive ways of responding to stimuli in the world around them. The goal of behavior therapy is to eliminate the maladaptive responses and replace them with useful responses. Cognitive treatments are founded on the knowledge that people interpret and think about stimuli in their environment, and that those interpretations and thoughts affect the way they feel and behave. The goal of cognitive therapy is to eliminate maladaptive ways of thinking and replace them with useful ways of thinking.

3. Psychotherapy and science Two questions can be asked about the relationship between psychotherapy and science: (a) Is psychotherapy a science? (b) Has science shown that psychotherapy works? These are fundamentally different questions.

The first question concerns the degree to which the techniques used in psychotherapy are based on scientific principles and can be described objectively. Most psychotherapists would respond that their practice is a blend of science and art—that it is based on theories that stem from scientific research, but that it also involves a great deal of intuition, not unlike the sort of intuition that is critical to any prolonged interaction between two human beings. Each client is a distinct individual with distinct problems and needs, who does not necessarily fit snugly with the statistically derived principles that have emerged from scientific research. One way to compare the various psychotherapy approaches is on the degree to which they emphasize empathy and intuition compared to the rigorous application of laboratory-derived principles. Rogers's humanistic therapy lies at one end of this spectrum and behavioral therapy lies at the other.

The second question concerns the use of scientific methods to evaluate psychotherapy. The history of psychotherapy has often been marked by feuds among advocates of one approach or another, each arguing that theirs is the only valid way. As increasingly well controlled outcome studies have been conducted, the feuds have died down somewhat. Evidence has mounted that all of the well-established psychotherapies work about equally well, on a statistical basis, though some may be more effective than others in treating certain kinds of problems. Such findings have led to increased recognition of the nonspecific therapeutic factors shared by the various approaches, and have also inspired a movement toward eclecticism, in which therapists draw from each tradition those methods that seem most appropriate to the client's specific needs.

Further Reading

John Q. La Fond & Mary L. Durham (1992). *Back to the Asylum.* New York: Oxford University Press.

This book describes the pendular swings that have occurred over the past 35 years in mental health policy and such legal issues as involuntary mental hospitalization and the insanity defense. The authors contend that policies arise not so much from scientific knowledge as from a blend of political ideology, self-interest, compassion, and fear.

Jeffrey Zeig (Ed.) (1987). *The evolution of psychotherapy.* New York: Brunner/Mazel.

Twenty-six well-known psychotherapists—representing psychodynamic, humanistic, cognitive, behavioral, family, and group approaches—describe here the rationale of their approach.

Danny Wedding & Raymond Corsini (Eds.) (1989). *Case studies in psychotherapy.* Itasca, IL: Peacock.

In each of these twelve case histories, a well-known psychotherapist describes the problems experienced by a particular client and the method through which the client was helped. Various versions of psychodynamic, humanistic, and cognitive-behavioral therapies are represented.

Aaron T. Beck (1976). *Cognitive therapy and the emotional disorders.* New York: International Universities Press.

The most notable development in psychotherapy in the past 2 decades has been the increased use of cognitive psychotherapeutic techniques. In this book, one of the leading founders of cognitive therapy describes the main principles of that approach and presents examples of its application in treating depression, generalized anxiety, phobias, and somatoform disorders.

Looking Ahead

I hope you have enjoyed this book and found it to be a useful survey of the vast field of psychology. Perhaps the book has helped you decide on areas of psychology that you would like to study further, either through additional courses or your own reading. If you look over the offerings of the Psychology Department at your college or university, you will probably find that the courses map quite readily onto the various parts of this book. I hope you pursue the areas that interest you most.

STATISTICAL APPENDIX

Organizing and Summarizing a Set of Scores

Converting Scores for Purposes of Comparison

Calculating a Correlation Coefficient

Supplement on Psychophysical Scaling

Statistical procedures are tools for dealing with data. Some people find them fascinating for their own sake, just as some become intrigued by the beauty of a saw or a hammer. But most of us, most of the time, care about statistics only to the extent that they help us answer questions. Statistics become interesting when we want to know our batting average, or the chance that our favorite candidate will be elected, or how much money we'll have left after taxes. In psychology, statistics are interesting when they are used to analyze data in ways that help answer important psychological questions.

Some of the basics of statistics are described in Chapter 2. The main purpose of the first three sections of this appendix is to supplement that discussion and make it more concrete by providing some examples of statistical calculations. The second section (Converting Scores for Purposes of Comparison) also contains information that is relevant to the discussions of IQ measurement in Chapter 11 and meta-analysis in Chapter 18. The final section of this appendix (Supplement on Psychophysical Scaling) supplements the discussion of Fechner's and Stevens's work in the section on psychophysics in Chapter 8.

Organizing and Summarizing a Set of Scores

This section describes some basic elements of descriptive statistics: the construction of frequency distributions, the measurement of central tendency, and the measurement of variability.

Ranking the Scores and Depicting a Frequency Distribution

Suppose you gave a group of people a psychological test of introversion-extroversion, structured such that a low score indicates introversion (a tendency to withdraw from the social environment) and a high score indicates extroversion (a tendency to be socially outgoing). Suppose further that the possible range of scores is from 0 to 99, that you gave the test to twenty people, and that you obtained the scores shown in the left-hand column of Table A.1. As presented in that column, the scores are hard to describe in a meaningful way; they are just a list of numbers. As a first step toward making some sense of them, you might rearrange the scores in *rank order*, from lowest to highest, as shown in the right-hand column of the table. Notice how the ranking facilitates your ability to describe the set of numbers. You can now see that the scores range from a low of 17 to a high of 91 and that the two middle scores are 49 and 50.

A second useful step in summarizing the data is to divide the entire range of possible scores into equal intervals and determine how many scores fall in each in-

Table A.1 ***Twenty scores unranked and ranked***

Scores in the order they were collected	The same scores ranked
58	17
45	23
23	31
71	36
49	37
36	41
61	43
41	45
37	45
75	49
91	50
54	54
43	57
17	58
63	61
73	63
31	71
50	73
45	75
57	91

Table A.2 ***Frequency distribution formed from scores in Table A.1***

Interval	Frequency
0– 9	0
10–19	1
20–29	1
30–39	3
40–49	5
50–59	4
60–69	2
70–79	3
80–89	0
90–99	1

terval. Table A.2 presents the results of this process, using intervals of 10. A table of this sort, showing the number of scores that occurred in each interval of possible scores, is called a ***frequency distribution***. Frequency distributions can also be represented graphically, as shown in Figure A.1. Here, each bar along the horizontal axis represents a different interval, and the height of the bar represents the frequency (number of scores) that occurred in that interval.

As you examine Figure A.1, notice that the scores are not evenly distributed across the various intervals. Rather, most of them fall in the middle intervals (centering around 50), and they taper off toward the extremes. This pattern would have been hard to see in the original, unorganized set of numbers.

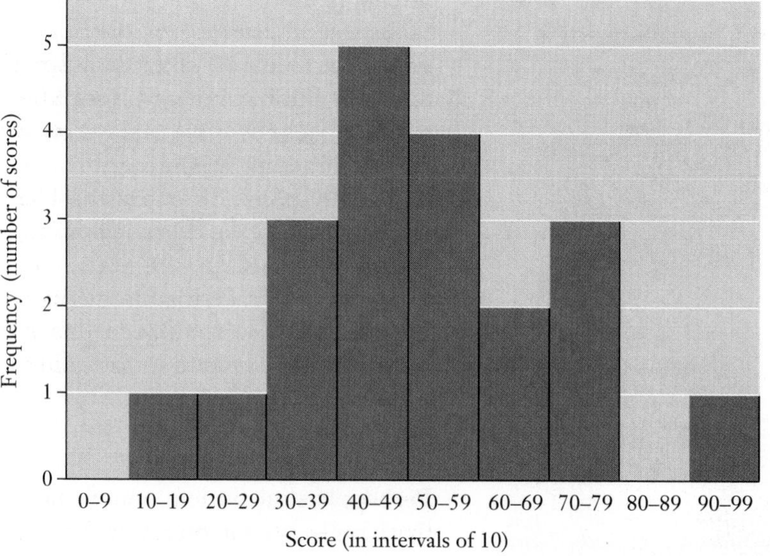

Figure A.1 ***A frequency distribution depicted by a bar graph***

This graph depicts the frequency distribution shown in Table A.2. Each bar represents a different interval of possible scores, and the height of each bar represents the number of scores that occurred in that interval.

Shapes of Frequency Distributions

The frequency distribution in Figure A.1 roughly approximates a shape that is referred to as a ***normal distribution*** or *normal curve*. A perfect normal distribution (which can be expressed by a mathematical equation) is illustrated in Figure A.2a. Notice that the maximum frequency lies in the center of the range of scores and that the frequency tapers off—first gradually, then more rapidly, and then gradually again—symmetrically on the two sides, forming a bell-shaped curve. Many measures in nature are distributed in accordance with a normal distribution. Height (for people of a given age and sex) is one example. A variety of different factors (different genes and nutritional factors) go into determining a person's height. In most cases, these different factors—some promoting tallness and some shortness—average themselves out, so that most people are roughly average in height (accounting for the peak frequency in the middle of the distribution). A small proportion of people, however, will have just the right combination of factors to be much taller or much shorter than average (accounting for the tails at the high and low ends of the distribution). In general, when a measure is determined by several independent factors, the frequency distribution for that measure at least approximates the normal curve. The results of most psychological tests also form a normal distribution if the test is given to a sufficiently large group of people.

But not all measures are distributed in accordance with the normal curve. Consider, for example, the set of scores that would be obtained on a test of English vo-

Normal, unimodal distribution

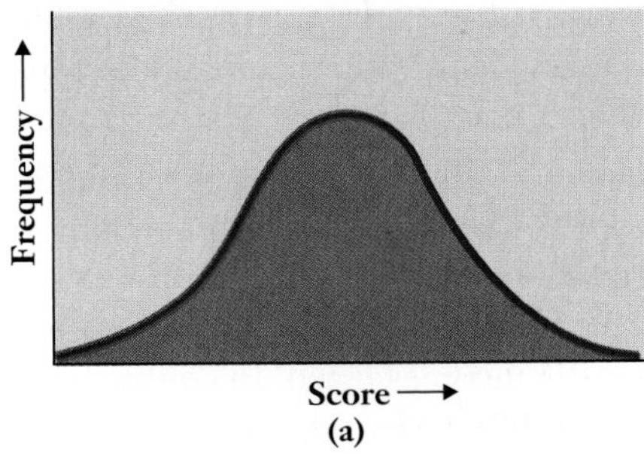

Bimodal distribution

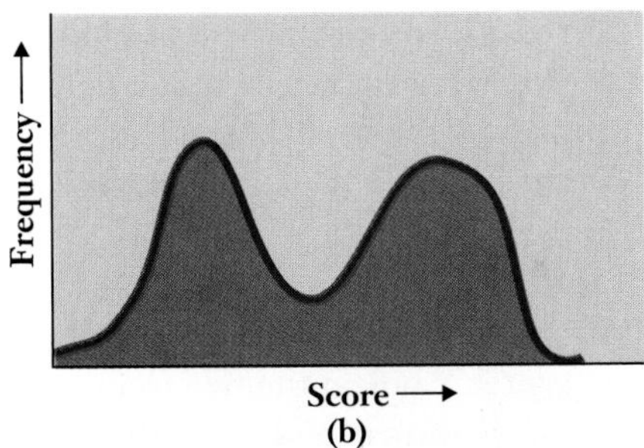

Positively skewed, unimodal distribution

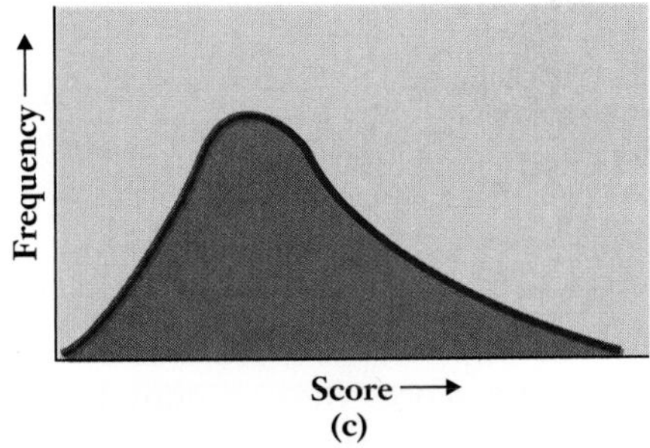

Negatively skewed, unimodal distribution

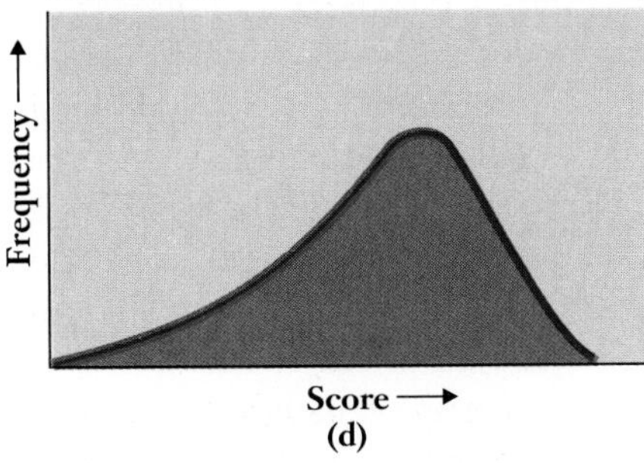

Figure A.2 ***Four differently shaped frequency distributions***

You can imagine that each of these curves was formed from a set of bars similar to those in Figure A.1, but the bars would be narrower and more numerous (the intervals would be smaller) and the data sets would be much larger.

cabulary if some of the people tested were native speakers of English and others were not. You would expect in this case to find two separate groupings of scores. The native speakers would score high and the others would score low, with relatively few scores in between. A distribution of this sort, illustrated in Figure A.2b, is referred to as a *bimodal distribution.* The ***mode*** is the most frequently occurring score or range of scores in a frequency distribution; thus, a bimodal distribution is one that has two separate areas of peak frequencies. The normal curve is a *unimodal distribution,* because it has only one peak in frequency.

Some distributions are unimodal, like the normal distribution, but are not symmetrical. Consider, for example, the shape of a frequency distribution of annual incomes for any randomly selected group of people. Most of the incomes might center around, let's say, $20,000. Some would be higher and some lower, but the spread of higher incomes would be much greater than that of lower incomes. No income can be less than $0, but no limit exists to the high ones. Thus, the frequency distribution might look like that shown in Figure A.2c. A distribution of this sort, in which the spread of scores above the mode is greater than that below, is referred to as a *positively skewed distribution.* The long tail of the distribution extends in the direction of high scores.

As an opposite example, consider the distribution of scores on a relatively easy examination. If the highest possible score is 100 points and most people score around 85, the highest score can only be 15 points above the mode, but the lowest score can be as much as 85 points below it. A typical distribution obtained from such a test is shown in Figure A.2d. A distribution of this sort, in which the long tail extends toward low scores, is called a *negatively skewed distribution.*

Measures of Central Tendency

Perhaps the most useful way to summarize a set of scores is to identify a number that represents the center of the distribution. Two different centers can be determined—the median and the mean (both described in Chapter 2). The ***median*** is the middle score in a set of ranked scores. Thus, in a ranked set of nine scores, the fifth score in the ranking (counting in either direction) is the median. If the data set consists of an even number of scores, determining the median is slightly more complicated because two middle scores exist rather than one. In this case, the median is simply the midpoint between the two middle scores. If you look back at the list of twenty ranked scores in Table A.1, you will see that the two middle scores are 49 and 50; the median in this case is 49.5. The ***mean*** (also called the *arithmetic average*) is found simply by adding up all of the scores and dividing by the total number of scores. Thus, to calculate the mean of the twenty introversion-extroversion scores in Table A.1, simply add them (the sum is 1020) and divide by 20, obtaining 51.0 as the mean.

Notice that the mean and median of the set of introversion-extroversion scores are quite close to one another. In a perfect normal distribution, these two measures of central tendency are identical. For a skewed distribution, on the other hand, they can be quite different. Consider, for example, the set of incomes shown in Table A.3 (on page A-4). The median is $19,500, and all but one of the other incomes are rather close to the median. But the set contains one income of $900,000, which is wildly different from the others. The size of this income does not affect the median. Whether the highest income were $19,501 (just above the median) or a trillion dollars, it still counts as just one income in the ranking that determines the median. But this income has a dramatic effect on the mean. As shown in the table, the mean of these incomes is $116,911. Because the mean is most affected by extreme scores, it will always be higher than the median in a positively skewed dis-

Table A.3 ***Sample incomes, illustrating how the mean can differ greatly from the median***

Rank	Income
1	$15,000
2	16,400
3	16,500
4	17,700
5	(19,500)
6	21,200
7	22,300
8	23,600
9	900,000
	Total: $1,052,200

Mean = $1,052,200 ÷ 9 = $116,911
Median = $19,500

tribution and lower than the median in a negatively skewed distribution. In a positively skewed distribution, the most extreme scores are high scores (which raise the mean above the median), and in a negatively skewed distribution they are low scores (which lower the mean below the median).

Which is more useful, the mean or the median? The answer depends on one's purpose, but in general the mean is preferred when scores are at least roughly normally distributed, and the median is preferred when scores are highly skewed. In Table A.3 the median is certainly a better representation of the set of incomes than is the mean, because it is typical of almost all of the incomes listed. In contrast, the mean is typical of none of the incomes; it is much lower than the highest income and much higher than all the rest. This, of course, is an extreme example, but it illustrates the sort of biasing effect that skewed data can have on a mean. Still, for certain purposes, the mean might be the preferred measure even if the data are highly skewed. For example, if you wanted to determine the revenue that could be gained by a 5 percent local income tax, the mean income (or the total income) would be more useful than the median.

Measures of Variability

The mean or median tells us about the central value of a set of numbers, but not about how widely they are spread out around the center. Look at the two frequency distributions depicted in Figure A.3. They are both normal and have the same mean, but they differ greatly in their degree of spread or variability. In one case the scores are clustered near the mean (low variability), and in the other they are spread farther apart (high variability). How might we measure the variability of scores in a distribution?

One possibility would be to use the *range*—that is, simply the difference between the highest and lowest scores in the distribution—as a measure of variability. For the scores listed in Table A.1, the range is 91 – 17 = 74 points. A problem with the range, however, is that it depends on just two scores, the highest and lowest. A better measure of variability would take into account the extent to which all of the scores in the distribution differ from each other.

One measure of variability that takes all of the scores into account is the ***variance.*** The variance is calculated by the following four steps: (1) Determine the mean of the set of scores. (2) Determine the difference between each score and

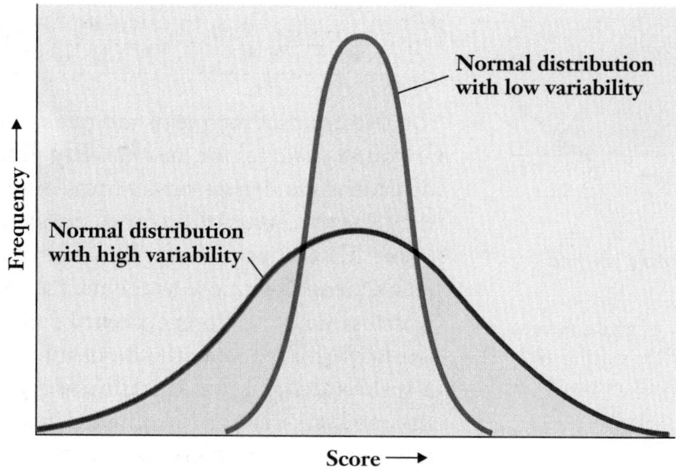

Figure A.3 ***Two normal distributions***

These normal distributions, superimposed on one another, have identical means but different degrees of variability.

Table A.4 ***Calculation of the variance and standard deviation for two sets of scores that have identical means***

First set of scores			*Second set of scores*		
Score	**Deviation (Score – 50)**	**Squared deviation**	**Score**	**Deviation (Score – 50)**	**Squared deviation**
42	–8	64	9	–41	1681
44	–6	36	19	–31	961
47	–3	9	31	–19	361
49	–1	1	47	–3	9
52	+2	4	56	+6	36
54	+4	16	70	+20	400
55	+5	25	78	+28	784
57	+7	49	90	+40	1600
Total = 400		Total = 204	Total = 400		Total = 5832
Mean = 400/8 = 50		Mean = 204/8 = 25.5	Mean = 400/8 = 50		Mean = 5832/8 = 729
Variance = Mean squared deviation = 25.5			**Variance = Mean squared deviation = 729**		
Standard deviation = $\sqrt{\text{Variance}}$ = $\sqrt{25.5}$ = 5.0			**Standard deviation = $\sqrt{\text{Variance}}$ = $\sqrt{729}$ = 27.0**		

the mean; this difference is called the *deviation.* (3) Square each deviation (multiply it by itself). (4) Calculate the mean of the squared deviations (by adding them up and dividing by the total number of scores). The result—the mean of the squared deviations—is the variance. This method is illustrated for two different sets of scores in Table A.4. Notice that the two sets each have the same mean (50), but most of the scores in the first set are much closer to the mean than are those in the second set. The result is that the variance of the first set (25.5) is much smaller than that of the second set (729).

Because the variance is based on the squares of the deviations, the units of variance are not the same as those of the original measure. If the original measure is points on a test, then the variance is in units of squared points on the test (whatever on earth that might mean). To bring the units to their original form, all we need to do is take the square root of the variance. The square root of the variance is the ***standard deviation***, which is the measure of variability that is most commonly used. Thus, for the first set of scores in Table A.4, the standard deviation = $\sqrt{25.5}$ = 5.0; for the second set, the standard deviation = $\sqrt{729}$ = 27.0.

Converting Scores for Purposes of Comparison

Are you taller than you are heavy? That sounds like a silly question, and it is. Height and weight are two entirely different measures, and comparing them is like the proverbial comparison of apples and oranges. But suppose I worded the question this way: Relative to other people of your gender and age group, do you rank higher in height or in weight? Now that is an answerable question. Similarly, consider this question: Are you better at mathematical or at verbal tasks? This, too, is meaningful only if your mathematical and verbal skills are judged relative to those of other people. Compared to other people, do you rank higher in mathematical or in verbal skills? To compare different kinds of scores with each other, we must convert each score into a form that expresses directly its relationship to the whole distribution of scores from which it came.

Percentile Rank

The most straightforward way to see how one person compares to others on a given measure is to determine the person's ***percentile rank*** for that measure. The percentile rank of a given score is simply the percentage of scores that are equal to that score or lower, out of the whole set of scores obtained on a given measure. For example, in the distribution of scores in Table A.1, the score of 37 is at the 25th percentile, because five of the twenty scores are at 37 or lower ($5/20 = 1/4 = 25\%$). As another example in the same distribution, the score of 73 is at the 90th percentile because eighteen of the twenty scores are lower ($18/20 = 9/10 = 90\%$). If you had available the heights and weights of a large number of people of your age and gender, you could answer the question about your height compared to your weight by determining your percentile rank on each. If you were at the 39th percentile in height and the 25th percentile in weight, then, relative to others in your group, you would be taller than you were heavy. Similarly, if you were at the 94th percentile on a test of math skills and the 72nd percentile on a test of verbal skills, then, relative to the group who took both tests, your math skills would be better than your verbal skills.

Standardized Scores

Another way to convert scores for purposes of comparison is to *standardize* them. A ***standardized score*** is one that is expressed in terms of the number of standard deviations that the original score is from the mean of original scores. The simplest form of a standardized score is called a ***z score***. To convert any score to a *z* score, you first determine its deviation from the mean (subtract the mean from it), and then divide the deviation by the standard deviation of the distribution. Thus,

$$z = \frac{\text{score} - \text{mean}}{\text{standard deviation}}$$

For example, suppose you wanted to calculate the *z* score that would correspond to the test score of 54 in the first set of scores in Table A.4. The mean of the distribution is 50, so the deviation is $54 - 50 = +4$. The standard deviation is 5.0. Thus, $z = 4/5 = +0.80$. Similarly, the *z* score for a score of 42 in that distribution would be $(42 - 50)/5 = -8/5 = -1.60$. Remember, the *z* score is simply the number of standard deviations that the original score is away from the mean. A positive *z* score indicates that the original score is above the mean, and a negative *z* score indicates that it is below the mean. As *z* score of +0.80 is 0.80 standard deviations above the mean, and a *z* score of −1.60 is 1.60 standard deviations below the mean.

Other forms of standardized scores are based directly on *z* scores. For example, Scholastic Aptitude Test (SAT) scores were originally (in 1941) determined by calculating each person's *z* score, then multiplying the *z* score by 100 and adding the result to 500 (DuBois, 1972). That is,

$$\text{SAT score} = 500 + 100(z)$$

Thus, a person who was directly at the mean on the test ($z = 0$) would have an SAT score of 500; a person who was 1 standard deviation above the mean ($z = +1$) would have an SAT score of 600; a person who was 2 standard deviations above the mean would have 700; and a person who was 3 standard deviations above the mean would have 800. (Very few people would score beyond 3 standard deviations from the mean, so 800 was set as the highest possible score.) Going the other way, a person who was 1 standard deviation below the mean ($z = -1$) would have an SAT score of 400, and so on.

Today, SAT scores are still based on the original standardization made in 1941. The test has been updated by means designed to keep the difficulty the same, but the scoring system has not been restandardized. Thus, a person today who scores

500 has performed average compared to people who took the test in 1941, not average compared to people taking the test today. Since 1941, average SAT scores have drifted downward; in 1992, the average scores were 423 for the verbal portion and 476 for the math portion. This means that the average person who took the SAT test in 1992 performed 0.76 standard deviations below the 1941 average on the verbal portion and 0.24 standard deviations below the 1941 average on the math portion. The decline is caused at least in part by the broader range of people taking the test now than in 1941, when only a relatively elite group applied to college. In addition, the greater decline on the verbal portion than on the math portion may be partly due to television and other cultural changes that have led young people today to read less than did young people in 1941 (Eckland, 1982).

Wechsler IQ scores (discussed in Chapter 11) are also based on *z* scores. They were standardized—separately for each age group—by calculating each person's *z* score on the test, multiplying that by 15, and adding the product to 100. Thus,

$$IQ = 100 + 15(z)$$

This process guarantees that a person who scores at the exact mean achieved by people in the standardization group will have an IQ score of 100, that one who scores 1 standard deviation above that mean will have a score of 115, that one who scores 2 standard deviations above that mean will have a score of 130, and so on.

Relationship of Standardized Scores to Percentile Ranks

If a distribution of scores precisely matches a normal distribution, one can determine percentile rank from the standardized score, or vice versa. As you recall, in a normal distribution the highest frequency of scores occurs in intervals close to the mean, and the frequency declines with each successive interval away from the mean in either direction. As illustrated in Figure A.4, a precise relationship exists between any given *z* score and the percentage of scores that fall between that score and the mean.

As you can see in the figure, slightly more than 34.1% of all scores in a normal distribution will be between a *z* score of +1 and the mean. Since another 50% will fall below the mean, a total of slightly more than 84.1% of the scores in a normal distribution will be below a *z* score of +1. By using similar logic and examining the figure, you should be able to see why *z* scores of –3, –2, –1, 0, +1, +2, and +3, respectively, correspond to percentile ranks of about 0.1, 2.3, 15.9, 50, 84.1, 97.7, and 99.9, respectively. Detailed tables have been made that permit the conversion of any possible *z* score in a perfect normal distribution to a percentile rank.

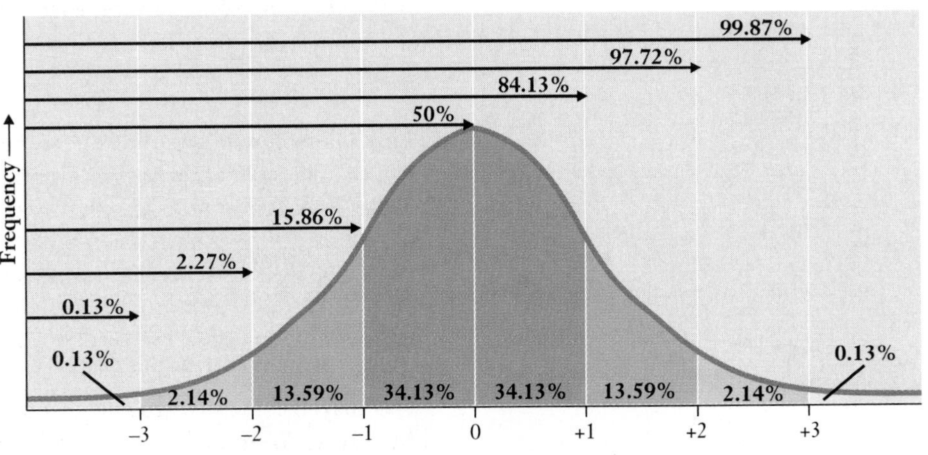

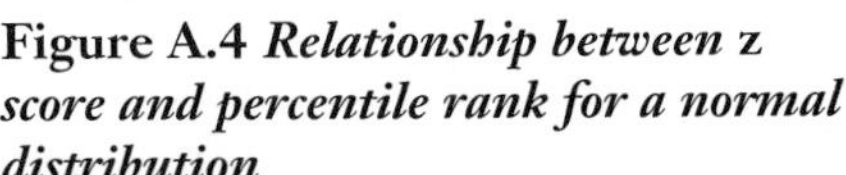

Figure A.4 ***Relationship between* z *score and percentile rank for a normal distribution***

Because the percentage of scores that fall between any given *z* score and the mean is a fixed value for data that fit a normal distribution, it is possible to calculate what percentage of individuals would score less than or equal to any given *z* score. In this diagram, the percentages above each arrow indicate the percentile rank for *z* scores of –3, –2, –1, 0, +1, +2, and +3. Each percentage is the sum of the percentages within the portions of the curve that lie under the arrow.

Calculating a Correlation Coefficient

The basic meaning of the term *correlation* and how to interpret a correlation coefficient are described in Chapter 2. As explained there, the correlation coefficient is a mathematical means of describing the strength and direction of the relationship between two variables that have been measured mathematically. The sign (+ or –) of the correlation coefficient indicates the direction (positive or negative) of the relationship; and the absolute value of the correlation coefficient (from 0 to 1.00, irrespective of sign) indicates the strength of the correlation. To review the difference between a positive and negative correlation, and between a weak or strong correlation, look back at Figure 2.4 and the accompanying text. Here, as a supplement to the discussion in Chapter 2, is the mathematical means for calculating the most common type of correlation coefficient, called the *product-moment correlation coefficient.*

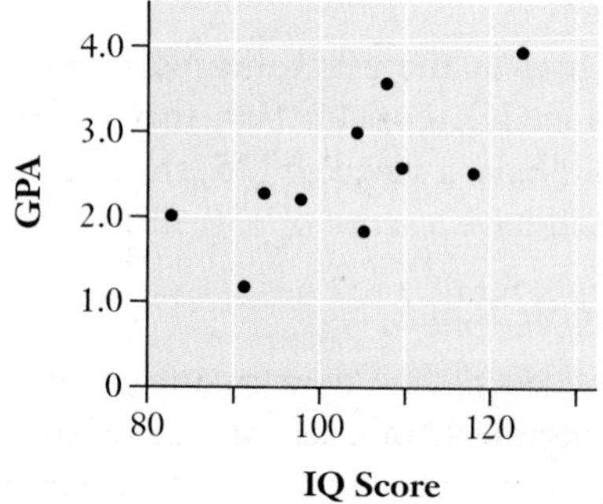

Figure A.5 ***Scatter plots relating GPA to IQ***

Each point represents the IQ and the GPA for one of the ten students whose scores are shown in Table A.5. (For further explanation, refer to Figure 2.4 in Chapter 2.)

To continue the example described in Chapter 2, suppose you collected both the IQ score and GPA (grade point average) for each of ten different high-school students and obtained the results shown in the "IQ score" and "GPA" columns of Table A.5. As a first step in determining the direction and strength of correlation between the two sets of scores, you might graph each pair of points in a *scatter plot,* as shown in Figure A.5 (compare this figure to Figure 2.4). The scatter plot makes it clear that, in general, the students with higher IQs tended to have higher GPAs, so you know that the correlation coefficient will be positive. However, the relationship between IQ and GPA is by no means perfect (the plot does not form a straight line), so you know that the correlation coefficient will be less than 1.00.

The first step in calculating a correlation coefficient is to convert each score to a z score, using the method described in the section on standardizing scores. Each z score, remember, is the number of standard deviations that the original score is away from the mean of the original scores. The standard deviation for the ten IQ scores in Table A.5 is 11.88, so the z scores for IQ (shown in the column marked z_{IQ}) were calculated by subtracting the mean IQ score (103) from each IQ and dividing by 11.88. The standard deviation for the ten GPA scores in Table A.5 is 0.76, so the z scores for GPA (shown in the column marked z_{GPA}) were calculated by subtracting the mean GPA (2.5) from each GPA and dividing by 0.76.

Table A.5 ***Calculation of a correlation coefficient*** **(r)**

Students (ranked by IQ)	IQ score	GPA	z_{IQ}	z_{GPA}	Cross-products $(z_{IQ}) \times (z_{GPA})$
1	82	2.0	–1.77	–0.66	1.17
2	91	1.2	–1.01	–1.71	1.73
3	93	2.3	–0.84	–0.26	0.22
4	97	2.2	–0.51	–0.39	0.20
5	104	3.0	+0.08	+0.66	0.05
6	105	1.8	+0.17	–0.92	–0.16
7	108	3.5	+0.42	+1.32	0.55
8	109	2.6	+0.51	+0.13	0.07
9	118	2.5	+1.26	0.00	0.00
10	123	3.9	+1.68	+1.84	3.09
	Sum = 1030	Sum = 25.0			Sum = 6.92
	Mean = 103	**Mean = 2.5**			**Mean = 0.69 = *r***
	SD = 11.88	**SD = 0.76**			

To complete the calculation of the correlation coefficient, you multiply each pair of z scores together, obtaining what are called the *z-score cross-products*, and then determine the mean of those cross-products. The product-moment correlation coefficient, r, is, by definition, the mean of the z-score cross-products. In Table A.5, the z-score cross-products are shown in the right-hand column, and the mean of them is shown at the bottom of that column. As you can see, the correlation coefficient in this case is +0.69—a rather strong positive correlation.

Supplement on Psychophysical Scaling

This section should *not* be read as a supplement to Chapter 2. It concerns two issues discussed in the section on psychophysical scaling in Chapter 8.

Derivation of Fechner's Law from Weber's Law

In Chapter 8, I described Ernst Weber's law, according to which the just-noticeable difference (jnd) between a comparison stimulus and a standard stimulus is directly proportional to the physical magnitude of the standard stimulus (M). As a formula, this is

$$\text{jnd} = kM$$

I then noted that Gustav Fechner used Weber's law to derive a law of psychophysical scaling, according to which the magnitude of a sensory experience (S) is directly proportional to the logarithm of the physical magnitude of the stimulus (M). As a formula, this is

$$S = c \log M$$

Here I will use the numbers shown in Table A.6 to demonstrate the logic of Fechner's derivation of his law from Weber's. The logic begins with the assumption that every jnd is subjectively equal to every other jnd. Thus, the sensory scale in the left-hand column of the table is a jnd scale, and each step in that scale produces an equal change in the magnitude of sensory experience (S). The example is for loudness of a 2000 Hz sound, for which the Weber fraction (k) is $\frac{1}{10}$ and the minimal intensity that can be heard is 1 sound-pressure unit. With these assumptions, Weber's law predicts that the intensity that will be 1 jnd above the minimum will be 1.10 units (1 + $\frac{1}{10}$th of 1 = 1.10). Similarly, the intensity that will be 2 jnd's above threshold will be 1.21 units (1.10 + $\frac{1}{10}$th of 1.10 = 1.21).

Continuing in this way, it is possible to derive the physical intensity of the stimulus that would be any given number of jnd's above threshold. The results, for

Table A.6 ***Demonstration that a jnd sensory scale is linearly related to the logarithm of the physical stimulus (log M)***

S in jnd units	M in sound-pressure units if $k = \frac{1}{10}$	Log M
0	1.00	0
1	1.10	0.041
2	1.21	0.082
3	1.33	0.123
4	1.46	0.164
5	1.61	0.205

5 jnd's, are shown in the middle column of the table. Notice that each successive jnd step involves a greater increase in the physical intensity than did the step before. For example, going from 0 to 1 jnd above threshold requires an addition of 0.10 physical units, whereas going from 4 to 5 jnd's requires an addition of 0.15 physical units (1.61 – 1.46 = 0.15). Thus, the relationship between the first and second columns is not linear. The third column of the table shows the logarithms (to base 10) of the numbers in the middle column. (If you have a calculator, you can check them yourself. The logarithm of 1 is 0, that of 1.1 is 0.041, and so on.) Notice that now, after the logarithmic transformation, the numbers do form a linear relationship with the numbers in the first column. Each jnd step corresponds with an increase of approximately 0.041 log units. Thus, in line with Fechner's law, each constant step in sensory magnitude corresponds with a constant step in the logarithm of the physical intensity of the stimulus.

Illustration Showing That Stevens's Power Law Preserves Sensory Ratios

At the end of Chapter 8, I described Stevens's power law, which states that the magnitude of a sensory experience (S) is directly proportional to the physical magnitude of the stimulus (M) raised by a constant power (p). As a formula, this is

$$S = cM^p$$

I then pointed out (as had Stevens) that our sensory systems may have evolved to operate according to a power law because such a law preserves constant sensory ratios as the overall physical intensity of stimulation waxes or wanes. For example, as a sound becomes closer (and therefore more intense), we hear its various pitches as maintaining the same ratios of intensity to each other as before, and thus we hear it as the same sound. As another example, as light fades in the evening, the relative brightness of one object compared to another in the visual scene remains constant. To make this more concrete, I mentioned in Chapter 8 that, according to Stevens's power law, every eightfold change in light intensity causes a twofold change in apparent brightness, no matter where on the intensity continuum we start from. Following are calculations proving that point.

For brightness estimations, $p = 1/3$ (as shown in Table 8.4). Let S_1 be the sensory magnitude for a stimulus whose physical magnitude is M, and let S_2 be the sensory magnitude for a stimulus that is physically eight times as intense as S_1 (that is, whose physical magnitude is $8M$). In accordance with the power law,

$$S_1 = cM^{1/3} \text{ and } S_2 = c(8M)^{1/3}$$

The ratio of S_2/S_1 can now be calculated as follows:

$$\frac{S_2}{S_1} = \frac{c(8M)^{1/3}}{cM^{1/3}} = \frac{(8M)^{1/3}}{M^{1/3}} = (8M/M)^{1/3} = 8^{1/3} = 2$$

Thus, regardless of the value of the original stimulus magnitude (M), an eightfold increase in that magnitude will produce a doubling of the sensory magnitude, or an eightfold decrease will produce a halving of the sensory magnitude. So, if the physical intensity of each part of a visual scene decreases to one-eighth what it was before, the sensory intensity experienced from each part of the scene will be cut in half and each part of the scene will maintain the same ratio of sensory intensity to each other part as it had before.

GLOSSARY

absolute threshold In psychophysics, the faintest (lowest-intensity) stimulus of a given sensation (such as sound or light) that an individual can detect. For contrast, see *difference threshold.* (p. 274)

accommodation In Piaget's theory of cognitive development, the change that occurs in an existing mental scheme or set of schemes as a result of the assimilation of the experience of a new event or object. See also *assimilation.* (p. 437)

action potentials Neural impulses; the all-or-nothing electrical bursts that begin at one end of the axon of a neuron and move along the axon to the other end. (p. 165)

actor-observer discrepancy The observation that a person who performs an action (the actor) is likely to attribute the action to the environmental situation, whereas the person who observes the same action (the observer) is likely to attribute it to the actor's inner characteristics (personality). See also *attribution, fundamental attribution error.* (p. 499)

adapt To change to suit new conditions of the environment. (p. 85)

adaptation See *adapt, sensory adaptation.*

additive color mixing The mixing of colored lights (lights containing limited ranges of wavelengths) by superimposing them to reflect off the same surface. It is called *additive* because each light adds to the total set of wavelengths that are reflected to the eye. For contrast, see *subtractive color mixing.* (p. 260)

adoptive method A method for studying the heritability of a characteristic, in which the similarity of adoptive relatives is compared with that of biological (birth) relatives. See *heritability.* (p. 68)

algorithm A rule specifying a set of steps that, if followed correctly, is guaranteed to solve a particular class of problem. For contrast, see *heuristic.* (p. 395)

alleles Different genes that can occupy the same locus on a pair of chromosomes and thus can potentially pair with one another. (p. 54)

altruism In sociobiology, a type of helping behavior in which an individual increases the survival chance or reproductive capacity of another individual while *decreasing* its own survival chance or reproductive capacity. For contrast, see *cooperation.* (p. 111)

amplitude The amount of physical energy or force exerted by a physical stimulus at any given moment; for sound, this physical measure is related to the psychological experience of loudness. (p. 246)

amygdala A brain structure that is part of the limbic system and is particularly important for evaluating the emotional and motivational significance of stimuli and generating emotional responses. (p. 236)

analogue theory of visual memory The theory that memories for visual scenes are functionally equivalent to pictures, that is, that such memories preserve the spatial gradients of the original scene in such a way that its recall is an experience similar to looking at a picture. For contrast, see *propositional theory of visual memory.* (p. 344)

analogy In ethology and comparative psychology, any similarity among species that is not due to common ancestry, but rather has evolved independently in the species because of some similarity in their habitat or lifestyle. For contrast, see *homology.* (p. 93)

antithesis principle In Darwin's theory of the origin of nonverbal signals, the idea that, as a result of natural selection or learning or both, opposite emotions of behavioral intentions will be expressed by opposite movements or postures. (p. 98)

anxiety disorders The class of mental disorders in which fear or anxiety is the most prominent symptom. It includes *generalized anxiety disorder, obsessive-compulsive disorder, panic disorder, phobias,* and *post-traumatic stress disorder.* (p. 617)

aphasia Any loss in language ability due to brain damage. See also *Broca's aphasia, Wernicke's aphasia.* (p. 402)

arousal response A pattern of measurable physiological changes (including tense muscles, increased heart rate, and secretion of certain hormones) that helps prepare the body for the possible expenditure of a large amount of energy. (p. 230)

artificial selection The deliberate selective breeding of animals or plants by humans for the purpose of modifying the genetic makeup of future generations. See *selective breeding.* For contrast, see *natural selection.* (pp. 81–82)

assertiveness training In behavior therapy, a direct method of training people to express their own desires and feelings and to maintain their own rights in interactions with others, while at the same time respecting the others' rights. (p. 673)

assessment In clinical practice, the process by which a mental health professional gathers and compiles information about a client for the purpose of describing the person's problems or disorder and developing a plan of treatment. (p. 651)

assessment interview A dialogue through which a mental health professional learns about a client. (p. 652)

assimilation In Piaget's theory of cognitive development, the process by which experiences are incorporated into the mind, or, more specifically, into mental schemes. See also *accommodation.* (p. 436)

assimilation theory Theory of size illusions postulating that the visual system tends to incorporate nearby elements into an object's boundaries when assessing the object's size. (p. 316)

association areas Areas of the cerebral cortex that receive input from the primary or secondary sensory areas for more than one sensory modality (such as vision and hearing) and are involved in associating this input with stored memories, in the processes of perception, thought, and decision making. (p. 174)

association by contiguity See *law of association by contiguity.*

association by similarity See *law of association by similarity.*

attachment The long-lasting emotional bonds that infants develop toward their principal caregivers. More broadly, the long-lasting emotional bonds that any individual develops toward any other individual or object. (p. 454)

attention In perception, the process or set of processes by which the mind chooses from among the various stimuli that strike the senses at any given moment, allowing only some of those stimuli to enter into higher stages of information processing. (p. 299) In the modal model of the mind, the process that controls the flow of information from the sensory store to the short-term store. More broadly, any focusing of mental activity along a specific track, whether that track consists purely of inner memories and knowledge or is based on external stimuli. (pp. 332–333)

attitude Any belief or opinion that has an evaluative component—a belief that something is good or bad, likable or unlikable, attractive or repulsive. (p. 514)

attribution In social cognition, any inference about the cause of a person's behavioral action or set of actions. More generally, any inference about the cause of any observed action or event. (p. 497)

auditory masking The phenomenon by which one sound (usually a lower-frequency sound) tends to prevent the hearing of another sound (usually a higher-frequency sound). (p. 251)

auditory nerve The cranial nerve that contains the sensory neurons for hearing and the vestibular sense (important for balance). (p. 249)

auditory neurons The sensory neurons for hearing, which run from the cochlea of the inner ear, through the auditory nerve, into the brain. (p. 249)

autonomic motor system The set of motor neurons that act upon visceral muscles and glands. (p. 167)

autosomes All of the chromosomes other than the sex chromosomes; that is, all of the chromosomes that are possessed in equal number by males and females. (p. 51)

aversion treatment In behavior therapy, a method for eliminating an undesired habit by applying some painful or unpleasant stimulus immediately after the unwanted response occurs or immediately after the person has experienced stimuli that would normally elicit the response. (p. 672)

avoidance response A response that occurs *before* the onset of an aversive (unpleasant) stimulus, preventing that stimulus from occurring for some period of time. (p. 140)

axon A thin, often very long, tubelike extension from a neuron that is specialized to carry neural impulses (action potentials) to other cells. (p. 165)

axon terminal A swelling at the end of an axon that is designed to release a chemical substance (neurotransmitter) onto another neuron, muscle cell, or gland. (p. 165)

---

basal ganglia The large masses of gray matter in the brain that lie on each side of the thalamus; they are especially important for the initiation and coordination of deliberate movements. (p. 172)

basilar membrane A flexible membrane in the cochlea of the inner ear; the wavelike movement of this structure in response to sound stimulates the receptor cells for hearing. See also *hair cells.* (p. 249)

behavior The observable actions of an individual person or animal. (p. 3)

behavior therapy The psychotherapy approach based on the philosophy of behaviorism and rooted in basic behavioral research on learning. In this approach, psychological problems are considered to stem from learned habits, and learning techniques are used to treat them. (p. 669)

behavioral genetics The study of the effects of genes on behavior. (p. 49)

behavioral monitoring Any assessment procedure that involves counting or recording actual instances of desired or undesired behaviors. (p. 655)

behaviorism A school of psychological thought that holds that the proper subject of study is observable behavior, not the mind, and that behavior should be understood in terms of its relationship to observable events in the environment rather than in terms of hypothetical events within the individual. (pp. 13, 121)

bias A technical term referring to nonrandom (directed) effects on research results, caused by some factor or factors that are extraneous to the research hypothesis. For contrast, see *error.* (p. 38)

biased sample A subset of the population under study that is not representative of the population as a whole. (p. 41)

binocular disparity The cue for depth perception that stems from the separate (disparate) views that the two eyes have of any given visual object or scene; the farther away the object is, the more similar are the two views of it. (p. 310)

biofeedback training A variety of operant conditioning in which a signal, such as tone or light, is made to come on whenever a certain desirable physiological change occurs, and the person is instructed to try to keep the signal on for increasing periods of time. It is used as a treatment for such problems as headaches and high blood pressure. (p. 134)

bipolar cells The class of neurons in the retina that receive input from the receptor cells (rods and cones) and form synapses on ganglion cells (which form the optic nerve). (p. 257)

bipolar disorder A mood disorder characterized by episodes of extreme depression alternating with episodes of extreme mania. (pp. 621, 625)

bipolar disorders The class of mental disorders characterized by mood swings in both directions—downward toward depression and upward toward mania. See *bipolar disorder*, *cyclothymia*. (pp. 621, 625)

blaming the victim The tendency to seek out flaws in the behavior or character of people who have suffered some misfortune. (p. 502)

blend The simultaneous, nonverbal expression of two or more emotions by mixing the muscle movements or postures that express one emotion with those that express the other. (p. 99)

blind In scientific research, the condition in which those who collect the data are deliberately kept uninformed about aspects of the study's design (such as which subjects have had which treatment) that could lead them either unconsciously or consciously to bias the results. See also *bias*, *observer-expectancy effect*. (p. 40)

blind spot The place in the retina of the eye where the axons of visual sensory neurons come together to form the optic nerve. Because the blind spot lacks receptor cells, light that strikes it is not seen. (pp. 254–255)

blocking effect In classical conditioning, the failure of a new stimulus to become a conditioned stimulus if it is accompanied by an already-effective conditioned stimulus during the conditioning trials. (p. 146)

blood-brain barrier The tight capillary walls and the surrounding glial cells that prevent many chemical substances from entering the brain from the blood. (p. 194)

bottom-up processes In theories of perception, mental processes that begin with the individual stimulus features recorded by the senses and then bring them together to form a perception of the larger object or scene. For contrast, see *top-down processes*. (p. 288)

brainstem The primitive, stalklike portion of the brain that can be thought of as an extension of the spinal cord into the head; it consists of the medulla, pons, and midbrain. (p. 170)

Broca's aphasia A specific syndrome of loss in language ability that occurs due to damage in a particular part of the brain called *Broca's area;* it is characterized by telegraphic speech in which the meaning is usually clear but the small words and word endings that serve grammatical purposes are missing. For contrast, see *Wernicke's aphasia*. (p. 402)

---

cell body The widest part of a neuron, which contains the cell nucleus and other basic machinery common to all cells. (p. 165)

cell membrane The thin, porous outer covering of a neuron or other cell, which separates the cell's intracellular fluid from extracellular fluid. (p. 183)

central drive system According to the central-state theory of drives, a set of neurons in the brain that, when active, most directly promotes a specific motivational state, or drive. (p. 204)

central nervous system The brain and spinal cord. (p. 164)

central route to attitude construction The logical analysis of available information for the purpose of developing or modifying an attitude. For contrast, see *peripheral route to attitude construction*. (p. 517)

central-state theory of drives The theory that the most direct physiological bases for motivational states, or drives, lie in neural activity in the brain. According to most versions of this theory, different drives correspond to activity in different, localizable sets of neurons. See also *central drive system*. (p. 204)

cerebellum The relatively large, conspicuous, convoluted portion of the brain attached to the rear side of the brainstem; it is especially important for the coordination of rapid movements. (p. 172)

cerebral cortex The outermost, evolutionarily newest, and (in humans) by far the largest portion of the brain; it is divisible into two hemispheres (right and left), and each hemisphere is divisible into four lobes, the occipital, temporal, parietal, and frontal. (pp. 173–174)

chromosomes The structures within the cell nucleus that contain the genetic material (DNA). (p. 51)

chunking A strategy for improving the ability to remember a set of items by grouping them mentally to form fewer items. (p. 339)

circadian rhythm Any cyclic physiological or behavioral change in a person or other living thing that has a period of about one day even in the absence of external cues signaling the time of day. (p. 225)

classical conditioning A training procedure or learning experience in which a neutral stimulus (the conditioned stimulus) comes to elicit a reflexive response through its being paired with another stimulus (usually an unconditioned stimulus) that already elicits that reflexive response; originally studied by Pavlov. See also *conditioned response*, *conditioned stimulus*, *unconditioned response*, *unconditioned stimulus*. (p. 124)

client-centered therapy The humanistic approach to psychotherapy developed by Rogers, in which the therapist refrains from offering advice or leading the course of therapy, but rather listens to the client with empathy and respect and reflects the client's thoughts and feelings back to him or her. (p. 662)

closure principle See *Gestalt principles of grouping*.

cochlea A coiled structure in the inner ear in which the receptor cells for hearing are located. (pp. 248–249)

cochlear implant A type of hearing aid used, experimentally, to treat sensorineural deafness; it transforms sounds into electrical impulses and directly stimulates the tips of auditory neurons within the cochlea. (pp. 249–250)

coding In sensation, the process by which information about the quality and quantity of a stimulus is preserved in the pattern of action potentials sent through sensory neurons to the central nervous system. (p. 245)

cognitive-behavior therapy The psychotherapy approach that stems from a union of cognitive and behavioral theory; it usually characterizes psychological problems as learned habits of thought and action, and its approach to treatment is to help people change those habits. See also *behavior therapy*, *cognitive therapy*. (p. 669)

cognitive dissonance The discomfort associated with the awareness of disagreement or lack of harmony between two or more of one's own cognitions (beliefs or bits of knowledge). (p. 519)

cognitive map The mental representation of the spatial layout of a familiar environment, inferred from the individual's ability to move in that environment as if guided by a map. (pp. 20, 149)

cognitive psychology The study of the ability to acquire, organize, remember, and use knowledge to guide behavior; it involves the construction of hypothetical mental processes to explain observable behavior. (pp. 19, 142)

cognitive therapy An approach to psychotherapy that begins with the assumption that people disturb themselves through their own thoughts and that they can overcome their problems through changing the way they think about their experiences. (p. 665)

common movement principle See *Gestalt principles of grouping.*

comparative psychology The field of psychological research that compares the behaviors of various animal species (including humans) with one another. The term is sometimes used to encompass all research with nonhuman animals. See *zoological psychology.* (p. 12)

concept A rule or other form of mental information for categorizing stimuli into groups. (p. 143)

conceptual priming The class of priming in which the priming stimulus makes certain mental concepts more accessible to one's flow of thoughts. See *priming.* For contrast, see *perceptual priming.* (p. 362)

concordance In behavioral genetics research, an index of heritability that is found by identifying a set of individuals who have a particular trait or disorder and then determining the percentage of some specific class of their relatives (such as identical twins) who have the same trait or disorder. (p. 75)

concrete-operational stage In Piaget's theory of cognitive development, the third stage (about 7 to 12 years old), in which the child can think logically about reversible actions (operations), but only when applied to objects with which the child has had direct (concrete) experience. See also *operations.* (p. 435)

conditioned reflex In classical conditioning, a reflex that occurs only because of previous conditions in the individual's experience; a learned reflex. For contrast, see *unconditioned reflex.* (p. 124)

conditioned response In classical conditioning, a reflexive response that is elicited by a stimulus (the conditioned stimulus) because of the previous pairing of that stimulus with another stimulus (the unconditioned stimulus) that already elicits a reflexive response. For contrast, see *unconditioned response.* (p. 124)

conditioned stimulus In classical conditioning, a stimulus that comes to elicit a reflexive response (the conditioned response) because of its previous pairing with another stimulus (the unconditioned stimulus) that already elicits a reflexive response. For contrast, see *unconditioned stimulus.* (p. 124)

conduction deafness Deafness that occurs when the ossicles of the middle ear become rigid and cannot carry sounds inward from the tympanic membrane to the cochlea. (p. 249)

cones The class of receptor cells for vision that are located in and near the fovea of the retina, operate in moderate-to-bright light, and are most important for the perception of color and fine detail. For contrast, see *rods.* (p. 254)

cone vision The high-acuity color vision that occurs in moderate-to-bright light and is mediated by cones in the retina; also called photopic or bright-light vision. See *cones.* For contrast, see *rod vision.* (p. 255)

content words Words, including nouns, verbs, adjectives, and adverbs, that are most essential to the meaning of a sentence. For contrast, see *grammatical morphemes.* (p. 397)

context-dependent memory The improved ability to retrieve information for memory that occurs when an individual is in the same environment as that in which the memory was originally encoded. (p. 354)

contingency contract In behavior therapy, a formal, usually written agreement in which certain specified services or rewards, provided by one party, are made contingent upon the actions of the other party. (p. 673)

continuity theories of development In developmental psychology, theories that maintain that psychological development is a gradual, continuous process. For contrast, see *stage theories of development.* (p. 415)

continuous measure In psychology, a measure of behavior or personality in which all possible gradations can occur within an observed range. (p. 62)

control processes In the modal model of the mind, the mental processes that operate on information in the memory stores and move information from one store to another. See *attention, encoding, retrieval.* (p. 328)

convergence See *neural convergence.*

cooperation In sociobiology, a type of helping behavior in which interaction among two or more individuals increases the survival chance or reproductive capacity of each individual involved in the interaction. For contrast, see *altruism.* (p. 111)

cornea The curved, transparent tissue at the front of the eyeball, which helps to focus light rays as they first enter the eye. (p. 254)

corpus callosum A massive bundle of axons connecting the right and left hemispheres of the higher parts of the brain, including the cerebral cortex. (p. 180)

correlates of structure Darwin's term for changes in a species that occur as nonadaptive side effects of other, adaptive changes. (pp. 87–88)

correlation coefficient A numerical measure of the strength and direction of the relationship between two variables. (pp. 36, A-7)

correlational study Any scientific study in which the researcher observes or measures (without directly manipulating) two or more variables to find relationships between them. Such studies can identify lawful relationships, but cannot determine whether change in one variable is the cause of change in another. (pp. 31–32)

counter-conditioning A behavior therapy technique for eliminating an undesired conditioned response (such as a conditioned fear response) by pairing the conditioned stimulus for the undesired response with an unconditioned stimulus for a new response (such as pleasure) that is incompatible with the undesired response. (p. 670)

cranial nerve A nerve that extends directly from the brain. See *nerves.* For contrast, see *spinal nerve.* (p. 167)

creole language A new language, with grammatical rules, that develops from a pidgin language in colonies established by people who had different native languages. See *pidgin language.* (p. 427)

critical period A relatively restricted time period in an individual's development during which a particular form of learning can best occur. See *imprinting.* (p. 156)

cross-sectional method In developmental psychology, the procedure for studying the effects of age, in which people of different ages are compared with one another. For contrast, see *longitudinal method.* (p. 414)

crossing over During meiosis, the random interchange of DNA sections between chromosomes within each set of four. (pp. 52, 53)

cultural psychology The study of the relationship between the culture in which a person develops and the person's thoughts, feelings, and behavior. Cultural psychologists may focus on just one culture or may compare people living in different cultures. (p. 18)

cyclothymia A mood disorder similar to bipolar disorder by involving less extreme depression and mania. See *bipolar disorder.* (p. 625)

---

dark adaptation The increased visual sensitivity that occurs when the eyes are exposed for a period of time to dimmer light than was present before the adaptation period. For contrast, see *light adaptation.* (p. 256)

deductive reasoning Logical reasoning from the general to the specific; the reasoner begins by accepting the truth of one or more general premises or axioms and uses them to assert whether a specific conclusion is true, false, or indeterminate. For contrast, see *inductive reasoning.* (p. 390)

deep structure In Chomsky's theory of language, the abstract, mental representation of the meaning of a sentence, organized in the simplest possible grammatical form consistent with that meaning. For contrast, see *surface structure.* (p. 399)

defense mechanisms In psychoanalytic theory, self-deceptive means by which the mind defends itself against anxiety. See *displacement, projection, rationalization, reaction formation, repression.* (p. 571)

deindividuation The reduced sense of personal responsibility that can occur when in a crowd or when distracted by highly arousing external stimulation, which can lead a person to perform actions that run counter to his or her personal beliefs or morals. (p. 546)

delusion A false belief that is maintained despite compelling evidence to the contrary. (p. 638)

dendrites The thin, tubelike extensions of a neuron that typically branch repeatedly near the neuron's cell body and are specialized for receiving signals from other neurons. (p. 165)

dependence See *drug dependence.*

dependent variable In any experiment, the variable that is believed to be dependent upon (affected by) another variable (the independent variable). In psychology, it is usually some measure of behavior. (p. 30)

depressive disorders The class of mood disorders characterized by prolonged or frequent bouts of depression. See *dysthymia, major depression.* (p. 621)

deprivation experiment An experiment in which animals are raised in ways that deprive them of some of their usual experiences in order to determine what experiences are essential (or not) for a particular species-specific behavior to develop. (p. 91)

descriptive statistics Mathematical methods for summarizing sets of data. (p. 35)

descriptive study Any study in which the researcher describes the behavior of an individual or set of individuals without systematically investigating relationships between specific variables. (p. 32)

developmental psychology The branch of psychology that charts changes in people's abilities and styles of behaving as they get older and tries to understand the factors that produce or influence those changes. (p. 413)

difference threshold In psychophysics, the minimal difference that must exist between two otherwise similar stimuli for an individual to detect them as different; also called the *just-noticeable difference (jnd).* (p. 276)

direct-perception theory The theory that perceptual mechanisms register directly the critical stimulus relationships that are present in the external environment, such that perception is not dependent upon mental inference. For contrast, see *unconscious-inference theory of perception.* (p. 321)

discrimination training The procedure, in both classical and operant conditioning, by which generalization between two stimuli is diminished or abolished by reinforcing the response to one stimulus and extinguishing the response to the other. See *extinction, generalization, reinforcement.* (pp. 127, 138)

discriminative stimulus In operant conditioning, a stimulus that serves as a signal that a particular response will produce a particular reinforcer. (p. 138)

displacement The defense mechanism by which a drive is diverted from one goal to another that is more realistic or acceptable. Also called *sublimation* in cases where the goal toward which the drive is diverted is highly valued by society. (p. 571)

dissociation A process by which some portion of a person's experiences are cut off mentally from the rest of his or her experiences, such that they cannot be recalled or can only be recalled under special conditions. (p. 635)

dissociative disorders The class of mental disorders that are characterized by dissociation. It includes *multiple personality disorder, psychogenic amnesia,* and *psychogenic fugue.* (p. 635)

distinctive features In Eleanor Gibson's theory of perceptual learning, those stimulus features of an object (or class of objects) that best distinguish it from other objects (or classes) with which it might be confused. (p. 298)

dizygotic twins See *fraternal twins.*

dominance hierarchy The ranking of individuals within a colony or group according to the degree to which others refrain from challenging that individual when their interests conflict. (p. 111)

dominant gene A gene that will produce its observable effects in either the *homozygous* or the *heterozygous* condition. (p. 54)

door-in-the-face technique A technique for gaining compliance in which one first asks for a large contribution or favor before asking for a smaller one. Hearing the first request, and refusing it, predisposes the person to comply to the second. (p. 537)

dopamine theory of schizophrenia The theory that the symptoms of schizophrenia arise from overactivity at synapses in the brain where dopamine is the neurotransmitter. (p. 640)

double blind experiment An experiment in which both the observer and the subjects are blind with respect to the subjects' treatment conditions. See also *blind.* (p. 41)

Down syndrome A chromosomal disorder, usually involving an entire extra chromosome 21, which is typified by a specific set of physical problems and by low-normal or retarded intellectual functioning; also called *trisomy-21.* (pp. 60–61)

drive See *motivational state.*

drug abuse The persistent taking of a drug in a way that is harmful to the self or that causes one to behave in a way that is harmful or threatening to others. (p. 632)

drug dependence The condition, which may or may not stem from physiological withdrawal symptoms, in which a person feels compelled to take a particular drug on a regular basis; also called *drug addiction.* (p. 632)

drug tolerance The phenomenon by which a drug produces successively smaller physiological and behavioral effects, at any given dose, if it is taken repeatedly. (p. 196)

DSM-IV The commonly used abbreviation for the *Diagnostic and Statistical Manual of Mental Disorders, Fourth Edition*, published by the American Psychiatric Association, which defines a wide variety of mental disorders and establishes criteria for diagnosing each. (p. 610)

dualism Descartes' theory that two distinct systems—the material body and the immaterial soul—are involved in the control of behavior; also called *interactionism.* For contrast, see *materialism.* (p. 4)

dysthymia A mental disorder characterized by feelings of depression that are less severe than those in major depression, but which last for at least a 2-year period. See also *major depression.* (p. 622)

---

early-selection theories Theories of attention, such as Broadbent's *filter theory* and Treismans's *attenuation theory,* according to which the selective process of attention occurs relatively early in the mind's analysis of sensory information, before the information has been analyzed for meaning. For contrast, see *late-selection theories.* (p. 307)

echoic memory Sensory memory for the sense of hearing. (p. 330)

ecological perspective (or approach) In research on learning, the view that different learning mechanisms have developed through natural selection to serve different survival needs, and that these mechanisms are best understood in relation to daily life in the natural environment. (p. 152) More generally, the view that behavioral or mental capacities are best understood by considering how they serve the individual's needs in the environment. (p. 385)

EEG See *electroencephalogram.*

ego In Freud's three-part division of the mind, the source of logical thought and realistic compromise among the various forces that act within the mind; the division of the mind that enables the person to function in the real world. See also *id, superego.* (p. 569)

elaboration (elaborative rehearsal) The process of thinking about an item of information in such a way as to tie the item mentally to other information in memory, which helps to encode the item into long-term memory. (p. 337)

electroencephalogram (EEG) A record of the electrical activity of the brain that can be obtained by amplifying the weak electrical signals picked up by recording electrodes pasted to the person's scalp. It is usually described in terms of wave patterns. (p. 221)

emotion A subjective feeling, the intensity of which is typically related to the degree of physiological arousal that accompanies it. (p. 231)

empiricism The idea that all human knowledge and thought ultimately comes from sensory experience; the philosophical approach to understanding the mind that is based on that idea. For contrast, see *nativism.* (p. 6)

encoding In the modal model of the mind, the mental process by which long-term memories are formed. See also *long-term memory.* (p. 333)

encoding rehearsal Any active mental process by which a person strives to encode information into long-term memory. For contrast, see *maintenance rehearsal.* (p. 337)

encoding-specificity principle The principle that the stimuli which were most prominent in a person's experience at the time of encoding a specific item of information into long-term memory are powerful cues for subsequent retrieval of that item from long-term memory. (p. 353)

endocrine glands Glands that are specialized to secrete hormones into the circulatory system. (p. 191)

endorphins Chemical substances produced in the body that act both as hormones and as neurotransmitters and are important for reducing the experience of pain. (pp. 192, 272)

environmentality The proportion of the variability in a particular characteristic, in a particular group of individuals, that is due to environmental compared to genetic differences among the individuals. For contrast, see *heritability.* (p. 65)

episodic memory Explicit memory of past events (episodes) in one's own life. For contrast, see *semantic memory, implicit memory.* (p. 359)

error A technical term referring to random variability in research results. For contrast, see *bias.* (p. 38)

escape response An operant response that is reinforced by the removal of a negative reinforcer. See *negative reinforcer.* (p. 140)

ethnocentrism The tendency for people to view and act toward their ingroups more favorably than they do toward their outgroups. (p. 502)

ethology The study of animal behavior in the natural environment, which uses evolutionary adaptation as its primary explanatory principle. (pp. 14, 89)

excitatory synapse A synapse at which the neurotransmitter increases the likelihood that an action potential will occur, or increases the rate at which they are already occurring, in the neuron on which it acts. For contrast, see *inhibitory synapse.* (p. 186)

experiment A research design for testing hypotheses about cause-effect relationships, in which the researcher manipulates one variable (the independent variable) in order to assess its effect on another variable (the dependent variable). (p. 30)

explicit memory The class of memory that can be consciously recalled and used to answer explicit questions about what one knows or remembers. See *episodic memory, semantic memory.* For contrast, see *implicit memory.* (p. 359)

exposure treatment Any method of treating fears—including flooding counter-conditioning, and systematic desensitization—that involves exposing the client to the feared object or situation (either in reality or imagination) so that the process of extinction or habituation of the fear response can occur. (p. 670)

extinction In classical conditioning, the gradual disappearance of a conditioned reflex that results when a conditioned stimulus occurs repeatedly without the unconditioned stimulus. (p. 126) In operant conditioning, the decline in response rate that results when an operant response is no longer followed by a reinforcer. (p. 135) See *classical conditioning, operant conditioning.*

eyebrow flash A momentary raising of the eyebrows, lasting about ⅙ of a second, which is a nonverbal sign of either greeting or flirtation in cultures throughout the world. (p. 101)

---

factor analysis A statistical procedure for analyzing the correlations among various measurements (such as test scores) taken from a given set of individuals; it identifies hypothetical, underlying variables called *factors* that could account for the observed pattern of correlations and assesses the degree to which each factor is adequately measured by each of the measurements that was used in the analysis. (p. 375)

feature theory of schemas The theory that a schema (the mental representation of a concept) is best characterized as a set of separate, discrete propositions that define the category of object or event that the schema represents. For contrast, see *prototype theory of schemas.* (p. 346)

Fechner's law The idea that the magnitude of the sensory experience of a stimulus is directly proportional to the logarithm of the physical magnitude of the stimulus. For contrast, see *power law.* (p. 278)

field study Any scientific research study in which data are collected in a setting other than the laboratory. (p. 34)

field theory Lewin's broad social psychological theory that each person exists in a field of psychological forces—made up of the person's own desires, goals, and abilities and the person's perceptions of others' expectations or judgments—that act simultaneously to push or pull the person in various directions. (pp. 19, 531)

figure In perception, the portion of a visual scene that draws the perceiver's attention and is interpreted as an object rather than as the background. For contrast, see *ground.* (p. 290)

fixation In Freud's psychoanalytic theory, the failure of some portion of the mind to advance beyond a particular childhood stage of psychosexual development, so that the person goes through life attempting to achieve pleasure in ways that are symbolically equivalent to the ways that pleasure is normally acheived in that stage. See also *psychosexual stages.* (p. 572)

fixed action pattern Ethologists' term for a behavior that occurs in essentially identical fashion among most members of a species (though it may be limited to one sex or the other), is elicited by a specific environmental stimulus, and is typically more complex than a reflex. (p. 89)

fixed-interval (FI) schedule In operant conditioning, a schedule of reinforcement in which a fixed period of time must elapse after each reinforced response before another reinforcer can be obtained. (p. 136)

fixed-ratio (FR) schedule In operant conditioning, a schedule of reinforcement in which the response must be emitted a certain fixed number of times (more than once) before it produces a reinforcer. (p. 136)

flexion reflex The reflexive folding of a limb (leg or arm) toward the body, usually in response to a potentially damaging stimulus to the limb. (p. 170)

flooding A behavior therapy technique for treating phobias, in which the person is presented with the feared object or situation until the fear response is extinguished or habituated. (p. 670)

foot-in-the-door technique A technique for gaining compliance in which one first asks for some relatively small contribution or favor before asking for a larger one. Complying to the first request predisposes the person to comply to the second. (p. 535)

formal-operational stage In Piaget's theory of cognitive development, the fourth stage (about 12 years old through adulthood), in which the individual is capable of reasoning about abstract concepts and hypothetical ideas. (p. 435)

formal thought disturbance A breakdown in the form or pattern of logical thinking, which often characterizes schizophrenia. (p. 639)

founder effect The genetic difference between two populations of the same species that results when one of the populations was founded by a small group of individuals that migrated to a new area and happened to have some unusual genes; a form of *genetic drift.* (p. 87)

four-walls technique A sales trick in which the salesperson asks a set of leading questions that cause the potential customer to say things that would contradict (and cause cognitive dissonance with) a subsequent refusal to purchase the product that the salesperson is trying to sell. (p. 535)

fovea The pinhead-sized area of the retina of the eye in which the cones are concentrated and that is specialized for high visual acuity. (p. 254)

fragile X syndrome A genetic disorder involving moderate to severe mental retardation accompanied by an observable break or tear on the X chromosome. (p. 59)

frame illusion The illusion by which a frame around the outside of an object makes the object look larger, and a frame placed within the border of an object makes the object look smaller. (p. 316)

fraternal twins Two individuals who developed simultaneously in the same womb, but who originated from separate zygotes (fertilized eggs) and are therefore no more genetically similar to one another than are ordinary siblings; also called *dizygotic twins.* For contrast, see *identical twins.* (p. 54)

free association In psychoanalysis, the procedure in which a patient relaxes, frees his or her mind from the constraints of conscious logic, and reports every image and idea that enter his or her awareness. (p. 567)

free nerve endings The sensitive tips of sensory neurons, located in the skin and other peripheral tissues, that are *not* surrounded by specialized end organs and are involved in the sense of pain. (p. 270)

frequency For any form of energy that changes in a cyclic or wavelike way, the number of cycles or waves that occur during a standard unit of time. For sound, this physical measure is related to the psychological experience of pitch. (p. 246)

frequency distribution A table or graph depicting the number of individual scores, in a set of scores, that fall within each of a set of equal intervals. (p. A-2)

Freudian symbols In psychoanalytic theory, objects or concepts that appear in a person's dreams or free associations and stand for other objects or concepts that exist in the person's unconscious mind. (p. 568)

frontal lobe The frontmost lobe of the cerebral cortex, bounded in the rear by the parietal and temporal lobes; it contains the motor area and parts of the association areas involved in planning and making judgments. (pp. 174, 236)

functionalism A school of psychological thought, founded by William James and others, that focuses on understanding the functions, or adaptive purposes, of mental processes. For contrast, see *structuralism.* (p. 9)

functionalist approach In psychology, the general approach that emphasizes the functions of behavior or mental processes. Whereas *functionalism* was a discrete school of thought in the early history of psychology, the *functionalist approach* has been integrated into many areas of psychology. (p. 85)

fundamental attribution error The tendency to attribute a person's behavior too much to the person's inner characteristics (personality) and not enough to the environmental situation. See also *attribution.* (p. 498)

---

g See *general intelligence.*

ganglion cells The sensory neurons for vision; their cell bodies are located in the retina, and their axons run by way of the optic nerve into the brain. (p. 257)

gate-control theory Melzack and Wall's theory that pain will be experienced only if the input from peripheral pain neurons passes through a "gate" located at the point that the pain-carrying neurons enter the spinal cord or lower brainstem. (p. 272)

gender identity A person's subjective sense of being male or female. (p. 470)

general intelligence In Spearman's theory of intelligence (and in other theories based on Spearman's), the underlying mental ability that affects performance on a wide variety of mental tests and accounts for the statistical correlation among scores on such tests; also called *g.* (p. 375)

generalization In classical conditioning, the phenomenon by which a stimulus that resembles a conditioned stimulus will elicit the conditioned response even though it has never been paired with the unconditioned stimulus. (p. 127) In operant conditioning, the phenomenon by which a stimulus that resembles a discriminative stimulus will increase the rate at which the animal produces the operant response, even though the response has never been reinforced in the presence of that stimulus. (p. 138)

generalized anxiety disorder A mental disorder characterized by prolonged, severe anxiety that is not consistently associated in the person's mind with any particular object or event in the environment or any specific life experience. (p. 617)

generative-transformational theory of language Chomsky's theory that the ability to produce and understand language can be specified as a set of rules for generating deep-structure sentences *(generative rules)* and another set of rules for transforming deep-structure sentences into any of various surface structures *(transformational rules).* See also *deep structure, surface structure.* (p. 400)

genetic drift All forms of chance events, other than natural selection, that can cause different populations of a given species to be genetically different (to have different gene pools). See also *founder effect.* (p. 87)

genotype The set of genes inherited by the individual. See also *phenotype.* (p. 50)

Gestalt principles of grouping The rules, proposed by Gestalt psychologists, concerning that manner by which the perceptual system groups sensory elements together to produce organized perceptions of whole objects and scenes. They include the principles of (a) *proximity* (nearby elements are grouped together), (b) *similarity* (elements that resemble one another are grouped together), (c) *closure* (gaps in what would otherwise be a continuous border are ignored), (d) *good continuation* (when lines intersect, those segments that would form a continuous line with minimal change in direction are grouped together), (e) *common movement* (elements moving in the same direction and velocity are grouped together), and (f) *good form* (elements are grouped in such a way as to form percepts that are simple and symmetrical). (p. 290)

Gestalt psychology A school of psychological thought, founded in Germany, which emphasizes the idea that the mind must be understood in terms of organized wholes, not elementary parts. For contrast, see *structuralism.* (pp. 11, 289)

gland Any bodily structure designed to secrete a chemical substance. See also *endocrine glands.* (p. 167)

glial cells Any of various non-neural cells in the nervous system, which help protect neurons from damage or in other ways facilitate neural functioning. (p. 166)

good continuation principle See *Gestalt principles of grouping.*

good form principle See *Gestalt principles of grouping.*

grammar The entire set of rules that specify the permissible ways that smaller units can be arranged to form morphemes, words, phrases, and sentences in a language. (p. 398)

grammatical morphemes The class of words, suffixes, and prefixes that serve primarily to fill out the grammatical structure of a sentence rather than to carry its main meaning. For contrast, see *content words.* (p. 397)

ground In perception, the portion of a visual scene that is interpreted as the background rather than as the object of attention. For contrast, see *figure.* (p. 290)

group polarization The tendency for a group of people who already share a particular opinion to hold that opinion more strongly—or in a more extreme form—after discussing the issue among themselves. (p. 550)

groupthink A model of thinking in which members of a group are more concerned with group cohesiveness and unanimity than with realistic appraisal of the actions being considered. (p. 552)

---

habituation The decline in the magnitude or likelihood of a reflexive response that occurs when the stimulus is repeated several or many times in succession. (p. 123)

hair cells The receptor cells for hearing, which are arranged in rows along the basilar membrane of the cochlea in the inner ear. (p. 249)

hallucination A false sensory perception; the experience of seeing, hearing, or otherwise perceiving something and believing it to be present, when in fact it is not present. (p. 638)

helping In sociobiology, any behavior that increases the survival chance or reproductive capacity of another individual. See also *altruism, cooperation.* (p. 111)

heritability The proportion of the variability in a particular characteristic, in a particular group of individuals, that is due to genetic compared to environmental differences among the individuals. For contrast, see *environmentality.* (p. 62)

heritability coefficient A measure of heritability, which can vary from 0 (no heritability) to 1 (complete heritability); specifically, variance due to genes divided by total variance. See *heritability.* (p. 62)

heterozygous The condition in which a pair of genes occupying the same locus on a pair of chromosomes are different from one another. For contrast, see *homozygous.* (p. 54)

heuristic A shortcut in problem solving; a rule for reducing the number of mental operations (or information-processing steps) taken to solve a problem. For contrast, see *algorithm.* (p. 395)

higher-order conditioning A classical-conditioning procedure in which a stimulus becomes a conditioned stimulus through being paired with a previously conditioned stimulus, rather than through being paired with an unconditioned stimulus. (p. 128)

holism In humanistic psychology, the view that a person must be understood as a whole entity and not as the sum of separate psychological components. (p. 581)

holistic perception The tendency, emphasized by Gestalt psychologists, to perceive whole patterns, objects, and scenes, and to ignore the smaller parts of which they are composed; the concept that wholes take precedent over parts in perceptual experience. (p. 289)

homeostasis The constancy in the body's internal environment that must be maintained through the expenditure of energy. (p. 203)

homology In ethology and comparative psychology, any similarity among species that exists because of the species' common ancestry. For contrast, see *analogy.* (p. 93)

homozygous The condition in which a pair of genes occupying the same locus on a pair of chromosomes are identical to one another. For contrast, see *heterozygous.* (p. 54)

hopelessness theory of depression The theory that depression stems from the sense of hopelessness that occurs when a person with a pessimistic attributional style is confronted with a series of negative experiences. (p. 624)

hormone Any chemical substance that is secreted naturally by the body into the blood and can influence physiological processes at specific target tissues (such as the brain) and thereby influence behavior. (p. 191)

humanistic psychology An approach to understanding the human personality that emphasizes (a) the person's subjective mental experiences, (b) a holistic view of the person, and (c) the person's inner drive toward higher psychological growth. (pp. 17, 580–581)

hypnosis A social interaction in which one person (the subject) voluntarily experiences a loss of control over his or her own perceptions, thoughts, or actions, and instead perceives, thinks, or acts in accordance with another person's (the hypnotist's) suggestions. (p. 357)

hypothalamus A small brain structure lying just below the thalamus, connected directly to the pituitary gland and to the limbic system, that is especially important for the regulation of motivation, emotion, and the internal physiological conditions of the body. (p. 173)

---

iconic memory Sensory memory for the sense of vision. (p. 329)

id In Freud's three-part division of the mind, the source of instincts and mental energy. See also *ego, superego.* (p. 569)

identical twins Two individuals who are genetically identical to one another because they originated from a single zygote (fertilized egg); also called *monozygotic twins.* For contrast, see *fraternal twins.* (p. 53)

implicit memory Memory that influences one's behavior or thought but does not itself enter consciousness. See *priming, procedural memory.* For contrast, see *explicit memory.* (p. 360)

impression management The entire set of ways by which people either consciously or unconsciously attempt to influence other people's impressions (perceptions and judgments) of them. (p. 510)

imprinting Ethologists' term for a relatively sudden and irreversible form of learning that can occur only during some critical period of the individual's development. See *critical period.* (p. 156)

incentive Any object or end that exists in the external environment and toward which behavior is directed. Also called *a reinforcer, reward, or goal.* (p. 202)

independent variable In an experiment, the condition that the researcher varies in order to assess its effect upon some other variable (the dependent variable). In psychology, it is usually some condition of the environment or of the organism's physiology that is hypothesized to affect the individual's behavior. (p. 30)

individual development The unique sequence of developmental changes, and the age at which each change occurs, that differentiate one person's development from that of others. For contrast, see *normative development.* (p. 414)

induction In Hoffman's typology of discipline styles, a form of verbal reasoning in which a parent (or other caregiver) induces the child to think about his or her actions and the consequences they have for other people. (p. 462)

inductive reasoning Logical reasoning from the specific to the general; the reasoner begins with a set of specific observations or facts and uses them to infer a more general rule to account for those observations or facts; also called *hypothesis construction.* For contrast, see *deductive reasoning.* (p. 387)

inferential statistics Mathematical methods for helping researchers determine how confident they can be in drawing general conclusions (inferences) from specific sets of data. (p. 35)

informational influence The class of social influence that derives from the use of others' behavior or opinions as information in forming one's own judgment about the objective nature of an event or situation. For contrast, see *normative influence.* (pp. 545, 560)

information-processing approach (or perspective) The general approach in psychological research and theory that begins with the premise that the mind is a device that acquires, stores, and analyzes information and uses information to control behavior. The goal of this approach is to explain behavior in terms of the steps in the decision-making process that lead the individual to respond in one way and not another under specific conditions. (p. 378)

ingroup A group to which an individual belongs or has the subjective sense of belonging. For contrast, see *outgroup.* (p. 502)

inhibitory synapse A synapse at which the neurotransmitter decreases the likelihood that an action potential will occur, or decreases the rate at which they are already occurring, in the neuron upon which it acts. For contrast, see *excitatory synapse.* (p. 186)

inner ear The portion of the ear lying farthest inward in the head; it contains the cochlea (for hearing) and the vestibular apparatus (for the sense of balance). (pp. 248–249)

insufficient-justification effect A change in attitude that serves to justify an action that seems unjustified in the light of the previously held attitude. (p. 521)

interneuron A neuron that exists entirely within the brain or spinal cord and carries messages from one set of neurons to another. (p. 164)

interview A self-report method of data collection in which the individual being studied (or assessed) answers questions in an oral dialogue; often used for clinical assessment. (p. 33)

intoxicating effects of a drug The relatively short-term effects on mood and behavior that stem from the immediate physiological effects of a drug, and that subside as the amount of the drug in the body diminishes. (p. 632)

introspection The process of looking inward to examine one's own conscious experience; the method used by Titchener and other structuralists. (p. 9)

iris The colored (usually brown or blue), doughnut-shaped, muscular structure in the eye, located behind the cornea and in front of the lens, that controls the size of the pupil and in that way controls the amount of light that can enter the eye's interior. (p. 254)

---

just-noticeable difference (jnd) See *difference threshold.*

just-world bias The tendency to believe that life is fair, which can lead people to assume that individuals who suffer misfortune deserve their misfortune. (p. 503)

---

karyotype The photographic representation of the chromosomes in a cell of an individual, organized in accordance with a standard numbering system. (p. 51)

kin selection theory of altruism The sociobiological theory that apparent acts of altruism have come about through natural selection because such actions are disproportionately directed toward close genetic relatives and thus promote the survival of others who have the same genes. See also *altruism.* (p. 112)

---

laboratory study Any research study in which the subjects are brought to a specially designated area (laboratory) that has been set up to facilitate the researcher's ability to control the environment or collect data. (p. 34)

language-acquisition device (LAD) Chomsky's term for the special, innate characteristics of the human mind that allow children to learn their native language; it includes innate knowledge of basic aspects of grammar that are common to all languages and an innate predisposition to attend to and remember the critical, unique aspects of the language. (p. 427)

language-acquisition support system (LASS) The term used by social learning theorists to refer to the simplification of language, and the use of gestures, that occur when parents or other language users speak to young children, which helps children learn language; developed as a complement to Chomsky's concept of the LAD (language-acquisition device). (p. 428)

late-selection theories Theories of attention that maintain that the selective process of attention occurs relatively late in the mind's analysis of sensory information, after the information has been analyzed for meaning. For contrast, see *early-selection theories.* (p. 307)

latent learning Learning that is not demonstrated in the subject's behavior at the time that the learning occurs, but can be inferred from its effect on the subject's behavior at some later time. (p. 150)

law of association by contiguity Aristotle's principle that if two environmental events (stimuli) occur at the same time or one right after the other (contiguously), those events will be linked together in the mind. (pp. 125, 348)

law of association by similarity Aristotle's principle that objects, events, or ideas that are similar to one another become linked (associated) in the person's mind (structure of memory), such that the thought of one tends to elicit the thought of the other. (p. 348)

law of complementarity The observation that certain pairs of limited-wavelength lights that produce different colors (such as red and green) alone will produce the perception of white (no color) when mixed. See also *additive color mixing.* (p. 260)

law of effect Thorndike's principle that responses that produce a satisfying effect in a particular situation become more likely to recur in that situation, and responses that produce a discomforting effect become less likely to recur in that situation. (p. 132)

learned helplessness theory of depression The theory that depression is a psychological giving up of the attempt to control one's own fate, brought on by repeated negative experiences over which the person has no control. (p. 623)

learning The process or set of processes through which sensory experience at one time can affect an individual's behavior at a future time. (p. 121)

lens In the eye, the transparent structure behind the iris that helps focus light that has passed through the pupil. (p. 254)

lesion Any localized area of damage in biological tissue, such as in the brain. (p. 205)

libido The instinctive force that underlies the sex drive; in Freud's psychoanalytic theory, the main life force. (p. 567)

light adaptation The decreased visual sensitivity that occurs when the eyes are exposed for a period of time to brighter light than was present before the adaptation period. For contrast, see *dark adaptation.* (p. 256)

lightness constancy The tendency to perceive a surface as having the same degree of lightness or darkness regardless of the amount of light that illuminates it. (p. 320)

limbic system An interconnected set of brain structures (including the amygdala and hippocampus) that form a circuit wrapped around the thalamus and basal ganglia, underneath the cerebral cortex. These structures are especially important for the regulation of emotion and motivation and are involved in the formation of long-term memories. (pp. 172–173)

linguistic relativity Whorf's theory that people who have different native languages perceive the world differently and think differently from each other because of their different languages. (p. 404)

localization of function The concept that different, localizable parts of the brain serve different, specifiable functions in the control of mental experience and behavior. (p. 6)

locus In genetics, a position on a chromosome that contains the DNA of a single gene. (p. 54)

locus of control According to Rotter, a person's perception of the typical source of control over rewards. *Internal locus of control* refers to the perception that people control their own rewards through their own behavior, and *external locus of control* refers to the perception that rewards are controlled by external circumstances or fate. (p. 587)

longitudinal method In developmental psychology, the procedure in which the same individuals are studied at different ages, so that each individual's ability or characteristic can be compared at one age with his or her ability or characteristic at another age. For contrast, see *cross-sectional method.* (p. 414)

long-term memory In the modal model of the mind, information that is retained in the mind for long periods (often throughout life). For contrasts, see *sensory memory, short-term memory.* (p. 333)

long-term store The third memory store in the modal model of the mind; the hypothetical place in the mind that retains information for long periods (often throughout life). (p. 333)

loudness That quality of the psychological experience (sensation) of a sound that is most directly related to the amplitude of the physical sound stimulus. (p. 246)

low-ball technique A sales trick in which the salesperson suggests a low price for the item being sold, and then, when the potential customer has agreed to buy it at that price, pretends to discover that the item cannot be sold for that price. The customer's earlier agreement to buy the item may cause him or her to exaggerate mentally the item's worth and therefore to be more likely than before to buy it at the higher price. (p. 535)

---

maintaining causes of a mental disorder Those consequences of a mental disorder—such as the way other people treat the person who has it—that help keep the disorder going once it begins. See also *precipitating* and *predisposing causes of a mental disorder.* (p. 609)

maintenance rehearsal Any active mental process by which a person strives to hold information in short-term memory for a period of time. For contrast, see *encoding rehearsal.* (p. 337)

major depression A mental disorder characterized by severe depression that lasts essentially without remission for at least two weeks. (p. 622)

materialism Hobbes's theory that nothing exists but matter and energy. For contrast, see *dualism.* (p. 6)

mean The arithmetic average of a set of scores, determined by adding the scores and dividing the sum by the number of scores. (pp. 35, A-3)

median The center score in a set of scores that have been rank-ordered. (pp. 35, A-3)

medical model In clinical psychology or psychiatry, the view that mental disorders either *are*, or *are analogous to*, physical diseases. (p. 606)

medulla The lowest portion of the brainstem, bounded at one end by the spinal cord and at the other by the pons, which is responsible, with the pons, for organizing reflexes more complex than spinal reflexes. (pp. 170–171)

meiosis The form of cell division involved in producing egg or sperm cells, which results in cells that are genetically dissimilar and that each have half the number of chromosomes of the original cell. (p. 52)

memory 1. The mind's ability to retain information over time. 2. Information retained in the mind over time. (p. 327)

memory stores In cognitive psychology, hypothetical constructs that are conceived of as places where information is held in the mind. See also *long-term store, sensory store, short-term store.* (p. 328)

mental disorder A disturbance in a person's emotions, drives, thought processes, or behavior that (a) involves serious and relatively prolonged distress and/or impairment in ability to function, (b) is not simply a normal response to some event or set of events in the person's environment, and (c) is not explainable as an effect of poverty, prejudice, or other social forces that prevent the person from behaving adaptively, nor as a deliberate decision to act in a way that is contrary to the norms of society. (p. 605)

mental set A habit of perception or thought, stemming from previous experience, that can either help or hinder a person in solving a new problem. (p. 393)

metacomponents In Sternberg's information-processing model of intelligence, the mental components (processes) that regulate and coordinate the activities of the various lower-level mental components in solving a problem or choosing a course of action. See also *performance components.* (p. 380)

method of magnitude estimation Stevens's psychophysical method in which people are asked to estimate the magnitude of a subjective experience (such as the perceived loudness of a sound), usually by assigning a number to it. (p. 278)

midbrain The upper portion of the brainstem, bounded at its lower end by the pons and at its upper end by the thalamus, which contains neural centers that organize basic movement patterns. (pp. 170–171)

middle ear The air-filled cavity, separated from the outer ear by the eardrum; its main structures are three ossicles (tiny bones), which vibrate in response to sound waves and stimulate the inner ear. (p. 248)

mind 1. The entire set of an individual's sensations, perceptions, memories, thoughts, dreams, motives, emotional feelings, and other subjective experiences. (p. 3) 2. In cognitive psychology, the set of hypothesized information-processing steps that analyze stimulus information and organize behavioral responses. (pp. 17–18)

mitosis The form of cell division involved in normal body growth, which produces cells that are genetically identical to each other. (p. 52)

MMPI The *Minnesota Multiphasic Personality Inventory.* A psychometric personality test that is commonly used for clinical assessment. See *assessment, psychometric personality test.* (p. 653)

modal model of the mind In cognitive psychology, the information-processing model that divides the mind into three *memory stores* (sensory, short-term, and long-term) and a set of mental processes (called *control processes*) that operate on information within the stores and move information from one store to another. (pp. 327–328)

mode The most frequently occurring score in a set of scores; in a frequency distribution, the interval that contains the highest frequency of scores. (p. A-3)

modeling The process of teaching a person what to do, or how to do it, by having the person watch another person (the model) engage in that behavior. (p. 674)

modern synthesis In evolutionary theory, the ideas that have resulted from combining Darwin's principle of natural selection with a modern understanding of genes. (p. 82)

modulatory neuron A neuron that produces relatively long-lasting changes in the responsiveness or effectiveness of other neurons. (pp. 188–189)

monoamine theory of depression The theory that the feeling of depression stems from too little activity at synapses in the brain where monoamines (norepinephrine, dopamine, and sertonin) are the neurotransmitters. (p. 622)

monogamy A mating system in which one female and one male bond only with each other. See *mating bond*. For contrast, see *polyandry, polygyny, polygynandry*. (p. 104)

monozygotic twins See *identical twins*.

mood disorders A class of mental disorders characterized by prolonged or extreme disruptions in mood. It includes the *depressive disorders* and *bipolar disorders*. (p. 621)

moon illusion The illusion by which the moon appears larger when seen near the horizon and smaller when seen near the zenith, even though it is objectively the same size and distance from the viewer in either location. (p. 315)

morphemes The smallest meaningful units of a verbal language; words, prefixes, or suffixes that have discrete meanings. (p. 397)

motion parallax The cue for depth perception that stems from the changed view one has of a scene or object when one's head moves sideways to the scene or object; the farther away an object is, the smaller is the change in view. (p. 311)

motivation The entire constellation of factors, some inside the organism and some outside, that cause an individual to behave in a particular way at a particular time. See also *incentive, motivational state*. (p. 201)

motivational state An internal, reversible condition in an individual that orients the individual toward one or another type of goal (such as food or water). This condition is not observed directly but is inferred from the individual's behavior; also called a *drive*. (p. 201)

motor neuron A neuron that carries messages from the brain or spinal cord, through a nerve, to a muscle or gland. (p. 164)

Müller-Lyer illusion A visual size illusion in which a horizontal line looks longer if attached at each end to an outward-extending, V-shaped object, and looks shorter if attached at each end to an inward-extending, V-shaped object. (p. 314)

multiple personality disorder A mental disorder in which two or more distinct personalities or self-identities are manifested by the same person at different times. (p. 635)

mutations Errors that occasionally and unpredictably occur during DNA replication, producing a "replica" that is different from the original. Mutations are believed to be the original source of all genetic variability. (p. 82)

myelin sheath A casing of fatty cells wrapped tightly around the axon of some neurons. (p. 165)

---

nativism The idea that certain elementary ideas are innate to the human mind and do not need to be gained through experience; the philosophical approach to understanding the mind that is based on that idea. For contrast, see *empiricism*. (p. 6)

natural selection The selective breeding that results from the obstacles to reproduction that are imposed by the natural environment; it is the driving force of evolution. See *selective breeding*. For contrast, see *artificial selection*. (p. 82)

naturalistic observation Any data-collection procedure in which the researcher records subjects' ongoing behavior in a natural setting, without interfering with that behavior. (p. 33)

nature An individual's biological (genetic) endowment. For contrast, see *nurture*. (p. 49)

nature-nurture debate The long-standing controversy as to whether the differences among people are principally due to their genetic differences (nature) or differences in their past and present environment (nurture). (p. 49)

negative contrast effect In operant conditioning, the decline in response rate, when the size of a reinforcer (or reward) is reduced, to a rate below that which occurs for subjects that had been receiving the smaller reinforcer all along. For contrast, see *positive contrast effect*. (p. 147)

negative interdependence A condition that engenders competition because the structure of rewards is such that each individual (or group) can obtain a reward only by preventing another individual (or group) from obtaining a reward. For contrast, see *positive interdependence*. (p. 553)

negative reinforcement In operant conditioning, the condition in which a response results in *removal* of a negative reinforcer. See *negative reinforcer*. (p. 140)

negative reinforcer In operant conditioning, a stimulus (such as electric shock or loud noise) that is *removed* after a response, and whose removal increases the likelihood that the response will recur. (p. 140)

negative symptoms The class of symptoms of schizophrenia that are characterized by the absence of, or reduction in, expected behaviors, thoughts, feelings, and drives. (p. 639)

nerves Large bundles containing the axons of many neurons. Located in the peripheral nervous system, they connect the central nervous system with muscles, glands, and sensory organs. (p. 166)

neural convergence In a sensory system, the funneling of the activity of many receptor cells upon fewer sensory neurons; high convergence increases sensitivity at the expense of acuity. More generally, any case in which a single neuron receives synaptic input from more than one other neuron. (p. 258)

neural network modeling Computer simulation of the netlike interconnections among neurons and the lawful means to modify the strength of the connections, for the purpose of developing theories of learning and other psychological processes. (p. 190)

neurohormone A chemical substance that is similar to a neurotransmitter in that it is secreted from the axon terminals of neurons, but is classed as a hormone because it is secreted into blood vessels rather than onto other neurons. (p. 192)

neuromodulator Neurotransmitter released from a modulatory neuron. Its effect on postsynaptic neurons lasts longer than does that of other neurotransmitters. (p. 189)

neurons Single cells in the nervous system that are specialized for carrying information rapidly from one place to another and/or integrating information from various sources; also called *nerve cells*. (p. 164)

neurotransmitter A chemical substance released from the axon terminal of a neuron, at a synapse, which influences the activity of another neuron, a muscle cell, or a glandular cell; also called a *transmitter*. (p. 165)

nonregulatory drive Any motivational state (such as the sex drive) that serves some function *other than* that of preserving some constancy of the body's internal environment. For contrast, see *regulatory drive*. (p. 204)

nonspecific factors In psychotherapy, those aspects of the therapist's interaction with the client that are not derived from the specific principles on which the therapy is based, but which may play an important role in the therapy process. (p. 676)

nonverbal communication Communication through bodily postures, movements, and facial expressions, that is, through means other than words or symbols that stand for words. (p. 96)

normal distribution A bell-shaped frequency distribution in which the mean, median, and mode are identical and the frequency of scores tapers off symmetrically on both sides, as defined by a specific mathematical equation. See *frequency distribution*. (pp. 62, A-2)

normative development The typical sequence of developmental changes, and the typical ages at which each change occurs, that are found for a given group of people. For contrast, see *individual development*. (p. 413)

normative influence The class of social influence that derives from people's concern about what others will think of them if they behave in a certain way or express a certain belief. For contrast, see *informational influence*. (pp. 545, 560)

nucleus In neuroanatomy, a cluster of cell bodies of neurons within the central nervous system (not to be confused with the cell nucleus within each cell). (p. 169)

nurture The entire set of environmental conditions that affect an individual's development. See also *nature*, *nature-nurture debate*. (p. 49)

---

object permanence Piaget's term for the understanding that an object still exists even when it is out of view. (p. 420)

objective questionnaire In clinical assessment or in personality research, a questionnaire on which a client or research subject checks off adjectives or statements that describe his or her own behaviors, thoughts, or feelings. (p. 652)

observational learning Learning by watching others. See also *modeling*. (p. 150)

observational method Any data-collection procedure in which the researcher directly observes the behavior of interest rather than relying on subject's self-descriptions. (p. 33)

observer-expectancy effect Any bias in research results that derives from the researcher's desire or expectation that a subject or set of subjects will behave in a certain way. See *bias*, *subject-expectancy effect*. (pp. 29, 40)

obsessive-compulsive disorder A mental disorder characterized by a repeated, disturbing, irrational thought (the *obsession*) that can only be terminated (temporarily) by performing some action (the *compulsion*). (p. 619)

occipital lobe The rearmost lobe of the cerebral cortex, bounded in front by the temporal and parietal lobes; it contains the visual area of the brain. (p. 174)

oedipal crisis In Freud's psychoanalytic theory, the mental conflict that occurs during the phallic stage of development, which stems from the child's feeling of sexual attraction to the opposite-sex parent and consequent fear of resentment of the same-sex parent. For the girl, this crisis is sometimes called the *electra crisis*. (p. 573)

operant conditioning A training or learning process by which the consequence of a behavioral response affects the likelihood that the individual will produce that response again; also called *instrumental conditioning*. (pp. 130, 132)

operant response Any behavioral response that produces some reliable effect on the environment, which influences the likelihood that the individual will produce that response again; also called *instrumental response*. (pp. 13, 130, 132)

operation Piaget's term for a reversible action that can be performed either in reality or mentally upon some object or set of objects. For example, rolling a clay ball into a clay sausage is an operation, because the sausage can be rolled back again to form the ball. (p. 435)

opponent-process theory of color vision Designed by Hering to explain the law of complementarity, this theory holds that units (neurons) that mediate the perception of color are excited by one range of wavelengths and inhibited by another (complementary) range of wavelengths. According to the theory, such units cancel out the perception of color when two complementary wavelength ranges are superimposed. See also *law of complementarity*. (p. 263)

optic nerve The cranial nerve that contains the sensory neurons for vision, which run from the eye's retina into the brain. (p. 254)

ossicles Three tiny bones (the hammer, anvil, and stirrup) in the middle ear, which vibrate in response to sound waves and stimulate the inner ear. (p. 248)

outer ear The pinna (the visible, external portion of the ear) and the auditory canal (the air-filled opening that extends inward from the pinna to the middle ear). (p. 248)

outgroup A group to which an individual does not belong or has the subjective sense of not belonging. For contrast, see *ingroup*. (p. 502)

outgroup homogeneity effect The tendency of people to perceive members of an outgroup as more similar to each other than they actually are. See *outgroup*. (p. 502)

overjustification effect The phenomenon in which a person who initially performs a task for no reward (except the enjoyment of the task) becomes less likely to perform that task for no reward after a period during which he or she has been rewarded for performing it. (p. 148)

---

panic disorder A mental disorder characterized by the repeated occurrence of panic attacks at unpredictable times and with no clear relationship to environmental events. Each attack involves an intense feeling of terror, which usually lasts several minutes and is accompanied by signs of high physiological arousal. (p. 620)

parallel processing In perception, the early (unconscious) steps in the analysis of sensory information that act simultaneously on all (or at least many) of the stimulus elements that are available at any given moment. For contrast, see *serial processing*. (p. 294)

parasympathetic division of the autonomic motor system The set of motor neurons that act upon visceral muscles and glands and mediate many of the body's regenerative, growth-promoting, and energy-conserving functions. For contrast, see *sympathetic division of the autonomic motor system*. (p. 168)

parental investment The time, energy, and risk to survival involved in producing, feeding, and otherwise caring for each offspring. (p. 104)

parietal lobe The lobe of the cerebral cortex that lies in front of the occipital lobe, above the temporal lobe, and behind the frontal lobe; it contains the somatosensory area of the brain. (p. 174)

partial reinforcement In operant conditioning, any condition in which the response sometimes produces a reinforcer and sometimes does not. See *reinforcer*. For contrast, see *continuous reinforcement*. (p. 135)

percentile rank For any single score in a set of scores, the percentage of scores in the set that are equal to or lower than that score. (p. A-6)

perception The recognition, organization, and meaningful interpretation of sensory stimuli. For contrast, see *sensation*. (pp. 241, 287)

perceptual priming The class of priming in which the priming stimulus improves one's ability to identify a specific test stimulus based on its physical features. See *priming*. For contrast, see *conceptual priming*. (p. 361)

perceptual set An expectation, established from prior experience, that leads a person to interpret an ambiguous stimulus in one way and not another. (p. 291)

performance components In Sternberg's information-processing model of intelligence, the mental components (processes) that act most directly on information when solving a problem or choosing a course of action. See also *metacomponents*. (p. 380)

peripheral nervous system The entire set of cranial and spinal nerves, which connect the central nervous system (brain and spinal cord) to the body's sensory organs, muscles, and glands. (p. 164)

peripheral route to attitude construction Any method for modifying or developing an attitude that does not entail logical analysis of the available information. For contrast, see *central route to attitude construction*. (p. 517)

permanent effects of a drug Irreversible forms of bodily damage, including brain damage, that result from drug use. (p. 633)

person schema The organized set of mental information that one has about a particular person, set of people, or people in general. See also *schema*. (p. 494)

personality The relatively consistent patterns of thought, feeling, and behavior that characterize each person as a unique individual. (p. 565)

personality theory A formal attempt to describe and explain the ways in which people differ from one another in their characteristic patterns of thought, feeling, and behavior. (p. 565).

phenomenology The study of subjective mental experiences; a theme of humanistic theories of personality. (p. 580)

phenotype The observable properties of an individual's body and behavior. See also *genotype*. (p. 50)

phobia Any mental disorder characterized by a strong, irrational fear of some particular category of object or event. (p. 618)

phonemes The various vowel and consonant sounds that provide the basis for a spoken language. (pp. 293, 398)

physiological psychology The study of the physiological mechanisms, in the brain and elsewhere, that mediate behavior and psychological experiences. (p. 16)

pictorial cues for depth perception The depth cues that operate not only when viewing real scenes, but can also operate when viewing pictures. They include occlusion, relative image size for familiar objects, linear perspective, texture gradient, and (for outdoor scenes) position relative to the horizon. (pp. 311–312)

pidgin language A primitive system of communication that emerges when people with different native languages colonize the same region; it uses words from the various native languages and has no or minimal grammatical structure. See also *creole language*. (p. 427)

pitch The quality of the psychological experience (sensation) of a sound that is most related to the frequency of the physical sound stimulus. (p. 246)

pituitary An endocrine gland that is located directly beneath the hypothalamus and is controlled by neural activity in that structure. Its hormones control the activity of many other endocrine glands, and for that reason it is sometimes called the "master endocrine gland." (p. 193)

PKU Abbreviation for *phenylketonuria*, a genetic disorder caused by a recessive gene and characterized by the body's inability to break down phenylalanine (an amino acid found in most protein-containing foods). (p. 58)

placebo In drug studies, an inactive substance given to subjects assigned to the nondrug group. (p. 41)

placebo effect In psychological research, any effect on a subject's behavior or feelings that stems from the subject's expectations as to how he or she should behave or feel as a result of a particular treatment. (p. 677)

polyandry A mating system in which one female bonds with more than one male. For contrast, see *monogamy, polygyny, polygynandry*. (p. 104)

polygenic characteristic Any trait or characteristic for which the observed variation is affected by many genes. (p. 62)

polygynandry A mating system in which a group consisting of more than one male and more than one female mate with one another. (p. 104) For contrast, see *monogamy, polygyny, polyandry.*

polygyny A mating system in which one male bonds with more than one female. For contrast, see *monogamy, polyandry, polygynandry.* (p. 104)

pons The portion of the brainstem bounded at its lower end by the medulla and its upper end by the midbrain, which is responsible, with the medulla, for organizing reflexes more complex than spinal reflexes. (pp. 170–171)

Ponzo illusion A visual size illusion in which two converging lines cause objects between the two lines to look larger near the converging ends of the lines and smaller near the diverging ends. (p. 314)

positive contrast effect In operant conditioning, the increase in response rate, when the size of the reinforcer (or reward) is increased, to a rate that increases above that which occurs for subjects that had been receiving the larger reinforcer all along. For contrast, see *negative contrast effect.* (p. 147)

positive interdependence A condition that engenders cooperation because the structure of rewards is such that each individual (or group) can best obtain a reward through actions that simultaneously help another individual (or group) obtain a reward. For contrast, see *negative interdependence.* (p. 553)

positive reinforcement In operant conditioning, the condition in which a response results in a positive reinforcer. (pp. 139–140)

positive reinforcer In operant conditioning, a stimulus (such as food or money) that is presented after a response and that increases the likelihood that the response will recur. (p. 140)

post-hypnotic amnesia The inability, after awakening from hypnosis, to remember specific items of information that were presented during hypnosis; it occurs in response to the hypnotist's suggestion during hypnosis that the information will not be remembered. (p. 358)

post-traumatic stress disorder A mental disorder that is directly and explicitly tied to a particular traumatic incident or set of incidents (such as torture) that the affected person has experienced. (p. 621)

power law In psychophysics, Stevens's idea that the intensity of a sensation is directly proportional to the intensity of the physical stimulus raised by a constant power. For contrast, see *Fechner's law.* (p. 279)

precipitating causes of a mental disorder The events that most immediately bring on a mental disorder in a person who is sufficiently predisposed for the disorder. See also *maintaining* and *predisposing causes of a mental disorder.* (p. 609)

predisposing causes of a mental disorder Those conditions that are in place well before the onset of a mental disorder and that make the person susceptible to the disorder. They may include genetic predisposition, early childhood experiences, and the sociocultural environment in which one develops. See also *maintaining* and *precipitating causes of a mental disorder.* (p. 609)

preoperational stage In Piaget's theory of cognitive development, the second stage (from about 2 to 6 years of age), in which the child can appreciate the stable, identifying features of objects and think about them when they are absent, but lacks the ability to think logically about reversible actions (operations) that can be performed on objects. See also *operations.* (p. 433)

primacy effect In list-learning experiments, the greater ability to recall items from the beginning of the list (those that were rehearsed first) than other items in the list. See also *recency effect.* (p. 334) In person perception, the tendency for information received early to carry more weight than information received later in one's final assessment of a person. (p. 495)

primary motor area An area in the rear part of the frontal lobe of the cerebral cortex that is directly involved in the control of movements, especially finely coordinated movements of small muscles, as in the fingers and vocal apparatus. (p. 174)

primary process In Freud's psychoanalytic theory, the kind of thinking that characterizes the id, in which reality and fantasy are not differentiated and the goal is to seek pleasure through the most direct routes. For contrast, see *secondary process.* (p. 569)

primary reinforcer In operant conditioning, a stimulus, such as food or water, that is innately reinforcing; also called an *unconditioned reinforcer.* See *reinforcer.* For contrast, see *secondary reinforcer.* (p. 139)

primary sensory areas Specialized areas of the cerebral cortex that receive input from sensory nerves and tracts by way of the relay nuclei in the thalamus. They include the visual area (in the occipital lobe), auditory area (in the temporal lobe), and somatosensory area (in the parietal lobe). (p. 174)

priming The implicit memory process by which a stimulus (the priming stimulus) activates (makes more retrievable) one or more that already exist in a person' s mind. See *conceptual priming, implicit memory, perceptual priming.* (p. 361)

prisoner's-dilemma games A class of laboratory game in which the tendency to compete can be pitted against the tendency to cooperate. In such games, the highest combined payoff to the two players occurs if both choose the cooperative response, but the highest individual payoff goes to a player who chooses the competitive response on a play in which the other chooses the cooperative response. (p. 554)

proactive interference The loss of memory for one set of information that results from the prior learning of another (usually similar) set of information. For contrast, see *retroactive interference.* (p. 351)

procedural memory The class of implicit memory that enables a person to perform specific learned skills or habitual responses. See *implicit memory.* (p. 360)

projection The defense mechanism by which a person consciously experiences his or her own unconscious emotion or wish as though it belongs to someone else or to some part of the environment. (p. 572)

projective tests Psychological tests involving free association, in which the person being tested is presented with an ambiguous stimulus and is asked to say quickly, without logical explanation, what the stimulus looks like or what ideas it brings to mind. See also *free association, projection.* (p. 654)

propositional theory of visual memory The theory that memories for visual scenes are stored in essentially the same way as verbal memories are stored, as sets of discrete units of information (propositions). For contrast, see *analogue theory of visual memory.* (p. 344)

prototype theory of schemas The theory that a schema (the mental representation of a concept) is best characterized as a holistic, picturelike representation of a typical or average member of the category of object or event that the schema represents. For contrast, see *feature theory of schemas.* (p. 346)

proximate explanations Explanations of behavior that state the immediate environmental conditions or the mechanisms within the individual that cause the behavior to occur. For contrast, see *ultimate explanations.* (p. 86)

proximity principle See *Gestalt principles of grouping.*

psychoactive substance-use disorder The class of mental disorders characterized by drug abuse or dependence. (p. 632)

psychoanalysis 1. The theory of personality developed by Freud that emphasizes the roles of unconscious mental processes, early childhood experiences, and the drives of sex and aggression in personality formation; also called *psychoanalytic theory.* (pp. 16, 566) 2. Freud's therapy technique in which such methods as free association, dream analysis, and analysis of transference are used to learn about the person's unconscious mind; the goal is to make the unconscious conscious. (p. 656)

psychodynamic theories of personality Any theory that describes personality and its development in terms of inner mental forces that are often in conflict with one another and are shaped by experiences in early childhood. (p. 566)

psychodynamic therapy Any approach to psychotherapy that is based on the premise that psychological problems are manifestations of inner mental conflicts and that conscious awareness of those conflicts is a key to recovery. See also *psychoanalysis.* (p. 656)

psychology The science of behavior and the mind. (p. 3)

psychometric personality test An objective questionnaire that has been developed through systematic, statistically based methods (usually involving factor analysis) to assess a wide range of personality characteristics. See *MMPI.* (p. 653)

psychometrics The systematic measurement of psychological differences among people and the statistical analysis of those differences as a way of learning about the structure of the human mind. (p. 370)

psychophysics The scientific study of the relationship between physical characteristics of stimuli and the psychological (sensory) experiences that the stimuli produce. (p. 243)

psychosexual stages In Freud's psychoanalytic theory, the life stages—oral, anal, phallic, latency, and genital—through which personality is formed and expressed; in each stage, sexual energy centers around a different purpose. (p. 572)

psychotherapy Any formal, theory-based, systematic treatment for mental problems or disorders that uses psychological means (such as dialogue or training) rather than physiological means (such as drugs) and is conducted by a trained therapist. (p. 656)

punishment In operant conditioning, the process through which the consequence of a response *decreases* the likelihood that the response will recur. For contrast, see *reinforcement.* (p. 142)

pupil The hole in the center of the iris of the eye through which light passes. See *iris.* (p. 254)

---

questionnaire A self-report method of data collection or clinical assessment method in which the individual being studied (or assessed) checks off items on a printed list, answers multiple-choice questions, or writes out answers to essay questions aimed at producing a self-description. (p. 33)

---

rational-emotive therapy A type of cognitive therapy developed by Albert Ellis, based on the idea that people's irrational interpretations of their experiences, not the experiences themselves, cause their negative emotions. (p. 665)

rationalization The defense mechanism by which a person uses conscious reasoning to justify or explain away his or her harmful or irrational behaviors or thoughts. (p. 572)

reaction formation The defense mechanism by which the mind turns a frightening wish into its safer opposite. (p. 572)

recency effect In list-learning experiments, the greater ability to recall items from the end of the list (those most recently rehearsed) than other items in the list. See also *primacy effect.* (p. 334)

recall test Test in which the person must generate the answer from memory rather than select it from a set of choices. For contrast, see *recognition test.* (p. 353)

receptive field For any neuron in the visual system, that portion of the retina that, when stimulated by light, results in a change in electrical activity in the neuron. More generally, a property of a neuron in any sensory system; it is the area of sensory tissue (or set of receptor cells) that, when stimulated by an appropriate stimulus, produces an electrical change in the neuron in question. (p. 257)

receptor potential The electrical change that occurs in a receptor cell (such as a rod or cone in the eye, or a hair cell in the inner ear) in response to the energy of a physical stimulus (such as light or sound). (p. 245)

receptors Specialized biological structures—which in some cases are separate cells and in other cases are the sensitive tips of sensory neurons—that respond to physical stimuli by producing electrical changes that can initiate neural impulses. (p. 244)

recessive gene A gene that will produce its observable effects only in the homozygous condition, that is, only when paired with a gene that is identical to it. (p. 54)

reciprocity norm The widespread sense of obligation that people have to return favors. (p. 536)

reciprocity theory of altruism The sociobiological theory that apparent acts of altruism have come about through natural selection because they are actually forms of long-term cooperation rather than true altruism. See also *altruism, cooperation.* (p. 112)

recognition test Test in which the person must use memory to decide which of several designated choices is the correct answer. For contrast, see *recall test.* (p. 353)

red-green color blindness Color blindness that is characterized by difficulty in distinguishing among the colors of the spectrum ranging from green through red; it is caused by the lack of one of the two cone types that are maximally sensitive to light in the long-wavelength end of the spectrum. (p. 262)

reference group A group of people with whom an individual compares himself or herself for the purpose of self-evaluation. See also *social comparison.* (p. 508)

reflex A simple, relatively automatic, stimulus-response sequence mediated by the nervous system. See *response, stimulus.* (p. 6)

reflexology An approach to understanding human behavior, developed by physiologists in the nineteenth century, that was based on the premise that all behavior occurs through reflexes. (p. 6)

regulatory drive Any motivational state (such as hunger or thirst) that helps maintain some constancy of the body's internal environment that is necessary for survival. For contrast, see *nonregulatory drive.* (p. 204)

reinforcement In operant conditioning, the presentation of a positive reinforcer or removal of a negative reinforcer when a response occurs, which increases the likelihood that the subject will repeat the response. See *negative reinforcer, positive reinforcer.* For contrast, see *punishment.* (p. 139)

reinforcer In operant conditioning, any stimulus change that occurs after a response and tends to *increase* the likelihood that the response will be repeated. See *negative reinforcer, positive reinforcer.* (p. 133)

reliability The capacity of a measurement system to produce similar results each time it is used with a particular subject or set of subjects under a particular set of conditions. (p. 39)

REM (rapid eye movement) sleep The recurring stage of sleep during which the EEG resembles that of an alert person, rapid eye movements occur, the large muscles of the body are most relaxed, and true dreams are most likely to occur. It is sometimes called *emergent stage 1.* For contrast, see *slow-wave sleep.* (pp. 222–223)

repression The defense mechanism by which the mind prevents anxiety-provoking ideas from becoming conscious. (p. 571)

research hypothesis The guess, or inference, that a researcher attempts to test in a scientific study. (p. 37)

resistance In psychotherapy, the client's conscious or unconscious attempts to block the course of therapy. Psychodynamic therapists interpret it as a defense against the anxiety that accompanies the discovery of previously unconscious memories or wishes in the course of therapy. (p. 658)

resting potential The constant electrical charge that exists across the membrane of an inactive neuron. (p. 184)

retina A thin membrane of cells that lines the rear interior of the eyeball; it contains the receptor cells for vision (rods and cones). (p. 254)

retrieval In the modal model of the mind, the mental process by which long-term memories are brought into the short-term (working) memory store where they become part of the flow of thought. See also *long-term memory, short-term memory.* (p. 333)

retrieval cue A word, phrase, or other stimulus that helps one retrieve a specific item of information from long-term memory. (p. 353)

retroactive interference The loss of memory for one set of information that results from the subsequent learning of another (usually similar) set of information. For contrast, see *proactive interference.* (p. 351)

reversible figure A visual stimulus (usually a picture) in which any given part is seen sometimes as the *figure* and other times as the *ground.* (p. 291)

rhodopsin The photochemical in rods that undergoes structural changes in response to light and thereby initiates the transduction process for rod vision. (p. 254)

ritualization An evolutionary process by which behaviors that originally served some noncommunicative function are modified so that they serve primarily a communicative role. (p. 97)

rods The class of receptor cells for vision that are located in the peripheral portions of the retina (away from the fovea) and are most important for seeing in very dim light. For contrast, see *cones.* (p. 254)

rod vision The low-acuity, high-sensitivity, noncolor vision that occurs in dim light and is mediated by rods in the retina of the eye. For contrast, see *cone vision.* (p. 255)

---

schema The mental representation of a concept; the information stored in long-term memory that allows a person to identify a group of different events or items as members of the same category. (p. 346)

schemes Piaget's term for the mental entities that provide the basis for thought and that change in a stagelike way through development. They contain information about the actions that one can produce on objects, either in reality or symbolically in the mind. (pp. 21, 433)

schizophrenia A serious class of mental disorder that is characterized by disrupted perceptual and thought processes, often including hallucinations and delusions. (pp. 73, 637)

science An approach to answering questions that is based on the systematic collection and logical analysis of objectively observable data. (p. 3)

script A variety of schema that represents in memory the temporal organization of a category of event (such as the sequence of occurrences at a typical birthday party). (p. 347)

seasonal affective disorder (SAD) A mood disorder characterized by severe depression in the fall and winter, apparently caused by reduced daylight. (p. 626)

secondary process In Freud's psychoanalytic theory, the kind of thinking that characterizes the ego, which involves the person's logical thought and understanding of reality. For contrast, see *primary process.* (p. 569)

secondary reinforcer In operant conditioning, a stimulus that has acquired reinforcing capacity through previous training, usually through serving as a discriminative stimulus for some other reinforced response. See *reinforcer.* For contrast, see *primary reinforcer.* (p. 139)

secondary sensory areas Specialized areas of the cerebral cortex, each of which receives input from a single primary sensory area and presumably contains neural mechanisms that analyze that input and help extract useful information from it. See also *primary sensory areas.* (p. 174)

selective breeding The mating of those members of a strain of animals or plants that manifest a particular characteristic, which may or may not be done deliberately to affect the genetic makeup of future generations of that strain; can be used to assess *heritability.* (p. 65)

self-actualization In humanistic psychology, the fulfillment of drives that go beyond one's survival needs and pertain to psychological growth, creativity, and self-expression. (pp. 581, 583–584)

self-effacing bias The tendency, more common in non-Western than in Western cultures, for people to underrate their own abilities in comparison to the abilities of others. For contrast, see *self-enhancing bias.* (p. 510)

self-efficacy A person's subjective sense of his or her own ability to perform a particular task or set of tasks. (p. 589)

self-enhancing bias The tendency for people to overrate their own abilities in comparison to those of others, and to attribute their own successes to their inner qualities and their failures to external circumstances beyond their control. For contrast, see *self-effacing bias.* (p. 509)

self-handicapping An impression-management strategy in which a person gives himself or herself an obvious handicap in a task in order to provide an excuse for anticipated poor performance. (p. 512)

self-monitoring A personality characteristic defined as sensitivity to other people's immediate reactions to oneself, combined with a desire and ability to control those reactions. (p. 512)

self-report method A data-collection method in which the people being studied are asked to rate or describe their own behaviors or mental states. See also *interview, questionnaire.* (p. 33)

semantic memory One's storehouse of explicit general knowledge, that is, of knowledge that can be expressed in words and is not mentally tied to specific experiences in one's own life. Semantic memory includes, but is not limited to, one's knowledge of word meanings. For contrasts, see *episodic memory, implicit memory.* (pp. 359–360)

sensation The psychological experience associated with a sound, light, or other simple stimulus, and the initial information-processing steps by which sense organs and neural pathways take in stimulus information from the environment. For contrast, see *perception.* (p. 241)

sensitivity The capacity of a measurement system to detect fine differences among individuals in the characteristic being measured. (p. 39)

sensorimotor stage In Piaget's theory of cognitive development, the first stage (birth to about 2 years old), in which the child lacks well-developed mental symbols, so thought is limited primarily to the child's actual actions on objects and the sensory feedback that comes from those actions. (pp. 420, 433)

sensorineural deafness Deafness due to damage to the cochlea, the hair cells, or the auditory neurons. (p. 249)

sensory adaptation The temporary decrease in sensitivity to sensory stimulation that occurs when a sensory system is stimulated for a period of time, and the temporary increase in sensitivity that occurs when a sensory system is not stimulated for a period of time. See also *dark adaptation, light adaptation.* (p. 245)

sensory areas of the cerebral cortex See *primary sensory areas, secondary sensory areas.*

sensory memory In the modal model of the mind, the memory trace that preserves the original information in a sensory stimulus for a brief period (less than 1 second for sights and up to 3 seconds for sounds) following the termination of the stimulus; it is experienced as if one is still sensing the original stimulus. For contrasts, see *long-term memory, short-term memory.* (p. 328)

sensory neuron A neuron that carries messages from a sensory organ, through a nerve, into the brain or spinal cord. (pp. 164, 244)

sensory physiological psychology The scientific study of the relationship between physiological responses in sensory organs and the nervous system and the psychological (sensory) experiences that accompany those responses. (p. 243)

sensory physiology The scientific study of the relationship between environmental stimuli and the physiological responses they produce in sensory organs and the nervous system. (p. 243)

sensory store The first memory store in the modal model of the mind; the hypothetical place in the mind where information is retained in its original sensory form for a very brief period; also called the *preattentive store.* (p. 328)

serial processing The steps in the processing of sensory information that operate sequentially, an item at a time, on the available sensory information. For contrast, see *parallel processing.* (p. 294)

set point The body weight that is most easily maintained by an individual person or animal. (p. 209)

sex chromosomes Those chromosomes that provide the genetic basis for the difference between males and females for the species. See also *X chromosome, Y chromosome.* For contrast, see *autosomes.* (p. 51)

sex-linked trait Any phenotypic trait whose development depends upon a recessive gene located on the X chromosome; they are more likely to occur in men than in women. (p. 59)

shape constancy The tendency to perceive an object as having the same shape even though the retinal image changes shape when the object is viewed from different positions. (p. 230)

shaping An operant-conditioning procedure in which successively closer approximations to the desired response are reinforced until the response finally occurs. See *reinforcement.* (p. 135)

short-term memory In the modal model of the mind, information that is retained in the mind as long as conscious thought is devoted to it, but which then fades relatively quickly (in a matter of seconds); also called *working memory.* For contrast, see *sensory memory, long-term memory.* (p. 330)

short-term store The second memory stored in the modal model of the mind; the hypothetical place in the mind that retains information to which conscious attention is being devoted. (p. 330)

sign stimulus Ethologists' term for any stimulus (well-defined environmental event) that elicits a fixed action pattern. See *fixed action pattern.* (p. 89)

similarity principle See *Gestalt principles of grouping.*

simple phobia Any phobia in which the feared object is a well-defined category of object (such as snakes) or environmental situation (such as heights) *other than* other people. See also *phobia.* For contrast, see *social phobia.* (p. 618)

size constancy The perceptual ability to see an object as the same size despite change in image size as it moves farther away or closer. (pp. 12, 320)

skeletal motor system The set of motor neurons that act upon skeletal muscles. (p. 167)

skeletal muscles The muscles attached to bones, which produce externally observable movements of the body when contracted. For contrast, see *visceral muscles.* (p. 167)

sleep thought A mental experience during sleep that lacks the vivid sensory and motor hallucinations of a *true dream* and is typically experienced as similar to daytime thought. (p. 227)

slow-wave sleep Stages 2, 3, and 4 of sleep characterized by the prominent occurrence of slow (delta) waves in the EEG. For contrast, see *REM (rapid eye movement) sleep.* (p. 223)

social clock A culture's set of expectations concerning the appropriate activities of people at various ages or life stages, which in turn affect the life course of people within that culture. (p. 452)

social cognition The mental processes that are involved in people's perceptions of, and reactions to, other people and the social environment; also the study of those mental processes. (p. 493)

social comparison Any process in which an individual evaluates his or her own abilities, characteristics, ideas, or achievements by comparing them with those of other people. See also *reference group.* (p. 508)

social development The person's developing capacity for social relationships and the effects of those relationships on further development. (p. 449)

social dilemma A situation in which a particular action will (a) benefit the individual who takes it; (b) harm the individuals who don't; and (c) cause more harm than benefit to everyone if everyone takes it. See *prisoner's dilemma games.* (p. 554)

social facilitation The tendency to perform a task better in front of others than alone. For contrast, see *social interference.* (p. 543)

social forces The demands, requests, expectations, judgments, and other psychological pressures, real or imagined, that people perceive to be directed toward them from other people. (p. 531)

social impact theory Latané's social psychological theory concerning the amount of social impact that the actual or imagined presence of others will have on a person. (p. 532)

social interference The tendency to perform a task worse in front of others than alone. For contrast, see *social facilitation.* (p. 543)

social phobia Any phobia in which the basic fear is of being scrutinized or evaluated by other people. For contrast, see *simple phobia.* (p. 618)

social psychology The branch of psychology that attempts to understand how the behavior and subjective experiences of individuals are influenced by the actual or imagined presence of other people. (pp. 19, 493)

social referencing The process by which infants use the nonverbal emotional expressions of a caregiver as cues to guide their behavior. (p. 455)

social skills training In behavior therapy, a direct method for training people to interact more effectively with other people. See also *assertiveness training.* (p. 673)

sociobiology The study of social systems in animals from an evolutionary perspective. (p. 104)

sociocultural perspective The general approach to psychological research and theory that emphasizes the role of culture and social interactions in the development and manifestation of behavioral or psychological characteristics. (pp. 442, 607)

somatoform disorders The class of mental disorders in which the person experiences bodily ailments in the absence of any physical disease that could cause them. It includes *conversion disorder, somatoform pain disorder,* and *somatization disorder.* (p. 627)

somatosensation The set of senses that derive from the whole body, such as from the skin, muscles, and tendons, as opposed to those senses that come from the special sensory organs of the head. (p. 167)

source traits In trait theories of personality, the relatively small set of basic traits (personality characteristics) that are inferred from statistical intercorrelations among various surface traits. See also *surface traits, trait.* (p. 592)

span of short-term memory The number of items of information (such as single, randomly chosen digits) that a person can retain in short-term memory at any given time through rote rehearsal; also called *memory span.* (p. 331)

spatial frequency The number of repetitions, per unit distance, of the repeating elements of the image of a pattern on the retina of the eye. (p. 267)

species-specific behavior Any behavior pattern that is so characteristic of a given species of animal that it can be used to help identify that species. (p. 89)

spinal nerve A nerve that extends directly from the spinal cord. See *nerve.* For contrast, see *cranial nerve.* (p. 167)

spinal reflex A reflex that is organized by neurons within the spinal cord, and that therefore can be elicited even if the spinal cord is no longer connected to the brain. (p. 170)

spontaneous recovery In both classical and operant conditioning, the return—due to passage of time with no further testing or training—of a conditioned response that had previously undergone extinction. (pp. 126–127)

spoonerisms Speech errors in which two elements of a sentence (phonemes, syllables, or morphemes) are accidentally interchanged in position. (p. 400)

stage theories of development In developmental psychology, theories that maintain that psychological development is discontinuous, with plateaus (periods of relative stability) separated by periods of rapid change. For contrast, see *continuous theories of development.* (p. 415)

standard deviation A measure of the variability in a set of scores, determined by taking the square root of the variance. (pp. 33, A-5)

standardized score A score that is expressed in terms of the number of standard deviations the original score is from the mean of the original scores. (p. A-6)

state-dependent memory The improved ability to retrieve information from memory that occurs when a person is in the same physiological condition (such as that induced by a drug) that he or she was in when the memory was originally encoded. (p. 354)

statistical significance A statistical statement of how small the likelihood is that an obtained result occurred by chance. By convention, research findings are said to be *statistically significant* if the probability is less than 5 percent that the data could have come out as they did if the research hypothesis were wrong. (p. 37)

stereotypes Mental concepts that people have for particular groups of people (such as races or ethnic groups) that exaggerate the differences between groups, minimize the differences among individual members of the same group, and may provide a basis for prejudice and discrimination. (p. 500)

strange-situation test A test of an infant's attachment to a particular familiar person, in which the infant's behavior is observed in an unfamiliar room while the familiar person and a stranger move in and out of the room in a preplanned way. (p. 456)

stress-induced analgesia The reduced sensitivity to pain that occurs when one is subjected to highly arousing (stressful) conditions. (p. 272)

Stroop interference effect Named after J. Ridley Stroop, the effect by which a printed color word (such as the word *red*) interferes with a person's ability to name the color of ink in which the word is printed, if the ink color is not the color named by the word. (p. 305)

structuralism A school of psychological thought, founded principally by Titchener, whose goal was to identify the basic elements of the mind and to determine how those elements combine with one another to produce more complex thoughts. For contrast, see *functionalism.* (p. 9)

subject-expectancy effect Any bias in research results that derives from subjects' expectations or beliefs about how they should feel or behave in response to the variables imposed in the study. See also *bias, observer-expectancy effect, placebo effect.* (p. 41)

sublimation See *displacement.*

subtractive color mixing The mixing of pigments whereby each pigment absorbs a different set of wavelengths of light that would otherwise be reflected to the eye. For contrast, see *additive color mixing.* (p. 259)

superego In Freud's three-part division of the mind, the source of morality and guilt. See also *ego, id.* (p. 570)

surface structure In Chomsky's theory of language, the specific wording of an uttered or written sentence. For contrast, see *deep structure.* (p. 399)

surface traits Traits (personality characteristics) that are most directly inferred from a person's external behavior. See also *source traits.* (p. 592)

syllogism A type of deductive-reasoning problem that contains a major and a minor premise, from which the reasoner must test the truth, falsity, or indeterminacy of a specific conclusion. (p. 390)

sympathetic division of the autonomic motor system The set of motor neurons that act upon visceral muscles and glands and mediate many of the body's responses to stressful stimulation, preparing the body for possible "fight or flight." For contrast, see *parasympathetic division of the autonomic motor system.* (p. 167)

symptom In clinical psychology or psychiatry, any characteristic of a person's actions, thoughts, or feelings that could be a potential indicator of a mental disorder. (p. 605)

synapse The functional connection through which neural activity in the axon of one neuron influences the action of another neuron, a muscle cell, or a glandular cell, and the structures most directly associated with that connection. (pp. 165–166)

syndrome In clinical psychology or psychiatry, the entire pattern of symptoms manifested in an individual's behavior and self-statements, which, collectively, may constitute evidence of a mental disorder. (p. 605)

syntax The set of grammatical rules for a given language that specifies how words can be arranged to produce phrases and sentences. (p. 398)

systematic desensitization A behavior therapy technique for eliminating phobias or fears, in which the client is first trained to relax and then to imagine various versions of the feared object or scene, progressing from weak to stronger forms of it, while remaining relaxed. (p. 671)

---

temporal lobe The lobe of the cerebral cortex that lies in front of the occipital lobe and below the parietal and frontal lobes, which contains the auditory area of the brain. (p. 174)

temporal lobe amnesia The loss in memory abilities that occurs as a result of damage to structures in the limbic system that lie under the temporal lobe of the cerebral cortex. (p. 363)

test A stimulus or problem, or set of these, that a researcher or clinician presents to a subject or client for the purpose of collecting information about that individual's behavioral or psychological state or capacities. (p. 33)

thalamus The brain structure that sits directly atop the brainstem; it functions as a sensory relay station, connecting incoming sensory tracts to special sensory areas of the cerebral cortex. (p. 171)

theory of planned behavior The theory that a person's behavioral intention, and hence behavior, is influenced by (a) the person's own attitude toward the behavior, (b) the person's belief about other's attitudes toward the behavior, and (c) the person's sense of his or her own ability to carry out the behavior. (p. 524)

three-primaries law The observation that one can choose three limited-wavelength lights (called *primaries*) and, by mixing them in differing proportions, match any color that the human eye can see. See also *additive color mixing.* (p. 260)

token In operant conditioning, a secondary reinforcer (such as money) that can be saved and turned in later for another reinforcer. See *secondary reinforcer.* (p. 139)

token economy An exchange system, adapted for use in a mental hospital or other institution, in which tokens are awarded for behaving in specific ways deemed desirable and the tokens can in turn be exchanged for goods or privileges. (p. 673)

tolerance See *drug tolerance.*

top-down processes In theories of perception, mental processes that bring preexisting knowledge or expectations about an object or scene to bear upon the perception of that object or scene. For contrast, see *bottom-up processes.* (p. 288)

tract A bundle of neural axons coursing together within the central nervous system; analogous to a *nerve* in the peripheral nervous system. (p. 169)

trait A hypothetical, relatively stable, inner characteristic that influences the way a person responds to various environmental situations. (p. 592)

trait theories of personality Theories of personality that are based on the idea that people can be described and differentiated in terms of hypothetical underlying personality dimensions, called *traits,* which can be measured by questionnaires or other quantitative means. (p. 592)

transduction The process by which a receptor cell (such as a rod or cone in the eye, or a hair cell in the inner ear) produces an electrical change in response to the energy of a physical stimulus (such as light or sound). (p. 244)

transference In psychotherapy (especially psychoanalysis), the phenomenon by which a patient's unconscious feelings about a significant person in his or her life are experienced consciously as feelings about the therapist. (p. 659)

transmitter See *neurotransmitter.*

trichromatic theory of color vision Proposed independently by Young and Helmholtz to explain the three-primaries law of color vision, this theory holds that the human ability to perceive color is mediated by three different types of receptors, each of which is most sensitive to a different range of wavelengths. See also *three-primaries law.* (p. 261)

true dream A mental experience during sleep in which the person has the feeling of actually seeing or in other ways sensing various scenes and objects, and of actually moving and behaving in the dream environment. For contrast, see *sleep thought.* (p. 227)

twin method A method for studying the heritability of a characteristic, in which the similarity between identical twins is compared with that between fraternal twins. See *heritability.* (p. 68)

---

ultimate explanations Explanations of behavior that state the role that the behavior plays or once played in survival and reproduction, that is, explanations of why the potential for the behavior was favored by natural selection. For contrast, see *proximate explanations.* (p. 86)

unconditioned reflex A reflex that does not depend upon previous conditions in the individual's experience; an unlearned reflex. For contrast, see *conditioned reflex.* (p. 124)

unconditioned response A reflexive response that does not depend upon previous conditioning, or learning. For contrast, see *conditioned response.* (p. 124)

unconditioned stimulus A stimulus that elicits a reflexive response without any previous training, or conditioning. For contrast, see *conditioned stimulus.* (p. 124)

unconscious-inference theory of perception The theory that perception is the end result of unconscious reasoning processes in which the mind uses sensory information as cues to infer the characteristics of objects or scenes that are being perceived. For contrast, see *direct-perception theory.* (p. 309)

unresponsive-bystander phenomenon The tendency for bystanders not to help the victim of an emergency if other bystanders are present. (p. 544)

---

validity The degree to which a measurement system actually measures the characteristic that it is supposed to measure. (p. 39)

variable-interval (VI) schedule In operant conditioning, a schedule of reinforcement in which an unpredictable amount of time, varying around some average, must elapse between the receipt of one reinforcer and the availability of another. (p. 137)

variable-ratio (VR) schedule In operant conditioning, a schedule of reinforcement in which the response must be emitted a certain *average* number of times before a reinforcer will appear, but the number needed on any given instance varies randomly around that average. (p. 136)

variance A measure of the variability of a set of scores, determined by obtaining the difference (deviation) between each score and the mean, squaring each deviation, and calculating the mean of the squared deviations. (p. A-4)

vestigial characteristics Inherited characteristics of anatomy or behavior that are no longer useful to the species, but were presumably useful at an earlier time in evolution. (p. 96)

visceral muscles Internal muscles, such as those of the heart, arteries, and gastrointestinal tract. For contrast, see *skeletal muscles.* (p. 167)

visual constancies Those characteristics of objects or scenes that remain constant in our visual perception of them despite changes in the retinal image. They include size constancy, shape constancy, and position constancy. (p. 320)

---

wavelength The physical length of one complete cycle of a wave; for light, this physical measure is related to the psychological (sensory) experience of color. (p. 253)

Weber fraction In Weber's law, the proportionality constant that relates the difference threshold to the magnitude of the original stimulus. (p. 277)

Weber's law The idea that, within a given sensory modality (such as vision), the difference threshold (amount that the stimulus must be changed in magnitude to be perceived as different) is a constant proportion of the magnitude of the original stimulus. (p. 277)

Wernicke's aphasia A specific syndrome of loss of language ability that occurs due to damage in a particular part of the brain called *Wernicke's area.* Speech in a person with this disorder typically retains its grammatical structure, but loses its meaning due to the speaker's failure to provide meaningful content words (nouns, verbs, adjectives, and adverbs). For contrast, see *Broca's aphasia.* (p. 402)

Westermarck effect The tendency of people to feel an aversion toward sexual involvement with anyone with whom they had prolonged, intimate contact in early childhood. Sociobiologists suggest that this effect is an evolved adaptation that serves the function of incest avoidance. (p. 117)

withdrawal symptoms The physiological, mental, and behavioral disturbances that can occur when a long-term user of a drug stops taking the drug. (pp. 196, 633)

working memory See *short-term memory.*

X chromosome The human sex chromosome that normally exists in duplicate in the female and in single (unpaired) fashion in the male. See also *sex chromosomes.* (p. 51)

Y chromosome The human sex chromosome that normally exists in single (unpaired) fashion in the male and is absent in the female. See also *sex chromosomes.* (p. 51)

Yerkes-Dodson law The idea that the optimal degree of arousal for performing a task depends on the nature of the task. High arousal is best for easy tasks and low arousal is best for difficult tasks. (p. 230)

---

z score The simplest form of a standardized score; it is the score minus the mean divided by the standard deviation. (p. A-6)

zoological psychology Term proposed to replace *comparative psychology* as a descriptive label for all psychological research on nonhuman animals. See *comparative psychology.* (p. 12)

zygote The single cell that is formed when an egg and sperm cell unite; the first, single-cell form of a newly developing individual. (p. 53)

REFERENCES

Abbey, S. E., & Garfinkel, P. E. (1991). Neurasthenia and chronic fatigue syndrome: The role of culture in the making of a diagnosis. *American Journal of Psychiatry, 148*, 1638–1646. (p. 629)

Abram, K. M., & Teplin, L. A. (1991). Co-occurring disorders among mentally ill jail detainees. *American Psychologist, 46*, 1036–1045. (p. 648)

Abramson, L. Y., Matelsky, G. I., & Alloy, L. B. (1989). Hopelessness depression: A theory-based subtype of depression. *Psychological Review, 96*, 358–372. (p. 624)

Adams, D. B., Gold, A. R., & Burt, A. D. (1978). Rise in female-initiated sexual activity at ovulation and its suppression by oral contraceptives. *The New England Journal of Medicine, 299*, 1145–1150. (p. 217)

Adamson, R. E. (1952). Functional fixedness as related to problem solving. *Journal of Experimental Psychology, 44*, 288–291. (p. 393)

Adelson, J. (1986). *Inventing adolescence: The political psychology of everyday schooling.* New Brunswick, NJ: Transaction. (p. 472)

Adelson, J., & Hall, E. (1987). Children and other political naïfs. In E. Hall (Ed.), *Growing and changing.* New York: Random House. (p. 483)

Ader, R., & Cohen, N. (1993). Psychoneuroimmunology: Conditioning and stress. *Annual Review of Psychology, 44*, 53–85. (p. 631)

Adkins-Regan, E. (1981). Early organizational effects of hormones: An evolutionary perspective. In N. T. Adler (Ed.), *Neuroendocrinology of reproduction.* New York: Plenum. (p. 214)

Adler, A. (1930). Individual psychology. In C. Murchison (Ed.), *Psychologies of 1930.* Worcester, MA: Clark University Press. (p. 576)

Agras, S., Sylvester, D., & Oliveau, D. (1969). The epidemiology of common fears and phobias. *Comprehensive Psychiatry, 10*, 151–156. (p. 619)

Aiken, L. R. (1991). *Psychological testing and assessment*, 7th edition. Boston: Allyn & Bacon. (pp. 372, 373)

Ainsworth, M. D. S. (1979). Attachment as related to mother-infant interaction. *Advances in the Study of Behaviour, 9*, 2–52. (p. 457)

Ainsworth, M. D. S. (1982). Attachment: Retrospect and prospect. In C. M. Parkes & J. Sevenson-Hinde (Eds.), *The place of attachment in human behavior.* New York: Basic Books. (p. 457)

Ainsworth, M. D. S. (1989). Attachments beyond infancy. *American Psychologist, 44*, 709–716. (p. 458)

Ainsworth, M. D. S., Blehar, M. C., Waters, E., & Wall, S. (1978). *Patterns of attachment: A psychological study of the strange situation.* Hillsdale, NJ: Erlbaum. (p. 456)

Ajzen, I. (1985). From intentions to actions: A theory of planned behavior. In J. Kuhl & J. Beckmann (Eds.), *Action control: From cognition to behavior.* Heidelberg: Springer. (p. 524)

Ajzen, I. (1987). Attitudes, traits, and actions: Dispositional prediction of behavior in personality and social psychology. In L. Berkowitz (Ed.), *Advances in experimental social psychology* (Vol. 20). New York: Academic Press. (p. 524)

Ajzen, I. (1991). The theory of planned behavior. *Organizational Behavior and Human Decision Processes, 50*, 179–211. (p. 524)

Ajzen, I., & Fishbein, M. (1980). *Understanding attitudes and predicting social behavior.* Englewood Cliffs, NJ: Prentice Hall. (p. 526)

Akerstedt, T., & Fröberg, J. E. (1977). Psychophysiological circadian rhythms in women during 72 hours of sleep deprivation. *Waking and Sleeping, 1*, 387–394. (p. 226)

Alexander, R. D. (1987). *The biology of moral systems.* New York: Aldine de Gruyter. (p. 114)

Allison, T., & Cicchetti, D. V. (1976). Sleep in mammals: Ecological and constitutional correlates. *Science, 194*, 732–734. (p. 223)

Allport, D. A., Antonis, B., & Reynolds, P. (1972). On the division of attention: A disproof of the single channel hypothesis. *Quarterly Journal of Experimental Psychology, 24*, 225–235. (p. 303)

Allport, F. H. (1920). The influence of the group upon association and thought. *Journal of Experimental Psychology, 3*, 159–182. (p. 543)

Allport, G. W. (1935). Attitudes. In C. Murchison (Ed.), *Handbook of social psychology.* Worcester, MA: Clark University Press. (p. 522)

Allport, G. W. (1968). The historical background of modern social psychology. In G. Lindzey & E. Aronson (Eds.), *The handbook of social psychology* (2nd ed., Vol 1). Reading, MA: Addison-Wesley. (pp. 19, 493)

Ambelas, A. (1987). Life events and mania: A special relationship? *British Journal of Psychiatry, 150*, 235–240. (p. 626)

American Psychiatric Association (1987). *Diagnostic and statistical manual of mental disorders (third edition, revised).* New York: Author. (pp. 605, 616)

American Psychiatric Association (1993): *DSM-IV draft criteria.* Washington, D. C.: American Psychiatric Association Press. (pp. 605, 616)

American Psychological Association (1981). Ethical principles of psychologists. *American Psychologist, 36*, 633–638. (p. 44)

American Psychological Association (1982). *Ethical principles in the conduct of research with human participants.* Washington, DC: Author. (p. 44)

Amsel, A. (1986). Developmental psychobiology and behaviour theory: Reciprocating influences. *Canadian Journal of Psychology, 40*, 311–342. (p. 148)

Anderson, J. R. (1985). *Cognitive psychology and its implications* (2nd ed.). New York: Freeman. (p. 344)

Anderson, R. H., Fleming, D. E., Rhees, R. W., & Kinghorn, E. (1986). Relationships between sexual activity, plasma testosterone, and the volume of the sexually dimorphic nucleus of the preoptic area in prenatally stressed and non-stressed rats. *Brain Research, 370*, 1–10. (p. 214)

Anderson, S., & Bem, S. L. (1981). Sex typing and androgyny in dyadic interaction. *Journal of Personality and Social Psychology, 41*, 74–86. (p. 505)

Anderson, V. N. (1992). For whom is this world just? Sexual orientation and AIDS. *Journal of Applied Social Psychology, 22*, 248–259. (p. 503)

Andreasen, N. C. (1978). Creativity and psychiatric illness. *Psychiatric Annals, 8*, 113–119. (p. 626)

Andreasen, N. C. (1987). Creativity and mental illness: Prevalence rates in writers and their first-degree relatives. *American Journal of Psychiatry, 144*, 1288–1292. (p. 626)

Andreasen, N. C., Flaum, M., Swayze, V. W., Tyrrell, G., & Arndt, S. (1990). Positive and negative symptoms of schizophrenia. *Archives of General Psychology, 47*, 615–621. (p. 641)

Anglin, J. M. (1977). *Word, object, and conceptual development.* New York: Norton. (p. 425)

Archer, S. L. (1985). Identity and the choice of social roles. In A. S. Waterman (Ed.), *Identity in adolescence: Processes and contents. New directions in child development* (Vol. 30). San Francisco: Jossey-Bass. (p. 477)

Archer, S. L., & Waterman, A. S. (1990). Varieties of identity diffusions and foreclosures: An exploration of the subcategories of the identity statuses. *Journal of Adolescent Research, 5*, 96–111. (p. 476)

Ardrey, R. (1961). *African genesis.* New York: Atheneum. (p. 114)

Arieti, S. (1966). Schizophrenic cognition. In P. Hook & J. Zubin (Eds.), *Psychopathology of schizophrenia.* New York: Grune & Stratton. (p. 639)

Arnold, A. P., & Jordan, C. L. (1988). Hormonal organization of neural circuits. In L. Martini & W. F. Ganong (Eds.), *Frontiers in neuroendocrinology*, Vol. 10. New York: Raven. (p. 213)

Aronson, E. (1992). The return of the repressed: Dissonance theory makes a comeback. *Psychological Inquiry, 3*, 303–311. (p. 523)

Aronson, E., Blaney, N., Stephan, C., Sikes, J., & Snapp, M. (1978). *The jigsaw classroom.* Beverly Hills, CA: Sage. (p. 558)

Asanuma, H., & Sakata, H. (1967). Functional organization of a cortical efferent system examined with focal depth stimulation in cats. *Journal of Neurophysiology, 30*, 35–54. (p. 176)

Asarnow, J. R. (1988). Children at risk for schizophrenia: Converging lines of evidence. *Schizophrenia Bulletin, 14*, 613–631. (p. 77)

Asch, S. E. (1946). Forming impressions of personality. *Journal of Abnormal and Social Psychology, 41*, 258–290. (pp. 494, 495)

Asch, S. E. (1952). *Social psychology.* Englewood Cliffs, NJ: Prentice Hall. (p. 547)

Asch, S. E. (1956). Studies of independence and conformity: I. A minority of one against a unanimous majority. *Psychological Monographs: General and Applied, 70* (9, Whole no. 416). (pp. 547, 548, 549)

Aschoff, J. (1969). Desynchronization and resynchronization of human circadian rhythms. *Aerospace Medicine, 40*, 844–849. (p. 225)

Ash, M. G. (1985). Gestalt psychology: Origins in Germany and reception in the United States. In C. E. Buxton (Ed.), *Points of view in the modern history of psychology.* New York: Academic Press. (p. 12)

Ashton, H. (1987). *Brain systems, disorders, and psychotropic drugs.* Oxford: Oxford University Press. (p. 679)

Aspinwall, L. G. & Taylor, S. E. (1992). Modeling and cognitive adaptation: A longitudinal investigation of the impact of individual differences and coping on college adjustment and performance. *Journal of Personality and Social Psychology, 63*, 989–1003. (p. 590)

Astley, S. L., & Wasserman, E. A. (1992). Categorical discrimination and generalization in pigeons: All negative stimuli are not created equal. *Journal of Experimental Psychology: Animal Behavior Processes, 18*, 193–207. (p. 143)

Atkin, O. (1980). *Models of architectural knowledge.* London: Pion. (p. 340)

Atkinson, R. C. (1975). Mnemotechnics in second-language learning. *American Psychologist, 30*, 821–828. (p. 342)

Atkinson, R. C., & Shiffrin, R. M. (1968). Human memory: A proposed system and its control processes. In K. W. Spence & J. T. Spence (Eds.), *The psychology of learning and motivation: Advances in research and theory* (Vol. 2). New York: Academic Press. (pp. 328, 334, 335, 337)

Atkinson, R. C., & Shiffrin, R. M. (1971, August). The control of short-term memory. *Scientific American*, 82–90. (p. 335)

Avery, D. H., Bolte, M. A., Dager, S. R., Wilson, L. G., Weyer, M., Cox, O. B., & Dunner, D. L. (1993). Dawn stimulation treatment of winter depression: A controlled study. *American Journal of Psychiatry, 150*, 113–117. (p. 626)

Axelrod, R. (1984). *The evolution of cooperation.* New York: Basic Books. (pp. 112, 555)

Ayllon, T., & Azrin, N. H. (1968). *The token economy: A motivational system for therapy and rehabilitation.* New York: Appleton-Century-Crofts. (p. 673)

Baddeley, A. (1986). *Working Memory.* Oxford: Clarendon. (p. 352)

Baddeley, A. (1990). *Human memory: Theory and practice.* Boston: Allyn and Bacon. (p. 332)

Bahrick, H. P., Bahrick, P. O., & Wittlinger, R. P. (1975). Fifty years of memory for names and faces. *Journal of Experimental Psychology: General, 104*, 54–75. (p. 350)

Bailey, C. H., & Chen, M. (1991). The anatomy of long-term sensitization in *Aplysia:* Morphological insights into learning and memory. In L. R. Squire, N. M. Weinberger, G. Lynch, & J. L. McGaugh (Eds.), *Memory: Organization and locus of change.* Oxford: Oxford University Press. (pp. 188, 189)

Bailey, J. M., & Pillard, R. C. (1991). A genetic study of male sexual orientation. *Archives of General Psychiatry, 48*, 1089–1096. (p. 215)

Baillargeon, R. (1987). Object permanence in 3½- and 4½-month-old infants. *Developmental Psychology, 23*, 655–664. (pp. 421, 422)

Banaji, M. R., & Crowder, R. G. (1989). The bankruptcy of everyday memory. *American Psychologist, 44*, 1185–1193. (p. 366)

Bancroft, J. (1978). The relationship between hormones and sexual behavior in humans. In J. B. Hutchinson (Ed.), *Biological determinants of sexual behavior.* New York: Wiley. (p. 217)

Bandura, A. (1969). *Principles of behavior modification.* New York: Holt, Rinehart & Winston. (p. 151)

Bandura, A. (1977). *Social learning theory.* Englewood Cliffs, NJ: Prentice Hall. (pp. 150, 151)

Bandura, A. (1982). Self-efficacy mechanisms in human agency. *American Psychologist, 37*, 122–147. (pp. 589, 590)

Bandura, A. (1986). *Social foundations of thought and action: A social cognitive theory.* Englewood Cliffs, NJ: Prentice Hall. (pp. 151, 586, 587, 589)

Bandura, A. (1989). Human agency in social cognitive theory. *American Psychologist, 44*, 1175–1184. (p. 589)

Bandura, A., Adams, N. E., & Beyer, J. (1977). Cognitive processes mediating behavioral change. *Journal of Personality and Social Psychology, 35*, 125–139. (p. 589)

Bandura, A., & Cervone, D. (1983). Self-evaluative and self-efficacy mechanisms governing the motivational effects of goal systems. *Journal of Personality and Social Psychology, 45*, 1017–1028. (p. 589)

Bandura, A., Cioffi, D., Taylor, C. B., & Brouillard, M. E. (1988). Perceived self-efficacy in coping with cognitive stressors and opioid activation. *Journal of Personality and Social Psychology, 55*, 479–488. (p. 273)

Bandura, A., O'Leary, A., Taylor, C. B., Gauthier, J., & Gossard, D. (1987). Perceived self-efficacy and pain control: Opioid and nonopiod mechanisms. *Journal of Personality and Social Psychology, 53*, 563–571. (p. 273)

Bandura, A., Reese, L., & Adams, N. E. (1982). Microanalysis of action and fear arousal as a function of differential levels of perceived self-efficacy. *Journal of Personality and Social Psychology, 43*, 5–21. (p. 674)

Banks, W. P., & Krajicek, D. (1991). Perception. *Annual Review of Psychology, 42*, 305–331. (p. 330)

Barker, S. L., Funk, S. C., & Houston, B. K. (1988). Psychological treatment versus nonspecific factors: A meta-analysis of conditions that engender comparable expectations for improvement. *Clinical Psychology Review, 8*, 579–594. (p. 677)

Barlow, D. H. (1988). *Anxiety and its disorders: The nature and treatment of anxiety and panic.* New York: Guilford Press. (pp. 617, 619)

Barlow, D. H. (1991). Disorders of emotion. *Psychological Inquiry, 2*, 58–71. (pp. 617, 621)

Barlow, D. H., & Craske, M. G. (1988). The phenomenology of panic. In S. Rachman & J. D. Maser (Eds.), *Panic: Psychological perspectives.* Hillsdale, NJ: Erlbaum. (p. 620)

Barnett, R. C., & Baruch, G. K. (1987). Social roles, gender, and psychological distress. In R. C. Barnett, L. B. Biener, & G. K. Baruch (Eds.), *Gender and stress.* New York: Free Press. (p. 615)

Barry, H. III, & Paxson, L. (1971). Infancy and early childhood: Cross-cultural codes, 2. *Ethnology, 10*, 466-508. (p. 459)

Bartlett, F. C. (1932). *Remembering: A study in experimental and social psychology.* Cambridge: Cambridge University Press. (pp. 347, 355)

Bartol, C. R., & Costello, N. (1976). Extraversion as a function of temporal duration of electric shock: An exploratory study. *Perceptual and Motor Skills, 42*, 1174. (p. 596)

Baruch, G. K., Biener, L., & Barnett, R. C. (1987). Women and gender in research on work and family stress. *American Psychologist, 42*, 130–136. (pp. 484, 615)

Basbaum, A. I., & Fields, H. L. (1984). Endogenous pain control systems: Brainstem spinal pathways and endorphin circuitry. *Annual Review of Neuroscience*, 7, 309–338. (p. 272)

Basseches, M. (1984). *Dialectical thinking and adult development.* Norwood: Ablex. (p. 442)

Basseches, M. (1986). Dialectical thinking and young adult cognitive development. In R. A. Mines and K. S. Kitchener (Eds.), *Adult cognitive development: Methods and models.* New York: Praeger. (p. 442)

Bassuk, E. L., & Gerson, S. (1978, February). Deinstitutionalization and mental health services. *Scientific American*, 46–53. (p. 648)

Bates, E., O'Connell, B., & Shore, C. (1987). Language and communication in infancy. In J. D. Osofsky (Ed.), *Handbook of infant development* (2nd ed.). New York: Wiley. (p. 426)

Baumeister, R. F., & Showers, C. J. (1986). A review of paradoxical performance effects: Choking under pressure in sports and mental tests. *European Journal of Social Psychology, 16*, 361-383. (p. 544)

Baumeister, R. F., & Steinhilber, A. (1984). Paradoxical effects of supportive audiences on performance under pressure: The home field disadvantage in sports championships. *Journal of Personality and Social Psychology, 47*, 85–93. (p. 544)

Baumeister, R. F., & Tice, D. M. (1984). Role of self-presentation and choice in cognitive dissonance under forced compliance: Necessary or sufficient causes? *Journal of Personality and Social Psychology, 46*, 5–13. (p. 522)

Baumrind, D. (1964). Some thoughts on ethics of research: After reading Milgram's "Behavioral study of obedience." *American Psychologist, 19*, 421–423. (p. 540)

Baumrind, D. (1967). Child care practices anteceding three patterns of preschool behavior. *Genetic Psychology Monographs, 75*, 43–88. (p. 462)

Baumrind, D. (1971a). Current patterns of parental authority. *Developmental Psychology Monograph, 4,* 1–103. (pp. 32, 462)

Baumrind, D. (1971b). Harmonious parents and their preschool children. *Developmental Psychology, 4,* 99–102. (p. 463)

Baumrind, D. (1986). *Familial antecendents of social competence in middle childhood.* Unpublished monograph, Institute of Human Development, University of California, Berkeley. (p. 463)

Beaman, A. L., Klentz, B., Diener, E., & Svanum, S. (1979). Self-awareness and transgression in children: Two field studies. *Journal of Personality and Social Psychology, 37,* 1835–1846. (p. 524)

Beck, A. T. (1967). *Depression: Clinical, experimental, and theoretical aspects.* New York: Harper & Row. (p. 624)

Beck, A. T. (1976). *Cognitive therapy and the emotional disorders.* New York: International Universities Press. (p. 667)

Beck, A. T. (1978). *BDI.* New York: Harcourt Brace Jovanovich. (p. 652)

Beck, A. T. (1991). Cognitive therapy: A 30-year retrospective. *American Psychologist, 46,* 368–375. (p. 667)

Beck, A. T., Brown, G., Eidelson, J. I., Steer, R. A., & Riskind, J. H. (1987). Differentiating anxiety and depression: A test of the cognitive content-specificity hypothesis. *Journal of Abnormal Psychology, 96,* 179–183. (p. 621)

Beck, A. T., & Emery, G. (1985). *Anxiety disorders and phobias: A cognitive perspective.* New York: Basic Books. (pp. 618, 667)

Beck, A. T., & Young, J. E. (1985). Depression. In D. H. Barlow (Ed.), *Clinical handbook of psychological disorders: A step-by-step treatment manual.* New York: Guilford. (pp. 667, 668)

Beck, M., & Galef, B. G. (1989). Social influences on the selection of a protein-sufficient diet by Norway rats *Rattus norvegicus). Journal of Comparative Psychology, 103,* 132–139. (p. 154)

Becklen, R., & Cervone, D. (1983). Selective looking and the noticing of unexpected events. *Memory and Cognition, 11,* 601–608. (pp. 301, 302)

Beitman, B. D., Goldfried, M. R., & Norcross, J. C. (1989). The movement toward integrating the psychotherapies. An overview. *American Journal of Psychiatry, 146,* 138–147. (p. 678)

Bell, A. P., Weinberg, M. S., & Hammersmith, S. K. (1981). *Sexual preference: Its development in men and women.* Bloomington, IN: Indiana University Press. (pp. 214, 474)

Bell, R. Q., & Harper, L. V. (1977). *Child effects on adults.* Hillsdale, NJ: Erlbaum. (p. 463)

Bellugi, U., Poizner, H., & Klima, E. S. (1990). Language, modality and the brain. *Trends in Neuroscience, 12,* 380–388. (p. 427)

Belsky, J., & Rovine, M. (1988). Nonmaternal care in the first year of life and the security of infant-parent attachment. *Child Development, 59,* 157–167. (p. 458)

Bendor, J., Kramer, R. M., & Stout, S. (1991). When in doubt. . .: Cooperation and a noisy prisoner's dilemma. *Journal of Conflict Resolution, 35,* 691–719. (p. 556)

Bengston, V. L., Reedy, M. N., & Gordon, C. (1985). Aging and self-conceptions. In J. E. Birren & K. W. Schaie (Eds.), *Handbook of the psychology of aging* (2nd ed.). New York: Van Nostrand Reinhold. (p. 486)

Berghe, P. L. van den (1983). Human inbreeding avoidance: Culture in nature. *The Behavioral and Brain Sciences, 6,* 91–123. (p. 117)

Berglas, S., & Jones, E. E. (1978). Drug choice as a self-handicapping strategy in response to noncontingent success. *Journal of Personality and Social Psychology, 36,* 405–417. (p. 512)

Berko, J. (1958). The child's learning of English morphology. *Word, 14,* 150–177. (p. 426)

Bermond, B., Nieuwenhuyse, B. Fasotti, L., & Schuerman, J. (1991). Spinal cord lesions, peripheral feedback, and intensities of emotional feelings. *Cognition and Emotion, 5,* 201–220. (p. 234)

Berndt, T. J. (1992). Friendship and friends' influence in adolescence. *Current Directions in Psychological Science, 1,* 156–159. (p. 473)

Bernstein, I. L., & Borson, S. (1986). Learned food aversion: A component of anorexia syndromes. *Psychological Review, 93,* 462–472. (p. 152)

Bernstein, W. M., Stephan, W. G., & Davis, M. H. (1979). Explaining attributions for achievement: A path analytic approach. *Journal of Personality and Social Psychology, 37,* 1810–1821. (p. 510)

Berry, D. S., & McArthur, L. Z. (1985). Some components and consequences of a babyface. *Journal of Personality and Social Psychology, 48,* 312–323. (p. 496)

Berry, J. W. (1971). Ecological and cultural factors in spatial perceptual development. *Canadian Journal of Behavioural Science, 3,* 324–336. (p. 386)

Bertelsen, A. (1979). A Danish twin study of manic-depressive disorders. In M. Schou & E. Strömgren (Eds.), *Origin, prevention, and treatment of affective disorders.* Orlando, FL: Academic Press. (p. 626)

Bertenthal, B., & Campos, J. J. (1990). A systems approach to the organizing effects of self-produced locomotion during infancy. In C. Rovee-Collier & L. P. Lipsitt (Eds.), *Advances in infancy research* (Vol 6). Norwood, NJ: Ablex. (p. 419)

Bertenthal, B. I., Campos, J. J., & Barrett, K. C. (1984). Self-produced locomotion: An organizer of emotional, cognitive, and social development in infancy. In R. N. Emde & R. J. Harmon (Eds.), *Continuities and discontinuities in development.* New York: Plenum. (p. 419)

Betz, N. E., & Fitzgerald, L. F. (1993). Individuality and diversity: Theory and research in counseling psychology. *Annual Review of Psychology, 44,* 343–381. (p. 608)

Bever, T. (1970). The cognitive basis for linguistic structures. In J. R. Hayes (Ed.), *Cognition and the development of language.* New York: Wiley. (p. 426)

Bick, P. A. & Kinsbourne, M. (1987). Auditory hallucinations and subvocal speech in schizophrenic patients. *American Journal of Psychiatry, 144,* 222–225. (p. 639)

Bickerton, D. (1984). The language bioprogram hypothesis. *The Behavioral and Brain Sciences,* 7, 173–221. (p. 427)

Bickman, L. (1972). Social influence and diffusion of responsibility in an emergency. *Journal of Experimental Social Psychology, 8,* 438–445. (pp. 545, 546)

Biederman, I. (1985). Recognition-by-components: A theory of human image understanding. *Computer Vision, Graphics, and Image Processing* (Vol. 32), pp. 29–73. (pp. 296, 297)

Biederman, I. (1988). Aspects and extensions of a theory of human image understanding. In Z. W. Pylyshyn (Ed.), *Computational processes in human vision: an interdisciplinary perspective.* Norwood, NJ: Ablex. (pp. 297, 299)

Biederman, I. (1989). Higher-level vision. In N. Osherson, H. Lasnik, S. Kosslyn, J. Hollerbach, E. Smith, & N. Bloch (Eds.), *An invitation to cognitive science.* Cambridge, MA: MIT Press. (p. 296)

Biederman, I., & Shiffrar, M. M. (1987). Sexing day-old chicks: A case study and expert systems analysis of a difficult perceptual-learning task. *Journal of Experimental Psychology: Learning, Memory, and Cognition, 13,* 640–645. (p. 299)

Biernat, M., & Wortman, C. B. (1991). Sharing of home responsibilities between professionally employed women and their husbands. *Journal of Personality and Social Psychology, 60,* 844–860. (p. 484)

Billings, A. G., Cronkite, R. C., & Moos, R. H. (1983). Social-environmental factors in unipolar depression: Comparisons of depressed patients and nondepressed controls. *Journal of Abnormal Psychology, 92,* 119–133. (p. 623)

Binet, A., & Henri, V. (1896). La psychologie individuelle. *Année Psychologie, 11,* 163–169. (p. 371)

Binet, A., & Simon, T. (1916; reprinted 1973). *The development of intelligence in children.* New York: Arno Press. (p. 371)

Bishop, J. A., & Cook, L. M. (1975, January). Moths, melanism and clean air. *Scientific American,* 90–99. (p. 83)

Bitterman, M. E. (1975). The comparative analysis of learning. *Science, 188,* 699–709. (p. 148)

Blakemore, C., & Sutton, P. (1969). Size adaptation: A new aftereffect. *Science, 166,* 245–247. (p. 267)

Blanchard-Fields, F. (1986). Reasoning on social dilemmas varying in emotional saliency. *Psychology and Aging, 1,* 325–333. (p. 442)

Blaney, P. H. (1986). Affect and memory: A review. *Psychological Bulletin, 99,* 229–246. (p. 354)

Blasi, A. (1980). Bridging moral cognition and moral action: A critical review of the literature. *Psychological Bulletin, 88,* 1–45. (p. 479)

Blazer, D., Hughes, D., & George, L. D. (1987). Stressful life events and the onset of a generalized anxiety syndrome. *American Journal of Psychiatry, 144,* 1178–1183. (p. 618)

Bleuler, E. P. (1911; reprinted 1950). *Dementia praecox, or the group of schizophrenias* (J. Zinkin, Trans.). New York: International Universities Press. (pp. 637, 639)

Bleuler, E. P. (1924; reprinted 1951). *Textbook of psychiatry* (A. A. Brill, Trans.). New York: Dover. (p. 642)

Bliss, E. L. (1986). *Multiple personality, allied disorders, and hypnosis.* Oxford: Oxford University Press. (pp. 635, 637)

Bloom, F. E., & Lazerson, A. (1988). *Brain, mind, and behavior* (2nd ed.). New York: Freeman. (p. 169)

Bloom, L. M., & Lahey, M. (1978). *Language development and language disorders.* New York: Wiley. (p. 424)

Blumenthal, A. L. (1985). Wilhelm Wundt: Psychology as the propaedeutic science. In C. E. Buxton (Ed.), *Points of view in the modern history of psychology.* New York: Academic Press. (pp. 9, 18, 20)

Blurton-Jones, N. G. (1967). An ethological study of some aspects of social behavior of children in nursery school. In D. Morris (Ed.), *Primate ethology.* Chicago: Aldine. (p. 103)

Blurton-Jones, N. G., & Konner, M. J. (1973). Sex differences in the behavior of Bushman and London two- to five-year-olds. In J. Crook & R. Michael (Eds.), *Comparative ecology and behavior of primates.* New York: Academic Press. (p. 460)

Bock, K. (1990). Structure in language: Creating form in talk. *American Psychologist, 45, 1221–1236.* (p. 401)

Bodenhausen, G. V. (1990). Stereotypes as judgmental heuristics: Evidence of circadian variations in discrimination. *Psychological Science, 1,* 319–322. (p. 500)

Bodenhausen, G. V. (1991). Identity and cooperative social behavior: Pseudospeciation or human integration? *World Futures, 31,* 95–106. (p. 558)

Bonanno, G. A., Davis, P. J., Singer, J. L., & Schwartz, G. E. (1991). The repressor personality and avoidant information processing: A dichotic listening study. *Journal of Research in Personality, 25,* 386–401. (p. 577)

Bond, M. H., & Cheung, T. (1983). College students' spontaneous self-concept: The effect of culture among respondents in Hong Kong, Japan, and the United States. *Journal of Cross-Cultural Psychology, 14,* 153–171. (p. 510)

Bonto, M. A., & Payne, D. G. (1991). Role of environmental context in eyewitness memory. *American Journal of Psychology, 104,* 117–134. (p. 356)

Boon, S., & Draijer, N. (1993). Multiple personality disorder in The Netherlands: A clinical investigation of 71 patients. *American Journal of Psychiatry, 150,* 489–494. (p. 637)

Boor, M. (1982). The multiple personality epidemic. *Journal of Nervous and Mental Disease, 170,* 302–304. (p. 636)

Booth-Kewley, S., & Friedman, H. S. (1987). Psychological predictors of heart disease: A quantitative review. *Psychological Bulletin, 101,* 343–362. (p. 630)

Borbély, A. (1986). *The secrets of sleep.* New York: Basic Books. (p. 226)

Borges, M. A., & Dutton, L. J. (1976). Attitudes toward aging. *The Gerontologist, 16,* 220–224. (p. 486)

Botwinick, J. (1984). *Aging and behavior: A comprehensive integration of research findings* (3rd ed.). New York: Springer-Verlag. (pp. 485, 486)

Bouchard, T. J. (1991). A twice-told tale: Twins reared apart. In W. M. Grove & D. Cicchetti (Eds.), *Thinking clearly about psychology. Volume 2: Personality and psychopathology.* Minneapolis: University of Minnesota Press. (p. 600)

Bouchard, T. J., Lykken, D. T., McGue, M., Segal, N. L., & Tellegen, A. (1990). Sources of human psychological differences: The Minnesota study of twins reared apart. *Science, 250,* 223–228. (pp. 70, 71, 72)

Bouchard, T. J., & McGue, M. (1981). Familial studies of intelligence: A review. *Science, 212,* 1055–1059. (pp. 69, 70)

Bower, G. H. (1981). Mood and memory. *American Psychologist, 36,* 129–148. (p. 354)

Bower, G. H., & Mayer, J. D. (1989). In search of mood-dependent retrieval. *Journal of Social Behavior and Personality, 4,* 121–156. (p. 354)

Bowlby, J. (1958). The nature of the child's tie to his mother. *International Journal of Psychoanalysis, 39,* 35–373. (p. 454)

Bowlby, J. (1973). *Attachment and loss, Vol. 2: Separation: anxiety and anger.* New York: Basic Books. (p. 458)

Bowlby, J. (1982). *Attachment and loss* (2nd ed.). New York: Basic Books. (pp. 451, 454, 455)

Bowmaker, J. K., & Dartnall, H. J. A. (1980). Visual pigments of rods and cones in a human retina. *Journal of Physiology, 298,* 501–511. (p. 262)

Boyes, M. C., & Walker, L. J. (1988). Implications of cultural diversity for the universality claims of Kohlberg's theory of moral reasoning. *Human Development, 31,* 44–59. (p. 479)

Bradshaw, G. L., & Anderson, J. R. (1982). Elaborative encoding as an explanation of levels of processing. *Journal of Verbal Learning and Verbal Behavior, 21,* 165–174. (p. 339)

Bransford, J. D., Stein, B. S., Vye, N. J., Franks, J. J., Auble, P. M., Mezynski, K. J., & Perfetto, G. A. (1982). Different approaches in learning: An overview. *Journal of Experimental Psychology: General, 111,* 390–398. (p. 337)

Braun, B. G. (Ed.) (1985). *Treatment of multiple personality disorder.* Washington, DC: American Psychiatric Press. (p. 636)

Bray, D. W., & Howard, A. (1983). The AT&T longitudinal studies of managers. In K. W. Schaie (Ed.), *Longitudinal studies of adult psychological development.* New York: Guilford. (p. 484)

Bray, G. A., & Gallagher, T. F., Jr. (1975). Manifestation of hypothalamic obesity in man: A comprehensive investigation of eight patients and a review of the literature. *Medicine, 54,* 301–330. (p. 208)

Breggin, P. R. (1991). *Toxic psychiatry.* New York: St. Martin's Press. (p. 678)

Bregman, E. (1934). An attempt to modify emotional attitude of infants by the conditioned response technique. *Journal of Genetic Psychology, 45,* 169–198. (p. 155)

Breier, A., Charney, D. S., & Heninger, G. R. (1986). Agoraphobia with panic attacks. *Archives of General Psychiatry, 43,* 1029–1036. (p. 620)

Breuer, G. (1982). *Sociobiology and the human dimension.* Cambridge: Cambridge University Press. (p. 115)

Breuer, J., & Freud, S. (1895; reprinted 1955). *Studies on hysteria.* In J. Strachey (Ed. & trans.), *The standard edition of the complete psychological works of Sigmund Freud.* London: Hogarth Press. (pp. 658, 671)

Briggs, S. R., & Cheek, J. M. (1986). The role of factor analysis in the development and evaluation of personality scales. *Journal of Personality, 51,* 106–148. (p. 513)

Broadbent, D. E. (1958). *Perception and communication.* London: Pergamon. (p. 306)

Broadhurst, P. L., Fulker, D. W., & Wilcock, J. (1974). Behavioral genetics. *Annual Review of Psychology, 25,* 389–413. (p. 66)

Broca, P. (1861; reprinted 1965). Paul Broca on the speech centers (M. D. Boring, Trans.). In R. J. Herrnstein & E. G. Boring (Eds.), *A source book in the history of psychology.* Cambridge, MA: Harvard University Press. (pp. 6, 180, 402)

Brody, N. (1985). The validity of tests of intelligence. In B. B. Wolman (Ed.), *Handbook of intelligence: Theories, measurements, and applications.* New York: Wiley. (p. 372)

Brody, N. (1988). *Personality: In search of individuality.* New York: Academic Press. (p. 589)

Brody, N. (1992). *Intelligence,* second edition. San Diego: Academic Press. (pp. 374, 380, 384)

Bronfenbrenner, U. (1979). *The ecology of human development.* Cambridge, MA: Harvard University Press. (pp. 451, 452)

Bronfenbrenner, U. (1986). Ecology of the family as a context for human development: Research perspectives. *Developmental Psychology, 22,* 723–742. (pp. 451, 452)

Brown, N. S., Curry, N. E., & Tittnich, E. (1971). How groups of children deal with common stress through play. In N. E. Curry & S. Arnaud (Eds.), *Play: The child strives toward self-realization.* Washington, DC: NAEYC. (p. 465)

Brown, R. (1973). *A first language.* Cambridge, MA: Harvard University Press. (p. 426)

Brown, R. (1986). *Social psychology: The second edition.* New York: Free Press. (pp. 432, 542)

Brown, R., & Hanlon, C. (1970). Derivational complexity and order of acquisition in child speech. In J. R. Hayes (Ed.), *Cognition and the development of language.* New York: Wiley. (p. 426)

Brownell, K., Greenwood, M. R. C., Stellar, E., & Shrager, E. E. (1986). The effects of repeated cycles of weight loss and regain in rats. *Physiology and Behavior, 38* 459–464. (pp. 211, 212)

Bruce, D. (1991). Integrations of Lashley. In G. A. Kimble, M. Wertheimer, & C. White (Eds.), *Portraits of pioneers in psychology.* Hillsdale, NJ: Erlbaum. (p. 16)

Bruner, J. S. (1983). *Child's talk: Learning to use language.* New York: Norton. (p. 428)

Buchsbaum, M. S. (1990). The frontal lobes, basal ganglia, and temporal lobes as sites for schizophrenia. *Schizophrenia Bulletin, 16,* 379–390. (p. 641)

Buehlman, K. T., Gottman, J. M., & Katz, L. F. (1992). How a couple views their past predicts their future: Predicting divorce from an oral history interview. *Journal of Family Psychology, 5,* 295–318. (p. 482)

Bushnell, I. W., R., Sai, F., & Mullin, J. T. (1989). Neonatal recognition of the mother's face. *British Journal of Developmental Psychology, 7,* 3–15. (pp. 417, 453)

Buss, A. H. (1980). *Self-consicousness and social anxiety.* San Francisco: Freeman. (p. 513)

Bussey, K., & Maughan, B. (1982). Gender differences in moral reasoning. *Journal of Personality and Social Psychology, 42,* 701–706. (p. 480)

Butcher, J. N. (1990). *The MMPI-2 in psychological treatment.* New York: Oxford University Press. (p. 653)

Butler, R. N. (1975). *Why survive?* New York: Harper & Row. (p. 488)

Butterfield, E. C., & Siperstein, G. N. (1974). Influence of contingent auditory stimulation upon non-nutritional suckle. *Proceed-*

ings of third symposium on oral sensation and perception: The mouth of the infant. Springfield, IL: Charles C. Thomas. (p. 422)

Byrne, J. H. (1990). Learning and memory in *Aplysia* and other invertebrates. In R. P. Kesner & D. S. Olton (Eds.), *Neurobiology of comparative cognition.* Hillsdale, NJ: Erlbaum. (p. 190)

Cacioppo, J. T., Berntson, G. G., & Klein, D. J. (1992, in press). What is an emotion? The role of somatovisceral afference, with special emphasis on somatovisceral "illusions." *Review of Personality and Social Psychology.* (p. 232)

Cacioppo, J. T., Rourke, P. A., Marshall-Goodell, B. S., Tassinary, L. G., & Baron, R. S. (1990). Rudimentary physiological effects of mere observation. *Psychophysiology, 27,* 177–186. (p. 543)

Caggiula, A. R., & Hoebel, B. G. (1966). "Copulation-reward site" in the posterior hypothalamus. *Science, 153,* 1284–1285. (p. 220)

Caldwell, J., Croft, J. E., & Sever, P. S. (1980). Tolerance to the amphetamines: An examination of possible mechanisms. In J. Caldwell (Ed.), *Amphetamines and related stimulants: Chemical, biological, clinical and social aspects.* Boca Raton, FL: CRC Press. (p. 197)

Callaway, M. R., & Esser, J. K. (1984). Groupthink: Effects of cohesiveness and problem-solving procedures on group decision making. *Social Behavior and Personality, 12,* 157–164. (p. 552)

Campbell, J. D., & Fairey, P. J. (1989). Informational and normative routes to conformity: The effect of faction size as a function of norm extremity and attention to the stimulus. *Journal of Personality and Social Psychology, 57,* 457–468. (p. 548)

Campbell, J. D., Tesser, A., & Fairey, P. J. (1986). Conformity and attention to the stimulus: Some temporal and contextual dynamics. *Journal of Personality and Social Psychology, 51,* 315–324. (p. 548)

Campbell, K. 1970). *Body and mind.* Notre Dame, IN: University of Notre Dame Press. (p. 5)

Campfield, L. A., & Smith, F. J. (1990). Systemic factors in the control of food intake: Evidence for patterns as signals. In E. M. Stricker (Ed.), *Handbook of behavioral neurobiology, Volume 10: Neurobiology of food and fluid intake.* New York: Plenum. (p. 209)

Campos, J. J., Bertenthal, B. I., & Kermoian, R. (1992). Early experience and emotional development: The emergence of wariness of heights. *Psychological Science, 3,* 61–64. (p. 419)

Campos, J. J., Hiatt, S., Ramsay, D., Henderson, C., & Svejda, M. (1978). The emergence of fear on the visual cliff. In M. Lewis & L. A. Rosenblum (Eds.), *The development of affect* (Vol. 1). New York: Plenum. (p. 419)

Cann, A., Sherman, S. J., & Elkes, R. (1975). Effects of initial request size and timing of a second request on compliance: The foot in the door and the door in the face. *Journal of Personality and Social Psychology, 32,* 774–782. (p. 537)

Cannon, W. B. (1927). The James-Lange theory of emotions: A critical examination and an alternative theory. *American Journal of Psychology, 39,* 106–124. (p. 236)

Cannon, W. B. (1932; reprinted 1963). *The wisdom of the body.* New York: Norton. (p. 203)

Card, J. J. (1987). Epidemiology of PTSD in a national cohort of Vietnam veterans. *Journal of Clinical Psychology, 43,* 6–27. (p. 621)

Carpenter, P. A., Just, M. A., & Shell, P. (1990). What one intelligence test measures: A theoretical account of the processing in the Raven Progressive Matrices Test. *Psychological Review, 97,* 404–431. (p. 380)

Carpenter, W. T., Jr., Heinrichs, D. W., & Alphs, L. D. (1985). Treatment of negative symptoms. *Schizophrenia Bulletin, 11,* 440–452. (p. 679)

Carroll, B. J. (1991). Psychopathology and neurobiology of manic-depressive disorders. In B. J. Carroll & J. E. Barrett (Eds.), *Psychopathology and the brain.* New York: Raven Press. (p. 626)

Carroll, M. A., Schneider, H. G., & Wesley, G. R. (1985). *Ethics in the practice of psychology.* Englewood Cliffs, NJ: Prentice Hall. (p. 43)

Case, R. (1992). Neo-Piagetian theories of intellectual development. In H. Beilin & P. B. Pufall (Eds.), *Piaget's theory: Prospects and possibilities.* Hillsdale, NJ: Erlbaum. (pp. 440, 442)

Case, R., Kurland, M., & Goldberg, J. (1982). Operational efficiency and the growth of short-term memory span. *Journal of Experimental Child Psychology, 33,* 386–404. (p. 439)

Casey, P. J. (1992). A reexamination of the roles of typicality and category dominance in verifying category membership. *Journal of Experimental Psychology: Learning, Memory, and Cognition, 18,* 823–834. (p. 347)

Cattell, R. B. (1950). *Personality: A systematic, theoretical, and factual study.* New York: McGraw-Hill. (p. 594)

Cattell, R. B. (1965). *The scientific analysis of personality.* Baltimore, MD: Penguin. (p. 594)

Cattell, R. B. (1973). *Personality and mood by questionnaire.* San Francisco: Jossey-Bass. (p. 594)

Cavanaugh, J. C. (1990). *Adult development and aging.* Belmont, CA: Wadsworth. (pp. 483, 484)

Ceci, S. J. (1990). *On intelligence . . . more or less: A bio-ecological treatise on intellectual development.* Englewood Cliffs, NJ: Prentice Hall. (p. 374)

Ceraso, J. (1967, October). The interference theory of forgetting. *Scientific American,* 117–124. (p. 351)

Chagnon, N. A. (1979). Mate competition, favoring close kin, and village fissioning among the Yanomamö Indians. In N. A. Chagnon & W. Irons (Eds.), *Evolutionary biology and human social behavior: An anthropological perspective.* North Scituate, MA: Duxbury Press. (p. 116)

Chagnon, N. A., & Irons, W. (1979). *Evolutionary biology and human social behavior: An anthropological perspective.* North Scituate, MA: Duxbury Press. (p. 115)

Chaiken, S. (1986). The heuristic model of persuasion. In M. P. Zanna, J. M. Olson, & C. P. Herman (Eds.), *Consistency in social behavior: The Ontario symposium, Vol. 2.* Hillsdale, NJ: Erlbaum, (p. 518)

Chandler, C. C. (1991). How memory for an event is influenced by related events: Interference in modified recognition tests. *Journal of Experimental Psychology: Learning, Memory, and Cognition, 17,* 115–125. (p. 356)

Chapman, J. (1966). The early symptoms of schizophrenia. *British Journal of Psychiatry, 112,* 225–251. (p. 642)

Chase, M. H., & Morales, F. R. (1987). Sleep states and somatomotor activity. In G. Adelman (Ed.), *Encyclopedia of neuroscience.* Boston: Birkhäuser. (p. 229)

Chase, W. G., & Simon, H. A. (1973). Perception in chess. *Cognitive Psychology, 4,* 55–81. (p. 340)

Chen, S. C. (1937). Social modification of the activity of ants in nest-building. *Physiological Zoology, 10,* 420–436. (p. 542)

Cherry, E. C. (1953). Some experiments on the recognition of speech, with one and with two ears. *Journal of the Acoustical Society of America, 25,* 975–979. (p. 300)

Cherry, E. C., & Taylor, W. K. (1954). Some further experiments on the recognition of speech with one and two ears. *Journal of the Acoustical Society of America, 26,* 554–559. (p. 300)

Chesler, P. (1969). Maternal influence in learning by observation in kittens. *Science, 166,* 901–903. (p. 150)

Chi, M. T. H. (1978). Knowledge structures and memory development. In R. S. Siegler (Ed.), *Children's thinking: What develops?* Hillsdale, NJ: Erlbaum. (p. 440)

Chi, M. T. H., & Glaser, R. (1985). Problem-solving ability. In R. J. Sternberg (Ed.), *Human abilities: An information-processing approach.* New York: Freeman. (pp. 392, 395, 396)

Chomsky, N. (1957). *Syntactic structures.* The Hague: Mouton. (pp. 21, 399)

Chomsky, N. (1965). *Aspects of a theory of syntax.* Cambridge, MA: MIT Press. (p. 427)

Chomsky, N. (1968). *Language and mind.* New York: Harcourt Brace Jovanovich. (p. 400)

Cialdini, R. B. (1985). *Influence: The new psychology of modern persuasion,* rev. ed. New York: Morrow. (pp. 534, 536, 537)

Cialdini, R. B. (1987). Compliance principles of compliance professionals: Psychologists of necessity. In M. Zanna, J. M. Olson, & C. P. Herman (Eds.), *Social influence: The Ontario symposium, Vol. 5.* Hillsdale, NJ: Erlbaum. (pp. 534, 535, 536)

Cialdini, R. B. (1988). *Influence: Science and practice* (2nd ed.). Glenview, IL: Scott, Foresman. (p. 534)

Cialdini, R. B., Cacioppo, J. T., Bassett, R., & Miller, J. A. (1978). The lowball procedure for producing compliance: Commitment then cost. *Journal of Personality and Social Psychology, 36,* 463–476. (p. 535)

Cicchetti, D., & Beeghly, M. (1988). *Down syndrome: A developmental perspective.* Cambridge: Cambridge University Press. (p. 61)

Clark, A. S., Pfeifle, J. K., & Edwards, D. A. (1981). Ventromedial hypothalamic damage and sexual proceptivity in female rats. *Physiology and Behavior, 27,* 597–602. (p. 213)

Clark, D. M. (1988). A cognitive model of panic attacks. In S. Rachman & J. D. Maser (Eds.), *Panic: Psychological perspectives.* Hillsdale, NJ: Erlbaum. (p. 620)

Clark, E. (1973). What's in a word? On the child's acquisition of semantics in his first language. In T. Moore (Ed.), *Cognitive development and the acquisition of language.* New York: Academic Press. (p. 425)

Clark, E. (1987). The principle of contrast: A constraint on language acquisition. In B. MacWhinney (Ed.), *Mechanisms of language acquisition.* Hillsdale, NJ: Erlbaum. (p. 425)

Clark, L. A., & Watson, D. (1991). Tripartite model of anxiety and depression: Psychometric evidence and taxonomic implications. *Journal of Abnormal Psychology, 100,* 316–336. (p. 621)

Clarke, J. C. (1988). *Alcoholism and problem drinking: Theories and treatment.* New York: Pergamon Press. (p. 672)

Clement, C. A., & Falmagne, R. J. (1986). Logical reasoning, world knowledge, and mental imagery: Interconnections in cognitive processes. *Memory and Cognition, 14,* 299–307. (p. 392)

Clifford, M. M., & Walster, E. (1973). The effects of physical attractiveness on teacher expectation. *Sociology of Education, 46,* 248–258. (p. 496)

Cloninger, C. R. (1990). Genetic epidemiology of alcoholism: Observations critical to the design and analysis of linkage studies. In C. R. Cloninger & H. Begleiter (Eds.), *Genetics and biology of alcoholism.* Plainview, NY: Cold Spring Harbor Laboratory Press. (p. 633)

Cloninger, C. R., Bohman, M., & Sigvardsson, S. (1981). Inheritance of alcohol abuse: Cross fostering analysis of adopted men. *Archives of General Psychiatry, 38,* 861–868. (p. 633)

Cohen, F. L. (1984). *Clinical genetics in nursing practice.* Philadelphia: Lippincott. (p. 61)

Cohen, R. A., & Albers, H. E. (1991). Disruption of human circadian and cognitive regulation following a discrete hypothalamic lesion: A case study. *Neurology, 41,* 726–729. (p. 229)

Cohen, S., Kaplan, J. R., Cunnick, J. E., Manuck, S. B., & Rabin, B. S. (1992). Chronic social stress, affiliation, and cellular immune response in nonhuman primates. *Psychological Science, 3,* 301–304. (p. 631)

Cohen, S., Tyrrell, D. A. J., & Smith, A. P. (1991). Psychological stress and susceptibility to the common cold. *The New England Journal of Medicine, 325,* 606–612. (p. 631)

Cohen, S., & Williamson, G. M. (1991). Stress and infectious disease in humans. *Psychological Bulletin, l09,* 5–24. (p. 631)

Colby, A., Kohlberg, L., Gibbs, J., & Lieberman, M. (1983). A longitudinal study of moral judgment. *Monographs of the Society for Research in Child Development, 48* (Whole nos. 1 & 2). (pp. 477, 479)

Cole, M., Gay, J., Glick, J., & Sharp, D. W. (1971). *The cultural context of learning and thinking.* New York: Basic Books. (p. 386)

Cole, M., & Means, B. (1981). *Comparative studies of how people think.* Cambridge, MA: Harvard University Press. (p. 385)

Collins, A., & Loftus, E. (1975). A spreading-activation theory of semantic processing. *Psychological Review, 82,* 407–428. (p. 349)

Commons, M. L., Grossberg, S., & Staddon, J. E. R. (Eds.) (1991). *Neural network models of conditioning and action.* Hillside, NJ: Erlbaum. (p. 146)

Condon, W. S., & Ogston, W. D. (1966). Sound film analysis of normal and pathological behavior patterns. *Journal of Nervous and Mental Disorders, 143,* 338–347. (p. 236)

Conley, J. J. (1984). The hierarchy of consistency: A review and model of longitudinal findings on adult individual differences in intelligence, personality, and self opinion. *Personality and Individual Differences, 5*, 11–26. (p. 599)

Conley, J. J. (1985). Longitudinal stability of personality traits: A multitrait-multimethod-multioccasion analysis. *Journal of Personality and Social Psychology, 49*, 1266–1282. (p. 599)

Connolly, J. A., & Doyle, A. (1984). Relation of social fantasy play to social competence in preschoolers. *Developmental Psychology, 20*, 797–806. (p. 465)

Conway, M. A. (1991). In defense of everyday memory. *American Psychologist, 46*, 19–26. (p. 366)

Cook, L. M., Mani, G. S., & Varley, M. E. (1986). Postindustrial melanism in the peppered moth. *Science, 231*, 611–613. (p. 83)

Cook, M., & Mineka, S. (1989). Observational conditioning of fear to fear-relevant versus fear-irrelevant stimuli in rhesus monkeys. *Journal of Abnormal Psychology, 98*, 448–459. (p. 155)

Cook, M., & Mineka, S. (1990). Selective associations in the observational conditioning of fear in rhesus monkeys. *Journal of Experimental Psychology: Animal Behavior Processes, 16*, 372–389. (p. 155)

Cooley, C. H. (1902; reprinted 1964). *Human nature and the social order*. New York: Schocken Books. (p. 504)

Coons, P. M., Bowman, E. S., & Milstein, V. (1988). Multiple personality disorder: A clinical investigation of 50 cases. *Journal of Nervous and Mental Disease, 176*, 519–527. (p. 636)

Cooper, H. M., & Good, T. L. (1983). *Pygmalion grows up: Studies in the expectation communication process*. New York: Longman. (p. 505)

Cooper, J., & Croyle, R. T. (1984). Attitudes and attitude change. *Annual Review of Psychology, 35*, 395–426. (p. 526)

Cooper, M. L., Russell, M., & George, W. H. (1988). Coping, expectancies, and alcohol abuse: A test of social learning foundations. *Journal of Abnormal Psychology, 97*, 218–230. (p. 634)

Cooper, R. M., & Zubek, J. P. (1958). Effects of enriched and restricted early environments on the learning ability of bright and dull rats. *Canadian Journal of Psychology, 12*, 159–164. (p. 67)

Coren, S. (1986). An efferent component in the visual perception of direction and extent. *Psychological Review, 93*, 391–410. (p. 317)

Coren, S., & Ward, L. M. (1989). *Sensation and perception* (3rd ed.). New York: Harcourt Brace Jovanovich. (p. 262)

Corey, S. M. (1937). Professed attitudes and actual behavior. *Journal of Educational Psychology, 28*, 271–280. (p. 523)

Cornblatt, B. A., & Erlenmeyer-Kimling, L. (1985). Global attentional deviance as a marker of risk for schizophrenia: Specificity and predictive validity. *Journal of Abnormal Psychology, 94*, 470–486. (p. 642)

Cosmides, L., & Tooby, J. (1992). Cognitive adaptations for social exchange. In J. H. Barkow, L. Cosmides, & J. Tooby (Eds.), *The adapted mind: Evolutionary psychology and the generation of culture*. Oxford: Oxford University Press. (p. 556)

Costa, P. T., & McCrae, R. R. (1980). Still stable after all these years: Personality as a key to some issues in adulthood and old age. In P. B. Baltes & O. G. Brim (Eds.), *Lifespan development and behavior* (Vol. 3). New York: Academic Press. (p. 486)

Costa, P. T., Zonderman, A. B., McCrae, R. R., Cornoni-Huntley, J., Locke, B. Z., & Barbano, H. E. (1987). Longitudinal analyses of psychological well-being in a national sample: Stability of mean levels. *Journal of Gerontology, 42*, 50–55. (p. 486)

Cottrell, N. B., Wack, D. L., Sekerak, G. J., & Rittle, R. H. (1968). Social facilitation of dominant responses by the presence of an audience and the mere presence of others. *Journal of Personality and Social Psychology, 9*, 245–250. (p. 543)

Cousins, N. (1977). Anatomy of an illness (as perceived by the patient). *Saturday Review*, May 23, 4–6, 48–51. (p. 590)

Cousins, S. D. (1989). Culture and self-perception in Japan and the United States. *Journal of Personality and Social Psychology, 56*, 124–131. (pp. 507, 508)

Cox, M. J., Owen, M. T., Henderson, V. K., & Margand, N. A. (1992). Prediction of infant-father and infant-mother attachment. *Developmental Psychology, 28*, 474–483. (p. 457)

Craik, F. I. M., & Tulving, E. (1975). Depth of processing and the retention of words in episodic memory. *Journal of Experimental Psychology: General, 104*, 268–294. (p. 339)

Craik, F. I., & Watkins, M. J. (1973). The role of rehearsal in short-term memory. *Journal of Verbal Learning and Verbal Behavior, 12*, 599–607. (pp. 336–337)

Crits-Christoph, P. (1992). The efficacy of brief dynamic psychotherapy: A meta-analysis. *American Journal of Psychiatry, 149*, 151–158. (p. 674)

Crow, T. J. (1980). Molecular pathology of schizophrenia: More than one process? *British Medical Journal, 280*, 66–68. (p. 639)

Crowne, D. P., & Liverant, S. (1963). Conformity under varying conditions of personal commitment. *Journal of Abnormal and Social Psychology, 66*, 547–555. (p. 588)

Culebras, A., & Moore, J. T. (1989). Magnetic resonance findings in REM sleep behavior disorder. *Neurology, 39*, 1519–1523. (p. 229)

Culp, R. E., Cook, A. S., & Housley, P. C. (1983). A comparison of observed and reported adult-infant interactions: Effects of perceived sex. *Sex Roles, 9*, 475–479. (p. 468)

Cumming, E., & Henry, W. (1961). *Growing old: The process of disengagement*. New York: Basic Books. (p. 486)

Curtiss, S. (1977). *Genie: A psycholinguistic study of a modern-day "wild child."* New York: Academic Press. (p. 428)

Curtiss, S. (1981). Dissociations between language and cognition: Cases and implications. *Journal of Autism and Developmental Disorders, 11*, 15–30. (p. 427)

Cutting, J. E., & Proffitt, D. R. (1982). The minimum principle and the perception of absolute, common, and relative motions. *Cognitive Psychology, 14*, 211–246. (p. 319)

Cutting, J. E., Proffitt, D. R., & Kozlowski, L. T. (1978). A biomechanical invariant for gait perception. *Journal of Experimental Psychology: Human Perception and Performance, 4*, 357–372. (p. 319)

Czeisler, C. A., Johnson, M. P., Duffy, J. F., Brown, E. N., Ronda, J. M., & Kronauer, R. E. (1990). Exposure to bright light and darkness to treat physiologic maladaptation to night work. *The New England Journal of Medicine, 322*, 1253–1259. (p. 225)

Czeisler, C. A., Kronauer, R. E., Allen, J. S., Duffy, J. F., Jewett, M. E., Brown, E. N., & Ronda, J. M. (1989). Bright light induction of strong (type O) resetting of the human circadian pacemaker. *Science, 244,* 1328–1333. (p. 225)

Daly, M., & Wilson, M. (1988). *Homicide.* New York: Aldine de Gruyter. (pp. 116, 117)

Damon, W., & Hart, D. (1992). Self-understanding and its role in social and moral development. In M. H. Bornstein & M. E. Lamb (Eds.), *Developmental psychology: An advanced textbook,* third edition. Hillsdale, NJ: Erlbaum. (pp. 473, 475)

Damsma, G., Pfaus, J. G., Wenkstern, D., Phillips, A. G., & Fibiger, H. C. (1992). Sexual behavior increases dopamine transmission in the nucleus accumbens and striatum of male rats: Comparison with novelty and locomotion. *Behavioral Neurosciences, 106,* 181–191. (p. 220)

Dance, K. A., & Kuiper, N. A. (1987). Self-schemata, social roles, and a self-worth contingency model of depression. *Motivation and Emotion, 11,* 251–268. (p. 507)

Darwin, C. (1859; reprinted 1963). *The origin of species.* New York: Washington Square Press. (pp. 7, 67, 81–82, 94–95)

Darwin, C. (1872; reprinted 1965). *The expression of the emotions in man and animals.* Chicago: University of Chicago Press. (pp. 7, 96–97, 98, 100, 102)

Darwin, C. T., Turvey, M. T., & Crowder, R. G. (1972). An auditory analogue of the Sperling partial report procedure: Evidence for brief auditory storage. *Cognitive Psychology, 3,* 255–267. (p. 330)

Dasen, P. R. & de Ribaupierre, A. (1988). Neo-Piagetian theories: Cross-cultural and differential perspectives. In A. Demetriou (Ed.), *The neo-Piagetian theories of cognitive development: Toward an integration.* Amsterdam: Elsevier. (p. 440)

Dasen, P. R., & Heron, A. (1981). Cross-cultural tests of Piaget's theory. In H. C. Triandis & A. Heron (Eds.), *Handbook of cross-cultural psychology: Vol. 4. Developmental psychology.* Boston: Allyn & Bacon. (p. 438)

Daum, I., Channon, S., & Canavar, A. (1989). Classical conditioning in patients with severe memory problems. *Journal of Neurology and Neurosurgery Psychiatry, 52,* 47–51. (p. 363)

Davidson, J. M. (1980). Hormones and sexual behavior in the male. In D. T. Krieger & J. C. Hughes (Eds.), *Neuroendocrinology.* Sunderland, MA: Sinauer Associates. (p. 216)

Davidson, J. M., Camargo, C. A., & Smith, E. R. (1979). Effects of androgen on sexual behavior in hypogonadal men. *Journal of Clinical Endocrinology and Metabolism, 48,* 955–958. (p. 216)

Davidson, J. M., & Myers, L. S. (1988). Endocrine factors in sexual psychophysiology. In R. C. Rosen & J. G. Beck (Eds.), *Patterns of sexual arousal: Psychophysiological processes and clinical applications.* New York: Guilford. (pp. 216, 217)

Davidson, R. J. (1992). Emotion and affective style: Hemispheric substrates. *Psychological Science, 3,* 39–43. (p. 237)

Davidson, R. J., Ekman, P., Saron, C. D., Senulis, J. A., & Friesn, W. V. (1990). Approach-withdrawal and cerebral asymmetry: Emotional expression and brain physiology I. *Journal of Personality and Social Psychology, 58,* 330–341. (p. 238)

Davies, K. (1991). Breaking the fragile X. *Nature, 351,* 439–440. (p. 59)

Davies, N. B. (1991). Mating systems. In J. R. Krebs & N. B. Davies (Eds.), *Behavioural ecology III.* Oxford: Blackwell Scientific Publications. (p. 105)

Davis, C. M. (1928). Self selection of diet in newly weaned infants: An experimental study. *American Journal of Diseases of Children, 36,* 651–679. (p. 154)

Davis, J. M. (1974). A two-factor theory of schizophrenia. *Journal of Psychiatric Research, 11,* 25–30. (p. 641)

Davis, M. (1992). The role of the amygdala in fear and anxiety. *Annual Review of Neuroscience, 15,* 353–375. (p. 237)

Davis, M. R. (1985). Perceptual and affective reverberation components. In A. B. Goldstein & G. Y. Michaels (Eds.), *Empathy: Development, training, and consequences.* Hillsdale, NJ: Erlbaum. (p. 236)

Davis, P. J., & Schwartz, G. E. (1987). Repression and the inaccessibility of affective memories. *Journal of Personality and Social Psychology, 52,* 155–162. (p. 577)

Dawes, R. M. (1991). Social dilemmas, economic self-interest, and evolutionary theory. In D. R. Brown & J. E. K. Smith (Eds.), *Frontiers of mathematical psychology.* New York: Springer-Verlag. (p. 556)

Deaux, K. (1984). From individual differences to social categories: Analysis of a decade's research on gender. *American Psychologist, 39,* 105–116. (p. 500)

Deaux, K. (1985). Sex and gender. *Annual Review of Psychology, 36,* 49–81. (p. 468)

DeCasper, A. J., & Fifer, W. P. (1980). Of human bonding: Newborns prefer their mothers' voices. *Science, 208,* 1174–1176. (p. 422)

DeCasper, A. J., & Spence, M. J. (1986). Prenatal maternal speech influences newborns' perception of speech sounds. *Infant Behavior and Development, 9,* 133–150. (p. 423)

de Groot, A. D. (1965). *Thought and choice in chess.* The Hague: Mouton. (p. 340)

DeJonge, F. H., Louwerse, A. L., Ooms, M. P., Evers, P., Endert, E., & Van de Poll, N. E. (1989). Lesions of the SDN-POA inhibit sexual behavior of male Wistar rats. *Brain Research Bulletin, 23,* 483–492. (p. 213)

Delabar, J.-M., Goldgaber, D., Lamour, Y., Nicole, A., Huret, J.-L., & others. (1987). ß amyloid gene duplication in Alzheimer's disease and karyotypically normal Down syndrome. *Science, 235,* 1390–1392. (p. 61)

Delay, J., & Deniker, P. (1952). Trente-huit cas de psychoses traitees par la cure prolongee et continue de 4560 RP. *Comptes Rendus Congrès des Médecins Aliénistes et Neurologistes de France et des Pays de Langue Française, 50,* 497–502. (p. 678)

DeLisi, L. E., Dauphinais, I. D., & Gershon, E. S. (1988). Perinatal complications and reduced size of brain limbic structures in familial schizophrenia. *Schizophrenia Bulletin, 14,* 185–191. (p. 641)

Dement, W. C. (1972). *Some must watch while some must sleep.* San Francisco: Freeman. (p. 226)

Dement, W. C. (1979). The relevance of sleep pathologies to the function of sleep. In R. Drucker-Colin, M. Shkurovich, & M. B.

Sterman (Eds.), *The functions of sleep*. New York: Academic Press. (p. 226)

Descartes, R. (1637; reprinted 1972). *Treatise of man* (T. S. Hall, Trans.). Cambridge, MA: Harvard University Press. (pp. 4, 5)

Deutsch, A. (1948). *The shame of the states*. New York: Harcourt, Brace. (p. 648)

Deutsch, J. A. (1990). Food intake: Gastric factors. In E. M. Stricker (Ed.), *Handbook of behavioral neurobiology, Volume 10: Neurobiology of food and fluid intake*. New York: Plenum. (p. 208)

De Valois, R. L., Abramov, I., & Jacobs, G. H. (1966). Analysis of response patterns of LGN cells. *Journal of the Optical Society of America, 56*, 96–977. (p. 264)

De Valois, R. L., & De Valois, K. K. (1988). *Spatial vision*. Oxford: Oxford University Press. (pp. 265, 267)

de Villiers, J. G., & de Villiers, P. A. (1979). *Language acquisition*. Cambridge, MA: Harvard University Press. (p. 426)

Devine, P. G. (1989). Stereotypes and prejudice: Their automatic and controlled components. *Journal of Personality and Social Psychology, 56*, 5–18. (p. 501)

Devine, P. G., Monteith, M. J., Zuwerink, J. R., & Elliot, A. J. (1991). Prejudice with and without compunction. *Journal of Personality and Social Psychology, 60*, 817–830. (p. 501)

Devocic, M., & Janssens, J. (1992). Parents' child-rearing style and child's sociometric status. *Developmental Psychology, 28*, 925–932. (p. 463)

DeWitt, L. A., & Samuel, A. G. (1990). The role of knowledge-based expectations in music perception: Evidence from musical restoration. *Journal of Experimental Psychology: General, 119*, 123–144. (p. 293)

Dewsbury, D. A. (1988). The comparative psychology of monogamy. In D. W. Leger (Ed.), *Comparative perspectives in modern psychology. Nebraska Symposium on Motivation, 1987*. Lincoln, NE: University of Nebraska Press. (pp. 106, 107, 116)

Dewsbury, D. A. (1992). What comparative psychology is about. *Teaching of Psychology, 19*, 4–11. (p. 12)

Dickinson, A. (1989). Expectancy theory in animal conditioning. In S. B. Klein & R. R. Mowrer (Eds.), *Contemporary learning theories: Pavlovian conditioning and the status of learning theory*. Hillsdale, NJ: Erlbaum. (pp. 146, 147)

Dickinson, A., & Dawson, G. R. (1987). The role of the instrumental contingency in motivational control of performance. *Quarterly Journal of Experimental Psychology, 39B*, 77–93. (p. 147)

Diener, E. (1977). Deindividuation: Causes and consequences. *Social Behavior and Personality, 5*, 143–155. (p. 546)

Diener, E. (1980). Deindividuation: The absence of self-awareness and self-regulation in group members. In P. B. Paulus (Ed.), *The psychology of group influence*. Hillsdale, NJ: Erlbaum. (p. 547)

Dienstfrey, H. (1991). *Where the mind meets the body*. New York: HarperCollins. (p. 630)

Digman, J. M. (1989). Five robust trait dimensions: Development, stability, and utility. *Journal of Personality, 57*, 195–214. (p. 596)

Digman, J. M., & Inouye, J. (1986). Further specification of the five robust factors of personality. *Journal of Personality and Social Psychology, 50*, 116–123. (p. 596)

DiMascio, A., Weissman, M. M., Prusoff, B. A., Neu, C., Zwilling, M., & Klerman, G. L. (1979). Differential symptom reduction by drugs and psychotherapy in acute depression. *Archives of General Psychiatry, 36*, 1450–1456. (pp. 31, 37, 42)

Dio, T. (1986). *The anatomy of self: The individual versus society*. Tokyo: Kodansha. (p. 514)

Dion, K. K. (1972). Physical attractiveness and evaluation of children's transgressions. *Journal of Personality and Social Psychology, 24*, 207–213. (p. 496)

Dion, K. K. (1986). Stereotyping based on physical attractiveness: Issues and conceptual perspectives. In C. P. Herman, M. P. Zanna, & E. T. Higgins (Eds.), *Physical appearance, stigma, and social behavior: The Ontario symposium, Vol. 3*. Hillsdale, NJ: Erlbaum. (p. 495)

Dobson, K. (1989). A meta-analysis of the efficacy of cognitive therapy for depression. *Journal of Consulting and Clinical Psychology, 57*, 414–429. (p. 675)

Donovan, J. M. (1975). Identity status and interpersonal style. *Journal of Youth and Adolescence, 4*, 37–55. (p. 476)

Doob, L. W. (1990). Forward. In M. H. Segall, P. R. Dasen, J. W. Berry, & Y. H. Poortinga, *Human behavior in global perspective: An introduction to cross-cultural psychology*. New York: Pergamon Press. (p. 18)

Dorman, M., Hannley, M., Dankowski, K., Smith, L., & McCandless, G. (1989). Word recognition by 50 patients fitted with the Symbion multichannel cochlear implant. *Ear and Hearing, 10*, 44–49. (p. 250)

Dorman, M., Smith, L., McCandless, G., Dunnavant, G., Parkin, J., & Dankowski, K. (1990). Pitch scaling and speech understanding by patients who use the Ineraid cochlear implant. *Ear and Hearing, 11*, 310–315. (p. 250)

Dovidio, J. F. (1984). Helping behavior and altruism: An empirical and conceptual overview. In L. Berkowitz (Ed.), *Advances in experimental social psychology* (Vol. 17). New York: Academic Press. (p. 545)

DuBois, P. H. (1972). College Board Scholastic Aptitude Test. In O. K. Buros (Ed.), *The seventh mental measurements yearbook* (2 vols.). Highland Park, NJ: Gryphon. (p. A-6)

Duckro, P. N. (1991). Biofeedback in the management of headache, part II. *Headache Quarterly, 2*, 17–22. (p. 135)

Duggan, J. P., & Booth, D. A. (1986). Obesity, overeating, and rapid gastric emptying in rats with ventromedial hypothalamic lesions. *Science, 231*, 609–611. (p. 208)

Duncan, B. L. (1976). Differential social perception and attribution of intergroup violence: Testing the lower limits of stereotyping of blacks. *Journal of Personality and Social Psychology, 34*, 590–598. (p. 500)

Duncan, J. (1984). Selective attention and the organization of visual information. *Journal of Experimental Psychology: General, 113*, 501–517. (p. 304)

Duncker, K. (1945). On problem-solving. *Psychological Monographs, 58* (Whole no. 270). (p. 393)

Dunham, P., & Dunham, F. (1992). Lexical development during middle infancy: A mutually driven infant-caregiver process. *Developmental Psychology, 28,* 414–420. (p. 429)

Dunn, J., & Plomin, R. (1990). *Separate lives: Why siblings are so different.* New York: Basic Books. (pp. 72, 600)

Dunphy, D. C. (1963). The social structure of urban adolescent peer groups. *Sociometry, 26,* 230–246. (p. 473)

Durham, W. H. (1991). *Coevolution: Genes, culture, and human diversity.* Stanford, CA: Stanford University Press. (p. 117)

Dweck, C. S., & Bush, E. S. (1976). Sex differences in learned helplessness: I. Differential debilitation with peer and adult evaluators. *Developmental Psychology, 12,* 147–156. (p. 469)

Dweck, C. S., Davidson, W., Nelson, S., & Enna, B. (1978). Sex differences in learned helplessness: II. The contingencies of evaluative feedback in the classroom. III. An experimental analysis. *Developmental Psychology, 14,* 268–276. (p. 469)

Dykens, E. M., & Leckman, J. F. (1990). Developmental issues in fragile X syndrome. In R. M. Hodapp, J. A. Burack, & E. Zigler (Eds.), *Issues in the developmental approach to mental retardation.* New York: Cambridge University Press. (p. 59)

Eagle, M., Wolitzky, D. L., & Klein, G. S. (1966). Imagery: Effect of a concealed figure in a stimulus. *Science, 151,* 837–839. (pp. 301, 302, 362)

Eagly, A. H., Ashmore, R. D., Makhijani, M. G., & Longo, L. C. (1991). What is beautiful is good, but . . .: A meta-analytic review of research on the physical attractiveness stereotype. *Psychological Bulletin, 110,* 109–128. (p. 495)

Eagly, A. H., & Chaiken, S. (1993). *The psychology of attitudes.* Orlando, FL: Harcourt Brace Jovanovich. (pp. 518, 519)

Ebbinghaus, H. (1885; reprinted 1913). *Memory: A contribution to experimental psychology* (H. A. Ruger & C. E. Bussenius, Trans.). New York: Teachers College Press. (pp. 332, 336, 350)

Eccles, J. (1985). Sex differences in achievement patterns. In T. B. Sonderegger (Ed.), *Nebraska symposium on motivation 1984.* Lincoln, NE: University of Nebraska Press. (p. 469)

Eckland, B. K. (1982). College entrance examination trends. In G. R. Austin & G. Garber (Eds.), *The rise and fall of national test scores.* New York: Academic Press. (p. A-7)

Edelman, G. M. (1987). *Neural Darwinism.* New York: Basic Books. (pp. 176, 227)

Eibl-Eibesfeldt, I. (1961, December). The fighting behavior of animals. *Scientific American,* 112–121. (p. 91)

Eibl-Eibesfeldt, I. (1975). *Ethology: The biology of behavior* (2nd ed.). New York: Holt, Rinehart & Winston. (pp. 96, 101, 102)

Eibl-Eibesfeldt, I. (1989). *Human ethology.* New York: Aldine de Gruyter. (pp. 98, 101, 116)

Eich, J. E. (1980). The cue-dependent nature of state-dependent retrieval. *Memory and Cognition, 8,* 157–173. (p. 354)

Eimas, P. D. (1975). Speech perception in early infancy. In L. B. Cohen & P. Salapafek (Eds.), *Infant perception.* New York: Academic Press. (p. 423)

Eisen, G. (1988). *Children and play in the Holocaust.* Amherst, MA: University of Massachusetts Press. (p. 465)

Ekman, P. (1973). Cross-cultural studies of facial expression. In P. Ekman (Ed.), *Darwin and facial expression.* New York: Academic Press. (p. 101)

Ekman, P. (1984). Expression and the nature of emotion. In K. R. Scherer & P. Ekman (Eds.), *Approaches to emotion.* Hillsdale, NJ: Erlbaum. (p. 234)

Ekman, P. (1992). Facial expressions of emotion: New findings, new questions. *Psychological Science, 3,* 34–38. (p. 102)

Ekman, P., & Friesen, W. V. (1975). *Unmasking the face.* Englewood Cliffs, NJ: Prentice Hall. (pp. 99, 100)

Ekman, P., & Friesen, W. V. (1982). Measuring facial movements with the facial action coding system. In P. Ekman (Ed.), *Emotion in the human face.* Cambridge: Cambridge University Press. (p. 99)

Ekman, P., Friesen, W. V., O'Sullivan, M., & many others (1987). Universals and cultural differences in the judgments of facial expressions of emotion. *Journal of Personality and Social Psychology, 53,* 712–717. (p. 101)

Ekman, P., Levenson, R. W., & Friesen, W. V. (1983). Autonomic nervous system activity distinguishes among emotions. *Science, 221,* 1208–1210. (p. 235)

Elliott, I. R., Witty, T. E., Herrick, S., & Hoffman, J. T. (1991). Negotiating reality after physical loss: Hope, depression, and disability. *Journal of Personality and Social Psychology, 61,* 608–613. (p. 590)

Ellis, A. (1962). *Reason and emotion in psychotherapy.* New York: Lyle Stuart. (p. 666)

Ellis, A. (1986). Rational-emotive therapy. In I. L. Kutash & A. Wolf (Eds.), *Psychotherapist's casebook.* San Franscisco: Jossey-Bass. (p. 665)

Ellis, A. (1993). Fundamentals of rational-emotive therapy for the 1990s. In W. Dryden & L. K. Hill (Eds.), *Innovations in rational-emotive therapy.* Newbury Park, CA: SAGE. (p. 665)

Ellis, L., & Ames, M. A. (1987). Neurohormonal functioning and sexual orientation: A theory of homosexuality-heterosexuality. *Psychological Bulletin, 101,* 233–258. (p. 215)

Ellis, L., Ames, M. A., Peckham, W., & Burke, D. (1988). Sexual orientation of human offspring may be altered by severe maternal stress during pregnancy. *Journal of Sex Research, 25,* 152–157. (p. 215)

Emlen, S. T. (1975, August). The stellar-orientation system of a migratory bird. *Scientific American,* 102–111. (pp. 92–93)

Endler, N. S. (1982). *Holiday of darkness: A psychologist's personal journey out of his depression.* New York: Wiley. (p. 622)

Enns, J. T., & Rensink, R. A. (1990). Sensitivity to three-dimensional orientation in visual search. *Psychological Science, 1,* 323–326. (p. 296)

Enright, R. D., Levy, V. M. Jr., Harris, D., & Lapsley, D. K. (1987). *Journal of Youth and Adolescence, 16,* 541–559. (p. 472)

Epstein, R. (1991). Skinner, creativity, and the problem of spontaneous behavior. *Psychological Science, 2,* 362–370. (p. 14)

Epstein, S. (1979). The stability of behavior: I. On predicting most of the people much of the time. *Journal of Personality and Social Psychology, 37*, 1097–1126. (p. 598)

Epstein, S., & O'Brien, E. J. (1985). The person-situational debate in historical and current perspective. *Psychological Bulletin, 98*, 513–537. (p. 598)

Erckmann, W. J. (1983). The evolution of polyandry in shorebirds: An evolutionary hypothesis. In S. K. Wasser (Ed.), *Social behavior of female vertebrates.* New York: Academic Press. (p. 106)

Erdelyi, M. H. (1985). *Psychoanalysis: Freud's cognitive psychology.* New York: Freeman. (pp. 22, 656)

Ericsson, K. A., & Chase, W. G. (1982). Exceptional memory. *American Scientist, 70*, 607–615. (p. 340)

Eriksen, C. W., & Collins, J. F. (1967). Some temporal characteristics of visual pattern perception. *Journal of Experimental Psychology, 74*, 476–484. (p. 329)

Erikson, E. (1959). *Identity and the lifecycle.* Monograph, *Psychological Issues, 1*, 1. (p. 450)

Erikson, E. H. (1963). *Childhood and society* (2nd ed.). New York: Norton. (pp. 450, 465, 481)

Erikson, E. H. (1968). *Identity: Youth and crisis.* New York: Norton. (p. 476)

Erlenmeyer-Kimling, L., Cornblatt, B. A., Rock, D., Roberts, S., Bell, M., & West, A. (1993). The New York high-risk project: Anhedonia, attentional deviance, and psychopathology. *Schizophrenia Bulletin, 19*, 141–153. (p. 642)

Errera, P. (1972). Statement based on interviews with forty "worst cases" in the Milgram obedience experiments. In J. Katz (Ed.), *Experimentation with human beings: The authority of the investigator, subject, professions, and state in the human experimentation process.* New York: Russell Sage Foundation. (p. 541)

Ervin-Tripp, S. (1964). An analysis of the interaction of language, topic, and listener. *American Anthropologist, 86* (6, Pt. 2), 86–102. (p. 406)

Essock-Vitale, S. M., & McGuire, M. T. (1980). Predictions derived from the theories of kin selection and reciprocation assessed by anthropological data. *Ethology and Sociobiology, 1*, 233–243. (p. 116)

Etscorn, F., & Stephens, R. (1973). Establishment of conditioned taste aversions with a 24-hour CS-US interval. *Physiological Psychology, 1*, 251–253. (p. 153)

Evans, J. A., Hamerton, J. L., & Robinson, A. (Eds.) (1991). *Children and young adults with sex chromosome aneuploidy: Follow-up, clinical, and molecular studies.* New York: Wiley-Liss. (p. 60)

Evarts, E. V. (1979, September). Brain mechanisms in movement. *Scientific American*, 164–179. (p. 176)

Eysenck, H. J. (1952). *The scientific study of personality.* London: Routledge & Kegan Paul. (p. 595)

Eysenck, H. J. (1973). *The inequality of man.* London: Temple Smith. (p. 69)

Eysenck, H. J. (1982). Development of a theory. In H. J. Eysenck (Ed.), *Personality, genetics, and behavior: Selected papers.* New York: Praeger. (pp. 593, 595)

Eysenck, H. J. (1990). Genetic and environmental contributions to individual differences: The three major dimensions of personality. *Journal of Personality, 58*, 247–261. (p. 599)

Eysenck, H. J., & Eysenck, M. W. (1985). *Personality and individual differences: A natural science approach.* New York: Plenum. (p. 595)

Eysenck, M. W. (1992). *Anxiety: The cognitive perspective.* Hillsdale, NJ: Erlbaum. (p. 618)

Eysenck, S. B. G., & Eysenck, H. J. (1967). Salivary response to lemon juice as a measure of introversion. *Perceptual and Motor Skill, 24*, 1047–1051. (p. 596)

Fagan, J. F. (1973). Infants' delayed recognition memory and forgetting. *Journal of Experimental Child Psychology, 16*, 424–450. (p. 418)

Fancher, R. E. (1985). *The intelligence men: Makers of the IQ controversy.* New York: Norton. (pp. 68, 69, 371)

Fantz, R. L. (1961). The origin of form perception. *Scientific American, 204*, 66–72. (p. 416)

Fantz, R. L. (1963). Pattern vision in newborn infants. *Science, 140*, 296–297. (p. 416)

Farah, M. J. (1989a). The neuropsychology of mental imagery. In J. W. Brown (Ed.), *Neuropsychology of visual perception.* Hillsdale, NJ: Erlbaum. (p. 345)

Farah, M. J. (1989b). The neural basis of mental imagery. *Trends in Neuroscience, 12*, 395–399. (p. 346)

Farina, A., Gliha, D., Boudreau, L. A., Allen, J. G., & Sherman, M. (1971). Mental illness and the impact of believing others know about it. *Journal of Abnormal Psychology, 77*, 1–5. (p. 616)

Faust, I. M. (1984). Role of the fat cell in energy balance physiology. In A. J. Stunkard & E. Stellar (Eds.), *Eating and its disorders.* New York: Raven. (pp. 210–211)

Fazio, R. H. (1986). How do attitudes guide behavior? In R. M. Sorrentino & E. T. Higgins (Eds.), *Handbook of motivation and cognition: Foundations of social behavior.* New York: Guilford. (p. 524)

Fazio, R. H. (1990). Multiple processes by which attitudes guide behavior: The mode model as an integrative framework. *Advances in Experimental Social Psychology, 23*, 75–109. (p. 524)

Fechner, G. T. (1860; translated edition 1966). *Elements of psychophysics.* (H. E. Alder, Trans.). New York: Holt, Rinehart & Winston. (p. 277)

Feder, H. H. (1984). Hormones and sexual behavior. *Annual Reviews of Psychology, 35*, 165–200. (pp. 192, 213, 216, 217)

Feeney, J. A., & Noller, P. (1990). Attachment style as a predictor of adult romantic relationships. *Journal of Personality and Social Psychology, 58*, 281–291. (pp. 458, 481)

Festinger, L. (1954). A theory of social comparison processes. *Human Relations, 7*, 117–140. (p. 516)

Festinger, L. (1957). *A theory of cognitive dissonance.* Stanford: Stanford University Press. (p. 519)

Festinger, L., & Carlsmith, J. M. (1959). Cognitive consequences of forced compliance. *Journal of Abnormal and Social Psychology, 58*, 203–210. (p. 521)

Field, T. (1990). *Infancy.* Cambridge, MA: Harvard University Press. (pp. 454, 458)

Field, T., Greenberg, R., Woodson, R., Cohen, D., & Garcia, R. (1984). Facial expressions during Brazelton neonatal assessments. *Infant Mental Health Journal, 5,* 61–71. (p. 454)

Field, T. M., Cohen, D., Garcia, R., & Greenberg, R. (1984). Mother-stranger face discrimination by the newborn. *Infant Behavior and Development, 7,* 19–25. (p. 417)

Fieve, R. R. (1975). *Mood swing.* New York: William Morrow. (p. 626)

Finkel, S. E., Guterbock, T. M., & Borg, M. J. (1991). Race-of-interviewer effects in a preelection poll. *Public Opinion Quarterly, 55,* 313–330. (p. 525)

Fiorito, G., & Scotto, P. (1992). Observational learning in *Octopus vulgaris. Science, 256,* 545–547. (p. 150)

Fischer, P. J., & Breakey, W. R. (1991). The epidemiology of alcohol, drug, and mental disorders among homeless persons. *American Psychologist, 46,* 1115–1128. (p. 648)

Fischler, M. A., & Firschein, O. (1987). *Intelligence: The eye, the brain, and the computer.* Reading, MA: Addison-Wesley. (p. 395)

FitzGerald, K. W. (1988). *Alcoholism: The genetic inheritance.* Garden City, NY: Doubleday. (p. 632)

Flaherty, C. F. (1982). Incentive contrast: A review of behavioral changes following shifts in reward. *Animal Learning and Behavior, 10,* 409–440. (p. 148)

Flourens, P. J. M. (1824; reprinted 1965). *Pierre Jean Marie Flourens on the functions of the brain* (M. D. Boring, Trans.). In R. J. Herrnstein & E. G. Boring (Eds.), *A source book in the history of psychology.* Cambridge, MA: Harvard University Press. (p. 16)

Foa, E. B., & Kozak, M. J. (1986). Emotional processing of fear: Exposure to corrective information. *Psychological Bulletin, 99,* 20–35. (pp. 670, 671)

Foa, E. B., Steketee, G. S., & Ozarow, B. J. (1985). In M. Mavissakalian, S. M. Turner, & L. Michelson (Eds.), *Obsessive-compulsive disorder.* New York: Plenum. (p. 620)

Fodor, I. G. (1982). Gender and phobia. In I. Al-Issa (Ed.), *Gender and psychopathology.* New York: Academic Press. (p. 619)

Ford, C. S., & Beach, F. A. (1951). *Patterns of sexual behavior.* New York: Harper & Row. (p. 475)

Ford, C. V. (1983). *The somatizing disorders: Illness as a way of life.* New York: Elsevier Biomedical. (p. 627)

Ford, M. R., & Lowery, C. R. (1986). Gender differences in moral reasoning: A comparison of the use of justice and care orientations. *Journal of Personality and Social Psychology, 50,* 777–783. (p. 480)

Ford, M. R., & Widiger, T. A. (1989). Sex bias in the diagnosis of histrionic and antisocial personality disorders. *Journal of Consulting and Clinical Psychology, 57,* 301–305. (pp. 614, 615)

Forrest, G. G. (1985). Antabuse treatment. In T. E. Bratter & G. G. Forrest (Eds.), *Alcoholism and substance abuse: Strategies for clinical intervention.* New York: Free Press. (p. 673)

Foss, J. D., & Hakes, D. T. (1978). *Psycholinguistics: An introduction to the psychology of language.* Englewood Cliffs, NJ: Prentice Hall. (p. 397)

Foulkes, D. (1985). *Dreaming: A cognitive-psychological analysis.* Hillsdale, NJ: Erlbaum. (p. 227)

Fowles, D. C. (1992). Schizophrenia: Diathesis-stress revisited. *Annual Review of Psychology, 43,* 303–336. (pp. 76, 77, 640, 641, 642, 679)

Fox, N. A., & Davidson, R. J. (1988). Patterns of brain electrical activity during facial signs of emotion in 10-month-old infants. *Developmental Psychology, 24,* 230–236. (pp. 102, 238)

Frandsen, A. N., & Holder, J. R. (1969). Spatial visualization in solving complex verbal problems. *Journal of Psychology, 73,* 229–233. (p. 392)

Frankel, K. A., & Bates, J. E. (1990). Mother-toddler problem solving: Antecedents of attachment, home behavior, and temperament. *Child Development, 61,* 810–819. (p. 458)

Franklin, B. (1818; reprinted 1949). *The autobiography of Benjamin Franklin.* Berkeley, CA: University of California Press. (p. 520)

Freedman, B., & Chapman, L. J. (1973). Early subjective experience in schizophrenic episodes. *Journal of Abnormal Psychology, 82,* 46–54. (p. 642)

Freedman, J. L., & Fraser, S. C. (1966). Compliance without pressure: The foot-in-the-door technique. *Journal of Personality and Social Psychology, 4,* 195–202. (p. 536)

Frenkel, O. J., & Doob, A. N. (1976). Post-decision dissonance at the polling booth. *Canadian Journal of Behavioural Science, 8,* 347–350. (p. 520)

Freud, A. (1936; reprinted 1946). *The ego and the mechanisms of defense* (C. Baines, Trans.). New York: International Universities Press. (p. 571)

Freud, S. (1900; reprinted 1953). *The interpretation of dreams* (J. Strachey, Ed. & trans.). London: Hogarth Press. (p. 568)

Freud, S. (1901; reprinted 1960). *The psychopathology of everyday life* (A. Tyson, Trans., & J. Strachey, Ed.). New York: Norton. (pp. 568, 569)

Freud, S. (1909; reprinted 1963). Notes upon a case of obsessional neurosis. In P. Rieff (Ed.), *Three case histories.* New York: Collier Books. (p. 660)

Freud, S. (1910; reprinted 1947). *Leonardo da Vinci: A study in psychosexuality.* New York: Random House. (p. 571)

Freud, S. (1912; reprinted 1932). A note on the unconscious in psychoanalysis. In J. Rickman (Ed.), *A general selection from the works of Sigmund Freud.* London: Hogarth Press. (p. 566)

Freud, S. (1923; reprinted 1963). [Note appended to the 1963 reprint of "Notes upon a case of obsession neurosis."] In P. Rieff (Ed.), *Three case histories.* New York: Collier Books. (p. 661)

Freud, S. (1926; reprinted 1964). Inhibitions, symptoms, and anxiety. In J. Strachey (Trans. & ed.), *The standard edition of the complete works of Sigmund Freud* (Vol. 20). London: Hogarth Press. (p. 570)

Freud, S. (1933; reprinted 1964). *New introductory lectures on psychoanalysis.* In J. Strachey (Trans. & ed.), *The standard edition of the complete works of Sigmund Freud* (Vol. 20). London: Hogarth Press. (pp. 569, 570)

Freud, S. (1935; reprinted 1960). *A general introduction to psychoanalysis.* New York: Washington Square Press. (pp. 480, 574)

Frey, D. (1986). Recent research on selective exposure to information. *Advances in Experimental Social Psychology, 19*, 41–80. (p. 519)

Friedman, H. S., & Booth-Kewley, S. (1987). Personality, Type A behavior, and coronary heart disease: The role of emotional expression. *Journal of Personality and Social Psychology, 53*, 783–792. (p. 630)

Friedman, H. S., & Miller-Harringer, T. (1991). Nonverbal display of emotion in public and private: Self-monitoring, personality, and expressive cues. *Journal of Personality and Social Psychology, 61*, 766–775. (p. 513)

Friedman, M., & Rosenman, R. H. (1974). *Type A behavior and your heart.* New York: Knopf. (p. 630)

Friedman, S. (1972). Habituation and recovery of visual response in the alert human newborn. *Journal of Experimental Child Psychology, 13*, 339–349. (p. 417)

Fromkin, V. A. (1973). *Speech errors as linguistic evidence.* The Hague: Mouton. (p. 400)

Fromkin, V. A. (1980). *Errors in linguistic performance: Slips of the tongue, ear, pen and hand.* New York: Academic Press. (p. 400)

Fuller, J. L., & Thompson, W. R. (1978). *Foundations of behavior genetics.* New York: Wiley. (p. 65)

Funder, D. C. (1991). Global traits: A neo-Allportian approach to personality. *Psychological Science, 2*, 31–39. (p. 598)

Furrow, D., Nelson, K., & Benedict, H. (1979). Mothers' speech to children and syntactic development: Some simple relationships. *Journal of Child Language, 6*, 423–442. (p. 428)

Futuyma, D. J. (1986). *Evolutionary biology* (2nd ed.). Sunderland, MA: Sinauer. (pp. 82, 83)

Gaertner, S. L., Mann, J. A., Dovidio, J. F., Murrell, A. J., & Pomare, M. (1990). How does cooperation reduce intergroup bias? *Journal of Personality and Social Psychology, 59*, 692–704. (p. 558)

Gaffan, E. A., Hansel, M. C., & Smith, L. E. (1983). Does reward depletion influence spatial memory performance? *Learning and Memory, 14*, 58–74. (p. 157)

Galambos, N. L. (1992). Parent-adolescent relations. *Current Directions in Psychological Science, 1*, 146–149. (p. 473)

Galef, B. G., Jr. (1985). Social learning in wild Norway rats. In T. D. Johnston & A. T. Pietrewicz (Eds.), *Issues in the ecological study of learning.* Hillsdale, NJ: Erlbaum. (p. 154)

Galef, B. G. (1990). An adaptationist perspective on social learning, social feeding, and social foraging in Norway rats. In D. A. Dewsbury (Ed.), *Contemporary issues in comparative psychology.* Sunderland, MA: Sinauer. (p. 154)

Galef, B. G. (1991). A contrarian view of the wisdom of the body as it relates to dietary self-selection. *Psychological Review, 98*, 218–223. (p. 154)

Galef, B. G. (1992). The question of animal culture. *Human Nature, 3*, 157–178. (p. 150)

Galef, B. G., Jr., & Clark, M. M. (1971). Social factors in the poison avoidance and feeding behavior of wild and domesticated rat pups. *Journal of Comparative and Physiological Psychology, 75*, 341–357. (p. 154)

Gallistel, C. R. (1990). *The organization of learning.* Cambridge, MA: MIT Press. (p. 150)

Gallup, G. G. (1970). Chimpanzees: Self-recognition. *Science, 167*, 86–87. (p. 503)

Gallup, G. G., McClure, M. K., Hill, S. D., & Bundy, R. A. (1971). Capacity for self-recognition in differentially reared chimpanzees. *Developmental Psychobiology, 10*, 281–284. (p. 504)

Galton, F. (1865). Hereditary talent and character. *Macmillan's Magazine, 12*, 157–166, 318–327. (p. 68)

Galton, F. (1869; reprinted 1962). *Hereditary genius: An inquiry into its laws and consequences.* Cleveland: World Publishing. (pp. 67, 68, 370)

Galton, F. (1876). The history of twins as a criterion of the relative powers of nature and nurture. *Royal Anthropological Institute of Great Britain and Ireland Journal, 6*, 391–406. (p. 68)

Galton, F. (1885). On the anthropometric laboratory at the late international health exhibition. *Journal of the Anthropological Institute, 14*, 205–219. (p. 370)

Galton, F. (1907). *Inquiries into human faculty and its development.* New York: Dutton. (p. 68)

Gantt, W. H. (1953). Principles of nervous breakdown—schizokinesis and autokinesis. *Annals of the New York Academy of Sciences, 56*, 143–163. (p. 127)

Gantt, W. H. (1975). Unpublished lecture on Pavlov given at Ohio State University, April 25. (p. 123)

Garcia, J., Brett, L. P., & Rusiniak, K. W. (1989). Limits of Darwinian conditioning. In S. B. Klein & R. R. Mowrer (Eds.), *Contemporary learning theories: Instrumental conditioning theory and the impact of biological constraints on learning.* Hillsdale, NJ: Erlbaum. (p. 153)

Garcia, J., McGowan, B. K., Ervin, F. R., & Koelling, R. A. (1968). Cues—their relative effectiveness as a function of the reinforcer. *Science, 160*, 794–795. (p. 153)

Garcia, J., McGowan, B. K., & Green, K. F. (1972). Biological constraints on conditioning. In A. H. Black & W. G. Prokasy (Eds.), *Classical conditioning II: Current research and theory.* New York: Appleton-Century-Crofts. (p. 152)

Gardner, H. (1974). *The shattered mind.* New York: Random House. (pp. 180, 383)

Gardner, H. (1985). *Frames of mind.* New York: Basic Books. (p. 383)

Gardner, L. I. (1972, July). Deprivation dwarfism. *Scientific American*, 76–82. (p. 454)

Gardner, R. A., & Gardner, B. T. (1978). Comparative psychology and language acquisition. In K. Salzinger & F. L. Denmark (Eds.), Psychology: The state of the art. *Annals of the New York Academy of Sciences, 309*, 37–76. (p. 429)

Gardner, R. A., & Gardner, B. T. (1989). A cross-fostering laboratory. In R. A. Gardner, B. T. Gardner, & T. E. Van Cantfort (Eds.), *Teaching sign language to chimpanzees.* Albany: State University of New York Press. (pp. 430, 431)

Garland, D. J., & Barry, J. R. (1991). Cognitive advantage in sports: The nature of perceptual structures. *American Journal of Psychology, 104*, 211–228. (p. 340)

Garman, M. (1990). *Psycholinguistics.* Cambridge: Cambridge University Press. (p. 402)

Garrett, M. F. (1975). The analysis of sentence production. In G. H. Bower (Ed.), *The psychology of learning and motivation* (Vol. 9). New York: Academic Press. (pp. 400, 401)

Garrett, M. F. (1982). Production of speech: Observations from normal and pathological language use. In A. W. Ellis (Ed.), *Normality and pathology in cognitive functions.* London: Academic Press. (p. 400)

Garrett, M. F. (1990). Sentence processing. In D. N. Osherson & H. Lasnik (Eds.), *Language: An invitation to cognitive science, volume 1.* Cambridge, MA: MIT Press. (p. 401)

Garvey, C. (1990). *Play: enlarged edition.* Cambridge, MA: Harvard University Press. (p. 465)

Gazzaniga, M. S. (1967, August). The split brain in man. *Scientific American,* 24–29. (pp. 181, 182)

Gazzaniga, M. S. (1970). *The bisected brain.* New York: Appleton-Century-Crofts. (p. 182)

Geen, R. G. (1980). The effects of being observed on performance. In P. B. Paulus (Ed.), *Psychology of group influence.* Hillsdale, NJ: Erlbaum. (p. 543)

Geen, R. G. (1984). Preferred stimulation levels in introverts and extraverts: Effects on arousal and performance. *Journal of Personality and Social Psychology, 45,* 1303–1312. (p. 596)

Geen, R. G. (1991). Social motivation. *Annual Review of Psychology, 42,* 377–399. (p. 543)

Geliebter, A., Westreich, S., Hashim, S. A., & Gage, D. (1987). Gastric balloon reduces food intake and body weight in obese rats. *Physiology and Behavior, 39,* 399–402. (p. 208)

Gelman, D., Foote, D., & Talbot, M. (1992). Born or bred? *Newsweek,* Feb. 24. (p. 215)

Gescheider, G. A. (1976). *Psychophysics: Methods and theory.* Hillsdale, NJ: Erlbaum. (p. 277)

Geschwind, N. (1972, April). Language and the brain. *Scientific American,* 76–83. (p. 403)

Ghez, C. (1991a). The control of movement. In E. R. Kandel, J. H. Schwartz, & T. M. Jessell (Eds.), *Principles of neural science, third edition.* New York: Elsevier. (p. 178)

Ghez, C. (1991b). Voluntary movement. In E. R. Kandel, J. H. Schwartz, & T. M. Jessell (Eds.), *Principles of neural science, third edition.* New York: Elsevier. (p. 176)

Gibbs, J. C., & Schnell, S. V. (1985). Moral development "versus" socialization. *American Psychologist, 40,* 1071–1080. (p. 479)

Gibson, E. J. (1969). *Principles of perceptual learning and its development.* Englewood Cliffs, NJ: Prentice Hall. (pp. 297–298)

Gibson, E. J. (1971). Perceptual learning and the theory of word perception. *Cognitive Psychology, 2,* 351–358. (p. 305)

Gibson, E. J., & Walk, R. D. (1960, April). The visual cliff. *Scientific American,* 64–71. (p. 418)

Gibson, J. J. (1966). *The senses considered as perceptual systems.* Boston: Houghton Mifflin. (p. 321)

Gibson, J. J. (1979). *The ecological approach to visual perception.* Boston: Houghton Mifflin. (p. 321)

Gilbert, C. D., & Wiesel, T. N. (1992). Receptive field dynamics in adult primary visual cortex. *Nature, 356,* 150–152. (p. 268)

Gilbert, D. T. (1989). Thinking lightly about others: Automatic components of the social inference process. In J. S. Uleman & J. A. Bargh (Eds.), *Unintended thought.* New York: Guilford. (pp. 498, 499)

Gilbert, D. T., & Hixon, J. G. (1991). The trouble of thinking: Activation and application of stereotypic beliefs. *Journal of Personality and Social Psychology, 60,* 509–517. (p. 500)

Gilbert, D. T., & Jones, E. E. (1986). Perceiver-induced constraint: Interpretations of self-generated reality. *Journal of Personality and Social Psychology, 50,* 269–280. (p. 498)

Gilligan, C. (1982). *In a different voice: Psychological theory and women's development.* Cambridge, MA: Harvard University Press (pp. 476, 480)

Gilligan, C. (1987). Adolescent development reconsidered. In C. E. Irwin, Jr. (Ed.), *Adolescent social behavior and health.* San Francisco: Jossey-Bass. (p. 480)

Gilligan, C., Lyons, N. P., & Hanmer, T. J. (Eds.) (1990). *Making connections: The relational worlds of adolescent girls at Emma Willard School.* Cambridge, MA: Harvard University Press. (pp. 476, 480)

Glanzer, M., & Cunitz, A. R. (1966). Two storage mechanisms in free recall. *Journal of Verbal Learning and Verbal Behavior, 5,* 351–360. (p. 334)

Gleitman, L. R., & Gleitman, H. (1992). A picture is worth a thousand words, but that's the problem: The role of syntax in vocabulary acquisition. *Current Directions in Psychological Science, 1,* 31–35. (p. 425)

Glisky, E. L., Schacter, D. L., & Tulving, E. (1986). Computer learning by memory-impaired patients: Acquisition and retention of complex knowledge. *Neuropsychologia, 24,* 313–328. (p. 363)

Godfray, H. C. (1992). The evolution of forgiveness. *Nature, 355,* 206–207. (p. 556)

Goffman, E. (1959) *The presentation of self in everyday life.* Garden City, NY: Doubleday. (p. 510)

Goldberg, L. R. (1990). An alternative "description of personality": The big-five factor structure. *Journal of Personality and Social Psychology, 59,* 1216–1229. (p. 596)

Goldberg, L. R. (1993). The structure of phenotypic personality traits. *American Psychologist, 48,* 26–34. (p. 596)

Goldenberg, G., Podreka, I., Steiner, M., Suess, E., Deeke, L., & Wilmes, K. (1988). Regional cerebral blood flow patterns in imagery tasks—Results of single photon emission computer tomography. In M. Denis, J. Englekamp, & J. T. E. Richardson (Eds.), *Cognitive and neuropsychological approaches to mental imagery.* Dordrecht, The Netherlands: Martinus Nijhoff. (p. 346)

Goldsmith, H. H., Bradshaw, D. L., & Riesser-Danner, L. A. (1986). Temperament as a potential developmental influence on attachment. In J. V. Lerner & R. M. Lerner (Eds.), *Temperament and social interaction in infants and children.* San Francisco: Jossey-Bass. (p. 456)

Goleman, D. (1992). Childhood trauma: Memory or invention? *New York Times,* July 21, pp. C1 and C5. (p. 356)

Golinkoff, R. M., Hirsh-Pasek, K., Bailey, L. M., & Wenger, N. R. (1992). Young children and adults use lexical principles to learn new nouns. *Developmental Psychology, 28,* 99–108. (p. 425)

Gonzalez, M. F., & Deutsch, J. A. (1981). Vagotomy abolishes cues of satiety produced by gastric distension. *Science, 212,* 1283–1284. (p. 208)

Good, T. L., & Findley, M. J. (1985). Sex role expectations and achievement. In J. B. Dusek (Ed.), *Teacher expectations.* Hillsdale, NJ: Erlbaum. (p. 469)

Goodale, M. A., Milner, A. D., Jakobson, L. S., & Carey, D. P. (1991). A neurological dissociation between perceiving objects and grasping them. *Nature, 349,* 154–156. (p. 308)

Goodall, J. (1986). *The chimpanzees of Gombe.* Cambridge, MA: Harvard University Press. (pp. 108, 109, 111, 112)

Goodall, J. (1988). *In the shadow of man* (rev. ed.). Boston: Houghton Mifflin. (p. 111)

Goodwin, D. W. (1976). *Is alcoholism hereditary?* New York: Oxford University Press. (p. 633)

Goodwin, D. W. (1979). Alcoholism and heredity. *Archives of General Psychiatry, 36,* 57–61. (p. 633)

Gopnik, M. (1990a). Feature-blind grammar and dysphasia. *Nature, 344,* 715. (p. 427)

Gopnik, M. (1990b). Feature-blindness: A case study. *Language Acquisition, 1,* 139–164. (p. 427)

Gopnik, M., & Crago, M. B. (1991). Familial aggregation of a developmental language disorder. *Cognition, 39,* 1–50. (p. 427)

Gordon, J. (1991). Spinal mechanisms of motor coordination. In E. R. Kandel, J. H. Schwartz, & T. M. Jessell (Eds.), *Principles of neural science, third edition.* New York: Elsevier. (p. 170)

Gordon, R. A. (1990). *Anorexia and bulimia: Anatomy of a social epidemic.* Cambridge, MA: Basil Blackwell. (p. 608)

Gordon, S., & Gilgun, J. F. (1987). *Adolescent sexuality.* In V. B. Van Hasselt & M. Hersen (Eds.), *Handbook of adolescent psychology.* New York: Pergamon. (p. 474)

Goren, C. C., Sarty, M., & Wu, P. Y. K. (1975). Visual following and pattern discrimination of face-like stimuli by newborn infants. *Pediatrics, 56,* 544–549. (p. 417)

Gorski, R. A., Harlan, R. E., Jacobson, C. D., Shryne, J. E., & Southham, A. M. (1980). Evidence for the existence of a sexually dimorphic nucleus in the preoptic area of the rat. *Journal of Comparative Neurology, 193,* 529–539. (p. 213)

Gotlib, I. H. (1992). Interpersonal and cognitive aspects of depression. *Current Directions in Psychological Science, 1,* 149–154. (p. 625)

Gottesman, I. I. (1991). *Schizophrenia genesis: The origins of madness.* New York: Freeman. (pp. 74, 75, 76, 640)

Gottesman, I. I., McGuffin, P., & Farmer, A. E. (1987). Clinical genetics as clues to the "real" genetics of schizophrenia (a decade of modest gains while playing for time). *Schizophrenia Bulletin, 13,* 23–47. (p. 640)

Gottesman, I. I., & Shields, J. (1966). Schizophrenia in twins: 16 years' consecutive admissions to a psychiatric clinic. *British Journal of Psychiatry, 112,* 809–818. (p. 75)

Gottman, J. M. (1979). *Marital interaction: Experimental investigations.* New York: Academic Press. (p. 482)

Gottman, J. M., & Krokoff, L. J. (1989). Marital interaction and satisfaction: A longitudinal view. *Journal of Consulting and Clinical Psychology, 57,* 47–52. (p. 482)

Gottman, J. M., & Porterfield, A. L. (1981). Communicative competence in the nonverbal behavior of married couples. *Journal of Marriage and the Family, 43,* 817–834. (p. 482)

Goudie, A. J. (1990). Conditioned opponent processes in the development of tolerance to psychoactive drugs. *Progress in Neuro-Psychopharmacology and Biological Psychiatry, 14,* 675–688. (p. 130)

Gould, J. L. (1982). *Ethology: The mechanisms and evolution of behavior.* New York: Norton. (p. 14)

Gould, S. J. (1983). Hyena myths and realities. In S. J. Gould (Ed.), *Hen's teeth and horse's toes: Further reflections in natural history.* New York: Norton. (p. 88)

Gould, S. J., & Eldredge, N. (1977). Punctuated equilibria: The tempo and mode of evolution reconsidered. *Paleobiology, 3,* 115–151. (p. 83)

Gouldner, A. W. (1960). The norm of reciprocity: A preliminary statement. *American Sociological Review, 25,* 161–178. (p. 536)

Graham, N. (1992). Breaking the visual stimulus into parts. *Current Directions in Psychological Science, 1,* 55–61. (pp. 268, 269)

Gray, P., & Chanoff, D. (1986). Democratic schooling: What happens to young people who have charge of their own education? *American Journal of Education, 94,* 182–213. (pp. 467, 583)

Green, D. M. (1964). Psychoacoustics and detection theory. In J. A. Swets (Ed.), *Signal detection and recognition by human observers.* New York: Wiley. (p. 276)

Green, M., & Walker, E. (1986). Attentional performance in positive- and negative-symptom schizophrenia. *The Journal of Nervous and Mental Disease, 174,* 208–213. (pp. 636, 637)

Green, M. F. (1993). Cognitive remediation in schizophrenia: Is it time yet? *American Journal of Psychiatry, 150,* 178–187. (p. 642)

Greenberg, D. (1992a). *The Sudbury Valley School experience* (3rd ed.). Framingham, MA: Sudbury Valley School Press. (pp. 444, 466)

Greenberg, D. (1992b). Sudbury Valley's secret weapon: Allowing people of different ages to mix freely at school. In *The Sudbury Valley School experience,* 3rd edition. Framingham, MA: The Sudbury Valley School Press. (pp. 444, 466)

Greenberg, D., & Sadofsky, M. (1992). *Legacy of trust: Life after the Sudbury Valley School experience.* Framingham, MA: The Sudbury Valley School Press. (p. 467)

Greenberg, J., & Kuczaj, S. A. (1982). Towards a theory of substantive word-meaning acquisition. In S. A. Kuczaj (Ed.), *Language development, vol. 1: Syntax and semantics.* Hillsdale, NJ: Erlbaum. (p. 347)

Greenberg, J. H. (1978). Generalizations about numeral systems. In J. H. Greenberg (Ed.), *Universals of human language: Volume 3, Word Structure.* Stanford, CA: Stanford University Press. (p. 405)

Greenfield, P. M., & Savage-Rumbaugh, E. S. (1991). Imitation, grammatical development, and the invention of protogrammar by an ape. In N. A. Karsnegor, D. M. Rumbaugh, R. L.

Schiefelbusch, & M. Studdert-Kennedy (Eds.), *Biological and behavioral determinants of language development.* Hillsdale, NJ: Erlbaum. (p. 432)

Greenfield, P. M., & Smith, J. H. (1976). *The structure of communication in early language development.* New York: Academic Press. (pp. 424, 426)

Greenough, W. T., & Black, J. E. (1992). Induction of brain structure by experience: Substrate for cognitive development. In M. R. Gunnar & C. A. Nelson (Eds.), *Developmental behavioral neuroscience: The Minnesota Symposia on Child Psychology, Vol. 24.* Hillsdale, NJ: Erlbaum. (p. 188)

Greenwald, A. G. (1992). New look 3: Unconscious cognition reclaimed. *American Psychologist, 47,* 766–779. (p. 360)

Gregory, R. L. (1968, November). Visual illusions. *Scientific American,* 66–76. (pp. 314, 315)

Griffith, J. D., Cavanaugh, J., Held, N. N., & Oates, J. A. (1972). Dextroamphetamine: Evaluation of psychotomimetic properties in man. *Archives of General Psychiatry, 26,* 97–100. (p. 641)

Grillner, S., & Wallén, P. (1985). Central pattern generators for locomotion, with special reference to vertebrates. *Annual Review of Neuroscience, 8,* 233–261. (p. 170)

Groos, K. (1898). *The play of animals.* New York: Appleton. (p. 464)

Groos, K. (1901). *The play of man.* New York: Appleton. (p. 464)

Gross, T. F. (1985). *Cognitive development.* Monterey, CA: Brooks/Cole. (p. 437)

Grossman, S. P. (1979). The biology of motivation. *Annual Review of Psychology, 30,* 209–242. (p. 207)

Groth-Marnat, G. (1990). *Handbook of psychological assessment* (2nd ed.). New York: Wiley. (pp. 654–655)

Grove, W. M. (1987). The reliability of psychiatric diagnosis. In C. G. Last & M. Hersen (Eds.), *Issues in diagnostic research.* New York: Plenum. (p. 610)

Grüsser, O. J., & Grüsser-Cornehls, U. (1986). Physiology of vision. In R. F. Schmidt (Ed.), *Fundamentals of sensory physiology* (3rd ed.). New York: Springer-Verlag. (pp. 256, 257)

Gusella, J. F., Wexler, N. S., Conneally, P. M., Naylor, S. L., Anderson, M. A., Tanzi, R. E., Watkins, P. C., Ottina, K., Wallace, M. R., Sakaguchi, A. Y., & others (1983). A polymorphic DNA marker genetically linked to Huntington's disease. *Nature, 306,* 234–238. (p. 57)

Guthrie, E. R. (1952). *The psychology of learning.* New York: Harper & Row. (p. 146)

Gutmann, D. L. (1975). Parenthood. In N. Datan & L. H. Ginsberg (Eds.), *Life-span development psychology.* New York: Academic Press. (p. 483)

Guyote, M. J., & Sternberg, R. J. (1981). A transitive-chain theory of syllogistic reasoning. *Cognitive Psychology, 13,* 461–525. (p. 392)

Gynther, M. D. (1972). White norms and black MMPIs: A prescription for discrimination? *Psychological Bulletin, 78,* 386–402. (p. 653)

Haan, N., Smith, M. B., & Block, J. (1968) The moral reasoning of young adults: Political-social behaviour, family background and personality correlated. *Journal of Personality and Social Psychology, 10,* 183–201. (pp. 479, 480)

Hagestad, G. O., & Neugarten, B. L. (1985). Age and the life course. In R. B. Binstock & E. Shanas (Eds.), *Handbook of aging and the social sciences* (2nd ed.). New York: Van Nostrand Reinhold. (p. 452)

Halpern, A. R. (1986). Memory for tune titles after organized or unorganized presentation. *American Journal of Psychology, 99,* 57–70. (p. 340)

Hamaguchi, E. (1985). A contextual model of the Japanese: Toward a methodological innovation in Japan studies. *Journal of Japanese Studies, 11,* 289–321. (p. 507)

Hamill, J. F. (1990). *Ethno-logic: The anthropology of human reasoning.* Urbana and Chicago: University of Illinois Press. (p. 385)

Hamilton, W. D. (1964). The genetical theory of social behaviour, I, II. *Journal of Theoretical Biology, 12,* 12–45. (p. 112)

Hardin, G. (1968). The tragedy of the commons. *Science, 162,* 1243–1248. (p. 554)

Harlow, H. F. (1959, June). Love in infant monkeys. *Scientific American,* 68–74. (pp. 454, 455)

Harper, L. V., & Sanders, K. M. (1975). The effect of adults' eating on young children's acceptance of unfamiliar foods. *Journal of Experimental Child Psychology, 20,* 206–214. (p. 155)

Harrington, D. M., Block, J. H., & Block, J. (1987). Testing aspects of Carl Rogers's theory of creative environments: Childrearing antecedents of creative potential in young adolescents. *Journal of Personality and Social Psychology, 52,* 851–856. (p. 583)

Harris, M. J., & Rosenthal, R. (1985). Mediation of interpersonal expectancy effects: 31 meta-analyses. *Psychological Bulletin, 97,* 363–386. (p. 505)

Hartshorne, H., & May, M. (1928). *Studies in deceit.* New York: Macmillan. (p. 597)

Hasler, A. D., & Larsen, J. A. (1955, August). The homing salmon. *Scientific American,* 72–76. (p. 157)

Hassett, J. (1978). *A primer of psychophysiology.* San Francisco: Freeman. (p. 221)

Hatfield, E., Cacioppo, J. T., & Rapson, R. (1992, in press). Primitive emotional contagion. *Review of Personality and Social Psychology.* (p. 236)

Hatfield, E., & Sprecher, S. 1986). *Mirror, mirror . . . The importance of looks in everyday life.* Albany, NY: State University of New York Press. (p. 482)

Hathaway, S. R., & McKinley, J. C. (1943). *MMPI manual.* New York: Psychological Corporation. (p. 653)

Hawkins, H. L., & Presson, J. C. (1986). Auditory information processing. In K. R. Boff, L. Kaufman, & J. P. Thomas (Eds.), *Handbook of perception and human performance, Vol. II: Cognitive processes and performance.* New York: Wiley. (p. 300)

Hay, D. (1985). *Essentials of behaviour genetics.* Melbourne: Blackwell. (p. 58)

Hayes, K. J., & Hayes, C. H. (1951). The intellectual development of a home-raised chimpanzee. *Proceedings of the American Philosophical Society, 95,* 105–109. (p. 429)

Hazen, C., & Shaver, P. (1987). Romantic love conceptualized as an attachment process. *Journal of Personality and Social Psychology, 52,* 511–524. (pp. 458, 481)

Heath, R. G. (1972). Pleasure and brain activity in man. *The Journal of Nervous and Mental Disease, 154,* 3–18. (p. 219)

Hebb, D. O. (1949). *The organization of behavior: A neuropsychological theory.* New York: Wiley. (p. 190)

Hebb, D. (1958). *A textbook of psychology.* Philadelphia: Saunders. (p. 63)

Hécaen, H., & Albert, M. L. (1978). *Human neuropsychology.* New York: Wiley. (p. 297)

Hecht, S., & Mandelbaum, M. (1938). Rod-cone dark adaptation and vitamin A. *Science, 88,* 219–221. (p. 257)

Hecker, J. E., & Thorpe, G. L. (1992). *Agoraphobia and panic: A guide to psychological treatment.* Boston: Allyn & Bacon. (p. 620)

Hefferline, R. F., Keenan, B., & Harford, R. A. (1959). Escape and avoidance conditioning of human subjects without their observation of the response. *Science, 130,* 1338–1339. (p. 133)

Heider, F. (1958). *The psychology of interpersonal relations.* New York: Wiley. (pp. 497, 498)

Heiman, M. (1987). Learning to learn: A behavioral approach to improving thinking. In D. N. Perkins, J. Lockhead, & J. Bishop (Eds.), *Thinking: The second international conference.* Hillsdale, NJ: Erlbaum. (p. 338)

Heimer, L., & Larsson, K. (1967). Impairment of mating behavior in male rats following lesions in the preoptic-anterior hypothalamic continuum. *Brain Research, 3,* 248–263. (p. 213)

Heinrichs, R. W. (1993). Schizophrenia and the brain: Conditions for a neuropsychology of madness. *American Psychologist, 48,* 221–233. (pp. 640, 641)

Helmholtz, H. von (1852). On the theory of compound colors. *Philosophical Magazine, 4,* 519–534. (p. 261)

Helmholtz, H. von (1867/1962). *Helmholtz's treatise on physiological optics.* (J. P. C. Southall, Ed. and trans.). New York: Dover Publications. (Originally published in the *Handbuch der physiologischen optik,* 1867.) (pp. 308, 309, 311, 315, 323)

Hendrick, C. (1977). Social psychology as an experimental science. In C. Hendrick (Ed.), *Perspectives in social psychology.* Hillsdale, NJ: Erlbaum. (p. 542)

Hendricks, B., Marvel, M. K., & Barrington, B. L. (1990). The dimensions of psychological research. *Teaching of Psychology, 17,* 76–82. (p. 30)

Henn, F. A. (1989). Animal models. In J. J. Mann (Ed.), *Models of depressive disorders: Psychological, biological, and genetic perspectives.* New York: Plenum Press. (p. 623)

Henry, J. L. (1986). Role of circulating opioids in the modulation of pain. In D. D. Kelly (Ed.), *Stress-induced analgesia* (Vol. 467 of the *Annals of the New York Academy of Sciences).* New York: New York Academy of Sciences. (pp. 192, 272)

Herek, G. M. (1986). The instrumentality of attitudes: Toward a neofunctional theory. *Journal of Social Issues, 42,* 99–114. (pp. 514, 516)

Herek, G. M. (1987). Can functions be measured? A new perspective on the functional approach to attitudes. *Social Psychology Quarterly, 50,* 285–303. (p. 516)

Herek, G. M., & Glunt, E. K. (1988). An epidemic of stigma: Public reactions to AIDS. *American Psychologist, 43,* 886–891. (p. 503)

Hering, E. (1878; translated edition 1964). *Outlines of a theory of the light sense.* (L. M. Hurvich and D. Jameson, Trans.) Cambridge, MA: Harvard University Press. (p. 263)

Herman, C. P. (1980). Restrained eating. In A. J. Stunkard (Ed.), *Symposium on obesity: Basic mechanisms and treatment.* Philadelphia: Saunders. (p. 210)

Herrnstein, R. J. (1971). *IQ in the meritocracy.* Boston: Little, Brown. (p. 69)

Herrnstein, R. J. (1979). Acquisition, generalization, and discrimination reversal of a natural concept. *Journal of Experimental Psychology: Animal Behavior Processes, 5,* 116–129. (p. 143)

Herrnstein, R. J. (1990). Levels of stimulus control: A functional approach. *Cognition, 37,* 133–166. (p. 143)

Hershenson, M. (1989). The most puzzling illusion. In M. Hershenson (Ed.), *The moon illusion.* Hillsdale, NJ: Erlbaum. (p. 316)

Hershman, D. J., & Lieb, J. (1988). *The key to genius.* Buffalo, NY: Prometheus. (p. 626)

Hess, E. H. (1958, March). "Imprinting" in animals. *Scientific American,* 81–90. (p. 156)

Hess, E. H. (1972, August). "Imprinting" in a natural laboratory. *Scientific American,* 24–31. (p. 156)

Hilgard, E. R. (1977). *Divided consciousness: Multiple controls in human action and thought.* New York: Wiley. (p. 635)

Hill, E. M. (1988). The menstrual cycle and components of human female sexual behaviour. *Journal of Social and Biological Structure, 11,* 433–455. (p. 217)

Hinson, R. E., Poulos, C. X., Thomas, W., & Cappell, H. (1986). Pavlovian conditioning and addictive behavior: Relapse to oral self-administration of morphine. *Behavioral Neuroscience, 100,* 368–375. (p. 129)

Hippocrates (1923). The sacred disease. In W. H. S. Jones (trans.), *Hippocrates, Vol. II.* London: Heinemann. (p. 163)

Hirsh-Pasek, K., & Golinkoff, R. M. (1991). Language comprehension: A new look at some old themes. In N. A. Karsnegor, D. M. Rumbaugh, R. L. Schiefelbusch, & M. Studdert-Kennedy (Eds.), *Biological and behavioral determinants of language development.* Hillsdale, NJ: Erlbaum. (p. 426)

Hirst, W., Spelke, E. S., Reaves, C. C., Caharack, G., & Neisser, U. (1980). Dividing attention without alternation or automaticity. *Journal of Experimental Psychology: General, 109,* 98–117. (p. 302)

Hobson, J. A. (1987). (1) Sleep, (2) Sleep, functional theories of, (3) Dreaming. All in G. Adelman (Ed.), *Encyclopedia of neuroscience.* Boston: Birkhäuser. (pp. 223, 227)

Hobson, J. A. (1988). *The dreaming brain.* New York: Basic Books. (pp. 227, 228)

Hochberg, J. (1971). Perception II: Space and movement. In J. W. Kling & L. A. Riggs (Eds.), *Woodworth & Schlosberg's experimental psychology* (3rd ed.). New York: Holt, Rinehart & Winston. (p. 310)

Hochschild, A. (1989). *The second shift: Working parents and the revolution at home.* New York: Viking Press. (p. 484)

Hoebel, B. G., Monaco, A. P., Hernandez, L., Aulisi, E. F., Stanley, B. G., & Lenard, L. G. (1983). Self-injection of amphetamine directly into the brain. *Psychopharmacology, 81,* 158–163. (p. 219)

Hoelter, J. W. (1985). The structure of self-conception: Conceptualization and measurement. *Journal of Personality and Social Psychology, 49,* 1392–1407. (p. 506)

Hoffman, C., Lau, I., & Johnson, D. R. (1986). The linguistic relativity of person cognition: An English-Chinese comparison. *Journal of Personality and Social Psychology, 51,* 1097–1105. (p. 406)

Hoffman, L. W., & Manis, J. D. (1979). The value of children in the United States. *Journal of Marriage and the Family, 41,* 583–596. (p. 483)

Hoffman, M. L. (1975). Developmental synthesis of affect and cognition and its implications for altruistic motivation. *Developmental Psychology, 11,* 607–622. (p. 477)

Hoffman, M. L. (1983). Affective and cognitive processes in moral internalization. In E. T. Higgins, D. N. Ruble, & W. W. Hartup (Eds.), *Social cognition and social development.* Cambridge: Cambridge University Press. (p. 461)

Hoffman, M. L. (1987). The contribution of empathy to justice and moral judgment. In N. Eisenberg & J. Strayer (Eds.), *Empathy and its development.* Cambridge: Cambridge University Press. (p. 477)

Hoffman, M. L., & Saltzstein, H. D. (1967). Parent discipline and the child's moral development. *Journal of Personality and Social Psychology, 5,* 45–57. (p. 462)

Hoffman, M. S. (Ed.), (1992). *The world almanac and book of facts 1993.* New York: Pharos Books. (pp. 468, 485)

Hofling, C. K., Brotzman, E., Dalrymple, S., Graves, N., & Pierce, C. M. (1966). An experimental study in nurse-physician relationships. *The Journal of Nervous and Mental Disease, 143,* 171–180. (p. 542)

Hofstadter, R. (1955). *Social Darwinism in American thought.* Boston: Beacon Press. (p. 113)

Hogarty, G. E., & Goldberg, S. C. (1973). Drug and sociotherapy in the aftercare of schizophrenic patients: One-year relapse rates. *Archives of General Psychiatry, 28,* 54–64. (p. 679)

Hogg, M. A., Turner, J. C., & Davidson, B. (1990). Polarized norms and social frames of reference: A test of the self-categorization theory of group polarization. *Basic and Applied Social Psychology, 11,* 77–100. (p. 552)

Hohmann, G. W. (1966). Some effects of spinal cord lesions on experienced emotional feelings. *Psychophysiology, 3,* 143–156. (pp. 233, 234)

Hollandsworth, J. G. (1990). *The physiology of psychological disorders: Schizophrenia, depression, anxiety, and substance abuse.* New York: Plenum. (pp. 618, 623)

Holway, A. F., & Boring, E. G. (1941). Determinants of apparent visual size with distance variant. *American Journal of Psychology, 54,* 21–37. (p. 313)

Honig, K. M., & Townes, B. D. (1976). Infants' attachment to inanimate objects: A cross-cultural study. *American Academy of Child Psychiatry Journal, 15,* 49–61. (p. 459)

Hooff, J. A. van (1972). A comparative approach to the phylogeny of laughter and smiling. In R. A. Hinde (Ed.), *Nonverbal communication.* Cambridge: Cambridge University Press. (p. 103)

Hooff, J. A. van (1976). The comparison of facial expression in man and higher primates. In M. von Cranach (Ed.), *Methods of inference from animal to human behaviour.* Chicago: Aldine. (pp. 102, 103)

Horne, J. A. (1979). Restitution and human sleep: A critical review. *Physiological Psychology, 7,* 115–125. (p. 226)

Horne, J. A. (1988). *Why we sleep: The functions of sleep in humans and other mammals.* Oxford: Oxford University Press. (p. 226)

Horney, K. (1937). *The neurotic personality of our time.* New York: Norton. (p. 575)

Horney, K. (1945). *Our inner conflicts.* New York: Norton. (p. 575)

Horney, K. (1950). *Neurosis and human growth: The struggle toward self-realization.* New York: Norton. (p. 576)

Hornik, R., Risenhoover, N., & Gunnar, M. (1987). The effects of maternal positive, neutral, and negative affective communications on infant responses to new toys. *Child Development, 58,* 937–944. (p. 455)

Hosobuchi, Y., Rossier, J., Bloom, F. E., & Guillemin, R. (1979). Stimulation of human periaqueductal gray for pain relief increases immunoreactive beta-endorphin in ventricular fluid. *Science, 203,* 279–281. (p. 272)

Hothersall, D. (1990). *History of psychology* (2nd ed.). New York: McGraw-Hill. (pp. 12, 123, 125)

Howes, C., & Matheson, C. C. (1992). Sequences in the development of competent play with peers: Social and pretend play. *Developmental Psychology, 28,* 961–974. (p. 465)

Hrdy, S. B. (1981). *The woman that never evolved.* Cambridge, MA: Harvard University Press. (pp. 107, 108)

Hubel, D. H., & Wiesel, T. N. (1962). Receptive fields, binocular interaction, and functional architecture of the cat's visual cortex. *Journal of Physiology* (London), *160,* 106–154. (p. 266)

Hubel, D. H., & Wiesel, T. N. (1979, September). Brain mechanisms of vision. *Scientific American,* 150–162. (p. 266)

Hudspeth, A. J. (1983, January). The hair cells of the inner ear. *Scientific American,* 54–64. (p. 249)

Huff, D. (1954). *How to lie with statistics.* New York: Norton. (p. 41)

Hunter, J. E., & Hunter, R. F. (1984). Validity and utility of alternative predictors of a job performance. *Psychological Bulletin, 96,* 72–98. (p. 374)

Husband, R. W. (1931). Analysis of methods in human maze learning. *Journal of Genetic Psychology, 39,* 258–278. (p. 543)

Huston, A. C., Carpenter, C. J., & Atwater, J. B. (1986). Gender, adult structuring of activities, and social behavior in middle childhood. *Child Development, 57,* 1200–1209. (p. 469)

Huxley, J. H., Mayr, E., Osmond, H., & Hoffer, A. (1964). Schizophrenia as a genetic morphism. *Nature, 204,* 220–221. (p. 87)

Hyde, J. S. (1986). Gender differences in aggression. In J. S. Hyde & M. C. Linn (Eds.), *The psychology of gender.* Baltimore, MD: Johns Hopkins University Press. (p. 614)

Inhelder, B., & Piaget, J. (1958). *The growth of logical thinking from childhood to adolescence.* New York: Basic Books. (p. 436)

Insko, C. A., Pinkley, R. L., Hoyle, R. H., Dalton, B., Hong, G., Slim, R. M., Landry, P., Holton, B., Ruffin, P. F., & Thibaut, J. (1987). Individual versus group discontinuity: The role of intergroup contact. *Journal of Experimental Social Psychology, 23,* 250–267. (p. 557)

Ironside, R., & Batchelor, I. R. C. (1945). The ocular manifestation of hysteria in relation to flying. *British Journal of Ophthalmology, 29,* 88–98. (p. 628)

Irwin, D. E., Zacks, J. L., & Brown, J. S. (1990). Visual memory and perception of a stable visual environment. *Perception and Psychophysics, 47,* 35–46. (p. 330)

Isen, A. M., Daubman, K. A., & Nowicki, G. P. (1987). Positive effect facilitates creative problem solving. *Journal of Personality and Social Psychology, 52,* 1122–1131. (p. 393)

Jablensky, A., Sartorius, N., Ernberg, G., Anker, M., Korten, A., Cooper, J. E., Day, R., & Bertelsen, A. (1992). Schizophrenia: Manifestations, incidence and course in different cultures. A World Health Organization ten-country study. *Psychological Medicine, Monograph Supplements,* whole volume *20.* (pp. 642, 643)

Jacklin, C. N., & Maccoby, E. E. (1978). Social behavior at 33 months in same-sex and mixed-sex dyads. *Child Development, 49,* 557–569. (p. 470)

Jackson, D. N., & Paunonen, S. V. (1985). Construct validity and the predictability of behavior. *Journal of Personality and Social Psychology, 49,* 554–570. (p. 598)

Jackson, J. M., & Latané, B. (1981). All alone in front of all those people: Stage fright as a function of number and type of co-performers and audience. *Journal of Personality and Social Psychology, 40,* 73–85. (p. 533)

Jacobson, J. L., & Wille, D. E. (1986). The influence of attachment pattern on developmental changes in peer interaction from the toddler to the preschool child. *Child Development, 57,* 338–347. (p. 458)

Jacoby, L. L. (1983). Remembering the data: Analyzing interactive processes in reading. *Journal of Verbal Learning and Verbal Behavior, 22,* 485–508. (p. 362)

James, W. (1884). Some omissions of introspective psychology. *Mind, 9* (January), 1–26. (p. 9)

James, W. (1890; reprinted 1950). *The principles of psychology.* New York: Dover. (pp. 9, 10, 25, 163, 232, 348, 394, 506, 509)

Jameson, D., & Hurvich, L. M. (1989). Essay concerning color constancy. *Annual Review of Psychology, 40,* 1–22. (p. 264)

Jamiesen, D. W., Lydon, J. E., & Zanna, M. P. (1987). Attitude and activity preference similarity: Differential bases of interpersonal attraction for low and high self-monitors. *Journal of Personality and Social Psychology, 53,* 1052–1060. (p. 513)

Janis, I. (1982). *Groupthink: Psychological studies of policy decisions and fiascoes* (2nd ed.). Boston: Houghton Mifflin. (p. 552)

Jaroff, L. (1992). Making the best of a bad gene. *Time,* Feb. 10, 78–79. (p. 58)

Jellison, J. M., & Green, J. (1981). A self-presentation approach to the fundamental attribution error: The norm of internality. *Journal of Personality and Social Psychology, 40,* 643–649. (p. 499)

Jenkins, H. M., Barrera, F. J., Ireland, C., & Woodside, B. (1978). Signal-centered action patterns of dogs in appetitive classical conditioning. *Learning and Motivation, 9,* 272–296. (p. 145)

Jenkins, J. G., & Dallenbach, K. M. (1924). Obliviscence during sleep and waking. *American Journal of Psychology, 35,* 605–612. (p. 351)

Jenkins, J. H., & Karno, M. (1992). The meaning of expressed emotion: Theoretical issues raised by cross-cultural research. *American Journal of Psychiatry, 149,* 9–21. (p. 643)

Jensen, A. R. (1969). How much can we boost IQ and scholastic achievement? *Harvard Educational Review, 39,* 1–123. (p. 72)

Jensen, A. R. (1980). *Bias in mental testing.* New York: Free Press. (pp. 37, 374)

Jensen, A. R. (1987). Individual differences in the Hick paradigm. In P. A. Vernon (Ed.), *Speed of information-processing and intelligence.* Norwood, NJ: Ablex. (p. 378)

Jensen, A. R. (1992). Commentary: Vehicles of *g. Psychological Science, 3,* 275–278. (p. 376)

Jerome, J. K. (1889; reprinted 1982). *Three men in a boat (to say nothing of the dog).* London: Pavilion Books. (p. 616)

Jessell, T. M., & Kelly, D. D. (1991). Pain and analgesia. In E. R. Kandel, J. H. Schwartz, & T. M. Jessell (Eds.), *Principles of neural science,* third edition. New York: Elsevier. (pp. 270, 272)

Johansson, G. (1975, June). Visual motion perception. *Scientific American,* 76–87. (p. 319)

Johnson, D. W., & Johnson, R. T. (1989). *Cooperation and competition: Theory and research.* Edina, MN: Interaction Book Company. (p. 553)

Johnson, J., & Newport, E. (1989). Critical period effects in second language learning: The influence of maturational state on the acquisition of English as a second language. *Cognitive Psychology, 21,* 60–99. (p. 428)

Johnson, J. E., Christie, J. F., & Yawkey, T. D. (1987). *Play and early childhood development.* Glenview, IL: Scott, Foresman. (p. 464)

Johnson, M. H., Dziurawiec, S., Ellis, H., & Morton, J. (1991). Newborns' preferential tracking of face-like stimuli and its subsequent decline. *Cognition, 40,* 1–19. (p. 417)

Johnson, M. H., & Horn, G. (1988). Development of filial preferences in dark-reared chicks. *Animal Behavior, 36,* 675–783. (p. 156)

Johnson-Laird, P. N. (1983). *Mental models: Towards a cognitive science of language, inference, and consciousness.* Cambridge, MA: Harvard University Press. (p. 392)

Johnson-Laird, P. N. (1985). Deductive reasoning ability. In R. J. Sternberg (Ed.), *Human abilities: An information-processing approach.* New York: Freeman. (p. 391)

Johnson-Laird, P. N., Byrne, R. M., J., & Schaeken, W. (1992). Propositional reasoning by model. *Psychological Review, 99,* 418–439. (p. 391)

Johnston, T. D., & Pietrewicz, A. T. (Eds.) (1985). *Issues in the ecological study of learning.* Hillsdale, NJ: Erlbaum. (p. 152)

Johnston, W. A., & Dark, V. J. (1986). Selective attention *Annual Review of Psychology, 37,* 43–75. (p. 306)

Jones, E. E., & Pulos, S. M. (1993). Comparing the process in psychodynamic and cognitive-behavioral therapies. *Journal of Consulting and Clinical Psychology, 61,* 306–316. (p. 661)

Jones, E. F., Forrest, J. D., Goldman, N., Henshaw, S. K., Lincoln, R., Rosoff, J. I., Westoff, C. F., & Wulf, D. (1985). Teenage pregnancy in developed countries: Determinants and policy implications. *Family Planning Perspectives, 1*[illegible] 53–63. (p. 474)

Jordan, K., & Randall, J. (1987). The effects of framing ratio and oblique length on Ponzo illusion magnitude. *Perception and Psychophysics, 41,* 435–439. (p. 317)

Jordan, N. (1972). Is there an Achilles' heel in Piaget's theorizing? *Human Development, 15,* 379–382. (p. 438)

Jouvet, M. (1967, February). The states of sleep. *Scientific American,* 62–70. (p. 229)

Jouvet, M. (1972). The role of monoamines and acetylcholine-containing neurons in the regulation of the sleep-waking cycle. *Ergebnisse der Physiologie, 64,* 166–307. (p. 229)

Judd, C. M., Ryan, C. S., & Park, B. (1991). Accuracy in the judgment of in-group and out-group variability. *Journal of Personality and Social Psychology, 61,* 366–379. (p. 502)

Julien, R. M. (1988). *A primer of drug action* (5th ed.). San Francisco: Freeman. (p. 196)

Jung, C. G. (1968). *Analytical psychology: Its theory and practice.* New York: Pantheon. (p. 576)

Jung, C. G. (1969). *The structure and dynamics of the psyche.* Princeton, NJ: Princeton University Press. (p. 486)

Jussim, L. (1986). Self-fulfilling prophecies: A theoretical and integrative review. *Psychological Review, 93,* 429–445. (p. 505)

Jussim, L. (1991). Social perception and social reality: A reflection-construction model. *Psychological Review, 98,* 54–73. (p. 505)

Kagan, J. (1976). Emergent themes in human development. *American Scientist, 64,* 186–196. (p. 455)

Kagan, J. (1984). *The nature of the child.* New York: Basic Books. (p. 438)

Kagan, J., Snidman, N., & Arcus, D. M. (1992). Initial reactions to unfamiliarity. *Current Directions in Psychological Science, 1,* 171–174. (p. 456)

Kahneman, D., & Treisman, A. (1984). Changing views of attention and automaticity. In R. Parasuraman & D. R. Davies (Eds.), *Varieties of attention.* New York: Academic Press. (p. 307)

Kail, R. (1984). *The development of memory in children* (2nd ed.). New York: Freeman. (p. 440)

Kail, R. (1991). Development of processing speed in childhood and adolescence. *Advances in Child Development and Behavior, 13,* 151–183. (p. 440)

Kamil, A. C., & Balda, R. P. (1985). Cache recovery and spatial memory in Clark's nutcrackers *(Nucifraga columbiana). Journal of Experimental Psychology: Animal Behavior Processes, 11,* 95–111. (p. 157)

Kamil, A. C., & Balda, R. P. (1990). Spatial memory in seed-catching corvids. *Psychology of Learning and Motivation, 26,* 1–25. (p. 157)

Kamin, L. J. (1969). Predictability, surprise, attention, and conditioning. In B. A. Campbell & R. M. Church (Eds.), *Punishment and aversive behavior.* New York: Appleton-Century-Crofts. (p. 146)

Kamin, L. J. (1974). *The science and politics of IQ.* New York: Wiley. (p. 70)

Kandel, E. R. (1991). Cellular mechanisms of learning and the biological basis of individuality. In E. R. Kandel, J. H. Schwartz, & T. M. Jessell (Eds.), *Principles of neural science, third edition.* New York: Elsevier. (pp. 188, 189)

Kane, J. M. (1992). Atypical neuroleptics for the treatment of schizophrenia. In J. Lindenmayer & S. R. Kay (Ed.), *New biological vistas on schizophrenia.* New York: Brunner/Mazel. (p. 680)

Kanizsa, G. (1976, April). Subjective contours. *Scientific American,* 48–52. (p. 292)

Kano, T. (1989). The sexual behavior of pygmy chimpanzees. In P. G. Heltne & L. A. Marquardt (Eds.), *Understanding chimpanzees.* Cambridge, MA: Harvard University Press. (p. 108)

Kano, T. (1990). The bonobos' peaceable kingdom. *Natural History,* Nov., 62–70. (pp. 108, 111)

Kanwisher, N., & Driver, J. (1992). Objects, attributes, and visual attention: Which, what, and where? *Current Directions in Psychological Science, 1,* 26–31. (p. 304)

Kaplan, M. (1983). A woman's view of DSM-III. *American Psychologist, 38,* 786–792. (p. 615)

Kaplan, M. F. (1987). The influencing process in group decision making. In C. Hendrick (Ed.), *Review of personality and social psychology, vol. 8: Group processes.* Newbury Park, CA: Sage. (p. 551)

Karádi, Z., Oomura, Y., Nishino, H., Scott, T. R., Lénárd, L., & Aou, S. (1990). Complex attributes of lateral hypothalamic neurons in the regulation of feeding of alert rhesus monkeys. *Brain Research Bulletin, 25,* 933–939. (pp. 207, 208)

Karasu, T. B. (1986). The specificity versus nonspecificity dilemma: Toward identifying therapeutic change agents. *American Journal of Psychiatry, 143,* 687–695. (p. 656)

Karon, B. P. (1989). Psychotherapy versus medication for schizophrenia: Empirical comparisons. In S. Fisher & R. P. Greenberg (Eds.), *The limits of biological treatments for psychological distress: Comparisons with psychotherapy and placebo.* Hillsdale, NJ: Erlbaum. (p. 679)

Karp, D. (1988). A decade of reminders: Changing age consciousness between fifty and sixty years old. *The Gerontologist, 28,* 727–738. (p. 487)

Kastenbaum, R. 1985). Dying and death. In J. E. Birren & K. W. Schaie (Eds.), *Handbook of the psychology of aging* (2nd ed.). New York: Van Nostrand Reinhold. (p. 488)

Katz, D. (1960). The functional approach to the study of attitudes. *Public Opinion Quarterly, 24,* 163–204. (p. 514)

Kaufman, A. S. (1990). *Assessing adolescent and adult intelligence.* Boston: Allyn & Bacon. (p. 382)

Kaufman, L., & Rock, I. (1962, July). The moon illusion. *Scientific American,* 120–130. (pp. 315, 316)

Kaufman, L., & Rock, I. (1989). The moon illusion thirty years later. In M. Hershenson (Ed.), *The moon illusion.* Hillsdale, NJ: Erlbaum. (pp. 315, 316)

Kaufmann, G. (1990). Imagery effects on problem solving. In P. J. Hampson, D. F. Marks, & J. T. E. Richardson (Eds.), *Imagery: Current developments.* London: Routledge. (p. 391)

Kay, S. R. (1990). Significance of the positive-negative distinction in schizophrenia. *Schizophrenia Bulletin, 16,* 635–652. (p. 640)

Kay, P., & Kempton, W. (1984). What is the Sapir-Whorf hypothesis? *American Anthropologist, 86,* 65–79. (p. 405)

Keenan, J. M., MacWhinney, B., & Mayhew, D. (1977). Pragmatics in memory: A study of natural conversation. *Journal of Verbal Learning and Verbal Behavior, 16,* 549–560. (p. 344)

Keesey, R. E. (1986). A set-point theory of obesity. In K. D. Brownell & J. P. Foreyt (Eds.), *Handbook of eating disorders.* New York: Basic Books. (p. 209)

Keesey, R. E., & Corbett, S. W. (1984). Metabolic defense of the body weight set-point. In A. J. Stunkard & E. Stellar (Eds.), *Eating and its disorders.* New York: Raven. (p. 211)

Keller, F. S., & Schoenfeld, W. N. (1950). *Principles of psychology: A systematic text in the science of behavior.* New York: Appleton-Century-Crofts. (p. 139)

Kelley, H. H. (1950). The warm-cold variable in first impressions of persons. *Journal of Personality, 18,* 431–439. (p. 495)

Kelley, H. H. (1967). Attribution theory in social psychology. In D. Levine (Ed.), *Nebraska symposium on motivation, 1967.* Lincoln, NE: University of Nebraska Press. (p. 497)

Kelley, H. H. (1973). The process of causal attribution. *American Psychologist, 28,* 107–128. (p. 497)

Kellogg, W. N. (1968). Communication and language in the home-raised chimpanzee. *Science, 162,* 423–427. (p. 429)

Kelly, G. A. (1958). The theory and technique of assessment. *Annual Review of Psychology, 9,* 323–352. (p. 652)

Kelly, J. A., & Hansen, D. J. (1987). Social interactions and adjustment. In V. B. Van Hasselt & M. Hersen (Eds.). *Handbook of adolescent psychology.* New York: Pergamon. (p. 473)

Kelman, H. C., & Hamilton, V. L. (1989). *Crimes of obedience: Toward a social psychology of authority and responsibility.* New Haven, CT: Yale University Press. (pp. 537, 546)

Kendler, H. H. (1987). *Historical foundations of modern psychology.* Philadelphia: Temple University Press. (pp. 8, 9)

Kendler, K. S., Neale, M. C., Kessler, R. C., Heath, A. C., & Eaves, L. J. (1992). Major depression and generalized anxiety disorder: Same genes, (partly) different environments? *Archives of General Psychiatry, 49,* 716–722. (p. 618)

Kendler, T. S. (1972). An ontogeny of mediational deficiency. *Child Development, 43,* 1–17. (p. 444)

Keppel, G., Postman, L., & Zavortink, B. (1968). Studies of learning to learn: VIII. The influence of massive amounts of training upon the learning and retention of paired-associate lists. *Journal of Verbal Learning and Verbal Behavior, 7,* 790–796. (p. 351)

Kessler, R. C., & McRae, J. A., Jr. (1981). Trends in the relationship between sex and psychological distress. *American Sociological Review, 46,* 443–452. (p. 615)

Kettlewell, B. (1973). *The evolution of melanism.* Oxford: Clarendon. (p. 83)

Kety, S. S. (1988). Schizophrenic illness in the families of schizophrenic adoptees: Findings from the Danish national sample. *Schizophrenia Bulletin, 14,* 217–222. (p. 75)

Kety, S. S., Rosenthal, D., Wender, P. H., Schulsinger, F., & Jacobson, B. (1976). Mental illness in the biological and adoptive families of adopted individuals who have become schizophrenic. *Behavior Genetics, 6,* 219–225. (pp. 74, 75)

Kiesler, C. A. (1993). Mental health policy and mental hospitalization. *Current Directions in Psychological Science, 2,* 93–95. (p. 650)

Kiesler, C. A., & Sibulkin, A. S. (1987). *Mental hospitalization: Myths and facts about a national crisis.* Newbury Park, CA: Sage. (p. 650)

Kihlstrom, J. F. (1985). Hynosis. *Annual Reviews of Psychology, 36,* 385–418. (pp. 357, 358)

King, B. M., Smith, R. L., & Frohman, L. A. (1984). Hyperinsulinemia in rats with ventromedial hypothalamic lesions: Role of hyperphagia. *Behavioral Neuroscience, 98,* 152–155. (p. 208)

Kinsey, A. C., Pomeroy, W. B., & Martin, C. E. (1948). *Sexual behavior in the human male.* Philadelphia: Saunders. (p. 214)

Kinsey, A. C., Pomeroy, W. B., Martin, C. E., & Gebhard, P. H. (1953). *Sexual behavior in the human female.* Philadelphia: Saunders. (p. 214)

Kirmayer, L. J. (1991). The place of culture in psychiatric nosology: *Taijin kyofusho* and *DSM-III-R. The Journal of Nervous and Mental Disease, 179,* 19–28. (p. 619)

Kirsch, I., Tennen, H., Wickless, C., Saccone, A. J., & Cody, S. (1983). The role of expectancy in fear reduction. *Behavior Therapy, 14,* 520–533. (p. 677)

Kissin, B. (1986). *Conscious and unconscious programs in the brain.* New York: Plenum. (p. 231)

Klayman, J., & Ha, Y. (1987). Confirmation, disconfirmation, and information in hypothesis testing. *Psychological Review, 94,* 211–228. (p. 390)

Klayman, J., & Ha, Y. (1989). Hypothesis testing in rule discovery: Strategy, structure, and content. *Journal of Experimental Psychology: Learning, Memory, and Cognition, 15,* 596–604. (p. 390)

Kleiman, D. G. (1977). Monogamy in mammals. *Quarterly Review of Biology, 52,* 39–69. (p. 107)

Klein, D. F., Gittelman, R., Quitkin, F., & Rifkin, A. (1980). *Diagnosis and drug treatment of psychiatric disorders: Adults and children* (2nd ed.). Baltimore, MD: Williams & Wilkins. (pp. 679, 680)

Kleinman, A. (1988). *Rethinking psychiatry: From cultural category to personal experience.* New York: Free Press. (p. 629)

Klemm, W. R. (1990). Historical and introductory perspectives on brainstem-mediated behaviors. In W. R. Klemm & R. P. Vertes (eds.), *Brainstem mechanisms of behavior.* New York: Wiley. (p. 171)

Klinke, R. (1986). Physiology of hearing. In R. F. Schmidt (Ed.), *Fundamentals of sensory physiology.* New York: Springer-Verlag. (p. 247)

Klüver H., & Bucy, P. C. (1937). "Psychic blindness" and other symptoms following temporal lobectomy in rhesus monkeys. *American Journal of Physiology, 119,* 352–353. (p. 236)

Knowlton, B. J., Ramus, S. J., & Squire, L. R. (1992). Intact artificial grammar learning in amnesia: Dissociation of classification learning and explicit memory for specific instances. *Psychological Science, 3,* 172–179. (p. 363)

Knox, R. E., & Inkster, J. A. (1968). Postdecision dissonance at post time. *Journal of Personality and Social Psychology, 8,* 319–323. (p. 520)

Koester, J. (1991). Membrane potential. In E. R. Kandel, J. H. Schwartz & T. M. Jessell (Eds.), *Principles of neural science, third edition.* New York: Elsevier. (p. 183)

Koffka, K. (1935). *Principles of Gestalt psychology.* New York: Harcourt Brace Jovanovich (p. 290)

Kohlberg, L. (1966). A cognitive-developmental analysis of children's sex-role concepts and attitudes. In E. E. Maccoby (Ed.), *The development of sex differences.* Stanford: Stanford University Press. (p. 470)

Kohlberg, L. (1975, June). The cognitive developmental approach to moral education. *Phi Delta Kappan,* 670–677. (p. 479)

Kohlberg, L. (1984). *The psychology of moral development.* San Francisco: Harper & Row. (p. 478)

Kohlberg, L., & Candee, D. (1984). The relationship of moral judgment to moral action. In W. M. Kurtines & J. L. Gewirz (Eds.), *Morality, moral behavior, and moral development.* New York: Wiley. (p. 479)

Kohlberg, L., Yaeger, J., & Hjertholm, E. (1968). Private speech: Four studies and a review of theories. *Child Development, 39,* 691–736. (p. 444)

Köhler, W. (1917; reprinted 1973). *Intelligenzprüfungen an Anthropoiden* (3rd ed.). Berlin: Springer. (p. 11)

Kohn, M. L. (1980). Job complexity and adult personality. In N. J. Smelser & E. H. Erikson (Eds.), *Theories of work and love in adulthood.* Cambridge, MA: Harvard University Press. (p. 484)

Kohn, M. L., & Schooler, C. (1983). *Work and personality: Inquiry into the impact of social stratification.* Norwood, NJ: Ablex. (p. 484)

Kolb, B., & Whishaw, I. Q. (1990). *Fundamentals of human neuropsychology* (3rd ed.). New York: Freeman, (pp. 173, 177, 237, 269, 297)

Komorita, S. S., Hilty, J. A., & Parks, C. D. (1991). Reciprocity and cooperation in social dilemmas. *Journal of Conflict Resolution, 35,* 494–518. (p. 556)

Konner, M. J. (1976). Maternal care, infant behavior and development among the !Kung. In R. B. Lee & I. DeVore (Eds.), *Kalahari hunter-gatherers: Studies of the !Kung San and their neighbors.* Cambridge, MA: Harvard University Press. (pp. 459, 460)

Konner, M. J. (1982). *The tangled wing: Biological constraints on the human spirit.* New York: Harper & Row. (pp. 459, 460)

Kornhuber, H. H. (1974). Cerebral cortex, cerebellum and basal ganglia: An introduction to their motor functions. In F. O. Schmitt & F. G. Worden (Eds.), *The neurosciences: Third study program.* Cambridge, MA: MIT Press. (pp. 172, 176)

Koss, M. P. (1990). The women's mental health research agenda: Violence against women. *American Psychologist, 45,* 374–380. (p. 615)

Kosslyn, S. M. (1973). Scanning visual images: Some structural implications. *Perception and Psychophysics, 14,* 90–94. (p. 345)

Kosslyn, S. M. (1980). *Image and mind.* Cambridge, MA: Harvard University Press. (p. 344)

Kosslyn, S. M. (1987). Seeing and imagining in the cerebral hemispheres: A computational approach. *Psychological Review, 94,* 148–175. (p. 344)

Kosslyn, S. M., Koenig, O., Barrett, A., Cave, C. B., Tang, J., & Gabrieli, J. D. E. (1989). Evidence for two types of spatial representations: Hemispheric specialization for categorical and coordinate relations. *Journal of Experimental Psychology: Human Perception and Performance, 15,* 723–735. (p. 382)

Kramer, F. M., Jeffrey, R. W., Foster, J. L., & Snell, M. K. (1989). Long-term follow-up of behavioral treatment for obesity: Patterns of weight regain among men and women. *International Journal of Obesity, 13,* 123–136. (p. 211)

Kramer, R. M., & Brewer, M. B. (1984). Effect of group identity on resource use in a simulated common dilemma. *Journal of Personality and Social Psychology, 46,* 1044–1057. (p. 556)

Kranzler, J. H., & Jensen, A. R. (1989). Inspection time and intelligence: A meta-analysis. *Intelligence, 13,* 329–347. (p. 379)

Krass, J., Kinoshita, S., & McConkey, K. M. (1989). Hypnotic memory and confident reporting. *Applied Cognitive Psychology, 3,* 35–51. (p. 358)

Kruuk, H. (1972). *The spotted hyena.* Chicago: University of Chicago Press. (p. 88)

Kryter, K. D. (1985). *The effects of noise on man* (2nd ed.). Orlando, FL: Academic Press. (p. 252)

Kübler-Ross, E. (1969). *On death and dying.* New York: Macmillan. (p. 487)

Kuczaj, S. A. (1977). The acquisition of regular and irregular past tense forms. *Journal of Verbal Learning and Verbal Behavior, 16,* 589–600. (p. 426)

Kuffler, S. W. (1953). Discharge patterns and functional organization of mammalian retina. *Journal of Neurophysiology, 16,* 37–68. (p. 264)

Kuhl, P. K. (1987). Perception of speech and sound in early infancy. In P. Salapatek & L. Cohen (Eds.), *Handbook of infant perception, Vol. 2: From perception to cognition.* New York: Academic Press. (p. 423)

Kurland, J. A. (1979). Paternity, mother's brother, and human sociality. In N. A. Chagnon & W. Irons (Eds.), *Evolutionary biology and human social behavior: An anthropological perspective.* North Scituate, MA: Duxbury Press. (p. 116)

Kyllonen, P. C., & Christal, R. E. (1990). Reasoning ability is (little more than) working-memory capacity?! *Intelligence, 14,* 389–433. (p. 380)

Lack, D. (1968). *Ecological adaptations for breeding in birds.* London: Methuen. (p. 107)

Lafferty, P., Beutler, L. E., & Crago, M. (1989). Differences between more and less effective psychotherapists: A study of select therapist variables. *Journal of Consulting and Clinical Psychology, 57,* 76–80. (p. 676)

La Freniere, P., Strayer, F. F., & Gauthier, R. (1984). The emergence of same-sex affiliative preferences among preschool peers: A developmental/ethological perspective. *Child Development, 55,* 1958–1965. (p. 470)

LaHoste, G. J., O'Dell, S. J., Widmark, C. B., Shapiro, R. M., Potkin, S. G., & Marshall, J. F. (1991). Differential changes in dopamine and serotonin receptors induced by clozapine and haloperidol. In C. A. Tamminga & S. C. Schulz (Eds.), *Advances in neuropsychiatry and psychopharmacology, volume 1: Schizophrenia research.* New York: Raven Press. (p. 680)

Laird, J. D. (1974). Self-attribution of emotion: The effects of expressive behavior on the quality of emotional experience. *Journal of Personality and Social Psychology, 29,* 475–486. (p. 234)

Lamb, M. E. (1986). *The father's role: Applied perspectives.* New York: Wiley. (p. 457)

Lamb, M. E., & Oppenheim, D. (1989). Fathers and father-child relationships: Five years of research. In S. H. Cath, A. Gurwitt, & L. Gunsberg (Eds.), *Fathers and their families.* Hillsdale, NJ: Erlbaum. (p. 457)

Lamb, M. E., Sternberg, K. J., & Prodromidis, M. (1992). Nonmaternal care and the secutity of infant-mother attachment. A reanalysis of the data. *Infant Behavior and Development, 15,* 71–83. (pp. 456, 458)

Lamborn, S. D., Mounts, N. S., Steinberg, L., & Dornbusch, S. M. (1991). Patterns of competence and adjustment among adolescents from authoritative, authoritarian, indulgent, and neglectful families. *Child Development, 62,* 1049–1065. (p. 463)

Langer, E. J., & Abelson, R. P. (1974). A patient by any other name. . .: Clinician group differences in labeling bias. *Journal of Consulting and Clinical Psychology, 42,* 4–9. (p. 616)

Langer, E. J., Beck, P., Weinman, C., Rodin, J., & Spitzer, L. (1979). Environmental determinants of memory improvement in late adulthood. *Journal of Personality and Social Psychology, 37,* 2003–2013. (p. 487)

Langer, E. J., Blank, A., & Chanowitz, B. (1978). The mindlessness of ostensibly thoughtful action. *Journal of Personality and Social Psychology, 36,* 635–642. (p. 534)

LaPiere, R. T. (1934). Attitude and actions. *Social Forces, 13,* 230–237. (p. 523)

Lashley, K. S. (1930). Basic neural mechanisms in behavior. *Psychological Review, 37,* 1–24. (p. 16)

Lashley, K. S. (1951). The problem of serial order in behavior. In L. A. Jeffress (Ed.), *Cerebral mechanisms in behavior.* New York: John Wiley. (p. 16)

Latané, B. (1981). The psychology of social impact. *American Psychologist, 36,* 343–356. (pp. 532, 533)

Latané, B., & Nida, S. (1981). Ten years of research on group size and helping. *Psychological Bulletin, 89,* 308–324. (p. 545)

Latané, B., & Rodin, J. (1969). A lady in distress: Inhibiting effects of friends and strangers on bystander intervention. *Journal of Experimental Social Psychology, 5,* 189–202. (p. 545)

Lauer, J., & Lauer, R. (1985, June). Marriages made to last. *Psychology Today,* 22–26, (pp. 482, 512)

Lazarus, A. A., Beutler, L. E., & Norcross, J. C. (1992). The future of technical eclecticism. *Psychotherapy, 29,* 11–20. (p. 678)

Lazarus, R. S. (1993). From psychological stress to the emotions: A history of changing outlooks. *Annual Review of Psychology, 44,* 1–21. (p. 609)

Leahey, T. H. (1992). *A history of psychology: Main currents in psychological thought,* 3rd ed. Englewood Cliffs, N. J.: Prentice Hall. (p. 18)

Leana, C. R. (1985). A partial test of Janis' groupthink model. Effects of group cohesiveness and leader behavior on defective decision making. *Journal of Management, 11,* 5–17. (p. 552)

Leary, M. R., & Kowalski, R. M. (1990). Impression management: a literature review and two-compartment model. *Psychological Bulletin, 107,* 34–47. (p. 511)

LeBon, G. (1896). *The crowd.* London: Ernest Benn. (p. 546)

LeDoux, J. E. (1989). Cognitive-emotional interactions in the brain. *Cognition and Emotion, 3,* 267–289. (pp. 236, 237)

LeDoux, J. E. (1992). Emotion and the amygdala. In J. P. Aggleton (Ed.), *The amygdala: Neurobiological aspects of emotion, memory, and mental dysfunction.* New York: Wiley-Liss. (pp. 236, 237)

LeDoux, J. E., Romanski, L., & Xagoraris, A. (1989). Indelibility of subcortical emotional memories. *Journal of Cognitive Neuroscience, 1,* 238–243. (p. 237)

Leinhardt, G., Seewald, A., & Engel, M. (1979). Learning what's taught: Sex differences in instruction. *Journal of Educational Psychology, 71,* 432–439. (p. 469)

Lenneberg, E. H. (1969). *Biological foundations of language.* New York: Wiley. (pp. 423, 428)

Lenzenweger, M. F., Dworkin, R. H., & Wethington, E. (1989). Models of positive and negative symptoms in schizophrenia: An empirical evaluation of latent structures. *Journal of Abnormal Psychology, 98,* 62–70. (p. 640)

Leon, G. R., Gillum, B., Gillum, R., & Gouze, M. (1979). Personality stability and change over a 30-year period—middle to old age. *Journal of Consulting and Clinical Psychology, 47,* 517–524. (p. 599)

Leonard, B. E. (1992). *Fundamentals of psychopharmacology:* New York: Wiley. (p. 680)

Lepper, M. R., & Greene, D. (1978). Overjustification research and beyond: Toward a means-ends analysis of intrinsic and extrinsic motivation. In M. R. Lepper & D. Greene (Eds.), *The hidden costs of reward: New perspectives on the psychology of human motivation.* New York: Wiley. (p. 148)

Lerner, M. J. (1980). *The belief in a just world: A fundamental delusion.* New York: Plenum. (p. 503)

Lerner, M. J., & Miller, D. T. (1978). Just world research and the attribution process: Looking back and looking ahead. *Psychological Bulletin, 85*, 1030–1051. (p. 502)

Lerner, M. J., & Simmons, C. H. (1966). The observer's reaction to the "innocent victim": Compassion or rejection? *Journal of Personality and Social Psychology, 4*, 203–210. (p. 503)

Lethmate, J., & Dücker, G. (1973). Untersuchungen zum Selbsterkennen im Spiegel bei Orang-utans und einigen anderen Affenarten. *Z. Tierpsychologie, 33*, 248–269. (pp. 503–504)

LeVay, S. (1991). A difference in hypothalamic structure between heterosexual and homosexual men. *Science, 253*, 1034–1037. (p. 215)

Levenson, J. L., & Bemis, C. (1991). The role of psychological factors in cancer onset and progression. *Psychosomatics, 32*, 124–132. (p. 631)

Levenson, R. W. (1992). Autonomic nervous system differences among emotions. *Psychological Science, 3*, 23–27. (p. 235)

Levenson, R. W., Ekman, P., & Friesen, W. V. (1990). Voluntary facial action generates emotion-specific nervous system activity, *Psychophysiology, 27*, 363–384. (p. 235)

Levine, J. D., Gordon, N. C., & Fields, H. L. (1979). The role of endorphins in placebo analgesia. *Advances in Pain Research and Therapy, 3*, 547–550. (p. 273)

Levine, M., Toro, P. A., & Perkins, D. V. (1993). Social and community interventions. *Annual Review of Psychology, 44*, 525–558. (p. 650)

LeVine, R. A. (1980). A cross-cultural perspective on parenting. In M. D. Fantini & R. Cardenas (Eds.), *Parenting in a multicultural society.* New York: Longman. (p. 461)

Levinger, G., & Schneider, D. J. (1969). Test of the "risk is a value" hypothesis. *Journal of Personality and Social Psychology, 11*, 165–169. (p. 551)

Levinson, D. J. (1978). *The seasons of a man's life.* New York: Ballantine. (p. 484)

Levinson, D. J. (1986). The conception of adult development. *American Psychologist, 41*, 3–13. (p. 481)

Levitt, M. J. (1991). Attachment and close relationships: A lifespan perspective. In J. L. Gewirtz & W. M. Kurtines (1991). *Intersections with attachment.* Hillsdale, NJ: Erlbaum. (p. 458)

Lewicki, P., Hill, T., & Czyzewska, M. (1992). *American Psychologist, 47*, 796–801. (p. 360)

Lewin, K. (1947). Frontiers in group dynamics: I. Concept, method and reality in social science. Social equilibria and social change. *Human Relations, 1*, 5–41. (p. 549)

Lewin, K. (1951). *Field theory in social science: Selected theoretical papers by Kurt Lewin* (D. Cartwright, Ed.). New York: Harper & Row. (pp. 19, 531)

Lewis, J. W., Cannon, J. T., & Liebeskind, J. C. (1980). Opioid and nonopioid mechanisms of stress analgesia. *Science, 208*, 623–625. (p. 273)

Lewis, M., & Brooks-Gunn, J. (1979). *Social cognition and the acquisition of self.* New York: Plenum Press. (p. 503)

Lewontin, R. (1970, March). Race and intelligence. *Bulletin of the Atomic Scientists*, 2–8. (p. 72)

Lewontin, R., & Gould, S. J. (1978). The spandrels San Marco and the Panglossian paradigm: A critique of the adaptationalist programme. *Proceedings of the Royal Society of London, 205*, 581–598. (p. 86)

Lewontin, R. C., Rose, S., & Kamin, L. J. (1984). *Not in our genes.* New York: Pantheon. (p. 69)

Lichtman, A. H., & Fanselow, M. S. (1990). Cats produce analgesia in rats on the tail-flick test: Naltrexone sensitivity is determined by the nociceptive test stimulus. *Brain Research, 553*, 91–94. (p. 273)

Lickey, M. E., & Gordon, B. (1991). *Medicine and mental illness: The use of drugs in psychiatry.* New York: W. H. Freeman. (pp. 679, 680, 681)

Lieberman, M. A., & Borman, L. D. (1981). Who helps widows: The role of kith and kin. *National Reporter, 4*, 2–4. (p. 487)

Liebert, R. (1984). What develops in moral development? In W. Kurtines & J. Gewirtz (Eds.), *Morality, moral behavior, and moral development.* New York: Wiley. (p. 479)

Liem, R. (1987). The psychological costs of unemployment: A comparison of findings and definitions. *Social Research, 54*, 319–353. (p. 485)

Liem, R., & Liem, J. H. (1988). Psychological effects of unemployment on workers and their families. *Journal of Social Issues, 44*, 87–105. (p. 485)

Light, W. J. H. (1986). *Neurobiology of alcohol abuse.* Springfield, IL: Charles C. Thomas. (p. 633)

Lin, K., & Kleinman, A. M. (1988). Psychopathology and clinical course of schizophrenia: A cross-cultural perspective. *Schizophrenia Bulletin, 14*, 555–567. (p. 643)

Linden, R., Davis, J. M., & Rubinstein, J. (1984). Antipsychotics in the maintenance treatment of schizophrenia. In H. C. Stancer, P. E. Garfinkel, & V. M. Rakoff (Eds.), *Guidelines for the use of psychotropic drugs: A clinical handbook.* New York: Spectrum. (p. 679)

Linder, D. E., Cooper, J., & Jones, E. E. (1967). Decision freedom as a determinant of the role of incentive magnitude in attitude change. *Journal of Personality and Social Psychology, 6*, 245–254. (pp. 521, 522)

Lindsay, D. S. (1990). Misleading suggestions can impair eyewitnesses' ability to remember event details. *Journal of Experimental Psychology: Learning, Memory, and Cognition, 16*, 1077–1083. (p. 357)

Lindsay, P. H., & Norman, D. A. (1977). *Human information processing,* 2nd ed. New York: Academic Press. (p. 247)

Lindsley, J. G. (1983). Sleep patterns and functions. In A. Gale & J. A. Edwards (Eds.), *Physiological correlates of human behavior (Vol. 1: Basic issues).* New York: Academic Press. (p. 229)

Linville, P. W. (1985). Self-complexity and affective extremity: Don't put all of your eggs in one cognitive basket. *Social Cognition, 3*, 94–120. (p. 507)

Linville, P. W. (1987). Self-complexity as a cognitive buffer against stress-related illness and depression. *Journal of Personality and Social Psychology, 52*, 663–676. (p. 507)

Lipman, R. S. (1989). Pharmacotherapy of the anxiety disorders. In S. Fischer & R. P. Greenberg (Eds.), *The limits of biological treatments for psychological distress: Comparisions with psychotherapy and placebo.* Hillsdale, NJ: Erlbaum. (p. 680)

Lipowski, Z. J. (1988). Somatization: The concept and its clinical application. *American Journal of Psychiatry, 145*, 1358–1368. (p. 627)

Lippmann, W. (1922; reprinted 1960). *Public opinion.* New York: Macmillan. (p. 500)

Littrell, J. (1991). *Understanding and treating alcoholism, volume 2: Biological, psychological and social aspects of alcohol consumption and abuse.* Hillsdale, NJ: Erlbaum. (p. 673)

Livingston, D. (1857). *Missionary travels and researches in South Africa.* London: J. Murray. (p. 272)

Livingstone, M., & Hubel, D. (1988). Segregation of form, color, movement, and depth: Anatomy, physiology, and perception. *Science, 240*, 740–749. (p. 269)

Locke, J. L. (1983). *Phonological acquisition and change.* New York: Academic Press. (p. 423)

Locksley, A., Ortiz, V., & Hepburn, C. (1980). Social categorization and discriminatory behavior: Extinguishing the minimal intergroup discrimination effect. *Journal of Personality and Social Psychology, 39*, 773–783. (p. 502)

Loeb, G. E. (1986, February). The functional replacement of the ear. *Scientific American*, 104–111. (p. 250)

Loehlin, J. C. (1992). *Genes and environment in personality development.* Newbury Park, CA: SAGE Publications. (p. 599)

Loehlin, J. C., Willerman, L., & Horn, J. M. (1988). Human behavior genetics. *Annual Review of Psychology, 39*, 101–133. (pp. 61, 70)

Loftus, E. F. (1992). When a lie becomes memory's truth: Memory distortion after exposure to misinformation. *Current Directions in Psychological Science, 1*, 121–123. (p. 355)

Loftus, E. F., & Loftus, G. R. (1980). On the permanence of stored information in the human brain. *American Psychologist, 35*, 409–420. (p. 356)

Loftus, E. F., & Palmer, J. C. (1974). Reconstruction of automobile destruction: An example of the interaction between language and memory. *Journal of Verbal Learning and Verbal Behavior, 13*, 585–589. (p. 355)

Logue, A. W. (1988). A comparison of taste aversion learning in humans and other vertebrates: Evolutionary pressures in common. In R. C. Bolles & M. D. Beecher (Eds.), *Evolution and learning.* Hillsdale, NJ: Erlbaum. (p. 152)

Lorenz, K. (1935; reprinted 1970). Companions as factors in the bird's environment (R. Martin, Trans.). In K. Lorenz (Ed.), *Studies in animal and human behavior (Vol. 1).* Cambridge, MA: Harvard University Press. (p. 156)

Lorenz, K. Z. (1966). *On aggression.* New York: Harcourt, Brace & World. (pp. 100, 110)

Lorenz, K. Z. (1974). Analogy as a source of knowledge. *Science, 185*, 229–234. (p. 94)

Lovelace, E. A., & Twohig, P. T. (1990). Healthy older adults' perceptions of their memory functioning and use of mnemonics. *Bulletin of the Psychonomic Society, 28*, 115–118. (p. 442)

Luchins, A. (1957). Primacy-recency in impression formation. In C. I. Hovland (Ed.), *The order of presentation in persuasion.* New Haven, CT: Yale University Press. (p. 495)

Luria, A. R. (1966). *Human brain and psychological processes.* New York: Harper & Row. (p. 181)

Luria, A. R. (1970, March). The functional organization of the brain. *Scientific American*, 66–78. (p. 181)

Luria, A. R. (1971). Towards the problem of the historical nature of psychological processes. *International Journal of Psychology, 6*, 259–272. (p. 386)

Lynch, G., Larson, J, Staubli, U., & Granger, R. (1991). Variants of synaptic potentiation and different types of memory operations in hippocampus and related structures. In L. R. Squire, N. M. Weinberger, G. Lynch, & J. L. McGaugh (Eds.), *Memory: Organization and locus of change.* Oxford: Oxford University Press. (p. 190)

Lynch, J. J. (1977). *The broken heart: The medical consequences of loneliness.* New York: Basic Books. (p. 487)

Maccoby, E. E. (1992). The role of parents in the socialization of children: An historical overview. *Developmental Psychology, 28*, 1006–1017. (p. 463)

Maccoby, E. E., & Jacklin, C. N. (1974). *The psychology of sex differences.* Stanford: Stanford University Press. (p. 468)

Maccoby, E. E. & Jacklin, C. N. (1987). Gender segregation in childhood. In H. W. Reese (Ed.), *Advances in child development and behavior, vol. 20.* New York: Academic Press. (pp. 467, 470, 471)

MacDonald, N. (1960). Living with schizophrenia. *Canadian Medical Association Journal, 82*, 218–221. (p. 642)

Macfarlane, A. J. (1975). Olfaction in the development of social preferences in the human neonate. *Ciba Foundation Symposia, 33*, 103–117. (p. 453)

MacKay, D. G. (1973). Aspects of the theory of comprehension, memory and attention. *Quarterly Journal of Experimental Psychology, 25*, 22–40. (p. 300)

Mackie, D. M. (1986). Social identification effects in group polarization. *Journal of Personality and Social Psychology, 50*, 720–728. (p. 551)

Mackintosh, N. J., & Dickinson, A. (1979). Instrumental (Type II) conditioning. In A. Dickinson & R. A. Boakes (Eds.), *Mechanisms of learning and motivation.* Hillsdale, NJ: Erlbaum. (p. 146)

Maier, N. R. F., & Solem, A. R. (1952). The contribution of a discussion leader to the quality of group thinking: The effective use of minority opinions. *Human Relations, 5*, 277–288. (p. 552)

Malcolm, J. R. (1985). Paternal care in Canids. *American Zoologist, 25*, 853–859. (p. 107)

Maltz, D. N., & Borker, R. A. (1982). A cultural approach to male-female miscommunication. In J. J. Gumperz (Ed.), *Language and social identity.* Cambridge: Cambridge University Press. (p. 471)

Mann, J. J. (1989). Neurobiological models. In J. J. Mann (Ed.), *Models of depressive disorders: Psychological, biological, and genetic perspectives.* New York: Plenum Press. (p. 623)

Mann, L. (1981). The baiting crowd in episodes of threatened suicide. *Journal of Personality and Social Psychology, 41*, 703–709. (p. 546)

Mäntylä, T. (1986). Optimizing cue effectiveness: Recall of 500 and 600 incidentally learned words. *Journal of Experimental Psychology: Learning, Memory, and Cognition, 12*, 66–71. (p. 353)

Manuck, S. B., Cohen, S., Rabin, B. S., Muldoon, M. F., & Bachen, E. A. (1991). Individual differences in cellular immune response to stress. *Psychological Science, 2*, 111–115. (p. 631)

Marcia, J. E. (1966). Development and validation of ego identity status. *Journal of Personality and Social Psychology, 3*, 551–558. (p. 476)

Marcia, J. E. (1980). Identity in adolescence. In J. Adelson (Ed.), *Handbook of adolescent psychology.* New York: Wiley. (p. 476)

Mark, V. H., Ervin, F. R., & Yakovlev, P. L. (1963). Stereotactic thalamotomy: III. The verification of anatomical lesion sites in the human thalamus. *Archives of Neurology, 8*, 528–538. (p. 271)

Marks, I. M. (1987). *Fears, phobias, and rituals: Panic, anxiety, and their disorders.* New York: Oxford University Press. (pp. 618, 620, 669)

Markus, H. R., & Kitayama, S. (1991). Culture and the self: Implications for cognition, emotion, and motivation. *Psychological Review, 98*, 224–253. (pp. 477, 507, 510, 514)

Marler, P. (1970). A comparative approach to vocal learning. Song development in white-crowned sparrows. *Journal of Comparative and Physiological Psychology, 7*, 1–25. (p. 91)

Marlowe, W. B., Mancall, E. L., & Thomas, J. J. (1975). Complete Klüver-Bucy syndrome in man. *Cortex, 11*, 53–59. (p. 237)

Marr, D. B., & Sternberg, R. J. (1987). The role of mental speed in intelligence. A triarchic perspective. In P. A. Vernon (Ed.), *Speed of information-processing and intelligence.* Norwood, NJ: Ablex. (p. 380)

Marschark, M., & Hunt, R. R. (1989). A reexamination of the role of imagery in learning and memory. *Journal of Experimental Psychology: Learning, Memory, and Cognition, 15*, 710–720. (p. 342)

Maslow, A. H. (1970). *Motivation and personality.* (2nd ed.). New York: Harper & Row. (pp. 17, 583, 584)

Masters, W. H., Johnson, V. E., & Kolodny, R. C. (1992). *Human sexuality*, 4th edition. New York: HarperCollins (p. 214)

Matarazzo, J. D. (1983). The reliability of psychiatric and psychological diagnosis. *Clinical Psychology Review, 3*, 103–145. (pp. 610, 610)

Matelsky, G. I., & Joiner, T. E. (1992). Vulnerability to depressive symptomatology: A prospective test of the diathesis-stress and causal mediation components of the hopelessness theory of depression. *Journal of Personality and Social Psychology, 63*, 667–675. (p. 625)

Matlin, M. W. (1988). *Sensation and perception* (2nd ed.). Boston: Allyn & Bacon. (p. 264)

Matlin, M. W., & Foley, H. J. (1992). *Sensation and perception*, 3rd ed. Needham Heights, MA: Allyn & Bacon. (pp. 246, 247)

Maurer, D., & Maurer, C. (1988). *The world of the newborn.* New York: Basic Books, (p. 416)

Mayer, R. E. (1992). *Thinking, problem solving, cognition*, second edition. New York: Freeman. (pp. 389, 392)

Mayeux, R., & Kandel, E. R. (1991). Disorders of language. The aphasias. In E. R. Kandel, J. H. Schwartz, & T. M. Jessell (Eds.), *Principles of neural science*, third edition. New York: Elsevier. (p. 403)

Mayr, E., & Provine, W. B. (Eds.) (1980). *The evolutionary synthesis: Perspectives on the unification of biology.* Cambridge, MA: Harvard University Press. (p. 82)

McArthur, L. Z. (1972). The how and what of why: Some determinants and consequences of causal attribution. *Journal of Personality and Social Psychology, 22*, 171–193. (p. 498)

McArthur, L. Z., & Berry, D. S. (1987). Cross-cultural agreement in perceptions of babyfaced adults. *Journal of Cross-Cultural Psychology, 18*, 165–192. (p. 496)

McCloskey, M., & Zaragoza, M. (1985). Misleading postevent information and memory for events: Arguments and evidence against memory impairment hypotheses. *Journal of Experimental Psychology: General, 114*, 1–16. (pp. 356, 357)

McCrae, R. R., & Costa, P. T. (1985). Updating Norman's "adequate taxonomy": Intelligence and personality dimensions in natural language and questionnaires. *Journal of Personality and Social Psychology, 49*, 710–721. (p. 596)

McCrae, R. R., & John, O. P. (1992). An introduction to the five-factor model and its applications. *Journal of Personality, 60*, 175–215. (p. 596)

McDuff, D. R. (1988). Presentation at the Annual Meeting of the American Psychiatric Association, as noted by Alison Bass in *Boston Globe*, May 5, p. 94. (p. 502)

McEwen, B. S. (1989). Endocrine effects on the brain and their relationship to behavior. In G. J. Siegel, B. W. Agranoff, R. W. Albers, & P. B. Molinoff (Eds.), *Basic neurochemistry: Molecular, cellular, and medical aspects* (4th ed.). New York: Raven Press. (p. 193)

McEwen, B. S., DeKloet, E. R., & Rostene, W. (1986). Adrenal steroid receptors and actions in the nervous sytem. *Physiological Review, 66*, 1121–1188. (p. 193)

McGuire, W. J. (1985). Attitudes and attitude change. In G. Lindzey & E. Aronson (Eds.), *Handbook of social psychology (Vol. 2)* (3rd ed.). New York: Random House. (p. 516)

McGuire, W. J., & McGuire, C. V. (1988). Content and process in the experience of self. In L. Berkowitz (Ed.), *Advances in experimental social psychology (vol. 21).* New York: Academic Press. (pp. 508, 509)

McKellar, P. (1979). *Mindsplit: The psychology of multiple personality and the dissociated self.* London: Dent & Sons. (p. 636)

McKenna, R. J. (1972). Some effects of anxiety level and food cues on the behavior of obese and normal subjects. *Journal of Personality and Social Psychology, 221*, 311–319. (p. 210)

McKim, W. A. (1991). *Drugs and behavior: An introduction to behavioral pharmacology* (2nd ed.). Englewood Cliffs, NJ: Prentice Hall. (p. 197)

McNally, R. J., & Steketee, G. S. (1985). Etiology and maintenance of severe animal phobias. *Behavioral Research and Therapy, 23*, 431–435. (p. 619)

McShane, D., & Berry, J. W. (1988). Native North Americans: Indian and Inuit abilities. In S. H. Irvine & J. W. Berry (Eds.), *Human abilities in cultural context.* Cambridge: Cambridge University Press. (p. 386)

Mead, M. (1935). *Sex and temperament in three primitive societies.* New York: William Morrow. (p. 468)

Meador, B. D., & Rogers, C. R. (1973). Client-centered therapy. In R. Corsini (Ed.), *Current psychotherapies.* Itasca, IL: Peacock. (p. 665)

Meddis, R. (1977). *The sleep instinct.* London: Routledge & Kegan Paul. (p. 226)

Mednick, S. A., Parnas, J., & Schulsinger, F. (1987). The Copenhagen high-risk project, 1962–1986. *Schizophrenia Bulletin, 13,* 485–495. (p. 642)

Melchior, C. L. (1990). Conditioned tolerance provides protection against ethanol lethality. *Pharmacology Biochemistry and Behavior, 37,* 205–206. (p. 130)

Meltzer, H. Y. (1992). The role of dopamine in schizophrenia. In J. Lindenmayer & S. R. Kay (Eds.), *New biological vistas on schizophrenia.* New York: Brunner/Mazel. (p. 641)

Meltzoff, A. N., and Moore, M. K. (1977). Imitation of facial and manual gestures by human neonates. *Science, 198,* 75–78. (p. 236)

Melzack, R. (1992). Phantom limbs. *Scientific American,* April, 120–126. (p. 271)

Melzack, R., & Wall, P. D. (1965). Pain mechanisms: A new theory. *Science, 150,* 971–979. (p. 272)

Melzack, R., & Wall, P. D. (1982). *The challenge of pain.* New York Basic Books. (pp. 269, 272, 273)

Merbs, S. L., & Nathans, J. (1992). Absorption spectra of human cone pigments. *Nature, 356,* 433–435. (p. 262)

Mercer, D. (1986). *Biofeedback and related therapies in clinical practice.* Rockville, MD: Aspen Systems. (p. 135)

Metzger, R. L., Boschee, P. F., Haugen, T., & Schnobrich, B. L. (1979). The classroom as a learning context: Changing rooms affects performance. *Journal of Educational Psychology, 71,* 440–442. (p. 354)

Meyering, T. C. (1989). *Historical roots of cognitive science: The rise of a cognitive theory of perception from antiquity to the nineteenth century.* Boston: Kluwer Academic Publishers. (p. 323)

Michaels, C. F., & Carello, C. (1981). *Direct perception.* Englewood Cliffs, NJ: Prentice Hall. (p. 319)

Michaels, J. W., Blommel, J. M., Brocato, R. M., Linkous, R. A., & Rowe, J. S. (1982). Social facilitation and inhibition in a natural setting. *Replications in Social Psychology, 2,* 21–24. (p. 543)

Miles, L. (1983). Apes and language: The search for communicative competence. In J. de Luce & H. T. Wilder (Eds.), *Language in primates.* New York: Springer-Verlag. (p. 429)

Milgram, S. (1963). Behavioral study of obedience. *Journal of Abnormal and Social Psychology, 67,* 371–378. (p. 540)

Milgram, S. (1964). Issues in the study of obedience: A reply to Baumrind. *American Psychologist, 19,* 848–852. (p. 541)

Milgram, S. (1974). *Obedience to authority: An experimental view.* New York: Harper & Row. (pp. 539, 540, 541)

Milinski, M. (1987). TIT FOR TAT in sticklebacks and the evolution of cooperation. *Nature, 325,* 433–435.

Mill, J. S. (1848; reprinted 1978). *Principles of political economy.* Toronto: University of Toronto Press. (p. 69)

Mill, J. S. (1869; reprinted 1980). *The subjection of women.* Arlington Heights, IL: Harlan Davidson. (p. 69)

Miller, A. G. (1986). *The obedience experiments: A case study of controversy in social science.* New York: Praeger. (p. 539)

Miller, G. A. (1981). *Language and speech.* San Francisco: Freeman. (p. 425)

Miller, G. E. (1956). The magic number seven plus or minus two: Some limits on our capacity for processing information. *Psychological Review, 63,* 81–97. (p. 339)

Miller, J. G. (1984). Culture and the development of everyday social explanations. *Journal of Personality and Social Psychology, 46,* 961–978. (p. 499)

Miller, J. G., & Bersoff, D. M. (1992). Culture and moral judgment: How are conflicts between justice and interpersonal responsibilities resolved? *Journal of Personality and Social Psychology, 62,* 541–554. (p. 480)

Miller, L. E., & Grush, J. E. (1986). Individual differences in attitudinal versus normative determination of behavior. *Journal of Experimental Social Psychology, 22,* 190–202. (p. 524)

Miller, L. T., & Vernon, P. A. (1992). The general factor in short-term memory, intelligence, and reaction time. *Intelligence, 16,* 5–29. (p. 380)

Miller, N. E. (1986). The morality and humaneness of animal research on stress and pain. In D. D. Kelly (Ed.), *Stress induced analgesia. Annals of the New York Academy of Sciences, Vol., 467.* (p. 43)

Miller, R. L., Brickman, P., & Bolen, D. (1975). Attribution versus persuasion as a means for modifying behavior. *Journal of Personality and Social Psychology, 31,* 430–441. (pp. 34, 505, 506)

Milner, B. (1965). Memory disturbance after bilateral hippocampal lesions. In P. Milner & S. Glickman (Eds.), *Cognitive processes and the brain.* Princeton, NJ: Van Nostrand. (pp. 335, 363)

Milner, B. (1970). Memory and the medial temporal regions of the brain. In K. H. Pribram & D. E. Broadbent (Eds.), *Biology of memory.* New York: Academic Press. (p. 335)

Milner, B. (1974). Hemispheric specialization: Scope and limits. In F. O. Schmitt & F. G. Worden (Eds.), *The neurosciences: Third research program.* Cambridge, MA: MIT Press. (p. 181)

Milner, B. (1984). Temporal lobes and memory disorders. Paper presented at the American Psychological Association Convention, Toronto, Canada. (p. 364)

Milner, P. M. (1991). Brain-stimulation reward: A review. *Canadian Journal of Psychology, 45,* 1–36. (p. 219)

Mineka, S., Davidson, M., Cook, M, & Keir, R. (1984). Observational conditioning of snake fear in rhesus monkeys. *Journal of Abnormal Psychology, 93,* 355–372. (p. 155)

Minix, D. A. (1976). *The role of the small group in foreign policy decision making: A potential pathology in crisis decisions?* Paper presented to the Southern Political Science Association. (For description, see D. G. Meyers, 1982.) (p. 550)

Mintz, L. B., & Betz, N. E. (1988). Prevalence and correlates of eating disordered behaviors among undergraduate women. *Journal of Counseling Psychology, 35,* 463–471. (p. 608)

Mischel, W. (1968). *Personality and assessment.* New York: Wiley. (pp. 586, 587, 597)

Mischel, W. (1984). Convergences and challenges in the search for consistency. *American Psychologist, 39,* 351–364. (pp. 597, 598)

Mischel, W., & Peake, P. K. (1982). Beyond déjà vu in the search for cross-situational consistency. *Psychological Review, 89,* 730–755. (p. 597)

Mishkin, M., & Appenzeller, T. (1987, June). The anatomy of memory. *Scientific American* 80–87. (p. 364)

Miyake, K., Chen, S., & Campos, J. (1985). Infant temperament, mother's mode of interaction, and attachment in Japan: an interim report. In I. Bretherton & E. Waters (Eds.), Growing points of attachment theory and research. *Monographs of the Society for Research in Child Development, 50* (1–2, Serial No. 209), 276–297. (p. 456)

Mogenson, G. J., & Yim, C. C. (1991). Neuromodulatory functions of the mesolimbic dopamine system: Electrophysiological and behavioral studies. In P. Willner & J. Scheel-Krüger (Eds.), *The mesolimbic dopamine system: From motivation to action.* New York: Wiley. (p. 207)

Money, J., & Ehrhardt, A. (1972). *Man and woman, boy and girl.* Baltimore: Johns Hopkins University Press. (p. 216)

Monteith, M. J., Devine, P. G., & Zuwerink, J. R. (1993). Self-directed versus other-directed affect as a consequence of prejudice-related discrepancies. *Journal of Personality and Social Psychology, 64,* 198–210. (p. 501)

Moore, H. T. (1917). Laboratory tests of anger, fear, and sex interests. *American Journal of Psychology, 28,* 390–395. (p. 543)

Moorhead, G., Ference, R., & Neck, C. P. (1991). Group decision fiascoes continue: Space shuttle *Challenger* and a revised groupthink framework. *Human Relations, 44,* 539–550. (p. 552)

Moray, N. (1959). Attention in dichotic listening: Effective cues and the influence of instructions. *Quarterly Journal of Experimental Psychology, 11,* 56–60. (p. 300)

Morelli, G. A. (1993). Growing up female in a farmer and forager community. M. E. Morbeck & A. L. Zihlman (Eds.), *Female biology, life history and evolution.* Princeton, NJ: Princeton University Press. (p. 469)

Morelli, G. A., Rogoff, B., Oppenheim, D., & Goldsmith, D. (1992). Cultural variation in infants' sleeping arrangements: Questions of independence. *Developmental Psychology, 28,* 604–613. (pp. 459, 460)

Morelli, G. A., & Tronick, E. Z. (1991). Parenting and child development in the Efe foragers and the Lese farmers of Zaïre. In M. H. Bornstein (Ed.), *Cultural approaches to parenting.* Hillsdale, NJ: Erlbaum. (p. 460)

Morgan, C. T. (1943). *Physiological psychology.* New York: McGraw-Hill. (p. 206)

Moriarty, T. (1975a). Crime, commitment and the responsive bystander: Two field experiments. *Journal of Personality and Social Psychology, 31,* 370–376. (p. 546)

Moriarty, T. (1975b, April). A nation of willing victims. *Psychology Today,* 43–50. (p. 534)

Morris, N. M., Udry, J. R., Khan-Dawood, F., & Dawood, M. Y. (1987). Marital sex frequency and midcycle female testosterone. *Archives of Sexual Behavior, 16,* 27–37. (p. 217)

Moscovici, S., Lage, E., & Naffrechoux, M. (1969). Influence of a consistent minority on the responses of a majority in a color perception task. *Sociometry, 32,* 365–380. (p. 549)

Moscovici, S., & Mugny, G. (1983). Minority influence. In P. B. Paulus (Ed.), *Basic group processes.* New York: Springer-Verlag. (p. 549)

Mowrer, O. H. (1960). *Learning theory and behavior.* New York: Wiley. (p. 146)

Mulcaster, R. (1582; reprinted 1929). *The first part of the elementarie, which intreateth of right writing of our English tung.* In R. H. Quick, *Essays on educational reformers.* London: Longmans, Green. (p. 49)

Mullen, B., Brown, R., & Smith, C. (1992). Ingroup bias as a function of salience, relevance, and status: An integration. *European Journal of Social Psychology, 22,* 103–122. (p. 502)

Mullen, B., & Hu, L. (1989). Perceptions of ingroup and outgroup variability: A meta-analytic integration. *Basic and Applied Social Psychology, 10,* 233–352. (p. 502)

Müller, J. (1838; reprinted 1842, 1965). *Elements of physiology* (Vol. 2) (W. Baly, Trans.). Excerpted in R. J. Herrnstein & E. G. Boring (Eds.), *A source book in the history of psychology.* Cambridge, MA: Harvard University Press. (p. 6)

Muntz, W. R. A. (1964, May). Vision in frogs. *Scientific American,* 110–119. (p. 281)

Murdock, G. P. (1981). *Atlas of world cultures.* Pittsburgh: University of Pittsburgh Press. (p. 116)

Murphy, G. E., Simmons, A. D., Wetzel, R. D., & Lustman, P. J. (1984). Cognitive therapy and pharmacotherapy: Singly and together in the treatment of depression. *Archives of General Psychiatry, 41,* 33–41. (p. 680)

Murray, E. J., & Foote, F. (1979). The origin of fear of snakes. *Behavioral Research and Therapy, 17,* 489–493. (p. 619)

Mussen, P., Eichorn, D. H., Honzik, M. P., Bieher, S. L., & Meredith, W. (1980). Continuity and change in women's characteristics over four decades. *International Journal of Behavioral Development, 3,* 333–347. (p. 599)

Myers, D. G. (1982). Polarizing effects of social interaction. In H. Brandstatter, J. H. Davis, & G. Stocker-Kreichgauer (Eds.), *Group decision making.* New York: Academic Press. (p. 551)

Myers, D. G., & Bishop, G. D. (1970). Discussion effects on racial attitudes. *Science, 169,* 778–779. (p. 550)

Myers, D. G., & Kaplan. M. F. (1976). Group-induced polarization in simulated juries. *Personality and Social Psychology Bulletin, 2,* 63–66. (p. 550)

Nathans, J. (1987). Molecular biology of visual pigments. *Annual Review of Neuroscience, 10,* 163–194. (p. 254)

Nathans, J., Piantanida, T. P., Eddy, R. L., Shows, T. P., & Hogness, D. S. (1986). Molecular genetics of inherited variation in human color vision. *Science, 232,* 203–210. (p. 262)

National Center for Health Statistics. (1985). Provisional data from the Health Promotion and Disease Prevention Supplement to the National Health Interview Survey: United States, Jan-March, 1985. *Advancedata,* November, 2–5. (p. 209)

National Institute of Alcohol Abuse and Alcoholism (1987). *Alcohol and health.* Rockville, MD: Author. (p. 632)

Nauta, W. J. H., & Feirtag, M. (1986). *Fundamental neuroanatomy.* New York: Freeman. (p. 164)

Neill, A. S. (1960). *Summerhill.* New York: Hart Publishing. (p. 466)

Neisser, U. (1976). *Cognition and reality.* San Francisco: Freeman. (p. 302)

Neisser, U. (1978). Memory: What are the important questions? In M. M. Gruneberg, P. E. Morris, & R. N. Sykes (Eds.), *Practical aspects of memory.* London: Academic Press. (p. 366)

Neisser, U. (Ed.) (1982). *Memory observed: Remembering in natural contexts.* New York: Freeman. (p. 366)

Nemeth, C. J. (1986). Differential contributions of majority and minority influence. *Psychological Review, 93,* 23–32. (p. 549)

Netley, C. (1983). Sex chromosome abnormalities and the development of verbal and nonverbal abilities. In C. L. Ludlow & J. A. Cooper (Eds.), *Genetic aspects of speech and language disorders.* New York: Academic Press. (p. 60)

Neugarten, B. L. (1974). Age groups in American society and the rise of the young-old. *Annals of the American Academy of Political and Social Sciences, 415,* 187–198. (p. 486)

Neugarten, B. L. (1979). Time, age, and the life cycle. *American Journal of Psychiatry, 136,* 887–894. (pp. 452, 481)

Neugarten, B. L. (1984). Interpretive social science and research on aging. In A. Rossi (Ed.), *Gender and the life course.* Chicago: Aldine. (p. 481)

Newcomb, T. M. (1943). *Personality and social change: Attitude formation in a student community.* New York: Dryden. (p. 516)

Newcomb, T. M. (1963). Persistence and repression of changed attitudes: Long-range studies. *Journal of Social Issues, 19,* 3–14. (p. 517)

Newcomb, T. M., Koenig, K., Flacks, R., & Warwick, D. (1967). *Persistence and change: Bennington College and its students after 25 years.* New York: Wiley. (p. 517)

Newman, J., & Layton, B. D. (1984). Overjustification: A self-perception perspective. *Personality and Social Psychology Bulletin, 10,* 419–425. (p. 148)

Newport, E. L. (1991). Contrasting conceptions of the critical period for language. In S. Carey & R. Gelman (Eds.), *The epigenesis of mind: Essays on biology and cognition.* Hillsdale, NJ: Erlbaum. (p. 428)

Newsom, C., Favell, J. E., & Rincover, A. (1983). Side effects of punishment. In S. Axelrod & J. Apsche (Eds.), *The effects of punishment on human behavior.* New York: Academic Press. (p. 141)

Nisbett, R. E., Caputo, C., Legant, P., & Marecek, J. (1973). Behavior as seen by the actor and as seen by the observer. *Journal of Personality and Social Psychology, 27,* 154–164. (p. 499)

Nishida, T. (Ed.) (1990). *The chimpanzees of the Mahale Mountains: Sexual and life history strategies.* Tokyo: University of Tokyo Press. (p. 112)

Nock, S. L. (1982). The life-cycle approach to family analysis. In B. B. Wolman (Ed.), *Handbook of developmental psychology.* Englewood Cliffs, NJ: Prentice-Hall. (p. 483)

Novin, D., Robinson, B. A., Culbreth, L. A., & Tordoff, M. G. (1983). Is there a role for the liver in the control of food intake? *American Journal of Clinical Nutrition, 9,* 233–246. (p. 208)

Nowak, M. A., & Sigmund, K. (1992). Tit for tat in heterogeneous populations. *Nature, 355,* 250–253. (p. 112)

Nowlis, G. H., & Frank, M. (1977). Qualities in hamster taste: Behavioral and neural evidence. In J. LeMagnen & P. MacLeod (Eds.), *Olfaction and taste* (Vol. 6). Washington, DC: Information Retrieval. (p. 245)

Nuechterlein, K. H., Dawson, M. E., Gitlin, M., Ventura, J., Goldstein, M. J., Synder, K. S., Yee, C. M., & Mintz, J. (1992). Developmental processes in schizophrenic disorders: Longitudinal studies of vulnerability and stress. *Schizophrenia Bulletin, 18,* 387–425. (p. 642)

Oetting, E. R., & Beauvais, F. (1988). Common elements in youth drug abuse: Peer clusters and other psychosocial factors. In S. Peele (Ed.), *Visions of addiction: Major contemporary perspectives on addiction and alcoholism.* Lexington, MA: Lexington Books. (p. 634)

Offer, D., & Schonert-Reichl, K. A. (1992) Debunking the myths of adolescence: Findings from recent research. *Journal of the American Academy of Child and Adolescent Psychiatry, 31,* 1003–1013. (pp. 472, 476)

Öhman, A. (1986). Face the beast and fear the face: Animal and social fears as prototypes for evolutionary analysis of emotion. *Psychophysiology, 23,* 123–145. (p. 156)

Okano, Y., Eisensmith, R. C., & many others (1991). Molecular basis of phenotypic heterogeneity in phenylketonuria. *The New England Journal of Medicine, 324,* 1232–1238. (p. 58)

Okin, R. L. (1983). On the future of state hospitals: Should there be one? *American Journal of Psychiatry, 140,* 577–581. (p. 648)

Olds, J. (1956, October). Pleasure centers in the brain. *Scientific American, 195,* 105–116. (p. 219)

Olds, J., & Milner, P. (1954). Positive reinforcement produced by electrical stimulation of the septal area and other regions of the rat brain. *Journal of Comparative and Physiological Psychology, 47,* 419–427. (p. 219)

Olds, M. E., & Fobes, J. L. (1981). The central basis of motivation: Intracranial self-stimulation studies. *Annual Review of Psychology, 32,* 523–574. (p. 220)

Olton, D. S. (1979). Mazes, maps, and memory. *American Psychologist, 34,* 583–596. (p. 157)

Orne, M. T., & Holland, C. G. (1968). On the ecological validity of laboratory deception. *International Journal of Psychiatry, 6,* 282–293. (p. 541)

Ornstein, R. (1977). *The psychology of consciousness,* second edition. New York: Harcourt Brace Jovanovich. (p. 382)

Öst, L. G. (1989). One-session treatment for specific phobias. *Behavioral Research and Therapy, 27,* 1–7. (p. 671)

O'Toole, R., & Dubin, R. (1968). Baby feeding and body sway: An experiment in George Herbert Mead's "taking the role of the other." *Journal of Personality and Social Psychology, 10,* 59–65. (p. 236)

Overmann, S. R. (1976). Dietary self-selection by animals. *Psychological Bulletin, 83,* 218–235. (p. 153)

Page, D., Mosher, R., Simpson, E. M., Fisher, E. M. C., Mardon, G., Pollack, J., McGillivray, B., Chapelle, A., & Brown, L. (1987). The sex-determining region of the human Y chromosome encodes a finger protein. *Cell, 51,* 1091–1104. (p. 213)

Paivio, A. (1971). *Imagery and verbal processes.* New York: Holt, Rinehart, and Winston. (Reprinted 1979, Hillsdale, NJ: Erlbaum). (p. 341)

Paivio, A. (1986). *Mental representations: A dual coding approach.* New York: Oxford University Press. (p. 341)

Paivio, A., Smythe, P. C., & Yuille, J. C. (1968). Imagery *versus* meaningfulness of nouns in paired-associate learning. *Canadian Journal of Psychology, 22,* 427–441. (p. 341)

Palmer, S. E. (1975a). The effects of contextual scenes on the identification of objects. *Memory and Cognition, 3,* 519–526. (p. 292)

Palmer, S. E. (1975b). Visual perception and world knowledge: Notes on a model of sensory-cognitive interaction. In D. A. Norman & D. E. Rumelhart (Eds.), *Explorations in cognition.* San Francisco: Freeman. (p. 291)

Papousek, H. (1969). Individual variability in learned responses in human infants. In R. J. Robinson (Ed.), *Brain and early behavior.* New York: Academic Press. (p. 420)

Park, B., & Rothbart, M. (1982). Perception of out-group homogeneity and levels of social categorization: Memory for the subordinate attributes of in-group and out-group members. *Journal of Personality and Social Psychology, 42,* 1031–1068. (p. 502)

Parkin, A. J. (1987). *Memory and amnesia: An introduction.* Oxford: Blackwell. (p. 363)

Parks, T. E., & Rock, I. (1990). Illusory contours from pictorially three-dimensional inducing elements. *Perception, 19,* 119–121. (p. 292)

Parmelee, A. H., Wenner, W. H., Akiyama, Y., Schultz, M., & Stern, E. (1967). Sleep states in premature infants. *Developmental Medicine and Child Neurology, 9,* 70–77. (p. 228)

Partridge, L., & Halliday, T. (1984). Mating patterns and mate choice. In J. R. Krebs & N. B. Davies (Eds.), *Behavioral ecology: An evolutionary approach.* Sunderland, MA: Sinauer. (p. 109)

Pascual-Leone, J. (1970). A mathematical model for the transition rule in Piaget's developmental stages. *Acta Psychological, 32,* 301–345. (p. 439)

Pashler, H. (1990). Do response modality effects support multiprocessor models of divided attention? *Journal of Experimental Psychology: Human Perception and Performance, 16,* 826–842. (p. 303)

Pashler, H. (1992). Attentional limitations in doing two tasks at the same time. *Current Directions in Psychological Science, 1,* 44–48. (p. 303)

Pashler, H. (1993). Doing two things at the same time. *American Scientist, 81,* 48–55. (p. 303)

Passingham, R. E., Perry, V. H., & Wilkinson, F. (1983). The long-term effects of removal of sensorimotor cortex in infant and adult rhesus monkeys. *Brain, 106,* 675–705. (p. 176)

Passman, R. H., & Weisberg, P. (1975). Mothers and blankets as agents for promoting play and exploration by young children in a novel environment: The effect of social and nonsocial attachment objects. *Developmental Psychology, 11,* 170–177. (p. 459)

Patterson, F., & Linden, E. (1981). *The education of Koko.* New York: Holt, Rinehart, and Winston. (p. 429)

Paul, G. L., & Lentz, R. J. (1977). *Psychosocial treatment of chronic mental patients: Milieu versus social-learning programs.* Cambridge, MA: Harvard University Press. (pp. 649, 673)

Pavlov, I. P. (1927; reprinted 1960). *Conditioned reflexes* (G. V. Anrep, Ed. & trans.). New York: Dover. (pp. 124, 125, 127, 128, 129, 144)

Peale, N. V. (1956). *The power of positive thinking.* Englewood Cliffs, NJ: Prentice-Hall. (p. 590)

Pearson, K. (1920). Notes on the history of correlation. *Biometrika, 13,* 25–45. (p. 370)

Peele, S. (1988). A moral vision of addiction: How people's values determine whether they become and remain addicts. In S. Peele (Ed.), *Visions of addiction: Major contemporary perspectives on addiction and alcoholism.* Lexington, MA: Lexington Books. (p. 635)

Penfield, W., & Perot, P. (1963). The brain's record of auditory and visual experience, *Brain, 86,* 595–696. (p. 227)

Perls, F. S., Hefferline, R. F., & Goodman, P. (1951). *Gestalt therapy.* New York: Julian. (p. 662)

Pervin, L. A. (1980). *Personality: Theory, assessment, and research* (3rd ed.). New York: Wiley. (p. 653)

Peterson, C. (1991). The meaning and measurement of explanatory style. *Psychological Inquiry, 2,* 1–10. (p. 590)

Peterson, C., & Seligman, E. P. (1984). Causal explanations as a risk factor for depression: Theory and evidence. *Psychological Review, 91,* 347–374. (p. 510)

Peterson, L. R., & Peterson, M. J. (1959). Short-term retention of individual verbal items. *Journal of Experimental Psychology, 58,* 193–198. (pp. 332, 359)

Peto, R., Lopez, A. D., Boreham, J., Thun, M., & Heath, C. (1992) Mortality from tobacco in developed countries: Indirect estimation from national vital statistics. *The Lancet, 339,* 1268–1278. (p. 485)

Pettito, L. A., & Marentette, P. F. (1991). Babbling in the manual mode: Evidence for the ontogeny of language. *Science, 251,* 1493–1496. (p. 424)

Petty, R. E., & Cacioppo, J. T. (1986). The elaboration likelihood model of persuasion. In L. Berkowitz (Ed.), *Advances in experimental social psychology* (Vol. 19). New York: Academic Press. (pp. 517, 518)

Petty, R. E., Cacioppo, J. T., & Goldman, R. (1981). Personal involvement as a determinant of argument-based persuasion. *Journal of Personality and Social Psychology, 41,* 847–855. (pp. 518, 519)

Petursson, H., & Lader, M. H. (1986). Benzodiazepine dependence. In J. Gabe & P. WIlliams (Eds.), *Tranquillisers: Social, psychological and clinical perspectives.* London: Tavistock. (p. 681)

Pfaff, D., & Modianos, D. (1985). Neural mechanisms of female reproductive behavior. In N. Adler, D. Pfaff, & R. W. Goy (Eds.), *Handbook of behavioral neurobiology (Vol. 7: Reproduction).* New York: Plenum. (p. 216)

Pfaff, D. W., & Sakuma, Y. (1979). Deficit in the lordosis reflex of female rats caused by lesions in the ventromedial nucleus of the hypothalamus. *Journal of Physiology, 288*, 203–210. (p. 213)

Pfungst, O. (1911; reprinted 1965). *Clever Hans: The horse of Mr. von Osten* (C. L. Rahn, Trans.). New York: Holt, Rinehart & Winston. (pp. 27, 28)

Phares, E. J. (1978). Locus of control. In H. London & J. E. Exner (Eds.), *Dimensions of personality.* New York: Wiley. (pp. 588, 589)

Phares, E. J. (1984). *Introduction to personality.* Columbus, OH: Merrill. (p. 589)

Phillips, A. G., Pfaus, J. G., & Blaha, C. D. (1991). Dopamine and motivated behavior: Insights provided by *in vivo* analyses. In P. Willner & J. Scheel-Krüger (Eds.), *The mesolimbic dopamine system: From motivation to action.* New York: Wiley. (p. 220)

Phillips, D. P. (1989). The neural coding of simple and complex sounds in the auditory cortex. In J. S. Lund (1989) (Ed.), *Sensory processing in the mammalian brain: Neural substrates and experimental strategies.* Oxford: Oxford University Press. (p. 252)

Piaget, J. (1923). *The language and thought of the child* (M. Worden, Trans.). New York: Harcourt, Brace & World. (p. 443)

Piaget, J. (1926). *Judgment and reasoning in the child* (M. Worden, Trans.). New York: Harcourt, Brace & World. (p. 434)

Piaget, J. (1927). *The child's conception of physical causality* (M. Worden, Trans.). New York: Harcourt, Brace & World. (pp. 434, 444)

Piaget, J. (1932; reprinted 1965). *The moral judgment of the child.* New York: Free Press. (pp. 453, 464)

Piaget, J. (1936; reprinted 1963). *The origins of intelligence in the child.* New York: Norton. (pp. 419, 420)

Piaget, J. (1962). *Play, dreams and imitation in childhood.* New York: Norton. (p. 433)

Piaget, J. (1970). *Genetic epistemology* (E. Duckworth, Trans.). New York: Norton. (p. 432)

Pick, A. D., Christy, M. D., & Frankel, G. W. (1972). A developmental study of visual selective attention. *Journal of Experimental Child Psychology, 14*, 165–175. (p. 440)

Pickens, R. W., Svikis, D. S., McGue, M., Lykken, D. T., Heston, L. L., & Clayton, P. J. (1991). Heterogeneity in the inheritance of alcoholism. *Archives of General Psychology, 48*, 19–28. (p. 633)

Pickles, J. O. (1988). *An introduction to the physiology of hearing* (2nd ed.). New York: Academic Press. (pp. 249, 251, 252)

Pierrel, R., & Sherman, J. G. (1963, February). Train your rat the Barnabus way. *Brown Alumni Monthly*, 8–14. (p. 138)

Pinker, S., & Bloom, P. (1992). Natural language and natural selection. In J. H. Barkow, L. Cosmides, & J. Tooby (Eds.), *The adapted mind-Evolutionary psychology and the generation of culture.* New York: Oxford University Press. (pp. 397, 398)

Pitman, R. K., van der Kolk, B. A., Orr, S. P., & Greenberg, M. S. (1990). Naloxone-reversible analgesic response to combat-related stimuli in posttraumatic stress disorder. *Archives of General Psychiatry, 47*, 541–544. (p. 273)

Plomin, R., & Daniels, D. (1987). Why are children in the same family so different from one another? *Behavioral and Brain Sciences, 10*, 1–60. (p. 71)

Plomin, R., & DeFries, J. C. (1985). *Origins of individual differences in infancy.* New York: Academic Press. (p. 468)

Plomin, R., DeFries, J. C., & McClearn, G. E. (1990). *Behavioral genetics: A primer* (2nd ed.). New York: Freeman. (pp. 53, 60, 62, 70, 76)

Plomin, R., & Foch, T. T. (1980). A twin study of objectively assessed personality in childhood. *Journal of Personality and Social Psychology, 39*, 680–688. (p. 601)

Polefrone, J., & Manuck, S. (1987). Gender differences in cardiovascular and neuroendocrine response to stressors. In R. C. Barnett, L. Biener, & G. K. Baruch (Eds.), *Gender and stress.* New York: Free Press. (p. 614)

Pomerantz, J. R., & Kubovy, M. (1986). Theoretical approaches to perceptual organization: Simplicity and likelihood principles. In K. R. Boff, L. Kaufman, & J. P. Thomas (Eds.), *Handbook of perception and human performance, Vol. II: Cognitive processes and performance.* New York: Wiley. (p. 292)

Powers, B., & Valenstein, E. S. (1972). Sexual receptivity: Facilitation by medial preoptic lesions in female rats. *Science, 175*, 1003–1005. (p. 213)

Powley, T. L. (1977). The ventromedial hypothalamic syndrome, satiety, and a cephalic phase hypothesis. *Psychological Review, 84*, 89–126. (p. 209)

Pratto, F., & Bargh, J. A. (1991). Stereotyping based on apparently individuating information. Trait and global components of sex stereotypes under attention overload. *Journal of Experimental Social Psychology, 27*, 26–47. (p. 500)

Prentice-Dunn, S., & Rogers, R. W. (1983). Deindividuation in aggression. In R. G. Geen & E. I. Donnerstein (Eds.), *Aggression: Theoretical and empirical reviews (Vol. 2).* New York: Academic Press. (p. 546)

Prentice-Dunn, S., & Spivey, C. B. (1986). Extreme deindividuation in the laboratory: Its magnitude and subjective components. *Personality and Social Psychology Bulletin, 12*, 206–215. (p. 547)

Pressin, J. (1933). The comparative effects of social and mechanical stimulation on memorizing. *American Journal of Psychology, 45*, 263–270. (p. 543)

Price, R. A., Cadoret, R. J., Stunkard, A. J., & Troughton, E. (1987). Genetic contributions to human fatness: An adoption study. *American Journal of Psychiatry, 144*, 1003–1008. (p. 210)

Price, R. H. (1992). Psychosocial impact of job loss on individuals and families. *Current Directions in Psychological Science, 1*, 9–11. (p. 484)

Provine, R. R. (1992). Contagious laughter: Laughter is a sufficient stimulus for laughs and smiles. *Bulletin of the Psychonomic Society, 30*, 1–4. (p. 236)

Pusey, A. E. (1980). Inbreeding avoidance in chimpanzees. *Animal Behaviour, 28*, 543–552. (p. 109)

Quattrone, A., & Jones, E. E. (1980). The perception of variability within in-groups and out-groups: Implications for the law of small numbers. *Journal of Personality and Social Psychology, 38,* 141–152. (p. 502)

Raaijmakers, J. G. W. (1991). The story of the two-store model: Past criticisms, current status, and future directions. D. E. Meyer & S. Kornblum (Eds.), *Attention and performance XIV: A silver jubilee.* Hillsdale, N. J: Erlbaum. (p. 328)

Rachman, S. J. (1985). An overview of clinical research issues in obsessional-compulsive disorders. In M. Mavissakalian, S. M. Turner, & L. Michelson (Eds.), *Obsessive-compulsive disorder.* New York: Plenum. (p. 620)

Rachman, S. J., & DeSilva, P. (1978). Abnormal and normal obsessions. *Behavioral Research and Therapy, 16,* 223–248. (p. 620)

Radke-Yarrow, M., Zahn-Waxler, C., & Capman, M. (1983). Children's pro-social dispositions and behavior. In P. H. Mussen & E. M. Hetherington (Eds.), *Handbook of child psychology: Vol. 4: Socialization, personality, and social development* (4th ed.). New York: Wiley. (p. 477)

Ramachandran, V. S. (1992). Blind spots. *Scientific American,* May, 84–91. (p. 268)

Ramachandran, V. S., & Gregory, R. L. (1991). Perceptual filling in of artificially induced scotomas in human vision. *Nature, 350,* 699–702. (p. 268)

Rank, S. G., & Jacobson, C. K. (1977). Hospital nurses' compliance with medication overdose orders: A failure to replicate. *Journal of Health and Social Behavior, 18,* 188–193. (p. 542)

Rapaport, J. L. (1989, March). The biology of obsessions and compulsions. *Scientific American,* 83–89. (p. 620)

Rapaport, J. L. (1991). Basal ganglia dysfunction as a proposed cause of obsessive-compulsive disorder. In B. J. Carroll & J. E. Barrett (Eds.), *Psychopathology and the brain.* New York: Raven Press. (p. 620)

Rasinski, K. A. (1989). The effect of question wording on public support for government spending. *Public Opinion Quarterly, 53,* 388–394. (p. 525)

Rasmussen, E. W. (1939). Social facilitation. *Acta Psychologica, 4,* 275–294. (p. 543)

Rasmussen, T., & Milner, B. (1977). The role of early left brain injury in determinating lateralizatin of cerebral speech functions. *Annals of the New York Academy of Sciences, 299,* 355–369. (p. 182)

Raugh, M. R., & Atkinson, R. C. (1975). A mnemonic method for learning a second-language vocabulary. *Journal of Educational Psychology, 67,* 1–16. (p. 343)

Raz, S., & Raz, N. (1990). Structural brain abnormalities in the major psychoses: A quantitative review of the evidence from computerized imaging. *Psychological Bulletin, 108,* 93–108. (p. 641)

Razran, G. A. (1939). A quantitative study of meaning by a conditioned salivary technique (semantic conditioning). *Science, 90,* 89–91. (p. 142)

Reber, A. S. (1989). Implicit learning and tacit knowledge. *Journal of Experimental Psychology: General, 118,* 219–235. (p. 360)

Recanzone, G. H., Merzenich, M. M., Jenkins, W. M., Grajski, K. A., & Dinse, H. R. (1992). Topographic reorganization of the hand prepresentation in cortical area 3b of owl monkeys trained in a frequency-discrimination task. *Journal of Neurophysiology, 67,* 1031–1056. (p. 176)

Redican, W. K. (1982). An evolutionary perspective on human facial displays. In P. Elkman (Ed.), *Emotion in the human face.* Cambridge: Cambridge University Press. (pp. 98, 103)

Ree, M. J., & Earles, J. A. (1992). Intelligence is the best predictor of job performance. *Current Directions in Psychological Science, 1,* 86–89. (p. 374)

Reed, T. E., & Jensen, A. R. (1991). Arm nerve conduction velocity (NCV), brain NCV, reaction time, and intelligence. *Intelligence, 15,* 33–47. (p. 379)

Reed, T. E., & Jensen, A. R. (1992). Conduction velocity in a brain nerve pathway of normal adults correlates with intelligence level. *Intelligence, 16,* 259–272. (p. 379)

Rees, J. A., & Harvey, P. H. (1991). The evolution of mating systems. In V. Reynolds & J. Kellett (Eds.), *Mating and marriage.* Oxford: Oxford University Press. (p. 104)

Reeves, R. A., Baker, G. A., Boyd, J. G., & Cialdini, R. B. (1991). The door-in-the-face technique: Reciprocal concessions vs. self-presentational explanations. *Journal of Social Behavior and Personality, 6,* 545–558. (p. 537)

Regier, D. A., Boyd, J. H., Burke, J. D., Rae, D. S., Myers, J. K., Kramer, M., Robins, L. N., George, L. K., Karno, M., & Locke, B. Z. (1988). One-month prevalence of mental disorders in the United States. *Archives of General Psychiatry, 45,* 977–986. (p. 613)

Reisberg, D., Smith, J. D., Baxter, D. A., & Sonenshine, M. (1989). "Enacted" auditory images are ambiguous; "pure" auditory images are not. *Quarterly Journal of Experimental Psychology: Human Experimental Psychology, 41,* 619–641. (p. 639)

Reiser, M. F. (1991). *Memory in mind and brain: What dream imagery reveals.* New York: Basic Books. (p. 228)

Reissland, N. (1988). Neonatal imitation in the first hour of life: Observations in rural Nepal. *Developmental Psychology, 24,* 464–469. (p. 236)

Reitan, R. M., & Wolfson, D. (1985). *The Halstead-Reitan neuropsychological test battery: Theory and clinical interpretation.* Tuscon: Neuropsychology Press. (p. 655)

Rende, R. D., Plomin, R., & Vandenberg, S. G. (1990). Who discovered the twin method? *Behavior Genetics, 20,* 277–285. (p. 68)

Rescorla, R. A. (1973). Effect of US habituation following conditioning. *Journal of Comparative and Physiological Psychology, 82,* 137–143. (p. 144

Rescorla, R. A. (1988). Pavlovian conditioning: It's not what you think it is. *American Psychologist, 43,* 151–160. (pp. 145, 146).

Rescorla, R. A. (1991). Associative relations in instrumental conditioning: The eighteenth Bartlett memorial lecture. *The Quarterly Journal of Experimental Psychology, 43B,* 1–23. (pp. 146, 147)

Rescorla, R. A., & Wagner, A. R. (1972). A theory of Pavlovian conditioning. Variations in effectiveness of reinforcement and nonreinforcement. In A. Black & W. F. Prokasky, Jr. (Eds.), *Classical conditioning II.* New York: Appleton-Century-Crofts. (p. 146)

Rest, J. R. (1986). *Moral development: Advances in research and theory.* New York: Praeger. (p. 478)

Reynolds, D. V. (1969). Surgery in the rat during electrical analgesia induced by focal brain stimulation. *Science, 164,* 444–445. (p. 272)

Rheingold, H., & Cook, K. (1975). The contents of boys' and girls' rooms as an index of parents' behavior. *Child Development, 46,* 459–463. (p. 468)

Rhodes, S. R. (1983). Age-related differences in work attitudes and behavior: A review and conceptual analysis. *Psychological Bulletin, 93,* 328–367. (p. 484)

Rhodewalt, F. (1990). Self-handicappers: Individual differences in the preference for anticipatory, self-protective acts. In R. L. Higgins, C. R. Snyder, & S. Berglas (Eds.), *Self-handicapping: The paradox that isn't.* New York: Plenum. (p. 512)

Richards, R., Kinney, D. K., Lunde, I., Benet, M., & Merzel, A. P. C. (1988). Creativity in manic-depressives, cyclothymes, their normal relatives and control subjects. *Journal of Abnormal Psychology, 97,* 281–288. (p. 626)

Richter, C. P. (1942–1943). Total self regulatory functions in animals and human beings. *Harvey Lecture Series, 38,* 63–103. (p. 154)

Richter, C. P., & Eckert, J. F. (1938). Mineral metabolism of adrenalectomized rats studied by the appetite method. *Endocrinology, 22,* 214–224. (p. 203)

Riley, J. W., Jr. (1970). What people think about death. In O.B. Brim, Jr., H. E. Freeman, S. Levine, & N. A. Scotch (Eds.), *The dying patient.* New York: Russell Sage Foundation. (p. 487)

Rime, B., Philippot, P., & Cisamolo, D. (1990). Social schemata of peripheral changes in emotion. *Journal of Personality and Social Psychology, 59,* 38–49. (p. 232)

Roberts, D., & Zito, K. (1987). Interpretation of lesion effects on stimulant self-administration. In M. A. Bozarth (Ed.), *Methods of assessing the reinforcing properties of abused drugs.* New York: Springer-Verlag. (p. 219)

Roberts, K. (1988). Retrieval of a basic-level category in prelinguistic infants. *Developmental Psychology, 24,* 21–27. (p. 418)

Robins, L. N., Helzer, J. E., Weissman, M. M., Orvaschel, H., Gruenberg, E., Burke, J. D., & Regier, D. A. (1984). Lifetime prevalence of specific psychiatric disorders in three sites. *Archives of General Psychiatry, 41,* 949–958. (pp. 613, 637)

Robinson, D. N., & Uttal, W. R. (1983). *Foundations of psychobiology.* New York: Macmillan. (p. 163)

Robinson, L. A., Berman, J. S., & Neimeyer, R. A. (1990). Psychotherapy for the treatment of depression: A comprehensive review of controlled outcome research. *Psychological Bulletin, 108,* 30–49. (p. 680)

Robinson, R. G., Kubos, K. L., Starr, L. B., Rao, K., & Price, T. R. (1984). Mood disorders in stroke patients: Importance of location of lesion. *Brain, 107,* 81–93. (p. 238)

Rock, I. (1984). *Perception.* New York: Scientific American Books. (pp. 301, 314, 315, 316, 317, 321)

Rock, I., & Gutman, D. (1981). The effect of inattention on form perception. *Journal of Experimental Psychology: Human Perception and Performance, 7,* 275–285. (pp. 300, 301)

Rodgers, D. A. (1972). Minnesota Multiphasic Personality Inventory. In O. K. Buros (Ed.), *The seventh mental measurements yearbook* (Vol 1). Highland Park, NJ: Gryphon. (p. 653)

Rodin, J. (1986). Aging and health: Effects of the sense of control. *Science, 233,* 1271–1276. (p. 487)

Rodin, J., & Ickovics, J. (1990). Women's health: Review and research agenda as we approach the 21st century. *American Psychologist, 45,* 1018–1034. (pp. 484, 485)

Rodin, J., Schank, D., & Striegel-Moore, R. (1989). Psychological features of obesity. *Medical Clinics of North America, 73,* 47–66. (pp. 209, 210, 211)

Roediger, H. L. (1990). Implicit memory: Retention without remembering. *American Psychologist, 45,* 1043–1056. (p. 362)

Roehling, P. V., Smith, G. T., Goldman, M. S., & Christiansen, B. A. (1987). *Alcohol expectancies predict adolescent drinking: A three year longitudinal study.* Paper presented at the 95th Annual Convention of the American Psychological Association, New York. (p. 634)

Rogers, C. R. (1951). *Client-centered therapy: Its current practice, implications, and theory.* Boston: Houghton Mifflin. (pp. 17, 662, 663)

Rogers, C. R. (1954). Toward a theory of creativity. *ETC: A Review of General Semantics, 11,* 249–260. (p. 583)

Rogers, C. R. (1959). A theory of therapy, personality, and interpersonal relationships, as developed in the client-centered framework. In S. Koch (Ed.), *Psychology: A study of a science* (Vol. 3). New York: McGraw-Hill. (p. 582)

Rogers, C. R. (1963). The actualizing tendency in relation to "motives" and to consciousness. In M. R. Jones (Ed.), *Nebraska symposium on motivation.* Lincoln, NE: University of Nebraska. (pp. 17, 582)

Rogers, C. R. (Ed.) (1967). *The therapeutic relationship and its impact: A study of psychotherapy with schizophrenics.* Madison, WI: University of Wisconsin Press. (pp. 664, 665)

Rogers, C. R. (1969). *Freedom to learn.* Columbus, OH: Merrill. (p. 583)

Rogers, C. R. (1977). *Carl Rogers on personal power.* New York: Delacorte Press. (p. 582)

Rogers, C. R., & Dymond, R. F. (1954). *Psychotherapy and personality change.* Chicago: University of Chicago Press. (p. 663)

Rogers, T. B., Kuiper, N. A., & Kirker, W. S. (1977). Self-reference and the encoding of personal information. *Journal of Personality and Social Psychology, 35,* 677–688. (p. 339)

Rogoff, B. (1990). *Apprenticeship in thinking: Cognitive development in social context.* New York: Oxford University Press. (pp. 444, 460, 461)

Rokeach, M. (1979). Change and stability in American value systems, 1968–1971. In M. Rokeach (Ed.), *Understanding human values.* New York: Free Press. (p. 526)

Rokeach, M. (1980). Some unresolved issues in theories of beliefs, attitudes, and values. In M. M. Page (Ed.), *1979 Nebraska symposium on motivation.* Lincoln, NE: University of Nebraska Press. (p. 527)

Roland, P. E., & Friberg, L. (1985). Localization of cortical areas activated by thinking. *Journal of Neurophysiology, 53,* 1219–1243. (p. 346)

Roland, P. E., Larsen, B., Larsen, N. A., & Skinhoj, E. (1980). Supplementary motor area and other cortical areas in organization of voluntary movements in man. *Journal of Neurophysiology, 43*, 118–136. (p. 176)

Rolls, E. T. (1982). Feeding and reward. In B. G. Hoebel & D. Novin (Eds.), *The neural basis of feeding and reward.* Brunswick, ME: Haer Institute. (pp. 207, 209)

Rolls, E. T., Murzi, E., Yaxley, S., Thorpe, S. J., & Simpson, S. J. (1986). Sensory-specific satiety: Food-specific reduction in responsiveness of ventral forebrain neurons after feeding in the monkey. *Brain Research, 368*, 79–86. (p. 207)

Rosch, E. (1973). On the internal structure of perceptual and semantic categories. In T. E. Moore (Ed.), *Cognitive development and the acquisition of language.* New York: Academic Press. (pp. 346–405)

Rosch, E. (1975). Cognitive representations of semantic categories. *Journal of Experimental Psychology: General, 104*, 192–223. (p. 346)

Rosch, E. (1977). Human categorization. In N. Warren (Ed.), *Advances in cross-cultural psychology* (Vol. 1). London: Academic Press. (p. 346)

Rose, S. (1973). *The conscious brain.* New York: Knopf. (p. 20)

Rosen, J. J., Glass, D. H., & Ison, J. R. (1967). Amobarbital sodium and instrumental performance changes following reward reduction. *Psychonomic Science, 9*, 129–130. (p. 148)

Rosenberg, S. (1988). Self and others: Studies in social personality and autobiography. In L. Berkowitz (Ed.), *Advances in experimental social psychology* (Vol. 21). New York: Academic Press. (p. 506)

Rosenhan, D. L. (1973). On being sane in insane places. *Science, 179*, 250–258. (p. 648)

Rosenhan, D. L., & Seligman, M. E. P. (1984). *Abnormal psychology.* New York: Norton. (p. 628)

Rosenqvist, G. (1990). Male mate choice and female-female competition for males in the pipefish *Norophis ophidion. Animal Behaviour, 39*, 1110–1115. (p. 106)

Rosenthal, N. E., Sack, D. A., Gillin, J. C., Lewy, A., Goodwin, F. K., Davenport, Y., Mueller, P., Newsome, D., & Wehr, T. (1984). Seasonal affective disorder: A description of the syndrome and preliminary findings with light therapy. *Archives of General Psychiatry, 41*, 72–80. (p. 626)

Rosenthal, R. (1965). Introduction to O. Pfungst, *Clever Hans: The horse of Mr. von Osten.* New York: Holt, Rinehart & Winston. (p. 29)

Rosenthal, R. (1976). *Experimenter effects in behavioral research* (enlarged ed.). New York: Irvington. (p. 29)

Rosenthal, R., & Jacobson, L. (1968). *Pygmalion in the classroom.* New York: Holt, Rinehart & Winston. (p. 505)

Rosenzweig, M. R. (1984). Experience, memory, and the brain. *American Psychologist, 39*, 365–376. (p. 188)

Rosenzweig, M. R., Bennett, E. L., & Diamond, M. C. (1972, February). Brain changes in response to experience. *Scientific American*, 22–29. (p. 188)

Ross, A. O. (1992). *The sense of self: Research and theory.* New York: Springer-Verlag. (p. 512)

Ross, C. A., Norton, O. R., & Wozney, K. (1989). Multiple personality disorder: An analysis of 236 cases. *Canadian Journal of Psychiatry, 34*, 413–418. (p. 637)

Ross, L. (1977). The intuitive psychologist and his shortcomings: Distortions in the attribution process. In L. Berkowitz (Ed.), *Advances in experimental social psychology.* New York: Academic Press. (p. 498)

Roth, M. (1957). Interaction of genetic and environmental factors in the causation of schizophrenia. In D. Richter (Ed.), *Schizophrenia: Somatic aspects.* New York: Pergamon. (p. 76)

Rotter, J. B. (1954; reprinted 1973, 1980). *Social learning and clinical psychology.* New York: Johnson Reprint Co. (p. 586)

Rotter, J. B. (1966). Generalized expectancies for internal versus external locus of control of reinforcement. *Psychological Monographs: General and Applied, 80* (Whole no. 609). (pp. 587, 588)

Rotter, J. B. (1982). Brief autobiography of the author. In J. B. Rotter (Ed.), *The development and application of social learning theory: Selected papers.* New York: Praeger. (p. 586)

Rotter, J. B., Liverant, S., & Crowne, D. P. (1961). The growth and extinction of expectancies in change controlled and skilled tasks. *Journal of Psychology, 52*, 161–177. (p. 587)

Rozée, P. D., & Van Boemel, G. V. (1989). The psychological effects of war trauma and abuse on older Cambodian refugee women. *Women & Therapy, 8*, 23–50. (p. 629)

Rozin, P., & Kalat, J. (1971). Specific hungers and poison avoidance as adaptive specializations of learning. *Psychological Review, 78*, 459–486. (p. 153)

Rozin, P., & Schull, J. (1988). The adaptive-evolutionary point of view in experimental psychology. In R. L. Atkinson, R. J. Herrnstein, G. Lindzey, & R. D. Luce (Eds.), *Steven's Handbook of Experimental Psychology*, 2nd edition. New York: Wiley. (p. 153)

Rubin, J. Z., Provenzano, F. J., & Luria, Z. (1974). The eye of the beholder: Parents' views on the sex of newborns. *American Journal of Orthopsychiatry, 44*, 512–519. (p. 468)

Ruff, H. A. (1986). Components of attention during infants' manipulative exploration. *Child Development, 57*, 105–114. (p. 420)

Ruff, H. A. (1989). The infant's use of visual and haptic information in the perception and recognition of objects. *Canadian Journal of Psychology, 43*, 302–319. (p. 420)

Rumelhart, D. E., & McClelland, J. L. (1986). *Parallel distributed processing: Explorations in the microstructure of cognition: Vol. 1. Foundations.* Cambridge, MA: MIT Press. (p. 190)

Runeson, S., & Frykholm, G. (1986). Kinematic specification of gender and gender expression. In V. McCabe & G. J. Balzano (Eds.), *Event cognition: An ecological perspective.* Hillsdale, NJ: Erlbaum. (p. 319)

Rupniak, N. M. J., Kilpatrick, G., Hall, M. D., Jenner, P., & Marsden, C. D. (1984b). Differential alterations in striatal dopamine receptor sensitivity induced by repeated administration of clinically equivalent doses of haloperidol, sulpiride or clozapine in rats. *Psychopharmacology, 84*, 512–519. (p. 679)

Rupniak, N. M. J., Mann, S., Hall, M. D., Fleminger, S., Kilpatrick, G., Jenner, P., & Marsden, C. D. (1984a). Differential effects of continuous administration of haloperidol or sulpiride on striatal dopamine function in the rat. *Psychopharmacology, 84,* 503–511. (p. 679)

Russek, M. (1971). Hepatic receptors and the neurophysiological mechanisms controlling feeding behavior. In S. Ehrenpreis (Ed.), *Neurosciences research* (Vol. 4). New York: Academic Press. (p. 208)

Rutberg, A. T. (1983). The evolution of monogamy in primates. *Journal of Theoretical Biology, 104,* 93–112. (p. 107)

Rutkowski, G. K., Gruder, C. L., & Romer, D. (1983). Group cohesiveness, social norms, and bystander intervention. *Journal of Personality and Social Psychology, 44,* 545–552. (p. 546)

Ryan, W. (1971). *Blaming the victim.* New York: Pantheon. (p. 503)

Rymer, R. (1993). *Genie: An abused child's flight from silence.* New York: HarperCollins. (p. 428)

Sachs, G. S., & Gelenberg, A. J. (1988). Adverse effects of electroconvulsive therapy. In A. J. Frances & R. E. Hales (Eds.), *Review of psychiatry, Vol,* 7. Washington, DC: American Psychiatric Press. (p. 682)

Sachs, J. S. (1967). Recognition memory for syntactic and semantic aspects of connected discourse. *Perception & Psychophysics, 2,* 437–442. (p. 343)

Sackeim, H. A. (1988). Mechanisms of action of electroconvulsive therapy. In A. J. Frances & R. E. Hales (Eds.), *Review of psychiatry, Vol.* 7. Washington, DC: American Psychiatric Press. (p. 681)

Sackeim, H. A. (1989). The efficacy of electroconvulsive therapy in the treatment of major depressive disorder. In S. Fisher & R. P. Greenberg (Eds.), *The limits of biological treatments for psychological distress.* Hillsdale, NJ: Erlbaum. (p. 682)

Sacks, O. (1970). *The man who mistook his wife for a hat, and other clinical tales.* New York: Harper & Row. (p. 269)

Sagi, A., Van Ijzendoorn, M. H., & Koren-Karie, N. (1991). Primary appraisal of the strange situation: A cross-cultural analysis of the preseparation episodes. *Developmental Psychology, 27,* 587–596. (p. 456)

Sajwaj, T., Lipert, J., & Agras, S. (1974). Lemon-juice therapy: The control of life-threatening rumination in a six-month-old infant. *Journal of Applied Behavior Analysis,* 7, 557–563. (p. 141)

Salthouse, T. A. (1991). Mediation of adult age differences in cognition by reduction in working memory and speed of processing. *Psychological Report, 2,* 179–183. (p. 442)

Samuel, A. G. (1991). A further examination of attentional effects in the phonemic restoration illusion. *The Quarterly Journal of Experimental Psychology,* 1991, *43A,* 679–699. (p. 293)

Sande, G. N., Goethals, G. R., & Radloff, C. E. (1988). Perceiving one's own traits and others': The multifaceted self. *Journal of Personality and Social Psychology, 54,* 13–20. (pp. 499, 507)

Sanford, E. C. (1917/1982). Professor Sanford's morning prayer. In U. Neisser (Ed.), *Remembering observed: remembering in natural contexts.* New York: Freeman. (Originally written as a letter in 1917; published in Neisser's book in 1982). (p. 336)

Sanna, L. J. (1992). Self-efficacy theory: Implications for social facilitation and social loafing. *Journal of Personality and Social Psychology, 62,* 774–786. (p. 543)

Sanna, L. J., & Shotland, R. L. (1990). Valence of anticipated evaluation and social facilitation. *Journal of Experimental Social Psychology, 26,* 82–92. (p. 543)

Savage-Rumbaugh, E. S. (1984). Verbal behavior at a procedural level in the chimpanzee. *Journal of the Experimental Analysis of Behavior, 41,* 223–250. (p. 431)

Savage-Rumbaugh, E. S., McDonald, K., Sevcik, R., & Hopkins, B. (1985). Language acquisition and use by a pygmy chimpanzee. *American Journal of Primatology, 8,* 362. (p. 431)

Savage-Rumbaugh, E. S., McDonald, K., Sevcik, R. A., Hopkins, B., & Rupert, E. (1986). Spontaneous symbol acquisition and communicative use by pygmy chimpanzees. *Journal of Experimental Psychology: General, 115,* 211–235. (p. 431)

Savage-Rumbaugh, S., Murphy, J., Sevcik, R. A., Brakke, K. E., Williams, S., & Rumbaugh, D. M. (1993). Language comprehension in ape and child. *Monographs of the Society for Research on Child Development.* (In press; will comprise issues 2 and 3, 1993). (pp. 431, 432)

Savage-Rumbaugh, S., Sevcik, R. A., Brakke, K. E., & Rumbaugh, D. M. (1990). Symbols: Their communicative use, comprehension, and combination by bonobos (*Pan paniscus*). In C. Rovee-Collier & L. P. Lipsitt (Eds.), *Advances in infancy research* (Vol 6). Norwood, NJ: Ablex. (p. 430)

Scarborough, E., & Furumoto, L. (1987). *Untold lives: The first generation of American women psychologists.* New York: Columbia University Press. (p. 10)

Scarr, S., & Carter-Saltzman, L. (1983). Genetics and intelligence. In J. L. Fuller & E. C. Simmel (Eds.), *Behavior genetics: Principles and applications.* Hillsdale, NJ: Erlbaum. (p. 73)

Scarr, S., & McCartney, K. (1983). How people make their own environments: A theory of genotype—environment effects. *Child Development, 54,* 424–435. (pp. 71, 72)

Scarr, S., Weber, P. L., Weinberg, R. A., & Wittig, M. A. (1981). Personality resemblance among adolescents and their parents in biologically related and adoptive families. *Journal of Personality and Social Psychology, 40,* 885–898. (p. 600)

Scarr, S., & Weinberg, R. A. (1977). Intellectual similarities within families of both adopted and biological children. *Intelligence, I,* 170–191. (p. 71)

Scarr, S., & Weinberg, R. A. (1983). The Minnesota adoption studies: Genetic differences and malleability. *Child Development, 54,* 260–267. (p. 71)

Schab, F. R. (1990). Odors and remembrance of things past. *Journal of Experimental Psychology: Learning, Memory, and Cognition, 16,* 648–655. (p. 354)

Schacter, D. L. (1992). Understanding implicit memory. *American Psychologist, 47,* 559–569. (p. 359)

Schacter, D. L., Harbluk, J. L., & McLachlan, D. R. (1984). Retrieval without recollection: An experimental analysis of source amnesia. *Journal of Verbal Learning and Verbal Behavior, 23,* 593–611. (p. 365)

Schachter, S. (1970). Some extraordinary facts about obese humans and rats. *American Psychologist, 26*, 129–144. (pp. 209–210)

Schachter, S. (1971). *Emotion, obesity, and crime.* New York: Academic Press. (p. 233)

Schaie, K. W. (1984). Midlife influences upon intellectual function in old age. *International Journal of Behavioral Development, 7*, 463–478. (p. 442)

Schaie, K. W. (1989). Perceptual speed in adulthood: Cross-sectional and longitudinal studies. *Psychology and Aging, 4*, 443–453. (p. 442)

Schank, R. C., & Abelson, R. P. (1977). *Scripts, plans, goals and understanding.* Hillsdale, NJ: Erlbaum. (p. 347)

Scharf, B. (1964). Partial masking. *Acustica, 14*, 16–23. (p. 251)

Scheier, M. F., & Carver, C. S. (1993). On the power of positive thinking: The benefits of being optimistic. *Current Directions in Psychological Science, 2*, 26–30. (p. 590)

Scheier, M. F., Matthews, K. A., Owens, J. F., Magovern, G. J., Lefebvre, R., Abbott, R. C., & Carver, C. S. (1989). Dispositional optimism and recovery from coronary artery bypass surgery: The beneficial effects of optimism on physical and psychological well-being. *Journal of Personality and Social Psychology, 57*, 1024–1040. (p. 590)

Scher, S. J., & Cooper, J. (1989). Motivational basis of dissonance: The singular role of behavioral consequences. *Journal of Personality and Social Psychology, 56*, 899–906. (p. 522)

Schieffelin, B., & Ochs, E. (1983). A cultural perspective on the transition from prelinguistic to linguistic communication. In R. Golinkoff (Ed.), *The transition from prelinguistic to linguistic communication.* Hillsdale, NJ: Erlbaum. (p. 429)

Schiff, M., Duyme, M., Dumaret, A., Stewart, J., Tomkiewicz, S., & Feingold, J. (1978). Intellectual status of working-class children adopted early into upper-middle-class families. *Science, 200*, 1503–1504. (p. 72)

Schifter, D. E., & Ajzen, I. (1985). Intention, perceived control, and weight loss: An application of the theory of planned behavior. *Journal of Personality and Social Psychology, 49*, 849–851. (p. 524)

Schildkraut, J. J. (1965). The catecholamine hypothesis of affective disorders: A review of supporting evidence. *American Journal of Psychiatry, 122*, 509–522. (p. 622)

Schlenker, B. R. (1980). *Impression management: The self-concept, social identity, and interpersonal relations.* Monterey, CA: Brooks/Cole. (p. 510)

Schmidt, F. L., & Hunter, J. E. (1992). Development of a causal model of processes determining job performance. *Current Directions in Psychological Science, 1*, 89–92. (p. 374)

Schmidt, F. L., Ones, D. S., & Hunter, J. E. (1992). Personnel selection. *Annual Review of Psychology, 43*, 627–670. (p. 374)

Schmidt, R. F. (1986). Motor systems. In R. F. Schmidt (Ed.), *Fundamentals of neurophysiology* (3rd ed.). New York: Springer-Verlag. (pp. 171, 178)

Schnapf, J. L., & Baylor, D. A. (1987, April). How photoreceptor cells respond to light. *Scientific American*, 40–47. (p. 254)

Schneider, J. M. (1972). Relationship between locus of control and activity preferences: Effects of masculinity, activity, and skill. *Journal of Consulting and Clinical Psychology, 38*, 225–230. (p. 588)

Schneider, J. W., & Hacker, S. L. (1973). Sex role imagery and use of the generic "man" in introductory texts: A case of the sociology of sociology. *The American Sociologists, 8*, 12–18. (p. 407)

Schneider, W., Dumais, S. T., & Shiffrin, R. M. (1984). Automatic and control processing and attention. In R. Parasuraman & D. R. Davies (Eds.), *Varieties of attention.* New York: Academic Press. (pp. 304–305)

Schopler, J., Insko, C. A., Graetz, K. A., Drigotas, S. M., & Smith, V. A. (1991). *Personality and Social Psychology Bulletin, 17*, 612–624. (p. 557)

Schunk, D. H. (1984). Self-efficacy perspective on achievement behavior. *Educational Psychologist, 19*, 48–58. (p. 590)

Schunk, D. H., & Hanson, A. R. (1985). Peer models: Influence on children's self-efficacy and achievement. *Journal of Educational Psychology, 77*, 313–322. (p. 589)

Schwartz, B. & Reisberg, G. (1991). *Learning and memory.* New York: Norton. (pp. 144, 145)

Schwartz, M. F. (1987). Patterns of speech production deficit within and across aphasia syndromes: Application of a psycholinguistic model. In M. Coltheart, G. Sartori, & R. Job (Eds.), *The cognitive neuropsychology of language.* Hillsdale, NJ: Erlbaum. (pp. 402, 403)

Schwartz, S. H., & Gottlieb, A. (1980). Bystander anonymity and reactions to emergencies. *Journal of Personality and Social Psychology, 39*, 418–430. (p. 546)

Schwartz-Giblin, S., McEwen, B. S., & Pfaff, D. W. (1989). Mechanisms of female reproductive behavior. In F. R. Brush & S. Levine (Eds.), *Psychoendocrinology,* New York: Academic Press. (pp. 216, 217)

Schwartzman, H. (1978). *Transformations: The anthropology of children's play.* New York: Plenum. (p. 464)

Scott, J. P. (1963). The process of primary socialization in canine and human infants. *Monograph of the Society for Research in Child Development, 28*, 1–47. (p. 57)

Scott, J. P., & Fuller, J. L. (1965). *Genetics and the social behavior of the dog.* Chicago: University of Chicago Press. (p. 56)

Scribner, S. (1977). Modes of thinking and ways of speaking: Culture and logic reconsidered. In P. N. Johnson-Laird & P. C. Wason (Eds.), *Thinking: Readings in cognitive science.* Cambridge: Cambridge University Press. (p. 385)

Scribner, S. (1986). Thinking in action: Some characteristics of practical thought. In R. J. Sternberg & R. K. Wagner (Eds.), *Practical intelligence: Nature and origins of competence in the everyday world.* Cambridge: Cambridge University Press. (p. 385)

Searle, L. V. (1949). The organization of hereditary maze-brightness and maze-dullness. *Genetic Psychology Monographs, 39*, 279–325. (p. 67)

Sears, R. R. (1936). Experimental studies of projection: I. Attributions of traits, *Journal of Social Psychology, 7*, 151–163. (p. 577)

Sechenov, I. M. (1863; reprinted 1935). Reflexes of the brain. In A. A. Subkow (Ed. & trans.), *I. M. Sechenov: Selected works.* Moscow:

State Publishing House for Biological and Medical Literature. (p. 6)

Sedikides, C., & Jackson, J. M. (1990). Social impact theory: A field test of source strength, source immediacy and number of targets. *Basic and Applied Social Psychology, 11,* 273–281. (p. 534)

Seeman, P., & Lee, T. (1975). Antipsychotic drugs: Direct correlation between clinical potency and presynaptic action on dopamine neurons, *Science, 188,* 1271–1219. (p. 641)

Segall, M. H., Dason, P. R., Berry, J. W., & Poortinga, Y. H. (1990). *Human behavior in global perspective: An introduction to cross-cultural psychology.* New York: Pergamon Press. (p. 438)

Sejnowski, T. J., & Tesauro, G. (1990). Building network learning algorithms from Hebbian synapses. In J. L. McGaugh, N. M. Weinberger, & G. Lynch (Eds.), *Brain organization and memory: Cells, systems, and circuits.* Oxford: Oxford University Press. (p. 190)

Seligman, M. E. P. (1971). Phobias and preparedness. *Behavior Therapy, 2,* 307–320. (pp. 155, 619)

Seligman, M. E. P. (1990). *Learned optimism.* New York: Knopf. (p. 590)

Seligman, M. E. P., Castellon, C., Cacciola, J., Schulman, P., Luborsky, L., Ollove, M., & Downing, R. (1988). Explanatory style change during cognitive therapy for unipolar depression. *Journal of Abnormal Psychology, 97,* 13–18. (p. 624)

Seligman, M. E. P., Maier, S. F., & Geer, J. H. (1968). Alleviation of learned helplessness in the dog. *Journal of Abnormal Psychology, 73,* 256–262. (p. 623)

Selkoe, D. J. (1991). Amyloid protein and Alzheimer's disease. *Scientific American, 265* (Nov.), 68–78. (p. 61)

Semmel, A. K. (1976). *Group dynamics and foreign policy process: The choice-shift phenomenon.* Paper presented to the Southern Political Science Association. (For description, see D. G. Myers, 1982.) (p. 550)

Serbin, L., Sprafkin, C., Elman, M., & Doyle, A. B. (1984). The early development of sex differentiated patterns and social influence. *Canadian Journal of Social Science, 14,* 350–363. (p. 470)

Shapiro, C. M., Bortz, R., Mitchell, D., Bartell, P., & Jooste, P. (1981). Slow-wave sleep: A recovery period after exercise. *Science, 214,* 1253–1254. (p. 223)

Shapiro, L. R. (1991). The fragile X syndrome, *The New England Journal of Medicine, 325,* 1736–1738. (p. 60)

Shapiro, S., Skinner, E. A., Kessler, L. G., Von Korff, M., German, P. S., Tischler, G. L., Leaf, P. J., Lee, B., Cottler, L., & Reiger, D. A. (1984). Utilization of health and mental health services: Three epidemiologic catchment area sites. *Archives of General Psychiatry, 41,* 971–978. (p. 650)

Shaver, P., Hazen, C., & Bradshaw, D. (1988). Love as attachment: The integration of three behavioral systems. In R. J. Sternberg & M. L. Barnes (Eds.), *The psychology of love.* New Haven, CT: Yale University Press. (p. 481)

Sheehan, P. W., Statham, D., & Jamieson, G. A. (1991). Pseudomemory effects and their relationship to level of susceptibility to hypnosis and state instruction. *Journal of Personality and Social Psychology, 60,* 130–137. (p. 357)

Sherif, M. (1966). *In common predicament: Social psychology of intergroup conflict and cooperation.* Boston: Houghton Mifflin. (p. 557)

Sherif, M., Harvey, O. J., White, B. J., Hood, W. E., & Sherif, C. S. (1961). *Intergroup conflict and cooperation: The Robbers Cave experiment.* Norman, OK: University of Oklahoma Book Exchange. (p. 557)

Sherman, P. W. (1977). Nepotism and the evolution of alarm calls. *Science, 197,* 1246–1253. (pp. 111, 112)

Shettleworth, S. J. (1972). Constraints on learning. In D. S. Lehrman, R. A. Hinde, & E. Shaw (Eds.), *Advances in the study of behavior* (Vol. 4). New York: Academic Press. (p. 15)

Shettleworth, S. J. (1983, March). Memory in food-hoarding birds. *Scientific American,* 102–110. (p. 157)

Shiffrin, R. M., & Schneider, W. (1977). Controlled and automatic information processing: II. Perceptual learning, automatic attending, and a general theory. *Psychological Review, 84,* 127–190. (p. 307)

Shimamura, A. P., & Squire, L. R. (1991). The relationship between fact and source memory: Findings from amnesic patients and normal subjects. *Psychobiology, 19,* 1–10. (p. 364)

Shoda, Y., Mischel, W., & Wright, J. C. (1989). Intuitive interactionism in person perception: Effects of situation-behavior relations on dispositional judgments. *Journal of Personality and Social Psychology, 56,* 41–53. (p. 598)

Shorter, E. (1992). *From paralysis to fatigue: A history of psychosomatic illness in the modern era.* New York: The Free Press. (p. 629)

Shweder, R. A. (1982). Fact and artifact in trait perception: The systematic distortion hypothesis. In B. A. Maher & W. B. Maher (Eds.), *Progress in experimental personality research, Vol. 11: Normal personality process.* New York: Academic Press. (p. 600)

Shweder, R. A. (1990). Cultural psychology—what is it? In J. W. Stigler, R. A. Shweder, & G. Herdt (Eds.), *Cultural psychology: Essays on comparative human development.* Cambridge: Cambridge University Press. (p. 18)

Sibley, C. G., & Ahlguist, J. E. (1984). The phylogeny of the hominoid primates, as indicated by DNA-DNA hybridization. *Journal of Molecular Evolution, 20,* 2–15. (p. 108)

Siegel, S. (1976). Morphine analgesia tolerance: Its situation specificity supports a Pavlovian conditioning model. *Science, 193,* 323–325. (p. 130)

Siegel, S. (1984). Pavlovian conditioning and herion overdose: Reports by overdose victims. *Bulletin of the Psychonomic Society, 22,* 428–430. (p. 130)

Siegel, S., Krank, M. D., & Hinson, R. E. (1988). Anticipation of pharmacological and nonpharmacological events. Classical conditioning and addictive behavior. In S. Peele (Ed.), *Visions of addiction: Major contemporary perspectives on addiction and alcoholism.* Lexington, MA: Lexington Books. (pp. 129, 634)

Siegler, R. S. (1983). How knowledge influences learning. *American Scientist, 71,* 631–638. (pp. 440, 441)

Siegler, R. S., & Jenkins, E. (1989). *How children discover new strategies.* Hillsdale, NJ: Erlbaum. (p. 440)

Simon, H. A. (1992). What is an explanation of behavior? *Psychological Science, 3,* 150–161. (pp. 20, 22)

Simpson, E. L. (1974). Moral development research: A case of scientific cultural bias. *Human Development, 17,* 81–106. (p. 479)

Sims, J. H., & Baumann, D. D. (1972). The tornado threat: Coping styles of the north and south. *Science, 176,* 1386–1392. (p. 588)

Singer B., & Benassi, V. A. (1981). Occult beliefs. *American Scientist, 69,* 49–55. (p. 29)

Singer, J. E., Brush, C. A., & Lublin, S. C. (1965). Some aspects of deindividuation and conformity. *Journal of Experimental Social Psychology, 1,* 356–378. (p. 547)

Siqueland, R. R., & Lipsitt, L. P. (1966). Conditioned headturning in human newborns. *Journal of Experimental Child Psychology, 3,* 356–376. (p. 138)

Sizemore, C. C. (1989). *A mind of my own,* New York: William Morrow. (p. 636)

Skinner, B. F. (1938). *The behavior of organisms.* New York: Appleton-Century-Crofts. (pp. 13, 122, 130, 133)

Skinner, B. F. (1953). *Science and human behavior.* New York: Macmillan. (pp. 133, 136, 141)

Skinner, B. F. (1957). *Verbal behavior.* New York: Appleton-Century-Crofts. (p. 522)

Skinner, B. F. (1966). The phylogeny and ontogeny of behavior. *Science, 153,* 1205–1213. (p. 133)

Skinner, B. F. (1971). *Beyond freedom and dignity.* New York: Knopf. (p. 14)

Skinner, B. F. (1974). *About behaviorism.* New York: Alfred A. Knopf. (p. 14)

Skinner, R. D., & Garcia-Rill, E. (1990). Brainstem modulation of rhythmic functions and behaviors. In W. R. Klemm & R. P. Vertes (Eds.), *Brainstem mechanisms of behavior.* New York: Wiley. (p. 171)

Skov, R. B., & Sherman, S. J. (1986). Information-gathering processes: Diagnosticity, hypothesis confirmation strategies and perceived hypothesis confirmation. *Journal of Experimental Social Psychology, 22,* 93–121. (p. 390)

Slater, E. (1975). The diagnosis of "hysteria." *British Medical Journal, 1,* 1395–1399. (p. 627)

Slavin, R. E. Sharan, S., Kagan, S., Hertz-Lazarowitz, R., Webb, C., & Schmuck, R. (1985). *Learning to cooperate, cooperating to learn.* New York: Plenum. (p. 559)

Slavney, P. R., & Teitelbaum, M. L. (1985). Patients with medically unexplained symptons: *DSM-III* diagnoses and demographic characteristics. *General Hospital Psychiatry, 7,* 25–35. (p. 627)

Sloane, M. C. (1981). *A comparison of hypnosis vs. waking state and visual vs. non-visual recall instructions for witness/victim memory retrieval in actual major crimes.* Unpublished doctoral dissertation, Florida State University, Tallahassee. (p. 358)

Sloane, R. B., Staples, F. R., Cristo, A. H., Yorkston, N. J., & Whipple, K. (1975). *Psychotherapy versus behavior therapy.* Cambridge, MA: Harvard University Press. (p. 675)

Slobin, D. I. (1973). Cognitive prerequisites for the development of grammar. In C. H. Ferguson & D. I. Slobin (Eds.), *Studies of child language development.* New York: Holt, Rinehart & Winston. (p. 427)

Slobin, D. I. (1985). Introduction: Why study acquisition crosslinguistically? In D. I. Slobin (Ed.), *The crosslinguistic study of language acquisition, Vol. I: The data.* Hillsdale, NJ: Erlbaum. (p. 427)

Small, M. (1992). The evolution of female sexuality and mate selection in humans. *Human Nature, 3,* 133–156. (pp. 116, 218)

Smetana, J. G., Yau, J., Restrepo, A., & Braeges, J. L. (1991). Adolescent-parent conflict in married and divorced families. *Developmental Psychology, 27,* 1000–1010. (p. 473)

Smith, J. D. (1992). The auditory hallucinations of schizophrenia. D. Reisberg (Ed.), *Auditory imagery.* Hillsdale, NJ: Erlbaum. (p. 638)

Smith, D. (1982). Trends in counseling and psychotherapy. *American Psychologist, 37,* 802–809. (pp. 662, 678)

Smith, E. A. (1989). A biosocial model of adolescent sexual behavior. In G. R. Adams, R. Montemayor, & T. P. Gullota (Eds.), *Biology of adolescent behavior and development.* Newbury Park, CA: SAGE Publications. (p. 474)

Smith, E. E., Shoben, E. J., & Rips, L. J. (1974). Structure and process in semantic memory: A feature model for semantic decision. *Psychological Review, 81,* 214–241. (p. 347)

Smith, M. B., Bruner, J. S., & White, R. W. (1956). *Opinions and personality.* New York: Wiley. (p. 514)

Smith, M. L., Glass, G. V., & Miller, T. I. (1980). *The benefits of psychotherapy.* Baltimore: Johns Hopkins University Press. (pp. 674, 675, 676)

Smith, S. M., Brown, H. O., Toman, J. E. P., & Goodman, L. S. (1947). The lack of cerebral effects of d-tubercurarine. *Anesthesiology, 8,* 1–14. (p. 404)

Smuts, B. (1992). Male aggression against women. An evolutionary perspective. *Human Nature, 3,* 1–44. (pp. 113, 218)

Smyth, M. M., Morris, P. E., Levy, P., & Ellis, A. W. (1987). *Cognition in action.* Hillsdale, NJ: Erlbaum. (p. 401)

Snarey, J. R. (1985). Cross-cultural universality of social-moral development: A critical review of Kohlbergian research. *Psychological Bulletin, 97,* 202–232. (p. 480)

Snow, C. P. (1961, February). Either-or. *Progressive,* 24. (p. 537)

Snow, C. E. (1984). Parent-child interaction and the development of communicative ability. In R. L. Schiefelbusch & J. Pickar (Eds.), *The acquisition of communicative competence.* Baltimore: University Park Press. (p. 428)

Snyder, C. R., Harris, C., Anderson, J. R., Holleran, S. A., Irving, L. M., Sigmon, S. T., Yosinobu, L., Gibb, J., Langelle, C., & Harney, P. (1991). The will and the ways: Development and validation of an individual-differences measure of hope. *Journal of Personality and Social Psychology, 60,* 570–585. (p. 590)

Snyder, F., & Scott, J. (1972). The psychophysiology of sleep. In N. S. Greenfield & R. A. Sternbach (Eds.), *Handbook of psychophysiology.* New York: Holt, Rinehart & Winston. (pp. 223, 228)

Snyder, M. (1974). Self-monitoring of expressive behavior. *Journal of Personality and Social Psychology, 30,* 526–537. (pp. 512, 513)

Snyder, M. (1979). Self-monitoring processes. In L. Berkowitz (Ed.), *Advances in experimental social psychology* (Vol. 12). New York: Academic Press. (p. 513)

Snyder, M. (1981). Seek and ye shall find: Testing hypotheses about other people. In E. T. Higgins, C. P. Herman, & M. P. Zanna (Eds.), *Social cognition: The Ontario symposium on personality and social psychology.* (pp. 277–303). Hillsdale, NJ: Erlbaum. (p. 390)

Snyder, M., & DeBono, K. G. (1987). A functional approach to attitudes and persuasion. In M. P. Zanna, J. M. Olson, & C. P. Herman (Eds.), *Social influence: The Ontario symposium, Vol. 5.* Hillsdale, NJ: Erlbaum. (pp. 516, 518)

Snyder, M., & DeBono, K. G. (1989). Understanding the functions of attitudes: Lessons from personality and social psychology. In A. R. Pratkanis, S. J. Breckler, & A. G. Greenwald (Eds.), *Attitude structure and function.* Hillsdale, NJ: Erlbaum. (p. 516)

Snyder, M., & Monson, T. C. (1975). Persons, situations, and the control of social behavior. *Journal of Personality and Social Psychology, 32,* 637–644. (p. 513)

Snyder, M., & Smith, D. (1986). Personality and friendship: The friendship worlds of self-monitoring. In V. Derlega & B. A. Winstead (Eds.), *Friendship and social interaction.* New York: Springer-Verlag. (p. 513)

Snyder, M., & Swann, W. B. (1976). When actions reflect attitudes: The politics of impression management. *Journal of Personality and Social Psychology, 34,* 1032–1042. (p. 523)

Snyder, M., Tanke, E. D., & Berscheid, E. (1977). Social perception and interpersonal behavior: On the self-fulfilling nature of social stereotypes. *Journal of Personality and Social Psychology, 35,* 656–666. (p. 505)

Snyder, S. H. (1985, October). The molecular basis of communication between cells. *Scientific American,* 132–141. (pp. 191, 192, 195)

Snyderman, M., & Rothman, S. (1987). Survey of expert opinion on intelligence and aptitude testing. *American Psychologist, 42,* 137–144. (p. 369)

Solomon, G. F., Amkraut, A. A., & Rubin, R. T. (1985). Stress hormones, neuroregulation, and immunity. In S. R. Burchfield (Ed.), *Stress: Psychological and physiological interactions.* Washington, DC: Hemisphere. (p. 231)

Sorce, J. F., Emde, R. N., Campos, J., & Klinnert, M. D. (1985). Maternal emotional signaling: Its effect on the visual cliff behavior of 1-year-olds. *Developmental Psychology, 21,* 195–200. (p. 455)

Sorokin, P. (1956). *Fads and foibles in modern sociology.* Chicago: H. Regnery Co. (p. 374)

Sourkes, T. L. (1989). Disorders of the basal ganglia. In G. J. Siegel, B. W. Agranoff, R. W. Albers, & P. B. Molinoff (Eds.), *Basic neurochemistry: Molecular, cellular, and medical aspects* (4th ed.). New York: Raven Press. (p. 172)

Spalding, D. A. (1873; reprinted 1954). Instinct with original observations on young animals. *British Journal of Animal Behavior, 2,* 2–11. (p. 156)

Spanos, N. P., Weekes, J. R., & Bertrand, L. D. (1985). Multiple personality: A social psychological perspective. *Journal of Abnormal Psychology, 94,* 362–376. (p. 636)

Spearman, C. (1904). The proof and measurement of association between two things. *American Journal of Psychology, 15,* 72–101. (p. 375)

Spearman, C. (1927). *The abilities of man.* New York: Macmillan. (pp. 375, 376)

Spelke, E. S., Breinlinger, K., Macomber, J., & Jacobson, K. (1992). Origins of knowledge. *Psychological Review, 99,* 605–632. (p. 422)

Spelke, E. S., Hirst, W. C., & Neisser, U. (1976). Skills of divided attention. *Cognition, 4,* 215–230. (p. 302)

Spence, K. W. (1956). *Behavior theory and conditioning.* New Haven, CT: Yale University Press. (p. 146)

Sperling, G. (1960). The information available in brief visual presentations. *Psychological Monographs, 74,* (Whole no. 498). (p. 329)

Spiegel, D., Bloom, J. R. Kraemer, H. C., & Gottheil, E. (1989). Effect of psychosocial treatment on survival of patients with metastic breast cancer. *The Lancet, 1989 ii,* 888–891. (p. 631)

Spiro, M. E. (1979). *Gender and culture: Kibbutz women revisited.* Durham, NC: Duke University Press. (p. 116)

Spitzer, L., & Rodin, J. (1983). Arousal-induced eating: Conventional wisdom or empirical finding? In J. T. Cacioppo & R. E. Petty (Eds.), *Social psychophysiology.* New York: Guilford. (p. 210)

Spitzer, R. L., & Fleiss, J. L. (1974). A reanalysis of the reliability of psychiatric diagnosis. *British Journal of Psychiatry, 125,* 341–347. (p. 610)

Spitzer, R. L., Williams, J. B. W., & Gibbon, M. (1987). *Instruction manual for the structured clinical interview for the DSM-III-R (SCID, 4/1/87 Revis.).* New York: NY State Psychiatric Institute. (p. 611)

Spock, B., & Rothenberg, M. B. (1985). *Dr. Spock's baby and child care* (rev. & updated ed.). New York: Pocket Books. (p. 460)

Spohn, H., & Patterson, T. (1980). Recent studies of psychophysiology in schizophrenia. *Schizophrenia-1980.* Washington, DC: NIMH. (p. 641)

Springer, S. P., & Deutsch, G. (1989). *Left brain, right brain* (3rd ed.). New York: Freeman. (pp. 182, 382)

Squire, L. R. (1992). Memory and the hippocampus: A synthesis from findings with rats, monkeys, and humans. *Psychological Review, 99,* 195–231. (pp. 335, 359, 363, 364)

Sroufe, L. A., & Fleeson, J. (1986). Attachment and the construction of relationships. In W. H. Hartup & Z. Rubin (Eds.), *Relationships and development.* Hillsdale, NJ: Erlbaum. (p. 457)

Stapp, J., Tucker, A. M., & VandenBos, G. R. (1985). Census of psychological personnel: 1983. *American Psychologist, 40,* 1317–1351. (p. 23)

Steele, C. M., & Josephs, R. A. (1990). Alcohol myopia: Its prized and dangerous effects. *American Psychologist, 45,* 921–933. (pp. 632–633)

Steen, S. N., Oppliger, R. A., & Brownell, K. D. (1988). Metabolic effects of repeated weight loss and regain in adolescent wrestlers. *Journal of the American Medical Association, 260,* 47–50. (p. 211)

Steinberg, L. D. (1981). Transformations in family relations at puberty. *Developmental Psychology, 17,* 883–840. (p. 473)

Steinberg, L. (1989). Pubertal maturation and parent-adolescent distance: An evolutionary perspective. In G. R. Adams, R. Montemayor, & T. P. Gullota (Eds.), *Biology of adolescent behavior and development.* Newbury Park, CA: SAGE Publications. (p. 473)

Steinberg, L., & Silverberg, S. B. (1986). The vicissitudes of autonomy in early adolescence. *Child Development, 57,* 841–851. (p. 473)

Steketee, G., & Foa, E. B. (1985). Obsessive-compulsive disorder. In D. H. Barlow (Ed.), *Clinical handbook of psychological disorders: A step-by-step treatment manual.* New York: Guilford. (p. 620)

Stellar, E. (1954). The physiology of emotion. *Psychological Review, 61,* 5–22. (p. 206)

Stellar, J. R., & Stellar, E. (1985). *The neurobiology of motivation and reward.* New York: Springer-Verlag. (pp. 204, 207)

Stelmack, R. M. (1990). Biological bases of extraversion: Psychophysiological evidence. *Journal of Personality, 58,* 293–311. (p. 596)

Sternberg, R. J. (1985a). *Beyond IQ: A triarchic theory of human intelligence.* Cambridge: Cambridge University Press. (pp. 322, 380, 381)

Sternberg, R. J. (1985b). General intellectual ability. In R. J. Sternberg (Ed.), *Human abilities: An information-processing approach.* New York: Freeman. (pp. 378, 381)

Sternberg, R. J. (1986a). *Intelligence applied: Understanding and increasing your intellectual skills.* San Diego: Harcourt Brace Jovanovich. (pp. 382, 392)

Sternberg, R. J. (1986b). Intelligence is mental self-government. In R. J. Sternberg & D. K. Detterman (Eds.), *What is intelligence? Contemporary viewpoints on its nature and definition.* Norwood, NJ: Ablex. (p. 380)

Sternberg, R. J. (1986c). A triangular theory of love. *Psychological Review, 93,* 119–135. (pp. 481, 482)

Sternberg, R. J. (1988). Triangulating love. In R. J. Sternberg & Michael Barnes (Eds.), *The psychology of love.* New Haven, CT: Yale University Press. (p. 481)

Sternberg, R. J., & Gardner, M. K. (1983). Unities in inductive reasoning. *Journal of Experimental Psychology: General, 112,* 80–116. (p. 381)

Stevens, C. F. (1979, September). The neuron. *Scientific American,* 54–65. (pp. 184, 186)

Stevens, S. S. (1962). The surprising simplicity of sensory metrics. *American Psychologist, 17,* 29–39. (p. 280)

Stevens, S. S. (1975). *Psychophysics: Introduction to its perceptual, neural, and social prospects.* New York: Wiley. (pp. 278, 279, 280)

Steward, O. (1989). *Principles of cellular, molecular, and developmental neuroscience.* New York: Springer-Verlag. (p. 166)

Stewart, R. B., & Marvin, R. S. (1984). Sibling relations: The role of conceptual perspective-taking in the ontogeny of sibling caregiving. *Child Development, 55,* 1322—1332. (p. 477)

Stigler, J. W., & Perry, M. (1990). Mathematics learning in Japanese, Chinese, and American classrooms. In J. W. Stigler, R. A. Shweder, & G. Herdt (Eds.), *Cultural psychology: Essays on comparative human development.* Cambridge: Cambridge University Press. (p. 466)

Stiles, W. B., Shapiro, D. A., & Elliott, R. (1986). Are all psychotherapies equivalent? *American Psychologist, 41,* 165–180. (pp. 674, 676)

Storms, M. D. (1973). Videotape and the attribution process: Reversing actors' and observers' points of view. *Journal of Personality and Social Psychology, 27,* 165–175. (p. 500)

Straube, E. R. & Oades, R. D. (1992). *Schizophrenia: empirical research and findings.* San Diego: Academic Press. (p. 637)

Stricker, E. M. (1973). Thirst, sodium appetite, and complementary physiological contributions to the regulation of intravascular fluid volume. In A. N. Epstein, H. R. Kissileff, & E. Stellar (Eds.), *The neuropsychology of thirst: New findings and advances in concepts.* Washington, DC: Winston. (p. 203)

Stricker, E. M. (1982). The central control of food intake: A role for insulin. In B. G. Hoebel & D. Novin (Eds.), *The neural basis of feeding and reward.* Brunswick, ME: Haer Institute. (p. 206)

Strickland, B. R. (1992). Women and depression. *Current Directions, 1,* 132–135. (p. 615)

Stroop, J. R. (1935). Studies of interference in serial verbal reactions. *Journal of Experimental Psychology, 18,* 643–662. (p. 305)

Struch, N., & Schwartz, S. H. (1989). Intergroup aggression: Its predictors and distinctness from in-group bias. *Journal of Personality and Social Psychology, 56,* 364–373. (p. 559)

Strupp, H. H. (1989). Psychotherapy: Can the practitioner learn from the researcher? *American Psychologist, 44,* 717–724. (p. 677)

Strupp, H. H. & Hadley, S. W. (1979). Specific vs. nonspecific factors in psychotherapy: A controlled study of outcome. *Archives of General Psychiatry, 36,* 1125–1136. (p. 677)

Susman, R. L. (Ed.) (1984). *The pygmy chimpanzee: Evolutionary biology and behavior.* New York: Plenum. (p. 430)

Sutherland, S. (1991). Only four possible solutions. *Nature, 353,* 389–390. (p. 383)

Svartberg, M., & Stiles, T. C. (1991). Comparative effects of short-term psychodynamic psychotherapy: A meta-analysis. *Journal of Consulting and Clinical Psychology, 59,* 704–714. (p. 675)

Swann, W. B. (1985). The self as architect of social reality. In B. R. Schlenker (Ed.), *The self and social life.* New York: McGraw-Hill. (p. 511)

Swann, W. B. (1987). Identity negotiation: Where two roads meet. *Journal of Social Psychology, 53,* 1038–1051. (p. 511)

Swann, W. B. (1992). Seeking "truth," finding despair: Some unhappy consequences of a negative self-concept. *Current Directions in Psychological Science, 1,* 15–18. (p. 511)

Swann, W. B., & Ely, R. J. (1984). A battle of wills: Self-verification versus behavioral confirmation. *Journal of Personality and Social Psychology, 46,* 1287–1302. (p. 512)

Swann, W. B., & Hill, C. A. (1982). When our identities are mistaken: Reaffirming self-conceptions through social interaction. *Journal of Personality and Social Psychology, 43,* 59–66. (p. 512)

Sweeney, P. D., & Gruber, K. L. (1984). Selective exposure: Voter information preferences and the Watergate affair. *Journal of Personality and Social Psychology, 46,* 1208–1221. (p. 519)

Symons, D. (1979). *The evolution of human sexuality.* Oxford: Oxford University Press. (pp. 116, 117, 218)

Tajfel, H. (1982). Social psychology of intergroup relations. *Annual Review of Psychology, 33,* 1–39. (p. 502)

Takahashi, J. S., & Zatz, M. (1982). Regulation of circadian rhythmicity. *Science, 217,* 1104–1111. (pp. 224, 229)

Tandon, R., & Kane, J. M. (1993). Neuropharmacologic basis for clozapine's unique profile. *Archives of General Psychiatry, 50,* 158–159. (p. 641)

Taylor, H. F. (1980). *The IQ game.* New Brunswick, NJ: Rutgers University Press. (p. 710)

Teigen, K. H. (1984). A note on the origin of the term "nature and nurture": Not Shakespeare and Galton, but Mulcaster. *Journal of the History of the Behavioral Sciences, 20,* 363–364. (p. 49)

Tellegen, A., Lykken, D. T., Bouchard, T. J., Wilcox, K. J., Segal, N. L., & Rich, S. (1988). Personality similarity in twins reared apart and together. *Journal of Personality and Social Psychology, 54,* 1031–1039. (p. 600)

Terman, G. W., Shavit, Y., Lewis, J. W., Cannon, J. T., & Liebeskind, J. C. (1984). Intrinsic mechanisms of pain inhibition: Activation by stress. *Science, 226,* 1270–1277. (p. 273)

Terman, L. M. (1954). The discovery and encouragememt of exceptional talent. *American Psychologist, 9,* 221–230. (p. 374)

Terman, M., Schlager, D., Fairhurst, S., & Perlman, B. (1989). Dawn and dusk stimulation as a therapeutic intervention. *Biological Psychiatry, 25,* 966–970. (p. 626)

Terrace, H. S. (1985). In the beginning was the "name." *American Psychologist, 40,* 1011–1028. (p. 430)

Terrace, H. S., Petitto, L. A., Sanders, R. J., & Bever, T. G. (1980). On the grammatical capacity of apes. In K. Nelson (Ed.), *Children's language* (Vol. 2). New York: Gardner Press. (pp. 430, 431)

Test, M. A. Knoedler, W. H., Allness, D. J., Burke, S. S., Brown, R. L., & Wallisch, L. S. (1991). Long-term community care through an assertive continuous treatment team. In C. A. Tamminga & S. C. Schulz (Eds.), *Advances in neuropsychiatry and psychopharmacology, volume 1: Schizophrenia research.* New York: Raven Press. (p. 650)

Tetlock, P. E. (1984). Cognitive style and political belief systems in the British House of Commons. *Journal of Personality and Social Psychology, 46,* 365–375. (p. 527)

't Hart, P. (1990). *Groupthink in government: A study of small groups and policy failure.* Amsterdam: Swets & Zeitlinger. (p. 552)

Therman, E. (1986). *Human chromosomes: Structure, behavior, effects.* New York: Springer-Verlag. (pp. 60, 61)

Thigpen, C. H., & Cleckley, H. M. (1957). *The three faces of Eve.* New York: Popular Library. (p. 636)

Thompson, R. F. (1985). *The brain: An introduction to neuroscience.* New York: Freeman. (p. 172)

Thorndike, E. L. (1898). Animal intelligence: An experimental study of associative processes in animals. *The Psychological Review Monograph Supplements, 2,* 4–160. (pp. 130, 131, 132, 137)

Thorndike, E. L. (1913). *Educational psychology.* New York: Teachers College Press. (p. 350)

Thorne, B. (1986). Girls and boys together . . . but mostly apart: Gender arrangements in elementary schools. In W. H. Hartup & Z. Rubin (Eds.), *Relationships and development.* Hillsdale, NJ: Erlbaum. (p. 471)

Thorne, B. (1990). Children and gender: Constructions of the difference. In D. L. Rhode (Ed.), *Theoretical perspectives on sexual difference.* New Haven, CT: Yale University Press. (p. 471)

Thornhill, R., & Thornhill, N. W. (1987). In C. Crawford, M. Smith, & D. Krebs (Eds.), *Sociobiology and psychology: Ideas, issues, and applications.* Hillsdale, NJ: Erlbaum. (p. 117)

Thornton, B. (1984). Defensive attribution of responsibility: Evidence from an arousal-based bias. *Journal of Personality and Social Psychology, 46,* 721–734. (p. 503)

Thurstone, L. L. (1938). *Primary mental abilities.* Chicago: University of Chicago Press. (pp. 376, 377)

Thurstone, L. L. (1947). *Multiple factor analysis.* Chicago: University of Chicago Press. (p. 376)

Tienari, P., Lahti, I., Sorri, A., Naarala, M., Moring, J., & Karl-Erik, W. (1989). The Finnish adoptive family study of schizophrenia: Possible joint effects of genetic vulnerability and family environment. *British Journal of Psychiatry, 155* (suppl. 5), 29–32. (p. 77)

Tiger, L., & Shepher, J. (1975). *Women in the kibbutz.* New York: Harcourt Brace Jovanovich. (p. 117)

Tilker, H. A. (1970). Socially responsible behavior as a function of observer responsibility and victim feedback. *Journal of Personality and Social Psychology, 14,* 95–100. (p. 540)

Tinbergen, N. (1951). *The study of instinct.* Oxford: Oxford University Press. (pp. 89–90)

Tinbergen, N. (1952, December). The curious behavior of the stickleback. *Scientific American,* 22–26. (p. 89)

Tinbergen, N. (1960, December). The evolution of behavior in gulls. *Scientific American,* 118–130. (p. 98)

Tinbergen, N. (1968). On war and peace in animals and man. *Science, 160,* 1411–1418. (p. 115)

Tizard, B., & Hodges, J. (1978). The effect of early institutional rearing on the development of eight-year-old children. *Journal of Child Psychology and Psychiatry, 19,* 99–118. (p. 458)

Tolman, E. C. (1948). Cognitive maps in rats and men. *The Psychological Review, 55,* 189–208. (pp. 20, 149)

Tolman, E. C. (1959). Principles of purposive behavior. In S. Koch (Ed.), *Psychology: A study of a science* (Vol. 2). New York: McGraw-Hill. (p. 146)

Tolman, E. C., & Honzik, C. H. (1930a). "Insight" in rats. *University of California Publications in Psychology, 4,* 215–232. (p. 149)

Tolman, E. C., & Honzik, C. H. (1930b). Introduction and removal of reward, and maze performance in rats. *University of California Publications in Psychology, 4,* 257–275. (pp. 149, 150)

Torgersen, S. (1986). Childhood and family characteristics in panic and generalized anxiety disorder. *American Journal of Psychiatry, 143,* 630–639. (p. 618)

Torgersen, S. (1990). Genetics of anxiety and its clinical implications. In G. D. Burrows, M. Roth, & R. Noyes (Eds.), *Handbook of anxiety, vol. 3: The neurobiology of anxiety.* Amsterdam: Elsevier. (p. 620)

Torrance, E. P. (1954). Some consequences of power differences on decision-making in permanent and temporary three-man groups. *Research Studies, State College of Washington, 22,* 130–140. (p. 552)

Torrey, E. F. (1988). Stalking the schizovirus. *Schizophrenia Bulletin, 14,* 223–229. (p. 641)

Townshend, B., Cotter, N., Van Compernolle, D., & White, R. L. (1987). Pitch perception of cochlear implant subjects. *Journal of the Acoustical Society of America, 82,* 106–115. (p. 252)

Travis, L. E. (1925). The effect of a small audience upon eye-hand coordination. *Journal of Abnormal and Social Psychology, 20,* 142–146. (p. 542)

Treisman, A. (1969). Strategies and models of selective attention. *Psychological Review, 76,* 282–299. (p. 317)

Treisman, A. (1986, November). Features and objects in visual processing. *Scientific American,* 114B–125. (pp. 294, 295)

Treisman, A. (1991). Search, similarity, and integration of features between and within dimensions. *Journal of Experimental Psychology: Human Perception and Performance, 17,* 652–676. (pp. 294, 296)

Treisman, A., & Gormican, S. (1988). Feature analysis in early vision: Evidence from search asymmetries. *Psychological Review, 95,* 15–48. (p. 295)

Triplett, N. (1898). The dynamogenic factors in peacemaking and competition. *American Journal of Psychology, 9,* 507–533. (p. 542)

Trivers, R. L. (1971). The evolution of reciprocal altruism. *Quarterly Review of Biology, 46,* 35–57. (pp. 112, 556)

Trivers, R. L. (1972). Parental investment and sexual selection. In B. Campbell (Ed.), *Sexual selection and the decent of man.* Chicago: Aldine. (pp. 104, 105, 106)

Tronick, E. Z., Morelli, G. A., & Ivey, P. K. (1992). The Efe forager infant and toddler's pattern of social relationships: Multiple and simultaneous. *Developmental Psychology, 28,* 568–577. (p. 460)

Troutt-Ervin, E. D. (1990). Application of keyword mnemonics to learning terminology in the college classroom. *Journal of Experimental Education, 59,* 31–41. (p. 343)

Tryon, R. C. (1942). Individual differences. In F. A. Moss (Ed.), *Comparative psychology* (rev. ed.). New York: Prentice Hall. (pp. 65, 66)

Tseng, W., Mo, K., Li, L., Chen, G., Ou, L., & Zheng, H. (1992). Koro epidemics in Guangdong, China. *The Journal of Nervous and Mental Disorders, 180,* 117–123. (p. 608)

Tucker, J. A., Vucinish, R. E., & Sobell, M. B. (1981). Alcohol consumption as a self-handicapping strategy. *Journal of Abnormal Psychology, 90,* 220–230. (p. 512)

Tulving, E. (1974). Recall and recognition of semantically encoded words. *Journal of Experimental Psychology, 102,* 778–787. (p. 353)

Tulving, E. (1985). How many memory systems are there? *American Psychologist, 40,* 385–398. (pp. 359, 365)

Tulving, E., Hayman, C. A., & Macdonald, C. A. (1991). Long-lasting perceptual priming and semantic learning in amnesia: A case experiment. *Journal of Experimental Psychology: Learning Memory, and Cognition, 17,* 595–617. (p. 364)

Tulving, E., & Schacter, D. L. (1990). Primary and human memory systems. *Science, 247,* 301–306. (pp. 359, 361, 362)

Turner, A. M., & Greenough, W. T. (1985). Differential rearing effects on rat visual cortex synapses. I. Synaptic and neuronal density and synapses per neuron. *Brain Research, 329,* 195–203. (p. 188)

Turner, J. C. (1985). Social categorization and the self-concept: A social cognitive theory of group behavior. In E. J. Lawler (Ed.), *Advances in group processes: Theory and research* (Vol. 2). Greenwich, CT: JAI Press. (p. 552)

Tversky, A., & Kahneman, D. (1973). Availability: A heuristic for judging frequency and probability. *Cognitive Psychology, 5,* 207–232. (p. 389)

Tversky, A., & Kahneman, D. (1974). Judgment under uncertainty: Heuristics and biases. *Science, 185,* 1124–1131. (pp. 388, 389)

Uttal, W. R. (1973). *The psychobiology of sensory coding.* New York: Harper & Row. (p. 243)

Vaillant, G. E. (1977). *Adaptation to life.* Boston: Little, Brown. (pp. 481, 577, 578)

Vaillant, G. E. (1983). *The natural history of alcholism.* Cambridge, MA: Harvard University Press. (p. 635)

Vaillant, G. E., & Vaillant, C. O. (1992). Empirical evidence that defensive styles are independent of environmental influence. In G. E. Vaillant (Ed.), *Ego mechanisms of defense: A guide for clinicians and researchers.* Washington, DC: American Psychiatric Press. (p. 578)

Valenstein, E. S. (1973). *Brain control: A critical examination of brain stimulation and psychosurgery.* New York: Wiley. (p. 219)

Valenstein, E. S. (Ed.) (1980). *The psychosurgery debate: Scientific, legal, and ethical perspectives.* San Francisco: Freeman. (p. 682)

Valenstein, E. S. (1986). *Great and desperate cures: The rise and decline of psychosurgery and other radical treatments for mental illness.* New York: Basic Books. (p. 682)

Vance, E. B., & Wagner, N. N. (1976). Written descriptions of orgasm: A study of sex differences. *Archives of Sexual Behavior, 5,* 87–98. (p. 214)

Van Dis, H., & Larsson, K. (1971). Induction of sexual arousal in the castrated male rat by intracranial stimulation. *Physiology and Behavior, 6,* 85–86. (p. 213)

Van Essen, D. C., Anderson, C. H., & Felleman, D. J. (1992). Information processing in the primate visual system: An integrated systems perspective. *Science, 255,* 419–423. (pp. 268, 269)

VanItallie, T. B., & Kissileff, H. R. (1990). Human obesity: A problem in body energy economics. In E. M. Stricker (Ed.), *Handbook of behavioral neurobiology, Volume 10: Neurobiology of food and fluid intake.* New York: Plenum. (p. 212)

Vanneman, R. D., & Pettigrew, T. F. (1972). Race and relative deprivation in the urban United States. *Race, 13*, 461–486. (p. 559)

Verkerk, A., Pieretti, M., & many others (1991). Identification of a gene (FMR-1) containing a CGG repeat coincident with a breakpoint cluster region exhibiting length variation in fragile X syndrome. *Cell, 65*, 905–914. (p. 59)

Vernon, P. A. (1987). New developments in reaction time research. In P. A. Vernon (Ed.), *Speed of information-processing and intelligence*. Norwood, NJ: Ablex. (p. 379)

Vernon, P. A., & Kantor, L. (1986). Reaction time correlations with intelligence test scores obtained under either timed or untimed conditions. *Intelligence, 9*, 357–374. (p. 379)

Vernon, P. E. (1961). *The structure of human abilities* (2nd ed.). London: Methuen. (p. 377)

Vinogradov, S., Gottesman, I. I., Moises, H. W., & Nicol, S. (1991). Negative association between schizophrenia and rheumatoid arthritis. *Schizophrenia Bulletin, 17*, 669–678. (p. 87)

Vinokur, A., & Burnstein, E. (1974). Effects of partially shared persuasive arguments on group-induced shifts: A group problem-solving approach. *Journal of Personality and Social Psychology, 29*, 305–315. (p. 551)

Volkova, V. D. (1953). On certain characteristics of the formation of conditioned reflexes to speech stimuli in children. *Fiziologicheskii Zhurnal USSR, 39*, 540–548. (p. 143)

Voss, J. F., & Post, T. A. (1988). On the solving of ill-structured problems. In M. T. H. Chi, R. Glaser, & M. J. Farr (Eds.), *The nature of expertise*. Hillsdale, NJ: Erlbaum. (p. 396)

Vygotsky, L. S. (1933; reprinted 1978). Play and its role in the mental development of the child. In M. Cole, V. John-Steiner, S. Scribner, & E. Sourberman (Eds.), *Mind and society*. Cambridge, MA: Harvard University Press. (p. 464)

Vygotsky, L. S. (1934; reprinted 1962). *Thought and language* (E. Haufmann & G. Vaker, Eds. & trans.). Cambridge, MA: MIT Press. (pp. 404, 443, 444)

Wade, N. J., & Swanston, M. (1991). *Visual perception: An introduction*. London: Routledge. (p. 254)

Wagstaff, G. F. (1984). The enhancement of witness memory by hypnosis: A review and methodological critique of the experimental literature. *British Journal of Experimental and Clinical Hypnosis, 2*, 3–12. (p. 357)

Wahl, O. F. (1976). Monozygotic twins discordant for schizophrenia: A review. *Psychological Bulletin, 83*, 91–106. (pp. 76, 641).

Wainwright, P. E., Simpson, J. R., Cameron, R., Hoffman-Goetz, L., Winfield, D., McCutcheon, D., & MacDonald, M. (1991). Effects of treadmill exercise on weight cycling in female mice. *Physiology and Behavior, 49*, 639–642. (p. 212)

Wakefield, J. C. (1992). Disorder as harmful dysfunction: A conceptual critique of *DSM-III-R*'s definition of mental disorder. *Psychological Review, 99*, 232–247. (p. 611)

Walden, T. A. (1991). Infant social referencing. In J. Garber & K. A. Dodge (Eds.), *The development of emotion regulation and dysregulation*. Cambridge: Cambridge University Press. (p. 455)

Walker, L. J. (1984). Sex differences in the development of moral reasoning: A critical review. *Child Development, 55*, 677–691. (p. 480)

Walker, L. J., de Vries, B., & Treverthan, S. D. (1987). Moral stages and moral orientations in real-life and hypothetical dilemmas. *Child Development, 58*, 842–858. (p. 480)

Walker, W. I. (1973). Principles of organization of the ventrobasal complex in mammals. *Brain Behavior and Evolution, 7*, 253–336. (p. 175)

Wallach, H. (1948). Brightness constancy and the nature of achromatic colors. *Journal of Experimental Psychology, 38*, 310–324. (p. 322)

Wallen, K. (1990). Desire and ability: Hormones and the regulation of female sexual behavior. *Neuroscience and Biobehavioral Reviews, 14*, 233–241. (p. 217)

Wallerstein, R. S. (1989). The psychotherapy research project of the Menninger Foundation: An overview. *Journal of Consulting and Clinical Psychology, 57*, 195–205. (p. 676)

Walster, E., Aronson, V., Abrahams, D., & Rottman, L. (1966). Importance of physical attractiveness in dating behavior. *Journal of Personality and Social Psychology, 4*, 508–516. (p. 482)

Ward, I. L., & Ward, O. B. (1985). Sexual behavior differentiation: Effects of prenatal manipulation in rats. In N. T. Adler, D. Pfaff, & R. Goy (Eds.), *Handbook of behavioral neurobiology (Vol. 7: Reproduction)*. New York: Plenum. (p. 214)

Warner, R. (1985). *Recovery from schizophrenia*. London: Routledge & Kegan Paul. (pp. 643, 679)

Warren. R. M. (1970). Perceptual restoration of missing speech sounds. *Science, 167*, 392–393. (p. 293)

Warren, R. M. (1984). Perceptual restoration of obliterated sounds. *Psychological Bulletin, 96*, 371–383. (pp. 293, 330)

Warrington, E. K., & Weiskrantz, L. (1968). New method of testing long-term retention with special reference to amnesic patients. *Nature, 217*, 972–974. (p. 363)

Warrington, E. K., & Weiskrantz, L. (1970). Amnesic syndrome: Consolidation or retrieval? *Nature, 228*, 628–630. (p. 363)

Wason, P. C. (1960). On the failure to eliminate hypotheses in a conceptual task. *Quarterly Journal of Experimental Psychology, 12*, 129–140. (p. 389)

Waterman, A. S. (1982). Identity development from adolescence to adulthood: An extension of theory and review of research. *Developmental Psychology, 18*, 341–358. (pp. 476, 477)

Waterman, A. S. (1985). Identity in the context of adolescent psychology. In A. S. Waterman (Ed.), *Identity in adolescence: Processes and contents. New directions in child development* (Vol. 30). San Francisco: Jossey-Bass. (p. 476)

Watson, J. B. (1913). Psychology as the behaviorist views it. *Psychological Review, 20*, 158–177. (pp. 13, 122)

Watson, J. B. (1924). *Behaviorism*. Chicago: University of Chicago Press. (pp. 13, 122, 128, 144, 404, 619, 670)

Watson, J. B. (1936). John Broadus Watson. In C. Murchison (Ed.), *A history of psychology in autobiography* (Vol. 3). New York: Russell & Russell. (p. 13)

Watson, J. B., & Rayner, R. (1920). Conditioned emotional reactions. *Journal of Experimental Psychology, 3*, 1–14. (p. 128)

Watson, J. S. (1972). Smiling, cooing, and "the game." *Merrill-Palmer Quarterly, 18*, 323–339. (p. 420)

Watson, R. I. (1973). Investigation into deindividuation using a cross-cultural survey technique. *Journal of Personality and Social Psychology, 25*, 342–345. (p. 546)

Watt, R. J. (1988). *Visual processing: Computational psychophysical, and cognitive research.* Hillsdale, NJ: Erlbaum. (p. 288)

Waugh, N. C., & Norman, D. A. (1965). Primary memory. *Psychological Review, 72*, 89–104. (pp. 328, 337)

Webb, W. B. (1982). Some theories about sleep and their clinical implications. *Psychiatric Annals, 11*, 415–422. (p. 223)

Weber, E. H. (1834). *De pulen, resorptione, auditu et tactu: Annotationes anatomicae et physiologicae.* Leipzig: Koehler. (p. 277)

Weinberg, R. A., Scarr, S., & Waldman, I. D. (1992). The Minnesota transracial study: A follow-up of IQ test performance at adolescence. *Intelligence, 16*, 117–135. (p. 73)

Weinberger, D. A. (1990). The construct validity of the repressive coping style. In J. L. Singer (Ed.), *Repression and dissociation: Implications for personality theory, psychopathology, and health.* Chicago: University of Chicago Press. (p. 577)

Weinberger, D. A., Schwartz, G. E., & Davidson, R. J. (1979). Low-anxious, high-anxious, and repressive coping styles: Psychometric patterns and behavioral and physiological responses to stress. *Journal of Abnormal Psychology, 88*, 369–380. (p. 577)

Weiner, R. D., & Coffey, C. E. (1988). Indications for use of electroconvulsive therapy. In A. J. Frances & R. E. Hales (Eds.), *Review of psychiatry, Vol.* 7. Washington, DC: American Psychiatric Press. (p. 681)

Weingartner, H., Miller, H., & Murphy, D. L. (1977). Mood-state-dependent retrieval of verbal associations. *Journal of Abnormal Psychology, 86*, 276–284. (p. 354)

Weinstein, C. S. (1991). The classroom as a social context for learning. *Annual Review of Psychology, 42*, 493–525. (p. 465)

Weiskrantz, L. (1956). Behavioral changes associated with ablation of the amygdaloid complex in monkeys. *Journal of Comparative Physiology and Psychology, 49*, 381–391. (p. 236)

Weiss, J. M., Glazer, H. I., & Pohoresky, L. A. (1976). Coping behavior and neurochemical change in rats: An alternative explanation for the "learned helplessness" experiments. In G. Serban & A. King (Eds.), *Animal models in human psychobiology.* New York: Plenum. (p. 623)

Wellman, H. M. (1990). *The child's theory of mind.* Cambridge, MA: MIT Press. (p. 443)

Welsh, M. C., Bennington, B. F., Ozonoff, S., Rouse, B., & McCabe, E. R. B. (1990). *Child Development, 61*, 1697–1713. (p. 58)

Werker, J. F., & Tees, R. C. (1992). The organization and reorganization of human speech perception. *Annual Review of Neuroscience, 15*, 377–402. (p. 423)

Werker, J. J., Gilbert, J. H. V., Humphrey, K., & Tees, R. C. (1981). Developmental aspects of cross-language speech perception. *Child Development, 52*, 349–355. (p. 423)

Werner, H. (1948). *Comparative psychology of mental development* (rev. ed.). Chicago: Follet. (p. 386)

Wernicke, C. (1874; reprinted 1977). The aphasia symptom complex: A psychological study on an anatomical basis. In G. H. Eggard (Ed. & trans.), *Wernicke's works on aphasia.* The Hague: Mouton. (p. 402)

Wertheimer, M. (1912; reprinted 1965). Experimentelle Studien über das Sehen von Bewegung (M. D. Boring, Trans.). In R. J. Herrnstein & E. G. Boring (Eds.), *A source book in the history of psychology.* Cambridge, MA: Harvard University Press. (p. 10)

Wertheimer, M. (1923; reprinted 1938). Principles of perceptual organization. In W. D. Ellis (Ed. & trans.), *A source-book of Gestalt psychology.* New York: Harcourt Brace. (pp. 289, 290)

West, S. G., & Graziano, W. G. (1989). Long-term stability and change in personality: An introduction. *Journal of Personality, 57*, 175–192. (p. 599)

Westermarck, E. (1891). *The history of human marriage.* London: Macmillan. (p. 117)

White, N. M. & Milner, P. M. (1992). The psychobiology of reinforcers. *Annual Review of Psychology, 43*, 443–471. (p. 219)

Whiten, A. (Ed.) (1991). *Natural theories of mind: Evolution, development, and simulation of everyday mindreading.* Cambridge, MA: Basil Blackwell. (p. 443)

Whiting, B. B., & Edwards, C. P. (1988). *Children of different worlds: The formation of social behavior.* Cambridge, MA: Harvard University Press. (pp. 461, 466, 469, 470, 471)

Whiting, J. W. M. (1971). Causes and consequences of the amount of body contact between mother and infant. Paper read at the American Anthropological Association Annual Meetings. New York. (p. 460)

Whorf, B. (1956). *Language, thought, and reality.* New York: Wiley. (p. 404)

Wickens, D. D. (1972). Characteristics of word encoding. In A. W. Melton & E. Martin (Eds.), *Coding processes in human memory.* Washington, DC: Winston & Sons. (p. 352)

Wicker, A. W. (1969). Attitudes versus actions: The relationship of verbal and overt behavioral responses to attitude objects. *Journal of Social Issues, 25*, 41–78. (p. 523)

Wicker, A. W. (1971). An examination of the "other variable" explanation of attitude-behavior inconsistency. *Journal of Personality and Social Psychology, 19*, 18–30. (p. 523)

Wicklund, R. A., & Frey, D. (1980). Self-awareness theory: When the self makes a difference. In D. M. Wegner & R. R. Vallacher (Eds.), *The self in social psychology.* New York: Oxford University Press. (p. 523)

Wiggins, S., Whyte, P., Huggins, M., Adam, S., Theilmann, J., Bloch, M., Sheps, S. B., Schechter, M. T., & Hayden, M.R. (1992). The psychological consequences of predictive testing for Huntington's disease. *The New England Journal of Medicine, 327*, 1401–1405. (p. 58)

Wiley, M. G., Crittenden, K. S., & Birg, L. D. (1979). Why a rejection? Causal attributions of a career achievement event. *Social Psychology Quarterly, 42*, 214–222. (p. 510)

Wilkins, L., & Richter, C. P. (1940). A great craving for salt by a child with cortico-adrenal insufficiency. *Journal of the American Medical Association, 114*, 866–868. (pp. 203–204)

Wilkinson, G. S. (1988). Reciprocal altruism in bats and other mammals. *Ethology and Sociobiology, 9*, 85–100. (p. 112)

Wilkinson, G. S. (1990). Food sharing in vampire bats. *Scientific American, 262*, 76–82. (p. 112)

Willerman, L. (1979). *The psychology of individual and group differences*. San Francisco: Freeman. (p. 72)

Williams, J. B. W., & Spitzer, R. L. (1983). The issue of sex bias in *DSM-III*. *American Psychologist, 38*, 793–798. (p. 615)

Williams, J. E., & Best, D. L. (1990). *Measuring sex stereotypes: a multination study, revised edition*. Newbury Park, CA: SAGE Publications. (p. 470)

Williams, R. (1989). *The trusting heart*. New York: Times Books. (p. 630)

Willner, P. (1985). *Depression: A psychobiological synthesis*. New York: Wiley. (p. 623)

Wilson, M. (1989). Marital conflict and homicide in evolutionary perspective. In R. W. Bell & N. J. Bell (Eds.), *Sociobiology and the social sciences*. Lubbock, Texas: Texas University Press. (p. 116)

Wilson, M. (1993). *DSM-III* and the transformation of American psychiatry: A history. *American Journal of Psychiatry, 150*, 399–410. (p. 611)

Wimer, R. E., & Wimer, C. C. (1985). Animal behavior genetics: A search for the biological foundations of behavior. *Annual Review of Psychology, 36*, 171–218. (p. 66)

Wise, R. A. (1989). Opiate reward: Sites and substrates. *Neuroscience and Biobehavioral Reviews, 13*, 129–133. (p. 219)

Wise, R. A., & Rompre, P. (1989). Brain dopamine and reward. *Annual Review of Psychology, 40*, 191–225. (pp. 219, 220)

Wise, R. A., Spindler, J., & Legault, L. (1978). Major attenuation of food reward with performance-sparing doses of pimozide in the rat. *Canadian Journal of Psychology, 32*, 77–85. (p. 220)

Wishart, J. G., & Bower, T. G. R. (1984). Spatial relations and the object concept: A normative study. In L. P. Lipsitt & C. Rovée-Collier (Eds.), *Advances in infancy research* (Vol. 3). Norwood, NJ: Ablex. (p. 421)

Wissler, C. (1901). The correlation of mental and physical tests. *Psychological Review, 3* (Whole no. 6). (p. 371)

Witty, P. A., & Jenkins, M. D. (1935). Intra-race testing and Negro intelligence. *The Journal of Psychology, 1*, 179–192. (p. 73)

Wolfe, J. B. (1936). Effectiveness of token-rewards for chimpanzees. *Comparative Psychology Monographs*, 12 (Whole no. 60). (p. 139)

Wolfe, J. M. (1992). The parallel guidance of visual attention. *Current Directions in Psychological Science, 1*, 124–128. (p. 295)

Wolpe, J. (1958). *Psychotherapy by reciprocal inhibition*. Stanford: Stanford University Press. (p. 671)

Wood, D. M., & Emmett-Oglesby, M. W. (1989). Mediation in the nucleus accumbens of the discriminative stimulus produced by cocaine. *Pharmacology, Biochemistry, and Behavior, 33*, 453–457. (p. 219)

Woods, P. J. (Ed.) (1987). *Is psychology the major for you?* Washington, DC: American Psychological Association. (p. 24)

World Almanac (1992). *The World Almanac and Book of Facts, 1993*. New York: World Almanac. (p. 468)

Wright, E. F., Jackson, W., Christie, S. D., McGuire, G. R., & Wright, R. D. (1991). The home-course disadvantage in golf championships: Further evidence for the undermining effect of supportive audiences on performance under pressure. *Journal of Sport Behavior, 14*, 51–60. (p. 544)

Wyndbrandt, J., & Ludman, R. D. (1991). *The encyclopedia of genetic disorders and birth defects*. New York: Facts on File. (p. 57)

Yasukawa, K. (1981). Song repertoires in the red-winged blackbird *(Agelaius phoeniceus)*: A test of the Beau Geste hypothesis. *Animal Behaviour, 29*, 114–125. (p. 86)

Yerkes, R. M., & Dodson, J. D. (1908). The relation of strength of stimulus to rapidity of habit-formation. *Journal of Comparative and Neurological Psychology, 18*, 459–482. (p. 230)

Yerkes, R. M., & Morgulis, S. (1909). The method of Pavlov in animal psychology. *Psychological Bulletin, 6*, 257–273. (p. 123)

Yuodelis, C., & Hendrickson, A. (1986). A qualitative and quantitative analysis of the human fovea during development. *Vision Research, 26*, 847–856. (p. 417)

Zahn-Waxler, C., Radke-Yarrow, M., Wagner, E., & Chapman, M. (1992). Development of concern for others. *Developmental Psychology, 28*, 126–136. (p. 477)

Zajonc, R. B. (1965). Social facilitation. *Science, 149*, 269–274. (p. 543)

Zajonc, R. B. (1980). Compresence. In P. B. Paulus (Ed.), *Psychology of group influence*. Hillsdale, NJ: Erlbaum. (p. 543)

Zajonc, R. B., Murphy, S. T., & Inglehart, M. (1989). Feeling and facial efference: Implications of the vascular theory of emotion. *Psychological Review, 96*, 395–416. (p. 235)

Zebrowitz, L. A., & McDonald, S. M. (1991). The impact of litigants' baby-facedness and attractiveness on adjudications in small claims courts. *Law and Human Behavior, 15*, 603–623. (p. 496)

Zelig, M., & Beidelman, W. B. (1981). The investigative use of hypnosis: A word of caution. *International Journal of Clinical and Experimental Hypnosis, 29*, 401–412. (p. 357)

Zelnick, M., & Kantner, J. F. (1980). Sexual activity, contraceptive use and pregnancy among metropolitan area teenagers: 1970–1979. *Family Planning Perspectives, 12*, 230–237. (p. 474)

Zelnick, M., Kantner, J. F., & Ford, K. (1981). *Sex and pregnancy in adolescence*. Beverly Hills, CA: Sage. (p. 474)

Zigler, E., & Hodapp, R. M. (1991). Behavioral functioning in individuals with mental retardation. *Annual Review of Psychology, 42*, 29–50. (p. 59)

Zimbardo, P. G. (1970). The human choice: Individuation, reason, and order versus deindividuation, impulse, and chaos. In W. J. Arnold & D. Levine (Eds.), *Nebraska symposium on motivation, 1969*, Lincoln, NE: University of Nebraska Press. (p. 546)

Zinbarg, R. E., Barlow, D. H., Brown, T. A., & Hertz, R. M. (1992). Cognitive-behavioral approaches to the nature and treatment of anxiety disorders. *Annual Review of Psychology, 43*, 235–267. (pp. 621, 671)

Zucker, R. A., & Gomberg, E. S. L. (1986). Etiology of alcoholism reconsidered: The case for a biopsychosocial process. *American Psychologist, 41*, 783–793. (p. 634)

Zurif, E. B. (1980). Language mechanisms: A neuropsychological perspective. *American Scientist, 68*, 305–311. (p. 403)

Zurif, E. B. (1990). Language and the brain. In D. N. Osherson & H. Lasnik (Eds.), *Language: An invitation to cognitive science, volume 1.* Cambridge, MA: MIT Press. (pp. 402, 403)

Zwislocki, J. J. (1981). Sound analysis in the ear: A history of discoveries. *American Scientist, 69*, 184–192. (p. 250)

ILLUSTRATION CREDITS

PART OPENERS

1 Ben Shahn, *In Rooms Withdrawn and Quiet* (Rilke Portfolio), 1968. Lithograph on paper. New Jersey State Museum Collection. Purchase, FA1970.1780 © Estate of Ben Shahn/VAGA, New York, 1993.

2 Mary Cassatt, *Mother & Child*, ca. 1890. Wichita Art Museum. The Roland P. Murdock Collection.

3 Pablo Picasso, *Fauteuil Rouge (The Red Armchair)*, 1931. Oil on cradled panel, 51.5" x 39". Art Institute of Chicago. Gift of Mr. & Mrs. Daniel Saidenberg. Photograph Art Institute of Chicago. All rights reserved. © 1993 A.R.S. NY/S.P.A.D.E.M.

4 Jacob Lawrence, *The Library* (detail), 1960. National Museum of American Art, Washington, D.C. Photo Art Resource

5 Zinaida Serebriakova, *The House of Cards* (detail), Russian State Museum, St. Petersburg. Photo Scala/Art Resource

6 Franz-Josef Grimmeisen, *Bicycle Racing in the Ruhr* (detail), Private Collection. Photo Bridgeman/Art Resource

7 Ben Shahn, *Conversations*, 1958. Watercolor on paper, 39.25" x 27" (99.7 cm x 68.6 cm). Collection of Whitney Museum of American Art. Purchase, with funds from the Friends of the Whitney Museum of American Art, 58.21. Photography by Geoffrey Clements, N.Y. © Estate of Ben Shahn/VAGA, New York, 1993.

FRONT MATTER

p. iv Johannes Vermeer, *Head of a Young Girl*, 17th century. Oil on canvas. Mauritshuis, The Hague. Photo The Granger Collection, New York City. **p. vii** © Linda Haas Photography

CHAPTER 1

Opener Musée Bourdelle, Paris/Giraudon/Art Resource **p. 4** The Bettmann Archive **p. 5 (top)** Historical Picture Service **p. 5 (bottom)** Descartes, R. (1972) *Treatise of man.* Cambridge, MA: Harvard University Press **p. 7** Paul Fusco/Magnum Photos **p. 8** National Library of Medicine **p. 9 (top)** Archives of the History of American Psychology, University of Akron **p. 9 (bottom)** Courtesy of the Harvard University Archives **p. 10** Wellesley College Archives **p. 11** Giuseppe Arcimboldo (1527–1593), *The Garden.* Scala/Art Resource **p. 12** Archives of the History of American Psychology, University of Akron **p. 14 and p. 15** Nina Leen, *LIFE Magazine*, © Time Warner, Inc. **p. 17** Edmund Engelman **p. 21** Adapted from Rose, S. (1973). *The conscious brain.* New York: Alfred A. Knopf, Inc. Copyright by Stephen Rose. Reprinted by permission of Alfred A. Knopf, Inc.

CHAPTER 2

Opener Will & Deni McIntyre/Science Source/Photo Researchers **p. 28** Pfungst, O. (1965). *Clever Hans: The horse of Mr. von Osten.* New York: Holt, Rinehart & Winston **Fig. 2.2** Hendricks, B., et al. (1990). The dimensions of psychological research. *Teaching of Psychology, 17*, 76–82. **Fig. 2.3** Di Mascio, A., et al. (1979). Differential symptom reduction by drugs and psychotherapy in acute depression. *Archives of General Psychiatry, 36*, 1453. Copyright © 1979, American Medical Association **p. 32** Peter Byron/Monkmeyer Press Photo **p. 33** Jeff Greenberg/The Picture Cube **p. 34** Michael Abramson/Gamma Liaison **p. 39** Peter Menzel **p. 42 (left)** Cary Wolinski/ Stock, Boston **p. 42 (right)** Paul Barton/The Stock Market **p. 43** Joel Gordon

CHAPTER 3

Opener Kindra Clineff/The Picture Cube **p. 51 (left)** Van Bucher/Photo Researchers **p. 51 (right)** Science Photo Library/Photo Researchers. **Fig. 3.4** From: *Behavioral Genetics: A Primer* by Robert Plomin, J. C. De Fries, and G. E. McClearn. Copyright © 1990 by W. H. Freeman and Company. Reprinted with permission **p. 56 (left and right)** Scott, J. P., & Fuller, J. L. (1965). *Genetics and social behavior of the dog.* Chicago: University of Chicago Press. **p. 57** Peter Ginter. Courtesy of the Hereditary Disease Foundation **p. 58** Hay, D. (1985). *Essentials of behaviour genetics.* Boston: Blackwell Scientific Publications **p. 60** Linda Haas Photography **p. 61** Courtesy of Marian Burke **p. 65** Ted Levin/Earth Scenes/Animals Animals **p. 68** AP/Wide World Photos **Table 3.2** T. J. Bouchard & M. McGue, 1981. Familial studies of intelligence: A review, *Science, 212*, pp. 1056–1057. Copyright © 1981 by the AAAS **p. 72** Jeff Albertson/Stock, Boston **p. 77 (left and right)** Courtesy of the Genain family

CHAPTER 4

Opener Tom McHugh/Photo Researchers **p. 83 (left)** W. F. Tweedie/Bruce Coleman, Inc. **p. 83 (right)** W. F. Tweedie/Photo Researchers **p. 85** E. R. Degginger/Bruce Coleman, Inc. **p. 86** S. Nielson/Bruce Coleman, Inc. **p. 88** Raymond Attuil/Agence Vandystadt/Photo Researchers **Figs. 4.2 and 4.3** Tinbergen, N. (1951). *The study of instinct.* Oxford: Oxford University Press. Copyright © by N. Tinbergen **p. 91** Eibl-Eibesfeldt, I. (1961, December). The fighting behavior of animals. *Scientific American, 205*, 7. Copyright 1961 by Scientific American, Inc. All rights reserved. **p. 92** Bill Dyer/Photo Researchers **Fig. 4.5** Adapted from: Emlen, S. T. (1975, August). The stellar orientation of a migrating bird. *Scientific American, 233*, 111 Copyright © 1975 by Scientific American, Inc. All rights reserved **p. 94 (left)** Joe McDonald/Animals Animals **p. 94 (center)** M. Tuttle/Photo Researchers **p. 94 (right)** James Carmich/Bruce Coleman, Inc. **Fig. 4.7** Lorenz, K. (1974). Analogy as a source of knowledge. *Science, 185*, 229–234. Copyright © 1974 The Nobel Foundation **p. 95 (left)** M. A. Chappell/Animals Animals **p. 95 (right)** D. M. Shale/Oxford Scientific Films/Animals Animals **p. 96** Eibl-Eibesfeldt, I. (1975). *Ethology.* New York: Holt, Rinehart & Winston **p. 97** Dr. Eckart Pott/Bruce Coleman, Inc. **p. 98 (left and right)** General Research Division, The New York Public Library, Astor, Lenox and Tilden Foundations. **p. 99 (all photos)** Ekman, P., & Friesen, W. (1975). *Unmasking the face.* Englewood Cliffs, NJ: Prentice Hall. **p. 100 (left and right)** Ekman, P., & Friesen, W. (1975). *Unmasking the face.* Englewood Cliffs, NJ: Prentice Hall. **Fig. 4.14** Lorenz, K. (1966). *On Aggression.* New York: Harcourt Brace & World. Copyright © 1963 by Dr. G. Borotha-Schoeller Verlag, Wein. English translation copyright © 1966 by Konrad Lorenz. Copyright © 1983 by Deutscher Taschcenbuch Verlag GmbH & Co. KG, Munchen. Reprinted by permission of Harcourt Brace Jovanovich, Inc. **p. 101 (top left)** Eibl-Eibesfeldt, I. (1989). *Human ethology.* Hawthorne, NY: Walter de Gruyter, Inc. **p. 102** Eibl-Eibesfeldt, I. (1975). *Human ethology.* Hawthorne, NY: Holt, Rinehart & Winston. **p. 103 (left and right)** Heltne, P. G., & Marquardt, L. (1989). *Understanding chimpanzees.* Cambridge, MA: Harvard University Press. **p. 105** Ben Osborne/Oxford Scientific Films/Animals Animals **p. 106** Jane Burton/Bruce Coleman, Inc. **p. 109** Ken Regan/Camera Five, Inc. **p. 110** Zig Leszczynski/Animals Animals **p. 111** L. & D. Klein/Photo Researchers **p. 114** Bruce Coleman, Inc. **p. 115** Victor Englebert/Black Star

CHAPTER 5

Opener Comstock **p. 123** Archives of the History of American Psychology, University of Akron **p. 125** Ben Mitchell/The Image Bank **Fig. 5.4** Pavlov, I. P. (1927/1960). *Conditioned reflexes.* New York: Dover **p. 129** D. K. Herschkowitz/Bruce Coleman, Inc. **Figs. 5.5 and 5.6** Thorndike, E. L. (1898). Animal intelligence: An experimental study of the associate processes in animals. *The Psychological Review Monograph Supplements, 2,* 4–160 **p. 132** Sybil Shelton/Monkmeyer Press Photo **p. 134** Dan McCoy/Rainbow **p. 135 (top)** Bob Daemmrich/The Image Works **p. 135 (bottom)** Richard Hutchings/Photo Researchers **p. 138** New York Times Pictures **p. 139** Joel Gordon **p. 143 (top)** Michael S. Thompson/Comstock **p. 143 (bottom)** Naoki Okamoto/The Stock Market **p. 145** Mark Sherman/Bruce Coleman, Inc. **Fig. 5.15** Dickinson, A., & Dawson, G. R. (1987). The role of the instrumental contingency in motivational control of performance. *Quarterly Journal of Experimental Psychology, 39B,* 77–93. Reproduced with permission. Copyright ©1987 by the Experimental Psychology Society and Lawrence Erlbaum Associates Ltd, Hove, UK **p. 148** Mark Antman/The Image Works **p. 150** Tom McHugh/Photo Researchers **p. 154** Joel Gordon

CHAPTER 6

Opener Richard Martin/Agence Vandystadt/Allsport USA **p. 165** Manfred Kage/Peter Arnold, Inc. **p. 167** © Lennart Nilsson, from *Behold man,* Little, Brown & Co. Photo courtesy Bonnier Fakta **Figs. 6.6, 6.7 and 6.8** Illustrations by David Macaulay from *The Amazing Brain* by Robert Ornstein and Richard Thompson. Illustrations copyright © 1984 by David A Macaulay. Reprinted by permission of Houghton Mifflin Co. All rights reserved. **p. 173** A. Gluberman/Photo Researchers **Fig. 6.10** From: *The conscious brain* by Steven Rose. Copyright © 1973 by Steven Rose. Reprinted by permission of Alfred A. Knopf, Inc. **Fig. 6.11** Reprinted with the permission of Macmillan College Publishing Company from *The cerebral cortex of man* by Wilder Penfield and Theodore Rasmussen. Copyright © 1950 Macmillan College Publishing Company; copyright renewed © 1978 Theodore Rasmussen **Fig. 6.12** Ghez, C. (1985). Voluntary movement. In E. R. Kandel & J. H. Schwartz (Eds.), *Principles of neural science* (3rd ed.). Norwalk, CT: Appleton & Lange **p. 180** Martin Rotker **Fig. 6.16** Adapted from: Gazzaniga, M. S. (1967, August). The split brain in man. *Scientific American,* 24–27. Copyright © 1967 by Scientific American, Inc. All rights reserved **p. 182** Dan McCoy/Rainbow **p. 187** E. R. Lewis **p. 188** Adrian Davies/Bruce Coleman, Inc.

CHAPTER 7

Opener Stephanie Maze/Woodfin Camp & Associates **p. 203 (left)** Culver Pictures **p. 203 (right)** Ted Spiegel/Black Star **p. 204** AP/Wide World Photos **p. 205** Courtesy Bart Hoebel, Department of Psychology, Princeton University **p. 206** Courtesy of Neal E. Miller, Yale University **p. 210** Alan Carey/The Image Works **p. 212** Barnett, S. A. (1975). *The rat: A study of behavior* (rev. ed.). Chicago: University of Chicago Press **p. 218 (left)** Lynn McLaren/The Picture Cube **p. 218 (center)** David Lissy/ThePicture Cube **p. 218 (right)** Daniele Pellegrini/Photo Researchers **p. 219** Olds, J. (1956) Pleasure centers in the brain. *Scientific American,* October 1956, 112. **p. 221** Pat Pfister/Medichrome **Figs. 7.9 and 7.10** Snyder, F., & Scott, J. (1972). The psychophysiology of sleep. In N. S. Greenfield & R. A. Sternbach (Eds.), *Handbook of psychophysiology.* New York: Holt, Rinehart & Winston. Copyright © 1972 by Holt, Rinehart and Winston, Inc., reproduced by permission of the publisher. **p. 225** *Boston Globe* **Fig. 7.14** Askerstedt, T., & Froberg, J. E. (1977). Psychophysiological circadian rhythms in women during 72 hours of sleep deprivation. *Waking and Sleeping, I,* 387–394 **p. 228** Petit Format/Nestle/Science Source/Photo Researchers **Fig. 7.15** Snyder, F., & Scott, J. (1972). The psychophysiology of sleep. In N. S. Greenfield & R. A. Sternbach (Eds.), *Handbook of psychophysiology.* New York: Holt, Rinehart & Winston. Copyright © 1972 by Holt, Rinehart and Winston, Inc., reproduced by permission of the publisher. **Fig. 7.19** Laird, J. D. (1974). Self-attribution of emotion: The effects of expressive behavior on the quality of emotional experience. *Journal of Personality and Social Psychology, 29,* 475–486. Copyright © 1974 by the American Psychological Association. Reprinted by permission **Fig. 7.21** Ekman, P., et al. (1983). Autonomic nervous system activity distinguishes among emotions. *Science, 221,* 1208–1210. Copyright © 1983 by the AAAS **p. 235 (left, center, and right)** Paul Ekman **p. 236** James Sugar/Black Star

CHAPTER 8

Opener Wayne Hoy/The Picture Cube **p. 242** Alexander Tsaras/Medichrome **Fig. 8.1** Uttal, W. R. (1973). *The psychobiology of sensory coding.* New York: Harper & Row **Fig. 8.2** Nowlis, G. H., & Frank, M. (1977). Qualities in hamster taste: Behavioral and neural evidence. In J. LeMagnen & P. MacLeod (Eds.), *Olfaction and taste* (Vol. 6). Washington, DC: Information Retrieval. By copyright permission of the Rockefeller University Press **p. 246** Sabine Weiss/Photo Researchers **Fig. 8.3** Klinke, R. (1986). Physiology of hearing. In R. F. Schmidt (Ed.), *Fundamentals of sensory physiology.* New York: Springer-Verlag **Fig. 8.8** Scharf, B. (1964). Partial masking. *Acustica, 14,* 16–23 **p. 250 (left and right)** Robert S. Preston. Courtesy of J. E. Hawkins, Kresge Hearing Research Institute, University of Michigan Medical School **p. 252** Jeff Albertson/The Picture Cube **p. 254** E. R. Lewis **Fig. 8.13** Lindsay, P. H., & Norman, D. A. (1977). *Human information processing* (2nd ed.). New York: Harcourt Brace Jovanovich **Fig. 8.15** Grusser, O. J., & Grussser-Cornehls, U. (1986). Physiology of vision. In R. F. Schmidt (Ed.), *Fundamentals of sensory physiology.* New York: Springer-Verlag **p. 260** Fritz Goro, *LIFE Magazine,* © 1944, Time Warner, Inc. **p. 262** Courtesy of Richmond Products, Boca Raton, Florida **Fig. 8.21** Bowmaker, J. K., & Dartnall, H. J. A. (1980). Visual pigments of rods and cones in a human retina. *Journal of Physiology, 298,* 501–511 **Fig. 8.23** Matlin, M. W. (1988). *Sensation and perception* (2nd ed.). Boston: Allyn & Bacon. Copyright © 1988 by Allyn and Bacon. Adapted by permission. **Fig. 8.24** De Valois, K. (1988). *Spatial vision.* New York: Oxford University Press **Fig. 8.29** Blakemore, C., & Sutton, P. (1969). Size adaptation: A new aftereffect. *Science, 166,* 245–247. Copyright © 1969 by the AAAS **p. 273** Marty Cooper/Peter Arnold, Inc. **p. 274** Dion Ogust/The Image Works **Fig. 8.36** Stevens, S. S. (1962). The surprising simplicity of sensory metrics. *American Psychologist, 17,* 29–39. Copyright © 1962 by the American Psychological Association. Reprinted by permission

CHAPTER 9

Opener Mark Romine/Superstock **p. 289** Ottmar Bierwagen/Black Star **Fig. 9.4** Rubin, EE. (1915/1958). *Synoplevede figurer.* Copenhagen: Cyldendalske. Abridged trans. by M. Wertheimer in C. C. Bearslee & M. Wertheimer (Eds.), *Readings in perception.* Princeton, NJ: Van Nostrand **Fig. 9.5** From: *Exploration in cognition* by Donald A. Norman and David E. Rumelhart. Copyright © 1975 by W. H. Freeman and Company. Reprinted with permission **p. 292** Pablo Picasso, *Assemblage/Flayed Head* (1943). *Cliché des Musées Nationaux–Paris Service photographie de la Reunion des Musées Nationaux, Paris. © 1993 A.R.S. NY/S.P.A.D.E.M. **Fig. 9.6** From Kanizsa, G. (1976). Subjective contours. *Scientific American, 234,* 48. Copyright © 1976 by Scientific American , Inc. All rights reserved **Fig. 9.9** Enns, J. T., & Rensink, R. A. (1990). Sensitivity to three-dimensional orientation in visual search. *Psychological Science, 1,* 323–326. Reprinted with the permission of Cambridge University Press **Figs. 9.10 and 9.11** Biederman, I. (1985). Recognition-by-components: A theory of human image understanding. *Computer Vision, Graphics, and Image Processing* (Vol. 32), pp. 29–73. **p. 298** Albert Normandin/The Image Bank **p. 300** Kay Chernush/The Image Bank **Fig. 9.12** Rock, I., & Gutman, D. (1981). The effect of inattention on form perception. *Journal of Experimental Psychology: Human Perception and Performance, I,* 275–285. Copyright © American Psychological Association. Reprinted by permission **Fig. 9.13** Becklen, R., & Cervone, D. (1983). Selective looking and the noticing of unexpected events. *Memory and Cognition, 11,* 601–608. Reprinted by permission of Psychonomic Society, Inc. **Fig. 9.14** Eagle, M., et al. (1966). Imagery: Effect of a concealed figure in a stimulus. *Science, 151,* 838. Copyright © 1966 by the AAAS **Fig. 9.15** Pashler, H. (1992). Attentional limitations in doing two tasks at the same time. *Current Directions in Psychological Science, 1,* 44–48. Reprinted with the permission of Cambridge University Press **p.304** Joel Gordon **p. 308** The Granger Collection **p. 309** Kindra Clineff/The Picture Cube **p. 311** J. R. Eyerman, *LIFE Magazine,* © Time Warner, Inc. **p. 313** S. Schwartzenberg/The Exploratorium **p. 314** Joel Gordon **p. 315** Peter Van Rhijn/Superstock **Fig. 9.25** Kaufman, L., & Rock, I. (1962, July). The moon illusion. *Scientific American,* 120–130. Copyright © 1962 by Scientific American, Inc. All rights reserved **Fig. 9.27** Coren, S. (1986). An efferent component in the visual perception of direction and extent. *Psychological Review, 93,* 399 & 401. Copyright © 1986 by the American Psychological Association. Adapted by permission **Fig. 9.28** From: *Perception* by Irvin Rock. Copyright © 1984 by Scientific American Books, Inc. Reprinted with permission of W. H. Freeman and Company **Fig. 9.29** Cutting, J. F., & Proffitt, D. (1982). The minimum principle and the perception of absolute, common, and relative motions. *Cognitive Psychology, 14,* 221 **Fig. 9.30** Michaels, C. F., & Carello, C. (1981). *Direct perception.* Englewood Cliffs, NJ: Prentice Hall. Copyright © 1981. Reprinted by permission of Prentice Hall, Inc. **p. 322** Comstock

CHAPTER 10

Opener H. Dratch/The Image Works **p. 329** Erich Hartmann/Magnum Photos **Fig. 10.2** Erickson, C. W., and Collins, J. F. (1967). Some temporal characteristics of visual pattern perception. *Journal of Experimental Psychology,* Vol. 74, No. 4, 476–484. Copyright © 1967 by the American Psychological Association. Reprinted by permission **p. 331 (top)** Barbara Alper/Stock, Boston **p. 331 (bottom)** Susan Lapides/Design Conceptions **Fig. 10.3** Peterson, L. R., & Peterson, M. J. (1959). Short-term retention in individual verbal items. *Journal of Experimental Psychology, 58*, 195 **Fig. 10.4** Glanzer, M., & Cunitz, A. R. (1966). Two storage mechanisms in free recall. *Journal of Verbal Learning and Verbal Behavior, 5*, 358 **p. 335** Eve-Lucie Bourque **p. 337** Robert McElroy/Woodfin Camp & Associates **Fig. 10.5** Craik, F. I. M., & Watkins, M. J. (1973). The role of rehearsal in short-term memory. *Journal of Verbal Learning and Verbal Behavior, 12*, 602 **p. 338 (left)** Tony O'Brien/Picture Group **p. 338 (right)** Joel Gordon **Fig. 10.6** Craik, F. I., & Tulving, E. (1975). Depth of processing and the retention of words in long-term memory. *Journal of Experimental Psychology: General, 104*, 274 **p. 340** UPI/The Bettmann Archive **p. 342 (left)** Bloom, F. E., & Lazerson, A. (1988) *Brain, mind and behavior* (2nd ed.). New York: Freeman **p. 342 (right)** The Bettmann Archive **Fig. 10.8** Atkinson, R. C. (1975). Mnemotechnics in second language learning. *American Psychologist, 30*, 822. Copyright © 1975 by the American Psychological Association. Adapted by permission **Fig. 10.9** Kosslyn, S. M. (1980). *Image and mind.* Cambridge, MA: Harvard University Press **p. 345 (top)** Hayne Lankinen/Bruce Coleman, Inc. **p. 345 (bottom)** Tom McHugh/Photo Researchers **Fig. 10.10** Collins, A., & Loftus, E. (1975). A spreading-activation theory of semantic processing. *Psychological Review, 82*, 407–428 Copyright © 1975 by the American Psychological Association. Reprinted by permission **Fig. 10.11 (b)** Bahrick, H. P., et al. (1975). Fifty years of memory for names and faces. *Journal of Experimental Psychology, 104*, 54–75. Copyright © 1975 by the American Psychological Association. Adapted by permission **Fig. 10.12** Keppel, G., et al. (1968). Studies of learning to learn: **VIII**. The influence of massive amounts of training upon learning and retention of paired-associate lists. *Journal of Verbal Learning and Verbal Behavior, 7*, 790–796 **p. 352** Jeff Dunn/The Picture Cube **Fig. 10.13** Mantyla, T. (1986). Optimizing cue effectiveness: Recall of 500 and 600 incidentally learned words. *Journal of Experimental Psychology: Learning, Memory, and Cognition, 12*, 69. Copyright © 1986 by the American Psychological Association. Reprinted by permission **p. 355** The Granger Collection **p. 358** Ernest Hilgard **Fig. 10.16** Jacoby, L. L. (1983). Remembering the data: Analyzing interactive processes in reading. *Journal of Verbal Learning and Verbal Behavior, 22*, 485–508

CHAPTER 11

Opener Bob Daemmrich/The Image Works **p. 370** The Bettmann Archive **p. 371** The Bettmann Archive **p. 372 (top right)** From *L'annee psychologique*, Paris, 1905. General Research Division, The New York Public Library, Astor, Lenox and Tilden Foundations. **p. 372 (bottom left)** R. L. Thorndike, E. P. Hagen, & J. M. Sattler, Riverside Publishing Co., Chicago **p. 378 (left)** AP/Wide World Photos **p. 378 (right)** NASA **p. 379** Michael L. Abramson/Woodfin Camp & Associates **p. 380** Dawson Jones/Stock, Boston **Fig. 11.6** Sternberg, R. J., & Gardner, M. K. (1983). Unities in inductive reasoning. *Journal of Experimental Psychology: General, 112*, 80–116. Copyright © 1983 by the American Psychological Association. Adapted by permission **p. 383** Selfe, L. (1979). *Nadia.* New York: Academic Press. Reprinted by permission. **p. 384 (left and right)** Rick Friedman/Black Star **p. 386** Rick Smolan/Stock, Boston **p. 388** The Granger Collection **p. 391** Sidney Harris **p. 394** Richard Hutchings/Info Edit **p. 397** Christopher Morris/Black Star **p. 398** Stephanie Maze/Woodfin Camp & Associates **p. 399** John F. Cook. Courtesy of Noam Chomsky **Fig. 11.15** Smyth, M. M., et al. (1987). *Cognition in action.* Hillsdale, NJ: Erlbaum **p. 404** Pro Pix **p. 407 (left)** Scarry, R. (1963). *Best word book ever.* © 1963 by Western Publishing Company, Inc. **p. 407 (right)** Scarry, R. (1980). *Best word book ever.* © 1980 by Western Publishing Company, Inc. Used by permission.

CHAPTER 12

Opener Martin Miller/Positive Images **p. 414 (left)** Nancy Sheehan/The Picture Cube **p. 414 (right)** Richard Hutchings/Info Edit **p. 416 (left)** Lawrence Migdale/Stock, Boston **Fig. 12.2** Johnson, M. H., Dziurawiec, S., Ellis, H., & Morton, J. (1991). Newborns' preferential tracking of face-like stimuli and its subsequent decline. *Cognition, 40*, 1–19 **Fig. 12.4** Wishart, J. G., & Bower, T. G. R. (1984). Spatial relations and the object concept: A normative study. In L. P. Lipsitt & C. Rovee-Collier (Eds.), *Advances in Infancy Research*, Vol. 3. Norwood, NJ: Ablex. Reprinted with permission from Ablex Publishing Corporation. **Fig. 12.5** Baillargeon, R. (1987). Object permanence in 3½ and 4½ month old infants. *Developmental Psychology, 23*, 655–664. Copyright © 1987 by the American Psychological Association. Adapted by permission **p. 423 (left and right)** Professor Peter McLeod, Acadia University **p. 424** Laura Dwight/Peter Arnold, Inc. **Fig. 12.7** Berko, J. (1958). The child's learning of English morphology. *Word, 14*, 150–177 **p. 428** Novosti from Sovfoto **p. 429** Susan Kuklin/Photo Researchers **p. 430** Courtesy of Sue Savage-Rumbaugh/Yerkes Language Research Center **p. 433** Anderson/Monkmeyer Press Photo **p. 434 (left, center, and right)** Hazel Hankin **p. 435** Susan Lapides/Design Conceptions **p. 436** Amy Zuckerman/Impact Visuals **p. 437** Bruce Plotkin/The Image Works **p. 439** Paul Conklin/Monkmeyer Press Photo **Fig. 12.10** Chi, M. T. H. (1978). Knowledge structures and memory development. In R. S. Siegler (Ed.), *Children's thinking: What develops.* Hillsdale, NJ: Erlbaum **Fig. 12.11** Siegler, R. S. (1983). How knowledge influences learning. *American Scientist, 71*, 631–638. Reprinted by permission of American Scientist, Journal of Sigma Pi and The Scientific Research Society **p. 445 (left)** Herbert Lanks/Monkmeyer Press Photo **p. 445 (right)** Beryl Goldberg

CHAPTER 13

Opener Elizabeth Crews **p. 451** Harvard University News Office, Cambridge, MA **Fig. 13.1** Bronfenbrenner, U. (1979). Nature and nurture: A reinterpretation of the evidence. In A. Montagu (Ed.), *Race and IQ.* New York: Oxford University Press **p. 454 (top)** Courtesy of University of Wisconsin Primate Lab, Madison, WI **p. 454 (bottom)** Monkmeyer Press Photo **Fig. 13.3** Harlow, H. (1959). Affectional responses in the infant monkey. *Science, 130*, 421–432. Copyright © 1959 by the AAAS **p. 456 (top)** Courtesy of Mary Ainsworth **p. 456 (bottom left)** Karen Webster, Psychology Department, University of Virginia **p. 457 (top)** Julie O'Neil/The Picture Cube **p. 457 (bottom)** Carol Palmer/The Picture Cube **p. 460 and p. 464** Courtesy of Gilda Morelli **p. 465** Laura Dwight **p. 467** Courtesy of Peter Gray/The Sudbury Valley School **p. 468** Courtesy of Chuck Painter, News and Publication Services, Stanford University **p. 469** Tom McCarthy/The Picture Cube **Fig. 13.7** Jacklin, C. N., & Maccoby, E. E. (1978). Social behavior at 33 months in same-sex and mixed-sex dyads. *Child Development, 49*, 557–569. Copyright © 1978 by The Society for Research in Child Development, Inc. **Fig. 13.8** Steinberg, L., & Silverberg, S. B. (1986). The vicissitudes of autonomy in early adolescence. *Child Development, 57*, 841–851. Copyright © 1986 by The Society for Research in Child Development, Inc. **p. 475** Emily Stong/The Picture Cube **p. 477** Willie Hill, Jr./The Image Works **Fig. 13.9** Colby, A., et al. (1983). A longitudinal study of moral judgement. *Monographs for the Society for Research in Child Development, 148*, 1–2. Copyright © 1983 by The Society for Research in Child Development, Inc. **p. 481** Carol Halebian/Gamma Liaison **p. 482** Joel Gordon **Fig. 13.10** Sternberg, R. J. (1986). A triangular theory of love. *Psychological Review, 93*, 119–135. Copyright © 1986 by the American Psychological Association. Adapted by permission **p. 483 (left)** Frank Siteman/Stock, Boston **p. 483 (right)** T. J. Florian/Rainbow **p. 484** Jodi L. Buren Photo **p. 485** Anthony Jalandoni/Monkmeyer Press Photo **p. 486** Joel Gordon

CHAPTER 14

Opener Patricia J. Bruno/Positive Images **p. 496 (top right)** Sandra Johnson/SAGA/Woodfin Camp & Associates **Fig. 14.2** Zebrowitz, L.A., & McDonald, S. M. (1991). The impact of litigants' baby-facedness and attractiveness on adjudications in small claims courts. *Law and Human Behavior, 15*, 603–623 **Fig. 14.4** Miller, J. G. (1984). Culture and the development of everyday social explanation. *Journal of Personality and Social Psychology, 46*, 961–978. Copyright © 1984 by the American Psychological Association. Reprinted by permission **p. 501** AP/Wide World Photos **p. 503** Lee Snider/The Image Works **p. 504 (top right)** Laura Dwight **p. 504 (bottom left)** Robert Brenner/Photo Edit **Fig. 14.5** Miller, R. L., et al. (1975). Attribution versus persuasion as a means for modifying behavior. *Journal of Personality and Social Psychology, 31*, 430–441. Copyright © 1975 by the American Psychological Association. Adapted by permission **p. 507** Noboru Hashimoto/Sygma **Fig. 14.8** McGuire, W. J., & McGuire, C. V. (1988). Content and process in the experience of self. In L. Berkowitz (Ed.), *Advances in experimental social psychology* (Vol. 21). New York: Academic Press **p. 511** Reuters/Bettmann **Table 14.1** Snyder, M. (1974). Self-monitoring of expressive behavior. *Journal of Personality and Social Psychology, 30*, 526–537. Copyright © 1974 by the American Psychological Association. Reprinted by permission **p. 515** Featured with permission of Buick Motor Division **Fig. 14.9** Petty, R. E., et al. (1981). Personal involvement as a determinant of argument-based persuasion. *Journal of Personality and Social Psychology, 41*, 847–855. Copyright © 1981 by the American Psychological Association. Reprinted by permission **Fig. 14.10** Azjen, I. (1987). Attitudes, traits, and actions: Dispositional prediction of behavior in personality and psychology. In L. Berkowitz (Ed.), *Advances in experimental social psychology* (Vol. 20). New York: Academic Press

CHAPTER 15

Opener Frank Siteman/The Picture Cube **p. 532** Archives of the History of American Psychology, University of Akron **Figs. 15.2 and 15.3(a)** Latané, B. (1981). The psychology of social impact. *American Psychologist, 36*, 343–356. Copyright © 1981 by the American Psychological Association. Reprinted by permission **Fig. 15.3(b)** Jackson, J. M., & Latané, B. (1981). All alone in front of all those people. *Journal of Personality and Social Psychology, 40,* 73–85. Copyright © 1981 by the American Psychological Association. Reprinted by permission **Fig. 15.4** Adapted from Freedman, J. L., & Fraser, S. C. (1966). Compliance without pressure: The foot-in-the-door technique. *Journal of Personality and Social Psychology, 4,* 195–202 **p. 538 and p. 540** © 1965 Stanley Milgram. From the film "Obedience" distributed by the Pennsylvania State University, PCR. **p. 542** Gerard Vandystadt/Agence Vandystadt/Allsport USA **p. 545** Hector Delgado/Impact Visuals **p. 547** Parker/Gamma Liaison **p. 548** William Vandivert/*Scientific American* **p. 552** Gerry Gropp/Sipa Press **p. 553** A. Tannenbaum/Sygma **p. 557** *From Social psychology* by Muzafer Sherif and Carolyn W. Sherif, Fig. 11.18a (p. 258): Copyright 1969 by Muzafer Sherif & Carolyn W. Sherif, by permission of Harper Collins, Inc. **p. 559** Mary Kate Denny/Photo Edit

CHAPTER 16

Opener Joel Gordon **p. 567** Mike Milkovich/The Picture Group **p. 568** Hieronymos Bosch (1450–1516), *The Garden of Earthly Delights* (detail of Hell). Prado/Art Resource. **Fig. 16.2** From THE COLLECTED PAPERS, VOLUME 1 by Sigmund Freud. Authorized translation under the supervision of Joan Riviere. Published by Basic Books, Inc., by arrangement with Hogarth Press, Ltd. and the Institute of Psycho-Analysis, London. Reprinted by permission of Basic Books, a division of HarperCollins Publishers, Inc. **p. 571** Bob Daemmrich **p. 573** Jeff Myers/Stock, Boston **p. 574 and p. 575** Culver Pictures **p. 580** Charles Gupton/Stock, Boston **p. 581** Courtesy of Peter Gray/The Sudbury Valley School **p. 582** S. Nozizwe, Center for the Study of the Person **p. 585** Alex Stewart/The Image Bank **p. 588** Paul Cézanne, *The Card Players,* 1892. Paris, Musée d'Orsay, Photo Erich Lessing/Art Resource **p. 590** UPI/Bettmann **Fig. 16.5** Eysenck, H. J. (1982). Development of a theory. In H. J. Eysenck (Ed.), *Personality, genetics, and behavior: Selected papers.* New York: Praeger. Copyright © 1982 by Praeger Publishers, an imprint of Greenwood Publishing Group, Inc., Westport, CT. Reprinted with permission **Fig. 16.6** Cattell, R. B. (1965). *The scientific analysis of personality.* Baltimore: Penguin **Fig. 16.7** Eysenck, H. J. (1982). Development of a theory. In H. J. Eysenck (Ed.), *Personality, genetics, and behavior: Selected papers.* New York: Praeger. Copyright © 1982 by Praeger Publishers, an imprint of Greenwood Publishing Group, Inc., Westport, CT. Reprinted with permission **p. 597** (both) Elizabeth Crews **p. 600** Aaron Haupt/Stock, Boston

CHAPTER 17

Opener Joel Gordon **p. 606** Cleo Freelance/Jeroboam, Inc. **p. 607** Dan McCoy/Rainbow **p. 608** William Thompson/The Picture Cube **Fig. 17.3** Regier, D. A., et al. (1988). One-month prevalence of mental disorders in the United States. *Archives of General Psychiatry, 45,* 977–986. Copyright © 1988 by the American Medical Association **p. 614** Comstock **Fig. 17.4** Adapted from Ford, M. R., & Widiger, T. A. (1989). Sex bias in the diagnosis of histrionic and antisocial personality disorders. *Journal of Consulting and Clinical Psychology, 57,* 301–305 **p. 619** Nubar Alexanian/Stock, Boston **p. 620** Will McIntyre/Photo Researchers **Table 17.2** Beck, A. T., Brown, G., Eidelson, J. I., Steer, R. A., & Riskind, J. H. (1987). Differentiating anxiety and depression: A test of the cognitive content-specificity hypothesis. *Journal of Abnormal Psychology, 96,* 181. Copyright © 1987 by the American Psychological Association. Reprinted by permission **p. 622** Edvard Munch (1863–1944), *Melancholia,* Art Resource **p. 628** Bart Bartholemew/New York Times Pictures **p. 630** Joel Gordon **Fig. 17.7** Cohen, S., Tyrell, D. A. J., & Smith, A. P. (1991). Psychological stress and susceptibility to the common cold. *The New England Journal of Medicine, 325,* 606–612. Reprinted with permission from *The New England Journal of Medicine* **p. 633** APN Illustrations/Wide World Photos **Fig. 17.8** Cooper, M. L., et al. (1988). Coping, expectancies and alcohol abuse: A test of social learning foundations. *Journal of Abnormal Psychology, 97,* 218–230. Copyright © 1988 by the American Psychological Association. Used by permission **p. 636** Gerald Martineau/*The Washington Post* **p. 638 (bottom left)** I. Klinger/Prinzhorn-Sammlung der Psychiatrischen Universitätsklinik Heidelberg **p. 638 (bottom right)** I. Klinger/Prinzhorn-Sammlung der Psychiatrischen Universitätsklinik Heidelberg **p. 639** Grunnitus/Monkmeyer Press Photo **p. 640** NIH/Science Source/Photo Researchers **Fig. 17.10** Seeman, P., & Lee, T. (1975). Antipsychotic drugs: Direct correlation between clinical potency and presynaptic action on dopamine neurons. *Science, 188,* 1217–1219. Copyright © 1975 by the AAAS

CHAPTER 18

Opener Tree **p. 648** Mary Evans Picture Library/Photo Researchers **p. 649** Culver Pictures **Table 18.1** Beck, A. T. (1978). *BDI.* New York: Harcourt Jovanovich. From the Beck Depression Inventory. Copyright © 1987 by Aaron T. Beck, M.D. Reproduced by permission of the publisher, The Psychological Corporation. All rights reserved **p. 654 (left)** Lew Merrim/Monkmeyer Press Photo **p. 654 (right)** Sing-Si Schwartz (c/o Betty Dornhein Co.) **p. 656** Stacy Pick/Stock, Boston **p. 657** The Bettmann Archive **p. 659 (top)** Edmund Engelman **p. 659 (bottom)** Michael Heron/Woodfin Camp & Associates **p. 662** Michael Rougier, *LIFE Magazine,* © Time Warner, Inc. **Fig. 18.2** Beck, A. T., & Young, J. E. (1985). Depression. In D. H. Barlow (Ed.), *Clinical handbook of psychological disorders: A step-by-step treatment manual.* New York: Guilford **p. 669** Spencer Grant/Stock, Boston **p. 670** Rick Friedman/Black Star **p. 672** Lester Sloan/Woodfin Camp & Associates **p. 673** Alvis Upitis/The Image Bank **Fig. 18.5** Redrawn with permission of the publishers from *Psychotherapy versus behavior therapy* edited by R. Bruce Sloane, Fred R. Staples, Allan H. Cristol, Neil J. Yorkston and Katherine Whipple, Cambridge, Mass.: Harvard University Press, Copyright © 1975 by the Commonwealth Fund **p. 677** Joel Gordon **Fig. 18.6** Adapted from Smith, D. (1982). Trends in counseling and psychotherapy. *American Psychologist, 37,* 802–809. **Fig. 18.7** Hogarty, G. E., & Goldberg, S. C. (1973). Drug and sociotherapy in the aftercare of schizophrenic patients: One year relapse rates. *Archives of General Psychiatry, 28,* 54–64 **p. 681** Will McIntyre/Photo Researchers

NAME INDEX

SUBJECT INDEX